Machine Learning for Trading

Third Edition

A disciplined workflow from research to live execution, with nine case studies and AI agents

Stefan Jansen

<packt>

Machine Learning for Trading

Third Edition

Portfolio Director: Sunith Shetty
Relationship Lead: Tushar Gupta and Apeksha Shetty
Project Manager: Shashank Desai
Content Engineer: David Sugarman
Technical Editor: Seemanjay Ameriya
Copy Editor: David Sugarman
Indexer: Tejal Soni
Production Designer: Ganesh Bhadwalkar
Growth Lead: Anjitha Murali

First published: December 2018

Second edition: July 2020

Third edition: July 2026

Production reference: 1160726

Published by Packt Publishing Ltd.

Grosvenor House

11 St Paul's Square

Birmingham

B3 1RB, UK.

ISBN 978-1-80324-697-0

www.packt.com

I would like to dedicate this book to Mariana and Bastian, who are my source of happiness and who put up with me and the many hours I missed while I wrote this book.

– Stefan Jansen

Foreword

I've read a lot of quant finance books, and most of them fall into the same trap: pile on the algorithms, sprinkle in some market data, and call it a day. Stefan Jansen's third edition of *Machine Learning for Trading* doesn't do that. It's grounded in a way that's almost refreshing—more of a working practitioner's notebook than a textbook. The whole thing assumes markets are messy, non-stationary, and out to ruin your backtest, and it builds from there.

A few things stuck with me.

The book cares about workflow more than algorithms. Jansen treats ML in trading as a lifecycle, not a model hunt. There's a clear line drawn between building your data infrastructure and the day-to-day grind of researching strategies. That separation sounds obvious until you realize how many people skip it.

The data chapters don't pull punches. The section on data quality is the part I'd hand to anyone starting out. Point-in-time errors, survivorship bias, the headache of corporate actions—Jansen walks through exactly how each one fabricates "alpha" that was never really there.

Microstructure is explained like it matters, because it does. The breakdown of the limit order book and how prices actually form connects the tidy theory to the ugly reality of execution. Spreads, queue position, the friction that quietly eats your returns—it's all here, and it changes how you think about whether a strategy is even tradable.

Alternative data gets sober treatment. Instead of breathless hype, you get a checklist: Is there real signal? Is the data clean? Are there legal landmines? What's it going to cost to engineer? Useful questions to ask before you sink three months into a dataset.

The synthetic data chapter is the one I keep thinking about. GANs, diffusion models, LLMs—all aimed at the quant's oldest problem: we only get one history to test against. Jansen is genuinely curious about generating more, but he never lets you forget that a generator's biases become your biases.

Three ideas actually shifted how I think:

Process beats the "perfect" model. Markets drift, break, and shift regimes. The edge isn't some pristine model you discover once—it's a research process disciplined enough to notice when your signal is decaying and flexible enough to change course.

Lookahead bias quietly kills everything. Future information sneaks into the past in ways you won't see: restated macro numbers, ignored SEC filing lags, a universe filtered down to the companies that happened to survive. Each one prints fake profits that vanish the moment real money is on the line.

Clock time is the wrong clock. A one-minute bar at the open and a one-minute bar at lunch are not the same animal, because activity isn't constant. Sampling by volume, dollars, or imbalance instead gives you return distributions that are far better behaved—and far better food for a model.

I definitely recommend this book if you want to understand Finance in the modern AI and Agentic world. It's a definitive guide.

Antonio Gulli

Sr. Engineering Director, Distinguished Engineer, Office of the CTO, Google

Contributors

About the author

Stefan Jansen is the founder of Applied AI and the author of *Machine Learning for Trading*. For over a decade, he has built production machine learning systems across finance, insurance, and healthcare—from contract intelligence that turns legacy insurance documents into structured logic; to forecasting at scale; to live trading infrastructure; and beyond, into LLMs and agents. He maintains the open-source `ml4t-*` libraries and the book's companion repository, which has drawn more than 19,000 GitHub stars. He holds a master's in economics from Harvard, an MS in computer science from Georgia Tech, and the CFA charter.

Writing a book is never a solo effort. My deepest thanks go to my friends and family, who supported me throughout and put up with the long hours this book demanded. I am grateful, too, to the team at Packt who brought this third edition to life: to David Sugarman, who edited the manuscript, and to Apeksha Shetty, Shashank Desai, and Yash Basil, who guided the project through to publication—along with everyone in editorial, production, and design whose work turned a draft into a finished book. My thanks also to the technical reviewer for feedback that improved the book, and to Antonio Gulli for his generous foreword.

About the reviewer

Haitam Borqane is an AI engineer, open source advocate, and huge coffee enthusiast. He has a vast array of experience in AI application across a variety of fields, from sustainability and agriculture to finance and innovation. Professionally, he develops and deploys robust AI solutions and systems for clients to enhance their processes; on the side, he is an AI fanatic who contributes to open source models for low resource languages, while also raising awareness on the state of AI across different conferences. When not working, you can find him at your nearest cozy specialty coffee spot.

I would like to thank the Packt team and author for this opportunity on this amazing book, and I would like to thank my parents and my sister for their constant support.

Table of Contents

Chapter 14: Latent Factor Models 347

Chapter 20: Strategy Synthesis 541

Chapter 21: Reinforcement Learning 579

Chapter 24: Autonomous Agents 659

Preface

Machine learning has changed what is possible in systematic trading, and it has changed how easily you can fool yourself. The same tools that surface a genuine edge will, used carelessly, manufacture one that exists only in your backtest. This book is about the difference between careful and careless tool use: how to take a research idea all the way to a strategy you can run, and keep running, in a live market without mistaking noise for signal along the way.

The third edition is a ground-up rebuild, organized around a single end-to-end workflow. Earlier editions moved technique by technique. This edition runs one process from start to finish: from data infrastructure and strategy research, across an *evidence boundary* that separates tuning from evaluation, to deployment and monitoring, with a feedback loop that retrains, pauses, or retires a strategy as its edge decays. Nine case studies run throughout the book, from raw data through features, models, backtests, costs, and risk to a deployment assessment. ETFs, crypto perpetuals, intraday equities, options, FX, futures, and equity factor panels each go through the *same* pipeline, which lets you see where a disciplined process works, where it breaks down, and why.

Two strands are new and run deliberately *across* the workflow rather than sitting at a single stage. **Generative AI** brings retrieval-augmented generation grounded in filings, knowledge graphs, and multi-agent research systems. **Causal machine learning** brings the tools for separating a real effect from a spurious correlation. Alongside them, the edition adds a full production track, a wider model toolkit ranging from gradient boosting to modern time-series and tabular architectures, reinforcement learning for execution and hedging, and synthetic data generators for validation when history is short. Throughout, methodological rigor is treated as a first-class subject: walk-forward validation, the multiple-testing and overfitting problems that quietly invalidate most backtests, and the tools that confront them, from the Deflated Sharpe Ratio to conformal prediction.

If there is one claim the book defends from beginning to end, it is the title's: the process is your edge. Markets drift, break, and change regime. A pristine model you discover once is not an edge; a research process disciplined enough to notice when a signal is decaying and flexible enough to change course is.

A book and a living repository

This edition is designed to be read alongside its code. The book contains the concepts, reasoning, and results; the **GitHub repository contains everything you run**. There are no code listings in these pages. That is deliberate. Code printed in a book is frozen the day it goes to press, and trading code ages badly: libraries move, data sources change, and a subtle bug found after publication can only be errata. The repository does not have that problem.

So the complete, runnable implementation of every method, every figure, and all nine case studies lives in the repository at:

`https://github.com/stefan-jansen/machine-learning-for-trading`

The repository is alive. It is version-controlled, continuously tested, and maintained past the print date. When a library changes or a reader finds a problem, the fix lands there, and everyone gets it. It can hold far more than a book can: full pipelines, intermediate artifacts, reproducible Docker environments, and material that grows over time. And it makes the subject what it has to be: hands-on. You are meant to clone it, run it, break it, and change it. The book tells you *what* a method does and *why* it matters; the repository is where you watch it work on real data and make it your own.

Read the two together. Each chapter in the book corresponds to a numbered directory in the repository, and the most productive way through the material is to read a chapter, then open its directory and run the notebooks that implement it.

How each chapter maps to the repository

Every chapter has its own directory, and each directory opens with a `README` that serves as the hub for that chapter's hands-on work. Each one gives you:

- Learning objectives, outlining what you should be able to do after the chapter
- A section-by-section guide to how the chapter's ideas map onto the notebooks
- The notebooks to run, with the exact commands, from the repository root
- References to the primary sources behind the chapter—the foundational papers and books worth reading next if you want to go deeper than the chapter goes

The notebooks themselves are paired Jupytext files: a `.py` source you edit and a generated `.ipynb` you run. Each notebook states in its preamble which environment it needs and any parameters worth changing. Start a chapter from its `README`, and the chapter's structure and its code stay in step.

The companion ecosystem at ml4trading.io

The book and the repository are anchored by a companion site, `ml4trading.io`, that extends both:

- **Primers:** Focused introductions to the financial, statistical, and machine-learning background the chapters build on. If a chapter assumes something you would like to firm up, the primer for it is the place to start; new readers should start there before *Chapter 1*.
- **Agent skills:** A library of skills that teach AI coding assistants the ML4T workflow. Each one packages a reviewer-grade check that keeps a coding agent from shipping the field's expensive mistakes—data leakage, lookahead bias, overfit backtests, unrealistic costs—so the agent you build with applies the book's discipline by default.
- **A page for every chapter:** A detailed table of contents, the full bibliography, and write-ups of all nine case studies: the online counterpart to the printed book.
- **Courses:** Guided paths through the material, including a research-to-production course that works the end-to-end workflow and a course on autonomous and multi-agent systems for financial research. *(See* `maven.com/stefan-jansen`*.)*

- **ML4T Insights:** An ongoing newsletter with new research, methods, and developments in machine learning for trading, well beyond the book itself.

The book is the durable spine. The repository, the primers, the coding skills, and the newsletter are how the subject keeps moving after the spine is solidified.

Who this book is for

This book is for anyone who wants to apply machine learning to trading as a disciplined, end-to-end practice rather than a collection of models: quantitative researchers and traders, data scientists and ML engineers moving into finance, advanced students, and technically minded investors who want to build and evaluate strategies seriously.

You should be comfortable reading and writing Python and at ease with the core ideas of probability, statistics, and linear algebra. Prior exposure to machine learning and to financial markets helps but is not assumed. Where a chapter leans on background you would like to shore up, the **primers at ml4trading.io** are there to fill the gap. You do not need a trading background to start; you do need a willingness to run the code.

What this book covers

An introduction and a closing chapter bracket six workflow-aligned parts.

Chapter 1, The Process Is Your Edge, opens the book by making the case that process discipline beats model sophistication and introduces the ML4T workflow and the evidence boundary that separates exploration from confirmation.

Part I — Financial Data (Chapters 2–5) covers the markets, instruments, and infrastructure that the rest of the book builds on.

Chapter 2, The Financial Data Universe, lays out a taxonomy of market, fundamental, and alternative data across eight asset classes, quantifies survivorship bias, and benchmarks storage formats and the data-quality framework used throughout.

Chapter 3, Market Microstructure, goes from raw exchange messages to feature-ready bars: parsing NASDAQ ITCH, reconstructing the limit order book, trade classification, and bar-sampling methods.

Chapter 4, Fundamental and Alternative Data, builds point-in-time pipelines for SEC EDGAR filings, entity resolution, macro and commodity fundamentals, and alternative-data evaluation, including on-chain crypto data and prediction markets.

Chapter 5, Synthetic Financial Data, generates alternative market histories for robust validation with TimeGAN, Tail-GAN, Sig-CWGAN, diffusion models, and LLM-based generation, evaluated through a fidelity–utility–privacy framework.

Part II — Research Design and Feature Engineering (Chapters 6–10) defines the trading problem, then turns data into the labels, features, and evaluation that determine what any model can learn.

Chapter 6, Strategy Research Framework, defines the trading game before any model is built—universe rules, decision schedule, cost model, evaluation protocol, and run logging—and introduces the nine case studies alongside the walk-forward discipline that anchors *Chapters 7–20*.

Chapter 7, Defining the Learning Task, covers label engineering, univariate feature evaluation with information coefficients, multiple-testing control, and causal plausibility checks.

Chapter 8, Financial Feature Engineering, builds five feature families from price data along with structural, cross-instrument, and contextual features, and covers feature selection with robustness testing.

Chapter 9, Model-Based Feature Extraction, derives features from fitted models—Kalman filters, spectral methods, GARCH volatility, and HMM regime probabilities—with point-in-time correctness enforced throughout.

Chapter 10, Text Feature Engineering, moves from bag-of-words through to transformers: TF-IDF, word embeddings, sequence models, FinBERT sentiment, financial NER, and news-return signals.

Part III — Model Development (Chapters 11–15) applies five model families to the same nine case studies, each building on the linear baseline.

Chapter 11, The ML Pipeline, establishes regularized linear models as the baseline every later model must beat, with SHAP interpretability, conformal prediction, and a cross-dataset comparison.

Chapter 12, Advanced Models for Tabular Data, covers gradient boosting (XGBoost, LightGBM, CatBoost) with multi-objective tuning and deep-learning tabular alternatives, with explainability and cross-dataset results.

Chapter 13, Deep Learning for Time Series, surveys LSTM, N-BEATS, Transformers, TSMixer, TCN, and Mamba against the LTSF-Linear debate, with evidence on when deep learning helps.

Chapter 14, Latent Factor Models, covers PCA eigenportfolios, IPCA, conditional and supervised autoencoders, and adversarial SDF estimation, with results on when latent factors add value.

Chapter 15, Causal Machine Learning, applies Double Machine Learning, Bayesian Structural Time Series, and causal discovery to isolate real effects from spurious correlation across the case studies.

Part IV — Strategy Implementation (Chapters 16–20) turns predictions into deployable strategies through backtesting, portfolio construction, costs, risk, and synthesis.

Chapter 16, Strategy Simulation, treats backtesting as falsification: protocol specification, vectorized versus event-driven engines, metric reporting, and strategy-level overfitting control.

Chapter 17, Portfolio Construction, goes from scores to portfolios with mean-variance optimization and its pitfalls, Hierarchical Risk Parity, Kelly sizing, conformal position sizing, and a controlled allocator comparison.

Chapter 18, Transaction Costs, covers the cost taxonomy, spread and market-impact estimation, execution algorithms, transaction-cost analysis, and breakeven costs that vary widely by asset class.

Chapter 19, Risk Management, covers VaR/CVaR, drawdown controls, factor and sector decomposition, stress testing, adaptive overlays, deep hedging, and kill switches.

Chapter 20, Strategy Synthesis, draws together what nine experiments reveal about turning predictions into strategies: IC–Sharpe decorrelation, the model-family cascade, cost-survival analysis, and a practitioner's decision framework.

Part V — Advanced AI (Chapters 21–24) covers reinforcement learning, large language models, knowledge graphs, and autonomous agents for finance.

Chapter 21, Reinforcement Learning, formulates execution and hedging as Markov decision processes and applies DQN, PPO, and SAC to optimal execution, market making, and deep hedging.

Chapter 22, RAG for Financial Research, builds retrieval-augmented generation grounded in SEC filings, from ingestion and domain embeddings through hybrid retrieval, evaluation, and the transition to agentic workflows.

Chapter 23, Knowledge Graphs, covers KG construction from filings, Graph RAG for multi-hop reasoning, graph features for ML, and temporal-leakage prevention.

Chapter 24, Autonomous Agents, covers agent architectures, memory and tools, the engineering stack, a stateful equity-research agent, and multi-agent forecasting with adversarial debate.

Part VI — Production (Chapters 25–26) takes strategies live, with the systems and operational infrastructure that this requires.

Chapter 25, Live Trading Systems, presents a unified framework bridging research and production with Interactive Brokers, Alpaca, and managed platforms, order lifecycle management, and operational readiness.

Chapter 26, MLOps and Governance, covers an ML failure taxonomy, drift detection, safe rollout, circuit breakers, feature stores, and experiment tracking.

Conclusion brackets the opening chapter: having run the full workflow, the book returns to where it began.

Chapter 27, The Systematic Edge, closes with the systematic philosophy, career paths, learning resources, research frontiers, and how to build your own edge.

To get the most out of this book

Read each chapter with its repository directory open beside you, and run the notebooks as you go. The workflow is cumulative: the case studies introduced in *Chapter 6* are carried through every chapter that follows, so the value compounds when you run them rather than only read about them. You should:

- **Set up the environment once.** Clone the repository and use the **Docker images** to ensure results are reproducible across machines, or set up a local environment with `uv`. Run everything **from the repository root**, never from a chapter directory.
- **Start small with data.** Most notebooks need datasets; begin with the free tier (no API keys), documented in the repository's `data/` directory.
- **Start with the ETF case study.** It uses free data, requires no API keys, and runs fast, so it is the quickest way to see the whole pipeline end-to-end before you commit to a larger dataset.

- **Fill gaps from the companion site.** If a chapter assumes background you would like to firm up, use the **primers at ml4trading.io**.

You will get the most from the book if you treat the code as the main focus rather than an appendix. The repository `README` documents installation for Linux, Windows (WSL2), and macOS, including GPU setup.

Download the example code

All of the book's code lives in the GitHub repository, which is the primary and continuously maintained source:

`https://github.com/stefan-jansen/machine-learning-for-trading`

```
git clone https://github.com/stefan-jansen/machine-learning-for-trading.git
cd machine-learning-for-trading
```

Packt also distributes a downloadable code bundle for the book. The GitHub repository is the authoritative, up-to-date version; prefer it, and use the `README`'s quick-start instructions to set up and run the notebooks.

Conventions used

`CodeInText` indicates code words in text: module, function, and variable names, file and directory names, and dataset and notebook names. For example: "run the `01_process_is_edge/factor_regimes.py` notebook from the repository root."

Bold indicates a new term or an important word.

A data convention worth knowing up front: across every dataset and chapter, the code uses a single canonical schema, with `symbol` identifying an instrument and `timestamp` identifying time, for both daily and intraday data. Notebooks and case studies share that vocabulary so results carry cleanly from one chapter to the next.

Note/Tip/Warning callouts appear throughout, flagging respectively something to be aware of, a useful shortcut, and a step where it is easy to go wrong.

Get in touch

Feedback from our readers is always welcome.

General feedback: Email `feedback@packtpub.com` and mention the book's title in the subject of your message. If you have questions about any aspect of this book, please email us at `questions@packtpub.com`.

Errata: Although we have taken every care to ensure the accuracy of our content, mistakes do happen. If you have found a mistake in this book, we would be grateful if you reported this to us. Please visit `http://www.packtpub.com/submit-errata`, click **Submit Errata**, and fill in the form.

Piracy: If you come across any illegal copies of our works in any form on the internet, we would be grateful if you would provide us with the location address or website name. Please contact us at `copyright@packtpub.com` with a link to the material.

If you are interested in becoming an author: If there is a topic that you have expertise in and you are interested in either writing or contributing to a book, please visit `http://authors.packtpub.com/`.

Free benefits with your book

This book includes free benefits designed to support your learning and help you apply what you learn effectively. Activate them now for instant access (see the *How to unlock* section for instructions).

Here's a quick overview of what you can instantly unlock with your purchase:

How to unlock

Scan the QR code (or go to `packtpub.com/unlock`). Search for this book by name, confirm the edition, and then follow the steps on the page.

UNLOCK NOW

Note: Have your invoice handy. Purchases made directly from the Packt website don't require an invoice.

Share your thoughts

Once you've read *Machine Learning for Trading, Third Edition*, we'd love to hear your thoughts! Please `click here to go straight to the Amazon review page` for this book and share your feedback.

Your review is important to us and the tech community and will help us make sure we're delivering excellent quality content.

1

The Process Is Your Edge

Machine learning (**ML**) now reaches every stage of systematic trading, from feature engineering and portfolio construction to execution and monitoring. However, the fundamental challenge remains unchanged: markets are dynamic, competitive, and unforgiving of undisciplined research.

The ML4T Workflow aims to help you meet that challenge as a systematic process for generating, testing, and deploying strategies that adapt to evolving markets. The workflow draws from quantitative finance practice, industrial ML deployment frameworks, and lessons repeatedly learned through market regime shifts.

By the end of this chapter, you will be able to:

- Distinguish structural breaks, regimes, and drift, and explain why static trading models degrade.
- Understand the ML4T Workflow, with its foundation layer (data infrastructure) and iterative research modules (scoping, features, modeling, strategy, deployment), and how each module's artifacts flow into the next.
- Explain the evidence boundary that separates exploration from confirmation, and how logging trials and selection-adjusted inference maintain research integrity.
- Recognize where modern tools like *causal inference* and *generative AI* fit within a disciplined workflow.
- Apply *regime thinking* to diagnose strategy vulnerabilities across different market states.

The chapter is grounded in process discipline, followed by a vocabulary for market change, the workflow's structure, the place of causal inference and generative AI within it, regime change as an engineering constraint, and the contrast between institutional and independent contexts, before closing with takeaways.

1.1 Why process discipline matters

Financial markets exact a high price for undisciplined inference. They also expose every weakness in a research workflow: an unquestioning reliance on unstable relationships or small, noisy effects, and insufficient consideration of real-world frictions such as liquidity, trading costs, execution timing, and capacity constraints. These challenges are not new, but three developments have increased the value of process discipline relative to model sophistication:

- **Market behavior changes**—sometimes abruptly and sometimes gradually—so assumptions that are held in one period can fail in the next
- **Modeling capacity has grown**, increasing the degrees of freedom available to the researcher and making overfitting easier to produce and harder to diagnose
- **Tooling has accelerated research**, amplifying both good practices (faster iteration, better monitoring) and bad ones (faster data mining, faster deployment of brittle systems)

Recent disruptions did not create these dynamics; they made their consequences more visible. Our core claim is that **durable performance depends at least as much on a disciplined, adaptive workflow steeped in trading reality** as on choosing an especially sophisticated model.

Four shockwaves and the fragility of assumptions

Between 2020 and 2025, markets experienced a sequence of disruptions that stressed assumptions calibrated to the 2010s. The catalysts differed, but the shared effect was the same: relationships learned from recent data proved unreliable when the environment changed. The major catalysts include:

- **The 2020 pandemic (liquidity shock):** Treasury intermediation strained (Duffie, 2020), and correlations shifted abruptly, weakening diversification assumptions and revealing that cross-asset relationships are regime-dependent rather than structural.
- **The 2021 meme-stock episode (sentiment shock):** Sentiment- and positioning-driven flows dominated fundamentals long enough to break short-horizon strategies—especially mean-reversion systems whose holding periods and risk limits assumed faster normalization.
- **The 2021–2023 inflation surge (macro regime shift):** The return of high inflation coincided with higher volatility and altered equity–bond co-movement, stressing models calibrated to a low-inflation decade and destabilizing common portfolio hedging heuristics (Marshall, 2023)
- **An equity concentration episode (crowding shock):** Index returns became unusually concentrated in a small set of mega-cap names, degrading strategies sensitive to breadth, diversification, and factor balance—and exposing how "market" exposure can become crowded exposure.

These are recent examples, not special cases. Liquidity crises, sentiment cascades, policy shifts, and crowding recur with different triggers. A workflow built for stable conditions is incomplete unless it includes explicit checks for instability and decay.

A vocabulary for change

Adaptive systems require precise language about how the data-generating process changes. Four concepts are commonly conflated but play different roles in research and production:

- **Structural break:** An abrupt change point where the process generating the data shifts. This concept is about *when* the system changed (for example, the onset of COVID-19).
- **Regime:** A persistent state in which market properties (for example, volatility or correlations) are relatively stable within the state but materially different across states (for example, a low-inflation regime versus a high-inflation regime).
- **Drift:** A model-centric description of change. Operationally, drift is not a diagnosis; it is a flag that triggers an investigation into data integrity, feature validity, execution conditions, and regime exposure:
    - **Data drift** occurs when the distribution of input features shifts.
    - **Concept drift** occurs when the relationship between features and the target changes. Concept drift is often a model-side manifestation of the same underlying change captured by a structural break; the distinction is a matter of perspective rather than substance (a statistical process versus model error).
    - **Online detection** is the operational task of identifying change in real time, using only information available at decision time. This differs from ex post labeling, which is easier but not actionable for trading.

This vocabulary clarifies what a monitoring system must do. A research backtest may tolerate ex post regime labeling; a live strategy cannot.

Why process trumps models

The shocks of the 2020s and many earlier episodes point to a practical constraint: **no single model remains optimal across regimes indefinitely**. The differentiator is not the ability to forecast regime transitions (which is often infeasible), but the ability to rigorously validate ideas, systematically monitor performance, and respond to deterioration without improvisation. As Fabozzi and Stenholm (2025) argue in the context of modern asset management, disciplined preparation and adaptation dominate impulse and overconfidence.

This claim is consistent with Andrew Lo's **Adaptive Markets Hypothesis** (2004), which reframes market efficiency as an evolutionary outcome rather than a permanent condition. In this view, markets consist of heterogeneous participants who learn, compete, and adapt. The degree of efficiency varies with "market ecology," including the mix of participants, capital, technology, regulation, and available opportunities. Under stable conditions, behavior can resemble a steady state; under changing conditions, temporary anomalies can emerge, persist, and disappear as the environment evolves.

For practitioners, the implication is operational rather than philosophical. **Key relationships are not structurally stable**: risk premia, correlations, and execution costs shift with the participant mix and constraints; profit opportunities decay as they are exploited; and strategies often wax and wane, sometimes reviving when conditions become favorable again. A durable **edge** (a repeatable source of profitable trades), therefore, depends less on selecting a "right model" and more on maintaining a research-to-production loop that detects decay early, distinguishes noise from regime change, and reallocates capital toward what remains robust.

Process as a research-to-production system

We treat machine learning for trading as a managed lifecycle rather than a sequence of disconnected experiments. López de Prado (2018) describes this industrialization as an "**alpha factory**": a repeatable pipeline that generates, evaluates, deploys, and monitors strategies under explicit constraints.

The underlying idea is broader than trading. In applied ML and quality engineering, **models are part of a lifecycle** that includes monitoring, diagnosis, and controlled interventions when performance degrades. Industry evidence indicates that **process failures predominate** over algorithmic failures. Gartner (2018) and RAND's more recent review of AI implementations (Ryseff et al., 2024) warned that many initiatives would deliver erroneous outcomes due to issues across data, modeling, and organizational practices.

Trading increases these risks because non-stationarity and transaction costs can turn small data or modeling errors into large financial losses. Trading also further complicates modeling "success" because the objective is not predictive accuracy but risk-adjusted performance after costs, under changing conditions.

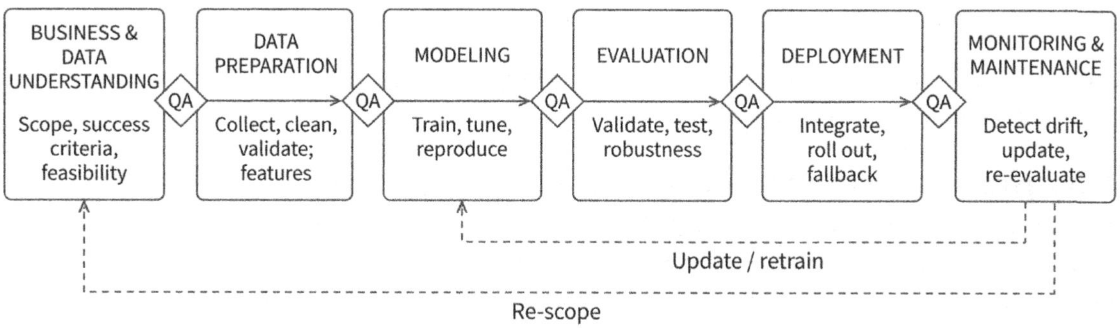

Figure 1.1: Cross-Industry Standard Process for ML with Quality Assurance CRISP-ML(Q)

The workflow introduced in the next section aligns with established engineering frameworks for addressing these failure modes. **CRISP-DM** (**Cross-Industry Standard Process for Data Mining**, 2000) provides a structured process from business understanding through deployment. **CRISP-ML(Q)** (Studer et al., 2021) adapts this logic to modern ML systems. It integrates the understanding of business and data realities, emphasizing explicit handoff checks and post-deployment monitoring (*Figure 1.1*).

We adopt this lifecycle discipline and adapt it to trading constraints: limited effective sample size under non-stationarity, pervasive opportunities for leakage and point-in-time errors, and objectives driven by transaction costs, market impact, and risk constraints rather than predictive accuracy. A disciplined workflow functions as a practical guardrail against common failure modes in quant research:

1. **Data mining and narrative overfitting:** Generating hypotheses after observing outcomes rather than pre-committing to what would falsify the idea.
2. **Leakage and non–point-in-time data:** Using information that was not available at decision time (revisions, survivorship effects, corporate actions, timestamp errors).
3. **Multiple testing and selection bias:** Searching across many variants until one "works," then treating noise as signal (Harvey, Liu, and Zhu, 2016).

4. **Ignoring implementability:** Confusing predictability with tradable edge after costs, constraints, and execution frictions.
5. **Sunk costs and delayed exits :** Maintaining a decaying strategy because it once worked, rather than because it remains supported by current evidence.

Undisciplined research tends to cycle through vague hypotheses, rapid backtests, and premature deployment, followed by post hoc explanations when performance breaks down. Disciplined research makes assumptions explicit, defines checks before optimization, and builds a feedback loop from hypothesis to validation to monitoring. Over time, both approaches require comparable effort. Only one produces a workflow that can compound learning and sustain performance in the face of change. Let's take a closer look at a workflow that leads to disciplined research.

1.2 Introducing the ML4T workflow

The instability described in *Section 1.1* makes any fixed model fragile. The practical response is workflow discipline: a lifecycle that separates data infrastructure from strategy research, and separates exploration from confirmation.

Figure 1.2 summarizes the ML4T workflow. It adapts standard process frameworks to systematic trading, where dominant constraints include limited effective history, point-in-time data integrity, time-aware evaluation, implementability after costs, risk limits, and monitoring that distinguishes signal decay from execution or risk-control failures.

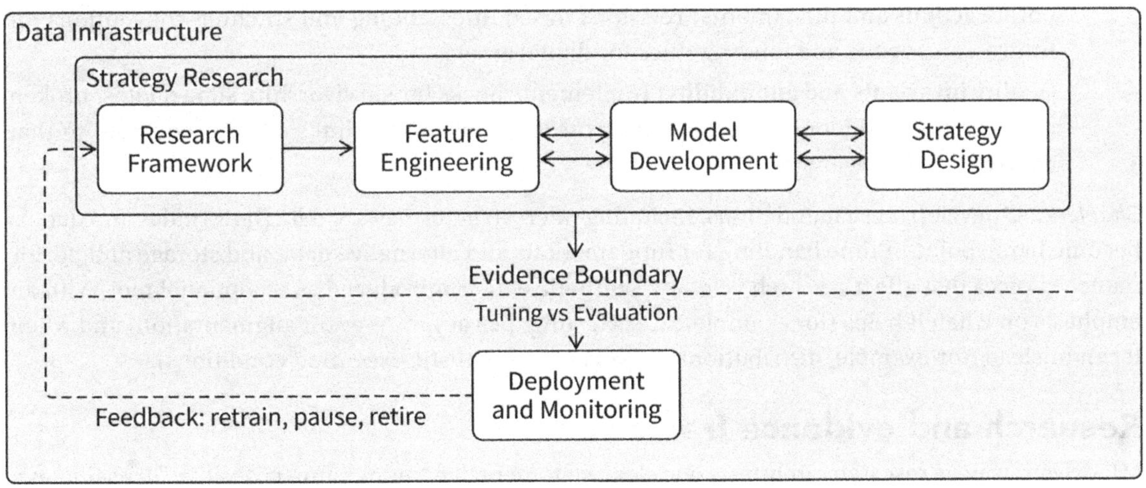

Figure 1.2: The ML for Trading workflow separates a foundational data-infrastructure layer from an iterative strategy-research loop, gated by an evidence boundary that reserves a holdout for confirmation

The workflow has two layers:

1. **Data infrastructure** (*Chapters 2–5*) provides reproducible, auditable, point-in-time-correct data that supports all research and live-trading.
2. **Strategy research** (*Chapters 6–21*) is an iterative loop that refines ideas into tradable systems.

The strategy-research boxes in *Figure 1.2* map to the subsections below: Research Framework, the combined Feature Engineering and Model Development pair, Strategy Design, and Deployment and Monitoring.

The workflow is cyclical and iterative rather than linear: each module produces artifacts used downstream, and live results feed back into revised hypotheses, data checks, and implementation assumptions.

The workflow does not require machine learning. Signals may come from discretionary research, rule-based systems, or learned models; the same structure applies.

Data infrastructure

Data infrastructure is an ongoing investment, not a one-time stage. In trading, the most damaging errors rarely crash code. They inflate backtests by leaking future information, mishandling revisions, or embedding unrealistic assumptions about execution. This layer establishes shared semantics and invariants so results are comparable across projects:

- **Data sourcing and coverage:** Select vendors and feeds, verify identifiers, address missing data, and document sampling and revision policies.
- **Time and availability semantics:** Define event time versus publish time, align features to what was knowable at decision time, and preserve ordering when events share timestamps.
- **Asset-class mechanics:** Apply rules that make data economically meaningful, including corporate actions and fundamental revisions for equities, rolling and stitching conventions for futures, and venue and funding rules for digital assets.
- **Quality invariants and auditability:** Implement checks for survivorship, stale quotes, broken adjustments, and identifier-mapping errors, and ensure pipelines are reproducible so that datasets can be regenerated exactly.

Chapters 2–5 develop these foundations, including microstructure-aware data (how trades and quotes become bars), point-in-time handling for fundamentals and alternative data, and storage and performance choices that affect research velocity. Synthetic data is introduced as an optional tool, with an emphasis on when it helps (for example, stress testing, privacy, rare-event augmentation) and when it can mislead (for example, distributional mismatch, unrealistic execution conditions).

Research and evidence framework

ML-driven strategy research rarely tests one clean statement like "momentum is positive." It evaluates a **research pipeline:** a set of data choices, feature families, model classes, and selection rules that together produce trades. That pipeline can surface relationships we did not anticipate, including interactions, regime dependence, or sign reversals. The practical question is not "did this one coefficient differ from zero?" but "will this pipeline produce tradable value when evaluated the way it would be run live?"

Many finance strategies are motivated by a **mechanism**—a plausible economic reason an effect might exist (for example, underreaction, liquidity provision, risk premia, or institutional flows). Mechanisms provide orientation and, later, help interpret performance and diagnose decay. In ML research, however, a mechanism is not a substitute for an explicit **trading specification**.

Credible evidence requires stating, up front, the decision point, the tradable universe, the target horizon, the cost assumptions, and the evaluation protocol that define what would count as success or failure.

Within those constraints, ML can be used as a flexible search tool. **Priors** guide where to look—candidate sources of edge and the measurable proxies that might capture them—while model training discovers the functional form. The core discipline is to fix the choices that determine what evidence means, then iterate downstream without revising the evaluation rules:

- **Decision-time correctness:** Specify the information available at each decision point and align each feature with its availability.
- **Tradability and universe rules:** Specify what can be traded and the constraints under which it can be traded. Fix liquidity and capacity screens and shorting rules up front.
- **Label and horizon definitions:** Define the target and the holding period. Labels define what the model optimizes and what counts as success.
- **Cost-model class:** Specify which frictions apply (such as spreads, slippage, financing, market impact). The class is fixed even if parameters are estimated from data.
- **Evaluation protocol:** Commit to how exploration is separated from confirmation, including the walk-forward structure, holdout design, and trial logging.

Iteration occurs in *feature engineering, model development*, and *strategy design*: diagnostics routinely prompt revisions to proxies, targets, model classes, and trading rules. The framework keeps that iteration honest by maintaining measurement conventions and evaluation rules, so improvements reflect stronger signals and better decisions rather than changes in definitions.

Feature engineering and model development

Signal research converts engineered datasets into decision inputs: forecasts, scores, rankings, or state estimates that can translate into trades. Feature engineering and modeling are best treated as a nested loop because diagnostics in each step should update the other:

- *Feature and label engineering* (*Chapters 7–10*) encodes market structure into measurable inputs and targets (such as forward returns, volatility, drawdown risk, and execution quality). Constraints include low signal-to-noise ratios, misalignment between model objectives and trading objectives, and false discoveries from extensive search. Lightweight evaluation methods such as information coefficients, rolling stability checks, and regime slicing can screen candidates before higher-capacity modeling.
- *Model design and evaluation* (*Chapters 11–15*) begins with strong baselines and transparent diagnostics, then increases capacity as warranted. As flexibility increases, the validation burden increases. Leakage checks, stability across regimes, and sensitivity to perturbations become requirements. Model diagnostics should also be treated as feature diagnostics, as failure modes often reflect data alignment problems, target leakage, unstable measurements, or a mismatch between the target definition and the trading objective. *Chapter 21* extends model development to reinforcement-learning agents that learn execution and allocation policies directly, placing RL alongside the supervised methods of *Chapters 11–15* rather than treating it as a deployment topic.

Time-aware validation is the core discipline. Evaluation must preserve temporal order through walk-forward splits and handle overlapping labels using cross-validation that prevents information leakage. Hyperparameter tuning must respect the same constraint. The objective is not only to estimate performance, but to characterize when a signal fails, why it appears to work, and whether it survives trading frictions.

Strategy design from signals to trades

A prediction is not a trade. Strategy design turns signals into an executable system by specifying how forecasts become positions, how positions become orders, and how the system behaves under constraints. The following must be considered:

- **Signal-to-trade translation:** Define the mapping from model outputs to actions: thresholds, ranks, position scaling, and entry and exit logic, including explicit "no trade" states.
- **Portfolio construction and constraints:** Convert decisions into target exposures while respecting leverage, concentration, liquidity, and risk limits. Portfolio design determines capacity and drawdown behavior and often dominates implementation feasibility.
- **Backtesting as falsification:** Use realistic assumptions about prices, fills, slippage, borrowing, fees, and turnover, and require stress tests across regimes and plausible operational failures.
- **Execution and risk controls:** Incorporate transaction-cost and market-impact models and define risk controls consistent with the scoping constraints position limits, kill switches, hedges, and drawdown-based de-risking.

Backtesting may show that statistically strong signals do not yield a tradable edge, prompting a return to modeling or feature engineering. *Chapters 16–20* expand strategy design across simulation, portfolio construction, transaction costs, risk management, and synthesis.

Deployment and monitoring

The final module connects research to live execution through deployment, monitoring, and feedback loops that enable adaptation. The transition from simulation to production introduces risks that backtests do not fully represent, including execution delays, queue effects, and liquidity shifts. The module covers:

- **Phased deployment:** Use a graduation process: shadow deployment (log orders but do not execute), canary deployment (trade with minimal capital to test the end-to-end pipeline), and full scale only after stability is demonstrated.
- **Monitoring and diagnosis:** Monitoring is a diagnostic system. It should distinguish data health (pipeline breaks, missing fields, timestamp misalignment), signal health (feature drift, label drift, calibration breakdown), execution health (slippage, fill rates, impact), and risk behavior (constraint breaches, exposure creep, drawdowns).
- **Decay detection and lifecycle rules:** Monitoring must detect systematic degradation and specify what actions follow. This includes both model performance (data drift and concept drift, as defined in *Section 1.1*) and strategy performance (profitability, risk profile, execution quality). Implement explicit retrain, pause, and retire triggers instead of ad hoc reactions, and treat these rules as part of the system specification rather than an afterthought.

These triggers make the workflow adaptive rather than linear. *Chapters 25–26* provide frameworks for live trading operations, market-adapted MLOps, and strategy lifecycle governance.

Beyond the iterative workflow, *Chapters 22–24* introduce research-tooling techniques—RAG, knowledge graphs, and autonomous agents—that augment the entire pipeline rather than fitting any single layer.

The evidence boundary

The central discipline mechanism in the workflow is the separation of exploration from confirmation. The goal is not to pre-commit to a fixed number of trials. The goal is to preserve the integrity of evidence despite iterative search. There are two modes:

- **Exploration mode** is where ideas develop. Use available data for diagnostics and iteration, and log trials in a research ledger so the search can be counted and characterized.
- **Confirmation mode** is where evidence is generated. Use a sealed holdout set that is not touched during exploration, evaluate a frozen specification, use predefined metrics, and apply selection-adjusted inference that accounts for the number of trials.

The evidence boundary is a transition, not a single event. Credibility comes from being able to count and characterize the search and from reserving untouched data for final evaluation. The workflow responds to a single fact: the environment changes. Later chapters treat change as an engineering constraint expressed through data availability, leakage risk, costs, and governance.

The next section locates two modern tools within the workflow and makes change tangible with a simple regime example used for risk framing and monitoring, not for regime timing.

1.3 Causal inference and generative AI in the workflow

The ML4T workflow is deliberately tool-agnostic: it is a lifecycle for turning ideas into tradable systems amid uncertainty, costs, and non-stationarity. What *has* changed is the toolkit. We add two families of methods that matter for modern practice, but for different reasons:

- **Causal inference** makes researchers more explicit about both the hypothesis they are advancing and the empirical evidence that would undermine it. It provides a framework for disciplined hypothesis formation, variable selection, and diagnosis when may be confounded by other variables.
- **Generative AI** broadens the range of data researchers can use, especially unstructured text and documents, and accelerates iteration across feature design, coding, analysis, and documentation. Without guardrails around data provenance, point-in-time availability, leakage, validation, and factual accuracy, it can also amplify errors by producing more unsupported signals, flawed code, and convincing but false explanations at greater speed.

These tools do not replace process discipline. They amplify the consequences of the workflow that employs them: used well, they reduce false discoveries and sharpen diagnosis; used poorly, they accelerate the production of plausible but unsupported results.

We also broaden the scope of "ML for trading." Beyond return prediction, we address forecasting and decision-making under uncertainty, end-to-end trading systems that run in real time, and richer market structures across asset classes. Concretely, we add:

- **Uncertainty quantification** using conformal prediction to turn model outputs into calibrated decisions
- **Stronger statistical hygiene** control for false discoveries in modeling and backtesting due to repeated experiments
- **Regime-aware modeling and monitoring**, including regime detection and HMMs
- **Modern deep learning for time series**, where it is empirically justified
- **Agentic automation** for research and operations

The workflow is the spine that places these additions into specific modules and shared safeguards, rather than treating them as a grab bag.

Two practical starting points and two deliverable types

Figure 1.3 describes two entry points into the research loop and two types of deliverables that can emerge. These are not mutually exclusive "modes"—most real projects blend elements of both, and some produce both types of deliverables. The distinction is practical: it clarifies *what artifact you make testable first* and *what "being wrong" would mean*. The two options are:

- **Prediction-first (complexity-tolerant)**: Start with a forecast target and broad feature set; allow high-capacity models when the objective is economic value (risk-adjusted returns, loss limitation, turnover, capacity). Recent work shows that high model complexity (many features) can coexist with strong out-of-sample performance through regularization and ensemble diversification (Kelly and Malamud, 2025; see *Chapter 9*). This entry point legitimizes high-dimensional forecasting, but only when leakage-resistant protocols, walk-forward validation, and statistical budgeting prevent "lucky" models from being promoted.
- **Mechanism-first (structure-imposing)**: Start with an economic rationale that bounds the search space and defines what should break in the presence of drift. This is not anti-ML; it is a response to limited effective sample sizes and winner's curse dynamics that make even cross-validated backtests vulnerable to false positives (Arnott et al., 2018). The mechanism imposes discipline: it filters nonsensical strategies, raises the evidentiary bar when the rationale is weak, and makes monitoring actionable when conditions change. Crucially, the "economic story" functions as a *search constraint and an aid to interpretability*, not necessarily as a claim of causal identification.

Both entry points can produce a *tradable signal*—a forecast that drives positions. mechanism-first work can also produce a *measurement deliverable*: a premia estimate, risk attribution, or exposure measurement used to constrain portfolios, construct hedges, or allocate risk budgets. When the deliverable is a measurement, specification correctness matters differently: misspecification (for example, missing variables) can produce "factor mirages"—estimates that appear precise but are causally wrong and fail in live markets (López de Prado and Zoonekynd, 2025).

A simple litmus test: if being wrong means "it doesn't make money after costs," you are in signal territory. If being wrong means "the estimate is biased or misleading," you are in measurement territory. Use this framing to decide what to freeze first (objective, constraints, and evaluation), not to label projects.

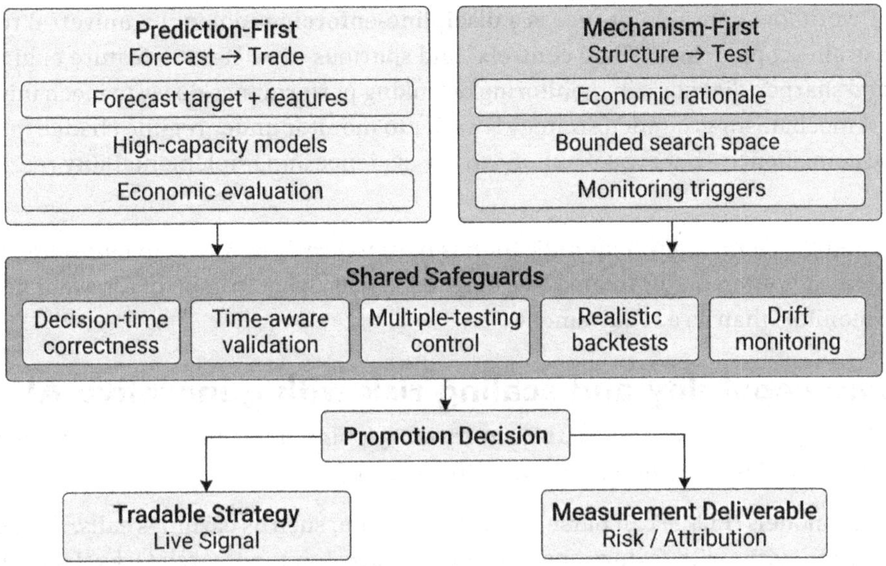

Figure 1.3: Two entry points into one trading research loop

Figure 1.3 shows that both entry points share the same safeguards: decision-time correctness, time-aware validation, multiple-testing control, robust backtests, and drift monitoring. Signal deliverables receive the larger share of treatment in subsequent chapters, which focus on forecasting-driven trading systems. Measurement deliverables—factor premia, risk attribution, hedging—appear primarily in *Chapter 19* and are not a prerequisite for tradable edge.

Causal inference as a discipline-enforcing tool

Causal inference matters here because it strengthens mechanism-first work—both signal and measurement deliverables—and improves diagnosis even when full identification is not feasible.

In trading, prediction alone is an unstable foundation: regimes shift, correlations invert, and the same feature can change meaning when market microstructure, policy, or participant composition changes. A mechanism-based view does not guarantee profits, but it makes research *testable* and monitoring *actionable*: you can state why the strategy should work, which assumptions must hold, and what evidence would invalidate the mechanism.

Stating *why* a strategy should work has always separated durable approaches from data-mined artifacts. In finance, that "why" is hard to establish because we rarely get clean experiments; we work with observational data shaped by confounding, selection, and market feedback. Modern causal inference provides a framework for reasoning under these constraints—using tools such as graphical models, instrumental variables, and causal machine learning—to move from "what predicts returns?" toward "what mechanism could plausibly generate them?", subject to explicit identification assumptions that must be defended and stress-tested (see *Chapters 9* and *15*; Pearl, 2019; Schölkopf et al., 2021).

Causal methods have become increasingly common in empirical finance and systematic investing—recognized by the 2021 Nobel Prize in Economics—but their conclusions remain conditional on identification assumptions that can fail under regime change (Fabozzi et al., 2024; López de Prado et al., 2025).

In the ML4T workflow, causal inference is a **discipline-enforcing tool**, not a universal requirement. It helps constrain scoping, avoid "bad controls" and spurious predictors in feature engineering and modeling, and sharpen diagnosis in monitoring by linking performance decay to mechanism-relevant conditions. A mechanism-grounded strategy is easier to monitor under regime change than one built on statistical coincidence—but robust out-of-sample evidence and implementability remain the final arbiters.

In many trading problems, causal identification is hard to justify and easy to overstate; when identification is weak, it is often better treated as a diagnostic lens (what to control for, what not to control for, what to monitor) than as a requirement.

Expanding capability and scaling risk with generative AI

Generative AI matters because it accelerates every entry point, but it also scales leakage, complexity, and confabulation unless the same safeguards are enforced.

Large language models (LLMs) can parse unstructured data, such as earnings calls, filings, and news sentiment at scale, assist with feature engineering, and accelerate research tasks (Luk, 2023). Within the workflow, generative AI can help with reasoning about trading strategies, improve productivity in data processing and feature generation, and support documentation throughout the process (see *Chapters 23* and *24*).

Automation introduces new failure modes. When models generate text, code, features, or even strategy variants, three risks become acute:

- **Hallucination and confabulation:** Plausible outputs that are wrong, especially in summaries of complex market events or in "explanations" of backtest results.
- **Leakage by construction:** Features, labels, or prompts that inadvertently incorporate future information, not only through subtle timestamp or revision errors but through inclusion in the LLM's training data.
- **Complexity inflation:** Strategy and pipeline bloat—more moving parts, more degrees of freedom, and more ways to overfit—without commensurate evidence of robustness.

The workflow response is the same: enforce decision-time correctness, pre-commit evaluation protocols, and treat automated outputs as candidates that must pass the same evaluation safeguards as any other research artifact. As automation increases, the practitioner's role shifts from "manual implementer" to **supervisor** and **validator**, with explicit governance in deployment (see *Chapter 26*).

Workflow stage	Machine learning	Generative AI
Strategy hypothesis	Anomaly detection and data-quality scoring	Synthesis and hypothesis checklists
Data and QA	Representation learning and embedding features	Document parsing and entity mapping
Feature and label design	Forecasting models and uncertainty calibration	Event extraction and feature ideation
Modeling and evaluation	Risk models and constrained optimization	Coding assistance and experiment summaries
Portfolio and constraints	Impact/cost models and execution policy tuning	Scenario enumeration and constraint encoding
Execution and costs	Drift detection and performance attribution	Venue-rule summaries and runbook assistance
Monitoring and operations	Shared with adjacent stages	Alert triage and incident summaries

Figure 1.4: ML/AI-augmented trading workflow

Figure 1.4 maps machine learning and generative AI contributions across the seven workflow stages: strategy hypothesis, data and QA, feature and label design, modeling and evaluation, portfolio and constraints, execution and costs, and monitoring and operations. At each stage, generative AI accelerates synthesis, documentation, and code production, while machine learning handles measurement: anomaly detection, forecasting, calibration, risk modeling, and drift attribution.

ML and generative AI can assist throughout, but automated outputs remain candidates that must pass the same evaluation safeguards as any other research artifact; monitoring closes the loop by triggering retraining or strategy revision when assumptions fail. We next turn to the challenges of constant change that any live strategy will inevitably face.

1.4 Keeping up with changing market regimes

The disruptions described earlier share a common feature: they reflect shifts in the market environment. A strategy should not try to predict specific events. It should answer an operational question: which market states are adverse for the strategy, and how can those states be detected in time to reduce exposure?

As defined in *Section 1.1*, a **regime** is a persistent market state in which the joint behavior of returns changes materially relative to other periods. Relevant dimensions include expected returns, volatility, cross-asset correlations, and liquidity. A strategy can be correct about its economic mechanism yet fail when its operating assumptions are violated. For example, a strategy calibrated to low volatility can break down when volatility rises, while correlations increase and liquidity deteriorates. Regime awareness is primarily a risk lens, not a return-timing tool.

Regime detection with labeling, conditioning, and monitoring

Regime methods support three tasks that share techniques but require different evaluation standards:

- **Ex post labeling (explanation):** Cluster historical data to build a vocabulary for when a strategy struggled and which market variables changed. This is descriptive and may use the full sample.
- **Backtest conditioning (robustness):** Evaluate performance conditional on labeled states. This is a stress test and must prevent leakage of regime labels into decision-time features or trading rules.
- **Live monitoring (operations):** Detect state changes using only information available at decision time, and evaluate performance using a walk-forward approach. The objective is early warning and risk control, not "regime-timing" alpha.

This separation matters because the most common misuse is to treat ex post labels as if they were known in real time. In this chapter, we use regimes to illustrate *diagnostic overlays* (what tends to break, and what risk action follows), not to propose regime-timing strategies. Throughout the book, regimes are used as *context* for stress testing and monitoring, not as signals that reliably forecast returns.

A practitioner literature applies unsupervised learning to construct regime maps of market history. For example, Two Sigma (Botte and Bao, 2021) applies **Gaussian mixture models (GMMs)** to investment-style returns. Horváth et al. (2021) use Wasserstein k-means (demonstrated in *Chapter 11*). Uysal and Mulvey (2021) use supervised learning to characterize regime-dependent behavior in risk-parity portfolios. The examples below follow this general approach.

Style regimes with century-long factor data

The notebook `factor_regimes.ipynb` uses the **Century of Factor Premia** dataset provided by AQR, one of the largest hedge funds managing over USD 100bn, which reports monthly returns for a broad equity market proxy and several factor portfolios (Ilmanen et al., 2021). These series represent **standardized systematic exposures**—that is, returns to broad, rule-based *styles* (such as value, momentum, carry, or defensive) that can be held across many securities and are designed to reflect common risk/return drivers in markets—rather than returns of individual stocks. The notebook standardizes the series and clusters their joint behavior to identify recurring states in how market and factor returns co-move across decades.

What the model estimates

The notebook fits GMMs with 2–6 components; a two-state specification is the most stable and interpretable in this dataset. AIC prefers K=6, but the silhouette at that choice is near zero and the partition fragments after 1950—a useful reminder that AIC alone is a poor model-selection criterion when the goal is an interpretable regime map. The clusters are then labeled ex post as "Risk-On" and "Risk-Off" based on which cluster coincides with worse equity-market outcomes. This labeling is a post hoc interpretation, not a tradable real-time signal.

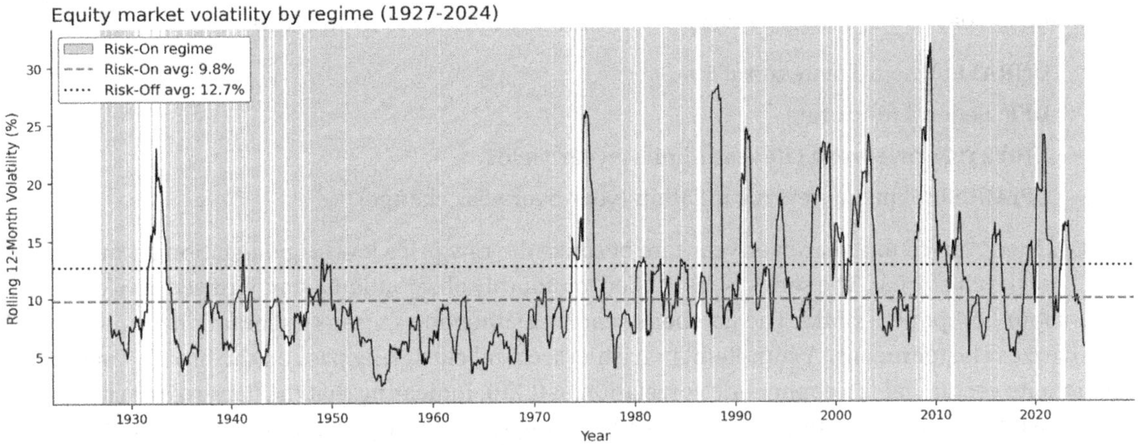

Figure 1.5: Equity market volatility by regime, 1927–2024

Figure 1.5 overlays regime membership with rolling 12-month equity volatility (annualized) and summarizes volatility by regime:

- Risk-Off volatility is 19.1% versus 8.6% in Risk-On (a 2.2× ratio), and the equity market Sharpe ratio drops from 1.11 to 0.12.
- Risk-Off also concentrates drawdown risk, with a maximum drawdown of −77% versus −23% in Risk-On.
- Factor behavior diverges across regimes as well: value is countercyclical (+5.3% annualized in Risk-Off versus +1.6% in Risk-On), while carry (−0.6%) and defensive (−0.5%) turn negative—precisely when diversification is most needed.

A coarse two-state map can separate risk environments in a way that supports concrete controls. The correct approach is not "buy when Risk-On," but to adjust the risk posture when the environment shifts. With 267 regime transitions over 98 years (roughly every 4 months on average), the model switches frequently enough to be noisy as a tactical signal—which reinforces the point that regimes are for risk management, not timing.

In workflow terms, this example illustrates what a regime overlay should provide:

- A compact vocabulary for "calm" versus "stressed" conditions
- A measurable link to risk (here, realized volatility, Sharpe ratio, and drawdown)
- Evidence that factor exposures behave differently across states
- A mapping to risk actions (position sizing, exposure caps, and buffers)

Macro regimes and volatility environments

The factor regime map is a "style" lens: it clusters systematic exposures by how they co-move. A macro regime map clusters *economic conditions* and then evaluates how market risk outcomes vary across those clusters.

The notebook `macro_regimes.ipynb` uses four monthly indicators from FRED:

- **UNRATE:** Unemployment rate
- **DFF:** Federal funds rate
- **T10Y2Y:** Term spread (10-year minus 2-year yield)
- **CPIAUCSL:** Consumer price inflation (year-over-year change)

The CPI is converted to a year-over-year rate because the raw price level is non-stationary and would dominate the clustering. The series is resampled to monthly observations, standardized, and clustered using a four-component GMM. The notebook reports a silhouette score as a separation diagnostic and summarizes cluster means. A complementary hierarchical clustering pass on the broader macroeconomic state vector yields a cophenetic correlation of 0.710, indicating that the dendrogram preserves the pairwise distance structure reasonably well—Ward, GMM, and K-Means give comparable regime structure on this panel.

Because unsupervised clusters are unlabeled, the notebook assigns short interpretive names based on cluster means (for example, high unemployment with near-zero rates suggests a "crisis" configuration; rising rates with a flatter curve and elevated inflation suggest "tightening"). These names are interpretations of the macro configuration, not claims about subsequent market performance.

Market validation – Volatility and drawdowns

To connect macroeconomic regimes to investable outcomes, the notebook uses monthly S&P 500 data evaluates regime-conditional realized volatility and maximum drawdown, with major episodes annotated (for example, the global financial crisis, COVID-19, and the inflation shock). In many applied settings, macro regimes separate *risk conditions* (volatility and drawdown) more cleanly than they separate average returns. Therefore, the notebook treats macro regimes as inputs to **risk management** rather than as return forecasts.

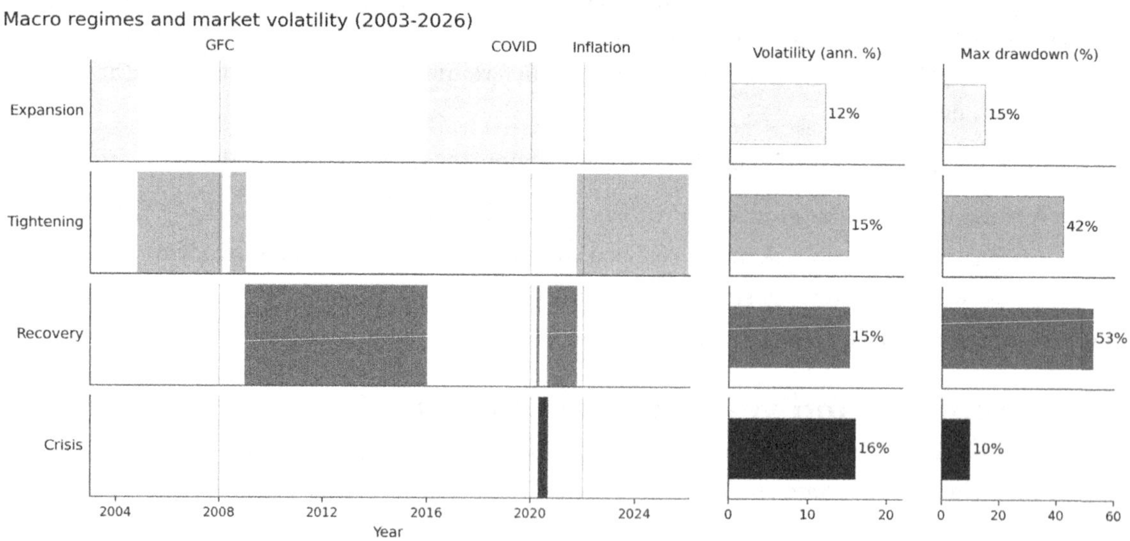

Figure 1.6: Macro regimes and market volatility, 2003–2026

Figure 1.6 shows regime membership over time and summarizes per-regime outcomes (annualized volatility and maximum drawdown), sorted by volatility. The goal is not to claim that macro regimes forecast returns, but to show that macro conditions provide an interpretable overlay for when risk tends to be higher and drawdowns deeper—conditions under which exposure caps, hedging triggers, or de-risking rules are most valuable.

The notebook also includes an extended analysis that expands the feature set to a broader collection of FRED series (for example, breakeven inflation, credit spreads, monetary aggregates, housing indicators, and volatility indices), subject to coverage filters. This yields a richer view of economic conditions at the cost of more noise and more modeling choices.

Real-time detection and risk management

Detecting regime changes as they occur is harder than labeling them after the fact. Sequential change-point tests and regime-switching models (*Chapter 11*) can help, but they must be evaluated strictly in a walk-forward design with decision-time features and out-of-sample monitoring metrics.

For the workflow in this chapter, the practical recommendation is narrower: monitoring should include indicators aligned with a strategy's known vulnerabilities, such as volatility spikes, correlation breaks, liquidity deterioration, or macro-policy pivots. The objective is not to perfectly classify a regime, but to trigger predefined risk actions when conditions that historically harmed the strategy reappear.

Regime models can create false confidence. Common pitfalls include:

- **Look-ahead bias:** Fitting or labeling on the full history and then using those labels in trading logic.
- **Degrees of freedom:** Results are sensitive to features, preprocessing, window lengths, and the number of states.
- **Over-interpretation:** Regimes summarize recurring patterns; they are not explanations.

Use regimes as a **risk lens:** identify which environments degrade the strategy and specify how risk controls will respond to them. The question is not "what regime is the market in?" but "how does this strategy behave when these conditions arise?" For example:

- **Momentum:** Does performance degrade when correlations spike or reversals cluster?
- **Carry:** What happens during funding stress and policy pivots?
- **Mean reversion:** how do drawdowns change when volatility rises and liquidity thins?

Process discipline requires that this environmental awareness be explicit. Pre-commit to regime-sensitive failure criteria, define the monitoring statistics that detect those conditions, and specify the risk actions that follow. We will discuss how to apply process discipline in different settings.

1.5 Independent versus institutional workflows in the real world

The workflow is universal, but the dominant failure modes differ by environment. In large institutions, specialization and independent review create natural friction: execution, risk, and data constraints are enforced by people whose incentives are not aligned with making the backtest look favorable. In a small team or solo practice, that friction is weaker. The primary risk is not insufficient sophistication—it is *unconstrained interpretation*: iterating until a result looks convincing, then treating it as evidence rather than as a candidate that emerged from search.

In the independent setting, we run the same lifecycle (see *Section 1.2*) without external gatekeepers. We must therefore supply our own governance through decision-making discipline: documentation, explicit assumptions, and checkpoints that make it easy to stop, revise, or retire ideas based on the evidence.

Solo failure modes that institutions partially avoid

Institutional infrastructure does not guarantee success, but it mitigates several predictable self-inflicted errors we must address deliberately:

- **Goalpost drift**: After seeing results, it becomes easy to redefine success—accepting lower Sharpe for smaller drawdown. The failure mode is not bad math; it is changing the question after observing outcomes.
- **Assumption stacking**: Strategies often appear profitable only because multiple small assumptions each lean favorably: optimistic fills, end-of-bar execution, understated costs, ignored capacity, or a favorable sample period. Each may seem harmless in isolation; together, they can manufacture performance.
- **Flexibility without accounting**: Large feature sets, extensive tuning, and flexible models increase the odds of finding a lucky winner unless the result is treated as conditional on the search that produced it. Without a research record, it becomes impossible to distinguish learning from selection effects.
- **Late tradability discovery**: Without a separate execution function, weeks of signal refinement can produce a result that cannot survive realistic spreads, slippage, latency, liquidity limits, or risk constraints.

These are not philosophical problems but workflow problems. We address them by making assumptions explicit early, recording the search, and requiring basic checks for implementability and robustness before investing in refinement.

Decision discipline through documentation and checkpoints

A practical solo process requires a small set of documented decisions and checks—not to discourage iteration, but to keep evidence interpretable after we iterate.

Scoping check (implementability first)

Write down the decision point and information set: what arrives when, why it might be slow to price, and what frictions plausibly prevent immediate arbitrage. Record a small number of "stop criteria" that justify ending the project early—turnover that makes costs dominant, capacity that is incompatible with the intended deployment size, or instability across obvious regime slices (see *Section 1.4*).

Data integrity check

Prefer definitions where "what the model knew at time *t*" is unambiguous. Messy point-in-time semantics, corporate actions, revisions, timestamps, or session alignment add uncertainty that can invalidate downstream results.

Signal check (robustness before cleverness)

As flexibility increases, the burden of validation increases. The key question is not "does it look significant," but "does it survive variation": different walk-forward splits, plausible regime slices, modest changes in preprocessing, and conservative cost assumptions. Signals that only work in a narrow configuration should remain in the exploration phase.

Tradability check (fragility audit)

For independent setups, sensitivity tests carry more information than point estimates:

- Does the edge persist if costs are doubled?
- If execution is delayed by seconds or minutes?
- If position sizes or participation are capped?
- If entry and exit timing shifts within the bar?

A strategy that degrades gracefully is more valuable than one that relies on a precise set of optimistic assumptions.

Monitoring check (diagnosis maps to action)

The minimum viable monitoring requirement is the ability to separate signal decay from operational failure. When performance drops, the diagnosis must distinguish a weakened signal, a degraded data pipeline, and rising execution costs, because each implies a different response. Without this separation, intervention reacts to noise, and intervention is itself a source of overfitting.

When failure rates are high, fast, well-documented rejection and clean post-mortems accelerate throughput more than any single refinement.

Constraints and asymmetric advantages

Independent researchers generally should not compete where institutional advantages are structural:

- **Speed and microstructure:** If the strategy depends on being first, it is unlikely to be viable. Favor strategies whose economics tolerate seconds-to-minutes of delay and still survive after costs.

- **High fixed-cost data as prerequisite:** If success requires expensive institutional datasets as a starting point, the capital and tooling gradient is steep. Prefer problems where information is accessible but interpretation and discipline are the differentiators.

Where independents can be advantaged:

- **Capacity-constrained opportunities:** Many effects do not scale. A large fund may ignore them because it cannot deploy size without excessive impact. Independents can operate below the capacity ceiling, provided capacity is modeled honestly and small-size viability is treated as a strategy class rather than a flaw.
- **Tighter iteration loops:** Faster movement from result to diagnosis to revision compounds. The advantage comes not from trying more configurations but from cleaner diagnostics and reusable tooling that lower the marginal cost of the next experiment.

Compounding returns with reusable infrastructure

For independents, the highest-leverage investment is reusable infrastructure that reduces the marginal cost of running disciplined experiments:

- Dataset versioning and point-in-time pipelines
- Standardized backtest and evaluation harnesses
- Shared cost and slippage models with sensitivity tests
- Monitoring templates that map failure modes to actions

Backtest harnesses (*Chapter 16*), cost models (*Chapter 18*), risk and monitoring (*Chapter 19*), and live-operations machinery (*Chapter 25*) develop these in depth. Every strategy we run correctly makes the next one faster, not through a learned trick but through accumulated machinery that makes discipline cheap and repeatable.

1.6 Summary

This chapter's core claim is that durable trading performance depends less on finding a "right model" and more on maintaining a disciplined research-to-production workflow that withstands non-stationarity, costs, and operational frictions. Market shocks are routine occurrences in which relationships shift, and assumptions fail; without disciplined iteration, backtests document narratives rather than supply evidence.

The ML4T Workflow provides that discipline: a persistent data-infrastructure foundation and an iterative research loop that moves from scoping invariants (decision-time correctness, tradability, labels, cost model, evaluation protocol) to features, models, strategy design, deployment, and monitoring. The evidence boundary formalizes the separation of exploration from confirmation through trial logging, sealed holdouts, and selection-aware inference. Causal inference and generative AI can strengthen this process, but in the absence of guardrails, they also amplify failure modes, especially for independent researchers who lack institutional friction.

Chapter 2, The Financial Data Universe, lays the foundation by introducing the asset classes, data structures, and storage choices that the workflow operates on.

2

The Financial Data Universe

The financial data landscape is expanding, and the surface area for analytical error grows in parallel. Alternative data providers have proliferated over the past decade alongside the broader expansion of large-scale data infrastructure, adding satellite imagery, credit card panels, and social sentiment feeds. Exchanges publish once-proprietary microstructure feeds. New providers are broadening access to institutional-grade market data. Prediction markets such as Polymarket and Kalshi add a new class of event-contract data. This expansion creates both opportunity and complexity.

Rigorous data management determines whether that complexity becomes insight or noise. Point-in-time errors, survivorship bias, and mishandled corporate actions have always invalidated backtests; each new source expands the failure surface. The value alternative data adds depends on the strategy, but it increases the number of ways a pipeline can fail. Vendor evaluation requires discipline across quality, legal, and technical dimensions. Storage decisions between parquet files, time-series databases, and lakehouse formats shape research velocity and production feasibility.

Chapter 1 established the ML4T workflow and emphasized process discipline. Before specifying strategies, we need to understand the data landscape—its possibilities, constraints, and failure modes. This chapter maps that universe, focusing on *three questions*: what kinds of data exist, which specific data challenges arise across asset classes, and which decisions matter along the dimensions of quality, sourcing, and storage. The following chapters deepen this foundation: market microstructure (*Chapter 3*), fundamental and alternative data (*Chapter 4*), and synthetic data generation (*Chapter 5*). Strategy specification (*Chapter 6*) builds on these data foundations. At the end of this chapter, you will be able to:

- Distinguish between Market, Fundamental, and Alternative data and their quality challenges.
- Evaluate the trade-offs between data availability and transparency across major asset classes.
- Apply a five-dimensional data-quality framework and identify specific failure modes in financial data.
- Conduct systematic vendor due diligence across technical, legal, and commercial factors.
- Select storage technologies based on access patterns and operational requirements.

This chapter and the next three focus on **dataset characteristics**—what data exists, how it behaves, and what can go wrong. They cover the raw material for strategy development, a process that begins in *Chapter 6*.

2.1 A Modern taxonomy of financial data

A dataset is a set of measurements, along with the rules that make those measurements comparable over time. It is a particular way of measuring real-world activity. That measurement comes with built-in definitions: timestamp conventions, trading calendars, adjustment policies, identifier schemes, and rules for revisions or restatements. These are not optional details; understanding them is necessary to understanding what the data *means*.

Because every dataset embeds definitions, the first question is what real-world process it measures: trading, fundamentals, or proxies. Financial data falls into three categories:

- **Market data:** Records what the market did—quotes, trades, and derived aggregates
- **Fundamental data:** Captures economic drivers of value (definitions vary by asset class)
- **Alternative data:** Signals not in standard market or fundamental feeds, often proxies for fundamentals

This taxonomy helps you reason about the kinds of real-world activity a dataset represents, what it omits, and the errors it can introduce. When you download "daily prices," you are adopting the provider's definitions. Define "close": last trade, auction close, or a timestamped snapshot (and in which timezone)? Are splits and dividends reflected point-in-time or back-adjusted? If you get any of these wrong, you may not see an obvious failure. Instead, you get silent misalignment and biased results that propagate through feature engineering, labels, and backtests.

Before you model anything, lock down four items: timestamp semantics, corporate-action adjustment methodology, identifier stability, and the handling of revisions and restatements. Make these choices explicit in your pipeline configuration and carry them forward as metadata, so downstream code cannot accidentally reinterpret the data. These issues are the focus of this chapter and the next two.

Market data – A hierarchy of aggregation

Market data reflects trading activity in financial markets. It embodies the institutional setting that shapes this activity, from centralized exchanges to over-the-counter environments. It originates in real time with message-level events related to individual orders and executions. Vendors typically aggregate this data in real time over a given interval to produce the familiar open, high, low, close, and volume summaries. Moving up the aggregation spectrum makes data easier to store and model, but discards micro-level information about supply and demand dynamics.

At the base, raw event streams reflect the mechanics of the trading venue: how orders are posted and matched, when trades are reported, and what trading rules apply. In modern markets, trading is split across multiple venues, including off-exchange venues such as dark pools, internalizing broker-dealers, and other alternative trading systems. As a result, "the best price" you see depends on which venues your feed covers and how it merges them.

Exchanges sell high-quality data products with strong completeness guarantees and validation fields; free feeds are often delayed, filtered, or missing metadata needed to verify correctness. Sourcing and validation discipline applies even to "basic" price data, regardless of cost.

Chapter 3 covers working with market data across levels of aggregation, including order-book reconstruction from tick data and the construction of analytical bars at multiple frequencies.

Fundamental data – Drivers of value with release lags

Fundamentals are economic variables that justify valuations. What counts as "fundamental" depends on asset class and institutional framework:

- **Equities:** Financial statements, corporate actions, guidance
- **Commodities:** Inventories, production, shipping, weather
- **Foreign Exchange (FX):** Interest rates, inflation, growth, policy
- **Crypto:** Issuance schedules, fees, on-chain activity, liquidity structure

Two properties drive most engineering errors:

- **Release-time data, not event-time data.** Fundamentals arrive with lags, schedules, embargoes, and revisions. The relevant question is not "what is the value," but "what was knowable at decision time."
- **Shaped by rules.** Accounting standards determine what equities disclose. Government agencies define commodity reporting. Statistical agencies revise macro series and publish vintages. Protocol rules govern which crypto variables are observable. Interpreting fundamentals requires understanding institutional constraints, not just downloading a series.

Chapter 4 works with three primary sources of fundamental data:

- For **equities**, we use regulatory filings to extract balance sheet and income statement data, using point-in-time filing dates to support bitemporal queries that respect announcement timing.
- For **macro**, we use the Federal Reserve's FRED data service to retrieve Treasury yields, unemployment claims, inflation measures, and volatility indices, with explicit handling of release schedules and vintage corrections.
- For **commodities**, we use CFTC Commitment of Traders reports to track institutional and speculator positioning in futures markets.

Alternative data – High variety, high validation burden

Alternative data extends observations beyond standardized price feeds and structured public information, such as regulatory filings. The rise of alternative data over the last decade reflects the broader trend toward digitalization (Ekster and Kolm, 2020).

Many categories of alternative data give timelier or more granular views of economic activity, which makes them useful complements to fundamental data:

- **Geospatial/mobility:** Satellite imagery, foot traffic, shipping AIS
- **Consumer analytics:** Credit/debit panels, app usage, web traffic
- **Corporate exhaust:** Job postings, procurement, supply-chain signals
- **Text/events:** News, earnings calls, filings, social media
- **ESG/disclosures:** Emissions, workforce metrics, governance ratings

While alternative data may provide novel measurements, it comes with its own interpretation challenges. For each category, the validation questions are: How stable is coverage over time? What selection effects exist in the sample? Can you reproduce the methodology? Do usage rights permit your intended deployment?

Chapter 4 applies the alternative data evaluation framework to three categories:

- **Prediction markets**—both CFTC-regulated Kalshi (economic events: Fed decisions, CPI, unemployment) and crypto-based Polymarket—show how to extract probability time series and engineer features from event contracts.
- **On-chain crypto data** from DeFi Llama provides Total Value Locked (TVL) metrics for protocol activity, evaluated as a forward-return predictor across major chains (see *Chapter 4* for the panel construction and IC analysis).
- **Text data** from SEC EDGAR filings demonstrate extraction pipelines that feed into NLP features, covered in more detail in *Chapter 10*.

The next section surveys market data across asset classes, lists the datasets used throughout the book, and points to the notebooks that explore them.

2.2 The asset-class market data landscape

Data characteristics vary across asset classes because market structures and economic determinants of value differ. The organization of trading—exchanges versus over-the-counter (OTC), electronic versus voice, consolidated versus fragmented—determines what market data you can obtain, how informative this data is, and where engineering choices affect results.

Table 2.1 summarizes observability, key failure modes, and engineering priorities across asset classes:

Asset Class	Observability	Key Failure Modes	Engineering Priority
Equities	High (consolidated)	Corp actions, fragmentation, identifiers	Adjustment methodology
Futures	High (exchange)	Roll rules, continuity method	Continuous series construction
Options	High (but sparse tails)	Illiquidity noise, surface construction	Surface representation
Digital Assets	Medium (venue-specific)	Volume integrity, 24/7 sessionization	Venue screening
FX	Low (OTC)	No consolidated tape, close conventions	Aggregation rule definition
Fixed Income	Low (OTC, sparse)	Matrix pricing, indicative versus firm	Liquidity inference

Asset Class	Observability	Key Failure Modes	Engineering Priority
Swaps/OTC	Low (reported)	Curve construction, convention mismatches	Curve-based representation
Commodities	Medium (futures high)	Spot ambiguity, delivery specs	Contract spec in metadata

Table 2.1: Asset class overview

The subsections move from exchange-traded instruments (equities, futures, options, digital assets), where data is richer and more standardized, to OTC markets (foreign exchange, fixed income, swaps, commodities), where data is sparser and conventions more fragmented.

Equities

Global equity market capitalization was approximately $126.7T (WFE, 2024); U.S. equity market cap was about $67.7T (SIFMA, Q3 2025). Listed equities trade on multiple lit exchanges and off-exchange venues (ATS/dark pools and retail wholesalers/internalizers). In the U.S., consolidated reporting defines a market-wide best bid and offer (NBBO) and publishes consolidated quotes and trades; direct venue feeds can be faster and expose richer detail, but cost more.

What you observe

Equity market structure varies along three axes that affect what you can observe and how you should define "the price":

- **Consolidation versus fragmentation.** Some jurisdictions provide consolidated reporting, while others have historically been fragmented across venues. The EU's consolidated tape for equities launches in 2026.
- **Auction intensity.** Many markets rely heavily on opening and closing auctions, which can dominate end-of-day liquidity and benchmark pricing. "Close" often means "auction close," not "last trade."
- **Trading constraints and conventions.** Tick sizes, short-selling constraints, price limits/volatility interruptions, and settlement conventions differ across markets and can alter the meaning of intraday liquidity measures and transaction cost estimates.

Quotes, trades, and derived bars are widely available for liquid names, but "best price" and "available liquidity" depend on feed scope and aggregation rules. Treat each venue feed as a partial view of the market; any consolidated view is a constructed aggregate with its own timestamps, inclusion rules, and latency profile.

Failure modes

Fragmentation creates ambiguity about timestamps and aggregation (especially when stitching venues or mixing consolidated and direct feeds). Corporate actions (splits, dividends, spinoffs) create discontinuities that require consistent adjustment and return definitions. International datasets add additional pitfalls: currency conversion and FX timestamps, withholding taxes for dividend-inclusive series, and cross-listing/ADR mapping that can break identifier joins.

Engineering decisions

Before research, clarify and document:

- Your definition of "close" (auction versus last trade; local close convention)
- Whether you use consolidated versus venue feeds for quotes
- Your corporate-action and total-return methodology
- Identifier policy for cross-listed names

These are dataset design choices with material impact on results.

Datasets

We use free daily data on 3,199 US equities (1962–2018) sourced from NASDAQ (the original Quandl WIKI price data, no longer updated after the Quandl acquisition). We also use two commercial datasets generously provided by Algoseek: daily OHLCV bars for S&P 500 constituents (2017-21) and minute bars for NASDAQ 100 constituents (2020-21), enriched with several dozen ML-focused market microstructure features.

Notebooks: `01_us_equities_eda` explores US equity characteristics; `02_corporate_actions` validates adjustment factors and compares unadjusted versus adjusted returns. We will explore the Algoseek NASDAQ 100 data in *Chapter 3* on Market Microstructure.

Exchange-traded products

Exchange-traded products (**ETPs**) are *exchange-listed wrappers that package exposures* to one or more underlying markets. They trade like equities—with quotes, trades, and order books—but holdings, index rules, and replication mechanics. ETPs may wrap bond, commodity, FX, volatility, or multi-asset exposures, so their trading and risk characteristics reflect both the wrapper and the underlying assets. ETPs also differ across common structures:

- **Exchange-traded funds (ETFs)** use a **creation/redemption** mechanism with authorized participants that links secondary-market prices to underlying asset values.
- **Exchange-traded notes (ETNs)** are unsecured debt instruments; they embed **issuer credit risk** and may track an index via an issuer promise rather than a fund structure.
- **Closed-end funds (CEFs)** generally lack continuous creation/redemption and can trade at **persistent premiums/discounts** to NAV.

What you observe

Consolidated quotes and trades, bars, and (from direct feeds) deeper order book information. Unlike single-name equities, ETP research requires a second layer of data:

- NAV (typically end-of-day) and, for many ETFs, an **intraday indicative value**.
- **Holdings and weights** (or index constituents) are often updated daily, but sometimes disclosed with or as representative baskets.

- **Fund actions** such as distributions, splits, and (for leveraged/inverse products) periodic rebalancing that alter exposure through time.

Failure modes

ETPs bundle a range of different products; therefore, the failure modes multiply:

- **Return definition.** Distributions like dividends or coupons are often material. Price-only series can understate returns and distort volatility; the "adjusted close" embeds vendor-specific adjustment methodology (see *Section 2.3* and *Chapter 4*). Be also explicit about (i) total versus price return, (ii) reinvested versus cash distributions, and (iii) taxes and currency treatment where relevant.
- **Premium/discount.** Traded prices can deviate from NAV, especially when the underlying market is closed, illiquid, or stressed. Avoid treating NAV returns as tradable.
- **Liquidity mismatch.** A liquid ETF can wrap illiquid underlyings. Secondary-market liquidity can overstate true capacity when flows are transmitted to constituents through creation/redemption or dealer hedging, particularly in stress regimes.
- **Look-through leakage.** Holdings and baskets change through rebalances and at the manager's discretion, and public holdings data may not be point-in-time. Using today's holdings to compute yesterday's exposures creates subtle forward-looking bias.
- **Replication complexity.** Many ETPs hold complex products: commodity products may be **futures-based**, leveraged/inverse products are **path-dependent** due to daily rebalancing, and options-overlay products embed *volatility surface* dynamics.

Engineering decisions

Treat ETPs as a distinct dataset type. At minimum, lockdown:

- **Return methodology:** Price versus total return; distribution handling; currency conversion.
- **Valuation anchor:** Price, NAV, or both, and which is used for signals versus evaluation.
- **Exposure mapping:** Holdings versus index constituents versus factor proxies; point-in-time and disclosure-lag policy.
- **Liquidity model:** ETF-level costs versus look-through capacity constraints for large orders/stress regimes.
- **Replication metadata:** Physical versus synthetic; futures-based; leveraged/inverse; options overlay.

> **Datasets and notebooks:** We use daily data on 100 ETFs (2006–2025) sourced from Yahoo Finance, with 50 categorized by asset class for the rotation case study. Liquidity spans a 23× range between SPY (126M shares/day) and the Commodities bucket (5.5M); 41 of the 100 ETFs launched after 2006, constraining lookback for features and evaluation. The notebook `03_etfs_eda` introduces this dataset.

Futures

Global exchange-traded futures volume in 2024 was about ~28B contracts (FIA). Futures trade on exchanges with transparent contract-level data. The complication is identity over time: a market is a sequence of expiring contracts with shifting liquidity.

What you observe

High-quality prices, volume, and open interest per contract. No perpetual ticker exists—you must construct one.

Failure modes

Roll rules (calendar, volume, open-interest) and continuity methods (ratio adjustment, difference adjustment) are backtest-defining choices. Different strategies need different roll logic.

Back-adjusted continuous series typically preserve futures price PnL but do not embed collateral return (margin interest). Back-adjusted continuous series often behave like **excess-return** proxies unless you explicitly model collateral return. When comparing to spot assets or total-return indices, be explicit about whether you model futures PnL, collateral return, or their sum.

Engineering decision

Store raw contract histories, along with one or more continuous variants so you can test and reconstruct roll decisions.

Datasets

We use hourly data on 30 CME futures for a diverse set of underlyings covering 2011-25, sourced from Databento.

> **Notebooks:** `04_cme_futures_eda` explores the futures data; `05_futures_session_aggregation` shows how to align the data with CME trading sessions; and `06_futures_continuous` demonstrates volume-based roll detection and the two mainstream back-adjustment methods (ratio and difference), validated against the vendor's pre-built continuous series.

Options

Global exchange-traded options volume in 2024 was about ~177B contracts (FIA). Listed options are electronically quoted, but the instrument space explodes across strikes, expiries, and types. Liquidity is highly uneven—concentrated in near-money, near-dated contracts.

What you observe

Rich quote and trade data for liquid strikes; sparse and noisy data elsewhere.

Failure modes

Storing and modeling the whole chain is expensive and mostly illiquid noise. Treating the chain as a single "dataset" conflates liquid and illiquid instruments.

Engineering decision

Represent options markets through derived surfaces—implied volatility surfaces, ATM vol, skew, term structure—rather than raw chains. This representation is a dataset design decision: the surface is the dataset, not a summary of it. Store volume and open interest for liquid contracts; ignore or aggregate the illiquid tail.

Datasets

S&P 500 daily options prices and analytics covering 2017-2021 provided by AlgoSeek. The notebook `07_sp500_options_eda` explores this dataset; the notebook `08_options_greeks_computation` derives Black-Scholes pricing and Greeks from first principles—Delta, Gamma, Vega, Theta, and Rho—and validates Delta, Gamma, Vega, and Theta against vendor-computed values; `09_options_continuous` demonstrates roll contamination in constant-maturity option series and constructs backtestable continuous returns.

Digital assets

Total crypto market capitalization was about ~$3T on 18 January 2026 (CoinMarketCap). Digital assets combine centralized exchanges (CEX) with familiar order books and decentralized exchanges (DEX) with automated market makers. The on-chain state is publicly observable, while exchange microstructure is venue-specific.

What you observe

CEX data resembles equities: spreads, depth, order flow—the microstructure concepts we will discuss in *Chapter 3* apply directly, and order book reconstruction works as expected. DEX data differs fundamentally: AMMs replace order books with reserve-based pricing (for example, constant-product AMMs; concentrated-liquidity designs generalize this), where price emerges from reserve ratios rather than bid-ask matching. There is no order book to reconstruct; "depth" becomes slippage at a given trade size, computable directly from pool reserves.

Failure modes

24/7 trading complicates sessionization. Reported volume on some venues is unreliable. **Maximal extractable value** (**MEV**) refers to the profit that validators or other actors can capture by reordering, inserting, or censoring transactions within a block; together with impermanent loss and on-chain latency, it materially affects DEX execution. Venue fragmentation makes cross-exchange comparison difficult.

Engineering decision

Screen venues for integrity before including them. Handle 24/7 timestamps explicitly. For DEXs, derive slippage and liquidity from reserves rather than treating AMM quotes as order-book depth.

Datasets

We use Perpetual Futures prices at hourly frequency and Premium Index at 8-hour intervals for 19 symbols covering 2020-25, sourced from Binance. The notebooks `10_crypto_perps_eda` and `11_crypto_premium_analysis` explore this data; the funding-rate premium analysis is relevant to funding arbitrage strategies.

Foreign exchange

Global daily average FX turnover was about ~$7.5T/day (April 2022, Fed NYC). FX is predominantly OTC with no single consolidated tape. Even "daily close" (for example, 5 pm New York) is a convention, not an exchange-defined event. Different platforms display different liquidity and spreads.

What you observe

Venue-specific quotes without centrally reported volume. In FX, "the price" is a convention: you choose a venue and an aggregation rule (mid, best-of, VW-mid).

Failure modes

Assuming a single authoritative price when none exists. Stale quotes, crossed markets, and outlier filtering all require explicit rules.

Concrete example

A "4 pm London close" and a "5 pm New York close" for EUR/USD often differ by several pips on volatile days. If your strategy mixes close conventions across currencies, you may be comparing non-comparable timestamps.

Engineering decision

Specify which price you can realistically trade: best-of aggregation, volume-weighted mid, or a specific venue. Document the close convention in your dataset metadata.

Datasets

We use 20 currency pairs at 4-hour intervals from 2011–2025 via OANDA and explore this data in the notebook `12_fx_pairs_eda`.

Fixed income

The outstanding amount in the global fixed-income market was approximately ~$145T (2024, SIFMA). Fixed income is predominantly OTC, with a vast instrument universe—thousands of corporate bonds and tens of thousands of municipal bonds. Many instruments trade infrequently; quoted markets may be indicative rather than firm.

What you observe

Sparse transaction prints, indicative quotes, and model-derived valuations. When the last trade is stale, research pipelines operate on yields, curves, and inferred prices rather than clean price series.

Failure modes

Liquidity estimation is an inference problem, not a measurement. Matrix pricing—mapping illiquid bonds to similar liquid instruments—introduces model assumptions. Still, any approach requires distinguishing between observed prints and indicative quotes, and between model outputs and model inputs.

Engineering decision

Decide how to handle illiquid instruments: exclude them, impute prices via matrix pricing, or model them separately. Document the methodology because "price" means different things for liquid treasuries versus thin municipals.

Swaps and OTC derivatives (rates, credit)

OTC derivatives notional amounts are enormous (~$846T in mid-2025, BIS), but **notional is not exposure**; it mainly reflects contract scaling. **Interest rate derivatives** accounted for ~79% of OTC derivatives notional (~$670T). Swaps markets sit "behind" much of modern fixed income and macro trading. Interest rate swaps, OIS, cross-currency swaps, and CDS are primarily OTC (with varying degrees of central clearing), and their data is shaped by reporting regimes and market conventions rather than a single consolidated tape.

What you observe

Post-trade reporting (where available), indicative dealer runs, cleared pricing where accessible, and curve-building inputs rather than a single authoritative "price series." Even when transactions are reported, timestamps, block-size masking, and venue fragmentation can affect what is observable at research granularity.

Failure modes

Treating OTC quotes as firm executable prices; mixing venues/reporting feeds with incompatible conventions; and building curves without consistent day-count, calendars, collateral/discounting conventions, or roll rules. Many downstream "returns" are artifacts of choices in curve construction.

Engineering decision

Decide whether your dataset is (1) transaction-based, (2) quote-based, or (3) curve/surface-based—and treat that choice as fundamental. For rates, store curve snapshots with explicit conventions; for credit, separate index products from single-name CDS; and keep a clear line between observed inputs and model-derived marks.

Commodities

Exchange-traded commodity derivatives volume was about ~8B contracts in 2024 (options and futures, FIA). Commodity datasets sit at the intersection of financial markets and physical constraints. "Spot" is often not a single tradable object (and can be reported, assessed, or location-specific), while futures curves are standardized, liquid, and exchange-observable for major commodities.

What you observe

Futures prices and term structures are typically the most reliable market data. Physical-market indicators (inventories, shipping, weather, refinery runs) often drive fundamentals but are subject to reporting lags and coverage bias.

Failure modes

Treating assessed spot series as if they were exchange-traded prices; ignoring contract specs (delivery location/grade) that determine basis; and mixing curve snapshots from different timestamps when computing roll yield or calendar spreads.

Engineering decision

Decide whether your "commodity price" is (1) a specific futures contract, (2) a continuous futures series (with explicit roll/adjustment), or (3) a curve representation (front-to-back term structure). Store the contract spec metadata in the dataset, not as documentation.

Microstructure tooling applicability

Chapter 3 discusses order-book reconstruction and bar-sampling methods. They apply directly to exchange-traded instruments (equities, futures, options, CEX crypto). They do not apply to OTC markets (much of fixed income many swaps) where quotes are indicative and fragmented across dealers, nor to DEX AMMs where no order book exists. For these markets, alternative approaches—such as quote aggregation, curve construction, matrix pricing, and reserve-based liquidity computation—are required.

Next, we discuss how to evaluate data sources and providers.

2.3 A due diligence framework for data sourcing

Data sourcing discipline catches defects before they become "alpha" (risk-adjusted trading gains) in a backtest and turn into production losses. Errors are systematic, not random: microstructure artifacts, reporting lags, revisions, corporate actions, and vendor backfills create error patterns that can inflate or deflate apparent performance. A single undetected defect can invalidate months of research. Luo et al. (2014) catalog systematic errors that inflate backtest returns; López de Prado (2018) emphasizes that many ML strategy failures trace to data issues rather than modeling.

General data quality dimensions

Data quality assessment typically spans five dimensions:

- **Timeliness:** Lag/latency from release/event to availability
- **Completeness:** Coverage gaps across instruments, dates, and fields
- **Accuracy:** Values match ground truth
- **Consistency:** Stable schemas and definitions over time
- **Validity:** Constraints satisfied (timestamps ordered; values within plausible bounds; field-level invariants hold)

Implementation: `13_data_quality_framework` implements an automated validation pipeline using the `ml4t-data` library to check these dimensions on OHLCV data. The 100-ETF panel from `03_etfs_eda` illustrates the scale to expect: 473 OHLC invariant violations (~0.1% of rows) trace to independent split and dividend adjustment of the four price fields, an artifact small enough to ignore for most uses but worth flagging in a vendor-comparison report. Prioritize checks that create lookahead bias (PIT, backfills, revisions) and universe leakage (survivorship).

This section covers data quality issues applicable to *all* financial data. For evaluation criteria specific to alternative data, see *Section 4.4*.

Finance-specific failure modes

Four failure modes commonly result in manufactured alpha:

Point-in-time correctness

Point-in-time (**PIT**) correctness means that every value used in historical research reflects what was *knowable at the time of the decision*, under the definitions and reporting conventions in force . PIT violations occur when datasets are revised after the fact, and you unknowingly train or backtest on the revised version.

Common culprits include revisions and restatements (fundamentals, macro), corporate action backfills, delayed or amended filings, and vendor database updates that overwrite history.

Example failure. A company reports Q4 2019 revenue as $91.8B in early 2020. By 2024, after a restatement, a vendor's database shows $92.3B for the same quarter. If you query "Q4 2019 revenue" today and use it in a 2020 backtest, you have introduced lookahead bias: the model is trained on information that did not exist at the time of the decision.

Fixing PIT requires **bitemporal storage** and **as-of queries**. A PIT-correct system stores values along with the period they refer to and when each value became publicly observable, so you can reconstruct the historical information set exactly as it existed at time t. We use the following terms to describe PIT correctness:

- **Event time:** When the economic event occurred (for example, end of Q4 2019)
- **Knowledge time:** When the information became publicly available (for example, filing acceptance time)
- **As-of time:** The historical moment being reconstructed in your analysis (the decision time)
- **Reference period:** What the value refers to (for example, "Q4 2019 revenue")

Figure 2.1 illustrates PIT correctness for fundamental data.

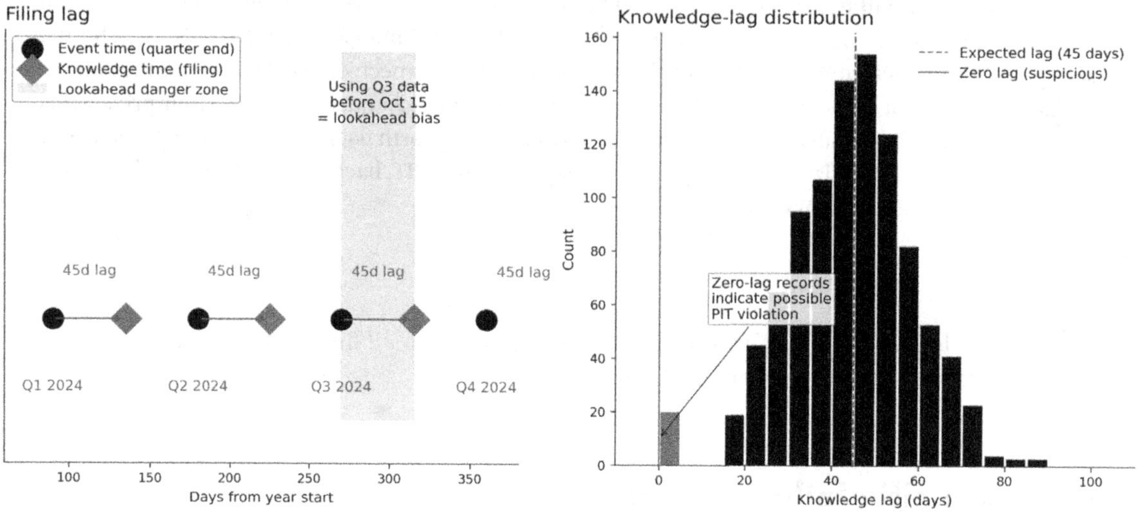

Figure 2.1: Point-in-time correctness for fundamental data

The left panel shows the "lookahead danger zone" between event time and knowledge time; the right panel highlights zero-lag records as a red flag. The companion notebook `14_point_in_time_validation` demonstrates bitemporal query patterns and produces *Figure 2.1*.

For any fundamental or alternative metric, store the *valid time interval* the value describes and the *availability* timestamp when that specific value became observable. Each record should also include a stable `source_id` (for example, SEC accession number or agency release identifier), an `entity_id` at the intended layer (issuer versus security), and a `version` identifier. A downstream feature at decision time *t* may use a record only if `available_at <= t`.

All joins across data sources must be constrained by `available_at <= decision_time`. For identifier mappings (for example, ticker→CIK, CUSIP→ISIN), also require that `effective_date <= decision_time < end_date`, so the mapping was valid at the decision point. Violating either constraint introduces lookahead bias—often silently—through "correct" joins that were impossible at the time.

Before using any dataset with fundamental-like inputs, verify PIT correctness across three dimensions:

Dimension	Question	Failure mode
Values	Does each data point have both a valid time and an availability (knowledge) time?	Using restated values for historical decisions
Universe	Is index/universe membership tracked historically?	Survivorship bias from current-day selection
Identifiers	Are entity mappings time-valid (ticker changes, mergers)?	Joining data across corporate events incorrectly

Table 2.2: PIT checklist

A dataset that passes value-level PIT but fails universe-level PIT can still produce biased backtests, especially for cross-sectional strategies and historical index universes.

Survivorship bias

Survivorship bias occurs when the historical universe is filtered using information from the future (for example, "still exists today"). Its effect can be positive or negative depending on what you exclude: excluding *bankruptcies* inflates returns (you miss losses), while excluding merger and acquisition (M&A) targets can deflate returns (because you may miss acquisition premiums). The missing names are not random: they include bankruptcies, delistings, acquisitions, and value traps—precisely the types of situations many strategies are exposed to. Therefore, the entities that "survive" are biased towards cases that did not experience such situations.

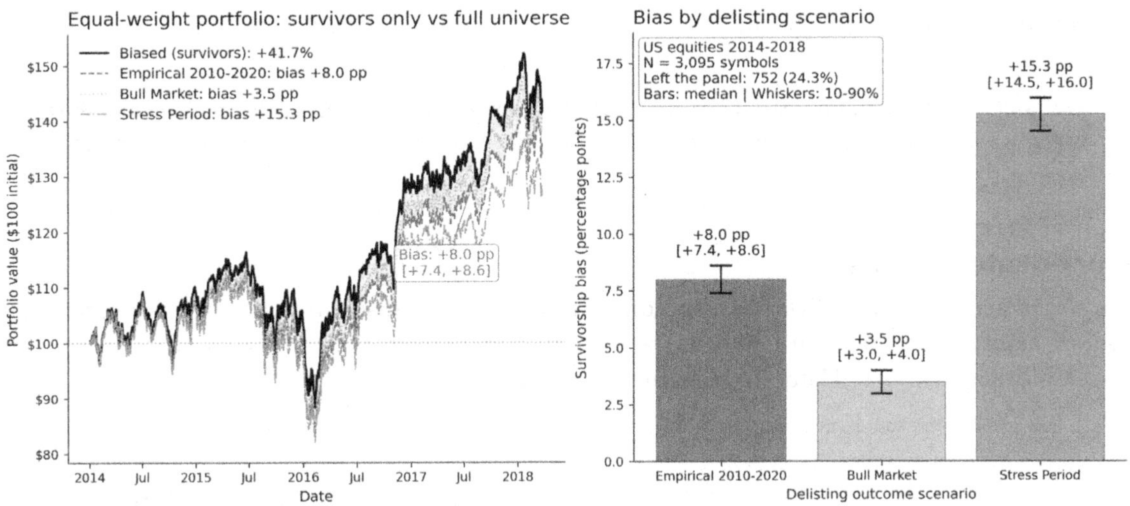

Figure 2.2: Survivors overstate the full-universe return (2014–2018 US equities panel)

The *US equities panel* contains 3,199 stocks, 777 of which (24.3%) were delisted before the dataset's end date—all after 2014, the only window in which the legacy Quandl WIKI feed captured delistings. Quantifying survivorship bias requires simulating terminal returns for delisted stocks by exit reason: distressed delistings, M&A, or voluntary exits, each with its own probability and terminal return. Eckbo and Lithell (2025) tabulate CRSP 2010–2020 outcome shares; the empirical scenario applies those tabulations, assuming 26% compliance failures at −60%, 65% acquisitions at +25%, and 9% other exits at 0%. Terminal returns are conservatively applied on the delisting date itself. In practice, acquisition premiums often materialize gradually as deal rumors circulate and the price converges toward the offer, so by delisting day, much of the +25% may already be priced in; bankruptcy losses, by contrast, tend to be more sudden. Therefore, this calibration overstates the magnitude of bias on M&A-heavy panels.

Figure 2.2 shows the results across Monte Carlo simulations with 1,000 draws per scenario. Over 2014–2018, survivorship bias inflated perceived returns by 3.5–15.3 percentage points across the three scenarios (+8.0 in the empirical scenario): dropping the delisted names removes the weaker half of the distribution, since the leavers returned a median +13.5% against the survivors' +30.8%. The sign of the bias depends on the dominant delisting cause: bankruptcy-heavy periods inflate survivor returns, while M&A-heavy periods can deflate them. Shumway (1997) and Beaver, McNichols, and Price (2007) document the underlying patterns of delisting returns.

The sign of the bias depends on the dominant delisting cause: bankruptcy-heavy periods inflate survivor returns, while M&A-heavy periods, such as the 2010–2017 sample, deflate them. Shumway (1997) and Beaver, McNichols, and Price (2007) document the underlying patterns of delisting returns.

Another source of bias is using today's S&P 500 constituents as the "universe" for a historical backtest. Even if those companies survive, the selection criterion is outcome-dependent: current members are firms that have grown large and successful enough to be included in the index. Backtesting on them retroactively bakes that success filter into the experiment.

The remedy: point-in-time universe construction. The 2010 backtest uses 2010 membership, with correct handling of delisting returns and corporate actions. CRSP is widely used as a benchmark for survivorship-aware U.S. equity data because it tracks delistings over long horizons, but many institutional vendors provide comparable histories.

> **Implementation:** `15_survivorship_bias_detection` quantifies delisting rates and shows how the composition of delisted names (M&A versus distress) affects the magnitude of the bias.

Corporate actions

Corporate actions—splits, dividends, spinoffs, mergers—create discontinuities in price series that require adjustment. The failure mode is the mixing of adjustment methodologies or the use of end-of-sample factors (covered later in this chapter) in historical research.

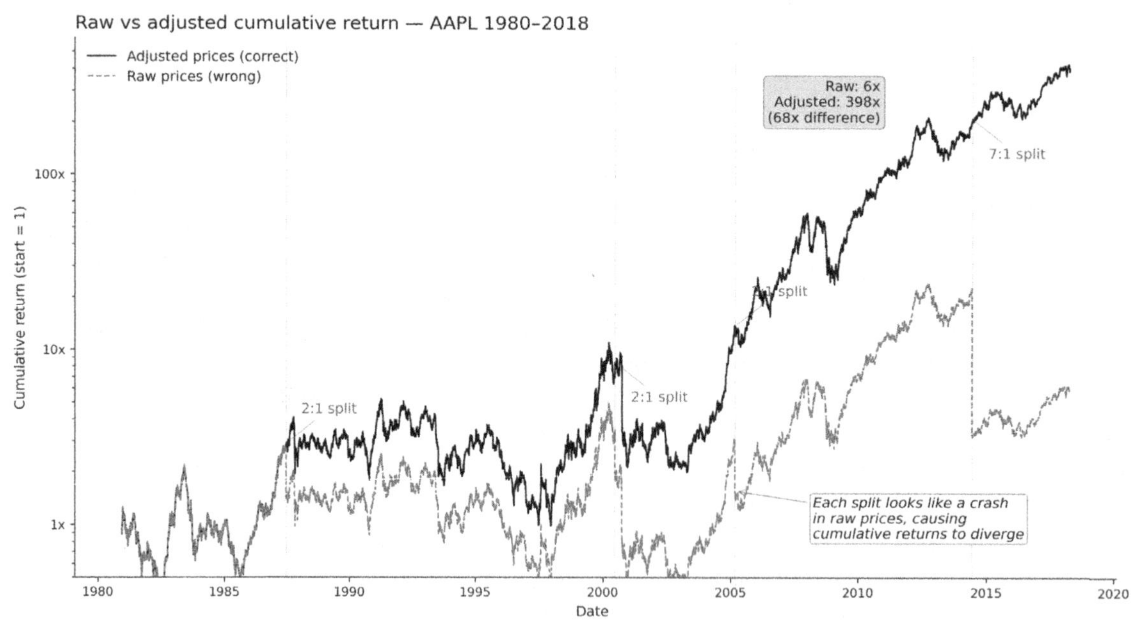

Figure 2.3: A graph comparing raw and adjusted prices impacted by corporate actions

A 7:1 stock split makes raw prices appear to have crashed by ~86%. Computing returns from unadjusted prices understates cumulative performance by a catastrophic margin. *Figure 2.3* illustrates this for AAPL: over its multi-decade price history (four splits plus dividends within the Wiki/Quandl panel through 2018), raw prices show a 5.9× cumulative return, while adjusted prices show a 398× return, a roughly 68× understatement.

Adjustment methodologies differ. Some vendors provide point-in-time adjustments (as-known-then factors); others offer back-adjusted series (end-of-sample factors applied retroactively). Mixing them introduces lookahead. Vendors also differ in how they handle dividends (total return versus price return), spin-offs, and rights issues.

The remedy: document and validate your adjustment methodology. `02_corporate_actions` validates adjustment factors against Apple's known historical splits. *Chapter 3* covers the mechanics in detail.

Identifier integrity

Identifier joins can align the wrong instrument. Ticker symbols get reused (when an old company delists, a new company takes the symbol). CUSIP changes through mergers. Vendor IDs have edge cases.

This creates fake alpha. Suppose your signal table has ticker "XYZ" from 2015, and your price table has "XYZ" from 2020, but these are different companies. The join succeeds; the signal now predicts the returns of a different company. If the second company happened to perform well, you have manufactured correlation from a data error.

The remedy: use permanent IDs with effective date ranges (vendor permanent IDs; FIGI/ISIN/CUSIP via crosswalks). `16_provider_comparison` demonstrates multi-source stitching with careful handling of identifiers; `17_complete_pipeline` shows Hive partitioning patterns that preserve identifier integrity across incremental writes.

The vendor ecosystem

Vendors span a wide range of cost and capability; key attributes that vary with cost include depth (intraday versus daily), history length, handling of corporate actions, PIT support, latency, redistribution rights, and methodology auditability.

Tier	Typical Profile	PIT Support	Survivorship-aware	Best For
Free/public	Easy access, limited guarantees	Rare (macro vintages via ALFRED)	Rare	Learning, prototypes, sanity checks
Prosumer (API-first)	Good coverage for liquid markets	Partial	Sometimes partial	Individual research
Institutional	Deeper history, documented methodology	Often available	Often available	Production, regulated environments

Table 2.3: Data provider tiers

When deciding what to buy and what to build, separate differentiating work (strategy-specific transforms) from commoditized work (clean histories, identifier crosswalks):

- *Build* the strategy-specific parts: ingestion pipelines, storage and versioning, validation checks, canonical identifiers, and the transformations that encode your assumptions (such as sessionization, adjustment policies, roll rules, PIT-aware features).
- *Buy* when the problem is non-differentiating or prohibitively expensive to reproduce: long-horizon cleaned histories, corporate action adjustments at scale, survivorship-aware universes, and standard identifier crosswalks (for example, FIGI mappings, Bloomberg identifiers).

Entity and identifier mapping is often a months-long effort: tracking an instrument across ticker changes, mergers, and cross-vendor conventions. Whether you buy vendor crosswalks or build your own, treat identifier integrity as core risk control.

Vendor due diligence checklist

Vendor selection is risk management. In practice, diligence comes down to three questions: Can you trust the numbers? Are you allowed to use them as intended? Will the vendor behave like a reliable dependency?

Data quality

The first task is to determine whether the dataset supports historically correct analysis rather than just convenient access to current values. That means checking not only what fields are available, but also how the vendor handles time, revisions, identifiers, and corporate events.

Key questions include:

- **PIT support**: Can the vendor provide snapshots or as-of queries? How are revisions handled?
- **Survivorship awareness**: Are delistings included with the correct final prices?
- **Adjustment methodology**: How are splits, dividends, and other corporate actions handled? Is the methodology documented and stable?
- **Coverage and definitions**: What is the true start date, instrument coverage, update cadence, and field definition?
- **Identifier integrity**: Which identifier scheme is used, and how are mappings handled through ticker reuse, mergers, and other entity changes?

These questions establish whether the dataset is analytically credible; the next step is to confirm that it is also permissible and defensible to use.

Legal and compliance

Even high-quality data can create problems if the rights and provenance are unclear. This review should establish that the data is lawfully sourced, that usage is permitted for the intended workflow, and that the vendor can document its methods if needed. Focus on four issues:

- **MNPI screening**: Does the vendor have documented provenance controls?

- **Privacy and consent:** For consumer data, is the collection compliant with GDPR, CCPA, and similar rules?
- **Usage rights:** What is permitted for backtests, live trading, redistribution, and model training?
- **Auditability:** Can the vendor provide documentation of its methodology for regulators, clients, or internal control functions?

Once the legal footing is clear, the practical question is whether the vendor can operate as a stable part of your research and production stack.

Technical and commercial

A vendor also needs to function as a dependable production dependency. Strong content is not enough if the delivery model is fragile, opaque, or difficult to integrate into research and live systems. In particular, assess the following:

- **Reliability:** Is there a status page, uptime history, or SLA?
- **Change management:** Are schema changes and methodology revisions versioned and communicated clearly?
- **Access patterns:** Are rate limits, bulk exports, and backfill mechanisms compatible with your pipelines?
- **Portability:** Can you export the data in a usable format, and are the exit terms reasonable?

If the vendor looks sound in principle, the next step is a short hands-on validation to confirm that the data behaves as expected in practice.

Minimum viable data validation checklist

Once a vendor passes initial due diligence, a brief validation pass should confirm that the dataset is usable for research. At a minimum, verify the following:

- **PIT:** No zero-lag records for delayed data
- **Survivorship:** Historical universe not filtered by future information
- **Corporate actions:** Adjustment methodology documented
- **Identifiers:** Join on permanent IDs + effective dates
- **Timestamps:** Timezone explicit, session assignment clear
- **Outliers:** Stale quote and anomaly detection in place
- **Versioning:** Reproducible as-of queries possible

Vendor diligence, however, is only part of the control framework; internal processes are also required to make data issues visible, traceable, and reversible.

Data governance

Good vendors do not replace internal governance, which makes problems discoverable and reversible across five areas:

- **Lineage:** Track where each dataset came from and how it was transformed.

- **Versioning:** Version data rather than overwriting. When you fix an error, preserve the ability to reproduce prior results.
- **Logging:** Log cleaning decisions so results are reproducible.
- **Validation automation:** Use tools like Great Expectations or Pandera; fail loudly on violations rather than silently dropping records. `13_data_quality_framework` provides the `AnomalyManager` toolkit, which produces JSON audit trails for each validation run.
- **Parallel runs:** When switching vendors or methodologies, run sources in parallel long enough to quantify differences. Preserve rollback options.

Treat sourcing as risk management: PIT and survivorship checks prevent the most expensive errors. The next section turns to efficient data storage.

2.4 Storing data

Storage is the foundation of research velocity and production reliability. There is no best solution independent of access patterns and operational constraints. The right choice depends on data volume, access patterns (scans, point lookups, range queries, joins), concurrency requirements, and operational maturity.

What we benchmark and why

These benchmarks address two distinct questions:

- **File formats:** If your data lives in files (the most common research pattern), which format gives the best trade-off between size, read speed, and write speed?
- **Database engines:** When you need SQL queries, concurrent access, or time-series operations like ASOF joins (see *ASOF join performance* in this chapter), which engines perform well for financial data workflows?

We separate these because most research workflows start with files (Parquet) and add databases only when the use case demands it. The benchmarks help you decide if and when to make that transition.

Benchmark context and caveats

The tables and figures in this section summarize benchmarks from the companion code at the L scale (approximately 1 million OHLCV rows, 64 MB of in-memory storage in Polars). The repository includes scripts to run at larger scales (XL: 10 million rows, XXL: 100 million rows) on your hardware.

Keep the following in mind when interpreting benchmark results:

- **Operation definitions matter.** "Read time" can mean opening a file handle, scanning a subset of columns, or fully scanning all data. Arrow IPC supports memory mapping, so opening the file does not necessarily load the entire file into RAM.
- **Warm versus cold cache.** A warm-up run often primes the OS page cache, making subsequent reads far faster than true cold reads.
- **Relative rankings are more portable than absolute times.** Treat the numbers as illustrative for your hardware and workload; use the companion scripts to generate benchmarks on your own systems.

File-based storage

We benchmarked file formats on a 1-million-row OHLCV dataset (100 symbols × 10,000 bars). *Figure 2.4* traces read-time scaling across formats as the row count grows; columnar formats hold their advantage as size increases, while CSV read time degrades linearly.

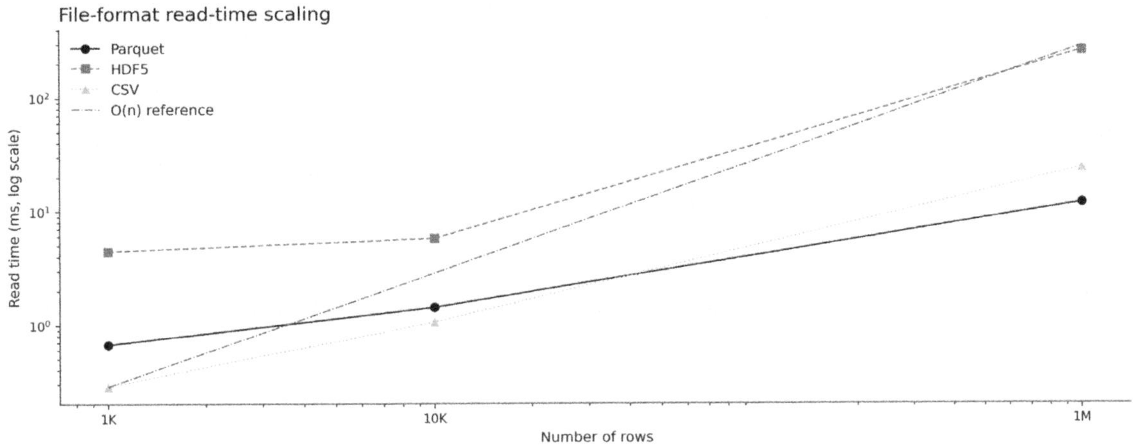

Figure 2.4: File format read-time scaling with dataset size

Table 2.4 summarizes file size, write time, and scan time at L scale for the three formats suitable for persistent storage. Rankings are often more stable than absolute timings, but ingestion paths and caching can materially affect results.

Format	File Size	Write Time	Full Scan	Notes
CSV	136 MB	0.13s	0.05s	Baseline: engine-dependent overhead
Parquet	40 MB	0.07s	0.02s	Columnar, compressed, selective reads
HDF5	71 MB	0.13s	0.40s	Performance depends on chunking

Table 2.4: File storage benchmark results

When choosing a format:

- **Parquet:** Recommended default for research and production: strong compression (3.4× versus CSV), efficient columnar reads, universal tool support across Python, R, Spark, and cloud platforms.
- **HDF5:** Still common in scientific and legacy finance stacks. It can work well for specific append-and-chunked access patterns, but read performance lags behind columnar formats.
- **CSV:** Use for exports and interoperability, not as a primary analytical store.

Note on Arrow IPC (Feather)

Arrow IPC is a fast serialization format optimized for interchange. It excels at moving data between notebooks and processes (including memory-mapped reads), but lacks key "data lake" features such as predicate pushdown, partition-aware layouts, and multi-file governance. Use it for short-lived interchange; use Parquet for persistent, queryable storage.

Lakehouse formats (such as **Delta Lake**, **Iceberg**, and **Hudi**) store data in Parquet and include a transaction log that provides ACID semantics, schema evolution, and multi-writer governance. Start with plain, partitioned Parquet; adopt a lakehouse format when you need update-heavy workflows, schema evolution with strong guarantees, or concurrent writes across multiple teams.

Implementation: `20_storage_benchmark_file` reproduces these benchmarks and extends them to larger scales.

Embedded analytics databases

Embedded databases provide SQL analytics without running a server:

- **DuckDB**: An in-process analytical database optimized for OLAP workloads. It can query Parquet directly and supports ASOF joins in SQL, making it a strong default for research workflows that want SQL semantics over a Parquet data lake.
- **SQLite**: A reliable embedded relational database for metadata, configuration, and small relational tables. Not competitive with DuckDB for analytical scans or time-series workloads.
- **ArcticDB**: A DataFrame-oriented store with versioning and time-travel. It is licensed under **BSL 1.1** (with time-based conversion to Apache 2.0 per release); verify licensing and operational constraints before adopting.

A useful default architecture:

1. Store raw and curated data as partitioned Parquet.
2. Use DuckDB for SQL analytics and quick joins over those files.
3. Use a DataFrame engine, such as Polars, for feature engineering. See `22_pandas_polars_benchmark` for an empirical pandas-versus-Polars comparison across read, groupby, join, and lazy-evaluation operations.

Server time-series databases

Server databases are valuable when you need concurrent access, centralized governance, strict durability, and production-service levels.

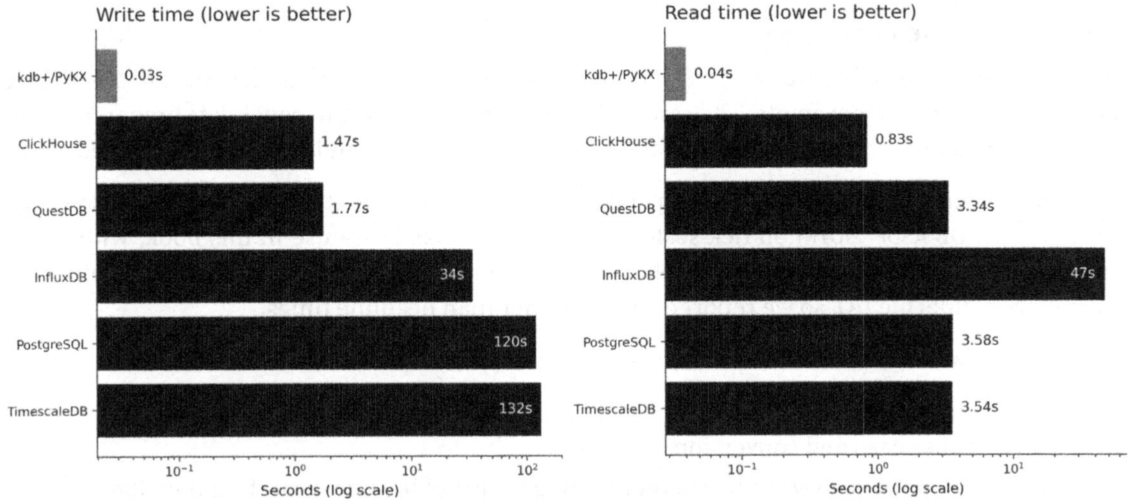

Figure 2.5: Server database comparison (1 million rows)

Figure 2.5 compares write and read performance across six server databases at L scale (kdb+/PyKX, ClickHouse, QuestDB, PostgreSQL, TimescaleDB, and InfluxDB). These results are directional; write time is sensitive to ingestion method, schema design, and durability settings. Rerun benchmarks using your intended ingestion path before making decisions.

Server time-series databases include:

- **kdb+/KDB X**: A highly optimized time-series and analytical engine widely used in market data contexts. KX offers free editions with material limits (often non-commercial); verify current license terms before committing.
- **ClickHouse**: A general-purpose OLAP database optimized for high-throughput columnar analytics, with strong SQL support and a large ecosystem.
- **QuestDB**: A time-series database optimized for ingestion and time-series SQL, including ASOF-style queries. Supports tiered storage patterns with Parquet for colder data.
- **PostgreSQL/TimescaleDB**: PostgreSQL is the default general-purpose relational database; TimescaleDB extends it with hypertables (automatic time partitioning) and continuous aggregates for time-bucketed rollups.
- **InfluxDB**: Designed for metrics and observability workloads. Flux supports equi-joins, but as-of style joins are not a native primitive; treat it as a monitoring database rather than a market microstructure engine.

Implementation: `21_storage_benchmark_database` provides reproducible server benchmarks. For production-grade orchestration, `18_data_management` composes the DataManager, Universe, and HiveStorage primitives into a working pipeline, while `19_incremental_updates` walks the daily-update lifecycle with weekend-aware gap detection and a health dashboard.

ASOF join performance

ASOF joins align events that are not perfectly time-synchronized—matching each trade to the most recent prevailing quote, for example. They are typically the dominant cost in panel-data preparation that mixes tick streams with slower-moving reference series. Both pandas and Polars require sorted inputs.

In-memory engines (Polars `join_asof` and pandas `merge_asof`) consistently outperform embedded-SQL engines (DuckDB `ASOF JOIN`) on tick-scale workloads at the sizes we use in this book, with Polars typically the fastest of the three. The absolute gap depends on hardware, sort state, and whether the benchmark counts file I/O, so we report ordering rather than headline times.

A few measurement caveats matter when comparing implementations:

- In-memory engines measure join execution when data is already loaded; SQL engines may include file scans and conversion overhead.
- For fair comparisons, decide whether sorting is part of the benchmark. If the pipeline maintains sorted data, exclude sorting consistently across engines.
- Tick-versus-quote ASOF performance is sensitive to the ratio of left- to right-side rows; benchmark at the ratio that matches the intended workload.

Strategic decision framework

The following matrix summarizes standard defaults by objective.

Objective	Strong default	Also consider
Research velocity	Parquet + Polars	Parquet + DuckDB
SQL analytics on files	DuckDB + Parquet	Polars lazy scans
Production reliability	PostgreSQL	TimescaleDB
Extreme time-series throughput	kdb+/KDB X	ClickHouse
High-throughput ingestion	QuestDB	ClickHouse
ASOF joins in memory	Polars	pandas
ASOF joins with SQL	DuckDB	QuestDB
Lowest operational burden	Parquet + DuckDB	Managed Postgres

Table 2.5: Recommended default and strong alternative by storage objective

Start with partitioned Parquet plus Polars or DuckDB. Add server databases when concurrency and governance requirements justify the operational overhead.

2.5 Summary

This chapter mapped the financial data universe and the decisions that make research reproducible. Use the taxonomy—market, fundamental, and alternative data—to match datasets to strategy horizons and to surface the assumptions embedded in timestamps, adjustments, identifiers, and revision rules.

Most alpha failures in production trace to a small set of data defects: point-in-time violations, survivorship bias, corporate action mistakes, and identifier join errors. Treat these as default risks rather than edge cases, and design validation checks to catch them early.

Market structure constrains what you can observe across asset classes: exchange-traded markets provide richer event data but require careful sessionization and adjustments; OTC markets often rely on indicative quotes and inferred prices; derivatives require explicit contract identity and roll logic; digital assets add 24/7 trading and venue-integrity concerns. Vendor selection is therefore a risk management process that involves evaluating quality, legal rights, and operational reliability.

Finally, storage choices determine iteration speed. A sensible default is partitioned Parquet queried DuckDB or Polars for most research; add specialized databases only when concurrency, governance, or latency requirements justify the operational cost.

Chapter 3 develops the details of market data—both as a key input to labels and features for modeling and as the basis for simulating historic strategy performance—and examines the institutional environment of exchanges that shapes how market data should be interpreted.

3

Market Microstructure

Market prices result from an engine that matches supply and demand under explicit rules. These matching engine rules determine what the data means (what counts as a trade, a quote, a "close"), and what a strategy can realistically earn once spreads, depth, and execution constraints come into play. We lay the foundation for working with modern market data, from parsing raw exchange messages to reconstructing order books and sampling tick-level data into bars whose statistical properties match how information arrives.

Consider a simple momentum rule: buy when the price rises above its 20-day moving average. A naïve backtest might use daily closes and assume immediate fills at the bar's end price. In live markets, execution is shaped by the order book:

- A market buy typically executes at the **ask** and a market sell at the **bid**, so traders pay the spread rather than transacting at the last price or a bar reference such as the "close."
- Execution quality depends on *available depth and queue position*. Larger or poorly timed orders can walk the book, fill partially, and move prices.
- In volatile periods, spreads widen and displayed depth becomes less reliable as cancellations accelerate, making "filled at the close" a fragile assumption even at daily horizons.

When backtests ignore spreads, depth, and queueing, the error is not just a "cost" but a mis-modeled price-formation process. Our goal is to make the price-formation process explicit so readers can (i) interpret market data correctly, (ii) choose sampling methods that respect how information arrives, and (iii) model execution and transaction costs in a way that survives contact with real markets. After completing this chapter, you will be able to:

- Explain how liquidity, order types, and price discovery shape market data (*Section 3.1*).
- Describe the main market data feed types from market-by-order to aggregated bars (*Section 3.2*).
- Parse exchange messages and reconstruct a limit order book (LOB) from an event stream (*Section 3.3*).
- Build time- and information-driven bars to reduce noise and improve statistical properties (*Section 3.4*).

- Detect price jumps in intraday returns and separate continuous from jump variance (*Section 3.5*).
- Apply data-quality and sessionization controls for intraday data (*Section 3.6*).

Section 3.2 introduces the five tick-level sources used in this chapter, positions each within the data hierarchy, and explains what analyses each enables.

3.1 How microstructure impacts price formation

Market data is the observable output of a matching engine: rules plus order flow produce quotes and trades. As O'Hara (1995) emphasizes, market structure choices have first-order effects on trading costs and price discovery. Without these mechanics, the data is easy to misread, strategies are mis-specified, and backtests do not survive contact with real execution.

At the core, trading coordinates latent supply and demand among anonymous counterparties. The **bid** is the highest price a buyer is willing to pay; the **ask** (or offer) is the lowest price a seller is willing to accept. Their difference, the **bid–ask spread**, is both a fundamental transaction cost and a primary measure of liquidity. For trading decisions, liquidity has three separable dimensions:

- **Spread:** The cost of immediate execution. Tighter spreads generally indicate more competitive markets.
- **Depth:** The quantity available at and away from the best prices. Depth determines how much can be traded before prices move.
- **Resiliency:** How quickly liquidity replenishes after trades consume it.

Together, these dimensions determine the feasibility of strategy: small signals cannot overcome wide spreads, and large positions require depth and resilience.

The frictions faced by liquidity providers

Participants either supply liquidity with resting orders or demand it with marketable orders:

- **Liquidity providers** (including market makers) post limit orders that supply quotes. They earn the spread *in expectation*, but only if they control selection risk and manage inventory.
- **Liquidity takers** demand immediacy by submitting marketable orders (market orders or aggressively priced limits). They incur spread costs and execution costs that depend on depth, volatility, and routing.

Two frictions drive quote formation and realized spreads:

1. **Adverse selection:** Liquidity providers quote under information asymmetry: if counterparties trade on information not yet reflected in prices, passive fills become losses. Providers respond by widening spreads, shading quotes, or reducing displayed depth to compensate for expected losses.

   Kyle (1985) formalizes this: price impact is proportional to net order flow, with **Kyle's lambda** measuring the strength of price responses to trade imbalances—a key input for the execution cost models we develop in *Chapter 18*. Glosten and Milgrom (1985) show that bid-ask spreads arise purely from adverse selection, even in the absence of transaction costs.

2. **Inventory risk:** Providing liquidity requires accumulating positions. A provider that becomes too long into a falling market, or too short into a rising one, can lose more on inventory than it earns from spread capture. Therefore, inventory constraints influence both quote placement and supply depth.

The spread compensates for **order processing** (fees, technology), **inventory holding**, and **adverse selection.** Madhavan (2002) shows that price impact has both temporary and permanent components, and is nonlinear in order size. In fast markets, adverse selection dominates; in calmer conditions, fee schedules and venue incentives matter more.

How order types express intent in the limit order book

Orders encode trading intent. Their details determine how a trade executes, what is paid in spreads and slippage, and what can be inferred from quotes and prints.

A **resting order** adds displayed depth; a **marketable order** removes it by crossing the spread.

- **Marketable orders** (market orders and marketable limit orders) execute immediately against the best available resting liquidity. Trade prints typically appear at the current best bid/ask, alongside a corresponding reduction in displayed size at that level (often followed by a price change if the level is exhausted).
- **Limit orders** specify a worst acceptable price. If priced to rest, they add liquidity at their price level (increasing displayed depth, and sometimes improving the best bid/ask). If priced to cross, they behave like marketable orders but with a price bound.
- **Stop and stop-limit orders** activate when a reference price crosses a threshold. Stops are often broker-managed and therefore absent from exchange-visible book data until triggered. Once triggered, a **stop-market** becomes a marketable order (often visible as a burst of executions and rapid top-of-book depletion near the trigger). In contrast, a **stop-limit** becomes a limit order that may not fill if the market moves past it quickly.

Modern venues also offer order types that reduce information leakage or automate repricing:

- **Hidden and iceberg orders** trade without fully displaying size, disguising intent. A common signature is repeated same-price prints with the displayed quote size refreshing rather than depleting.
- **Pegged orders** automatically reprice to a reference (often the midpoint or best quote). A common signature is prints inside the spread (for example, at the midpoint) without a corresponding displayed quote at that exact price.
- **Post-only orders** are designed to *rest* (maker behavior): they add liquidity and are rejected or repriced rather than executed immediately if they would cross the spread.

These signatures are useful diagnostics but only suggestive: hidden liquidity and routing can generate similar prints. Repeated fills with quote refresh suggest non-displayed supply; inside-the-spread prints suggest reference-priced liquidity that may never appear in the visible book.

Market design and intraday regimes

Markets match orders through different mechanisms, and microstructure varies predictably over the trading day; both dimensions shape what the data means and when signals are actionable.

Electronic limit order books dominate modern price formation, with orders executing under price-time priority across multiple venues. Quote-driven markets remain important in OTC, FX, and fixed income, where dealer inventory and relationship pricing shape execution. Periodic auctions—especially opening and closing—concentrate liquidity and set benchmark reference prices.

Intraday seasonality is a first-order confounder: the same "signal" can mean different things at 9:35 AM and 2:00 PM. Three regimes dominate:

- **Opening** (first 30–60 minutes): High volatility, wide spreads, heavy trading as overnight information is incorporated. Madhavan, Richardson, and Roomans (1997) show that information asymmetry—measured via the MRR model—starts high at the open and declines as prices are discovered, while inventory costs rise toward the close. Schwartz, Ross, and Ozenbas (2022) confirm that variance ratios remain elevated in the opening half-hour, indicating microstructure noise rather than fundamental information.
- **Midday**: Lower activity, thinner liquidity. Spreads may tighten, but depth is shallow—the same order size has greater price impact than during busier periods.
- **Closing** (final hour): Elevated volume as institutions complete programs and index funds rebalance. The closing auction concentrates substantial liquidity and sets reference prices for benchmarks and settlement.

These U-shaped patterns in volume, volatility, and spreads shape execution timing and signal interpretation. Across the 13-day ITCH sample, the first and final 30 minutes each account for roughly 15–17% of daily volume, compared with 2.6% at midday—about a 6× open-to-midday ratio (see `06_itch_intraday_patterns`).

O'Hara (2015) emphasizes that algorithmic trading has altered flow interpretation: institutional parent orders now break into many passive child orders so that a large buy may appear as a stream of sell-side prints (passive fills on the bid). This can confound naive trade-signing heuristics. The next section turns to the content of market data feeds.

3.2 The anatomy of modern market data feeds

Market data arrives through a hierarchy of feeds that differ in *latency, cost, coverage, and information content*. Reck (2022) offers a practitioner's view of how market design choices propagate into data products and, ultimately, what strategies are feasible. In practice, data decisions are part of strategy design: the feed you can afford and process determines what you can observe (and which information is not visible), how quickly you can observe it, and which research and backtesting assumptions are defensible.

The data hierarchy – From best quote to full order book

Vendor terminology varies; here, we define the distinctions among market data feeds by information content: top-of-book, price-level depth, and order-level events. Examples use U.S. equities, but the hierarchy generalizes across venues and asset classes:

Level 1 (L1): Top-of-book quotes

L1 provides the *best displayed prices* currently available.

- **What it is:** The highest bid and lowest ask at the top of the book.
- **BBO** is venue-specific (in other words, the best bid/offer for a given venue).
- **NBBO** is the national best bid/offer across protected exchanges via the SIP (top of book). It reflects protected quotations on exchanges (not dark pools/internalizers), and its construction depends on the prevailing lot/quotation rules.
- **What you can do with it:** Compute spreads and midprice, build basic **Trades and Quotes** (**TAQ**) signals, and define immediately actionable reference prices.
- **What it hides:** Depth beyond the top level and any queue dynamics that determine fill probability and slippage.

Level 2 (L2): Market-by-price depth (MBP)

L2 adds *displayed depth (number of resting limit orders) by price level* on each venue (often top N levels).

- **What it is:** Aggregated size at each price level (orders are combined by price).
- **What you can do with it:** Estimate displayed liquidity, depth imbalance, and execution difficulty beyond top-of-book.
- **What it hides:** Order count, queue position, and time priority within a price level.

Level 3 (L3): Market-by-order messages (MBO)

L3 provides *order-level events* that allow deterministic replay of the book state.

- **What it is:** Submissions, modifications, cancellations, and executions at the individual order level.
- **What you can do with it:** Reconstruct venue-level book state and measure order flow (cancellations, replenishment, event-by-event dynamics).
- **What it hides:** Nothing about displayed order flow on that venue—but it is more demanding operationally and typically more expensive than L1/L2.

Most commercial "tick" products are TAQ; deeper products add depth or order messages.

Trades and quotes – The standard data package

Most medium-horizon strategies can be built from TAQ alone (prices, spreads, volume, and basic liquidity proxies).

- **Trades** are completed transactions with price and size.

- **Quotes** summarize the displayed bid/offer (top-of-book); depth is provided separately in L2/MBP products.

In U.S. equities, consolidated infrastructure produces a market-wide view of top-of-book quotes and trades (including the official NBBO), while exchanges sell proprietary direct feeds with faster delivery and richer fields. Consolidated feeds prioritize coverage; direct feeds prioritize speed and venue-specific detail.

TAQ-style datasets are sufficient for many medium-horizon strategies, but they are limited for microstructure work. Without order-level messages, you cannot reconstruct the evolving book, estimate queue position, or directly measure liquidity replenishment and cancellation dynamics.

Enriched TAQ products (for example, minute bars with precomputed microstructure fields) can help bridge part of this gap by incorporating trade-direction buckets, quote-pressure proxies, or off-exchange activity. They are useful, but treat them as *derived features* with embedded assumptions. Understanding what they measure (see `13_algoseek_minute_bars_eda.py` for the 61-column schema) prepares the way for feature engineering in *Chapter 8*.

Price conventions in this chapter

Different data products expose different "prices," and they are not interchangeable. We use the following conventions and label them explicitly in figures and captions:

- **Midprice:** (bid + ask) / 2, computed from the relevant L1 quote (venue BBO or consolidated NBBO, depending on the feed). We use midprice changes as a default proxy for price discovery because it reduces bid–ask bounce relative to trade prices.
- **Last trade (print):** The most recent transaction price. It reflects a completed trade but includes microstructure noise from trade direction and execution venue.
- **Close:** In bar construction, typically the last trade within the bar interval; for daily bars, often the official closing price from the exchange's closing auction.

Rule of thumb: Use midprice for measuring short-horizon price response (signals); use executable prices (bid for sells, ask for buys) for PnL markouts; use last trade/close for standard OHLC bars unless stated otherwise.

These distinctions shape strategy feasibility. L1 signals are widely available and therefore more crowded. Strategies that depend on depth, queue dynamics, or very short-horizon order flow usually require L2 or L3—and that shift increases engineering requirements and data costs.

The feeds, books, and bars in this chapter are outputs of market microstructure mechanisms, not neutral measurements. That perspective helps you choose fit-for-purpose data, encode realistic backtest assumptions, and make sampling decisions that reduce bias rather than create it.

Sample datasets – From MBO to enriched bars

This chapter uses five tick-level sources spanning the data hierarchy:

Market-by-order (L3):

- **NASDAQ ITCH** provides order-level events for LOB reconstruction and order-flow analysis (notebooks `01–07`, with bar sampling on the same source in notebooks `14–16`). Raw binary messages (>10GB/day uncompressed for our sample) require parsing but offer complete visibility into venue-level book dynamics.
- **DataBento MBO** offers similar granularity in a user-friendly format on a commercial basis (notebooks `08`, `09`, and `17`).

Market-by-price depth (L2):

- **IEX HIST** provides free, publicly accessible depth data aggregated by price level (L2). You can build a price-level book (aggregate size at each price level), but you can't track individual orders or queue positions. Simpler than MBO but sufficient for spread analysis and depth-based signals (notebook `10`).

Trades and quotes:

- **AlgoSeek TAQ** delivers nanosecond-precision trades and NBBO quotes without depth. Notebooks `11–12` analyze tick-level patterns during the March 2020 crash.
- **AlgoSeek minute bars** provide 61 precomputed microstructure columns derived from TAQ data—trade buckets, pressure indicators, and off-exchange volume—serving as input to *Chapter 7* feature engineering (notebook `13`).

These sources illustrate a practical reality: "tick data" is a family of products, not a single standard.

Message protocols – From human-readable to fast binary

The hierarchy maps directly to distribution protocols: TAQ-style consolidation vs. venue-direct binary feeds; crypto often via APIs:

- The **FIX** protocol remains central to *order entry* and many *post-trade workflows*, but it is not designed for high-rate public-market data distribution.
- Real-time exchange feeds typically use **binary protocols and multicast** for high throughput. Examples include NASDAQ ITCH (notebook `01_itch_parser`), NYSE XDP, and Cboe PITCH.
- Crypto markets often expose data through API-style access: **REST** for historical downloads and **WebSocket** streams for real-time updates. The barrier to entry is lower, but stability, rate limits, schema drift, and cross-venue timestamp synchronization become first-order data-quality problems.

Further reading: Novocin and Weber (2022) examine how blockchain, decentralized autonomous organizations, and generative AI are reshaping exchange platforms and the data products built on them.

Data integrity challenges

At high frequencies, infrastructure details become data-quality constraints:

- **Latency and co-location:** For sub-second strategies, *where* you ingest data, and *which feed you use* can change what you observe. SEC market structure work and SIP latency analyses (Holden et al., 2023) document that consolidation and distribution introduce delays, and that direct feeds can arrive earlier—differences that can range from hundreds of microseconds to single-digit milliseconds depending on network design and proximity. Aquilina et al. (2021) assert that latency arbitrage races occur roughly once per minute per liquid symbol (FTSE 100), with the modal race lasting just 5–10 microseconds, and impose an aggregate tax of approximately 0.5 basis points on trading—billions of dollars annually across global equity markets.
- **Timestamp semantics:** Vendors may normalize, truncate, or re-stamp timestamps. Verify whether a timestamp reflects the exchange event, SIP publication, vendor processing, or local arrival.
- **Exchange time versus decision time:** Treating exchange time as decision time creates look-ahead bias when observation and processing delays are ignored. Use arrival timestamps when available, or apply conservative lags when they are not—especially for event studies and sub-second strategies—depending on the estimated event travel time. Holden et al. (2023) emphasize that latency affects trade–quote alignment and can bias standard microstructure measures if handled incorrectly.
- **Corrections and cancellations:** Real feeds include corrections, cancellations, and late reports. For historical research, prefer vendor-cleaned end-of-day datasets over archived real-time captures, but confirm the provider's correction policy.
- **Fragmentation and normalization:** Modern equity markets span exchanges and off-exchange venues (ATSs, dark pools, internalizers). Off-exchange volume has grown steadily—from roughly 37% in 2019 (SEC 2020) to over 50% by the early 2020s (SIFMA US Equities Volume Summary)—which shapes data availability and price discovery. The burden is not just "more venues," but schema normalization, symbol handling, clock alignment, and deterministic replay across heterogeneous feeds.

Subscription, parsing, timestamping, and precision set up everything that follows. The next section turns to the most information-rich case, message-level events. The goal is not parsing for its own sake but making implicit market state explicit—a prerequisite for understanding what microstructure features measure and what backtests assume.

3.3 From raw messages to the limit order book

The limit order book (**LOB**) contains all active limit orders at any given point in time. Reconstructing the LOB turns message traffic into state: a time-indexed view of best prices, depth by level, and the event history that produced them. This is the core data-engineering step behind microstructure-aware research and execution modeling. Throughout this section, "LOB" refers to the *displayed, venue-local* book implied by the feed (not a consolidated market-wide book).

Practically, reconstruction follows a simple pipeline: parse messages, normalize fields, apply updates, enforce invariants, snapshot the state, and validate outputs against independent references (for example, BBO/NBBO time series). Gould et al. (2013) survey LOB modeling and empirical regularities, providing useful conceptual foundations. Zhang, Zohren, and Roberts (2019) apply convolutional neural networks (DeepLOB) and Zhang et al. (2025) apply clustering (ClusterLOB) to generate trading signals from LOB data.

NASDAQ TotalView-ITCH – A case study

NASDAQ's TotalView-ITCH data feed exemplifies modern, message-by-order exchange data. It publishes order-level events—adds, cancels, replaces, and executions—that let you reconstruct the visible book throughout the trading day and study how liquidity evolves at the venue.

NASDAQ also provides downloadable historical samples, making ITCH a practical learning resource for readers who want hands-on exposure to real exchange protocols. We use a single day of data (January 30, 2020) for the headline pipeline and detailed empirical work. The raw file contains 423 million messages and expands to roughly 13 GB uncompressed, which demands streaming I/O, memory discipline, and reproducible parsing.

Binary parsing at scale

Each message follows a precisely defined binary structure with nanosecond timestamps and fixed-point prices (four implied decimals). A single trading day contains hundreds of millions of messages, requiring streaming processing—parse sequentially and write to disk incrementally.

Processing hundreds of millions of binary messages exposes the performance gap between research and production systems. The companion repo provides two parsers: a **Python implementation** prioritizing readability (about 23 minutes for a full day via `01_itch_parser.py`) and a **Rust implementation** that uses memory-mapped I/O for roughly an order-of-magnitude faster parsing (well under five minutes).

Metric	Python	Rust	Notes
Wall-clock time	~23 min	< 5 min	~5–8× speedup
Memory footprint	~8 GB peak	< 500 MB	~16× smaller

Table 3.1: 13 GB ITCH file (423M messages). Timings are hardware-dependent and approximate; precise Rust benchmarks are pending a multi-machine benchmark notebook

Both parsers emit the same schema and are validated via checksum sanity checks, round-trip decoding tests, and consistency checks on downstream outputs (for example, identical BBO time series).

The parsed output—Parquet files partitioned by message type—serves as the stable input to all downstream notebooks. Whether the parse runs in Python, Rust, or a commercial service, the reconstruction logic below is unchanged.

The LOB state machine

A reconstructed order book is a state machine updated by each event. The implementation must maintain two related views of state:

- An **order registry** keyed by order reference number to track remaining size, price, and side. Later messages (cancel/execute/delete) refer to the original order ID.
- A **price-level view** for fast queries and snapshot generation.

The ITCH 5.0 specification defines 20+ message types; for LOB reconstruction, the essential ones are:

- **Add Order: A** (anonymous) and **F** (with MPID attribution)
- **Cancel/Delete/Replace:**
  - X (partial cancel)
  - D (delete)
  - U (replace: old order terminated, new order ID created)
- **Executions:**
  - E (executed at the order price)
  - C (executed with an explicit execution price)

System context messages (for example, **S** system events, **R** stock directory, **H** trading action) are required to correctly interpret the trading day. Trade-reporting messages such as **P** (trade) and **Q** (cross trade) are important for activity analysis and auctions, but they are not book-update events in the same way as adds, cancels, replaces, and executions.

The registry answers "what remains of order 123?", the price view answers "how many shares are bid at $101.23?" The core ITCH mechanics are:

- **Add (A, F)** creates a visible limit order: assert that the reference is new, insert it into the registry, and increase the depth at that price. **F** is "add with attribution" (MPID), not a different economic event.
- **Cancel/Delete/Replace** modifies or terminates liquidity: **X** reduces shares (partial cancel), **D** removes the order, **U** terminates the original and creates a new reference—correct handling of replace chains is essential.
- **Executions** reduce the remaining shares on a resting order: **E** executes at the order price, while **C** supplies the execution price when it differs from the order price. Trade-reporting messages such as **P** (trade) and **Q** (cross-trade) are useful for activity analysis and auctions, but they are not book-update events like adds, cancels, replaces, and executions.
- **Trade and cross messages (P, Q)** contribute to execution analytics but do not substitute for order-level book updates.

Figure 3.1 maps each ITCH message type to a state transition in the order lifecycle.

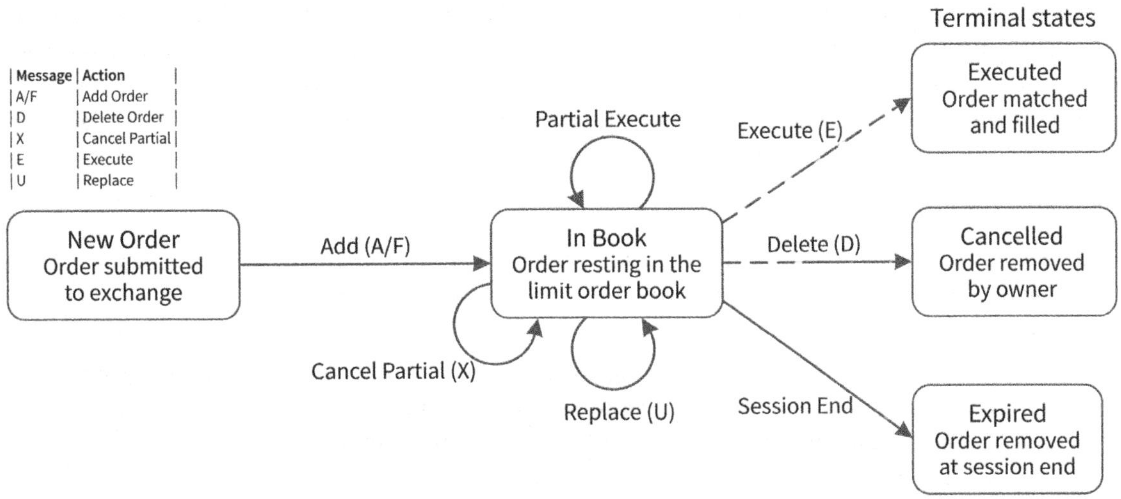

Figure 3.1: Order lifecycle state machine showing how ITCH message types drive transitions

On our sample day, roughly 96% of submitted orders are ultimately deleted; many never execute, while some execute partially and are later deleted (see `04_itch_order_lifecycle_analysis.py`).

Maintaining book integrity

LOB reconstruction is an accounting problem: every message updates the state, and small inconsistencies compound quickly. Cont, Kukanov, and Stoikov (2014) analyze how order book events translate into price movements, making accurate reconstruction a prerequisite for meaningful measurement of impact and liquidity. In practice, treat reconstruction as a state machine, as depicted in *Figure 3.1*, with explicit invariants. Our reference implementation fails fast when these invariants are violated; production pipelines often quarantine and count violations instead, then decide whether to drop symbol/time ranges or apply feed-specific repair rules. At a minimum, validation checks should enforce that:

- Order references exist before any modification, execution, or cancellation
- The remaining quantity is never negative (per order and per price level)
- Prices are valid for the instrument (tick size, auction bands where applicable) and remain within sanity bounds
- Aggregate depth by price level equals the sum of constituent orders at that price (within the reconstructed scope)

In addition, maintain *price-level totals* as a first-class state. Price-level cleanup is then a consequence of the accounting: decrement the size when trades execute, or orders are canceled; remove a level when its aggregate size reaches zero; and flag an error if a level would become negative. When the pipeline persists periodic snapshots, reconcile them against the event-driven state (for example, level totals, best bid/ask) to catch drift early.

Single-exchange data – A local view

A key limitation of direct feeds, such as Nasdaq TotalView-ITCH, is that they describe the state of a **single venue's order book** (Nasdaq's "single book") rather than a consolidated market-wide book across venues. In fragmented equity markets, the best price and deepest liquidity may reside on other exchanges or off-exchange at the same moment, so a single-venue book is an incomplete view of executable liquidity.

This matters in two ways:

1. *Venue-local best quotes* can differ materially from the NBBO, and the depth that looks "available" on one venue may be irrelevant if an order routes elsewhere (or if routing constraints prevent access).
2. Comparing a venue-local reconstruction with consolidated data can produce *apparent* locks or crosses at the market level (for example, a local best bid exceeding the consolidated best ask) due to timestamp differences, feed latency, and the fact that "market-wide" best quotes are assembled from multiple asynchronous sources.

Treat these as diagnostic signals: they can indicate real fragmentation and timing issues, but they can also surface clock alignment issues or message-handling bugs.

Market-wide best prices require consolidated top-of-book data (SIP/CTA/UTP) and, for depth, a **multi-venue aggregation pipeline** that normalizes timestamps and quote semantics across feeds. Single-venue books remain valuable for venue-level microstructure, queue dynamics, and building intuition about how order events translate into observed prices—provided the analysis is explicit about what the book does and does not represent.

Snapshots and analysis

Once reconstruction passes invariant checks, capture order-book snapshots either at a fixed clock interval (for example, every 100ms) or in event time (for example, every N book updates). The choice is part of the measurement design: clock-time snapshots align naturally with latency and execution constraints; event-time sampling aligns with information arrival but can over-represent active periods.

From snapshots, compute a small set of metrics that summarize liquidity and state:

- **Bid-ask spread** measures the cost of immediate execution in the displayed book. Track both the absolute spread and a relative measure (for example, spread divided by midprice) to compare instruments.
- **Displayed depth** measures available size by level. Top-of-book depth matters for short-horizon execution; deeper levels for capacity and impact.
- **Top-of-book imbalance** refers to the asymmetry in displayed depth at the best prices. This snapshot descriptor differs from event-based **order flow imbalance (OFI)** (Cont, Kukanov, and Stoikov, 2014). Hautsch and Huang (2012) show that limit orders, not just marketable orders, carry meaningful information for price discovery—challenging the view that only market orders drive prices.

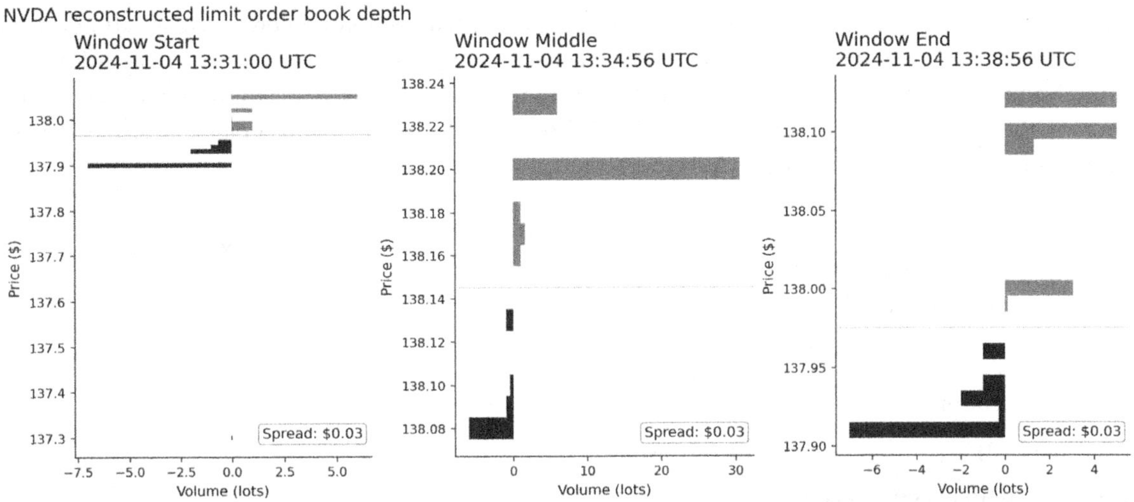

Figure 3.2: A reconstructed LOB showing bid (green, left) and ask (red, right) depth across price levels at three times during the trading day. Data: DataBento MBO for NVDA, regular session

In *Figure 3.2*, the Nasdaq-visible spread varies from \$0.01 at midday (when liquidity is deepest) to \$0.06 near close. This intraday pattern—tighter spreads during calm periods, wider at the open and close—reflects the changing cost of providing liquidity. These are venue-local measures from Nasdaq's single book and may differ from NBBO-based measures in fragmented markets (see `08_databento_lob_reconstruction.py`).

Empirical findings

Modern electronic markets are dominated by order updates and cancellations. Hasbrouck and Saar (2013) document that the vast majority of limit orders are canceled before execution and that median lifetimes are well under a second—"fleeting orders" probing for hidden liquidity. Our single-day NASDAQ ITCH snapshot (January 30, 2020) of 423 million messages includes 186.6 million add-order events and the following lifecycle counts (computed by `04_itch_order_lifecycle_analysis.py`):

Metric	Count
Add-order events (A + F)	186,610,705
Delete events (D)	180,285,101
Partial-cancel events (X)	4,990,972
Replace events (u)	36,777,372
Execute events (E + C)	8,555,084
Unique orders with a delete event	172,764,815
Unique orders with at least one execution	6,258,508
Cancellation rate (delete events/add events)	96.6%
Execution rate (orders with execution/add events)	3.4%

Table 3.2: Order Lifecycle Statistics (NASDAQ, January 30, 2020)

Rates are not complements: an order can be partially executed and later deleted. Cancellation rate is the fraction of submitted orders that receive at least one delete event in their lifecycle; execution rate is the fraction with at least one `E` or `C` execution. Counts of `D`/`X`/`U` events exceed unique-order counts because the same order can be partially canceled before being deleted, and replace messages create a new order reference whose lifecycle is then tracked separately.

Time to cancellation:

- 41% of cancellations occur within 500 milliseconds
- 50% within one second (median: 0.99 seconds)
- 80% within 10 seconds

Time to execution:

- 10% of executions occur within 1 millisecond
- Median execution time is 6.1 seconds
- 1% of orders wait over 40 minutes for execution

These patterns are consistent with algorithmic market making and automated order management. High cancellation and replacement activity is not, by itself, evidence of misconduct; it is a mechanical consequence of competitive quoting, inventory control, and rapid information incorporation—while still implying that displayed liquidity can be fleeting and must be modeled carefully. See `05_itch_trading_activity.py` for market-wide statistics.

Important caveat: Reconstruction systems show the *visible* order book. Hidden orders (icebergs) and internalized order flow remain invisible—a reconstructed LOB represents only displayed liquidity, not total available liquidity.

LOB stylized facts – Predictive patterns

Beyond reconstruction mechanics, LOB data reveals empirical patterns with predictive power. The companion notebooks demonstrate three well-documented regularities:

- **Top-of-book depth imbalance** measures the asymmetry between bid-side and ask-side volume at the best prices: `(bid_size - ask_size) / (bid_size + ask_size)`. When bids exceed asks, buying pressure often leads to short-term price increases—but the signal is weaker than often assumed.

  Our analysis of Nasdaq-book OFI across 50 stocks shows a *weak, noisy correlation* (cross-stock mean $\rho \approx 0.01$, $\sigma \approx 0.10$, range −0.35 to 0.16) with subsequent returns (*Figure 3.3*). Each point in *Figure 3.3* represents one stock; the x-axis shows activity level, and the y-axis shows the imbalance-return correlation; see `03_itch_lob_analysis` for details.

  The finding that naive imbalance metrics are not directly tradeable is consistent with the literature: raw microstructure signals require conditioning on context (spread dynamics, time of day, extreme events) to extract actionable edge. *Chapter 6*'s order flow reversal strategy demonstrates how conditional signals can work where unconditional ones fail.

Terminology note: This is a *state-based* measure from LOB snapshots. *Chapter 8* covers additional imbalance metrics, including *trade imbalance* (from signed trade volume) and *event-based OFI* (Cont, Kukanov, and Stoikov, 2014), which measure queue changes rather than queue levels.

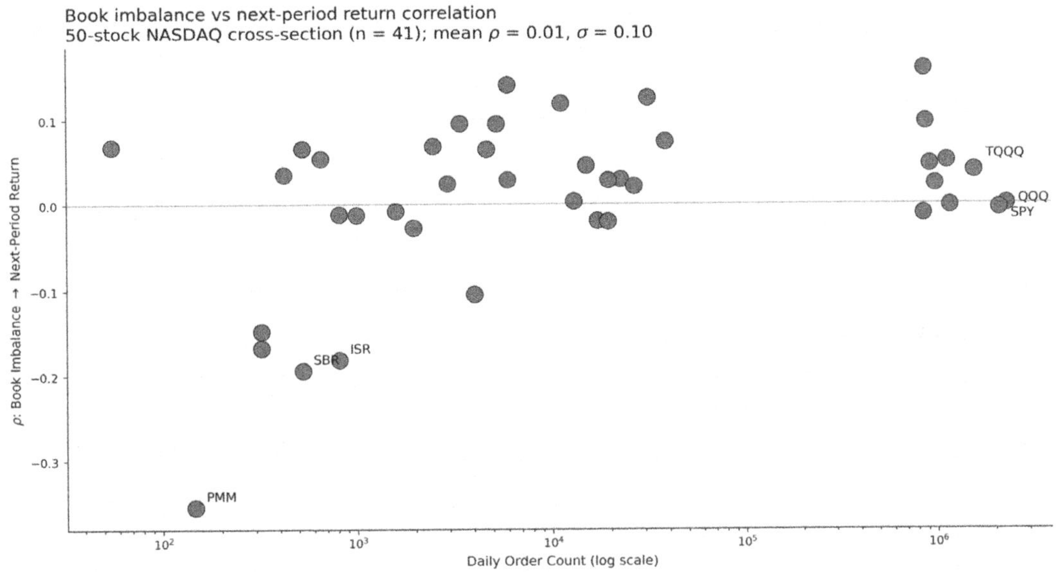

Figure 3.3: Naive imbalance shows weak predictive power. Data: NASDAQ ITCH, multiple symbols, January 30, 2020

Tradability caveat: A positive association at a one-second horizon is not a trading rule. At this horizon, spread and queue dynamics dominate PnL. The notebook `09_databento_mbo_analysis.py` reports both midprice and executable markouts (using bid/ask at decision time) to illustrate this gap.

- **Intraday U-shaped patterns** in volume and volatility are well established: trading activity peaks at the market open and close, with a lull in the middle of the day. This pattern persists across both liquid and illiquid stocks, though the magnitude varies. See `06_itch_intraday_patterns.py` for the aggregate cross-section.
- **Bid-ask bounce** manifests as negative first-order autocorrelation in tick-level returns. When trades alternate between hitting the bid and lifting the ask, sequential returns exhibit apparent mechanical mean reversion. Understanding this effect is essential for constructing return targets—naive tick-to-tick returns contain significant microstructure noise. See `07_itch_stylized_facts.py` for autocorrelation analysis.

The liquidity spectrum spans orders of magnitude. AAPL trades 50+ million shares daily; obscure ETFs like UGA may trade fewer than 100,000 shares. This dispersion in displayed depth is associated with differences in spread, volatility, and price impact—patterns we exploit when engineering features in *Chapters 8* and *9*, and modeling execution costs in *Chapter 18*. The next section addresses how to sample this high-frequency data into analytical bars.

Implementation: For LOB reconstruction across the four data sources surveyed in *Section 3.2*:

- `02_itch_lob_reconstruction.py` (ITCH MBO)
- `08_databento_lob_reconstruction.py` (DataBento MBO)
- `10_iex_lob_reconstruction.py` (IEX MBP)
- `12_algoseek_taq_lob_reconstruction.py` (AlgoSeek TAQ NBBO)

3.4 The art of sampling

Raw tick data is voluminous and noisy. The **bid-ask bounce** alone causes price oscillations as trade initiation alternates between buyers and sellers—a buy market order executes near the ask, a sell near the bid, creating apparent volatility that reflects microstructure mechanics rather than information.

Sampling ticks into analytical **bars** reduces noise, compresses data, aligns observations with a chosen notion of 'time' (clock time or activity time), and produces time series with statistical properties better suited to machine learning models. The choice of sampling method significantly affects model performance.

Standard aggregation methods

All bar types compute similar summary statistics over their respective intervals:

- **Open, High, Low, Close (OHLC):** First, maximum, minimum, and last prices
- **Volume:** Total shares or contracts traded
- **VWAP:** Volume-weighted average price
- **Trade count:** Number of individual transactions

The methods differ in how they define interval boundaries.

Time bars

Time bars aggregate trades within fixed calendar intervals (1-minute, 5-minute, daily). They are intuitive and ubiquitous, but they suffer from **unequal information content**: a minute during the opening rush can see hundreds of trades; a minute during lunch might see only a handful.

Tick, volume, and dollar bars

Several bar types aim to hold some proxy of trading activity, rather than time, constant:

- **Tick (or trade) bars** aggregate a fixed number of transactions regardless of size—equal transaction count, but ignoring trade magnitude.

- **Volume bars** aggregate until the total volume exceeds a threshold, thereby better capturing market activity because large trades carry more weight.
- **Dollar bars** aggregate by traded value (price × volume), providing more robust handling of price level changes than volume bars—the same shares at doubled price represent twice the economic activity.

Note: Dollar bars help capture organic price changes but still require attention to corporate actions; a 2-for-1 split doubles the share count while halving the price, so the dollar threshold must be rescaled or prices must be split-adjusted.

Easley, López de Prado, and O'Hara (2012) develop the "**volume clock**" concept, showing that sampling based on volume rather than calendar time yields more stable statistical properties—a key motivation for activity-time sampling methods such as volume and dollar bars. High-frequency trading is defined not by speed per se but by operating in "**event-based time**," which yields returns that are closer to a normal distribution and exploits traders who think in clock time.

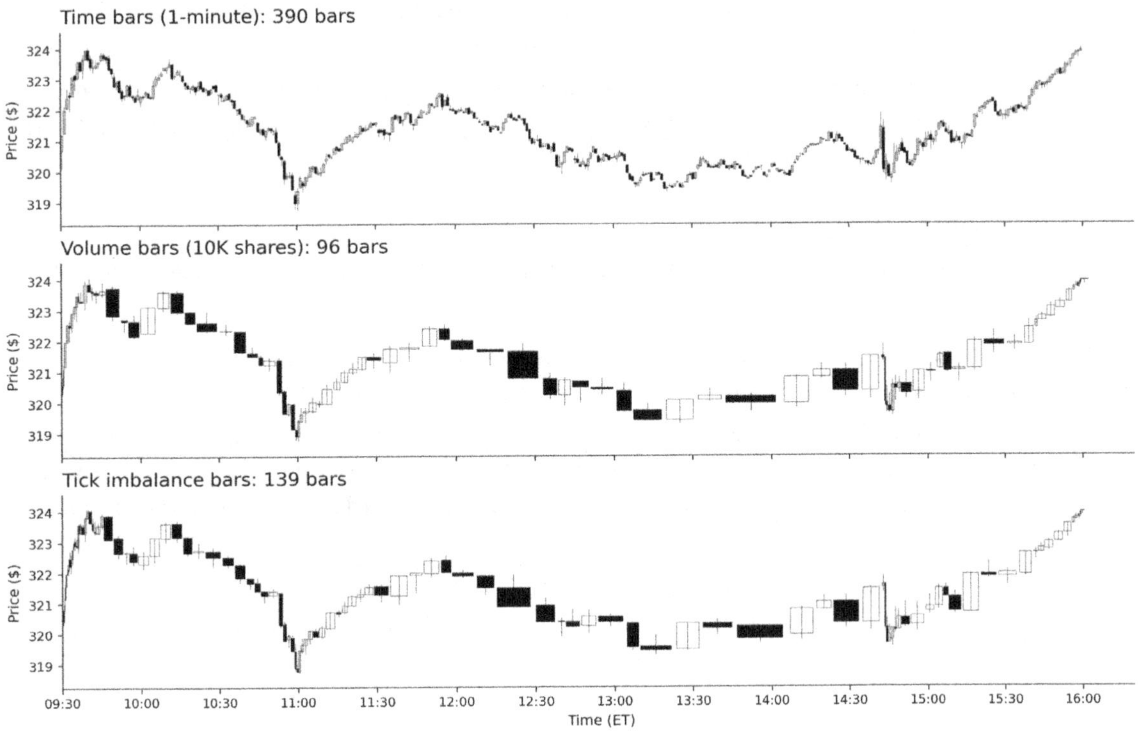

Figure 3.4: Comparison of bar sampling methods on the same underlying tick data

As shown in *Figure 3.4*, time bars produce a fixed sequence of intervals. In contrast, volume bars adapt to market activity, concentrating samples during high-activity periods and spacing them out during quiet periods. See `14_itch_bar_sampling.py` for the comparison code.

Information-driven bars

Standard time and volume bars summarize trading activity but don't explicitly target when new information arrives. *Information-driven bars* aim to identify when new information enters the market, drawing on concepts from market microstructure theory. Marcos López de Prado introduced these methods in *Advances in Financial Machine Learning* (López de Prado, 2018), building on research showing that sequences of trades consistently initiated by one side—buy or sell streaks—often signal informed trading.

Trade classification – Data sources matter

Information-driven bars require knowing the **aggressor side** of each trade—whether the buyer or seller initiated the transaction to identify when a buy or sell streak starts. López de Prado lists "Aggressor side" as standard market data in his taxonomy, and CME provides it directly via FIX tag 5797. The challenge is that not all data feeds include this field:

- **Some institutional MBO feeds** (for example, DataBento) provide the aggressor side directly. Most trades in our DataBento NVDA sample include aggressor-side labels (B=buy, A=sell), with a minority marked as neutral/unknown—enabling direct computation of imbalance bars without estimation. Other vendors (Refinitiv, Bloomberg) vary by product and entitlement.
- **ITCH Trade (P) messages**, while excellent for learning the protocol, do not include aggressor direction—each trade reports the same indicator regardless of which side initiated it. For the ITCH sample data, we must estimate direction.

The Lee-Ready algorithm

When the aggressor side is unavailable, the **Lee-Ready algorithm** (Lee and Ready, 1991) estimates it by combining quote and tick information:

1. **Quote (midpoint) test:** Compare trade price to the midpoint of the prevailing bid-ask spread. Trades above the midpoint are classified as buys; trades below as sells.
2. **Tick test fallback:** When trades occur exactly at (or extremely near) the midpoint, use the price change from the previous trade. An uptick (a price increase) indicates a buy; a downtick (a price decrease) indicates a sell. If unchanged, carry forward the last non-zero direction.

> **Practical note:** Lee-Ready is only as good as the **quote alignment.** If quotes and trades are not time-synchronized, define an "as-of" rule (or apply a small lag) to avoid using quotes that were not yet visible at the time of the trade.

Empirical validation – Classification accuracy

We validated classification methods using DataBento NVDA data, in which direct aggressor labels serve as the ground truth. The results reveal important differences between approaches:

Method	Coverage	Accuracy	Notes
Lee-Ready (quote plus tick)	100%	94.7%	Requires the best bid/ask quotes aligned with each trade
Tick test (continuous)	100%	80.0%	Carries forward the last direction
Tick test (non-zero)	19%	90.0%	Only classifies when the price changes

Table 3.3: Trade classification accuracy (NVDA, 742,527 trades across 5 DataBento days)

Table 3.3 shows validation results for NVDA trades using DataBento aggressor labels as the ground truth over five trading days (2024-11-04 to 2024-11-08). Accuracy is computed on trades with non-unknown ground-truth side; unknown/neutral trades are excluded, and quotes are aligned using an as-of rule with a small lag. Lee-Ready accuracy was stable across days (94.4–95.0%); the tick test averaged 80%. "Coverage" indicates what percentage of trades receive a classification. See `15_itch_lee_ready.py` for the full multi-day analysis.

The tick test faces a fundamental challenge: **most consecutive trades occur at the same price** (zero-tick)—across the five NVDA days, only about 19% of trades carry a non-zero price change. The continuous tick test handles this by carrying forward the last non-zero direction, reaching 80% accuracy—roughly 15 percentage points below Lee-Ready. When only non-zero ticks are classified, accuracy rises to 90%, but coverage drops to that same 19% of trades.

Lee-Ready achieves 95% accuracy by using the order book state (best bid/ask at trade time) for most classifications, falling back to the tick test only for trades at the midpoint. This exceeds the 70–90% range typically cited in academic literature, likely because modern markets with tighter spreads allow more precise quote-based classification.

The practical implication of the ~16-point improvement from the tick test (78%) to Lee-Ready (95%) matters for information bars. With ITCH data, the order book must be reconstructed to compute quote midpoints for Lee-Ready classification—worthwhile complexity for accurate trade-direction estimation. See `14_itch_bar_sampling.py` for a complete implementation.

With only trade prices and no order book reconstruction, the tick test provides reasonable (78%) but not optimal classification. For information bars where direction accuracy directly impacts signal quality, prefer Lee-Ready.

Volume imbalance bars

Volume imbalance bars (VIBs) close when cumulative signed volume exceeds an expected threshold:

- **Label each trade:** +1 if buyer-initiated, -1 if seller-initiated (via Lee-Ready or similar)
- **Compute signed volume:** Label × trade volume
- **Accumulate imbalance:** Running sum of signed volumes
- **Close bar:** When |accumulated imbalance| exceeds expected value

The expected imbalance is derived from historical bar characteristics, updated using an exponential moving average. The algorithm adapts: periods of balanced trading produce fewer, longer bars; periods of sustained buying or selling pressure produce more frequent bars.

Tick imbalance bars

Tick imbalance bars (TIB) accumulate signed trade direction rather than signed volume:

$$\theta_T = \sum_{t=1}^{T} b_t, \qquad E[|\theta_T|] \approx E[T] \cdot |2Pr(b_t = +1) - 1|$$

where $b_t \in +1, -1$ is the trade direction. TIBs count all trades equally regardless of size, while VIBs (above) weight by volume.

This means that when the order flow is close to balanced ($Pr(b_t = +1) \approx 0.5$), the expected imbalance $|2Pr(b_t = +1) - 1|$ becomes small and TIBs produce *many short bars*. When one side dominates, thresholds grow, and bars become longer. TIBs are therefore most interpretable as a *directional pressure sampler*, not as a fixed "bars-per-day" construction. Choose TIBs when trade count matters (detecting informed trading frequency); choose VIBs when volume flow matters (detecting institutional activity).

Run bars

Run bars form when one side of the market dominates, measured by cumulative trade counts within a potential bar:

$$\theta_T = max\left(N_T^{buy}, N_T^{sell}\right), \qquad E[\theta_T] = E[T] \cdot max\left(Pr(b_t = +1), 1 - Pr(b_t = +1)\right)$$

Run bars count *cumulative* trades on each side, not consecutive same-direction trades. The statistic is the maximum of cumulative buy versus sell counts within the bar, not the length of the longest consecutive streak. Direction changes within a bar do not reset the counts. This captures sustained directional pressure even when individual trades interleave.

Calibration – Avoiding threshold spiral

The adaptive **exponential weighted moving average** (**EWMA**) algorithm places greater weight on recent data points and is sensitive to persistent order-flow imbalances. When stocks show systematic buy/sell bias, the standard $\alpha = 0.1$ causes a **threshold spiral**, a positive feedback loop where bars grow progressively larger:

Symbol	**Buy Fraction**	**E[T] Drift ($\alpha = 0.1$)**	**E[T] Drift ($\alpha = 0.001$)**
NVDA	47%	17.5×	0.98× ✓

Table 3.4: Threshold behavior for NVDA

Even at a 47% buy fraction, $\alpha = 0.1$ inflates the expected bar size by 17.5× over the trading day—the runaway feedback loop that collapses the day into a handful of oversized bars—while $\alpha = 0.001$ holds it essentially flat (0.98×), avoiding the spiral.

Recommended settings: $\alpha = 0.1$ can be too reactive at the tick level for liquid equities; start with a much smaller α (for example, 0.001) and verify stability. Use warmup=100+ bars and monitor the `expected_imbalance` column for drift detection. For production use, consider fixed-threshold imbalance bars, which avoid adaptive feedback entirely. See `16_itch_information_bars.py` for formula verification and `17_databento_bar_sampling.py` for multi-day calibration analysis.

Information-driven bars pose several practical difficulties:

- **Trade classification:** The tick test (~78%) is roughly 16 points below Lee-Ready (~95%). For optimal quality, reconstruct the order book.
- **Circular initialization:** Expected bar length requires existing bars; initialize with reasonable estimates and update via EMA.
- **Parameter sensitivity:** Single trading days rarely suffice; multi-day data produces more robust thresholds.
- **Flow balance:** When P[buy] ≈ 0.5, the expected imbalance approaches zero, causing rapid bar formation.

Statistical properties comparison

Before the formal statistics, it helps to compare the bar constructions on three axes: the sampling clock, the quantity each method keeps approximately constant, and whether it depends on trade-direction classification (the first four don't, the last three do).

Bar Type	Clock	Target	Typical use
Time	Calendar	Time interval	Clock-time forecasting
Tick	Activity	Trade count	Equal trade frequency
Volume	Activity	Shares/contracts	Size-based activity
Dollar	Activity	Traded value	General ML default
Tick imbalance	Information	Signed trade count	Directional pressure
Volume imbalance	Information	Signed volume	Informed flow by size
Run	Information	Side dominance	Persistent one-sided flow

Table 3.5: Bar characteristics

Empirical testing reveals meaningful differences between bar types. Using NASDAQ ITCH trade data for AAPL (January 30, 2020), we compare standard bars and information-driven bars (with tick-test trade classification). Bar thresholds are noted in parentheses:

Bar Type	N Bars	Jarque-Bera Stat	Lag-1 Autocorrelation
Time (1 min)	390	609.0	-0.023
Volume (10K shares)	96	1.9	0.026
Dollar ($3M)	102	2.2	-0.027

Bar Type	N Bars	Jarque-Bera Stat	Lag-1 Autocorrelation
Tick imbalance	139	22.6	0.057
Tick Run	455	12.5	-0.007

Table 3.6: Bar Type Statistical Comparison (AAPL, 14,184 trades); higher Jarque-Bera values make a normal distribution less likely

Table 3.6 shows trade direction, classified using the tick test (~78% accuracy, per *Table 3.3*). Volume and dollar bar thresholds (10K shares, $3M) produce roughly 100 bars per day for AAPL; information-driven bars adapt to flow dynamics, with tick imbalance bars (139) concentrating during directional episodes and tick run bars (455) capturing persistent one-sided flow. The **Jarque-Bera (JB)** statistic measures how far a return distribution departs from normality by combining two features: **skewness** and **kurtosis**. A low JB suggests returns are closer to normal, while a high JB indicates greater asymmetry and/or fatter tails, making normality less plausible.

Using DataBento NVDA data with **direct aggressor labels** (100% accuracy), activity-driven bars achieve modestly better normality than time bars—Tick (500 trades/bar) JB=58.8 and Volume (50K shares/bar) JB=2.3 versus 132.8 for one-minute bars on the same day. The flow on this day was essentially balanced, marginally buy-tilted (P[buy]=0.426), so volume imbalance bars (calibrated to ~500 bars/day) produced 691 bars; dollar bars at $5M/bar yielded 519 bars. Autocorrelation remains small for all types—a desirable property for ML.

Bar Type	N Bars	Jarque-Bera Stat	Lag-1 Autocorrelation
Time (1 min)	390	132.8	0.014
Tick (500 ticks)	390	58.8	-0.061
Volume (50k shares)	380	2.3	-0.017
Dollar ($5M)	519	33.0	0.039
Vol Imbalance	691	51.0	0.035

Table 3.7: Bar type comparison with Direct Aggressor Labels (NVDA, 2024-11-04, 195,420 trades)

Table 3.7 shows trade direction from DataBento's side field. Activity-driven bars (tick and volume) achieve materially lower Jarque-Bera than time bars, while dollar and volume-imbalance bars remain far closer to normal than the one-minute clock.

Easley et al. (2021) revisit these dynamics in light of machine learning, arguing that information-based sampling remains relevant as algorithmic and ML-driven strategies have grown more prevalent.

Trade-offs and selection

Several trade-offs and selection decisions matter in practice:

- The default choice (most ML workflows) is to **use dollar bars**. They are simple to implement, require only trades, and, in practice, tend to produce more stable return distributions than time bars. They also scale naturally with the price level (define thresholds in notional terms). Adjust consistently for corporate actions (and contract multipliers/roll rules for futures).

- **Use time bars when the decision and label horizon are in clock time** (for example, "next 5 minutes," intraday seasonality features, session-aligned execution constraints). Time bars are intuitive but have uneven information per sample across the day; expect heteroskedasticity and regime-dependent sample quality.
- **Use volume bars when "activity" is naturally measured in shares/contracts** (and price level is relatively stable), but prefer dollar bars where robustness to price-level changes matters.
- **Use information-driven bars (imbalance/run) when order-flow dynamics are the object of measurement** (toxicity, informed trading, execution risk), not when the primary goal is "more normal" returns. These methods require reliable trade direction: use a direct aggressor field when available; otherwise, use Lee–Ready with aligned quotes. Tick-test-only classification is usable but materially noisier. Expect higher implementation and tuning overhead (for example quote alignment or book reconstruction, initialization, and stability monitoring).
- **With only trades and no quotes, prefer dollar (or volume) bars** and avoid imbalance/run bars unless the limitations of tick-test direction are acceptable and sensitivity has been validated.

For most applications, **dollar bars** are the best starting point: they exhibit good statistical behavior in many settings, handle price-level changes gracefully, and are not dependent on trade classification. Next, we turn to the role of price jumps.

> **Implementation:** `14_itch_bar_sampling.py` demonstrates how to construct bar types and compares them.

3.5 Detecting price jumps in intraday returns

Intraday returns mix two statistically distinct processes. A continuous component reflects the steady arrival of small order-flow innovations and is well approximated by a diffusion. A discrete component reflects scheduled news, unexpected announcements, and large block trades, and manifests as price moves that are too large to attribute to diffusion. Separating the two matters because realized variance, autocorrelation diagnostics, and label distributions all change shape once jumps are removed.

> **Implementation:** `18_algoseek_jump_detection` builds the full pipeline on AlgoSeek minute bars for AMD, AMZN, and FB across 2020. The results below are computed end-to-end in that notebook.

Continuous and jump variance

For a trading day with n intraday log returns $r_1, \dots, r_n$, the realized variance:

$$RV_d = \sum_{i=1}^{n} r_i^2$$

is a consistent estimator of total quadratic variation: continuous plus squared jumps. The bipower variation of Barndorff-Nielsen and Shephard (2004),

$$BV_d = \mu_1^{-2} \sum_{i=2}^{n} |r_i|\,|r_{i-1}|, \qquad \mu_1 = \sqrt{2/\pi}$$

is jump-robust: a single large $|r_i|$ is multiplied by its smaller neighbor and contributes negligibly to the sum.

Therefore, the non-negative gap $max(RV_d - BV_d, 0)$ estimates the jump-attributable variance on day d. In the notebook, the three names show annualized continuous volatility (from $\sqrt{BV}$) of 30% for AMZN, 34% for FB, and 45% for AMD; the jump component contributes roughly 6–10% of the annual realized variance (6.8% for AMD, 10.4% for AMZN, 6.2% for FB). The 2020 sample spans the March dislocation, and the jump share reflects that episode rather than a steady-state value.

The Lee–Mykland Test

To time individual jumps to the bar, Lee and Mykland (2008) form a standardized statistic

$$L_i = \frac{r_i}{\hat{\sigma}_i}, \qquad \hat{\sigma}_i^2 = \frac{1}{K-2} \sum_{j=i-K+2}^{i-1} |r_j|\,|r_{j-1}|$$

where $\hat{\sigma}_i$ is a local bipower volatility built from a trailing window of K prior returns. The window adapts to slow-moving volatility regimes and inherits the jump-robustness of bipower variation. Under the no-jump-at-i null and a continuous-diffusion alternative, the maximum of $|L_i|$ over n intraday bars converges to a Gumbel distribution.

The rejection rule at family-wise level α over n bars per day is:

$$|L_i| > S_n \beta^*(\alpha) + C_n, \qquad \beta^*(\alpha) = -log\big(-log(1-\alpha)\big)$$

with $C_n = (2logn)^{1/2}/\mu_1 - (log\pi + loglogn)/(2\mu_1(2logn)^{1/2})$ and $S_n = 1/(\mu_1(2logn)^{1/2})$.

The multiple-testing burden is borne by the n-dependent constants rather than by an ad hoc *Bonferroni adjustment* (see *Chapter 7* for more detail).

In the notebook, the test runs at $\alpha = 0.01$ with $K = 12$ (about an hour at the five-minute frequency, near Lee–Mykland's $\sqrt{n}$ recommendation for 78 bars per day), yielding a critical value of 5.10 and 0.37 jumps per symbol-day on average. The window is built strictly within session, so the first $K - 1$ bars of each day are not testable—the trade for removing overnight-gap contamination from the local-volatility denominator. Longer K is slower-adapting and burns more bars on warm-up; shorter K tracks the intraday shape more closely but is noisier.

What the data show

The daily jump-count distribution is right-skewed. Roughly a quarter to a third of symbol-days contain at least one jump (24% for AMD, 31% for AMZN, 34% for FB); the median day with any jumps has exactly one, and the maximum is three jumps in a single symbol-day.

The corresponding Q–Q plot in the notebook makes the diagnostic visible: standardized returns from all bars curve well above the normal-quantile line in the upper tail with a heavier lower-tail outlier, while standardized returns from jump-filtered bars track the normal line much more closely. Jumps are the source of most of the tail heaviness, not diffusion heterogeneity.

The time-of-day distribution shows a clear close-of-day cluster within the testable window: 27% of flagged jumps occur in the last thirty minutes of the session, where end-of-day rebalancing flows and the close auction produce sharp moves. The first thirty minutes fall within the $K - 1$ warm-up window, so the open-time rejection rate is zero by construction rather than an empirical finding; probing it at this frequency would require either finer-grained bars or a complementary estimator that pools cross-session information without overnight-gap contamination.

The year-2020 variance decomposition in the notebook (illustrated for AMD) stacks BV_d and the jump residual $RV_d - BV_d$ over time and shows that jump variance is episodic—concentrated around the March 2020 dislocation, a handful of earnings dates, and several macro-release days—rather than uniformly distributed.

Why a local volatility adjustment matters

A common shortcut flags any bar with $|r_i/\hat{\sigma}_d| > 4$, where $\hat{\sigma}_d$ is a single daily standard deviation. The notebook compares this rule with Lee–Mykland on the same data. The two disagree on most bars, and the disagreement is directional. The counts are 70 Lee–Mykland versus 55 naive jumps with 2 overlapping for AMD; 103 versus 48 with 6 overlapping for AMZN; 109 versus 49 with 6 overlapping for FB.

On stressed days, $\hat{\sigma}_d$ is dragged up by the jumps themselves so genuinely large bars no longer clear $4\hat{\sigma}_d$—the naive rule under-detects. On calm days, $\hat{\sigma}_d$ is small, and the same threshold is easy to clear, so the rule fires on borderline returns—over-detection. The bipower local estimator avoids both failure modes by ignoring its own large neighbors and tracking the intraday volatility shape.

Jumps as features

The notebook persists a per-symbol, per-day feature panel with the four columns that downstream chapters consume: `jump_count`, `signed_jump_var`, `jump_variance`, and `jump_share` (jump variance as a fraction of *RV*). The panel feeds two specific uses:

- In *Chapter 7*, jump indicators support *label conditioning*—skipping the first thirty minutes after a flagged jump removes a class of returns whose statistical properties differ sharply from the diffusive labels the model is trained on.
- In *Chapter 8*, the daily continuous and jump variances are features in their own right: separate volatility regimes (continuous-only days, jump-heavy days, blow-up days) are estimable rather than implicit.

The decomposition operates on the same bar grid as *Section 3.4*'s sampling pipeline; it adds an event-aware feature layer on top of it. The next section turns to issues in the quality of microstructure data.

3.6 Microstructure data quality and sessionization

Microstructure research depends on two forms of correctness: data-quality checks that keep corrupted records out of analysis, and session logic that prevents time-boundary mistakes from creating artificial returns and invalid state transitions. *Chapter 2* provides the general framework; here we focus on intraday-specific failure modes.

Many microstructure "errors" are not extreme values but inconsistencies: out-of-sequence events, invalid book transitions, stale quotes, or trades that qualifiers mark for exclusion. Prefer invariant checks and cross-field consistency over purely statistical filters.

Start with event sequencing, because everything downstream assumes a correct event order:

- **Enforce ordering per symbol and venue**: Check that timestamps are monotone within each stream, and use feed sequence numbers to break ties. If the provider offers both, treat the sequence as authoritative ordering and the timestamp as event time.
- **Be explicit about time semantics**: Confirm whether a timestamp reflects exchange event time, SIP publication time, vendor processing time, or local arrival time. Holden et al. (2014) show that misaligned trade and quote times can introduce systematic bias into standard microstructure measures.

Once ordering is trustworthy, double-check the two primary observables—trades and quotes:

- Validate basic fields (positive price and size, valid symbols, expected tick size where available), and flag impossible spreads and other violations of instrument constraints.
- Then, honor qualifiers and condition codes: many feeds mark late reports, corrected prints, auctions, and other non-standard trades. Default to excluding records that are explicitly out-of-sequence, corrected, or non-eligible for "last sale" style analytics unless your analysis intentionally models them.
- Finally, treat stale quotes and feed drops as first-class issues. Distinguish "no trades occurred" from "data is missing": long gaps are normal in illiquid names, but for liquid symbols, a long gap in quote updates often indicates a feed interruption.

If you reconstruct a LOB, quality control becomes an accounting problem: treat the book as a stateful system with explicit invariants—no negative depth at the order or price level; best bid ≤ best ask, with locks or crosses either forbidden or allowed only during explicitly modeled auction or transition states (open, close, halts) under documented rules; and order lifecycle consistency.

After aggregation, validate again at the derived data product level:

- Reconcile bars against the underlying events: bar volume matches summed trade size, VWAP equals the size-weighted mean of constituent trades, and OHLC matches first/max/min/last by the bar definition.
- When you have both venue-local and consolidated sources, expect differences in timing and conventions; treat large discrepancies as triggers for investigation rather than automatic errors. They may reflect real fragmentation, but they can also indicate clock misalignment, filtering differences, or a reconstruction bug.

Two AlgoSeek explorations make these failure modes concrete.

1. On AAPL during the March 16, 2020, COVID crash, median spread runs at 2.4 bps against a baseline closer to 1 bps, with a 9.9% intraday range—stress-day numbers that distinguish a real liquidity event from a feed glitch (see `11_algoseek_taq_eda`).
2. AlgoSeek's NASDAQ-100 minute panel runs continuously from 04:00 to 20:00 ET, so trade fields are null in 20–23% of bars (extended-hours intervals with no executions) while quote fields are never null; treating those nulls as missing data would silently bias any aggregate (see `13_algoseek_minute_bars_eda`).

Statistical outlier filters (MAD, rolling z-scores) remain useful mainly as triage to surface candidates for inspection. For ticks and quotes, the default treatment is flagging and exclusion rather than interpolation: interpolation fabricates market activity, blurs discontinuities, and breaks consistency with the event stream. If you winsorize (replace extremes with a fixed value, for example, the 5th/95th percentile), drop, or otherwise modify records, log the rule, and keep an audit trail so results remain reproducible.

Apply the same rigor to sessionization. Misclassifying weekends, holidays, early closes, or daylight-saving transitions creates artificial returns (for example, "overnight" returns inside the regular session) and invalid book states. A robust workflow looks as follows:

1. Build the schedule from the current exchange calendar, including early closes and special sessions.
2. Tag observations as pre-, regular-, or post-session using local exchange time.
3. Validate that closed dates contain no regular-session events, and that early closes end on schedule.
4. Define the session date explicitly (the trading day a timestamp belongs to) and apply it consistently across trades, quotes, and reconstructed book states.
5. Handle halts and auctions deliberately: exclude them from intraday modeling or treat them as distinct states with separate rules.

Run these checks after parsing, after reconstruction, and after bar aggregation, and use the data-quality and lineage framework from *Chapter 2* to keep QA rules and calendars configurable while preserving a consistent audit trail.

3.7 Summary

We treated market data as the output of a trading mechanism, not as a neutral time series. We connected market structure and feed design to the observables a researcher models: how quotes and trades encode liquidity provision, how order types and execution rules shape intraday patterns, and why message-level data enables analyses that are impossible with top-of-book snapshots. We also showed how this context matters operationally: reconstructing a limit order book requires enforcing book invariants and lifecycle consistency; sampling ticks into bars changes the statistical and economic meaning of each observation depending on the boundary rule.

The next step is to turn these clean, correctly sessionized observables into features. *Chapter 2* provided the general data-quality framework; *Chapters 8* and *9* use the bar- and book-derived outputs from this chapter to engineer predictive signals, including microstructure features that depend on order flow and depth dynamics. Disciplined parsing, validation, and sampling are not preliminaries; they determine what models can learn and what conclusions research can legitimately support.

The next chapter covers fundamental and alternative data across asset classes.

4

Fundamental and Alternative Data

While market data captures *what* happened in the market—prices, volume, and the mechanics of trading—fundamental and alternative data help explain *why*. Turning these sources into model-ready signals is less about clever algorithms than about disciplined pipelines: ingesting messy inputs, tracking revisions, validating identifiers, and producing time-consistent features that hold up in backtests and production.

Fundamental data is asset-specific information about the underlying economic drivers of value, rather than trading activity or market microstructure. In practice, fundamentals capture variables that influence expected cash flows, discount rates, or key constraints (for example, supply and demand), and they typically arrive through reporting or measurement rather than through markets. Examples include financial statements and filings for equities, issuer and covenant information for credit, supply-demand and inventory measures for commodities, and protocol and on-chain metrics for crypto. Alongside these sources, **alternative data** has expanded to include digital exhaust, such as web traffic, transactions, geolocation data, satellite imagery, and text, reflecting its growing use in active management (Green and Zhang, 2024).

In practice, two failures dominate the real-world use of fundamentals and alternative data: time consistency and entity consistency.

- **Point-in-time (PIT) accuracy** ensures that research uses only information *available* at the decision date. *Chapter 2* introduces the PIT vocabulary and the bitemporal data model; this chapter applies them to SEC filings, macroeconomic releases, and other revision-prone sources.
- **Entity resolution** ensures that records from disparate sources map to the same real-world issuer and tradable instrument despite naming variants, identifier changes, corporate actions, and mergers, and that the correct security identifier remains aligned over time.

This chapter provides the engineering playbook for both challenges; it will enable you to:

- Implement a bitemporal data model to distinguish valid time from knowledge time (*Section 4.1*).

- Parse SEC EDGAR filings and construct point-in-time corporate fundamental databases (*Section 4.1*).
- Apply various hierarchical entity resolution approaches (*Section 4.2*).
- Characterize fundamental data across asset classes (*Section 4.3*).
- Evaluate alternative data sources along signal, data quality, legal, and commercial/engineering dimensions (*Section 4.4*).
- Extract structured data from EDGAR text filings for NLP analysis (*Section 4.5*).

We'll start with the practical challenge of creating a data pipeline that is point-in-time correct.

4.1 The point-in-time pipeline

Chapter 2 introduced PIT correctness and the bitemporal vocabulary (valid time versus knowledge time). The question here is operational: given EDGAR filing histories, how do we build a dataset that returns the value eligible at decision time *t*, not the value that exists in a vendor database today? The core complications are amended filings, taxonomy changes, and corporate actions that create multiple "versions" of the same reporting period.

Why restatements create leakage

Consider a simple **P/E ratio strategy**. A company might report Q3 revenue of $95M in October, then restate it to $98M in the next 10-Q and again to $100M in the next 10-K. A backtest that uses $100M for October decisions has applied the *later* accounting view to an *earlier* decision—this is lookahead bias.

Luo et al. (2014) identify it as one of the "seven sins" of quantitative investing, showing how errors in data handling can completely reverse a strategy's performance. The others are survivorship bias, storytelling bias, overfitting and data snooping bias, turnover and transaction cost, outliers, and shorting cost.

Bitemporal storage and as-of queries

The implementation follows the *Chapter 2* PIT contract: each fact must carry both the period it describes and the timestamp when that specific version became observable. A single reporting period may therefore have multiple versions over time: the original filing, an amendment, or a later restatement.

For earnings, markets often react first to the earnings release, typically via Form 8-K Item 2.02, and only later to the detailed Form 10-Q or Form 10-K. Using the 10-Q or 10-K acceptance time as the availability timestamp is conservative for PIT backtests. If event-time precision matters, track both timestamps explicitly.

The **as-of query pattern** is straightforward:

1. Select the latest reporting period eligible at historical time t.
2. Within that period, select the latest version with an availability timestamp no later than t.

A practical caveat is the **SEC XBRL Frames API**. Frames returns the "last filed" value that best matches the requested period, which makes it useful for cross-sectional snapshots and prototyping, but not PIT-safe on its own. For PIT research, reconstruct the history from the filing-level records and timestamps.

The *Chapter 2* PIT checklist is a precondition here: values must be time-valid, the historical universe must be reconstructible, and identifier mappings must be valid at the decision date. The remainder of this section shows how to satisfy those requirements for large-scale fundamental sourcing.

Timestamp authority by modality

The authoritative availability timestamp varies by data source. The conventions below apply uniformly across pipelines:

Modality	Authoritative Timestamp	Notes
SEC	accepted_at (filing acceptance)	Optionally track earlier earnings releases if event-time matters
Macro	Official release timestamp (timezone-normalized)	Use ALFRED vintage data for historical accuracy
Commodities	Agency release timestamp + contract roll mapping	EIA, USDA, and CFTC each have specific release schedules
Crypto	Block time + confirmation/finality policy + vendor ingestion time	Treat observation as available only after N confirmations to avoid reorg lookahead

Table 4.1: Timestamp authority by source

The EDGAR sourcing pipeline

The SEC's **Electronic Data Gathering, Analysis, and Retrieval** (**EDGAR**) system provides free, comprehensive access to U.S. corporate filings. EDGAR's phase-in began in 1993 and became mandatory for domestic issuers by May 1996. The system now offers multiple access channels:

Bulk Downloads: The Financial Statement and Notes (FSN) datasets provide parsed XBRL data in tabular format. These cover all 10-K, 10-Q, and 8-K filings back to 2009, organized into eight related tables:

File	Description
SUB	Submission metadata—CIK, form type, filing date, accession number
NUM	Numeric values extracted from XBRL tags
TAG	Taxonomy tag definitions and descriptions
DIM	Dimensional breakdowns (by segment, geography, and so on)

Table 4.2: Selected FSN tables

The FSN dataset includes four additional files (TXT, PRE, CAL, REN) for text content and display formatting.

REST APIs: Real-time access to company filings, specific concepts, and submission histories. No authentication required—callers identify themselves via the user-agent header. The company-concept API returns all historical values for a specific metric (for example, `EarningsPerShareDiluted`) in JSON format.

Python Libraries: Packages such as `edgartools`, `sec-edgar`, and `sec-downloader` wrap the API complexity with convenient interfaces. `edgartools` provides direct access to parsed financial statements and text sections. For high-throughput applications, services like `datamule` offer bulk downloads via hosted archives, often with higher throughput than direct EDGAR access (check current rate limits and terms).

For systematic research, the bulk approach is often most efficient: download the compressed FSN archives, extract to columnar Parquet format for fast queries, then build the bitemporal database from the parsed content.

XBRL and taxonomy structure

The **eXtensible Business Reporting Language** (**XBRL**) standardizes electronic business reporting. Each numeric value in a filing is tagged with:

- **Concept:** What the number represents (for example, `us-gaap:RevenueFromContractWithCustomerExcludingAssessedTax`)
- **Period:** The time span covered (point-in-time for balance sheet items, duration for income statement)
- **Unit:** Measurement unit (USD, shares, USD/share)
- **Dimensions:** Optional breakdowns by segment, geography, or other categories

The U.S. GAAP taxonomy defines thousands of standardized concepts, but companies can extend it with custom tags. This flexibility enables precise reporting but complicates cross-company analysis—the same economic fact might appear under different tags.

For PIT reconstruction, the filing date (`knowledge_date`) is derived from the submission metadata rather than the financial data itself. For each filing, the valid period is derived from the XBRL content and paired with the filing date from the submission record. This separation makes PIT reconstruction possible.

Implementation:

- `01_academic_characteristics` introduces the academic-fundamentals panel and the long-run cross-section that motivates careful PIT construction.
- `02_sec_filing_explorer` introduces EdgarTools for interactive EDGAR exploration.
- `03_sec_form4_insider_transactions` demonstrates how to retrieve and parse Form 4 insider-transaction filings as an example of event-timestamped fundamental data.
- `04_sec_xbrl_fundamentals` consumes the materialized XBRL Frames output and demonstrates bitemporal query patterns.

Handling data inconsistency

Even with proper PIT tracking, fundamental data presents consistency challenges:

- **Accounting standard evolution:** U.S. GAAP changes over time. A tag like `RevenueFromContractWithCustomerExcludingAssessedTax` might replace `SalesRevenueNet` mid-series, requiring mapping between taxonomy versions.
- **Company-specific choices:** Within GAAP, companies have discretion in categorization. One firm's "Cost of Revenue" might include items another firm reports separately. Cross-company comparisons require careful normalization.
- **Restatements and amendments:** When companies file amended filings (10-K/A, 10-Q/A) or restate prior periods, multiple versions of the same reporting period coexist. A bitemporal model stores each version with its own availability timestamp; analysis code must be explicit about which version is eligible at each decision date.
- **Corporate actions:** Stock splits require retroactive adjustment of per-share metrics. A 3:1 split means historical EPS must be divided by 3 for comparability. Mergers and spin-offs create discontinuities that simple adjustment factors cannot resolve.

Leakage becomes visible when the same simple strategy is run twice: once using an as-of eligible ("as-known") fundamentals view and once using a naïve "latest available today" view. The second backtest often appears better—not because the signal is stronger, but because the dataset has silently incorporated information that arrived later.

In practice, even small amounts of leakage can swamp the true signal-to-noise ratio in fundamentals-based strategies. The lesson is methodological rather than a fixed percentage: if a vendor cannot explain how it handles revisions, amendments, and identifier history, presume the dataset is *not* PIT-correct until proven otherwise.

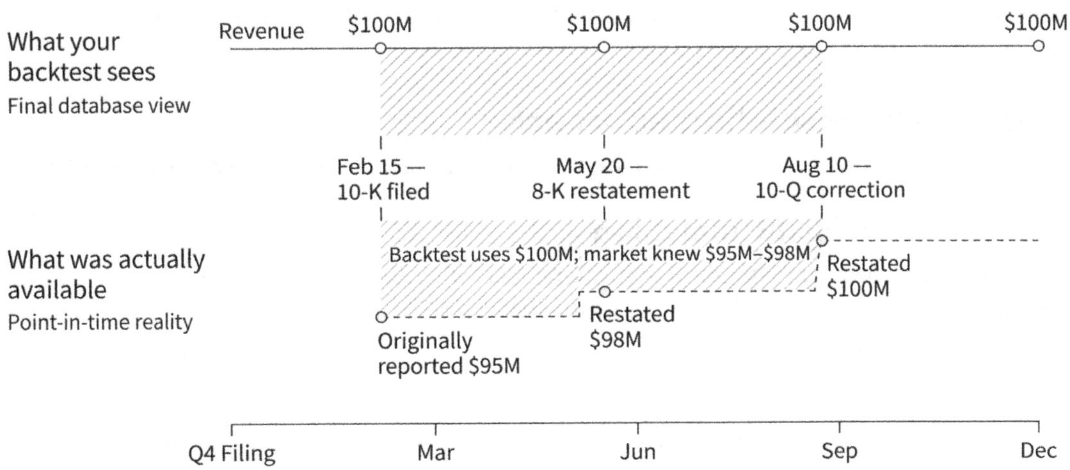

Figure 4.1: Lookahead bias from restated fundamentals

Figure 4.1 shows a naïve "latest value" fundamentals dataset that assigns the restated Q3 revenue ($100M) to dates before its public release. A point-in-time dataset keeps the original value ($95M) until the restatement date, preventing leakage at the strategy decision date. The next section discusses how to address entity resolution.

4.2 Entity resolution and mapping

Before we can combine any data from disparate sources, we must address the universal problem of **entity resolution**. Different data providers, regulatory systems, and internal databases all identify the same company differently. Ekster and Kolm (2020) identify entity mapping as one of the primary technical challenges in alternative data integration. Without correct mapping, any multi-source analysis is compromised from the start.

Why resolution is critical

Consider a strategy that combines SEC fundamental data with alternative data on government contracts. The SEC identifies companies by Central Index Key (CIK). Federal award data commonly includes the Unique Entity Identifier (UEI) (which replaced DUNS in April 2022), as well as legal names and address fields. Credit card transaction data might use proprietary merchant codes. None of these maps directly to stock tickers without crosswalks and a clear definition of the target layer (issuer, subsidiary, security).

A single false-positive match can poison every downstream join; prioritize precision and escalate uncertain matches. If "ZOOM VIDEO COMMUNICATIONS" (ticker ZM) is confused with "ZOOM TECHNOLOGIES INC" (formerly ticker ZOOM, now ZTNO), fundamental data from one company gets paired with alternative signals from another. The resulting "alpha" is noise.

The problem multiplies with corporate complexity. IBM's government contracts might be filed under "INTERNATIONAL BUSINESS MACHINES CORPORATION," "IBM CORP," "IBM GLOBAL SERVICES," or dozens of subsidiary names. These must all map to ticker IBM, but contracts from spun-off, now-independent units like Kyndryl should not.

A hierarchical resolution approach

Practical entity resolution proceeds in stages, from deterministic to probabilistic to model-based.

Stage 1: Deterministic matching

When a data source provides **standard identifiers**, start with deterministic joins. The main pitfall is resolving to the wrong *layer*, because "company identifiers" can refer to different things. More specifically, identifiers can point to:

- A **legal entity** (the corporate parent or filing entity)
- A **security** (a specific tradable instrument, such as a share class, bond, or ADR)
- A **derivatives contract** (a specific listed contract/expiration on an exchange)

Production systems typically maintain three linked master tables—**entities**, **securities**, and (when relevant) **contracts**—with **time-valid mappings** between them.

For instance, "Apple" can legitimately resolve to different objects depending on the question:

- A legal entity (via a **Legal Entity Identifier** or **Central Index Key**)
- A security (for example, the common stock versus a specific bond issuance, each with its own identifier)
- An exchange-listed contract (for futures/options)

So "identifier match succeeded" is not the same as "resolved correctly" unless the correct layer (entity, security, or contract) has been selected.

Common standardized identifiers (and what they identify):

- **Legal Entity Identifier (LEI)**: A 20-character identifier for *legal entities* used in financial transactions (ISO 17442).
- **Central Index Key (CIK)**: The SEC identifier for *filing entities* in EDGAR; mapping to traded instruments typically requires additional reference tables (for example, subsidiaries versus holding companies).
- **Financial Instrument Global Identifier (FIGI)**: An *instrument-level* identifier (security-level, not entity-level); OpenFIGI provides lookup and mapping APIs.
- **CUSIP/ISIN/SEDOL**: *Security-level* identifiers used in trading and settlement (CUSIP: U.S.; ISIN: global; SEDOL: U.K.).

When a source includes any of these, resolution is usually a straightforward join against the relevant crosswalk. The harder cases come from sources that omit institutional identifiers—or sources that include one but only at a different layer than the target.

A wrong-join example

Alternative data often arrives at the *issuer* level (for example, web traffic for "Amazon.com Inc"), while returns are measured at the *security* level (AMZN common stock). Without an effective-date security master, this join can fail silently: (1) joining issuer-level data to the wrong share class (Class A versus Class B with different voting rights and prices); (2) joining to an ADR instead of the ordinary share; (3) using a ticker that belonged to a different entity before a corporate action. The fix: maintain explicit issuer→security mappings with effective dates, and constrain all joins by `effective_date <= decision_time < end_date`.

Stage 2: Probabilistic matching

When identifiers are absent, text matching becomes necessary. String similarity algorithms handle variations in company names:

- **Levenshtein Distance**: Counts character edits (insertions, deletions, substitutions) to transform one string into another. "TESLA INC" and "TESLA, INC." are one edit apart.
- **Jaro-Winkler Similarity**: Weighted similarity favors matching prefixes. Handles abbreviations well—"INTERNATIONAL BUSINESS MACHINES" scores high against "INTL BUSINESS MACH".

- **Token-based methods:** Jaccard similarity on word tokens. "APPLE INC" and "APPLE INCORPORATED" share the important token despite different suffixes.

Libraries like `rapidfuzz` implement these algorithms efficiently, enabling fuzzy matching against reference lists with configurable similarity thresholds. A typical pattern extracts the best matches above a confidence threshold (often 85-90%), and flags lower-confidence matches for manual review.

Probabilistic matching benefits from human-in-the-loop QA because the failure mode is asymmetric: a missed match costs coverage, but a false match can corrupt every downstream join and backtest. The right objective is usually high precision first, then improved recall via escalation stages and better candidate generation.

The complicated cases tend to fall into repeatable buckets:

- Subsidiaries whose legal names are unrelated to the parent brand
- DBAs and trade names
- Joint ventures and consortia
- Generic names that collide across unrelated entities

For example, "Amazon Web Services" may not fuzzy-match to "Amazon.com Inc" despite the clear relationship, requiring either subsidiary lookup tables or embedding-based semantic matching. Name-only fuzzy matching is rarely sufficient for these cases.

For threshold selection, a tiered scheme is typical: auto-accept only at very high confidence (practitioner thresholds often sit around 95%); route a middle band (commonly 85-95%) to manual review; escalate the tail (below roughly 85%) to richer features such as addresses, websites, or descriptions. Calibrate these cutoffs against the empirical score distribution in a labeled sample rather than treating the numbers as universal constants. Track match quality over time—if post-hoc review reveals incorrect matches, adjust thresholds or add disambiguation features.

Stage 3: Manual review and QA

Records in the middle-confidence band—high enough that deterministic and probabilistic matching produced a credible candidate, but not high enough for auto-acceptance—escalate to a human-review queue. Effective workflows separate the queue by failure mode (ambiguous fuzzy match, missing identifier, candidate-set tie) so reviewers can apply the right disambiguation procedure rather than triaging case by case. Each decision is written back to the master entity table as a new alias or a rejection, with the reviewer, timestamp, and rationale. Hence, the audit trail supports both downstream debugging and periodic threshold recalibration.

Embedding-based semantic matching, useful when fuzzy and identifier matching both fail to disambiguate (for example, "Amazon Web Services" versus "Amazon.com Inc"), is covered in *Chapter 10* (text embeddings) and *Chapter 23* (knowledge graphs), where Chen et al. (2023) describe FinKG. This knowledge graph integrates SEC filings and market data for entity linking across U.S. companies.

Building a master security database

Production systems maintain a master entity table that serves as the canonical reference:

id	name	ticker	cik	lei	figi
1001	Tesla, Inc.	TSLA	1318605	54930043XZGB27CTOV49	BBG000N9MNX3
1002	Apple Inc.	AAPL	320193	HWUPKR0MPOU8FGXBT394	BBG000B9XRY4

Table 4.3: Master entity example

All incoming data—regardless of source identifier—resolves to this master `entity_id` before joining with other datasets. The master table accumulates name variants and identifier mappings over time, improving resolution accuracy as more data is processed.

Temporal entity mapping

Static mapping is a hidden source of lookahead and survivorship bias. Entity relationships are dynamic: tickers are reused (ZOOM belonged to Zoom Technologies before Zoom Video took the ticker ZM), and identities evolve through rebranding (FB → META) or mergers. A production system must be temporally aware, tracking when each identifier was valid:

id	identifier_type	identifier_value	effective_date	end_date
1095	ticker	FB	2012-05-18	2022-06-08
1095	ticker	META	2022-06-09	NULL

Table 4.4: Temporal mapping example

Without `effective_date` constraints, a backtest might join 2015 alternative data to 2024 ticker symbols—creating a dataset that could never have existed. Every cross-source join must be constrained by observation timestamp to ensure the mapping was valid at that historical moment.

Mapping quality assurance

Production entity resolution requires ongoing validation:

Check	Method	Frequency
Confidence Tiers	Segment mappings by confidence using calibrated cutoffs (commonly around 95% auto-accept, 85-95% review, below 85% use another method)	Per batch
Sampling Audit	Manually verify 1–5% of auto-accepted mappings for false positives	Monthly
Drift Monitoring	Track match rate and confidence distribution over time; investigate sudden changes	Weekly

Table 4.5: Quality assurance example

A declining match rate often signals changes in the data source (for example, new naming conventions or added subsidiaries). Rising false-positive rates indicate threshold drift or coverage gaps in the reference data.

Key QA metrics to track:

- **Match rate by tier:** Percentage of records resolved at each stage (deterministic, fuzzy, embedding, or unresolved)
- **Confidence score distribution:** Histogram of match scores; watch for bimodal patterns indicating threshold issues
- **False positive estimate:** From sampling audit—fraction of auto-accepted matches that are incorrect
- **Temporal drift:** Week-over-week change in match rate and mean confidence; sudden shifts warrant investigation

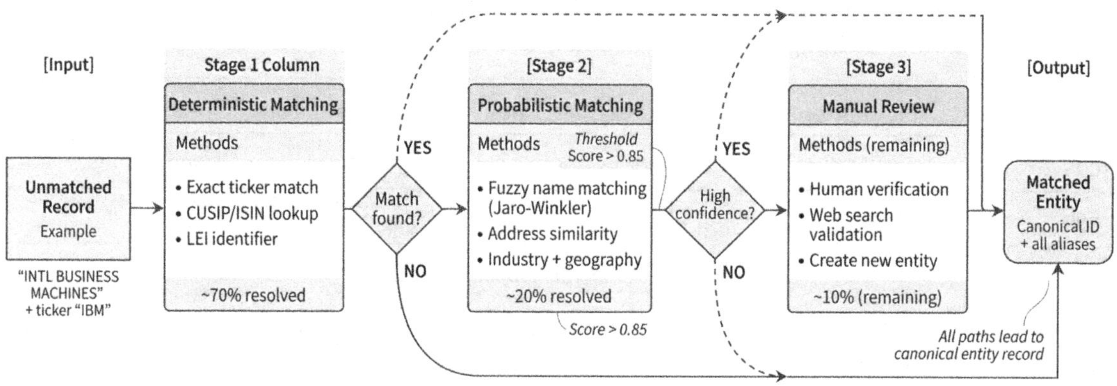

Figure 4.2: Hierarchical entity resolution pipeline

Figure 4.2 shows the entity-resolution pipeline. Deterministic identifier matching resolves the bulk of records; probabilistic record linkage absorbs name variants above a confidence threshold; the residual middle-confidence band escalates to manual review, with all decisions written back to a master entity table under time-valid mappings. The next section surveys the fundamental data landscape across asset classes.

Implementation: `05_entity_resolution` demonstrates deterministic joins, fuzzy string matching (with normalization), and a simple master database pattern in an end-to-end pipeline.

4.3 Fundamentals across the asset-class spectrum

Sections 4.1–4.2 established the PIT contract and entity mapping for equities. This section generalizes those concepts: every asset class has revision-prone fundamentals, but the *timestamp authority* and *instrument mapping* differ across asset classes. Getting these details wrong introduces the same lookahead bias—the failure mode is universal, even if the mechanics vary.

The idea of "fundamentals" extends well beyond corporate equities, but the meaning changes by asset class. Each domain has distinct economic drivers, publication mechanics, and revision behavior, so the engineering problem is not "collect more data"—it is building time-consistent inputs that respect release calendars, vintages, and instrument conventions.

Macro and sovereign data (FX/Rates)

Rates and FX are driven by macro fundamentals such as growth, inflation, labor conditions, monetary policy, and fiscal sustainability. The engineering challenge is that these series come from multiple agencies and are published on *release schedules* with **lags** and **revisions**, so what was known at each decision time must be modeled explicitly.

Key sources

Federal Reserve Economic Data (FRED) aggregates hundreds of thousands of time series from many sources and provides APIs for retrieval and vintage-aware workflows. For non-U.S. macro, primary sources include Eurostat, IMF/World Bank datasets, national statistics agencies, and central banks. (See *Chapter 2* for a complete data source inventory; this section focuses on timing and revisions.) FRED data show the U.S. 10y-2y yield curve has been inverted on 15.5% of days since 2000, including 36% of days since 2020—a regime-shift anchor for macroeconomic state variables.

Alignment challenges

Macro data presents several engineering challenges:

- **Release cadence variation:** Many key macro series are measured over a period (month/quarter) but published later on scheduled dates. GDP is published quarterly, with multiple monthly vintages (advance/second/third estimates), while claims are weekly and CPI is monthly. Aligning these to a daily decision grid requires a clear policy: treat releases as **event data** (timestamped) and carry forward only after they become available, or treat macro as a slowly evolving **state** updated at release times. Avoid interpolation methods that blend future values into the past.
- **Release time matters:** For daily or intraday models, the release *timestamp* (date, time, and time zone) determines eligibility; "same day" does not mean "pre-trade." Many U.S. releases are scheduled at 8:30 a.m. ET, but schedules can shift due to holidays or disruptions, so the pipeline should ingest and store the published release timestamp rather than hard-coding assumptions.
- **Time zones and calendars:** A global macro dataset must normalize timestamps (typically to UTC) and track the local release calendar. "Quarterly" series from different jurisdictions can be released on different local dates/times and revised on different schedules, so PIT correctness requires storing both the *period covered* and the *availability timestamp*.
- **Revision histories:** Many macro series are revised after initial release. Backtesting on today's "final" series gives the model information that was not available at the time. The correct input for realistic backtests is vintage data ("what was known when"), not the latest revision.

FRED supports **vintage-aware retrieval** through **ALFRED** (Archival FRED): observations have real-time validity windows (in other words, the value that was current between two vintage dates), and the API exposes vintage dates and vintage-specific downloads. The Philadelphia Fed Real-Time Data Set provides the canonical reference for vintage-aware macroeconomic research; Croushore (2008) surveys the methods and pitfalls. In practice, the two production patterns are (i) querying specific vintage dates to reconstruct what a model would have seen historically, or (ii) storing the revision ladder explicitly when the downstream strategy is revision-sensitive.

PIT requirements include storing the release timestamp and calendar; maintaining the vintage/revision ladder; normalizing time zones; and distinguishing the period covered from the availability time.

Implementation: `06_fred_macro_eda` introduces the macro data; `07_macro_data_alignment` illustrates how to load native-frequency series, model publication lag, and how vintage-aware inputs differ from "latest series" inputs.

Commodities – Physical market data

Commodity prices are anchored to physical supply-and-demand constraints. However, the data is often **domain-specific** (inventories, shipments, crop conditions, refinery utilization), and the tradable instruments are **contractual** (futures by delivery month). That creates a two-part engineering problem:

1. Ingest scheduled fundamental releases with correct timestamps.
2. Map them to the contract you could actually trade.

Energy and agriculture

U.S. government agencies anchor the calendar for energy and agricultural fundamentals. The U.S. Energy Information Administration (EIA), the U.S. Department of Agriculture's World Agricultural Supply and Demand Estimates (WASDE) report, and the U.S. Commodity Futures Trading Commission's (CFTC) Commitments of Traders (COT) report are timestamped events; joins should occur only after their published release times. The EIA's Weekly Petroleum Status Report follows a standard schedule (Wednesdays at 10:30 a.m. ET, with holiday exceptions); the release timestamp must be part of the dataset.

USDA's WASDE report is released at 12:00 p.m. ET on scheduled dates and is widely viewed as a risk event for grains and oilseeds. Use the release timestamp; avoid any workflow that implicitly treats pre-release expectations as published facts.

Meteorological data (for example, from NOAA) often enter as high-frequency state variables rather than as scheduled releases; treat it differently from "lock-up" economic reports.

Mapping to tradable instruments

Physical market data must be mapped **to the instrument you can trade**. When an inventory number is released, the relevant price response may concentrate in the actively traded front-month contract (or the most liquid point on the curve), not in an abstract "continuous series" that blends multiple delivery months.

This is where the *futures roll logic* from *Chapter 3* becomes an input dependency: a consistent mapping from calendar time to the active contract. Fundamental event timestamps should be joined to the active contract at their timestamp, then carried into any continuous-series representation using the same roll rules as prices.

Beyond the physical fundamentals, CFTC's COT reports provide a public snapshot of trader positioning by category. COT is a PIT dataset: positions are as of Tuesday. They are generally released on Friday at 3:30 p.m. ET (with holiday delays), so backtests must treat the report as **available only after the release time.** Positioning extremes and rapid changes are often used as sentiment-style features (contrarian or trend-confirming); any claim about predictability should be evaluated out-of-sample with the release lag enforced.

PIT requirements for this include tracking scheduled release timestamps; mapping fundamental events to the correct contract and curve point at event time; applying roll rules consistent with prices; and enforcing reporting lags.

Implementation: `08_futures_positioning` shows COT retrieval, PIT availability timestamps, and positioning z-scores.

Cryptocurrency and digital assets – On-chain fundamentals

Crypto markets introduce a new category of fundamentals: on-chain data is publicly observable and programmatically verifiable, often at high frequency—the engineering challenge shifts from access to interpretation. Different chains differ in how quickly transactions become final, how vulnerable recent blocks are to reorganization, which token standards they use, and how protocol events are represented in the data. As a result, even the same metric may need to be defined differently across ecosystems. Harvey et al. (2022) provide a practitioner-oriented investor guide that emphasizes that crypto is much broader than just spot bitcoin.

Core on-chain metrics

Core on-chain metrics include:

- **Network activity:** Active addresses, transaction counts, and transfer volumes provide a first view of protocol usage. These measures can signal adoption and engagement, but they require careful interpretation because bots, internal transfers, or address-reuse patterns may inflate activity.
- **Security metrics:** In proof-of-work networks, hash rate measures the total computational power securing the chain; in proof-of-stake networks, staked value measures the capital validators have committed and put at risk. In both cases, these are rough proxies for the economic cost of attacking the network, though their interpretation depends on the protocol design and market structure.

- **Economics:** Token supply schedules, inflation mechanics, issuance rules, and fee dynamics shape incentives for users, validators, and investors. These variables also influence valuation narratives by affecting scarcity, dilution, and the distribution of economic rewards. Separately, futures positioning data, including COT-style classifications, are often used to study who trades crypto futures and whether specific trader categories exhibit timing ability (Baur and Smales, 2022).
- **DeFi metrics:** Total value locked, or TVL, is widely used as a proxy for the capital committed to a protocol. It can be informative, but should be interpreted cautiously because it may reflect double-counting, leverage, or token price swings rather than net new economic activity. Protocol fees and revenue offer additional measures of usage and value capture, but definitions vary across aggregators—record the exact definition used.

Data sources

When it comes to cryptocurrency data sources, direct access (running nodes) provides maximum control but entails high operational costs. Indexing protocols and analytics platforms (for example, The Graph, Dune) make decoded blockchain data queryable without requiring full infrastructure maintenance.

Commercial aggregators provide curated metrics via API, but they should be treated like any vendor feed: document transformations, definitions, and backfills. Alexander and Dakos (2020) examine which cryptocurrency data sources scholars should use, finding that major aggregators provide statistically equivalent data for liquid assets but can diverge for illiquid tokens.

AMM and DEX data

Decentralized exchanges using AMMs generate transparent on-chain records of liquidity provision, swaps, and fees. Lehar and Parlour's (2021) empirical work on Uniswap illustrates how this transparency enables measurement of market structure that is hard to obtain in traditional venues.

PIT requirements include understanding finality and reorg policies; documenting metric definitions and provider transforms; tracking backfills and recomputations; and accounting for differences in chain and token standards. The next section explores alternative data and discusses how to work with this increasingly relevant source.

> **Implementation:** `09_onchain_fundamentals` illustrates how to query on-chain metrics and align them with traditional market data.

4.4 Understanding alternative data

Alternative data can be a genuine edge, but it is also a high-variance investment: noisy signals, unstable coverage, hidden backfills, and real legal and reputational risk. A disciplined evaluation process is what separates interesting datasets from production-worthy inputs.

In *Chapter 2*, we covered data quality issues such as PIT correctness, survivorship bias, and identifier integrity, which apply to *all* financial data. This section focuses on evaluation criteria for alternative data acquisition decisions—specifically, whether to invest in a new dataset.

The alternative data landscape

Alternative data encompasses information beyond traditional market and fundamental sources. Green and Zhang (2024) provide a useful taxonomy:

- **Text and attention data:** News articles, social media, earnings call transcripts, and search activity. Classic evidence shows that media tone can predict short-horizon market behavior, though effects are sensitive to leakage and model specification (Tetlock, 2007). The *engineering* of text data (extraction, cleaning, PIT storage) is covered in *Section 4.5*; the *featurization* of text (sentiment, embeddings, transformers) is covered in *Chapter 10*.
- **Business process data:** Credit card transactions, point-of-sale records, job postings, and hiring patterns. LinkedIn entry/exit data and Glassdoor ratings can predict operational health, though coverage is uneven and firm-reported numbers in 10-Ks are often too lagged to compete (Green and Zhang, 2024).
- **Sensor and geospatial data:** Satellite imagery of parking lots or construction sites, geolocation tracking, shipping vessel positions, and industrial sensor readings.
- **Prediction markets:** Platforms trading binary event contracts whose prices produce continuously updated probability proxies. Ng et al. (2025) document meaningful price discovery in modern prediction markets, finding that higher-liquidity venues incorporate information more quickly. Limitations include thin liquidity outside headline contracts and regulatory fragmentation.

On the demand side, evidence suggests sell-side analysts increasingly reference non-traditional datasets in their research workflows, and that this adoption is associated with improved forecast accuracy (Chi, Hwang, and Zheng, 2024).

The evaluation framework

Alternative datasets usually fail for predictable reasons: they are not incremental once existing features are controlled for, they cannot be reconstructed at decision time, or they introduce legal and operational risks that overwhelm their expected value. A practical due diligence focuses on signal content, data quality, legal risks, and commercial/engineering costs with an explicit bias toward stopping early on hard constraints rather than debating marginal score differences.

Signal content evaluation asks whether the dataset can plausibly deliver incremental, tradable information:

- **Uniqueness:** Specify the baseline feature set and test incremental value rather than raw correlations (for example, baseline-versus-baseline and dataset-versus-dataset-only). Improvements that vanish under reasonable controls are typically redundant proxies.

- **Decay and durability:** Treat half-life as a design constraint. McLean and Pontiff (2016) show that published stock return predictors lose ~58% of their performance post-publication—a useful baseline for how quickly signals erode. Whether a specific alternative dataset "accelerates diffusion" is an empirical question to test under realistic timestamps and costs (Hong et al., 2000).
- **Common failure modes:** (i) Real signal content but not tradable after costs/capacity, (ii) apparent performance created by revisions or look-ahead.

Data quality checks verify that we can reproduce results under production constraints, especially those related to point-in-time availability.

- **Quality and stability:** Verify versioning, revision exposure, and detectability of changes to the methodology. Backfills and vendor process changes can affect performance; ESG ratings illustrate how methodological differences drive disagreement, making "stability of measurement" central (Berg et al., 2022).
- **Coverage:** Evaluate representativeness across the tradable universe (names, regions, sectors) and across regimes; diagnose systematic bias or missingness (for example, low coverage of small-cap or non-U.S.).
- **Latency:** Align publication lag, cadence, and timestamp conventions with the decision process. If "first observable time" cannot be stated precisely, point-in-time backtests are not defensible.

Legal risks are a hard-fail gate: risk cannot be "optimized away" by model performance.

- **Compliance and rights:** Establish provenance, permitted uses, contractual restrictions, audit/deletion obligations, and downstream redistribution limits.
- **Red flags:** (i) Material Nonpublic Information (MNPI) by narrowness (small panels, constrained geographies, entity-specific "channel checks"), (ii) privacy risk through linkage even without explicit identifiers (device/ad IDs, granular location/event data) with GDPR/CCPA exposure.

Commercial and engineering gates ensure the dataset fits deployable capacity and does not impose disproportionate operational drag.

- **Technical friction and economics:** Evaluate total cost of ownership (integration, entity resolution, storage, monitoring, schema-change handling, incident load) and compare expected value to roadmap capacity.
- **Operationalization test:** Estimate one-time engineering lift, ongoing maintenance burden, and a conservative value range after realistic latency, costs, and capacity constraints.
- **Decision rule:** Privilege hard constraints (legal, point-in-time integrity) over marginal differences elsewhere; only compare "scores" among datasets that clear the hard-fail gates.

Build versus buy for alternative data

Chapter 2 discussed general build-versus-buy tradeoffs for financial data. For alternative data specifically, additional factors apply:

- **Alpha crowding:** Built pipelines using proprietary internal data remain differentiated; purchased datasets erode as adoption spreads.
- **Legal risk asymmetry:** Web scraping and data collection operate in legal gray areas; vendors may provide representations, but the buyer still owns compliance and the interpretation of what use is permitted.
- **Maintenance burden:** Alternative data sources change frequently (API breaks, coverage shifts, and methodology updates); vendors absorb these operational costs.

For most organizations, a hybrid approach works best: buy cleaned, validated data for mainstream alternative sources; build capabilities only for truly proprietary signals where internal data or relationships provide unique access.

Data sources and implementation

The ecosystem spans terminal platforms (Bloomberg, LSEG Workspace), vendors specializing in different modalities, such as payments, web data, or geospatial data, and marketplaces such as Nasdaq Data Link, Snowflake Marketplace, and AWS Data Exchange. Marketplaces can simplify procurement, but do not eliminate the need for PIT validation and methodology audits.

Several sources provide meaningful alternative data for experimentation (the chapter `README` lists additional sources):

- **GDELT Project:** Large-scale global news event data for geopolitical risk and event detection; just the 2015 dataset weighs 2.5TB; requires NLP pipelines to extract signals (see next section and *Chapter 10*).
- **SEC 13F filings:** Institutional holdings disclosed quarterly; useful for "smart money" positioning and crowded trade detection.
- **On-chain DeFi metrics:** Total Value Locked (TVL) and protocol revenue as crypto-native fundamentals.
- **Prediction markets:** Kalshi (CFTC-regulated) and Polymarket (crypto-based) provide time series of event probabilities.

Text data, including corporate filings, news, and earnings calls, represents the largest category of accessible alternative data—but requires substantial engineering before it becomes model-ready. The next section covers the extraction and storage pipeline, and *Chapter 10* covers featurization (sentiment dictionaries, embeddings, and fine-tuned transformers such as FinBERT).

Implementation:

- `10_institutional_holdings_13f` builds the 2024Q3 manager-stock graph from SEC 13F filings, computes manager-level concentration metrics and co-ownership edges, and surfaces the most widely held issuers.
- `11_defi_tvl_evaluation` walks the DeFi TVL panel (4 chains, 2017-2026) and tests TVL growth as a forward-return predictor (peak IC = 0.12; weak signal).
- `12_kalshi_prediction_markets` extracts event-prior probabilities from Kalshi markets and demonstrates the API pattern for prediction-market consumption.
- `13_polymarket_prediction_markets` covers the Polymarket equivalent, with notes on liquidity and contract-design differences.

4.5 Using text data for NLP features

SEC filings are *fundamental* data by source, but the unstructured text they contain, such as Management Discussion and Analysis, Risk Factors, and earnings call transcripts, is, by nature, *alternative* data: it requires NLP pipelines to extract signals that cannot be reduced to accounting line items. This section covers the engineering work that makes text usable: source selection, section extraction, cleaning, and PIT-correct storage.

Targeting MD&A and risk factors

SEC 10-K annual reports contain standardized narrative sections that provide rich signals about a company's outlook:

- **Management's Discussion and Analysis (MD&A, Item 7)**: Narrative discussion intended to provide material information for assessing financial condition, results of operations, liquidity, and cash flows (Regulation S-K Item 303).
- **Risk Factors (Item 1A)**: Required disclosure of *material* factors that make an investment speculative or risky, organized under relevant headings; the SEC discourages generic risk factors (Regulation S-K Item 105). Often lengthy and standardized, but *changes* in structure, emphasis, or newly introduced themes are frequently more informative than the level of boilerplate.

These sections contain information that cannot be reduced to numbers: qualitative context, forward-looking language, and explanations of changes that may not appear in line items. Tetlock (2014) surveys how textual information transmits to financial markets, establishing the theoretical foundation for extracting signals from corporate narratives. Modern NLP approaches (including finance-adapted BERT variants such as FinBERT) can extract more context-sensitive signals than dictionary methods, but only if extraction and timestamps are correct.

The engineering pipeline

Building a filing-based text dataset requires four engineering steps:

1. **Document selection**: Pick the primary filing document, not an exhibit.
2. **Section extraction**: Identify item boundaries robustly.
3. **Cleaning and normalization**: Remove markup and non-prose artifacts while preserving paragraph structure.
4. **Point-in-time storage**: Store availability timestamps and audit keys.

Step 1: Filing access and metadata

EDGAR provides filing packages plus submission metadata. Libraries such as `edgartools` can simplify retrieval, but the pipeline must still capture the filing's stable identifier (accession number), form type (10-K/10-Q, amendments), period end, and the **SEC acceptance timestamp** (when the filing became public). That metadata becomes part of the PIT contract for downstream NLP features. The accession number is the natural primary key because multiple filings can share the same date, and amendments require separate tracking.

Step 2: Section extraction

Extraction via document parsers should be layered (structured access when available; HTML-anchored boundaries otherwise) and instrumented with measurable quality checks (missing sections, collisions, length outliers). Item numbers label sections, but the same filing can contain multiple "Item 7" mentions (for example, in the Table of Contents and cross-references), and formatting varies across filers and over time. Amendments (10-K/A) and older filings can break naive boundary logic—treat extraction quality as a measurable output and sample failures for iterative rule refinement.

Step 3: Cleaning and normalization

Cleaning should remove markup and artifacts of repeated filing without destroying linguistic structure. Common issues include:

- **HTML remnants**: Unclosed tags, entity codes (` `, `&`), style attributes.
- **Table structures**: Financial tables embedded in narrative sections. May need separate handling or removal.
- **Boilerplate**: Safe-harbor statements, standard risk language, repeated cross-references. In many corpora, boilerplate accounts for a large fraction of the extracted text. The right approach is to *measure* it (for example, by comparing year-over-year text overlap) and decide whether to remove it (for novelty/change features) or keep it (for level-based sentiment features).

Cleaning should preserve paragraph boundaries (important for downstream chunking and change detection) while removing non-prose artifacts and normalizing whitespace.

Step 4: PIT-correct storage

Store each extracted section as a row keyed by a stable filing identifier (accession number) and include both the reporting period and the availability timestamp. The minimal schema includes:

- **Identifiers:** `cik` (company), `accession` (filing), and `section` (Item 7, Item 1A, and so on) together form the primary key—this triple uniquely identifies each extracted section, including amendments.
- **Timestamps:** `filing_date` and `accepted_at` (the SEC acceptance timestamp, to the second) determine *availability*—when this text became public. `period_end` indicates the fiscal period covered.
- **Content:** The `text` column stores the extracted section; optionally, store both raw and cleaned versions.
- **Metadata:** Form type (10-K, 10-Q, amendments), extraction method, pattern version, and character offsets enable auditing and re-extraction when rules change.

Following the bitemporal data model introduced above:

- `filing_date`/`accepted_at` (knowledge time) determines *availability*—when this text became public. Use `accepted_at` for intraday PIT correctness.
- `period_end` (valid time) indicates the reporting period covered.

Store both **the raw extracted text** and **the cleaned text**, along with extraction metadata (method, pattern version, offsets), so the extraction can be audited and rerun when rules change. Persist to Parquet for efficient filtering by section and time.

Output artifact

The pipeline produces a **text corpus** with the schema described above. Key fields:

- `cik + accession + section` uniquely identify an extracted section version (including amendments).
- `filing_date`/`accepted_at` enable PIT-correct feature construction.
- `section` enables targeted modeling (MD&A versus Risk Factors versus Business).

Text is most useful when aligned with numeric outcomes. The engineering requirement is that joins must be PIT-safe and audit-safe. The accession number is the natural primary key; keeping both `accepted_at` and `period_end` allows the same filing to be queried as of any historical date without leaking later revisions.

This corpus is the input for *Chapter 10*, which covers the full NLP feature engineering pipeline—dictionary-based sentiment, static word embeddings, and fine-tuned transformer models—and demonstrates a 'news surprise' alpha factor that measures semantic deviation of today's news from recent coverage, depending directly on the PIT-correct text storage established here.

Implementation: `14_text_data_extraction` shows the complete pipeline from EDGAR filings to a structured Parquet dataset. It demonstrates the year-over-year change-analysis primitive on Apple's 10-K: the 2025 filing's Risk Factors section runs 9,792 words with 92.9% word overlap relative to the prior year (Jaccard 0.31), surfacing 28 new risk-factor terms.

4.6 Summary

We have laid the data engineering foundations for working with fundamental and alternative data. The central theme is point-in-time correctness: every data source—whether SEC filings, macroeconomic releases, futures positioning, or blockchain metrics—must be timestamped with both the date it became available and the period it covers. The bitemporal model introduced here applies uniformly across asset classes and data types, enabling defensible backtests that avoid look-ahead bias.

The companion notebooks demonstrate these principles in practice: extracting XBRL fundamentals with proper vintage handling, aligning macro data by release schedule rather than reference period, building text corpora from SEC filings with robust section extraction, and evaluating alternative data sources through a systematic framework.

These PIT-correct artifacts become the inputs to *Chapter 8*'s feature engineering workflow. The EDGAR text corpus from *Section 4.5* feeds *Chapter 10*, where we build NLP-based features (sentiment, topics, and embeddings) on the storage pipeline established here.

Chapter 5 turns to synthetic financial data: generative models that augment scarce histories and stress-test backtests against unobserved scenarios.

5

Synthetic Financial Data

Every quantitative strategy depends on historical data, but history provides only one realized path through a large space of market outcomes. A backtest on a 2010–2025 sample can indicate a stable relationship, but it can also look strong simply because the realized path was favorable to the strategy's assumptions and parameter choices. One response is to augment the single realized history with additional, statistically consistent market paths sampled from a fitted generative model.

Those sampled paths are **synthetic data**, drawn from a model fitted to the empirical joint distribution of observed data, designed to preserve marginal behavior and dependence structure across time, assets, and regimes. Related terms include **simulated data** (typically parametric Monte Carlo under an assumed process) and **generated scenarios** (samples conditioned on a specified regime or state). All three supplement a single realized history with additional samples to assess robustness.

The objective is *robustness assessment*, not prediction. If generated paths reproduce key characteristics of financial time series, then strategy performance can be evaluated as a distribution under the learned model rather than as a single point estimate. Synthetic data can also support *model development* by augmenting real training samples. In these settings, the performance must still be assessed on real out-of-sample data, and generators must be treated as potential sources of bias.

Throughout this chapter, synthetic data is treated as a *decision-support tool* rather than as a substitute for historical evidence. Its value depends on whether it improves a downstream task. In finance, this standard is demanding: general distributional similarity is not enough if the generated data fails to preserve tail behavior, dependence, volatility clustering, or regime dynamics. By the end of this chapter, you will be able to:

- Diagnose when a historical backtest is underpowered and when synthetic generation is a reasonable supplement.
- Select a generative architecture based on data type and sampling frequency.
- Apply stylized-fact diagnostics to generated returns.
- Evaluate synthetic data using **Fidelity–Utility–Privacy criteria** and Train-on-Synthetic-Test-on-Real validation.

- Identify generator-specific risks, including bias amplification, generator overfitting, and missing novel scenarios.

The chapter first motivates the use of synthetic financial data, describes the stylized facts it needs to reproduce, and explains a practical evaluation framework. We then turn to classical simulation methods, before proceeding to learned generators, including GANs, diffusion models, and LLM-based generators for tabular financial data. The chapter closes by applying the evaluation framework across these methods.

5.1 The quant's dilemma

A quantitative strategy is developed and validated on a single realized history. This is true for discretionary rule-based systems and for machine-learning pipelines that fit predictive models and then backtest the implied trading rules. The historical record contains only a limited number of crises, regime shifts, and correlation breakdowns, so inference can be fragile because evidence is **path-limited**: apparent performance may be dominated by episodes that need not repeat.

The multiple testing challenge

This path limitation manifests as inflated performance when strategy research adapts as results emerge: strategy development is an iterative search over many coupled choices, including the universe and filters; signal and feature definitions; label horizons and sampling schemes; model class and regularization; cross-validation design; hyperparameters; risk controls; execution assumptions; and portfolio construction details. Each additional decision expands the search space and increases the chance of selecting an in-sample winner that reflects noise, data quirks, or favorable market episodes rather than a persistent edge.

Adaptive research creates a selection problem. As the number of tested variants grows, selection inflation becomes material: the best observed in-sample performance improves mechanically with the number of trials, even when true performance is zero. Bailey et al. (2015) formalize this risk and argue that the probability of backtest overfitting can exceed 50%: under independence and normal-error approximations, after testing 10 configurations, the expected maximum in-sample Sharpe, a measure of risk-adjusted performance, is 1.57, even when all configurations have a true Sharpe of 0; with 100 trials, the expected maximum exceeds 2.5.

Interpreted broadly, this is a statement about the end-to-end research process: the reported result is the output of a selection procedure operating on limited data. The implication is not that backtests, or predictive models, are useless, but that **performance estimates should be treated as conditional on the research path taken**. Bailey and Lopez de Prado (2014) propose the **Deflated Sharpe Ratio**, which adjusts performance inference for non-normality and the number of trials (see *Chapter 17*). We will encounter additional multiple-testing corrections throughout the book. However, selection-aware statistical corrections can only adjust inference to account for this effect; they do not create additional market histories to assess robustness.

Synthetic data as simulation infrastructure

Synthetic generation addresses path-limited evidence by turning a single realized history into a distribution of plausible histories. Cetingoz and Lehalle (2025) describe this as sampling additional trajectories from an estimated distribution to support robustness checks beyond a single realized path. In practice, the workflow fits a generative model to observed data, aiming to capture key **stylized facts of financial time series**, such as:

- **Heavy tails:** Extreme returns occur more frequently than under a Gaussian model.
- **Volatility clustering:** Large absolute returns cluster in time; the autocorrelation of squared or absolute returns decays slowly.
- **Leverage effect:** Negative returns are associated with higher subsequent volatility, especially in equity markets.
- **Weak return autocorrelation:** Linear autocorrelation in returns is typically small at daily horizons.

At a minimum, the resulting model should generate data that capture marginal distributions, temporal dependence, and cross-asset relationships, enabling it to produce alternative trajectories consistent with the learned structure.

However, a synthetic return generator is useful only if it reproduces empirical regularities that matter for downstream decisions (Takahashi and Mizuno, 2024). This limitation is especially acute in finance because the features that drive decisions are concentrated in the extremes. Risk management, leverage, and portfolio construction depend on tail outcomes, correlation breakdowns, and regime transitions that are rare and unstable. A method that produces samples that "look realistic" in the bulk of the distribution can still be useless if it understates drawdowns, misses volatility clustering, or fails to reproduce dependence in stress.

In this chapter, we therefore treat the generator as part of the modeling stack and evaluate it primarily by whether it supports downstream decisions, not by whether its samples are visually or marginally similar to historical returns.

Used carefully, synthetic data supports three practical capabilities:

- **Robust parameter selection:** Evaluate candidate parameters across many sampled trajectories rather than relying on a single realized history.
- **Regime stress testing:** Generate additional stress-like trajectories consistent with observed volatility and dependence to probe drawdowns, correlation breakdowns, and risk-control stability.
- **Privacy-preserving development:** When transaction-level data cannot be shared, synthetic data can support development and collaboration, provided it is subject to explicit privacy evaluation (*Section 5.8*).

Synthetic data does not remove selection bias. If strategies are tuned on synthetic trajectories, they can overfit to the generator's inductive biases and failure modes. The generator must therefore be treated as part of the modeling stack: fix it before strategy selection when possible, validate it on held-out real data, and use an outer validation loop when synthetic data affects model selection.

Before introducing specific generators, we first define the validation framework used throughout the chapter. The key question is not whether generated samples look realistic in isolation, but whether they preserve the structure required for the intended use case while controlling privacy and leakage risk.

5.2 Evaluating synthetic financial data

Synthetic data can appear plausible yet still be unsuitable for its intended use. In finance, this risk is acute because the economically relevant structure often lies in rare events, shifts in dependence, and conditional dynamics rather than at the center of the distribution. A generator that matches marginal returns but understates drawdowns, weakens volatility clustering, or misses stress-period correlations can produce misleading conclusions.

For this reason, the validation protocol often matters more than the generative architecture. Throughout this chapter, we evaluate synthetic data using three criteria: **fidelity**, **utility**, and **privacy**. These objectives typically trade off against one another. Improving privacy can reduce fidelity; improving distributional fidelity does not necessarily improve downstream task performance; and a generator that performs well for one use case may fail for another.

Does it preserve the relevant data structure?

Fidelity asks whether synthetic samples reproduce the empirical structure of the real data at the resolution required by the application. This includes marginal behavior, dependence, and time-series dynamics.

For tabular or cross-sectional data, start with feature-level distributions. Compare real and synthetic samples using statistics such as the Kolmogorov–Smirnov statistic or Wasserstein distance, and complement these with histograms, empirical CDFs, and QQ plots. Summary statistics alone can hide artifacts, especially in the tails.

Dependence must be tested separately. A generator can match each feature's marginal distribution while failing to preserve cross-feature relationships. For multivariate financial data, compare correlation or covariance matrices, rank correlations, sector- or regime-level relationships, and other dependence measures appropriate to the use case.

For financial time series, fidelity also requires stylized-fact diagnostics. At a minimum, test whether the generated series preserves heavy tails, weak raw-return autocorrelation, volatility clustering, leverage effects where relevant, and cross-asset dependence. The autocorrelation function of squared or absolute returns is a useful compact diagnostic because it summarizes volatility persistence, but it should be complemented with tail and dependence checks.

Does it support the intended use case?

Utility evaluates whether synthetic data improves or preserves performance on the downstream task. Fidelity is usually necessary but not sufficient: synthetic data can match broad distributional properties while missing the specific signal needed for forecasting, classification, risk estimation, or strategy evaluation.

A common benchmark is **train-on-synthetic, test-on-real (TSTR)**:

1. Train a model using synthetic data only.
2. Evaluate it on held-out real data.
3. Compare the result with **train-on-real, test-on-real** (**TRTR**) using the same model class, features, target, and evaluation period.

For error metrics such as MSE or MAE, a useful summary is:

$$TSTR\ error\ ratio = \frac{Error_{TSTR}}{Error_{TRTR}}$$

Values near 1 indicate that synthetic data preserves task-relevant information. Values above 1 indicate utility loss. Values below 1 can occur when synthetic data suppresses idiosyncratic noise. Still, they require careful interpretation, as they may also signal leakage, target simplification, or an evaluation design that is too narrow.

For score metrics where higher is better, such as AUC or accuracy, report the TSTR and TRTR scores directly, or use a score ratio with the direction clearly stated. Do not mix error ratios and score ratios without explaining the convention.

Utility is always use-case-specific. Tail-GAN should be evaluated on tail-risk metrics such as VaR and Expected Shortfall; Sig-CWGAN should be evaluated on path-wise criteria; diffusion models require temporal and dependence diagnostics; and tabular LLM generators require schema validity, distributional checks, and downstream predictive tests.

Does it leak training information?

Privacy validation tests whether synthetic samples reveal information about the records used to train the generator. This is especially important for transaction-level, customer-level, and proprietary institutional data.

At a minimum, check for exact or near duplicates between synthetic and training records. More informative diagnostics compare nearest-neighbor distances between synthetic records and well-trained and held-out real records. Membership-inference tests provide a stronger adversarial check by asking whether an attacker can infer whether a specific record was included in the training set.

When formal privacy guarantees are required, train the generator with a **differentially private mechanism**. Methods such as **Differentially Private Stochastic Gradient Descent** (DP-SGD, Abadi et al., 2016) clip per-sample gradients and add calibrated noise during training, with privacy loss summarized by a budget (ε, δ). Smaller values of ε imply stronger privacy but usually reduce fidelity and utility. Privacy should therefore be treated as a design constraint, not as an after-the-fact label attached to generated data.

Synthetic-specific failure modes

The fidelity–utility–privacy framework is necessary but incomplete. Synthetic data introduces failure modes that are specific to generated samples.

1. Generators can **amplify biases in the training data**. If the historical sample overrepresents one regime, one sector, or one market state, the generator may reproduce that imbalance more strongly.
2. Strategies can **overfit to the generator**. Selecting a strategy because it performs well across many synthetic paths can produce a solution tailored to the generator's assumptions rather than to the market. Finalists should always be evaluated on held-out real data that was not used to train the generator.
3. Synthetic data has **limited novelty**. Most generators are better at interpolating within the support of the training distribution than at producing genuinely unprecedented scenarios.

Synthetic data is therefore useful for robustness checks, stress testing, and model development. Still, it should not be treated as evidence about events outside the training regime unless the generator was explicitly designed and validated for that purpose.

Practical validation checklist

At a minimum, every synthetic-data experiment in finance should report:

- A **fidelity diagnostic**, such as marginal distribution error, correlation-matrix distance, tail statistics, or volatility-persistence error
- A **utility benchmark**, such as TSTR versus TRTR or a task-specific risk metric
- A **privacy check**, such as duplicate detection, nearest-neighbor analysis, membership inference, or a formal DP budget
- A **real-data holdout result**, especially when synthetic data is used for model selection or strategy development

Thresholds should be calibrated to the data frequency, sample size, asset class, and downstream objective. There is no universal synthetic-data score. The relevant question is whether the generated data preserves the structure on which the decision depends.

5.3 Classical simulation baselines

Classical simulation methods provide the first test of the evaluation framework. Before using learned generators, practitioners should compare them with transparent baselines that are easier to calibrate, diagnose, and govern.

These baseline models can be grouped into **bootstrap models**, which resample historical data, and **parametric models of stochastic processes** that generate new data based on model assumptions. Both families are limited, but their limitations are visible, which makes them valuable reference points for evaluating more flexible learned generators.

Bootstrap methods

Bootstrap methods generate new paths by resampling observed returns:

- Their main advantage is fidelity to the empirical marginal distribution: heavy tails and other non-Gaussian features present in the data are preserved by construction.
- The key limitation is equally direct: resampling cannot create fundamentally new events outside the historical record. If no crisis-scale move or correlation breakdown appears in the sample, bootstrapping cannot invent it.

Key bootstrap techniques include:

- **IID bootstrap** (IID means *independently and identically distributed*) draws individual returns with replacement. It preserves the marginal distribution but destroys temporal dependence, including volatility clustering. As a result, it is typically unsuitable for risk or sizing studies that require time-varying volatility.
- **Block bootstrap** resamples contiguous blocks of fixed length, preserving dependence within blocks. This recovers the short-horizon autocorrelation structure but can introduce artificial boundaries between blocks and tends to weaken long-range persistence when blocks are too short. Block length is therefore a bias–variance tradeoff: longer blocks preserve dependence better but reduce sample diversity. A common starting point is one month (about 22 trading days), then adjust based on diagnostics.
- The **stationary bootstrap** (Politis and Romano, 1994) uses random block lengths (geometric), thereby reducing boundary artifacts while preserving dependence in expectation. In practice, it is often a better default than fixed blocks when you want volatility clustering without imposing a parametric volatility model.

A high-value diagnostic for bootstrap methods is the **autocorrelation function** (**ACF**) of squared (or absolute) returns: the IID bootstrap collapses this structure toward zero, whereas block and stationary bootstrap retain a decaying pattern that is at least directionally consistent with volatility clustering.

Parametric price and volatility models

Parametric models simulate market data by specifying a stochastic process for prices or returns and sampling paths from that process. In continuous time, these models are written as **stochastic differential equations** (**SDEs**), where dt denotes a small time step, dW denotes a Brownian (Wiener) increment (random noise that scales with $\sqrt{dt}$), and dN denotes a Poisson jump-count increment.

Parametric models can generate paths "beyond history," which is useful for stress testing and scenario expansion, but the results are only as good as the assumptions; misspecification tends to show up in the tails and during regime transitions.

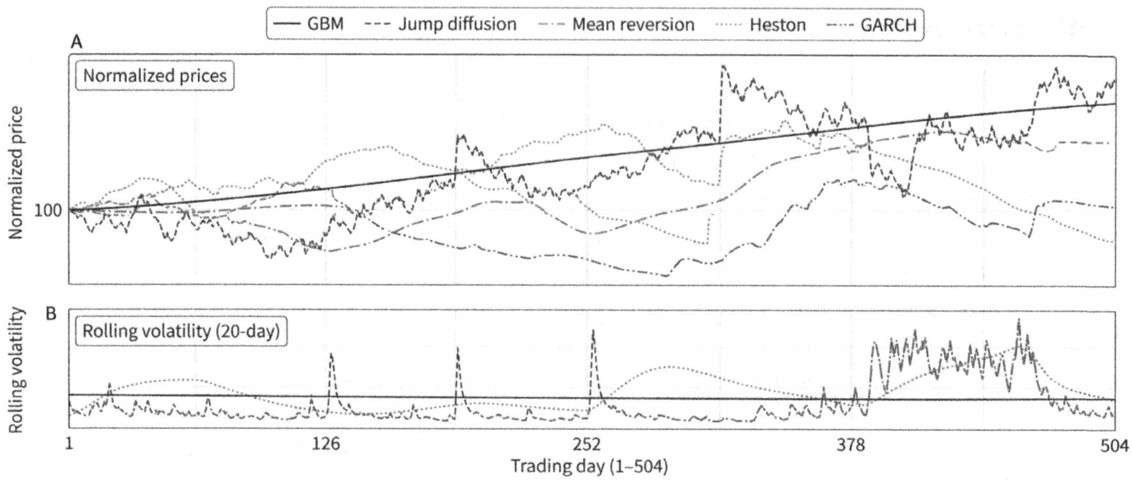

Figure 5.1: Parametric price and volatility models

Figure 5.1 compares stylized simulations from five stochastic time-series models over two years, with all prices normalized to 100 at the start. The top panel shows different price trajectories produced by each model; the bottom panel characterizes the distinct volatility patterns.

Geometric Brownian Motion (**GBM**) defines a foundational baseline. Price S follows a trajectory described as follows:

$$dS = \mu S, dt + \sigma S, dW$$

where μ is drift and σ is volatility. Log-price increments are Gaussian, and volatility is constant. GBM is analytically tractable (Black-Scholes) but fails core stylized facts: it produces no volatility clustering and tails that are too thin (no excess kurtosis).

Jump-Diffusion (**Merton model**) adds discontinuous moves via a compound Poisson process:

$$dS = \mu S, dt + \sigma S, dW + S, (e^Y - 1), dN$$

where dN is a Poisson increment with intensity λ and $Y \sim N(\mu_J, \sigma_J^2)$ is the log jump size. In practice, the drift is typically adjusted to account for the expected jump contribution; otherwise, the unconditional mean can be misstated. Jump diffusion generates fat tails and explicit crash-like moves, but in its basic form, jump arrivals are independent of the volatility state, unlike real markets, where jumps cluster during episodes of market stress.

Mean-Reversion (**Ornstein-Uhlenbeck**) models log-prices (or spreads) gravitating toward equilibrium:

$$d(logS) = \kappa(\theta - logS), dt + \sigma, dW$$

where κ is the mean-reversion speed and θ is the long-run level. The half-life is $ln(2)/\kappa$. This is appropriate for spreads and some rates/commodity settings, but it is not a general return model for trend-capable assets.

Stochastic volatility (**Heston**) introduces a separate variance process v:

$$dS = \mu S, dt + \sqrt{v}, S, dW_S$$

$$dv = \kappa(\theta - v), dt + \xi\sqrt{v}, dW_v$$

$$Corr(dW_S, dW_v) = \rho$$

Negative ρ produces a leverage effect (price drops increase volatility), and the model can generate fat tails and volatility clustering. Practical use depends on careful discretization (for example, full-truncation Euler or Andersen's QE) to maintain non-negative variance.

Generalized Autoregressive Conditional Heteroskedasticity, GARCH(p,q), models the variance of returns in discrete time, with parameters p and q denoting the numbers of lagged squared shocks and lagged conditional variances, respectively (see also *Chapter 9*). The most common specification is GARCH(1,1), which uses one lag of each:

$$r_t = \mu + \sigma_t\varepsilon_t, \quad \varepsilon_t \sim N(0,1)$$

$$\sigma_t^2 = \omega + \alpha(r_{t-1} - \mu)^2 + \beta\sigma_{t-1}^2$$

where α captures the reaction to recent return shocks and β captures volatility persistence; a common stationarity condition is $\alpha + \beta < 1$. GARCH is typically calibrated by maximum likelihood, making it a pragmatic bridge between theory and data. Basic GARCH often reproduces volatility clustering well in practice.

Limitations and how to use these baselines

Classical baselines make strong tradeoffs explicit. Bootstrap methods preserve the empirical distribution but are constrained to the historical record: they cannot generate truly novel extremes or structural breaks. Parametric models can generate paths "beyond history," but only along the dimensions implied by their dynamics; misspecification often shows up exactly where finance cares most (tails, stress dependence, regime transitions).

In this chapter, we use these methods as reference points. They provide sanity checks for learned generators (a deep model should at least outperform an appropriate baseline on the diagnostics that matter), and they remain useful when interpretability, small-sample robustness, or governance requirements dominate. The next section provides an overview of different generative models.

> **Implementation:** `00_classical_simulation.py` implements all methods with calibration diagnostics.

5.4 Generative model taxonomy

This section covers **learned generators**: models that approximate the joint distribution of the variables of interest (for example, financial returns of multiple assets) by optimizing a training objective rather than by specifying a parametric process or resampling scheme. The goal is not to produce "realistic-looking" samples, but to preserve the temporal structure, dependencies, and tail behavior required for downstream robustness analysis or model development.

A useful distinction is between **discriminative** models, which learn $p(y \mid X)$, and **generative** models, which learn $p(X)$ or $p(X, y)$ and can therefore produce new samples. In finance, learned generators are attractive because they can represent complex dependence structures that are difficult to write down parametrically. Still, they can also fail silently by smoothing tails, collapsing modes, or learning spurious regime structure.

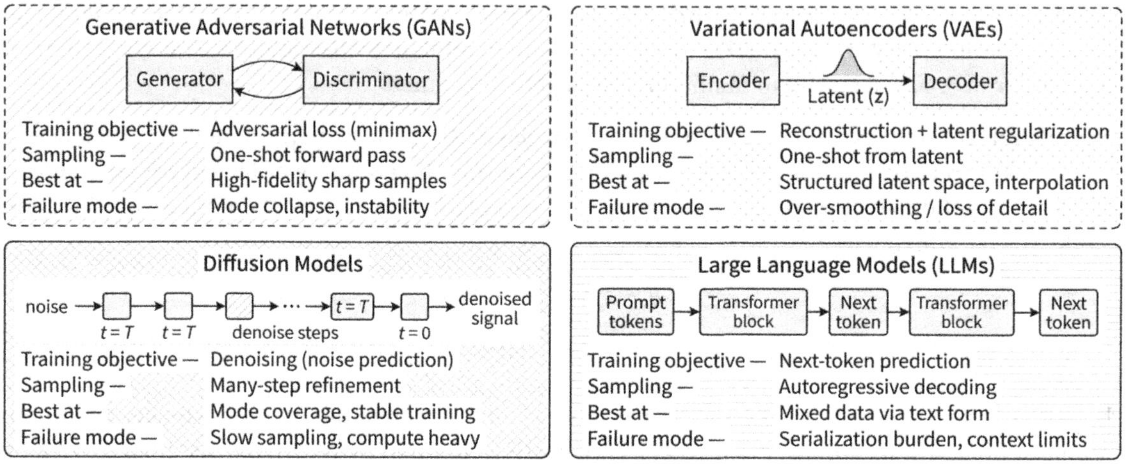

Figure 5.2: Comparing various deep generative models

The learned generators used in this chapter fall into four families:

- **Variational Autoencoders** (**VAE**) learn a latent-variable generative model that aims to both reconstruct the input and conform to certain distributional assumptions. VAEs often train more stably than adversarial models and can serve as strong baselines for mixed-type structured data. Still, they may oversmooth and require calibration or more expressive likelihoods to avoid underrepresenting rare categories and tail behavior.
- **Generative Adversarial Networks** (**GANs**) learn through adversarial training. They can produce sharp samples and capture complex dependence, but training can be unstable. *Section 5.5* focuses on GAN variants designed to reduce collapse and improve path-wise and tail fidelity.
- **Diffusion models** learn to generate by iteratively denoising. Training is typically stable, and the framework supports conditional generation. *Section 5.6* presents a diffusion model for regime-conditioned time-series generation.
- **LLM-based generators for tabular data** serialize records as text and generate rows autoregressively. This can work well for heterogeneous, mixed-type datasets, especially when conditional generation is important. *Section 5.7* covers this approach, along with faster specialized alternatives where appropriate.

The following sections focus on specific, finance-oriented instantiations of these families. These learned generators should be treated as part of the modeling stack: they can expand the space of plausible trajectories, but they can also introduce their own inductive biases.

Each model family below should be evaluated against the framework introduced in *Section 5.2*. GAN variants are useful when their objectives align with the desired notion of fidelity, such as temporal structure, tail risk, or path-wise similarity. Diffusion models often provide more stable training and stronger conditional generation, at the cost of slower sampling. LLM-based tabular generators can handle heterogeneous structured data, but they require strict schema validation and privacy checks.

The practical question is therefore not which generator is universally best, but which generator preserves the structure required by the downstream decision, performs competitively against classical baselines, and satisfies the applicable privacy constraints.

5.5 GANs for financial time series

GANs generate synthetic samples via an adversarial game between a **generator** and a **discriminator** (*Figure 5.3*). The generator maps random input to candidate samples, while the discriminator scores both real and generated samples as real or fake.

Training alternates between strengthening the discriminator and updating the generator to fool it. This setup provides a useful learning signal even when the data likelihood is hard to specify.

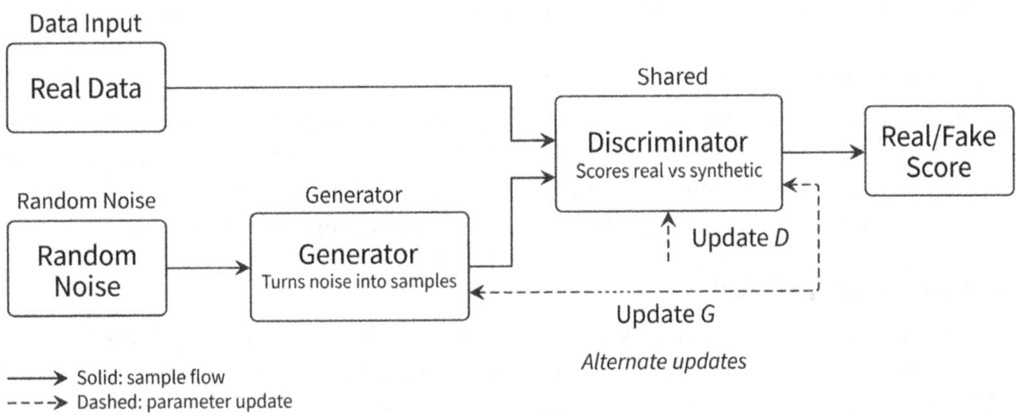

Figure 5.3: The GAN training workflow

Figure 5.3 illustrates the core loop without committing to any particular sequence model, loss function, or stabilization technique. In finance, however, vanilla GANs tend to prioritize the high-density "center" of the distribution and underrepresent rare but economically important tail events. The models that follow keep the adversarial loop but adapt it to what vanilla GANs miss: temporal dependence (**TimeGAN**), tail behavior and risk measures (**Tail-GAN**), path-wise similarity (**Sig-CWGAN**), and irregularly sampled continuous-time dynamics (**GT-GAN**).

Using TimeGAN for sequential data

TimeGAN (Yoon, Jarrett, and van der Schaar, 2019) adapts adversarial training to time series by adding supervised temporal objectives and by learning in an embedding space rather than directly on raw sequences.

Architecture

TimeGAN comprises five networks trained in stages:

1. **Embedding network** (e): maps a raw sequence x to a latent representation h.
2. **Recovery network** (r): reconstructs x from h; together, (e, r) form an autoencoder trained to minimize reconstruction error.
3. **Supervisor network** (s): predicts the next latent state h_{t+1} from h_t, adding a supervised loss that encourages temporal coherence in latent space.
4. **Generator** (g): produces synthetic latent paths from noise.
5. **Discriminator** (d): distinguishes real from synthetic latent trajectories.

Training

Training usually proceeds in three phases:

1. Pretrain the embedding and recovery networks as an autoencoder.
2. Train the supervisor on real embeddings.
3. Jointly optimize the full system under reconstruction, supervised, and adversarial losses.

Data requirements

Many reference implementations use sigmoid activations in the recovery network, constraining outputs to ([0,1]). This is convenient for normalized OHLCV inputs (see *Chapter 3*) but incompatible with unbounded return series unless returns are mapped to a bounded range or the output layer is modified. For returns, a linear output layer preserves the full real-valued support of the target.

When to use TimeGAN

TimeGAN is a strong baseline for multivariate sequence generation: it is well documented, has reference implementations, and provides a benchmark for comparing newer architectures. It does not explicitly target tail fidelity and assumes a regular sampling grid.

> **Implementation:** The notebook `01_timegan.py` trains TimeGAN on six stocks (BA, CAT, DIS, GE, IBM, KO) using 24-step windows. Discriminative accuracy is 68%, with ROC AUC 0.87, indicating residual separability between real and synthetic sequences.

The **TSTR** ratio for one-step forecasting is 1.76: training on TimeGAN-generated multi-stock adjusted-close data produces 76% higher one-step forecast error than training on real data, suggesting that synthetic data is informative but imperfect for downstream prediction.

Under the validation framework from *Section 5.2*, these results show partial utility but incomplete fidelity: the generated data contains enough structure to support a weak downstream forecasting task, yet the discriminator and dependence diagnostics indicate that real and synthetic sequences remain materially separable.

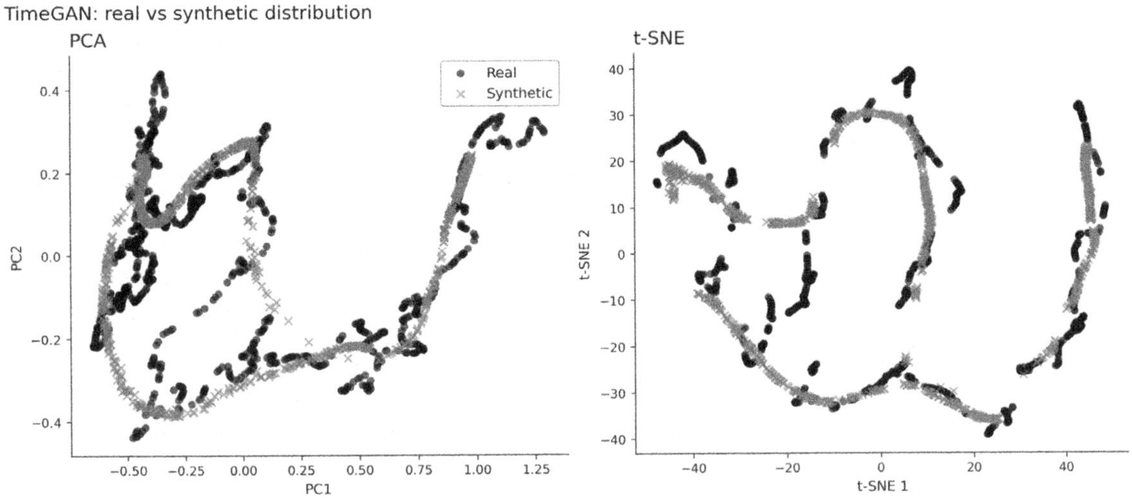

Figure 5.4: TimeGAN fidelity, showing how PCA and t-SNE overlap

In our analysis, synthetic sequences underrepresent temporal and cross-asset dependence relative to real data, consistent with TimeGAN's focus on overall distribution rather than fine-grained dynamics. On similar inputs, Diffusion-TS (*Section 5.6*) performs better in our experiments (TSTR ratio: 1.00 compared to 1.76).

Using Tail-GAN for risk-constrained generation

Tail-GAN (Cont et al., 2025) variants address a limitation of standard GAN objectives: optimizing for average distributional fidelity can underweight rare but consequential tail events. For risk management, matching tail risk measures such as **Value-at-Risk** (**VaR**) and **Expected Shortfall** (**ES**) is often more important than matching the distribution center.

Tail-GAN augments the generator loss with penalties that discourage discrepancies between real and synthetic tail risk measures:

$$L_{tail} = \lambda_1 \left| VaR_\alpha^{real} - VaR_\alpha^{synth} \right| + \lambda_2 \left| ES_\alpha^{real} - ES_\alpha^{synth} \right|$$

where α is the tail probability (often 1% or 5%), and (λ_1, λ_2) trade off tail matching against overall fit.

Portfolio focus

Tail constraints are typically computed on portfolio returns rather than on individual assets. This aligns the objective with risk management practice, where joint dependence drives drawdowns and limits are set at the portfolio level.

When to use Tail-GAN

Use Tail-GAN when the downstream task is risk measurement and tail accuracy dominates other fidelity notions. The method may sacrifice fit in the distribution center to improve VaR/ES matching.

Implementation: `02_tailgan_tail_risk.py` trains Tail-GAN on 5 ETFs using 32 random long-short portfolio strategies. At $\alpha = 5$, VaR relative error is 13% and ES error is 11%, illustrating that explicit tail penalties produce usable risk estimates. In this 32-strategy configuration, synthetic VaR is slightly more negative than real (synthetic ≈ -10.33 versus real ≈ -9.13), so the trained Tail-GAN modestly overstates loss magnitude rather than understating it.

Tail-GAN improves selected tail statistics, but the constraints are usually defined on specific benchmark portfolios and risk levels. Matching VaR and ES for those portfolios does not guarantee accurate tail dependence for other portfolios, individual assets, or path-dependent risk measures.

More generally, VaR and ES capture only part of the tail: two models can match these quantities yet differ in tail shape, clustering, and temporal dynamics. Performance, therefore, depends materially on the choice of tail probability α, the benchmark portfolios used during training, and the regimes represented in the data.

Using Sig-CWGAN for path signatures for temporal fidelity

Sig-CWGAN (Ni et al., 2020) replaces the learned discriminator with an analytic criterion based on **path signatures** from rough path theory. The objective reduces reliance on an adaptive discriminator and provides a structured notion of distance between path distributions.

A path signature is a **sequence of iterated integrals** that summarizes the shape of a path: not just where it starts and ends, but how it moves through its coordinates, in what order, and with what directional interactions.

Intuitively, the first level records the path's net increments, the second level records pairwise interaction effects between coordinates and the order in which moves occur, and higher levels capture progressively richer geometric structure.

A key mathematical property is that the signature depends on the path's traced-out shape rather than the speed at which the path is traversed, so it is **invariant to time reparameterization**. In financial applications, this is often useful but not always desirable, because elapsed time and observation spacing can themselves contain information. Therefore, implementation often augments X with time as an additional channel. For a path $X\colon [0,T] \to R^d$, a level-k term has the form:

$$S(X)^{i_1,\ldots,i_k} = \int_{0<t_1<\cdots<t_k<T} d\,X_{t_1}^{i_1} \cdots dX_{t_k}^{i_k}$$

and the depth-n signature collects all terms up to order (n). In practice, one can think of the truncated signature as a finite feature map that converts a sequential path into a set of statistics describing its geometry at increasing levels of detail. Implementations often augment (X) with time as an additional channel and use truncated signatures at modest depth.

Sig-CWGAN minimizes a signature-kernel **maximum mean discrepancy** (**MMD**) between real and synthetic path distributions, yielding a stable training signal without adversarial classification.

The number of signature terms grows as $O(d^n)$ in the path dimension d and truncation depth n. With two assets, time $d = 3$, and depth 3, the truncated signature has $1 + 3 + 9 + 27 = 40$ terms. By contrast, 50 assets at depth 3 would require over 125,000 terms, making straightforward scaling impractical without dimensionality reduction.

Use Sig-CWGAN when **path-wise fidelity** matters (for example, in path-dependent pricing or sequential decision problems) and the dimension is small enough to compute signatures reliably. The analytic objective can reduce failure modes driven by discriminator overfitting, but scalability is the binding constraint.

Implementation: `03_sigcwgan_signatures.py` reproduces the paper-exact setup: a single asset (S&P 500 index log returns, 2005–2020) at signature depth 4 over 16-day windows, trained for 2,500 generator steps.

- The Sig-W1 distance (RMSE of expected signatures) descends to 0.054 in training and 0.42 on the held-out window, and the train-on-synthetic, test-on-real ratio reaches 0.954—close to parity with the real data.
- Stylized facts are only partially captured: synthetic skewness and excess kurtosis fall far short of the empirical values, and the squared-return autocorrelation collapses to 0.05 (versus 0.49 in the data), so volatility clustering is not preserved.

Sig-CWGAN is most attractive in low-dimensional settings. Truncating the signature discards higher-order path information, while increasing depth quickly becomes computationally expensive and statistically harder to estimate. In practice, **the method is best viewed as a structured low-dimensional generator** rather than a general-purpose solution for broad multivariate market panels.

Using GT-GAN for irregular time series

GT-GAN (Jeon et al., 2022) extends adversarial generation to **irregularly sampled** time series, in which observations occur at non-uniform intervals (for example, tick data, event-driven bars, consolidated feeds).

GT-GAN models continuous-time dynamics with a neural **ordinary differential equation (ODE)** that parameterizes:

$$\frac{dx}{dt} = f_\theta(x, t)$$

and integrates the dynamics to generate values at arbitrary timestamps.

The discriminator evaluates both sampled values and their associated timestamps, and a supervised component encourages temporal coherence, analogous to TimeGAN's supervisor.

GT-GAN is designed for naturally irregular data, where observation times carry information (for example, trade arrivals or information events). Applying it to regularly sampled series with artificial irregularity (random subsampling) is unlikely to outperform simpler discrete-time generators.

Use GT-GAN when observation times carry information. For regularly sampled daily or minute bars, discrete-time generators are usually simpler and more efficient.

> **Implementation:** `04_gtgan_irregular.py` trains GT-GAN on NVDA dollar bars from *Chapter 3*. Reconstruction MSE is 0.026, and the interpolation/real smoothness ratio is 0.02—the ODE-driven paths are considerably smoother than real bars. Because the experiment uses only 446 bars from a single trading day, these results should be read primarily as an illustration of the continuous-time training procedure rather than as a competitive benchmark of distributional fidelity.

GT-GAN introduces substantially more modeling and optimization complexity than discrete-time generators. With limited data, a continuous-time generator may produce visually smooth paths without accurately matching the true event-time distribution, dependence structure, or regime behavior. The method is most compelling when irregular timing is economically meaningful; if irregularity mainly reflects sampling choices or microstructure noise, the additional continuous-time machinery may add complexity without improving fidelity.

GAN training challenges

GAN variants share recurring implementation risks:

- **Mode collapse:** The generator covers only a subset of regimes, underrepresenting rare states that matter for risk.
- **Training instability:** Optimization can oscillate or diverge; stabilization methods include spectral normalization, gradient penalties (WGAN-GP), and phased training (TimeGAN).
- **Hyperparameter sensitivity:** Learning rates, architectures, and regularization weights often require dataset-specific tuning.
- **Evaluation ambiguity:** There is no ground-truth label; evaluation relies on held-out distributional tests, downstream utility (TSTR), and diagnostics for temporal structure and cross-sectional dependence.

Kwon and Lee (2024) report that GANs can approximate marginal return distributions but often struggle with finer temporal structure and multivariate dependence; reported performance varies across architectures, and multivariate generation can collapse to a low-dimensional dependence structure. Passing marginal tests is therefore necessary but not sufficient; temporal dynamics and cross-sectional relationships require separate validation. *Section 5.6* turns to diffusion models.

5.6 Diffusion models for financial time series

Diffusion models have shown strong empirical performance on synthetic data, from images to financial time series.

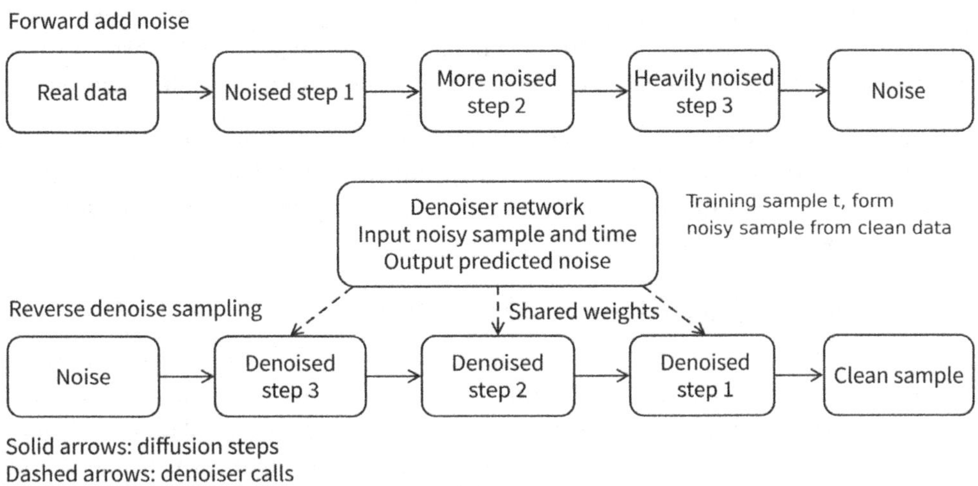

Figure 5.5: DDPM forward/reverse schematic

In *Figure 5.5*, the forward process progressively corrupts the real data into near-pure noise. During training, a timestep t is sampled, noise is added to the real data, and a single denoiser network is optimized to predict the added noise. At generation time, sampling starts from near-pure noise and iteratively applies the same denoiser to produce real data; the reverse chain is stochastic, injecting fresh noise at intermediate steps (except the final step), so each run can yield a different sample.

Their iterative denoising mechanism can reproduce non-Gaussian features of market data that simpler generators often miss, which makes them useful when sample fidelity is the primary objective (Takahashi and Mizuno, 2024). The main trade-off is computational cost: training and generation are typically slower than with one-shot generators.

The denoising diffusion framework

Diffusion models define a **forward process** that gradually corrupts an observed sequence with noise, and a **reverse process** that learns to remove it. Sampling starts from noise and applies learned reverse transitions to generate a synthetic sequence.

The forward process is a Markov chain that adds Gaussian noise over diffusion steps $t = 1, \ldots, T$. Given original data x_0, define:

$$q(x_t \mid x_{t-1}) = N\left(x_t; \sqrt{\alpha_t} x_{t-1}, (1 - \alpha_t) I\right)$$

where $\alpha_t = 1 - \beta_t$ and β_t is a noise schedule. With sufficiently many steps, x_T approaches an isotropic Gaussian. The schedule determines the signal-to-noise ratio across timesteps and shapes the difficulty of denoising.

The reverse process learns a conditional transition from x_t to x_{t-1}:

$$p_\theta(x_{t-1} \mid x_t) = N\left(x_{t-1}; \mu_\theta(x_t, t), \Sigma_\theta(x_t, t)\right)$$

The denoiser takes x_t and an embedding of t as inputs and outputs either parameters $\mu_\theta, \Sigma_\theta$ or an equivalent quantity such as the noise ε. Training samples diffusion steps and minimizes an expectation over timesteps, so the model learns to invert the corruption process at multiple noise levels.

The **Denoising Diffusion Probabilistic Model (DDPM)** (Ho et al., 2020) popularized a mean squared error loss between the realized forward-process noise ε and the network prediction $\varepsilon_\theta(x_t, t)$, avoiding direct reconstruction of x_0 during training. This objective is widely used because it is stable and maps directly to an iterative sampling procedure.

Why diffusion models fit financial returns

The stylized facts in *Section 5.1*—heavy tails, volatility clustering, leverage effects, and weak return autocorrelation—constrain generators for returns or return-like series. A useful generator must match both the marginal distribution and conditional dynamics, such as persistent volatility and time-varying tail risk. Diffusion models can capture such structure because the denoiser is trained across noise levels rather than being optimized to match only low-order moments.

The three families have distinct failure profiles. VAEs can produce overly smooth samples during decoding, as they average over uncertainty. GAN training can be unstable and may underrepresent tails or minority modes. Diffusion training is typically more stable, but sampling can be slow because it performs many reverse steps per generated sequence.

Conditional generation for regime stress testing

Conditional generation produces samples consistent with specified attributes. Two common approaches are:

- **Classifier guidance**, which trains a separate classifier on noised data and uses its gradient to steer sampling
- **Classifier-free guidance**, which embeds conditioning during training

Both can direct generation toward states such as "low volatility" or "crisis," enabling regime-specific scenario generation and stress testing.

A workflow that integrates with regime detection methods (discussed in more detail in *Chapter 9*) is:

1. Fit a regime model (for example, an HMM) to label historical periods.
2. Train a classifier to predict regime labels from noisy sequences across diffusion timesteps.
3. At generation time, compute $\nabla_{x_t} log p(regime \mid x_t)$, the gradient of the log-probability of the target regime with respect to the current noisy sample x_t, and use it to adjust the denoising update.

Classifier guidance (Dhariwal and Nichol, 2021) requires tuning. Strong guidance can reduce diversity and exaggerate rare regimes, producing unrealistic extremes. Temperature scaling and stochastic sampling (for example, Denoising Diffusion Implicit Models with $\eta > 0$) can help balance targeting and diversity. *Figure 5.6* shows the result: low- and high-volatility regime samples produce visibly separated paths, with a 2.1× regime-volatility ratio.

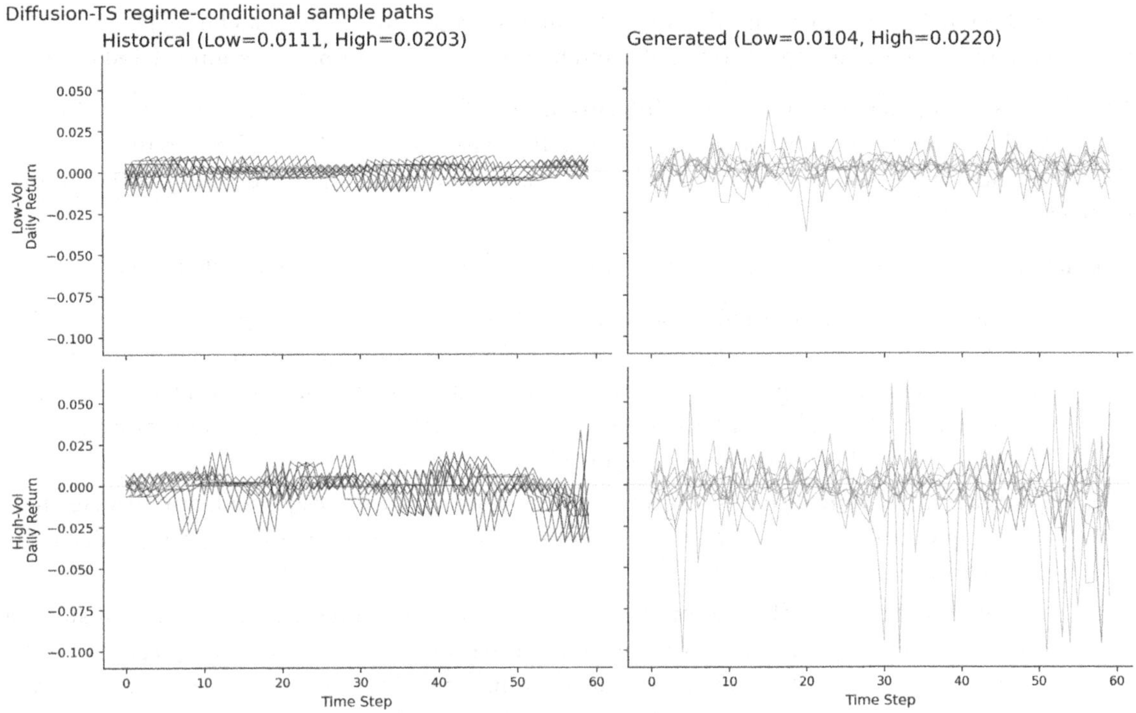

Figure 5.6: Diffusion-TS regime-conditional sample paths

Because regimes are model-derived, the conditional generator inherits errors from the regime detector. Misclassified periods become mislabeled training data, which can distort conditional samples. Use regime-conditioned sequences as model-based scenarios and validate them with regime-specific diagnostics before downstream use.

Applying Diffusion-TS with interpretable decomposition

Time-series generators must represent dependencies across the sequence, not just marginal distributions. Diffusion-TS (Yuan and Qiao, 2024) adapts the diffusion denoiser to sequential data by using an **encoder-decoder transformer** and explicitly decomposing the reconstructed sequence into low- and mid-frequency components.

The denoiser takes a noised sequence x_t and a timestep embedding t. An encoder produces a context representation of x_t, and a decoder uses cross-attention to predict the clean sequence $\hat{x}_0$.

Rather than predicting $\hat{x}_0$ directly, Diffusion-TS constrains the output to be a sum of two components:

$$\hat{x}_0 = trend + season$$

The **trend** component is parameterized as a low-order polynomial fit, intended to capture slow-moving drift over the generation horizon. The **seasonal** component is represented using a truncated Fourier basis (top-k modes), which targets periodic or quasi-periodic structure.

A **Fourier-domain loss** complements the time-domain loss by penalizing mismatches in the frequency representation, encouraging spectral fidelity, and helping preserve autocorrelation-related patterns.

This decomposition is not a guarantee of **interpretability** in the economic sense, but it provides an operational handle: when samples fail diagnostics, the error can often be localized to the slow component (trend), the periodic component (seasonality), or the residual high-frequency variation that neither component represents well.

In practice, Diffusion-TS shares training and evaluation challenges with other DDPM models:

- **Variance calibration:** A trend-plus-seasonal output can understate high-frequency variation and reduce realized return variance. In the reference implementation, raw unconditional samples understate variance by approximately one-third in the normalized space before post hoc rescaling. Downstream tasks that depend on volatility matching may require explicit variance-calibration terms during training.
- **Compute and latency:** DDPM sampling can be slow because it requires many reverse steps per sample. DDIM and distillation-style methods reduce the number of steps, typically at the expense of speed.
- **Temporal coherence:** Alternative approaches impose sequential structure via path summaries such as signatures, which are stable under reparameterization. For example, Sig-CWGAN uses a signature-based discrepancy in its training objective (*Section 5.5*). For diffusion models, include temporal diagnostics (ACF, volatility persistence, leverage proxies) in addition to marginal distribution tests.
- **Validation:** Matching stylized facts is necessary but not sufficient: a generator can satisfy distributional diagnostics yet fail to preserve task-relevant structure. *Section 5.8* presents validation aligned with the intended application.

> **Implementation:** `05_diffusion_ts.py` implements Diffusion-TS end-to-end with interpretable decomposition, Fourier loss, and classifier-guided regime-conditional generation.

For the 20 ETF daily return series (2018–2025), the implementation reports a KS statistic of 0.06, a correlation error of 0.04, and an ACF error of 0.05. Regime-conditional generation produces low-volatility samples at 0.93× historical volatility and high-volatility samples at 1.08× historical volatility.

Choosing between GANs and diffusion models

Diffusion models trade generation speed for training stability. GANs produce samples in a single forward pass; diffusion models require iterative denoising, though DDIMs reduce this cost to 50–100 steps. The GAN variants in *Section 5.5* each address a specific limitation: Tail-GAN targets risk measures, Sig-CWGAN targets path fidelity, and GT-GAN handles irregular timestamps. Diffusion-TS offers a more general-purpose alternative with built-in conditional generation, but specialized GANs remain appropriate when their design objective aligns with the evaluation target.

Direct comparison of these toy implementations would be misleading—each generator was designed for a different task with different data requirements. TimeGAN requires bounded data; Tail-GAN optimizes for portfolio-level tail metrics; Sig-CWGAN works only at low dimensionality; GT-GAN needs naturally irregular timestamps. The practical question is not "which generator is best?" but "which generator matches my use case?" For tabular data, large language models can be a good candidate, as we will see next.

5.7 LLMs for structured financial data

Large language models (**LLMs**) can generate realistic synthetic samples from tabular datasets when the table is represented as text. Although LLMs are trained on natural language, they can learn and reproduce complex cross-column dependencies in structured data, which is useful for financial tables that mix numerical, categorical, and occasional free-text fields.

Serialization converts each table row into a text record that explicitly encodes column–value pairs. A serialized table becomes a corpus of short records that an autoregressive model can learn to reproduce. Consider a credit application record:

income	debt_ratio	emp_length	home_status	approved
85000	0.32	7	MORTGAGE	1

Table 5.1: A table showing a record for a credit application

One serialized representation is:

```
income is 85000, debt_ratio is 0.32, emp_length is 7, home_status is MORTGAGE,
approved is 1
```

Training on many such records encourages the model to capture conditional structure across fields (for example, how income and debt ratio relate to approval, conditional on employment and housing status).

The GReaT framework

Generate Realistic Tabular Data (**GReaT**) formalizes a simple workflow (Borisov et al., 2023):

1. **Serialize the training data.** Convert each row into a text record of column–value pairs. To reduce sensitivity to a fixed presentation order, training often randomizes the column order.
2. **Fine-tune an autoregressive LLM.** Fine-tune a pre-trained language model (for example, GPT-2-scale) on the serialized corpus so it learns to predict the next token given the preceding tokens, thereby implicitly modeling a joint distribution over fields.
3. **Generate new samples.** Sample new text records and parse them back into rows. Filter invalid outputs (malformed records, missing fields, out-of-range values).

The framework can be useful for financial applications subject to some limitations and risks.

Financial applications

LLM-based tabular generation is well-suited to datasets with mixed field types and complex conditional dependencies:

- **Credit and loan data:** Application records with demographic variables, financial ratios, and categorical fields are natural candidates. Synthetic datasets can support model development while reducing exposure of sensitive customer data.
- **Customer profiles:** Retail banking and wealth datasets often combine transaction aggregates, account attributes, and occasional text fields. Serialization provides a uniform interface to this heterogeneity.
- **Corporate fundamentals:** Financial statements and derived ratios, together with industry codes and accounting flags, can be augmented or anonymized using LLM-based generators, subject to strict point-in-time and accounting-convention checks.

Limitations and risks

LLM-based generation introduces failure modes that require explicit mitigation:

- **Invalid records:** Autoregressive generation can produce internally inconsistent combinations (for example, an employment history that is incompatible with age). Post-generation validation is required.
- **Numerical fidelity:** LLMs optimize for token likelihood, not distributional accuracy. High-precision numeric strings are difficult to represent reliably; practitioners often discretize, bin, scale, or normalize numeric features before serialization. Even with preprocessing, marginal distributions and tail behavior can drift relative to the training data.
- **Compute cost:** Fine-tuning and inference add computational overhead. In many tabular settings, moderate-sized models can be sufficient, but cost should be evaluated relative to simpler tabular generators and classical baselines.
- **Privacy leakage:** Synthetic samples can memorize and reproduce rare training examples. Privacy evaluation (*Section 5.8*) is required before using generated data outside a controlled environment.

Serialized generation often violates domain constraints. To manage this risk, implement a **constraint layer** that validates each parsed row:

- **Type constraints:** Age is an integer; ratios are non-negative
- **Range constraints:** Employment years `< age - 16`
- **Logical constraints:** If `home_status = "RENT"`, then `mortgage_balance = 0`

Monitor rejection rates as a diagnostic. Sustained rejection rates above 10–15% suggest that the serialization format, preprocessing, or training protocol needs adjustment.

Implementation: `06_llm_tabular_great.py` fine-tunes `distilgpt2` on ETF-derived tabular features (returns, volatility, volume ratios, and categorical regime labels). Fifty epochs of fine-tuning on an RTX 3090 take roughly thirteen minutes—modest compared with training a dedicated tabular generator from scratch.

- On a held-out test set of 600 samples (extreme-move classification, $|fwd_r et_{5d}|$ above the 90th percentile), TSTR achieves an AUC-ROC of 0.70, close to the 0.74 TRTR baseline; the TSTR ratio is 92%, indicating that synthetic training data largely preserves downstream model utility for this task.
- Distributional fidelity is weaker than utility. Among numerical columns, only `volume_ratio` matches well (KS = 0.10); `volatility` and all four return features (1-, 5-, 20-day, and forward 5-day) sit in the 0.30–0.59 range with p-values below 0.001, so synthetic and real marginals are statistically distinguishable. The categorical distribution is heavily mode-collapsed: the model overgenerates the negative-return regime (`direction = down` 94% synthetic versus 45% real) and the no-trend regime (`momentum = flat` 69% versus 36%), and undergenerates strong-trend states (`momentum = strong` 10% versus 28%; `vol_regime = high` 1% versus 7%). This gap between high task utility and modest distributional fidelity is the practical limit of short LLM fine-tuning on small tabular datasets—longer fine-tuning, larger base models, or rejection sampling on schema constraints close it at the cost of compute, which is the trade-off *Section 5.2* formalized.

This result illustrates why utility and fidelity must be evaluated separately. The synthetic data preserves enough task-relevant structure to support the extreme-move classifier, but the marginal and categorical diagnostics reveal substantial distributional distortion. The next section presents the comprehensive evaluation framework recommended for practical use cases.

5.8 Applying the Fidelity–Utility–Privacy framework

The preceding sections show that the quality of synthetic data depends on the intended use case. No generator dominates across fidelity, utility, privacy, dimensionality, and computational cost. The Fidelity–Utility–Privacy framework from *Section 5.2* provides a common language for comparing methods without reducing them to a single score.

Reading the Diffusion-TS results

The Diffusion-TS reference run on 20 daily return series of ETFs illustrates how to interpret the framework in practice. The model reports a KS statistic of 0.06 for marginals, a correlation error of 0.04 for cross-asset dependence, and an ACF error of 0.05 for volatility persistence. These are **fidelity** diagnostics: they suggest that the generated samples preserve broad distributional and temporal structure in this configuration.

Utility is evaluated separately. For the extreme-move classification task, the TSTR result is approximately at parity with the TRTR benchmark, indicating that synthetic training data preserves the task-relevant signal for this specific prediction problem.

Privacy is not established by these results. Unless the generator is trained with a formal privacy mechanism or subjected to leakage tests, strong fidelity and utility do not imply privacy. A model can reproduce useful structure while still memorizing rare records or leaking proprietary information.

The interpretation is therefore conditional: Diffusion-TS is a strong, general-purpose generator in this experiment, especially in terms of broad fidelity and task utility. Tail-focused risk applications may still require explicit tail penalties, as in Tail-GAN. Low-dimensional path-dependent applications may benefit from signature-based objectives, as in Sig-CWGAN. Privacy-sensitive applications require a separate privacy mechanism and leakage evaluation.

Privacy–utility trade-off with DP-GAN

When formal privacy guarantees are required, differential privacy provides a mathematical bound on the influence of individual training records.

Implementation: The notebook `07_dp_gan.py` demonstrates this trade-off by training a GAN with DP-SGD using Opacus and sweeping across privacy budgets.

Privacy Budget	Mean Abs Diff	Correlation Distance	Interpretation
1.0	8.02	0.12	Strong privacy, poor utility
5.0	2.40	0.15	Good balance
10.0	2.67	0.06	Good utility
50.0	1.68	0.11	Best utility, weak privacy

Table 5.2: Privacy-utility tradeoff example

At $\varepsilon = 1$, the noise required for stronger privacy substantially degrades distributional fidelity. As the privacy budget increases, utility improves, but the formal privacy guarantee weakens. In this example, the middle range around $\varepsilon \in [5,10]$ offers a more practical trade-off, but the appropriate threshold depends on the data sensitivity, regulatory context, and intended use.

The important lesson is that **privacy cannot be inferred from realism**. Synthetic data may look different from the training data and still leak information; it may also satisfy privacy constraints while becoming too distorted for downstream modeling. Privacy-sensitive synthetic-data workflows therefore require explicit leakage tests or formal DP accounting in addition to fidelity and utility evaluation.

5.9 Summary

Synthetic data generation addresses a core limitation in quantitative finance: we only observe one realized market path, yet strategies must remain robust across many plausible alternatives. Modern generative models can produce "alternative histories" that preserve key statistical structure, enabling more rigorous robustness checks, stress testing, and parameter selection than a single backtest trajectory can support.

Effective use hinges on disciplined benchmarking and validation. Generators should reproduce core stylized facts, and classical models remain strong, interpretable baselines when transparency or data constraints matter.

Deep generative approaches (GAN variants, diffusion models, and LLMs for serialized tabular data) can target objectives such as tail risk, path-wise fidelity, irregular time sampling, and heterogeneous schema generation. Each must be evaluated against the Fidelity–Utility–Privacy triad and stress-tested for synthetic-specific failure modes such as bias amplification, limited novelty, and overfitting to the generator, with conclusions confirmed on held-out real data.

In *Chapter 6*, we present the strategy research framework that guides the ML4T workflow and our nine case studies.

6

Strategy Research Framework

Every trading strategy starts with an idea. The hard part is turning that idea into trustworthy evidence: results that survive realistic costs and constraints, remain interpretable after iterative search, and translate into a repeatable process that performs out-of-sample rather than a one-off in-sample backtest. We introduce the strategy research framework that anchors the ML4T workflow: a research loop we develop in *Chapters 7-20*, from feature engineering and modeling to strategy backtesting, before taking a strategy live in *Chapter 25*.

The framework requires us to define the trading setup early: what is traded, when decisions are made, how signals become positions, and how positions produce net outcomes after costs, constraints, and risk controls. Some parameters are known from the outset (for example, the universe of investable assets, or explicit fees); others require further research (for example, market impact or risk management). The goal is to make dependencies visible, state conservative assumptions for early feasibility screens, and record open issues for later chapters.

By the end of the chapter, you will be able to:

- **Place an idea on the strategy map,** connecting it to a strategy family, a plausible source of recurring profits, and the dominant feasibility constraints.
- **Specify the trading setup** in decision-time terms: what is tradable, when decisions are made, what is admissible, and how scores become positions.
- **Define "better" economically**, and separate metric roles so diagnostics guide iteration without substituting for strategy evaluation.
- **Adopt a time-series evaluation protocol** that separates selection from performance estimation.
- **Define a baseline checkpoint** that is narrow by design and supports early feasibility screens before broad search.
- **Keep search countable and recoverable** using automatic run logging and a simple trial taxonomy.

In practice, these choices live in code: a small set of versioned configuration objects and a pipeline that consumes them. Every run automatically emits a record (config, splits, metrics, outputs) so that results are reproducible and iterations are countable.

6.1 From idea to evidence with the ML4T workflow

A trading strategy is an executable process. Once live, it runs on a schedule, uses the information available at decision time to produce model inputs, converts model outputs into positions, and realizes outcomes after accounting for costs and constraints. This workflow is shown in *Figure 6.1*.

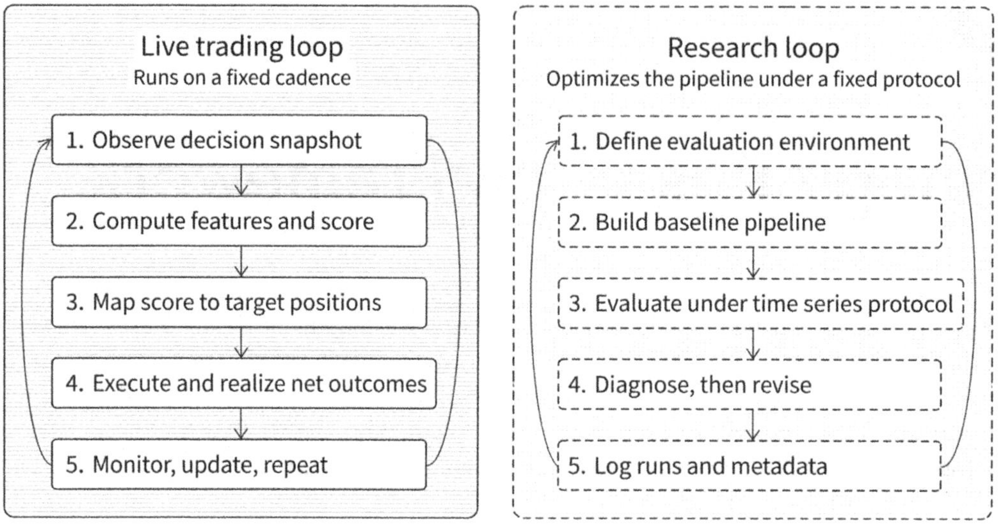

Figure 6.1: Live trading and the research loop

During research, we simulate this process using historical data. The goal is to optimize the process by iteratively refining each component while keeping comparisons meaningful and interpretable, so that historical simulation matches the live system's behavior at decision time.

The live trading loop

Every systematic strategy—whether it uses a hand-built signal or an ML model—can be described as a sequence of steps that repeat on a fixed cadence:

1. **Observe a decision snapshot.** At each decision time, the strategy takes a snapshot of the available information that defines what it "knows" when it commits to trades.
2. **Compute features and produce a score.** This data is transformed into a set of features for a model (or a rule-based signal) to predict rankings, probabilities, return forecasts, or other scores useful for trading decisions.
3. **Translate the score into positions.** A trading policy converts these predictions into target positions, subject to risk limits and constraints, and places orders accordingly.
4. **Execute and realize net outcomes.** Orders become fills (completed trades) with slippage, spreads, fees, financing, funding, roll costs, and other market-specific mechanics. Positions generate profit and loss (PnL) and exposures that are measured and monitored.
5. **Monitor, update, and repeat.** Performance, risk, and data quality are tracked; operational exceptions are handled; the loop repeats at the next decision time.

This loop is only meaningful when its timing is well defined. It is impossible to use information that is not available when trading live, but deceptively easy to do so during research on historical data. We must therefore clearly define the timing of trading decisions and keep these conventions stable, so that improvements can be attributed to deliberate changes rather than to shifting assumptions.

The research loop

Research builds evidence about how the live loop will behave without "moving the goalposts" as we iterate. We start with a baseline version of the live loop, evaluate it using a time-series protocol, diagnose weaknesses, and change one component at a time, while accounting for measurement noise. A practical research loop looks like this:

1. **Define the evaluation environment.** Declare the tradable universe, the decision cadence, basic constraints, and the cost components treated as material. This setup makes results comparable across iterations and avoids surprises during deployment.
2. **Build a baseline pipeline.** Implement the simplest end-to-end version that is consistent with the setup: minimal features, a baseline label, a baseline model class, and a simple mapping from scores to positions.
3. **Evaluate under a time-series protocol.** Compare candidates using time-aware validation and reserve a holdout test set for confirmation once the pipeline is stable. This is where we prevent leakage and selection bias from dominating conclusions.
4. **Diagnose, then revise.** Use diagnostics to decide what to change next: data definitions, feature families, model class, hyperparameters, mapping class parameters, constraints, or cost assumptions. Make changes deliberately and keep the rest fixed.
5. **Log what happened.** Record enough metadata to reproduce each run and to count the alternatives tried. Without this, iteration becomes untraceable, and selection bias becomes invisible.

The loop does not assume a single crisp hypothesis at the outset. In ML-driven research, we typically explore a **hypothesis class:** a family of measurements that might, in combination, yield better trading decisions. The discipline is not "never explore" but to explore within a stable setup and robust protocol so that results remain interpretable.

Illustrating the research framework with case studies

Nine case studies illustrate the strategy research workflow throughout our remaining chapters. Each is a scaffold for timing, feasibility, and evaluation, not a recommended trading system. They span multiple asset classes and data frequencies, drawing on the datasets from *Chapters 2* and *3*. For each case study, we highlight the asset class, data frequency, and coverage in terms of the number of symbols and the time period.

- `etfs`: *Multi-asset · Daily · ~100 symbols over 20 years.* Cross-asset rotation strategies that highlight turnover economics and regime dependence across equities, fixed income, and commodities.

- `us_equities_panel`: *Equities · Daily · ~3,000 symbols over 50 years.* The workhorse cross-sectional dataset for signal construction, universe filtering, and capacity analysis at scale.
- `us_firm_characteristics`: *Equities · Monthly · ~2,500 stocks · 1996-2016.* Factor models built on ~57 firm-level characteristics, emphasizing point-in-time discipline to avoid survivorship and lookahead bias.
- `fx_pairs`: *FX · 4-hour bars / daily NY 5PM decisions · 20 pairs · 2011-2025.* Currency strategies that confront close definitions, bar aggregation choices, and tradable return construction across time zones.
- `cme_futures`: *Futures · Daily · 30 contracts over 15 years.* Trend and carry strategies that require careful session alignment, roll mechanics, and term-structure modeling.
- `crypto_perps_funding`: *Crypto · 8-hour · ~20 symbols over 5 years.* Perpetual futures, where funding schedules, exchange-specific market mechanics, and transaction costs dominate signal economics.
- `nasdaq100_microstructure`: *Equities · Minute (downsampled to 15 Minutes) · ~114 symbols over 2 years.* High-frequency features that expose timing conventions, execution realism, and the gap between theoretical and realized fills.
- `sp500_equity_option_analytics`: *Equities + Options · Daily · S&P 500 over 5 years.* Equity strategies enriched with option-derived features such as implied volatility, skew, and put-call ratios.
- `sp500_options`: *Options · Daily · S&P 500 over 5 years.* Options strategies that foreground payoff accounting, hedging turnover, and the financing assumptions behind net returns.

The next section presents strategy families and sources of edge, using the case studies to make the strategy map concrete.

6.2 Mapping strategies and sources of edge

Most strategy ideas start as narratives: "prices underreact," "carry is a premium for bearing risk," or "flows create predictable pressure." A map turns those narratives into a usable design tool. Before building models or running large backtests, the map should answer two questions in operational terms:

- **What is the strategy's structure?** What is traded, how often are decisions made, how long is risk held, and which frictions dominate at that cadence?
- **Why should this earn net returns, and why should it persist?** What economic force could plausibly generate returns after costs and constraints, and what would have to remain true for the effect to survive competition and regime change?

The map uses two complementary lenses. **Strategy families** classify ideas by cadence, information source, and the frictions that become first order at that cadence. They identify what must be fixed early. **Sources of edge** are economic narratives about why a premium might exist and what persistence depends on. They guide stress tests and failure-mode hypotheses. A credible story with an infeasible implementation is not a strategy. A feasible implementation without a credible story is a backtest whose failure modes remain uninterpretable.

Box 6.1: Time notions to keep separate

The recurring activity of a trading strategy implies several periods and points in time that are important to define:

- **Decision cadence:** How often the strategy is allowed to change its position. This is the schedule for decisions and rebalancing. A strategy might enter only once per day, for example, but monitor exit signals intraday.
- **Holding period:** How long risk is typically held once a position is entered. It can be fixed (every 5 days, for example) or variable (exit on a signal or risk control).
- **Forecast horizon:** The future interval the model is trained to predict. It does not need to match the holding period when predictions span a given horizon and positions are held until a reason to exit manifests. A strategy can also use multiple models for entry and exit signals, each with a different horizon.
- **Lookback window:** How far back features look when formed at decision time. It determines the historical span available to features. Different model inputs can use different windows, irrespective of holding and forecast periods.

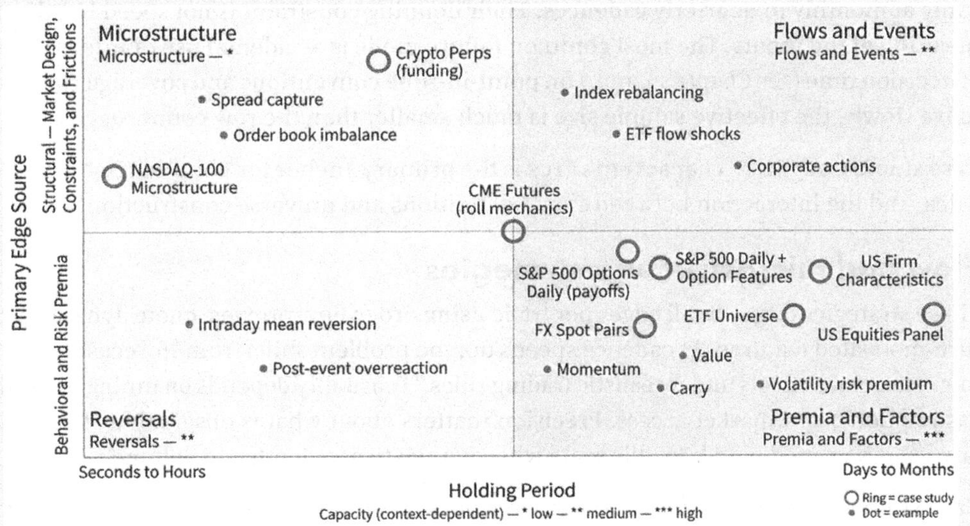

Figure 6.2: Strategies illustrated in edge and holding-period terms, spanning the strategy families (cadence axis) and sources of edge developed in the rest of this section

Strategy families as feasibility filters

Families overlap. The same label (for example, "momentum") can refer to both monthly cross-sectional sorting and intraday trend-following. The family does not uniquely determine the cadence; it identifies what will break first once one is chosen. Use the family whose dominant constraints match the intended cadence, and treat the family as a feasibility checklist: what must be fixed *early enough* to make results interpretable.

Price-based strategies

These strategies generate signals from past prices, returns, or realized volatility, including time-series trend-following, cross-sectional momentum, and short-horizon mean reversion (Moskowitz et al., 2012; Hurst et al., 2017; Jegadeesh and Titman, 1993; Asness, Moskowitz, and Pedersen, 2013). At short cadences, turnover and execution realism become first order. At longer cadences, risk concentrates in episodic drawdowns and regime shifts (momentum crashes are a known stress case; Daniel and Moskowitz, 2016).

To make a price-based idea testable, fix the holding horizon and rebalance cadence, lookback window, and score-to-position mapping. First screens: does performance hold up to modest changes in lookback/rebalance choices, and does it remain plausible under conservative, turnover-aware costs?

Case studies: `etfs`, `us_equities_panel`, and `fx_pairs` illustrate turnover economics, exposure control, and regime sensitivity at daily-to-monthly horizons.

Fundamental and valuation strategies

These strategies trade on cross-sectional differences in valuation, quality, growth, or profitability, typically at monthly to quarterly cadences. Their defining constraint is not speed but the **decision-time meaning** of the inputs. The most common failure mode is accidental use of information unavailable at decision time (see *Chapters 2* and *4* on **point-in-time conventions** and **coverage rules**). When signals move slowly, the **effective sample size** is much smaller than the row count suggests.

Case studies: `us_firm_characteristics` is the primary anchor for point-in-time discipline, coverage rules, and the interaction between signal definitions and universe construction.

Flow and microstructure strategies

These strategies target small edges per trade using order-flow proxies, quote dynamics, or microstructure-motivated features. As cadence speeds up, the problem shifts from "forecast returns" to "capture microstructure effects under realistic trading rules." Feasibility depends on timing discipline, execution assumptions, and market access. Precision matters about what is observable at decision time, what latency is assumed, and how fills scale with size relative to depth and volume.

Case studies: `nasdaq100_microstructure` prioritizes timing conventions and execution realism as first-order concerns.

Market mechanics and payoff strategies

These strategies depend on instrument mechanics that form part of the economic payoff: futures roll and term structure, perpetual funding, margin and financing, option payoffs and hedging turnover, settlement conventions, and contract eligibility rules. Testability requires an explicit **return decomposition** and explicit **lifecycle rules** (contract selection, roll schedule). First screens: component attribution, rule stability, and stress behavior under binding constraints (margin, funding, forced deleveraging).

Case studies: `cme_futures` and `crypto_perps_funding` are mechanics-first examples. `sp500_equity_option_analytics` and `sp500_options` anchor options research, where payoff accounting, surface timing/coverage, hedging turnover, and financing assumptions dominate interpretation.

> **A note on "machine learning strategies."**
>
> Machine learning is not a family of strategies. It is a modeling and decision-support layer that can be applied to any family. Because ML expands the effective degrees of freedom (more features, more model classes, more hyperparameters), it increases, rather than reduces, the value of a bounded strategy definition and disciplined evaluation.

Defining edge, alpha, and capacity

An **edge** is a repeatable advantage that makes the distribution of **net** trade outcomes favorable under a given strategy, reflecting both the likelihood of gains versus losses and their magnitudes after costs. Two related terms matter:

- **Alpha** is performance relative to a benchmark (an index or factor model) representing alternative opportunities or compensated risk exposures. A strategy that cannot outperform a passive baseline with similar exposures and constraints may not be worth pursuing.
- **Capacity** is the capital that can be deployed before the edge degrades from impact, fees, financing constraints, or opportunity-set limits. Capacity does not determine whether an edge exists, but often determines whether it is economically usable at scale.

Sources of edge as durability filters

Feasibility addresses whether the idea can be tested credibly. Durability addresses what must remain true for the edge to persist. McLean and Pontiff (2016) found that published predictors lose roughly half their predictive power post-publication, partly due to overfitting and partly to arbitrage. The implication: edges that depend on information alone tend to erode; edges that depend on risk tolerance, constraints, or capacity limits can persist even when widely known. Real strategies often combine multiple sources of edge; the goal is to be explicit about the dominant ones and to test their corresponding failure modes.

A useful organizing framework distinguishes six sources of excess returns based on *why* the opportunity persists (Paleologo, 2025):

Source	**Mechanism**	**Durability**	**ML4T examples**
Risk compensation	Bearing exposures others avoid (tail, volatility, illiquidity risk)	High — persists as long as investors are risk averse	cme_futures carry, sp500_options volatility risk premium
Liquidity provision	Earning a premium for supplying immediacy or absorbing inventory	High — structural demand for immediacy	nasdaq100_ microstructure intraday reversals
Funding constraints	Exploiting dislocations when capital is scarce or leverage is restricted	Moderate — episodic, strongest during stress	Short-horizon mean reversion after forced liquidations

Source	Mechanism	Durability	ML4T examples
Flow predictability	Front-positioning around mandated or rules-based demand (index rebalancing, hedging programs)	Moderate — erodes with crowding but recurs with each event	Index reconstitution trades, ETF creation/ redemption flows
Informational advantage	Better inference from public data: cleaner features, faster processing, superior models	Low to moderate — erodes as competitors replicate methods	ML-based feature engineering across case studies
Pure arbitrage	Exploiting identical-asset mispricing across venues or structures	Very low — fleeting, capacity-constrained, operationally intensive	Not represented in our case studies

Table 6.1: Comparing six sources of excess

The following subsections expand on several of these sources and related mechanisms. Most real strategies blend two or more; the table helps identify which ones anchor a thesis and which failure modes to test first.

Box 6.2: Why most published anomalies fail in practice

The academic literature documents hundreds of cross- al predictors, yet very few survive as tradable strategies. Three gaps account for most of the attrition:

- **Post-publication decay.** McLean and Pontiff (2016) show that anomaly alphas decline roughly 50% after publication, partly due to overfitting corrections, partly due to arbitrage capital flowing in.
- **Implementation gap.** Academic studies typically use simplified portfolio construction (equal-weight long-short deciles, monthly rebalancing, no costs), which overstates live performance. Turnover, bid-ask spreads, and borrow costs often consume the reported alpha.
- **Detail sensitivity.** Small definitional choices (universe filters, rebalancing timing, winsorization thresholds) can flip the sign of a backtest result. A backtested anomaly is a hypothesis, not evidence; the evidence comes from out-of-sample evaluation under a fixed protocol (*Sections 6.5* and *6.6*).

The defense is not to avoid published ideas but to treat them as starting points that require independent validation within a researcher's own trading setup and cost assumptions.

Slow adjustment and behavioral responses

Prices may incorporate information gradually due to limited attention, delegated decision-making, or slow portfolio rebalancing, motivating underreaction narratives behind momentum and intermediate-horizon trend effects (Jegadeesh and Titman, 1993).

Early failure-mode tests: Examine drawdown and rebound episodes (momentum crashes; Daniel and Moskowitz, 2016) and check whether performance concentrates under benign conditions but reverses when volatility spikes or liquidity dries up, a pattern that often reveals that alpha partly compensates for state-contingent risk.

Risk compensation

Some returns compensate for bearing exposures others avoid: liquidity risk, tail risk, volatility risk, or balance-sheet-intensive exposures. Persistence can coexist with widespread awareness because the constraint is risk tolerance and leverage capacity, not information.

Early failure-mode tests: Performance during tail episodes when constraints bind (margin/funding shocks, forced deleveraging) and performance conditional on volatility and liquidity proxies.

Market segmentation and limits to arbitrage

Segmented markets and institutional constraints create persistent wedges: funding differences, capital charges, short-selling constraints, inventory limits, and client-flow internalization. The edge persists because the arbitrage is balance-sheet intensive or operationally constrained.

Early tests: Stability under stressed financing and fee regimes, realism of access assumptions, and capacity/crowding behavior.

Box 6.3: Why prediction alone is insufficient

A correct forecast does not guarantee a profitable trade. When 3Com announced the IPO of its Palm subsidiary in 2000, Palm's implied valuation quickly exceeded that of the parent—a textbook mispricing visible to every market participant. Yet the trade was nearly impossible to execute: Palm shares available to borrow were scarce, borrowing fees spiked to extreme levels, and uncertainty about the spin-off timeline created open-ended funding risk. The mispricing persisted for months despite being obvious. For ML-driven research, the lesson is concrete: before engineering features for a mispricing hypothesis, verify that the short side is accessible, that borrowing and funding costs do not consume the spread, and that the holding-period risk is bounded. A model that identifies unexploitable opportunities is operationally useless regardless of its predictive accuracy.

Mechanical and institutional flows

Predictable demand from mandates, hedging, index rebalancing, roll schedules, or systematic execution programs creates transient or recurrent price pressure, driven by rules and constraints rather than beliefs.

Early tests: Calendar dependence and event alignment, decay under crowding, and execution sensitivity (flow edges often live near the spread).

Index reconstitution is the standard example. When an index provider announces an addition or deletion, passive funds tracking that index must trade by the effective date, creating a demand shock whose direction, approximate magnitude, and timing are publicly known in advance. The edge is not in having private information but in positioning ahead of the mandated flow: predicting *which* securities will be added or removed, and *when* the demand will materialize. The risk is real: holding-period exposure to company-specific losses, potential event cancellations, and crowding as more participants exploit the same signal. As passive investment continues to grow (estimated at 35-40% of U.S. equity market capitalization), these flow events create larger dislocations and attract more competition, illustrating the tension between opportunity size and crowding that recurs across flow-based strategies. In our case studies, futures roll effects in `cme_futures` and ETF creation/redemption dynamics in `etfs` create analogous flow-driven patterns at different cadences.

Information and measurement advantages

Net returns can come from better inference: cleaner definitions, better timing discipline, more reliable labeling, and a more faithful mapping from observables to actions. This is rarely "free money"; it is often what turns a fragile backtest into a robust implementation within another category.

Early tests emphasize robustness to definition choices and conservative timing, sensitivity to coverage/missingness, and the extent to which incremental signal quality survives realistic costs and constraints.

Using the map

A strategy is well posed when the following questions can be answered:

- **Family and cadence:** Which frictions dominate?
- **PnL decomposition:** Which payoffs generate returns, and which costs are first order?
- **Edge narrative:** What is the primary economic source, and why should it persist?
- **Top failure modes:** Two or three ways the strategy could fail.

Answering these before expanding the search helps focus the next design decision: what to fix in the trading setup, which diagnostics to run first, and which stress tests are non-negotiable. We discuss the trading setup components next.

6.3 Defining the trading setup

Comparability breaks when the evaluation environment drifts without notice: the instrument set changes, the rebalance snapshot shifts, execution timing moves, or costs are treated differently. The **trading setup** is the fixed part of that environment: the invariants the code treats as constant within a research line, and every run automatically records. We can explore aggressively inside those invariants, but changing them defines a new setup and requires bumping the version.

What the trading setup must fix

The trading setup fixes the decision-time snapshot, mapping form, and friction regime, rather than enumerating every lookback or threshold. It should cover the following topics:

Universe and tradability rules

Define eligibility and membership mechanics that make pricing and execution economically meaningful. Specify filters (liquidity, listing venue, contract type), and how listings, delistings, and stale or missing prices are handled. For example, `etfs` need explicit investability filters and rules for ETF launches and closures; `crypto_perps_funding` needs venue and contract eligibility and a rule for how convention changes (such as fees, funding caps, margining) are treated.

Decision schedule and admissible information

Specify the trading snapshot and what is knowable at that moment. This is the guardrail against leakage, so it must be explicit: the timestamp convention, the bar frequency (if any), and any mechanical execution delay. `etfs` might use a weekly or month-end snapshot; `crypto_perps_funding` aligns decisions with the funding timestamp; `nasdaq100_microstructure` requires a fixed bar schedule and a stated observation-to-execution delay because a one-bar shift can change results.

Cadence and horizon feasibility

The cadence choice is intimately linked to costs: at each horizon, what fraction of typical price moves exceeds round-trip transaction costs? This principle determines feasibility before considering any signal.

Each case study includes a setup notebook with a horizon feasibility analysis that shows return distributions across multiple cadences and a cost reference line. These identify three regimes:

- A **hard floor** where costs clearly dominate (for example, `nasdaq100_microstructure` at 15-minute bars)
- A **gray zone** where feasibility depends on signal strength and turnover (for example, `etfs` for daily trading)
- A **comfortable zone** where costs are not the binding constraint (for example, `etfs` with monthly rebalancing)

The cadence decision is made in the following chapters, when signal diagnostics reveal whether features are sufficiently predictive, either on a standalone basis or in a model context, to justify trading at a given frequency.

Score-to-trade mapping

Define how a model's score translates into orders, positions, and exits. This mapping determines trade frequency, holding-period distribution, and where costs and constraints bite. At a minimum, determine the following design parameters to ensure results are comparable:

- **Position state space:** For example, long-only, long/short, or multi-leg (spread/hedge).
- **Entry logic:** For example, rank selection or threshold gating.
- **Exit logic:** For example, time-, signal-, or risk-based exit.
- **Position sizing:** How scores translate into exposures (for example, equal weight, volatility targeting).
- **Order timing:** When orders are placed (at open, intraday window, execution delay).

The specifics will likely evolve, but when they do, the reference for comparison will as well.

Constraints and risk controls in scope

Specify the constraints treated as binding: exposure and leverage limits, concentration rules, and any liquidity or capacity limits enforced. Risk controls that alter trading actions (for example, a de-risking overlay or a kill switch) must be explicit and versioned, as they alter the effective strategy.

Cost model class and components

Early research does not need a perfect simulator, but it does require consistency about which frictions are treated as material. State the cost components included (fees, spreads, slippage/impact, financing or funding, borrow, roll) and how conservative the assumptions are. Later chapters expand the cost model; early screens use conservative, coarse assumptions.

Example (perpetual futures): in `crypto_perps_funding`, funding is a position-dependent cash flow that is part of the total return stream: a cost when paid and a benefit when received. Because it accrues only when a position is held at the funding timestamp and is settled under venue-specific conventions, the trading setup must specify (i) how trades and position changes are aligned to the funding snapshot, (ii) which pricing and funding formula (including any caps/floors) and fee schedule are assumed, and (iii) how convention changes are versioned. Otherwise, the same backtest can imply different effective exposures and produce materially different PnL.

Example: The **ETF cross-asset momentum setup (v1)** defines the following invariants:

- **Universe:** 100 cross-asset ETFs with point-in-time eligibility based on trailing annual ADV ≥ \$10M. The lenient threshold preserves cross-sectional breadth in early sample years (70–95 eligible ETFs per year). Note that the universe composition has survivorship bias that cannot be fully resolved without historical constituent data, while within-universe eligibility is point-in-time correct.
- **Decision schedule:** Monthly month-end close snapshot with execution at the next-day bar open. This aligns with momentum literature for benchmark comparability. Weekly (5-day) cadence is tested as a variant.
- **Mapping:** Long-only, rank-select top-N, equal-weight, rebalanced on cadence. Long-only because ETFs are expensive to short; equal-weight because it isolates the ranking signal from sizing optimization that would confound evaluation.
- **Constraints:** Fully invested long-only with no leverage, a minimal constraint set appropriate for a pedagogical baseline.
- **Cost model:** Material is a per-share commission (\$0.0035/share, IBKR Pro Tiered) plus tiered half-spread slippage (0.5¢ for the most liquid mega-ETFs, 1¢ for sector ETFs, 2¢ default for thematic and regional ETFs). The horizon feasibility analysis uses a 5–15 bps-per-leg reference cost line to screen cadences and confirms that monthly moves exceed 30 bps round-trip costs in over 90% of observations; daily trading operates in the gray zone where feasibility depends on signal strength and turnover.

The setup notebook writes these choices to versioned YAML artifacts (`setup.yaml`) that downstream chapters consume programmatically. Changing the mapping from long-only to long/short would require `setup_version: v2` and a new baseline checkpoint; parameter changes, such as adjusting top-N from 10 to 20, remain within `v1`.

When a change requires a new setup version

Treat the trading setup as versioned. Bump the setup version on any change that alters the strategy's decision-time meaning or shifts its dominant frictions and constraints. Parameter tuning stays within a setup; changes to mechanics define a new setup. A change is a new setup version if it changes at least one of:

- **Universe or tradability rules**, for example, eligibility, membership mechanics, instrument scope.
- **Decision schedule or admissible information**, for example, rebalance snapshot, cadence, execution delay, and input availability rules.
- **Score-to-trade mapping** at the level of state space, entry or exit form, sizing normalization, or order timing.
- **Constraint regime**, such as binding exposure/leverage limits, concentration rules, capacity or liquidity constraints, action-changing overlays.
- **Cost model class or included components**, for example, adding funding or roll mechanics, or changing the slippage model in a way that affects feasibility.

To keep this boundary unambiguous, separate **mechanics** from **parameters:**

Same setup version (parameter tuning)	New setup version (mechanics changed)
Threshold 1.8 → 2.0	Rank selection → threshold gating
Top 10% → top 20%	Long-only → long/short
20-day → 60-day normalization window	Adding a stop rule when none existed
Different lookback horizon	Changing rebalance cadence or execution delay
Cost assumption 10 bps → 15 bps per leg	Adding funding/roll as a cost component

Table 6.2: Comparing mechanics and parameters

Results across setup versions can still be informative, but they are not direct competitors within a single research program. The next section defines what counts as improvement within a fixed setup, separating development diagnostics from strategy-level evaluation.

Implementation: `02_case_study_overview` inventories the trading setup for each of the nine case studies (universe, decision schedule, mapping, constraints, cost model) and is the source of the worked examples above.

6.4 Setting objectives and evaluation metrics

A research program needs an explicit definition of "better" before running large experiment grids. Here, "better" means **economic value under a fixed trading setup**: portfolio returns produced by mapping model outputs into positions and applying constraints and costs. This section specifies three important rules:

- Evaluate strategy candidates in **economic terms**, based on a consistent PnL definition
- **Keep metric roles separate** for model and strategy evaluation
- Choose **one primary selection metric for development** and a **separate reporting set** for strategy outcomes

Specific metrics appear in later chapters on features, models, and backtests; here, we establish the framework for how these metric layers interact.

Three metric layers, each with a different role

Confusion in ML-driven strategy research often arises from relying on a single metric to address multiple questions. Treat metrics as three distinct layers, each tied to a specific decision:

- **Model diagnostics** answer a narrow question: can the model learn the label in a way that generalizes across time splits? Typical checks include loss or error, calibration, and stability across folds. If these fail, treat downstream trading results as difficult to interpret because the predictor is unstable. These checks do not require a cost model, position sizing, or portfolio simulation; they serve as an early gate that prevents overinterpreting noise.
- **Signal diagnostics** test whether the model output behaves like a tradable signal under the chosen mapping class. A common choice is the **information coefficient (IC)**, the Spearman rank correlation between predicted scores and subsequent realized returns (see *Chapter 7*). Signal diagnostics treat the output **as a score to be traded**; model diagnostics treat it **as a predictor to be trusted**. *Chapter 7* covers both in detail.
- **Strategy outcomes** evaluate the end-to-end process under costs and constraints, in terms of risk and return. Typical reporting includes risk-adjusted returns, volatility and drawdowns, exposure and concentration behavior, and realized turnover (see *Chapter 17*). The failure mode is to use these outcomes as the objective for every small design choice during development, which encourages overfitting to the simulator's degrees of freedom and will likely disappoint out-of-sample.

A complementary diagnostic, **conformal prediction intervals**, provides calibrated uncertainty estimates without distributional assumptions. *Chapter 11* introduces conformal methods for time-series prediction; here, note that well-calibrated prediction intervals can flag when a model's confidence is misaligned with realized outcomes, serving as an early warning alongside the three layers mentioned earlier.

Use model diagnostics to assess learnability, signal diagnostics to assess tradability under the mapping, and strategy outcomes to determine whether the declared setup produces economic value. Keep strategy outcomes "late-stage": when they drive every micro-decision, the risk of overfitting to implementation details rises, masking a robust edge. We now turn to evaluating our target metrics in a time-series context.

6.5 Evaluation protocol for time series

Evaluation answers a simple question: how will a procedure learned from historical data behave on data it has not seen? We estimate this by testing decisions on data unavailable when those decisions were made. The notebook `01_cv_foundations` illustrates these concepts using the `ml4t-diagnostic` library. The core discipline: separate selection from performance estimation, and enforce a fixed decision time so no future information leaks into training or simulation.

Data leakage and estimation bias

Look-ahead bias occurs when any component of the pipeline uses information that would not have been available at the time of the trading decision. It is the most dangerous form of data leakage because it produces spectacular backtest results that cannot be replicated in live trading. Look-ahead bias manifests in several forms in the context of time-series evaluation (in addition to source data problems like survivorship bias or point-in-time errors, as discussed in *Chapters 2* and *4*):

- **Label leakage:** Using future returns in the same observation's features (for example, computing 5-day-forward returns and accidentally including next-day returns in a feature).
- **Standardization leakage:** For derived features, computing inputs on the full dataset, instead of the training set alone. For example, using the mean and standard deviation to compute z-scores from the full data may reveal a distribution shift during the validation period.
- **Threshold leakage:** Setting thresholds using statistics computed from validation or test data. For example, choosing "enter when the z-score exceeds 2.0" after observing that 2.0 maximizes returns on the test period embeds future information in the trading rule.

Every component of the ML pipeline must respect point-in-time constraints: labels (*Chapter 7*), features (*Chapters 8-10*), validation splits, and signal calibration. A backtest that assumes access to information before it was knowable produces fictional performance.

From k-fold cross-validation to time series evaluation

Standard *k-fold cross-validation* trains on, say, 80% of randomly selected observations and validates on the remaining 20%, repeating k times (Kohavi, 1995). This works when observations are IID, which implies they are exchangeable draws from a stable distribution. Financial time series break that assumption in two ways:

- **The live procedure is directional.** In production, at time t, only information available at or before *t* can be used. A random split almost always trains on timestamps after the validation point, which means it estimates a procedure that cannot be executed in real time. Nearby observations are also dependent due to autocorrelation and slow-moving regimes, so random shuffling inflates apparent performance.

- **Rows are coupled through windows.** Features and labels are computed from lookback and forward windows (rolling volatility, trailing returns, h-day forward returns). Even with chronological splits, overlapping windows across the boundary can leak information.

Time-series evaluation requires split rules that preserve chronology and prevent window overlap, matching a decision-time procedure that could actually be run. Bergmeir, Hyndman, and Koo (2018) show that standard k-fold CV can produce unbiased error estimates for autoregressive models when residuals are uncorrelated, a condition that often fails when model misspecification leaves exploitable structure in the errors.

Walk-forward cross-validation as the baseline

Walk-forward CV mirrors deployment: fit on a past window, predict on a future window, score, roll forward, and repeat. *Figure 6.3* compares k-fold with walk-forward CV. A minimal CV design:

1. Choose a **training window**.
2. Choose a **validation window** (a future block for prediction).
3. Enforce **decision-time admissibility** at the boundary: training data must end early enough that every training label is already resolved before validation begins.
4. Fit on the admissible training window.
5. Predict on the validation window.
6. Score with the selection metric.
7. Advance by a fixed step and repeat.

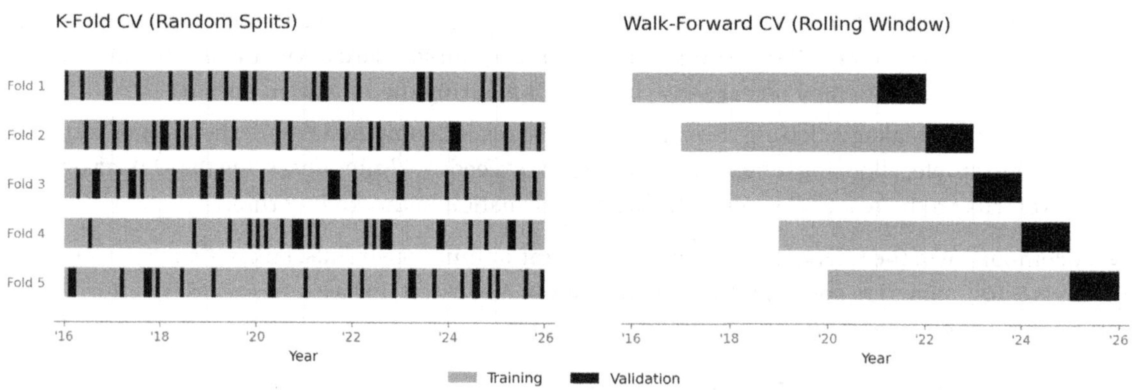

Figure 6.3: Comparing k-fold and walk-forward cross-validation

The protocol can be checked with one question: *At decision time t, which labeled samples were actually available?* A sample indexed at time τ is admissible for training at decision time t only if its:

- **Features** are computable using information available at or before t
- The **label** is already known by t

Example (FX 4-hour bars): For an FX strategy that decides on 4-hour bars, "the close" depends on the venue and bar construction. If the decision snapshot is the 4-hour bar close, features must be computable from prices available at that close, and the execution assumption must specify whether the trade fires at the same close, the next bar open, or with a fixed delay. A one-bar shift can turn a realistic rule into leakage.

The second condition is a common failure mode. If the label is an h-day forward return, then the label for τ is not known until $\tau + h$. So, training "as of t" must exclude the most recent h timestamps. This is the **label buffer** (called "purging" by López de Prado, 2018). For example, with 5-trading-day forward-return labels and a five-day trading week, suppose decision time is Tuesday, Feb 10. Then, the latest eligible training timestamp is Tuesday, Feb 3. Interim timestamps are ineligible because their labels have not yet resolved as of Feb 10.

Walk-forward evaluation uses either an **expanding window** (all admissible history, which may have lower variance but may introduce bias from stale data) or a **rolling window** (the most recent L admissible observations, which offers faster adaptation but may produce higher variance).

Retraining frequency

Retrain when new data represents at least 1–5% of the training window, or when out-of-sample performance degrades systematically. With a 10-year window, monthly or quarterly retraining suffices; with 20-day windows, daily retraining captures meaningful change. These design choices materially affect results and must be logged.

Temporal buffers – Label buffer and feature buffer

Walk-forward validation eliminates the grossest form of leakage—training on the future—but leaves a subtler problem. Training observations can "see" validation data through two channels:

- **Labels look forward:** A 20-day return label period begins on the observation date. If a training observation occurs 15 days before validation starts, its label overlaps with five validation days.
- **Features look backward:** A 20-day momentum feature uses data from the past 20 days. If training *follows* validation (as in k-fold or combinatorial schemes; see Combinatorial methods and path dependence below), a training observation immediately after the validation period computes features using prices from the validation period.

The solution is **temporal buffers:** gaps that prevent labels and features from reaching across the boundary. In practice, always count buffer gaps in **trading days**, not calendar days. The difference is material. For example, a 21-trading-day label buffer in January 2024 spans 30–32 calendar days; a naive 21-*calendar*-day purge covers only 15 trading days, leaving 6 days of label leakage (see `01_cv_foundations`):

- The **label buffer** removes training observations whose labels overlap with those in the validation set. Its size equals the label horizon: for 20-day forward returns, exclude training observations within 20 (trading) days of the validation boundary. For one-day-ahead forecasts on daily data, no buffer is needed. López de Prado (2018) calls this **purging**.

- The **feature buffer** removes training observations whose feature lookback windows overlap with the validation period. This buffer is only needed when training data appear after the validation period, which does not occur in standard walk-forward CV but does occur in k-fold and combinatorial schemes. López de Prado (2018) calls this an **embargo** and proposes 1% of the sample length as a rule of thumb; the appropriate size depends on the strategy's horizon and the strength of temporal dependence.

Holdout test set and rolling retuning

Walk-forward splits reveal how choices behave when the "fit on the past, predict the future" pattern is repeated. But they do not, by themselves, answer the governance question: *when do we stop selecting and start measuring?*

To make that boundary operational, reserve a **sealed holdout test set**: a final time block that plays no role in any development decision (signal definition, feature selection, hyperparameter tuning, model selection, or reporting choices). The holdout may be inspected only after the pipeline is frozen. During development, we select using the primary development metric computed on walk-forward validation; we report strategy outcomes after freezing the pipeline; and we use the sealed holdout only once for confirmation.

With that rule in place, two distinct evaluation modes are useful:

- **Fixed holdout (tune once, test once)**: Use walk-forward validation on the development period to select a single configuration, freeze the full pipeline (including the score-to-trade mapping and cost/constraint assumptions), and evaluate it once on the sealed holdout to estimate out-of-sample performance.
- **Rolling retuning**: To estimate the performance of a procedure that regularly retunes as new data arrives, split the overall test period into smaller windows and repeat the "fixed holdout" procedure for each window. At each test step, tune using only data strictly prior to the next test window, refit on admissible history, and then score on the next test window. Each test window is used for measurement only. This approach is called **nested walk-forward** because it uses an outer test loop and an inner model-selection loop. Bates et al. (2021) show that confidence intervals computed from nested CV have superior statistical properties. *Figure 6.4* illustrates this procedure with expanding and rolling windows.

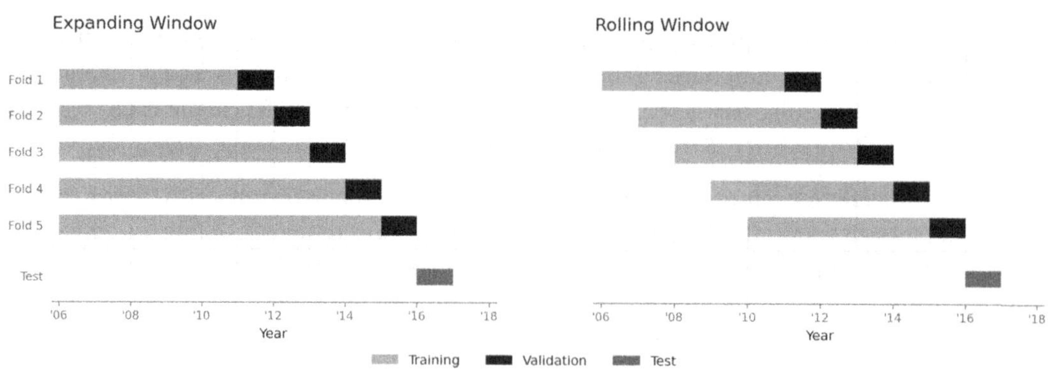

Figure 6.4: Nested walk-forward CV with rolling windows

Nested walk-forward can capture when model configurations change and can be more realistic. For example, with a two-year test period and a five-year lookback, a live strategy would likely retune the model more than once as assumed by the fixed-holdout approach. Nested walk-forward with many feature sets is computationally demanding; parallelized evaluation, incremental retraining, and feature caching are standard optimizations. The key invariant remains: tuning never uses future data relative to the outer test window.

Combinatorial methods and path dependence

A standard walk-forward yields a single sequence of out-of-sample windows: a single historical path. **Combinatorial methods** partition time into blocks and evaluate many train–test combinations, producing a distribution of out-of-sample outcomes rather than a single trajectory. The motivation is **path dependence**: a strategy may appear unusually strong or weak depending on which regimes fall along the single test path.

López de Prado (2018) proposes **Combinatorial Purged Cross-Validation** (CPCV), which selects k groups of contiguous observations from n total groups, creating $\binom{n}{k}$ distinct train/test configurations. Each configuration applies both label and feature buffers—necessary because validation groups can appear anywhere relative to training blocks.

Combinatorial evaluation is most useful when comparing many variants and seeking a more stable view of selection risk. It does not replace decision-time discipline: overlap leakage must still be prevented using the buffers described above, and each test block must be treated as "future" relative to its paired training blocks. Combinatorial evaluation is computationally expensive—$\binom{n}{k}$ configurations grow quickly—and offers diminishing returns when the time series is short or when most blocks share the same regime. We will discuss CPCV in more detail in *Chapter 17*.

Design commitments

Before running experiments, specify and log the evaluation design:

- **Window lengths:** Training, validation (if used), and test
- **Step size:** How far the splits roll forward each iteration
- **Retraining cadence:** How often the model is refit
- **Label horizon:** The forward window used to define labels, which determines the label buffer size
- **Longest feature lookback:** The maximum lookback across all features, which determines the feature buffer size
- **Test period:** The dates reserved for final evaluation, not used for any development decision

These are design commitments, not tuning parameters. Changing them mid-research defines a different evaluation procedure rather than an "improved" result under the same evaluation. Throughout, we encode these commitments in the `setup.yaml` configuration that each setup notebook writes; downstream chapters convert it to a `WalkForwardConfig` object for the ml4t-diagnostic splitters. This makes the evaluation design both explicit and executable. Logging these choices before experimentation enables reproducibility and makes "the same strategy" operationally well-defined.

Figure 6.5 shows the prediction coverage across the case studies. Coverage varies substantially; this heterogeneity motivates strategy-specific protocol choices, and the figure serves as a reference for understanding the statistical depth available for each case study.

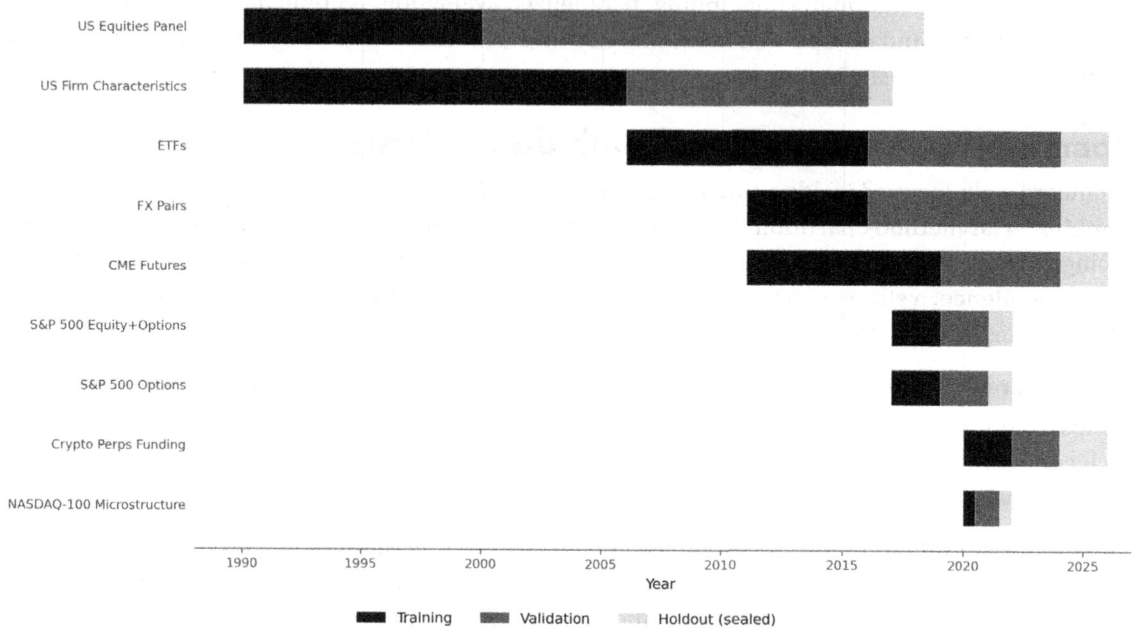

Figure 6.5: Training, validation, and holdout periods for the nine case studies

The notebook `02_case_study_overview.py` shows the trading setups and time-series validation configurations for all case studies; the underlying analysis is in the `01_setup.py` notebooks in each case study directory. Next, we discuss how to start research with a focused baseline.

6.6 Establishing a baseline checkpoint

Before running large experiment grids, we need a **baseline checkpoint**: the smallest runnable specification that answers an early governance question: under the trading setup and evaluation protocol, is there enough stable structure to justify deeper work, or should the setup itself be revised?

Three preflight sanity checks

Before investing in feature engineering and model search, run three checks that catch common failures early. These are not evidence of an edge. They are sanity checks that the checkpoint is well-posed. Here are the three checks:

1. **Timing sanity.** Confirm that the baseline measurement and label can be computed using only information available at the declared decision snapshot, respecting data and model pipeline timelines, and execution delays.
2. **Coverage sanity.** Report how much of the intended universe is actually tradable at each decision time under the eligibility rules, and whether that coverage changes materially across history.

3. **Trading-intensity sanity.** Use a coarse proxy for how often the mapping would trade. The goal is to detect definitions that implicitly demand unrealistic turnover before building a detailed cost model.

If these checks fail, the right response is usually to revise the trading setup conventions (snapshot, eligibility, mapping class) rather than to "optimize around" a brittle definition.

The first reference run is narrow by design

The first reference run produces comparable, interpretable output under the declared setup and protocol. Its inputs (labels, features, and a baseline model) arrive across the next five chapters. Keep it narrow:

- **One label and horizon.** Choose a single forward horizon aligned with the strategy cadence and mapping class. This horizon determines the label buffer required by *Section 6.5*.
- **Compact feature families.** Use a small set of feature families that represent the narrative at the correct cadence. The goal is representative coverage, not exhaustiveness.
- **One simple baseline model class.** Use a stable baseline with minimal tuning. At this stage, the objective is a comparable reference point, not peak performance.
- **One walk-forward design.** Specify training and test window lengths, step size, and the purging rule implied by the label horizon. Reserve the sealed holdout for later confirmation.

The reference run answers a narrow question: Given the declared setup and evaluation protocol, does a simple baseline produce stable, non-pathological behavior without relying on fragile timing conventions or extreme implied turnover?

If the answer is "no," the next step is often to revisit the setup (cadence, mapping class, tradability filters, or the measurement/label alignment). If the answer is "yes," the information set and the model class can be expanded in later chapters, while keeping the baseline comparable. The next section addresses the bookkeeping that makes this comparison trustworthy: how to log every run so that search breadth is countable and selection bias is visible.

6.7 Search accounting and run logging

A **run log** is automatic metadata, along with pointers to the artifacts produced by each execution. When the same configuration can be rerun and the same inputs, splits, metrics, and outputs recovered, results can be compared reliably. Otherwise, the discussion of outcomes proceeds without verifying what produced them. The multiplication of research opportunities, amplified by LLM-assisted hypothesis generation (*Chapters 22–24*), further strengthens the case for countable search. A run log supports three practical needs:

- **Comparability:** Performance differences can be attributed to a change in the pipeline only when everything else is held constant and recorded, including the trading setup version, data snapshot, split design, and cost model class.

- **Selection transparency:** Once variants are compared, selection bias enters. We must know how many alternatives were tested, which metric was used to choose among them, and whether any results were used solely for confirmation. Bailey and López de Prado (2014) introduced the Deflated Sharpe Ratio, which adjusts performance metrics to account for the probability of overfitting, based on the number of trials. Applying these corrections requires knowing the trial count, which, in turn, requires logging.
- **Recovery:** A figure, a backtest, or a table can be reproduced from a concrete run identifier, without guessing which notebook cell or intermediate file produced it.

Trial taxonomy

Use a small, consistent taxonomy so the search is countable without being bureaucratic. A workable four-level structure is:

1. **Strategy.** A named trading setup and objective with fixed invariants (universe, decision cadence, position mapping class, and cost model class), for example, `etfs`.
2. **Trial family.** A group of comparable alternatives that share the same setup and evaluation design but differ along one intended axis, for example, baseline signal definitions for the same horizon, or alternative feature sets for the same model class.
3. **Trial.** One fully specified pipeline configuration within a family, including the exact signal definition, feature specification, model class, hyperparameters (if any), and position-sizing rules.
4. **Run.** One execution of a trial tied to a concrete code version, data snapshot, random seed, and compute environment, producing metrics and artifacts.

This taxonomy answers "how many signal definitions did we compare?" and "which run produced *Figure 6.3*?" without turning research into a document workflow.

Minimum contents of the run log

The goal of a run log is to make results **reproducible, comparable, and gateable**. There is no single way to organize research. However, the following five categories of records are non-negotiable, while the specific representations may vary:

- **Provenance (what ran):** Strategy setup version, trial IDs, code revision (git hash), timestamp, random seeds.
- **Data and evaluation (what was tested):** Dataset and point-in-time conventions, dev and holdout ranges, split scheme (windowing, step, label, and feature buffers), label horizon, and admissibility constraints.
- **Configuration (how it was produced):** Baseline definition and timing, feature and preprocessing spec, model class and hyperparameters, position mapping, plus risk and cost model parameters.
- **Artifacts (where outputs live):** References to features and labels, predictions, and backtest outputs (positions, trades, PnL, diagnostics).
- **Decision and gates (why it was kept):** Selection metric and rule, reported acceptance metrics, and the holdout gate outcome.

This list is intentionally small. If a field does not affect reproducibility, comparability, or the holdout rule, do not add it by default. Tools such as MLflow and Weights & Biases automate much of this logging; *Chapter 26* discusses MLOps governance in detail (*Section 26.6*).

One structural way to reduce the effective number of strategies tested is to pre-register the hypothesis: specify the economic thesis, signal definition, and evaluation criteria before running the backtest. Pre-registration does not preclude exploration, but it draws a clear line between confirmatory tests (which count toward the deflation adjustment) and exploratory analyses (which inform future hypotheses). *Chapter 16* formalizes this idea via the Rademacher Anti-Serum, which quantifies the penalty for searching over multiple strategies (*Section 16.7*). The summary draws these commitments together into the research contract that *Chapters 7-20* will carry forward.

6.8 Summary

We have turned a strategy idea into a research program that produces trustworthy evidence under iterative search. We distinguished the live trading loop from the research loop, then used a strategy map, built from families (dominant frictions by cadence) and sources of edge (durability requirements and failure modes), to force early clarity on the strategy's structure and what must remain true for an effect to persist.

Discipline rests on four commitments: a versioned trading setup that fixes the evaluation environment; explicit economic objectives that separate development metrics from reporting outcomes; a time-series evaluation protocol that enforces chronology and decision-time admissibility with a sealed holdout; and a compact baseline checkpoint with run logging that keeps the search auditable, reproducible, and countable.

The next chapter is devoted to defining our learning task.

7

Defining the Learning Task

A machine learning model can only be as good as the learning problem you define. Before you select an algorithm, you need a label that captures an outcome relevant to your strategy, preprocessing conventions that keep inputs comparable across trials, and an evaluation framework that can distinguish genuine signal from artifacts of timing, overlap, or search. This chapter builds that scaffolding.

Chapters 8–10 provide the candidate features (financial, model-based, and text-derived) that this framework evaluates. The definitions, diagnostics, and decision gates built here govern every candidate in that sequence.

After completing this chapter, you will be able to:

- Build a split-aware preprocessing pipeline that produces stable, auditable inputs for label and feature computation.
- Define execution-consistent labels and diagnose their overlap and implied trading intensity.
- Evaluate feature–label bundles using fold-aware diagnostics for continuous and binary targets.
- Apply feasibility screens to filter out candidates who cannot survive implementation costs.
- Account for selection bias by defining searched sets, separating exploration from confirmation, and adjusting fold-level summaries.
- Apply mechanism plausibility checks to distinguish stable mechanisms from confounded proxies.

Throughout, diagnostics are computed within each walk-forward fold and aggregated across folds to surface instability that pooled statistics hide.

7.1 Data preprocessing and encodings

Data preprocessing turns validated datasets into stable inputs for label and feature computation. Earlier chapters handled point-in-time correctness, corporate actions, and calendar alignment; *Chapter 6* defined tradeable universes. This section covers the steps that are new at the feature-engineering stage: split-aware fitting, outlier treatment, representation choices, and missing-data protocols.

Box 7.1: Protocol-safe definitions and computation

This chapter treats labels, features, and preprocessing transforms as data products. To keep results comparable across iterations and to prevent silent leakage, every run must satisfy five invariants:

- **Observability:** Every raw input must be observable under the trading setup at decision time. Reporting lags, update times, eligibility rules, and calendar conventions are part of the definition.
- **Train-only fitting:** Transforms that estimate parameters from data must be fit using only the training portion of each walk-forward split.
- **Overlap-aware evaluation:** Overlapping label horizons induce dependence. Handle this using a split design (*Chapter 6*) and report overlap diagnostics alongside the metrics.
- **Versioned metadata:** A "feature" or "label" is a fully specified recipe. Log the definition with the run record; changes create new trial families.
- **Auditable masks:** Eligibility masks are part of the learning problem. Store the mask definition (not just the resulting rows) and report effective sample sizes by fold and asset group.

Split-aware preprocessing

Any preprocessing step that estimates parameters from data (means, standard deviations, quantiles, imputed values) must be fit only to the training split. Fitting on the full dataset before splitting leaks future information into the training representation, inflating performance.

In walk-forward evaluation (*Chapter 6*), this means refitting the preprocessor at each fold boundary using only data available up to that point. Steps that are **stateless** (dropping rows with invalid values, applying a fixed unit conversion, computing a boolean calendar flag) do not require split-aware fitting, but anything that computes a summary statistic from a population of observations does.

When in doubt, treat the step as fitted. Record which preprocessing steps are fitted and which are stateless in the pipeline configuration. Ensure that the same pipeline object handles both training and inference, so that no transform is accidentally omitted or double-applied (*Box 7.1*, invariant 2). See `02_preprocessing_pipeline` for a `SplitAwarePreprocessor` that enforces train-only fitting and shows the consequences of leakage: test mean 0.110 under train-only fitting versus 0.101 with full-panel fit.

Outliers and heavy tails

The first distinction is between **invalid** and **rare**. Invalid observations violate domain constraints (negative volume, impossible timestamps, or crossed bid-ask quotes) and should be removed. Single-interval spikes that revert immediately are often data errors; field-aware spike checks that compare the magnitude of the change and reversion pattern against the field's distribution help separate errors from genuine moves.

Valid observations that fall in the tails require a different treatment. Aggressive truncation discards real information; the goal is to limit the influence of extreme values on downstream transforms without eliminating them. **Winsorization** or clipping at a fixed percentile prevents single-point blowups during scaling and normalization. **Robust scaling** (centering on the median and dividing by the interquartile range) is generally more stable than mean-variance standardization when the distribution is skewed or leptokurtic. `02_preprocessing_pipeline` applies winsorization and domain filters to the US Equities panel, with before-and-after diagnostics.

The important exception: when the label itself targets extreme moves or barrier events, clipping returns removes precisely the outcomes the model is meant to learn. Preserve tails when tails are the prediction target.

Scaling and representation choices

Representation is part of the definition of a learning task. For level-like series (prices, yields, spreads), models learn more reliably from changes (returns or differences) than from raw levels. Stationarity diagnostics and the transformations that enforce it are covered in *Chapter 9*; return calculations for labels follow in *Section 7.2*.

Risk scaling (dividing by realized volatility) stabilizes features and labels across regimes. Treat the volatility estimate (its definition and lookback) as a fixed part of the representation rather than a parameter tuned between trials.

Ranks and percentile ranks are often the most robust encoding for cross-sectional features because they reduce sensitivity to outliers and vendor-specific units. Specify whether you rank across assets at each timestamp (cross-sectional) or within an asset's history (time-series percentile), and keep that choice stable.

For **categorical encodings**, use one-hot encoding for low-cardinality fields, ordinal encoding when ordering is meaningful (for example, credit rating tiers), and hashing or learned embeddings for high-cardinality identifiers. Fit the encoder on the training split.

Handling missing data

Missing values are not one problem but three. Your response depends on *why* the data is missing and what your model can accept:

- **Missing values as noise.** Values are absent for reasons unrelated to the asset, the time, or the value itself (random gaps). If your model requires complete inputs, fill in a robust default (for example, the cross-sectional median). If your model can handle missing values, you can often leave them missing.
- **Missing values due to observed coverage rules.** Missingness is explained by fields you do observe (for example, vendor coverage depends on size, exchange, region, or listing age). Either impute from the observed fields and add a "was missing" indicator, or keep the missing values and rely on a model that can handle missingness and the indicator.

- **Missing values that are themselves informative.** Absence is linked to the unobserved value or an unobserved driver (for example, non-reporting when metrics are poor; sparse prints precisely when liquidity is low). Here, "missing" can be signal or bias. Preserve it explicitly (using an indicator or a separate "not reported" category), and treat imputation as a modeling assumption, not a default.

Two practical defaults include

- If the model requires complete inputs, impute robustly and add a missingness indicator
- Use models that handle missingness natively (for example, tree-based methods, see *Chapter 12*)

Avoid silent imputations that make missingness disappear without a trace. *Table 7.1* lists some dataset-specific considerations:

Dataset	Key preprocessing concerns
ETF Universe	Adjustment artifacts, ticker changes, coverage gaps
Crypto Premium/Perps	Funding rate alignment, liquidation outliers, delistings mid-panel
CME Futures	Roll-adjusted continuity, vacation calendar alignment
FX Pairs	Weekend gaps, rollover liquidity, timezone conventions
US equities	Survivorship bias, split/dividend adjustments, penny-stock filtering
Firm Characteristics	Pre-cleaned panel; missingness patterns and structural breaks
NASDAQ-100 Bars	Session boundaries, auction prints (pre-cleaned by AlgoSeek)
S&P 500 Bars	Index rebalancing effects, consistency with ETF universe
S&P 500 Options	Moneyness/expiry filtering, Greeks checks, alignment with underlying

Table 7.1: Case study preprocessing concerns

Implementation:

- `01_data_quality_diagnostics` summarizes distribution characteristics across all datasets, including tail statistics that inform the choice between scaling methods.
- `02_preprocessing_pipeline` reports coverage by column, asset, and time period, and shows cross-dataset alignment.

The next section turns to engineering labels.

7.2 Label engineering

Labels define the learning task: what outcome you want to predict, over what horizon, and when that outcome becomes known. A label that is even slightly misaligned (starting or ending at an untradeable price) can create "predictability" that disappears in live trading. Label definitions must be **execution-consistent** and evaluated under the time-series protocol from *Chapter 6*; see also *Figure 7.1*.

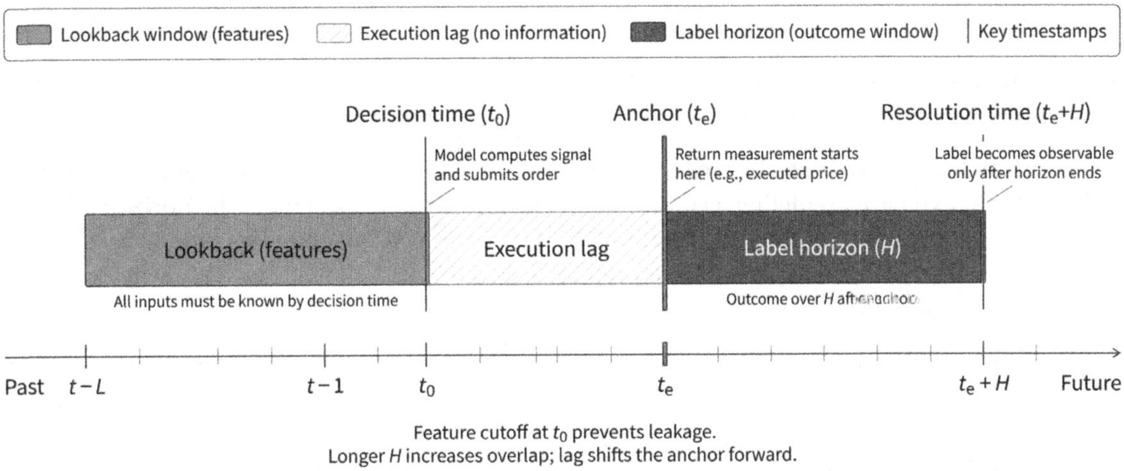

Figure 7.1: Label and Feature Horizons

Let t denote the decision time, t_e the anchor at which the position is established, a the asset, and $p_{t,a}$ the tradable price at t; every price in a label formula must be tradable under the chosen execution assumption. The horizon H counts forward bars from t_e to the resolution time $t_e + H$, in time or volume-related units (*Chapter 3*). `03_label_methods` demonstrates the methods in this section.

Execution conventions

The execution convention determines which prices are tradable at the start and end of the label window. For bar data, two conventions dominate:

- **Close-to-close:** The signal is generated at the close of bar t; the return is measured from $close_t$ to $close_{t+H}$. This is the simplest convention and the default in most academic work.
- **Next-open-to-open:** The signal is generated at the close of bar t, but the position is entered at the open of bar $t + 1$ and exited at the open of bar $t + H + 1$. This reflects the fact that most end-of-bar signals cannot be executed at the closing price.

The difference is not cosmetic. On daily equity data, the close-to-close label can differ from the next-open-to-open label by 50–100 basis points per trade in either direction, depending on overnight moves and opening gaps. The effect is large: over the past 30 years, nearly all U.S. equity market returns have accrued overnight rather than intraday (Glasserman et al., 2025).

Choose the convention that matches your execution assumption, document it, and keep it consistent between label computation and backtest PnL. `03_label_methods` quantifies the close-to-close versus next-open gap on SPY for a 21-day horizon.

Fixed-horizon labels

The default label is a forward return computed over a fixed number of bars H. Two common return conventions are:

- *Simple (arithmetic) return:* $r^s_{t,t+H,a} = \frac{p_{t+H,a}}{p_{t,a}} - 1$

- *Log return:* $r^{log}_{t,t+H,a} = log\left(\frac{p_{t+H,a}}{p_{t,a}}\right)$

For small moves, the two are nearly identical. Log returns are additive across periods; simple returns align with PnL arithmetic. Choose one, use it consistently, and record the choice.

Fixed-horizon labels align best with strategies that act on a stable cadence with a roughly fixed holding period, whether you are predicting a continuous value or a discrete direction. The horizon need not be measured in calendar time: you can define H in bar counts over volume bars or information bars (*Chapter 3*), so the horizon adapts to activity rather than the clock. The outcome is always known at $t + H$, which simplifies overlap analysis and fold construction.

The key decision is whether to train on a continuous metric or discrete categories. Many long/flat/short strategies model continuous returns and discretize model scores using a threshold to generate entries.

Continuous targets

The most common continuous target is the raw forward return $r_{t,t+H,a}$ itself. Alternative representations include **transformations** that are robust to outliers, such as (percentile) ranks relative to the cross-section or an asset's own history, **excess returns** relative to a peer group, a benchmark, or a financing series, and risk measures such as realized volatility. The choice depends on the task: directional prediction, ranking, or risk estimation.

Discrete targets

Discrete labels are useful when small returns are economically irrelevant relative to costs, when you want to learn a directional or event-like outcome, or when your evaluation and model selection benefit from classification metrics:

- **Binary labels:** The simplest discretization flags a directional outcome: set $y_{t,a} = 1$ if $r_{t,t+H,a} > \tau_t$, else 0. Common variants include flagging extreme returns (top decile, meaning values above the top 10 percent of historical returns), volatility spikes, or drawdown events.
- **Multi-class labels:** A common three-class construction assigns +1 (long), 0 (neutral), and −1 (short) based on upper and lower thresholds:

$$y_{t,a} = \{+1\ r_{t,t+H,a} > \tau_t\ 0\ |r_{t,t+H,a}| \le \tau_t\ -1\ r_{t,t+H,a} < -\tau_t$$

The threshold τ_t controls two things simultaneously: the **magnitude** of the event being labeled and the **base rate** (fraction of positives). A threshold that is too tight produces a near-50/50 split and labels noise; one that is too wide produces a rare-event problem and implies a trading frequency that may be infeasible. Choose thresholds that are economically meaningful and consistent with your turnover and cost budget. Three rules cover most cases:

1. **Fixed absolute threshold:** Set τ to a constant (for example, 1%). Simple and interpretable, but the implied base rate drifts with volatility.
2. **Volatility-scaled threshold:** Set $\tau_t = k\, \hat{\sigma}_{t,a}\sqrt{H}$ or $\tau_t = k\, \widehat{ATR}_{t,a}$, where the volatility estimate uses past-only inputs. This stabilizes the base rate across regimes.

3. **Percentile thresholds:** Time-series percentiles set τ_t to be the rolling percentile of the asset's recent return distribution (for example, the 75th percentile of $|r|$ over the past 252 bars), adapting to asset-specific volatility. Cross-sectional percentiles rank all assets by forward return at each t and assign labels by quantile membership (for example, top quintile = +1, bottom = −1). Cross-sectional labels have the useful property that *class proportions are stable by construction*. Time-series percentiles must be estimated within the training fold; global percentiles leak information about the future distribution.

Most multi-asset strategies use cross-sectional percentiles; single-asset strategies favor volatility-scaled or time-series percentile thresholds. Treat threshold selection as part of the label definition.

Variable-horizon labels

Fixed horizons are simple and well-behaved, but many real trading problems do not have a single natural horizon.

Adaptive horizons via trend scanning

When the appropriate horizon is uncertain, **trend scanning** provides an adaptive alternative: for each observation, it evaluates candidate horizons (typically 5–60 bars) and selects the one with the highest t-statistic for a linear trend fit (López de Prado, 2018).

The adaptive horizon introduces **selection bias:** by picking the "best" horizon for each observation, trend scanning systematically selects extreme outcomes that may not persist outside the sample. You can mitigate this by applying **Bonferroni correction** to the selected t-statistic (dividing by the number of candidate horizons) or by constraining the horizon range to match strategy turnover constraints. *Section 7.4* generalizes this per-observation correction to the search-level problem of evaluating many candidates.

Because the prediction horizon varies across observations, you cannot compute a single IC. Report the distribution of selected horizons alongside performance metrics, and verify that the distribution is stable across folds.

> **Implementation:** `03_label_methods` demonstrates trend scanning on SPY using 5–20-bar windows and compares raw versus Bonferroni-corrected t-statistics.

Event-style labels

Event-style labels let the price **path** determine when the outcome resolves. The broader risk-management context—stop-loss design, position sizing, execution—is in *Chapter 20*; here, the goal is a precise, auditable label definition.

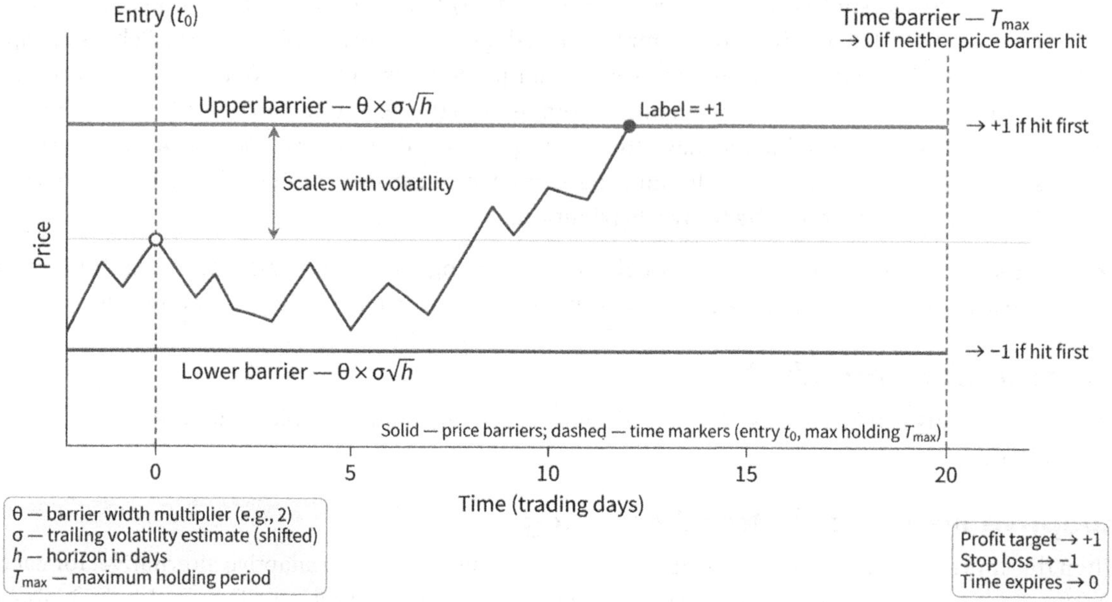

Figure 7.2: Triple barrier labels

The standard construction is the **triple-barrier label** (López de Prado, 2018). Starting from the tradable price at t, define an upper barrier $\pi_t > 0$, a lower barrier $\ell_t > 0$, and a vertical barrier at $t + H_{max}$. The cumulative return from the entry at t to any subsequent bar u is $r_{t,u,a}$. Assign the event label as follows:

- $+1$ if $r_{t,u,a}$ first reaches $+\pi_t$
- -1 if $r_{t,u,a}$ first reaches $-\ell_t$
- 0 if neither barrier is hit before $t + H_{max}$

Unlike fixed-horizon labels, where the outcome is always known at $t + H$, event labels resolve at a variable **resolution time**, namely the moment a price barrier is hit, or $t + H_{max}$ otherwise. We denote this as t^{res} when we need to refer to it explicitly—it becomes the key quantity in the overlap analysis later in this chapter.

With bar data, when both barriers are crossed in the same bar, specify a resolution rule and log it: for example, consider the event a loss (conservative) or exclude ambiguous bars.

Barrier widths can be set using the same volatility-scaling logic as threshold design, with asymmetric multipliers when the strategy has directional conviction.

Maximum favorable and adverse excursion diagnostics

Barrier widths are not arbitrary. They shape class balance, time to resolution, and the amount of label overlap. A practical way to calibrate them is to examine **the maximum favorable** and **adverse excursions** (**MFE/MAE**) over the candidate holding period:

- MFE measures the best return reached before the event resolves

- MAE measures the worst drawdown over the same window

Together, they show how far prices typically move for and against a position before a barrier is hit or the horizon expires. These diagnostics help set profit-taking and stop-loss barriers at levels that are economically sensible rather than arbitrary:

- Narrow barriers tend to resolve quickly but can be dominated by noise
- Wide barriers increase time to resolution, reduce the number of usable observations, and create more overlap across labels

In practice, the goal is to choose widths that yield a workable class balance, plausible upper- and lower-barrier hit rates, and reasonable resolution-time distributions.

Implementation: `04_maximum_favorable_adverse_excursion` demonstrates MFE/MAE visualizations, barrier calibration, and validation using hit fractions and resolution-time distributions.

Overlap, sample dependence, and effective sample size

Overlap is structural: adjacent H-bar labels share most of the same price increments, and event-style labels overlap irregularly because resolution times vary. Any price shock affects every label alive at that moment, creating mechanical dependence.

A label generated at time t is alive from t until its resolution time t^{res}—the interval $L_{t,a} = [t, t^{res}]$. The **concurrency** at bar u, denoted $c(u)$, counts how many labels are alive at u. The **average uniqueness** of a label summarizes its overlap:

$$w_{t,a} = \frac{1}{|L_{t,a}|} \sum_{u \in L_{t,a}} \frac{1}{c(u)}$$

where $|L_{t,a}|$ is the number of bars in the label's lifetime. A uniqueness of 1.0 means no overlap; values near $1/H$ indicate near-maximal overlap. The **effective sample size** is approximately $N_{eff} = \sum_{t,a} w_{t,a}$. For fixed-horizon labels sampled at every bar, $N_{eff} \approx N/H$ (ignoring cross-section and time-series correlation that may further reduce the effective sample size).

As a concrete example, `03_label_methods` measures uniqueness for SPY with $H = 21$ over roughly 10 years: 248,436 nominal observations collapse to an effective sample size of about 11,830, so confidence intervals based on the nominal count are roughly 4.6 × too narrow. Standard errors should use N_{eff}, not N.

Overlap creates three distinct problems:

1. Training and test labels that share price increments leak information across the split.
2. Gradient updates and evaluation metrics overweight high-concurrency periods.
3. Serial dependence in labels inflates apparent statistical significance.

The **time-series protocol** (*Chapter 6*) addresses problem 1 through purge gaps; sample weighting addresses problem 2; and reporting N_{eff} (or block-bootstrap standard errors) addresses problem 3.

Dealing with overlap

Four complementary strategies address overlap:

- **Protocol-correct splits** are non-negotiable: leave at least H_{max} bars between training and validation/test windows (*Chapter 6*).
- **Sample weighting** assigns a uniqueness weight $w_{t,a}$ to each observation, so that high-concurrency periods do not dominate loss or metrics.
- **Subsampling** reduces overlap by sampling every H bars or starting a new label only after the previous one resolves.
- A more data-efficient alternative is the **sequential bootstrap** (López de Prado, 2018). Instead of drawing each index with equal probability, the sequential bootstrap updates selection probabilities after every draw so that observations with higher expected uniqueness, that is, with less overlap with the labels already selected, become more likely to enter the sample. Intuitively, labels that overlap heavily with the current sample contribute less new information and are less likely to be drawn, while labels from less crowded periods are more likely to be selected. The result is a resampled dataset with lower effective redundancy, even though the original labels may overlap substantially.

Weighting retains all data; subsampling is simpler but discards information. Most setups combine at least two of these four.

Label diagnostics before modeling

Before training, verify labels are correctly defined and stable. Inspect distribution and tail behavior by time and asset group. Outliers often signal broken adjustments. Track base rates over time (class fractions should be stable across regimes), examine resolution-time distributions for event labels, and compute implied trading intensity. If trading intensity is infeasible, revise the label before modeling.

Close each label definition with a short audit record: anchor convention, horizon definition, resolution-time rule (including bar-data tie-breaking), overlap summary, and base-rate summary. These fields keep trials comparable under the *Chapter 6* research ledger (see `03_label_methods` and `04_maximum_favorable_adverse_excursion` for reusable diagnostics).

Meta-labels for confidence-weighted sizing

A different way to structure the labeling problem is to **decompose direction and confidence** into two stages (López de Prado, 2018). A primary model (often a simple rule or an existing strategy) generates entry signals; the secondary label records only whether each signal was profitable after costs. A separate **meta-model** then learns *when* the primary signal is trustworthy, and its calibrated probability is mapped to a position size, for example through a sigmoid that scales conviction into a fraction of the maximum bet.

`03_label_methods` includes a self-contained illustration: a 20-day-momentum signal on SPY is meta-labeled by its forward-return outcome, and a sigmoid bet-size mapping converts the confidence score into a position. The case studies in this book do not adopt this two-stage structure: each case study trains a single model on a single label horizon and sizes positions via an allocator (*Chapter 17*). The technique is most useful when a directional model is already in place and the goal is to filter weak signals rather than re-engineer the entry rule.

Label diagnostics here focus on *the quality of definitions*; the next section shows how to evaluate the relationship between a label and a candidate feature.

7.3 Univariate feature–label evaluation

The first layer of evaluation is univariate feature–label screening: each candidate is assessed against the label one at a time. Preprocessed inputs and execution-consistent labels are described in *Sections 7.1–7.2*; candidate features appear in *Chapters 8–10*. The screens apply in rough order:

1. **Correctness:** Can you trust the definition at decision time?
2. **Association:** Does the feature carry information about the label?
3. **Shape:** Is the relationship compatible with a plausible mapping from signal to positions?
4. **Feasibility:** Could anything implementable survive the trading setup's cost and capacity constraints?

A feature must clear each screen to advance to the next. All diagnostics are computed within each fold and aggregated across folds: medians, interquartile ranges, and worst-fold views rather than a single pooled statistic.

Univariate triage is necessary but not sufficient. A feature that looks promising in isolation may duplicate another candidate, and a feature with weak marginal association may become valuable once conditioned on the right companion. Multivariate model selection (*Chapters 11–12*) makes the decisive judgments. *Section 7.4* addresses the multiple-testing problem that arises when many candidates pass screening.

Correctness screens – The non-negotiable first pass

Before evaluating predictive power, verify that the feature and label are usable under the stated protocol. Run these checks on each feature–label bundle:

1. **Coverage:** What fraction of eligible (asset, decision-time) pairs have non-null feature values? Sparse coverage changes the effective sample size and may indicate stale or lagged inputs.
2. **Timing and lag consistency:** Verify that the feature uses only information available at the time of decision. Check reporting lags for fundamental data, publication times for third-party signals, and update schedules for derived quantities.
3. **Mask alignment:** Confirm that the eligibility mask is applied identically to feature computation, label computation, and evaluation. Misaligned masks are a common source of leakage.
4. **Staleness:** For features that update infrequently (for example, quarterly fundamentals), check that the feature value changes at appropriate intervals. A feature that never updates may be dominated by asset-specific intercepts rather than a time-varying signal.

These checks do not establish economic value; they prevent the costliest research failure: promoting a definition you cannot trust. See `05_signal_evaluation` for reusable diagnostics of correctness and coverage applied to the case-study ETF universe.

Evaluating continuous labels

For continuous labels (forward returns, excess returns, realized risk targets), the workhorse diagnostic at triage is the **information coefficient** (IC): the cross-sectional association between a feature observed at decision time and a label that resolves later.

The Information Coefficient

The default is **rank IC** (Spearman), which equals the Pearson correlation of cross-sectional ranks:

$$IC_t \; := \; corr_a\left(rank(x_{t,a}),\; rank(y_{t,a})\right)$$

where $x_{t,a}$ is the feature value for asset a at time t, $y_{t,a}$ is the label anchored at t, and $corr_a(\cdot)$ denotes correlation across assets at time t. Computing IC_t for each decision time yields an IC time series $\{IC_t\}_t$.

IC is a learnability diagnostic for the definition bundle (feature, label, masks) under the evaluation protocol. It is not, by itself, a claim about tradable performance.

> **Rank IC versus Pearson IC**
>
> Rank IC is the conservative default: it aligns with ranking-based portfolio construction and is less sensitive to heavy tails and nonlinear monotone relationships. Pearson IC is appropriate when you care about linear association on raw values—for example, a signal that will enter a linear forecast where scale matters. Keep the representation consistent: if you store a feature as ranks, evaluate it with rank IC.

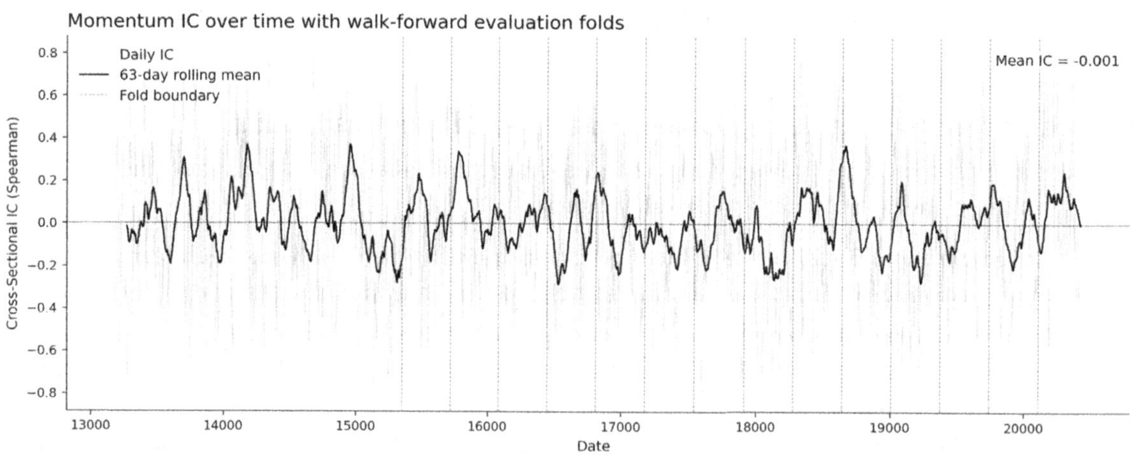

Figure 7.3: IC time series with fold boundaries

Figure 7.3 shows IC_t over the full sample period. Vertical dashed lines mark fold boundaries. A centered rolling average highlights the trend. Two patterns to watch for: (i) IC that concentrates in a single episode—the feature may be exploiting a transient shock or protocol artifact; (ii) IC that flips the sign across folds—the feature's usefulness depends on state variables not yet modeled.

Fold-level summarization – ICIR and sign consistency

Because IC_t observations are not IID, overlapping horizons induce serial dependence, and cross-sectional universes share common shocks—treat the fold as the unit of summary. Within each fold k, compute a fold mean $IC^{-(k)}$ and a dispersion estimate $\sigma^{(k)}$. Summarize across folds using the median and interquartile range (IQR) of $IC^{-(k)}$ plus a worst-fold view (see also *Figure 7.3*).

If you want a compact stability ratio, compute a fold-level IC information ratio:

$$ICIR^{(k)} := \frac{IC^{-(k)}}{\sigma^{(k)}}$$

and report it by fold rather than as a single pooled statistic. **Sign consistency**—the fraction of folds where $IC^{-(k)}$ shares the sign of the overall median—is the key stability gate. A momentum feature might show a mean IC of 0.04 across five folds but achieve 0.08 in two trending folds and −0.02 in three mean-reverting folds—the aggregate masks a regime switch that would devastate a static allocation. In the ETF universe, 21-day momentum has a pooled IC of 0.001 (near zero) but a fold-level mean IC of 0.064 with ICIR of 0.79 and 75% of folds positive—the pooled statistic hides a signal that is real in most regimes but cancelled by a few adverse episodes (see `05_signal_evaluation`).

IC across horizons and rebalancing frequency

Computing IC across a grid of forward-return horizons reveals the signal's useful life. A signal that peaks at 5 days and halves by 10 should not be held for a month; one flat from 5 to 21 days offers rebalancing flexibility. Report the IC decay curve alongside fold-level statistics (see `05_signal_evaluation` for the ETF momentum signal).

Inference at triage

If you use inference, apply it to fold summaries, not daily IC_t: (1) **block bootstrap** within each fold, with block lengths reflecting horizon overlap; (2) **within-time permutation** that shuffles the asset–label assignment within each cross-section, preserving cross-sectional dependence while breaking feature–label pairing. Treat p-values as descriptive at this stage; *Section 7.4* covers multiplicity adjustment.

`05_signal_evaluation` demonstrates walk-forward fold construction and reports per-fold IC, spread, and monotonicity. See `06_ic_inference` for HAC-adjusted inference and block bootstrap confidence intervals applied to IC time series. For the 21-day ETF momentum IC, HAC inflates the naive standard error by 2.54× and effective sample size drops from 4,989 to 773, an 85% efficiency loss that anchors minimum-track-record planning.

Box 7.3: IC and portfolio performance

Under simplifying assumptions, Grinold's Fundamental Law of Active Management (1989) suggests an approximate relation between forecast skill and portfolio performance:

$$IR \approx IC \times \sqrt{B}$$

where IC measures forecast skill and B is the effective number of independent bets ("breadth"). The approximation is not a performance forecast—bets are rarely independent, and a universe of 100 ETFs with shared sector exposure may offer effective breadth of 20–30. The triage lesson: small but persistent ICs matter when breadth is genuinely large; peak IC is less informative than stable IC across folds.

Kendall's τ and mutual information

Kendall's τ and **mutual information** (MI) measure different kinds of dependence. Kendall's τ is a **rank-based measure of association:** it assesses whether pairs of assets are consistently ordered by the signal and the realized outcome. More formally, it compares the number of *concordant* and *discordant* pairs, so it is interpretable as a measure of **monotone association.** Like Spearman's rank correlation, it is insensitive to scale, but it is often more stable in very small cross-sections ($n < 30$) because it is built directly from pairwise orderings rather than rank moments. In practice, τ is usually smaller in magnitude than Spearman for the same relationship, so the two should not be compared numerically as if they were interchangeable.

Mutual information (MI) is different: it is an **information-theoretic measure of dependence**, not a rank correlation. MI asks how much knowing the signal reduces uncertainty about the outcome. As a result, it can detect **nonlinear** and **non-monotonic** relationships that Kendall's τ, Spearman's, or Pearson's may miss. However, MI is harder to estimate reliably in finite samples, typically requires discretization or other density-estimation choices, and is less directly interpretable than a rank IC. It is also nonnegative, so unlike Kendall's τ, it does not indicate direction.

For routine triage of large cross-sections with a monotone prior, rank IC remains the default. Use **Kendall's** τ when cross-sections are small, and you want a robust monotone dependence check based on pairwise ordering. Use MI only when quantile plots or other diagnostics suggest a clear nonlinear or non-monotone pattern that rank-based measures miss. `05_signal_evaluation` computes cross-sectional IC at multiple horizons and visualizes the resulting time series.

Discrete labels – Evaluating features as classifiers

For binary labels with $y_{t,a} \in \{0,1\}$, evaluate whether a feature can act as a score that separates positives from negatives. As with continuous labels, all metrics should be computed fold-by-fold, respecting masks.

Threshold-dependent evaluation

Given a score threshold or top-k action set, report precision, recall, and specificity. In trading terms, **false positives** are costly entries (round-trip costs plus adverse move); **false negatives** are foregone gains.

Threshold-free metrics

Start with the **Receiver Operating Characteristic** (ROC) area under the curve (AUC), which measures how well the feature ranks positives above negatives across decision thresholds, and the **Precision-Recall** (PR) AUC. PR AUC is often more informative when the positive class is rare because precision directly reflects how many predicted positives are true positives.

Under strong **class imbalance**, a feature can have a high ROC AUC while still producing many false positives relative to true positives at practically relevant thresholds, which the PR curve makes more visible. Compute both metrics fold-by-fold and report the median and inter-quartile range (IQR).

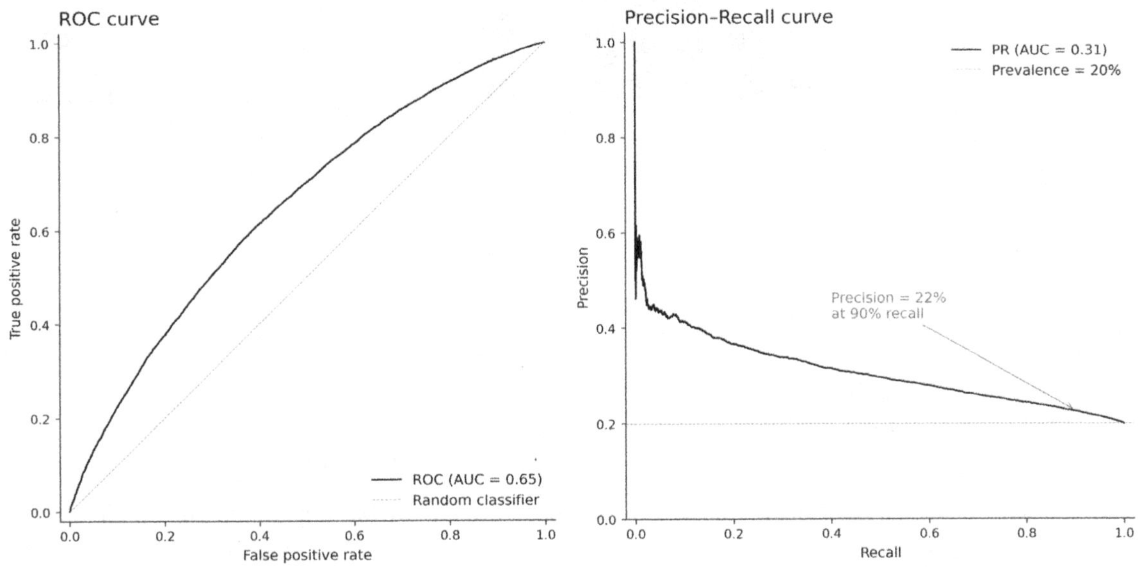

Figure 7.4: ROC and PR curves, side by side. Left: ROC curve for a feature with moderate discrimination (AUC ≈ 0.65), with the diagonal reference. Right: PR curve for the same feature, baseline at the prevalence rate.

As shown in *Figure 7.4*, the PR curve reveals that at high-recall operating points, precision drops sharply, a pattern hidden by the ROC curve when the base rate is low.

For multi-class event labels (profit, stop, time-out), report base rates by class and fold, which shift across regimes. If you collapse multi-class labels into binary actions, explicitly record the collapse rule and verify that it aligns with your intended action set.

Implementation: `05_signal_evaluation` computes ROC AUC and PR AUC with fold-level breakdowns and Wilson confidence intervals for precision and recall.

Nonparametric diagnostics – Quantile and decile analysis

Correlation is compact, but it can hide non-monotone structure. At each decision time t, sort assets by $x_{t,a}$ within the eligibility mask, split into Q bins, and compute the mean label per bin $\mu_{t,q}$. Track the spread $S_t := \mu_{t,Q} - \mu_{t,1}$ and summarize within folds.

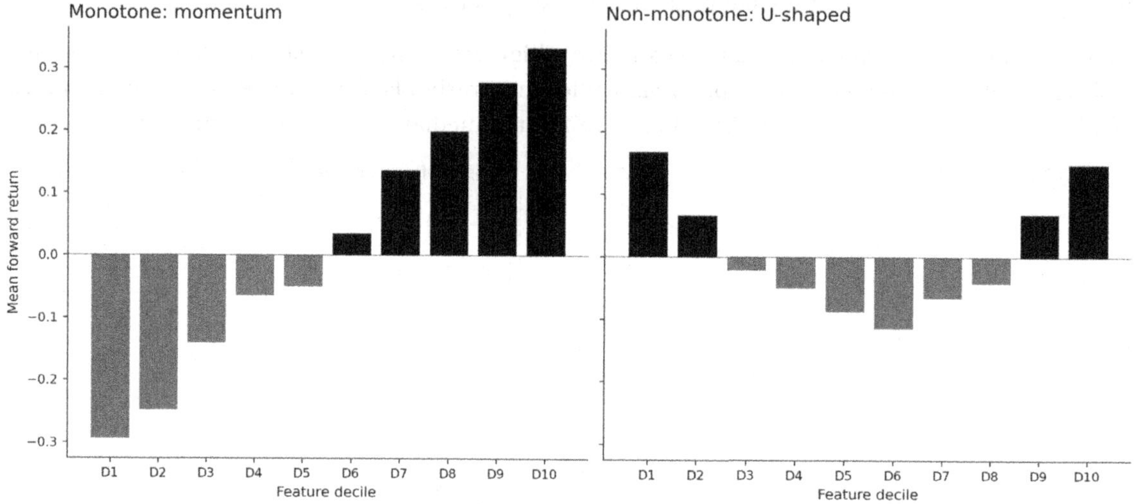

Figure 7.5: Quantile bar charts: monotone versus non-monotone. Left: mean forward return by feature decile increases monotonically, consistent with a ranking-based mapping. Right: a U-shaped pattern where both extreme deciles show elevated returns.

Figure 7.5 shows that a monotone mapping will miss the signal in the bottom decile; this implies either a nonlinear mapping or a confounder.

Monotone increasing patterns are compatible with ranking-based approaches (top-k selection, long-short spreads). Non-monotone patterns may require nonlinear mappings or suggest an interaction with market state. At this stage, you are validating shape, not designing the mapping.

Preliminary feasibility checks

Feasibility screens ask whether any plausible mapping could survive implementation. These use the simplest possible mapping—rank assets by score and select the top k—as a stress test. Three checks cover most early failures:

1. **Turnover proxies**: Measure entry and exit rates in the top-k set across decision times within each fold. A feature in which the top-k set turns over completely at each rebalance is a warning; one in which positions persist has a structural cost advantage.
2. **Break-even cost sanity checks**: Compare typical fold spreads to conservative cost estimates. If the median fold spread is 20 basis points (0.2 %, bps) and round-trip costs are 15 bps, the net spread is 5 bps—barely above noise. A signal whose gross spread does not clear 2 × estimated costs warrants caution; one that fails to clear the cost hurdle is a stop.

3. **Capacity warnings:** Recompute IC or spreads by liquidity bucket. A signal confined to the least liquid bucket is a stop for the current setup; smooth degradation from liquid to illiquid suggests the signal is broad-based.

Standardize triage decisions so later stages can trust the results:

Decision	Condition	Action
Proceed	Correctness screens pass; primary diagnostic directionally consistent across folds; quantile/confusion-matrix supports plausible mapping	Hand off to the modeling chapters
Revise	Idea plausible, but definition flawed (anchor mismatch, horizon mismatch, unstable base rates)	Change definition, re-run triage, record delta
Stop	Sign unstable across folds; spread too small to survive costs; signal confined to untradeable liquidity	Archive and document the failure mode

Table 7.2: Triage decisions standards

Read triage output in order: correctness first, then association, then shape and feasibility, then search accounting. Record the decision, diagnostic summaries, and searched-set metadata in the research ledger alongside the definition bundle (see *Box 7.1*).

Feature evaluation is not model selection, hyperparameter search, or a backtest. Its output is an auditable decision (proceed, revise, or stop) supported by fold-level summaries and plots that can be regenerated from the run record. The next section addresses the risks associated with an extensive search for predictive features.

> **Implementation:** `05_signal_evaluation` covers correctness screens, fold-level IC and ICIR, IC decay, turnover, and break-even costs for the ETF momentum signal. `06_ic_inference` covers HAC inference, stationary block bootstrap, and minimum-track-record planning.

7.4 Search accounting and multiple testing

Trend scanning (*Section 7.2*) applied Bonferroni correction to a single observation's t-statistic when the best horizon is selected from many candidates. The same logic (correcting for the number of comparisons made) applies at the search level. When triage screens many candidate features, labels, or variants, the best-observed IC, spread, or AUC come with a positive bias: some candidates will look good by chance.

Define the searched set

The starting point is to record what you actually evaluated. Define the **search set** as all candidates tested under the same decision rules. This typically includes

- Label-definition variants (anchor, horizon, threshold, or barrier rules)
- Feature-family variants (lookbacks, transforms, reference frames)
- Any conditioning templates you have tried

Record the searched-set size and the generation rules (grid, deduplication, exclusions). Without this, "significance" claims are uninterpretable.

For example, evaluating 5 label horizons × 3 threshold rules × 10 feature variants gives 150 bundles. Even if each bundle has only a 5% chance of passing a naive significance test under the null, we would expect roughly 7—8 false positives. The searched-set size is 150, and that number must accompany any reported p-value. See `07_multiple_testing` for a simulation showing how selection bias inflates the best IC when all factors are noise.

Separate exploration from confirmation

There are two phases to evaluation:

1. **Exploration pass:** Evaluate many candidates, but promote primarily on fold stability rather than peak performance (sign consistency, lack of single-episode dominance, robustness to timing and coverage checks).
2. **Confirmation pass:** Freeze promoted candidates and re-run triage with a minimized comparison set to produce the summaries you will cite later.

The exploration pass is where we learn; the confirmation pass is where we commit. Mixing the two is the most common cause of failure in multiple testing: promoting on peak performance, then "confirming" on the same data.

Adjustment methods

If you report p-values or confidence intervals, compute them on fold summaries and adjust over the searched set you actually evaluated. Two families of correction dominate:

Family-wise error rate (**FWER**) controls the probability of *at least one* false positive across all tests. Use FWER when promoting a small number of candidates from a large pool: the cost of a single false positive (a strategy built around a spurious feature) is high.

The standard procedure is **Holm–Bonferroni:** sort the m p-values in ascending order, $p_{(1)} \leq p_{(2)} \leq \cdots \leq p_{(m)}$, and reject $p_{(i)}$ only if $p_{(i)} \leq \alpha/(m-i+1)$ for all $j \leq i$. This is uniformly more powerful than the original Bonferroni ($p_{(i)} \leq \alpha/m$) while controlling the same error rate.

False discovery rate (**FDR**) controls the expected fraction of false positives among all rejections. FDR is appropriate for large screens where you expect many true positives and can tolerate some false discoveries: for example, when screening 200 feature variants and expecting to advance 20–30.

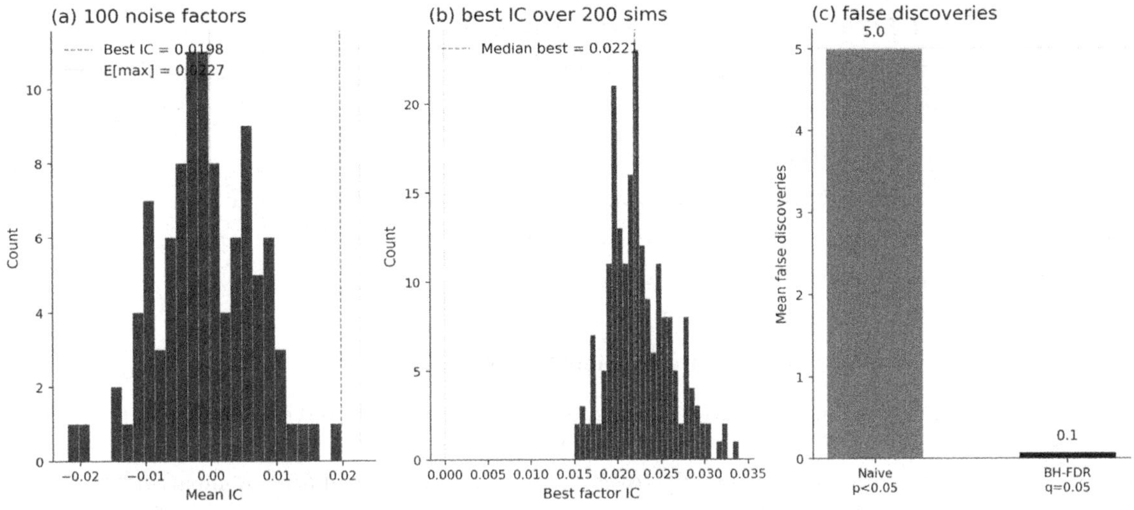

Figure 7.6: Selection bias under the null

Figure 7.6 shows three graphs. (a) Among 100 noise factors (50 assets, 252 days), the best achieves an IC of 0.020, close to the theoretical maximum of 0.023. (b) Across 200 simulations, the median best-factor IC is 0.022 — a spurious signal that would pass most screens. (c) Naive testing ($p < 0.05$) yields 5 false discoveries per simulation; BH-FDR control reduces this to near zero.

The standard procedure is **Benjamini–Hochberg:** sort p-values and reject $p_{(i)}$ if $p_{(i)} \leq (i/m) \cdot q$, where q is the target FDR (for example, 0.05). The notebook `07_multiple_testing` applies both BH and Holm–Bonferroni to a simulated factor zoo and compares discovery rates, false-positive counts, and statistical power. Applied to 13 ETF features, zero survive BH-FDR or Holm-Bonferroni at $\alpha = 0.05$: RVol 10d leads with HAC $t = 2.36$ but is rejected after correction.

The choice depends on the **downstream cost structure**:

- If each promoted feature incurs expensive modeling and backtesting costs, prefer FWER
- If you are building a feature pool where a few false positives are tolerable because model selection will weed them out, FDR is more practical

Harvey, Liu, and Zhu (2016) surveyed over 300 published factors and recommended raising the significance threshold to $t > 3.0$ (from 2.0) for new factor discovery — a practical shortcut that accounts for the accumulated search across the literature.

When candidates are correlated (lookback variants or parameter sweeps around a single factor), independence-based corrections overstate the penalty. **Rademacher complexity** provides sharper bounds by measuring the effective richness of the hypothesis class (see *Chapter 16*).

Report effect sizes, not only significance

Adjustment methods control error rates but say nothing about economic magnitude. For any candidate carried forward, report:

- Searched-set size and generation rules
- Fold-level summaries (median and worst fold) for the primary diagnostic
- A stability indicator, such as sign consistency and time concentration
- Whether the numbers come from the exploration or confirmation pass

> **Box 7.4: Adaptive choices are additional trials**
>
> If a threshold, lookback grid, missingness rule, or interaction was chosen or modified after reviewing results, treat it as a new trial family and include it in the search-set accounting. These are legitimate research moves, but they increase the multiple-comparison burden. This is the single most common accounting failure: optimizing a parameter after peeking at results and not counting it as a trial.

Strategy-level selection-bias diagnostics

When the outcome is a Sharpe ratio rather than an IC, three analogous diagnostics apply:

- The **Deflated Sharpe Ratio** (Bailey and López de Prado, 2014) estimates the probability that the best Sharpe exceeds chance
- the **Probability of Backtest Overfitting** (Bailey et al., 2015) measures how often the in-sample best-ranked configuration becomes the out-of-sample worst
- **Minimum Track Record Length** quantifies the amount of data required before promoting a strategy

> **Implementation:** `07_multiple_testing` implements the full pipeline: HAC-adjusted p-values, BH-FDR, and Holm–Bonferroni. It also previews Rademacher adjustments and the Deflated Sharpe Ratio (for more detail, see *Chapter 16*).

The next section provides a first introduction to causality.

7.5 From correlation to causality

The association diagnostics in *Section 7.3* establish that a feature carries information about the label. They do not explain why. A feature can appear predictive because it proxies for a market state characterized by volatility, liquidity, or risk appetite that also drives returns, rather than because it captures a stable, exploitable relationship.

This section introduces causal thinking as a **falsification filter**: state a mechanism, encode it as a graph, and then check whether the data are consistent with the assumptions implied by the mechanism.

The point is not to prove causality but to rule out stories that fail to meet their own basic implications before committing to more complex modeling.

In practice, this means asking whether the observed association survives simple checks suggested by the assumed mechanism, or whether it disappears once plausible confounders, timing effects, or selection effects are taken into account. These are robustness diagnostics guided by **mechanism reasoning**; they test one feature at a time and cannot detect multivariate confounding. *Chapter 15* supplies that more comprehensive toolkit.

Why causal thinking matters for features

Most trading data is observational. Nobody runs randomized experiments on asset prices. A feature that correlates with future returns may do so for reasons that will not persist. Causal thinking surfaces three common traps:

- **Confounding:** A feature and a label share a common driver; the correlation disappears when that driver shifts. For example, both momentum and forward returns may respond to the volatility regime: the observed correlation reflects a shared exposure, not a direct link.
- **Conditioning traps:** Adding the wrong "control" can create spurious relationships (collider bias) or remove the effect you care about (conditioning on a mediator). Whether a variable should be included as a control depends on the causal structure, not on its statistical significance.
- **Construction artifacts:** The pipeline inadvertently encodes information about selection or timing rather than about the market: for example, a rolling window that overlaps the label horizon, creating spurious correlation through shared data points.

What is a directed acyclic graph?

A **directed acyclic graph** (DAG) is a diagram that encodes causal assumptions. Each node represents a variable (a feature, a label, or a third quantity), and each arrow represents a hypothesized direction of influence, one variable affecting another. "Acyclic" means no path through the arrows leads back to its starting point; there are no feedback loops. *Figure 7.7* illustrates the basic anatomy.

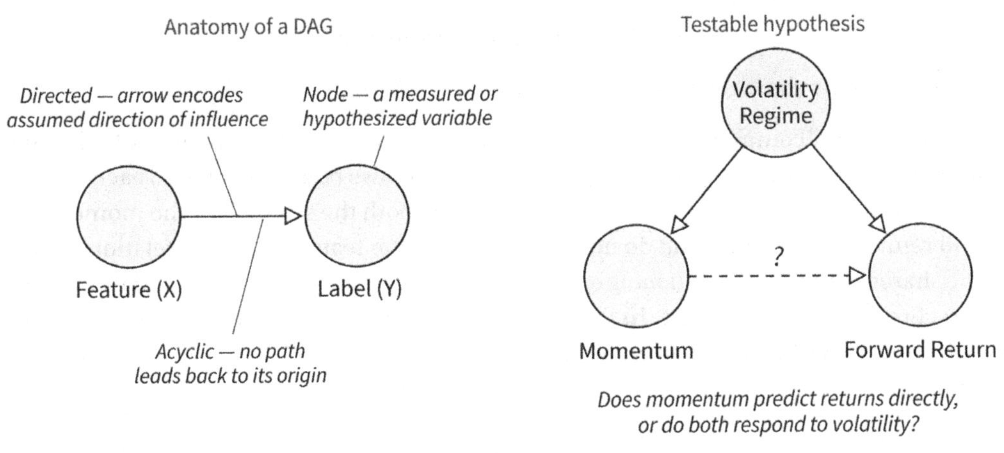

Figure 7.7: Directed Acyclic Graph

Why draw a DAG? Because it forces you to state your assumptions explicitly. A claim that "momentum predicts returns" is vague; a DAG that places an arrow from momentum to returns—and specifies that volatility regime affects both—is a testable structure. The arrows commit you to specific implications: which variables should be correlated, which should become independent once you condition on a third, and which conditioning choices are safe. If the data contradict those implications, the assumed mechanism is wrong, and you have saved yourself from modeling a spurious relationship.

In financial applications, DAGs are typically small (three to five nodes) and encode a single hypothesis about one feature. The goal is not a comprehensive model of the economy but a minimal structure sufficient to identify what could go wrong with a specific feature-label association. Three recurring patterns—confounders, mediators, and colliders—determine what you should and should not condition on.

Three structural roles

Every variable adjacent to a feature-label pair plays one of three structural roles. Getting this right determines whether conditioning on a variable clarifies or distorts the relationship you are trying to evaluate. *Figure 7.8* illustrates each pattern with a minimal DAG:

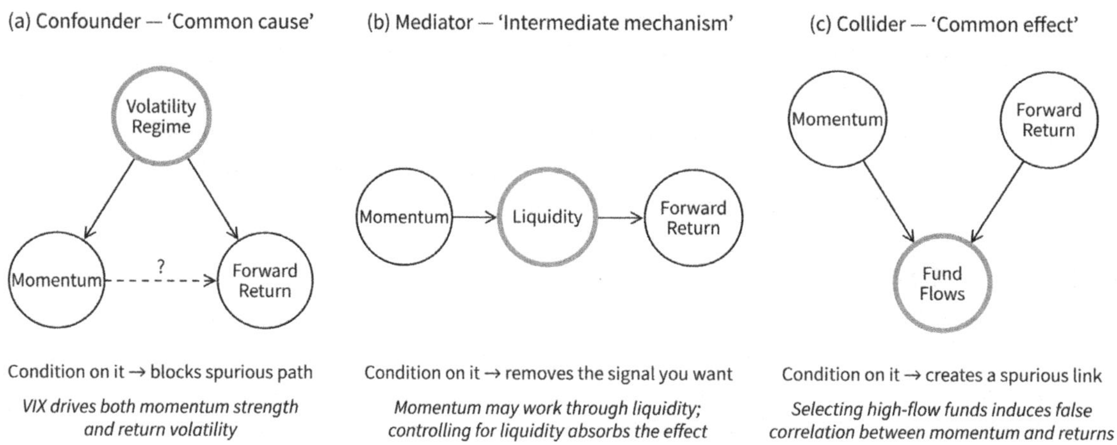

Figure 7.8: Fundamental causal relationships

The three components shown in this diagram are:

- **Confounder: A common cause.** A confounder is a variable that influences both the feature and the label. In the DAG, it sits above both, with arrows pointing down to each. For example, the volatility regime (measured by the VIX) affects both the strength of the momentum signal and return dispersion. If you do not account for it, the feature-label correlation is inflated by the shared exposure. *Conditioning on a confounder blocks the spurious path* and isolates whatever direct relationship may exist. In the worked example below, the regime heterogeneity check partitions by VIX precisely to assess this.

- **Mediator: An intermediate mechanism.** A mediator lies on the causal chain between feature and label: the feature affects the mediator, which in turn affects the label. For example, momentum may partly operate through liquidity: past winners attract flows, improving liquidity and supporting further price appreciation. If you condition on liquidity, you remove the indirect channel and may eliminate the very signal you are measuring. *Do not condition on a mediator* unless your goal is specifically to test whether the feature has any effect beyond the mediated path.
- **Collider: A common effect.** A collider is a variable caused by both the feature and the label. In the DAG, arrows from both the feature and the label converge on it. For example, both momentum and forward returns drive fund flows: strong-momentum funds with high returns attract the most capital. Unconditionally, there is no distortion. But if you *condition on the collider* (say, by restricting your analysis to high-flow funds) you induce a spurious negative correlation between momentum and returns that does not exist in the full population. The notebook `08_causal_sanity_checks` includes a synthetic simulation showing this effect: conditioning on fund flows (the collider) creates an approximately −0.25 correlation between two independent variables.

Before controlling for any variable, decide which role it plays. If you cannot decide, flag the feature for the multivariate toolkit in *Chapter 15*.

From DAG vocabulary to falsification checks

Drawing a DAG is the first step; testing its implications is the payoff. Each arrow in a DAG implies specific, testable patterns in the data: for example, that conditioning on a confounder should reduce a correlation, or that shifting a feature in time should cause its predictive power to decay. The four checks below probe these implications cheaply, using tools you already have from *Section 7.3*.

The diagnostics produce one of three outcomes, matching the triage gates introduced in *Section 7.3*:

- **PROCEED** (the mechanism survives all checks)
- **REVISE** (partial survival: the feature has a signal, but with caveats that inform downstream modeling)
- **STOP** (the mechanism fails: redirect effort to other features)

In efficient markets, cross-sectional ICs are small, and few single features will cleanly pass every check. REVISE is the expected and most informative outcome: it tells you *where* and *when* a feature works, which is precisely what downstream model design needs to know.

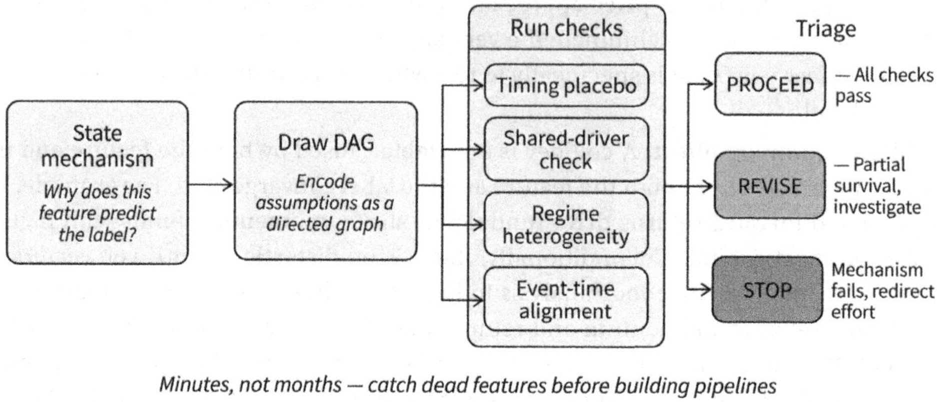

Figure 7.9: The mechanism plausibility workflow from hypothesis to triage decision

Mechanism plausibility checks

Each check has a clear protocol: what you compute, what you expect if the mechanism is real, and what constitutes a red flag. The notebook `08_causal_sanity_checks` first runs a feature × horizon scan—expanding on the null result from *Section 7.4*—and then applies the first three checks to two selected features.

Try a **timing placebo.** Shift the feature backward by Δ bars (for example, 5, 21, 63, 126, 252 days) and recompute IC at each lag. If the feature contains timely information, IC should be strongest near lag 0 and decay as the feature becomes stale. For a rolling-window feature with lookback L, a Δ-shifted version shares roughly $(L - \Delta)/L$ of its inputs with the original, creating a mechanical floor on IC persistence; focus on decay at lags beyond the lookback window. A red flag: IC that remains flat or *increases* at distant lags suggests the feature proxies a slow-moving state variable rather than timely information.

A **shared-driver check** replaces the label with an outcome that has no plausible link to the feature's mechanism: for example, Treasury returns for a microstructure-driven equity feature, or a shuffled cross-sectional assignment. IC should be indistinguishable from zero. This tests whether the feature's information is specific to the hypothesized channel or leaks into unrelated outcomes via a shared driver. A second control uses permutation: shuffling forward returns cross-sectional data at each date, producing a null distribution; the observed IC should lie far outside it.

Regime heterogeneity is important. Partition the sample by a candidate state variable (for example, VIX terciles) and recompute IC within each partition. IC may attenuate in some regimes, but should maintain sign and rough magnitude. If IC flips sign across partitions—with a significant opposite-sign partition (HAC $|t| > 2$) and a near-zero unconditional IC—the unconditional association is a pure aggregation artifact. This check cannot distinguish confounding from genuine effect modification; a feature whose IC varies by regime may be confounded or may have a mechanism that operates differently across states.

For features motivated by a discrete event (earnings, FOMC, rebalancing), compute IC in event-time windows. IC should concentrate where the mechanism predicts an effect. Symmetric pre- and post-event ICs, or ICs peaking before the event, usually indicate anticipation, leakage, or a confound. The example below omits this check because neither feature is event-driven.

Worked example – 12-1 momentum versus short-term reversal

The multiple-testing scan in *Section 7.4* found that no short-lookback feature survived BH-FDR at a 5-day horizon on ETFs. The notebook expands the search: a scan of 10 features across three horizons (5d, 21d, 63d) reveals that long-lookback momentum features (126d+) carry significant cross-sectional information at monthly horizons, confirming academic findings on cross-asset momentum (Asness et al., 2013). Two features are selected for the mechanism checks, using a 21-day forward return label.

Feature A: 12-1 Momentum (REVISE)

Check	Result	Interpretation
Timing placebo	IC peaks at lag 0 (0.053); persists to lag 252d (0.034), HAC $t_0 = 3.5$	IC strongest at lag 0—partly mechanical for 231d lookback, but timely
Shared-driver check	Treasury HAC $t = 0.2$	
perm $p < 0.001$	No shared driver; IC well above permutation null	
Regime heterogeneity	Low-VIX IC = +0.086 (HAC $t = 3.9$); high-VIX IC = +0.017 ($t = 0.6$)	Sign stable; magnitude varies 5× across VIX regimes

Table 7.3: Momentum analysis

Momentum earns REVISE: only the shared-driver check passes cleanly. It carries genuine cross-sectional information (IC = 0.053, HAC $t = 3.5$) that does not predict Treasury returns, but the timing placebo and regime heterogeneity checks both flag caution—IC persists without clear decay, and the effect concentrates in low-volatility markets, attenuating during high-VIX episodes, consistent with the well-documented "momentum crash" phenomenon (Daniel and Moskowitz, 2016). This is an actionable finding that motivates regime-conditional modeling in later chapters.

Feature B: 1-day Reversal (STOP)

Check	Result	Interpretation
Timing placebo	No timely signal ($IC_0 = 0.002$, HAC $t_0 = 0.4$)	Near-zero IC at all lags – no information to decay
Shared-driver check	Treasury HAC $t = 0.1$; perm $p = 0.38$	IC indistinguishable from shuffled noise
Regime heterogeneity	Low-VIX IC = −0.019 (HAC $t = -2.6$); high-VIX IC = +0.028 ($t = 2.5$)	Sign flips (HAC sig.) with near-zero unconditional IC – aggregation artifact

Table 7.4: Reversal analysis

Reversal earns STOP: all three checks fail. The unconditional IC is near zero (0.002, HAC $t = 0.4$) with no timely signal at any lag, and the regime heterogeneity check reveals a textbook aggregation artifact—the feature encodes opposite information in low-VIX and high-VIX markets, producing a near-zero unconditional IC.

Plausibility scorecard

The following table summarizes the decision criteria for each check:

Check	Pass	Caution	Stop
Timing placebo	IC significant (HAC) with meaningful decay	IC persists without clear decay	No timely signal; IC increases at distant lags
Shared-driver check	IC ≈ 0 on control outcome (HAC)	IC is small but nonzero	IC is significant on control (HAC)
Regime heterogeneity	IC is stable across partitions	IC varies; sign flip not sig. (HAC)	Sign flip sig. (HAC) AND unconditional IC ≈ 0
Event-time alignment	IC concentrates post-event	IC spread across windows	IC peaks pre-event

Table 7.5: Plausibility scorecard

This is visualized in the following figure:

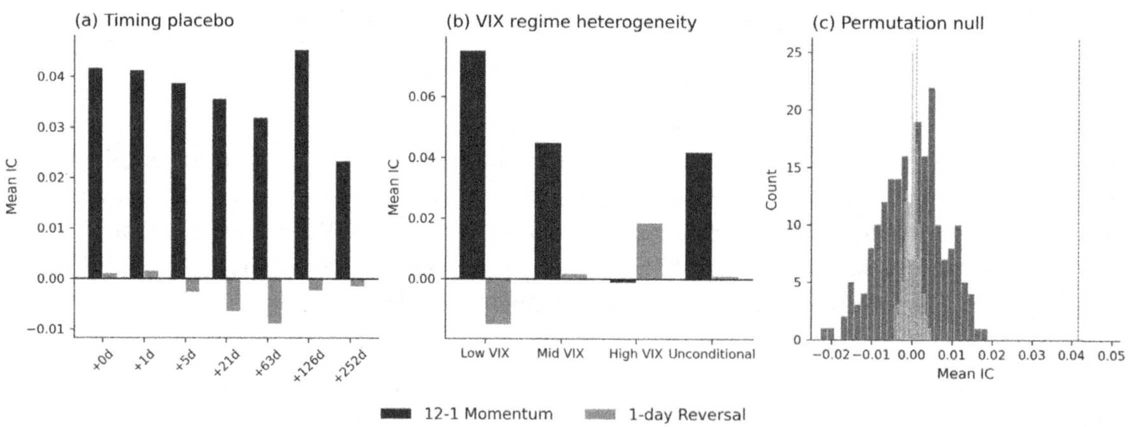

Figure 7.10: Mechanism plausibility scorecard

Figure 7.10 shows the timing placebo decay curves, regime-conditional IC, and permutation null for the two features. Momentum IC decays gradually from 0.053 to 0.034 over 252 days, consistent with a slow-moving signal that is still strongest when most current. Momentum IC concentrates in low-volatility markets (IC = 0.086 in low-VIX versus 0.017 in high-VIX). Momentum IC of 0.042 (permutation $p < 0.001$) lies far outside the permutation null; reversal IC of 0.002 (permutation $p = 0.535$) is indistinguishable from noise.

All t-statistics use **Newey–West** (**HAC**) standard errors to account for serial dependence in overlapping IC series. Features that fail multiple checks should be investigated before proceeding; features that pass all checks have survived a first filter but have not been shown to be causal: these are bivariate diagnostics that cannot detect multivariate confounding.

These checks can reject proposed mechanisms but cannot confirm them. The natural next step is to move from single-feature diagnostics to the multivariate toolkit: structural models, double- or debiased machine learning, and sensitivity analysis. That machinery is reserved for the survivors and lives in *Chapter 15*.

> **Implementation:** `08_causal_sanity_checks` runs the collider simulation, the feature × horizon scan, and the timing-placebo, shared-driver, and regime-heterogeneity checks on ETF returns.

7.6 Summary

Defining the learning task well is one of the highest-leverage steps in the quantitative workflow. This chapter developed five interlocking disciplines that aim to separate reliable features from research noise. Clean, auditable preprocessing (*Section 7.1*) ensures that every input is comparable across trials and free of encoding surprises. Execution-consistent labels (*Section 7.2*) anchor predictions to tradeable prices with explicit timing, lag, and horizon conventions; a mismatch of even one bar can fabricate or erase a possible edge. Fold-aware evaluation (*Section 7.3*) surfaces instability that pooled statistics hide: a feature whose IC flips sign across walk-forward folds is a lot less useful, regardless of its aggregate statistic. Search accounting (*Section 7.4*) records the number of candidates tested and applies multiple-testing corrections so that the best-observed IC is not simply the luckiest. Finally, mechanism plausibility checks (*Section 7.5*) encode causal assumptions as directed acyclic graphs and test their implications cheaply—catching confounded proxies and aggregation artifacts before they consume modeling effort.

Together, these disciplines feed a single decision framework. The triage gates (proceed, revise, or stop) convert diagnostics into auditable decisions at every stage. A candidate that advances carries a definition bundle (label specification, feature configuration, preprocessing choices), fold-level diagnostics (IC, ICIR, sign consistency, quantile spreads), a searched-set record (how many variants were tested, which correction was applied), and a mechanism assessment (which plausibility checks it passed and where its signal concentrates). This documentation also serves as the minimum audit trail to make results reproducible and failures diagnosable.

The shared `ml4t.*` ecosystem wires this framework together under the canonical `timestamp + symbol` schema: `ml4t.data` for loaders, `ml4t.engineer` for feature recipes, `ml4t.diagnostic` for evaluation utilities, and `ml4t.backtest` for execution; see `10_ml4t_library_ecosystem` for the API tour.

With the framework set, *Chapter 8* translates strategy hypotheses into concrete feature specifications and applies the evaluation and triage gates built here to each family.

8

Financial Feature Engineering

Feature engineering is where our trading setup becomes learnable. A model can only exploit relationships that the dataset makes visible at decision time, at the relevant horizon, and in a representation consistent with how we trade.

Starting from the *Chapter 7* label, we propose economic drivers and express them as feature families with design choices and failure modes.

After completing this chapter, you will be able to:

- Translate a strategy hypothesis into a feature specification using the three-step filter.
- Select appropriate design choices for each feature family and distinguish meaning-changing from noise-reduction ones.
- Distinguish signal features from state features and understand when each applies.
- Construct interaction features and evaluate whether they add incremental information.
- Apply degrees-of-freedom discipline to prevent spurious discovery from search.
- Connect feature specifications to the triage protocol from *Chapter 7*.

The chapter is organized into four stages:

1. *Section 8.1* introduces the three-step filter (horizon alignment, driver hypothesis, role separation) that turns a strategy narrative into a feature specification, as well as three design choices that configure each family.
2. *Section 8.2* develops price-derived families that apply to all nine case studies, and *Section 8.3* adds families that require multi-instrument data.
3. *Section 8.4* covers slow-moving contextual features (fundamentals, calendars, macro state) where point-in-time correctness is the binding constraint.
4. *Section 8.5* surveys cross-cutting feature types and the limits of direct aggregation, and *Section 8.6* addresses how to combine signals with state variables and control the resulting degrees of freedom.

We begin in *Section 8.1* by formalizing the hypothesis → driver → measurement filter that turns an idea into a tested feature.

8.1 Capturing and configuring the economic drivers

A **feature** encodes a claim about why an observable variable should shift the conditional distribution of the predictive target (a return, a volatility measure, or an event). The claim should be consistent with the strategy narrative from *Chapter 6*: the strategy family indicates which information is relevant, and the edge hypothesis explains why. A feature is the *computable expression* of that reasoning: a point-in-time transformation of data, aggregated over a lookback window and expressed in a chosen reference frame, intended to add incremental predictive content given the label definition from *Chapter 7*.

Move from labels to features using three filters (depicted in *Figure 8.1*):

1. **Horizon alignment:** Match lookback, sampling cadence, and aggregation to the label horizon and execution lag. Strategy families provide useful defaults: very short horizons motivate microstructure and order-flow features; medium horizons motivate trend, reversal, volatility state, and event drift; slow horizons motivate carry, term structure, and fundamentals. This is not a rigid partition; mismatches between feature and label horizons are a common source of unstable estimates. Document the implied update frequency and turnover so the design remains compatible with the trading setup.
2. **Driver hypothesis:** When predicting returns, most feature hypotheses map to a small set of economic mechanisms:
   - **Persistence (trend/momentum):** Information is incorporated gradually due to attention limits or slow institutional flows.
   - **Reversion (microstructural or behavioral):** Predictable flows (hedging, rebalancing, inventory management) create transient pressure and subsequent reversal.
   - **Risk compensation (carry and state variables):** Returns compensate for exposures others avoid, such as liquidity, tail, or funding risk.
   - **Predictable clocks:** Calendar effects, roll schedules, funding resets, and scheduled events can generate rule-driven patterns tied to market structure. If we cannot name a plausible mechanism, the result is a data pattern rather than a feature hypothesis (*Box 8.1*).
3. **Role separation:** Classify each feature as a **signal** (intended to predict the conditional mean or direction) or a **state variable** (intended to condition when signals work, how aggressively to trade, and how costly or risky trading will be). State variables such as volatility, liquidity, and funding conditions often matter through interactions (gating or scaling signals) rather than strong marginal association.

The workflow is shown in *Figure 8.1*:

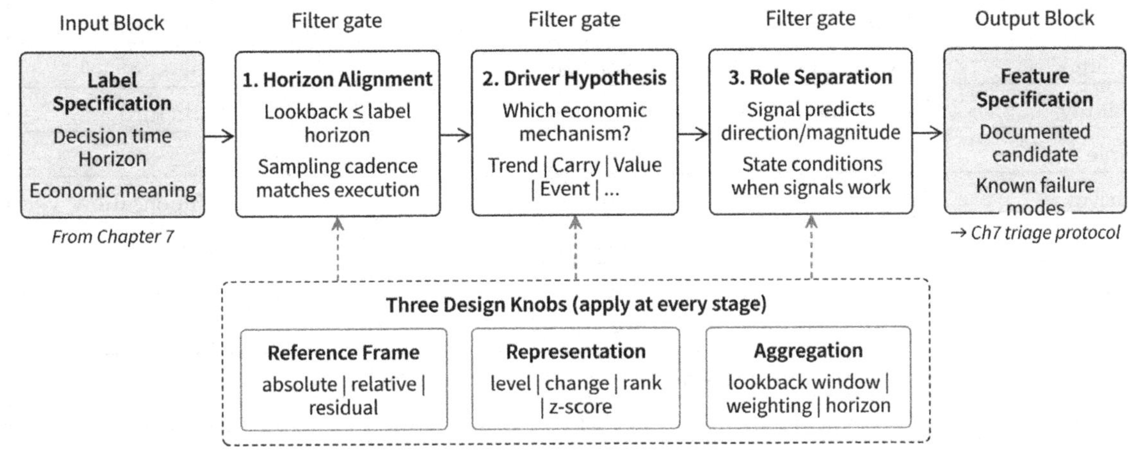

Figure 8.1: The three-step filter

Box 8.1: Patterns without a mechanism

Regularities without an economic explanation require a higher evidentiary standard because they provide no guidance on failure modes or regime dependence. Treat them as provisional:

- Apply stricter multiple-testing discipline and reserve untouched out-of-sample holdouts beyond cross-validation folds.
- Check robustness across related instruments, regimes, and small variants of the definition.
- Monitor decay after deployment and retire the feature when evidence weakens.

Across these steps, most feature designs can be configured using three choices:

- **Reference frame:** Absolute time-series measurements per asset versus relative cross-sectional ranks or peer-set comparisons, depending on whether the hypothesis concerns the time series' own dynamics or relative positioning.
- **Representation:** Raw values versus transformed values such as ranks, volatility scaling, winsorization, or residualization; choose transforms that match the hypothesis.
- **Aggregation:** How raw inputs are summarized to trade responsiveness against variance reduction. Aggregation sets the feature's effective bandwidth and should be guided by horizon alignment.

Treat the resulting choices as part of a **feature specification**. At minimum, we record the name, family, signal-versus-state role, driver hypothesis, and edge source; inputs and observability constraints; lookback and aggregation; reference frame; representation; and expected failure modes.

If we cannot fill in these fields, we have an input awaiting a hypothesis. *Table 8.1* provides three examples. In production systems, this specification corresponds to a feature-registry entry that supports versioning, auditability, and consistent reuse across trials.

Field	21-Day Momentum	Realized Volatility	Carry (Roll Yield)
Name	mom_21d	rvol_20d	carry_roll
Family	Trend/momentum	Volatility	Term structure
Role	Signal	State	Signal
Driver	Persistence	Risk state	Risk compensation
Inputs	Close prices	Close prices	Near/far futures
Lookback	21 days	20 days	Current contracts
Reference frame	Time series	Time series	Cross-section
Representation	Volatility-scaled return	Annualized standard deviation	Annualized percent
Failure modes	Crowding, regime shift	Stale in low-vol regimes	Roll-date artifacts

Table 8.1: Feature specification template

A feature is well posed when it operationalizes one element of the strategy narrative as a computable, testable input, with explicit timing and failure modes. The remainder of this chapter develops the main feature families, organized by the economic mechanisms they target.

Each feature specification becomes a trial entry in the *Chapter 7* workflow. Evaluate candidates at the label horizon using fold-aware diagnostics (cross-sectional IC, decile spreads). Conditional diagnostics (for example, momentum IC stratified by volatility terciles) test whether conditioning adds information or merely fragments the sample.

Sections 8.2-8.4 construct features by aggregating observable inputs using rolling windows, cross-sectional ranks, and simple formulas. *Chapter 9* extends the approach to features extracted from fitted objects. We start by looking at price-derived features.

8.2 Price-derived features

This section covers families computed from an asset's own price, volume, and trade data, the minimum dataset available for any traded instrument:

Family	Economic claim	Primary role	Typical horizons
Trend/momentum	Recent performance persists	Signal	Hours to months
Reversal	Prices revert to an anchor	Signal	Seconds to days
Volatility/tail risk	Risk conditions sizing and gating	State	All horizons
Liquidity/tradability	Costs and capacity gate signals	State	All horizons
Microstructure/order flow	Informed flow moves prices	Signal/state	Seconds to hours

Table 8.2: Overview of common features

Other families (carry/funding, cross-asset relative value, options-implied state, fundamentals, calendar effects, and macro shocks) appear later in this chapter sequence.

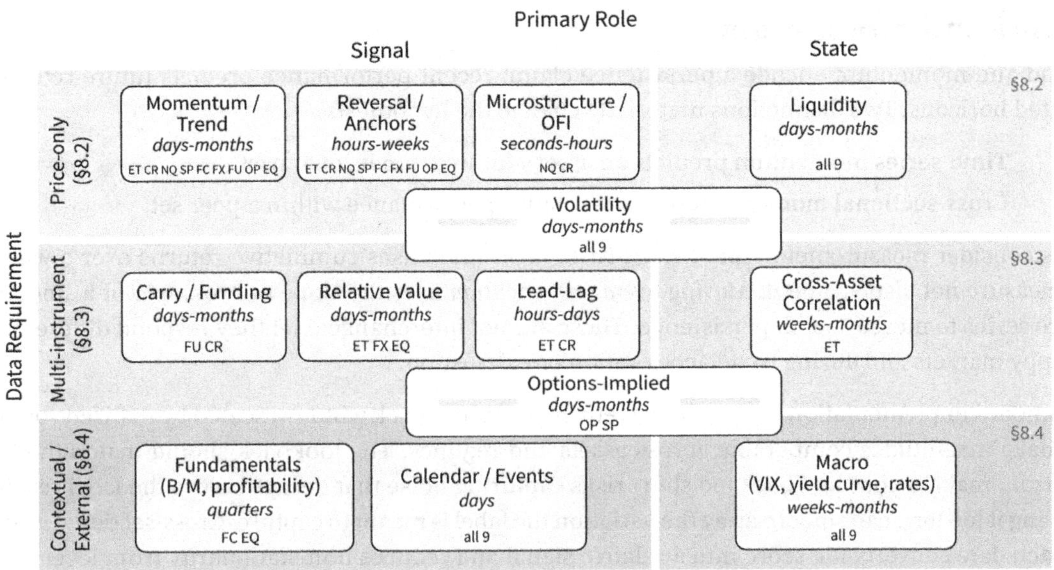

Figure 8.2: Feature families

For each family, use the same four questions:

1. What is the economic claim, and is the feature used primarily as a **signal** or a **state** variable?
2. At what horizons can the claim plausibly operate under your execution assumptions?
3. Which design choices change the hypothesis (not just the noise level)?
4. How does the feature typically fail in backtests and live trading?

Two constraints apply across families:

- **Horizon alignment**: lookback, sampling cadence, and smoothing must be commensurate with the label horizon and execution lag.
- **Distributional stability**: prefer representations whose distributions drift slowly; use level-based features only with an explicit rationale and diagnostics.

Most price-derived features can be reduced to a few primitives: changes over a window, distances to an anchor, gain–loss asymmetries, and cross-sectional comparisons. The practical discipline is to separate **meaning-changing choices** (reference frame, anchor definition, peer set, estimator choice) from **noise-reduction choices** (smoothing, shrinkage, winsorization). The former create new hypotheses; the latter trade variance for bias. All nine case studies support the families in this section; differences come from cadence, market structure, and whether overnight gaps matter.

Implementation:

- `01_price_volume_features` creates trend, reversal, and volatility features.
- `02_microstructure_features` implements trade-based liquidity proxies and order-flow imbalance.

Trend and momentum

Trend and momentum encode a **persistence** claim: recent performance predicts future returns at related horizons. Two distinctions materially change the hypothesis:

- **Time-series momentum** predicts an asset's future from its own past
- **Cross-sectional momentum** predicts relative performance within a peer set

Let's consider measurement type. *Return-based momentum* uses cumulative returns over a window to measure net displacement. *Moving-average momentum* uses the slope or crossover of a smoothed price series to measure path persistence. These are not interchangeable: they respond differently in choppy markets and during trend acceleration or exhaustion.

A standard implementation is cumulative return over a lookback window, scaled by realized volatility to make magnitudes comparable across assets and regimes. The lookback should match the label horizon: making your lookback too short risks capturing noise that decays before the label resolves; making it too long can smooth away the variation the label is meant to capture. Cross-sectional ranking at each date converts the score into a relative signal and reduces non-stationarity from level effects. In time-series use, volatility scaling carries most of the normalization.

Key characteristics for this feature family:

- **Role and horizons:** Primarily signal; hours to months.
- **Meaning-changing choices:** Time-series versus cross-sectional framing; lookback and holding horizon; decay profile; benchmark/sector residualization; volatility scaling and risk targeting.
- **Typical implementations:** Cumulative-return momentum, rank momentum, moving-average slope/crossover, residual momentum (persistence after factor adjustment).
- **Failure modes:** Regime concentration (trend versus mean-reverting regimes), misalignment between the lookback and label horizons, and search inflation from scanning many windows without selection correction.

Implementation: The same templates appear with cadence-appropriate windows in `etfs` (cross-sectional and daily), `crypto_perps_funding` (time-series and 8-hour), `cme_futures` (time-series across products), and `fx_pairs` (cross-sectional currency momentum).

Reversal and mean reversion to an anchor

Reversion features claim that prices return **to an anchor**, and the anchor defines the economic content.

At short horizons, reversal is often microstructure-driven: bid–ask bounce, inventory effects, and short-lived overreaction. The implicit anchor is a "fair" mid-price or a short-run equilibrium of the quote process. Longer-horizon mean reversion relies on more economically grounded anchors, such as **volume-weighted average price** (**VWAP**), moving averages, peer means, or spread equilibria.

A standard template is a normalized distance-to-anchor statistic, often a z-score:

- An **anchor** determines **where the price should revert**: a moving average, VWAP, cross-sectional peer mean, or a fundamental parity level encodes different hypotheses.
- **Normalization** determines **what "extreme" means:** z-scoring by the asset's own recent volatility measures abnormality relative to its history; cross-sectional ranking measures abnormality relative to peers. (Keep the anchor window and deviation window separate: they control different aspects of the hypothesis.)

Key characteristics for this feature family:

- **Role and horizons:** Signal; seconds to days (longer when the anchor is economically grounded).
- **Meaning-changing choices:** Anchor definition (statistical versus economic); extremeness definition (z-score versus percentile); clock-time versus event-time sampling; conditioning on spread and liquidity.
- **Typical implementations:** Last-k return reversal, bounded-oscillator templates (for example, RSI), explicit distance-to-anchor with a stated normalization.
- **Failure modes:** Edges that vanish after costs and execution delays, instability due to poorly estimated anchors, and "reversion" signals that are actually liquidity proxies.

Implementation:

- `nasdaq100_microstructure` implements bid–ask bounce at minute frequency.
- `fx_pairs` shows parity or moving-average equilibria.
- `sp500_equity_option_analytics` shows implied–realized spread reversion.

Volatility and tail-risk state

Volatility features are usually **state** variables: they summarize dispersion, regime, and tail risk that determine whether directional signals should be trusted and how aggressively to trade. If the label is itself a volatility target, the same measurements become **signals**, and you should evaluate them against a volatility label rather than against returns.

A standard volatility measure is **realized volatility**, which is the square root of the sum of squared returns over a time window (often annualized). The lookback controls the responsiveness–stability tradeoff: short windows react quickly but are noisy; long windows are smooth but can miss transitions. Converting volatility levels to percentiles of the asset's historical distribution (or cross-sectional ranks) often improves stability, as downstream models typically require a relative "high/low volatility" state rather than a drifting level.

Key characteristics for this feature family:

- **Role and horizons:** Primarily state (often via signal interaction); all horizons.
- **Meaning-changing choices:** Estimator; lookback and smoothing; downside emphasis (semi-variance, drawdown depth); level versus change versus rank.

- **Typical implementations:** Realized volatility, range-based estimators, volatility percentiles, and drawdown summaries.
- **Failure modes:** Single shocks dominate short windows, smoothing that masks spikes, and estimator–cadence mismatch.

Efficient volatility estimation from OHLC data

Close-to-close volatility uses only closing prices. When open, high, and low prices are available, range-based estimators extract more information per bar and can deliver comparable precision with shorter windows.

Estimator	Inputs	Efficiency versus close-to-close	Best when
Close-to-close	Close	1×	Only closes are available
Parkinson	High, Low	~5×	Daily bars with negligible overnight effects
Garman-Klass	OHLC	~7×	Full OHLC with small gaps
Yang-Zhang	OHLC	~8–14×	Overnight gaps are material

Table 8.3: Volatility estimators compared to close-to-close standard deviation

Here, "relative efficiency" refers to the **precision gain per observation**, commonly reported as the ratio of the close-to-close variance to the estimator's variance under the model assumptions. A 5× efficiency factor means that, for the same target variance, you need roughly one-fifth as many observations:

- The **Parkinson** estimator uses only the range:

$$\hat{\sigma}_P^2 = \frac{1}{4ln2}(lnH_t - lnL_t)^2.$$

- **Garman-Klass** adds open and close for higher efficiency:

$$\hat{\sigma}_{GK}^2 = 0.5(lnH_t - lnL_t)^2 - (2ln2 - 1)(lnC_t - lnO_t)^2.$$

- The **Yang-Zhang** estimator decomposes volatility into overnight (close-to-open) variation, intraday variation, and a Rogers-Satchell term. This is valuable when opening gaps are nontrivial, since a meaningful share of total variance may occur outside regular trading hours.

These formulas produce single-bar variance estimates. In practice, use a rolling mean over n bars, for example:

$$\hat{\sigma}_P(n) = \sqrt{\frac{1}{n}\sum_{i=0}^{n-1} \hat{\sigma}_{P,t-i}^2}$$

This is visualized in the following chart:

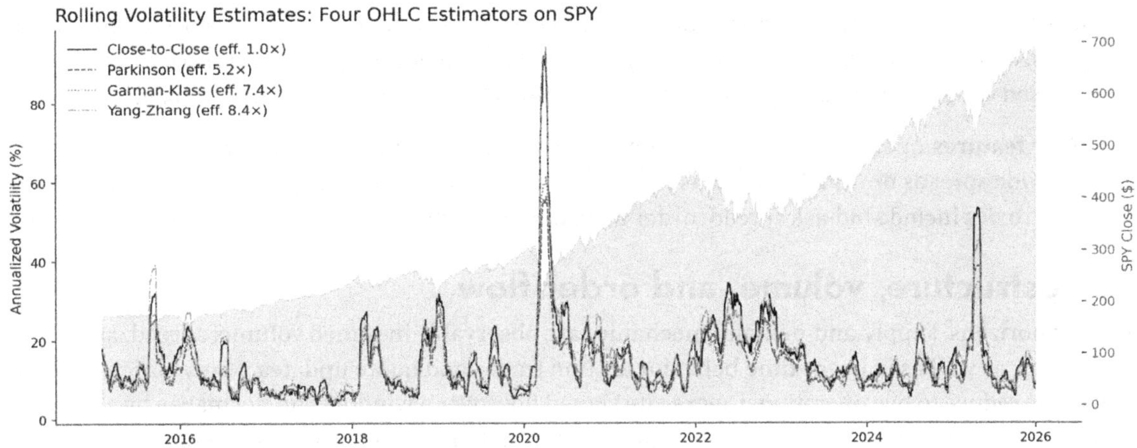

Figure 8.3: Volatility estimators

Implementation:

- `crypto_perps_funding` uses close-to-close on 8-hourly returns; 24/7 trading makes the overnight decomposition unnecessary.
- `etfs` and `us_equities_panel` use close-to-close as the variance estimator and add NATR as a price-denominated range indicator for gating and sizing rather than for variance measurement.
- `fx_pairs` and `sp500_equity_option_analytics` compute Garman-Klass alongside close-to-close, exploiting the full OHLC bar when overnight gaps are small at the chosen cadence.
- `cme_futures` compute Yang-Zhang alongside close-to-close; overnight session moves around the U.S. open are material for the bulk of the contract set.
- `nasdaq100_microstructure` computes realized volatility at minute frequency from intraday returns rather than applying daily OHLC estimators.

Tail-risk and regime indicators

Tail-risk measures extend the volatility state beyond dispersion. **Value-at-Risk** (**VaR**) and **Conditional VaR** (**CVaR, expected shortfall**) quantify losses beyond a given percentile (for example, the 95th percentile). Downside deviation (volatility on negative returns only) and tail ratios summarize asymmetry.

Regime indicators summarize path character. The **variance ratio** compares long-horizon variance to the scaled short-horizon variance: values below 1 suggest mean reversion, values above 1 suggest persistence. **Fractal efficiency** (net displacement divided by path length) makes a related "trending versus choppy" distinction. Parametric regime models are discussed in *Section 9.5*.

Average True Range (ATR) measures the typical price range. It is useful for execution rules (stop distances, dollar risk scaling, breakout filters) but is not a statistical estimator of return variance. Use range-based variance estimators to measure volatility and ATR for price-denominated sizing and gating.

Liquidity features operationalize expected costs and capacity. They are usually used as masks (excluding wide spreads or thin depth) or as interaction terms (downweighting signals when liquidity is scarce). Proxies include bid-ask spread, order book depth, turnover, and price impact per unit volume.

Microstructure, volume, and order flow

At short horizons, supply-and-demand mechanics are observable in signed volume, spread, and depth conditions, as well as in event-time behavior around trades and quote updates. Many "price+volume" indicators reduce to two operations: aggregate signed flow over a window and normalize by a liquidity scale. The binding constraint is delay sensitivity: test whether the effect survives a realistic execution latency before optimizing the details.

A standard feature is **order-flow imbalance** (**OFI**; see *Chapter 3*): the signed trade volume accumulated over a window, with the sign indicating whether trades are buyer- or seller-initiated:

- The first meaning-changing choice is the trade-signing rule (tick rule, quote-midpoint comparisons such as Lee–Ready-style methods, venue aggressor flags).
- The second is the aggregation structure. Simple OFI sums signed trades; order-book OFI (Cont, Kukanov, and Stoikov, 2014) uses changes in best-bid/ask quantities and is cleaner when full depth is available, but it requires limit order book reconstruction (*Chapter 3*).

Normalization determines portability across assets and regimes: divide OFI by total volume (fraction), by depth (liquidity-scaled), or by a z-score relative to the asset's own history (rarity). Volume-normalized and depth-normalized OFI can diverge sharply in thin markets, and the divergence can itself be informative.

Key characteristics for this feature family:

- **Role and horizons:** Signal or state; seconds to hours.
- **Meaning-changing choices:** Clock-time versus event-time sampling; trade-signing rule; trade-based OFI versus order-book OFI; normalization (volume, depth, volatility); conditioning on spread/depth regimes.
- **Typical implementations:** Signed volume imbalance, order-book OFI, spread/depth proxies, queue imbalance when available, Kyle's λ (price impact per unit of flow).
- **Failure modes:** Latency sensitivity (predictive at $t + \varepsilon$ but not at $t + 5min$), venue and data artifacts (mis-signed trades, crossed quotes, reporting delays), and execution assumptions that do not hold up in real order routing.

Venue structure constrains implementation. Central limit order books (for example, CME and major crypto venues) expose depth and queue state; RFQ/dealer markets typically expose flow only through transactions; AMMs expose pool state but not a traditional order book. The claim "informed flow moves prices" must be expressed in the venue-provided data structure.

Implementation:

- `02_microstructure_features` constructs trade-sign OFI, Kyle's λ, Amihud illiquidity, and Roll-spread features, and tests delay sensitivity by comparing the contemporaneous and lagged OFI relationship with returns. TSLA shows the highest Kyle lambda (0.003), indicating the greatest price impact per unit of volume. However, contemporaneous OFI-return correlation (+0.053) substantially exceeds lagged OFI-return correlation (-0.011).
- The `nasdaq100_microstructure` pipeline combines quote-based liquidity, signed-volume order flow, price impact, and dark-pool proxies.

8.3 Structural and cross-instrument features

The three families in this section require data beyond a single asset's price series: term structures, cross-instrument relationships, and derivatives-implied quantities. They encode information that is invisible in any individual price history: the cost of carrying a position, an asset's relative position within its peer group, and the market's probabilistic assessment of future outcomes.

Carry, funding, and term structure

Carry features encode **risk compensation**: the return from holding a position in the absence of a price change, measured by roll yield, basis, funding rates, and curve shape.

The standard feature is **roll yield**: the annualized price difference between two futures contracts of different maturities, measuring the return earned or paid to maintain exposure over time. The choice of maturity pair determines what part of the curve the signal represents:

- Comparing the **front-month** with the **second-month** contract captures conditions at the very front of the curve and is most sensitive to short-term supply-and-demand imbalances
- Comparing the **front** contract with a more deferred **back** contract measures the broader slope of the term structure and often reflects more persistent market conditions

Annualizing by the number of days between expirations makes roll yields comparable across contracts with different maturities. Cross-sectional ranking within a commodity sector then converts the raw level into a relative carry signal, separating assets whose curves reward holders from those whose curves impose a cost.

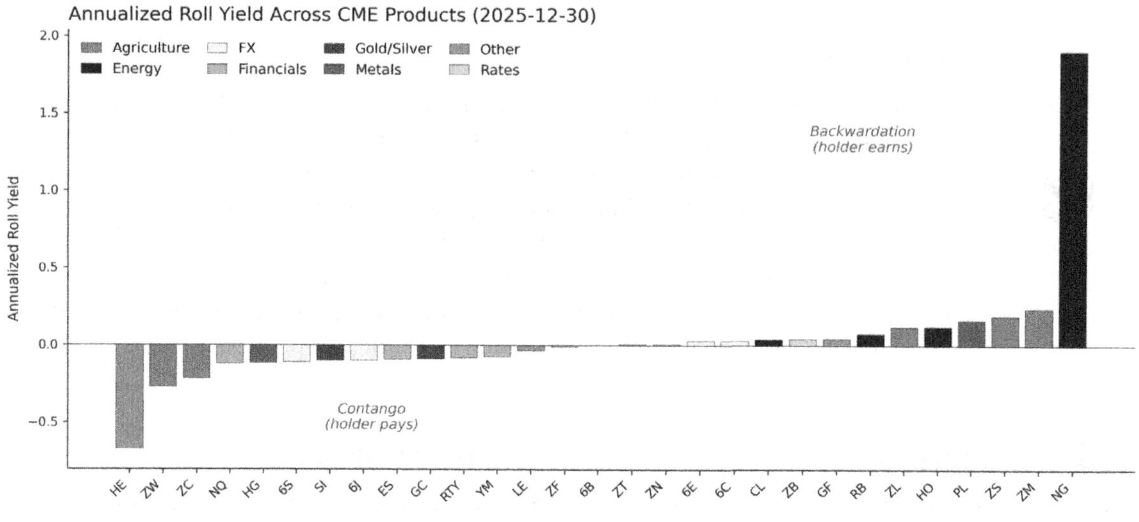

Figure 8.4: Annualized roll yield across 29 CME products on 2025-12-30, sorted by sector. Negative bars (Contango) indicate carry cost; positive bars (Backwardation) indicate carry earned

The curve itself contains more than a single slope. Level, slope, and curvature (the butterfly spread between short, mid, and long maturities) capture parallel shifts, tilt, and non-parallel movements, three independent dimensions driven by different economic forces.

Box 8.2: Crypto perpetuals — A distinct carry regime

Perpetual futures exchange funding at fixed intervals, meaning periodic cash payments between longs and shorts that keep the perpetual price anchored to spot, rather than rolling on monthly or quarterly expiry dates like standard futures. This poses a distinct feature-engineering problem. Most major exchanges (such as Binance, OKX, and Bybit) use 8-hour funding intervals (00:00, 08:00, 16:00 UTC), but some venues use 4-hour or 1-hour funding intervals. The interval should be verified per venue; using 8-hour windows on 4-hour funding data mixes settlements. Three design choices matter:

- **Clock alignment:** Funding rates reset at fixed UTC times (typically 00:00, 08:00, 16:00). Features built on non-aligned windows mix pre- and post-settlement observations. Use 8-hour windows that respect the funding clock, or explicitly model the intra-window dynamics.
- **Basis-funding decomposition:** The perpetual's deviation from spot has two components: the *basis* (the price difference) and the funding rate (the mechanism that anchors the perpetual to spot). These encode different information. The basis reflects the immediate supply-demand imbalance; the funding rate reflects the cost of maintaining positions. Treat them as separate features with distinct horizons and failure modes.

- **Signal versus state:** The funding rate plays a dual role. As a *signal*, extreme funding predicts mean reversion: high positive funding tends to precede perpetual underperformance as longs pay shorts. As a *state*, funding proxies crowding: when funding is persistently elevated, directional signals become less reliable because one-sided positioning creates fragility. Log both roles explicitly.

A common mistake is treating the funding rate as equivalent to traditional roll yield. Roll yield is a known mechanical cost; funding rate is market-determined and can swing by 100 bps within hours during periods of volatility. Features that assume stable funding regimes fail during the regime transitions that matter most.

Key characteristics for this feature family:

- **Role and horizons:** Signal or state; days to months.
- **Meaning-changing choices:** Roll and funding clock alignment; curve representation; maturity alignment to the label horizon; levels versus changes versus ranks.
- **Typical implementations:** Futures roll yield, spot–future basis, funding-rate level and change (perpetuals), term-structure slopes and butterfly spreads.
- **Failure modes:** Roll discontinuities when contract definitions change, calendar misalignment between roll dates and feature windows, and hidden assumptions about which contract month is “front.”

Implementation: The `cme_futures` case study computes carry features across 30 products; `crypto_perps_funding` uses funding rates as the carry analog for perpetual futures.

Cross-asset structure and relative value

Cross-asset features exploit relationships across instruments rather than relying only on each asset’s own history. They ask three related but distinct questions: what exposure should be treated as common and removed, whether one market leads another, and how the relationship between assets changes over time.

The first class is **relative-value features**. Neutralization is not cleanup; it defines the hypothesis. These features remove what should be common, such as market, sector, or factor exposure, and focus on what remains: spreads, deviations, and residuals. Peer-set stability and refresh cadence are first-order design choices because a shifting peer set changes the hypothesis mid-backtest.

The standard feature is deviation from a peer mean, z-scored by the asset’s own volatility: how far this asset has moved relative to its reference group, measured in units of its own noise. The peer-set definition is the meaning-changing choice. Sector peers, factor-model residuals, and statistical clusters encode different theories of what “common” means, and each produces a different residual.

Factor-neutral residual returns deserve particular attention. **Residual momentum**, defined as the persistence of factor-model residuals after neutralizing market and sector exposures, aims to capture stock-specific information that common factors miss. By construction, it is less exposed to broad market direction than raw momentum.

A second cross-asset hypothesis is that some markets lead others. Credit spreads may lead equity drawdowns, FX volatility may anticipate rate volatility, and in crypto markets, BTC moves may lead altcoin positioning at intraday frequencies. Unlike relative-value features, which usually assume contemporaneous relationships, **lead-lag features** model temporal cross-asset structure. They require careful treatment of time zones, trading hours, settlement conventions, and stale prices. Their main failure mode is mistaking delayed price discovery, low liquidity, or nonsynchronous trading for genuine information flow.

A third and often more robust class of cross-instrument features captures **how the relationship between assets changes over time**. These features are usually better interpreted as state variables than as direct trading signals. For example, the 63-day rolling correlation between SPY and TLT returns measures the equity-bond relationship. When this correlation remains negative, diversification is working, and flight-to-safety dynamics are operative. When it moves toward zero or turns positive, the usual stock-bond hedge weakens, as in 2022, and other signals may behave differently.

This type of cross-asset state variable can have substantial conditioning power. The `etfs` case study computes the 63-day rolling SPY-TLT correlation as `corr_spy_tlt_63d` and supplies it to the LightGBM momentum model alongside other regime features. Aggregated across the 120-fold × config observations on the 21-day momentum label, the feature has the highest stable (non-NaN-aggregating) fold-normalized importance among the 27 inputs, with a mean of 0.73, ahead of `yield_curve_zscore` and the momentum-slope features. While this does not isolate the feature's stand-alone predictive content, it confirms that the tree-based model is repeatedly choosing the equity-bond correlation as a node-split criterion, which is consistent with the state-variable interpretation: when the usual stock-bond hedge weakens, the relative attractiveness of momentum versus reversal shifts.

Key characteristics for this feature family:

- **Role and horizons:** Signal or state; hours to months.
- **Meaning-changing choices:** Peer-set definition; spreads versus residualization; neutralization strength; reference-set stability and refresh cadence.
- **Typical implementations:** Pair spreads, deviation from peer mean, z-scored peer deviations, factor-neutral residual returns, within-peer momentum, residual momentum.
- **Failure modes:** Universe drift, moving targets due to frequent peer-set redefinitions, and estimation noise introduced by the neutralization step itself.

Implementation:

- `03_structural_cross_instrument_features` implements rolling beta and relative-value features and tests SPY-to-sector ETF lead-lag relationships. It finds uniformly negative lag-1 correlations, ranging from approximately -0.06 to -0.13, indicating short-term reversal rather than continuation. At daily frequency, highly liquid instruments trading in the same venue show no exploitable lead-lag effect in this test; the negative correlations likely reflect microstructure effects such as bid-ask bounce, ETF rebalancing, or short-horizon flow reversal. This negative result is useful because it illustrates why lead-lag claims require careful validation before they can be promoted to features.
- The `etfs` case study contains the production SPY-TLT correlation computation; `13_model_analysis` reports the feature-importance evidence cited above, while `06_robustness_sensitivity` evaluates regime-conditioning of momentum IC using SPY realized-volatility terciles (see *Section 8.6*).

Options-implied features

Option prices are useful because they not only reflect what the underlying asset has done in the past but also what the market is willing to pay for protection and upside exposure going forward. Inverting an option price through an option-pricing model yields **implied volatility** (**IV**): the volatility input that makes the model match the observed market price. Repeating this across strikes and maturities produces the **implied volatility surface**, which summarizes how the market prices expected volatility, downside risk, and event uncertainty.

These features are often more forward-looking than realized volatility or return-based measures, but they only make sense if the surface is constructed consistently. In practice, this requires a stable **surface policy**: how moneyness is defined (whether an option's strike price is equal or very close to the underlying's price), which quotes are accepted, whether mid or last prices are used, how to interpolate across strikes and maturities, and how to map observed maturities to standardized horizons such as 30 days. If this policy changes over time, the feature may start tracking construction artifacts rather than changes in market beliefs.

Two definitions matter throughout:

- **ATM (at the money)** means an option whose strike is near the current spot or, more precisely, near the current forward price for the maturity in question. ATM options are the standard reference for the overall level of implied volatility because they are usually among the most liquid contracts.
- **OTM (out of the money)** means an option with no intrinsic value at the current price. For equity or index options, an **OTM put** has a strike below the current price, and an **OTM call** has a strike above the current price. OTM options, especially puts, are often used to measure tail-risk pricing because they become valuable only after sufficiently large moves.

Five features capture most of the economically relevant information in the volatility surface:

- **ATM implied volatility** (often mapped to a constant 30-day maturity) measures the market's baseline expectation of future dispersion. It is the primary state variable for the volatility regime: high ATM IV usually indicates elevated uncertainty, while low ATM IV is characteristic of calmer periods.
- **Implied-realized spread** compares today's implied volatility to the **subsequent realized volatility** over a matching horizon. This difference is a practical measure of the **variance risk premium:** investors often pay more for option protection than the volatility that is later realized. Historically, for index options such as the S&P 500, implied volatility has, on average, exceeded realized volatility, though the gap varies substantially across regimes. The spread can serve as a direct signal for volatility-selling strategies and as a conditioning variable for other strategies.
- **Risk reversal** is commonly defined as the implied volatility of a 25-delta put minus that of a 25-delta call at the same maturity. It measures the asymmetry of downside versus upside pricing. In equity index markets, puts usually trade at higher implied volatility than calls, so a larger put-minus-call spread indicates stronger demand for downside protection and greater perceived fragility.
- **Volatility term-structure slope** compares implied volatility at a short maturity with implied volatility at a longer maturity, for example, front-month versus 3-month IV. This feature distinguishes near-term stress from more persistent uncertainty. When short-dated IV rises above long-dated IV, the term structure inverts, often signaling an imminent event or market stress.
- **Put-call skew** compares the implied volatility of **OTM puts** with that of **OTM calls**, holding maturity and distance from the money fixed as closely as possible. It isolates how expensively the market prices downside tails relative to upside tails, rather than the overall ATM volatility level.

These features define the economic content. In practice, however, their meaning still depends on several construction choices, so the implementation needs to be specified just as carefully as the feature definition itself.

Key characteristics for this feature family:

- **Role and horizons:** Usually regime or state variables; sometimes direct signals around earnings, macro announcements, or crisis periods; typical holding horizons range from days to months.
- **Meaning-changing choices:** ATM convention (spot-based, forward-based, or delta-based), delta choice for skew measures, quote filter rules, mid versus last prices, interpolation and extrapolation method, constant-maturity mapping, and whether the feature is used in levels, changes, z-scores, or cross-sectional ranks.
- **Typical implementations:** 30-day ATM IV, IV minus matched-horizon future realized volatility, 25-delta risk reversals, front-versus-back term-structure slopes, and OTM put-minus-call skew measures.
- **Failure modes:** Stale or wide quotes on illiquid strikes distorting the surface; inconsistent moneyness conventions across data vendors; survivorship bias when options expire or series are delisted; look-ahead bias when the "realized" leg of IV-minus-RV uses future data that overlaps the label horizon; and regime-dependent feature meaning—a risk reversal of −5 vol points carries different information in a VIX-15 environment than in a VIX-35 environment.

Implementation:

- `03_structural_cross_instrument_features` illustrates key calculations.
- `sp500_equity_option_analytics` constructs the full feature set (ATM IV, risk reversals, IV-RV spread at multiple horizons, and cross-sectional ranks) from S&P 500 constituent options.
- `sp500_options` works at the contract level, computing VRP features directly from straddle-level implied and realized volatility.

We turn next to features that capture changing state, which conditions how the signals built so far should be interpreted.

8.4 Contextual and slow-moving features

This section covers three feature families that are external to market prices: financial statements, macroeconomic releases, and deterministic calendars. They share a low update frequency (monthly, quarterly, or scheduled), strict *point-in-time correctness* requirements (*Chapter 4*), and a primary role as state variables that condition faster signals.

In practice, these features enter as controls, regime indicators, or conditioning variables in models that also use faster market-derived signals. The limiting factor is data integrity: each observation must reflect only what was available at the time of the trading decision. The `us_firm_characteristics` and `us_equities_panel` case studies are the main testbeds; calendar features apply to both.

Fundamentals and characteristics

Fundamental features are primarily designed to capture **long-horizon premia**. Because accounting variables such as earnings, book equity, leverage, or profitability update slowly, they are usually informative about return drivers that play out over months or quarters rather than days. They can also condition short-horizon signals: a tactical signal like momentum, reversal, or volatility may have different reliability depending on valuation, profitability, or balance-sheet strength.

The central risk is point-in-time error: using backfilled revisions or treating slowly updated fields as if they were new information every day. Repeating a quarterly value across daily rows also inflates the nominal sample size without adding information and creates strong within-period dependence. For example, quarterly book equity, repeated over roughly 63 trading days, multiplies the nominal N by about 63. When evaluating such features, apply the effective-sample-size and uniqueness-weighting logic from *Section 7.2* so repeated values do not dominate fold-level diagnostics.

Per *Section 8.1*'s measurement filter, the feature definition must specify reporting lags, revision policy, and availability rules. A standard example is the **book-to-market ratio**: book equity from the most recent reported quarter (lagged to account for reporting delays) divided by current market capitalization. The numerator updates quarterly and must use the vintage available at the time of the decision; the denominator updates daily. Cross-sectional ranking (often expressed as percentiles and often sector- or industry-neutral) converts the raw ratio into a relative-value signal comparable across firms. The assumed lag is meaning-changing: a 60-day versus 90-day lag defines a different feature with different lookahead risk.

Standard characteristic families map directly to the `us_firm_characteristics` dataset. They fall into four broad categories: value (book-to-market, earnings yield), profitability (operating profitability, gross margins), investment (asset growth, capital expenditure), and quality (accruals, leverage), which match the factor-zoo literature developed in depth in *Chapter 14*.

Key characteristics for this feature family:

- **Role and horizon:** Signal or state; weeks to years.
- **Meaning-changing choices:** Reporting lag; revision and restatement policy; update cadence; cross-sectional ranking/normalization; sector/industry neutralization; "surprise" definitions that depend on what was known when.
- **Typical implementations:** Valuation ratios, profitability and quality proxies, balance-sheet growth, and point-in-time surprises, where supported.
- **Failure modes:** Lookahead via revised fundamentals, inflated nominal sample size due to repeated values, and stale fundamentals treated as fresh daily observations.

Time, calendar, and event encodings

Calendar features encode **predictable clocks**: sessions, auctions, roll and funding windows, and scheduled events such as earnings or macro releases. Encode **phase and proximity**, not outcomes. Use time-to-event and post-event decay indicators, not realized post-event quantities in pre-event windows.

A standard feature is **time-to-event**: the number of periods until a scheduled event, capped at a maximum horizon. Optional binning (pre, event, post) turns a countdown into a regime indicator. Time-to-event should be computed in the same time zone and trading calendar as the strategy, using the same session boundaries and holiday rules used for bar construction. For earnings, use confirmed announcement dates from a point-in-time calendar; treating estimated dates as confirmed can create lookahead. Post-event decay features represent a separate hypothesis about information absorption after the event.

For periodic patterns (time-of-day, day-of-week, month-of-year), cyclical encodings using *sin* and *cos* terms, or low-order Fourier terms, preserve circular structure. The number of harmonics is a noise-control parameter; the choice of which clocks to encode is meaning-changing.

Key characteristics for this feature family:

- **Role and horizon:** Typically state; sometimes a direct signal for known clocks; minutes to months.
- **Meaning-changing choices:** Event windows (pre/post boundaries); proximity caps and binning; decay shape; release-time alignment; encoding choice and number of harmonics.
- **Typical implementations:** Cyclical time encodings, Fourier seasonality terms, time-to-event proximity features, post-event decay indicators.
- **Failure modes:** Time zone and holiday misalignment, non-vintage calendar data, leakage from post-event realized quantities used in pre-event windows.

Calendar features are central in `crypto_perps_funding` (8-hour funding resets) and `cme_futures` (roll schedules that shift basis, volume, and liquidity).

Macro and policy state

In most trading setups, macro data is best treated as a **state:** it conditions when trend, carry, and relative-value signals work and how correlations and drawdowns behave. The feature definition must specify vintage series, release timestamping, and how values persist between releases (*Chapter 4*).

A standard feature is the **yield-curve slope,** such as the spread between long-term and short-term government yields (often 10-year minus 2-year), optionally smoothed and standardized against its own recent history. Standardization turns the level into a statement about how unusual the current regime is relative to a recent baseline. The maturity choice is meaning-changing (10Y-2Y versus 10Y-3M, or a principal-component representation) because it selects different aspects of the term structure. Smoothing and standardization horizons are noise-control parameters.

Related state variables include credit spreads, funding-stress proxies (for example, TED spread, cross-currency basis), and volatility regime indicators such as VIX level or percentile. **Macro surprise** features (realized value minus a consensus proxy) capture news flow, but the expectations series is itself a modeling choice and can be unstable across time and vendors.

Key characteristics for this feature family:

- **Role and horizon:** Primarily state; days to years, with discontinuities around releases and policy events.
- **Meaning-changing choices:** Release-time alignment and revision policy; level versus change versus surprise; smoothing and decay; global versus local panels; normalization (z-scores or ranks).
- **Typical implementations:** Yield-curve slope/curvature, policy-rate summaries, credit and funding-stress spreads, volatility regime indicators, nowcasts, macro surprise indices.
- **Failure modes:** Lookahead via revised data (use ALFRED or equivalent vintage series), incorrect release timestamping, stale values treated as daily-fresh observations, unstable expectations proxies.

> **Implementation:** `04_fundamentals_macro_calendar` shows representative constructions across these families, including book-to-market with simulated reporting lags, cyclical time encodings, and time-to-event features, and macro-state features such as yield-curve slope and VIX-based regimes.

8.5 Cross-cutting feature types and the limits of direct aggregation

Two cross-cutting feature types deserve explicit treatment because they do not fit neatly into a single family:

- **Learned representations:** Latent factors from correlated inputs, such as principal components, autoencoders, and time-series foundation models (TimesFM, Chronos, Moirai). These representations are fitted objects: they are trained inside folds, persist versioned parameters, and log training windows alongside downstream trials. *Chapter 9* covers model-based feature extraction; *Chapter 13* develops the transformer architectures behind foundation-model embeddings.
- **Flows and positioning:** Proxies for crowding and constraints (for example, the Commitment of Traders report; *Chapter 4*), typically used as a **state** that conditions trend, carry, and mean reversion. Positioning proxies can become unstable when definitions, reporting conventions, or sources change; treat them as first-class hypotheses and apply the same discipline to timestamps, reference sets, and failure modes.

For crypto assets, blockchain data provides direct observability of exchange reserve flows, whale wallet movements, stablecoin supply shifts, and protocol-level metrics (TVL, liquidity pool composition). *Chapter 4* covers the data infrastructure and sourcing for these signals. From a feature-engineering perspective, on-chain data represents a positioning family with novel failure modes: addresses can be relabeled, protocols can fork, and definitions (what counts as a "whale") are researcher-imposed. We log the classification logic and version it alongside the features.

The cross-case diagnostic in `case_study_feature_summary` makes the breadth-versus-skill tension concrete: across the nine case studies, feature counts range from 39 to 66, with deliberate per-asset-class specialization, and past-return windows are the one family universal to every case study. Plotting universe size against best in-sample |IC|, with bubble area proportional to the Fundamental Law's IR estimate ($IC \times \sqrt{N}$), shows `us_firm_characteristics` as the dominant outlier with an estimated IR near 4 on its 2,483-stock universe—breadth, not a marginally higher IC, is what separates a thin signal from an investable one.

When direct aggregation is not enough

Every feature in *Section 8.2–8.4* is a deterministic formula applied to a trailing window of observable data. This works when the structure we care about is visible in the raw series: trend direction, deviation from an anchor, relative rank, range. But some structure is hidden:

- **Conditional dynamics.** How quickly does a volatility shock decay? A rolling standard deviation shows the current level; it cannot indicate persistence. A fitted model (GARCH) is required to estimate that.
- **Latent states.** Is the market in a trending or mean-reverting regime? No observable variable answers this directly. A regime model, such as an HMM or Markov-switching model, is required to infer the state probabilities.
- **Cyclical structure.** Is there a weekly pattern in this volume series, or is it noise? A spectral decomposition (for example, an FFT) is required to measure cycle strength.
- **Path geometry.** Two 20-day windows with identical returns but different paths (one smooth, one jagged) may predict different outcomes. A sequential encoding (path signatures) is required to distinguish them.

Chapter 9 discusses model-based features designed to capture such hidden structure.

8.6 Combining features and controlling search

Much of the practical improvement in feature-based strategies does not come from individual features but from combining a signal feature with a state feature. The signal carries the directional view (momentum, carry, mean reversion); the state describes the environment in which the signal operates (volatility regime, liquidity conditions, market breadth).

Three **interaction templates** cover most combinations:

Template	What it does	Example	Effect on strategy
Gating	Trade only when the state is favorable; otherwise, go flat	Trade momentum only when volatility is below its 67th percentile	Changes the active sample—and therefore turnover and capacity
Scaling	Adjust signal strength continuously by state	Divide momentum by realized volatility to get a risk-adjusted signal	Changes position size conditionally on state
Conditional variant	Log "signal in regime" as a separate, versioned feature	Momentum-in-low-vol and momentum-in-high-vol as distinct candidates	Turns the interaction into separately testable hypotheses

Table 8.4: Common interaction patterns

Start with one signal and one state, and vary one template at a time. Record each combination as an explicit trial (see *Section 7.3*) so every interaction is traceable in searched-set accounting.

Not all combinations deserve testing. Prioritize interactions where:

- **The state is economically relevant:** Volatility can condition trend capture; liquidity conditions effective costs.
- **The interaction is asymmetric:** Conditional IC differs meaningfully across state values, rather than a constant rescaling of the average.
- **The state is observable at decision time:** Avoid definitions that depend on contemporaneous information unavailable at execution, or on revised data.

Interaction diagnostics

Because interactions multiply the searched set, evaluate each with three diagnostics (computed within each walk-forward fold, summarized using medians and worst-fold views):

- **Structure:** Conditional IC varies systematically with the state; irregular patterns suggest overfitting or unstable binning.
- **Fold stability:** Conditional effects do not repeatedly flip sign across folds.
- **Real-time robustness:** Noisy, delayed, or revised state estimates reduce transfer from backtest to live, especially for hard gates.

Common interaction patterns

Dividing a signal by a positive state variable yields risk-adjusted variants:

Ratio feature	Formula	Interpretation
Risk-adjusted momentum	momentum/volatility	Risk scaling
Carry-to-vol	carry/implied_vol	Risk-adjusted carry
Momentum-to-spread	momentum/bid-ask spread	Cost-adjusted signal

Table 8.5: Feature interaction examples

Ratio definitions implicitly assume the denominator is strictly positive and meaningfully estimated at decision time. Handle edge cases explicitly: clip near-zero volatility, and set the ratio to zero (or missing) when the denominator is undefined.

Discretize the state into bins (for example, terciles), compute the IC within each bin, and compare ICs across bins. This tests whether information content depends on the state and identifies the direction of the dependence.

Worked example – Momentum × volatility-regime terciles

The `etfs` case study illustrates conditional IC analysis using 126-day momentum as the signal and 42-day realized volatility as the state. Volatility is proxied by SPY to define a market-wide regime.

At each decision time t:

1. Compute cross-sectional 126-day momentum ranks for all ETFs.
2. Compute 42-day realized volatility for SPY and assign t to a volatility tercile using expanding-window percentiles (low: <33rd; medium: 33rd–67th; high: >67th). Expanding-window thresholds avoid look-ahead bias.
3. Compute the IC between momentum rank and 20-day forward return, separately within each volatility tercile.

Results (full sample; HAC-adjusted for serial correlation):

Volatility tercile	Momentum IC	HAC t-statistic	p-value
Low	+0.071	2.8	0.006
Medium	+0.025	1.3	0.21
High	−0.034	−1.1	0.26

Table 8.6: Feature interaction example

Momentum is strongest in low volatility and weakens as volatility rises. The monotonic decay across terciles is the relevant pattern. This motivates a **gating** rule: take the momentum signal only when volatility is not in the top tercile.

Implementation: `06_robustness_sensitivity` partitions SPY's 42-day realized volatility into terciles (expanding-window thresholds) and reports HAC-adjusted IC by regime. The 10.5pp IC swing between low-vol (+0.071) and high-vol (−0.034) regimes is the empirical evidence for the regime-conditioning hypothesis tested in this section. The notebook also runs parameter sweeps over lookback windows and interaction features to test signal stability.

Each tested interaction increases the search set. For example, 5 signals × 3 states × 3 templates yields 45 interactions. Apply the controls from *Section 7.4*: report the number of interactions searched, use Benjamini–Hochberg false discovery rate (FDR) control, and treat "best-in-search" results as exploratory unless confirmed on held-out folds.

Event studies

A complementary diagnostic asks whether a feature-defined event is followed by abnormal returns in the direction implied by the signal. Following MacKinlay (1997), define an event date $\tau = 0$, estimate normal returns over a pre-event estimation window, compute abnormal returns during the event window, and aggregate them into cumulative abnormal returns. In feature research, the "event" is usually not a corporate announcement but a rule-based signal: for example, an ETF momentum breakout, a transition into the top momentum decile, or a volatility regime change. The event definition must use only information available at the time of the decision; otherwise, the event study inherits look-ahead bias.

Formally, estimate a normal-return model on a window that ends before the event window begins, such as a market-adjusted return, market model, or factor model. The abnormal return is:

$$AR_{i,\tau} = R_{i,\tau} - \hat{E}\left(R_{i,\tau} \mid X_\tau\right)$$

where $R_{i,\tau}$ is the realized return for asset i at event time τ, and the conditional expectation is the benchmark return implied by the fitted normal-return model. The cumulative abnormal return over event window $[\tau_1, \tau_2]$ is:

$$CAR_i(\tau_1, \tau_2) = \sum_{\tau=\tau_1}^{\tau_2} AR_{i,\tau}$$

and averaging across events gives the average abnormal return (AAR) or cumulative average abnormal return (CAAR). The key diagnostic is whether the abnormal-return path continues after the event rather than merely reflecting the price movement used to define the breakout. Because feature-generated events often overlap, and because assets share common risk exposures, inference should use HAC or clustered standard errors rather than assuming independent event returns.

Implementation: `07_event_studies` applies this framework to ETF momentum breakouts. The event date is the breakout signal, abnormal returns are measured relative to an explicit benchmark model, and the event window runs from day -3 to day +10. The mean CAR of 1.11% is statistically significant (t=3.28, p=0.001), and CAAR builds from day -3 to day +10 without a pre-event reversal. This pattern supports the hypothesis that the breakout captures continuation rather than a mechanical rebound.

Signal-conditioned analysis reveals an important asymmetry: long momentum signals are validated (CAAR=0.87%, t=3.30), while short signals are not (CAAR=-0.25%, t=-1.31). This asymmetry is consistent with the broader empirical pattern that long and short momentum signals need not be equally reliable after costs, constraints, and market frictions. More importantly, it illustrates the role of event studies as a falsification tool: a candidate feature should not merely produce a significant average effect; it should exhibit the correct event-time shape, withstand reasonable benchmark choices, and behave consistently in the signal direction it claims to capture.

Degrees of freedom discipline

Dense grids over lookbacks, transforms, and interactions create spurious winners and reduce interpretability. Three controls keep feature search disciplined:

- **Budget by family and by role:** Allocate variants within a hypothesis class (for example, momentum signals) separately from state features (for example, volatility, liquidity).
- **One choice at a time by default:** Fix the driver and representation, vary one choice (often the lookback), keep a small set of survivors, then consider a second.
- **Deduplicate within families first:** Cluster by correlation (or rank correlation) computed within folds to remove near-duplicates before modeling, preserving diversity across families.

When search produces many near-equivalent variants, deduplication reduces redundancy before the model stage. Here, "near-equivalent" means features that move so similarly that they contribute little distinct information, while "stability" refers to how consistently a feature performs across validation folds rather than how well it does in a single split:

- **Pairwise dependence:** Within each fold, compute rank correlations ρ over the training window, producing a p × p dependence matrix for p features.
- **Clustering:** Apply hierarchical clustering using distance $1 - |\rho|$, which groups features that are highly similar up to sign. The cut level is a tuning choice rather than a rule; thresholds in the range $|\rho| \approx 0.6$ to 0.8 are common starting points.
- **Representative selection:** Choose one feature per cluster using a transparent rule, such as the highest median IC with low fold-to-fold IC dispersion, simplest construction, or lowest implementation burden. When these criteria conflict, favor stability across folds over a small gain in a single summary metric.

Deduplication reduces redundancy within a family but does not replace model-stage selection or importance analysis. MDI and permutation feature importance can disagree substantially, so the choice of importance method materially affects feature selection outcomes.

Implementation: `05_feature_selection` runs the full pipeline for the `etfs` case study: starting from 57 candidate features, correlation filtering (threshold 0.9) removes 14, IC ranking retains 18 above the significance threshold, and final selection produces 10 features, an 82.5% reduction. The strongest single feature is distance-to-52-week-low (IC=0.076). After BH-FDR correction, four of the 34 features significant at the raw 5% level no longer survive the multiple-testing adjustment. MDI and permutation feature importance agree on only 49% of rankings.

Three implementation choices that change the hypothesis

Three implementation choices change the economic claim, not just the noise level:

- **Residualization:** Removing market or sector components defines a different question and introduces a fitted model that must be handled inside the walk-forward protocol.
- **Winsorization:** Clipping at the 1st/99th versus 5th/95th percentiles changes which observations drive the signal. Fit clipping bounds on training data and apply them to the corresponding validation window.
- **Stationarity–memory trade-off:** First-differencing ($d = 1$) removes long-range dependence; fractional differencing with $d \in (0,1)$ preserves more memory while improving stationarity. A feature with $d = 0.4$ encodes a different hypothesis than one with $d = 1.0$ (see *Section 9.1*). The stationarity–memory trade-off applies across all families in *Section 8.2–8.4*; fractional differencing with a data-driven d is developed in *Section 9.1*.

Operationally, fit any transform with learned parameters on walk-forward training splits and apply it to the corresponding validation splits. When a feature depends on a fitted object (for example, a neutralization model, scaling estimator, or learned representation), log the fitted parameters and the training window to support reproducibility.

8.7 Summary

We turned trading hypotheses into a disciplined feature design process. The three-step filter (horizon alignment, driver hypothesis, role separation) ensures every feature encodes a testable economic claim. The feature families in *Section 8.2* are reusable hypothesis classes, not ad hoc indicators: many named technical indicators are parameterizations of the same underlying claim, and recognizing this prevents indicator sprawl. Within each family, the distinction between meaning-changing choices (reference frame, anchor definition, peer set) and noise-reduction choices (smoothing, shrinkage) determines whether we are testing a new hypothesis or merely smoothing the same one.

Our second theme is combination and control. Signal × state interactions (gating, scaling, conditional variants) are where much of the practical improvement comes from, but they multiply the search space geometrically. The deduplication workflow and one-choice-at-a-time discipline from *Section 8.6* keep the search disciplined, and every interaction enters the trial taxonomy from *Chapter 7* as a distinct hypothesis with its own multiple-testing burden.

The deliverable is a documented, reproducible candidate feature set with clear economic meaning and known failure modes, ready for the triage protocol in *Chapter 7* and the modeling pipeline in *Chapters 11-16*.

Direct aggregation has limits. When the structure we need is hidden (conditional dynamics, latent states, cyclical patterns, path geometry), we must fit a model and extract features from the fitted object. That is the subject of *Chapter 9*, where the point-in-time obligation tightens: a GARCH parameter or HMM state probability depends on an estimation window that must be confined to each walk-forward training fold, versioned, and monitored for drift.

9

Model-Based Feature Extraction

In *Chapter 8*, we built financial features by aggregating and applying deterministic transformations to observed data. This chapter turns to **model-based features**, produced by estimated procedures. Some take the form of structural quantities, such as coefficients, persistence measures, or latent states. Many others are operational outputs, including filtered estimates, innovations, forecasts, conditional variances, regime probabilities, and posterior uncertainty summaries. The common idea is simple: fit a procedure to the training data and use its outputs as features.

These procedures add value in two related ways. Some forecast quantities that matter for downstream prediction, especially volatility and other state variables that condition expected returns. Others do not forecast the target directly, but instead infer hidden structure in the data, such as trend, persistence, break risk, or regime membership. In both cases, the fitted procedure can summarize historical information more effectively with respect to the predictive target than a direct backward-looking formula, yielding features that can be more informative, more stable, or more interpretable than raw transformations alone.

The chapter is organized by extraction method rather than by economic family because a single fitted procedure can generate several distinct feature types. A Kalman filter yields level, trend, innovation, and uncertainty features; a GARCH model yields both conditional-volatility outputs and persistence parameters; a regime model yields probabilities, expected durations, and transition structure. Whatever form the feature takes, the point-in-time requirement remains unchanged. Every estimate, state, forecast, and probability must be generated using only information available at the time of decision, re-estimated within the walk-forward protocol, and versioned alongside the features it produces. After completing this chapter, you will be able to:

- Distinguish direct features from model-based features and judge when a fitted procedure adds useful information.
- Use fitted procedures to extract forecasts, filtered states, residuals, conditional volatility, regime probabilities, and uncertainty summaries as downstream features.
- Design a compact, interpretable set of model-based features from diagnostics, signal transforms, volatility models, uncertainty summaries, and regime models.

- Enforce point-in-time correctness by fitting and selecting models within training windows, using filtered rather than future-informed outputs, and aligning refit cadence and online updates with the walk-forward protocol.
- Transform asset-level temporal outputs into cross-sectional, benchmark-adjusted, pairwise, and universe-level features for multi-asset prediction tasks.
- Distinguish between exploratory time-series methods that are useful for research diagnosis and deployable features that are safe for live, point-in-time use.
- Use uncertainty and regime outputs primarily as conditioning features, and recognize when they should not be treated as stand-alone trading signals.

We begin with diagnostics and stationarity features. *Section 9.2* turns to signal transforms, including Kalman filters, spectral methods, wavelets, and signatures, which expose temporal structure that rolling statistics miss. *Section 9.3* focuses on volatility features, and *Section 9.4* treats uncertainty itself as a feature. *Section 9.5* develops regime features from threshold rules, HMMs, Markov-switching models, and distribution-based clustering. *Section 9.6* shows how to convert these temporal outputs into cross-sectional and panel features.

9.1 Diagnostics and stationarity features

Model-based features often begin as diagnostics. Before fitting a forecasting or state-space model, inspect the series to understand what kind of temporal structure it contains, what transformations it may require, and which outputs may themselves be useful downstream features. In this section, diagnostics play both roles. They guide preprocessing decisions and produce quantities that can be used directly as features. A rolling stationarity statistic can serve as a regime indicator; a detected break date can become a conditioning variable; a persistence estimate can summarize how quickly shocks decay.

A practical workflow begins with a small set of **visual diagnostics**. A plot of the series itself shows whether the level drifts over time, whether volatility changes across subsamples, and whether large moves cluster. Autocorrelation plots summarize lag dependence:

- The **autocorrelation function** (ACF) shows how strongly current values move with past values at different lag lengths
- The **partial autocorrelation function** (PACF) shows the incremental contribution of each lag after controlling for shorter lags
- A **Q-Q plot** compares the empirical distribution with a reference distribution, typically the normal, and quickly reveals skewness, fat tails, and outliers

These plots do not prove stationarity or non-stationarity, but they indicate which questions to ask next and which formal tests are worth running.

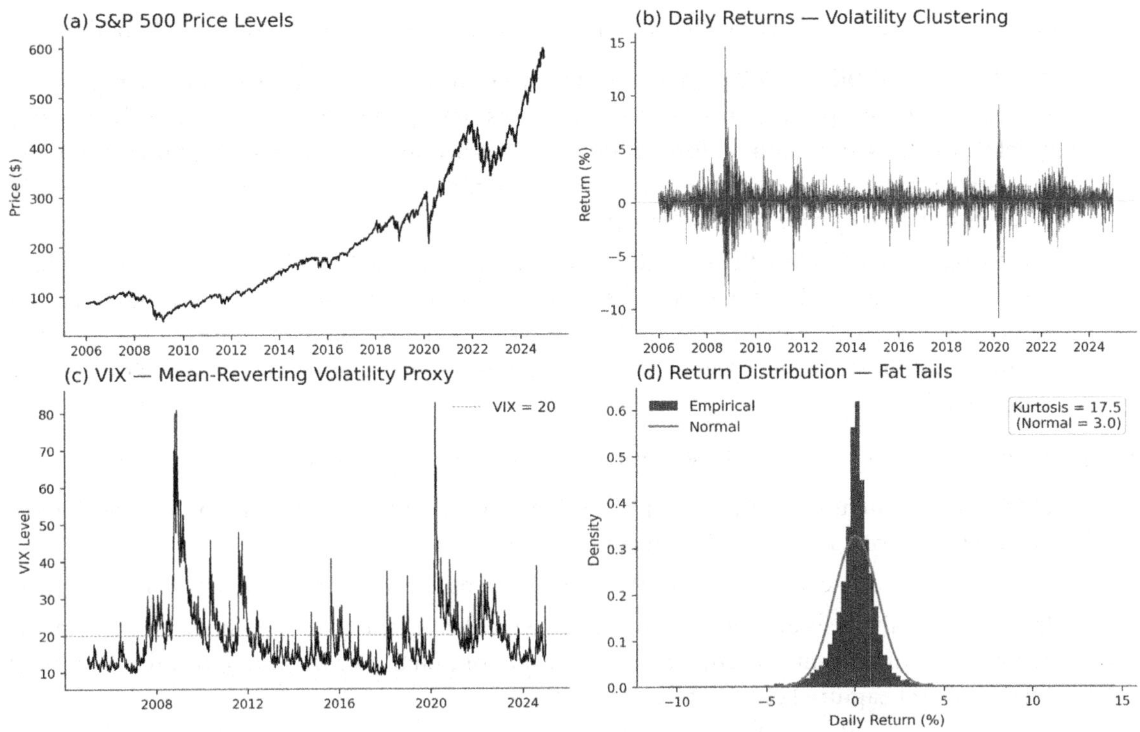

Figure 9.1: A set of four graphs, demonstrating different ways of looking at the data distribution

Figure 9.1 illustrates this first pass for S&P 500 data. The level series trends and is therefore an obvious candidate for non-stationarity. Returns fluctuate around a more stable mean but show volatility clustering. VIX behaves more like a persistent, mean-reverting state variable than a drifting price series. The return distribution departs visibly from normality, especially in the tails. Together, these views suggest three follow-up questions. Is the series stationary? Has it changed regime? If it is non-stationary, what is the least destructive transformation that makes it usable?

Implementation: See `01_visual_diagnostics` for the full workflow, including visual inspection, stationarity tests, autocorrelation diagnostics, distribution diagnostics, and rolling stationarity features.

Stationarity tests as features

Many time series methods assume that the object being modeled has reasonably stable statistical properties over time. In the simplest case, this means that the mean, variance, and dependence structure do not drift in ways the model cannot absorb. Prices often violate this requirement because shocks to the level can persist for long periods. Returns, spreads, volatility measures, and some alternative data series are more likely to exhibit approximate stationarity, though this varies across assets, horizons, and regimes.

Two complementary tests are especially useful because they begin from opposite null hypotheses:

1. The **Augmented Dickey-Fuller** (**ADF**) test takes a **unit root** as its null hypothesis. In practical terms, a unit root means that shocks to the series have persistent effects rather than fading quickly, which is one common form of non-stationarity. Rejection of the ADF null is therefore evidence against a unit root and, under the chosen deterministic specification, evidence in favor of stationarity or trend-stationarity.
2. The **Kwiatkowski-Phillips-Schmidt-Shin** (**KPSS**) test reverses the null. Depending on the specification, it tests whether the series is stationary around a constant level or around a deterministic trend. Rejecting the KPSS null is therefore evidence against that form of stationarity. Running both tests reduces the asymmetry that arises when inference depends on a single null hypothesis.

The **joint interpretation** is useful but should not be treated mechanically:

- If ADF rejects the unit-root null and KPSS does not reject the stationarity null, the evidence favors stationarity under the chosen specifications
- If ADF does not reject the null and KPSS rejects the null, the evidence favors non-stationarity
- If both reject, the tests are sending conflicting signals: the series may contain a deterministic trend, structural breaks, nonlinear mean reversion, changing volatility, or other forms of instability not captured cleanly by either test
- If neither rejects, the result is best treated as inconclusive, often because the window is short, the process is highly persistent, or the tests have limited power

For feature engineering, the test outputs matter as much as the final label. The ADF and KPSS statistics, along with their p-values, can be tracked over rolling windows:

- An ADF statistic moving upward toward zero, or an ADF p-value rising, suggests weaker evidence against a unit root
- A rising KPSS statistic or a declining p-value suggests weaker evidence for stationarity

These diagnostics are therefore not just gatekeepers for preprocessing. They are model-based summaries of persistence and regime stability that can be used as lagged inputs to downstream models.

In **cross-sectional settings**, these tests are often most informative when applied to spreads, valuation ratios, volatility proxies, residualized returns, and slowly evolving firm characteristics rather than to raw daily equity returns. Returns are usually closer to stationary than prices because differencing removes much of the persistence in levels, but volatility clustering, changing liquidity, and regime shifts can still violate strict stationarity. The feature is therefore not simply "stationary versus non-stationary" but a time-varying measure of how stable the underlying process appears at the time of decision.

Implementation: `01_visual_diagnostics` shows rolling ADF and KPSS computation, joint interpretation, and examples of time-varying stationarity features.

Structural break features

A series can fail a stationarity test for different reasons. It may drift continuously, as prices often do, or it may be mostly stable but interrupted by one or more regime changes. Break diagnostics focus on the second case.

The **Zivot-Andrews** test (Zivot and Andrews, 1992) extends the unit-root framework by allowing one break to be chosen endogenously from the data. It is useful when a single major discontinuity is plausible, and a genuine unit root must be distinguished from a broken but otherwise stable process. For longer samples, multiple breaks are often more realistic. In that setting, **Bai-Perron** (Bai and Perron, 1998) segmentation is more appropriate because it identifies several candidate break dates rather than forcing the sample into a single break or none at all.

For online monitoring, the problem is different. The goal is not to explain the full sample retrospectively, but to detect instability as it develops. **CUSUM** statistics accumulate deviations from a target level and trigger when sustained drift becomes too large to ignore. This makes them useful monitoring features even when the exact break date will only be clear in hindsight.

A complementary approach treats break detection as a supervised classification problem. Instead of relying on a single statistic, combine weak signals from several sources, such as shifts in location, scale, dependence, or distributional shape, and let the classifier aggregate them. This approach is often more effective when labeled break examples are available and when no single classical test is decisive across all regimes.

As with stationarity tests, the outputs become features. Break dates, time since the most recent break, pre- and post-break means, CUSUM statistics, and classifier probabilities can all be used as conditioning information for later models. A break detector is therefore both a diagnostic tool and a feature generator.

Implementation: `02_structural_breaks` shows classical break tests, online monitoring, and the classification-based break-detection pipeline.

Fractional differencing features

When diagnostics indicate non-stationarity, the standard response is **differencing**. Ordinary first differencing applies $(1-L)x_t = x_t - x_{t-1}$, which is effective but blunt because it removes the low-frequency component in one step. Fractional differencing generalizes this operator by allowing the differencing order to be real:

$$(1-L)^d x_t = \sum_{k=0}^{\infty} \omega_k \, x_{t-k}, \qquad \omega_0 = 1, \qquad \omega_k = -\omega_{k-1}\frac{d-k+1}{k} = (-1)^k \binom{d}{k}$$

For $0 < d < 1$, the filter applies a slowly decaying sequence of lag weights, so persistence is attenuated more gradually than under ordinary first differencing. The transformed series is therefore not simply "between levels and returns" in an informal sense; it occupies the continuum between no differencing and first differencing defined by the fractional integration order.

In the **fractional ARIMA** (**ARFIMA**) literature, this same operator allows the integration parameter to be non-integer. For the stationary long-memory case, typically $0 < d < 0.5$, autocorrelations decay hyperbolically rather than at the exponential rate associated with short-memory ARMA models (Granger and Joyeux, 1980; Hosking, 1981).

In practice, fractional differencing is implemented with a finite lookback rather than the full infinite sequence of weights. The transform combines the current observation with past values whose weights decay with lag; weights beyond a truncation threshold or fixed maximum lookback are dropped. Two boundary conventions then differ on what to do at the start of the sample:

- A **full-window** implementation treats the first observations as unavailable until the required lookback period has accumulated, resulting in a warmup period and a corresponding validity mask. This is the convention used by fixed-width fractional differencing implementations inspired by López de Prado.
- A **boundary-partial** implementation, such as the truncated-weights approach used in `ml4t.engineer.features.fdiff.ffdiff`, applies whatever weights are available near the start of the sample. This preserves the row count but means that early observations are produced by a shorter effective filter than later observations.

Either convention is defensible, but the choice is part of the feature definition. Downstream models should know which observations rely on a partial filter and how many observations would be lost under the corresponding full-window convention.

That mask, and the associated loss of observations, are part of the feature definition. Changing d changes how slowly the weights decay, and changing the truncation rule changes how much history must be retained. Both, therefore, affect two things at once: how much persistence remains in the transformed series, and how many observations are usable for modeling.

This also clarifies what it means to choose or estimate d. The question is not whether fractional differencing is mathematically elegant, but how much persistence must be removed to obtain a usable representation of the series.

A **practical workflow**:

1. Evaluates a bounded grid of d values over the training window.
2. Computes a stationarity diagnostic, such as the ADF statistic, for each transformed series.
3. Assesses how much correlation with the original series is retained.

The target is usually the smallest d that yields an acceptable stationarity diagnostic while preserving as much memory as possible, rather than a globally "optimal" value computed on the full sample.

Implementation: `03_fractional_differencing` illustrates fixed-width fractional differencing, bounded d-grids, walk-forward-safe d-selection, ADF-based diagnostics, and validity-mask handling.

When it works well, fractional differencing yields a more stable representation than raw levels without paying the full information cost of ordinary first differencing. The next section moves from preprocessing transforms to a richer class of signal decompositions—Kalman filters, spectral methods, wavelets, and path signatures—that expose latent structure rolling statistics cannot reach.

9.2 Transforming signals to uncover hidden structure

Signal transforms can be grouped by the kind of **hidden structure** they recover: latent state, recurring frequency, time scale, and path shape. Rolling statistics summarize what happened over a window, but they compress away much of the structure that may matter for prediction. A moving average captures the average level, and rolling volatility captures dispersion, but neither tells us whether the path was smooth or jagged, whether fluctuations occurred early or late in the window, or whether a regular cycle was present beneath the noise. Signal transforms address this limitation by mapping the raw series into a new representation and then extracting features from it.

The methods in this section serve different purposes, but they share the same logic:

- **Kalman filters** summarize the hidden state that may underlie noisy observations
- **Spectral methods** summarize how variation is distributed across frequencies
- **Wavelets separate** the series into components at different scales
- **Path signatures** summarize the ordered geometry of a path rather than just its endpoints or moments

In each case, the goal is to convert raw sequential data into summaries that may be more informative than simple rolling statistics.

Kalman filter features

A simple moving average uses a fixed window and fixed weights. That makes it easy to interpret, but also rigid. In a strong trend, it may react too slowly, while in a noisy sideways market, it may react too quickly. A Kalman filter takes a different approach. Instead of mechanically averaging past observations, it maintains a running estimate of an underlying latent state and updates it each time a new observation arrives. Unlike an exponential moving average or a rolling linear trend regression, a Kalman filter does not commit to a fixed lookback period; its gain **adapts to the estimated signal-to-noise ratio.**

The key idea is to distinguish between what we observe and what we are trying to infer. The observed series may be a price, return, spread, or other market variable. The latent state is the smoother or more persistent object we believe generated those observations, such as an underlying level and trend. In a **state-space model**, the hidden state evolves over time, and the observed series is treated as a noisy measurement of that state.

In a local linear trend model, the state contains both a level and a slope. The filter alternates between two steps:

1. In the **predict** step, it projects the state forward using the model's transition rule.
2. In the **update** step, it revises that projection using the new observation.

The result is a feature extraction procedure that balances persistence against surprise. When the series behaves smoothly relative to the assumed noise level, the estimated state moves steadily. When observations become erratic, the filter becomes more cautious.

Originally developed for navigation and control (Kalman, 1960), the model can be written as:

$$x_t = Fx_{t-1} + w_t, \qquad y_t = Hx_t + v_t$$

where x_t is the hidden state, y_t is the observed value, F governs how the state evolves, and w_t and v_t represent process and observation noise.

This representation yields several useful features:

- The **Kalman level** is the filtered estimate of the underlying level and serves as an adaptive trend anchor
- The **Kalman trend** is the slope component of the state and serves as a momentum feature without requiring a fixed lookback
- The **innovation** is the prediction error, that is, the gap between what the filter expected and what it observed; it is a natural surprise variable
- The **state uncertainty** is the estimated variance of the state and measures how confident the filter currently is in its own estimate

These outputs often carry more information than a conventional moving-average crossover because they distinguish direction, surprise, and confidence rather than collapsing everything into a single smoothed line. The same state-space logic also extends naturally from single-series trend extraction to dynamic hedge-ratio estimation, where coefficients such as β_t are allowed to evolve over time rather than being treated as fixed constants.

For the `etfs` case study, applying a local-linear-trend Kalman filter to daily returns produces a trend feature that is more stable than 20-day momentum during choppy markets (fewer whipsaws) and comparably responsive during sustained trends.

On SPY, the Kalman slope achieves an information coefficient of -0.16 with 5-day forward returns, roughly nine times stronger than a 20-day rolling OLS slope (-0.02); both are negative, consistent with short-term mean reversion, but the adaptive filter separates signal from noise far more effectively. The innovation feature shows elevated values around earnings seasons and macro releases—periods when the filter's smooth model is repeatedly surprised, which can condition the triage of other signals.

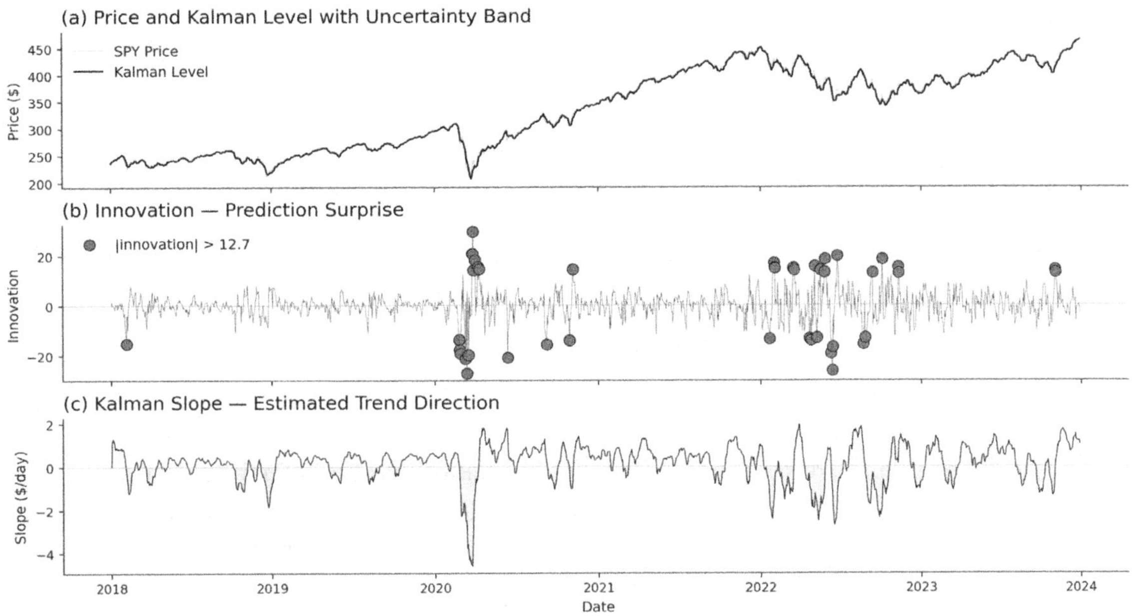

Figure 9.2: Kalman filter smoothing

> **Implementation:** `04_kalman_filter` shows Kalman filter feature extraction, including MLE-based noise covariance estimation, walk-forward refitting, and a dynamic hedge-ratio application for pairs trading.

Spectral features

Kalman filters work in the time domain: they update estimates one observation at a time. Spectral methods answer a different question. Instead of asking how the series evolved day by day, they ask whether part of the variation is organized around **recurring cycles**. A weekly trading rhythm, a monthly rebalance effect, or a quarterly earnings pattern may be difficult to see directly in the raw series but may become more visible when the series is decomposed by frequency.

A **frequency** is simply a rate of repetition, measured in cycles per unit time. Its reciprocal is the **period**. A weekly cycle in daily data has a period of 5 and a frequency of 1/5; a monthly cycle has a period of about 21 and a frequency of 1/21. The **discrete Fourier transform** converts a finite time series into a set of sinusoidal components at different frequencies. The **fast Fourier transform** (**FFT**) is the standard algorithm used to compute that transform efficiently. The resulting **power spectrum** shows how much of the series' variance is associated with each frequency band.

The basic transform is:

$$X_k = \sum_{t=0}^{N-1} x_t \, e^{-2\pi ikt/N}$$

but for feature engineering, the interpretation matters more than the formula. A large value of $|X_k|^2$ at a weekly frequency means that the series contains a strong weekly component; a diffuse spectrum means that no single frequency dominates. The spectrum, therefore, summarizes how structured or noisy the series appears when viewed through the lens of periodic repetition.

Several features follow directly from this representation:

- **Spectral energy** measures total power, or power in a target band, and captures the strength of cyclical structure.
- The **dominant period** is the period associated with the largest peak in the rolling spectrum.
- **Spectral entropy** measures how concentrated or diffuse the normalized power spectrum is: low entropy implies a small number of strong periodic components, while high entropy implies a flatter, more noise-like distribution of energy.
- The **low-frequency ratio** measures the fraction of energy below a chosen cutoff, such as (1/21), and provides a compact indicator of whether variation is concentrated in slower trend-like components or faster noisy ones.

These features must be computed causally. At time t, the transform should use only a trailing window such as $[t - W, t]$, not the full sample. Window length matters because frequency resolution depends on it: a quarterly cycle cannot be resolved well in a very short window. In practice, these features are often built on returns or other approximately stationary inputs, and several window lengths are useful; for example, 21-, 63-, and 126-day windows capture different cycles in daily data.

Spectral features complement the deterministic calendar features from *Chapter 8*. Calendar encodings impose known cycles through sine and cosine pairs. Spectral features ask whether a cycle is actually present in the data and whether its strength is rising, stable, or fading. That distinction matters whenever cyclical structure is itself time-varying.

Implementation: See `05_spectral_features` for rolling FFT feature extraction, Welch PSD estimation, and a time-frequency heatmap that tracks spectral regime shifts.

Wavelet features

Fourier methods identify which frequencies are present, but they are much less effective at telling us when those frequencies were active. Wavelets address that limitation by providing a **multi-resolution** representation of the series. A wavelet decomposition separates the series into coarse components that capture slower variation and finer components that capture short-lived detail, while retaining temporal localization. The detail bands provide a rough horizon map, from very short 2- to 4-day fluctuations through 32- to 64-day components, while the approximation term captures the slower trend.

This makes wavelets useful for structures that are localized in time, such as a volatility burst that lasts only a few days or a cycle that appears only during a particular regime. In contrast to the Fourier transform, which is naturally global, the wavelet transform can preserve both scale and timing.

In feature engineering, wavelets are especially helpful for **horizon discovery**. They can show whether the informative structure in a series lives mainly at very short horizons, intermediate horizons, or slower trend-like scales. That information can then guide the design of simpler causal features built on trailing windows, fitted filters, or band-limited transforms.

A **practical caution** is important here. Standard wavelet decompositions are often not causal in their usual offline form because coefficients at time t may depend on observations on both sides of t. That makes them well-suited to exploratory analysis and offline diagnostics, but not automatically safe for live production pipelines. When wavelets reveal that a particular scale is informative, the usual next step is to build a causal proxy at that horizon rather than to deploy the raw offline coefficients directly.

Wavelets are therefore best viewed as a bridge between raw data and deployable features. They help answer the question, "At what horizons does the relevant structure live?"

Implementation: See `05_spectral_features` for wavelet multi-resolution decomposition as a research diagnostic, including scale-variance analysis and the translation of wavelet insights into causal rolling-window proxies.

Path signature features

Spectral methods summarize cycles, and wavelets summarize variation by scale. Path signatures address a different problem: they summarize **path shape**. Two windows can have the same start, end, and realized volatility, yet differ materially in how the path got there. A steady rise followed by a sharp reversal is not the same pattern as an early selloff followed by a gradual recovery. Traditional lag features often treat those two paths as more similar than they really are because they compress the window into endpoint and dispersion summaries. Signatures are designed to preserve more of the ordered geometry.

A path signature, rooted in **rough path theory** (see Chevyrev et al., 2016, for an accessible introduction), is a collection of ordered integrals that summarize how a path evolves through time:

- At *depth-1*, the signature records total displacement, which is essentially net change
- At *depth-2*, it begins to capture interactions between coordinates, including lead-lag structure
- Higher depths capture increasingly fine geometry, but the number of terms grows rapidly

For feature engineering, the main intuition is that signatures preserve sequence information that ordinary lag stacks often discard.

For financial series, **time augmentation** is especially important. Without an explicit time coordinate, two paths with the same geometric trace but different ordering may look too similar at low depth. By adding a monotone time coordinate, the signature can distinguish "rose early, then faded" from "fell early, then recovered." This is one reason signatures can be useful when the order itself contains a signal.

A second practical distinction is between full signatures and **log-signatures**. The full signature contains algebraic redundancy. The log-signature is a more compact representation that removes much of that redundancy while preserving the expressive information needed for prediction tasks. In practice, low-depth log-signatures are often the most sensible starting point because they balance expressiveness against dimensionality.

Path signatures are **not a general replacement for simpler features**. They are most useful when path shape genuinely matters, when ordering contains signal beyond endpoint summaries, or when we want a compact representation of a multi-dimensional path. In those settings, they complement standard return, volatility, and momentum features rather than displacing them. For most daily applications, depth-2 log-signatures are the sensible starting point; higher depths quickly increase dimensionality and are most defensible when path shape is central to the problem.

The same general principle will reappear in later chapters in learned form. Temporal convolutional networks, recurrent models, and transformer encoders also transform raw sequences into richer internal representations and then expose hidden states, embeddings, or forecasts as features.

Implementation: See `06_path_signatures` for the mathematical formulation (iterated integrals, log-signatures, time augmentation), computation using the `esig` library, and a head-to-head comparison against traditional lag features.

With latent state, frequency, scale, and path structure now available as features, the next section turns to volatility—the single most predictable property of financial time series—and shows how fitted models such as GARCH, EGARCH, HAR, and rough-volatility estimators convert that predictability into production features.

9.3 Volatility Features

Chapter 8 introduced direct volatility measures built from observed prices, including close-to-close realized volatility and range-based estimators such as Parkinson (1980), Garman and Klass (1980), and Yang and Zhang (2000). Those measures efficiently summarize price variation, but they remain backward-looking summaries. This section turns to fitted volatility models and treats their outputs as features. The aim is not to replace the direct measures from *Chapter 8*, but to model how volatility evolves through time and to extract point-in-time safe summaries from that fitted dynamics.

Fitted volatility models provide three kinds of information that direct aggregation does not:

- They produce **conditional volatility** estimates that update as new shocks arrive
- Some models separate short-, medium-, and long-horizon contributions to current volatility
- They expose parameters that describe persistence and asymmetry, which are often informative in their own right

Throughout this section, the model is the feature extractor. Conditional variance paths, persistence measures, leverage parameters, and horizon-specific components are incorporated into later machine learning pipelines alongside the direct features from *Chapter 8*.

Autoregressive integrated moving average features

Autoregressive integrated moving average (**ARIMA**) plays a supporting role in this section. Its main use is to remove simple linear structure from a series before volatility modeling or to generate fitted features for ancillary series that are more predictable than daily returns. In practice, residuals are often the most useful output because they provide a de-meaned or de-trended input for later volatility models. For series such as realized volatility, bid-ask spreads, funding rates, or futures basis, the one-step forecast can also be used directly as a feature. For liquid daily returns, however, low-order ARIMA models usually add little as standalone predictors, so ARIMA belongs here mainly as a preprocessing and auxiliary-feature tool.

This distinction matters. For many liquid return series, the direct predictive value of a low-order ARIMA mean equation is modest at best. In those cases, the residual is usually more useful than the forecast because it removes whatever linear dependence is present before the conditional variance model is fit. For series with a clearer autoregressive structure, the fitted ARIMA model can generate two practical features:

- The residual, which measures deviation from the model's expected path
- The one-step forecast, which provides a model-based estimate of the next period's level

Order selection should remain conservative. For stationary inputs, low-order models such as ARIMA(1,0,1) or ARIMA(2,0,1) are usually sufficient; for trending inputs, differencing may be required. Automated selection by information criteria can be useful, but any search over orders must be repeated inside each walk-forward training window. Otherwise, the lag structure itself is chosen with knowledge of later data. In this section, the key outputs are therefore `arima_residual` and, where the series supports it, `arima_forecast`.

> **Implementation:** See `07_arima_features` for ARIMA order selection, residual extraction, and walk-forward evaluation.

Generalized autoregressive conditional heteroskedasticity features

The standard workhorse is the **generalized autoregressive conditional heteroskedasticity** (**GARCH**) model, introduced by Engle (1982) for the ARCH case and generalized by Bollerslev (1986). In a GARCH(1,1) specification, today's conditional variance depends on a constant term, yesterday's squared innovation, and yesterday's conditional variance:

$$\sigma_t^2 = \omega + \alpha\epsilon_{t-1}^2 + \beta\sigma_{t-1}^2$$

For feature engineering, the model matters less as a forecasting object than as a structured decomposition of volatility dynamics. The fitted conditional standard deviation, often stored as `cond_vol`, is the central output. It is a model-based estimate of the volatility state at time t and is often more responsive than a fixed-window realized-volatility estimate because it updates recursively as new shocks arrive.

- The coefficient α summarizes how strongly volatility reacts to recent shocks; this is the natural `shock_impact` feature
- The coefficient β summarizes persistence in the volatility process and becomes a `vol_persistence` feature

Their sum, $\alpha + \beta$, is especially useful because it captures how slowly a volatility shock decays. When $\alpha + \beta$ is close to one, volatility is highly persistent.

That persistence can be translated into a more intuitive quantity. In a stationary GARCH model, the approximate half-life of a volatility shock is $log(0.5)/log(\alpha + \beta)$. For SPY, a GARCH(1,1) fit yields $\alpha \approx 0.17$ and $\beta \approx 0.80$, giving $\alpha + \beta = 0.97$ and an implied half-life of about 23 trading days. This helps explain why volatility models often contribute useful features even when mean-return models do not: volatility clusters, and that clustering can be summarized parsimoniously.

The model also implies a long-run variance level:

$$\frac{\omega}{1 - \alpha - \beta}$$

which can be used as a `long_run_vol` feature when the fit is covariance-stationary. That restriction matters. If $\alpha + \beta \geq 1$, the model behaves like an **integrated GARCH** (**IGARCH**) process and does not imply a finite unconditional variance. In that case, the long-run variance should not be interpreted as a valid feature. In practice, it is safer either to constrain estimation to stationary fits or to explicitly flag nonstationary estimates.

Implementation: See `08_garch_volatility` for GARCH estimation, ARCH-effect testing, and conditional volatility extraction.

Asymmetric volatility – Exponential GARCH features

Standard GARCH treats positive and negative shocks symmetrically because it depends on squared innovations. Financial markets often do not behave that way. In many equity markets, negative returns are followed by larger increases in volatility than positive returns of the same magnitude.

The **exponential GARCH** (**EGARCH**) model captures this asymmetry by modeling log variance:

$$log(\sigma_t^2) = \omega + \alpha\frac{|\epsilon_{t-1}|}{\sigma_{t-1}} + \gamma\frac{\epsilon_{t-1}}{\sigma_{t-1}} + \beta log(\sigma_{t-1}^2)$$

The asymmetry enters through γ. When γ is negative, negative shocks raise future volatility more than positive shocks do (Nelson, 1991). That parameter is the natural `leverage_effect` feature. Its sign and magnitude summarize whether the asset exhibits the familiar equity-style leverage pattern and how strong that pattern is in the current estimation window.

This is often more useful as a conditioning variable than as a forecast on its own. A strongly negative leverage parameter indicates that downside shocks have disproportionate consequences for the volatility state. That can matter for risk controls, for feature interactions with momentum or carry signals, and for interpreting whether a recent increase in volatility reflects generic turbulence or specifically downside stress.

An alternative is the **Glosten-Jagannathan-Runkle GARCH (GJR-GARCH)** model (Glosten et al., 1993), which introduces asymmetry through an indicator for negative shocks rather than through the EGARCH log-variance form. For feature extraction, the two models serve a similar purpose: they add a parameter that distinguishes symmetric persistence from downside-sensitive persistence. The choice between them is usually empirical.

Implementation: See `08_garch_volatility` for GARCH, EGARCH, and GJR-GARCH estimation and comparison.

Heterogeneous autoregressive volatility features

The **Heterogeneous Autoregressive (HAR) model** (Corsi, 2009) captures daily volatility persistence across different horizons. A standard specification is:

$$RV_{t+1}^{(d)} = c + \beta_d RV_t^{(d)} + \beta_w RV_t^{(w)} + \beta_m RV_t^{(m)} + \epsilon_{t+1}$$

where $RV_t^{(d)}$, $RV_t^{(w)}$, and $RV_t^{(m)}$ denote daily, weekly, and monthly averages of **realized volatility (RV)**.

The horizon-specific volatility measures are inputs of the kind introduced in *Chapter 8*. What HAR adds is a fitted layer on top of them. The coefficients β_d, β_w, and β_m measure how strongly short-, medium-, and longer-horizon volatility contribute to the next day's volatility forecast. A larger monthly coefficient indicates more persistent volatility conditions, whereas a larger daily coefficient indicates greater sensitivity to recent shocks.

HAR is naturally specified on a daily realized-volatility series, ideally constructed from intraday returns. When only daily open-high-low-close-volume data are available, range-based estimators such as Garman-Klass or Yang-Zhang can serve as practical proxies. The model remains the same; only the volatility input changes.

On SPY, the weekly component dominates ($\beta_w \approx 0.43$), consistent with institutional-frequency dynamics driving index volatility. In an out-of-sample comparison, HAR achieves roughly half the RMSE of GARCH (0.061 compared to 0.111), confirming that the multi-horizon decomposition captures persistence structure that a single-lag recursion misses.

Implementation: See `09_har_rough_volatility` for HAR estimation, rolling coefficient tracking, and comparison with GARCH.

Re-estimation cadence and online updates

Volatility features are only useful if they reflect the current volatility environment. That requires two separate decisions: how often to re-estimate model parameters, and how to update features between refits.

The **refit cadence** should match the stability of the parameters and the model's cost:

- GARCH parameters often move slowly enough that weekly or monthly re-estimation is sufficient.
- EGARCH asymmetry parameters usually do not need to be refitted daily either.
- HAR coefficients can be somewhat more regime-sensitive because they summarize changing horizon contributions, but they are still typically re-estimated on a rolling schedule rather than every day.

By contrast, **stochastic volatility (SV)** (see *Chapter 5*) models estimated via **Markov chain Monte Carlo (MCMC)** are usually computationally expensive enough that monthly, or even less frequent, full re-estimation is more realistic.

Between refits, however, many features can still be updated online. In GARCH, the conditional variance recursion updates daily using fixed parameter estimates. In HAR, the daily, weekly, and monthly realized-volatility inputs update as new realized-volatility observations arrive. In stochastic-volatility settings, filtering updates can refresh latent-state estimates without rerunning the full posterior.

For large panels, the practical workflow matters as much as the choice of model. A common approach is to re-estimate parameters overnight across the universe and update the recursive features during the next trading day. Where even that is too expensive, an exponential-smoothing approximation can be a reasonable operational substitute, though at the cost of a less interpretable parameterization. Marra (2023) compares these estimators in practice, and Moreira and Muir (2017) show that even simple volatility-managed strategies improve Sharpe ratios across asset classes.

Rough volatility and the Hurst exponent

GARCH and HAR describe persistence well, but they impose relatively smooth volatility dynamics. Rough-volatility methods start from a different empirical observation: volatility is persistent in level, yet the changes in volatility can be much more irregular than standard diffusion models imply. In that sense, volatility can be persistent and rough at the same time.

A compact way to summarize this behavior is the **Hurst exponent**, H. In broad terms:

- $H = 0.5$ corresponds to Brownian scaling
- $H > 0.5$ indicates persistence in increments
- $H < 0.5$ indicates anti-persistence in increments

For log-volatility, Gatheral et al. (2014) documented Hurst exponents around $H \approx 0.1$ for equity indices—well below 0.5—suggesting that volatility shocks are bursty and mean-revert in their increments more quickly than a smooth Brownian specification would imply. The SPY data confirm this pattern: returns show $H \approx 0.5$ (consistent with a random walk), while log-volatility increments give H between 0.12 and 0.23 depending on the estimator—squarely in the rough regime.

For feature engineering, the Hurst exponent is best treated as a **slow-regime descriptor** rather than as a high-frequency signal. A rolling estimate based on log-volatility can indicate whether the current environment is smoother or rougher than usual. When the estimate falls well below 0.5, standard volatility recursions may understate how abruptly volatility can spike and then decay. This does not invalidate GARCH-style features, but it does change how they should be interpreted.

These estimates are noisy, so they should be updated over relatively long windows and interpreted with caution. A 252-day rolling window, refreshed weekly, is often more useful than daily re-estimation. Large one-day moves in the estimate usually reflect estimation noise rather than a genuine structural break. If the Hurst exponent is used on return series rather than on log-volatility, it should be interpreted even more cautiously.

Implementation: See `09_har_rough_volatility` for rescaled-range and detrended-fluctuation-analysis implementations, rolling Hurst estimation, and cross-asset roughness analysis.

This section treated volatility models as feature generators: ARIMA residuals for prewhitening, GARCH/EGARCH estimates for conditional variance and asymmetry, HAR components for horizon-specific structure, and Hurst-based measures for roughness. The next section turns from volatility itself to uncertainty about fitted states and forecasts.

9.4 Uncertainty features

Model-based features need not stop at point estimates. A fitted procedure also tells us how certain it is about the current state or the next forecast. That uncertainty can be informative in its own right. A narrow posterior or prediction interval indicates a stable estimate; a wide one indicates that the model sees several plausible outcomes. In trading applications, these uncertainty summaries can help condition signal strength, exposure, risk buffers, and the interpretation of other features.

Two distinctions matter:

- First, **uncertainty about a latent state is not the same as uncertainty about a forecast.** A stochastic-volatility model can be uncertain about the current volatility state even before we ask it to predict the next period. An ARIMA model can be relatively certain about the current level of a series while remaining uncertain about its next-step forecast.
- Second, **uncertainty can come from different estimation traditions. Bayesian methods** produce posterior distributions directly, whereas **frequentist models** often provide forecast standard errors and prediction intervals.

For feature engineering, both can be useful.

The uncertainty-as-feature principle

Once a fitted model produces a distribution rather than a single value, several additional features become available. Common examples include:

- Posterior standard deviations
- Credible interval widths (the Bayesian version of the frequentist confidence interval)
- Tail probabilities
- Forecast standard errors
- Prediction interval widths

These quantities do not replace the underlying point estimate. They complement it by describing how reliable that estimate appears at decision time.

This perspective is especially useful when two observations share the same point forecast but differ in uncertainty. A volatility forecast of 20 % with a narrow interval carries a different operational meaning from the same 20% forecast with a wide interval. The first suggests a relatively well-identified state; the second suggests that the model sees materially more ambiguity. The uncertainty summary can therefore serve as a conditioning feature even when the central estimate itself is already included elsewhere in the model.

Implementation: See `10_uncertainty_features` for posterior uncertainty from a stochastic-volatility model and forecast uncertainty from ARIMA applied to log realized volatility.

Stochastic volatility features

GARCH models treat conditional volatility as a deterministic recursion once the parameters and past data are given. Stochastic-volatility (SV) models (Taylor, 1982) take a different view. They treat volatility itself as a latent process that evolves with its own shock term, so the current **volatility state is not observed directly** but inferred from the data. Estimation, therefore, yields a distribution over the latent state rather than only a single filtered path.

That distribution produces several useful features:

- The posterior mean of current volatility is the central state estimate
- The posterior standard deviation and the credible interval width quantify the uncertainty of the estimate
- A parameter governing the innovation variance of the log-volatility process summarizes volatility of volatility, and the persistence parameter summarizes how slowly volatility states decay

Together, these quantities distinguish three cases that a single volatility estimate would conflate: volatility is low and well identified; volatility is high and well identified; or volatility is high but poorly identified.

For downstream models, uncertainty about volatility often matters most when it rises independently of the volatility level itself. A large posterior standard deviation means the model is not only detecting elevated risk but is also less certain about where that risk state actually sits. That can be a stronger warning signal than high volatility alone.

Point-in-time handling is critical. For feature extraction, use filtered posteriors rather than smoothed full-sample state estimates that borrow information from the future. In practice, stochastic-volatility models are usually re-estimated less frequently than simpler volatility models because posterior sampling is expensive.

> **Implementation:** `10_uncertainty_features` fits a Student-t stochastic-volatility model in a walk-forward setting, extracts the filtered final-state posterior at each refit, and carries those features forward between refits.

ARIMA forecast uncertainty features

ARIMA models produce more than fitted values and residuals. They also produce forecast distributions that can be used as features to capture the model's confidence in the next step. For volatility-like series, this is often more useful than applying ARIMA directly to returns, because realized volatility, spreads, funding rates, and similar ancillary series tend to have clearer serial structure.

When the target is strictly positive, such as realized volatility, it is often preferable to model log volatility rather than the raw level. The log transform stabilizes scale and avoids negative back-transformed forecasts. It also yields prediction intervals on the original scale that are asymmetric, which is often more realistic for volatility because the downside is bounded near zero, while upside spikes can be large.

Three uncertainty features are especially practical:

- The forecast standard error summarizes uncertainty on the modeled scale
- The prediction-interval width summarizes uncertainty on the original scale
- Their ratio, such as the interval width divided by the forecast level, provides a relative measure of how uncertain the forecast is relative to its central value

High relative uncertainty indicates that the model's forecast is weakly identified even if the point forecast itself looks large.

These features are often better used as conditioning variables than as stand-alone signals. A directional or allocation model may respond differently when its volatility input is estimated precisely than when the same input is surrounded by a wide interval.

> **Implementation:** `10_uncertainty_features` notebook fits rolling ARIMA models to log Garman-Klass realized volatility, back-transforms the interval to the original scale, and tracks forecast-standard-error and interval-width features over time.

As in earlier sections, the fitted-object discipline remains unchanged. Any order selection, interval estimation, and refitting must remain inside the walk-forward protocol. Uncertainty features are only useful when the uncertainty itself is measured without look-ahead bias.

Regime models generate analogous summaries, including uncertainty about the current state assignment and the persistence of transitions. We turn to these next.

9.5 Regime features

Many financial series are better described as moving among recurring market environments than as fluctuating around one stable distribution. Volatility can remain low for extended periods and then shift abruptly into a stressed state. Trend-following signals can work well in persistent markets and fail in choppy ones. Correlations that appear stable in one macro environment can reverse in another (Ang and Bekaert, 2002; see Ang and Timmermann, 2011, for a comprehensive survey of regime-change models in finance). A regime feature attempts to summarize the changing environment.

This differs from a structural break in one important respect:

- A **structural break** marks a discrete change in the data-generating process
- A **regime model** instead assumes that the series can revisit earlier states

A calm market can give way to stress and later return to calm; a trend regime can alternate with a range-bound regime several times within the same sample.

Observable regime rules

The simplest regime features are **deterministic rules** applied to observed data. These remain useful because they are transparent, require no latent-state estimation, and are easy to audit in production. For equities, a volatility threshold, such as the VIX above a fixed level, can indicate a stressed market. A trend rule, such as price above or below a long moving average, can separate upward-trending from downward-trending or range-bound conditions. Other deterministic indicators, such as the choppiness index or a trend-efficiency measure, further refine this classification.

These rules are often dismissed as crude, but they **solve a real problem.** A threshold feature fails transparently. If VIX ceases to be informative for a particular universe or horizon, the failure is easy to diagnose. A more flexible latent-state model can represent richer dynamics, but it also introduces more assumptions and more failure modes. For this reason, deterministic regime indicators are often good **baseline features** even when more elaborate models are added later.

A useful way to think about these features is that they **encode a market context** rather than a forecast. A volatility threshold does not predict returns by itself. It tells the downstream model whether other features should be interpreted in a calm or stressed environment. In practice, this **conditioning role** is often the most important function of regime features more broadly.

Hidden Markov model features

The standard latent-state approach is the **Hidden Markov Model** (HMM; Rabiner, 1989, provides a standard tutorial). An HMM assumes that an unobserved state variable follows a **Markov chain**, so the probability of tomorrow's state depends only on today's state. Conditional on that hidden state, the observed data are generated from a state-specific distribution. In finance, the observations are often returns, realized volatility, or a small vector of market variables, and the hidden states are interpreted as regimes such as calm and stressed volatility or low- and high-dispersion return environments (Uysal and Mulvey, 2021).

The most important output is the **filtered state probability**, $P(S_t = k \mid y_{1:t})$, which measures the probability that the system is in state k given only information available through time t. This is the central object for feature engineering. By contrast, the smoothed probability, $P(S_t = k \mid y_{1:T})$, uses future observations and is therefore suitable only for retrospective analysis. *Figure 9.3* illustrates the HMM architecture: hidden states generate observed returns through regime-specific emissions.

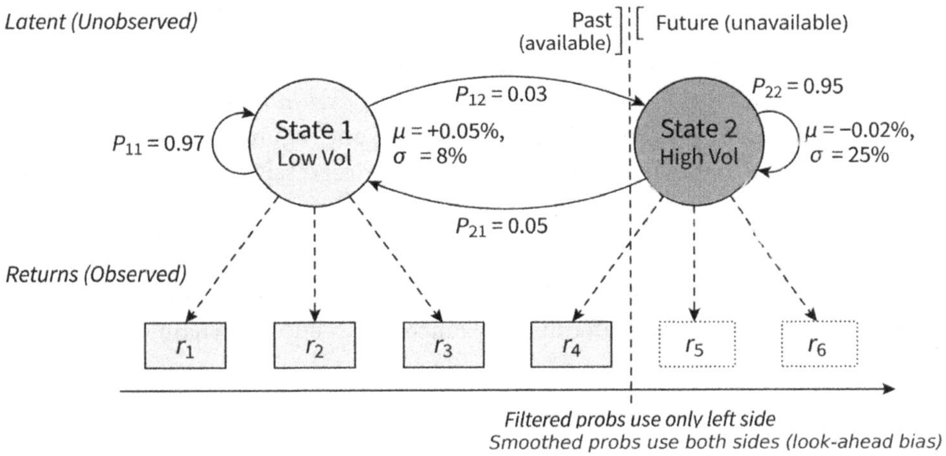

Figure 9.3: Hidden Markov Model architecture

Several other features follow naturally from the fitted model:

- The filtered probability of each state preserves uncertainty and is usually more useful than a hard state label.
- The **transition matrix** provides quantities such as the probability of moving from a low-volatility state to a high-volatility state in the next step.
- The **expected duration** of state k, $\frac{1}{1-p_k}$, summarizes regime persistence, where p_k is the probability of remaining in that state.
- The **entropy** of the filtered probability vector quantifies classification uncertainty: it is low when a single state dominates and high when the model is uncertain among states.

Two implementation issues deserve explicit attention:

- The states are unlabeled. What one estimation window calls "state 0" may correspond to "state 1" in the next window. To keep features comparable over time, relabel the fitted states using a stable characteristic, such as variance, if the states primarily differ in volatility.
- The number of states should remain modest unless there is a strong reason to do otherwise. Two-state specifications are often easier to interpret and more stable out-of-sample than richer models that fit historical noise.

Implementation: `11_hmm_regimes` walks through the forward-filtering logic, contrasts filtered and smoothed probabilities, and extracts transition, duration, and entropy features from HMM fits.

Markov-switching autoregressive features

An HMM with simple state-specific emissions is useful when the main difference across regimes lies in the unconditional distribution of the observations. Sometimes the dynamics themselves also change across states. Hamilton's (1989) **Markov-switching autoregressive** (**MS-AR**) model addresses this by allowing the autoregressive process to vary by regime.

This produces a different class of features. In addition to regime probabilities and regime-specific variances, the fitted model yields **regime-specific autoregressive coefficients**. These coefficients summarize whether persistence, mean reversion, or short-horizon momentum differs across states. A market can, for example, display stronger continuation in one regime and weaker or negative serial dependence in another. In that case, the regime-specific autoregressive coefficient becomes a natural conditioning feature for downstream return models.

MS-AR models are most useful when the question is not only which regime the market is in but also how the series' behavior changes across regimes. If the regimes primarily differ in volatility, a simpler HMM may be sufficient. If they also differ in persistence or directional dynamics, the autoregressive extension can add useful structure.

> **Implementation:** `11_hmm_regimes` includes a Markov-switching autoregression alongside the HMM, so the differences in the extracted features are visible within the same workflow.

Distribution-based regime features

Moment-based regime models, including many HMM specifications, distinguish states through quantities such as the mean and variance. That is often appropriate, but it can miss cases where the main difference lies in distributional shape, especially in skewness and tail behavior. Two return windows can have similar means and volatilities while differing materially in downside concentration or upside convexity.

A distribution-based approach addresses this by treating each rolling window as an empirical distribution and clustering those windows directly. The **Wasserstein distance** is a natural metric for this task because it measures the cost of reshaping one distribution into another. In one dimension, it can be interpreted as the distance between quantile functions, making it sensitive to differences across the entire distribution rather than only at a few summary moments.

This changes both the regime definition and the resulting features. The basic output is the **cluster assignment**, which acts as a regime label. The distance from the current window to its assigned cluster center measures how typical or atypical the current regime instance is. A window that lies far from every centroid may indicate an unusual environment, even if it is still assigned to the nearest cluster.

A further feature can be obtained by comparing distribution-based and moment-based classifications. When a Wasserstein-based assignment differs from a moment-based regime label, the disagreement itself is informative, suggesting that tails or skewness matter more than the mean and variance alone.

This type of feature is especially relevant when the trading problem is sensitive to downside asymmetry, jump risk, or changing tail exposure rather than just to volatility level.

Implementation: On a synthetic two-regime benchmark, Wasserstein K-means achieves an adjusted Rand index of 0.87, compared with 0.31 for moment-based K-means—a large gap that confirms the distributional metric captures regime structure that summary statistics miss. `12_wasserstein_regimes` applies this to S&P 500 returns using the stream-lift methodology of Horvath et al. (2021).

Using regime features downstream

Regime features are usually more effective as **conditioning variables** than as hard switches between separate predictive models. The central reason is that regime inference is uncertain precisely when regime information matters most. Near transitions, the model may assign meaningful probabilities to several states simultaneously. A hard-switching system must still commit to one regime-specific model, which creates instability when small changes in regime probability lead to large changes in the active predictor.

A single predictive model that receives regime features as inputs handles this more gracefully. Filtered state probabilities, regime entropy, duration measures, and regime-conditioned interaction terms enable the model to learn that a signal behaves differently in calm and stressed environments without forcing an abrupt change in the model. As regime certainty falls, the regime inputs naturally become less decisive. The system degrades smoothly instead of switching discontinuously at the boundary between two estimated states. Shu and Mulvey (2025) show a similar approach to factor allocation, confirming that regime probabilities, treated as continuous features, outperform hard regime-switching rules.

This does not make separate regime-specific models useless. They can still be informative when there is a strong economic reason to believe that distinct mechanisms operate in different states and when each regime contains enough data to support separate estimation. But they impose a cost in sample size, increase operational complexity, and are often fragile near the boundary cases that matter most in live trading.

Implementation: `13_regime_as_feature` constructs both unified and regime-conditioned designs and shows how regime probabilities and entropy can be incorporated directly into a downstream gradient-boosting workflow.

All features developed so far—diagnostics, signal transforms, volatility models, uncertainty measures, and regime indicators—are computed asset-by-asset from each series' own history. The next section shows how to convert these temporal outputs into cross-sectional and panel features that place each asset in the context of its peers and the broader universe, completing the bridge to the multi-asset modeling workflow used in later chapters.

9.6 Cross-sectional and panel features

A conditional volatility estimate of 25 % annualized means something different for a utility stock than for a biotech. The same is true for a Kalman trend, a regime probability, or a spectral-energy measure. Temporal features are first computed asset by asset from each series' own history. They become more useful in multi-asset settings when placed in a cross-sectional context or combined across related assets. The result is a second layer of feature engineering: transform temporal outputs into **relative, pairwise, and universe-level signals.**

Cross-sectional transforms of temporal features

Cross-sectional ranking is the simplest and often the most useful transform. At each date, take a temporal feature already finalized for each asset and replace its raw value with a rank, percentile, or z-score relative to the eligible universe. A raw Kalman trend then becomes a universe-relative momentum signal, a conditional-volatility estimate becomes a volatility percentile, and a regime probability becomes a measure of whether the asset looks more stressed or calmer than its peers.

These transforms solve two problems. They reduce the importance of absolute scale and align the feature with cross-sectional prediction tasks, where the objective is to sort assets rather than forecast their standalone levels. Ranking is often the most robust choice because it is less sensitive to outliers than z-scores and remains comparable across heterogeneous assets. Z-scores retain more information about cross-sectional distance and are often preferable when dispersion itself matters. Percentiles provide a bounded compromise that is easy to interpret.

The temporal model still does the primary extraction. The cross-sectional transform does not create the signal from scratch; it re-expresses an already meaningful temporal quantity in a form suited to multi-asset decisions.

Implementation: See `14_panel_features` for cross-sectional ranking of 60-day momentum and volatility across an ETF universe and how those relative positions evolve over time.

Relative and benchmark-adjusted features

Some temporal features become more informative when expressed relative to a benchmark rather than the full cross-section. Subtracting market or sector momentum from an asset's momentum isolates the idiosyncratic component. Dividing an asset's conditional volatility by market volatility distinguishes asset-specific risk from market-wide stress. Subtracting an asset's stress probability from the universe average shows whether it is unusually defensive or unusually exposed relative to the current environment.

This distinction matters because many temporal features mix systematic and idiosyncratic variation. An oil-sector ETF can show strong absolute momentum simply because the entire equity market is rising. Once broad-market momentum is removed, the residual measures whether the asset is outperforming or lagging that common trend. The same logic applies to volatility, drawdown risk, and regime indicators.

Benchmark choice should follow the economic question. For broad equity universes, a market index is often the natural first benchmark. Sector, country, duration-bucket, or commodity-sleeve benchmarks can be more appropriate when the goal is to separate local structure from a narrower common factor.

> **Implementation:** `14_panel_features` constructs market-relative momentum and relative volatility for ETFs by subtracting or scaling with SPY-based benchmarks.

Pairwise temporal features

Multi-asset feature engineering also includes relationships between assets. Some of the most useful features are defined in terms of spreads, hedge ratios, or rolling dependence measures rather than in terms of a single series. Cointegration diagnostics summarize whether two prices share a stable long-run relationship. A time-varying hedge ratio from a Kalman filter summarizes how that relationship changes through time. The spread built from that hedge ratio can then produce standardized deviation measures, such as z-scores, and mean-reversion summaries, such as an estimated half-life.

These pairwise features are most natural in relative-value and statistical-arbitrage settings, but their usefulness is broader. A rolling beta to a benchmark, a rolling correlation regime indicator, or a cointegration score can all serve as conditioning features in a larger predictive model. They describe whether an asset is moving with, away from, or back toward a related instrument or common factor.

Interpret these quantities as state summaries, not trading rules. A short half-life does not by itself justify a trade, and a cointegration test does not guarantee a robust spread after costs. The important point is that the pairwise model produces temporally structured features that are unavailable from single-asset transformations alone.

> **Implementation:** `14_panel_features` screens ETF pairs with Engle-Granger and Johansen tests, compares static and Kalman-filtered hedge ratios, and derives spread z-scores and half-life estimates from the resulting spreads.

Universe-level aggregation

Once asset-level temporal features are available, they can be aggregated across the universe to summarize market-wide conditions. The cross-sectional mean of conditional volatility measures the overall volatility state. Cross-sectional dispersion shows whether assets are behaving similarly or differentiating sharply. The fraction of assets with elevated stress probability becomes a breadth measure of instability. An asset's deviation from the universe average then measures whether it is moving with the market-wide regime or against it.

These aggregates are especially useful for regime features. A high average stress probability suggests that pressure is broad rather than idiosyncratic. High breadth indicates that many assets are simultaneously under stress. High dispersion, by contrast, indicates disagreement across the universe and often accompanies rotation, segmentation, or selective risk-taking. The combination is often more informative than any single asset-level regime label.

The same aggregation logic applies beyond regime models. Cross-sectional averages of Kalman trends, volatility forecasts, or forecast-interval widths can summarize the market's prevailing direction, risk state, or level of uncertainty.

> **Implementation:** `14_panel_features` constructs `universe_crisis_prob`, `crisis_breadth`, and `regime_dispersion` to show how such aggregates behave through time.

Point-in-time handling in panels

The **order of operations** is non-negotiable. First, compute each asset's temporal feature from its own trailing history. Then align those asset-level outputs at the decision date. Only after that step should the cross-sectional rank, benchmark adjustment, pairwise transform, or universe aggregation be applied. Reversing the order leaks information across assets or across time.

The **universe definition** matters as well. When assets enter or leave the tradable set, cross-sectional ranks shift even if no underlying signal changes. Fixed-composition checks, eligibility filters defined in advance, and explicit handling of missing values help separate genuine signal movement from composition effects. Benchmark mappings require the same discipline: sector, country, or market assignments should be those known at the time of decision, not later classifications.

Cross-sectional and panel transforms add a final layer of structure to model-based features. They turn asset-level temporal estimates into relative signals, pairwise states, and market-wide summaries that can be consumed directly by downstream models.

9.7 Summary

This chapter expanded feature engineering from direct transformations to features produced by fitted procedures. Diagnostics contribute rolling measures of stability and break risk. Signal transforms recover latent state, frequency structure, scale, and path geometry. Volatility models add conditional variance, persistence, asymmetry, and horizon-specific components. Uncertainty models turn interval width and posterior dispersion into usable conditioning variables. Regime models summarize market state through thresholds, filtered probabilities, durations, and distribution-based clusters. In multi-asset settings, these temporal outputs become more useful once ranked, benchmarked, paired, or aggregated across the universe.

The practical challenge is not to include every feature a method can generate, but to keep the set interpretable and nonredundant. Many families overlap, so a compact baseline often works better than a maximal catalog: one or two volatility features, one regime feature, one signal-transform feature, and a limited set of cross-sectional transforms are usually enough to establish what the fitted methods add. From there, feature selection can decide whether additional structure improves the model or only increases complexity.

Chapter 10 applies the same fitted-object discipline to text features, in which timing, decay, and embedding-model dependencies serve as the binding constraints.

10

Text Feature Engineering

Quantitative investors have always sought informational edges. Yet the richest source of financial insight—text—has historically resisted systematic analysis. Earnings calls, analyst reports, regulatory filings, news articles, and social media posts contain forward-looking statements, management sentiment, and market-moving revelations that no price chart can capture.

The challenge is scale and structure. Most enterprise information is not stored in clean relational tables; it appears in text, audio, images, presentations, logs, filings, transcripts, and messages. Common industry estimates put the unstructured share of enterprise data around 80-90%, but the exact number matters less than the practical implication: much of the information relevant to investors arrives in forms that require representation, extraction, and timestamp discipline before it can become a tradable feature.

An earnings call transcript arrives at 4:30 PM. We extract a "guidance confidence" feature by comparing current language to the prior quarter. The feature becomes tradable only after we verify (a) when we received it, (b) that our embedding model was trained before the call date, and (c) that no revisions contaminate the historical series. These constraints—not the NLP model—often determine whether a text signal survives backtesting.

Investor attention to corporate filings is now measurable at internet scale, and the volume of text long ago outgrew manual analysis.

By the end of this chapter, you will be able to:

- Distinguish lexical features, static embeddings, sequential models, and transformers in terms of the information each representation preserves and loses.
- Explain how transformer self-attention produces contextual embeddings and why this mitigates key limitations of earlier NLP methods, including polysemy, weak context handling, and long-range dependence.
- Apply a practical financial NLP workflow that combines pre-trained checkpoints, domain adaptation when needed, and task fine-tuning for classification or extraction tasks.

- Design text-derived features such as sentiment, narrative surprise, or structured event signals using point-in-time-safe timestamps, model cutoffs, and aggregation rules.
- Evaluate text-derived signals using horizon-aware diagnostics, coverage-aware analysis, and event-time alignment rather than benchmark accuracy alone.
- Use token-level attribution and related diagnostics to audit, debug, and stress-test NLP features before deployment.

We begin by covering lexical and statistical baselines to establish what simple methods can and cannot capture. *Section 10.2* introduces static embeddings that learn semantic relationships from co-occurrence patterns. *Section 10.3* traces the development of sequential models to motivate the transformer revolution. *Section 10.4* covers the transformer architecture, self-attention, and domain-specific variants like FinBERT, with empirical comparisons across paradigms. *Section 10.5* assembles the production workflow: pipeline contracts, fine-tuning, embedding-based factor construction, structured extraction, and signal evaluation.

Figure 10.1 previews this progression from lexical methods to contextual transformers. The structure traces an increasingly sophisticated search for *context*: lexical methods treat documents as unordered collections of terms; static embeddings capture semantic similarity but assign a single vector per word; sequential models introduce memory but process words one at a time; and transformers enable parallel processing with contextual embeddings that dynamically adjust to surrounding text.

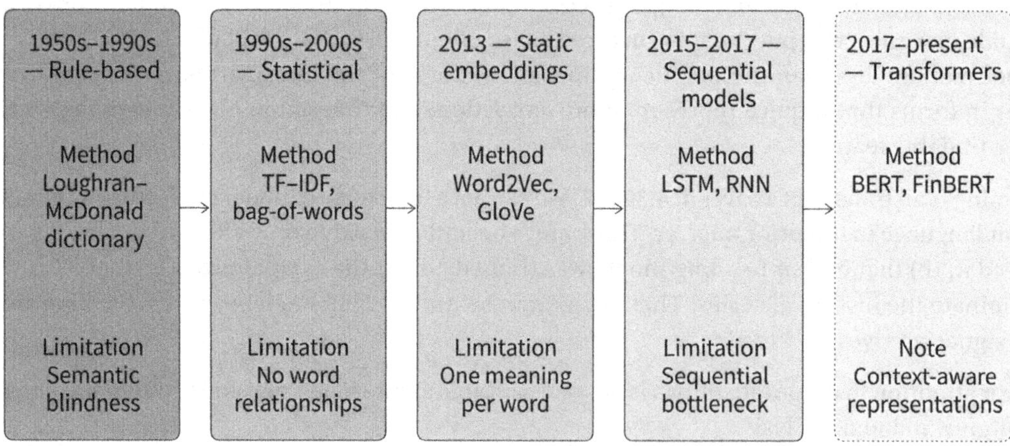

Figure 10.1: From rule-based to data-driven text understanding

The first step in this progression—lexical and statistical models—provides the baselines against which all subsequent methods are measured.

10.1 Lexical and statistical models

The earliest text analysis methods treat documents as collections of terms, extracting features by counting and weighting them. These approaches remain useful baselines, but their semantic blindness motivates the embedding methods that follow.

Financial text analysis progressed through several iterations. Tetlock (2007) established that the tone of news predicts market outcomes under event-time framing. Loughran and McDonald (2011) showed that general sentiment dictionaries misclassify financial language, motivating the development of domain-specific lexicons. More recent work uses unsupervised representations (topics, embeddings) to build "narrative" signals; reported performance varies with corpus choice, coverage bias, and evaluation protocol. This chapter focuses on representations and leakage-safe pipelines for turning text into features that can be evaluated like any alpha factor.

Lexicon-based sentiment

Sentiment measures have a long history in markets, but large-scale systematic extraction became practical only with digitized corpora and modern NLP (Loughran and McDonald, 2020). The intuition is straightforward: count positive and negative words and compute a polarity score. But whose word lists?

General-purpose dictionaries designed for psychology or product reviews fail in finance. Loughran and McDonald (2011) found that nearly three-quarters of "negative" words in the Harvard General Inquirer are *not* negative in financial contexts. "Liability"—unambiguously negative in everyday language—is a neutral accounting term on a balance sheet. Similarly, "tax," "vice," and "capital" carry negative connotations in general dictionaries yet appear neutrally in corporate filings.

The Loughran-McDonald Master Dictionary addresses this mismatch. Built for 10-Ks and related filings, it provides six curated word lists:

Category	Example Terms	Financial Interpretation
Negative	loss, impairment, termination	Adverse events
Positive	gain, favorable, improved	Favorable developments
Uncertainty	may, possible, approximate	Hedging, risk disclosure
Litigious	litigation, court, lawsuit	Legal exposure
Strong modal	will, must, always	Commitment
Weak modal	could, might, may	Hedging intent

Table 10.1: Loughran-McDonald word list examples

The Strong/weak modal distinction is particularly valuable: executives who consistently use "will" versus "might" reveal different levels of confidence in forward-looking statements.

Statistical representations using bag-of-words

Beyond sentiment dictionaries, machine learning requires general-purpose document representations. The **bag-of-words** (BoW) model represents each document as a vector of term counts, ignoring word order entirely.

The process involves several steps: **tokenization** splits text into terms; **normalization** converts text to lowercase and removes punctuation; stop-word removal filters out uninformative terms ("the," "is," "and"); and a **vocabulary** of unique terms maps each document to a count vector.

Raw counts have an obvious problem: common words dominate regardless of informativeness. **Term Frequency–Inverse Document Frequency (TF-IDF)** weights each term's frequency by its rarity across documents:

$$TF - IDF(t, d) = TF(t, d) \times log\frac{N}{DF(t)}$$

where $TF(t, d)$ is term frequency in document d, N is total documents, and $DF(t)$ is documents containing term t. Implementations typically use smoothed IDF variants and L2-normalize vectors. BM25 (Robertson and Zaragoza, 2009), a probabilistic extension used in search engines, incorporates document-length normalization and term saturation.

Critical limitations

These lexical methods establish useful baselines—simple, interpretable, and computationally cheap. But their limitations are severe:

- **Semantic blindness:** Bag-of-words cannot distinguish "assets exceed liabilities" from "liabilities exceed assets." Word order carries meaning that counting destroys.
- **No synonym awareness:** "Buyout," "acquisition," and "takeover" are synonyms, but TF-IDF treats them as distinct features.
- **Polysemy ignored:** "Interest" means something different in "interest rate" versus "interest in the company." Context determines meaning; lexical models lack it.
- **Negation handling:** "Not profitable" contains a positive word but conveys negative sentiment. Simple counting fails.
- **Sparsity:** With 50,000+ term vocabularies, most documents contain tiny fractions of all words. The resulting high-dimensional, sparse vectors pose challenges for many algorithms—the curse of dimensionality.
- **Boilerplate dilution** (finance-specific): 10-K risk factor sections contain boilerplate that dominates term frequencies, drowning out incremental disclosure.
- **Amendment leakage** (finance-specific): Document revisions (amended filings, updated articles) contaminate historical features without careful timestamp handling.

These limitations do not make lexical baselines obsolete. In small samples, narrow domains, and highly formulaic document types, well-regularized lexical models often remain difficult to beat. They are also valuable diagnostics: if a complex encoder fails to outperform a strong TF-IDF baseline, the problem may lie in label quality, temporal alignment, or task definition rather than model capacity.

But lexical models memorize fixed vocabulary and scoring rules. They cannot *learn* that semantically related words should produce similar features, *generalize* to new terminology, or resolve context-dependent meanings. This problem has motivated a shift from counting words to learning **representations**—dense, low-dimensional vectors that capture semantic relationships through distributional patterns.

Lexical models with the right dictionary (Loughran-McDonald) are interpretable, fast, and domain-specific, but they remain semantically blind: no synonym awareness, no context, no negation handling. A lexical model cannot learn that "shortfall" and "miss" mean the same thing.

The next section takes the first step beyond counting: learning dense vectors that encode semantic similarity from distributional patterns in text.

Implementation: `03_sentiment_evolution.py` compares TF-IDF baselines against embedding approaches.

10.2 Static embeddings

Bag-of-words reached its limits: treating words as atomic symbols with no relationships. The **distributional hypothesis** offered a path forward: words that appear in similar contexts tend to have similar meanings. "You shall know a word by the company it keeps" (Firth, 1957). This principle enabled models that *learn* semantic representations directly from text.

Instead of sparse, high-dimensional count vectors, embedding models produce dense, low-dimensional representations—typically 100-300 real values per word. These vectors occupy a semantic space where geometry captures meaning: "earnings" near "profit," "equity" near "stock," "volatility" near "risk."

Embeddings encode analogical relationships through vector arithmetic:

$$v_{king} - v_{man} + v_{woman} \approx v_{queen}$$

This reflects consistent directional patterns in the appearance of gendered and royal terms in context. In finance, embeddings place "equity" near "stock" and "volatility" near "risk," reflecting co-occurrence structure, though analogies are less stable than the standard "king/queen" example.

Learning from local context with Word2Vec

Word2Vec (Mikolov et al., 2013) trains a shallow neural network on a simple task: predicting a word from its context or predicting context from a word. Two architectures accomplish this:

- **Skip-Gram:** Given a target word, predict surrounding context words within a window (typically 5-10 words). Better for rare words and smaller datasets.
- **CBOW (Continuous Bag-of-Words):** Given the surrounding words, predict the central target word. Faster to train, works well for frequent terms.

Words that can substitute for each other in similar contexts develop similar vectors. Training on billions of words from news, Wikipedia, or corporate filings produces vectors capturing subtle semantic relationships.

For financial applications, domain-specific training matters. Word2Vec trained on 10-K filings captures relationships invisible to general-purpose embeddings—for example, "risk factors" associate differently when trained on SEC filings versus Wikipedia.

Global co-occurrence statistics with GloVe

Global Vectors for Word Representation (**GloVe**) (Pennington et al., 2014) takes a different approach: rather than predicting context word by word, GloVe factorizes a global co-occurrence matrix that counts how often each word pair appears together across the corpus.

The model learns word and context vectors whose inner products, together with bias terms, fit the logarithm of global co-occurrence counts. The resulting geometry captures ratios of co-occurrence probabilities, which helps distinguish terms that appear in systematically different contexts. These ratios are embedded in the vector space.

Both methods produce high-quality embeddings with similar downstream performance. The choice often depends on implementation convenience and the availability of pre-trained models.

Asset embeddings from portfolio data

Embedding techniques generalize to any domain with meaningful co-occurrence patterns—including financial data. Word2Vec's core assumption—items in similar contexts share similar properties—applies wherever meaningful co-occurrence exists. Portfolio holdings offer a compelling application: stocks that institutions consistently hold together are likely to share characteristics relevant to asset pricing.

We train Word2Vec on data from SEC Form 13F filings, which disclose the long U.S. equity positions of large institutional investment managers each quarter. We treat each portfolio as a "sentence" and each stock as a "word." When funds repeatedly hold NVIDIA alongside other semiconductor stocks, the model learns that these stocks occupy similar positions in the institutional investment space. Portfolios encode implicit views about stock relationships that no fundamental database captures directly.

Gabaix et al. (2025) show practical value on 500 institutional portfolios (6,343 stocks): on the **masked asset prediction** benchmark—predicting which stocks belong in a portfolio given its other holdings—Word2Vec embeddings substantially outperform random baselines. The resulting embeddings complement traditional factor exposures. Two stocks may have similar market betas yet occupy different positions in institutional portfolio space—information useful for portfolio construction, risk decomposition, or similarity-based analysis.

Implementation: `02_asset_embeddings.py` replicates this approach on the largest 500 institutions in the 2024 Q3 13F bulk filing (1.32 million holdings, 9,167 stocks after a min-count filter of 5):

- Trained Word2Vec embeddings place Apple nearest to Microsoft (0.914), Amazon (0.913), and NVIDIA (0.906) — the institutional-ownership analog of "you shall know a stock by the company it keeps."
- On the masked-asset benchmark, embeddings reach 30.6 % Hits@5 on top-decile portfolio positions versus a 0.055 % analytical random baseline (a 229× lift, 95 % CI 217–241×, bootstrap over 1,000 iterations); the lift attenuates to ~6 % on positions 11–50 and below 1 % on positions 51–200, where individual fund preference dominates the co-occurrence signal.

The polysemy problem

Static embeddings advance beyond bag-of-words—they capture similarity, analogy, and semantic relationships. But they share a critical limitation: **each word gets exactly one vector, regardless of context.**

Consider the word "bear" in the following sentences:

- "Bear market conditions persist."
- "The bear wandered into the campsite."

In each case, the word "bear" has a different meaning, but Word2Vec assigns identical vectors to both. For financial NLP, this polysemy problem—words with multiple context-dependent meanings—pervades investor communication:

- **"Prime"**: prime broker versus subprime mortgage (opposite connotations)
- **"Interest"**: interest rate versus interest in acquiring (different concepts)
- **"Guidance"**: earnings guidance versus regulatory guidance (different domains)
- **"Margin"**: operating margin versus margin loan (different financial concepts)

Static embeddings conflate these usages into a single representation, typically dominated by the most frequent sense. They cannot dynamically adjust to surrounding words.

This is not merely academic. A sentiment model that cannot distinguish "growth slowed" (negative) from "tumor growth" (irrelevant) produces unreliable signals. Context determines meaning; static embeddings ignore it at inference time.

Resolving polysemy requires models that read the surrounding words before committing to a representation, which motivates contextual embeddings and transformers.

Static embeddings deliver semantic similarity, dense representations, and vector arithmetic; synonyms cluster together and generalize to new vocabulary. They remain weak on polysemy, however, because a single vector per word ignores context: "margin" in "operating margin expanded" and "margin call triggered" is represented identically. The next section traces the brief era of sequential models and the limitations that led directly to the transformer architecture.

> **Implementation:** For Word2Vec training, see `01_word2vec_training.py`, and `03_sentiment_evolution.py` for GloVe, TF-IDF, and transformers.

10.3 Sequential models

Static embeddings ignore the surrounding context. **Recurrent Neural Networks (RNNs)** addressed this by processing text word by word, maintaining a hidden state that acts as a compressed memory of the sequence so far. In principle, an RNN's representation of "growth" differs depending on whether it follows "revenue" or "tumor"—a step towards resolving the polysemy problem.

In practice, RNNs suffer from vanishing gradients: error signals can shrink rapidly over long sequences, making it difficult for vanilla RNNs to learn dependencies that span many tokens. **Long Short-Term Memory (LSTM)** networks (Hochreiter and Schmidhuber, 1997) mitigate this by using gated cell states that selectively preserve and discard information, enabling the modeling of longer-range dependencies. Three learned gates—forget, input, and output—regulate what the cell state retains, incorporates, and exposes at each step. LSTMs were the dominant sequence models in NLP through approximately 2018 and were used for sentiment analysis, named entity recognition, and time-series state extraction.

Three limitations drove the transition to transformers:

- The **sequential bottleneck**: processing the 100th word requires completing words 1–99, preventing parallelization on GPU hardware designed for massively parallel computation.
- **Imperfect long-range memory**: despite gating, information still decays over hundreds of words, making full 10-K processing (50,000+ words) impractical.
- **Unidirectional bias**: standard LSTMs read left-to-right only; bidirectional variants double computation without enabling parallelism.

The transformer architecture removes the recurrent bottleneck and gives tokens direct access to other eligible tokens through self-attention. This substantially improves contextual modeling, although sequence length remains constrained by the quadratic cost of standard attention.

10.4 Transformers

In 2017, Vaswani et al. introduced the **transformer**, a sequence model built around self-attention rather than recurrence or convolution. This design enabled processing all positions in sequence in parallel during training, while allowing each token representation to depend directly on other relevant tokens in the same sequence. The result was a simpler and more scalable architecture that quickly became the foundation for modern language models.

For feature engineering, the key idea is not that the model reads text "word by word," but that it learns a contextual representation for each token. In the phrase "revenue growth slowed," the representation of "growth" can incorporate information from "revenue" and "slowed" in the same layer. In "operating margin expanded" versus "margin call triggered," the token "margin" receives different contextual representations because the surrounding tokens change the representation the model computes.

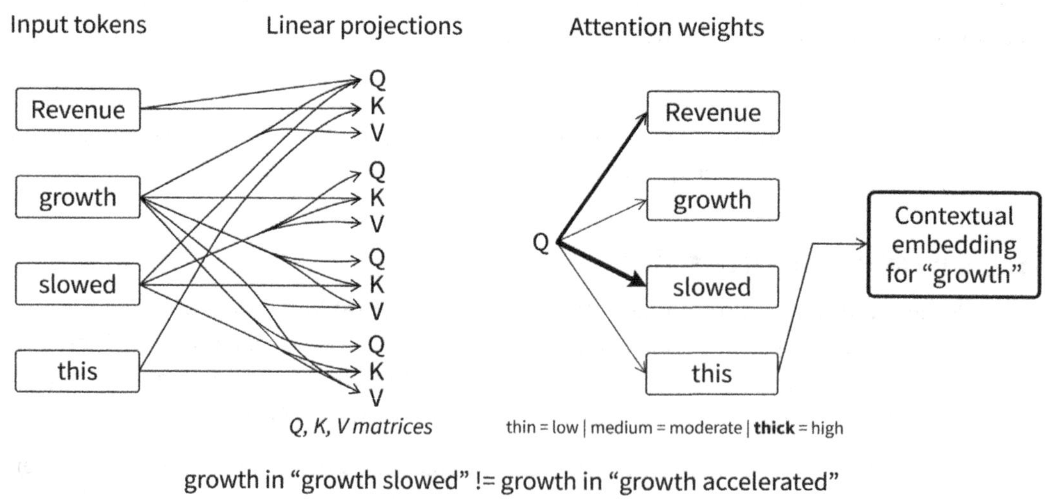

Figure 10.2: The self-attention mechanism

Attention, therefore, helps with lexical ambiguity, but it does not by itself solve meaning or provide an explanation of the model's decision. Attention weights are internal routing weights; they can be informative, but they should not be treated as faithful explanations without additional validation.

Query, key, value, and the attention mechanism

Self-attention begins by projecting each token representation into three learned vectors:

- **Query (Q):** the representation used to search for relevant context
- **Key (K):** the representation used by other tokens to decide whether this token is relevant
- **Value (V):** the information this token contributes when it is attended to

For each token, the model compares its query with the keys of all eligible tokens in the sequence. The resulting similarity scores are normalized to attention weights, which determine the weighted average of the value vectors. The output is a new contextual representation for the token.

For example, when processing "growth" in "Revenue growth slowed," the query for "growth" may assign higher weights to "revenue" and "slowed" than to less informative tokens. The resulting representation combines what the token is, what it modifies, and what happened to it. In deeper layers, repeated attention and feed-forward transformations allow the model to build more abstract syntactic, semantic, and discourse-level representations.

Multi-head attention and positional information

A single attention operation gives each token one learned way to aggregate context. **Multi-head attention** runs several attention operations in parallel, each with its own learned projections. Different heads can learn different relationship patterns, such as local syntax, longer-range dependencies, or repeated references, although head specialization is an empirical tendency rather than a design guarantee. The head outputs are concatenated and projected back into the model dimension.

Self-attention alone is permutation-invariant: without positional information, the model would not know whether "assets exceed liabilities" or "liabilities exceed assets" came first. Transformers, therefore, add positional information to token representations or to the attention computation itself. Original transformers used sinusoidal positional encodings, BERT used learned absolute position embeddings, and many modern architectures use relative position methods or rotary position embeddings to improve length generalization.

Box 10.1 Scaled dot-product attention

The query-key-value description above can be written compactly as:

$$Attention(Q, K, V) = softmax\left(\frac{QK^{\top}}{\sqrt{d_k}}\right)V$$

Here, Q, K, and V are the query, key, and value matrices for a sequence of length T. Each row corresponds to one token. For each query token, the model computes dot products against all eligible key tokens, divides by $\sqrt{d_k}$ to stabilize the scale of the scores, and applies a row-wise softmax to obtain attention weights that sum to one. These weights are then used to average the value vectors.

In encoder self-attention, Q, K, and V are derived from the same input sequence, so each token can attend to the rest of the sequence, subject to padding masks. In decoder-only language models, a causal mask prevents each token from attending to future tokens. In cross-attention, the queries come from one sequence while the keys and values come from another, as in an encoder-decoder model.

The attention matrix has size $T \times T$, so standard self-attention scales quadratically with sequence length. This is acceptable for short sequences but becomes the main bottleneck for long financial documents, such as earnings call transcripts, 10-K filings, and research reports. Modern implementations reduce this cost through better kernels, sparse or local attention patterns, longer-context positional schemes, and document chunking strategies. These engineering choices do not change the basic attention equation, but they determine which documents can be processed efficiently in practice.

Transformer architectures

Transformer models appear in three common configurations:

- **Encoder-only models** such as BERT, FinBERT, DeBERTa, and ModernBERT use bidirectional self-attention. They are well-suited for embeddings, classification, retrieval, entity extraction, and regression features built from text.
- **Decoder-only models** such as GPT-style and LLaMA-style models use causal self-attention, so each position attends only to earlier positions. They are the dominant architecture for open-ended generation and increasingly also support extraction, classification, and reasoning workflows through prompting or fine-tuning.
- **Encoder-decoder models** such as T5 and BART combine a bidirectional encoder with an autoregressive decoder. They remain natural choices for translation, conditional generation, and some summarization tasks.

For financial feature engineering in this chapter, encoder-only models remain the most direct choice because they produce stable document-, sentence-, or token-level representations that can feed downstream models. *Chapters 22-24* return to decoder-only LLMs for retrieval-augmented generation, knowledge-graph workflows, and agentic research systems.

Bidirectional transformers

Bidirectional Encoder Representations from Transformers (**BERT**) stacks transformer encoder layers with a powerful pre-training objective: **Masked Language Modeling** (**MLM**). Random words are masked; the model predicts them from *both* directions (Devlin et al., 2019).

Bidirectional training produces representations that capture richer meaning than unidirectional approaches. Pre-training on massive corpora (Wikipedia, BooksCorpus) gives BERT a general understanding of language that transfers to specific tasks through fine-tuning.

Domain-Specific Variants for Finance

General-purpose encoders learn broad linguistic patterns, but financial text has domain-specific vocabulary, genres, and label conventions. Words such as "liability," "guidance," "impairment," "beat," "miss," and "margin" can carry meanings that differ from everyday usage. **Domain adaptation** addresses this gap by continuing pre-training on financial corpora before task-specific fine-tuning.

Model families, pre-training corpora, and task heads are distinct. **FinBERT** refers to several checkpoints, not a single model:

- `ProsusAI/finbert`, based on Araci (2019), adapts BERT to Reuters TRC2 financial text and fine-tunes it for Financial PhraseBank sentiment.
- `yiyanghkust/finbert-tone`, associated with Huang, Wang, and Yang (2023), targets analyst-report tone using different training data and labels.

These models should not be treated as interchangeable: the correct checkpoint depends on the document genre and label definition.

More recent general-purpose encoders can also be strong starting points when finance-specific labels are available:

- **DeBERTa-v3** improves on the BERT family with stronger pre-training and disentangled attention mechanisms, making it a competitive supervised baseline.
- **ModernBERT** (Warner et al., 2024) updates the encoder architecture for contemporary training and inference, including an 8,192-token native context window. This makes it better suited than classic BERT for longer financial passages, although full 10-K filings and many complete earnings-call transcripts still require chunking or hierarchical aggregation.

The practical rule is simple: use domain-specific checkpoints when their corpus and labels match the target task; otherwise, start from a strong modern encoder and fine-tune on task-specific financial labels. For long documents, context length and aggregation strategy are part of the modeling design, not implementation details.

Beyond BERT in the LLM Era

Encoder-only transformers remain the default for high-throughput text feature extraction, but **decoder-only LLMs** have changed how financial NLP systems are designed. Their advantage is not only generation. They can perform tasks as diverse as:

- Extraction-by-prompt
- Document question answering
- Table-to-text reasoning
- Multi-document synthesis
- Workflow orchestration

These capabilities matter when the task is ambiguous, rare, or schema-rich enough that building a separate supervised model is uneconomical.

The trade-off is reliability. LLM outputs can be sensitive to prompts, retrieval context, decoding parameters, and model version. They are also more expensive to run than compact encoders and harder to audit at scale. For systematic strategies, this means LLMs are often best used as controlled components in a larger pipeline: generating labels for supervised distillation, extracting rare events under schema constraints, summarizing evidence for human review, or supporting research workflows. High-volume daily features should still prefer encoders or distilled models unless the LLM adds measurable incremental value after realistic latency, cost, and validation constraints.

BloombergGPT (Wu et al., 2023) was an early finance-specific LLM milestone: a 50-billion-parameter decoder-only model trained on a large mixed corpus that combined Bloomberg financial data with general-purpose text. BloombergGPT no longer defines the default for financial NLP; its importance is that it showed the value of combining domain-specific financial corpora with general language modeling at LLM scale.

Benchmarks should match the use case:

- **FinBen** evaluates LLMs across a broad range of financial tasks, including information extraction, textual analysis, question answering, generation, risk management, forecasting, and decision-making.
- **FinMTEB** is more relevant when the problem is embedding quality, retrieval, or semantic similarity in financial corpora.
- General retrieval benchmarks such as MTEB and RTEB are useful reference points, but they should not substitute for domain-specific evaluation on the documents, labels, and retrieval tasks that define the investment use case.

To measure the progression concretely, we classify sentences from **Financial PhraseBank** into three sentiment categories—positive, neutral, and negative. The full Financial PhraseBank contains 4,846 English-language sentences drawn from financial news on LexisNexis, each labeled by 5–8 finance professionals. We evaluate on the `sentences_allagree` subset (2,264 sentences; 3-class label distribution: 1,391 neutral, 570 positive, 303 negative; majority-class baseline: 61.4%), which retains only sentences in which all annotators agreed. This is a common high-precision benchmark for financial sentiment models.

Method	Accuracy	F1 (macro)	Key Characteristic
TF-IDF + Logistic Regression	83.2%	0.742	Lexical features only
GloVe + Logistic Regression	80.6%	0.709	Static document averages
FinBERT-tone (zero-shot, no PhraseBank training)	93.2%	0.917	Pre-trained classification head
FinBERT (fine-tuned on PhraseBank)	97.1%	0.955	Domain-specific fine-tuning
DeBERTa-v3 (fine-tuned on PhraseBank)	94.4%	0.932	Disentangled attention
ModernBERT (fine-tuned on PhraseBank)	96.5%	0.962	General-purpose, long context

Table 10.2: Financial Phrasebank sentiment classification results

Three patterns emerge:

- On the high-precision `all_agree` subset, GloVe averages give up about 2.6% points to TF-IDF (80.6 % versus 83.2 %)—averaging GloVe vectors discards order and negation, which the bigram TF-IDF representation partially recovers, so the gain from semantic similarity is more than offset by the loss of word order.
- Zero-shot FinBERT-tone leads both lexical baselines by roughly 10% (93.2% compared to 83.2%)—the analyst-report → financial-news distribution shift is mild enough on `all_agree` that the pre-trained classification head transfers cleanly.
- Task-specific fine-tuning further lifts accuracy to 94–97%: FinBERT 97.1%, ModernBERT 96.5%, DeBERTa-v3 94.4%, all on roughly 1,600 fine-tuning examples.

The order is informative—domain-adapted FinBERT and long-context ModernBERT are within a percentage point, suggesting that on a clean, short-sentence sentiment benchmark, the gain from domain pre-training is small once a strong base encoder has been fine-tuned.

Transformers deliver context-dependent representations that address polysemy, pre-trained checkpoints that transfer to specific tasks, and strong accuracy with modest fine-tuning data. The costs are higher compute per document, attention patterns that are harder to audit than dictionaries, and sequence limits of 512 to 8,192 tokens that remain inadequate for full 10-Ks.

Implementation:

- See `04_bert_finetuning.py` for fine-tuned results on a 70/15/15 train/val/test split. "FinBERT-tone (zero-shot)" applies `yiyanghkust/finbert-tone`, already fine-tuned on analyst-report sentiment, to PhraseBank without further training; the 93.2 % accuracy shows that the distribution shift from analyst-report to news is small enough on this dataset that the zero-shot head transfers cleanly.
- See `06_finbert_cross_dataset.py` for cross-dataset evaluation on FinMarBa market-labeled headlines: FinBERT, fine-tuned on Financial PhraseBank in its release form (ProsusAI's published in-domain accuracy 87.0%), scores only 49.4% on FinMarBa—a 37.6% drop confirming that the same labels across different text distributions produce near-random performance.

With representation methods established, the next section turns to the harder problem: converting these models into reliable, backtestable trading signals without introducing look-ahead bias.

10.5 The modern feature extraction workflow

The preceding sections traced a progression in how models represent text—from term counts to contextual embeddings. Representation quality, however, is only half the problem. A FinBERT embedding of an earnings call is not yet a tradable signal. It becomes one only after you define when the embedding was available, how it maps to a tradable entity, and what temporal constraints prevent leakage. This section covers the conversion from a pre-trained model to a backtestable alpha factor.

Text-to-signal pipeline contract

Before selecting a model or writing any extraction code, define the data contract that determines whether a text feature is tradable. In *Chapter 6* terms, this means specifying the observation timestamp, the entity mapping, and the admissible information set for each text-derived feature.

The following items form a text-feature checklist:

- **Timestamp definition:** Publication time, scrape time, and vendor timestamp are three different quantities—only one defines when you could have acted. Choose it explicitly and use it to index backtests.
- **Publication lag:** SEC filings depend on the form type and the filer's status (large accelerated filers have shorter deadlines). News arrives in seconds to hours; transcripts are same-day to next-day. Measure the lag empirically for your data source.
- **Entity resolution:** Map every mention to a tradable identifier—ticker, CIK, FIGI. Handle ambiguous names ("Apple" the company rather than the word), subsidiaries, and M&A transitions where identifiers change mid-series (see *Chapter 4*).
- **Deduplication:** Syndicated news, wire updates, and editorial revisions count information multiple times. TF-IDF similarity within (ticker, date) groups removes near-duplicates; see `07_news_return_signals.py`.
- **Sampling unit:** Sentence, paragraph, or full document? Define per-firm-day aggregation rules before modeling, not after.
- **Universe construction:** News coverage is endogenous—heavily covered firms differ systematically from lightly covered ones. Coverage itself may predict returns.
- **Pre-training horizon:** Verify that every model's training cutoff predates your backtest period. A model trained on 2024 web crawls has "seen" news you are using to predict 2023 returns.

A text feature is valid only if every upstream step respects an availability timestamp. That timestamp—not the document's date label—indexes backtests.

Walk-forward testing for text signals requires four additional safeguards beyond the standard cross-validation protocol defined in *Chapter 6*:

- **Purged cross-validation:** Exclude documents within k days of the prediction boundary to prevent information leaking across folds. The gap k depends on the signal's decay horizon—a 1-day sentiment signal needs $k \geq 1$; a topic-drift signal operating at monthly frequency may need $k \geq 20$.
- **Rolling fine-tuning windows:** When fine-tuning on recent labeled data, ensure no test-period documents appear in any training window. Track both document dates and model training dates—a model retrained on January data cannot score December documents in a backtest.
- **Revision leakage:** Amended filings, corrected transcripts, and updated articles can silently alter historical features. Snapshot documents at first availability; flag and exclude revisions. The `amendment_leakage` field in your data contract should default to "reject" unless you explicitly verify the revision timeline.
- **Event-study alignment:** A document arriving at time t predicts returns over $[t + \Delta, t + H]$. Verify that Δ accounts for actual availability, not publication date. For earnings calls, Δ may be minutes; for 10-K filings, hours to days depending on the vendor's processing pipeline.

The pre-train, adapt, fine-tune cascade

Training a transformer from scratch requires thousands of GPU-hours and billions of tokens. The three-stage cascade lets practitioners build powerful text features without that cost. *Figure 10.3* visualizes the workflow.

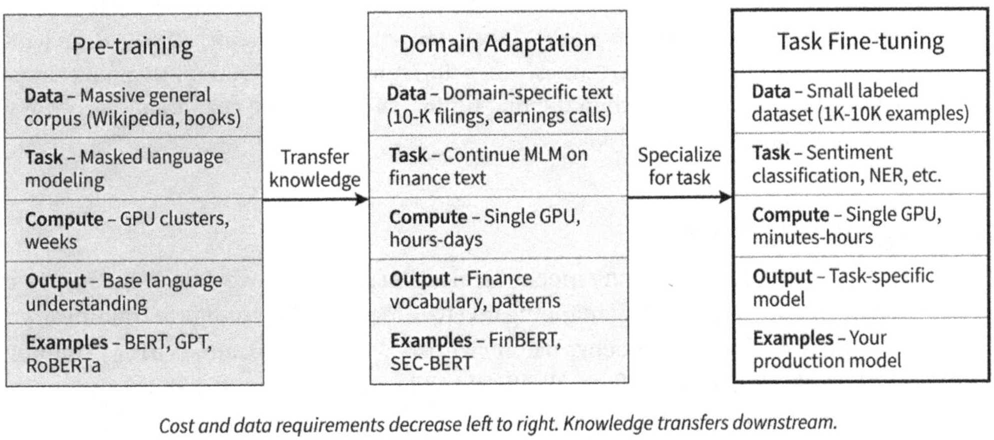

Figure 10.3: From pre-training to fine-tuning

Stage 1: General pre-training

Models like BERT train on massive corpora—Wikipedia, web crawls, books—learning syntax, semantics, and world knowledge through masked language modeling. You never run this stage yourself. You download a checkpoint.

Stage 2: Domain adaptation

Resume masked language modeling on domain-specific text: 10-K filings, earnings call transcripts, analyst reports, and financial news. The model learns vocabulary ("EBITDA," "covenant"), phrasing patterns ("guidance raised to"), and domain-specific co-occurrence relationships ("margin expansion" near "operating leverage"). This stage requires hours of GPU time, not days, and produces checkpoints like FinBERT.

Stage 3: Task fine-tuning

Add a task-specific output head—classification layer, regression head, token-level tagger—and train on labeled examples. For sentiment: sentences labeled positive, neutral, or negative. Fine-tuning requires thousands of examples, not millions, because the model already understands both language (*Stage 1*) and financial vocabulary (*Stage 2*).

This cascade explains why FinBERT outperforms general BERT on financial sentiment: broad language understanding, plus domain knowledge, plus task specialization.

The complementary failure mode is **distribution shift**. A model fine-tuned on one text source may fail when applied to another source with a different language, label conventions, or market context.

> **Implementation:** `06_finbert_cross_dataset.py` illustrates this failure mode. FinBERT—with ProsusAI's published in-domain accuracy of 87.0% on PhraseBank—scores only 49.4% on the FinMarBa market-labeled headline benchmark, a 37.6% drop with the same model, the same label names, and a different text distribution. Domain adaptation does not rescue a model when the fine-tuning and inference corpora disagree on what counts as positive or negative.

Fine-tuning in practice

The Hugging Face Trainer API handles the mechanical boilerplate. The workflow: load a pre-trained model and its tokenizer, prepare a dataset mapping text to integer labels, configure training arguments (learning rate around 2×10^{-5}, 3–5 epochs, batch size 16–32), call `trainer.train()`, and evaluate on held-out data. For BERT-style classifiers, the final hidden state of the ([CLS]) token is commonly passed to the classification head. During fine-tuning, this representation is adapted to summarize the information needed for the supervised task. For retrieval and similarity tasks, mean pooling over token embeddings often performs better than raw ([CLS]) pooling unless the model has been trained specifically for sentence embeddings.

For limited GPU memory, LoRA (Low-Rank Adaptation; Hu et al., 2022) updates only a small fraction of model weights while freezing the rest. This reduces memory by 60–80% with modest quality loss—often acceptable for production pipelines where hundreds of task-specific models must coexist.

The following table offers some example scenarios of when to fine-tune:

Scenario	Recommendation	Rationale
A few hundred labeled examples	Start with frozen embeddings, prompt-based labels, or parameter-efficient tuning	Full fine-tuning may overfit without careful validation
1,000–10,000 labeled examples	Fine-tune with early stopping	Sweet spot for adaptation
Domain-specific vocabulary	Prefer domain adaptation or supervised fine-tuning	Depends on whether the gap is vocabulary, document genre, or label definition
Real-time latency-critical	Fine-tune a smaller model	FinBERT-base over LLMs
Nuanced reasoning required	Consider LLM + prompting	Fine-tuning may not capture complex logic

Table 10.3: Fine-tuning scenarios

The "few hundred examples" limitation has a practical workaround: use an LLM (GPT-4, Claude) to synthetically label thousands of examples, then fine-tune a smaller encoder on the resulting labels. This converts the first row into the second—see *Chapter 5* for synthetic data generation pipelines and quality validation.

Practitioner warning: Look-ahead bias in pre-trained models

A model trained on 2024 web crawls may have "seen" the news you are using to predict 2023 returns. Topic models like batch LDA pose the same risk: they estimate topics over the entire corpus, incorporating future documents. Online LDA (Bybee et al., 2023) processes documents sequentially using only past data. Verify every pipeline component—not just the final model—uses only information available at prediction time.

Tokenization pitfalls

Financial text contains terms unseen during pre-training: tickers (NVDA, TSLA), acronyms (EBITDA, YoY), and composite expressions ($94.8B). Subword tokenizers (WordPiece, BPE) break unknown words into known pieces, increasing sequence length and potentially reducing numeric precision. "Non-GAAP" becomes three tokens; "$94.8B" may split into five or more, fragmenting the number across subwords.

There are two consequences for pipeline design. First, documents that approach the 512-token limit after tokenization may lose content at truncation—switch to ModernBERT's 8,192-token context or explicitly chunk the document. Second, numeric expressions that span multiple tokens are poorly represented; consider extracting numbers separately before embedding the text.

From tokens to document embeddings

Transformers produce one embedding per token. Many applications—such as factor construction, similarity search, and clustering—require a single vector per document. Four pooling strategies:

- **[CLS] pooling** uses the classification token's embedding. Standard for classification tasks where the [CLS] token is trained to aggregate sequence information.
- **Mean pooling** averages all token embeddings (weighted by the attention mask to exclude padding). Typically stronger for retrieval and similarity because it incorporates information from every token.
- **Max pooling** takes the element-wise maximum across tokens. Captures the most activated feature per dimension.
- **Attention pooling** learns a weighted combination of token embeddings. More expressive but requires task-specific training.

For classification, [CLS] is the default. For similarity and retrieval, Sentence-BERT (Reimers and Gurevych, 2019) with mean pooling consistently outperforms [CLS].

Embedding selection and long documents

Three trade-offs dominate the selection of embedding models in practice.

One trade-off involves **retrieval architecture.** Bi-encoders (Sentence-BERT, E5, BGE, GTE) embed documents independently—encode once, compare via cosine similarity. This scales linearly: encode n documents, then compare any pair in constant time. Cross-encoders (reranking models) jointly process document pairs, yielding higher accuracy for pairwise judgments but at $O(n^2)$ cost. Production systems use bi-encoders for candidate retrieval and cross-encoders for reranking small candidate sets (typically the top 50–100).

Another key issue is *context length*. Standard encoders handle 512 tokens—sufficient for headlines, abstracts, and short paragraphs. Earnings call transcripts (8,000–12,000 words) and 10-K sections require either chunking or long-context models: ModernBERT, GTE-large, and BGE-M3 support 8,192 tokens. Longer context increases compute cost per document; justify the cost with a measurable improvement in quality on your evaluation set.

For high-volume pipelines processing millions of documents daily, *distilled models* (MiniLM, all-MiniLM-L6-v2) offer 5× faster inference with modest quality loss. Reserve larger encoders (E5-large, BGE-large) for high-value extraction tasks where accuracy is more important than latency. The MTEB benchmark provides standardized quality comparisons across model families, while retrieval- and finance-specific benchmarks, such as RTEB and FinMTEB, offer more targeted evaluation for financial retrieval use cases.

Modern embedding families such as E5, BGE, and GTE often use instruction-tuning, meaning they are trained to produce embeddings that depend on the task prompt, such as "represent this query for retrieval" or "represent this passage for search." This helps the model place queries and documents in a vector space that better reflects their intended use, especially for retrieval. Many of these families also support multiple languages. For English financial text, appropriately sized models from these families will generally outperform older Sentence-BERT checkpoints. Pin model versions: when an embedding model changes, the meaning of its vectors can shift, potentially silently invalidating cached embeddings and downstream models trained on them.

Handling long documents

Financial documents routinely exceed model limits. A 10-K filing spans 50,000+ words; even an earnings call runs 8,000–12,000. Three strategies handle this:

- **Chunking and pooling**: Split documents into overlapping chunks (typically 256–512 tokens with 64-token overlap), encode each chunk independently, and aggregate via mean or attention-weighted pooling. Simple, robust, and easy to parallelize. The overlap prevents information loss at chunk boundaries (see *Chapter 22* for more detail).
- **Hierarchical encoding:** Encode sentences or paragraphs individually, then feed the resulting sequence of embeddings to a lightweight document-level model (an LSTM, a small transformer, or learned attention pooling). This preserves intra-document structure that flat pooling discards.
- **Long-context models:** ModernBERT handles 8,192 tokens, a major improvement over classic 512-token encoders, enabling it to cover longer passages or shorter transcripts. Full 10-K filings and many complete earnings calls still require chunking, section selection, or hierarchical aggregation. For longer documents, retrieval-augmented approaches identify relevant passages before encoding; *Chapter 22* covers RAG pipelines in detail.

Verify that chunking does not introduce look-ahead bias by mixing sentences from different time periods within a single chunk. When processing a sequence of quarterly filings, chunk within each filing, not across them.

Text signal families and factor construction

Production text pipelines generate multiple signal families, each capturing different information from the same documents:

- **Sentiment** measures positive, negative, or neutral tone. Valuable but increasingly commoditized—most edge comes from speed and coverage breadth rather than model sophistication (baseline signal in `07_news_return_signals.py`).
- **Novelty and surprise** measure semantic distance from a recent baseline. A firm whose news embedding suddenly diverges from its 20-day average is experiencing a narrative shift—a topic change invisible to sentiment. This narrative-surprise factor is developed in the next subsection.
- **Attention** captures coverage intensity, source diversity, and headline prominence. Attention predicts volatility even when tone is neutral: a stock mentioned in 50 articles generates different risk dynamics than one mentioned in 2, regardless of whether coverage is positive.
- **Events** are structured extractions: guidance changes, buyback announcements, litigation disclosures, and executive departures. Schema-based extraction enables reliable aggregation (see *Extract-to-Schema Feature Engineering* below).
- **Entity relations** map who is mentioned with whom: supply chain links, competitive mentions, and regulatory exposure. These relational features feed *Chapter 23*'s knowledge graph pipelines.
- **Topic exposure** categorizes documents by subject (earnings, M&A, regulatory, litigation, macro). Topic attention series—how much coverage each topic receives over time—aggregate into tradable factors. Bybee et al. (2023) construct narrative factors from 180 news topics that explain approximately 25% of aggregate return variance.

Embedding-based factor construction

Embeddings are now the default substrate for systematic text features. An embedding becomes a tradable factor after you define two things:

- **Aggregation unit:** Compute one embedding per document. For a given firm on a given day, aggregate all document embeddings—mean pooling weighted by recency or source reliability. This produces a firm-day embedding vector.
- **Baseline:** The rolling-average embedding over the prior 20 news days serves as the firm's expected narrative. Any distance measure between the current firm-day embedding and this baseline produces a signal.

Three factor patterns cover most production use cases:

- **Semantic novelty (the news surprise metric):** The cosine distance between a firm's daily embedding and its 20-day rolling baseline captures topic shifts that are invisible to sentiment. The signal:

  $$surprise_t = 1 - cosine\_similarity\big(e_t,; mean(e_{t-20:t-1})\big)$$

  When a company's news coverage shifts abruptly—sudden regulatory mentions after months of growth discussion—the surprise signal spikes regardless of whether the new coverage is positive or negative. Bhargava et al. (2023) find that unexpected narrative shifts predict returns at short horizons.

- **Peer-relative positioning:** Measure the distance between a firm's embedding and the centroid of its peer group (industry, supply chain, or similarity-based neighbors). A firm whose narrative differs from peers may be experiencing idiosyncratic developments that the market has not yet priced in. Cross-sectional dispersion in this distance serves as a second factor.
- **Narrative drift:** Treat the embedding series as a time series and compute standard features: period-over-period changes, rolling volatility of the embedding trajectory, and decay rate of similarity to older embeddings. Drift in narrative framing often matters more than levels—markets adapt to stable narratives but respond when the framing changes.

Take these two safeguards for research integrity. First, do not fit global transforms (PCA, clustering) on the full corpus without walk-forward implementation—this leaks future distributional information into past features. Second, version the embedding model and preprocessing pipeline. Embeddings change meaning when models change. Pin versions and cache embeddings indexed by document hash and model identifier.

Practitioner warning: Coverage bias

The 20-day lookback counts news-days, not trading days. Tickers with fewer than 21 days of coverage in the lookback window are dropped, biasing the resulting factor toward high-attention stocks. Handle sparse coverage explicitly: impute with sector-level baselines, flag as missing, or model coverage itself as a separate signal.

Implementation:

- `07_news_return_signals.py` builds the deduplication pipeline, FinBERT scoring, and surprise factor at daily granularity—suitable for daily or longer holding periods.
- `09_filing_text_signals.py` applies sentiment and narrative-change signals to quarterly SEC 10-Q filings, showing how the same factor patterns work at lower frequency with point-in-time availability anchored to filing dates.

Intraday news-to-return alignment requires second-level timestamp precision, latency modeling, and venue-specific microstructure considerations, all of which are beyond the scope of this chapter.

Evaluating text-derived signals

Standard diagnostics apply—IC, ICIR, *t*-statistics, quintile spreads—following the framework in *Chapter 7*. Text signals introduce three additional evaluation dimensions:

- **Decay analysis**: Compute IC at multiple horizons (1-day, 5-day, 20-day). Text signals typically decay faster than fundamental signals. Strong 1-day IC with negligible 5-day IC suggests the signal captures short-term attention rather than fundamental information—useful for short-horizon strategies but misleading for monthly rebalancing.
- **Coverage-conditional performance**: Evaluate IC separately for high-coverage and low-coverage stocks. If the signal works only for stocks with dense news flow, it is capturing attention dynamics rather than fundamental information—a distinction that affects portfolio construction.
- **Event-time alignment**: Verify that performance persists when you shift the availability timestamp by realistic amounts (for example, 30 minutes, 1 hour, or next-day open). A signal whose IC collapses with a 1-hour delay is pricing speed, not information.

Implementation: `08_text_feature_evaluation.py` provides IC/ICIR computation, decay curves across horizons, and coverage-conditional diagnostics. The notebook `09_filing_text_signals.py` illustrates decay analysis concretely on a 50-symbol 10-Q sample (cluster bootstrap by symbol, $B = 1{,}000$ iterations):

- Narrative change (embedding cosine distance between consecutive filings) shows IC = −0.151 (95% CI [−0.226, −0.074], $p < 0.001$ cluster bootstrap, $n = 671$ across 47 symbols) at the 5-day horizon, attenuating to IC = +0.059 (95% CI [−0.021, +0.138], $p = 0.154$, $n = 670$) at 20 days — the significant short-horizon negative signal does not reverse into a significant medium-term positive on this universe.
- FinBERT sentiment on 10-Q MD&A sections shows no predictive power at the 5-day horizon (IC = +0.055, 95% CI [−0.036, +0.160], $p = 0.264$, $n = 720$) and a directionally contrarian signal at 20 days (IC = −0.082, 95% CI [−0.195, +0.034], $p = 0.172$, $n = 719$) that does not clear conventional significance under cluster bootstrap by symbol.

These profiles illustrate why horizon selection matters: the same document source produces a statistically significant short-horizon negative signal on narrative change and a directional but inconclusive medium-horizon signal on sentiment — suited to different research questions and trading directions, but only the narrative-change signal clears conventional significance on this 50-symbol universe.

Extract-to-schema feature engineering

Embeddings measure similarity and change. Many questions require explicit structure—not how similar today's language is to yesterday's, but whether the company announced a buyback and, if so, for how much.

Start with the output. A press release states: "Board authorizes $10B share repurchase program through 2027." A well-designed extraction pipeline produces:

```
{event: "buyback", magnitude: 10e9, currency: "USD", horizon: "2027",
confidence: 0.95}
```

The factor pipeline aggregates these records by firm: buyback intensity equals announced buyback divided by market capitalization over the trailing 90 days. This structured signal is testable with standard IC analysis, combinable with other factors, and fully auditable—properties that raw sentiment scores lack.

The schema that makes this possible contains four field groups:

- **Entity fields:** Issuer and counterparties mapped to stable identifiers (CIK, FIGI, ticker). Entity resolution must handle subsidiaries, M&A transitions, and ambiguous mentions.
- **Event fields:** Controlled vocabulary, such as guidance, buyback, issuance, litigation, regulatory action, executive change. Fixed vocabularies enable reliable aggregation across documents and time.
- **Attribute fields**: Direction, magnitude, units, and time horizon. These transform qualitative events into quantitative features.
- **Uncertainty fields**: Modality (hedging language), confidence score, and an abstention flag. When the model's confidence falls below the threshold, emit no record rather than a noisy one.

Implement extraction with fine-tuned encoder models for high-throughput tasks, prompt-constrained LLMs with JSON-mode decoding for complex or rare event types, or a cascade that uses cheap encoders for broad coverage and reserves LLM extraction for high-novelty or low-confidence regions. For LLM-based extraction, prefer constrained or schema-guided decoding when available. Modern inference stacks can restrict generation to JSON schemas, enumerated choices, regular expressions, or grammars, reducing the need for brittle post-processing. Schema guidance improves format reliability, but it does not guarantee factual correctness: extracted entities, dates, magnitudes, and units still require validation against the source text and downstream sanity checks.

Two **safeguards** for systematic use:

- Enforce **schema validation** at the pipeline boundary—reject records with missing required fields, out-of-vocabulary event types, or magnitudes that fail sanity checks. Invalid extractions that slip through corrupt aggregated features silently.

- **Separate extraction from aggregation.** Extraction operates at the document level with a deterministic model version and an availability timestamp. Aggregation operates at the firm-day level using only records available at that point in time. This separation simplifies backtesting, failure auditing, and model upgrades—you can re-extract documents with a new model without rebuilding the entire feature history.

> **Implementation:** See `05_financial_ner_finetuning.py` for token-level entity extraction from financial text using fine-tuned encoders, including downstream feature engineering from extracted entities. *Chapters 22–24* extend these extraction patterns to agentic workflows with LLM-based structured extraction and schema validation.

Model interpretability

For risk-managed strategies, opacity is a liability. Regulators may require explainability, and production failures are harder to diagnose without inspecting the factors that drove a prediction.

SHAP (Lundberg and Lee, 2017) computes the marginal contribution of each input token to a model's output. Positive SHAP values push toward one class; negative values push toward another. The resulting attribution map shows which words mattered and in which direction.

Consider the sentence: "Net loss narrowed significantly from the prior year." A dictionary-based model flags "loss" as negative. Fine-tuned FinBERT correctly classifies the sentence as positive with 69.7% confidence. SHAP reveals why: " narrowed" carries the highest positive attribution (+0.373), dominating the negative contribution of "loss." The model learned that *improving* losses signals positive sentiment—a contextual judgment that no word list can replicate.

Token attributions serve three functions in a systematic workflow:

- **Risk management:** Before deploying a text signal, inspect SHAP attributions on a sample of high-confidence and low-confidence predictions. If the model relies on boilerplate phrases, ticker symbols, or formatting artifacts rather than substantive language, the signal is fragile.
- **Debugging:** When a text signal's IC degrades, SHAP attributions during the degraded period often reveal the cause—a new phrasing pattern the model misinterprets, a shift in boilerplate that the model overweights, or a data quality issue that introduces spurious tokens.
- **Alpha discovery:** Systematic analysis of high-attribution tokens across thousands of documents reveals which linguistic patterns consistently predict returns. Modal verbs ("will" versus "might"), hedging phrases, and specific financial terms may retain predictive power that is worth engineering into dedicated features.

A caveat: token-level attributions can be noisy, particularly for long documents where many tokens contribute small amounts. Treat SHAP as an audit and diagnostic tool, not as a source of causal explanations. For full implementation details, including batched attribution computation and visualization, see *Chapter 12*.

This workflow delivers production pipelines with proper temporal alignment, fine-tuning recipes that adapt pre-trained models, embedding factors that capture semantic information beyond sentiment, structured extraction for reliable downstream aggregation, and interpretability diagnostics that make transformer-based signals auditable.

The cost is operational complexity. Text pipelines demand careful attention to deduplication, coverage bias, look-ahead leakage, and model versioning. Every shortcut in the pipeline contract—an approximate timestamp, an unversioned embedding model, a schema without validation—introduces a failure mode that may not surface until live trading.

> **Implementation:** Notebooks `04_bert_finetuning.py` through `09_filing_text_signals.py` cover every major workflow step discussed in this section. Start with the pipeline contract checklist above; no notebook output is trustworthy until you can answer all seven questions for your specific data source.

The following summary consolidates the trade-offs across all four representation families to guide model selection in practice.

10.6 Summary

Text feature engineering has progressed primarily through improvements in how models represent *context*. Lexical methods (dictionaries, bag-of-words, TF-IDF) are simple and interpretable, but they discard word order and cannot resolve polysemy or negation. Static embeddings (Word2Vec, GloVe) move from sparse counts to dense vectors that capture semantic similarity, yet still assign one representation per word regardless of usage. Sequential models (RNNs/LSTMs) incorporate preceding context, but their sequential computation and difficulty with long-range dependencies make them impractical for long financial documents.

Transformers address these limits with self-attention: each token can condition on all others, producing contextual embeddings that adapt to surrounding text. In practice, performance depends on matching the model to the domain and task: continue pre-training on financial corpora when needed, and fine-tune on labeled data to achieve measurable gains over lexical baselines. Because text arrives in real time, pipelines must also guard against look-ahead bias by respecting data availability and model training cutoffs.

For systematic trading, representation quality is only half the problem. The resulting embeddings must be turned into time-aligned, backtestable features (including factors based on narrative surprise or topic drift), and models must be auditable: interpretability tools such as SHAP help verify that predictions rely on sensible language cues rather than spurious artifacts. The next chapter shifts from representation to evaluation, situating these text features inside the broader ML pipeline that turns features into validated predictions; LLM-based generative workflows return in *Chapters 22–24*.

11

The ML Pipeline

Previous chapters constructed features across the case studies and evaluated their predictive power through information coefficients, factor spreads, and the triage framework of *Chapter 7*. Now we will take the next step: transforming those features into trading signals using machine learning.

This chapter introduces regularized linear models (Ridge, LASSO, and Elastic Net) as interpretable baselines that introduce the ML signal-generation workflow within the trading setup defined in *Chapter 6*. We will build the walk-forward validation pipeline to prevent look-ahead bias, the interpretability tools to verify economic sensibility, and a conformal prediction framework to quantify uncertainty, foundations that carry forward to every model in *Chapters 12–15* and translate into positions in *Chapters 16–19*.

By the end of this chapter, you will be able to:

- Choose between *regression and classification* formulations based on how predictions will be translated into trading decisions.
- Fit regularized linear models, including Ridge, LASSO, Elastic Net, and logistic regression, using point-in-time preprocessing and standardization.
- Tune and evaluate linear models with walk-forward validation, temporal buffers, and, when needed, nested cross-validation to reduce selection bias.
- Interpret model behavior with SHAP-based diagnostics to assess feature importance, economic plausibility, and stability across refits.
- Construct and evaluate conformal prediction intervals or prediction sets, and monitor where coverage degrades under non-stationary market conditions.
- Use cross-case-study evidence to judge when linear models provide a strong baseline and when a weak linear signal motivates more flexible models.

We will begin by motivating the use of regularization for prediction, then introduce linear regression and classification, show how to use SHAP values for explainability, and present conformal predictions to quantify uncertainty. We conclude by presenting insights from the case studies.

Chapters 12–14 extend the models introduced here. Every model must beat the regularized linear baseline from this chapter. A gradient-boosting model that underperforms Ridge has added complexity without improving predictive power. Each modeling chapter loads the linear baseline automatically and reports the improvement (or lack thereof) alongside the candidate model.

11.1 From inference to prediction

Classical **econometrics** (the application of statistics to economic data) and machine learning approach the same data with different objectives. Econometrics asks: "What is the relationship between these variables, and is it statistically reliable?" Machine learning asks: "Given inputs, what is the best forecast of the outcome?" This chapter develops linear models for this exact predictive task. The shift from inference to prediction changes which properties of an estimator matter and motivates the regularization methods that follow.

Two modeling cultures

Leo Breiman's 2001 paper "Statistical Modeling: The Two Cultures" formalized a distinction that had long been implicit:

- The *data modeling culture*, dominant in econometrics, posits a stochastic model for the data-generating process (DGP) and estimates its parameters
- The *algorithmic modeling culture*, dominant in machine learning, treats the DGP as unknown and evaluates models solely by their predictive accuracy on data not used to develop the model

The distinction is not about complexity. A linear regression can serve either culture: used for inference, it recovers coefficient estimates and tests hypotheses about them; used for prediction, it generates forecasts evaluated by out-of-sample error. The distinction is about the *success criterion*. In the data modeling culture, a model succeeds when it recovers interpretable, statistically significant parameters under a correctly specified model. In the algorithmic culture, a model succeeds when it predicts well. As Breiman argued, predictive accuracy should serve as the primary check on whether it has captured meaningful structure in the data.

For algorithmic trading, the more relevant criterion is predictive accuracy (generating stable, profitable forecasts), not unbiased parameter recovery (Simonian, 2024).

What inference requires

The inferential framework is powerful but demanding. **Ordinary Least Squares (OLS)** regression (the estimator behind models from the CAPM to Fama-French-Carhart) recovers coefficient estimates $\hat{\beta}_j$ that, under certain conditions, are unbiased estimates of the true *ceteris paribus* effects of each feature x_j on the outcome. Those conditions are the **Gauss-Markov assumptions** that require:

- **Linearity** in the parameter vector $\beta\beta$, implying the functional form$y = X\beta + \varepsilon$
- **Strict exogeneity**: $E[\varepsilon \mid X] = 0$, which implies that regressors contain no information about the error term (no omitted variables or lagged dependent variables)
- **No perfect multicollinearity**, meaning no regressor is an exact linear combination of the others, so β is identifiable

- **Spherical errors,** $\mathrm{Var}(\varepsilon \mid X) = \sigma^2 I$, which assumes errors have constant variance and are uncorrelated across observations

When all four hold, the Gauss-Markov theorem guarantees that OLS is the **Best Linear Unbiased Estimator (BLUE)**: among all unbiased linear estimators, OLS has the smallest variance.

The linearity and exogeneity assumptions require that the model include the right variables in the right functional form. This is a strong requirement when the true DGP is unknown. In financial markets, the DGP almost certainly involves nonlinearities, regime changes, and time-varying parameters. When the model is misspecified, the unbiasedness guarantee fails, and the coefficient estimates become difficult to interpret as causal or structural parameters.

Given a correctly specified model, hypothesis testing evaluates whether a coefficient is distinguishable from zero. A p-value measures the probability of observing a test statistic as extreme as the one computed, assuming the null hypothesis ($\beta_j = 0$) is true. This is useful for inference (determining whether a variable has a statistically reliable relationship with the outcome), but it does not measure predictive power. A coefficient can be highly significant yet economically negligible (for example, a large sample size with a tiny effect), or insignificant yet genuinely predictive when combined with other features.

The Gauss-Markov optimality of OLS is defined within the class of unbiased estimators. But for prediction, unbiasedness is not inherently desirable. What matters is total prediction error, which decomposes as:

$$\mathrm{MSE} = \mathrm{Bias}^2 + \mathrm{Variance} + \sigma_\varepsilon^2$$

An estimator that introduces some bias but substantially reduces variance can achieve lower MSE than an unbiased estimator, particularly when the number of features is large relative to the number of observations. The Gauss-Markov theorem does not claim that OLS minimizes MSE; it claims that OLS minimizes variance **subject to the constraint of unbiasedness**. Relaxing that constraint opens a path to lower total error.

Why prediction demands a different approach

Consider a strategy research problem: predicting next-month returns using 100 features from momentum, valuation, and sentiment feature families across 240 monthly observations. OLS will fit this model. Under the Gauss-Markov assumptions, the resulting coefficient estimates are unbiased. But **unbiasedness alone does not ensure good predictions.** With 100 parameters estimated from 240 observations, estimation variance is large: small changes in the training sample produce large swings in $\hat{\beta}$, and therefore in predictions. The model fits training data well (it has enough free parameters to absorb idiosyncratic patterns), but those patterns do not generalize.

This is not a failure of OLS as an inferential tool. It is a consequence of using an estimator optimized for unbiased parameter recovery in a setting where predictive stability matters more. **OLS has no mechanism to trade bias for variance**, because doing so would compromise the inferential guarantees that justify its use in econometrics.

Three aspects make the problem particularly acute in finance:

- **High dimensionality relative to observations.** As p/n grows, OLS estimates become unstable; when $p > n$, they are not uniquely defined.
- **Multicollinearity.** Financial features are pervasively correlated: momentum overlaps with trend, valuation ratios share accounting inputs. OLS assigns arbitrary weights to correlated features, producing offsetting coefficients that amplify noise.
- **Low signal-to-noise ratio.** Cross-sectional return regressions typically achieve R^2 of 1–3% in-sample and lower out-of-sample. Variance dominates MSE: an unconstrained model fits noise, while a constrained model sacrifices modest signal to suppress far more spurious patterns.

Regularization addresses this tradeoff directly. It adds a penalty to the OLS loss function that increases with the magnitude of the coefficients, shrinking estimates toward zero. This introduces bias (penalized estimates no longer center on the true β), but it reduces variance by preventing the model from assigning extreme weights to any feature or distributing weight erratically across correlated features.

The form of the penalty encodes a *prior about the structure of the signal*:

- **Ridge** (L_2) shrinks all coefficients proportionally, which is suited to diffuse signals with pervasive multicollinearity
- **LASSO** (L_1) drives coefficients to zero, performing automatic selection when the signal concentrates in a sparse subset
- **Elastic Net** combines both, retaining correlated feature groups while still shrinking toward sparsity, a common requirement when momentum, trend, and mean-reversion indicators overlap

These are principled responses to the **bias-variance tradeoff**, not ad hoc corrections. The tuning parameter λ controls the tradeoff, and cross-validation selects the degree of shrinkage that minimizes out-of-sample error. *Section 11.2* develops each method formally.

The label families defined in *Chapter 7* (continuous returns, thresholded direction, quantile membership) map to regression (predicting magnitudes) and classification (predicting categories). The choice depends on alignment with the trading setup and the data. We first discuss regularized regression, then classification in more practical detail.

Implementation: `01_ols_inference` shows OLS summary tables, the Gauss-Markov diagnostic battery, variance inflation factors, and robust standard errors on the ETFs case study.

11.2 Regularized regression

Ridge, LASSO, and Elastic Net each encode a different assumption about how the signal is distributed across features. This section presents their formal objectives, the geometry that gives each method its distinctive behavior, and the practical machinery (standardization, hyperparameter optimization, and loss function choice) required to deploy them within the walk-forward protocol of *Chapter 6*.

Ridge regression for distributed signal

Ridge regression augments the OLS objective with an L_2 penalty on the coefficient vector:

$$\min_{\beta} \sum_{i=1}^{n} (y_i - X_i\beta)^2 + \lambda|\beta|_2^2$$

where $\lambda > 0$ controls regularization strength and $|\beta|_2^2 = \sum_j \beta_j^2$. The penalty increases with the sum of squared coefficients, discouraging large values but never forcing any coefficient exactly to zero.

The closed-form solution reveals the mechanism. OLS solves $\hat{\beta}_{\text{OLS}} = (X^\top X)^{-1} X^\top y$; Ridge solves $\hat{\beta}_{\text{Ridge}} = (X^\top X + \lambda I)^{-1} X^\top y$.

Adding λI to $X^\top X$ stabilizes the inversion, shrinking coefficient estimates, and bounding their variance. When $\lambda = 0$, the solution reduces to OLS; as $\lambda \to \infty$, all coefficients shrink toward zero.

The geometry is instructive. In the **singular value decomposition** (**SVD**) of the feature matrix, each singular value corresponds to a direction in the feature space and measures the amount of variance the data exhibit along that direction:

- OLS estimates are least stable along directions of low variance: small denominators in the inversion produce large, noisy coefficients
- Ridge adds λ to every singular value before inverting, which disproportionately shrinks coefficients along low-variance directions while leaving well-identified directions largely intact (Hastie, Tibshirani, and Friedman, 2009)

The practical consequence: strong signals supported by substantial variation in the data survive with modest shrinkage; weak signals in poorly identified directions (precisely the ones most likely to reflect noise) are heavily attenuated.

This makes Ridge well-suited to settings where many features contribute modestly to the signal and multicollinearity is pervasive. If momentum, trend-following, and relative-strength indicators capture overlapping information, OLS assigns weights in an erratic manner; Ridge retains all of them with reduced, stabilized weights. `02_regularization_paths` traces Ridge coefficient paths across regularization strengths and compares IC against the OLS baseline.

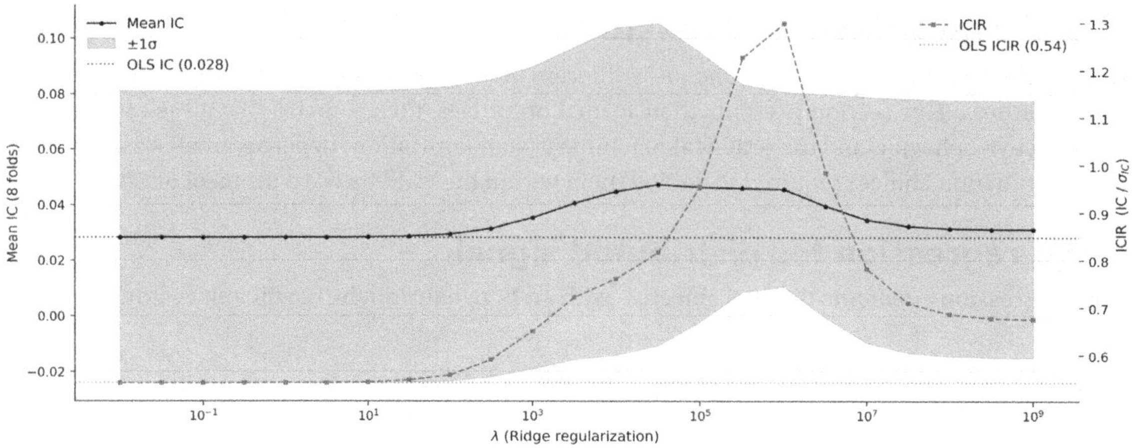

Figure 11.1: Ridge etfs performance for increasing regularization

Figure 11.1 traces Ridge prediction quality across ten orders of magnitude in penalty strength α, using the `etfs` case study with 21-day return labels (n≈394,000):

- Below α≈100, the penalty is negligible, and Ridge is indistinguishable from OLS (IC≈0.028, ICIR≈0.54, right-hand scale).
- Between 10^3 and 10^6, both IC and ICIR improve as shrinkage suppresses noisy coefficient directions; the peak ICIR of 1.30 at α≈10^6 represents a 2.4× improvement over the OLS baseline, driven by a 60% increase in mean IC (0.046 versus 0.028) combined with a 33% reduction in the IC standard deviation across folds.
- Mean IC peaks earlier at α≈3×10^4 (IC=0.047) and declines slightly thereafter, but IC variance keeps shrinking faster, so ICIR continues improving until α≈10^6, where it plateaus.

LASSO regression for sparse signal

LASSO replaces the L_2 penalty with an L_1 penalty:

$$\min_{\beta} \sum_{i=1}^{n} (y_i - X_i\beta)^2 + \lambda|\beta|_1$$

where $|\beta|_1 = \sum_j |\beta_j|$. Unlike Ridge, the L_1 penalty produces *sparse* solutions: some coefficients are exactly zeroed, performing automatic feature selection. This encodes a prior that the signal concentrates in a small subset of features: only a handful of the candidate indicators truly predict returns, and the rest are noise.

The **sparsity** arises from the geometry of the L_1 constraint set. The absolute-value penalty creates a diamond-shaped feasible region with corners on the coordinate axes. The OLS objective's contours typically intersect these corners, setting some coefficients exactly to zero (Tibshirani 1996). The L_2 penalty's circular constraint set has no corners, which is why Ridge shrinks but never zeros.

Sparsity has practical appeal: fewer active features mean fewer data pipelines to maintain and clearer PnL attribution. However, LASSO is **unstable when features are correlated.** Among a set of similar indicators, LASSO selects one at random and sets the others to zero. Which indicator survives can change with minor perturbations in training data, making the active feature set unstable across walk-forward windows. This instability does not necessarily harm predictive accuracy because the selected feature may serve as a reasonable proxy for the group. However, it complicates interpretation and can increase turnover if the trading signal depends on which specific features are active.

The LASSO coefficient path in `02_regularization_paths` shows which features enter the model first as λ decreases and how the active set shifts across walk-forward folds (see *Figure 11.2*).

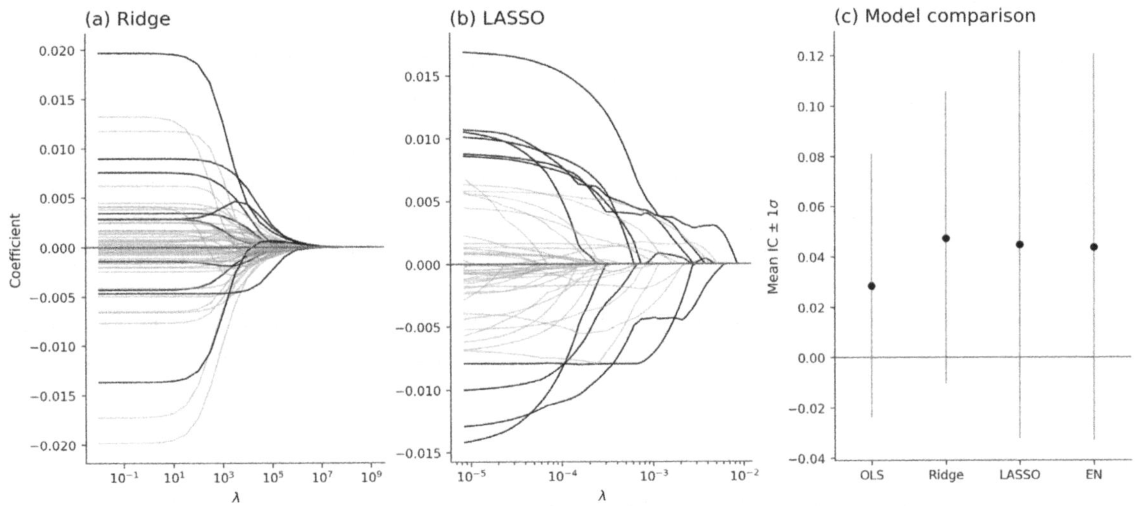

Figure 11.2: Ridge (a) shrinks all 57 coefficients smoothly toward zero as λ increases, retaining every feature; LASSO (b) eliminates features sequentially, snapping coefficients to exactly zero at different λ thresholds. The 10 largest-magnitude features are highlighted, the remaining 47 in gray. Panel (c) compares mean out-of-sample IC (±1σ) for OLS, Ridge, LASSO, and Elastic Net. All panels use standardized features from the etfs case study (21-day returns, single training fold).

For the `etfs` case study, LASSO tells a different story than Ridge: even mild sparsity ($\alpha \approx 0.0001$) zeros out roughly a quarter of features, and stronger penalties *reduce* IC below OLS, while $\alpha \geq 0.01$ eliminates virtually all coefficients.

With 57 correlated momentum and volatility features, the ETF signal is diffusely distributed: Ridge's uniform shrinkage preserves it, while LASSO's variable selection discards informative features along with noise.

Combining both priors with elastic net

Elastic Net blends the L_1 and L_2 penalties:

$$\min_{\beta} \sum_{i=1}^{n} (y_i - X_i\beta)^2 + \lambda\left[\alpha|\beta|_1 + \frac{1-\alpha}{2}|\beta|_2^2\right]$$

where $\lambda > 0$ controls overall regularization strength and $\alpha \in [0,1]$ controls the mixing ratio: $\alpha = 1$ recovers LASSO, $\alpha = 0$ recovers Ridge.

The combination produces a distinctive grouping behavior (Zou and Hastie, 2005). The L_2 component encourages correlated features to receive similar coefficients; the L_1 component then performs group-level selection, keeping or discarding entire clusters. For financial feature sets with many correlated indicators (momentum variants, overlapping sentiment measures, related valuation ratios), this grouping is more stable than LASSO's arbitrary within-cluster selection and more selective than Ridge's retention of everything.

Scikit-learn's `ElasticNet` parameterizes the objective as $\frac{1}{2n}|y - X\beta|^2 + \alpha\left[\ell_1\text{\_ratio} \cdot |\beta|_1 + \frac{1-\ell_1\text{\_ratio}}{2}|\beta|_2^2\right]$, where `alpha` controls overall penalty strength, and `l1_ratio` controls the L1/L2 mix (`1.0` = pure LASSO, `0.0` = pure Ridge). Note the $1/2n$ normalization: `ElasticNet` averages the loss, unlike `Ridge`, which uses the unnormalized **sum-of-squares error (SSE)**, so the `alpha` scales are not directly comparable between the two.

To begin, cross-validate over a grid of `l1_ratio` values (for example, 0.1,0.3,0.5,0.7,0.9) and `alpha` values log-spaced over the range appropriate to n (see the scaling heuristic in the Optuna section below, adjusting for the $1/2n$ normalization). If the optimal `l1_ratio` consistently lands near 1.0 across walk-forward windows, the data favor sparsity; near 0, the signal is diffuse across features. Unstable `l1_ratio` across windows reflects genuine variation in which feature relationships dominate. Consider averaging predictions across several mixing ratios rather than selecting a single point estimate. The case study pipeline runs this grid search (see `06_linear` in each case study directory).

Standardization

Regularization penalties penalize all coefficients equally, whereas raw coefficients depend on the units of the features. A momentum signal, measured in percentage points, and a volume indicator, measured in millions of shares, have vastly different magnitudes. Without standardization, the penalty shrinks large-scale features more aggressively, a result driven by unit choices rather than predictive importance.

Standardize each feature to zero mean and unit variance:

$$x_j^{(\text{std})} = \frac{x_j - \mu_j}{\sigma_j}$$

After standardization, coefficient magnitudes are directly comparable: a coefficient of 0.3 on standardized momentum and 0.1 on standardized volume means the model assigns three times as much weight to momentum, regardless of the original scales.

Two implementation details are critical:

- **Fit on training data only.** Compute μ_j and σ_j from the training fold, then apply those parameters to transform validation and test data. Using full-sample moments introduces look-ahead bias. In a walk-forward protocol, recompute standardization parameters at every refit.

- **Winsorize before standardizing.** A single extreme observation can inflate σ_j, compressing all other observations toward zero. Clip at the 1st and 99th percentiles (computed from training data) before standardizing. Both errors (leaking moments and skipping winsorization) are silent: no error is raised, but the model benefits from information unavailable at prediction time.

The walk-forward pipeline in `02_regularization_paths` applies `StandardScaler`, fitted only to the training data, at every fold, implementing the leakage-safe workflow described here.

Hyperparameter optimization with Optuna

Ridge, LASSO, and Elastic Net each introduce hyperparameters (regularization strength and, for Elastic Net, the mixing ratio) that control the bias-variance tradeoff. Grid search over a pre-specified schedule works for one or two parameters but scales poorly to joint optimization and does not adapt to the loss surface.

Optuna (Akiba et al. 2019) provides **sequential, model-based hyperparameter optimization** through a define-by-run API: the objective function samples parameters from distributions, evaluates walk-forward cross-validation performance, and Optuna's **Tree-structured Parzen Estimator** (TPE) sampler steers subsequent trials toward promising regions of the search space.

The critical risk is **validation overfitting**: running many trials on the same validation folds can select hyperparameters that exploit idiosyncrasies of the validation period rather than a durable signal. Nested cross-validation, with an inner loop for hyperparameter optimization and an outer loop for evaluation, is the cleanest correction, although it increases computation. For time series, the same principle requires nested walk-forward validation, with each outer walk-forward split evaluated only after tuning inside the corresponding training window (see *Chapter 6*).

A useful diagnostic is to examine the full distribution of validation ICs, the stability of trial rankings across folds, and the uncertainty around the selected trial's IC. A best trial that materially exceeds the rest of the search but owes its advantage to outliers in a single fold, regime, or random seed is a warning sign. Report the number of trials, the search space, the selected hyperparameters, and the fold-level dispersion of the selected configuration. *Chapter 12* develops Optuna's advanced features (pruning, multi-objective optimization, and time-series-aware tuning) for the larger hyperparameter space of gradient boosting.

Before launching an adaptive search, the search space must be calibrated to span substantively different model regimes.

This is especially important for the regularization strength because the penalty's numerical scale depends on the estimator's loss convention and feature scaling. With standardized features, `sklearn.Ridge` uses an unnormalized sum-of-squares objective, so values of alpha that materially affect the solution often scale with the sample size through the eigenvalues of $X^\top X$. By contrast, `sklearn.ElasticNet` averages the loss over observations, absorbing a factor of n; comparable penalties therefore differ by roughly this factor when translating between conventions.

In the ETF case study, with approximately 400,000 observations, a Ridge search that stopped at $\lambda = 10^2$ would mostly explore the near-OLS region and could falsely suggest that regularization has little effect.

The notebook therefore maps a wider range, from 10^{-2} to 10^9, to include both the under-regularized plateau and the strongly regularized regime.

Implementation: `04_nested_cv_hpo` sweeps λ from 10^{-2} to 10^9 across walk-forward folds. Mean IC stays mildly negative across most of the range, troughs near $\lambda \approx 10^3$ at -0.039, recovers monotonically as regularization tightens, and only crosses zero at $\lambda \gtrsim 10^7$ to reach a noisy peak of $\approx +0.007$ at the top of the search range. The fold-level standard deviation ranges from roughly 0.04 to 0.10 across the grid and dwarfs the cross-λ mean, flagging the landscape as noise-dominated. The notebook then implements both single-loop and nested cross-validation with Optuna, quantifying the selection-bias inflation (Cawley and Talbot, 2010).

When the underlying signal is weak, the protocol distinction is exactly when selection bias matters most. Here, it is large enough to flip the reported sign: single-loop CV reports a positive mean IC of +0.028; nested CV returns -0.032 on identical splits. We illustrate these principles by first optimizing a single hyperparameter (Ridge λ); *Chapter 12* extends to the joint tuning of multiple hyperparameters.

Box 11.1: Incremental updates

The walk-forward protocol above retrains from scratch at every refit. For high-frequency case studies, such as Crypto (8-hour) and NASDAQ-100 (minute bars), full retraining is computationally expensive.

Scikit-learn's `SGDRegressor` and `SGDClassifier` support `partial_fit` for incremental updates: present a single mini-batch of new observations and update the coefficients via one gradient step, rather than re-solving the full optimization. This is the fastest for online deployment but introduces sensitivity to the learning rate schedule and can drift without periodic full retraining. *Chapter 25* develops the full online learning framework for live trading systems.

Loss function choice

The regularizers above are usually paired with **mean squared error** (**MSE**) by default, especially in standard Ridge and Lasso regression. But the penalty does not require MSE: you can combine the same regularization idea with other loss functions when a different target (such as a median, a robust central tendency, or a tail quantile) better matches the trading objective.

MSE is a natural choice when the goal is to estimate the conditional mean of the return distribution, but the conditional mean may not be the right target:

- **MSE** penalizes errors quadratically, forcing the model to accommodate extreme observations that may reflect idiosyncratic events rather than systematic patterns.
- **Mean absolute error** (MAE) penalizes linearly and estimates the conditional *median* rather than the mean. Because outliers shift the median far less than the mean, MAE produces more stable coefficients when a few large moves dominate.

- **Huber loss** transitions from quadratic for small errors (like MSE) to linear for large errors (like MAE) at a threshold δ, chosen as a tuning parameter or scaled to a robust estimate of the residual dispersion, preserving MSE's efficiency for typical observations while limiting outlier influence (Huber, 1964).

All three losses estimate a location parameter of the conditional return distribution. Scikit-learn's `SGDRegressor` provides a unified interface: `loss='squared_error'`, `loss='epsilon_insensitive'` (MAE proxy), and `loss='huber'` all accept the same regularization penalties and `sample_weight` parameter. `02_regularization_paths` compares all three at the best Ridge alpha, isolating the loss function's effect on IC.

Quantile regression changes the estimand entirely, predicting specified percentiles rather than a central tendency. If a long-short strategy trades only the top and bottom deciles, the conditional mean is the wrong target: most of the model's capacity is spent distinguishing among assets that will never be traded. *Section 11.5* develops quantile regression as the foundation for conformalized prediction intervals.

Evaluating regression models

Training losses determine what the model optimizes; evaluation metrics determine how we judge the result. The appropriate metric depends on how predictions map to trades:

- **Information Coefficient (IC).** Spearman's rank correlation between predicted and realized returns is the primary metric for cross-sectional models that generate ranked signals. IC captures monotonic association without assuming linearity. In general, the coefficient of variation is the ratio of the mean to the standard deviation for a given metric; for the IC, this measure is also called the **IC Information Ratio** (**ICIR**; see *Chapter 7*).
- **RMSE and MAE.** RMSE, the square root of the MSE, measures the standard deviation of prediction errors; MAE measures the average absolute error and is less sensitive to outliers. Both are useful for relative model comparison within the same dataset and label definition, but neither has a standalone threshold for "good" performance: the relevant benchmark is always a naive model that, for example, predicts the cross-sectional mean.
- **Turnover.** No statistical metric measures tradability: a model that improves IC by 20% but triples turnover may degrade net performance after transaction costs. Report turnover alongside every metric. *Section 11.6* examines this tradeoff empirically across all nine case studies; *Chapter 17* formalizes the turnover-adjusted evaluation framework.

Since IC measures global ranking quality, strategies that trade only the extremes should also track quintile or decile spreads to verify that ranking accuracy translates into separation in the traded tails.

Implementation: `02_regularization_paths` reports IC, RMSE, and R^2 across all four model types for the `etfs` case study. The stability of predicted rankings for the same test data, measured as the correlation between cross-sectional rankings from models trained on consecutive windows, diagnoses signal robustness to retraining; `02_regularization_paths` computes this for Ridge across all fold pairs.

Sample weighting

Most scikit-learn estimators accept a `sample_weight` parameter, allowing observations to contribute unequally to the loss function. Two weighting schemes from *Section 7.2* apply directly:

- **Uniqueness weighting** ($w_{t,a}$ = average inverse concurrency) corrects for label overlap when using the $\bar{H}$-bar labels defined in *Chapter 7*. Overlapping labels violate the independence assumption implicit in the sum-of-squared-errors objective; down-weighting observations with high concurrency partially mitigates this.
- **Recency weighting** ($w_t^{\text{recency}} = e^{-\lambda(T-t)}$) gives more influence to recent observations, adapting the model to regime evolution. The decay rate λ controls the effective lookback horizon.

The two compose multiplicatively: $w_{t,a}^{\text{combined}} = w_{t,a}^{\text{uniqueness}} \cdot w_t^{\text{recency}}$. Report the effective sample size $N_{\text{eff}} = \sum w_{t,a}^{\text{combined}}$ alongside performance metrics. A small N_{eff} relative to the nominal sample size signals that a few observations dominate the fit, increasing the risk of overfitting to those observations.

Implementation: `02_regularization_paths` shows recency weighting with exponential decay in the final walk-forward fold and reports the effective sample size.

Training loss versus trading objective

A model can reduce MSE while degrading PnL if the improvement comes from fitting the middle of the cross-section (assets that are never traded) or from increasing turnover. We therefore maintain a strict separation between *model selection* (validation loss and rank metrics within the leakage-safe walk-forward protocol) and *strategy evaluation* (turnover- and cost-adjusted returns, *Chapter 18*). Without this separation, in-sample statistical improvements masquerade as trading value. We now turn to a different prediction task that focuses on direction, or extreme moves.

11.3 Predicting direction with logistic regression

The previous section treated the label as a continuous return. Many trading setups, however, operate on discrete decisions (go long, go short, or stay flat), and the label families defined in *Chapter 7* include binary up/down flags, three-class directional labels, and quantile memberships. For these setups, classification models that directly predict discrete outcomes are the natural choice, and logistic regression is the regularized baseline.

Classification is not universally superior to regression. Direction prediction can misalign with PnL when payoffs are asymmetric: a model that correctly predicts direction 55% of the time but systematically misses large moves may underperform a regression model that captures magnitude in the tails.

The choice should follow from the *signal-to-trade mapping* defined in *Chapter 7*. If the mapping applies a threshold or quantile rule to convert predictions into positions, classification fits naturally because the model directly optimizes the decision that matters. If the mapping scales position size in proportion to the predicted return, regression preserves the magnitude information that classification discards. Ultimately, however, what works better in a given case is an empirical matter.

Binary logistic regression

Logistic regression models the probability that the outcome belongs to the positive class:

$$P(y = 1 \mid X) = \frac{1}{1 + e^{-X\beta}} = \sigma(X\beta)$$

where $\sigma(\cdot)$ is the sigmoid function, mapping any real-valued linear combination to the (0,1) interval. The model learns β by maximizing the **log-likelihood** of the observed labels, or equivalently by minimizing the **cross-entropy** (log-loss) between predicted probabilities and observed outcomes.

The key difference from linear regression is that logistic regression produces a *probability estimate* rather than a point forecast of the return. A prediction of 0.65 means that, under the fitted logistic specification, the model assigns a 65% probability to an up move. This interpretation is justified by the log-loss objective: in population, cross-entropy is minimized by the true conditional probability $P(y = 1 \mid X)$, provided the model class is rich enough and the data-generating process is stable.

In practice, however, the fitted probabilities *may not be well calibrated* due to misspecification, finite sample size, regularization, class weighting, resampling, noisy labels, or distribution shift. The output should therefore be treated as a probability estimate, not automatically as a calibrated empirical frequency. Calibration diagnostics or post-hoc calibration may be needed before using these probabilities for risk-adjusted position sizing (discussed later in this section).

Each coefficient β_j represents the change in log-odds per unit change in x_j. After standardization, a coefficient of 0.5 on momentum means that a one-standard-deviation increase in momentum raises the log-odds of an up move by 0.5. At a baseline probability of 50, this changes the predicted probability to $\sigma(0.5) \approx 62$. At a baseline probability of 90, the same log-odds increase changes the predicted probability to approximately 94. The probability-point effect is therefore not constant: **coefficients are linear on the log-odds scale**, not on the probability scale.

Classification labels collapse return magnitudes into categories: a 50% return and a 2% return both count as "up." This is simultaneously a strength and a limitation. It prevents extreme observations from dominating the loss function, as they would with MSE in regression, producing more stable coefficient estimates in the presence of fat tails. But it discards valuable magnitude information. The trade-off may favor classification when the trading decision is binary (long or short) and regression when position size varies with the predicted magnitude.

Implementation: `03_logistic_classification` traces the full walk-forward binary logistic regression pipeline on ETF data, including the label construction and the L2/L1 regularization sweeps described below.

Multi-class extension

The binary model extends to K classes via **multinomial logistic regression (softmax)**. For the three-class label, with classes long (+1), neutral (0), and short (−1), the model estimates:

$$P(y = k \mid X) = \frac{e^{X\beta_k}}{\sum_{j=1}^{K} e^{X\beta_j}}$$

Each class receives its own coefficient vector β_k, and probabilities sum to one across classes (`multi_class='multinomial'` in scikit-learn). The neutral zone filters observations near the zero-return boundary, reducing label noise, but each additional class adds a full coefficient vector, increasing parameter count by roughly $K - 1$.

For quantile strategies trading only the extremes, a binary framing (top decile versus bottom decile, discarding the middle) is typically more efficient than a multi-class model that must also learn middle categories.

Regularization

The L_1, L_2, and Elastic Net penalties from *Section 11.2* apply identically in form, added to the negative log-likelihood rather than the sum of squared residuals:

$$\min_{\beta} - \sum_{i=1}^{n} \left[y_i \log\sigma(X_i\beta) + (1 - y_i)\log\left(1 - \sigma(X_i\beta)\right) \right] + \lambda |\beta|_2^2$$

Scikit-learn's `LogisticRegression` uses $C = 1/\lambda$ (higher C means less regularization), with `penalty` and `l1_ratio` controlling the penalty type. All guidance from *Section 11.2* carries over.

Regularization is more critical here than in regression: the maximum likelihood objective diverges when classes are perfectly or nearly separable. In high-dimensional feature spaces where p approaches n, a separating hyperplane almost always exists, driving coefficients toward $\pm\infty$ and producing arbitrarily confident predictions that fail out of sample. Regularization bounds coefficients, ensuring finite solutions, a concern absent from OLS, which has a closed-form solution whenever $X^\top X$ is invertible.

Probability calibration

Under correct specification, logistic regression is calibrated by construction: if the model predicts $P(y = 1 \mid X) = 0.7$ for a set of observations, approximately 70% of them will have $y = 1$. In practice, two forces distort this correspondence:

- **Regularization** systematically compresses predicted probabilities toward the base rate. Shrinking coefficients toward zero flattens the sigmoid, pulling extreme predictions toward 0.5. This is a predictable, directional distortion: the model becomes systematically underconfident in its predictions.
- **Misspecification** introduces less predictable distortions. If the true decision boundary is nonlinear but the model is linear, calibration breaks in ways that depend on the specific form of the misspecification.

Calibration matters when position sizes depend on predicted probability levels: if a probability of 0.7 triggers a larger position than 0.6, miscalibrated probabilities translate directly into misallocated capital:

- **Platt scaling** (fitting a logistic function to the model's raw outputs on a held-out set) corrects for the systematic compression caused by regularization.
- **Isotonic regression** (fitting a non-parametric monotone function) handles more complex miscalibration patterns but requires more data to estimate reliably (Niculescu-Mizil and Caruana, 2005).

Both must use data not used for training: the validation fold in the walk-forward protocol serves this purpose. Scikit-learn's `CalibratedClassifierCV` automates the procedure.

Bin predictions by predicted probability (for example, [0.5, 0.55), [0.55, 0.6), ...) and compute accuracy within each bin. Monotonically increasing hit rates as predicted probability moves away from 0.5 indicate well-calibrated confidence; non-monotonic patterns (high-confidence predictions performing worse than moderate-confidence ones) suggest overfitting or misspecification.

For threshold-based and rank-based signal generation, calibration is less critical because only the *ordering* of predictions matters. Assess whether the signal-to-trade mapping depends on probability levels or only on ranks before investing effort in calibration.

> **Implementation:** `03_logistic_classification` produces calibration curves for the walk-forward predictions and compares them against perfect calibration.

From probabilities to trading signals

The conversion from predicted probabilities to positions should match the trading setup defined in *Chapter 7*. Common approaches include:

- **Threshold-based:** Go long if $P(y = 1 \mid X) > \tau_{\text{upper}}$, short if $P(y = 1 \mid X) < \tau_{\text{lower}}$, flat otherwise. The thresholds control selectivity: $\tau_{\text{upper}} = 0.6$ and $\tau_{\text{lower}} = 0.4$ is a common starting point, but optimal values depend on transaction costs and the base rate. Asymmetric thresholds accommodate asymmetric costs of long versus short positions.
- **Probability-weighted:** Position size is proportional to the distance from 0.5, expressing graduated confidence. This requires calibrated probabilities: if the model systematically underestimates confidence (as regularization tends to do), positions will be systematically undersized relative to the true signal.
- **Rank-based:** Within a cross-section, rank assets by predicted probability and go long the top decile, short the bottom decile. This ensures a fixed number of positions regardless of the probability distribution and depends only on ordering, making it robust to miscalibration.

Thresholds and quantile cutoffs must use only information available at decision time: the walk-forward protocol (*Chapter 6*) enforces this by recomputing them within each training window.

Implementation: `03_logistic_classification` compares all three conversion methods on the same fold, showing that identical predictions yield substantially different portfolios. *Chapter 16* extends this comparison across full backtests.

Handling class imbalance

When predicting rare events (the 5% of stocks exceeding two standard deviations, or the minority class in an asymmetrically thresholded label), the minority class contributes little to the log-likelihood. The model minimizes loss by predicting the majority class for all observations, achieving high accuracy but generating no trading signal.

Class weighting scales each class's loss contribution inversely to its frequency, ensuring that minority-class errors carry proportionally more weight. Scikit-learn's `class_weight='balanced'` computes these weights automatically. This does not change the decision boundary's location in feature space but adjusts how aggressively the optimizer penalizes errors on each side. `03_logistic_classification` compares default and balanced class weighting on the last fold, confirming that the effect is modest when classes are roughly balanced.

When combining class weights with the uniqueness and recency weights from *Section 11.2*, monitor N_{eff}: a sharp drop below the nominal sample size signals that a few observations dominate the fit. This risk is acute when minority-class observations cluster in crisis periods. Verify that reweighted training sets span multiple market conditions rather than concentrating on a single regime.

Evaluating classification models

Classification evaluation requires metrics suited to the probabilistic and discrete nature of the outputs. As with regression (*Section 11.2*), the appropriate metric depends on how predictions map to trades:

- **AUC (area under the ROC curve)** measures the quality of ranking across all possible classification thresholds. An AUC of 0.5 indicates random ranking; values of 0.55–0.60 represent meaningful predictive power for financial applications, where signal-to-noise ratios are low. Values above 0.65 on out-of-sample financial data warrant scrutiny: they may indicate data leakage or an evaluation window that happens to align with a strong trend.
- **Precision and recall.** Precision (fraction of predicted positives that are true positives) guards against wasted trades; recall (fraction of true positives that are predicted) guards against missed opportunities. The trade-off depends on costs: high transaction costs favor precision (fewer, more accurate trades); strategies with capacity constraints favor recall (capturing all available opportunities). The F1 score balances both but assigns equal weight to each, which may not reflect the trade-offs in economics.
- **Log-loss.** If the signal-to-trade mapping uses probability levels rather than ranks, log-loss directly evaluates the quality of the probability estimates. It penalizes confident wrong predictions heavily, making it a useful complement to AUC in settings where calibration matters. The Brier score (the mean squared difference between predicted probabilities and binary outcomes) provides a complementary calibration-sensitive metric.

Turnover

As with regression, report turnover alongside every classification metric. A model that improves AUC by shifting the decision boundary (changing which assets are traded each period) may increase turnover beyond what the strategy can absorb.

Now that we have familiarized ourselves with the inner workings of the most popular linear models, let us take a closer look at model interpretability.

Implementation: `03_logistic_classification` shows the full workflow on the ETF case study. The per-case-study notebooks apply both regression and classification pipelines across all nine datasets.

11.4 Interpreting models with SHAP

A model that predicts returns but cannot explain why offers limited value. Understanding which features drive predictions (and whether those relationships make economic sense) separates robust signals from spurious curve-fitting. **SHapley Additive exPlanations** (SHAP) is the primary interpretability framework, embedded in the walk-forward pipeline as a continuous diagnostic.

The case for interpretability rests on three pillars:

- **Diagnosis**: When a model fails in production, you need to know why. A Ridge model that suddenly underperforms might be responding to a vendor data migration that changed how momentum is computed, or to genuine decay in the momentum premium. SHAP analysis of recent versus historical predictions can distinguish these scenarios.
- **Economic sanity-checking**: A momentum feature should positively contribute to high-momentum stocks; a volatility feature should reflect the expected risk-return relationship. When attributions contradict established theory, the model is more likely to fit noise than capture signal.
- **Governance**: Model risk frameworks such as SR 11-7 (Federal Reserve) and SS1/23 (Bank of England) require that firms understand and justify algorithmic outputs. Even without regulatory obligations, "the model said so" does not explain a drawdown.

For standardized linear models, coefficient magnitudes offer a tempting shortcut, but shrinkage entangles importance with the penalty strength, correlated features split or steal credit depending on the penalty type, and coefficient interpretation does not generalize beyond linear models.

SHAP supplies a unified attribution language: it disentangles regularization distortion, allocates credit fairly among correlated features, and carries forward unchanged to trees (*Chapter 12*) and deep learning (*Chapter 13*).

Game-theoretic attribution with SHAP

SHAP builds on **Shapley values** from cooperative game theory, which determine each player's contribution to the outcome. Here, the "players" are features, the "payoff" is the gap between a specific prediction and the model's average prediction (the baseline), and the question is: how much did each feature contribute to moving this prediction away from baseline?

The *Shapley value* for feature j averages its marginal contribution across all orderings in which features could enter the model:

$$\phi_j = \sum_{S\subseteq F\setminus\{j\}} \frac{|S|!\,(|F|-|S|-1)!}{|F|!}[f(S\cup\{j\}) - f(S)]$$

where F is the full feature set, S ranges over subsets excluding j, and $f(S)$ is the expected prediction when only features in S are known.

Shapley (1953) proved that this is the **unique allocation satisfying four axioms**:

- Efficiency: attributions sum exactly to the prediction minus baseline
- Symmetry: identically contributing features receive equal credit
- Null player: irrelevant features receive zero credit
- Linearity: attributions for a sum of models equal the sum of attributions

Lundberg and Lee (2017) unified **LIME, DeepLIFT**, and classic Shapley regression within this framework, showing that SHAP is the unique additive attribution method that satisfies all four axioms.

Efficient computation

Exact computation requires evaluating $2^{|F|}$ subsets, which is intractable for realistic feature sets. Model-specific algorithms make it practical:

- **LinearSHAP** exploits the closed form for linear models: $\phi_j = \beta_j \cdot (x_j - E[x_j])$, computed over the training set. This is exact and $O(F)$ per observation, the right choice for this chapter.
- **TreeSHAP** (*Chapter 12*) and **KernelSHAP** (*Chapter 13*) extend the framework to nonlinear models.

> **Implementation:** `05_shap_analysis` shows LinearSHAP end-to-end on the ETF case study, including verification that SHAP values match the closed-form coefficient attribution.

Practical application in global and local analysis

SHAP supports both global views (feature importance summarized across all predictions) and local views, decomposing the contribution of each feature to a single model score.

Global feature importance

SHAP summary plots rank features by mean $|\phi_j|$ across all test observations. Each point represents the SHAP value for one observation, colored by its feature value. The plot reveals which features matter most, the direction of effects, and whether importance is consistent or conditional.

In the `etfs` case study, volatility horizons dominate the top of the ranking: six-month volatility (`vol_126d`) contributes most, with a positive feature-to-SHAP relationship, while three-month volatility (`vol_63d`) is the second-most important and pulls in the opposite direction. Risk-adjusted return appears next (`sharpe_63d`, positive), followed by `vol_ratio_medium` and `yield_curve_slope`.

SHAP importance can differ from coefficient rankings: a feature with a moderate coefficient but high variance at informative observations can have a higher mean $|\phi_j|$ than a feature with a larger coefficient but lower variance. *Figure 11.3* shows the beeswarm summary for the ETF case study.

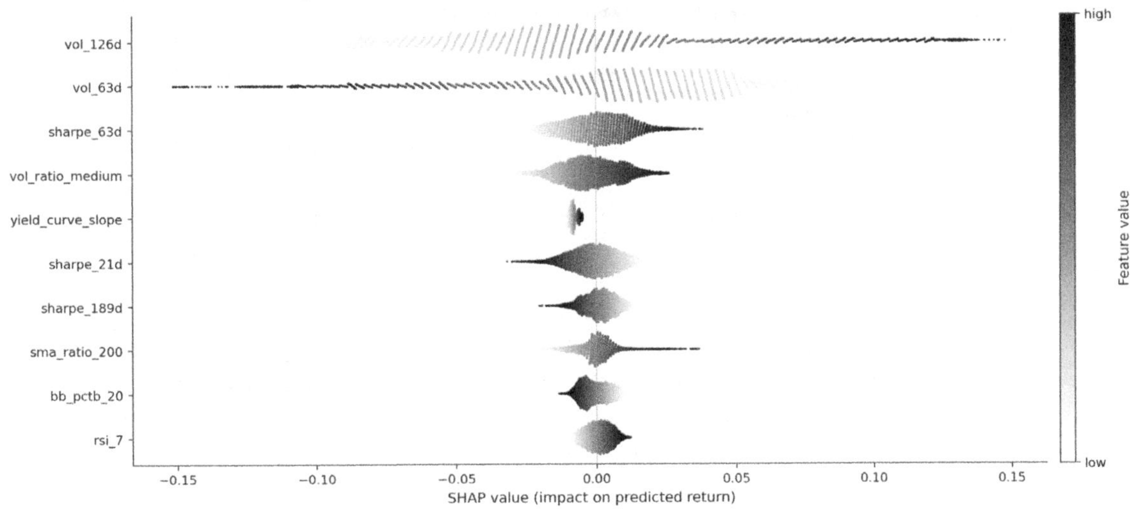

Figure 11.3: Importance of the top 20 etfs features

Local explanations

Waterfall plots decompose a single prediction from baseline to final value, feature by feature. For a high-conviction stock: baseline of 0.5% → momentum adds +0.8% → mean reversion subtracts −0.3% → volatility adds +0.2% → final prediction of 1.4%. This enables two checks:

1. An *attribution audit*: is outperformance driven by trusted features or suspicious ones (an illiquidity proxy reflecting data staleness)?
2. A *concentration-risk flag*: a prediction dominated by a single feature is fragile.

In practice, flagging predictions in which a single feature accounts for more than a certain threshold of the total $|\phi_j|$ could provide an automated alert for manual review or position-size reduction. *Figure 11.4* contrasts a correct high-conviction prediction whose attribution spreads across ten features with an incorrect one in which a single liquidity-proxy feature carries most of the model's conviction; the right-panel pattern is exactly what the concentration-risk flag is designed to catch.

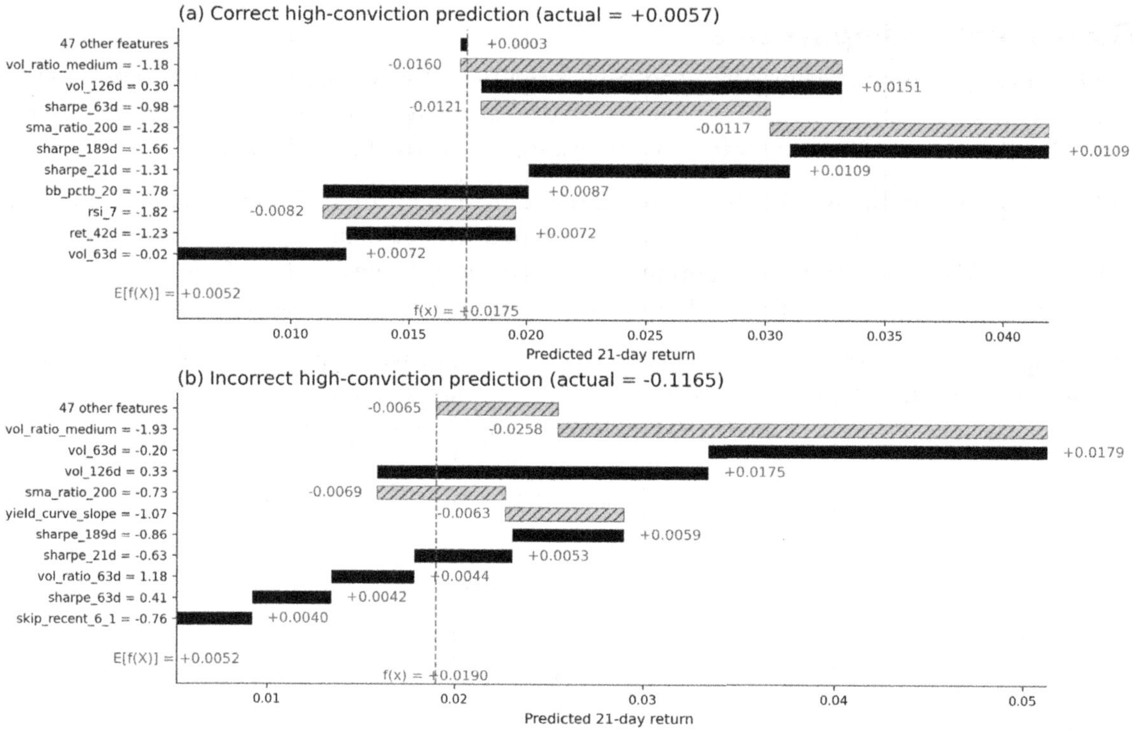

Figure 11.4: SHAP waterfall decomposition of two high-conviction predictions from the `etfs` *case study (Ridge, 21-day forward returns). Both predictions sit in the top 5% by predicted magnitude. Panel (a): a correct call where ten features contribute roughly evenly, and the prediction reflects diversified evidence. Panel (b): an incorrect call where* `vol_63d` *(volume ratio) alone contributes +0.018, yet the realized return was −11.7%*

Implementation: `05_shap_analysis` includes waterfall decompositions for both correct and incorrect high-conviction predictions.

Feature dependence

SHAP dependence plots show how a feature's SHAP value varies with its own value, colored by an interacting feature. For linear models, the relationship is linear by construction, but the plot still serves as a sanity check for sign consistency and outlier behavior.

For tree-based and neural network models (*Chapters 12* and *13*), dependence plots reveal threshold effects, saturation, and interaction structures that are invisible in coefficient tables.

Building an economic narrative

SHAP's primary value for systematic investing is epistemic: it provides a structured protocol for distinguishing genuine signal from overfitting, organized in four layers:

- **Sign consistency:** does each feature's contribution have the expected sign? A model that has learned the opposite of every documented factor relationship is almost certainly fitting noise.
- **Magnitude plausibility:** Does a single feature imply a 5% monthly return contribution in a universe where median monthly returns are 0.8%? If so, the model is extrapolating.
- **Stability across walk-forward windows:** Compute SHAP values per fold and track whether the same features rank in the top five, maintain consistent signs, and show stable magnitudes. Plotting mean $|\phi_j|$ over time produces a "SHAP stability chart," one of the most informative validation diagnostics (*Figure 11.5*).
- **Regime-conditional analysis:** Partition test data by volatility tercile or regime label (*Chapter 7*) and compute SHAP summaries within each partition. A model that shifts from momentum to mean reversion across regimes may be economically sensible, but only if regime identification is itself robust.

A refinement: fold-to-fold variation in SHAP rankings conflates temporal regime shifts (interesting) with finite-sample estimation noise (uninteresting). Bootstrapping SHAP values within a single fold provides confidence intervals on feature importance, separating the two sources.

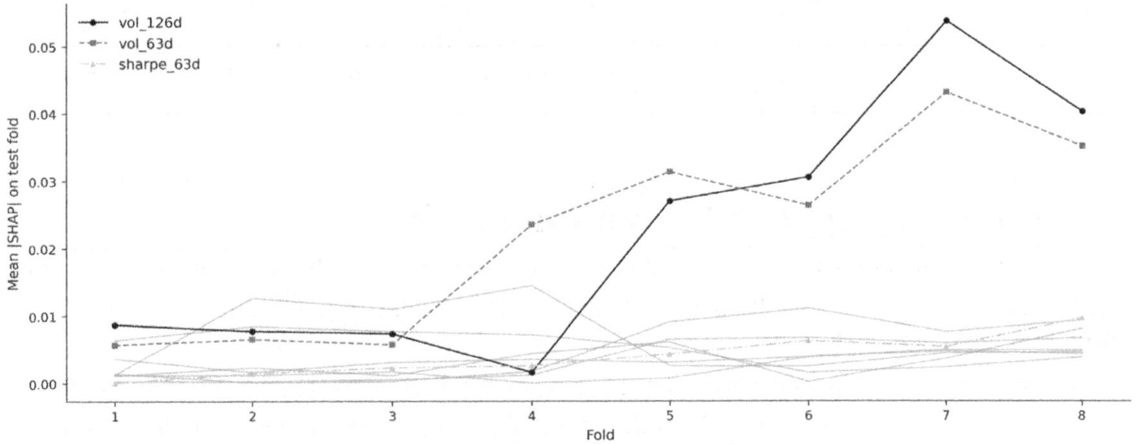

Figure 11.5: SHAP stability across folds

A complementary diagnostic compares SHAP **profiles for high-conviction predictions** that were directionally correct versus those that were incorrect. Features where the model relied heavily on wrong predictions (measured by the ratio of mean $|\phi_j|$ for incorrect to correct cases, or by large directional differences in mean signed SHAP) are candidates for re-engineering or nonlinear modeling. This right-versus-wrong decomposition targets the predictions that matter most for PnL.

Limitations and failure modes

Causal misinterpretation is a major risk. A high SHAP value for feature j means it contributed to *this model's prediction*, not that it caused the return. A feature such as `obv_zscore_63d` with high SHAP importance could reflect genuine predictive power, correlation with an omitted predictor, or a pipeline confound. Kumar et al. (2020) formalize how Shapley-based explanations can mislead when features are correlated or when they are interpreted causally. Use SHAP for descriptive attribution ("what is the model responding to?"), not causal claims.

Feature dependence and *impossible coalitions* are also significant issues. Standard SHAP marginalizes out absent features independently, creating impossible feature combinations when features are correlated. For linear models, this is manageable; for nonlinear models, Aas et al. (2021) propose **conditional SHAP**, which requires estimating conditional distributions. **Permutation importance** and LIME lack SHAP's axiomatic guarantees: permutation importance inflates scores for correlated features; LIME attributions need not sum to the prediction.

Integration with the walk-forward pipeline

The SHAP stability chart across folds serves as a model-selection tool alongside IC and coverage metrics, providing qualitative evidence that the model has learned stable, economically sensible relationships.

The SHAP stability chart in `05_shap_analysis` tracks mean $|\phi_j|$ across all walk-forward folds for the top features. Models that pass quantitative hurdles yet exhibit unstable or economically implausible SHAP patterns warrant skepticism, regardless of their reported performance.

> **Implementation:** `05_shap_analysis` implements SHAP computation within the walk-forward framework, including summary plots, waterfall decompositions, and right-versus-wrong diagnostic comparisons for high-conviction predictions. *Section 11.5* turns from explaining individual predictions to bounding them: how to attach calibrated uncertainty to each forecast.

11.5 Quantifying predictive uncertainty

A point forecast is incomplete because it suppresses information about the reliability of the estimate. In trading, this matters directly: the same predicted return can imply very different decisions depending on how uncertain the forecast is.

Consider a Ridge regression model that predicts a 2% return for two ETFs. For the first ETF, the current feature values lie near the center of the training distribution. For the second, volatility has spiked, liquidity has deteriorated, and several features sit near their historical extremes. The point forecast is the same, but the second prediction is much less reliable. Treating both forecasts as equivalent inputs to portfolio construction would overstate the precision of the second signal.

Classical **prediction intervals** often rely on assumptions that are fragile in financial data. Gaussian intervals of the form $\hat{y} \pm z_{\alpha/2}\hat{\sigma}$ assume a useful residual scale estimate and often rely, explicitly or implicitly, on approximately normal, homoskedastic errors. Asset returns instead exhibit heavy tails, volatility clustering, nonlinear residual dispersion, and regime dependence. The uncertainty around a forecast is rarely constant across assets, horizons, or market states.

Conformal prediction offers a model-agnostic alternative. It acts as a calibration layer placed on top of an existing forecasting model. After fitting the base model, we evaluate its forecast errors on a held-out calibration set and use the empirical distribution of those errors to construct prediction intervals or prediction sets for future observations. Because the procedure uses observed forecast errors rather than a parametric error model, it does not require normal residuals, homoskedasticity, or a correctly specified likelihood.

The key assumption behind the formal guarantee is **exchangeability**. A sequence of observations is exchangeable if its joint distribution is unchanged by reordering the observations. Independent and identically distributed observations are exchangeable, but exchangeability is weaker than independence. This assumption matters because conformal prediction relies on the rank of the next observation's calibration score among the scores already observed. If the calibration scores and the next test score are exchangeable, the future score is equally likely to occupy any rank, which yields finite-sample marginal coverage.

Under exchangeability, conformal prediction delivers a finite-sample **marginal coverage guarantee**. For example, a 90% conformal interval will contain the realized outcome at least 90% of the time over repeated samples. This guarantee is distribution-free: it does not depend on the correctness of the base model, the shape of the return distribution, or the sample size. It is, however, a marginal guarantee. It does not imply that coverage is exactly 90% within every asset, fold, volatility regime, or predicted-return bucket.

Financial time series are not exchangeable in the strict sense because order matters. Autocorrelation, volatility clustering, changing liquidity, and structural breaks mean that calibration residuals from one period may not represent those in the next. Conformal prediction remains useful in this setting, but the theorem no longer mechanically justifies coverage. In financial applications, conformal intervals should therefore be treated as empirically calibrated uncertainty estimates whose coverage must be monitored, stress-tested, and adapted over time.

Split-conformal prediction

The simplest practical variant is split-conformal prediction (Papadopoulos et al., 2002; Lei et al., 2018). It separates model fitting from uncertainty calibration:

1. **Partition the data.** Divide the available training observations into a proper training set and a calibration set. The proper training set fits the model and selects any hyperparameters. The calibration set must remain untouched until the fitted model is evaluated for uncertainty calibration.
2. **Compute calibration scores.** For each calibration observation i, compute a nonconformity score. For a symmetric regression interval, the usual score is the absolute residual:$s_i = |y_i - \hat{f}(x_i)|$.

   These scores estimate the empirical distribution of the model's out-of-sample forecast errors.
3. **Compute the conformal quantile.** Let n_{cal} be the number of calibration observations, and let:

   $$s_{(1)} \le s_{(2)} \le \cdots \le s_{(n_{\text{cal}})}$$

   denote the sorted calibration scores. For target miscoverage rate α, define:

   $$k = \lceil (n_{\text{cal}} + 1)(1 - \alpha) \rceil$$

   The conformal correction is the conservative order statistic $\hat{q} = s_{(k)}$. This corresponds to using the higher empirical quantile rather than an interpolated quantile. If $k > n_{\text{cal}}$, the calibration set is too small to provide a finite conformal quantile at the desired coverage level.

4. **Construct prediction intervals.** For a new observation x, the split-conformal interval is:

$$C(x) = \left[\hat{f}(x) - \hat{q}, \hat{f}(x) + \hat{q}\right]$$

This interval has fixed width $2\hat{q}$ for every observation. That simplicity is useful: split conformal is easy to implement, easy to audit, and robust to misspecification of the base model. Its limitation is equally clear: it cannot vary the interval width across market regimes, assets, or feature configurations. A forecast made during a volatility spike receives the same residual correction as one made during a quiet regime.

Under exchangeability of the calibration observations and the next test observation, split-conformal prediction provides **finite-sample marginal coverage:**

$$P\left(Y_{n+1} \in C(X_{n+1})\right) \geq 1 - \alpha$$

This guarantee holds for any fitted base model and any outcome distribution, provided the calibration set was not used to fit or tune the model whose scores are being calibrated. The guarantee is marginal: it averages over the joint distribution of future observations. It does not ensure correct coverage conditional on a particular date, asset, volatility state, sector, or signal-strength bucket.

Implementation: `06_conformal_prediction` implements split-conformal prediction with Ridge regression on the ETF case study.

The exchangeability problem

The exchangeability assumption is fragile in financial time series. The order of observations carries information: volatility clusters, correlations change, liquidity varies, and regimes shift. Randomly permuting daily returns or cross-sectional residuals would destroy part of the data-generating structure. As a result, the rank argument behind the conformal guarantee no longer applies exactly. Yesterday's calibration residuals may not be representative of tomorrow's forecast errors.

This does not make conformal prediction unusable. It changes how the method should be interpreted. In finance, conformal prediction is best viewed as a disciplined empirical calibration procedure whose formal guarantee is exact under exchangeability and approximate under sufficiently stable nonexchangeable conditions. Coverage should therefore be measured out of sample, monitored by regime, and updated when the calibration distribution becomes stale.

Several adaptations are useful in practice:

- **Rolling calibration windows.** Instead of using all historical calibration scores, compute $\hat{q}$ from a recent window, such as the most recent 250 trading days. This makes the score distribution more responsive to current volatility and liquidity conditions. The trade-off is higher estimation noise because fewer calibration observations are used.

- **Weighted conformal calibration.** Assign larger weights to more recent or more relevant calibration observations. Exponential time decay is a practical heuristic for nonstationary time series. More formal weighted conformal methods are justified under specific distributional shift assumptions, such as covariate shift, when the relative likelihoods of calibration and test covariates can be estimated.
- **Regime-conditional calibration.** Partition the calibration scores by pre-specified market states, such as realized-volatility quantiles, VIX terciles, liquidity buckets, or macro regimes, and compute separate conformal corrections within each state. This can improve conditional coverage when residual dispersion differs sharply across regimes. The partition should be defined ex ante, and each regime must contain enough calibration observations to estimate a stable quantile.
- **Online coverage feedback.** Adaptive conformal methods monitor realized coverage as outcomes arrive and adjust the effective miscoverage rate or calibration threshold. Recent misses widen subsequent intervals; persistent overcoverage narrows them. This provides a practical feedback mechanism when the historical calibration distribution no longer matches current conditions.

These adaptations do not fully restore the original exchangeability theorem. They make the calibration layer more responsive to the types of drift and dependence that matter in financial forecasting.

Adaptive conformal inference

Adaptive Conformal Inference (ACI) (Gibbs and Candès, 2021, 2023) modifies conformal calibration for online, nonstationary environments. Rather than fixing the miscoverage level α once, ACI updates an effective miscoverage parameter α_t after each realized outcome.

At time t, the model constructs a conformal set $C_t(X_t)$ using the current value α_t. After observing Y_t, the update is:

$$\alpha_{t+1} = \alpha_t + \gamma(\alpha - \mathbf{1}\{Y_t \notin C_t(X_t)\})$$

where α is the target miscoverage rate and $\gamma > 0$ is the learning rate.

The sign of the update is intuitive. If the interval misses, then $\mathbf{1}\{Y_t \notin C_t(X_t)\} = 1$, so α_{t+1} decreases. A lower miscoverage level produces a wider next interval. If the interval covers, then the indicator equals zero, so α_{t+1} increases and the next interval narrows. Undercoverage triggers expansion; persistent overcoverage triggers contraction.

ACI provides a long-run coverage control mechanism for nonstationary sequences. Its guarantee is weaker than the finite-sample marginal guarantee of split conformal under exchangeability: it targets average empirical coverage over time rather than exact coverage for each time point, subgroup, or regime. This distinction is important in trading. ACI can help the interval sequence recover after drift, but it does not eliminate the need to inspect coverage by fold, volatility regime, asset group, and signal bucket.

The *learning rate* γ controls the speed-stability trade-off. Larger values adapt faster after misses but can make interval widths oscillate. Smaller values produce smoother intervals but may respond too slowly to abrupt changes in volatility. TheT notebook tunes values such as $\gamma \in [0.005, 0.05]$ within the walk-forward framework. In implementation, the adaptive miscoverage level α_t should be clipped to a bounded range, such as $[0.001, 0.999]$, to avoid degenerate intervals.

Implementation: `06_conformal_prediction` shows the ACI online update, the resulting α_t trajectory, and the effect of adaptive feedback on coverage and interval width.

Conformalized quantile regression

Split-conformal intervals have constant width, which is often unrealistic in financial data. **Conformalized Quantile Regression** (CQR; Romano et al., 2019) addresses this limitation by combining conditional quantile models with conformal calibration.

For target coverage $1 - \alpha$, CQR proceeds as follows:

1. Train lower and upper quantile models. On the proper training set, estimate conditional quantiles:

   $$\hat{q}_{\alpha/2}(x) \quad \text{and} \quad \hat{q}_{1-\alpha/2}(x)$$

   For 90% coverage, these correspond to the 5th and 95th conditional quantiles.

2. Compute CQR calibration scores. On the calibration set, compute:

   $$s_i = \max\{\hat{q}_{\alpha/2}(x_i) - y_i,\ y_i - \hat{q}_{1-\alpha/2}(x_i)\}$$

   A positive score indicates that the realized outcome fell outside the estimated quantile band. A negative score indicates that the outcome fell inside the band, with room to spare.

3. Compute the conformal correction. Sort the calibration scores and compute the same conservative conformal order statistic $\hat{q}_{\text{CQR}}$ used in split conformal.
4. Construct calibrated intervals. For a new observation x, define:

   $$C(x) = \left[\hat{q}_{\alpha/2}(x) - \hat{q}_{\text{CQR}},\ \hat{q}_{1-\alpha/2}(x) + \hat{q}_{\text{CQR}}\right]$$

CQR retains the adaptive shape of the quantile model: intervals widen where the model predicts greater conditional dispersion and narrow where the model predicts lower uncertainty. The conformal correction then calibrates the empirical coverage of these intervals. Unlike split conformal, the interval width can vary across assets, dates, regimes, and feature configurations.

CQR is often preferable when residual dispersion is visibly heterogeneous, and enough calibration data is available. For cross-sectional financial models with many assets and regime-dependent uncertainty, it is usually more informative than a fixed-width split conformal. However, CQR depends on the quality of the underlying quantile model. If the quantile estimates are unstable, the calibration sample is small, or the regime shifts sharply, rolling split conformal or ACI may be more robust.

This uncertainty estimate also has a direct **interpretation in terms of allocation.** A simple preview is to scale the position size inversely with the interval width:

$$w_i \propto \frac{1}{\text{width}\big(C(x_i)\big)}$$

so that forecasts with tighter calibrated intervals receive larger allocations, all else equal. A stock with a 50 basis point interval receives twice the uncertainty-adjusted weight of one with a 100 basis point interval before applying volatility, correlation, turnover, and portfolio-level constraints. *Chapter 17* develops this idea within a full-allocation framework.

Implementation: `06_conformal_prediction` implements CQR with native quantile models and compares its interval-width distribution with split conformal. Ridge-based results should be interpreted as a baseline comparison unless the model explicitly estimates lower and upper conditional quantiles.

Conformal prediction sets for classification

Conformal prediction also applies to classification. Instead of producing a prediction interval for a continuous return, it produces a prediction set: a subset of labels that contains the true class with probability at least $1 - \alpha$ under exchangeability.

For a classifier with predicted class probabilities $\hat{p}(y \mid x)$, a simple nonconformity score is:

$$s_i = 1 - \hat{p}(y_i \mid x_i)$$

where y_i is the true class for calibration observation i. Large scores indicate that the model assigned low probability to the realized class. After computing the conformal quantile $\hat{q}$ from the calibration scores, the prediction set for a new observation is:

$$C(x) = \{y: 1 - \hat{p}(y \mid x) \leq \hat{q}\} = \{y: \hat{p}(y \mid x) \geq 1 - \hat{q}\}$$

The result is a set of plausible labels rather than a single forced classification. For three-class direction labels such as long, neutral, and short, a singleton set such as {long} conveys greater directional confidence than a wider set such as {long,neutral}. A full set containing all classes indicates that the classifier cannot distinguish the alternatives at the desired coverage level.

This maps naturally to trading decisions. One conservative rule is to trade only singleton prediction sets and abstain when the conformal set contains multiple labels. This can reduce exposure when the model is uncertain about direction. However, the conformal guarantee applies to the prediction sets over all evaluated observations, not automatically to the subset of observations selected for trading. Coverage, hit rate, abstention rate, turnover, and realized performance should therefore be reported separately for singleton and non-singleton cases.

Conformal classification calibrates set coverage, not the probability estimates themselves. Poorly calibrated probabilities can still produce valid conformal sets under the required assumptions, but inefficient probability estimates may lead to unnecessarily large sets. Probability calibration and conformal set calibration are related diagnostics, but they are not the same object.

Evaluating calibration quality

A conformal method should be evaluated by whether its realized coverage matches its claimed coverage and whether the resulting intervals are useful for decision-making. A nominal 90% interval that covers only 70% of realized outcomes is overconfident: it claims a 10% failure rate but delivers a 30% failure rate. Conversely, a method that covers 99% of outcomes at a 90% target may be too conservative, producing intervals too wide to support meaningful allocation decisions.

A calibration plot summarizes this relationship. For target coverage levels:

$$1 - \alpha \in \{0.10, 0.20, \ldots, 0.90\}$$

plot nominal coverage against empirical coverage. Points below the diagonal indicate overconfidence; points above the diagonal indicate conservatism.

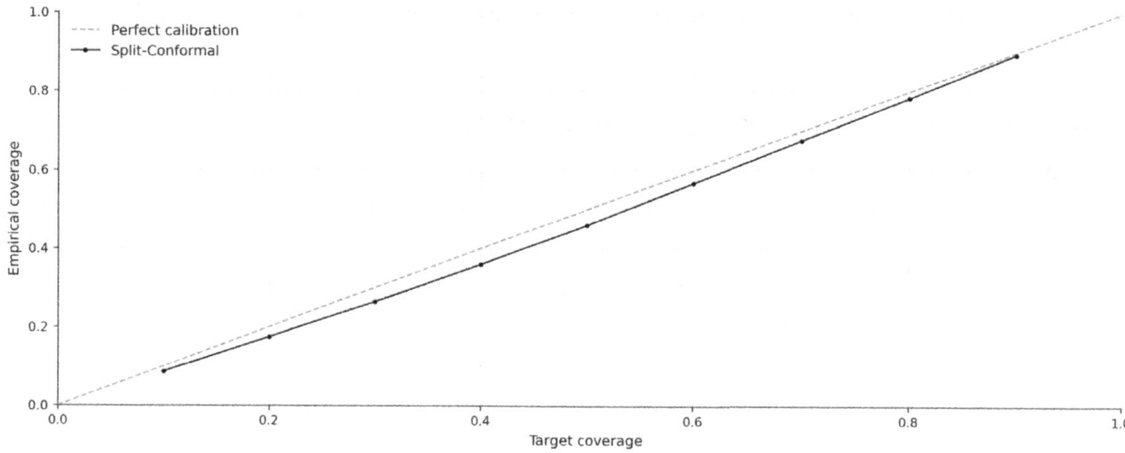

Figure 11.6: Conformal prediction calibration

Marginal coverage can hide failures that matter for trading. Conditional coverage should therefore be evaluated by stratifying observations by:

- **Walk-forward fold**, to test whether coverage is stable through time
- **Predicted return magnitude**, to test whether intervals fail in the signal tails
- **Market regime**, to test whether coverage deteriorates during high volatility or low liquidity
- **Asset characteristics**, to test whether coverage varies systematically by sector, liquidity, volatility, or instrument type

Coverage estimates should be reported with uncertainty. A realized coverage rate of 89.9% may be statistically indistinguishable from a 90% target, while 88.4% may or may not be material depending on the effective sample size, serial dependence, and cross-sectional clustering. Fold-level dispersion, block-bootstrap confidence intervals, or cluster-robust standard errors make the comparison more informative than a single pooled number.

On the `etfs` case study, conformal prediction is evaluated using daily data for 99 ETFs over 2006–2025, with out-of-sample evaluation across eight walk-forward folds spanning 2015–2023. Within each fold, the model uses an 80/20 proper-training/calibration split. The base model is Ridge regression.

Method	**Target**	**Marginal Coverage**	**Mean Width (%)**	**Width σ (%)**
Split-Conformal	90%	88.4%	16.9%	3.3
CQR	90%	89.9%	15.7%	7.5
ACI on SC base ($\gamma = 0.01$)	90%	89.5%	16.3%	6.8

Table 11.1: Conformal evaluation results

The results illustrate the trade-offs among the three methods:

- Split conformal is simple and auditable but produces fixed-width intervals and undercovers relative to the 90% target
- CQR comes closest to the target and produces the narrowest average interval, while allowing interval width to vary substantially across observations
- ACI improves the static split-conformal baseline by adapting interval width over time, though its realized coverage remains slightly below target in this run

The width dispersion is also informative. Split conformal has relatively low width variation because all observations in a fold receive the same conformal correction. CQR has higher width dispersion because its quantile models adapt to the conditional uncertainty of each observation. ACI also produces more variable widths because recent coverage errors feed back into the effective miscoverage level.

These results are consistent with the challenges posed by nonexchangeable financial data, but they should not be mechanically attributed solely to exchangeability violations. Undercoverage can also arise from calibration leakage, overly small calibration windows, unstable quantile estimates, inappropriate score definitions, or implementation choices such as interpolated quantiles. The correct diagnostic response is to inspect coverage by fold, regime, and asset group before changing the method.

Several warning signs deserve attention. Coverage below 80% during volatility spikes, for a 90% target, indicates that the calibration distribution is stale or poorly stratified. Monotonically deteriorating coverage over the backtest suggests drift in the calibration scheme's tracking. Asymmetric violations, with many more outcomes above or below the interval, indicate a directional bias or residual skewness. Symmetric split conformal can widen intervals but cannot recenter a biased forecast. CQR can represent asymmetric conditional tails if the quantile models learn them, but the conformal correction itself calibrates coverage rather than correcting the predictive center.

> **Implementation:** `06_conformal_prediction` shows the full calibration comparison, including marginal coverage, per-fold coverage, interval-width distributions, conditional coverage diagnostics, and ACI adaptation dynamics.

11.6 Case study insights

One regularized linear pipeline, run unchanged across all case studies, lets us ask a single question nine times: when does a linear model turn off-the-shelf features into a useful ranking of forward returns, and when does it not? Most of the time it does not. The linear model is the baseline the more flexible families in *Chapters 12* through *14* have to beat, so it matters as much where it fails as where it succeeds. Throughout, the measure of success is the average daily information coefficient (IC) between the predicted score and the realized return, read together with its 95% confidence interval (CI); all *t*-statistics use the Newey–West (HAC) correction. The full evidence is in `07_case_study_insights`.

The signal is real in three of the nine case studies and absent in the other six. *Table 11.4* sorts the case studies by whether the confidence interval around their IC clears zero. Three intervals exclude zero, three are positive but wide enough to contain it, and three sit below it. Reliable cross-sectional ranking from a linear model on engineered features is therefore the exception rather than the rule, even before any of the frictions of trading enter the picture.

Category	Count	Case studies
CI excludes zero	3	ETFs, US Equities, NASDAQ-100
CI overlaps zero (positive)	3	Crypto, SP 500 Options, FX
CI overlaps zero (negative)	3	CME Futures, SP 500 Eq+Opt, US Firms

Table 11.4: Case studies by whether the regression IC confidence interval excludes zero

All nine case studies are scored this way on a regression label. Four of them also carry a direction label, which is a classification problem scored differently; those results are held back to the dedicated comparison near the end of the section, so that the regression picture stays clean first.

Where the signal is

ETFs, US equities, and intraday NASDAQ-100 are the three case studies whose linear models rank returns with an IC that is reliably positive. *Table 11.5* lists the best configuration, and its IC for each case study at its primary label, and *Figure 11.7* plots the same estimates so that the intervals clearing zero are visible at a glance. The prose below reads the pattern; the numbers live in the table.

Case study	Horizon	IC	t	95% CI	n
ETFs	21 days	+0.054	2.4	[+0.009, +0.098]	2,016
US Equities	1 day	+0.016	9.1	[+0.012, +0.019]	4,018
NASDAQ-100	15 min	+0.005	4.3	[+0.003, +0.007]	64,580
Crypto	8 hours	+0.009	1.4	[−0.003, +0.020]	1,956
SP 500 Options	~30 days	+0.007	0.6	[−0.015, +0.029]	502
FX	1 day	+0.005	0.6	[−0.012, +0.022]	2,064

Case study	Horizon	IC	t	95% CI	n
CME Futures	5 days	−0.000	−0.0	[−0.034, +0.034]	1,290
SP 500 Eq+Opt	5 days	−0.006	−0.4	[−0.033, +0.022]	502
US Firms	1 month	−0.005	−0.6	[−0.022, +0.011]	120

Table 11.5: Best linear configuration for the primary regression label measured on the validation set

The interval is the HAC 95% CI; n is the number of trading periods over which the daily IC is averaged. The labels correspond to the total forward return over the given horizon, except for S&P 500 options, where the label is the per-position profit and loss of an at-the-money short straddle held from formation to expiry (25–35 days), following the hold-to-maturity construction of O'Donovan and Yu (2024). See case study `README` for more details.

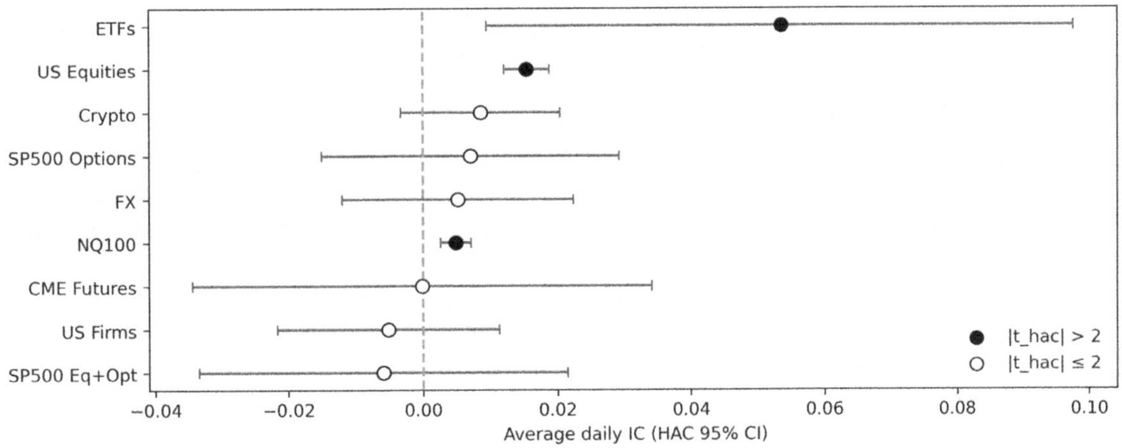

Figure 11.7: Best daily IC per case study at the primary regression label, with HAC 95% CI. Filled markers mark intervals that exclude zero; open markers mark intervals that overlap it

Two things separate these three from the rest. The first is that their features genuinely align with the cross-section of returns: momentum and value carry ranking information in equities and ETFs in ways that engineered features do not for currencies or futures. The second is statistical, not economic. Whether an IC clears zero depends as much on how many independent observations support it as on its size and variance. NASDAQ-100 reaches significance on the smallest IC of the three because its intraday history is large. Sample size, not effect size, is doing much of the work, which is worth remembering before reading a small but significant IC as a strong signal; both statistical and economic significance matter.

Choice of regularization

Each linear model is fit over a grid of regularization strengths, with the strength chosen by cross-validation, under three penalties: Ridge, which shrinks every coefficient toward zero; LASSO, which drives some coefficients to exactly zero; and Elastic Net, which blends the two. All three are fit on seven of the nine case studies.

Ridge gives the highest IC on every case study where the linear model has measurable signal. LASSO and Elastic Net match it elsewhere, and edge it on CME Futures, but the IC there is indistinguishable from zero under any penalty, so the gap is noise rather than a finding. Ridge holds up because of how the features are built: momentum at several horizons, volatility at several scales, and cross-sectional ranks are correlated by construction, so a penalty that keeps all of them and shrinks them together discards less information than one that zeroes some out. The gain from regularizing at all, relative to an unpenalized fit, is small, and it is largest exactly where the unpenalized fit lands far from the best strength. Regularization here buys numerical stability; it does not manufacture signal the features do not carry.

Ridge, LASSO, and Elastic Net are all fit on seven of the nine case studies. NASDAQ-100 and US Equities are represented by their best Ridge fit in *Table 11.5*; LASSO and Elastic Net add nothing to the comparison on those two and are not reported.

Whether the signal persists

A positive IC averaged over the whole validation period can still come from a few good stretches, so the more demanding question is whether the signal holds up over time. The clearest way to see this is a rolling three-month average of the daily IC, which traces how ranking quality evolves rather than collapsing it to a single number. Because each case study covers a different validation window, the view is most informative for case studies with overlapping periods. *Figure 11.8* shows ETFs and FX over the same 2016–2023 span: the ETF signal spends most of the period above zero, with sharp but temporary drawdowns, while the FX signal is split almost evenly across zero with no persistent sign. The ETF edge is a property of the whole period; the FX entry in *Table 11.5* averages a series that is positive and negative in roughly equal measure, which is why its interval includes zero.

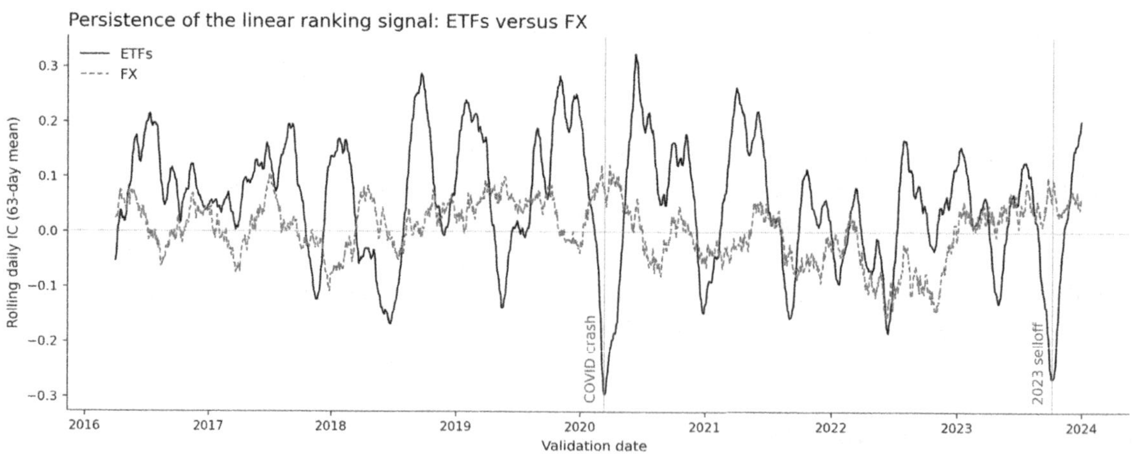

Figure 11.8: Three-month rolling average of the daily IC for the ETF and FX case studies over their common 2016–2023 validation window. The ETF series holds a positive level; the FX series crosses zero repeatedly

A second, simpler check guards against the opposite error: reading a near-zero IC as the symptom of an unstable fit rather than a genuine absence of signal. Across folds, the model keeps the sign of its coefficients in the vast majority of cases for each case study, even when the IC overlaps zero. The fits are stable; what the flat case studies lack is ranking content in the features, not a settled model.

Horizon effects

The horizon at which a label is defined affects how much signal a linear model can extract, and the effect varies by case study (*Figure 11.9*). For ETFs, US equities, and SP 500 Eq+Opt the IC rises with horizon, as the day-to-day noise averages out and a slower cross-sectional signal shows through. NASDAQ-100 is flat across its intraday horizons: a linear read of microstructure features carries the same ranking content at five, fifteen, and sixty minutes. Crypto behaves the same way across its eight- and twenty-four-hour labels, consistent with a funding-rate signal that does not decay over a day.

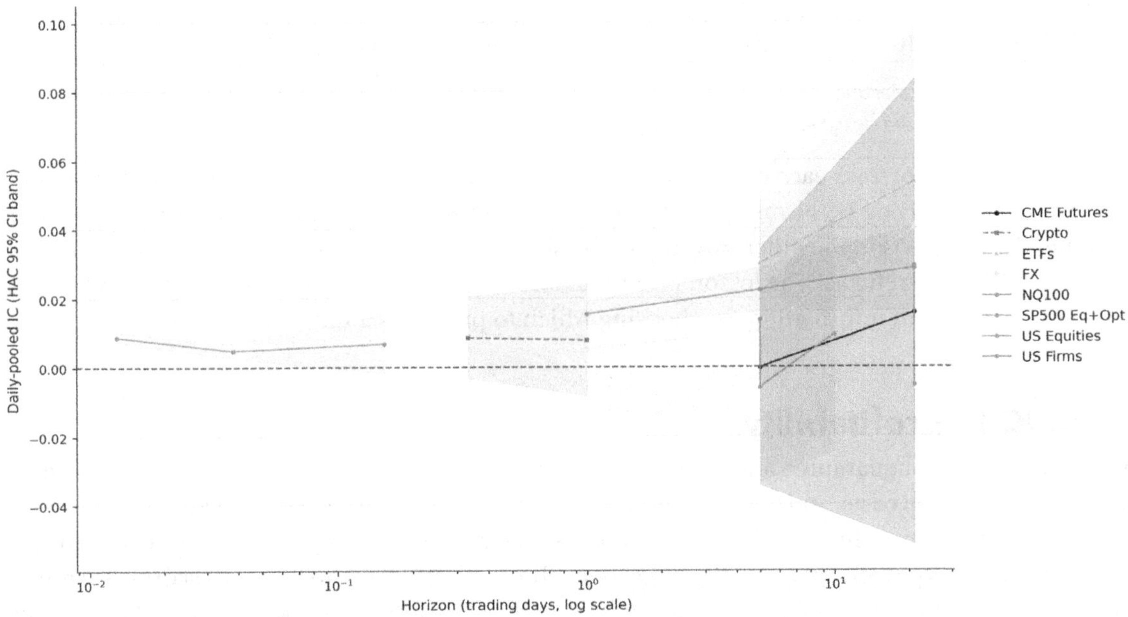

Figure 11.9: Best daily IC per case study and regression label, with HAC 95% CI bands, on a log-horizon axis. Only case studies with two or more regression labels appear

The practical reading is to match the horizon to the signal: where information accumulates slowly, a longer holding period yields a higher IC; where it lives inside the window, a shorter horizon captures as much. A single model trained jointly on several horizons can pool this structure, an idea *Chapter 14* develops in latent-factor form.

Direction versus magnitude

Predicting the sign of a return and ranking its size are different problems, and a model can be good at one while indifferent to the other. Three case studies (Crypto, SP 500 Eq+Opt, and US Firms) train both a regression model on continuous returns and a classifier on binary direction over the same horizon, allowing us to score each model on both targets. The classifier is read by its AUC against the direction; the regression model by its IC against the return; and each is also cross-evaluated on the other's target (*Table 11.6*).

Case study	Horizon	Native AUC	Cross-IC (t)	Cross-AUC (regression)
Crypto	8 hours	0.509 [0.498, 0.521]	+0.033 (5.3)	0.498
US Firms	1 month	0.539 [0.528, 0.550]	+0.074 (6.8)	0.494
SP 500 Eq+Opt	5 days	0.510	overlaps zero	0.496
SP 500 Eq+Opt	10 days	0.507	overlaps zero	0.523

Table 11.6: Classifier and regression scores at matched horizons. Native AUC scores the classifier on direction; cross-IC scores the classifier on the continuous return; cross-AUC scores the regression model on direction

The two targets do not track each other. On Crypto and US Firms the classifier's score ranks continuous returns well, yet only on US Firms does its AUC separate direction from chance with any confidence. Running the comparison the other way, the regression score barely moves AUC away from one-half even where it ranks returns. The lesson is not that one target is better, but that direction and magnitude encode different information, so choosing which to predict is a modeling decision rather than a formality.

From IC to profitability

A higher IC does not guarantee a more profitable strategy because realized returns also depend on turnover, transaction costs, and position sizing. `08_ml_backtest_intro` makes the gap concrete on the ETF case study, where a simple 126-day momentum signal carries a lower IC than Ridge yet matches or beats it on net Sharpe ratio, because the Ridge portfolio trades far more to act on its scores. Turning a ranking into a return is the subject of *Chapters 16* through *19*: strategy simulation, portfolio construction under turnover constraints, transaction-cost modeling, and risk management.

11.7 Summary

This chapter established the end-to-end ML pipeline for translating alpha factors into trading signals. Regularized regression (Ridge, LASSO, and Elastic Net) provides the first rung of the baseline ladder: interpretable models whose coefficients reveal which features the model relies on and how strongly. Logistic regression extends the framework to direction prediction, offering an alternative when continuous return signals are weak. SHAP attributions verify that the model's reasoning aligns with economic intuition and remains stable across walk-forward folds. Conformal prediction wraps any base model in calibrated uncertainty bands, enabling position sizing that reflects prediction confidence rather than treating all forecasts as equally reliable.

The cross-dataset evaluation in *Section 11.6* reveals where linear models work and where they do not. These results define the baseline for *Chapter 12* (gradient boosting), *Chapter 13* (deep learning), and *Chapter 14* (latent factors), which test whether nonlinear models can extract signal on the datasets where the linear baseline runs out.

12

Advanced Models for Tabular Data

Gradient Boosting Machines (**GBMs**) dominate tabular prediction in both academic research and production trading systems, combining predictive power with computational efficiency. While *Chapter 11*'s linear models assume additive feature relationships, GBMs capture the interaction effects and threshold dynamics that financial data exhibit, without manual feature engineering.

This chapter covers the three industry-standard GBM libraries (XGBoost, LightGBM, and CatBoost) and the techniques that make them production-ready. By the end of this chapter, you will be able to:

- Explain how boosting differs from bagging and why sequential error correction makes GBMs effective for financial tabular prediction.
- Select among XGBoost, LightGBM, and CatBoost based on categorical structure, compute environment, latency needs, and leakage risk.
- Choose appropriate GBM objectives and constraints for financial tasks, including pointwise regression, learning to rank, and monotonic constraints.
- Tune GBMs efficiently with Optuna using pruning, multi-objective search, and time-series-aware validation.
- Use TreeSHAP to analyze feature effects, interactions, instability, and drift in deployed tree-based models.
- Evaluate when tabular deep learning alternatives such as TabPFN, TabM, and TabR are worth considering relative to GBMs.
- Interpret cross-case-study evidence to decide when nonlinear tree models earn their added complexity relative to linear baselines

We progress from the shared boosting framework through Bayesian hyperparameter optimization with Optuna, TreeSHAP-based interpretation and drift monitoring, and learning-to-rank objectives for quantile strategies. We then evaluate deep learning alternatives (TabPFN and TabM) using decision criteria for when added complexity pays off, and conclude with a cross-case study comparison that benchmarks GBMs against the linear baselines from *Chapter 11*.

12.1 From decision trees to ensembles

Gradient boosting rests on three building blocks: how decision trees partition feature space, how Random Forests reduce variance by averaging independent trees, and why averaging alone cannot correct systematic bias.

A **decision tree** makes predictions by recursively partitioning the feature space into regions. At each node, the algorithm selects the feature and threshold that best separate the data, typically using information gain for classification or variance reduction for regression.

Decision trees handle mixed feature types (continuous returns, categorical sectors) without encoding, capture non-linear relationships through hierarchical splits, and need no feature scaling. Their critical weakness is high variance: a small change in training data can produce a dramatically different tree structure, making individual predictions unstable. Yet individual trees can learn that momentum is predictive only when volatility is below a threshold, an interaction that linear models require explicit engineering to capture. The question is how to harvest this flexibility without the instability.

Random forests – Reducing variance with bagging

Random forests (Breiman, 2001) apply the bagging principle to decision trees with an additional twist: at each split, only a random subset of features is considered. This feature randomization decorrelates the trees, making the variance reduction from averaging more effective.

For a regression task, a Random Forest prediction is simply the average of all individual tree predictions:

$$\hat{y} = \frac{1}{M}\sum_{m=1}^{M} T_m(x)$$

where M is the number of trees and $T_m(x)$ is the prediction from tree m.

Random forests require minimal hyperparameter tuning and rarely overfit, even with many trees. In the model comparison notebooks for this chapter, Random Forests serve as a baseline whose accuracy GBMs must materially improve upon to justify their additional complexity. *Figure 12.1* illustrates the contrast between bagging (averaging independent trees) and boosting (sequential error correction).

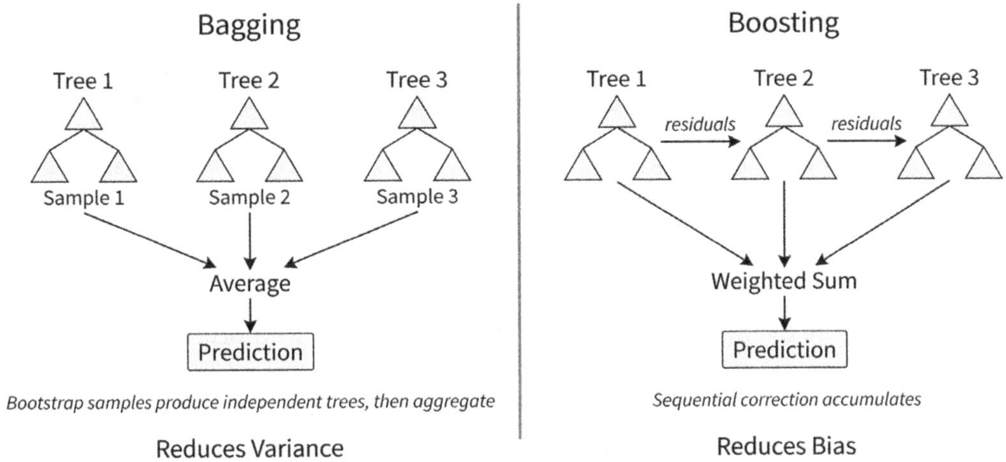

Figure 12.1: Bagging versus boosting

However, because trees are trained independently, they cannot correct each other's systematic errors. If all trees share a consistent bias (for example, underestimating extreme returns), averaging does not help. This limitation motivates the boosting paradigm covered next.

The path to boosting

Boosting builds models sequentially, so each new model targets the errors of the current ensemble. If the current prediction is 2% but the true return is 5%, the next tree learns to predict the 3% residual. Adding that correction to the ensemble gradually eliminates systematic under-prediction, the bias that averaging independent trees cannot address.

This sequential error correction, combined with shrinkage and regularization, forms the foundation of gradient boosting machines, which we detail in the next section. The notebook `01_ensemble_foundations` benchmarks Random Forests against XGBoost, LightGBM, and CatBoost on the Chen–Pelger–Zhu firm characteristics dataset (414K train/307K valid/497K test observations across 1967–2016) and finds a consistent ordering on this benchmark: each GBM achieves higher out-of-sample test IC than the Random Forest baseline (0.058–0.060 versus 0.056), with library-to-library differences (~0.002 IC) smaller than the boosting-versus-bagging gap.

12.2 Gradient boosting machines

The three dominant GBM libraries (XGBoost, LightGBM, and CatBoost) share the core boosting algorithm but differ in tree construction, categorical handling, and regularization. This section covers the shared framework, then examines each library's distinctive innovations.

High performance with boosting

Gradient boosting, formalized by Friedman (2001), frames model training as iterative optimization in function space. Rather than fitting a single complex model, we construct an additive ensemble in which each new component explicitly targets the errors in the current prediction.

The algorithm proceeds as follows:

1. Initialize with a constant prediction (typically the target mean).
2. For each boosting iteration $m = 1,2,\dots,M$:
   a. Compute the negative gradient of the loss function with respect to the current predictions.
   b. Fit a weak learner (typically a shallow tree) to these "pseudo-residuals."
   c. Add the new tree's predictions to the ensemble, scaled by a learning rate η.

The update at each iteration is:

$$F_m(x) = F_{m-1}(x) + \eta \cdot h_m(x)$$

where h_m is the tree fitted in iteration m. The final GBM prediction after M boosting rounds can be written as:

$$\hat{y} = F_M(x) = F_0(x) + \eta \sum_{m=1}^{M} h_m(x)$$

where $F_0(x)$ is the initial constant prediction, often the training-set mean for squared-error regression, and each $h_m(x)$ is a shallow tree fitted to the loss gradient implied by the current ensemble. This expression highlights the key difference from the Random Forest prediction above. A Random Forest averages independently trained trees, whereas a GBM starts with a baseline prediction and iteratively adds targeted corrections. Each tree is therefore not a standalone forecast of $\hat{y}$, but an incremental adjustment to the current prediction. For classification, the same additive structure applies to the model's raw score scale, such as log-odds for binary classification, before applying the appropriate link function to obtain probabilities.

The **learning rate** η (typically 0.01–0.3) controls how aggressively each tree's contribution is added. Smaller values require more trees but often yield better generalization: a GBM with 100 trees is not averaging 100 predictions but accumulating 100 incremental corrections.

The **choice of loss function** determines what "errors" the algorithm targets. In *Chapter 11*, we discussed mean squared error, mean absolute error, and Huber loss:

- **Quantile loss** predicts specific quantiles rather than the conditional mean, enabling direct estimation of prediction intervals.
- All three GBM libraries support **custom objectives**, enabling asymmetric losses (for example, penalizing under-prediction more than over-prediction) as long as you can provide stable first and second derivatives with respect to the model's predictions (or use a smooth approximation when the loss is non-smooth).

The next section explains why this blend of flexibility and regularization gives GBMs such a strong track record on tabular data.

Why GBMs excel on tabular data

Gradient boosted decision trees have an **inductive bias** well-matched to financial tabular data:

- Financial datasets mix continuous variables (returns, volatility), categorical features (sector, exchange), and derived indicators. Tree-based methods accommodate **heterogeneous tabular inputs** well: continuous variables can be split by thresholds, while categorical variables are handled through library-specific encodings or native categorical split mechanisms. The details differ materially across libraries.
- Financial relationships often exhibit **discontinuities** (a P/E ratio above a threshold may trigger fundamentally different investor behavior than just below it), and trees capture these non-smooth boundaries directly. Unlike neural networks that impose smoothness through continuous activation functions, trees partition the feature space into discrete regions. Trees also discover feature interactions through hierarchical splits: a sufficiently deep tree learns that "high momentum is predictive only when volatility is moderate" without manual interaction engineering.

Several practical advantages compound this expressive power:

- Boosted trees rely on **threshold splits**, so they are typically more robust to extreme feature values than models that depend directly on magnitudes or distances
- Modern GBM implementations **handle missing values** by learning the optimal split direction for missing features, rather than requiring imputation
- Trees can also operate on raw feature values without normalization, eliminating a class of preprocessing bugs

The next section examines the most widely used libraries that implement these ideas: XGBoost, LightGBM, and CatBoost.

Inside the engines – XGBoost, LightGBM, and CatBoost

XGBoost, LightGBM, and CatBoost share the gradient boosting framework but differ in key algorithmic innovations that affect their performance characteristics.

XGBoost – Regularization and sparsity

XGBoost (eXtreme Gradient Boosting), introduced by Chen and Guestrin (2016), brought several innovations that shaped current gradient boosting practice.

Regularized objective: Unlike earlier implementations that relied primarily on early stopping and shrinkage, XGBoost explicitly adds regularization terms to the objective function:

$$\mathcal{L} = \sum_i l\left(y_i, \hat{y}_i\right) + \sum_k \Omega\left(f_k\right)$$

where:

$$\Omega(f_k) = \gamma T + \frac{1}{2}\lambda \sum_{j=1}^{T} w_j^2$$

penalizes both tree complexity and the magnitude of the model's leaf scores. Here, T is the number of leaves in tree k, w_j is the prediction assigned to leaf j, γ controls the penalty for adding additional leaves, and λ controls the L2 penalty on leaf weights. Larger values of γ encourage simpler trees, while larger values of λ shrink leaf predictions toward zero. This regularization directly limits overfitting rather than relying only on heuristic stopping rules:

- **Sparsity-aware split finding:** Real-world data often contains extensive missing values or zero entries. XGBoost learns a default direction for each tree node: when a sample has a missing value for the split feature, it follows this learned default path. This eliminates the need for imputation while often improving predictive performance.
- **Second-order approximation:** XGBoost uses a second-order Taylor expansion of the loss function, incorporating both the gradients and the Hessian, which contains the second derivatives. This provides more accurate updates than first-order methods, particularly for loss functions with significant curvature.
- **Cache-aware access patterns:** XGBoost optimizes how data is laid out and accessed in memory to make repeated computations better use of the CPU cache. This improves training speed, especially on large tabular datasets where inefficient memory access can become a bottleneck.

LightGBM – Speed through sampling and bundling

LightGBM (Ke et al., 2017), developed by Microsoft, focuses on dramatically improving training speed while maintaining or improving accuracy. On large, sparse datasets, LightGBM used to train 5–10× faster than pre-histogram XGBoost, but the CPU speed advantage has narrowed as XGBoost has adopted the histogram mode introduced by LightGBM, which added several innovations:

- **Histogram-based learning:** Instead of sorting feature values for exact split finding, LightGBM discretizes continuous features into histograms. Split finding then examines only histogram bin boundaries. Histogram construction still requires scanning the data, but once the histogram is built, split gain can be evaluated over bin boundaries rather than all distinct feature values. The split-evaluation step, therefore, scales with the number of bins, which is typically far smaller than the number of observations.
- **Leaf-wise tree growth:** LightGBM is best known for leaf-wise, best-first tree growth. At each step, it splits the leaf with the largest loss reduction. This can reduce training loss faster with a fixed number of leaves than depth-wise growth does, but it also increases the risk of overfitting on small or noisy datasets unless constrained by `num_leaves`, `max_depth`, `min_data_in_leaf`, or related regularization parameters.

- **Gradient-based One-Side Sampling (GOSS):** The key insight is that samples with large gradients (those that the model is currently getting wrong) contribute more to information gain than samples with small gradients (those that are already well-predicted). GOSS keeps all large-gradient samples but randomly samples only a fraction of small-gradient samples (and reweights them to preserve a good estimate of split quality), significantly reducing computational cost without sacrificing split quality.
- **Exclusive Feature Bundling (EFB):** In high-dimensional sparse data (common after one-hot encoding categorical variables), many features are mutually exclusive: they never take non-zero values simultaneously. EFB identifies and bundles such features into combined features, reducing the effective number of features to evaluate when finding splits.

CatBoost – State-of-the-art categorical handling

CatBoost (Prokhorenkova et al., 2018), developed by Yandex, addresses a critical challenge: **how to handle categorical features without introducing target leakage.**

Standard target encoding (replacing a category with the mean target value of samples in that category) creates a subtle form of data leakage. When computing the encoded value for a training sample, that sample's target value influences its feature value, inflating the model's apparent performance.

CatBoost's solution is "**ordered target statistics.**" For each training sample, target statistics are computed using only samples that appear earlier in a random permutation of the data. This ensures no sample's target value influences its own features. Multiple permutations are used and averaged to reduce variance.

Unlike XGBoost and LightGBM, where each node can split on a different feature, CatBoost uses symmetric, or **"oblivious" decision trees,** by default, where all nodes at the same depth use the same split condition. This simplicity enables extremely fast prediction (often the fastest inference among the three libraries) because the prediction path can be computed as a bitwise operation rather than a sequential tree traversal. This makes CatBoost particularly well-suited for latency-sensitive applications where inference speed matters.

While one-hot encoding becomes impractical for high-cardinality categoricals with thousands of unique values, CatBoost's ordered encoding naturally handles any cardinality. Features such as individual stock identifiers, analyst IDs, and detailed sector codes can be used directly.

Practical comparison – Which GBM to choose?

Scikit-learn's `HistGradientBoostingRegressor` provides a no-dependency baseline. It uses the same histogram-based splitting as the specialized libraries and is often the fastest option on CPU for small-to-medium datasets. However, it lacks GPU support and the tuning ecosystem (Optuna callbacks and early stopping flexibility) that specialized libraries provide. We include it in the `02_gbm_comparison` benchmark alongside the three specialized libraries.

Table 12.1 summarizes the library selection decision points. The specialized libraries still differ in what they optimize for. XGBoost is the most general-purpose option of the three: it supports both CPU and CUDA-based GPU training, includes native categorical support, and remains a strong default when you want one library that covers a wide range of production and research settings. The choice between XGBoost, LightGBM, and CatBoost depends on your specific constraints and data characteristics:

Criterion	XGBoost	LightGBM	CatBoost
CPU training (4.9M rows, 8 threads)	~100s	~50s — fastest (~2× XGBoost)	~135s — slowest
GPU training (4.9M rows, CUDA)	~14s (~7× its CPU)	~14s (~3.5×; FP64-only, see below)	~10s (~14×) — fastest
Prediction speed (heavy preset, 24K test rows)	0.5M rows/s CPU; 1.7M rows/s GPU	0.07M rows/s CPU (slowest)	6.5M rows/s CPU; symmetric trees → bitwise path, ~12× faster than XGBoost on CPU
High-cardinality categoricals	Native support	Native support	Ordered target statistics avoid leakage
Default performance	Good	Good	Often strong, especially with many categorical variables
Tuning sensitivity	Moderate	Moderate-high (leaf-wise growth requires depth/leaf constraints)	Often lower, but data-dependent
Memory efficiency	Moderate	Often best (histogram bins reduce memory)	Moderate

Table 12.1: GBM library characteristics

The `02_gbm_comparison` notebook benchmarks all four libraries on CPU and GPU with light, medium, and heavy presets, measuring accuracy, training time, and memory usage.

LightGBM remains especially attractive in CPU-first tabular workflows. Its leaf-wise tree growth can reduce training loss quickly, but it also makes the library somewhat more sensitive to parameters such as `num_leaves`, `min_data_in_leaf`, and sometimes `max_depth`

All three libraries support **GPU-accelerated training**, but the speedup depends on dataset size and numerical precision:

- On the **US equities panel** (4.92M training rows, 72 features, 8 threads), CatBoost achieves the largest GPU speedup at ~14× with `task_type='GPU'` (~135s CPU → ~10s GPU), and XGBoost ~7× using `device='cuda'` (~100s → ~14s). LightGBM trains in ~50s on CPU (the fastest CPU configuration in the scale benchmark) and ~14s on GPU with `device='cuda'`, a more modest ~3.5× speedup; its GPU wall time matches XGBoost's but not CatBoost's, for the FP64 reason discussed below.

- On the smaller **ETF dataset** (227K rows), launch overhead compresses the speedups: for XGBoost and CatBoost the gain ranges from ~2.4× (XGBoost light) to ~5.2× (CatBoost heavy). LightGBM is the exception: its FP64 CUDA path is counterproductive at this scale, training *slower* on GPU than on CPU (about ~9.5s CPU versus ~48s GPU on the heavy preset), so LightGBM should stay on CPU for datasets this size. For XGBoost and CatBoost the GPU still helps, but the relative advantage is roughly an order of magnitude smaller than at the 4.9M-row scale.

LightGBM's CUDA speedup is modest even though its GPU wall time (~14s at the 4.9M-row scale) matches XGBoost's: its **CUDA backend uses double precision (FP64) exclusively**: the `gpu_use_dp` toggle that enables single-precision training "can be used only in OpenCL implementation (`device_type='gpu'`), in CUDA implementation only double precision is currently supported." Note that:

- **Consumer GPUs** have an FP32:FP64 throughput ratio of roughly 64:1 (the RTX 3090 delivers 35.6 TFLOPS FP32 but only ~0.6 TFLOPS FP64), so LightGBM's GPU histogram computation runs at a fraction of the available throughput.
- **Data center GPUs** with better FP64 ratios (A100: 2:1) would show a different result.

LightGBM also offers a separate OpenCL backend (`device='gpu'`) that defaults to single precision, but it requires an OpenCL SDK and produces slightly different results due to the precision difference. The CUDA build requires compilation from source with `USE_CUDA=ON`, which is the build that produces the GPU times reported here; CUDA-enabled conda packages are now available on supported systems.

The practical picture at scale is therefore:

- **CatBoost GPU delivers the largest training speedup** (~14× at the 4.9M-row scale), making it the clear choice when GPU-accelerated training time matters. At that scale CatBoost finishes GPU training in ~10s, with XGBoost and LightGBM together at ~14s. On CPU, LightGBM is the fastest at ~50s, the fastest CPU configuration in the scale benchmark.
- CPU times at the 4.9M-row scale (8 threads) spread from LightGBM (~50s) to XGBoost (~100s) to CatBoost (~135s); LightGBM's histogram plus leaf-wise growth has the best parallel efficiency at this thread count and dataset size.

In practice, the accuracy gap between libraries is smaller than the gap between good and bad hyperparameter configurations of any single library. The four libraries fall within a narrow IC band after tuning, and their fold-level rankings vary over time.

The real selection criteria are therefore operational: CatBoost's GPU backend delivers the fastest training at scale, CatBoost's ordered encoding eliminates subtle leakage bugs when working with sector codes or analyst identifiers, and XGBoost's mature ecosystem provides the best integration with SHAP, Optuna callbacks, and deployment tooling. On CPU at the 4.9M-row scale, LightGBM is the fastest of the three (roughly 2× XGBoost and 2.7× CatBoost at 8 threads). For readers with CUDA-capable GPUs and large datasets, CatBoost's GPU acceleration offers the most substantial training-time savings.

This book's nine **case study pipelines use LightGBM** as the default library because its CPU speed is particularly advantageous when running walk-forward cross-validation across multiple hyperparameter configurations. Readers with access to **CUDA-capable GPUs** should consider switching to **XGBoost** for the larger case studies (US equities, S&P 500 equity-option analytics) where GPU acceleration provides meaningful time savings.

Native feature importance and its limitations

Every GBM library reports feature importance after training: typically either the total gain from splits on each feature or the number of times each feature is used for splitting. These metrics are fast to compute and provide a quick first look at which features the model relies on. However, they have well-documented failure modes:

- **Gain-based importance** is biased toward high-cardinality features because more unique values create more candidate splits.
- **Split-count importance** is biased toward continuous features over categoricals for the same reason.

Both metrics are *unstable*: retraining with a different random seed can substantially change importance rankings, especially for correlated features where the model can substitute one for another.

These limitations motivate the SHAP-based analysis in *Section 12.5*, which provides consistent, theoretically grounded attributions. Use native importance for quick screening during development and SHAP for any analysis that informs decisions: feature selection, model monitoring, or risk committee reporting.

Learning to rank

Standard GBM training minimizes pointwise losses (MSE or log-loss), treating each prediction independently. But a long-short portfolio that buys the top decile and sells the bottom profits from correct *ranking*, not accurate magnitude. When MSE is dominated by large absolute errors in the middle of the distribution, the model sacrifices ranking accuracy in the tails where trading actually occurs.

Learning-to-Rank (**LTR**) objectives directly optimize ranking quality. LightGBM supports the `lambdarank` objective, which implements LambdaMART, a gradient boosting algorithm where the loss function is defined implicitly through the gradients (the "lambdas") that would improve pairwise ordering. Each gradient accounts for the change in a ranking metric when two samples swap positions, weighted by the metric's sensitivity at that position. The result is a model trained to produce well-ordered predictions rather than accurate point estimates.

The standard target metric is **Normalized Discounted Cumulative Gain (NDCG)**, which assigns exponentially higher value to correctly ranking items near the top of the list. This aligns naturally with quantile strategies: correctly identifying the best and worst stocks matters far more than distinguishing between the 40th and 50th percentiles.

When LTR outperforms pointwise regression

LTR provides the largest gains in high-breadth cross-sections where only the tails are traded. Consider a universe of 500 stocks ranked monthly: a long-short decile strategy trades only the top and bottom 50 names. MSE-trained models optimize prediction accuracy across all 500 stocks equally, including the 400 in the middle that generate no trading signal. LambdaMART concentrates its fitting capacity on correctly separating the extremes.

The advantage diminishes for strategies that trade the full cross-section (for example, rank-weighted portfolios) or for low-breadth universes where most assets enter positions. It also diminishes when the signal-to-noise ratio is so low that ranking and pointwise objectives converge to the same solution.

A practical consideration: LTR models produce scores that are well-ordered but not calibrated to return magnitudes. If downstream portfolio construction requires return forecasts (for example, mean-variance optimization in *Chapter 17*), either calibrate the LTR scores post-hoc or use pointwise predictions. For strategies that simply go long the top quintile and short the bottom quintile, uncalibrated ranking scores suffice.

A worked example – LambdaMART versus Pointwise MSE

In the notebook `02_gbm_comparison`, we compare LambdaMART against standard MSE regression on the ETF dataset using the same feature set and train/test fold. The key configuration difference is minimal:

- **Pointwise:** `objective='regression'`, optimizing MSE
- **LTR:** `objective='lambdarank'`, with `label_gain` mapping within-date return quintiles to relevance grades and `ndcg_eval_at=[10]` targeting top-of-rank quality

Both models produce ranked predictions, but they differ in where they spend fitting capacity. The notebook evaluates mean group-wise NDCG@10 (ranking quality by date) alongside IC against raw returns. This makes the objective–metric alignment explicit: LambdaMART is optimized for ordering, while pointwise regression is optimized for magnitude fit. For tail-trading strategies, ranking quality is usually the more relevant diagnostic.

LightGBM's `lambdarank` objective requires grouping samples by cross-section (date), specified via the `group` parameter. Each group defines the set of assets ranked against each other. XGBoost provides equivalent functionality through its `rank:ndcg` objective. CatBoost supports ranking via `YetiRank` and `YetiRankPairwise` objectives, which use their own gradient formulations optimized for CatBoost's symmetric tree architecture.

The worked example is implemented in `02_gbm_comparison`, including date-group construction, relevance labeling, LambdaMART training, and NDCG@10 comparison against a regression baseline.

Enforcing economic logic with monotonic constraints

While GBMs excel at discovering non-linearities, they are blind to economic theory. A purely data-driven model might learn that higher P/E ratios generally predict lower returns, but due to noise in specific training regions, it might predict a spike in returns for extremely high P/E values, almost certainly an artifact rather than a structural signal.

Monotonic constraints enforce directional relationships: a positive constraint (+1) requires that the prediction not decrease as the feature increases; a negative constraint (–1) requires the opposite.

Monotonic constraints serve as theory-driven regularization: in low-signal-to-noise environments, enforcing a sign (for example, higher-value scores predict higher returns) prevents the model from fitting non-monotonic artifacts in noisy regions. The constraint also improves deployability (risk committees accept strategies with directional logic they can audit) and robustness to regime shifts, because the model cannot learn complex, non-monotonic patterns that are unlikely to repeat.

All three libraries support monotonic constraints via a parameter-mapping feature that maps names to their intended directions.

SHAP dependence plots (*Section 11.4*) make the effect of constraints immediately visible. An unconstrained model's dependence plot for a value feature might show a generally downward slope with local reversals, regions where higher value scores paradoxically predict lower returns. The same model with a negative monotonic constraint produces a strictly monotone dependence curve, eliminating these artifacts while preserving the overall relationship. When the constrained model's IC is comparable to the unconstrained version (as it typically is for economically motivated constraints), the constraint is acting as regularization rather than information loss. This provides a concrete implementation of the economic sanity-checking framework in *Section 11.4*.

See `02_gbm_comparison` for constrained versus unconstrained SHAP dependence plots on the ETF case study.

We now turn to a more recent addition: deep learning models for tabular data.

12.3 Deep learning alternatives for tabular data

GBMs remain the defensible default for tabular financial data, but the landscape shifted materially between 2024 and 2026. Tabular foundation models, led by TabPFN's Nature publication (Hollmann et al., 2025), moved from research curiosity to frontier baseline, matching or exceeding tuned GBMs on small-to-medium datasets without task-specific training. Parameter-efficient neural ensembles like TabM have shown that well-engineered MLPs, rather than exotic architectures, can compete with GBMs when given equivalent tuning budgets. Retrieval-augmented models like TabR showed that hybridizing deep learning with nearest-neighbor lookups improves predictions when local similarity matters.

The **TabArena** living benchmark (Erickson et al., 2025), evaluating 16 model families across 51 curated datasets, formalized a key finding: with sufficient tuning and ensembling, deep learning can match or exceed GBMs, but the practical winner depends on dataset size, feature composition, and compute budget.

For finance, a critical caveat applies: most major tabular benchmarks assume IID splits and exclude temporal dependence. The *TabReD* benchmark (Rubachev et al., 2024), which tested models under temporal distribution shift, found that attention-heavy architectures degraded faster than GBMs and simple MLPs, directly relevant to non-stationary financial data. Benchmark wins do not imply trading profitability without walk-forward validation.

Tabular foundation models

The most conceptually striking development is the rise of **tabular foundation models** (**TFMs**) that use **in-context learning** (**ICL**). Unlike conventional models that train on a specific dataset via gradient descent, a TFM is pre-trained once on millions of synthetic datasets generated from structural causal models. At inference time, it uses the training data as context to produce predictions for test samples in a single forward pass: no gradient updates, no hyperparameter tuning on the target dataset. The model has already learned *how to learn* from tabular structure during pre-training.

The interface is deceptively simple: given `(X_train, y_train, X_test)`, the model returns predictions immediately. Training is replaced by in-context computation, where the transformer's attention mechanism identifies patterns in the provided context that generalize to query samples.

TabPFN pioneered this paradigm for tabular data. The original version (Hollmann et al., *Nature*, 2025) validated the approach on curated benchmarks: datasets of up to 10,000 samples and 500 features, where the default TabPFN outperformed tuned baselines without any task-specific optimization. **TabPFN v2.5** (Grinsztajn et al., 2025) substantially expanded the practical envelope (to approximately 50,000 rows and 2,000 features) through sketching and feature selection. A separately released distillation tooling path converts the TFM's predictions into compact MLPs or tree ensembles for production deployment, addressing the inference latency bottleneck that limited earlier versions to batch-only workflows.

There are several known **limitations for financial applications**. TabPFN performs best on numeric-only data and degrades on purely categorical datasets (Ye et al., 2024). IID pretraining on synthetic data does not capture temporal dependence or regime shifts. Per-sample inference latency exceeds that of optimized tree libraries at high throughput, though TabPFN 2.5's distillation path mitigates this in batch workflows. Calibration depends on similarity between the target data structure and the synthetic pretraining distribution; structural breaks absent from the synthetic priors may degrade zero-shot predictions.

There is a practical role that TabPFN can play. For financial ML, TabPFN's strongest use case is **rapid prototyping**: test whether a feature set contains predictive signal before investing in GBM tuning. If TabPFN achieves non-trivial IC on a subsample, the features warrant deeper investigation with production-grade models. The distillation engine now makes deployment feasible by converting the TFM's predictions into a tree ensemble that inherits the foundation model's accuracy while achieving GBM-class inference speed. TabPFN 2.5 weights are released under a non-commercial license by default; readers working in production trading systems should treat them as a research prototyping tool unless a commercial license is secured.

The notebook `03_dl_vs_gbm` includes TabPFN as an optional model in the walk-forward comparison; if installed, it runs alongside GBMs and TabM on the ETF case study with per-fold IC reporting.

Modern neural baselines – TabM and strong defaults

A quieter but arguably more impactful development than foundation models is the rehabilitation of simple neural architectures through better training recipes and engineering.

Holzmüller et al. (2024) showed that **meta-tuned MLP defaults** (training recipes optimized across hundreds of datasets) can make neural networks competitive with GBMs without any architectural novelty. Their **RealMLP** achieves a strong time-accuracy trade-off on medium-to-large datasets by improving defaults rather than inventing new layers. The implication is that many older "DL loses to trees" conclusions reflected weak neural baselines rather than fundamental architectural limits.

TabM (Gorishniy et al., 2025) takes this further with parameter-efficient ensembling. Rather than training M independent MLPs (which is computationally prohibitive for large financial datasets), TabM maintains a shared weight backbone and applies rank-1 adapters (scaling parameters) to create M diverse ensemble members, all trained simultaneously in a single forward pass. Each individual member's predictions are noisy: the rank-1 perturbations introduce enough diversity that individual members overfit in different directions. Averaging cancels these uncorrelated errors while preserving the shared signal, achieving the generalization benefits of deep ensembles at the computational cost of a single network.

In evaluations across 46 benchmarks, TabM achieved the strongest performance among deep learning models, including on domain-aware temporal splits, which are historically challenging for neural networks. This temporal robustness is directly relevant to financial applications in which the training distribution shifts across walk-forward folds.

TabM represents the most practical case for "deep learning a practitioner can actually use on tabular financial data." It is architecturally simple, well-documented, and competitive without transformer-scale complexity. Interpretability uses standard model-agnostic methods (permutation importance and KernelSHAP) at a moderate computational cost. Training is slower than GBMs but does not require the multi-GPU infrastructure of large transformer models.

The notebook `03_dl_vs_gbm` compares LightGBM, a vanilla MLP, and a TabM rank-1 adapter ensemble on the ETF case study across walk-forward folds, reporting per-fold IC and training time.

Retrieval-augmented models – TabR

TabR (Gorishniy et al., 2024) hybridizes a deep encoder with k-nearest-neighbor retrieval. At prediction time, the model retrieves similar training instances from a learned embedding space and uses an attention-like mechanism to extract signals from their features and labels. The retrieved neighbors effectively provide local context that the base model can exploit, a principled way to help neural networks with the kind of local pattern recognition that trees perform naturally through hierarchical splitting.

The conceptual appeal for finance is immediate: "these neighbors drove the prediction" aligns with intuitions about regime similarity and peer-relative valuation. If the current market environment resembles a historical period, retrieval surfaces that analogy explicitly rather than requiring the model to encode it implicitly in fixed weights.

Benchmark evaluations show that TabR consistently outperforms non-retrieval deep baselines, and it is included as a first-class method in modern tabular toolkits (Ye et al., 2024). The trade-off is operational complexity: retrieval adds memory overhead for the neighbor index and increases inference latency in proportion to the database size.

Box 12.1: Lookahead bias in retrieval-augmented models

Standard TabR implementations build a retrieval index over the entire training set without temporal constraints. In a walk-forward setting, the model can retrieve neighbors from time periods that overlap with or follow the prediction target, a form of lookahead bias that standard implementations do not prevent. Any deployment must enforce temporal isolation: neighbors must come strictly from periods before the prediction date, with the same purging and embargo logic applied to the walk-forward splits. Implementing this remains an open engineering challenge; treat TabR results without temporal isolation as upper bounds, not production estimates.

When to look beyond GBMs – A decision framework

The choice between GBMs and neural alternatives for tabular (cross-sectional) prediction is regime-dependent. *Table 12.2* summarizes the decision framework for this class of problems, synthesizing the benchmark evidence with the operational constraints that matter in production financial ML. Sequential models (LSTMs, transformers, temporal convolutional networks) add a temporal dimension to this decision; *Chapter 13* covers that extension.

Data regime	Recommended	Rationale
Fewer than 10K effective samples, rapid signal testing	TabPFN (v2.5; distilled)	Strong "no-tuning" baseline for small data; fast iteration. Distillation engine enables deployment.
10K–100K samples, production tabular	LightGBM (or XGBoost)	Strong default accuracy/robustness; efficient training; TreeSHAP explanations are practical for tree ensembles.
10K–100K samples, DL warranted by complexity	TabM (rank-1 adapter ensemble)	Strongest tabular DL baseline in recent evaluations; validate under walk-forward temporal splits.
More than 100K samples, heavy categoricals	CatBoost (or LightGBM)	CatBoost's ordered scheme prevents leakage with categoricals; LightGBM supports categoricals via integer codes.
More than 1M samples, GPU available	LightGBM and TabM (or TabR)	No reliable crossover point. Trees often remain competitive; validate both families under your constraints.
Multi-modal inputs (text and tabular)	End-to-end DL (transformers)	Joint representation learning across modalities requires DL; GBMs don't natively fuse modalities.
Local similarity/regime matching matters	TabR	Nearest-neighbor retrieval improves on some benchmarks; enforce temporal isolation to avoid leakage.

Table 12.2: Heuristics for model selection

For readers who want a performance ceiling rather than a single production model, **AutoGluon Tabular** (Erickson et al., 2020) provides a useful reference. Its "best quality" preset blends GBMs, neural networks, and TabPFN into a multi-layer stacking ensemble with automated hyperparameter selection. These stacks frequently achieve the best benchmark results by exploiting complementary model strengths. The cost (multi-hour training budgets and operational overhead) makes direct deployment burdensome.

In our workflow, AutoGluon serves as a "ceiling sanity check": if your tuned LightGBM or TabM is within striking distance, you have extracted most of the available signal. If AutoGluon dramatically outperforms your single-model baseline, inspect which model family in the stack contributes the lift. This diagnoses whether you are leaving signal on the table that a different architecture could capture.

For the medium-sized datasets typical of financial ML (where walk-forward splits reduce effective training size, signal-to-noise ratios are low, and features exhibit heavy tails), well-tuned GBMs remain a strong default. The gap is narrowing, and the regime map above identifies where neural alternatives are most likely to pay off.

The notebook `03_dl_vs_gbm` provides a systematic comparison of LightGBM, TabM, TabPFN, and a vanilla MLP on the ETF case study under walk-forward splits. LightGBM achieves competitive IC at a fraction of neural network training time, while TabM's rank-1 adapter ensemble provides the strongest neural baseline, consistent with its showing across the broader case study comparison in *Section 12.6*, where TabM beats GBM on 3 of the 8 case studies with TabM coverage.

Box 12.2: Reading tabular benchmarks critically

The tabular ML literature now includes several large-scale benchmarks. Before transferring their conclusions to financial applications, four methodological issues deserve scrutiny:

- *IID assumptions.* TabArena (Erickson et al., 2025) and TALENT (Ye et al., 2024) focus on IID classification and regression. Both explicitly exclude temporal dependence from their current scope. Conclusions about model rankings under IID splits may not hold under walk-forward evaluation.
- *Tuning budget inequity.* Results depend heavily on whether models receive equal time for hyperparameter optimization. A tuned GBM versus a default neural network (or vice versa) proves nothing about the model families. Fair comparisons must specify and equalize the compute budget.
- *Post-hoc ensembling.* TabArena reports that cross-model ensembles (stacking GBMs with neural methods) often produce the best results. This changes the definition of "baseline" and complicates single-model comparisons. If your production constraint is a single model family, ensemble results are aspirational rather than actionable.
- *Dataset leakage.* Multiple benchmark studies have identified leakage in popular tabular datasets: features that encode the target, mislabeled tasks, or timestamp columns that enable lookahead. Curated subsets exist for a reason: TabArena retained 51 datasets from an initial pool of 1,053.

Regardless of the model family, performance depends heavily on hyperparameter configuration. The next section introduces Optuna's Bayesian approach to efficiently navigating that search space.

12.4 Advanced hyperparameter tuning with Optuna

GBMs introduce tree depth, learning rate, regularization strength, sampling ratios, and leaf counts into the hyperparameter search space, making Bayesian optimization essential for cost-effective parameter optimization rather than just convenient.

The tree-structured Parzen Estimator

Optuna implements hyperparameter optimization (HPO) using sampling methods to learn the relationship between parameter configurations and objective values. The default **Tree-structured Parzen Estimator** (**TPE**, Bergstra et al., 2011) maintains two density estimators: $l(x)$ for hyperparameters that yielded good objective values, and $g(x)$ for those that yielded poor objective values. The acquisition function maximizes $l(x)/g(x)$, concentrating evaluations on promising regions. As trials accumulate, the density estimators sharpen, concentrating proposals on regions that have historically produced strong validation metrics.

TPE is particularly effective for the discrete and conditional parameter spaces common in GBM tuning. It handles integer parameters, categorical choices, and conditional dependencies naturally, for example, sampling `num_leaves` only when tree growth is leaf-wise. The notebook `04_optuna_tuning` shows TPE-based optimization on the ETF case study, with emphasis on search-space design and early-stopping integration.

The define-by-run API

Optuna's define-by-run API defines the search space dynamically within the objective function. During each trial, calls to `trial.suggest_int()` or `trial.suggest_float()` request parameter values based on Optuna's current model of the objective landscape. This enables conditional parameters to sample regularization strength only for certain model types, hierarchical search to select a library, then tune its specific parameters, and dynamic stopping via pruning.

For iterative models like GBMs, we can evaluate intermediate performance after each boosting iteration. Optuna's **pruners automatically terminate trials** that appear unpromising:

- **MedianPruner** prunes trials worse than the median at each step
- **HyperbandPruner** uses adaptive resource allocation for more aggressive early pruning

Pruning can reduce total computation by 50% or more without sacrificing optimization quality.

For production-scale tuning, studies can be backed by a shared database (PostgreSQL, MySQL) so that multiple workers evaluate trials in parallel across machines.

GBM-specific tuning strategy

GBM hyperparameters fall into three families with distinct effects:

- **Tree structure** parameters (max depth, number of leaves, min samples per leaf) control model complexity: deeper trees capture more interactions but carry a higher risk of overfitting.
- **Boosting parameters** (learning rate, number of iterations, subsampling ratios) control training dynamics: lower learning rates with more iterations generally produce better results but increase training time.
- **Regularization parameters** (L1/L2 penalties, min child weight) directly penalize complexity.

A common pitfall is tuning the tree structure extensively while neglecting regularization. Regularization parameters (`reg_alpha`, `reg_lambda`) often have the greatest impact on out-of-sample performance because they directly address overfitting in low-signal-to-noise regimes. Set the learning rate at a low value (0.01–0.05) and let Optuna determine the optimal number of rounds via early stopping. This is generally more efficient than tuning both jointly. Start with 100–200 trials; beyond this range, marginal improvement tends to diminish while the risk of validation overfitting increases (*Box 12.3*).

> **Box 12.3: Validation overfitting in hyperparameter search**
>
> Validation overfitting is the primary risk of automated tuning. In low-signal-to-noise environments like daily return prediction, 500 TPE trials will find hyperparameters that exploit validation-set noise rather than genuinely better configurations: the 0.02 IC improvement vanishes on truly held-out data.
>
> Defenses: limit trials to 50–100, use coarser parameter grids, and always evaluate final candidates on data untouched during optimization. This is not a theoretical concern; it is the most common source of backtest-to-live performance degradation.

Multi-objective optimization

Financial models often face competing objectives that cannot be collapsed into a single metric. Optuna supports multi-objective optimization through its `NSGAIISampler` (Deb et al., 2002), which finds the **Pareto frontier** of non-dominated solutions, configurations where improving one objective necessarily harms another.

Optimizing IC versus turnover in practice

The notebook `06_optuna_multi_asset` tunes a LightGBM model on the ETF case study with two objectives: maximize rank IC and minimize portfolio turnover. Aggressive hyperparameters (deeper trees, lower regularization, more boosting rounds) tend to increase both IC and turnover simultaneously, because the model fits finer-grained patterns that change more frequently across rebalancing periods.

The Pareto frontier on this dataset is tight. NSGA-II finds two non-dominated solutions, one at IC≈0.029 with normalized turnover ≈0.004 and one at IC≈0.030 with turnover ≈0.005, both at similarly conservative parameter ranges with modest depth and sample weights. Single-objective optimization on IC alone, run with TPE on the same search space, converges to IC≈0.010, substantially below either Pareto solution; the multi-objective NSGA-II search reached a region of the parameter space that the single-objective search did not.

The multi-objective approach also reveals when objectives are less conflicted than assumed. If the Pareto frontier is nearly flat in one region, for example, high IC with only modestly higher turnover, you can claim both objectives without significant compromise. Conversely, a steeply curved frontier signals that marginal IC improvements come at rapidly increasing turnover costs, warranting careful analysis of transaction-cost sensitivity.

Other common multi-objective pairs include return versus drawdown (aggressive models achieve higher returns while experiencing larger peak-to-trough declines) and Sharpe ratio versus capacity (strategies with higher Sharpe often trade in smaller, less liquid names).

Implementation:

- `04_optuna_tuning` demonstrates HPO on the ETF case study.
- `05_cross_library_hpo` compares the three GBM libraries XGBoost, LightGBM, and CatBoost with loss type as a tunable hyperparameter on the firm characteristics dataset.
- `06_optuna_multi_asset` compares single-objective and multi-objective approaches across asset classes.
- `07_hpo_comparison` compares the efficiency of grid search and Optuna on the same tuning problem, including empirical evidence of validation overfitting as trial budgets increase.

Well-tuned models need interpretation before deployment. The next section covers TreeSHAP as the primary tool for explaining GBM predictions and detecting feature drift.

12.5 Model explainability with SHAP

Chapter 11 introduced SHAP values (Lundberg and Lee, 2017) as sanity checks for economic models. TreeSHAP (Lundberg et al., 2020) makes this framework routine for GBMs by computing exact Shapley values in $O(TLD^2)$ time per prediction, where T, L, and D are the number of trees, leaves per tree, and average tree depth. For a 500-tree LightGBM model on 100K samples, computation takes seconds, fast enough to run on every walk-forward fold as standard diagnostic infrastructure. By contrast, neural networks require approximate methods (for example, KernelSHAP, sampling) that are orders of magnitude slower and introduce approximation errors.

Dependence and interaction effects

Section 11.4 covered SHAP dependence plots and their use for identifying feature interactions. For GBMs, TreeSHAP additionally provides exact *interaction values* that decompose each prediction into main effects and pairwise interactions:

$$f(x) = E[f(X)] + \sum_j \phi_j^{\text{main}} + \sum_{j<k} \phi_{jk}^{\text{interaction}}$$

This decomposition quantifies how much of each prediction comes from features acting independently versus in combination, a capability unique to tree-based SHAP that approximate methods do not provide efficiently.

In our ETF case study, the strongest interaction ($H \approx 0.43$) is between the yield-curve z-score and the short-horizon volatility ratio, the top pair among 29 statistically strong interactions identified by the H-statistic. The SHAP interaction matrix shows that the yield-curve signal carries most of its predictive content when short-term volatility deviates meaningfully from its longer-horizon baseline; the interaction contribution can shift sign across volatility regimes. This conditional structure is invisible in standard feature-importance rankings, which rank the yield-curve z-score as a top feature regardless of regime, one reason the same model can look stable on average while its mechanism shifts beneath the surface. `08_shap_analysis` shows TreeSHAP computation, dependence plots, and the full interaction decomposition on the ETF case study.

SHAP-based drift monitoring

The SHAP stability chart from *Section 11.4* (tracking feature importance across walk-forward folds) extends naturally to production drift monitoring, as illustrated in *Figure 12.2*, where the comparison shifts from training folds to rolling prediction windows.

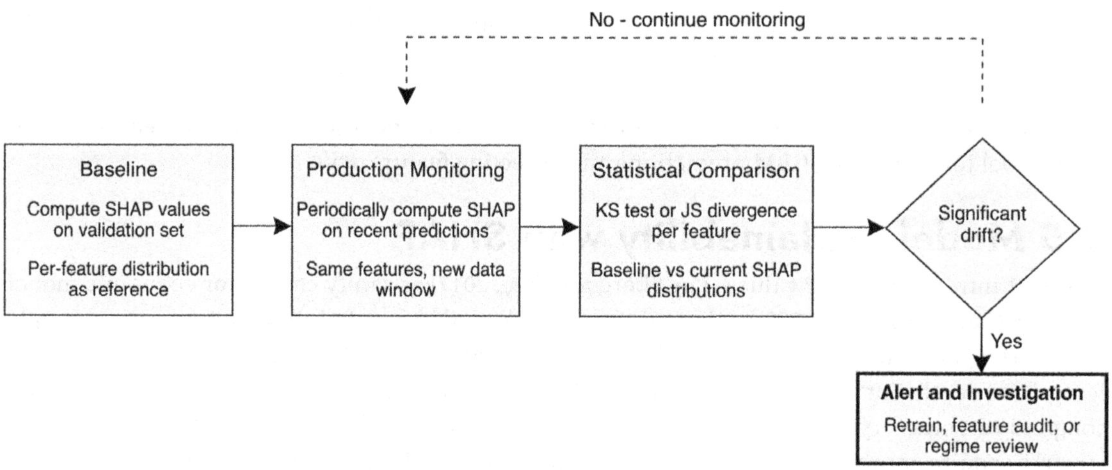

Figure 12.2: SHAP-based drift detection

Comparing SHAP distributions between a baseline period and recent predictions detects changes in mechanisms before they manifest in performance metrics. When features that were predictive lose their SHAP importance (or when previously irrelevant features gain prominence), investigate before performance deteriorates. This provides an earlier warning than outcome-based monitoring (rolling IC, Sharpe ratio) because it detects changes in the model's *reasoning*: by the time returns degrade, the damage is done. `08_shap_analysis` implements this comparison by tracking the mean |SHAP| across walk-forward folds and flagging features whose importance changes exceed 50%.

Critically, SHAP drift is a *diagnostic signal* warranting investigation, not proof of concept drift. Feature distributions can shift without affecting predictions if the model does not rely heavily on those features. Validate with downstream metrics (rolling IC, residual patterns) before acting. *Chapter 19* covers risk monitoring infrastructure; *Chapter 26* covers production alert thresholds and automated response protocols.

The Rashomon Effect – When equally good models disagree

Models with similar predictive performance can produce strikingly different explanations, a phenomenon known as the Rashomon Effect, after *Rashomon*, the 1950 film directed by Akira Kurosawa, in which witnesses give contradictory accounts of the same event. If a Random Forest and a gradient boosting ensemble both achieve 0.05 IC but attribute predictions to different features, each explanation reveals model-specific logic, not ground truth about the data-generating process. This multiplicity is inherent and should temper confidence in any single model's explanation. When SHAP attributions matter for downstream decisions such as feature pruning, risk allocation, or regulatory reporting, validate findings across multiple model specifications.

In practice, when a GBM and a TabM disagree on which features drive predictions, this disagreement is a signal to investigate the underlying relationship in the data rather than declare one correct. Features that both model families rank as important are more likely to reflect genuine structure; features that only one family highlights may reflect architecture-specific fitting patterns. `09_xai_limitations` shows explanation instability: predictions that differ by roughly 1.3% can yield entirely different top-three SHAP contributors.

SHAP also applies to token-level attributions for NLP models. The notebook `10_shap_nlp_sentiment` shows this for FinBERT sentiment predictions; *Chapter 10* covers the text feature-engineering pipeline in detail.

Using SHAP for feature selection and pruning

TreeSHAP's efficiency enables SHAP-based feature selection as a practical workflow step. Compute mean absolute SHAP values across the training set, rank features by importance, and retrain on the top-k features. This approach can produce models with comparable or improved out-of-sample performance when the removed features primarily contribute noise, though the improvement depends on the original feature set's redundancy and the signal-to-noise ratio. Unlike wrapper methods that require retraining for each feature subset, SHAP importance from a single trained model provides a strong initialization for the feature selection search.

For financial models with dozens of features, SHAP-based pruning improves interpretability and reduces the risk of spurious correlations. Features with consistently near-zero SHAP values across walk-forward folds are strong candidates for removal. Features with high SHAP variance across folds (important in some periods but not others) may indicate regime-dependent signals worth investigating rather than discarding.

Comparing SHAP rankings against permutation importance (PFI) and mean decrease in impurity (MDI), as shown in `08_shap_analysis`, identifies features that are robustly important across methods, and helps filter out artifacts of any single technique.

From explanation to uncertainty and robustness

Conformal prediction (*Chapter 11*) applies directly to GBM residual workflows. The notebook `11_conformal_gbm` implements four variants side by side: split conformal, quantile regression, **conformalized quantile regression** (CQR), and an **adaptive conformal** (ACI-style) online update loop. Split conformal provides the finite-sample coverage guarantee under exchangeability; CQR preserves asymmetric intervals while restoring calibration; ACI targets stable coverage under non-stationary residual dynamics through online alpha updates. When drift monitoring flags a regime change, these interval diagnostics typically widen, creating a feedback loop between explainability and uncertainty quantification. *Chapter 19* covers the position-sizing implications.

With the model-building and explanation toolkit in place, we now benchmark GBMs against the linear baselines from *Chapter 11* across all nine case studies to assess where nonlinear models earn their additional complexity.

12.6 Case study insights

Chapter 11 fit a linear baseline to nine case studies and asked each one question: does the model turn engineered features into a cross-sectional ranking that survives out-of-sample? The question and the case studies stay fixed; the two more flexible families introduced in this chapter (gradient-boosted trees and the TabM tabular network) now sit beside that baseline. The `12_case_study_insights` notebook fits all three families to every case study at its primary regression label and reads the results from the locked registry. Each model is summarized by its average daily information coefficient (IC), the mean of the daily cross-sectional rank correlations between prediction and realized return. The uncertainty around it is the 95% confidence interval computed with a HAC correction for the autocorrelation in that daily series. An interval that excludes zero is the bar for distinguishable cross-sectional signal.

Added flexibility does not win by default. Gradient boosting's interval clears zero on five of the nine case studies, against three for the linear baseline; TabM clears it on three of the eight it covers. The flexible families widen the set of case studies with measurable signal, but only modestly, and on no case study do they manufacture a ranking where the linear model found none.

Where flexibility adds ranking content

Figure 12.3 places the three families side by side: for each case study, the highest-IC configuration of each family at the primary label, with its HAC interval. *Table 12.3* holds the underlying numbers. Read together, they separate three situations, beginning with the numbers in the table.

Case study	Horizon	Target	Linear	GBM	TabM
US Firms	1 month	forward return	−0.005	+0.080	+0.031
ETFs	21 days	forward return	+0.054	+0.037	+0.041
CME Futures	5 days	forward return	−0.000	+0.032	+0.004
US Equities	1 day	forward return	+0.016	+0.032	+0.017
SP500 Options	to expiry	straddle return	+0.007	+0.018	+0.002

Case study	Horizon	Target	Linear	GBM	TabM
Crypto	8 hours	forward return	+0.009	+0.011	+0.003
NASDAQ-100	15 minutes	forward return	+0.005	+0.006	—
SP500 Eq+Opt	5 days	forward return	−0.006	+0.006	+0.011
FX	1 day	forward return	+0.005	+0.003	+0.007

Table 12.3: Average daily IC at each case study's primary regression label, for the highest-IC configuration of each family. Bold marks a HAC 95% confidence interval that excludes zero. TabM has no NASDAQ-100 coverage. The SP500 Options target is the return of a hold-to-maturity at-the-money straddle; shorter-horizon and delta-hedged alternatives post higher in-sample IC but, as O'Donovan and Yu (2024) document, do not survive realistic option transaction costs, so each case study is held at its primary label

Figure 12.3 then presents the same comparison visually:

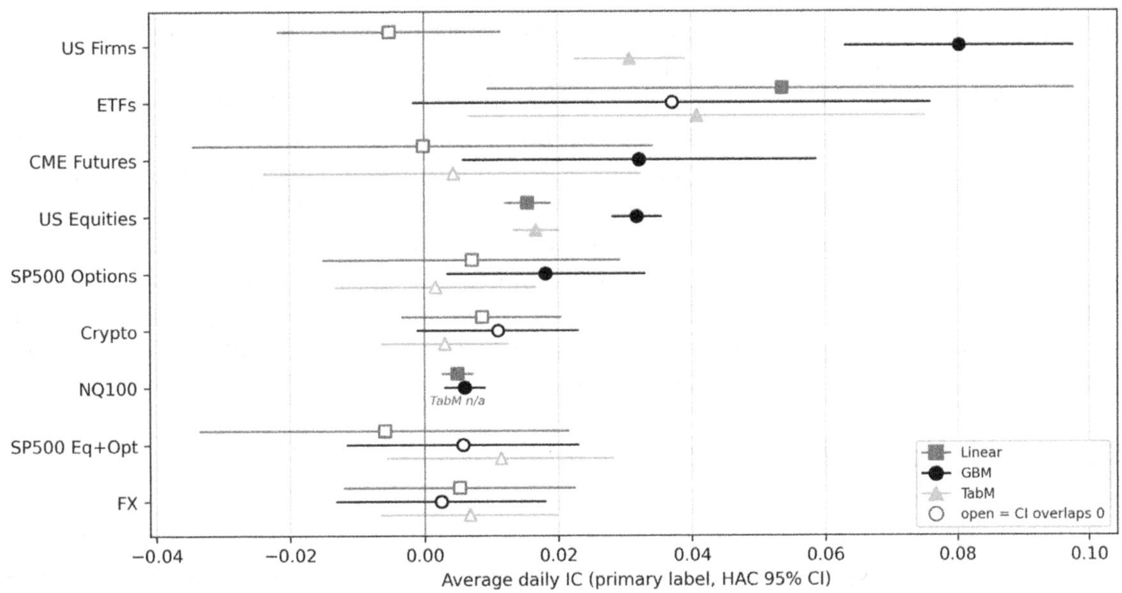

Figure 12.3: Highest-IC configuration of each family per case study at the primary regression label, with HAC 95% confidence intervals. Filled markers indicate an interval that excludes zero; open markers indicate one that overlaps zero

On the case studies where the linear model already found signal, the flexible families match or extend it. US Equities and NASDAQ-100 microstructure carry signal under all three families; on US Equities gradient boosting raises the daily IC from +0.016 to +0.032 with a tight interval, and on the NASDAQ-100 all three agree at a small but well-resolved value near +0.005. Gradient boosting then crosses the significance line on three case studies whose linear interval overlapped zero: US Firms (+0.080), CME Futures (+0.032), and the SP500 Options straddle (+0.018). This is the clearest sign that nonlinear structure carries ranking content the linear projection cannot reach.

The reverse also happens. On ETFs the linear model posts the highest IC of the three (+0.054) and is the only family whose interval clears zero; gradient boosting (+0.037) and TabM (+0.041) order the cross-section slightly worse and less certainly. Cross-asset momentum is close to linear in these features, and tree splits spend capacity on interactions that do not survive out of sample. Where the linear baseline was flat (FX and the combined SP500 equity-and-options case study), all three families stay within noise of zero. Added capacity moves the point estimate without moving the interval off zero.

TabM follows gradient boosting in sign more than in magnitude: when boosting adds content, TabM usually does too, but the two disagree on which case study each serves best. TabM edges boosting on ETFs and FX; boosting is far ahead on US Firms and the SP500 Options straddle. The two encode nonlinearity through different inductive biases (axis-aligned tree splits against learned dense embeddings), and neither dominates across the case studies.

What the lift rests on

The interval comparison in *Figure 12.3* already marks where boosting genuinely improves: on US Equities its interval clears the linear one outright, and on US Firms, CME Futures, and the SP500 Options straddle it crosses zero over a linear baseline whose own interval overlapped it. Where the two families' intervals overlap (the NASDAQ-100, where both sit near +0.005), there is nothing to separate. Where boosting does add content, the mechanism is nonlinear conditioning: splits encode regime indicators, volatility-rank crossings, and cross-asset correlations whose predictive value depends on conditional structure a linear model cannot express. On the case studies with both saved linear coefficients and a stored booster, the most important features reorder substantially between the linear coefficient ranking and the boosting gain ranking, and the per-fold feature ranking is far more stable on US Firms than on US Equities even though US Equities carries the tighter IC. Credible cross-sectional signal does not require a stable top-feature set.

Choosing the configuration

The registry grid crosses three loss functions (squared error, absolute error, and Huber) with leaf budgets from 7 to 127. This is a deliberately small slice of the hyperparameter space: it varies the loss and the leaf budget but leaves at their defaults the regularization controls that usually accompany tree complexity, namely maximum depth, the L1 and L2 leaf penalties, and feature and row subsampling (LightGBM documentation, *Parameters Tuning*). A production model would search those jointly; the goal here is to compare the families on equal footing, not to wring out every last basis point, and the book returns at the end to how lightly these demonstrations are tuned relative to a deployment workflow. On most case studies the loss changes the IC by less than one interval half-width: absolute error (MAE) posts the highest IC on eight of the nine primary labels and squared error (MSE) on the remaining one, ETFs, with Huber competitive but never highest. US Firms is the exception that shows why the default matters. *Figure 12.4* contrasts it with US Equities on shared axes. On US Firms the MAE curve sits near +0.080 across every leaf budget while Huber and MSE bunch around +0.030 to +0.035, a gap of two to three interval half-widths that absolute error opens by refusing to chase the heavy-tailed extreme returns squared error spends capacity on. On US Equities the same three losses fall within a single half-width at every depth; the configuration barely resolves and the operative choice lies elsewhere.

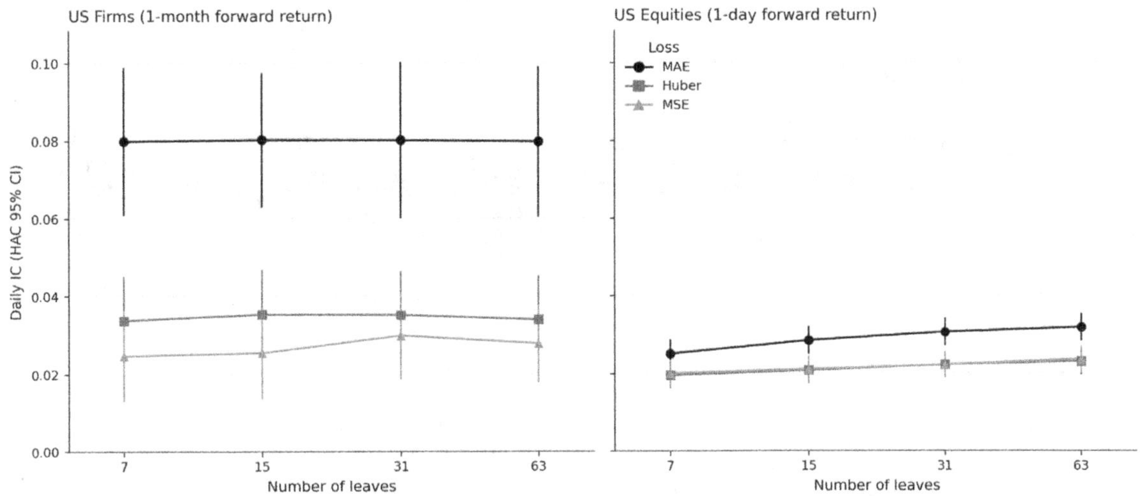

Figure 12.4: Daily IC by loss function and leaf budget for the GBM grid, on US Firms and US Equities, with HAC 95% confidence intervals and shared axes. The configurations spread widely on US Firms but fall within a single interval half-width on US Equities

Tree depth is the least consequential of these hyperparameters. The highest-IC leaf budget scatters across the interior of the grid (seven leaves on three case studies, 63 on three others), and within any case study the depth profiles differ by less than one interval half-width, so depth rarely changes whether the interval clears zero. The hyperparameter that pays operationally is early stopping. The boosting trajectories peak across a wide range: SP500 Options and ETFs by 50 trees, CME Futures and Crypto by 100, FX by 150, while US Firms peaks near 350 and US Equities, the NASDAQ-100, and the SP500 equity-and-options case study are still climbing at the 500-tree budget cap. Early stopping should be a tuning outcome rather than a fixed prior: a coarse checkpoint grid retires a large fraction of the trees on the early-peaking case studies and is simply inactive where IC keeps rising.

Ranking each case study's grid by HAC-corrected significance (t_{HAC}) rather than by IC selects the same configuration on seven of the nine case studies, and on the two exceptions (US Equities and the NASDAQ-100) both choices sit far inside the region where the interval excludes zero ($t_{HAC} \approx 17$ and ≈ 4), so the substitution never changes whether a case study's interval clears zero. The two rankings nearly coincide because the HAC standard error varies little across configurations within a case study and family; scoring by IC and by significance reorders only configurations whose ICs are already statistically indistinguishable.

Whether the lift persists

A single-period IC can hide a signal that lived in a few windows. *Figure 12.5* tracks the rolling three-month daily IC of gradient boosting relative to the linear baseline across two contrasting case studies, with walk-forward fold boundaries marked. On US Equities, across 2000–2015, the boosting curve sits above the linear curve through most of the fifteen-year span, including the 2008–2009 dislocation. The improvement is a standing feature, not a one-window artifact. On ETFs, across 2015–2023, the two curves cross repeatedly and neither holds a durable margin, consistent with the linear model being the better-resolved choice there. Persistence, not the point estimate, is what separates a deployable edge from a lucky window.

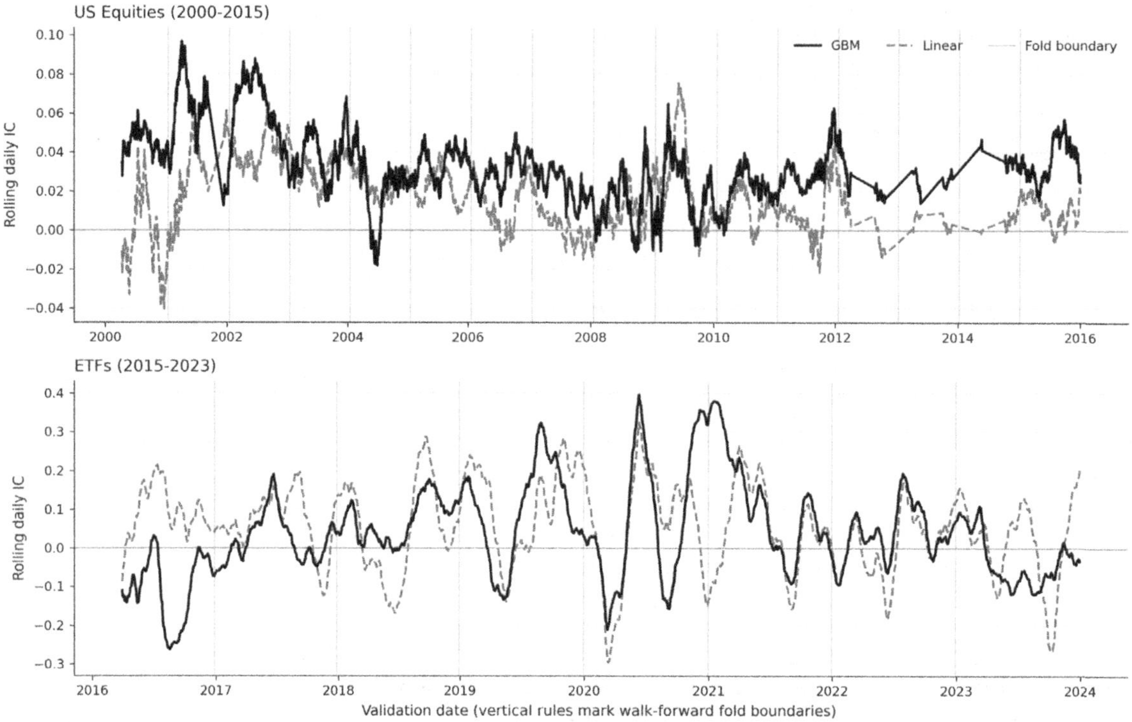

Figure 12.5: Rolling three-month daily IC for gradient boosting and the linear baseline on US Equities (2000–2015) and ETFs (2015–2023). Vertical rules mark walk-forward fold boundaries

Regression versus classification

Three case studies (Crypto, the SP500 equity-and-options case study, and US Firms) train gradient boosting on both the continuous return and the binary direction over the same horizon, allowing the two targets to be compared directly. Each model emits a continuous score, but they are trained and evaluated against different targets: the regression score is read by IC against the continuous return, and the classifier score by AUC against the realized direction (*Chapter 7*). *Table 12.4* cross-evaluates them, asking whether the scores are interchangeable: whether the classifier also ranks magnitudes, and whether the regression score also separates signs.

Case study	Horizon	Classifier score → IC	Classifier → AUC	Regression score → AUC
Crypto	8 hours	+0.020	0.513	0.502
US Firms	1 month	+0.084	0.543	0.540
SP500 Eq+Opt	5 days	+0.004	0.507	0.489
SP500 Eq+Opt	10 days	−0.010	0.505	0.498

Table 12.4: GBM regression-versus-classification cross-evaluation. "Classifier score→IC" reads the binary-direction model's score by IC against the continuous return; "Classifier→AUC" scores that model against its own direction label; "Regression score→AUC" reads the continuous-return model's score against direction. Bold marks an interval that excludes the null (zero for IC, one-half for AUC)

They are not interchangeable. On Crypto the classifier's eight-hour score reaches an IC of +0.020 against the continuous return, with an interval excluding zero, and its direction AUC of 0.513 clears one-half: the gradient-boosted classifier recovers directional content on Crypto that the linear classifier in *Chapter 11* did not. On US Firms the classifier score reaches IC +0.084 with a direction AUC of 0.543. On the SP500 equity-and-options case study neither target separates at either horizon: the classifier IC overlaps zero and its AUC sits at one-half. Read the other way, the regression score's AUC against direction stays within ±0.04 of one-half on every pairing, so a model tuned to rank magnitudes is close to uninformative about sign. The same lesson held in *Chapter 11*; the loss function, logistic against squared, decides which discriminative content the score carries. Both views feed downstream: *Chapter 16*'s signal stage ranks on the IC view, and the direction-aware classifiers continue to drive long–short construction in the case-study chapters.

Reading the model

Native gain and split-count importances rank features differently (gain rewards large conditional effects, split count rewards features used for fine partitioning), so neither alone explains a booster. TreeSHAP resolves the disagreement by decomposing each prediction into exact per-feature contributions. *Figure 12.6* shows the SHAP beeswarm for the ETFs and SP500 Options boosters: on ETFs the yield-curve slope and its z-score dominate the spread of contributions, while on the SP500 straddle the GARCH variance-risk-premium and the realized-volatility ratios lead. The fold-level view in the notebook shows some features contributing consistently and others only in particular regimes; monitoring the regime-dependent features for drift, as *Section 12.5* develops, is the operational implication.

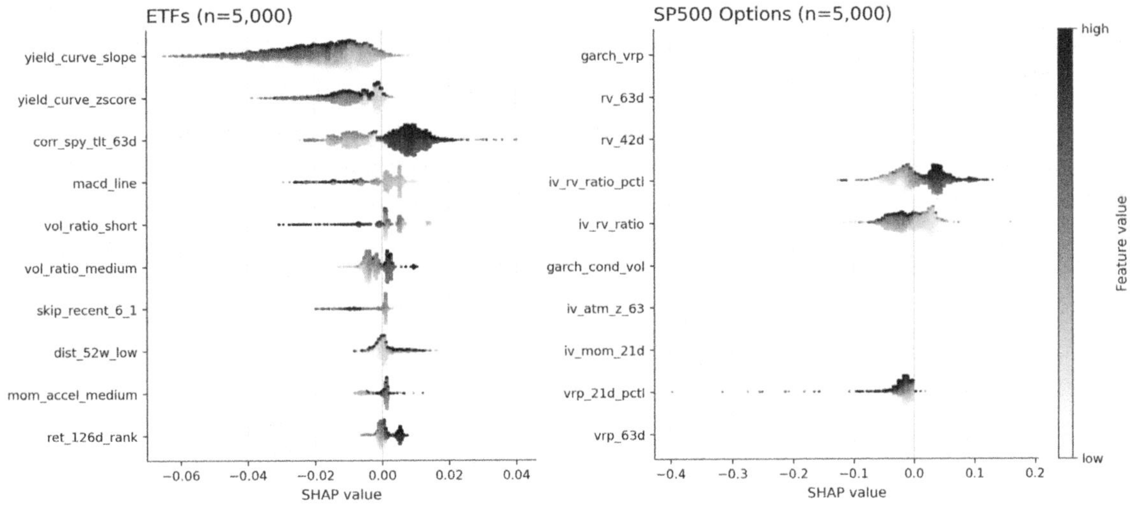

Figure 12.6: SHAP beeswarm of per-feature contributions for the GBM boosters on ETFs and SP500 Options. Each dot is one prediction; shade encodes the feature value; horizontal position is the SHAP value

From IC to profitability

An interval that clears zero certifies a ranking, not a return. On five case studies (US Firms, US Equities, CME Futures, the SP500 Options straddle, and the NASDAQ-100) gradient boosting supplies the cross-sectional ordering that the portfolio-construction and simulation chapters turn into positions. Where boosting does not clear zero, another family may still carry the ranking (the linear model does so on ETFs), so a null for boosting is not a null for the case study. *Chapters 16* through *19* take these ranked predictions through execution, cost, and risk, to ask which of the statistically distinguishable signals survives as economic profit.

12.7 Summary

Gradient boosting machines are the defensible default for tabular financial prediction. XGBoost, LightGBM, and CatBoost achieve similar accuracy after tuning. The real selection criteria are operational: training speed (LightGBM), categorical integrity (CatBoost), or ecosystem maturity (XGBoost). The cross-case study evaluation confirms that shallow trees with MAE loss and early stopping constitute a strong starting configuration, while monotonic constraints encode economic logic as regularization without sacrificing predictive power. TreeSHAP provides the interpretability infrastructure (dependence analysis, interaction decomposition, and drift monitoring) that production deployment demands.

Deep learning alternatives are narrowing the gap. TabPFN enables rapid signal testing without tuning; TabM provides a practical neural baseline competitive with GBMs on medium datasets. TabPFN degrades faster than GBMs under temporal distribution shift, and all benchmark claims must be validated under walk-forward protocols with purging and embargo before they translate to trading decisions. The regime-dependent decision framework in *Section 12.3* identifies where neural alternatives are most likely to pay off.

Chapter 13 extends to sequential data, covering deep learning architectures (transformers, state-space models, and temporal convolutional networks) for time-series prediction, in which the temporal structure that GBMs treat as features becomes the model's native input format.

13

Deep Learning for Time Series

Deep learning enters time-series prediction when the ordering of observations may carry information beyond the most recent datapoint. *Chapters 11* and *12* treated prediction mainly as a cross-sectional problem: given today's features, forecast a future label. This chapter asks when the sequence history itself adds incremental signal, which architectures can extract it, and how the formulation of the forecast target changes the answer.

That formulation choice matters. Some models generate a future path one step at a time; others predict the entire future path in a single forward pass; many financial ML pipelines skip the path and predict only a horizon label, such as a 5-day return, 21-day return, direction, or cross-sectional rank. This chapter focuses on the architectures and evaluates them in terms of predictive performance, in line with the other modeling chapters. *Chapter 17* then returns to the trading objective itself, showing how deep learning can learn positions or portfolio weights directly under allocation-level losses, such as the Sharpe ratio, drawdown, and cost-aware objectives.

The answer to the architecture choice is not "use Transformers." Modern time-series modeling is better understood as a competition among inductive biases: recurrence, explicit decomposition, attention, convolutions, state-space models, and strong linear baselines. Each makes different assumptions about temporal structure, covariates, and forecast horizon. The practical task is to decide when sequence-model complexity is warranted, when a direct horizon-label model is the cleaner formulation, and when the problem should be moved downstream into an allocation objective.

By the end of this chapter, you will be able to:

- Explain why recurrent networks became a bottleneck for long-context forecasting tasks.
- Compare the main temporal modeling philosophies and explain when each is most appropriate.
- Use strong baselines and diagnostics to judge whether sequence-model complexity is warranted.
- Distinguish the design logic of modern time-series Transformer variants and relate those choices to multivariate structure, covariates, and forecast horizon.
- Distinguish recursive one-step forecasting, direct multi-horizon path forecasting, and direct horizon-label prediction, and explain why the distinction matters.

- Evaluate time-series foundation model adaptation modes for financial applications, including the implications of transfer mismatch and pretraining contamination.
- Apply practical uncertainty estimation methods, including MC Dropout and deep ensembles, to support risk-aware trading decisions.

Figure 13.1 lays out the timeline of the architecture evolution. We begin with Long Short-Term Memory (LSTM) networks and the limitations that created space for both N-BEATS and Transformer-based architectures. A pivotal 2022 critique by Zeng et al. showed that simple linear models often outperform complex Transformers, challenging assumptions about the need for architectural sophistication. Modern architectures like PatchTST and iTransformer respond through stronger temporal inductive biases. The chapter concludes with a practitioner's framework for selecting architectures based on problem characteristics rather than research hype.

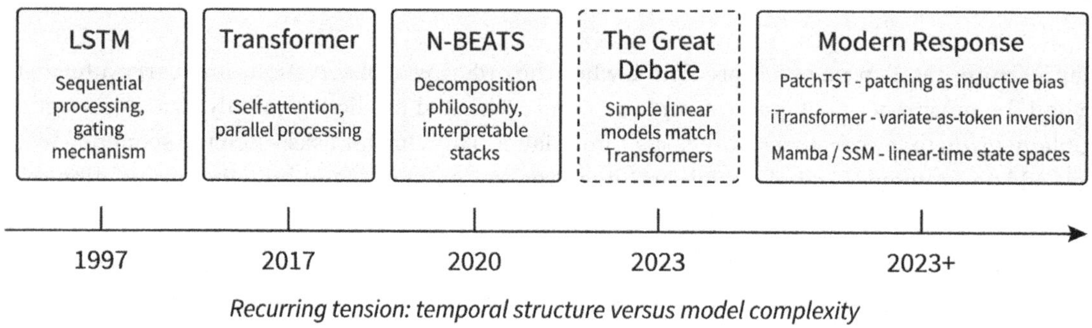

Figure 13.1: Timeline of time-series architecture evolution

Recurrent networks come first; their limitations motivated every architecture that follows.

13.1 Recurrent networks and their limits

Recurrent neural networks (RNNs) maintain a **hidden state** that evolves as the network processes each element of a sequence. This design made them the default architecture for time series forecasting through the mid-2010s.

Long Short-Term Memory (LSTM) networks (Hochreiter and Schmidhuber, 1997) addressed the problem that limited vanilla RNNs: **vanishing gradients** prevented the model from learning long-range dependencies (Hochreiter et al., 2001). The LSTM introduced a cell state that acts as a conveyor belt, allowing information to flow across many time steps with minimal degradation.

The LSTM gating mechanism

The LSTM's power derives from three gates (forget, input, and output) that regulate information flow (*Figure 13.2*). The cell state update combines their decisions:

$$C_t = f_t \odot C_{t-1} + i_t \odot \tanh(W_C \cdot [h_{t-1}, x_t] + b_C)$$

where f_t and i_t are sigmoid-gated functions of the previous hidden state and current input. This gating mechanism allows LSTMs to selectively remember or forget information, theoretically capturing dependencies spanning hundreds of time steps. In financial applications, LSTMs have been used for volatility forecasting, return prediction, and limit order book modeling (Zhang, Zohren, and Roberts, 2019).

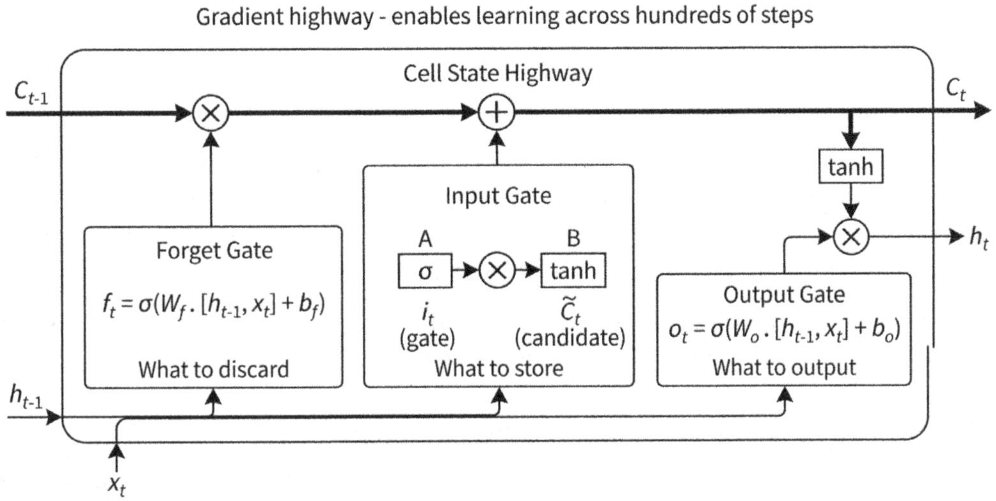

Figure 13.2: LSTM cell with forget, input, and output gates

Two limitations

LSTMs have two limitations that motivated the search for alternatives.

- **The sequential computation bottleneck.** The hidden state at time t depends on the hidden state at time $t - 1$, creating an inherent computational dependence on the sequence's length. LSTMs still benefit from GPU acceleration, but their recurrence limits *temporal* parallelism compared with attention-based models discussed in *Section 13.3*. For high-frequency data with tens of thousands of observations, this bottleneck can become prohibitive. Transformers process all time steps simultaneously through matrix operations, often yielding substantially faster training at similar sequence lengths.
- **Gradient flow challenges.** While LSTMs were designed to address vanishing gradients, they do not eliminate the problem entirely. For very long sequences, gradients must still flow through many gating operations during backpropagation through time (Werbos, 1990). In practice, long nominal lookbacks do not guarantee that the model effectively uses distant information; they often increase noise, training instability, and sensitivity to hyperparameters. For financial series, where the signal is weak and non-stationary, that distinction matters more than the architecture's theoretical capacity.

`01_core_architectures` illustrates the **computation-versus-signal trade-off** on a deliberately simple ETF task: pooled univariate 60-day return windows predict the same ETF's next-day return. On this noisy objective the LSTM trains about twice as slowly as a comparable MLP (32 versus 17 seconds) yet ranks next-day returns no better: both models post a cross-sectional Spearman IC near zero.

The **Gated Recurrent Unit** (**GRU**) simplifies the LSTM by merging the forget and input gates into a single update gate and eliminating the separate cell state, reducing parameters by roughly one-quarter in the `01_core_architectures` implementation. This streamlining can reduce model size and sometimes improve generalization on smaller datasets. However, the GRU inherits both fundamental limitations: sequential computation remains $O(T)$, and gradient flow through the merged gating mechanism still degrades over long sequences. The GRU trains slightly faster, and its IC is also near zero: a lighter recurrent cell does not solve the return-prediction problem.

The comparison shows architecture, not strategy: recurrence adds sequential computation without improving next-day return ranking, which reflects the weak signal in return sequences.

Some financial processes exhibit **long-memory** properties, such as volatility clustering (*Chapter 9*), persistent order flow, and calendar effects, in which dependencies span multiple trading days or longer. These long-range dependencies can exceed what LSTMs reliably capture through gradient-based learning, especially when the useful signal is weak and non-stationary.

These limits motivated parallel architectures along two lines: embedding classical decomposition into neural networks (*Section 13.2*) and importing attention from NLP (*Section 13.3*).

13.2 N-BEATS and explicit decomposition

N-BEATS (Oreshkin et al., 2019) encodes a specific inductive bias: time series are compositions of interpretable components (trend and seasonality) that neural networks should decompose explicitly rather than discover implicitly.

Blocks, stacks, and doubly residual learning

The N-BEATS architecture builds complexity from simple components through a hierarchical structure.

- **The basic block**. The fundamental unit is a fully-connected block that takes a lookback window of historical data as input. The input passes through several dense layers with ReLU activations. The block produces two outputs: a *forecast* for the future horizon and a *backcast* that reconstructs the historical input. The backcast represents what the block has "understood" about the input signal.
- **Residual stacking**. Multiple blocks connect sequentially within a stack. The first block receives the original input. Each subsequent block receives the *residual* from its predecessor: the original input minus the previous block's backcast. This forces each block to focus on what earlier blocks failed to capture, progressively extracting finer patterns from the signal.
- **Doubly residual architecture**. The full model chains multiple stacks together, applying the same residual principle at a higher level. The second stack receives the residual from the entire first stack. This creates a deep, hierarchical decomposition in which early stacks capture dominant patterns, and later stacks refine the details. The final forecast is the sum of all block-level forecasts across all stacks. This progressive refinement acts as a strong regularizer, paralleling boosting in tree-based methods (*Chapter 12*), since each block must explain only what its predecessors missed.

Figure 13.3 illustrates the complete block-stack-doubly-residual structure.

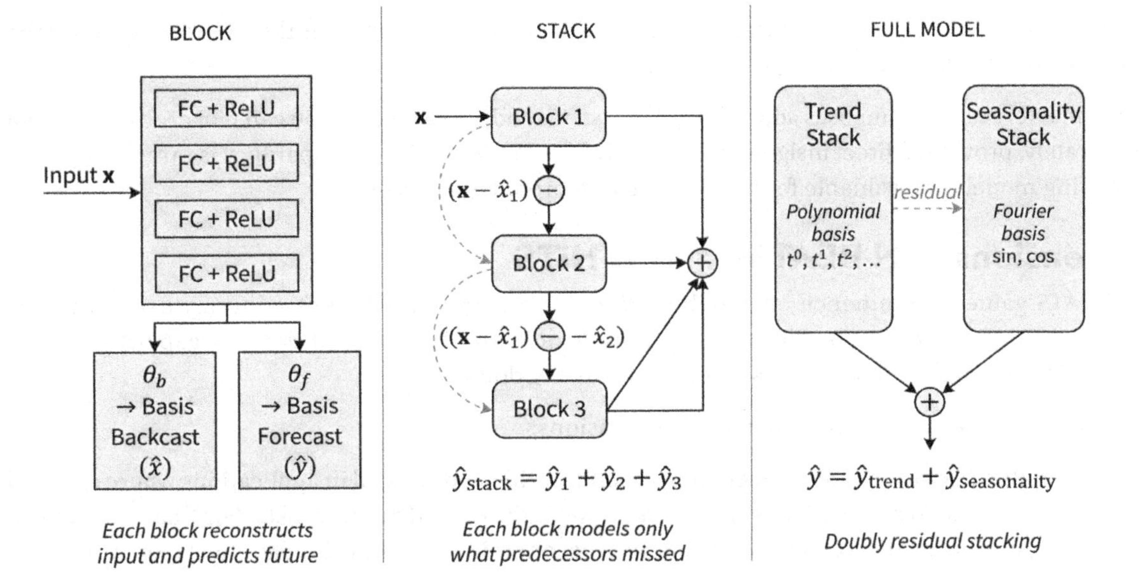

Figure 13.3: N-BEATS block-stack doubly-residual architecture

Basis expansion

The mechanism by which N-BEATS generates its outputs distinguishes it from generic neural networks. Rather than directly outputting forecast values, each block's final layers produce *expansion coefficients* that weight the *basis functions*.

For the forecast, the block outputs coefficients θ_f that combine with basis vectors g_f:

$$\hat{y} = \sum_{i=1}^{|\theta_f|} \theta_{f,i} \cdot g_{f,i}$$

This approach generalizes classical decomposition. Fitting a trend is equivalent to finding coefficients for a polynomial basis; modeling seasonality is equivalent to finding coefficients for a Fourier basis. In the generic N-BEATS configuration, the model learns suitable basis functions from data. In the interpretable configuration, these bases are explicitly constrained.

Making N-BEATS interpretable

The interpretable configuration, **N-BEATS-I**, constrains each stack to model a specific component.

The *Trend Stack* uses a polynomial basis. For a polynomial of degree p, the trend forecast becomes:

$$\hat{y}_{trend}(t) = \sum_{i=0}^{p} \theta_{trend,i} \cdot t^i$$

The neural network learns the optimal polynomial coefficients that capture the underlying trend component.

The *Seasonality Stack* uses a Fourier basis of sine and cosine terms, with the network learning the coefficients that best represent periodic patterns.

The final forecast decomposes additively: Forecast = Trend + Seasonality. You can plot each component separately, providing direct insight into what drives predictions. This transparency is rare among deep learning models and valuable for building trust in production systems.

Extensions – N-BEATSx and N-HiTS

N-BEATS gained prominence by matching the M4 competition winner's accuracy using a purely deep-learning approach, showing that appropriate inductive biases could close the gap between neural and traditional methods across diverse forecasting domains.

The architecture has inspired two notable extensions:

- **N-BEATSx** incorporates exogenous variables, which are crucial in applications where external factors, such as weather or macroeconomic indicators, drive forecasts. For financial applications, this enables conditioning on macroeconomic releases, calendar effects, or cross-asset signals.
- **N-HiTS** (Challu et al., 2022) introduces hierarchical interpolation and multi-rate signal processing, improving long-horizon forecasting accuracy by capturing patterns at multiple temporal resolutions simultaneously. Its MaxPool downsampling reduces input dimensionality for long-range stacks while preserving detail in short-range ones.

Both extensions preserve the core philosophy of structured decomposition while expanding the model's applicability.

Practical caveats

N-BEATS is sensitive to the **lookback-to-horizon ratio**: too short a lookback starves the decomposition of context, while very long horizons can destabilize training. The interpretable configuration can underperform the generic variant when the true generating process does not decompose cleanly into polynomial trend and Fourier seasonality, a common situation in financial data where regime changes violate both assumptions. N-BEATS-I should therefore be benchmarked against N-BEATS-G on the target data before committing to the interpretable variant.

Decomposition is one escape from sequential processing; importing the attention mechanism from language models is another, and it changes how models relate distant time steps.

Implementation: `02_nbeats_interpretable` implements this architecture from scratch in PyTorch, building blocks, stacks, and the doubly-residual connections step by step. It also trains and evaluates both configurations on SPY data.

13.3 Attention for time series

While N-BEATS evolved classical decomposition principles, a more radical approach came from natural language processing. The Transformer architecture (Vaswani et al., 2017) dispensed with recurrence entirely in favor of self-attention, a mechanism that models relationships between all pairs of sequence elements simultaneously. Its adaptation for time series represents a bet that a sufficiently general mechanism can learn all temporal structure from data alone, without decomposition priors.

Adapting Transformers for temporal data

Applying Transformers to time series requires addressing the architecture's origin in discrete token sequences. Three key adaptations bridge this gap:

- **Tokenization via patching.** Unlike words, which are natural discrete units, time series values are continuous and densely sampled. A naive approach treats each time step as a token, but this creates prohibitively long sequences for the attention mechanism. The modern solution is *patching*: segmenting the input window into fixed-length subsequences that become input tokens. A lookback window of 512 time steps might yield 32 patches, each of length 16. Patching reduces computational cost while preserving local temporal patterns within each patch.

> **Caution: Data leakage in patching**
>
> Patching can introduce data leakage if normalization statistics are computed across the full window rather than causally. Practitioners must ensure that all preprocessing respects temporal boundaries: either by normalizing each patch independently or by using only backward-looking statistics.

- **Positional encoding.** Self-attention is *permutation-invariant*: without additional information, it cannot distinguish the sequence (x_1, x_2, x_3) from (x_3, x_1, x_2). For time series, where temporal order is essential, this is a critical deficiency. Positional encodings inject order information by adding position-dependent vectors to each token's embedding. The original Transformer used fixed sinusoidal encodings; many time series variants learn these encodings during training.
- **Encoder-decoder structure.** The standard Transformer comprises an encoder that processes the historical lookback window to create contextual representations, and a decoder that generates forecasts. Time-series adaptations use several variants of that template, including encoder-only and direct multi-horizon heads.

Forecast formulation is a separate design choice from architecture. A model can be recurrent, attention-based, decomposition-based, or linear, but it still needs a target definition. Three formulations matter in this chapter (see *Figure 13.4*):

1. Recursive one-step forecasting learns a one-period-ahead model and rolls it forward. The model predicts y_{t+1} from the past window, appends that prediction to the input, predicts y_{t+2}, and repeats until y_{t+H}. This is the natural extension of one-step statistical forecasting, including the ARIMA-style models used in *Chapter 9* for model-based features, but forecast errors can compound across the horizon.

2. Direct multi-horizon path forecasting predicts the entire future path in a single forward pass $(y_{t+1}, y_{t+2}, \ldots, y_{t+H})$. Many deep forecasting architectures, including sequence-to-sequence models and multi-horizon heads, are designed for this task. They avoid recursive error propagation, but they still model the future path and must learn the joint structure of all intermediate steps.
3. Direct horizon-label prediction skips the path and predicts only the final label used by the investment problem: a 5-day return, 21-day return, direction, volatility premium, or cross-sectional rank. This is the dominant formulation in *Chapters 11, 12, 13,* and *14*. The model may use sequential inputs, but the target is a supervised horizon-label problem rather than a time-series path forecast.

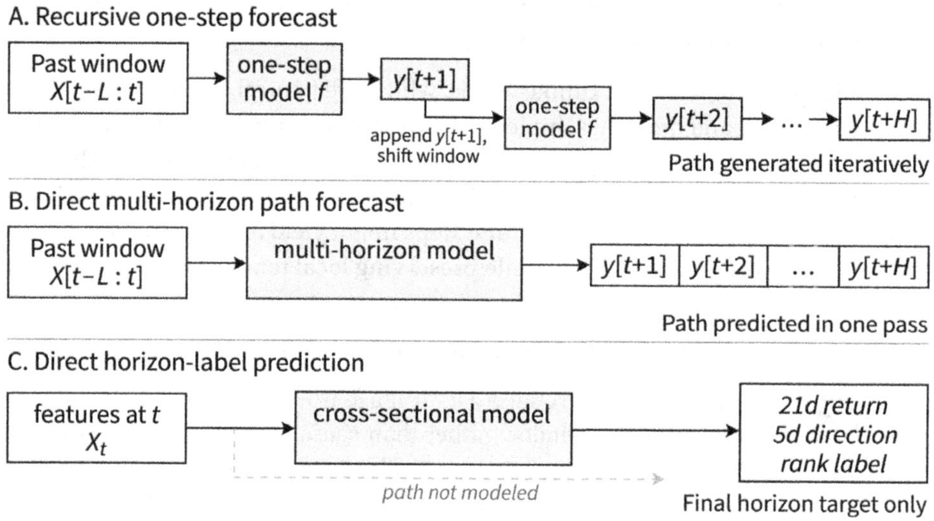

Figure 13.4: Three forecast formulations for financial time series

Recursive forecasting generates the path one step at a time, direct multi-horizon forecasting predicts the path in one pass, and direct horizon-label prediction skips the path and predicts only the final target.

All three formulations recur in this chapter, but the case-study evaluation focuses on how sequence architectures perform under direct horizon-label prediction.

The self-attention mechanism

The **self-attention mechanism**, introduced in *Chapter 10* for language applications, operates identically when applied to time series tokens. Each position attends to all others via Query, Key, and Value projections (see *Figure 13.5*):

$$\text{Attention}(Q, K, V) = \text{softmax}\left(\frac{QK^T}{\sqrt{d_k}}\right)V$$

Unlike RNNs, which must pass information sequentially through hidden states, self-attention creates direct connections between any two positions, regardless of distance. Multiple **attention heads** learn different relationship types in parallel (local trends, seasonality, regime shifts), and their outputs combine through a learned projection.

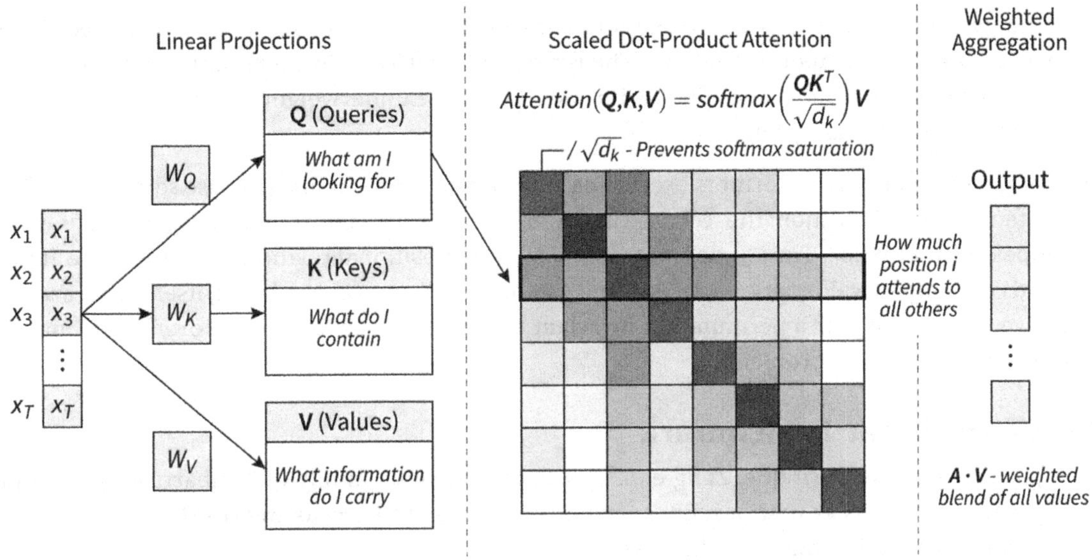

Figure 13.5: Self-attention via query, key, and value projections

The vanilla Transformer's $O(L^2)$ (quadratic) attention complexity motivated several *efficiency-focused variants*, including **Informer**, **Autoformer**, **FEDformer**, and **Pyraformer**, each reducing cost through sparse or frequency-domain attention. All shared a *common assumption*: time series should be tokenized like language, with attention computing relationships between temporal positions. Whether attention genuinely extracted temporal structure (or merely overfitted to patterns that simpler models could match) remained an open question until the empirical challenge the next section takes up.

13.4 Linear baselines versus Transformers

Zeng et al. (2022) showed that simple linear models can outperform several Transformer-based architectures on standard long-term forecasting benchmarks. The result changed the field's baseline expectations: a new architecture should not be taken seriously unless it improves on strong linear benchmarks.

At the same time, these results do not establish that attention is ineffective for time-series modeling in general. They show, rather, that on widely used benchmark tasks, additional architectural sophistication often failed to improve predictive accuracy.

The practical implication is clear: begin with strong, simple baselines, then add complexity only when it delivers robust out-of-sample gains.

Permutation-invariance and temporal order

The core argument against using Transformers for time-series targets the mathematical properties of self-attention. The mechanism is **permutation-invariant**: without positional encodings, attention treats input sequences as unordered sets. The dot product between a query at position i and keys at all other positions produces the same values regardless of how those positions are arranged.

Positional encodings inject order information, but Zeng et al. argue this is a patch on a mechanism that may underutilize temporal structure. The issue is not that Transformers *cannot* represent order (they can) but that order must be explicitly injected. It may be underweighted in practice depending on architecture and training dynamics.

There is a deeper point. Transformers excel in natural language processing because semantic relationships often transcend position: the words "king" and "queen" relate conceptually regardless of where they appear in a sentence. Time series forecasting is about positional relationships: the value at time t depends causally on values at $t - 1$, $t - 2$, and so on, so the temporal ordering itself may carry the predictive signal. Applying a permutation-invariant architecture to a task where order is paramount is a mismatch of tool and problem.

The LTSF-Linear benchmark

To empirically test their critique, Zeng et al. (2022) introduced a family of "embarrassingly simple" one-layer linear models as new baselines for **Long-Term Series Forecasting** (LTSF), the task of predicting many steps rather than just the next value:

- **Linear** maps the lookback window directly to the forecast horizon via a single matrix multiplication, with no hidden layers, nonlinearities, or attention.
- **D-Linear** first decomposes the series into trend and seasonal components using a simple moving average, then applies separate linear layers to each component, and finally sums them. This adds minimal complexity while incorporating the decomposition insight that N-BEATS had validated.
- **N-Linear** normalizes for distribution shift: subtract the last input value before the linear layer, add it back to the output. This simple trick stabilizes predictions when test-time statistics differ from those used during training. `03_great_debate` implements all three LTSF-Linear variants, along with a vanilla Transformer encoder, for direct comparison.

The models require seconds to train on standard hardware. Their total parameter counts are orders of magnitude smaller than those of Transformer variants.

Results and diagnostic evidence

In the Zeng et al. (2022) experiments, these linear models outperformed Transformer architectures across all nine LTSF benchmark datasets, achieving 20-50% improvements over Informer, Autoformer, and FEDformer. Perceived progress had been illusory, driven by comparisons against weak baselines rather than genuine architectural advances.

Diagnostic experiments revealed specific failure modes. Forecasting error *increased* for most Transformers as the lookback window grew: they were confused by additional noise rather than extracting useful signals. When input sequences were randomly shuffled (destroying all temporal structure), D-Linear's MSE more than quadrupled (0.345 to 1.406), while the Transformer's barely changed (0.379 to 0.391; *Figure 13.6*). D-Linear exploits temporal structure and collapses without it; the Transformer relies primarily on channel correlations, so removing the time axis incurs little cost. Attention was not learning temporal patterns.

Implementation: `03_great_debate` replicates these diagnostics for ETF return data.

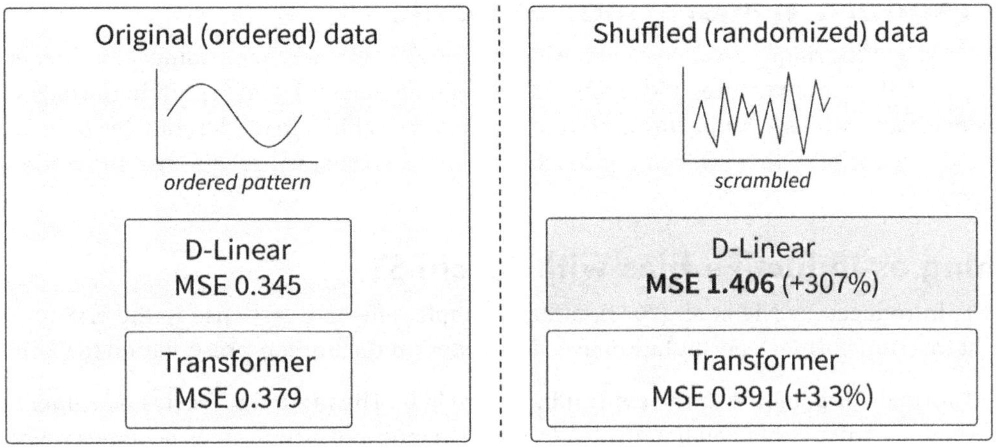

Figure 13.6: The Shuffle experiment: D-Linear versus Transformer under shuffled inputs

Counterpoints and caveats

The paper by Zeng et al. (2022) is not the final word. The original study focused on univariate forecasting; Transformers may do better in *multivariate settings* with rich covariates, where cross-series attention can extract meaningful relationships (see the next section). The comparison may also understate the Transformer's potential: with careful *hyperparameter tuning*, attention-based models can match or exceed linear baselines on some of the same datasets, indicating sensitivity to the training budget. Finally, **the benchmarks are small** by language model standards. Time-series foundation models trained on millions of diverse series might unlock scaling benefits. However, *Section 13.6* indicates that the evidence regarding financial data is mixed.

Subsequent large-scale evaluations reinforce this message while generalizing it. Small experimental changes (hyperparameter budgets, train/test splits, metric choice) can flip model rankings on standard LTSF suites; across multiple cross-domain forecasting benchmarks, statistical and linear baselines frequently match or beat deep models deemed state-of-the-art on individual datasets. The problem extends beyond "Transformers versus Linear" to the **fragility of benchmark conclusions** themselves.

A closer look at *why* some Transformers succeed reveals that **tokenization and normalization choices matter more than the attention mechanism itself.** Performance on these benchmarks is largely driven by intra-variate dependencies and dataset stationarity, partially explaining why shuffle critiques hold on standard suites yet prove less predictive on harder tasks. The practical comparison is not "Transformers versus Linear" but "strong linear baselines versus time-series-aware tokenization with careful tuning," and the latter's advantage is conditional on problem characteristics.

The paper served as a reset rather than an indictment. Any new architecture must now show clear improvement over LTSF-Linear, not just over previous Transformers. The goal shifted from making Transformers bigger to making them *smarter*, and the next generation of architectures, from **PatchTST**'s temporal patching to **iTransformer**'s variate inversion, responded directly to this challenge.

13.5 Modern Transformer variants

The Zeng et al. (2022) critique catalyzed a new wave of innovation rather than ending Transformer-based forecasting. Modern architectures address the identified weaknesses by incorporating stronger temporal inductive biases while retaining the attention mechanism's ability to model complex dependencies. Three models exemplify this evolved approach: PatchTST, iTransformer, and the Temporal Fusion Transformer (TFT).

Patching as inductive bias with PatchTST

PatchTST, introduced by Nie et al. (2023), offers a simple, effective response to the critique: rather than fight the Transformer's permutation invariance, design the input representation to work with it.

PatchTST formalizes patching as the central inductive bias. The input time series is segmented into non-overlapping patches of fixed length P. A lookback window of L time steps becomes roughly L/P patches, each treated as a single token. This design has several implications:

- **Computational efficiency**: Attention complexity is $O\left(N_{patches}^2\right)$ rather than $O(L^2)$, a large reduction that enables much longer lookback windows
- **Local pattern preservation**: Each patch encapsulates local temporal structure, information that raw pointwise tokenization would scatter across the attention mechanism
- **Semantic coherence**: Patches represent meaningful units of temporal evolution, more analogous to words in language than individual characters

For *multivariate time series*, PatchTST ignores cross-channel dependencies during training. Each channel (each time series in a multivariate set) is processed independently through shared Transformer weights. Forecasts are generated per-channel without attempting to model correlations between variables.

This seems counterintuitive, since multivariate data presumably contains cross-series information worth exploiting. But channel-independence acts as a regularizer. On many benchmarks, cross-channel attention overfits to spurious correlations in the training data that do not generalize. By forcing the model to predict each series solely from its own history, PatchTST avoids this trap while still benefiting from shared representations learned across all channels.

PatchTST often employs **Reversible Instance Normalization** (RevIN) to handle distribution shifts, neutralizing local distributional shifts before the attention mechanism processes the data. This normalization trick (subtracting the instance mean and dividing by the instance standard deviation, then reversing the transformation on the outputs) is crucial for time series that wander across different statistical regimes over time.

The combination of patching, channel-independence, and RevIN allowed PatchTST to achieve state-of-the-art results on LTSF benchmarks, outperforming both earlier Transformer variants and the linear models that had previously matched them.

Inverting the dimensions with iTransformer

Where PatchTST preserves the standard Transformer structure while changing its inputs, iTransformer (Liu et al., 2024) takes a more radical approach: it **inverts the dimensions on which attention operates.**

In a standard multivariate Transformer, each token represents a time step containing values from all variables. Attention operates across time, relating different moments to each other. iTransformer inverts this: **each token represents an entire univariate series** (or a substantial portion of it), and attention operates across variables.

Concretely, given a multivariate series with *N* variables, iTransformer creates *N* tokens, each embedding the full temporal history of one variable. Attention then learns relationships between variables: how one asset's behavior relates to another's, how a leading indicator connects to a lagging one.

Why does inversion work? This design sidesteps the temporal order critique entirely. The model does not apply permutation-invariant attention to time steps; temporal patterns within each variable are captured by the initial embedding process, which can use any time-aware architecture (such as an MLP or convolution applied along the time axis). Attention instead **models cross-variable dependencies,** a domain where permutation invariance is less problematic since there is often no intrinsic ordering among variables.

For *financial applications* involving portfolios of correlated assets, iTransformer offers a natural fit. The model can learn that technology stocks move together, that gold inversely correlates with the dollar, or that volatility spikes in one market presage spikes in others. These cross-asset dynamics represent the type of complex, non-local relationships that attention mechanisms excel at capturing.

Covariate-rich forecasting with Temporal Fusion Transformers

While PatchTST and iTransformer optimize for pure time-series forecasting, the **Temporal Fusion Transformer** (TFT) addresses a different challenge: forecasting when rich metadata and known future inputs are available (Lim et al., 2021). Financial applications often include:

- Static covariates (sector, exchange, asset class)
- Time-varying observed inputs (volume, volatility, macroeconomic indicators)
- Known future inputs (calendar features, scheduled events, options expiry dates)

TFT provides a principled architecture for integrating all three: its distinguishing features are *learned variable selection* (a gating mechanism that assigns time-varying importance weights to inputs, providing interpretability absent from PatchTST and iTransformer) and multi-horizon quantile output, producing *calibrated prediction intervals* rather than point forecasts. For risk management and position sizing, this native uncertainty quantification is more principled than post-hoc methods applied to point-forecast architectures.

When is TFT the right choice? It is strongest in covariate-rich settings with heterogeneous input types, such as portfolio forecasting that incorporates sector metadata, macro indicators, and calendar effects. For pure time series without covariates, PatchTST's simpler design typically matches or exceeds TFT.

Covariate-aware forecasting is a design axis. TFT's covariate handling is no longer unique. Recent benchmarks formalize covariate categories (static, past-only, dynamic, known-future) as a primary axis of evaluation. An emerging result shows that reframing forecasting as a tabular regression with temporal features achieves competitive covariate-aware performance without a time-series-specific architecture, which connects directly to the tabular methods of *Chapters 11–12*.

Table 13.1 summarizes the comparison.

Model	Key Innovation	Attention Domain	Best For
Vanilla Transformer	Self-attention	Time steps	Short sequences, simple baselines
TFT	Variable selection + covariates	Time steps	Covariate-rich, multi-horizon with uncertainty
PatchTST	Patching + Channel-independence	Time patches	Long-horizon univariate/multivariate LTSF
iTransformer	Variate-as-token inversion	Variables	Cross-asset dynamics, portfolio forecasting

Table 13.1: Transformer summary

There is no benchmark substitute for validation on the target data: ETTh1 electricity demand has little in common with cryptocurrency returns.

Transformers are far from the only response to the recurrent bottleneck: temporal convolutions, state-space models, and pretrained foundation models each offer distinct trade-offs that the next section surveys.

Implementation: `04_transformers` benchmarks PatchTST, iTransformer, and Ridge on ETF return prediction. On a 60/20/20 temporal split with cross-sectional IC, Ridge sits at +0.010, a stable anchor across reruns at the same random seed. Both Transformers clear that anchor by a small margin, but their relative ordering (PatchTST versus iTransformer) drifts across reruns of the same code on the same data. Single-split point estimates at this signal-to-noise ratio are not sufficiently stable to rank the architectures; the cuDNN non-determinism in the attention path is large relative to the ETF-panel IC scale. The walk-forward case studies in *Section 13.9* are the authoritative ranking. There, the marginal benefit of temporal modeling depends on how much signal the feature pipeline has already extracted.

13.6 Alternative architectures and foundation models

Beyond decomposition and attention, **several architectures address specific forecasting requirements:**

- **Temporal Convolutional Networks** (TCNs; Bai, Kolter, and Koltun, 2018) enforce causality through dilated causal convolutions, offering a middle ground between RNNs and Transformers with efficient parallelism and explicit temporal ordering.

- **TSMixer** (Chen et al., 2023) shows that well-designed MLPs that alternate time-mixing and feature-mixing layers can compete with attention on standard benchmarks.
- **CNN-based approaches** (Jiang et al., 2020) convert price histories into images using Gramian Angular Fields (GAFs), which transform a time series into a matrix capturing pairwise temporal relationships. This lets CNNs detect recurring market patterns by treating price dynamics as visual texture.

Hybrid statistical-neural models represent a design philosophy rather than a single architecture: let a classical model handle known structure such as level, seasonality, and trend, while a neural network learns residuals or time-varying parameters. The ES-RNN (Smyl, 2020), winner of the M4 forecasting competition, combines Holt-Winters exponential smoothing with an RNN. Holt-Winters is a classical forecasting method that recursively updates estimates of level, trend, and seasonality; ES-RNN uses this decomposition to remove non-stationary structure before the RNN learns multiplicative corrections.

Deep state space models (Rangapuram et al., 2018) take the probabilistic variant: neural networks generate time-varying parameters for a linear state space model, with inference performed via Kalman filtering (see *Chapter 9* for details), embedding well-understood Bayesian filtering structure while allowing non-stationary parameterization.

This hybrid philosophy lives on in N-BEATS's decomposition priors (*Section 13.2*), TFT's structured covariate handling (*Section 13.5*), and the modern SSMs below, but the explicit approach remains relevant in low-data regimes where pure neural networks overfit, and classical structure provides essential regularization (Lim and Zohren, 2021).

Three developments warrant deeper treatment: state space models for their different approach to sequence processing, foundation models for their implications about transfer learning in finance, and the emerging evaluation infrastructure that determines whether any claimed advance can be trusted.

State space models

State Space Models (SSMs) have become a primary alternative to Transformers for sequence modeling. SSMs are inspired by **continuous-time dynamical systems** and are discretized for sequential processing. A latent state evolves according to learned dynamics:

$$h_t = Ah_{t-1} + Bx_t$$

$$y_t = Ch_t + Dx_t$$

In a conventional SSM, the matrices A, B, C, and D are learned during training but then applied uniformly across sequence positions.

The **Mamba** architecture, introduced by Gu and Dao (2023), achieves linear $O(L)$ complexity while maintaining the ability to model long-range dependencies. Mamba's innovation is **selective state spaces:** the model learns functions that generate input-dependent SSM coefficients for each time step. In particular, B_t, C_t, and the discretization step Δ_t depend on the current input x_t; the base transition matrix A remains learned and shared, while the effective discretized transition varies through Δ_t.

This makes the recurrence content-aware, allowing the model to retain relevant information and filter out contextually noisy inputs. Mamba therefore combines the temporally structured memory of recurrent models with hardware-aware parallelization, making it efficient on very long sequences where even patched Transformers can become costly.

A limitation of base SSMs is their reliance on a single temporal resolution. Financial data contains signals across multiple timescales: microstructure dynamics within minutes, momentum over days, regime shifts over months. The **Multi-scale Mamba** architecture (**ms-Mamba**) addresses this by deploying parallel Mamba blocks operating at different sampling rates, capturing high-frequency and low-frequency patterns simultaneously without the quadratic cost of multi-scale attention (Karadag et al., 2025). This directly targets the long-memory properties discussed in *Section 13.1*: volatility clustering and persistent order flow produce dependencies spanning dozens or more trading days across multiple temporal granularities, precisely the setting where a single-resolution model loses information.

SSMs are best understood as part of a **sequence-mixing primitives toolkit** rather than an outright attention replacement. The practical question is: what is my context length, latency budget, and maintenance burden? For sequences exceeding 10,000 time steps, such as tick-level or minute-bar data spanning minutes to weeks, SSMs offer clear efficiency advantages because their linear complexity avoids the memory exhaustion that quadratic attention methods encounter. For shorter sequences with rich cross-variate structure, attention-based models retain their edge because cross-variable attention captures portfolio dynamics that SSMs do not natively model.

Hybrid architectures that interleave attention and SSM layers are an active research direction, but lack broad independent validation. The most promising finance-specific work, **FinMamba** (Hu et al., 2025), combines market-aware graph construction with multi-level Mamba blocks for stock movement prediction, but remains a single-paper result awaiting replication.

We evaluate each architecture for ETF return prediction against a Ridge baseline. On the single 60/20/20 split, Ridge anchors the comparison with a cross-sectional Spearman IC of +0.016 (MSE 0.0035), stable across reruns with the same seed. TCN and TSMixer point estimates sit within the rerun noise of Ridge: TCN has flipped from +0.051 to -0.013 across reruns of identical code, TSMixer from +0.013 to +0.001, with MSEs (TCN 0.0043, TSMixer 0.0039) close to Ridge's. Single-split IC at this signal-to-noise ratio is an architectural sanity check, not a ranking signal; *Section 13.9*'s case studies offer a more thorough walk-forward comparison, and TSMixer reaches IC +0.029 at the 21-day horizon on the ETF panel under multi-step Darts retraining.

Implementation:

- `05_tcn` implements dilated causal convolutions with a receptive field spanning the full lookback window
- `06_tsmixer` alternates time-mixing and feature-mixing MLP layers
- `07_mamba_ssm` for a Mamba/SSM implementation on ETF data
- `08_cnn_image_encoding` converts price histories into Gramian Angular Field images and applies convolutional feature extraction

Time series foundation models

Foundation models (**FMs**) for time series follow the LLM playbook: pretrain on massive corpora to learn universal temporal representations, then adapt to downstream tasks.

The first generation, comprising **Chronos** (Amazon), **TimesFM** (Google), **Lag-Llama**, and **MOMENT**, shared a common limitation: univariate-only inference with no native support for exogenous covariates or multivariate structure, making them poorly suited to quantitative finance where assets coevolve, and external signals are central.

Time-series foundation models import the *pretrain-then-adapt* logic of large language models into forecasting. Early systems showed that large pretrained models could produce useful zero-shot forecasts. However, many were evaluated primarily in univariate settings and were not designed for the multivariate, covariate-rich structure common in real applications.

The second generation addresses this directly. **Chronos-2** (Ansari et al., 2025) introduces a group attention mechanism that processes multivariate series and exogenous covariates through a unified pipeline, enabling covariate-informed zero-shot forecasting via in-context learning. By assigning group identifiers to targets and their associated covariates, the model shares dynamic information across related series without requiring task-specific fine-tuning. **Moirai-MoE** (Liu et al., 2024) replaces static frequency-based input projections with sparse **Mixture-of-Experts** routing, in which token-level gating automatically specializes to the data's heterogeneous characteristics.

The result is **competitive performance with a fraction of the active parameters** of dense models: 11 million active parameters, achieving accuracy that previously required billion-parameter architectures. These advances do not invalidate the first-generation negative results discussed in this chapter, but they do substantially change the adaptation calculus.

Adaptation modes

How a foundation model is deployed matters as much as which model is chosen. The literature has converged on four adaptation modes, each with distinct compute, data, and maintenance requirements:

- **Zero-Shot Inference**: Deploy the pretrained model directly without weight updates. Viable when the target domain resembles the pretraining corpus: energy demand, retail sales, and weather. Empirical evidence suggests that TSFMs help most in data-scarce regimes but do not reliably dominate specialized models when sufficient training data is available, and that scaling laws are not strictly monotonic. For financial returns, zero-shot performance is unreliable (see below).
- **In-Context Learning (ICL)**: Feed historical reference series and covariates alongside the target within the context window; the model infers the current distribution without weight updates. Chronos-2's group attention natively enables this. Recent work demonstrates that training TSFMs to use multiple related series in context at inference time can sometimes match the performance of explicit fine-tuning on target domains. ICL is most valuable for cold-start scenarios and rapid prototyping where gradient-based adaptation is impractical.

- **Parameter-Efficient Fine-Tuning (PEFT):** Adapt a subset of model weights (LoRA adapters, low-rank projections) on domain-specific data. Standard PEFT can lock adapters into suboptimal minima near initialization, particularly on noisy financial data. Two directions show promise: progressive training that stochastically deactivates adapters to encourage broader exploration, and prune-then-finetune, where removing up to 90% of parameters before adaptation yields superior accuracy. Both exploit the same insight: foundation models are overparameterized for any single task, and constraining the adaptation surface improves generalization.
- **Test-Time Model Selection** and **Ensembling:** Rather than fine-tuning one large model, build a portfolio of smaller pretrained models and combine them via selection or ensembling at inference time. Recent work demonstrates that this approach can match single-model accuracy while reducing inference cost, and can be more compute-efficient than test-time fine-tuning. This pathway suits production environments where latency, maintenance burden, and reproducibility matter more than marginal gains in accuracy.

The practical implication is to treat foundation models as *initializations* rather than solutions. The adaptation mode should match the compute budget, data availability, and deployment constraints, not the model's marketing materials.

The limits of scaling

The NLP-imported assumption that performance scales monotonically with parameters does not hold for time series. Evidence from the **GIFT-Eval benchmark** (Aksu et al., 2024), which enforces strict pretrain/test separation across 28 datasets and 177 million data points, bears this out: hybrid architectures interleaving Fast-Fourier Transform (FFT) based long convolutions with linear RNNs achieve competitive zero-shot performance with under 3 million parameters, matching the accuracy of dense models with 1.5 billion parameters.

Independent evaluations confirm that a strict scaling law does not consistently hold for forecasting and that smaller models can occupy favorable positions on the accuracy-efficiency Pareto frontier. In practice, this means high-performance zero-shot forecasting is feasible on standard hardware without debilitating inference latency. The right evaluation metric is the **accuracy-efficiency frontier**, not the raw parameter count. When comparing TSFMs, report active parameter counts, wall-clock inference times, and memory footprints alongside predictive metrics.

The finance transfer gap

Despite these advances, foundation models face persistent challenges in financial applications. The gap between benchmark performance on standard forecasting tasks and actual utility for trading signals remains the central tension in applying TSFMs to finance.

Rahimikia et al. (2025) provide a *large-scale evaluation of TSFMs* in financial forecasting, covering daily excess returns across 94 countries over 34 years. Off-the-shelf TSFMs underperform tree-based ensembles on both statistical and economic metrics:

- In the U.S. zero-shot setting with a 512-day input window, Chronos Large achieves an out-of-sample R^2 of -1.37%, while TimesFM 500M reaches -2.80%; by comparison, CatBoost achieves -0.03% for the same window size, and -0.10% when averaged across all window sizes.

- **Directional accuracy remains close to random**. Chronos large is just above 51%, TimesFM is just below 50%, and CatBoost reaches 51.16% in the 512-day setting. Even the tree ensembles therefore operate close to the noise floor, reinforcing the weak-signal-plus-non-stationarity premise that runs throughout this book.
- Pretraining TSFMs on financial data substantially improves economic performance: the paper reports, for example, annualized returns and Sharpe ratios of 36.84% and 5.42 for Chronos small, and 30.36% and 3.66 for TimesFM 20M, both with a 512-day window, supporting the view that **domain-specific adaptation is required** rather than optional.

This poor transfer stems from a *distributional mismatch*: general time-series corpora emphasize seasonality, trend, and clear patterns that are largely absent in financial returns. The heavy tails, low signal-to-noise ratio, and non-stationarity of asset prices differ from the electricity demand, weather, and traffic data that dominate pretraining corpora.

TSFMs show promise in risk forecasting. The return-prediction results do not generalize to all financial tasks. For volatility and Value-at-Risk forecasting, where the target exhibits stronger and more transferable structure (volatility clustering, persistence, and mean reversion), TSFMs show credible evidence. Studies evaluating TimesFM against econometric baselines such as GARCH report that fine-tuned foundation models rank among the top performers across multiple VaR quantiles. Statistical forecast-comparison tests support these gains:

- The **Diebold-Mariano** test evaluates whether two models have equal average predictive accuracy under a chosen loss function
- The **Giacomini-White** test evaluates conditional predictive ability, asking whether performance differences remain significant given the information available at the time of forecasting

Zero-shot forecasting is insufficient even for these more structured targets; incremental fine-tuning is essential to learn volatility dynamics specific to the asset class and evaluation period.

Leakage risks specific to pretrained models are a concern. When evaluating TSFMs on financial data, standard temporal train/test splits are necessary but not sufficient. The pretraining corpus becomes a new leakage channel: if the TSFM was pretrained on data that overlaps with or is correlated with the evaluation period, zero-shot claims are compromised.

The **TIME** benchmark (Zou et al., 2025) formalizes this using "fresh datasets" and a human-in-the-loop construction pipeline designed to ensure strict zero-shot integrity. The growing training corpora used by TSFMs make test-set integrity increasingly difficult, analogous to the contamination challenges facing LLM evaluation. Practitioners must verify that evaluation data postdate the pretraining corpus or are excluded from it, and that no proxy leakage occurs via correlated series.

For return prediction, tree-based ensembles with engineered features (*Chapter 12*) remain a hard baseline; for risk forecasting (volatility, VaR), fine-tuned TSFMs are a credible addition to the toolkit. Prefer models with Student-t or mixture output distributions for financial data.

With this many architectures available, the question shifts from which model is best to which model fits the problem. The next section gives a decision framework for matching architecture to data characteristics, computational budget, and deployment constraints.

Implementation: `09_foundation_models` compares zero-shot Chronos and TTM against trained baselines on ETF return prediction. Chronos achieves IC of −0.015, and TTM reaches −0.017, both worse than random, while a task-specific LSTM (50K parameters) achieves IC +0.025, and even Ridge regression (60 parameters) reaches +0.022. Chronos carries roughly 20 million parameters, and TTM 1–5 million, yet both produce negative zero-shot signals, confirming the distributional mismatch between general pretraining corpora and financial returns.

13.7 A practical framework

The chapter's evidence and trade-offs translate into a practical model-selection process.

Step 1: Establish strong baselines

Before evaluating any deep learning model, establish a baseline performance that any complex architecture must beat. The following models form a baseline ladder: each rung represents a stronger comparison that must be surpassed before adding complexity is justified:

1. **Seasonal naive:** For data with a seasonal pattern (not the case for, for example, return series), predict using the value at the same point in the previous cycle.
2. **LTSF-linear:** The D-Linear variant decomposes before applying linear layers; N-Linear normalizes by the last input value to handle distribution shift. If a sophisticated model cannot outperform D-Linear, its complexity is unjustified.
3. **Statistical models:** ARIMA and ETS remain strong baselines for univariate series with clear trend and seasonality (*Chapter 9*). For multivariate settings, VAR provides a comparable baseline.
4. **Gradient boosting models:** LightGBM or XGBoost with lagged features often match neural approaches, particularly with limited data. Applying GBMs to time series requires transforming the sequential problem into a tabular regression problem that includes lag features ($t-1$, $t-2$, ..., $t-k$), rolling statistics, and calendar features. GBMs excel at learning complex nonlinear relationships in these engineered features but cannot extrapolate beyond the training range.

When does DL outperform GBMs? Chapters 11 and *12* showed that gradient boosting tops many tabular cross-sectional problems. In the case study comparison, the paired daily IC delta between the DL and best-tabular models, with a HAC interval on the common-date difference, excludes zero on three of eight DL-covered case studies: Crypto perpetuals funding, where NLinear at IC +0.029 sits credibly above GBM at +0.011; US Equities, where LSTM at +0.007 sits credibly below GBM at +0.032; and CME Futures, where the LSTM near zero sits credibly below GBM at +0.032. The DL point estimate also exceeds the best tabular baseline on ETFs and FX, but the paired interval overlaps zero on both. On the remaining three panels, the baselines are comparable or stronger. In *Section 13.9, Table 13.4* reports the per-case-study evidence. The practical decision rule is unchanged: test whether temporal ordering adds incremental signal beyond lag-feature engineering, and keep the simpler model unless gains are robust out-of-sample.

TabM (*Chapter 12*) extends tabular deep learning with batch-level feature interactions, offering a middle ground between GBMs and sequence architectures. On cross-sectional panels without a strong sequential structure, it is a useful additional baseline alongside LightGBM and Ridge.

Sample size thresholds are calibrated on the book's daily-frequency, moderate-SNR case studies and should be adjusted for the target data's signal strength and feature dimensionality:

- **Fewer than 5,000 samples:** Ridge regression or LightGBM. Deep learning risks overfitting with insufficient data.
- **5,000–20,000 samples:** LightGBM typically offers the best accuracy-to-compute ratio. Deep learning may match but rarely exceeds.
- **More than 20,000 samples:** LSTM and other deep architectures can be *tested at scale*, but superiority is not guaranteed. A large sample size should trigger model comparison, not model replacement.

Once established baselines are beaten, **foundation models offer a progressive adaptation ladder**:

1. Zero-shot inference (free but unreliable for financial returns).
2. In-context learning with domain examples.
3. PEFT/LoRA adaptation on target data.
4. Full domain-specific training.

Each step adds compute and data requirements and improves domain fit (*Section 13.6*). For covariate-rich problems, the chosen model should be verified to handle the relevant covariate types natively: TFT and Chronos-2 support static, past-only, and known-future covariates, while sequence-only models (PatchTST, Mamba) require feature engineering to incorporate external signals.

Step 2: Diagnose the problem

The problem is likely to belong to one of the following categories:

- **Univariate versus multivariate.** For univariate forecasting, N-BEATS and TCNs are natural choices. For multivariate forecasting, the choice depends on whether cross-series dependencies are known or must be learned.
- **Known versus unknown relationships.** If the relationship structure is known (for example, a physical network or supply chain), GNNs (*Chapter 23*) exploit it directly. If relationships must be learned, iTransformer's cross-variate attention or PatchTST's channel independence is appropriate.
- **Forecast horizon.** For long-horizon (weeks to months), PatchTST and modern Transformers are appropriate. For short-horizon (minutes to days), performance gaps narrow, favoring simpler approaches.
- **Interpretability.** N-BEATS-I provides trend/seasonal decomposition; TFT offers learned variable importance; GBMs offer feature importance. Standard Transformers are black boxes. Note that post hoc methods such as SHAP and LIME (*Chapter 11*) typically ignore sequential dependencies among inputs, making them unreliable for attributing importance in recurrent or attention-based architectures (Lim and Zohren, 2021).

- **Covariate richness.** If the problem includes static metadata, known future inputs, or heterogeneous feature types, TFT's variable selection architecture is purpose-built for this setting.
- **Sequence length.** For extremely long sequences (more than 10K steps), Mamba's linear complexity is necessary. PatchTST handles moderately long sequences via patching.

Step 3: Apply the selection matrix

With the problem diagnosed, match characteristics to recommended architectures (*Table 13.2*):

Scenario	Primary Choice	Alternative	Baseline
Univariate, interpretability required	N-BEATS-I	Autoformer	Seasonal ARIMA
Univariate, black-box acceptable	PatchTST	N-BEATS (generic)	D-Linear
Multivariate, known graph structure	GNN (Ch. 23)	-	VAR
Multivariate, unknown correlations	PatchTST	iTransformer	D-Linear
High dimensionality (>50 series)	iTransformer	PatchTST	Linear
Long horizon LTSF task	PatchTST	D-Linear	Naive Repeat
Covariate-rich, multi-horizon	TFT	PatchTST	LightGBM
Extremely long sequences (more than 10K steps)	Mamba	TCN	Rolling statistics and GBM
Limited data, need robustness	ARIMA/LightGBM	N-Linear	Seasonal Naive
Zero adaptation budget	D-Linear	Zero-shot TSFM	Seasonal Naive
Moderate adaptation budget (PEFT)	PatchTST and LoRA	TSFM ensemble	LightGBM

Table 13.2: Architecture selection matrix. Match problem characteristics to recommended architectures

Apply the walk-forward protocol (*Chapter 6*) for validation and evaluation. Always include non-deep baselines: omitting them inflates perceived gains. For TSFM evaluation, verify pretrain/test data separation to rule out leakage through pretraining corpora (*Section 13.6*). Report bootstrapped confidence intervals alongside economic metrics (IC, Sharpe, maximum drawdown).

Forecasting paths versus predicting horizon labels

The architectures in this chapter originate in time-series forecasting, predicting future values of a series from its history. Our case study pipelines solve a related but distinct problem: given a lookback window of time series values and features for each asset, predict the forward return as a scalar. This is direct panel regression with sequential inputs, not classical forecasting. In other words, the model sees a sequence, but the supervised target is a scalar label at horizon H, often multiple time steps ahead, not the full path from $t + 1$ to $t + H$.

The distinction matters in practice:

- True forecasting predicts a path (daily returns over a multi-day horizon), then maps that path to a label
- Direct regression skips the path and predicts the label itself

For the cross-sectional ranking task central to this book, direct regression has two advantages: it matches the evaluation metric (Spearman IC on the predicted labels), and it avoids compounding prediction errors over the horizon.

This differs from both recursive and direct multi-horizon forecasting (see *Figure 13.4*):

- Recursive forecasting generates the path one step at a time
- Direct multi-horizon forecasting predicts the path in one pass
- Direct horizon-label prediction skips the intermediate path entirely

That last formulation is often the right choice for cross-sectional ranking because the evaluation metric is defined on the final label, not on the intermediate daily path. If we care about the path, say from a risk perspective, the choice might change.

We tested the forecasting formulation directly. For N-BEATS and TSMixer, we ran the faithful library implementations (via Darts), which predict daily return paths and compound them to the horizon label, the task these architectures were designed for. For ETFs (21-day horizon) and CME futures (5-day horizon), the forecasting formulations produced substantially weaker signals than the direct regression models (LSTM, NLinear) on the same data. The long horizons amplified per-step errors, and the forecasting objective was misaligned with the ranking metric.

This finding carries a practical lesson: architecture selection is necessary but not sufficient. The formulation of the prediction problem itself (direct regression versus multi-step forecasting, cross-sectional ranking versus per-series prediction) determines whether temporal modeling adds value. N-BEATS and TSMixer are faithful forecasting models for forecasting a future path. LSTM and NLinear can be better matched to the book's direct horizon-label prediction task because they learn the scalar ranking target directly. The sophisticated forecasting components of N-BEATS, TSMixer, and PatchTST are valuable when the path matters; they can add unnecessary complexity when only the horizon label is evaluated.

There is a fourth formulation that we cover in *Chapter 17: direct learning of portfolio allocation*. Instead of predicting a path or horizon label, the model outputs positions or portfolio weights and is trained on an economic objective such as Sharpe ratio, drawdown, turnover, or transaction-cost-adjusted return.

Forecasting libraries

This chapter implements architectures directly in PyTorch for demonstration. For standard forecasting tasks, several mature libraries reduce implementation effort substantially:

- **Darts** (Unit8) provides the broadest model coverage with a unified `fit()`/`predict()` API spanning classical and deep learning methods. Darts is the appropriate choice for rapidly benchmarking diverse approaches on standard forecasting tasks.
- **NeuralForecast** (Nixtla) offers native panel-data support and optimized training loops. Choosing NeuralForecast is the primary requirement when training a shared model across multiple related time series.
- **PyTorch Forecasting** (maintained under the sktime umbrella) is built around the Temporal Fusion Transformer. It is the appropriate choice when the problem involves rich covariates: static metadata, known future inputs, and multiple target variables.

- **GluonTS** (Amazon) anchors the foundation model ecosystem around Chronos and Chronos-2 with native probabilistic outputs. Choose GluonTS when zero-shot or fine-tuned foundation models are the deployment target.
- **sktime** provides a scikit-learn-compatible meta-framework that wraps Darts, NeuralForecast, HuggingFace, and classical methods under a single `fit/predict/score` API. sktime is the appropriate choice for swapping backends without rewriting data pipelines.

For standard per-series forecasting, Darts or NeuralForecast will save significant implementation time. For cross-sectional panel prediction (ranking N assets by predicted return and evaluating via Spearman IC, as our case studies require), raw PyTorch with custom training loops remains the most natural fit. Our case study experiments illustrate this directly: running N-BEATS and TSMixer through Darts's forecasting formulation produced a substantially weaker signal than the direct regression adaptations (see *Forecasting paths versus predicting horizon labels* above), confirming that library choice implies a modeling choice.

Library	Strengths	Panel Support	Foundation Models
Raw PyTorch	Full control, custom losses, cross-sectional	Manual	Manual
Darts	Broad model coverage, unified API	Limited	TimesFM
NeuralForecast	Speed, native multi-series	Native (unique_id)	No
PyTorch Forecasting	TFT, rich covariates	Via TimeSeriesDataSet	No
GluonTS / AutoGluon	Chronos-2, probabilistic	Via DeepAR / Chronos-2	Yes
sktime	Composable pipelines, wraps backends	Via reduction	Via wrappers

Table 13.3: DL for time series library overview

Selecting the right architecture and library is only the first step: a point forecast without a confidence measure gives no guidance on how aggressively to trade the signal. The next section addresses uncertainty quantification, the bridge between prediction and position sizing.

Implementation: `11_library_landscape` provides a hands-on comparison of raw PyTorch, sktime, and Darts on the same forecasting task, with per-library API details and code-effort metrics.

13.8 Quantifying prediction uncertainty

Point forecasts are only part of the signal (see *Chapter 11*). For risk management, portfolio construction, and position sizing, the uncertainty surrounding a prediction is often as important as the prediction itself. A forecast of +2% warrants a different response when accompanied by a narrow predictive interval than when surrounded by wide uncertainty bands. In practice, useful uncertainty estimates can often be obtained from standard deep learning models without moving to fully Bayesian neural networks or other specialized probabilistic architectures.

Estimating uncertainty with MC dropout and deep ensembles

Deep learning models can provide useful uncertainty estimates without requiring fully Bayesian neural networks. Two practical approaches are **Monte Carlo (MC) dropout** (Gal and Ghahramani, 2016) and **deep ensembles** (Lakshminarayanan et al., 2017). Both start from the same idea: instead of relying on a single deterministic prediction, generate several plausible predictions from closely related models and use both their average and their spread.

The average prediction often improves accuracy because idiosyncratic errors partially cancel out. The spread across predictions then serves as an uncertainty signal. When many plausible versions of the model produce similar forecasts, confidence is higher. When they disagree substantially, the prediction is less reliable. For trading applications, the main practical value is that uncertainty estimates help distinguish forecasts that warrant larger positions from those that call for smaller positions, tighter risk limits, or no trade at all.

MC dropout obtains this distribution from a single trained model. Dropout remains active during inference, and the model is evaluated repeatedly, typically over 50-100 forward passes. Each pass samples a different subnetwork, producing a distribution of predictions rather than a single output. The sample mean becomes the point forecast, and the sample standard deviation provides a simple measure of predictive uncertainty. This uncertainty is commonly interpreted as reflecting uncertainty in the fitted model itself: the model's forecast changes because different plausible subnetworks produce different answers.

Deep ensembles generate the same kind of distribution in different ways. Instead of sampling many subnetworks from one trained model, they train several independent models, typically 3 to 10, with different random initializations and sometimes different data orderings or bootstrap samples. Each model converges to a somewhat different solution, so the ensemble captures a range of plausible predictive functions. Averaging across ensemble members often improves predictive performance, while disagreement among members provides a natural estimate of uncertainty.

In practice, **deep ensembles are often more robust than MC dropout**, but they also cost more because both training and inference scale approximately linearly with the number of ensemble members. The tradeoff is straightforward:

- MC dropout is cheaper and easier to add to an existing model because it requires little architectural change
- Deep ensembles usually demand more compute, but they often provide stronger predictive performance and better-calibrated uncertainty estimates

In many applied settings, an ensemble of about five models offers a reasonable compromise between performance and computational cost.

A more elaborate variant extends deep ensembles by having each model predict not only a mean forecast but also a variance through a **heteroscedastic output head**. This aims to capture the idea that some observations are intrinsically noisier than others: even a well-specified model may be less certain for some assets, horizons, or market regimes than for others.

This extension can produce richer predictive intervals, but it also increases modeling complexity and is not necessary to obtain the main practical benefit of ensembles. The essential point is simpler: model averaging can improve forecasts, and model disagreement can identify less trustworthy predictions.

Whatever method is used, uncertainty estimates should be evaluated empirically rather than accepted at face value. Useful diagnostics include empirical coverage, interval width, sharpness, and reliability plots for predictive intervals. In trading applications, the most important test is whether forecasts flagged as more uncertain actually produce larger out-of-sample errors, and whether any chosen interval target achieves its intended coverage (see *Section 11.5*). Where nominal coverage is poor, conformal calibration on a held-out window can improve interval validity.

Implementation: `10_uncertainty` illustrates both MC dropout and a five-member LSTM ensemble on ETF data, together with **split-conformal calibration** on a held-out window. Without calibration, Gaussian intervals from either method are under-covered by roughly an order of magnitude at the 95% nominal level. After split-conformal post-processing, empirical coverage lands within about three percentage points of nominal at the 50, 80, and 95% levels for both methods. At the 95% target, MC dropout reaches 0.97 and the ensemble 0.97. The calibration step recovers interval validity without retraining the base model. Across reruns at the same random seed, the ensemble's uncertainty-error rank correlation exceeds MC dropout's, but the precise magnitudes drift; the *qualitative ordering* (ensemble disagreement tracks error better than dropout-subnetwork variance on this LSTM) is the result that survives rerunning.

Foundation model calibration

Uncertainty estimation becomes more challenging for foundation models, especially under the regime shifts, heavy tails, and volatility clustering that characterize financial data. A model pretrained on broad time-series or textual corpora may produce useful point forecasts in finance, yet still be poorly calibrated in the tails or during market stress. In these settings, nominal predictive intervals may be too narrow exactly when risk control matters most.

Conformal calibration (see *Chapter 11*) offers a practical post hoc correction. By calibrating on a held-out window, conformal methods can improve empirical coverage without retraining the base model. This is particularly valuable when the pretraining distribution differs materially from the target financial environment.

For risk-sensitive tasks such as **Value-at-Risk** or **Expected Shortfall**, calibration is not secondary to point accuracy. A time-series foundation model may predict the conditional mean reasonably well while still understating tail risk. In such cases, *domain-specific fine-tuning* and *post-hoc calibration* are often essential not only for improving accuracy but also for obtaining usable uncertainty estimates.

With architectures selected and uncertainty estimates evaluated, the question becomes empirical: which approaches actually deliver useful signals across asset classes, horizons, and data regimes? The next section synthesizes the evidence from the case studies to answer that question.

13.9 Case study insights

Chapters 11 and *12* measured how far regularized linear models, gradient boosting, and the TabM tabular network turn engineered features into a cross-sectional ranking. The deep sequence models of this chapter join that running comparison under the same test: reading the return sequence directly, do they rank assets better than the tabular families already do? The deep architectures cover eight of the nine case studies (all but US Firms) at each case study's primary regression label, with NLinear fit on every one, the LSTM on all but the SP500 Options straddle, and TCN, TSMixer, and PatchTST contributing on a further subset. Each model is summarized by its average daily Spearman information coefficient (IC) and the 95% confidence interval around it, computed with a HAC correction for the autocorrelation in the daily series. An interval that excludes zero is the bar for distinguishable signal.

Where the sequence models add ranking content

Two questions separate here. The first is whether a deep model clears zero; the second, sharper one is whether it clears the tabular baseline. *Table 13.4* reports, for each case study, the highest-IC deep architecture for the primary label, alongside the strongest tabular model from *Chapters 11* and *12*. The deep family's interval excludes zero on four case studies (ETFs, Crypto, US Equities, and the NASDAQ-100). It overlaps zero on the SP500 Options straddle, CME Futures, the SP500 equity-and-options case study, and FX.

Case study	Horizon	Best deep model	Deep IC (t)	Best tabular	Tabular IC	Δ IC
ETFs	21 days	NLinear	+0.062 (3.0)	Ridge	+0.054	+0.009
Crypto	8 hours	NLinear	+0.029 (4.6)	GBM	+0.011	+0.018
SP500 Options	to expiry	PatchTST	+0.013 (1.8)	GBM	+0.018	−0.005
FX	1 day	NLinear	+0.011 (1.3)	TabM	+0.007	+0.004
SP500 Eq+Opt	5 days	PatchTST	+0.011 (1.1)	TabM	+0.011	≈ 0
US Equities	1 day	LSTM	+0.007 (5.4)	GBM	+0.032	−0.025
NASDAQ-100	15 minutes	NLinear	+0.005 (2.3)	GBM	+0.006	−0.001
CME Futures	5 days	LSTM	−0.001 (−0.1)	GBM	+0.032	−0.033

Table 13.4: Highest-IC deep architecture per case study at the primary regression label, with its HAC t-statistic, beside the strongest tabular baseline (Ridge, GBM, or TabM) from Chapters 11 and 12. Δ IC is the deep-model point estimate minus the best tabular point estimate

Clearing zero is not the same as improving on the baseline, and the two come apart sharply. On US Equities, the LSTM's IC is credibly above zero yet, at +0.007, sits far below gradient boosting's +0.032 on the same data. To compare the families, we compute the average difference between the two daily IC series and an HAC interval around this mean difference, pairing the models day by day. On this measure, the deep-minus-tabular delta excludes zero on three case studies (*Figure 13.7*): Crypto, where the deep model adds +0.018 in daily IC over a baseline near zero; US Equities, where it trails gradient boosting by 0.025; and CME Futures, where it trails by 0.033. On the other five case studies, the paired interval overlaps zero, so the deep model is statistically indistinguishable from the strongest tabular alternative.

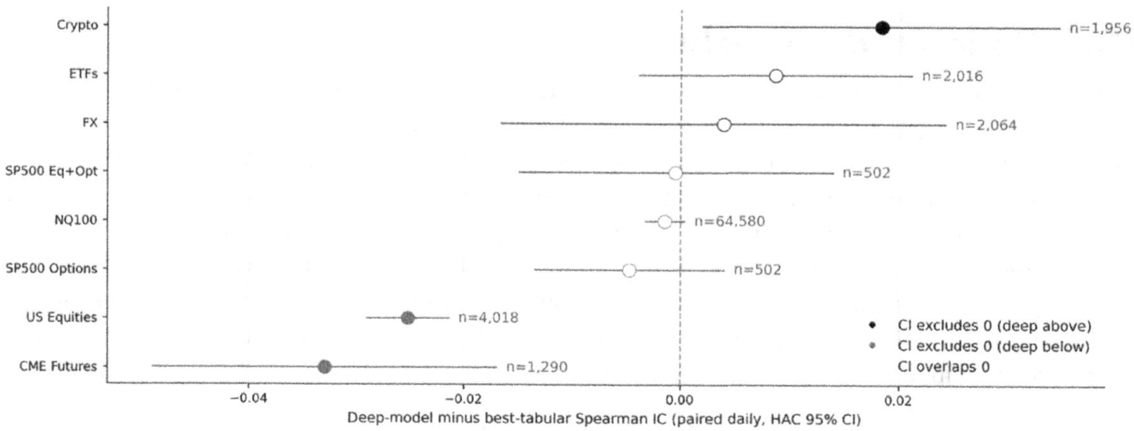

Figure 13.7: Deep-model-minus-best-tabular daily IC delta per case study, with paired HAC 95% confidence intervals on the common-date difference. The three intervals that exclude zero are Crypto (deep model above) and CME Futures and US Equities (deep model below)

The result, stated plainly: across eight case studies, direct sequence modeling credibly improves the ranking on one, Crypto; credibly trails on two, US Equities and CME Futures; and matches the tabular families on the other five, at substantially higher training cost.

Which architectures carry the signal

NLinear reaches the highest deep-model IC on four case studies (ETFs, Crypto, the NASDAQ-100, and FX), the LSTM on two (CME Futures and US Equities), and PatchTST on two (the SP500 Options straddle and the SP500 equity-and-options case study); the temporal convolutional network leads on none. That ordering follows from how the architectures are used here. The case studies frame each model as a direct predictor of the horizon-label return (see *Section 13.7*), rather than as a classical multi-step path forecaster. In that role, NLinear's normalize-and-project structure and the LSTM's gating retain enough temporal information to rank the cross-section without incurring the error-compounding cost of a multi-step objective. N-BEATS, TSMixer, PatchTST, and iTransformer carry inductive biases designed for path forecasting or cross-variate modeling, and those biases do not align with a cross-sectional rank label.

Training-budget trajectories fall into two regimes. On the high-frequency case studies (the NASDAQ-100, SP500 Options, and Crypto), daily IC peaks early and then decays. On the daily and longer-horizon case studies (FX, CME Futures, and US Equities), it drifts upward as training progresses. The late-trajectory spread is tightest where coverage is widest, so early stopping is best treated as a per-case-study tuning outcome rather than a fixed rule.

Whether the predictive uncertainty is reliable

A credible ranking and a reliable uncertainty estimate are separate properties, and the deep models earn them unevenly. Calibrating a single split-conformal layer on one fold's residuals and reading empirical coverage against the 90% nominal level splits the eight case studies three ways. On CME Futures, ETFs, and US Equities coverage lands near nominal, close to 0.90.

The two SP500 case studies over-cover, returning intervals wider than the data warrant. The rest under-cover by varying margins: Crypto returns intervals well short of nominal, FX modestly short of it, and the NASDAQ-100 falls to near-zero empirical coverage. The spread reflects the fragility of a single calibration split in finite samples, whose validity rests on the calibration and evaluation residuals remaining exchangeable, something a stationary label does not guarantee.

Coverage refines the IC reading rather than restating it. A case study with a credibly nonzero IC and near-nominal coverage, such as ETFs or US Equities, sits in a different operational position from one with a credibly nonzero IC but unreliable coverage, such as Crypto or the NASDAQ-100, where the model may still rank assets while its uncertainty layer cannot yet be trusted. Multi-fold conformal calibration is the natural response where split noise dominates, and Mondrian, group-conditional calibration where coverage fails along known groupings (asset class, horizon, or volatility regime) at the cost of fewer calibration points per group.

Direct prediction versus forecasting

The case studies treat sequence models as direct horizon-label predictors, and a controlled comparison shows why. Trained instead as a multi-step forecaster through Darts, TSMixer reaches an IC of +0.029 on ETFs at the 21-day horizon—real signal, but below both the direct-regression NLinear and Ridge on the same data (*Table 13.4*), because errors compound over the forecast path and degrade the eventual ranking. To remove compounding from the comparison, the US Equities case study was resampled to weekly, non-overlapping returns, in which predicting the five-day-ahead return becomes a single step.

Model	Approach	Mean IC (4 folds)
NLinear	Direct regression	+0.018
LSTM	Direct regression	+0.006
N-BEATS (Darts)	One-step forecasting	–0.013

Table 13.5: Weekly-frequency US Equities experiment on non-overlapping Friday-to-Friday returns, where the five-day horizon reduces to a single forecast step

Matching the data frequency to the horizon removes one source of error. However, it does not salvage the forecasting objective: direct regression still ranks better than one-step forecasting (*Table 13.5*), and both trail the daily tabular baselines, with gradient boosting reaching +0.032 on the primary one-day label. The finding restates *Section 13.7*: cross-sectional ranking is a direct prediction problem, not a path-forecasting one. It is also specific to this objective. Evaluating deep models for risk-adjusted position sizing instead and scoring on Sharpe ratio, downside risk, and cost robustness, Saly-Kaufmann et al. (2026) find hybrid recurrent and feature-selection architectures more competitive, a reminder that the target and the metric, not the architecture alone, determine what is being tested. *Chapter 17* returns to that risk-aware framing.

Implementation: `case_studies/us_equities_panel/12_dl_weekly` produces the results in this section.

From IC to profitability

The case studies where the deep and tabular models part ways carry that result into the portfolio-construction and simulation chapters: Crypto, where the deep model adds content the tabular families miss, and US Equities and CME Futures, where gradient boosting holds the edge. On the rest, the choice between a deep and a tabular model is a choice between roughly equal ICs at very different training and inference costs. *Chapters 16* through *19* weigh that trade-off against turnover, capacity, and transaction costs to determine which ranking yields economic profit.

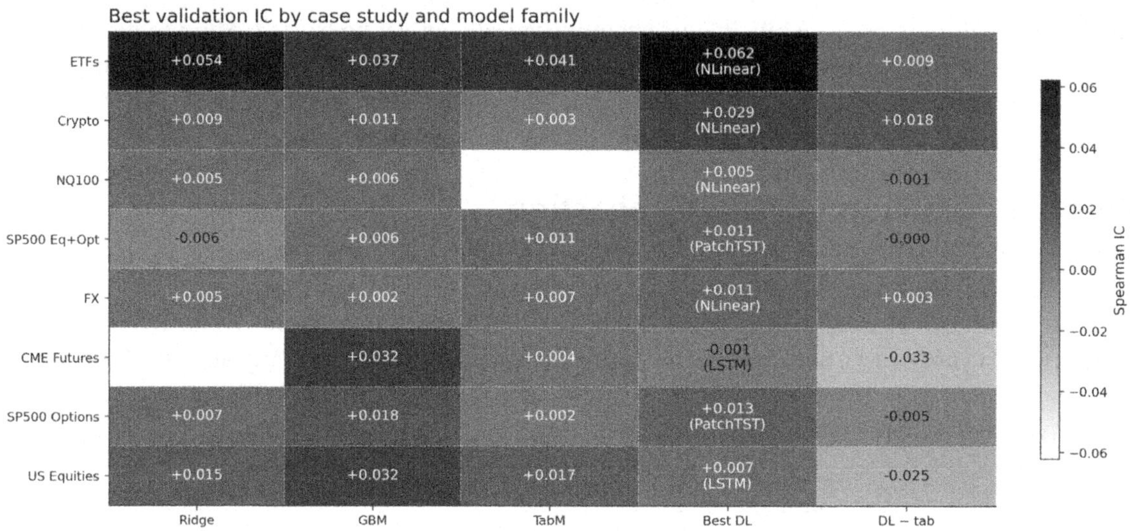

Figure 13.8: Best validation IC by family (Ridge, GBM, TabM, and the best deep model) for each case study, with the deep-minus-best-tabular delta in the final column. Shade encodes IC magnitude

13.10 Summary

Deep learning for time series has evolved from sequential RNNs through two competing philosophies, namely decomposition (N-BEATS) and attention (Transformers), into a mature toolkit where architecture choice depends on data characteristics, not benchmark rankings. The Zeng et al. critique remains a central lesson: any architecture must justify its complexity against a one-layer linear baseline. Modern responses like PatchTST and iTransformer succeed precisely because they embed stronger inductive biases rather than relying on raw model capacity.

Foundation models extend this toolkit with pretrained representations. However, in finance, they generally require domain adaptation: zero-shot inference on returns is limited, whereas parameter-efficient fine-tuning appears more promising for tasks such as volatility and risk forecasting. Evaluation also remains fragile because leakage, tuning budgets, and benchmark design can easily distort rankings. As a result, rolling-origin validation, strong non-deep baselines, and economic performance metrics remain essential.

The cross-dataset case study experiments reinforce a practical point: in the book's horizon-label, prediction-first setting, deep learning clearly beat the best tabular baseline in only one of eight case studies, while several others were statistically indistinguishable. This does not show that deep learning fails in finance; it shows that performance depends heavily on how the problem is formulated.

That leads to the chapter's central conclusion: **architecture matters only after the target is defined correctly**. Recursive one-step forecasting, direct multi-horizon forecasting, horizon-label prediction, and direct allocation learning solve different problems.

In practice, begin with Ridge and LightGBM, test whether temporal structure is genuinely informative, and only then choose a more complex architecture that matches the data and objective. Uncertainty methods such as MC Dropout and Deep Ensembles can improve calibration for sizing and risk control. At the same time, generative and graph-based models extend the framework to scenario generation and relational data. *Chapter 14* next turns to latent factor models, which use dimensionality reduction to extract the underlying drivers of returns.

14

Latent Factor Models

Hundreds of return predictors have been proposed in the empirical asset-pricing literature. The question is not how many exist but which of them reflect a stable common structure, which are priced, and which are artifacts of specification search or portfolio construction.

This chapter approaches that problem from the perspective of latent-factor estimation. It begins with Principal Component Analysis (PCA), then moves to Instrumented PCA (IPCA) and Risk-Premium PCA (RP-PCA), and finally to conditional autoencoders (CAE) and related stochastic-discount-factor (SDF) approaches. The unifying theme: use the data to summarize high-dimensional return variation with fewer factors, while being explicit about what each method can and cannot identify.

These methods differ because they optimize different objects. PCA maximizes explained covariance variation. IPCA allows factor loadings to vary with observable characteristics. RP-PCA trades off variance fit against cross-sectional pricing performance. Conditional autoencoders generalize the loading function nonlinearly, and adversarial SDF methods target pricing restrictions more directly. Keeping these objectives distinct is essential: a factor that explains covariation is not necessarily a priced factor, and a factor that helps price assets need not be the one that explains the most variance.

By the end of this chapter, you will be able to:

- Distinguish covariance-explaining attribution factors from priced factors, and explain why that distinction matters for prediction, risk decomposition, and trading applications.
- Implement PCA on asset returns, interpret principal components as latent risk dimensions or eigenportfolios, and diagnose key practical issues including covariance noise, component selection, and loading instability.
- Explain how IPCA and RP-PCA extend PCA by introducing time-varying characteristic-based betas and pricing-error penalties, and evaluate when these extensions are preferable to plain variance maximization.
- Implement and evaluate Conditional Autoencoders using walk-forward validation, ensemble averaging, and interpretability diagnostics such as SHAP, while recognizing their main failure modes.

- Explain how adversarial SDF estimation enforces no-arbitrage restrictions, how its objective differs from CAE reconstruction, and when direct pricing-error minimization is likely to add value.
- Compare latent factor methods across datasets and modeling objectives, and choose among PCA, IPCA, RP-PCA, CAE, and SDF approaches based on dimensionality, economic goal, and evaluation design.
- Move from the from-scratch teaching implementations to the `ml4t-models` library's `LatentFactorForecastPipeline` for production use, and recognize when a model (SDF, SAE) does not fit that pipeline.

A **stochastic discount factor** (SDF), also called a **pricing kernel**, is the object that links future payoffs to today's asset prices. An asset's price equals the expected value of its future payoff weighted by the SDF, so states of the world in which wealth is especially valuable receive a higher weight. Formally, for a gross return $r_{i,t+1}$, the no-arbitrage condition is $E_t[M_{t+1}r_{i,t+1}] = 1$, or equivalently $E_t[M_{t+1}r^e_{i,t+1}] = 0$, for excess returns.

The methods in this chapter pursue three different objectives, and the predictive workflow differs accordingly. PCA is a covariance-decomposition tool; eigenportfolios and yield-curve PCA inherit that role. IPCA and CAE are conditional latent-factor models that estimate factor returns together with characteristic-conditioned loadings. RP-PCA also estimates latent factors but tilts the criterion toward priced variation through a pricing-error penalty. The adversarial SDF estimates a pricing kernel directly from no-arbitrage moment restrictions, and the supervised autoencoder learns a return forecast end-to-end without an intermediate factor representation.

Several of these models share a predictive workflow that *Section 14.5* develops as the **three-stage latent-factor forecasting adapter:**

1. **Estimate a factor representation** from realized returns and, where applicable, conditioning information.
2. **Forecast the factor premia** from the estimated factor-return history.
3. **Map factor-premium forecasts to asset-level expected returns** using current exposures.

If stages 2 and 3 are grouped as the forecasting layer, the same workflow can also be described as a two-block structure: factor estimation followed by forecasting and mapping. IPCA, RP-PCA, and CAE pass through the adapter as a matter of routine; PCA can be wrapped in it when factor-timing is the goal, but its main use in this chapter is risk decomposition. The adversarial SDF and the supervised autoencoder sit entirely outside the adapter: the SDF learns a discounting object directly, and the SAE predicts returns end-to-end. The `ml4t-models` library packages the adapter as a single composable object; the teaching notebooks derive each stage from scratch.

Section 14.1 frames latent factor models as a response to the factor zoo. *Sections 14.2–14.4* develop the linear foundation (PCA on equities, eigenportfolios, yield curves). *Section 14.5* introduces IPCA and RP-PCA and operationalizes the three-stage adapter. *Section 14.6* extends it to the nonlinear CAE and clarifies why the SDF requires a different design. *Section 14.7* walks through a full from-scratch CAE implementation and contrasts it with the supervised autoencoder. *Section 14.8* compares results across five case studies, and *Section 14.9* distills the lessons.

14.1 Making the case for latent factors

Empirical asset pricing started with a single 'market' factor (CAPM), grew to three (Fama and French, 1993) and then five (Fama and French, 2015), and eventually became what John Cochrane called the "factor zoo" in his 2011 AFA Presidential Address: hundreds of published factors, each claiming to explain the cross-section of expected returns (Cochrane, 2011). By the mid-2010s, the count exceeded 400 (Harvey and Liu, 2019). The question facing every practitioner is how much of this proliferation reflects genuine economic content and how much is a statistical artifact (*Figure 14.1*).

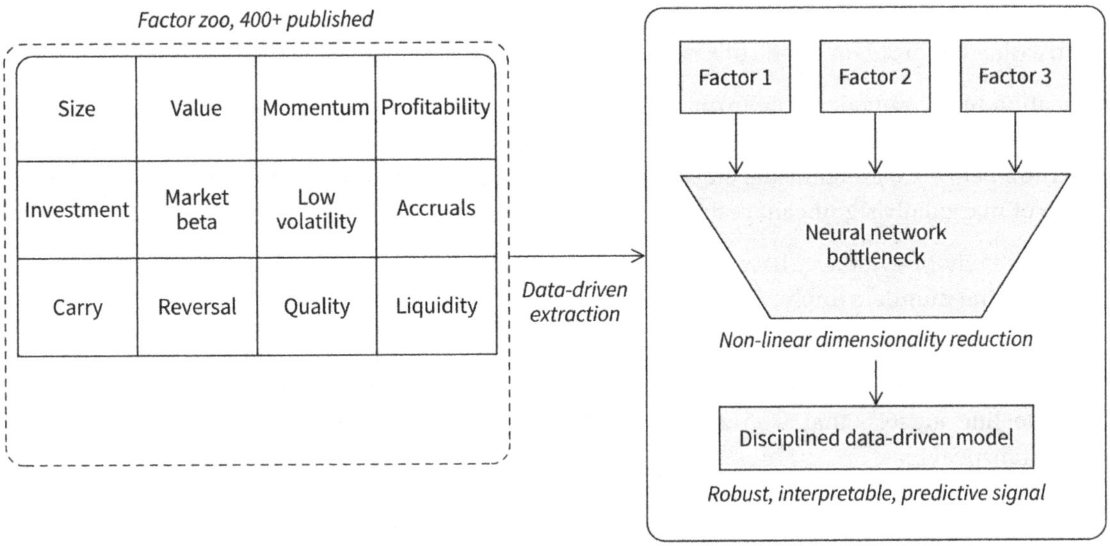

Figure 14.1: From Factor Zoo to Latent Factor Models

Academic research does not support a single, settled verdict on the factor zoo. One strand emphasizes multiple testing, publication bias, and the proliferation of published factors. Another emphasizes that replication rates can remain high once factors are evaluated within consistent frameworks and across broader datasets.

A balanced summary would be: the field has genuine false-positive and specification-risk problems, but the strongest conclusion is not that the entire factor zoo is illusory. Rather, the evidence points to a smaller, more robust set of recurring factor themes embedded in a much larger set of fragile or implementation-sensitive results.

Three axes of the factor zoo debate

The controversy runs along three axes (statistical validity, identification, and economic interpretation), drawing on work that includes Harvey (2017), Hou, Xue, and Zhang (2020), and Cochrane (2011).

Axis 1 – Statistical validity

The primary culprit is **data mining.** Harvey, Liu, and Zhu (2016) quantified the damage. When hundreds of factors have been tested across the literature, the conventional t-statistic threshold $t > 2.0$ is far too lenient. This threshold implies an estimated effect at least two standard errors away from zero, which, in turn, for large samples, corresponds to a (two-sided) p-value below 0.05. Equivalently, if the true effect were zero, the probability of observing an effect this or more extreme would be less than 5%. Instead, the authors suggest a multiple-testing adjustment (see *Chapter 7*) of around $t > 3.0$ for newly proposed factors, a rule of thumb that, if applied retroactively, eliminates a large share of published results. Harvey later stresses that even this threshold may be insufficient when effects are rare, treating the problem as one of research culture rather than a simple threshold correction.

Publication bias compounds the problem: the publication process creates strong incentives toward significant results and selective reporting. The resulting distribution of published t-statistics shows truncation below 2.0 and unusual clustering in the ranges just above it, consistent with selective reporting of marginally significant results.

A growing body of evidence, however, suggests the data-mining problem may be less severe than these headline numbers imply:

- McLean and Pontiff (2016) find that predictor returns decline by about 26% beyond the original sample period (consistent with modest overfitting), while a further 58% post-publication decline suggests that arbitrage erodes returns after discovery, a separate mechanism from statistical bias.
- Jensen et al. (2022) mount the most comprehensive challenge, developing a hierarchical Bayesian replication framework across 153 factors in 93 countries. Testing CAPM alpha rather than raw returns (the theoretically correct benchmark), they find an 82% replication rate, show that the factors cluster into roughly 13 themes that hold up globally out-of-sample, and that the evidence is *strengthened*, not weakened, by the large number of observed factors.
- Chen (2024) arrives at a consistent conclusion from a different direction, developing false-discovery bounds showing that at least 75–91% of published predictors are statistically valid and demonstrating that Harvey, Liu, and Zhu's high false-discovery estimates stem from misinterpreting statistical insignificance as falsity.

The emerging picture is that most published factors reflect genuine statistical regularities, but whether they survive trading costs and market learning is a distinct and often more demanding question.

Axis 2 – Identification and measurement

Hou, Xue, and Zhang (2020) show why construction choices matter so much. They define **microcaps** using the 20th percentile of NYSE market equity, and when that breakpoint is applied to the full stock universe, these firms represent a majority of listed names but only a very small share of total market capitalization. Therefore, equal-weighted anomaly portfolios give microcaps disproportionate influence. Under NYSE breakpoints and value-weighted returns, they report that 65% of 452 anomalies fail even the conventional $|t| > 1.96$ hurdle, with especially severe attrition in trading-frictions variables.

Anomaly evidence is therefore highly sensitive to the definition of the universe and portfolio construction, so any comparison between named and latent factors must keep those choices fixed.

Axis 3 – Risk versus mispricing

Even among factors that survive statistical and methodological filters, the field remains divided on *why* they work: whether the return premium compensates for systematic risk or reflects persistent behavioral mispricing sustained by limits to arbitrage. Cochrane (2011) frames this as modern finance's "dark matter" problem: we observe the gravitational pull of risk premia but cannot directly identify the specific macroeconomic shocks that cause them. This risk-versus-mispricing distinction has direct consequences for model design and evaluation, a theme that recurs throughout *Sections 14.5–14.6*.

The recurring core

Recent replication and model-selection work repeatedly returns to a compact core of factors (Hou, Xue, and Zhang, 2020; Fama and French, 2015; Barillas and Shanken, 2018):

- **Market**: The equity risk premium
- **Value**: Buying cheap assets, potentially proxying for distress or duration risk
- **Momentum**: Trend-following, reflecting behavioral underreaction or liquidity cascades
- **Profitability**: Buying productive assets, central to both the Fama-French five-factor model and the q-factor model
- **Investment**: Buying conservative assets, consistent with low discount rates in production models

This compact set is not a definitive list, but it is striking that independent lines of research converge on it. Fama and French's five-factor model derives its factors from the dividend discount model; Hou, Xue, and Zhang's (2015) q-factor model derives its factors from the firm's investment optimization (the Investment CAPM), later augmented with an expected-growth factor (Hou et al., 2021). Both arrive at overlapping empirical predictions centered on profitability, investment, and valuation.

Model-comparison work by Barillas and Shanken (2018) finds that both factor families are dominated by specifications that include momentum, further reinforcing the recurrence of this core. Jensen et al. (2022) find that their 153-factor universe clusters into roughly 13 themes, and Swade et al. (2023) show that about 15 factors suffice to span the alpha of the full set, consistent with a true dimensionality much smaller than the zoo but somewhat larger than the five highlighted above.

Machine learning reinforces this picture. Gu, Kelly, and Xiu (2020) found that neural networks' dominant predictive inputs are familiar (price trends, liquidity, accounting quality), and that gains come from nonlinear interactions among core factors rather than esoteric new signals. Feng et al. (2020) use a double-selection LASSO (*Chapter 15*) to show that most proposed new factors are redundant relative to the existing menu, with profitability and investment retaining the clearest incremental content, a finding about disciplined testing rather than a definitive reduction to a handful of labels.

From the zoo to latent factors

A key conceptual distinction clarifies what latent factor models can and cannot resolve. Following Idzorek, Kaplan, and Ibbotson (2024):

- **Attribution factors** explain co-movement among assets but may carry zero expected return
- **Priced factors** emanate from asset pricing models and carry genuine risk premia

PCA is designed to extract common variation in returns, which may or may not line up with priced expected-return factors. The three objectives introduced previously organize methods that progressively tighten this link: variance maximization (*Sections 14.2–14.4*), variance plus pricing errors (*Section 14.5*), and direct pricing-error minimization (*Section 14.6*).

Latent factor models do not make the factor-zoo debate disappear. They change the object of selection. Instead of proposing and testing a long list of named characteristics one at a time, they infer a low-dimensional structure directly from returns, sometimes augmented by pricing restrictions or observable characteristics. This reduces one source of researcher discretion, but it does not, by itself, guarantee that the extracted factors are priced, economically interpretable, or stable out-of-sample.

The methods that follow are complementary responses to factor proliferation: powerful tools for discovering structure, not clean escape hatches from the data-mining problem.

14.2 Extracting latent factors with PCA

PCA solves the first of the three latent factor objectives introduced in *Section 14.1*: maximizing explained variance. It transforms a set of correlated asset returns into uncorrelated components that capture maximum variance (Goyal, 2012).

The transformation relies on eigendecomposition of the return covariance matrix, a standard linear algebra operation with direct financial interpretation. As a pure variance-maximization method, PCA finds the dominant directions of co-movement but is agnostic to whether those dimensions carry risk premia, a limitation that *Section 14.5* addresses.

The mechanics of eigendecomposition

The PCA procedure begins with a matrix of asset returns (time periods as rows, assets as columns). Returns are demeaned; standardizing to unit variance is optional but standard for cross-sectional work (see *Assumptions and design choices*, the following subsection).

From the standardized return matrix, we compute an $N \times N$ covariance matrix Σ. When inputs are standardized to unit variance, this yields the correlation matrix, a distinction that matters for interpretation, taken up in the next subsection. PCA then solves the eigenvalue problem: finding all pairs (λ, v) such that $\Sigma v = \lambda v$.

The solution yields two key outputs. **Eigenvalues** (λ_i) are scalars representing the magnitude of variance explained by each corresponding principal component. They are ranked in descending order, so $\lambda_1 \geq \lambda_2 \geq \ldots \geq \lambda_n$. The proportion of total variance explained by the i-th component equals $\lambda_i / \Sigma\lambda$. A "scree plot" shows eigenvalues in descending order; the "elbow," where explained variance levels off, suggests how many components to retain (*Figure 14.2*).

`01_pca_equity_sectors` constructs this scree plot for sector ETFs and adds bootstrap confidence intervals on the loadings to assess which sector exposures are statistically reliable.

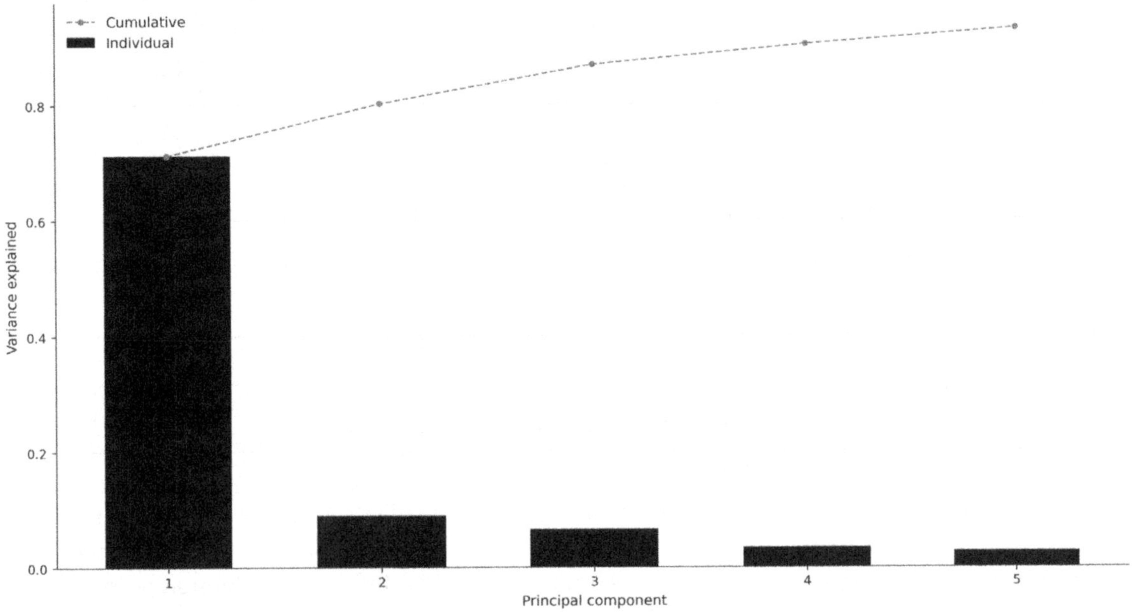

Figure 14.2: Variance explained by the top 5 principal components

Eigenvectors (v_i) are vectors of "loadings" that define each principal component as a linear combination of the original asset returns. These vectors are mutually orthogonal, meaning the resulting principal components are uncorrelated with one another. In finance, each eigenvector can be interpreted as portfolio weights, a concept we develop fully in the next section on eigenportfolios. `02_eigenportfolios` demonstrates this interpretation on a broad US equity universe.

Assumptions and design choices

PCA is a useful tool, but its interpretation in finance depends on several important assumptions.

- **Linearity.** PCA captures only linear patterns of co-movement. In financial markets, however, relationships often change across regimes, especially during stress, and many interactions among characteristics are non-linear. For example, the effect of momentum may depend on volatility or liquidity. Rolling-window PCA can partially adapt to temporal variation, but it does not address the underlying linearity constraint. *Section 14.6* returns to this limitation when we introduce autoencoders. The notebook `01_pca_equity_sectors` illustrates rolling PCA for sector ETFs.
- **Variance is not the same as pricing relevance.** PCA is designed to explain as much return variation as possible, not to identify factors with high expected returns. A factor can explain a large share of covariance yet earn little or no risk premium; conversely, a factor with modest variance can be economically important if it commands a large premium. This gap between covariance structure and pricing relevance motivates RP-PCA in *Section 14.5*.

- **Focus on second moments.** PCA works entirely through the covariance matrix of centered returns, so it uses only second-moment information. Under Gaussian assumptions, this aligns with the maximum-likelihood estimation of a linear factor model. Financial returns, however, are rarely Gaussian: they are often skewed, heavy-tailed, and prone to jumps. In those settings, PCA still finds directions of maximum variance, but it may miss structure that appears in higher moments and may still matter economically.

Two key design choices deserve a closer look.

Covariance or correlation?

A basic implementation choice is whether to apply PCA to the covariance matrix or the correlation matrix.

- Using the **covariance matrix** preserves the natural scale of returns, so more volatile assets receive more weight in the decomposition
- Using the **correlation matrix** first standardizes each asset to unit variance, preventing high-volatility assets from dominating the results

For cross-sectional equity analysis, correlation-based PCA is usually preferred because it emphasizes common structure rather than differences in raw volatility. For multi-asset portfolios with markedly different volatilities, the choice should be deliberate rather than by default. The notebook `01_pca_equity_sectors` uses correlation-PCA for the sector ETF example.

Idiosyncratic volatility normalization

A useful third option goes beyond the simple covariance-versus-correlation choice: normalize each asset's returns by its lagged idiosyncratic volatility before running PCA.

This adjustment targets a specific problem. In raw covariance PCA, high-volatility assets can dominate the decomposition. Correlation PCA solves that problem by forcing all assets to have equal total variance, but that is often too strong: it removes not only idiosyncratic volatility differences but also meaningful differences in common-factor exposure. Idiosyncratic volatility normalization is more selective. It scales returns only by the diversifiable component of volatility, leaving common variation more intact.

In practice, this often leads to cleaner separation between signal and noise, more stable eigenvectors over time, and more parsimonious factor structures, meaning that fewer components explain the same share of variation. To implement this correctly, idiosyncratic volatility must be estimated from residuals in a prior estimation window, and current returns must be normalized using only that lagged information. This preserves the point-in-time structure and avoids lookahead bias.

Covariance estimation quality

A practical warning: PCA is only as reliable as the covariance matrix it decomposes. When the number of assets N, approaches or exceeds the number of time periods, T, the sample covariance matrix becomes difficult to estimate. In that regime, sample eigenvalues are distorted upward, weak factors become hard to distinguish from noise, and estimated eigenvectors can become unstable across samples.

Random matrix theory provides a useful benchmark for separating signal from noise in large covariance matrices. In particular, the **Marchenko-Pastur distribution** characterizes the range of eigenvalues that can arise from noise alone, given the N/T ratio. Eigenvalues that fall within this range should be treated cautiously, since they may not reflect genuine common structure.

A common remedy is to use **shrinkage estimators**, with the **Ledoit-Wolf** family being the best-known example. These methods pull extreme sample eigenvalues toward a more structured target, reducing estimation error and improving stability. For large equity cross-sections, applying shrinkage before PCA is often advisable; otherwise, the leading eigenportfolios may reflect sampling noise rather than persistent market structure. See the Primer for a fuller discussion of the Marchenko-Pastur benchmark and shrinkage-based covariance estimation.

How many PCA factors are real?

When the number of assets, N, is large relative to the number of time periods, T, PCA starts to pick up noise as well as signal. In this high-dimensional setting, sample eigenvalues are biased upward, and weak factors can become indistinguishable from random variation (noise).

The **Baik-Ben Arous-Péché (BBP)** phase transition (Baik et al., 2005; see Paleologo, 2025, Ch. 7) quantifies this: a factor is recoverable only if its population eigenvalue exceeds $1 + \sqrt{\gamma}$, where $\gamma = N/T$ and eigenvalues are normalized to unit idiosyncratic variance. Below this threshold, no estimation technique can separate signal from noise.

The practical message is simple: the larger n/T becomes, the harder it is to recover anything except the strongest factors. In our case studies, this works out quite differently across datasets. For ETFs, where $\gamma \approx 0.2$, the threshold is relatively low, so several components can be retained. For a 500-stock equity panel with only one year of daily data, $\gamma \approx 2.0$, and only the market plus a few dominant sector factors are likely to survive. For CME futures, where $\gamma \approx 0.06$, most factors remain identifiable.

A good rule of thumb is therefore to keep n modest relative to T whenever possible. If that is not feasible, expect PCA to recover only the dominant part of the factor structure. When γ becomes moderately large, eigenvalue shrinkage is usually more reliable than a visual scree-plot rule for deciding how many components to keep. See the Primer for details on the BBP threshold, the Marchenko-Pastur benchmark, and shrinkage-based alternatives.

> **Implementation:** See `01_pca_equity_sectors` for rolling PCA and bootstrap stability analysis.

Next, we discuss how to use the eigendecomposition techniques to construct equity portfolios.

14.3 Eigenportfolios for equity strategies

Reading eigenvectors as portfolio weights yields uncorrelated "eigenportfolios," building blocks for risk management and systematic trading (Avellaneda and Lee, 2010). See `02_eigenportfolios` for the full PCA pipeline, including universe selection, variance decomposition, and market factor validation.

Constructing and interpreting eigenportfolios

The first eigenportfolio, corresponding to the largest eigenvalue, captures the dominant source of variance. Empirically, nearly all weights are positive: it acts as a data-driven proxy for the broad market portfolio.

In our analysis of the 500 most liquid stocks by dollar volume from the US Equities Panel dataset, the first principal component (PC1) correlates with the equal-weighted market return by 0.99, confirming that it serves as a data-driven market proxy. Each stock's loading on PC1 measures its exposure to this statistically extracted market mode. This is analogous to the **CAPM beta** in the sense that both quantify sensitivity to a common factor. Unlike CAPM beta, however, the PC1 loading is not estimated relative to a prespecified market portfolio and does not carry an asset-pricing interpretation; it follows mechanically from the sample covariance matrix and the PCA normalization.

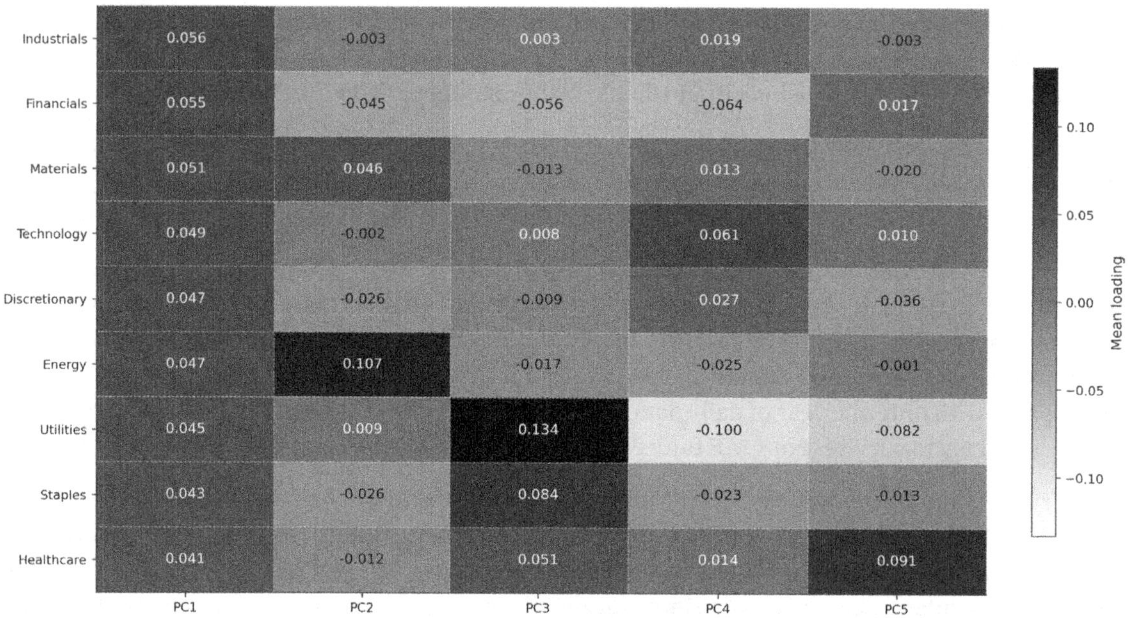

Figure 14.3: Eigenportfolio loadings across sectors

Whereas the first eigenportfolio $PC1$ loads positively on all sectors, PC2 reveals a growth-versus-value rotation, loading positively on Technology and Communication Services while negatively on Financials and Energy. PC3 captures defensive-versus-cyclical dynamics (see *Figure 14.3*). These **interpretable patterns** emerge purely from the return covariance structure, without any imposed economic labels.

Higher-order eigenportfolios are, by mathematical construction, orthogonal to each other. **Orthogonality** ensures that the extracted component returns are uncorrelated in the sample. Higher-order eigenportfolios are often approximately market-neutral in practice, but they are not automatically dollar- or beta-neutral. These portfolios are typically long-short in nature (positive weights in some stocks, negative in others) and often capture intuitive economic exposures such as sector rotations or style tilts. For example, the second eigenportfolio might represent a long position in growth stocks against a short in value stocks, or a long in technology against a short in utilities.

Stationarity is one caveat to consider. Eigenportfolio loadings can rotate significantly across estimation windows. The second component might capture growth-versus-value in one decade and defensive-versus-cyclical in the next, as sector correlations shift with the macroeconomic regime. This instability limits the use of eigenportfolios in live trading without periodic re-estimation, and it means that economic interpretations of higher-order components should be treated as descriptive rather than structural.

Statistical factors can also be interpreted via regression. Statistical PCA factors are abstract by construction: they maximize variance explained but carry no economic label. A practical interpretation method: regress each eigenvector's loadings cross-sectionally on observable firm characteristics such as sector indicators, market capitalization, momentum, and book-to-market ratio (Connor and Korajczyk, 2009). The regression R^2 indicates how much of the variation in each statistical factor is explained by known fundamentals. If PC1 loadings correlate strongly with sector dummies, it is effectively a sector factor under a different name. If PC4 shows low R^2 against all available characteristics, it may capture a genuinely novel latent risk dimension, precisely the type of structure that justifies data-driven factor discovery over pre-specified models.

Applications in quantitative finance

Annualized return, volatility, and Sharpe ratio statistics for each eigenportfolio quantify the risk-return profile of each latent factor: the first component typically shows the highest volatility while higher-order components may offer modest risk-adjusted returns.

Any portfolio's risk decomposes into exposures to these orthogonal factors, revealing concentrations that pre-specified factor models miss: a manager might discover that apparent sector diversification masks exposure to a single statistical factor. This decomposition feeds directly into *Chapter 17*'s portfolio construction: eigenportfolio betas serve as the risk dimensions over which position sizing is optimized.

Regressing stock returns on the top K eigenportfolios isolates residuals that are hypothesized to mean-revert; the eigenportfolio return series can also serve as inputs for factor-timing models. Both applications face practical headwinds: mean-reversion parameters are unstable out-of-sample, and evidence for reliable short-horizon factor timing remains mixed.

Improving interpretability with hierarchical PCA

A common critique of standard PCA is that higher-order factors lack a clear economic interpretation and can be statistically unstable across different time periods. Marco Avellaneda's **Hierarchical PCA (HPCA)** addresses this by injecting known economic structure into the analysis (Avellaneda, 2019).

HPCA proceeds in two steps. First, PCA is performed independently *within* each known economic grouping, such as GICS sectors. This identifies the dominant factor for technology stocks, another for financials, and so forth. Second, another PCA is applied to the correlation matrix of these sector-level factors to capture cross-sector dynamics. The resulting factors are much easier to interpret: they correspond to clear inter-sector bets (long financials versus short industrials) or intra-sector momentum effects, resolving much of the ambiguity of standard PCA. The notebook `02_eigenportfolios` demonstrates both standard eigenportfolio construction and the HPCA two-step procedure on GICS sectors.

Fixing eigenvector instability

A persistent practical challenge with rolling PCA is that factor loadings can change abruptly between adjacent estimation windows, not because the underlying factor structure has shifted, but because of a mathematical pathology. Understanding and correcting this instability is essential before using PCA loadings for portfolio allocation or performance attribution.

Consider the problem of near-degenerate eigenvalues. When two eigenvalues are close in magnitude, the corresponding eigenvectors become poorly identified. A small perturbation (adding or removing a single day of returns, or changing one stock in the estimation universe) can cause the eigenvectors to rotate within their shared subspace or swap entirely. In rolling PCA on equity returns, this manifests as factor loadings that "flip sign" between adjacent estimation windows: sector exposures suddenly invert, creating phantom turnover in downstream portfolio weights. The first principal component is typically immune (its eigenvalue is well-separated), but components 3 and beyond frequently exhibit this instability (Paleologo, 2025).

Measuring instability is vital. Cosine similarity between consecutive eigenvectors provides a simple diagnostic. For eigenvectors $v(t)$ and $v(t+1)$, cosine similarity equals $|v(t)^T v(t+1)|$ (taking the absolute value because eigenvectors are identified only up to sign). A value of 1 indicates stable loadings; values near 0 indicate rotation into a different subspace. Track this metric for each principal component across estimation windows. Components with frequent drops below 0.8 are unreliable for attribution or allocation without correction.

A practical fix is to align loading matrices across adjacent windows by an **orthogonal Procrustes rotation:**

- Let B_t and B_{t+1} denote the $N \times K$ loading matrices from two consecutive estimations
- Compute the singular value decomposition of $B_t^\top B_{t+1} = USV^\top$
- The orthogonal matrix that best aligns the two loading spaces is $R^* = VU^\top$, and the aligned next-window loadings are $\tilde{B}_{t+1} = B_{t+1}R^*$

This transformation preserves orthogonality and factor span, but it removes arbitrary rotations within nearly degenerate eigenspaces. The result is not a different covariance model; it is the same model written in a temporally smoother coordinate system.

Always check eigenvector stability before using PCA loadings for allocation or attribution:

- If the top 3–5 principal components have well-separated eigenvalues (ratios exceeding 2:1 between consecutive eigenvalues), Procrustes rotation is unnecessary: the loadings are naturally stable
- If eigenvalues are clustered, which is common for equity returns beyond the third component, always apply Procrustes

The stability diagnostic connects directly to *Chapter 17*'s portfolio construction: unstable loadings produce an unstable covariance matrix, which generates unnecessary turnover, and that turnover incurs real transaction costs.

Practitioner recipe for two-stage production PCA

The notebooks in this chapter demonstrate PCA on a single estimation window with uniform time weighting. Risk models used by institutional investors apply a more sophisticated procedure that separates two empirical facts about financial markets: volatility changes quickly (days to weeks), while the correlation structure changes slowly (months to quarters). Mixing both dynamics in a single estimation window either overreacts to volatility spikes or underreacts to shifts in correlation.

The following two-stage procedure, formalized by Paleologo (2025), addresses this separation:

1. **Capture volatility dynamics.** Apply exponentially-weighted time weighting (half-life ~20 days) to emphasize recent volatility. Run a preliminary PCA ($p \approx 5$ components), compute residuals, and estimate per-asset idiosyncratic volatility.
2. **Estimate the correlation factor structure.** Normalize returns by Stage 1's idiosyncratic volatility, apply slow exponential weighting (half-life ~120 days), and perform the production PCA. Apply BBP-informed eigenvalue shrinkage (*Section 14.2*) and Procrustes rotation to stabilize loadings. Reconstruct the full covariance matrix: $\Omega = D_\sigma(B\Omega_f B^T + \Omega_\varepsilon)D_\sigma$, where D_σ restores the original volatility scale.

This procedure matters for the ML4T pipeline because it produces the covariance matrix that feeds directly into the portfolio construction methods of *Chapter 17*. Mean-variance optimization, hierarchical risk parity, and risk budgeting all consume a covariance estimate as their primary input. The separation of volatility and correlation estimation also connects to *Chapter 18*'s short-term volatility updating for transaction cost models. The two-stage structure ensures that a sudden volatility spike (for example, a VIX event) immediately updates risk estimates without destabilizing the slower-moving factor structure that determines diversification benefits. Next, we apply Principal Component Analysis to the yield curve to identify fixed income factors.

> **Implementation:** See `02_eigenportfolios` for eigenportfolio construction, including sector loading heatmaps, HPCA, and cumulative return visualization.

14.4 Decoding the yield curve

PCA's clearest success is in fixed income. Litterman and Scheinkman (1991) showed that three factors explain 95–99% of variation in the Treasury yield curve, a result that has been replicated across decades and markets.

Level, slope, and curvature

When PCA is applied to daily or monthly changes in Treasury yields across maturities (from 1-month bills through 30-year bonds), studies consistently find that 95–99% of variation can be attributed to three orthogonal principal components, each with a widely-accepted economic interpretation (*Figure 14.4*):

- **Level:** Explains over 90% of the total variance. Loadings are nearly uniform across maturities, so a level shock corresponds to a parallel shift, all rates moving up or down together. Economically, this reflects broad changes in inflation expectations and real growth prospects.

- **Slope:** Explains 5–8% of variance. Loadings have opposite signs at short and long maturities, so a slope shock steepens or flattens the curve. This factor is closely tied to monetary policy: rate hikes compress the short-long spread, flattening the curve.
- **Curvature:** Captures 1–2% of variance. Mid-curve maturities move opposite to both ends, creating a "butterfly" twist. This factor is linked to rate volatility and path uncertainty. Observing it clearly requires at least 5–7 maturities spanning the curve; with fewer, the third component captures residual variation rather than a clean butterfly.

Three principal components are shown in *Figure 14.4*:

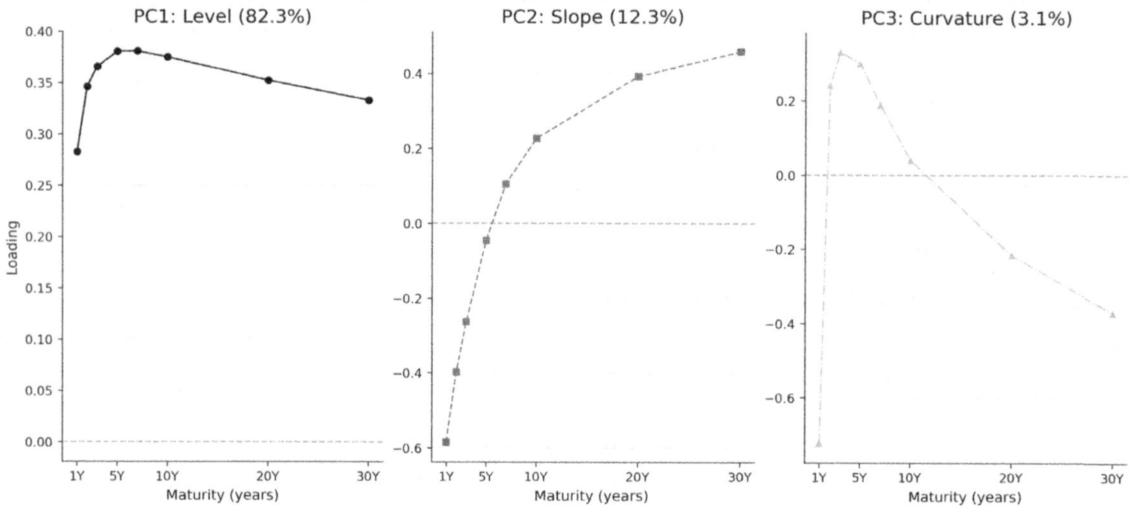

Figure 14.4: Principal component analysis on yield curve components

> **Implementation:** `03_yield_curve_decomposition` applies PCA to daily changes in eight Treasury constant-maturity yields (1Y, 2Y, 3Y, 5Y, 7Y, 10Y, 20Y, 30Y), which recovers the classical Level/Slope/Curvature decomposition with variance shares of 82.3%, 12.3%, and 3.1% (97.8% cumulative). Each maturity is reconstructed from the three factors, and the generalized-duration hedging framework is illustrated on the resulting exposures.

Why PCA works for yield curves

The yield curve is the rare case where the variance objective and the pricing objective largely coincide: no-arbitrage constraints in fixed income aim to ensure that variance-explaining factors are also priced. The contrast with equities highlights a structural difference:

- Interest rate drivers are low-dimensional and persistent: inflation expectations, real growth, and monetary policy affect all bonds simultaneously, with sensitivity varying by maturity. At the same time, PCA on yield changes is a descriptive decomposition of curve movements, not a proof that the same components are the uniquely priced term-premium factors. No-arbitrage term-structure models and return-predictive term-premium models add further structure that PCA alone does not impose.

- Equities are the opposite: thousands of stocks driven by idiosyncratic news, sector effects, macro shocks, and behavioral factors produce a covariance structure that is complex, time-varying, and regime-dependent, explaining why PCA on equities yields less interpretable and less stable factors.

Practical application for efficient hedging

This low-dimensional structure enables efficient hedging. Rather than managing exposure to dozens of individual bonds, a manager neutralizes three factor exposures, namely level, slope, and curvature, using liquid instruments (Treasury futures, interest rate swaps). This **generalized duration** approach is more precise, cheaper in transaction terms, and grounded in the yield curve's empirical low-rank structure.

Factor	Variance Explained	Movement Pattern	Standard Interpretation
Level (PC1)	>90%	Parallel shift	Inflation, growth expectations
Slope (PC2)	~5-8%	Steepening/flattening	Monetary policy stance
Curvature (PC3)	~1-2%	Butterfly twist	Rate volatility, uncertainty

Table 14.1: Principal components of the yield curve

Economic interpretations are widely used heuristics, not definitive causal mappings, as shown in *Table 14.1*. Exact percentages depend on the maturity set, sample period, and whether PCA is applied to the correlation or covariance matrix of yield changes.

Next, we explore how to enrich the statistical techniques introduced so far with economic data to make them more useful in practice.

14.5 Bridging economics and statistics with advanced models

The yield curve's low-dimensional success highlights PCA's limitations for equities: high dimensionality, weak structural constraints, and time-varying relationships produce factors that explain variance but not necessarily returns. Two innovations address this:

- **IPCA** (Kelly, Pruitt, and Su, 2019) makes factor loadings dynamic through observable characteristics
- **RP-PCA** (Lettau and Pelger, 2020) explicitly targets pricing-relevant factors

Before deriving either model, we explain the predictive structure they share.

The three-stage latent-factor forecasting adapter

Several factor-representation models in this chapter can be used for prediction by adding a forecasting layer. PCA, RP-PCA, IPCA, and CAE all estimate latent factors, but they do so for different purposes: PCA explains covariance, RP-PCA tilts factor extraction toward priced variation, IPCA estimates linear characteristic-conditioned loadings, and CAE generalizes that loading map nonlinearly. To turn these representations into ex-ante asset-level forecasts, the **three-stage latent-factor forecasting adapter** wraps each estimator in the same workflow (*Figure 14.5*):

1. **Stage 1: Factor estimation.** Compress the $T \times N$ excess-return panel R^e into a $T \times K$ factor history F and a per-asset loading map. PCA solves this by SVD on R^e; RP-PCA modifies the criterion by adding a pricing-error penalty; IPCA and CAE parameterize the loading map $\beta_{i,t}$ as a function of lagged characteristics. Stage 1's training objective (variance, variance-plus-pricing-error, or cross-sectional reconstruction) uses contemporaneous returns; this is what the structural model is for.
2. **Stage 2: Factor-premium forecaster.** Predict $\hat{\lambda}_{t+1} \in \mathbb{R}^K$ from the training-window factor history $F_{1:t}$. The simplest choice, used implicitly by KPS (2019) and GKX (2020) and labeled "IID-BS" by Engel et al. (2025), is the training-sample mean. The library's `ExpandingMeanFactorForecaster` implements this baseline. AR(1), EWMA, gradient-boosted regression (LightGBM, an analog to Engel et al.'s Q-Boost), and pretrained foundation models (their ZS-Chronos) are drop-in alternatives that target the same object with progressively richer representations of factor dynamics. *Figure 14.6* catalogs the forecasters used in this chapter.
3. **Stage 3: Asset map.** Combine today's exposures with the forecast premium: $\hat{\mu}_{i,t+1} = \beta_{i,t} \cdot \hat{\lambda}_{t+1}$

If Stages 2 and 3 are grouped as a single forecasting layer, the same workflow reads as a two-block structure: factor estimation followed by forecasting and mapping. The numbered three-stage formulation is the one used consistently throughout this chapter.

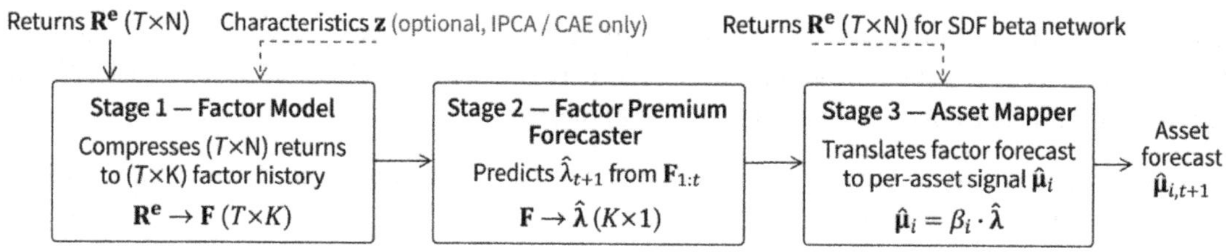

PER-METHOD INSTANTIATION

PCA	SVD of centred $\mathbf{R^e}$	Constant / AR(1) / EWMA	Static $\mathbf{B}$
RP-PCA	Eigendecomp of $\boldsymbol{\Sigma} + \gamma \cdot \boldsymbol{\mu\mu}$ (γ>0)	Constant / AR(1) / EWMA	Static $\mathbf{B}$
IPCA	ALS on $\mathbf{z}_t\,\boldsymbol{\Gamma} \rightarrow \mathbf{R^e}$	Constant / AR(1) / EWMA	$\mathbf{z}_{i,t} \cdot \hat{\boldsymbol{\Gamma}}$
CAE	Encoder $\mathbf{g}_\theta(\mathbf{z})$ + managed portfolios	Constant / AR(1) / Q-Boost (Engel '25)	$\mathbf{g}_\theta(\mathbf{z}_{i,t})$
SDF	Conditional weight network $\hat{\omega}_{t,i}$	(no separate stage)	Beta network on $\mathbf{R^e} \cdot \hat{\mathbf{F}}$

Figure 14.5: The three-stage latent-factor forecasting adapter. Stage 1 compresses the excess-return panel into a factor history and a per-asset loading map; Stage 2 forecasts the next-period factor premium from that history; Stage 3 combines current loadings with the forecast premium to produce asset-level expected returns. RP-PCA, IPCA, and the CAE differ only in Stage 1

Two design properties follow. First, Stage 1 and Stage 2 are *separable*: the same structural model can pair with any forecaster, and the same forecaster works across structural models. The chapter notebooks exploit this by sharing the Stage 2 catalog across IPCA, RP-PCA, and CAE. Second, forecast quality enters at Stage 2: better forecasts of the factor premium translate directly into better asset-level signals through Stage 3.

The adversarial SDF and the supervised autoencoder do not pass through this adapter. The SDF estimates a pricing kernel directly from no-arbitrage moment restrictions and produces pricing-error diagnostics rather than a factor-return history; *Section 14.7* shows why a separate Stage 2 forecast is not the natural output. The supervised autoencoder predicts returns end-to-end and has no factor-return intermediate to forecast; *Section 14.7* presents it as a direct-prediction contrast.

Engel et al. (2025) extend the adapter by ranking factors by forecast *uncertainty* and using only the most predictable ones in tangency portfolios; that extension lives at Stage 2 and is also a natural place to plug in modern probabilistic forecasters.

The `ml4t-models` library packages the adapter as a single composable object, `LatentFactorForecastPipeline(model, forecaster, mapper)`. The teaching notebooks are built from scratch at each stage; the library is the production format used by the case-study runners.

Dynamic betas with instrumented PCA

Standard PCA estimates a single, static beta per asset, an unrealistic assumption when risk profiles evolve. Instrumented PCA (IPCA; Kelly, Pruitt, and Su, 2019) makes betas time-varying by modeling them as functions of observable characteristics: size, book-to-market, momentum, and others.

The IPCA model specifies excess returns as:

$$r^e_{i,t+1} = z^\top_{i,t}\Gamma f_{t+1} + \varepsilon_{i,t+1}$$

where $z_{i,t}$ is a $P \times 1$ vector of characteristics observed at time t, Γ is a $P \times K$ matrix, and f_{t+1} is the $K \times 1$ vector of latent factor returns. Equivalently, $\beta_{i,t} = \Gamma^\top z_{i,t}$, so characteristics govern time-varying loadings rather than expected returns directly. This timing matters. Characteristics must be lagged relative to returns, and the interpretation is conditional risk exposure rather than a reduced-form anomaly regression.

The central insight is that *characteristics are covariances*: firm characteristics predict returns not because they represent standalone anomalies but because they proxy for time-varying exposures to latent risk factors. A small-cap value stock loads on different factors than a large-cap growth stock, and loadings update as characteristics change.

This interpretation enables a direct empirical test of risk versus mispricing:

- If characteristics primarily explain returns through their role in shaping risk exposures, IPCA identifies strong latent factors and insignificant pricing errors (alphas)
- If characteristics represent pure mispricing independent of risk, the model attributes their effect to a significant alpha term

Kelly, Pruitt, and Su (2019) report that a five-factor IPCA model explains cross-sectional returns far more accurately than existing models, with characteristic effects almost entirely absorbed by their role as instruments for risk exposures.

The original Kelly, Pruitt, and Su (KPS) study uses 94 characteristics; our `us_firm_characteristics` dataset provides 57 after filtering. Missing characteristics should be imputed (using the cross-sectional median is standard) rather than dropping observations, since missingness is informative: smaller firms tend to have fewer available characteristics.

IPCA estimation uses **Alternating Least Squares** (**ALS**), iterating between updating Γ (the mapping from characteristics to loadings) and updating f_t (the latent factors). The number of characteristics P matters: too few limit the model's ability to capture time-varying loadings; too many introduce estimation noise.

Three sensitivities regarding identification recur across post-2019 replications:

- Results depend on the number of latent factors K; report a range (typically 3–8) rather than selecting a single optimum, since the standard out-of-sample pricing-error rule is sensitive to the test-asset set (Didisheim et al., 2023, show that more complex factor models can outperform out-of-sample).
- Missing characteristics are absorbed into residuals rather than systematic risk. The 57 characteristics in our `us_firm_characteristics` implementation (down from 94 in the original KPS study) are a floor, not a ceiling.
- The linear map $\beta = \Gamma^\top z$ cannot capture interactions (momentum's behavior conditional on volatility, size effects conditional on liquidity); *Section 14.6*'s non-linear extensions trade identification clarity for expressive power.

> **Implementation:** `04_ipca` includes a parameter-recovery exercise on synthetic data that confirms ALS estimation recovers the true Γ before applying the model to real data, and directly demonstrates K-sensitivity.

Finding priced factors with risk-premium PCA

The second PCA flaw (focusing on variance rather than expected returns) is addressed by RP-PCA (Lettau and Pelger, 2020). The defining feature of RP-PCA is not a different loading map but a different objective: standard PCA is augmented with a pricing-error penalty so that factors that explain small amounts of variance yet carry meaningful risk premia are not overlooked.

RP-PCA minimizes a weighted combination of unexplained variance and cross-sectional pricing errors:

$$\min_{\Lambda,F} \frac{1}{NT}\sum_{i,t} \left(\tilde{X}_{i,t} - \tilde{F}_t^\top \Lambda_i\right)^2 \; + \; \kappa \frac{1}{N}\sum_{i} (\bar{X}_i - \bar{F}^\top \Lambda_i)^2$$

where the first term is the usual reconstruction loss on time-demeaned returns and the second term penalizes pricing errors in mean returns.

The parameter κ controls the trade-off. At $\kappa = 0$, RP-PCA reduces to standard PCA, which maximizes pure variance with no regard for pricing. As κ increases, the objective shifts toward factors that explain cross-sectional return differences, even if they explain little of the total variance. In the limit $\kappa \to \infty$, the method focuses entirely on pricing and ignores variance altogether.

The objective is solved by applying standard PCA to a modified matrix, $\left((1/T)X^\top X - \bar{X}\bar{X}^\top\right) + \kappa\,\bar{X}\bar{X}^\top$, the sample covariance plus a penalty that overweights the mean-return information (so $\kappa = 0$ recovers ordinary covariance PCA). The result is factors that are both statistically significant (explaining co-movement) and economically significant (carrying high Sharpe ratios).

A factor capturing credit risk might explain only 2% of the return variance yet have a Sharpe ratio of 0.8, remaining invisible to standard PCA, which ranks it below the 15th component. RP-PCA with $\kappa = 5$ elevates it to the 3rd. Lettau and Pelger (2020) report out-of-sample Sharpe ratios more than double those of standard PCA on US equities, 1963–2017; results are sample-dependent and require out-of-sample validation.

Note that **double-selection LASSO** (Feng, Giglio, and Xiu, 2020), the modern standard for testing new candidate factors against an existing zoo, is a special case of the debiased ML framework developed in *Chapter 15*, applied to the factor returns from this chapter's case studies.

Implementation: `05_rp_pca` for a comparison of standard PCA against RP-PCA across multiple penalty values. The notebook's `gamma` parameter is this κ, and `gamma=0` reproduces standard PCA. Lettau and Pelger write the penalty weight as $1 + \gamma$ with PCA recovered at $\gamma = -1$; the chapter's $\kappa = 1 + \gamma$ shifts this so that $\kappa = 0$ is the no-penalty case.

Test assets as a design choice

Test assets are a design choice, not a neutral backdrop. Recent work shows that factor strength depends on the span of the test assets used in estimation and evaluation:

- Giglio, Xiu, and Zhang (2021) emphasize this point and propose **supervised PCA** to select informative assets when weak factors are present
- Bryzgalova, Pelger, and Zhu (2025) take a complementary route, building test assets endogenously with trees so that the resulting basis assets better span the stochastic discount factor

The practical implication is straightforward: compare methods on a common benchmark set of test assets, but also report how results change when the test-asset span is enriched or redesigned.

All methods in this section share a limitation: factor loadings are linear functions of characteristics. Momentum behaves differently at high versus low volatility, size effects vary with liquidity, and linear models cannot capture these interactions without manual feature engineering. *Section 14.6* addresses this with deep learning models that learn non-linear mappings while retaining the economic structure developed here.

Model	Estimation objective	Loading structure	Forecast adapter	Best use
PCA	Maximize covariance explained	Static loadings	Optional	Risk decomposition
RP-PCA	Variance plus pricing-error penalty	Static latent loadings	Yes, as factor extractor	Priced-factor discovery
IPCA	Conditional latent factor model	Linear characteristic-conditioned betas	Yes	Interpretable conditional betas
CAE	Nonlinear conditional latent factor model	Neural characteristic-conditioned betas	Yes	Nonlinear conditional betas

Model	Estimation objective	Loading structure	Forecast adapter	Best use
Adversarial SDF	No-arbitrage moment restrictions	Pricing-kernel weights	No	Direct pricing-error minimization
SAE	Supervised return prediction plus reconstruction regularizer	Bottleneck representation	No	Predictive benchmark

Table 14.2: Latent-factor and related models: estimation objective, loading structure, and relationship to the three-stage forecasting adapter

RP-PCA, IPCA, and CAE pass through the adapter as a matter of routine; PCA can be wrapped in it for factor-timing, but is used here for risk decomposition. The adversarial SDF and the SAE sit outside the adapter. The CAE is introduced in *Section 14.6*; the SDF and the SAE in *Section 14.7*.

The shared adapter, therefore, covers PCA (optionally), RP-PCA, IPCA, and CAE; the differences between these four models live in Stage 1. *Figure 14.6* catalogs the three-tier Stage 2 forecaster ladder (Tier 1: Constant, AR(1), EWMA; Tier 2: Ridge, LightGBM; Tier 3: LSTM, TCN) that the teaching notebooks make swappable; *Section 14.8* reports how the choice interacts with the structural estimator. The next section introduces non-linear techniques for dimensionality reduction.

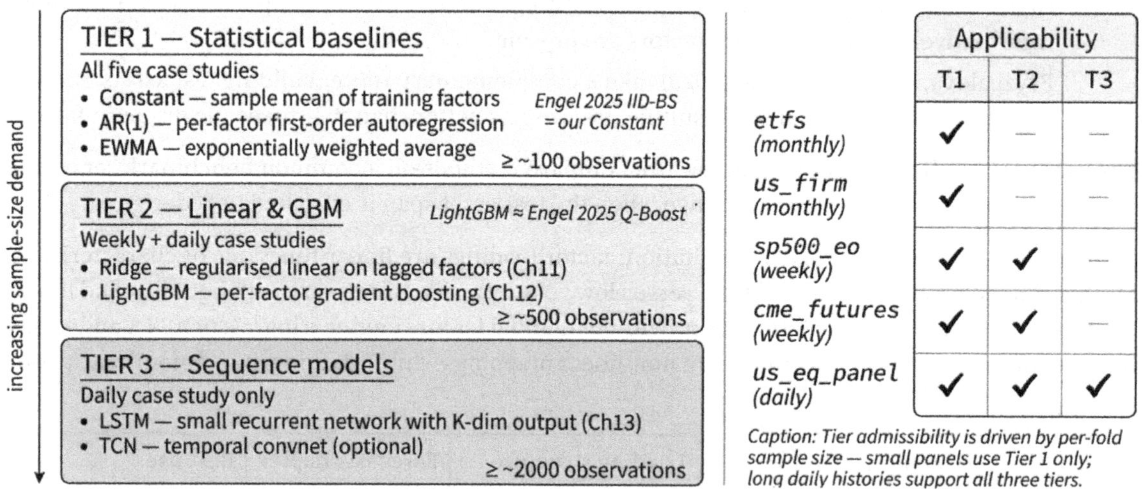

Figure 14.6: The Stage 2 factor-premium forecaster catalog. Tier 1 holds the constant, AR(1), and EWMA baselines; Tier 2 adds ridge and gradient-boosted regressions; Tier 3 adds LSTM and TCN sequence models. Any forecaster pairs with any Stage 1 estimator without retraining the factor model

Implementation: `04_ipca` demonstrates ALS estimation with recovery on synthetic data plus the swappable Stage 2 forecaster catalog; `05_rp_pca` compares standard PCA against RP-PCA across κ values within the same framework. For real-data applications with walk-forward validation, see applicable case study notebooks.

14.6 The conditional autoencoder

Section 14.5 operationalized the three-stage forecasting adapter with linear loading maps: IPCA ties conditional betas to characteristics through a single matrix, and RP-PCA tilts the factor-extraction criterion toward priced variation. Both keep the map between characteristics and loadings linear. The **conditional autoencoder** (CAE; Gu, Kelly, and Xiu, 2019) is the nonlinear member of the same family: it keeps the conditional-factor structure and replaces only the linear loading map with a neural network.

The CAE is a strict nonlinear generalization of IPCA. Both start from the same conditional factor representation:

$$r_{i,t+1} = \beta_{i,t}^{\top} f_{t+1} + \varepsilon_{i,t+1}$$

and differ only in the loading map. IPCA restricts conditional betas to be linear in lagged characteristics, $\beta_{i,t} = \Gamma^{\top} z_{i,t}$, whereas the CAE replaces this map with a neural network, $\beta_{i,t} = g(z_{i,t}; W)$. With a single linear layer and no nonlinear activation, the CAE collapses to IPCA, so it is best understood as the same conditional-factor idea with a more expressive loading map, rather than a separate direct-prediction architecture.

That placement is what keeps the CAE inside the adapter. Its training objective reconstructs realized returns from conditional betas and latent factor returns; it does not directly optimize next-period expected returns. The fitted model is nevertheless a conditional asset-pricing representation: covariates guide the dimension reduction, and nonlinear interactions among characteristics shape the factor exposures. Once estimated, the CAE supplies the same two objects as IPCA, namely current conditional betas and a history of latent-factor returns, so the Stage 2 forecaster catalog from *Section 14.5* carries over unchanged. The training-sample mean of factor returns gives the baseline forecast, while AR(1), EWMA, Q-Boost, and ZS-Chronos replace it without retraining the CAE. The CAE therefore changes only Stage 1: the beta network learns nonlinear characteristic-to-loading relationships, and the factor side extracts latent factor returns from characteristic-managed portfolios.

This also locates the CAE relative to the time-series models of *Chapter 13*. Those models capture temporal patterns in realized return histories; the CAE captures cross-sectional structure at each point in time. Temporal features derived from *Chapter 13* models can enter the CAE as additional characteristics, but the CAE itself is not primarily a sequence model.

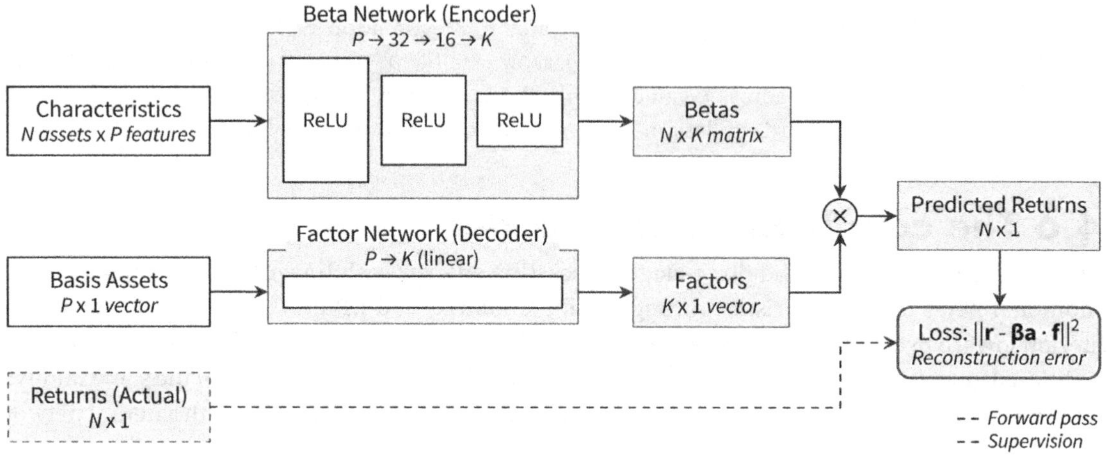

Figure 14.7: The conditional autoencoder. A beta network maps each asset's lagged characteristics to conditional factor loadings; a factor side extracts latent factor returns from characteristic-managed portfolios; their inner product reconstructs the contemporaneous cross-section

Preparing the characteristic panel

The `us_firm_characteristics` case study (*Section 14.1*) provides the main dataset. Custom panels should apply the same survivorship-bias-free, point-in-time requirements introduced in *Chapter 4*: characteristics must be observable before the return they explain or forecast, and universe membership must be defined without future information. The investable universe should be fixed before estimation, because microcap and illiquidity filters determine which firms contribute to the estimated factor structure and which premia the model can learn. Since characteristic-based predictability is often concentrated among smaller and less liquid firms, report results both with and without the smallest 20% of firms by market capitalization to separate tradable signal from microcap and liquidity artifacts.

The dataset used here contains 63 precomputed features: the 57 fundamental characteristics from *Section 14.5* plus six temporal features. The original CAE study uses a larger set, but the implementation logic is unchanged. Neural networks are sensitive to input scale, and firm characteristics often carry extreme outliers, so we rank stocks by each characteristic each month and rescale the ranks to $[-1,1]$. This cross-sectional transformation reduces the influence of outliers, makes characteristics comparable across units, and preserves the relative information available at each date.

Specifying the dual-network architecture

The CAE contains two linked components: a beta network and a factor side.

The **beta network** maps each stock's P lagged characteristics into K conditional factor loadings. In the PyTorch implementation, it is a feed-forward network with ReLU activations and batch normalization, typically pyramidal (for example, 64 → 32 → 16 → 8). For each date t, it produces an $N_t \times K$ matrix of conditional exposures:

$$B_t = g(Z_{t-1}; W)$$

where $Z_{t-1} \in \mathbb{R}^{N_t \times P}$ holds lagged characteristics for the N_t firms observed at date t.

The **factor side** estimates the latent factor returns used to reconstruct the cross-section. Let $r_t \in \mathbb{R}^{N_t}$ collect contemporaneous excess returns. The first step forms characteristic-managed portfolio returns by projecting realized returns on the lagged characteristic matrix:

$$x_t = (Z_{t-1}^{\top} Z_{t-1})^{-1} Z_{t-1}^{\top} r_t$$

where $x_t \in \mathbb{R}^P$ summarizes how the cross-section of returns loads on each characteristic at date t; a pseudo-inverse or regularized inverse replaces the inverse when $Z_{t-1}^{\top} Z_{t-1}$ is ill-conditioned. The resulting vector reads as returns on characteristic-managed basis portfolios. This is a cross-sectional projection rather than a univariate sort: the sorting interpretation is useful intuition, but the formal object is the projection coefficient vector x_t. A simple factor network, often a single linear layer, maps these managed-portfolio returns into K latent factor returns:

$$f_t = h(x_t; \Theta)$$

The beta network and factor side are estimated jointly so that the model reconstructs realized returns as:

$$\hat{r}_{i,t} = \beta_i\left(z_{i,t-1}; W\right)^{\top} f_t$$

This is the central difference between the CAE and a direct prediction network. The CAE does not map characteristics to next-period returns; it estimates a conditional factor representation and then uses it as input to a separate forecasting step.

Estimating the CAE

For each training window, the CAE minimizes the cross-sectional reconstruction loss:

$$\sum_{t,i} \left(r_{i,t} - \beta_i\left(z_{i,t-1}; W\right)^{\top} f_t\right)^2$$

with regularization and early stopping. This objective estimates the latent factor structure and should not be confused with the final forecasting objective. The implementation uses L1 regularization to encourage sparse weights and early stopping to limit overfitting. Deep networks are sensitive to random initialization, so the notebook trains an ensemble across seeds and averages the predictions; ensemble averaging reduces the variance of the fitted loading map and yields more stable downstream forecasts than a single initialization.

From the `us_firm_characteristics` case study, effective beta-network ranges are two to three hidden layers, widths from 32 to 128 in a pyramidal structure, learning rates from 10^{-4} to 10^{-2}, L1 regularization from 10^{-5} to 10^{-3}, and batch sizes of 1,000–5,000 observations, typically close to a full monthly cross-section. Dropout above 0.3 tends to underfit; below 0.05, overfitting becomes more likely. The factor network is simpler, usually a single linear layer. The identification caveats from *Section 14.5* apply here too: the number of latent factors K should be large enough to capture persistent cross-sectional structure but small enough to avoid redundant or unstable factors. Start with $K = 3$–10 for equity models; after applying the model's normalization conventions, highly correlated learned factors signal that K is too large or that regularization is too weak.

Turning latent factors into forecasts

After Stage 1 estimation, the CAE provides current conditional betas and a historical series of latent factor returns. Forward prediction requires the Stage 2 factor-premium forecast. The simplest rule uses the training-sample mean of each latent factor return, recovering the baseline GKX-style setup; AR(1), EWMA, Q-Boost, or ZS-Chronos replace only this factor-premium forecaster. Given a forecast $\hat{\lambda}_{t+1}$, the asset-level expected return is:

$$\hat{r}_{i,t+1} = \beta_i(z_{i,t}; W)^\top \hat{\lambda}_{t+1}$$

The decomposition is useful because the CAE estimates the cross-sectional structure, while the forecasting rule specifies how much compensation each latent factor is expected to earn in the next period. A CAE can reconstruct realized returns well and still forecast weakly if the extracted factors carry little persistent premium, which is why model selection rests on downstream forecast quality rather than reconstruction loss alone.

Tuning, validation, and failure modes

Reconstruction loss is an optimization diagnostic: it shows whether the model can fit the training cross-section, not that the learned factors earn stable out-of-sample premia. The validation protocol therefore evaluates the complete forecasting workflow. At each walk-forward origin, fit the characteristic transformation, CAE parameters, regularization choices, and factor-premium forecaster on the training window only; then freeze those components, generate forecasts for the next validation period, and evaluate the asset-level predictions. Compare configurations on validation IC, IC information ratio, quintile spreads, turnover, and portfolio-level performance, reserving reconstruction loss for diagnosing optimization failure or underfitting. Optuna's Bayesian optimization (*Section 12.4*) can explore the architecture and regularization space, using downstream validation IC or IC information ratio as the objective, with at least 50 trials to ensure a stable search.

The common failure modes are visible in the estimated factors, betas, and validation behavior. Diverging reconstruction loss usually indicates either too high a learning rate or insufficient gradient control; strong seed sensitivity argues for a larger ensemble; highly correlated latent factors point to an oversized K model or weak regularization; near-identical betas across assets indicate beta-network collapse, diagnosed by cross-sectional beta dispersion. Statistical performance must also withstand economic checks: a high-IC signal with high turnover may be untradeable after costs are deducted. Quintile spreads, turnover, and factor decay across horizons indicate whether predictability is economically meaningful, and gross and net performance should both be stated. A simple approximation is net return $\approx$ gross return $-2 \times$ turnover $\times$ one-way cost, with cost assumptions matched to the universe: 5–10 basis points one-way for large-cap equities, 50 or more for microcaps.

Empirical evidence and replication caveats

In the original GKX study of US equities, long-short portfolios built on CAE predictions outperformed linear IPCA benchmarks, with the gains driven by nonlinear interactions among firm characteristics. The economics are intuitive: the effect of momentum, value, size, volatility, or liquidity need not be additive or constant across the cross-section, and a neural loading map can represent interactions such as momentum behaving differently between high- and low-volatility stocks without the researcher pre-specifying those terms.

The gains are not mechanical, and our `us_firm_characteristics` implementation illustrates the difficulty of replication. On the primary one-month label, the CAE flips negative at −0.030 in IC, well below the supervised autoencoder treated in *Section 14.7*, a result not directly comparable to the predictive R^2 metrics reported by GKX. It still points to the same conclusion as the literature: latent-factor signals are modest in absolute terms and sensitive to sample period, universe definition, characteristic coverage, and validation design. The case study uses a shorter and more recent sample, a smaller universe, and fewer characteristics than the original, which likely accounts for much of the gap.

Neural factor loadings lack the eigenvector interpretation available for PCA. SHAP (*Section 11.4*) provides a partial diagnostic by attributing each asset's learned loadings to its input characteristics: a high loading on a learned factor may be associated with momentum and low volatility, while size contributes negatively; aggregating SHAP values across assets yields factor-level importance rankings. Two caveats are essential. SHAP explains how the fitted beta network uses characteristics; it does not prove those characteristics causally drive returns, and with correlated inputs the attribution can be unstable across samples. It is an interpretability diagnostic, not an independent validation of the economic mechanism.

Recent extensions modify Stage 1 while preserving the broader adapter. Self-attention lets the beta network condition each asset's loading on the broader cross-section, capturing sector, peer, and supply-chain relationships that per-asset feed-forward networks miss (Kelly et al., 2025), and text embeddings from earnings calls, filings, and news (*Chapter 10*) can enter as additional characteristics. In each case, the Stage 2 forecaster and Stage 3 asset map stay conceptually unchanged. Engel et al. (2025) push the idea further, using a CAE to extract latent factor portfolios and then training separate time-series models on each factor, with predictive uncertainty used to select the most forecastable factors for tangency-portfolio construction.

Implementation: `06_conditional_autoencoder` builds the full workflow in PyTorch: characteristic preprocessing, dual-network estimation, ensemble training, three Stage 2 forecasters (Constant, AR(1), EWMA), the Stage 3 asset map, SHAP interpretability, and beta-dispersion diagnostics.

14.7 The stochastic discount factor and the supervised autoencoder models

The adapter of *Section 14.5* separates factor estimation from factor-premium forecasting, and PCA, RP-PCA, IPCA, and the CAE all fit it: each estimates a factor representation that a Stage 2 model then forecasts. Two deep models break that pattern for opposite reasons. The **stochastic discount factor** (SDF; Chen, Pelger, and Zhu, 2021) collapses the stages by learning the pricing object directly from no-arbitrage conditions, leaving no factor-return history to hand to a separate forecaster. The **supervised autoencoder** (SAE) skips the structure altogether, mapping characteristics to forward returns end-to-end with no factor intermediate. They are grouped here by that shared trait: each bypasses the three-stage adapter, one because it prices directly and one because it predicts directly. This architecture is shown in *Figure 14.8*:

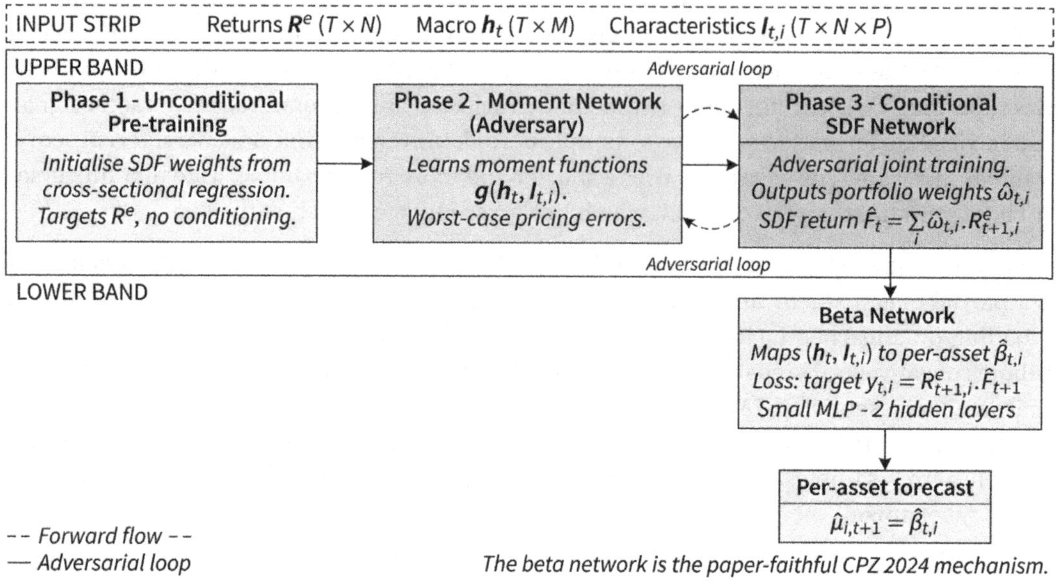

Figure 14.8: Where the SDF and the supervised autoencoder sit relative to the three-stage adapter

The SDF learns the pricing kernel directly from no-arbitrage moment conditions and emits pricing-error diagnostics rather than a factor-return history; the supervised autoencoder maps characteristics to forward returns end-to-end. Neither exposes a factor premium for a separate Stage 2 forecaster.

The stochastic discount factor

The Chen-Pelger-Zhu (CPZ, 2021) framework operationalizes the third objective introduced in *Section 14.1*: minimizing pricing errors directly through conditional moment restrictions. No-arbitrage is naturally written one step ahead. For gross returns $r_{i,t+1}$ the stochastic discount factor M_{t+1} satisfies $E_t[M_{t+1} r_{i,t+1}] = 1$, or equivalently $E_t[M_{t+1} r^e_{i,t+1}] = 0$ for excess returns. CPZ parameterize M_{t+1} with a flexible network of firm characteristics and macro-state variables, and estimate it by minimizing violations of these conditional moment restrictions. The output is a learned pricing kernel $\widehat{M}_t$ and the associated pricing-error diagnostics, not a factor-return history designed for a downstream premium forecaster, which is why the model has no natural Stage 2 hook.

Building the SDF with adversarial deep learning

The conditional moment set is effectively infinite, so evaluating every restriction is infeasible; the adversarial mechanism is how CPZ make the problem tractable. A second network learns to construct the worst-case test portfolio, the linear combination of assets that the current SDF estimate would most misprice. Training then alternates between two objectives. The SDF network updates to minimize pricing errors on the adversary's portfolio, and the adversary updates to find new portfolios the improved SDF still misprices. This minimax structure disciplines the SDF against the hardest cases rather than the average ones, the crucial difference from the CAE's average reconstruction loss. The `07_stochastic_discount_factor` notebook implements this as a three-phase training loop with configurable adversarial rounds.

The state variables enter through a recurrent macro encoder. A MacroLSTM learns a low-dimensional state from FRED indicators (yield spreads, inflation, volatility) so the kernel adapts to the regime without the researcher pre-specifying which macro variables matter, the time-series analog of letting the beta network discover characteristic interactions in the CAE.

Evaluation differs from the CAE because the object being estimated is different. Report the SDF-implied maximum Sharpe ratio, which the Hansen-Jagannathan bound ties to the magnitude of pricing errors; the pricing errors against benchmark factor models; and the worst-case adversarial portfolio at each step. One caveat warrants close attention: cross-sectional GMM can yield spuriously high fit through weighting-matrix choices when the model is misspecified (Gospodinov, Kan, and Robotti, 2014), so rerun under alternative weightings and across both fixed and adaptive test-asset sets. The teaching and case-study notebooks run these diagnostics by default. For comparability with the other model families, the case study selects the reported SDF checkpoint on the validation IC rather than the validation-Sharpe criterion used in the original CPZ protocol.

The supervised autoencoder

The supervised autoencoder is the other model outside the adapter, but it sits there as a practical benchmark rather than a structural asset-pricing object. It is the useful direct-prediction alternative when the goal is a strong tabular signal rather than a factor decomposition. An encoder compresses characteristics to a bottleneck, a decoder reconstructs the inputs as a regularizer, and a supervised prediction head maps the bottleneck to forward returns. The architecture is best known as the winning entry in the Jane Street-sponsored Kaggle market-prediction competition (2020–2021), which motivates its inclusion as a strong baseline; the chapter README links the original write-up.

There is no Stage 1/Stage 2/Stage 3 separation. The supervised loss shapes the bottleneck, and the prediction head is the asset mapper, so evaluation follows direct-prediction conventions, cross-sectional IC and AUC for directional labels, rather than the pricing-error or factor-premium diagnostics that suit the SDF. The contrast with the CAE is the point worth carrying forward: both compress characteristics through a network, but the CAE's bottleneck is a conditional factor structure disciplined by reconstruction, while the SAE's bottleneck is whatever representation best predicts the label. The first is interpretable as risk; the second is not, and is not meant to be.

Implementation:

- `07_stochastic_discount_factor` builds the adversarial SDF with MacroLSTM and three-phase minimax training on a top-200 US equities universe with eight characteristics
- `08_supervised_autoencoder` implements the supervised variant with purged cross-validation, performing direction classification (AUC scoring) with characteristic-reconstruction regularization; `ml4t.models.SAEModel` is the production form

14.8 Case study insights

Chapters 11 through *13* trained models directly on the forward-return label, from regularized linear regressions to gradient boosting and deep sequence networks. The latent-factor estimators reach the same cross-sectional ranking from the other side: they recover structure from the joint behavior of returns and characteristics with little or no return supervision, then score assets on it. The question here is whether that structure ranks assets as well as the supervised families already do.

Five of the nine case studies have cross-sections sufficiently balanced to fit the full latent menu: ETFs, the S&P 500 equity-and-options study, US Equities, US Firm Characteristics, and CME Futures. The five estimators differ in what they optimize: PCA takes the leading variance directions, IPCA fits conditional linear betas from characteristics, the conditional autoencoder (CAE) minimizes reconstruction error, the stochastic discount factor (SDF) targets a no-arbitrage pricing error, and the supervised autoencoder (SAE) adds a return-prediction task to the reconstruction.

Coverage is uneven: ETFs and the equity-and-options study run all five estimators; US Firm Characteristics drops PCA, because anonymized firm identifiers are not stable from month to month and break the balanced panel PCA requires; CME Futures runs PCA and the SDF, and US Equities runs PCA and IPCA. Each estimator is summarized by its average daily information coefficient (IC) and a 95% confidence interval computed with a HAC correction for the autocorrelation in the daily series; an interval that excludes zero is the bar for significant signal.

Where latent factors add ranking content

The strongest latent estimator clears zero on four of the five case studies (ETFs, US Firm Characteristics, CME Futures, and US Equities) and overlaps zero on the equity-and-options study. *Table 14.3* places each one beside the strongest model from *Chapters 11* through *13*. Neural objectives carry the latent result almost everywhere: the SDF leads on ETFs and CME Futures and the SAE on US Firm Characteristics, while IPCA, the conditional linear estimator, carries US Equities at a small but credibly positive value. PCA, the unconditioned baseline, reaches the highest latent IC on none of the five.

Case study	Horizon	Best latent model	Latent IC (t)	Strongest prior model	Prior IC	Δ IC
ETFs	21 days	SDF	+0.085 (4.9)	NLinear	+0.062	+0.023
US Firm Characteristics	1 month	SAE	+0.062 (5.5)	GBM	+0.080	-0.018
CME Futures	5 days	SDF	+0.037 (2.8)	GBM	+0.032	+0.005
S&P 500 Eq+Opt	5 days	SDF	+0.012 (0.7)	TabM	+0.011	+0.001
US Equities	1 day	IPCA	+0.005 (2.2)	GBM	+0.032	-0.027

Table 14.3: Highest-IC latent estimator at each case study's primary forward-return label, with its HAC t-statistic, beside the strongest supervised model from Chapters 11 through 13 (a regularized linear model, gradient boosting, TabM, or a deep sequence network). Δ IC is the latent point estimate minus that of the strongest prior model

Clearing zero is not the same as improving on the best model already in hand, and the Δ column shows the two apart. To compare each latent estimator directly against the strongest prior model, we compute the daily IC series difference on the dates they share and place a HAC interval around the mean difference, the paired counterpart of the single-model intervals in *Table 14.3*.

On this measure, the latent estimator credibly leads the strongest prior model on ETFs, where the SDF sits 0.023 above NLinear, and credibly trails on two case studies: US Equities, where IPCA sits 0.027 below gradient boosting, and US Firm Characteristics, where the SAE sits 0.019 below it. On CME Futures and the equity-and-options study, the latent point leads in expectation, but the interval spans zero. Latent factors therefore match or beat the strongest supervised family on three of the five case studies and credibly trail on two, a substantial showing for estimators that lean on structure rather than direct return supervision.

The equity-and-options study is the one case where the primary label hides the signal rather than lacking it. Every estimator overlaps zero at the 5-day return, but IPCA on the risk-adjusted 5-day label reaches +0.041 with an interval clear of zero, the only credibly nonzero latent point on that study.

Which objective extracts the signal

The estimator that does best is the one whose objective matches what the cross-section rewards, and the case studies do not agree on which that is. *Figure 14.9* sets the five estimators against the five case studies; conditioning and supervision help where unconditioned variance does not. PCA recovers the directions of largest return variance, which need not price the cross-section, and it ranks no case study best. The SDF and SAE, which add a pricing constraint or a prediction task on top of the factor structure, reach the highest latent IC on four of the five; IPCA's characteristic-conditioned betas carry the fifth.

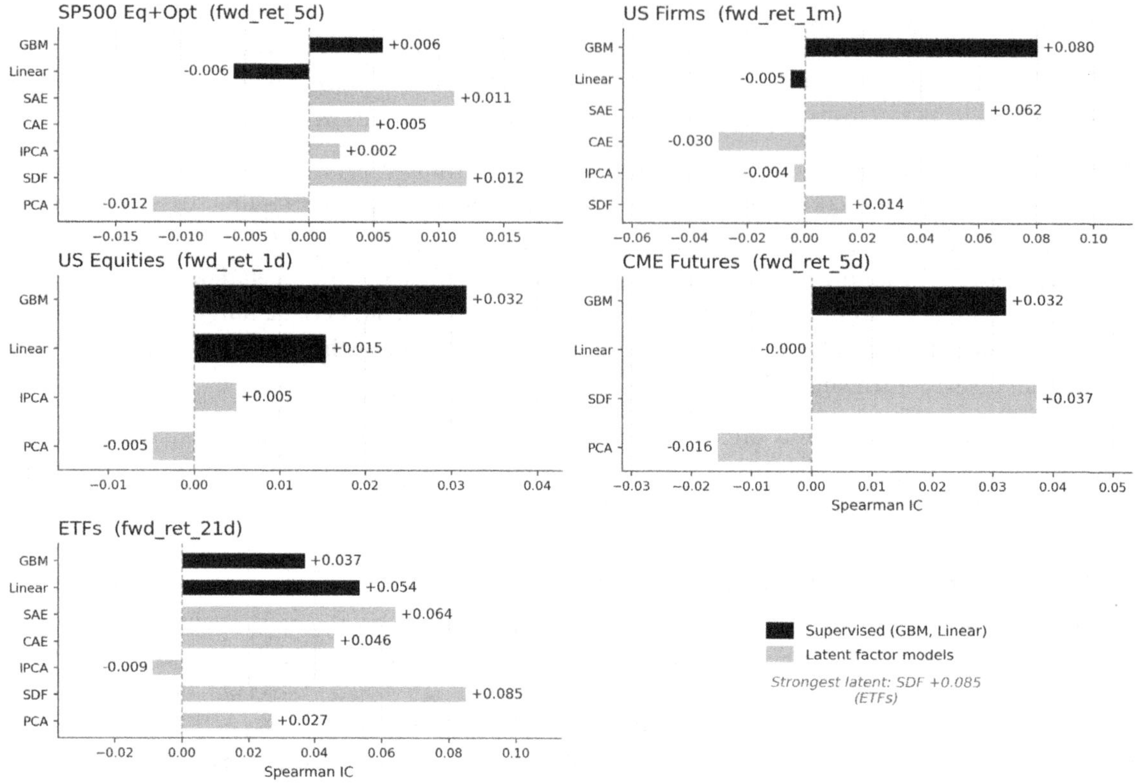

Figure 14.9: IC by latent estimator across the five case studies at the primary label. Shade encodes IC magnitude

US Firm Characteristics shows the spread most cleanly because it runs four objectives on a single monthly cross-section. At the one-month label, the SAE reaches +0.062 while the CAE lands at −0.030, with the SDF and IPCA bunched near zero between them (*Figure 14.10*). Both extremes clear their intervals and carry opposite signs: a multi-task objective that uses the return label yields a positive ranking, while a pure reconstruction objective, which fits contemporaneous factors with no forward target, points in the wrong direction. This is the prediction-protocol caveat from *Section 14.5*: contemporaneous-factor reconstruction is a poor proxy for one-step-ahead forecasting on monthly characteristics.

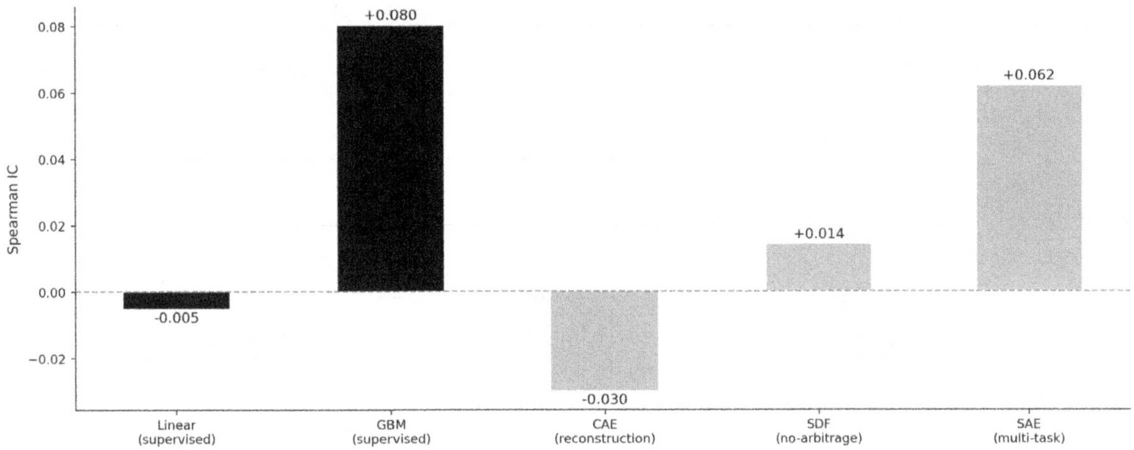

Figure 14.10: Objective ladder on US Firm Characteristics: SAE highest, CAE negative, SDF and IPCA near zero between them

Because the objectives capture different structure, their predictions disagree. Across the three neural estimators for US Firm Characteristics, the pairwise rank correlations have different signs, so the models are not near-duplicates of a single latent signal. That disagreement is the empirical opening for the multi-objective averaging *Chapter 20* builds on.

Dimensionality and stability

The latent estimators face markedly different estimation problems across the five case studies, and panel dimensionality accounts for much of the spread. CME Futures and ETFs sit in a favorable regime, with far more time periods than assets, so the signal eigenvalues cleanly separate from the noise floor predicted by random-matrix theory. US Equities and US Firm Characteristics are severely high-dimensional (US Firm Characteristics carries roughly nine times as many assets as time periods), where the sample return covariance is too noisy to invert directly. The estimators that still resolve a credible IC there, IPCA on US Equities and the SAE on US Firm Characteristics, both sidestep that covariance by mapping characteristics to factor loadings rather than estimating loadings from returns.

Stability over the walk-forward folds tracks the resolution of the label. *Figure 14.11* plots the per-fold ICs against their means; even the case studies whose intervals exclude zero with margin show wide fold-to-fold variation, which is why the HAC interval, not the point estimate, is the threshold throughout. The monthly US Firm Characteristics result, built on a structural cross-sectional edge, is positive on every fold; the daily US Equities result, built on a thin per-day edge, is positive on about three folds in five. The first is a small effect measured cleanly; the second a smaller effect measured against more noise.

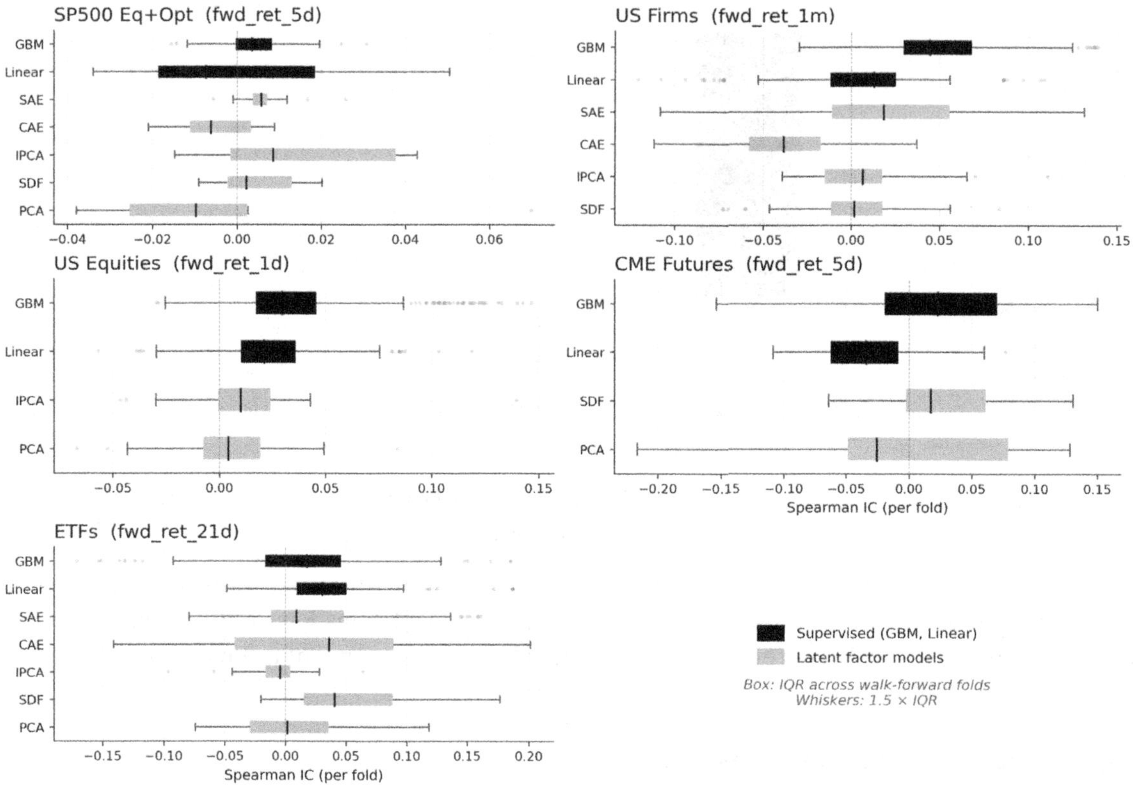

Figure 14.11: Per-fold IC distribution against fold means across the five case studies

Regression versus classification

Only US Firm Characteristics carries a classification label through the latent stack, the one-month direction label. Under the symmetric metric introduced in *Section 11.6* (IC for a regression score against the continuous return, AUC for a classifier against the binary direction), IPCA's continuous score reaches an IC of +0.010 against the realized return, a low-margin result whose interval spans zero. It neither confirms nor contradicts the ordering established by the regression labels, which remains the more informative reading for this monthly cross-section.

Choosing a method

These estimators are complements rather than substitutes. PCA focuses on risk decomposition, with its eigenportfolios supporting position sizing in *Chapter 17* and risk management in *Chapter 19*; IPCA, the CAE, the SDF, and the SAE add conditioning, non-linearity, a no-arbitrage discipline, and a supervised task. Estimating several under one walk-forward protocol, then reading agreement as a likely signal and divergence as model risk, is what carries forward.

The case studies where a latent estimator clears zero (ETFs, US Firm Characteristics, and CME Futures most clearly) take that ranking into *Chapters 16* through *19*, which weigh it against turnover and cost, while the disagreement measured here is what *Chapter 20* turns into a multi-objective ensemble.

14.9 Summary

The four latent-factor methods of this chapter share a common predictive workflow, the three-stage forecasting adapter. Stage 1 estimates a factor representation, Stage 2 forecasts the factor premium, and Stage 3 combines today's exposures with that forecast. RP-PCA, IPCA, and the CAE pass through the adapter as a matter of routine, and PCA can be wrapped in it for factor-timing. The four differ in Stage 1 alone: PCA maximizes covariance explained, RP-PCA adds a pricing-error penalty, IPCA estimates linear characteristic-conditioned betas, and the CAE generalizes that map nonlinearly.

The adversarial SDF and the supervised autoencoder sit outside the adapter. The SDF estimates a pricing kernel directly under no-arbitrage moment restrictions; the SAE predicts returns end-to-end and earns its place as a neural-network benchmark rather than a structural factor model. The `ml4t-models` library packages the adapter as a composable pipeline, while the chapter notebooks derive every stage from scratch.

Across the five case studies, the objective that matches what the cross-section rewards reaches the highest information coefficient, and the case studies disagree on which objective that is. The SDF reaches the highest latent IC on three of them, the supervised autoencoder on US Firm Characteristics, and IPCA on US Equities; unconditioned PCA leads on none. The clearest case is ETFs, where the SDF clears the HAC threshold with an IC of +0.085. The strongest latent estimator meets that threshold in four of the five case studies, overlapping zero only in the equity-and-options study.

Clearing zero is not the same as improving on the supervised families of *Chapters 11* through *13*. Compared with the strongest prior model on shared dates, the latent estimator matches or beats it in three case studies (credibly leading on ETFs and statistically indistinguishable on CME Futures and the equity-and-options study) and credibly trails in two, US Equities and US Firm Characteristics, where gradient boosting ranks clearly higher. That is a substantial showing for estimators that lean on structure rather than direct return supervision, though not a wholesale improvement over models that learn the label directly.

The practical lesson is that latent-factor models compete where the panel carries more periods than assets and genuine cross-sectional structure, fall behind where richly featured supervised models dominate, and stay useful as risk-decomposition tools regardless of predictive ranking (*Chapters 17* and *19*). *Chapter 15* moves from prediction to causal estimation; *Chapter 16* turns the predictions from *Chapters 11* through *14* into trading signals.

15

Causal Machine Learning

We introduced causal thinking as a falsification filter in *Chapter 7*: directed acyclic graphs (DAGs) to encode mechanism assumptions, the three structural roles of confounders, mediators, and colliders to guide conditioning decisions, and four plausibility checks to triage features before committing to heavier modeling. Those diagnostics are bivariate – they test one feature at a time and cannot detect multivariate confounding. This chapter provides the multivariate estimation machinery that the survivors require.

Feature-level triage asked whether a single feature's association with the label is consistent with a proposed mechanism. The methods here ask harder questions:

- What is the magnitude of a treatment effect after orthogonalizing against high-dimensional confounders?
- Did a discrete event actually move prices relative to a data-driven counterfactual?
- Which variables in a multivariate system cause which, and at what lags?

Each question demands a different estimator, and each estimator rests on assumptions that must be stated and tested. After completing this chapter, you will be able to:

- Define a **causal research question** in terms of treatment, outcome, estimand, and counterfactual, and use DAGs to justify an admissible adjustment set.
- Apply validation and refutation tools, including placebo tests, sensitivity analysis, and subset-stability checks, to assess whether a causal claim is robust enough to inform trading research.
- Use Double Machine Learning (DML) to **estimate causal effects of continuous treatments** in the presence of high-dimensional confounders, while respecting temporal cross-fitting and pre-treatment timing discipline.
- Use Bayesian Structural Time-Series (BSTS) to **estimate the impact of discrete events** by constructing data-driven counterfactuals and evaluating spillover risk in control series.
- **Use causal discovery methods** such as PCMCI, NOTEARS, and VAR-LiNGAM to generate candidate structures and interpret them as hypotheses requiring further validation rather than as definitive causal truth.

- Distinguish predictive signal from causal effect, and interpret cross-dataset evidence with attention to confounding bias, multiple testing, and the gap between statistical significance and refutation survival.

The chapter begins with the conceptual bridge from predictive features to causal estimands, then develops the identification framework in *Section 15.2* and the validation and refutation toolkit in *Section 15.3* that every causal claim must survive. *Section 15.4* applies Double Machine Learning to continuous treatment-effect estimation across the case studies, while *Section 15.5* shifts to discrete-event impact measurement using BSTS. *Section 15.6* reverses the direction of inquiry, using causal discovery algorithms to infer structure from data rather than imposing it. *Section 15.7* synthesizes the cross-dataset evidence, and *Section 15.8* distills the practical guidelines.

15.1 From theory to estimation

The conceptual toolkit from *Section 7.5* (DAGs, structural roles, mechanism plausibility checks) establishes *whether* a causal story is worth pursuing. This section bridges from that qualitative assessment to quantitative estimation: given a DAG and an identification strategy, how do we measure causal effects with valid uncertainty quantification?

The causal estimation challenge

Classical causal designs begin with a research design, not with an algorithm. They ask **what source of variation could identify the effect of interest:**

- Backdoor adjustment with observed controls
- An instrument that shifts treatment without directly affecting the outcome
- A before-and-after comparison with a credible control group
- A threshold that approximates random assignment
- A counterfactual path constructed from an untreated series

In each case, the central question is the same: *why should the observed data isolate the causal effect rather than reflect confounding, selection, anticipation, or spillover?*

In finance, these designs remain essential, but they are often difficult to apply cleanly. Confounders are numerous, nuisance relationships are nonlinear, effects vary across regimes, events propagate across assets, and treated units are often few. Machine learning helps estimate these **nuisance components** more flexibly, but it does not create identification where none exists. The methods in this chapter, therefore, combine causal design with modern predictive tools:

- **Double Machine Learning** (DML) for continuous treatments under backdoor-style adjustment
- **Bayesian Structural Time-Series** (BSTS) for event-level counterfactual construction
- **Causal discovery** methods for generating structural hypotheses when the graph is not known in advance

Before we make these design families concrete, we need to distinguish identification from estimation, and clarify where the chapter's three main methods fit.

Three estimation problems

The chapter is organized around **three distinct causal questions** within that broader design landscape, each requiring a different estimator:

1. Does momentum *cause* forward returns after controlling for volatility and regime? **DML** orthogonalizes the treatment against confounders using flexible ML models, yielding debiased effect estimates with valid confidence intervals.
2. How much did a Fed rate decision move bond ETF prices relative to what would have happened absent the announcement? **BSTS** constructs a synthetic counterfactual from the control series and measures the gap.
3. Which cross-asset return series actually drive others, and which merely co-move? **PCMCI** tests conditional independence at multiple lags, recovering a time-lagged causal graph; neural methods (NOTEARS, VAR-LiNGAM) scale discovery to higher dimensions.

Table 15.1 maps research questions to estimators and Python libraries.

DAG known?	Treatment type	Method	Library
Yes	Binary/Cont.	Backdoor adj.	DoWhy
Yes	Continuous	DML	EconML
Yes	Binary (event)	BSTS	tfp-causalimpact
No	N/A (discovery)	PCMCI	Tigramite
No	N/A (discovery)	NOTEARS	causal-learn
No	N/A (discovery)	VAR-LiNGAM	causal-learn

Table 15.1: Method selection guide, from research question to Python library

A sophisticated estimator cannot rescue an identification failure. The pipeline runs: DAG specification → adjustment-set identification → estimand derivation → ML-based estimation → refutation testing. *Section 15.2* covers the shared identification and validation framework that precedes all three estimation strategies; the method-specific sections that follow assume valid identification is in place.

The goal is not to prove causation from observational data but to distinguish robust claims from those that collapse under scrutiny. A key step in this regard is identifying the causal mechanism, to which we turn next.

Implementation: `01_library_overview` compares the libraries in *Table 15.1*.

15.2 Identification and validation

Causal estimation is only as credible as the design that supports it. Estimation asks how to compute an effect once the causal question has been defined. Identification asks the prior question: whether the effect can be learned from the available data under explicit assumptions.

This distinction matters in financial markets because prediction, correlation, and causation often point in different directions. A variable may predict returns because it captures risk, proxies for a hidden market state, is downstream of the outcome, or reflects a genuine causal mechanism. Causal analysis begins by separating these possibilities before fitting a model.

From outcome and intervention to estimand

Every causal question requires specifying what is being varied, what is being measured, and what comparison defines the effect. These choices should be made before fitting a model.

The **intervention**, or treatment, is the exposure whose effect we want to estimate. In markets, treatments are rarely interventions that a researcher can assign. They are usually events, rules, or shocks that approximate interventions: a change in index membership, a regulatory change, an earnings surprise, or a revision to a portfolio allocation rule. The *treatment definition* should specify the treated units, the timing of treatment, and the relevant treatment horizon.

The **outcome** is the variable whose response defines the question. It should match both the proposed mechanism and the decision problem. Depending on the application, the outcome may be a forward return, volatility, drawdown, liquidity measure, or risk exposure. Outcome choice is part of the research design because it defines the estimand and affects the plausibility of the identifying assumptions. A mechanism closely related to the outcome may support a more credible causal claim than a broad trading outcome that is influenced by many other forces. This does not make the broader outcome irrelevant; it means the causal claim is likely harder to defend.

The **estimand** is the causal quantity to be estimated. Common examples include:

- **Average Treatment Effect (ATE)**: the average effect across the target population
- **Average Treatment Effect on the Treated (ATT)**: the average effect for the units that actually received treatment, often the relevant estimand in event studies
- **Conditional Average Treatment Effect (CATE)**: the effect conditional on observed state variables, such as volatility regime, liquidity, or valuation conditions

The estimand also fixes the target population, treatment timing, outcome horizon, and comparison being made. For example, the effect of a funding-rate shock on next-period premium reversion is not the same estimand as the effect of the same shock on multi-day forward returns. The first asks whether the funding premium itself mean-reverts after the shock. The second asks whether that shock translates into a broader trading outcome after other return drivers have also acted.

Several closely related terms recur throughout the chapter and are easy to conflate. The following definitions are used consistently in the sections and notebooks that follow.

Term	Definition
ATE	Average marginal treatment effect across the target population, under the specified controls
Subgroup ATE	The ATE re-estimated within a stratum, such as a volatility regime
CATE	A covariate-conditional effect from a single heterogeneity model (causal forest, X-learner)

Term	Definition
Effect modifier	A variable along which the treatment effect is allowed to vary
Confounder (control)	A pre-treatment variable used for adjustment to block a backdoor path
Refutation	A diagnostic that can weaken a causal claim but cannot prove it

Table 15.2: Definitions for key terms

The distinction between a subgroup ATE and a CATE matters in practice. Splitting the sample by regime and re-estimating the ATE within each stratum yields subgroup ATEs; it does not fit a model of how the effect varies with covariates. A CATE requires a heterogeneity estimator that directly learns the effect surface. Likewise, a confounder and an effect modifier play different roles: a confounder is adjusted for to remove bias, whereas an effect modifier defines how the effect changes. Many estimators, including the double machine learning interface used later in this chapter, expose these two roles through separate arguments, and using the wrong one changes the quantity being estimated.

Several assumptions are required before an estimand can be interpreted causally:

- **Consistency** means that the observed outcome under the observed treatment corresponds to the relevant potential outcome
- **Overlap** means that the data support the comparison, so both treated and untreated observations are available for the relevant covariates
- **No interference**, or **Stable Unit Treatment Value Assumption (SUTVA)**, means that one unit's treatment does not change another unit's outcome
- **Conditional exchangeability** means that, after conditioning on an admissible set of pre-treatment variables, treatment assignment is as good as random with respect to the potential outcomes

These assumptions are **demanding in financial markets.** Prices aggregate information quickly, assets interact through common factors and portfolio flows, and treatment timing is often ambiguous. The point is not to pretend these assumptions are automatically satisfied. The point is to state the causal question precisely enough that the assumptions can be inspected.

Define the treatment, outcome, estimand, target population, and timing before fitting any model. Without this discipline, causal analysis degenerates into post-hoc rationalization, which is another form of the selection bias it aims to eliminate. We will use T to denote the treatment, Y the outcome, and W a set of pre-treatment covariates.

Directed acyclic graphs and adjustment sets

A directed acyclic graph, or DAG, makes the identification assumptions explicit. *Section 7.5* introduced confounders, mediators, and colliders as structural roles in a causal graph. Here, those roles become rules for deciding which variables belong in the adjustment set, a specific group of covariates conditioned on to estimate the causal effect of an intervention.

The central problem is confounding. A **confounder** is a common cause of treatment and outcome. If market stress affects both funding rates and future returns, then a raw association between funding rates and returns may partly reflect a common driver rather than a causal effect of funding rates. **Adjustment** aims to compare treated and untreated observations that are similar with respect to such common causes.

The **backdoor criterion** formalizes the conditions under which this comparison is valid. A set of variables W is an admissible adjustment set for the effect of T on Y if it blocks every noncausal path from T to Y that begins with an arrow into T, and if it contains no descendants of T. Under consistency, overlap, no interference, and conditional exchangeability given W, the interventional distribution for a discrete treatment can be written as:

$$P\big(Y = y \mid do(T = t)\big) = \sum_{w} P\,(Y = y \mid T = t, W = w)\,P(W = w)$$

For a continuous outcome, the same idea is often more useful in expectation form:

$$\mathbb{E}[Y \mid do(T = t)] = \sum_{w} \mathbb{E}\,[Y \mid T = t, W = w]\,P(W = w)$$

When W is continuous, the corresponding expression is:

$$\mathbb{E}[Y \mid do(T = t)] = \int \mathbb{E}[Y \mid T = t, W = w]\,dF_W(w)$$

Adjustment compares treated and untreated observations within strata of admissible covariates W, where the relevant backdoor paths have been blocked, and then averages those conditional comparisons over the population distribution of W. In words, it asks what the outcome would look like if everyone were set to treatment level t, while the distribution of pre-treatment covariates remained unchanged.

This expression defines the estimand implied by the DAG assumptions. Estimation methods differ in how they approximate the conditional expectation $\mathbb{E}[Y \mid T = t, W = w]$. Linear regression imposes a parametric form. Matching and weighting more directly approximate the comparison. Double machine learning uses flexible models for the nuisance functions. The identification question comes first in all cases: is W an admissible adjustment set?

The answer depends on **causal structure**, not predictive power. True confounders are good controls because conditioning on them blocks spurious association. Strong pre-treatment predictors of Y may also improve precision, provided they are not colliders, mediators, treatment descendants, or selection variables. By contrast, poor controls can worsen a causal estimate. Conditioning on a mediator removes part of the pathway through which treatment affects the outcome, thereby changing the estimand. Conditioning on a collider opens a noncausal path that was previously closed. Conditioning on a treatment descendant introduces post-treatment bias.

This is why **kitchen-sink regression is dangerous** in causal work. Adding more variables does not automatically make an estimate safer. It may do the opposite if some of those variables sit downstream of treatment or are common effects of treatment and outcome. The DAG determines which variables belong in the adjustment set. Statistical significance, feature importance, and predictive accuracy do not.

Timing discipline is the most practical screen in trading applications. Every control in W should be known before treatment is realized. Event studies should avoid variables that may react contemporaneously to the event, especially when macro announcements move broad markets immediately. Factor studies should avoid realized performance, portfolio outcomes, or variables mechanically constructed from future returns. This timing rule implements the requirement that the adjustment set contain no treatment descendants.

Timing discipline is necessary, but not sufficient. A variable observed before treatment can still be a collider, a selection variable, or a proxy for a conditioning event that changes the population being analyzed. For example, filtering on liquidity, analyst coverage, or fund flows may appear harmless because these variables are observed before the outcome horizon. Yet they can still create bias if they are common effects of prior performance, investor attention, and treatment exposure. The DAG remains the governing object.

This also clarifies the relationship to the simpler checks from *Section 7.5*. The timing placebo and shared-driver checks introduced there were informal, single-feature versions of the same logic. A feature that survives those checks has passed an initial plausibility screen. The adjustment-set problem asks the harder multivariate question: whether the apparent effect survives conditioning on a causally admissible set of pre-treatment confounders.

In practice, the DAG should be written down before the estimator is chosen. Libraries such as `DoWhy` make this discipline operational by requiring the researcher to specify the graph, declare the treatment and outcome, and identify the estimand implied by the assumptions. The software does not remove judgment; it exposes where judgment enters. If identification fails, the problem is not that the estimator is weak. The problem is that the research design has not justified a causal interpretation.

Once the DAG has been translated into an admissible adjustment set and an explicit estimand, the next question is whether adjustment on observed controls is credible. When important confounders may be unobserved, poorly measured, or impossible to condition on without introducing new bias, identification must come from a different source of variation.

Alternative identification designs

Backdoor adjustment identifies a causal effect by conditioning on observed confounders. When that strategy is not credible, the design problem changes. The question is no longer only which controls to include, but which source of variation can plausibly separate treatment from the factors that would otherwise confound the comparison.

Each alternative design uses a different comparison. Instrumental variables use variation in treatment induced by an external instrument. Difference-in-differences uses changes over time between treated and untreated groups. Regression discontinuity uses assignment rules near a threshold. Event-study counterfactual methods use pre-event dynamics and control series to estimate a no-event path. These designs differ in implementation, but they serve the same purpose: they replace broad unconfoundedness with a narrower assumption about the source of identifying variation.

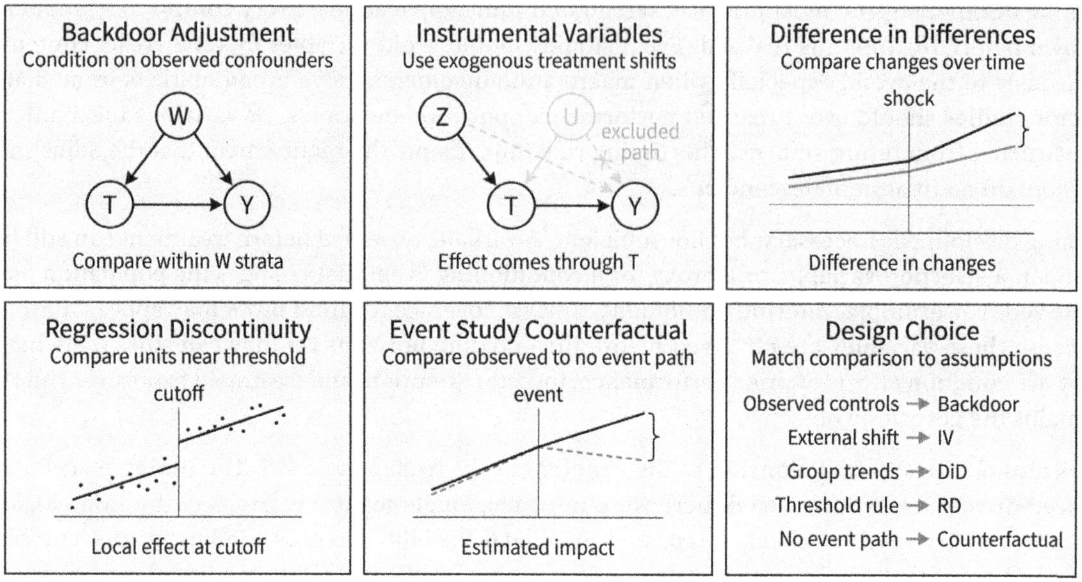

Figure 15.1: Alternative identification designs isolate causal effects using different comparisons

Instrumental variables

Instrumental variables use a variable Z that shifts treatment T but affects the outcome Y only through that treatment. The instrument must satisfy three conditions:

1. **Relevance** requires that Z meaningfully moves T.
2. **Independence** requires that Z is unrelated to the unobserved causes of Y.
3. **Exclusion** requires that Z has no direct path to Y except through T.

The exclusion restriction is usually the hardest condition to defend. A policy announcement, an index assignment rule, or a change in market structure may shift the treatment of interest, but it may also affect attention, liquidity, risk appetite, funding conditions, or other channels that directly influence the outcome. If those channels cannot be ruled out, the IV estimate should not be interpreted as the causal effect of T alone.

IV estimates also require careful interpretation. When treatment effects vary across units, the design often identifies a local effect for the units whose treatment status is shifted by the instrument, rather than an average effect for the entire population. This may still be the relevant estimand, but it should be stated explicitly. We do not implement IV estimation in this chapter; for applied work, the `linearmodels` library provides standard estimators.

Difference in differences

Difference in differences (**DiD**) identifies effects from differential changes over time. It compares treated and control units before and after an event, asking whether treated units changed more than comparable untreated units. The identifying assumption is that, absent treatment, the treated and control groups would have followed parallel trends.

A typical finance example is a short-selling ban that applies to one group of stocks but not to another. The relevant comparison is not simply whether treated stocks moved after the ban. The question is whether their returns, spreads, or volatility differed from those of a comparable control group exposed to the same broad market conditions.

The main threat is that treated and control assets may not share the same counterfactual trend. Sector shocks, time-varying betas, liquidity regimes, or macro news can all generate differential movements unrelated to the treatment. Pre-trend checks, narrow event windows, and economically justified controls can make the design more credible, but they do not prove parallel trends. In panel settings with staggered treatment timing, simple fixed-effects implementations also require care, as heterogeneous treatment effects can distort the resulting estimate.

Regression discontinuity

Regression discontinuity exploits treatment assignment rules with sharp thresholds. If units just above and just below a cutoff are otherwise comparable, the discontinuous change in treatment at the threshold can approximate local randomization.

In finance, thresholds arise in index inclusion rules, credit ratings, eligibility constraints, regulatory categories, and portfolio mandates. The identifying comparison is local: units close to the cutoff are compared with nearby units on the other side of the cutoff. The resulting estimate applies to the margin around the threshold, not necessarily to the full population.

The key assumption is continuity. In the absence of treatment, potential outcomes should evolve smoothly through the cutoff. Credibility is weakened if units can manipulate their position around the threshold, if other rules change at the same cutoff, or if too few observations lie near the boundary. RD can be highly persuasive when the assignment rule is transparent and difficult to manipulate, but its strength comes from its locality.

Event study counterfactuals

Event-study counterfactual methods identify effects by comparing the observed path after an event with an estimated no-event path. The source of the identified variation is event timing, combined with the assumption that pre-event dynamics and unaffected control series can predict what would have happened without the event.

BSTS, discussed in *Section 15.5*, implements this logic with a Bayesian time-series model. It estimates a counterfactual path from pre-event behavior and contemporaneous controls, then attributes the gap between the observed and counterfactual paths to the event. The design is synthetic-control-like because it uses control series to model the untreated trajectory, but it remains a model-based counterfactual rather than a randomized experiment.

The main threat is contamination. Controls must help predict the treated series while remaining unaffected by the event. This is difficult for macro events because the same announcement may move nearly all plausible control assets. For example, an unexpected Fed decision may affect a bond ETF, related rates instruments, credit spreads, equity indices, and risk sentiment at the same time. In such settings, the estimate should be interpreted as model-dependent and supported with placebo dates, alternative control sets, and sensitivity checks.

Choosing among designs

The right design is the one whose identifying variation is most credible for the question. Backdoor adjustment is appropriate when the main confounders are observed and can be conditioned on without introducing post-treatment or selection bias. IV is useful when an external source shifts treatment but does not otherwise affect the outcome. Difference-in-differences is appropriate when treated and control units plausibly share a counterfactual trend. Regression discontinuity is strongest when a threshold creates locally comparable treated and untreated units. Event-study counterfactuals are useful when the no-event path can be modeled from stable pre-event relationships and uncontaminated controls.

No design is automatically superior. Each exchanges one set of assumptions for another. The research task is to choose the comparison whose assumptions are most defensible, state the corresponding estimand, and then test whether the resulting claim is fragile under plausible perturbations.

15.3 Validation and refutation

Identification follows from assumptions. Validation asks whether the resulting claim is fragile, contradicted by placebo evidence, or dependent on implausibly strong relationships with omitted confounders. These checks do not prove causality. They test whether the design behaves as it should if the identifying assumptions are credible.

A useful validation workflow separates three questions:

- First, does the method detect effects where none should exist? This is the role of placebo and negative-control tests.
- Second, how much omitted confounding would be required to overturn the result? This is the role of sensitivity analysis.
- Third, does the estimated effect persist across reasonable samples, specifications, and outcome definitions? This is the role of stability checks.

Placebo and negative control tests

Placebo tests ask whether the pipeline produces an effect when the treatment, timing, or outcome should not generate one. A credible design should estimate near-zero effects in these settings. If placebo effects are large or frequent, the model is likely capturing confounding, leakage, overfitting, or contaminated controls.

A **placebo treatment** replaces the actual treatment with a randomized, shifted, or otherwise irrelevant treatment assignment. For example, an event-study pipeline can be rerun by moving event dates to periods when no event occurred. A backdoor adjustment design can be tested using a treatment variable that should not affect the outcome once the same controls are applied. The goal is not to obtain exactly zero in finite samples, but to verify that the method does not systematically discover effects where the design says none should exist.

A **placebo date** is especially useful for event studies. The same counterfactual model is applied to dates without the event. If the model repeatedly finds large effects on non-event dates, the estimated event effect may reflect model instability or contaminated controls rather than the event itself.

A **negative control** is an outcome that should not respond to the treatment. If the treatment appears to affect such an outcome, the result points to residual confounding, timing leakage, or misspecified adjustment. Negative-control outcomes are especially useful when the proposed mechanism is specific. They test whether the estimated effect appears only where the mechanism predicts it should appear.

Sensitivity to omitted confounding

Adjustment only addresses confounders that are measured and included in an admissible way. Even after careful DAG design, unobserved confounding may remain. Sensitivity analysis asks how strong an omitted confounder would need to be to materially change the conclusion.

A practical implementation perturbs the design by adding synthetic confounding, varying assumed confounder strength, or measuring how the estimate changes under alternative assumptions about hidden common causes. `DoWhy` supports refutation tests and sensitivity checks that probe this kind of robustness. These diagnostics do not prove that omitted confounding is absent. They quantify how dependent the conclusion is on the assumption that remaining confounding is limited.

The interpretation should be conservative. If a small omitted-confounder perturbation changes the sign, magnitude, or significance of the estimate, the result is not separable from the assumed confounder structure at the strengths tested. It should be treated as a hypothesis rather than as evidence for a causal effect. If the estimate remains stable under large and economically plausible perturbations, the claim becomes more credible, but still conditional on the design assumptions.

Stability across samples, specifications, and outcomes

Stability checks assess whether the estimated effect is specific to a single sample, model, or outcome definition. They are not substitutes for identification, but they reveal whether the claim depends on narrow modeling choices:

- **Subsample stability** checks whether the effect persists across time periods, regimes, assets, or market conditions. A funding-rate effect that appears only in one short volatility regime, for example, may still be real, but the estimand should then be described as regime-specific rather than general.
- **Specification stability** checks whether the effect survives reasonable alternative adjustment sets, nuisance-function models, or estimator choices. In DML, this includes varying the models used for the treatment and outcome nuisance functions. In event-study counterfactuals, it includes using alternative control series and model windows. A claim that depends on one narrow specification is weaker than a claim that survives a defensible range of specifications.
- **Outcome triangulation** assesses whether the pattern of effects aligns with the proposed mechanism. The same treatment need not affect every outcome in the same direction or with the same strength. A mechanism-near outcome may show a clearer effect than a broad trading outcome influenced by many other forces. The relevant question is whether the estimated effects appear where the mechanism predicts they should appear, weaken where the mechanism is indirect, and disappear for outcomes that should not respond.

Taken together, placebo tests, sensitivity analysis, and stability checks define the evidentiary status of the result. A claim that passes these checks is not proven causal. It is credible under the stated assumptions and tested perturbations. A claim that fails them should not be discarded automatically; rather, it should be downgraded from a causal conclusion to a research hypothesis that requires a stronger design.

Implementation: `02_dowhy_causal_graph` walks through the full validation workflow (DAG specification, identification, estimation with temporal splits, placebo and refutation checks) for the crypto funding-rate two-outcome contrast (premium reversion against forward returns). We develop the quantitative diagnostics in the next section.

15.4 Isolating factor effects with DML

Double/Debiased Machine Learning (**DML**) bridges modern machine learning and causal inference (Chernozhukov et al., 2018). It estimates the causal effect of a factor while controlling for many potential confounders, using flexible ML models for the nuisance components and a debiased score for the target parameter.

The *identification checklist* for DML, based on *Section 15.2*, reads as follows:

- Treatment T timing is fixed; covariates X are strictly pre-treatment
- Estimand declared (ATE, ATT, or CATE)
- Unconfoundedness argued: X blocks all backdoor paths from T to Y
- Cross-fitting respects time ordering (expanding or rolling windows, not random folds)
- Sensitivity analysis probes robustness to omitted confounders

The intuition behind double machine learning

DML estimates a *low-dimensional set of causal parameters* while using flexible machine learning models to capture the high-dimensional nuisance relationships among covariates, treatment, and outcome (Chernozhukov et al., 2018).

In this chapter, the relevant setting is a *backdoor-style design*: after specifying treatment T, outcome Y, and an admissible pre-treatment adjustment set X (the covariate set W from *Section 15.2*), DML estimates the effect of T on Y while allowing the relationships involving X to be nonlinear and high-dimensional.

In its most intuitive form, DML proceeds in three steps (see *Figure 15.2*):

1. **Predict the outcome from the controls.** Estimate the nuisance function $g(X) = \mathbb{E}[Y \mid X]$. This captures the part of the outcome predictable from the controls. The residual $\tilde{Y} = Y - \hat{g}(X)$ is the part of the outcome not explained by X.
2. **Predict the treatment from the controls.** Estimate the nuisance function $m(X) = \mathbb{E}[T \mid X]$. The residual $\tilde{T} = T - \hat{m}(X)$ is the part of the treatment not explained by X.

3. **Estimate the causal effect from the residualized variables.** Regress $\tilde{Y}$ on $\tilde{T}$. In the partially linear case, the slope from this final-stage regression is the DML estimate of the causal effect of T on Y.

This three-step workflow is the machine-learning analog of the **Frisch-Waugh-Lovell** logic from econometrics: remove the variation explained by admissible controls, then estimate the relationship in the remaining variation. It also generalizes the partial-IC idea from *Section 7.5*, in which known drivers were partialled out before examining the residual signal.

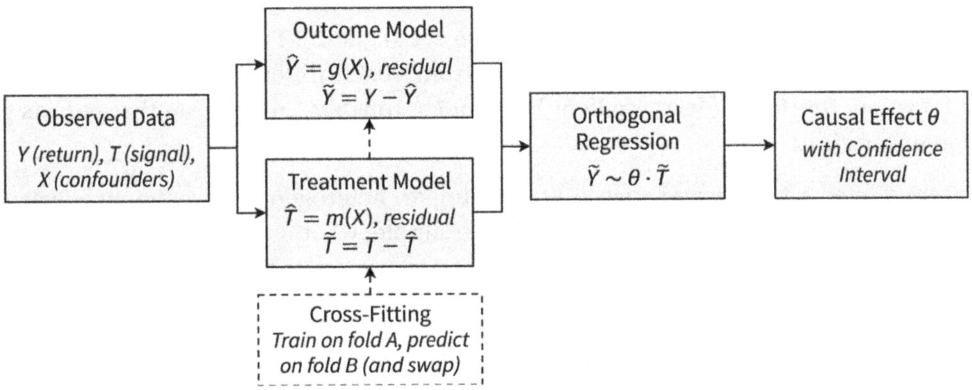

Figure 15.2: The Double ML workflow: orthogonalize both treatment and outcome against confounders, then regress the residuals

What makes DML statistically useful, however, is not residualization alone. The key idea is that DML uses an **orthogonal score**, meaning an estimating equation constructed so that small errors in the nuisance models have only a second-order effect on the target causal parameter. This makes it possible to use flexible machine learning models for the nuisance functions without letting regularization bias dominate inference on the treatment effect (Chernozhukov et al., 2018).

DML also uses **cross-fitting**. Nuisance models are trained on one fold and evaluated on another, so the same observations are not used for both learning the nuisance structure and scoring the causal effect. This reduces overfitting bias in the final estimate. For time-series data, cross-fitting must respect temporal ordering: use expanding or rolling windows rather than random folds, and include a temporal gap when needed to avoid leakage from overlapping forward returns.

This point is important for interpretation. The three-step residualization picture is the clearest intuition for the *partially linear ATE-style setup* used in this section. More general DML-style estimators extend the same logic to treatment effects on the treated and to heterogeneous treatment effects, but they do so using different orthogonal scores and specialized learners rather than a single generic regression recipe.

DML, therefore, depends on two ingredients:

1. **Credible identification**: the covariates (X) must form an admissible adjustment set under the causal design described in *Section 15.2*.

2. **Adequate nuisance estimation:** if the nuisance models (the ML models used in steps 1 and 2) are too weak, unstable, or poorly tuned, the resulting causal estimate may be noisy or fragile even when the design itself is sound.

For this reason, nuisance-model sensitivity is part of the empirical diagnosis: poorly specified nuisance models produce biased causal estimates. Mitigate nuisance-model dependence by using flexible learners (gradient boosting, random forests), tuning via cross-validation, and comparing estimates across at least two different model classes.

Large changes in the estimated effect across reasonable nuisance learners should be treated as evidence that the causal conclusion is unstable (Chernozhukov et al., 2018). The ETF momentum analysis in `03_econml_dml` illustrates this: the DML ATE ranges from -0.055 (linear nuisance) to -0.060 (shallow gradient boosting) to -0.088 (deep gradient boosting), a roughly $1.6\times$ spread that reflects genuine estimation uncertainty.

Beyond average effects, frameworks such as `EconML` support **heterogeneous treatment effects:** estimating how causal impacts vary across conditions (for example, whether momentum works differently in high- and low-volatility regimes). `EconML` provides metalearners and causal forests for this purpose.

A closely related application is *post-double-selection LASSO* for factor-zoo validation. Adapting Belloni, Chernozhukov, and Hansen (2014) following Feng, Giglio, and Xiu (2020), one tests whether candidate factors retain marginal pricing power after controlling for the existing factor zoo. Among the four managed-portfolio factors examined in `11_factor_zoo_validation`, only MeanRev clears the naive significance bar at $t \approx +2.6$; that signal collapses to insignificance once the first ten principal components of the asset universe are included as controls: the BCH/FGX correction substantively changes the inferential conclusion.

Implementation:

- `03_econml_dml`: DML for ETF momentum, manual and EconML implementations; nuisance-model sensitivity sweep across linear and gradient-boosting specifications; block-permutation refutation.
- `11_factor_zoo_validation`: post-double-selection LASSO applied to four managed-portfolio factors, with principal-component controls.

Measuring the causal impact of momentum

We apply DML to the ETF Rotational Momentum strategy to estimate the causal effect of momentum on forward returns, controlling for volatility and market regime, two confounders that affect both the treatment and the outcome.

The causal framework is:

- **Treatment (T):** Momentum score (risk-adjusted 6-month return)
- **Outcome (Y):** 21-day forward return
- **Confounders (X):** Realized volatility, yield curve regime

The naive approach (regressing returns on momentum) produces a biased estimate because volatility and regime affect both treatment and outcome.

Applied to ETF momentum data in `03_econml_dml` under a strict temporal train/test split, the naive OLS slope is -0.0385 with HAC-corrected 95% confidence interval $[-0.0484, -0.0285]$, a negative relationship consistent with reversal at the 21-day horizon. The HAC bandwidth matches the 21-day forward outcome, since overlapping returns induce autocorrelation that a shorter bandwidth would understate. After orthogonalization, the EconML DML estimate is -0.0537 with 95% confidence interval $[-0.0613, -0.0462]$, which excludes zero; a manual DML implementation with walk-forward cross-fitting agrees at -0.0494. The causal effect of momentum on forward returns becomes *more* negative once volatility and regime confounders are controlled for. The naive slope understates the DML magnitude by roughly 28%, so naive factor research misses part of the effect rather than overstating it. The confounders enter the estimator as controls used for residualization, not as effect modifiers, the distinction that separates a single average effect from a model of how the effect varies.

On crypto perpetual funding rates, the picture is reversed: in `04_dml_crypto_regime`, the naive and DML estimates keep the same sign, but confounders suppress roughly 90 percent of the effect magnitude, so the naive estimate captures only a fraction of the DML-estimated signal. A block-permutation test that shuffles treatment in seven-day blocks passes ($z = -4.1$), confirming the effect is distinguishable from placebo; shortening the blocks to one day inflates the statistic to $z = -6.2$, an illustration that too-short blocks understate the autocorrelation null. Neither estimate is statistically significant, however (naive $t = -0.44$, DML $t = -1.23$): even DML cannot guarantee robustness when the underlying signal is weak.

Confounders distort the naive estimate through two channels: high volatility weakens momentum signals and increases return dispersion, and regime transitions affect both the treatment and the outcome. In the crypto configuration, regime-stratified estimates remain directionally similar, and a single-model interaction test finds the high-vol versus low-vol difference statistically insignificant ($t = -0.63$, $p = 0.53$), so the dominant lesson is that the effect magnitude is confounded rather than that regime heterogeneity is strong.

When evaluating any factor, the workflow proceeds as follows:

1. Identify potential confounders based on domain knowledge.
2. Apply DML to estimate the causal effect after controlling for confounders.
3. Compare to the naive estimate to quantify confounding bias.
4. Examine confidence intervals to assess statistical certainty.
5. Test robustness using refutation tests (placebo treatments, random common causes, data subsets) and block-permutation tests.

A narrow confidence interval that excludes zero, combined with stable estimates in sensitivity analyses, provides stronger evidence of factor robustness than correlation-based approaches. Robust estimates change minimally when synthetic confounders are added or when the estimator is run on data subsets; fragile estimates flip sign under small perturbations. This qualitative difference determines which causal claims can support trading decisions.

Outcome choice shapes causal credibility

A key lesson from the crypto funding-rate analysis is that causal credibility depends not only on the treatment and estimator, but also on the outcome being analyzed. The same treatment can support a more or less plausible causal interpretation depending on whether the outcome is tightly connected to the proposed mechanism or exposed to many broader market forces.

We define the treatment as episodes of extremely high funding-rate premiums: observations where the funding-rate z-score exceeds 2. We then compare two outcomes: subsequent forward returns and subsequent premium reversion. These are related but distinct causal questions. Forward returns are a broad market outcome. Extreme funding rates may contain information about future returns, but the relationship is exposed to common drivers such as speculative demand, leverage, volatility, liquidity conditions, and market-wide risk appetite. These forces may influence both the treatment and the outcome, making the causal interpretation fragile.

Premium reversion is more closely tied to the institutional mechanism of perpetual futures. Funding is designed to help anchor the perpetual contract price to the spot price. When the perpetual trades at a large premium, positive funding makes long positions more expensive and short positions more attractive. This creates an incentive, subject to trading costs, liquidity, and limits to arbitrage, to sell the perpetual contract and buy the spot asset. The proposed treatment-outcome link is therefore narrower and easier to connect to an explicit market mechanism.

This does not mean that premium reversion is automatically causal. Because the treatment is defined by an extreme value of the same funding-rate process, subsequent reversion may partly reflect ordinary mean reversion after an extreme observation. The stronger claim is therefore not that premium reversion proves an arbitrage effect, but that it is a more mechanism-consistent outcome than broad forward returns.

`DoWhy`'s *refutation checks* help summarize this distinction. Here, we report two diagnostics derived from the refutation results:

1. **Out-of-sample drift** (OOS) measures how much the estimated effect changes when the model is refitted or evaluated across alternative sample splits; larger drift indicates lower stability.
2. **Placebo ratio** reports the share of placebo refutations in which the placebo estimate is large enough to challenge the original effect; a higher ratio suggests that comparable effects are easier to reproduce under falsified conditions.

These diagnostics do not establish identification and do not rule out omitted confounding. They provide narrower evidence: whether the estimate remains stable across resamples and whether similar effects appear under placebo treatments or outcomes.

Outcome	Mechanism	OOS Drift	Placebo Ratio
Forward returns	Broad market outcome exposed to sentiment, positioning, and risk appetite	85%	12.7%
Premium reversion	Mechanism-adjacent outcome linked to funding incentives and arbitrage pressure	51%	5.7%

Table 15.3: Refutation diagnostics for two outcome choices

The results are consistent with this interpretation. The forward-return estimate is substantially more fragile: its estimated effect changes more across out-of-sample configurations, and placebo tests more often produce effects resembling the original estimate. This is unsurprising for a broad market outcome. Extreme funding rates may predict returns, but the same latent forces that produce extreme funding may also drive subsequent returns. Unless these forces are adequately measured and adjusted for, the estimated effect remains vulnerable to confounding.

The premium-reversion estimate is less fragile, but not conclusive. Its lower OOS drift and placebo ratio suggest that the result is more stable and less easily reproduced under falsified conditions. This is consistent with the proposed mechanism: high funding premiums alter the relative attractiveness of long and short positions in the perpetual market and can create pressure for the premium to compress. At the same time, the remaining 51% drift is not small, and the outcome is mechanically close to the treatment definition. The evidence, therefore, supports a *cautious conclusion*: premium reversion is a more credible outcome for this causal question than forward returns, but the refutation checks do not by themselves prove a causal arbitrage effect.

The broader methodological lesson is that causal estimation should begin with the treatment-outcome pair, not the estimator. Before applying DML or any other causal method, ask whether the outcome is connected to a plausible, testable mechanism. A narrow, mechanism-consistent outcome is not automatically valid, and a broad market outcome is not automatically invalid. But broad outcomes usually require stronger assumptions, richer controls, and more careful sensitivity analysis. A simple estimator applied to a well-chosen outcome can support a more credible claim than a sophisticated estimator applied to an outcome only weakly connected to the treatment.

Implementation: `02_dowhy_causal_graph` shows the full two-outcome comparison, including sensitivity and placebo-refutation tests.

Regime-conditional position sizing – A case study

The preceding sections establish DML methodology. The case study tests whether the estimated causal effects translate into improved position sizing on out-of-sample data; see `05_momentum_causal_trading` for implementation details.

ETF rotational momentum (buying recent winners and selling losers) has historically generated positive returns. Standard implementations apply uniform position sizing regardless of regime. The CATE estimates from DML offer a candidate alternative: scale exposure by the regime-conditional causal strength of the signal.

To avoid in-sample overfitting, we implement a strict *temporal split*:

- Training period (2007-01 to 2022-11): Estimate all causal effects, learn regime scaling
- Test period (2022-12 to 2025-12): Apply learned scaling to held-out data
- No leakage: Regime thresholds, CATE estimates, and position rules are fixed before the test period begins

`CausalForestDML` from `EconML` is fit on training data with market volatility and the regime indicators as effect modifiers (EconML's `X` argument) and the volatility-horizon panel plus yield-curve slope as controls (EconML's `W` argument, which together with the effect modifiers form the adjustment set), using the same walk-forward folds as the LinearDML stage. The CATE varies in *sign* across regimes: $+0.019$ in low volatility, $+0.043$ in mid volatility, and -0.066 in high volatility. The ATE is -0.0097 with 95% CI $[-0.0138, -0.0055]$, against a naive OLS coefficient of -0.0037, a 61% bias once the controls are absorbed.

The sizing rule applies a regime multiplier to a gross-normalized portfolio weight. Let $w_{i,t}^{\text{base}}$ denote the long-short quintile weight for asset i at date t, rescaled so $\sum_i |w_{i,t}^{\text{base}}| = 1$. The regime-scaled weight is:

$$w_{i,t} = w_{i,t}^{\text{base}}\, s(r_t)$$

where $s(r_t)$ uses the signal-to-noise ratio CATE/std within each regime, clipped to $[0.5,1.5]$ so that imprecise estimates shrink toward neutral exposure. The resulting factors are 0.50 in high volatility, 1.09 in low volatility, and 1.28 in mid volatility: exposure is cut by half where the effect reverses sign and rises where the signal is both strong and precisely estimated.

The companion notebook compares three strategies during the test period:

1. **Naive:** Uniform momentum, no regime adjustment.
2. **Causal-Informed:** Scale by training-period CATE estimates, shrunk by their estimation uncertainty.
3. **Simple Heuristic:** Reduce exposure in high-vol (no causal machinery).

Results include transaction costs (10 basis points), with a sweep over the 5–20 basis-point range. Sharpe ratios are positive in training (Naive $+0.12$, Causal $+0.23$, Heuristic $+0.20$) and negative in holdout (Naive -0.18, Causal -0.05, Heuristic -0.11). Causal is the best of the three in holdout, but does not deliver positive risk-adjusted returns:

- Causal scaling reduces exposure in high volatility, where the training-period CATE was negative, and increases it in mid volatility, where the effect was largest and most precisely estimated. That heterogeneity partly persists, which is why the causal strategy degrades least.
- Momentum IC drops from $+0.023$ in training to -0.053 in holdout: the base signal inverts post-2022. No sizing rule rescues a treatment whose relationship to forward returns flips sign; the negative holdout Sharpes reflect that signal failure rather than a failure of the causal machinery.

Causal analysis reduces out-of-sample degradation when training-period heterogeneity carries information; it does not guarantee alpha when the underlying signal breaks down.

All estimates use only training data; the test period remains untouched. Cross-fitting uses walk-forward folds within training (no random folds). Regime classification uses pre-treatment volatility. Transaction costs are included. Results are sample-dependent and may not generalize.

The workflow differs from correlation-based analysis in two ways. First, CATE estimates measure the causal strength of momentum after controlling for the volatility and regime confounders, rather than the unconditional statistical correlation. Second, the test period is held out before any estimation choice is made, so the reported Sharpe ratios reflect post-decision behavior rather than in-sample fit.

DML handles continuous treatment effects: how a *dose* of factor exposure causally affects returns. Many financial questions instead involve discrete events: a specific Fed announcement, a regulatory change, a CEO departure. These require explicit counterfactual construction rather than averaging across treatment intensities, which we will discuss next.

15.5 Measuring event impact with Bayesian structural time-series

While DML addresses continuous treatment effects, many financial questions involve discrete events: Did the Fed's surprise rate hike affect bond prices? What was the impact of a CEO's departure on the stock? Bayesian Structural Time-Series (BSTS) models provide a rigorous framework for answering such questions by constructing data-driven counterfactuals (Brodersen et al., 2015).

The identification checklist for BSTS, applying *Section 15.2*, is:

- Estimand is the post-period counterfactual difference (ATT on the treated series)
- Control series selection rule defined; spillover risk assessed
- Pre-period relationship stability verified via fit diagnostics
- Placebo dates tested to validate model specification
- Robustness checked across alternative control sets

The intuition behind BSTS

BSTS constructs a counterfactual: a model of what the target series would have done in the absence of the event. The difference between the observed series and this "synthetic twin" is the estimated causal impact, illustrated by *Figure 15.3*.

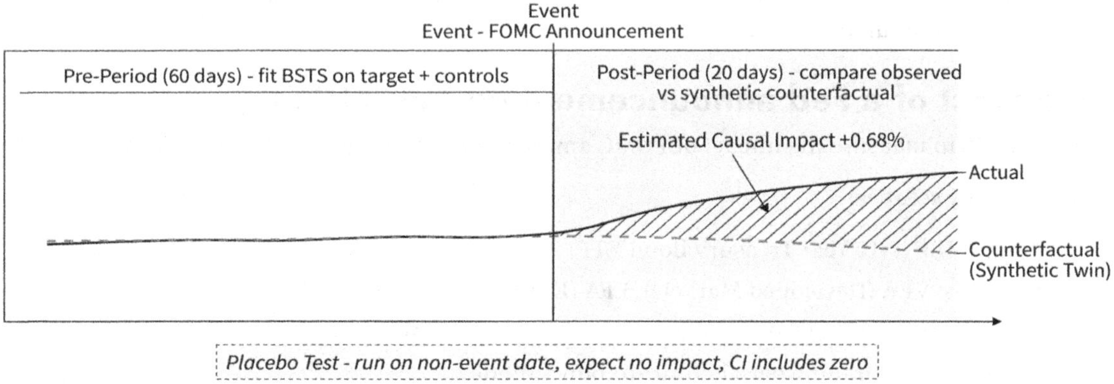

Figure 15.3: BSTS constructs a counterfactual from pre-event control relationships, then measures the gap between observed and projected series as the causal impact

The workflow involves three steps:

1. Learn target-control relationships in the pre-event period.
2. Project the counterfactual "business as usual" path using post-event control movements.

3. Take the difference between actual and counterfactual as the causal impact.

Bayesian methods provide posterior distributions with credible intervals. Unlike traditional event studies, which assume constant expected returns, BSTS adapts to changing market conditions through control series.

Two assumptions underlie BSTS event studies:

- **Stable relationships:** The target-control relationship learned in the pre-period must hold in the post-period, absent the event.
- **No spillover:** The event must not affect the control series. If a Federal Reserve Open Market Committee (FOMC) monetary policy announcement moves both IEF and SPY, using SPY as a control corrupts the counterfactual.

Spillover is the most common failure mode in financial event studies. Mitigate it by choosing controls from asset classes with weak fundamental linkages to the event (for example, agricultural commodities for banking regulation). A useful diagnostic is to run BSTS on an asset the analyst believes is unaffected: if it shows a "significant" effect, the control group is contaminated.

`06_fed_announcement_bsts` automates this by running BSTS with each control as the target; any control showing significant impact is flagged for exclusion. For macro events where truly unaffected controls may not exist, rely on placebo-date validation and robustness across alternative control sets rather than assuming the problem away.

These assumptions cannot be tested directly: they must be justified by domain knowledge and validated indirectly through placebo tests.

The original Google R package (Brodersen et al., 2015) uses Bayesian structural time-series. We use `tfcausalimpact`, the actively maintained TensorFlow-Probability port that computes posterior credible intervals for the cumulative event effect.

The impact of a Fed announcement on bond ETFs

We apply BSTS to measure the impact of FOMC announcements on the IEF Treasury bond ETF.

The event-study setup is:

- **Target:** IEF (7-10 Year Treasury Bond ETF)
- **Controls:** VEA (Developed Markets), EFA (EAFE), DBC (Commodities)
- **Event:** March 2023 FOMC announcement (25bp hike amid banking stress)
- **Pre-period:** 60 trading days before announcement
- **Post-period:** 20 trading days after announcement

The controls are correlated with bond prices through macro factors, but should not be directly affected by the FOMC decision.

Illustrative results

BSTS analysis of four FOMC announcements (March 2023, July 2023, November 2023, March 2024) in `06_fed_announcement_bsts` runs on log-price indexes anchored to the start of each window. Hence, the cumulative effect reads as a cumulative abnormal log return rather than a dollar quantity that depends on the ETF's price level. The estimated effects on IEF carry signs consistent with the macro context:

- The March 2023 announcement (a 25bp hike amid banking stress) produced a positive cumulative effect of +0.59 over the post-window, consistent with flight-to-quality demand for Treasuries.
- The July 2023 announcement (a 25bp hike in calmer conditions) produced a cumulative effect of −0.28: the same policy action, an opposite market response.
- The November 2023 hold and the March 2024 hold-with-revised-projections both produced negative cumulative effects (−0.09 and −0.29).

All four events have 95% credible intervals on the cumulative effect that exclude zero. Taken at face value, that would mean every announcement had a significant impact on IEF. The validation tests below show why the model in its current form does not support that reading.

Placebo test validation

We re-run the same BSTS specification on twelve trading days with no Fed announcement. A well-specified model should flag very few of these as "significant." In the companion notebook, seven of twelve placebo dates yield credible intervals that exclude zero, corresponding to a *placebo false-positive rate of* 58%. With only twelve placebo dates, this is a coarse estimate, and these dates are not screened against other macro releases such as CPI prints, payrolls, or Treasury refunding announcements, so the rate is illustrative rather than precise. Even so, the magnitude is large enough to indicate that the model finds "significant" effects on arbitrary non-event dates at over half the rate it finds them on FOMC dates. Under that condition, the apparent significance of the four FOMC events cannot be attributed to the announcements themselves.

The control-as-target spillover check uses BSTS to ask whether each control series shows a significant response on each FOMC date. Running the check per event, rather than assuming the verdict from a single date transfer, shows the contamination is pervasive: all three control ETFs (VEA, EFA, DBC) respond on the March 2023, November 2023, and March 2024 dates, and DBC alone responds in July 2023. A control is flagged solely when its own post-period cumulative-effect credible interval excludes zero. For macro events such as FOMC announcements, this is not surprising (the same policy shock propagates across global equities, developed-market bonds, and commodities through the dollar and global risk-appetite channels). Still, it means the counterfactual constructed from these controls absorbs the announcement effect rather than isolating it. The control set is the plausible choice, not an unaffected one; a more conservative design would use duration-matched non-US sovereign bonds or a local-level model with no cross-asset controls.

Taken together, the validation tests indicate that BSTS on log-price indexes with global cross-asset controls is not a credible event-study design for FOMC announcements. The four reported event impacts should not be read as each Fed announcement moving IEF by a known cumulative amount; the placebo and spillover checks reject the design before any individual finding can be taken seriously.

Posterior probability versus credible intervals

A common source of confusion is how different libraries report uncertainty. A true **posterior probability of a causal effect** is the integral of the posterior distribution above or below zero, a Bayesian tail probability over the parameter, not over time. The fraction of point-effect rows whose mean is positive is not such a probability; it is a sample frequency over the post-period that can be high or low for reasons unrelated to whether the effect is real. The reliable diagnostic is whether the **credible interval for the cumulative effect** excludes zero, supported by placebo tests with a low false-positive rate. When the placebo rate is high, neither the credible interval nor any derived sign frequency is trustworthy.

Both DML and BSTS require specifying the causal structure. When the structure is unknown, we turn to *causal discovery*: learning the DAG from data.

Implementation: `06_fed_announcement_bsts` covers the spillover diagnostics, the four-FOMC main analysis, and twelve placebo dates.

15.6 Causal discovery from observational data

The methods discussed so far (DML and BSTS) begin with a specified causal question: treatment, outcome, and identification strategy are declared in advance. **Causal discovery** addresses a different problem: when the structure is not known, can observational data suggest a plausible causal graph? In finance, the answer is only provisional. Discovery methods can generate hypotheses about lead-lag structure, indirect pathways, and candidate controls, but they do not convert observational market data into causal truth.

All causal discovery methods rely on strong assumptions. Depending on the method, these include some combination of:

- **Causal sufficiency**: There are no unobserved common causes
- **Faithfulness**: Observed independences reflect the graph rather than the exact cancellation of effects
- **Stationarity**: Structural stability over time

These assumptions are demanding in financial markets, where omitted macro drivers, regime changes, simultaneous feedback, and evolving market structure are common. For that reason, discovered edges should be treated as **hypotheses for validation** rather than as deployable trading signals (Spirtes, Glymour, and Scheines, 2000; Runge et al., 2019b).

Time-series discovery with Granger, PCMCI, and VAR-LiNGAM

A natural baseline is **Granger causality**. Granger asks whether past values of one series improve the prediction of another beyond that series' own history. This makes it intuitive and useful for preliminary screening. Still, it remains limited: standard implementations are often pairwise, typically linear, and do not by themselves distinguish direct effects from common drivers or indirect paths (Shojaie and Fox, 2022).

A more ambitious time-series method is **PCMCI**, implemented in the **Tigramite** library. PCMCI is designed for multivariate time series with autocorrelation and potentially nonlinear dependence. It proceeds in two stages, which also explain what the acronym stands for:

1. **PC (Peter and Clark) Phase:** This step uses a modified version of the PC algorithm to identify a "superset" of potential causal parents for each variable. It acts as a fast condition-selection step to reduce high dimensionality by filtering out irrelevant variables.
2. **MCI (Momentary Conditional Independence) Phase:** This second step performs more rigorous conditional independence tests to prune the remaining links. It specifically addresses the challenges of autocorrelation and time-delayed influences, which often cause standard methods to produce false positives.

This is more informative than pairwise Granger testing because it accounts for autocorrelation, indirect links, and common drivers, rather than testing each pair in isolation (Runge et al., 2019b). This distinction is important. PCMCI does not simply condition on all other variables. Its advantage is that it reduces the conditioning problem to relevant parent sets, which improves statistical power and tractability in sparse systems. The output is a **time-lagged graph of candidate dependencies** that can be interpreted causally only under the method's assumptions.

A second time-series causal discovery method is **VAR-LiNGAM** (Hyvärinen et al., 2010). VAR-LiNGAM combines vector autoregression (VAR) with the Linear Non-Gaussian Acyclic Model (LiNGAM) framework to estimate the lagged and contemporaneous causal structure within a linear, non-Gaussian model. Identification rests on the *assumptions* that:

- The structural errors are non-Gaussian
- Acyclicity of the contemporaneous structure
- The absence of hidden common causes

These are strong assumptions, but the non-Gaussianity requirement is often more plausible in finance than Gaussianity because returns, flows, and volatility measures frequently exhibit skewness and fat tails.

VAR-LiNGAM is therefore best understood as a **structured alternative to PCMCI** rather than as a universally stronger method. PCMCI is built around conditional independence testing in multivariate time series; VAR-LiNGAM is more model-based and derives its identification from distributional structure. When the two disagree, the disagreement usually indicates assumptions rather than evidence that one graph is simply correct.

Cross-sectional DAG learning with NOTEARS

NOTEARS addresses a different problem from PCMCI and VAR-LiNGAM. Its original contribution is to reformulate cross-sectional DAG learning as a continuous optimization problem subject to an exact, differentiable acyclicity constraint (Zheng et al., 2018). In its original form, NOTEARS is a linear structure-learning method that has since been extended.

That distinction matters because the appeal of NOTEARS is conceptual as much as practical. Classical DAG learning often involves combinatorial search over graph structures. NOTEARS replaces that discrete search with smooth constrained optimization. For an adjacency matrix W, the graph is acyclic if and only if:

$$h(W) = \text{tr}(e^{W \circ W}) - d = 0$$

where d is the number of variables and $\circ$ denotes the element-wise product. This constraint allows DAG learning to be cast as an optimization problem rather than a graph-search problem.

NOTEARS is most naturally applied to *cross-sectional or contemporaneous* structure, not to lagged time-series discovery. That is why it should be distinguished from PCMCI and VAR-LiNGAM. Later work extends the basic idea to *nonlinear and temporal settings,* but those extensions are separate developments. The core NOTEARS formulation should therefore be presented as a method for sparse DAG learning in a linear, contemporaneous setting (Zheng et al., 2018).

Empirical method comparison

These methods answer related but distinct questions:

- **Granger causality** is best viewed as a predictive screening tool
- **PCMCI** is a multivariate time-series discovery method that attempts to control for indirect paths and common drivers
- **VAR-LiNGAM** is a time-series method that exploits linear structure and non-Gaussian errors for identification
- **NOTEARS** is a cross-sectional or contemporaneous DAG-learning method based on differentiable optimization

This distinction helps explain why their outputs can diverge materially on the same financial universe.

All four methods are applied to a daily ETF panel spanning 2015–2024. The seven assets cover distinct market segments:

- **SPY** (S&P 500), **QQQ** (NASDAQ-100), **IWM** (Russell, 2000): US large-cap, tech-heavy, and small-cap equities
- **TLT**: Long-term US Treasuries
- **GLD**: Gold
- **EEM**: Emerging-market equities
- **XLF**: US financials sector

This mix includes assets with plausible lead-lag relationships (financials and broad equities) and macro-diversified pairs (bonds and gold) where temporal structure is less expected. *Table 15.4* compares the discovered structure:

Method	Result	Key Characteristics
Granger	26 FDR-significant edges	Pairwise only, ignores multivariate confounding
PCMCI	42 lagged links ($p < 0.05$)	Multivariate; conditions on other variables
NOTEARS	5 contemporaneous edges (all 5 stable under bootstrap)	Continuous optimization, cross-sectional sparsity
VAR-LiNGAM	1 lagged edge (causal-learn); 11 (from scratch)	Time series native, requires non-Gaussian residuals

Table 15.4: Causal discovery method comparison on daily ETF returns (7 assets, 2015–2024)

The spread from a single edge to 42 edges on identical data is the central lesson of this comparison. On daily financial returns, method outputs diverge materially because each method operationalizes different assumptions and responds differently to noise, dimensionality, and weak dependence. The four methods answer different questions and produce different graphs; the candidate causal structure is **assumption-sensitive.**

PCMCI discovers substantial temporal structure on the seven-asset panel, identifying 42 significant lagged links at $p < 0.05$ out of 147 possible (7 variables × 7 targets × 3 lags). XLF (financials) emerges as the dominant causal driver, with its one-day lag on SPY, QQQ, and EEM among the strongest links (absolute partial correlation greater than 0.10). Most of the 42 links, however, have small effect sizes (median absolute value ≈ 0.06), statistically distinguishable from zero but not necessarily economically meaningful.

This **contrast between statistical significance and effect size** is itself a useful lesson: practitioners should examine effect magnitudes, not just p-values, when deciding which edges warrant further investigation.

This result contrasts with the 4-asset analysis in `07_tigramite_time_series`, which finds zero significant lagged links among SPY, IEF (intermediate-term US Treasuries), GLD, and VIX. Block-bootstrap stability confirms the null: the most stable edge (IEF→VIX) appears in only 37% of resamples, below the 50% robustness threshold. The difference from the 7-asset VAR-LiNGAM result is not a contradiction: the 4-asset universe primarily comprises macro-diversified assets with little lead-lag structure at the daily frequency, whereas adding sector ETFs (especially XLF) introduces genuine temporal dependencies. The sensitivity to universe composition reinforces the need to interpret discovery results conditionally on the assets, frequency, and sample period used.

The VAR-LiNGAM row illustrates implementation sensitivity. VAR-LiNGAM is implemented twice on this panel: first from scratch (VAR via Ridge regression, then raw ICA on residuals) and then using the `causal-learn` library, which applies DirectLiNGAM (a more principled ordering algorithm) with statistical pruning. The from-scratch version finds 11 lagged edges; the library version retains only 1 (XLF→SPY). The same algorithm, under different estimation and pruning strategies, can produce radically different graphs. The shared edge (financials leading the broad market by one day) is the most robust signal precisely because it survives both implementations and is also the dominant driver in the PCMCI graph.

NOTEARS, applied to contemporaneous standardized returns rather than lagged links, recovers a sparse same-day structure of five edges, all of which survive in at least half of the block-bootstrap resamples. The strongest is SPY→QQQ, present in every resample, followed by IWM→SPY and IWM→XLF at above 80%. The edge XLF→SPY, stable in 69% of resamples, corroborates the financials-leading-the-market signal that PCMCI and VAR-LiNGAM also surface, here as a within-day rather than lagged relationship. Because NOTEARS targets cross-sectional sparsity, its graph is best read as a hypothesis about which assets share contemporaneous structural dependence, not as evidence of temporal lead-lag.

Granger causality finds 26 FDR-significant edges out of 42 directed pairs, comparable in density to PCMCI despite testing only pairwise. While Granger cannot distinguish direct from indirect effects, its agreement with PCMCI on the densest links (especially XLF→equity) provides additional evidence for the strongest signals. The practical implication is that edges confirmed by multiple methods carry more weight than those that depend on a specific specification.

Table 15.5 summarizes the typical use and the central limitation of each method.

Method	Typical use	Main strength	Key limitation
Granger causality	Preliminary time-series screening	Simple and intuitive	Pairwise and predictive rather than fully causal
PCMCI	Multivariate lagged discovery	Controls for autocorrelation and indirect links	Strong assumptions; can be conservative
VAR-LiNGAM	Temporal discovery with structural assumptions	Uses non-Gaussianity for identification	Linear model; assumes no hidden common causes
NOTEARS	Cross-sectional or contemporaneous DAG learning	Converts DAG search into continuous optimization	Original formulation is linear and not time-series specific

Table 15.5: Causal discovery methods and their typical use cases

Box 15.1: What the ADIA Lab challenge does and does not show

The ADIA Lab Causal Discovery Challenge is best read as a **benchmark for a special supervised setting**, not as evidence that causal discovery from observational data has been solved. Participants were given many synthetic datasets together with their true DAGs, and the organizers explicitly allowed either unsupervised discovery methods or supervised prediction models. The scoring rule then reduced each predicted graph to the local causal role of every node relative to a designated treatment X and outcome Y and evaluated multiclass balanced accuracy (Olivetti et al., 2026).

On this task, **supervised and hybrid methods dramatically outperformed** classical discovery baselines. That result is real, but its interpretation is narrow. The benchmark shows that when many labeled dataset-graph pairs are available from a stable simulator family, a supervised model can learn the mapping from statistical patterns to causal-role labels better than a stand-alone discovery algorithm. This is a legitimate result about amortized inference under a known synthetic regime, not a general result about causal discovery in realistic financial settings.

That distinction matters in finance. In practice, **researchers rarely have a labeled training set of true causal graphs,** and market data are shaped by latent confounding, structural breaks, simultaneity, equilibrium feedback, and endogenous sampling. For that reason, the ADIA result should not be read as "supervised causal discovery is the new default." Its real value is cautionary: benchmark success may reflect the structure of the benchmark itself more than transferable causal competence. Synthetic benchmarks can still be useful, especially as sandboxes for experimentation, but their outputs remain proposals to be validated rather than truths to be deployed (Reisach, Seiler, and Weichwald, 2021).

Implementation:

- `07_tigramite_time_series`: PCMCI on a four-asset macro panel (SPY, IEF, GLD, VIX); produces the null result discussed above.
- `08_neural_causal_discovery`: seven-asset daily ETF panel with PCMCI, NOTEARS, VAR-LiNGAM, and Granger causality side by side; produces the values in *Table 15.4*.
- `09_adia_causal_benchmark`: reproduces the ADIA Lab supervised-versus-unsupervised contrast in a simplified setting and shows how a supervised classifier exploits regularities in synthetic graph-generated data.

15.7 Case study causal evidence

Estimating one causal treatment effect per case study with Double Machine Learning applies a single identification standard to the cross-section of factor claims. Most primary-label effects turn out to be small once observed confounders are controlled for; the gap between the naive and orthogonalized coefficients is wide, and only a few estimates survive both credibility checks applied here. Each case study estimates one primary treatment (momentum on ETFs, US Equities, and FX; the funding-premium z-score on Crypto; an order-flow microstructure effect on the NASDAQ-100; the IV–RV spread on SP500 Eq+Opt; a monthly momentum factor on US Firms; carry on CME Futures; and the variance risk premium on SP500 Options) and reports the orthogonalized coefficient with heteroskedasticity- and autocorrelation-consistent (HAC) inference alongside a block-permutation refutation p-value. Two gates summarize each estimate at its primary label: HAC significance at $|t| > 1.96$, and a refutation pass at $p_{\text{ref}} < 0.05$. *Table 15.6* lists the results:

Case	Treatment	DML effect	t_{HAC}	HAC p	Bias	p_{ref}	Both gates
ETFs (21d)	momentum	-0.058	-9.84	<0.001	+33.2%	0.00	yes
US Firms (1m)	factor	+0.007	+1.98	0.048	+42.8%	0.03	yes
SP500 Options	VRP, HTM	-0.123	-4.69	<0.001	+49.8%	0.03	yes

Case	Treatment	DML effect	t_{HAC}	HAC p	Bias	p_{ref}	Both gates
US Equities (1d)	momentum	-0.001	-2.16	0.031	+68.8%	0.00	yes
NASDAQ-100 (15m)	microstructure	0.00	+2.52	0.012	-9.9%	0.11	HAC only
Crypto (8h)	premium z	-0.001	-1.03	0.303	+68.3%	0.00	refutation only
SP500 Eq+Opt (5d)	IV–RV spread	-0.002	-1.50	0.135	+86.5%	0.00	refutation only
FX Pairs (1d)	momentum	+0.0004	+0.42	0.675	-213.5%	0.30	neither
CME Futures (5d)	carry	+0.0003	+0.75	0.454	-59.7%	0.19	neither

Table 15.6: Primary-label DML estimate with HAC significance ($|t| > 1.96$) and a block-permutation refutation gate ($p_{\text{ref}} < 0.05$). Bias is $(\text{naive} - \text{DML})/|\text{DML}|$, signed: positive when the naive coefficient exceeds the DML estimate in signed terms, negative when it falls below. Where the effect is negative, this runs counter to a magnitude reading: a positive signed bias means the DML estimate is more negative than the naive estimate, so the naive coefficient understates the magnitude

These are conditional estimates under the stated causal models, not proof of causation: DML requires that all confounders be observed and that the nuisance models be well specified. A refutation pass strengthens the evidence but does not close the unconfoundedness gap.

The two gates

The two gates rarely agree. Four case studies clear both (ETFs, US Firms, SP500 Options, and US Equities), one clears HAC significance alone, the NASDAQ-100; two clear refutation alone, Crypto and SP500 Eq+Opt; and two clear neither, FX and CME Futures. *Figure 15.4* places each case study on the two axes.

The disagreement is informative because the gates probe different properties. Refutation asks whether the point estimate is distinguishable from a placebo-generated artifact under the chosen null; HAC significance asks whether it is distinguishable from zero under inference robust to heteroskedasticity and serial correlation. A treatment can pass one and fail the other. The NASDAQ-100 microstructure effect is significant under HAC inference yet does not separate from a placebo-permuted treatment, the pattern expected when autocorrelation or specification structure carries part of the apparent signal. Crypto and SP500 Eq+Opt show the reverse: both reproduce above the placebo background, but their HAC standard errors are wide enough that the estimate is not distinguishable from zero. Neither gate alone suffices.

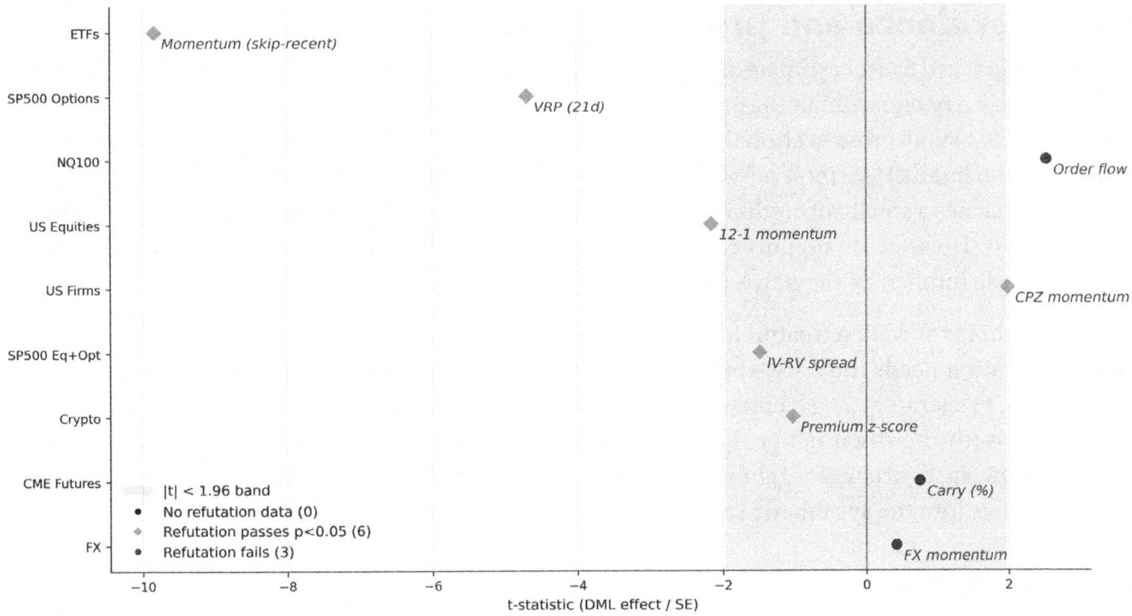

Figure 15.4: Causal credibility dashboard: refutation p-value versus HAC $|t|$ across the nine case studies, with the two gates ($p_{\text{ref}} < 0.05$ and $|t_{HAC}| > 1.96$) marked

Confounding bias

Orthogonalization moves the estimate substantially. The median absolute gap between the naive OLS coefficient and the DML estimate is 59.7% and exceeds 50% in five of the nine case studies. FX is the only case study where naive and DML disagree on sign, though with $t_{HAC} = +0.42$ and $p_{\text{ref}} = 0.30$ the reversed estimate is itself indistinguishable from noise. The implication reaches past these case studies: a factor evaluation that skips orthogonalization draws its conclusions from systematically distorted coefficients, which is how much of the backtesting literature reports factor premia.

Variation across horizons

Horizon and label specification move the causal estimate as much as they move the predictive IC of the same treatment. ETFs momentum is the clearest case. At the five-day horizon, the orthogonalized effect is positive and HAC-significant; at the 21-day horizon, it is negative and larger in magnitude (−0.058 against +0.025), and only the longer horizon clears both gates. SP500 Options reports five horizons, all negative, but only the hold-to-maturity return (the option held to expiry, abbreviated HTM in *Table 15.6*) clears both gates; the raw ten-day horizon is HAC-significant without refutation, and the shorter and delta-hedged variants carry intervals that overlap zero. The same sensitivity appears within US Firms, where winsorizing the monthly label raises the HAC t-statistic, but the estimate then fails to be refuted. The lesson from the predictive chapters carries over: label engineering is a first-order decision for the causal estimate, not a preprocessing detail.

Causal evidence and predictive signal

The orthogonalized causal estimate and the cross-sectional prediction signal are different objects, and a feature can carry one without the other. SP500 Eq+Opt is the clearest illustration: the predictive case study extracts a small cross-sectional IC from the IV–RV spread, while the causal estimate reproduces above placebo but its HAC interval overlaps zero. Crypto sits in the same cell: *Chapter 12*'s predictive case study reaches a small but credibly positive IC, while the causal premium-z estimate's HAC interval includes zero. These cases support continued predictive use of the feature without a causal claim of the magnitude implied by the naive coefficient.

The reverse holds as well. A treatment that clears both causal gates is not, on its own, a tradable signal: alpha generation needs the cross-sectional ranking machinery developed in *Chapters 11* through *14*, and *Chapter 16*'s strategy stack consumes predictions, not causal coefficients. The cross-case-study DML analysis (the per-treatment t_{HAC} and refutation distributions, and the bias decomposition) is assembled in `10_case_study_insights`. These findings distill into practical guidelines for incorporating causal analysis into the systematic trading research workflow.

15.8 Summary

The methods in this chapter (DML for continuous treatments, BSTS for discrete events, PCMCI and neural methods for structure discovery) share a discipline: make assumptions explicit, test them where possible, and know when conclusions are fragile. Method selection follows the assumption-fragility ordering: where a DAG and a valid adjustment set are defensible, DML estimates a continuous treatment effect with the strongest finite-sample guarantees; where the treatment is a discrete event, BSTS shifts the burden onto control-series stability and spillover testing; and where neither condition holds, PCMCI for time series or PC/NOTEARS/FCI for cross-sections generate candidate structures whose credibility scales with the strength of their stationarity and confounding assumptions.

The right method is the one whose assumptions best match the data and question, not the most sophisticated one available. DML with a well-specified DAG on a clean panel will produce more credible results than PCMCI applied to a short, noisy time series, even though PCMCI is technically more ambitious.

Causal effect estimates feed directly into downstream chapters: portfolio construction (*Chapter 17*) can weight factors by causal confidence, and risk management (*Chapter 19*) can account for effect uncertainty when sizing positions. The progression from *Section 7.5*'s single-feature plausibility checks through this chapter's multivariate estimation provides a complete pipeline: screen features cheaply, then invest in formal causal analysis for the survivors.

In the next chapter, we will move from machine learning to strategy development and introduce the historical simulation of trading strategies to evaluate how model outputs translate into entry and exit signals.

16

Strategy Simulation

The predictive models developed in earlier chapters produce forecasts: expected returns, scores, rankings, or directional signals. Those outputs acquire economic meaning only when they are translated into trades governed by explicit rules for timing, position sizing, cost, and accounting. Backtesting is the discipline that bridges this gap, turning a predictive claim into a falsifiable statement about realized portfolio behavior under a trading protocol.

That translation is consequential. A strong signal can disappear once fills are delayed, turnover is penalized, cash is tracked correctly, or a benchmark is included for comparison. Conversely, a modest signal can remain useful when the protocol is carefully specified and evaluated without optimistic shortcuts. This chapter, therefore, treats strategy simulation as a falsification exercise rather than as a search for the smoothest equity curve.

After completing this chapter, you will be able to:

- Formalize a backtest as an explicit trading protocol covering timing, execution, costs, sizing, data availability, and benchmark choice.
- Distinguish vectorized and event-driven engines in terms of assumptions, use cases, and parity requirements rather than caricaturing them as realistic or unrealistic by default.
- Build and interpret a simple non-ML ETF baseline to provide a concrete reference point for the methods in later chapters.
- Evaluate a strategy using the core reporting stack: gross and net performance, drawdowns, regime behavior, baseline comparisons, and cost survival.
- Apply strategy-level inference tools, including search-aware significance checks, before treating a selected Sharpe ratio as evidence of genuine skill.

We will begin with the falsification mindset and then specify the trading protocol that a credible backtest must declare. Next, we will distinguish between vectorized and event-driven backtesting in terms of representation and simulation semantics, including the practical execution choices that cause ostensibly similar backtests to diverge. We will develop an ETF baseline strategy, cover performance reporting and regime diagnostics, and close with strategy-level overfitting and multiple-testing controls. The summary then positions allocation, transaction costs, and risk overlays as the next layers of realism.

16.1 Backtesting as falsification

A common error in quantitative trading is overestimating the ability of a backtest to predict future strategy performance. A backtest is evidence to be considered, not a verdict. It is a historical simulation used to test whether a strategy survives realistic assumptions about data timing, execution, and costs. Bailey et al. (2015) show how easily selection effects can produce strong in-sample results that fail out of sample.

This framing changes the default interpretation of every equity curve. A good curve is not confirmation; it is a claim that now needs deliberate attempts to break it. López de Prado (2018) argues that the purpose of backtesting is to reject fragile ideas early, not to certify strategies that look good under one historical path.

The verification mindset asks whether performance looks attractive. The **falsification mindset** asks what would disprove the result. That shift forces three questions:

1. Is the signal genuine, or is it an artifact of leakage, data errors, or selection?
2. Is the execution model feasible at the assumed timing, liquidity, and market impact?
3. Is performance stable across regimes and small specification changes?

A strategy that cannot survive these questions is not ready for capital.

This perspective also changes how negative outcomes are treated. Failed tests are the main product of disciplined research. The faster a weak idea is falsified, the more resources remain for hypotheses that can survive scrutiny.

Failure modes and diagnostic design

Bailey et al. (2014a) describe recurrent sources of backtest failure, and each has a direct diagnostic implication.

Failure Mode	Description	Diagnostic Test
Lookahead bias	Using information unavailable at decision time	Walk-forward validation; point-in-time data audit
Survivorship bias	Testing only on assets that survived	Include delisted securities; verify universe construction
Data snooping	Selecting strategies that worked ex post	Deflated Sharpe Ratio; hold-out validation
Unrealistic execution	Assuming perfect fills at unrealistic prices	Slippage modeling; capacity analysis
Cost underestimation	Ignoring or minimizing trading frictions	Cost sensitivity analysis across realistic ranges
Regime fragility	Strategy works only under specific conditions	Regime-sliced performance diagnostics

Table 16.1: Backtest failure modes

ML workflows add **leakage channels** of their own. Common examples include fitting transformations to full samples, leaking future information through target construction, or using cross-validation splits that allow information to flow across folds. These are easy to miss because they often appear to be normal preprocessing.

White (2000) formalized data snooping as a **multiple-comparison problem**: when the same sample is used to evaluate many rules, models, or parameterizations, the selected winner can appear significant purely because it is the maximum of many noisy estimates. In trading applications, this means that the best reported Sharpe ratio is upward-biased when many effectively independent trials are searched.

Backtest frameworks and what they answer

Joubert et al. (2024a) distinguish **three simulation frameworks** with different inferential roles:

- **Walk-forward testing** preserves temporal ordering by training on a past window and testing on the next window as time advances. It is the most direct way to test implementable forecasting and execution logic, but its estimates can still be sample-specific.
- **Resampling methods** reuse historical data, often through block-bootstrap variants, to quantify uncertainty around performance statistics. They are useful for confidence intervals and robustness checks, but conclusions depend on the resampling assumptions used to preserve dependence structure.
- **Monte Carlo simulation** generates synthetic paths from an explicit data-generating model. This is valuable for stress analysis and edge-case exploration that may not be captured within finite historical windows. Its limitation is equally clear: results are only as credible as the structural assumptions behind the simulation engine.

A strong research process uses these frameworks as complements. Walk-forward establishes temporal plausibility, resampling characterizes uncertainty around observed outcomes, and Monte Carlo probes model-conditional stress behavior.

Practical workflow and decision standard

A practical **falsification workflow** starts by pre-specifying the claim and expected failure conditions, then mapping diagnostics to failure modes in signal quality, execution realism, cost assumptions, and capacity. Results are then interpreted with skepticism proportional to search breadth, and negative outcomes are recorded rather than discarded. Pre-specification is the anchor: without it, nearly any historical pattern can be rationalized post hoc.

Even with rigorous tests, the base-rate problem remains. If only a small fraction of candidate strategies has a true edge, false positives can rival or exceed true positives. In competitive markets, the prior belief regarding edge is plausibly low, so rejection standards should be stricter than most exploratory research practice would suggest. The implication is simple: the default posture is disbelief until evidence survives multiple, explicitly documented attempts at rejection.

16.2 Specifying your backtest protocol

A backtest is interpretable only after its trading protocol is fixed. The protocol states what information is available, when orders are generated, how fills are simulated, how positions are sized, which constraints bind, and how costs enter NAV. Two backtests of the same signal can reach different conclusions because they answer different protocol questions.

The protocol should be recorded before results are interpreted. At minimum, it must specify six components: signal timing, rebalance and holding rules, position sizing, fill assumptions, constraints, and costs. *Chapter 6* defines the setup-level configuration and validation split; here those choices become executable simulation semantics.

Signal generation timing

When does the signal become available relative to when trades execute? Common options include:

- **Close-to-next-open:** Signal computed on day t close prices; trades execute at day $t + 1$ open. This is conservative and realistic for most signals.
- **Close-to-close:** Signal computed on day t close; trades execute at day t close. This is only valid if the signal is computed before market close (for example, from intraday data).

Same-bar execution, where signal and execution occur at the same timestamp, is generally unrealistic. The rule is simple: the decision to trade, order placement, and fill are sequential events; assuming they occur simultaneously fuses past and future and, thus, introduces **lookahead bias.**

Strategy returns need to reflect order executions, not trade decisions. Deciding to enter at the close, and acting on this decision at the next ($t + 1$) open implies that the holding period return for a single-day position is:

$$r_{t+1} = \frac{P_{t+2}^{\text{open}} - P_{t+1}^{\text{open}}}{P_{t+1}^{\text{open}}}$$

This assumes entry at day $t + 1$ open and exit at day $t + 2$ open. For multi-day holds, adjust the exit price accordingly. The key point: signal computation (day t close) must be strictly separated from execution (day $t + 1$). Misspecifying this lag can dramatically inflate returns.

Score to signal conversion

Quantitative strategies often use continuous scores, whether based on custom metrics or ML predictions, and require an explicit conversion to an entry signal. Three common approaches trade off adaptiveness against complexity:

- **Fixed threshold:** Enter when the predicted score exceeds a static cutoff (for example, predicted return > 0). Simple and interpretable, but does not adapt to changing score distributions.
- **Rolling percentile:** Enter when the score exceeds its own recent distribution (for example, above the 90th percentile of the trailing 63-day window). Adapts to regime shifts, but higher turnover as the threshold moves.

- **Cross-sectional percentile:** At each rebalance, rank all assets and select the top N%. Controls position count exactly and ensures the portfolio is always invested, but ignores absolute signal strength.

The nature and calibration of the rules applied at this step significantly impact performance.

Rebalancing frequency and holding period

A rebalancing schedule needs to define the following items:

- **Frequency:** Daily, weekly, monthly, or event-driven rebalancing
- **Holding period:** Minimum time between entering and exiting a position
- **Calendar versus business days:** Whether schedules account for market holidays

A strategy designed for monthly rebalancing cannot be validated with daily returns unless the backtest enforces monthly position changes. Mixing frequencies—computing signals daily but rebalancing monthly—must be explicitly modeled.

The **rebalancing schedule** determines when the portfolio *can* change, but **exit rules** determine when individual positions *must* change before the next rebalance:

- **Strategic exits** include rules such as dropping a position when the signal weakens or a rank threshold is lost before the next rebalancing timestamp.
- **Protective exits** include stop-loss, trailing, and maximum-holding-period rules; see *Chapter 19* for risk overlays.

Position sizing

We will discuss common approaches to position sizing in the next chapter. The key categories for this section include:

- **Equal weight:** Each position receives $1/N$ of capital
- **Inverse volatility:** Position sizes inversely proportional to asset volatility

Here, the goal is to isolate the effects of signal quality from those of portfolio construction.

Futures require additional protocol detail. Position size is not shares times price, but contracts times notional value, where notional equals price times the contract multiplier. That multiplier also converts price moves into realized PnL, so omitting it can misstate profits and losses by orders of magnitude.

Order types and fill assumptions

We introduced different order types and motivations for using them in *Chapter 3*, and we will discuss strategies to manage execution cost in more detail in *Chapter 18*. For now, we consider these options:

- **Market orders at open/close:** Assume execution at the official price
- **Limit orders:** Require a fill model (partial fills, queue position)
- **VWAP/TWAP:** Assume execution at time-weighted or volume-weighted average price

Market order fills at the open or close are the simplest assumption, but can be optimistic for large positions. Conservative implementation assumptions and explicit documentation of fill logic are therefore part of the protocol, not an optional detail.

Constraints

Constraints determine not only which portfolio is desired but also which trades are actually admissible. Key constraints include:

- **Leverage limit:** Maximum gross exposure (for example, 100% = no leverage)
- **Short selling:** Whether shorting is permitted, the borrowing costs, and the availability
- **Minimum position size:** Regulatory or practical minimums
- **Sector/country limits:** Limits on the portfolio share in certain categories
- **Cash buffer:** Minimum cash held for redemptions or margin
- **Corporate actions:** How splits, dividends, delistings, and symbol changes are handled; use adjusted prices and include delisting returns

A constraint that is checked after returns are computed was not simulated. In practice, constraints interact with sizing, fill assumptions, and cost modeling. *Chapter 17* discusses constraints from a portfolio allocation perspective, and *Chapter 19* discusses them through a risk lens.

Cost model

Transaction costs are the largest source of backtest-to-live performance decay; *Chapter 18* discusses estimating costs in detail. The cost model must include:

- **Commissions and fees:** Broker commissions, exchange fees, and regulatory fees; vary by broker and order type and may be measured in monetary units or percentage terms.
- **Bid-ask spread:** The spread represents an immediate cost for market orders.
- **Market impact:** Large orders move prices against the trader. *Chapter 18* covers detailed market impact models.
- **Slippage:** The difference between expected and realized price due to delays, partial fills, or market impact.

In this chapter, we focus on testing performance robustness to cost assumptions; *Chapter 18* addresses estimating and refining the cost model itself.

Testing sensitivity to cost assumptions

Cost parameters beyond fees and commissions are estimates. **Sensitivity analysis** varies spread, slippage, commissions, and impact across plausible ranges, then reports break-even levels for Sharpe and net return. The question is whether profitability survives realistic costs. In practice, the procedure is straightforward:

1. Define a conservative grid for the main frictions.
2. Then, run the strategy across that grid, and identify the break-even region where net Sharpe or net return turns negative.

3. Finally, compare that break-even region with the realistic execution costs for the market and trading style under study.

If the strategy only works in the optimistic corner of the grid, the signal has not survived validation.

The thinner the edge of your strategy, the more important sensitivity becomes. If unsure about costs, use conservative estimates. It is better to reject a profitable strategy than to implement an unprofitable one. Document the cost assumptions that would make the strategy unprofitable because it defines the operational requirements for live trading.

Implementation:

- `01_backtest_first_principles.py` builds a complete ETF momentum backtest from scratch, making every protocol decision explicit.
- `02_futures_backtesting.py` illustrates how contract multipliers, per-contract fees, and session conventions affect the simulation contract.
- `08_signal_method_comparison.py` compares turnover, signal frequency, and risk-adjusted returns across all three score-to-signal methods.

The next section shows how backtesting engines differ in how they encode this trading flow and these constraints, and how this can affect measured performance.

16.3 Vectorized and event-driven backtesting

Backtesting engines differ less by programming style than by the **simulation semantics** they encode. A strategy can often be represented as timestamp-aligned arrays of signals, target weights, and returns. It can also be represented as a sequential process in which the engine observes market data, updates portfolio state, generates orders, processes fills, applies costs, and advances to the next bar.

Both representations can be correct. Both can also be misleading. The distinction that matters is not whether the implementation uses NumPy arrays or a loop internally. The distinction is whether the trading protocol is naturally a static array transformation or a state-transition system:

- In a **vectorized backtest**, you specify the inputs needed to compute the portfolio path in array form: signals, tradable universe, rebalance dates, and cost formulas. The backtest then evaluates the implied portfolio returns under a timing convention.
- In an **event-driven backtest**, you specify how the strategy behaves as the simulation unfolds. The engine maintains portfolio state: cash, positions, open orders, realized and unrealized PnL, margin usage, borrow constraints, risk flags, and possibly order history. Each bar updates that state, and the next action depends on the state produced by earlier actions.

The practical questions are therefore: Can the full trading protocol be expressed as timestamped signals, target exposures, and cost formulas without changing the strategy's meaning? Or does the strategy require an explicit simulation of orders, fills, cash, positions, and risk state?

That question is more useful than a generic preference for "fast vectorized research" or "realistic event-driven research." Vectorized backtests are not inherently naive, and event-driven backtests are not inherently realistic. Each is only as credible as the protocol it implements.

How vectorized backtesting works

A vectorized backtest treats the portfolio path as a transformation of aligned data arrays. The core inputs are usually:

- A price or return matrix
- A tradable-universe mask
- A signal or score matrix
- A rebalance schedule
- A target-weight or target-position matrix
- A transaction-cost model applied to changes in exposure

For example, a monthly long-short equity strategy can often be described in this form. At each rebalance date, rank stocks by a lagged signal, select the top and bottom quantiles, assign equal or volatility-scaled weights, apply turnover costs, and compound the resulting portfolio returns. The simulation does not need to know about individual order objects if the intended protocol is genuinely "rebalance to these weights at this price using this cost assumption."

The advantage is **computational efficiency**. Array-based research scales well across large universes, long histories, and many variants of the same idea, since NumPy arrays are usually much faster than Python loops. It is often the right tool for answering early research questions:

- Does the signal have any economically meaningful effect after plausible costs?
- Is performance robust across parameter values?
- Is the result concentrated in a small subset of assets or dates?
- Does the strategy survive different ranking, weighting, or rebalance rules?

The limitation is that many execution details must be compressed array transformations. A turnover penalty may approximate transaction costs, but it does not by itself model order rejection, partial fills, cash release, integer shares, short-sale constraints, borrow availability, or intrabar stop behavior. That compression is acceptable when those details are immaterial to the claim. It is dangerous when they determine the result.

The main failure mode of vectorized research is **semantic drift**: the arrays no longer correspond to a feasible trading protocol. Common examples include same-bar execution from close-to-close signals, implicit trading in assets with missing bars, forward-filled prices that create artificial tradability, target weights that ignore cash constraints, or cost formulas that penalize turnover without checking whether the trade could have been financed.

How event-driven backtesting works

An event-driven backtest models trading as a sequence of state updates. At each timestep, the engine performs some version of the following loop:

1. Ingest the next market event.
2. Update prices, valuations, and portfolio state.

3. Process open orders according to the fill model.
4. Apply commissions, slippage, and other cost components.
5. Call the strategy logic and create, modify, cancel, or defer orders.
6. Advance the simulation clock.

This is the natural representation when the strategy's next action depends on earlier simulated outcomes. The **relevant state** is not merely the signal value at time t, but the entire simulated trading context: current holdings, cash, unsettled orders, realized PnL, drawdown, margin, short exposure, and any risk flags triggered earlier in the run. Examples include:

- A drawdown circuit breaker that reduces exposure after the realized equity curve breaches a threshold
- A Kelly-style sizing rule that updates capital-at-risk based on realized gains and losses
- A stop-loss or trailing-stop rule that adjusts based on the path after entry
- A multi-leg strategy where the second leg depends on whether the first leg filled
- A futures strategy whose contract roll, margin usage, and available capital interact

The benefit is not that event-driven simulation automatically matches live trading. Bar data still hides the order book, queue position, intrabar path, and market impact unless these are modeled separately. The benefit is that event-driven simulation exposes the state variables and transition rules that the strategy actually uses. This makes the protocol inspectable.

The cost is complexity. Event-driven systems require more assumptions, more bookkeeping, and more validation. Defaults matter: when orders are evaluated, the price they are filled at, whether exits are processed before entries, whether cash is released immediately, how fractional shares are handled, how shorts are financed, and how missing data is treated. A poorly specified event-driven backtest can be less reliable than a disciplined vectorized one.

How to select a backtest methodology

Use a vectorized backtest when the portfolio path can be computed from timestamped signals, target exposures, rebalance dates, and explicit cost formulas without changing the strategy's meaning. Use an event-driven backtest when strategy behavior depends on simulated state that only materializes during the course of the simulations: fills, cash, margin, rejected orders, inventory, stops, drawdowns, or pending orders.

The distinction is semantic, not aesthetic. A vectorized backtest can be valid when the protocol is weight-based and path independent. An event-driven backtest can be invalid if its fill timing, cash accounting, or missing-data policy is wrong. The simulator is credible only when its state variables match the trading protocol.

How simulation semantics control results

Even when the same strategy can be implemented in both styles, different engines may produce different results because they encode different execution semantics. This is why comparisons among tools such as vectorBT, Zipline, backtrader, Lean, and `ml4t-backtest` are useful, but they should not be framed as a brand ranking. They reveal which assumptions control the result.

Simulation choice	Why it matters
Signal-to-fill timing	Same-bar close, next-bar open, and next-bar close imply different information sets and different look-ahead risks.
Fill price basis	Open, close, midpoint, stop, limit, and slippage-adjusted prices change both PnLn and trade feasibility.
Order sequencing	Processing sells before buys can release cash; processing buys first can cause rejection or resizing.
Target-weight translation	Target weights must be converted into orders using a portfolio value convention, which may be frozen or updated during the rebalance.
Cash accounting	Engines differ in how they handle cash release, unsettled proceeds, commissions, short sale proceeds, and margin requirements.
Fractional versus integer shares	Rounding creates residual cash, allocation drift, and sometimes small unintended trades.
Insufficient-cash behavior	Orders may be rejected, resized, partially filled, or allowed through margin. Each choice changes the path.
Short-sale rules	Short positions may generate cash, consume margin, require borrow availability, or incur financing costs.
Stop and limit semantics	Trigger timing and fill price assumptions can dominate results for path-dependent exits.
Missing bars and calendars	Sparse prices, late asset entry, delistings, holidays, and forward-filled data determine what is tradable.
Cost and slippage models	Costs affect not only net returns but also affordability, order size, and whether trades are executed.

Table 16.2: Simulation semantics that can change backtest results

Order sequencing is a useful example because it is easy to miss in weight-based research. Suppose a rebalance involves selling one asset and buying another. If the engine processes the sell first, the proceeds may finance the buy. If it processes the buy first, the buy may be rejected or resized because the cash has not yet been released. The difference is not philosophical. It is a concrete statement about the simulated trading process.

Timing conventions are even more consequential. A strategy that forms a signal using the close and also executes at the same close is usually using information that was not available before the trade. Shifting execution to the next bar may convert an attractive result into an unprofitable one. This is not an implementation detail. It is the difference between a valid and invalid information set.

Where the major libraries fit

The major Python and open-source backtesting libraries occupy different points in this design space:

- Array-first tools such as vectorBT and vectorBT PRO are especially strong for large-scale research and parameter sweeps (with due attention to multiple testing adjustments, see *Section 16.7*). They can be highly sophisticated and may include compiled order simulation, but their natural research interface is array-oriented.
- Zipline, backtrader, Lean, and `ml4t-backtest` expose the trading process more directly as a sequence of strategy decisions, orders, fills, and portfolio updates. They are therefore better suited when the strategy claim depends on explicit execution state, path-dependent risk management, cash constraints, or order-level behavior.

This distinction should not be overstated. A research workflow can use both. The right question is not which library is more realistic in general. The right question is which simulation contract matches the strategy being tested.

A practical workflow

A disciplined workflow begins with the protocol, not the engine:

- For **exploratory research**, use the cheapest representation that preserves the strategy's meaning. Many ranking, allocation, and factor-portfolio ideas can be tested efficiently with vectorized calculations, provided the timing convention, tradable universe, rebalance rule, weight construction, and cost model are explicit.
- For **strategies with a recursive state**, begin with sequential simulation. Do not force an array approximation when the strategy depends on fills, cash, margin, inventory, drawdown, or contingent orders. In these cases, the event loop is not incidental machinery. It is part of the strategy definition.
- For **validation**, make the simulation semantics explicit. Record the signal timestamp, execution timestamp, fill price, order sequencing rule, cash and margin treatment, share granularity, short-sale assumptions, missing-data behavior, and cost model. Then, verify that the backtester implements these choices as intended. Defaults should be treated as assumptions, not conveniences.

The broader lesson is that backtest credibility comes from aligning three objects:

- The economic claim
- The trading protocol
- The simulator's state and timing semantics

Implementation:

- `03_single_asset_vectorbt.py` shows a compact vectorized representation.
- `04_single_asset_ml4t_backtest.py` introduces sequential simulation.
- `05_stateful_strategies.py` shows when explicit state becomes the natural formulation of the strategy itself.
- `06_framework_parity.py` then shows how mismatched semantics create different results.
- `07_engine_divergence_anatomy.py` decomposes those differences in detail.

For comparison of `ml4t-backtest` with popular libraries, see:

- `15_lean_engine_parity.py`
- `16_case_study_lean_parity.py`
- `17_backtrader_zipline_engine_parity.py`
- `18_vectorbt_engine_parity.py`

We now turn to a key step in the backtest workflow: a trustworthy baseline.

16.4 An auditable non-ML baseline

Before evaluating machine learning models, we need a credible baseline – a non-ML strategy that is simple, interpretable, and difficult to "cheat" accidentally. This baseline serves two purposes:

- It establishes a performance yardstick for later chapters
- It forces us to build the full backtesting infrastructure before adding model complexity

McLean and Pontiff (2016) found that published anomalies lose approximately 26% of their magnitude out-of-sample after discovery, with another 32% decaying after publication. This pattern is consistent with in-sample overfitting and post-publication arbitrage. A robust baseline helps distinguish genuine signal from noise by providing:

- **A benchmark for improvement.** ML strategies must beat the baseline by a significant margin. Otherwise, the added complexity is not justified.
- **A sanity check on infrastructure.** Bugs in data pipelines, execution assumptions, or cost models affect all strategies equally. A baseline with known properties helps identify infrastructure problems before they contaminate model evaluations.
- **A template for the trading protocol.** Building the baseline forces us to make every protocol decision explicit. These decisions then apply consistently to all subsequent strategies.

A simple baseline – Momentum with risk filter

We can construct a baseline using two well-documented signals:

- **Cross-sectional momentum:** Rank assets by risk-adjusted trailing return over a lookback window. The academic standard is 12-minus-1-month momentum—ranking by trailing 12-month return, excluding the most recent month to avoid short-term reversal. Jegadeesh and Titman (1993) established this anomaly, which has been replicated across markets and time periods. For the ETF universe (see case study `README` for details), we adapt that idea to 6-month risk-adjusted momentum (cumulative return divided by realized volatility), which fits a smaller, cross-asset universe with widely differing volatility more naturally than a stock-level 12-minus-1 formulation.
- **Regime filter:** A yield-curve-based risk indicator determines whether to hold momentum positions or rotate to a defensive allocation. When the 10-year minus 2-year Treasury spread exceeds 0.5%, the strategy goes risk-on by holding the top 3 momentum ETFs equally weighted; otherwise, it shifts to a defensive sleeve of 60% AGG and 40% TLT.

The baseline is intentionally unsophisticated. We use no optimization, no machine learning, and only widely-known signals. `01_backtest_first_principles.py` implements this baseline from scratch—no frameworks, just NumPy and Pandas - so every protocol decision is visible. If this baseline underperforms expectations, the problem lies in our infrastructure, not our signals.

Step-by-step baseline construction

Let's build the baseline, step-by-step:

1. **Define the universe:** Our baseline uses ten liquid asset-class ETFs: SPY, QQQ, IWM, EFA, EEM, AGG, TLT, GLD, VNQ, and DBC. The universe is intentionally small, covering US and international equities, bonds, gold, real estate, and commodities, so the strategy can express cross-sectional momentum and regime rotation without introducing stock-level survivorship and delisting mechanics.
2. **Compute signals:** The teaching notebook computes a 6-month cumulative return and scales it by 6-month realized volatility.
3. **Apply filters and rank:** Rank the ten ETFs by the risk-adjusted momentum score. In risk-on regimes, select the top three ETFs and weight them equally. In risk-off regimes, ignore the cross-sectional ranking and move to the defensive AGG/TLT sleeve.
4. **Assign positions:** Equal-weight the selected momentum ETFs in risk-on states; in risk-off states, set $w_{\text{AGG}} = 0.60$ and $w_{\text{TLT}} = 0.40$.
5. **Apply the trading protocol:** Using the trading protocol defined in *Chapter 6*'s `setup.yaml` and detailed in *Section 16.2*:
    - Signal computed at the month-end close
    - Rebalance on the first trading day of next month
    - Monthly rebalancing frequency
    - 5 basis points per trade (10 bp round-trip)
    - No leverage

6. **Generate reports:** Produce a standardized tear sheet with:
    - Equity curve and drawdowns
    - Monthly return heatmap
    - Performance metrics (*Section 16.5*)
    - Regime-sliced diagnostics (*Section 16.6*)

The equity path, drawdown profile, monthly heatmap, and rolling diagnostics together make it harder to conflate a single favorable metric with a robust trading process.

Documenting baseline specification and performance

Running the ETF momentum baseline from January 4, 2010, through December 29, 2023, produces:

Metric	ETF Momentum	60/40 Benchmark
Total Return	171.4%	282.8%
CAGR	7.4%	10.1%
Volatility	11.4%	12.7%
Sharpe Ratio	0.65	0.80
Sortino Ratio	0.86	0.96
Max Drawdown	–31.9%	–26.9%

Table 16.3: ETF Momentum baseline backtest

Here, **the benchmark is a static 60/40 mix of 60% SPY and 40% AGG.** That is distinct from the strategy's risk-off sleeve, which rotates to 60% AGG and 40% TLT when the yield-curve filter turns defensive. The Sharpe ratios in this teaching notebook are computed against a zero cash rate, so they should be read as simple risk-adjusted summaries rather than as fully risk-free-adjusted institutional performance measures.

The baseline is still useful precisely because it is not flattering. It fails to beat the static 60/40 benchmark on total return and experiences a deeper maximum drawdown in this sample. That is a healthy outcome for a reference strategy: the baseline is transparent, easy to audit, and hard to romanticize. Any later ML strategy that claims progress must improve on an explicit, somewhat disappointing benchmark rather than on an unrealistically weak straw man.

If your baseline significantly exceeds these figures, investigate for bugs (lookahead, survivorship, cost omission). If it significantly underperforms, verify data quality and protocol implementation.

The baseline specification becomes a permanent reference:

Component	Specification
Universe	10 ETFs (SPY, QQQ, IWM, EFA, EEM, AGG, TLT, GLD, VNQ, DBC)
Signal	6-month risk-adjusted momentum (return/volatility)
Positioning	Top 3 momentum ETFs (risk-on) or 60% AGG / 40% TLT (risk-off)

Component	Specification
Regime	10Y–2Y Treasury spread greater than 0.5% = risk-on
Weighting	Equal weight among the selected assets
Rebalancing	Monthly, first trading day
Costs	5 bp per trade (10 bp round trip)
Benchmark	Static 60% SPY/40% AGG
Period	2010-01-04 to 2023-12-29

Table 16.4: Baseline backtest specification

The next section introduces key performance metrics.

Implementation: `01_backtest_first_principles.py` builds this baseline from scratch with full position accounting and a 60/40 benchmark comparison.

16.5 Understanding performance metrics

A backtest turns a trading rule into a history of portfolio values, returns, positions, trades, and costs. A tear sheet summarizes this history into a small set of metrics that describe the strategy's economic profile: how much capital it earned, how volatile and path-dependent those gains were, how much trading was required, and how sensitive the result is to implementation frictions.

This section defines the core metric set used throughout the book. The goal is not to prove that a strategy has skill, nor to compare every possible model variant. Those questions require uncertainty estimates, baseline comparisons, regime diagnostics, and multiple-testing controls. Here, we first define the reporting standards for a given backtest configuration; the next section uses these metrics for economic diagnostics across costs, baselines, and regimes. Finally, *Section 16.7* addresses statistical inference and strategy-level overfitting.

Design principles for backtest reporting

No single metric is sufficient. A strategy with high cumulative return may have unacceptable drawdowns. A strategy with a strong Sharpe ratio may require turnover that cannot survive realistic costs. A strategy with attractive average performance may earn all its profits in one favorable regime. A useful tear sheet, therefore, reports a compact but complete set of measures.

The core metric set follows three principles:

- **Completeness:** Report returns, risk, risk-adjusted performance, trading behavior, and implementation costs. Omitting any one category can make a fragile strategy appear robust.
- **Parsimony:** Include the metrics needed for the decision at hand. This chapter focuses on the credibility of strategy backtests. Later chapters add metrics specific to allocation, execution, capacity, and tail-risk overlays.

- **Comparability:** Use standardized definitions across strategies, datasets, and time periods. A metric whose definition changes across notebooks loses most of its diagnostic value.

The tear sheet should be read as an evidence summary, not as a verdict. It describes what the simulation produced under a specified protocol. Whether the result is statistically reliable, economically robust, and implementable requires the additional diagnostics developed in the following sections.

Return and compounding metrics

Return metrics describe the scale and path of capital growth. They answer the first question every backtest raises: what happened to invested capital over the evaluation period?

Let r_t denote the portfolio return in period t, and let W_t denote portfolio wealth or net asset value after period t. The **cumulative return** R over T periods is:

$$R = \prod_{t=1}^{T}(1 + r_t) - 1$$

Cumulative return is easy to interpret but depends heavily on sample length. A strategy tested over 20 years will, by definition, have more time to compound than one tested over 5 years. For cross-sample comparison, the **compound annual growth rate** (CAGR) reports the constant annual rate that would produce the same ending wealth:

$$\text{CAGR} = \left(\frac{W_T}{W_0}\right)^{A/T} - 1$$

where A is the number of return periods per year. For daily returns, $A = 252$, for monthly returns, $A = 12$; for 15-minute bars, A should reflect the number of tradable bars per year under the backtest calendar.

The **equity curve** plots W_t through time:

$$W_t = W_0 \prod_{s=1}^{t}(1 + r_s)$$

The equity curve is not a scalar metric, but it is often the most informative object in the tear sheet. It reveals whether performance was smooth or concentrated, whether losses clustered, and whether the strategy spent long periods below its prior peak.

A simple supplementary metric is the **hit rate**, the fraction of periods with positive returns. This metric is useful only with context. A strategy can have a high hit rate and still lose money if occasional losses are large. Conversely, trend-following and option-like strategies may have low hit rates but positive **expectancy** (expected net profit per trade) because gains are much larger than losses. Hit rate also varies with the measurement interval, so it should not be compared across daily, weekly, and monthly strategies without careful consideration.

Risk and drawdown metrics

Risk metrics describe the variability and path dependence of returns. Volatility measures dispersion around the mean. Drawdown metrics measure losses from prior peaks, which often matter more to investors than unconditional return variance.

The **annualized volatility** of periodic returns is:

$$\sigma_{\text{ann}} = \sqrt{A} \cdot \text{std}(r_t)$$

where A is the number of return periods per year. This square-root annualization assumes weak dependence across periods. When returns exhibit material serial correlation, volatility and Sharpe-ratio annualization require the adjustments discussed in *Section 16.7*.

Maximum drawdown is the largest percentage loss from a previous wealth peak. Define the running peak as:

$$\overline{W}_t = \max_{0 \le s \le t} W_s$$

and the drawdown at time t as:

$$D_t = \frac{W_t - \overline{W}_t}{\overline{W}_t}$$

The maximum drawdown is then:

$$\text{MDD} = \min_{0 \le t \le T} D_t$$

Some reports present maximum drawdown as a positive loss magnitude |MDD|, while others report it as a negative return. The convention should be explicit and consistent.

Maximum drawdown is highly sample-dependent because it is an extreme statistic. Longer samples have more opportunities to produce severe drawdowns, even for the same underlying strategy. This makes MDD useful for stress interpretation but unreliable as a stand-alone measure of strategy quality.

Drawdown duration measures how long capital remains below its prior high. A long drawdown duration is economically important because investors may redeem, reduce risk, or abandon a strategy before the eventual recovery. A strategy with moderate maximum drawdown but repeated multi-year underwater periods may be harder to hold than a strategy with a sharper but shorter loss.

The **Calmar ratio** divides compounded return by maximum drawdown:

$$\text{Calmar} = \frac{\text{CAGR}}{|\text{MDD}|}$$

The Calmar ratio is useful when drawdown risk is central, especially for directional or trend-following strategies. It should not be interpreted mechanically. A high Calmar ratio over a short sample can reflect a favorable period with no major stress event, while a low Calmar ratio may still be acceptable for a diversifying strategy that improves portfolio-level risk.

Risk-adjusted performance metrics

Risk-adjusted metrics relate returns to a measure of risk. They are useful because raw returns are not comparable across strategies with different volatility, leverage, or downside exposure.

The **Sharpe ratio** measures excess return per unit of return volatility:

$$\text{SR} = \frac{E[R - R_f]}{\sigma_R}$$

where R is the strategy return, R_f is the risk-free rate over the same period, and σ_R is the standard deviation of strategy returns. In implementation, the numerator and denominator must use the same return frequency before any annualization is applied.

The Sharpe ratio is the most common performance statistic because it is simple, comparable, and closely related to mean-variance portfolio theory. Its simplicity is also its weakness:

- It treats upside and downside volatility symmetrically
- It summarizes the full return distribution using only the mean and variance
- It is sensitive to serial dependence, non-normality, and sample size

A reported Sharpe ratio is therefore an estimate, not a property known with certainty. *Section 16.7* discusses confidence intervals, serial-correlation adjustments, Deflated Sharpe Ratios, and search-adjusted interpretation.

The **Sortino ratio** aims to address the Sharpe ratio's first weakness by replacing total volatility with downside deviation:

$$\text{Sortino} = \frac{E[R - R_f]}{\sigma_{\text{downside}}}$$

where downside deviation is computed from returns below a target threshold. Using the risk-free rate as the threshold:

$$\sigma_{\text{downside}} = \sqrt{E\left[\min(R - R_f, 0)^2\right]}$$

The Sortino ratio is useful when upside volatility should not be penalized. However, it is not automatically more reliable than the Sharpe ratio. It depends on the target threshold, can be unstable when the number of downside observations is small, and still does not fully characterize tail risk. It should be reported alongside drawdown and tail diagnostics rather than replacing them.

Trading and exposure metrics

Trading metrics describe how the return stream was produced. This matters because two strategies with similar returns and volatility can have very different implementation profiles. One may rebalance monthly with low cost and high capacity; another may require rapid turnover, leverage, and fragile execution assumptions.

Turnover measures the fraction of the portfolio traded during a period. Let $w_{i,t}$ denote the target weight of asset i after rebalancing at time t, and let $w_{i,t-1}^{\text{drift}}$ denote the previous portfolio weights after price movement but before the new rebalance. One-way portfolio turnover is:

$$\text{Turnover}_t = \frac{1}{2}\sum_i \left|w_{i,t} - w_{i,t-1}^{\text{drift}}\right|$$

The factor ½ avoids double-counting buys and sells when the portfolio is self-financing. For a long-only, fully invested strategy, a turnover of 0.10 means that roughly 10% of the portfolio's value was traded during the period. For long-short portfolios, turnover should be interpreted alongside gross exposure, as the capital base and traded notional may differ.

Average turnover is:

$$\overline{\text{Turnover}} = \frac{1}{T}\sum_{t=1}^{T} \text{Turnover}_t$$

Annualized turnover is approximately:

$$\text{Turnover}_{\text{ann}} = A \cdot \overline{\text{Turnover}}$$

where A is the number of rebalance periods per year. This approximation is most meaningful when turnover is measured at the strategy's native rebalance frequency.

Gross exposure measures total absolute portfolio exposure:

$$\text{Gross Exposure}_t = \sum_i \left|w_{i,t}\right|$$

A long-only fully invested portfolio has gross exposure near 1.0. A dollar-neutral long-short portfolio with 100% long and 100%short exposure has gross exposure near 2.0. Gross exposure above 1.0 indicates leverage or short exposure and increases sensitivity to financing costs, margin requirements, and position-level risk limits.

Net exposure measures directional market exposure:

$$\text{Net Exposure}_t = \sum_i w_{i,t}$$

A dollar-neutral long-short strategy should have net exposure near zero. Persistent positive or negative net exposure indicates directional bias, which may explain performance that appears to come from security selection. Net exposure should therefore be interpreted alongside benchmark returns and factor exposures.

Average holding period provides another view of trading intensity. A rough portfolio-level approximation is:

$$\text{Average Holding Period} \approx \frac{\overline{\text{Gross Exposure}}}{\text{Turnover}_{\text{ann}}}$$

expressed in years when turnover is annualized. This approximation is imperfect because positions enter and exit at different times, but it is useful for detecting mismatches between signal horizon and trading behavior. A strategy based on monthly features but turning over most of the book every few days requires explanation.

Cost and implementation metrics

Cost metrics connect simulated returns to implementability. They measure how much performance depends on assumptions about commissions, bid-ask spreads, market impact, financing, and slippage. A strategy that is attractive before costs but unattractive after realistic costs is not a trading strategy; it is an artifact of an incomplete simulation.

The first distinction is gross versus net return. Gross return measures portfolio performance before trading costs, r_t^{gross}, and net return subtracts implementation costs incurred during the period:

$$r_t^{\text{net}} = r_t^{\text{gross}} - c_t$$

where c_t includes the modeled cost of trading, financing, borrowing, and other implementation frictions included in the backtest protocol. Both gross and net returns should be reported. The difference between them is often as informative as the net result itself because it reveals whether performance is generated by forecast quality or consumed by trading intensity.

Cost capacity measures how much turnover-scaled implementation cost the strategy can absorb before its expected excess return is exhausted. It is not an estimate of realized cost. It is a diagnostic threshold that converts portfolio-level gross excess return into an implied maximum cost per dollar traded.

Let τ_t denote traded notional as a share of portfolio value, using a stated one-way or round-trip convention. Suppose trading costs are linear in traded notional, so that a cost of c per dollar traded reduces period return by $c\tau_t$. Then expected net excess return is:

$$E\left[r_t^{\text{net}} - r_t^f\right] = E\left[r_t^{\text{gross}} - r_t^f\right] - c\,E[\tau_t]$$

The turnover-scaled break-even threshold is therefore:

$$c^* = \frac{E\left[r_t^{\text{gross}} - r_t^f\right]}{E[\tau_t]}$$

In a finite sample, the corresponding estimate is:

$$\hat{c}^* = \frac{\sum_t \left(r_t^{\text{gross}} - r_t^f\right)}{\sum_t \tau_t}$$

The units are cost per dollar traded. If expected gross excess return is 1 per period and turnover is 10 of NAV, then $c^* = 10$ per dollar traded: a cost of ten cents on each dollar traded would consume the full 1% portfolio-level excess return. This is not a forecast of implementation cost; it is the maximum average linear trading cost consistent with non-negative expected excess return.

The convention for τ_t must be stated. If turnover is one-way traded notional, c^* is a one-way cost per dollar traded. If turnover is round-trip turnover, leverage-adjusted turnover, or half-turnover, the cost interpretation changes accordingly.

This threshold should not replace a realistic cost model. It is useful as an implementation-margin diagnostic. If plausible spread, commission, slippage, and market-impact costs exceed c^*, the strategy is unlikely to survive implementation. If realistic trading costs are well below c^*, the strategy has more cost capacity, although capacity, nonlinear impact, financing, borrow costs, and execution risk still require separate analysis.

Cost sensitivity reports key performance metrics over a range of cost assumptions. This is especially important for high-turnover strategies, intraday signals, less liquid assets, and strategies with short holding periods. A robust backtest should not depend on a single optimistic cost assumption.

Section 16.6 uses cost sensitivity, baseline comparison, and regime slicing to turn these metrics into economic diagnostics, where an acceptable aggregate report can still mask state dependence.

Implementation: `09_performance_reporting.py` computes core metrics using `ml4t-backtest` and `ml4t-diagnostic` and displays standard visual diagnostics, including equity curves, drawdown plots, rolling performance, and monthly return heatmaps.

16.6 Diagnosing the economic value

A tear sheet summarizes what the backtest produced. Economic diagnostics ask a different question: **Why did it produce these results, and under what conditions would they survive?**

The metrics in *Section 16.5* describe return, risk, trading activity, and implementation cost for a fixed backtest. Those metrics are necessary, but they are not sufficient. A strategy can have an attractive net Sharpe ratio while depending on optimistic cost assumptions. This section turns the tear sheet into a diagnostic framework. It focuses on three questions:

1. Does performance survive realistic costs and turnover?
2. Does the ML strategy add value relative to a simple baseline?
3. Is performance robust across economically meaningful regimes?

Statistical inference, Sharpe-ratio uncertainty, and search adjustments are deferred to *Section 16.7*. Here, the focus is on economic credibility.

From aggregate metrics to diagnostic decomposition

Aggregate metrics compress the backtest into a small number of statistics. This compression is useful, but it can obscure the underlying performance mechanism. A CAGR of 12%does not reveal whether returns came from broad market exposure, a few crisis months, or a small number of high-turnover trades. A Sharpe ratio of 1.0 does not reveal whether the strategy survives a slightly wider bid-ask spread. A maximum drawdown does not reveal whether losses occurred in expected failure modes or in supposedly favorable states.

Diagnostic decomposition separates **three layers of evidence:**

1. **Implementation robustness.** A strategy must survive plausible assumptions about commissions, spreads, slippage, financing, borrowing, and market impact. This is especially important when signals are short-lived, turnover is high, or the traded universe contains less liquid instruments.
2. **Incremental model value.** ML forecasts should be compared with simple, transparent baselines. A strategy that fails to beat equal-weight, inverse-volatility, buy-and-hold, or a naïve factor rule may still be useful as a component of a larger portfolio, but it has not been established that model complexity adds economic value.
3. **State dependence.** Performance should be sliced by regimes that correspond to economically meaningful states: high versus low volatility, uptrend versus downtrend, expansion versus contraction, or normal versus stressed liquidity. A strategy whose edge appears only in benign states may be fragile even if its full-sample performance looks acceptable.

These diagnostics change the role of the tear sheet. Rather than a conclusion, it serves as the starting point for assessing whether the backtest result is implementable, benchmark-relevant, and robust across states.

Cost sensitivity and turnover fragility

The first diagnostic is cost sensitivity. A strategy's gross return is the return before implementation frictions. Its net return is the return after costs. The gap between the two measures how much simulated performance is consumed by trading.

High-turnover strategies are especially vulnerable because small cost errors compound across many trades. A 5-basis-point mistake in the estimated round-trip cost may be tolerable for a monthly strategy. The same error can destroy an intraday strategy that rebalances thousands of times per year.

The *Section 16.4* ETF momentum baseline illustrates the cost-sensitivity diagnostic on a strategy whose protocol is already explicit. With monthly rebalancing and a 5 bp per-leg fee assumption, the baseline produces an annualized two-way turnover near 460%of portfolio value—the rotation between top-3 momentum ETFs and the defensive sleeve generates substantial trading on every rebalance. *Figure 16.1* sweeps the per-leg fee from 0 to 200 basis points, which moves net Sharpe from 0.68 to slightly negative and crosses zero net CAGR near a per-leg cost of about 166 basis points. That break-even is a fragility *ceiling*, not a target: the *Section 16.4* protocol's 5 bp assumption sits roughly thirty times below the ceiling, so realistic commission errors are unlikely to change the qualitative conclusion. A higher-frequency strategy with the same gross CAGR but ten times the turnover would have one tenth of the headroom.

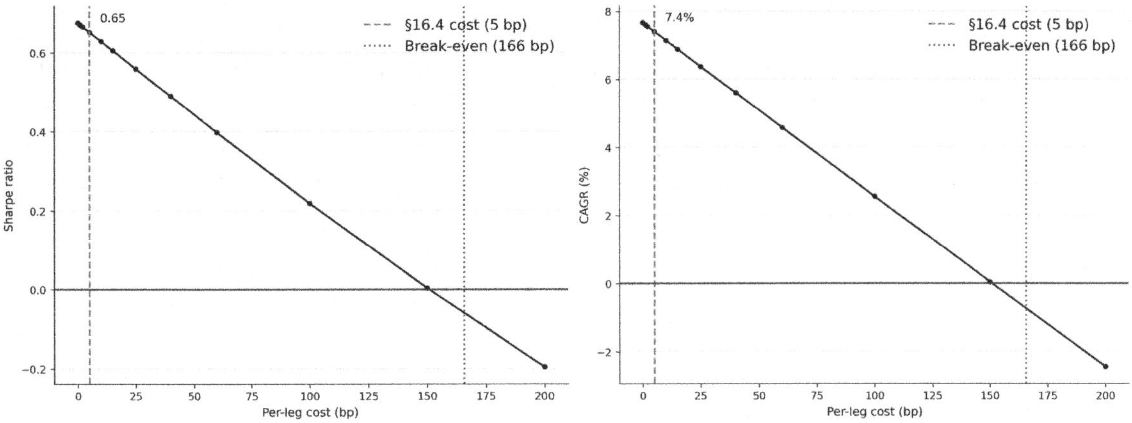

Figure 16.1: Net Sharpe and net CAGR for the Section 16.4 ETF momentum baseline as the per-leg fee sweeps from 0 to 200 basis points. Dashed line marks the Section 16.4 protocol's 5 bp assumption; dotted line marks the break-even cost where gross CAGR crosses zero. The slope of either curve is the strategy's marginal cost elasticity

This example clarifies the diagnostic role of cost sensitivity. Signal validity alone is not enough. Implementation assumptions can dominate model quality, and the cost-sensitivity sweep is what reveals it. The relevant quantities are the **gross-to-net Sharpe gap** at the protocol's cost assumption, the **break-even cost** at which gross return equals zero, and the **annualized turnover** that translates per-leg cost into annual return drag. A strategy whose break-even cost sits close to its assumed cost is fragile regardless of the headline net Sharpe that simulation produced.

A credible backtest should therefore report:

- Gross and net performance
- Average and annualized turnover
- Break-even cost per dollar traded
- Performance under conservative, baseline, and optimistic cost assumptions
- Sensitivity of Sharpe, CAGR, and drawdown to the cost model

For high-turnover strategies, the cost-sensitivity table is not supplementary. It is part of the core evidence. If a strategy survives only under the most favorable cost assumption, the correct conclusion is fragility, not success.

Baseline comparison and incremental model value

A backtest should not ask only whether the ML strategy made money. It should ask whether the ML strategy improved on a simple alternative available at the same time and under the same trading protocol.

The appropriate baseline depends on the strategy:

- For a long-only cross-sectional equity strategy, equal-weight, value-weight, or inverse-volatility weighting may be natural.
- For a long-short strategy, a dollar-neutral factor baseline may be more appropriate.
- For an asset-allocation strategy, risk parity or a static diversified portfolio may be the relevant comparator.

The important point is that the baseline should be simple, transparent, and implementable.

A baseline comparison protects against three common mistakes:

- It separates **model value** from **market exposure**. A strategy may look strong because the traded universe performed well, not because the model selected better assets.
- It separates **forecasting skill** from **portfolio construction effects**. A simple rank rule or equal-weight allocation may capture most of the available edge.
- It imposes an economic **opportunity cost**. Complexity is not free. ML pipelines require data engineering, feature maintenance, model monitoring, retraining, and governance. A complex strategy should justify this burden by improving net performance, risk, turnover, capacity, or diversification relative to a simpler alternative.

Section 16.4 already supplied the simplest version of this diagnostic. *Table 16.3* reports the *Section 16.4* top-3 momentum rule alongside a static 60% SPY/40% AGG benchmark on the same calendar, the same per-leg cost, and a matched monthly rebalance schedule. The static benchmark earns a meaningfully higher Sharpe (0.80 compared to 0.65) with a shallower max drawdown (−-26.9% compared to −31.9%) at a small fraction of the momentum strategy's turnover. The momentum rule has therefore not yet established that complexity earns incremental economic value on this sample. *Chapter 17* returns to the broader question of how to construct and compare allocators systematically; the *Section 16.6* diagnostic need only verify that the strategy clears one transparent benchmark before allocators are compared in detail.

A backtest report that omits the baseline comparison makes it too easy to confuse model sophistication with economic improvement. The relevant question is not whether the model is more advanced. The relevant question is whether the complete strategy earns a better net result than a lower-complexity alternative.

Regime-sliced performance

Aggregate performance metrics can mask state dependence. A strategy with a respectable full-sample Sharpe ratio may profit mostly during calm bull markets while losing heavily during crises. Regime diagnostics reveal whether performance is robust across economically meaningful states or concentrated in favorable environments.

Ang and Bekaert (2002) show that asset returns differ across regimes such as expansion and contraction, high and low volatility, and changing interest-rate environments. For backtesting, this implies that the same trading rule can exhibit different expected returns, volatility, turnover, and drawdown behavior across states.

Consider a momentum strategy that earns almost all of its lifetime profits during extended bull markets but loses during sharp reversals and liquidity stress. Its aggregate Sharpe ratio may be acceptable, but the strategy may fail precisely when investors most value diversification. Regime analysis turns this hidden dependence into explicit evidence.

Chapter 9 introduced several regime features. Here, we use simple threshold-based regimes because they are transparent, reproducible, and sufficient for diagnostic reporting.

A volatility regime classifies periods by trailing realized volatility relative to a point-in-time historical threshold. Let σ_t denote the trailing 60-day realized volatility of a market index, computed using information available by time t. Let m_t denote the expanding historical median of σ_s for $s < t$, or the median estimated on the training sample. Then:

$$\text{Vol State}_t = \begin{cases} \text{Low}, & \text{if } \sigma_t < m_t, \\ \text{High}, & \text{if } \sigma_t \geq m_t. \end{cases}$$

The key point is that the threshold must not be computed using the full test sample. A full-sample median would use future information to classify earlier periods, thereby contaminating the diagnostic.

A trend regime classifies periods by recent return relative to a point-in-time average of itself. Let $\rho_t = P_t/P_{t-126} - 1$ denote the trailing 6-month total return of the market index, and let $\tilde{\rho}_t$ denote the expanding median of $\{\rho_s : s < t\}$. Then:

$$\text{Trend State}_t = \begin{cases} \text{Uptrend}, & \text{if } \rho_t > \tilde{\rho}_t \\ \text{Downtrend}, & \text{if } \rho_t \leq \tilde{\rho}_t \end{cases}$$

Comparing ρ_t to its expanding median enforces a 50/50 split by construction, so each combination of volatility and trend states carries enough observations to make conditional metrics meaningful.

When the regime label is aligned with the next-period strategy return, use the lagged label implied by information known before that return is realized.

Crossing volatility and trend produces a four-state diagnostic:

State	**Volatility**	**Trend**
Risk-on	Low	Up
Caution	High	Up
Crisis	High	Down
Recovery	Low	Down

Table 16.5: Combined volatility and trend regimes

More sophisticated models, such as Hidden Markov Models or regime-switching VARs, can be useful, but they introduce estimation risk, parameter instability, and additional researcher discretion. For diagnostic reporting, simple regimes are often preferable because they are easy to audit and harder to overfit.

For each regime state s, compute the same metric family used in the tear sheet:

$$\text{Sharpe}_s = \frac{E[r_t \mid \text{State}_t = s] - r_{f,s}}{\text{std}(r_t \mid \text{State}_t = s)}$$

The regime table should include both performance and sample coverage. Applied to the *Section 16.4* ETF baseline over the 2010-01-04 to 2023-12-29 sample (3,395 active days after the 126-day trend warm-up), the four-state diagnostic produces the following picture:

Regime	Time %	Observations	CAGR	Vol	Sharpe	MDD
Risk-on	36.0%	1,223	1.6%	10.7%	0.15	-18.3%
Caution	13.4%	454	17.1%	14.0%	1.23	-13.9%
Crisis	33.8%	1,146	6.6%	11.9%	0.55	-24.0%
Recovery	16.8%	572	16.4%	9.9%	1.66	-10.9%
Overall	100%	3,395	7.7%	11.5%	0.67	-31.9%

Table 16.6: Regime-sliced performance for the Section 16.4 ETF momentum baseline. Computed by 10_regime_backtest_analysis.py from the same backtest used in Table 16.3. The Overall Sharpe of 0.67 differs from Table 16.3's 0.65 because this row covers active days only (3,395) after the 126-day trend warm-up, whereas Table 16.3 reports the full-sample 2010-01-04 to 2023-12-29 backtest including warm-up

The observation count matters. Regime slices are smaller than the full sample and often non-contiguous. Their Sharpe ratios are therefore noisier than the aggregate Sharpe ratio. The smallest slice (**Caution**, with 454 observations) is roughly an eighth of the full sample, so its conditional metrics carry more sampling variability than the aggregate.

Three observations follow. First, the two highest conditional Sharpes are in **Recovery** (1.66) and **Caution** (1.23): low-volatility post-decline mean reversion and the defensive AGG/TLT sleeve in high-vol uptrends together carry the strategy's risk-adjusted return. Second, **Risk-on** is the weakest slice (Sharpe 0.15, CAGR 1.6%)—when SPY is in a low-volatility uptrend, the top-3 momentum rotation captures only a fraction of the buy-and-hold return that an unfiltered allocator would earn. The aggregate Sharpe of 0.67 is therefore carried by Recovery and Caution, not by the high-frequency Risk-on state where most of the sample sits. Third, **Crisis** is where the deepest within-regime drawdown lives (−24.0): the binary yield-curve filter rotates to bonds only once the signal flips, leaving the strategy exposed when volatility spikes alongside a steep curve. The aggregate −31.9 drawdown is the path combination of those Crisis losses with the Risk-on shortfall; the regime table separates the two channels that aggregate metrics flatten.

Regime-sliced drawdowns and failure modes

Regime diagnostics should not stop at average returns or Sharpe ratios. Drawdowns are path-dependent and often reveal risks that conditional averages miss.

A useful regime-drawdown analysis reports three related measures:

- First, **regime-conditional drawdown** measures the maximum drawdown experienced during periods assigned to each regime. This shows whether losses are concentrated in specific states.

- Second, **drawdown attribution** decomposes the largest full-sample drawdowns into regime-specific components. A crisis may begin in a high-volatility downtrend but continue into a recovery or a state of caution. Attribution helps explain which states contributed most to the total loss.
- Third, **recovery time by regime** measures how long it takes to recover from drawdowns that began in each state. A strategy may suffer moderate losses in recessions but take years to recover, which can be more damaging than the initial drawdown magnitude suggests.

A direct way to surface this information is to compare the strategy's conditional metrics with those of a simpler allocator that lacks its risk filters. *Figure 16.2* applies that test against an unfiltered equal-weight allocation across the same 10-ETF universe. The comparison is unflattering. Equal-weight pulls ahead in Caution (1.50 versus 1.23), Recovery is essentially tied (1.74 versus 1.66), and **Crisis** turns against the strategy on both axes: equal-weight earns 0.78 conditional Sharpe versus 0.55 with a –20 within-regime drawdown versus −23. The binary yield-curve filter rotates to bonds late and incompletely; equal-weight's structural diversification across ten ETFs delivers a smoother defensive profile by construction. **Risk-on** is the one cell where the momentum rule outscores the benchmark (0.15 versus roughly zero), but the gap reflects how poorly both allocators capture buy-and-hold in the low-volatility uptrend rather than any genuine edge. The state-contingent risk profile is intentional, but on this sample the *Section 16.4* filter trails continuous diversification wherever the trail matters.

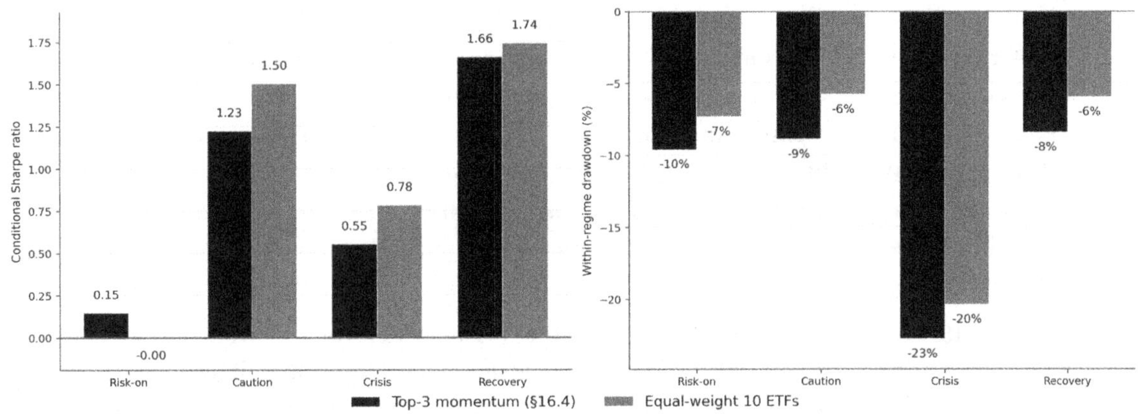

Figure 16.2: Conditional Sharpe and within-regime maximum drawdown for the Section 16.4 ETF momentum baseline versus equal-weight 10 ETFs, sliced by the four-state vol × trend regime. Equal-weight matches or beats the Section 16.4 baseline on Sharpe in Caution, Crisis, and Recovery, and its Crisis drawdown is shallower; the Section 16.4 rule outscores equal-weight only in Risk-on, where both allocators underperform buy-and-hold. Sample sizes per state are reported in the figure header

This distinction matters because not all regime dependence invalidates a strategy. Some strategies are designed to earn returns by bearing specific **state-contingent risks.** The diagnostic question is whether those risks are intentional, measured, and compensated. Unexpected regime losses require investigation before the strategy advances to allocation or live trading.

This is the economic mismatch that aggregate statistics can obscure. A strategy may be statistically attractive on average and still be economically unattractive if losses occur when capital is most valuable, when investors face liquidity needs, or when the strategy increases rather than reduces portfolio-level stress. Regime diagnostics bridge the gap between statistical performance and investor utility.

Regime snooping and diagnostic discipline

Regime analysis introduces its own risk of overfitting. Testing many regime definitions and reporting only the one that tells the most favorable story is another form of data snooping. The fact that the analysis is framed in economic language does not exempt it from multiple-testing logic. Regime snooping can enter through several choices, including, for example:

- Volatility lookback window
- Percentile threshold
- Macro variable selection and crisis definition
- Sample split and number of states
- Decision to combine or omit regimes

A researcher who tries enough combinations can usually find a regime definition under which the strategy looks robust. That is not evidence of robustness. It is another search path.

To reduce regime snooping, use four rules:

1. Pre-specify the main regime definitions before inspecting the strategy's conditional performance. The standard volatility and trend regimes should be part of the reporting protocol, not selected after seeing the result.
2. Prefer transparent definitions. A trailing-volatility split and a trailing-return split are easier to audit than a complex latent-state model with many tuning choices.
3. Report all standard regimes, including unfavorable ones. The purpose is to find where the strategy fails, not to find a flattering partition of the sample.
4. Treat exploratory regime searches as part of the strategy research record. If regime definitions influence strategy selection, risk overlays, or capital allocation, they belong in the trial accounting discussed in *Section 16.7*.

Bailey et al. (2015) emphasize that backtest overfitting arises whenever researchers search across many alternatives and report only selected successes. Regime definitions are alternatives in exactly this sense. They must be handled with the same discipline as signal parameters, cost assumptions, and model configurations.

Reporting economic diagnostics

Every backtest report should include the aggregate tear sheet from *Section 16.5* and the diagnostic evidence from this section, with at least four components:

- **Cost sensitivity**: gross performance, net performance, turnover, break-even cost, and performance under conservative, baseline, and optimistic cost assumptions.
- **Baseline comparison**: the ML strategy against a simple implementable benchmark under the same calendar, universe, constraints, costs, and rebalance schedule.
- **Regime-sliced performance**: time spent in each regime, observation count, CAGR, volatility, Sharpe ratio, maximum drawdown, and preferably confidence intervals or standard errors for the main conditional estimates.

- **Failure-mode reconciliation:** whether losses occur where the strategy design predicts they should occur. Expected weaknesses may be acceptable if compensated and controlled. Unexpected weaknesses require diagnosis before the strategy moves forward.

This diagnostic package sets a new standard for backtest credibility. A strong aggregate tear sheet is not enough. A credible strategy should survive plausible costs, improve on simple baselines, and disclose where its performance depends on market state. *Section 16.7* adds the final layer: whether the apparent performance remains statistically credible after accounting for estimation error, serial dependence, non-normality, and the full strategy search path.

Implementation: Each diagnostic has its own teaching notebook on the *Section 16.4* ETF baseline:

- `10_regime_backtest_analysis.py` builds point-in-time vol × trend regime labels, the regime-sliced tear sheet (*Table 16.6*), the within-regime drawdown attribution, and *Figure 16.2*.
- `14_cost_sensitivity.py` runs the per-leg cost sweep, reports turnover and break-even cost, and produces *Figure 16.1*.

The baseline-comparison diagnostic does not need a dedicated notebook: *Section 16.4*'s NB01 already simulates the *Section 16.4* top-3 momentum rule alongside the static 60/40 benchmark on the same calendar and the same per-leg cost (*Table 16.3*). *Chapter 17* picks up the broader allocator-comparison question.

16.7 Statistical inference and backtest overfitting

A backtest converts one historical path into a small set of estimates. The statistical question is whether these estimates provide evidence of an effect that is likely to persist, rather than a favorable realization of noise. Two issues matter. First, even a fixed strategy has sampling error. Second, most reported strategies are selected after many design choices, so fixed-strategy inference understates uncertainty unless it accounts for the search that produced the result.

Chapter 7 introduced this problem for feature and label evaluation: screening many horizons, thresholds, transforms, or conditioning templates inflates the best observed information coefficient (IC) or area under the curve (AUC). At the strategy level, the searched object expands to the full trading rule: signal definition, model class, hyperparameters, training window, portfolio construction rule, rebalance schedule, cost assumption, constraint set, risk overlay, and regime filter.

A backtest statistic is an estimate

A Sharpe ratio is a sample estimate of a population quantity. Let r_t, $t = 1, \dots, T$, denote excess strategy returns measured at a fixed frequency, and define:

$$\widehat{SR} = \frac{\hat{r}}{\hat{\sigma}_r}$$

Under independent, identically distributed normal returns, the approximate standard error of the per-period Sharpe ratio is:

$$\mathrm{SE}(\widehat{SR}) \approx \sqrt{\frac{1+\frac{1}{2}\widehat{SR}^2}{T}}$$

For small per-period Sharpe ratios, this is close to $1/\sqrt{T}$. If the Sharpe ratio is annualized, its standard error must be annualized on the same scale.

A strategy with an annualized Sharpe ratio 1.0 over five years of daily data has about $T = 1{,}260$ observations. With $A = 252$ trading days per year:

$$\widehat{SR}_d = \frac{1.0}{\sqrt{252}}$$

and the annualized standard error is approximately:

$$\mathrm{SE}(\widehat{SR}_{ann}) \approx \sqrt{252}\sqrt{\frac{1+\frac{1}{2}\widehat{SR}_d^2}{1{,}260}} \approx 0.45$$

A rough two-sided 95%confidence interval is therefore:

$$1.0 \pm 1.96 \times 0.45 \approx [0.12, 1.88]$$

Even under favorable independent and identically distributed assumptions, five years of daily returns do not precisely pin down the annualized Sharpe ratio.

The same logic determines how much history is needed to detect a given effect. For annualized Sharpe ratio SR_{ann}, one-sided significance level α, and power $1-\beta$, a simple approximation is:

$$Y_{\min} \approx \left(\frac{z_{1-\alpha} + z_{1-\beta}}{SR_{ann}}\right)^2$$

For $\alpha = 0.05$, $1-\beta = 0.80$, and $SR_{ann} = 0.5$:

$$Y_{\min} \approx \left(\frac{1.645 + 0.842}{0.5}\right)^2 \approx 24.7$$

This minimum-track-record-length calculation is implemented in `11_sharpe_ratio_inference.py`. Its practical message is that modest Sharpe ratios can be economically useful, especially as diversifiers, yet still require long sample sizes to establish statistical reliability.

Sharpe inference under serial dependence

Trading returns are rarely independent. Overlapping positions, persistent signals, stale prices, gradual rebalancing, and portfolio smoothing can all induce serial dependence. This matters because the usual square-root-of-time annualization is valid only when returns are uncorrelated.

Lo (2002) shows that if $\widehat{SR}(1)$ is the one-period Sharpe ratio and $\hat{\rho}_k$ is the return autocorrelation at lag k, then the implied q-period Sharpe ratio is:

$$\widehat{SR}(q) = \widehat{SR}(1)\sqrt{q}\left[1 + 2\sum_{k=1}^{q-1}\left(1 - \frac{k}{q}\right)\hat{\rho}_k\right]^{-1/2}$$

When all autocorrelations are zero, the bracketed term equals one, and the standard square-root rule is recovered. Positive autocorrelation typically overstates the naive annualized Sharpe ratio; negative autocorrelation can understate it.

The same dependence affects standard errors. Positive autocorrelation reduces the effective number of independent observations, while negative autocorrelation can increase it. Sharpe-ratio inference should therefore adjust standard errors for **heteroskedasticity and autocorrelation** (HAC), or use a dependence-aware bootstrap when serial dependence is material.

From strategy inference to search adjustment

Fixed-strategy inference assumes that the trading rule was specified before the evaluation. Research rarely works that way. A reported strategy is often the survivor of many variants. Once the best result is selected, the relevant null is no longer about one strategy in isolation. For a fixed strategy, a simple null is:

$$H_0: E[r_t] \leq 0$$

After a search over N candidate strategies, the null becomes:

$$H_0: \max_{j=1,\ldots,N} E\left[d_{t,j}\right] \leq 0$$

where $d_{t,j}$ is the benchmark-relative performance differential for candidate j. The selected strategy is the winner of the search, not a randomly chosen member of the family. Even if every candidate has zero true edge, the best observed candidate will usually look positive.

The *Chapter 7* accounting principle carries over directly: adaptive choices are trials. A threshold, universe filter, cost assumption, regime rule, or selection metric changed after observing performance belongs to the same search record.

Selection bias and White's reality check

If N independent strategy estimates have no true edge and standard deviation $\sigma_{\widehat{SR}}$ under the null, the expected maximum scales approximately as:

$$E\left[\max_{1\leq j\leq N} \widehat{SR}_j\right] \approx \sigma_{\widehat{SR}}\sqrt{2\log N}$$

This is only a scale argument, but it shows why the best Sharpe ratio rises mechanically with search breadth. The `12_dsr_validation.py` simulation makes this concrete: among 100 zero-skill candidate strategies, the best observed annualized Sharpe reaches 2.54 – an artifact of selection alone.

The **Reality Check** of White (2000) formalizes this data-snooping problem. Let $j = 1, \dots, N$ index candidate strategies and let strategy 0 denote the benchmark. Define the performance differential:

$$d_{t,j} = g(r_{t,j}) - g(r_{t,0})$$

where $g(\cdot)$ is the tested performance object. For return differences, $g(r) = r$. The sample mean differential is:

$$\bar{d}_j = \frac{1}{T}\sum_{t=1}^{T} d_{t,j}$$

The Reality Check tests:

$$H_0\colon \max_{1 \le j \le N} E[d_{t,j}] \le 0$$

using a statistic such as:

$$V = \sqrt{T} \max_{1 \le j \le N} \bar{d}_j$$

The reference distribution is obtained by resampling the joint differential process under the null. The bootstrap must preserve cross-strategy dependence; if the differential series are serially dependent, it should also preserve time dependence, for example, through a stationary or block bootstrap.

The result is not a p-value for the winning strategy as if it had been chosen in advance. It tests whether the best result in the searched family exceeds what the search itself could plausibly produce under the null. The **Superior Predictive Ability** test of Hansen (2005) refines the centering step to reduce the conservatism of White's test when the candidate set contains many poor models, but the searched family remains part of the evidence.

Deflated Sharpe ratio and search haircuts

The Deflated Sharpe Ratio (DSR), introduced by Bailey and López de Prado (2014b), asks whether an observed Sharpe ratio remains significant after accounting for non-normality, sample length, and multiple testing. It builds on the Probabilistic Sharpe Ratio (PSR) of Bailey and López de Prado (2012). Let $\widehat{SR}$ be the observed Sharpe ratio, SR^* a benchmark Sharpe threshold, T the number of observations, γ_3 sample skewness, and γ_4 sample kurtosis. Then:

$$PSR(SR^*) = \Phi\left(\frac{(\widehat{SR} - SR^*)\sqrt{T-1}}{\sqrt{1 - \gamma_3\widehat{SR} + \frac{\gamma_4 - 1}{4}\widehat{SR}^2}}\right)$$

where $\Phi(\cdot)$ is the standard normal cumulative distribution function. The denominator adjusts for skewness and kurtosis. When returns are serially dependent, T should be interpreted as an effective sample size or adjusted through a dependence-aware procedure.

The DSR evaluates the same probability at a threshold SR^* that reflects the expected best Sharpe ratio generated by the search. Under a simplified independent-trial null, the selection hurdle scales like:

$$SR^* \propto \sqrt{\frac{2\log N}{T}}$$

The implementation requires an effective number of independent trials, not just a raw count of configurations. One hundred adjacent lookback windows are not one hundred independent ideas, but they are not one idea either. The DSR is therefore a search-adjusted Sharpe diagnostic: it combines observed performance, sample length, non-normality, and the breadth of the research process that produced the selected strategy.

False discovery control and effective search complexity

Search adjustment can also be framed as a multiple testing problem. Family-wise error-rate control limits the probability of at least one false positive across a test family. Holm-Bonferroni (Holm, 1979) is appropriate when a single false discovery could promote a spurious strategy. False-discovery-rate control limits the expected fraction of false positives among declared discoveries. Benjamini-Hochberg (1995) is more natural for large signal libraries where later validation stages impose additional filters.

Harvey, Liu, and Zhu (2016) make the same point for published factors: accumulated testing raises the hurdle for declaring a new anomaly. A naive t-statistic near 2.0 is not enough when the literature, or an internal research program, has searched across many related hypotheses.

The hard part is dependence. Strategy candidates are usually correlated because they share signals, universes, horizons, cost models, and training samples. Counting every configuration as independent overstates the penalty; ignoring the search understates it.

Rademacher complexity provides a data-dependent measure of effective search richness. The **Rademacher Anti-Serum** of Paleologo (2025) starts from the performance matrix:

$$X \in \mathbb{R}^{T \times N}$$

where each column is a candidate strategy, and each row is an evaluation period. For strategy n:

$$\hat{\theta}_n = \frac{1}{T}\sum_{t=1}^{T} x_{t,n}$$

For Sharpe-like strategy evaluation, $x_{t,n}$ can be the volatility-scaled return:

$$x_{t,n} = \frac{w_{t,n}^{\top} r_t}{\sqrt{w_{t,n}^{\top} \Omega_t w_{t,n}}}$$

so that $\hat{\theta}_n$ is a non-annualized Sharpe-like estimate. For signal testing, $x_{t,n}$ can instead be a period-t information coefficient:

$$x_{t,n} = \frac{\alpha_{t,n}^{\top} \epsilon_t}{\| \alpha_{t,n} \| \| \epsilon_t \|}$$

where $\alpha_{t,n}$ is the signal vector and ϵ_t is the realized idiosyncratic return vector.

The empirical Rademacher complexity is estimated by drawing random sign vectors $\varepsilon_t \in \{-1, +1\}$ and recording the largest signed average across strategies:

$$\hat{R} = E_\varepsilon \left[\sup_n \frac{1}{T} \varepsilon^\top x^n \right]$$

If many strategies are nearly identical, random signs have few independent patterns to exploit, and $\hat{R}$ remains low. If the family spans many independent return patterns, some strategy will often align with random noise and $\hat{R}$ rises. The Rademacher Anti-Serum bound subtracts this data-snooping term, together with finite-sample uncertainty terms, from each $\hat{\theta}_n$ to produce simultaneous lower confidence bounds. Its validity depends on how X is constructed; material serial dependence requires a dependence-aware design, such as non-overlapping blocks.

The methods answer different questions. The DSR tests whether the selected Sharpe ratio clears a search-adjusted hurdle. Multiple-testing procedures control error rates across p-values. Rademacher Anti-Serum produces lower bounds for a correlated strategy family. They are complementary diagnostics, not substitutes for a disciplined search protocol.

Search budget, sample length, and trial accounting

Search breadth and sample length must be considered together. A short sample can support only a narrow search; a broad search requires stronger performance, longer history, or both. Under the same simplified independent-trial logic, the null hurdle for a per-period Sharpe ratio scales as:

$$\sqrt{\frac{2\log N}{T}}$$

Rearranging gives the rough requirement:

$$T_{\min} \gtrsim \frac{2\log N}{\widehat{SR}^2_{period}}$$

For annualized Sharpe ratios, with A periods per year and $T = AY$:

$$Y_{\min} \gtrsim \frac{2\log N}{\widehat{SR}^2_{ann}}$$

This is not a decision rule. It ignores non-normality, serial dependence, correlated trials, power, cost uncertainty, and benchmark choice. Its value is diagnostic: search consumes evidence. Two years of daily data cannot support as many adaptive modeling choices as twenty years of monthly data, unless the observed edge is unusually large and stable.

Trial accounting should include every adaptive choice that could have changed the selected strategy: features, labels, horizons, lookbacks, model class, hyperparameters, training window, rebalance rule, universe filter, cost model, risk overlay, constraint set, regime definition, and selection metric. The boundary is conceptual. Replacing invalid outputs caused by a bug is not a new hypothesis; changing the specification after observing performance is.

Exploration and confirmation should remain separate. Exploration identifies candidates. Confirmation evaluates a frozen candidate against a reduced and disclosed set of comparisons, preferably on data that did not guide the specification.

Reporting and decision standards

A credible backtest report should disclose the fixed-strategy estimate and the search path that produced it. The essential items are the selected specification, benchmark, searched-set size, and generation rule; selection rule; gross and net performance; confidence intervals; dependence adjustment; search-adjusted significance measure; sample-adequacy check; cost sensitivity; turnover; capacity; and regime stability.

Unadjusted Sharpe ratios remain useful descriptive statistics, but they are not standalone evidence. *Table 16.7* presents screening priors for diversified, multi-year, daily-to-monthly strategies after accounting for realistic costs.

Unadjusted Sharpe	Diagnostic Interpretation
Less than 0.5	Weak standalone evidence; potentially useful only with strong diversification, low costs, or high capacity.
0.5–1.0	Economically interesting if costs, drawdowns, and portfolio-level diversification are favorable.
1.0–1.5	Promising if net of costs, stable across regimes, superior to simple baselines, and supported by confidence intervals.
1.5–2.0	Strong for many medium-frequency strategies but requires careful checks for leakage, costs, sample selection, and search bias.
Greater than 2.0	Unusual for diversified, scalable strategies; requires aggressive scrutiny of implementation, capacity, leakage, and multiple testing.

Table 16.7: Diagnostic interpretation of unadjusted Sharpe ratios. These ranges are screening priors, not decision rules

Across the case-study sweeps, search adjustment changes the interpretation of several candidates. Some high raw Sharpe ratios do not survive correction. Others pass a DSR screen but fail minimum-track-record adequacy, HAC-adjusted IC significance, cost sensitivity, or regime stability. The pattern matters more than any single gate: IC, Sharpe ratio, baseline comparison, cost sensitivity, regime stability, and search-adjusted significance answer different questions. *Chapter 20* discusses these results in detail.

A strategy should advance only when four layers of evidence are coherent: measurement, economic diagnostics, fixed-strategy inference, and search-adjusted inference. DSR, Reality Check inference, false-discovery control, and Rademacher Anti-Serum reduce the risk of strategy-level overfitting, but they work best when paired with explicit hypotheses, constrained search budgets, complete trial logs, and inference that reflects the full selection path.

Implementation:

- `11_sharpe_ratio_inference.py` implements Probabilistic Sharpe Ratio calculations, minimum track-record length, confidence intervals, and Lo-style autocorrelation adjustments.
- `12_dsr_validation.py` implements Deflated Sharpe Ratio diagnostics and search-adjusted Sharpe hurdles.
- `13_ras_protocol.py` implements the Rademacher Anti-Serum workflow for correlated strategy families.

16.8 Summary

Backtesting converts forecasts into falsifiable trading claims. A credible simulation begins with a protocol that fixes signal timing, execution, sizing, costs, constraints, benchmark choice, and accounting before results are interpreted. Vectorized and event-driven engines are both useful when their simulation semantics match the strategy being tested.

Evaluation then proceeds in layers. First, compare the strategy with a transparent non-ML baseline. Next, report gross and net performance, drawdowns, turnover, and exposure. Then diagnose cost survival, benchmark-relative value, and regime dependence. Finally, treat the reported Sharpe ratio as an estimate selected from a research process, not as a known property of the strategy. Fixed-strategy inference, dependence-aware standard errors, and search-adjusted tools such as DSR, White's Reality Check, and Rademacher-style bounds reduce the risk of mistaking noise for skill.

The next chapters keep this simulation contract fixed while adding portfolio construction, transaction-cost modeling, risk overlays, and cross-case strategy synthesis.

17

Portfolio Construction

Portfolio construction translates forecasts into positions. The predictive models developed in *Chapters 11* to *14* produce expected returns, class probabilities, rankings, or alpha scores. These outputs become investable only after an allocator decides how much capital to assign to each asset, how much risk to concentrate, how often to rebalance, and which constraints must remain binding while the portfolio is held.

This translation is itself a model. It has inputs, assumptions, hyperparameters, and failure modes. A strong predictive signal can underperform when naive sizing concentrates risk, raises turnover, or amplifies estimation error. Conversely, a disciplined allocator can preserve the value of weak but diversified signals by controlling leverage, covariance exposure, and implementation costs.

After completing this chapter, you will be able to:

- Formalize the allocation problem in terms of inputs, constraints, and decision variables.
- Evaluate allocators across multiple dimensions rather than relying on the Sharpe ratio alone.
- Implement baseline heuristics and understand why they are surprisingly hard to beat.
- Apply mean-variance optimization with robust fixes and diagnose the Markowitz curse.
- Construct hierarchical risk-parity portfolios that avoid matrix inversion and yield stable allocations across regimes.
- Compare allocators under a common protocol without introducing a new source of overfitting.
- Explain how deep learning enables end-to-end portfolio weight prediction.

The chapter begins by defining the allocation problem and its inputs, then introduces a structured workflow. *Section 17.3* develops the multi-dimensional evaluation framework. *Sections 17.4–17.6* present classical allocators in order of complexity: baseline heuristics, mean-variance optimization with robust fixes, and hierarchical risk parity. *Section 17.7* compares them under a common protocol. *Section 17.8* turns to end-to-end deep learning, where a single network maps features to positions under a portfolio-level objective.

17.1 Defining the allocation problem

Portfolio allocators combine forecasts, risk estimates, and constraints to translate signals into position weights. The first input is a view on **expected returns**, represented in this book by model scores s_t, asset rankings, or return forecasts from *Chapters 11* to *14*. Allocators rarely use raw model output directly. Signals are typically standardized, winsorized, ranked, or decayed across horizons to prevent extreme predictions from dominating the portfolio. Rank transformations usually produce more even position sizes, while z-scores allow conviction to affect sizing but can concentrate risk in names with the most extreme forecasts. Even modest distortions in relative expected returns can materially change allocations (Lopez de Prado, 2016).

The second input is a description of **expected risk**. Even simple diversification rules require volatility estimates, while mean-variance and risk-budgeting methods rely explicitly on a covariance matrix, Σ_t. Its diagonal records individual asset risk; its off-diagonal elements describe how positions reinforce or offset one another.

The third input is the investor's definition of **admissible risk**. Volatility targets, leverage caps, position limits, concentration rules, drawdown tolerances, and liquidity requirements define the feasible region from the start. The same forecast can justify a very different portfolio for a long-only pension fund than for a leveraged market-neutral mandate. Constraints are therefore part of the allocation model, not an implementation afterthought.

The decision problem – Weights, exposure, and timing

The allocator's output appears simple: a vector of portfolio weights, $w_t = (w_t^1, w_t^2, \ldots, w_t^N)$ drawn from a feasible set W_t, where each w_t^i denotes the fraction of capital assigned to asset i at time t. Formally, the allocator aims to maximize investor utility U:

$$w_t \in \underset{w \in \mathcal{W}_t}{\operatorname{argmax}} U(w; s_t, \Sigma_t, w_{t-1})$$

But this weight vector w_t embeds several distinct decisions:

- **Long-only versus long-short.** A long-only constraint, $w_i \geq 0$, substantially shrinks the feasible region and often prevents the allocator from fully expressing relative views. A long-short mandate can hedge out market exposure and express cross-sectional signals more sharply, but it also introduces leverage, stock-borrow costs, and practical constraints on the short book. Even the scaling of the long and short legs matters. French (2024) argues that equal-notional dollar neutrality is usually not the best way to size long-short factor portfolios. In his sample, short legs are typically more volatile and less diversified than long legs, so volatility-matched scaling of the short side improves both absolute and risk-adjusted performance and yields market exposure closer to zero than standard equal-notional construction.
- **Gross and net exposure.** Gross exposure, $\sum_i |w_i|$,measures the total amount of risk taken, regardless of direction. Net exposure, $\sum_i w_i$,measures directional bias. A market-neutral portfolio may target zero net exposure while still maintaining substantial gross exposure through offsetting long and short positions. This distinction becomes especially important once leverage, margin requirements, or derivatives enter the problem.

- **Leverage.** Whenever gross exposure exceeds 100%, the portfolio is leveraged, whether through borrowing, derivatives, or embedded financing. Leverage can improve the use of weak but diversified signals, but it also amplifies estimation error, drawdowns, and implementation risk. Position sizing and leverage, therefore, cannot be separated.
- **Rebalance frequency.** More frequent rebalancing keeps the portfolio aligned with current signals but increases turnover and trading costs. Less frequent rebalancing reduces implementation costs but allows the actual holdings to drift away from target weights. There is no universal optimum. The right schedule depends on signal decay, market frictions, liquidity, and the rate at which the covariance structure itself changes.

Constraints as first-class modeling choices

Constraints are modeling choices with direct economic consequences:

- **Position limits** prevent excessive concentration in individual names. A maximum-weight constraint such as $w_i \leq w_{\max}$ protects the portfolio not only from estimation error but also from liquidity risk, if properly calibrated: a position in a small-cap stock that appears attractive may be difficult to enter or exit at scale.
- **Sector and factor caps** limit aggregate exposure to correlated groups of assets. Without such caps, an optimizer may present a highly concentrated macro or style bet as if it were diversified stock selection.
- **Turnover limits** make the path from yesterday's holdings to today's target explicit: $\sum_i \left|w_i^{\text{new}} - w_i^{\text{old}}\right| \leq T$. Once turnover is constrained, portfolio choice becomes path-dependent. Today's optimal allocation depends not only on today's signals, but also on the inherited portfolio and the cost of moving away from it.
- **Cash and leverage requirements** matter for the same reason. Minimum cash balances may be needed to meet redemptions, margin calls, or internal liquidity policies. Conversely, leverage caps limit how aggressively the allocator can scale a signal, even when the signal looks attractive in isolation.

The mathematical form of a constraint also changes behavior:

- A **hard cap** at 5% creates a literal boundary in the feasible region
- A **soft concentration penalty** merely makes large positions progressively more expensive

Hard constraints are appropriate when a limit reflects a true operational, regulatory, or mandated restriction. Soft penalties are better interpreted as preferences about diversification, turnover, or stability.

How signal quality becomes portfolio performance

The **Fundamental Law of Active Management** (FLAM) (Grinold and Kahn, 2000) links the quality of the ML signals produced by *Chapters 11* to *14* to the portfolio performance realized here:

$$\text{IR} \approx \text{IC} \times \sqrt{\text{BR}}$$

Where:

- IC is the information coefficient (see *Chapter 7*)
- BR is breadth, measured as the number of independent bets
- IR is the information ratio, the benchmark-relative performance per unit of benchmark-relative risk

When the benchmark is cash or a passive allocation, the IR is closely related to the Sharpe ratio; when the benchmark is an active reference portfolio, the distinction becomes more important.

The ETF case study's linear specification with the highest validation IC delivers a daily IC of about 0.054. On its own, this seems low. But with a universe of roughly 100 ETFs rebalanced monthly to 20 positions, **nominal breadth** is $BR = 20 \times 12 = 240$, which implies $IR \approx 0.054 \times \sqrt{240} \approx 0.84$ (before costs). Breadth compensates for weak individual forecasts: a small edge, repeated across many assets and many periods, can still support an attractive allocator.

The relevant concept, however, is **effective breadth**, not the naive count of assets times rebalancing periods. Correlated assets do not provide independent opportunities. If those 20 ETF positions are largely driven by roughly five common risk factors, effective breadth is closer to $5 \times 12 = 60$, which yields IR $\approx 0.054 \times \sqrt{60} \approx 0.42$. This gap between nominal and effective breadth is one of the main reasons realized performance falls short of naive FLAM projections.

In a univariate cross-sectional weighted regression with an intercept, the squared weighted Pearson IC equals the regression R^2. An IC of 0.03, therefore, explains only about 0.09% of the cross-sectional variation in returns: in terms of variance explanation, the raw signal is extremely weak. Its potential economic value comes not from single-name predictability, but from repeated application across many assets and periods: if the signal is sufficiently stable, diversified, and inexpensive to trade, portfolio construction can aggregate a small predictive edge into an investable strategy.

The FLAM should therefore be treated as a **mental model** and as an **order-of-magnitude calibration**. It assumes unbiased forecasts, a correct covariance model, independent bets, and negligible trading frictions. In practice, none of these conditions holds exactly. Still, the approximation provides the right intuition: doubling IC has the same effect as quadrupling breadth, and both benefits can easily be overwhelmed by high correlation among bets, poor risk estimation, or implementation costs. Allocation quality can amplify a weak signal, but it can also destroy it.

Implementation: `02_mean_variance_optimization` traces the efficient frontier and contrasts five objective functions (max-Sharpe, min-vol, ERC, inverse-volatility, equal-weight) on a 30-ETF universe, showing how each maps a noisy expected-return vector and covariance matrix into very different allocations.

17.2 A portfolio construction workflow

Portfolio construction requires a specification before it can use an optimizer. The allocator term sheet records the objective, inputs, constraints, rebalancing rule, cost treatment, and evaluation plan. It prevents allocation from becoming an unlogged search layer after model selection.

A structured workflow makes these allocation choices explicit and testable. *Figure 17.1* summarizes it: signals feed a risk-and-constraint layer, the allocator turns them into positions, and diagnostics feed back into the next specification pass.

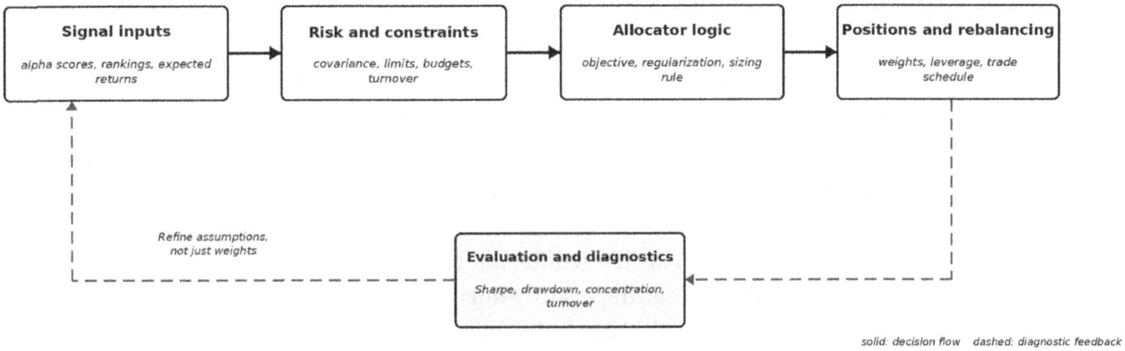

Figure 17.1: Portfolio-construction workflow. Allocation sits between signal generation and implementation, with diagnostics feeding back into the next specification pass

The allocator term sheet

Before implementing any allocation method, the specification should be documented in a compact term sheet that records the objective, inputs, constraints, trading protocol, and evaluation design.

The **objective function** should be explicit enough that two practitioners would produce the same optimizer from the same description. Mean-variance utility, maximum Sharpe, minimum variance, and risk parity all imply different trade-offs, and those trade-offs should not remain implicit in notebook code.

The same discipline applies to the **inputs**:

- **Expected returns** may come from predictive models developed in *Chapters 11-14*, historical averages, or equilibrium-style priors.
- **Covariance** may be estimated with a sample matrix, a shrinkage method, or a factor model.
- Each input also carries a **horizon choice**, and those choices shape behavior at least as much as the optimization routine itself.
- **Constraints** belong on the same term sheet with their numerical values and enforcement rules: long-only restrictions, maximum position sizes, sector caps, turnover penalties, leverage limits, and any distinction between hard feasibility constraints and soft objective penalties.

The documentation should also contain the **rebalancing protocol** and the **evaluation plan**. Rebalancing frequency, drift thresholds, and the treatment of transaction costs determine whether the allocator is testing a realistic implementation or an idealized exercise.

Evaluation rules determine which metrics, subperiods, and regime slices will be reported. Once these choices are written down in advance, poor performance can be traced to a forecast, a covariance estimate, a constraint set, or an execution assumption.

Estimation windows and leakage prevention

Allocation can leak future information just as easily as signal generation. A covariance matrix estimated on day t with data through day $t + k$ is enough to produce an invalid backtest. Three methods protect against leakage:

- **Strict temporal ordering**: expected returns, covariance estimates, risk budgets, and execution assumptions must all be constructed only from information available when the portfolio is formed.
- **Matched estimation windows**. An allocator that uses next-week forecasts and a 10-year covariance matrix combines a short-horizon view of expected return with a long-horizon view of risk structure. That mismatch can be defensible, but it should be a conscious modeling choice rather than an accident of default settings. Short-horizon signals usually call for shorter, more adaptive risk estimates, even though that choice increases estimation noise.
- **Out-of-sample validation** of the allocator itself. Shrinkage intensity, risk-aversion parameters, turnover penalties, and constraint values are hyperparameters in exactly the same sense as the model choices in the predictive pipeline. If those levers are tuned by repeatedly inspecting the final test sample, the allocator has been fitted to the answer key, even if the forecasting model was held fixed.

17.3 Portfolio evaluation metrics

Chapter 16 established the core backtest report: return, volatility, Sharpe, drawdown, turnover, and gross versus net performance. Allocator comparison requires an additional layer. Once the forecast stream and backtest protocol are held fixed, the main questions become benchmark-relative performance, concentration, diversification, and trading stability.

Benchmark-relative performance

The most important addition is the distinction between absolute and active performance. A new allocator is usually judged against a benchmark allocator rather than against cash. Equal weight, inverse volatility, or a strategic policy portfolio all serve as defensible references. In that setting, the key quantities are **active return, tracking error** (TE), and the **information ratio** (IR):

$$r_t^{\text{active}} = r_t^{\text{portfolio}} - r_t^{\text{benchmark}}$$

$$\text{TE} = \sqrt{\text{Var}\left(r_t^{\text{active}}\right)}$$

$$\text{IR} = \frac{E\left[r_t^{\text{active}}\right]}{\text{TE}}$$

The Sharpe ratio remains useful, but it no longer answers the full question. An allocator can improve Sharpe simply by lowering total risk, while still failing to add value relative to a simple benchmark. The information ratio asks the more relevant question: given the benchmark already available, did the new allocator earn enough active return to justify its deviations?

Tracking error makes the source of allocator risk visible. A high tracking error may reflect deliberate, well-paid active bets, or it may reflect unnecessary churn and unstable positions. That is why benchmark-relative metrics should be read together with concentration and trading metrics rather than in isolation.

For benchmarked portfolios, **active share** is often informative as well:

$$\text{Active Share} = \frac{1}{2}\sum_i \left|w_i^{\text{portfolio}} - w_i^{\text{benchmark}}\right|$$

Active share measures how different the holdings are from the benchmark in weight space. It does not replace tracking error because it ignores covariance, but together the two metrics distinguish a portfolio that is genuinely different from one that is only cosmetically active.

Concentration and diversification

Allocators also differ in how they distribute capital and risk across the investable universe. The **Herfindahl-Hirschman Index:**

$$\text{HHI} = \sum_{i=1}^{N} w_i^2$$

is a compact summary of **capital concentration.** Its reciprocal, often interpreted as the **effective number of bets** , gives an intuitive measure of how many meaningful positions the portfolio is really holding. Two allocators can hold the same number of names and still look very different on this metric if one spreads risk broadly while the other concentrates capital in a few dominant positions.

Capital concentration is only part of the picture. **Risk contribution** asks how much each position contributes to total portfolio volatility:

$$RC_i = w_i \cdot \frac{(\Sigma w)_i}{\sigma_p}$$

This quantity is especially important for allocators advertised as balanced or diversified. Equal capital weights do not imply equal risk contributions, and inverse-volatility weights do not imply equal portfolio-risk contributions once correlations are present. A portfolio that looks diversified in capital space can still be dangerously concentrated in risk space.

Stability and implementation metrics

Allocator comparisons also need metrics that connect portfolio design to implementation. *Chapter 16* introduced **turnover** as a trading-cost diagnostic; here, it takes on an additional interpretation. High turnover can mean that the allocator is unstable, reacting aggressively to small changes in forecasts or covariance estimates. That instability matters even before costs are modeled in detail because it signals that the portfolio may be fitting noise rather than a durable structure.

Realized gross exposure and leverage stability serve a similar role. A strategy with a modest average leverage target can still be fragile if it experiences sharp swings in gross exposure as market conditions change. Monitoring the time path of leverage, sector weights, or factor exposures often reveals behavior that a single summary statistic hides.

Diversification has a ceiling when assets share the same risk driver. In the stylized case where n assets have identical standalone Sharpe ratio s, identical volatility, and constant pairwise correlation ρ, the equal-weight portfolio has:

$$SR_n = s\sqrt{\frac{n}{1+(n-1)\rho}}$$

As n grows, this converges to $s/\sqrt{\rho}$. The calculation is not a trading rule; it is a diagnostic. When correlations are high, adding more assets from the same opportunity set contributes little independent risk. The allocator must either find less correlated bets, reduce concentration in the common factor, or accept that diversification cannot rescue the strategy.

This is also where *Chapter 16*'s **regime slicing** still matters, but only as a secondary view. The allocator-specific metrics above should be established first in aggregate. If an allocator then appears acceptable, the *Chapter 16* regime framework can be reused to ask whether concentration, leverage, or benchmark-relative losses deteriorate in stress periods.

Evaluating the risk model through the portfolio

Because covariance estimates drive many allocators, they should be judged by portfolio outcomes rather than by abstract matrix fit alone. A practical test is to form comparable minimum-variance or risk-budgeted portfolios using competing covariance estimates and then compare realized out-of-sample risk. If a covariance model is genuinely better for allocation, it should deliver lower realized variance or more stable risk contributions under the same target exposure.

A portfolio-based criterion can be more useful than a generic matrix norm because **the allocator never trades the covariance matrix** directly. It trades the portfolio implied by that matrix. *Chapter 19* returns to this issue when tail risk and stress constraints become explicit; the principle applies here as well – allocator inputs should be judged by the portfolios they generate.

Implementation: `01_portfolio_metrics` runs the full `ml4t.diagnostic` evaluation suite on the ETF case-study allocation backtest, resolved at runtime via `resolve_best_backtest_runs(...)` so the metrics always reflect the allocator that achieves the best Sharpe ratio during the validation period. The strategy series is benchmarked against SPY across alpha, beta, tracking error, information ratio, up/down capture, drawdown, VaR/CVaR, rolling metrics, and stress-period comparisons.

17.4 Defining baseline allocators

Before reaching for sophisticated optimization, consider what simple allocation rules can achieve. Equal weighting, inverse volatility, and score-based weighting require minimal estimation, are robust to input errors, and frequently outperform complex alternatives out of sample. These heuristics serve as rigorous baselines: any proposed allocator must improve on them to justify its complexity.

Figure 17.2 illustrates the methods discussed as a trade-off between information use and estimation sensitivity: methods relying on fewer inputs are typically more robust, while methods exploiting richer information pay for that expressiveness with increased noise. Risk parity and hierarchical risk parity occupy a middle ground: both consume the full covariance matrix but impose structural constraints that dampen sensitivity to estimates.

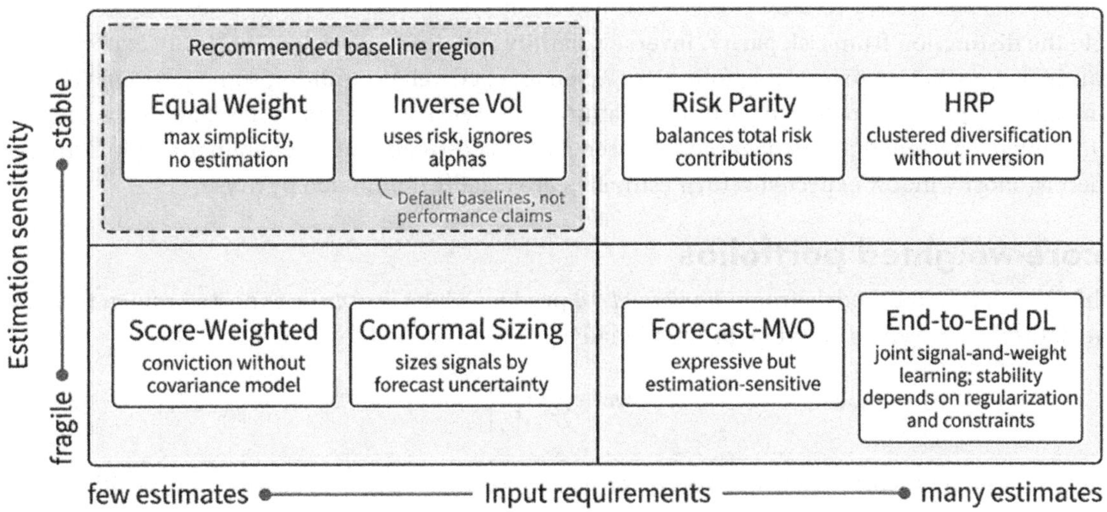

Figure 17.2: Allocation methods trade information use against estimation sensitivity

Equal weight – The null model

The equal-weight portfolio assigns identical weight to each of N assets:

$$w_i = \frac{1}{N}$$

This seemingly naive approach has surprising virtues. It requires no estimation of expected returns or covariance, eliminating the primary source of optimization error. It maintains maximum diversification across available assets. Empirically, equal-weight portfolios are famously hard to beat out of sample because **estimation error often overwhelms the theoretical gains from optimization** (DeMiguel, Garlappi, and Uppal, 2009).

Optimization trades diversification for concentration based on estimated inputs. When those estimates are noisy (and they always are), the concentration may add more risk than the "optimal" tilt adds return. In competitive markets where no asset offers an obvious free lunch, equal weighting's agnosticism is wisdom.

Inverse volatility weighting

Inverse volatility weighting scales positions inversely to an estimate of each asset's ex ante volatility:

$$w_i = \frac{1/\sigma_i}{\sum_{j=1}^{N} 1/\sigma_j}$$

where σ_i is the volatility estimate for asset i. Simple implementations base σ_i on recent realized returns. More generally, it can be any forward-looking estimate, including an exponentially weighted estimate, or a GARCH-style conditional volatility forecast. More volatile assets receive smaller weights, so the portfolio equalizes standalone volatility exposure, $w_i\sigma_i$, across assets. This approach sits between equal weighting and full optimization. It uses volatility estimates but ignores expected returns and, in its plain form, correlations.

Note the distinction from risk parity: inverse volatility equalizes standalone volatility exposure, not marginal contribution to total portfolio risk. When asset correlations differ, some positions can still contribute disproportionately to portfolio volatility. The appeal is in estimation reliability: volatility is sufficiently persistent that recent or model-based volatility estimates often contain useful information, whereas short-window expected-return estimates are usually dominated by noise.

Score-weighted portfolios

When the predictive models from *Chapters 11-14* produce alpha scores or expected return forecasts, one natural allocation is to weight proportionally:

$$w_i = \frac{s_i}{\sum_{j=1}^{N} |s_j|}$$

where s_i is asset i's score. Positive scores receive long positions; negative scores short positions. This formula normalizes gross exposure but not net exposure. Unless scores sum to zero by construction, the portfolio will have directional bias. For dollar-neutral portfolios, normalize long and short legs separately.

Score-weighted allocation works best when the predictive model already accounts for risk, and the correlation structure is relatively uniform. It fails when extreme scores concentrate exposure in correlated assets. Combining score-weighting with position limits or volatility targeting can address this weakness.

Conformal position sizing

Score-weighted portfolios use the *magnitude* of a point prediction to size a position. Conformal position sizing uses the *uncertainty* of that prediction instead. Conformal prediction (*Chapter 11*) wraps any forecaster in a calibration step that produces a prediction interval $[\hat{y}_i - q_i, \hat{y}_i + q_i]$ whose width $\Delta_i = 2q_i$ is calibrated so the realized return falls inside the interval at the chosen coverage level (80% in our implementation). Narrower intervals indicate higher model confidence for that asset at that time. Inverse-width weights translate that confidence directly into a position size:

$$w_{i,t} = \frac{1/\Delta_{i,t}}{\sum_{j=1}^{K} 1/\Delta_{j,t}}$$

For inverse-width weights to differ from equal weights, the widths Δ_i must vary across assets. Pooled split-conformal calibration produces a single quantile per fold and would collapse the rule to equal weight. The `07_conformal_position_sizing` notebook therefore uses **per-symbol Mondrian split-conformal calibration** under strict walk-forward ordering: fold-k's width uses only validation folds that end before fold k begins, and the chronologically earliest fold falls back to pooling residuals from all *other* folds for that symbol. On the holdout window, each symbol's width is the $(1-\alpha)$-quantile of $|y_{\text{true}} - y_{\text{score}}|$ over the full validation history, with the trailing h timestamps embargoed (where h is the forward-return horizon in data-step units) so the calibration cannot peek across the holdout boundary.

We compare the conformal allocator against the cross-stage validation baseline (the highest-Sharpe non-conformal configuration on the same label, pooling signal, allocation, and risk-overlay stages) across seven of nine engine case studies in *Table 17.1*. Two case studies are excluded for structural reasons. The S&P 500 options case study is excluded because its cohort engine realizes PnL on overlapping 30-day option positions, which the per-prediction Mondrian residual definition does not extend to. NASDAQ-100 microstructure is excluded because its selected configuration is a signal-stage slot strategy whose slot mechanism is itself the position-sizing rule, leaving no cross-sectional allocation step for the conformal inverse-width overlay to replace; for the same structural reason, its allocation stage is reported not applicable in *Chapter 20*. On validation, conformal sizing trails the baseline in all seven cases, by margins ranging from negligible to about 1.2 Sharpe, because the baseline is selection-maximized in-sample. On holdout, conformal sizing improves the comparison on four of six cases with a non-conformal comparator on the same prediction set, though only one move is material: it lifts Sharpe substantially on `sp500_equity_option_analytics` (−0.73 → +0.08) and is essentially flat on `etfs` (+1.00 → +1.02), `crypto_perps_funding` (−0.13 → −0.13), and `us_firm_characteristics` (+1.77 → +1.79). It trails `cme_futures` and `us_equities_panel` by 0.24 to 0.41 in Sharpe ratio.

The `fx_pairs` row illustrates the flat-signal case. The cross-stage baseline (HRP top-5 on the linear-ridge predictions) barely clears zero on validation (+0.05), and conformal sizing on the same thin signal is worse (−0.11): with no real dispersion in predictive confidence to exploit, the inverse-width weights only add noise. Only that baseline strategy was taken to the holdout, where it earns +0.19 yet remains statistically indistinguishable from an equal-weight book of the same currencies. Conformal sizing carries no embedded direction-of-effect (it amplifies whatever per-symbol confidence the underlying model reports), so it can neither rescue nor distort a signal that has no resolved edge to begin with.

Case study	**Label**	**Val baseline → conformal**	**Holdout baseline → conformal**	**Δ holdout**
etfs	fwd_ret_21d	+1.36 → +1.04	+1.00 → +1.02	+0.02
crypto_perps_funding	fwd_ret_24h	+2.57 → +2.41	−0.13 → −0.13	+0.00
sp500_equity_option_analytics	fwd_ret_risk_adj_5d	+2.39 → +1.23	−0.73 → +0.08	+0.81
us_firm_characteristics	fwd_ret_1m_win	+2.75 → +2.73	+1.77 → +1.79	+0.02

Case study	Label	Val baseline → conformal	Holdout baseline → conformal	Δ holdout
cme_futures	fwd_ret_5d	+1.36 → +1.07	+1.11 → +0.70	−0.41
us_equities_panel	fwd_ret_5d	+2.03 → +1.56	−0.49 → −0.73	−0.24
fx_pairs	fwd_ret_21d	+0.05 → −0.11	+0.19 → —	n/a

Table 17.1: Conformal sizing (the uncertainty-driven inverse-width overlay defined above) versus the cross-stage baseline across seven engine case studies. Sharpe ratios are queried from each case study's registry.db. The fx_pairs holdout has no conformal comparator because only the baseline HRP strategy was taken to the holdout

The pattern is consistent with the conformal allocator's mechanism: a position-sizing rule driven by calibrated uncertainty trades some in-sample Sharpe for tighter alignment between sizing and model confidence. It does not substitute for a properly tuned risk overlay, and it cannot rescue a selection signal whose predictive content decays out of sample.

Risk parity – Equal risk contribution

Risk parity allocates to equalize each asset's contribution to portfolio risk (Maillard, Roncalli, and Teiletche, 2008; for an accessible introduction, see Hurst, 2010). Traditional allocation concentrates risk in the most volatile assets: a 50/50 stock-bond portfolio typically carries most of its risk in equities rather than bonds. Risk contribution for asset i is:

$$RC_i = w_i \cdot \frac{(\Sigma w)_i}{\sigma_p}$$

Risk parity seeks weights to achieve equal risk contribution (ERC) across assets. Risk parity lies between minimum variance and equal weighting, with portfolio volatilities satisfying $\sigma_{MV} \leq \sigma_{ERC} \leq \sigma_{1/n}$. Risk parity proponents frame ERC as a practical compromise: less risk-concentrated than minimum variance, more risk-balanced than equal weighting, and often competitive on the diversification-turnover trade-off.

Risk parity requires leverage to achieve competitive returns; whether leveraged risk parity outperforms depends on financing costs and the stability of correlations.

Volatility targeting

Volatility targeting is an *overlay* that wraps any base allocator, not a standalone method. First, construct a base portfolio using a method of your choice, then scale its exposure to achieve a target volatility:

$$w_{\text{scaled}} = \frac{\sigma_{\text{target}}}{\sigma_{\text{portfolio}}} \cdot w_{\text{base}}$$

If the base portfolio has an annualized volatility of 15% and the target is 10%, scale all positions by 0.67. When realized volatility exceeds the target, reduce exposure; when volatility falls, increase it.

Volatility targeting produces a more stable risk profile over time, naturally reduces exposure during high-volatility periods, and prioritizes explicit control over portfolio risk, subject to the accuracy of estimates. The main design choice is how to estimate volatility: trailing windows are simple but slow to adapt; EWMA or GARCH models respond faster but introduce additional parameters.

The preceding allocation rules are deliberately simple. Equal weighting ignores both forecasts and covariance. Score-based weighting uses forecasts but does not define an explicit growth or utility objective. Volatility scaling and risk parity incorporate risk, but they largely avoid expected-return estimates. These heuristics are often robust precisely because they ask little of the data. The Kelly criterion introduces the missing optimization principle: when a signal implies a positive edge, how much capital should be committed to it?

The Kelly criterion – Optimal sizing from signal quality

The Kelly criterion starts from a repeated-betting problem. Suppose you stake a fixed fraction f of current wealth each round. Kelly's key insight is that the relevant objective is not expected wealth after one bet, but the expected growth rate of wealth over many repeated bets. Because wealth compounds, this objective is the expected change in log wealth.

For a binary bet that gains bf on a win and loses f on a loss, where b denotes the payoff odds and p the probability of winning, the expected log-growth rate is:

$$g(f) = p\log(1 + bf) + (1 - p)\log(1 - f)$$

Maximizing this expression gives the familiar **edge-over-odds Kelly fraction:**

$$f^* = \frac{bp - (1 - p)}{b}$$

The numerator is the expected advantage of the bet, while the denominator converts that edge into the appropriate fraction of wealth to stake. Betting too little leaves long-run growth on the table, while betting too much increases the probability of large losses enough to reduce expected log growth, even when the bet has positive expected value. If the edge is negative and shorting the bet is not allowed, the constrained Kelly stake is zero.

The same logic extends to financial returns. For one risky asset with excess return r, expected excess return μ, and variance σ^2, the expected log-growth objective is:

$$\mathbb{E}[\log(1 + fr)]$$

For small returns, a second-order approximation gives:

$$\mathbb{E}[\log(1 + fr)] \approx f\mu - \frac{1}{2}f^2\sigma^2$$

So the growth-maximizing exposure is:

$$f^* = \frac{\mu}{\sigma^2}$$

This expression is useful because it links signal quality directly to position size. A larger expected excess return increases the optimal exposure, while greater variance reduces it. The criterion, therefore, does not merely ask whether a signal is positive. It asks how large the edge is relative to the risk of harvesting it.

In a multi-asset setting, the same quadratic approximation yields:

$$\mathbb{E}[\log(1 + w^\top r)] \approx w^\top \mu - \frac{1}{2} w^\top \Sigma w$$

where w is the vector of risky-asset weights, μ is the vector of expected excess returns, and Σ is the covariance matrix. The unconstrained Kelly allocation is then:

$$w^* = \Sigma^{-1} \mu$$

The same result reappears in the next section on mean-variance optimization. Under the standard approximation, the Kelly portfolio points in the same direction as the tangency portfolio. Both reward higher expected excess returns and penalize covariance risk. The difference is that a normalized tangency portfolio typically fixes the scale of risky exposure, while the Kelly solution also determines the leverage implied by the estimated opportunity set. In that sense, Kelly is an integrated allocation criterion rather than just a forecasting rule.

Kelly gives a principled answer to the sizing problem when the return distribution is known (as in many games), but in trading applications, the inputs are estimated. Because full Kelly scales aggressively with the estimated edge, even modest overestimation of μ can produce excessive leverage and severe drawdowns. The criterion is therefore highly sensitive to the same estimation errors that make forecast-based (classical) mean-variance optimization unstable.

Practitioners usually treat full Kelly as an upper bound rather than as a literal operating rule. **Fractional Kelly** scales the theoretical allocation by a constant, such as one-half or one-quarter, to reduce leverage, drawdowns, and sensitivity to estimation error. This sacrifices some expected log growth under the assumed model, but it can improve robustness when the model is misspecified or the estimated edge is uncertain.

This connection makes Kelly a useful bridge from heuristic sizing rules to formal portfolio optimization. The same moment estimates that make Kelly allocations principled also make them fragile: expected returns and covariances must be estimated, and errors in those inputs are amplified when they are converted into portfolio weights. The next section turns this observation into the classical Markowitz framework and shows why regularization is essential in practice.

Implementation:

- `04_kelly_criterion` derives the binary, continuous, and multi-asset Kelly fractions in SymPy and shows the full-versus-fractional trade-off on real ETF returns, including raw Kelly's leverage (typically 30×+) before shrinkage.
- `05_factor_allocation_evidence` documents the empirical case for diversifying across factor sources using Fama-French and AQR Century-of-Premia data: Harvey-Liu-Zhu $t > 3$ thresholds, value-momentum negative correlation across asset classes, TSMOM crisis alpha, and crisis-period factor performance.
- `07_conformal_position_sizing` implements Mondrian split-conformal calibration on the ETF and CME-futures case-study GBM predictions and computes the inverse-width weights compared in this section.
- `09_allocator_comparison` provides the inverse-volatility, equal-weight, and score-weighted reference implementations used elsewhere in the chapter.

17.5 Mean-variance optimization and the Markowitz curse

Mean-variance optimization (**MVO**) remains the standard framework for portfolio construction. Markowitz (1952) showed that rational investors should choose portfolios on the **efficient frontier**: the set of allocations offering the highest expected return for each level of risk. The framework is elegant, but naïve implementations often produce unstable, concentrated portfolios that perform poorly out-of-sample.

The standard formulation is:

$$\max_{w} \mu^T w - \frac{\lambda}{2} w^T \Sigma w$$

subject to $\mathbf{1}^T w = 1$, where μ denotes expected returns, Σ the covariance matrix, w the portfolio weights, and λ risk aversion. Smaller values of λ tilt the solution toward return-seeking portfolios; larger values place more weight on risk control and move the solution toward the minimum-variance end of the frontier. Equivalent formulations maximize the Sharpe ratio or minimize variance for a target return, but all depend on the same estimated moments.

Figure 17.3 places the minimum-variance and maximum-Sharpe portfolios on the same frontier. The figure clarifies why the **tangency portfolio** is especially exposed to estimation error. The tangency point is determined by the slope of the capital allocation line, so small changes in estimated expected returns or covariances can materially shift the optimum and produce large changes in portfolio weights. Portfolios near the minimum-variance region are typically less fragile because they depend less on precise estimates of expected return.

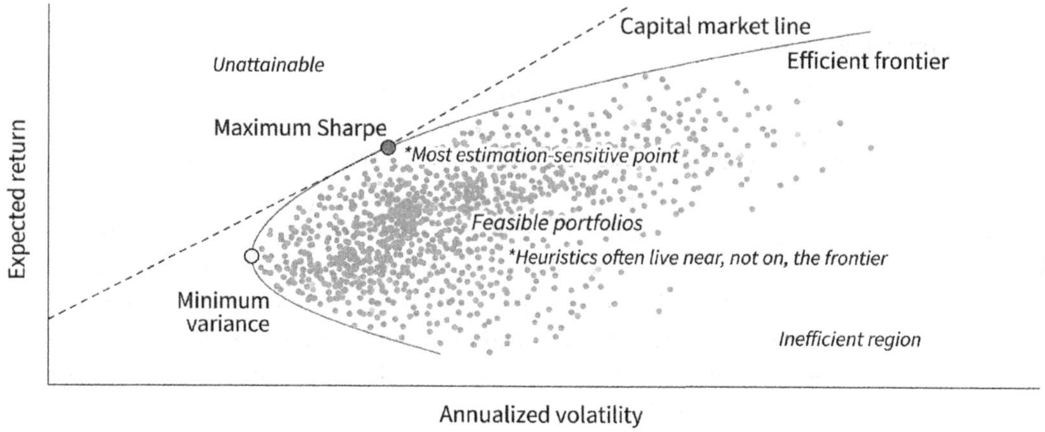

Figure 17.3: Efficient frontier with allocation zones

This quadratic objective is exact under **constant absolute risk aversion (CARA)** utility and normally distributed returns. Under CARA, an investor's aversion to a given dollar amount of risk does not vary with wealth. That assumption matters because, with normal returns, it implies that expected utility depends only on mean and variance, yielding the MVO objective directly. More generally, the same expression can be read as a second-order approximation to expected utility over moderate horizons.

In the unconstrained risky-asset formulation with excess returns and a second-order approximation to log utility, $\lambda = 1$ reproduces the full-Kelly scale. Larger λ values correspond to fractional-Kelly-style scaling.

The central implementation problem appears in the unconstrained solution:

$$w^* = \frac{1}{\lambda}\Sigma^{-1}\mu$$

Both μ and Σ must be estimated, and both are noisy. MVO combines these noisy inputs through the inverse covariance matrix, which can amplify small errors into large allocation changes. That sensitivity is the central practical weakness of the classical framework.

Why MVO fails out of sample

Antonov, Lipton, and Lopez de Prado (2024) argue that MVO underperforms out-of-sample for three linked reasons:

1. **Expected returns are hard to estimate**, so optimizer inputs carry substantial noise.
2. **Covariance inversion becomes unstable** when the sample size is not large relative to the universe size.
3. The optimizer tends to **concentrate on assets whose alphas are overestimated** by chance, creating an error-maximization effect (Lopez de Prado, 2016).

The practical symptom is familiar: strong in-sample Sharpe and weak out-of-sample stability. The `02_mean_variance_optimization` notebook reproduces this gap on the ETF universe.

A useful nuance is that allocation quality depends more on alpha ranking than on alpha calibration. If the forecast scale is uniformly miscalibrated, portfolio composition changes little, and leverage absorbs most of the error. Ranking mistakes, not pure scale error, do most of the damage.

Making MVO more robust with covariance shrinkage

In practice, the question is not whether MVO is theoretically correct, but how aggressively one should regularize it. One source of fragility is covariance estimation. **Ledoit-Wolf shrinkage** (Ledoit and Wolf, 2003) replaces the sample covariance matrix with a weighted average of the sample estimate and a structured target:

$$\hat{\Sigma} = (1 - \alpha)S + \alpha F$$

where S is the sample covariance, F is a structured target, and α is a data-driven shrinkage intensity. This trades a small amount of bias for a substantial reduction in estimation variance and numerical instability. A related approach models **covariance through factor structure:**

$$\Sigma = B\Omega_f B^T + \Omega_\varepsilon$$

thereby reducing dimensionality by separating common-factor risk from idiosyncratic residual risk. Shrinkage and factor structure are best viewed as complementary tools rather than competing alternatives.

Constraints play a similarly important role. Position caps limit concentration, long-only constraints suppress fragile short positions supported only by noisy return estimates, and turnover penalties reduce the tendency to convert forecast error into trading costs. In this sense, constraints are not secondary implementation details but part of the estimator itself: they regularize the mapping from noisy inputs to portfolio weights.

As Paleologo (2025) argues, many common constraints admit a robustness reading. Quadratic penalties reflect uncertainty about alpha magnitudes, sparse allocations reflect a preference for parsimony, conservative covariance treatments act like higher effective risk aversion, and turnover penalties reflect uncertainty about net alpha after costs. Framed this way, MVO is not a claim of precise optimality. It is a disciplined procedure for translating uncertain beliefs into tradable weights under explicit guardrails.

Accordingly, MVO is most defensible when the investable universe is modest, covariance estimation is tractable, and signal quality is strong enough that return tilts survive implementation costs. Under those conditions, shrinkage, realistic constraints, and turnover control often matter more than the particular form of the optimizer.

Shrinkage hedging as robust optimization

The same robustness logic applies when the optimizer is used to remove risk rather than to allocate toward expected return. **A hedge ratio is an allocation decision**: it chooses how much of a hedge instrument to add to an existing portfolio in order to reduce an unwanted exposure. If the exposure estimate is noisy, full neutralization can be as fragile as an unconstrained maximum-Sharpe portfolio.

Beta hedging provides the simplest example. With a known beta, the variance-minimizing hedge offsets the portfolio's exposure to the hedge instrument. In practice, however, beta is estimated from finite data. Paleologo (2025, *Chapter 12*) shows that when the beta estimate is noisy, full beta-neutral hedging can increase realized variance rather than reduce it. The hedge overreacts to estimation error: it trades against noise as if it were true exposure.

The remedy is shrinkage. The hedge ratio should be scaled down when the estimation error in beta is large relative to the portfolio's aggregate exposure. In Paleologo's formulation, the shrinkage factor declines with the portfolio-weighted covariance of beta-estimation errors and rises with the squared estimated aggregate beta. The intuition is the same as for robust MVO: when the signal-to-noise ratio is weak, the optimizer should move less.

This point is especially important for concentrated portfolios, where beta-estimation errors do not diversify across many positions. A concentrated book should usually hedge more conservatively, while a highly diversified book can move closer to full beta neutrality if the aggregate exposure is estimated with greater precision. The practical rule is therefore not "always hedge to zero," but "hedge in proportion to the reliability of the exposure estimate."

Viewed this way, hedging is not a separate topic from portfolio optimization. It is the defensive version of the same problem: translating uncertain estimates into tradable weights without letting estimation error dominate the allocation. The next subsection extends this idea from single hedge instruments to factor-mimicking portfolios.

Factor-mimicking portfolios

A **factor-mimicking portfolio (FMP)** isolates a single factor exposure with minimal residual risk. Grinold and Kahn (2000) give the active-management framing, and Paleologo (2025) provides a factor-model derivation in *Chapter 9*. Given factor loadings b and idiosyncratic covariance Ω_ε, the minimum-residual-risk factor-mimicking portfolio is:

$$w_{FMP} = \frac{\Omega_\varepsilon^{-1} b}{b^\top \Omega_\varepsilon^{-1} b}$$

FMPs are useful because they convert feature-level hypotheses into tradable portfolios and provide a direct portfolio-level test of the incremental value of factors. In practice, factors are evaluated by the out-of-sample marginal Sharpe of orthogonalized FMPs, which aligns factor admission with the same model-accounting discipline used elsewhere in the chapter.

Implementation:

- `02_mean_variance_optimization` traces the efficient frontier on a 30-ETF universe, and reproduces the Markowitz curse – the unconstrained max-Sharpe solution collapses to two assets (XLK 78.9%/GLD 21.1%) and the unconstrained min-variance solution to one (SHY ~98%).
- `03_robust_optimization` runs six allocators side-by-side via Riskfolio-Lib (max-Sharpe, min-variance, risk-parity, HRP, min-CDaR, equal-weight) on an 11-ETF multi-asset universe under Ledoit-Wolf covariance shrinkage, and quantifies the equal-capital-versus-equal-risk gap with risk-contribution diagnostics.

17.6 Optimizing for stability with Hierarchical Risk Parity

Hierarchical Risk Parity (**HRP**) takes a hierarchy-based approach to the same covariance-driven allocation problem that makes naïve MVO fragile. Rather than estimating expected returns and inverting the full covariance matrix, HRP uses hierarchical clustering to order assets based on the empirical correlation structure, then allocates capital through recursive inverse-variance splits (Lopez de Prado, 2016). HRP avoids covariance-matrix inversion and tends to produce less concentrated and more stable portfolios.

The intuition is that **not every asset should compete with every other asset for portfolio weight**. In MVO, small changes in expected returns or covariances can alter the entire allocation. HRP instead imposes a nested structure on the universe: assets that appear similar under the chosen distance metric are grouped together before capital is allocated. This does not eliminate estimation error, but it localizes much of its effect and reduces the chance that a small covariance perturbation produces a global reallocation.

Consider a portfolio containing technology and utilities stocks. MVO compares all names simultaneously. HRP uses the correlation structure to place similar names near one another, then allocates across and within the resulting branches. Errors in estimating the relationship between Apple and Microsoft primarily affect the technology branch and its estimated cluster variance; they are less likely to propagate through the entire portfolio through a global covariance inverse.

The hierarchical structure also follows a simple rule: diversify first across dissimilar groups, then within similar ones. This produces portfolios that better capture true diversification rather than the spurious diversification MVO often creates.

From correlations to weights – The HRP algorithm

HRP has three computational steps. First, **convert correlations into distances**, commonly:

$$d_{ij} = \sqrt{\frac{1-\rho_{ij}}{2}}$$

Second, **apply hierarchical clustering** to this distance matrix and order assets by traversing the dendrogram. This quasi-diagonalization places similar assets near one another, making the covariance matrix more block-like.

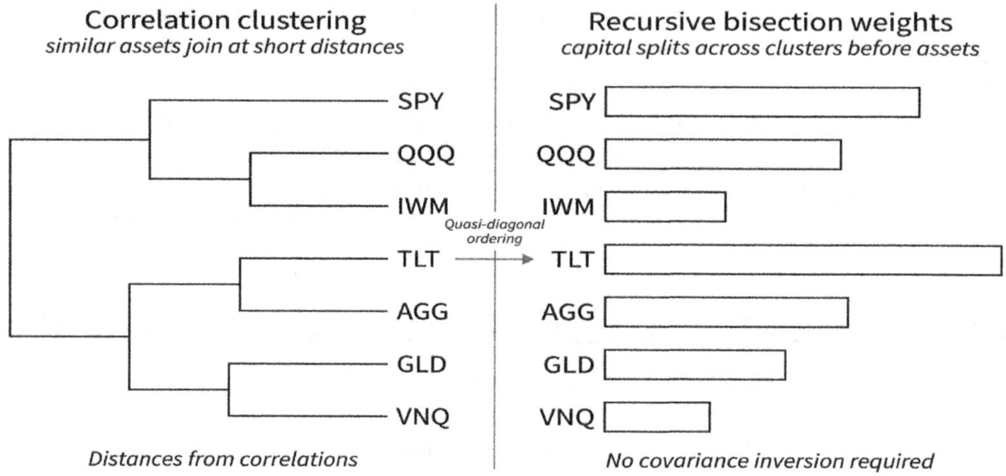

Figure 17.4: HRP workflow from clustering to recursive allocation. The hierarchy stabilizes diversification by grouping similar assets before assigning weights

Third, allocate capital by recursive bisection. Start from the whole universe, repeatedly split each cluster into two sub-clusters and allocate capital between them in inverse proportion to the variance of the cluster. The lower-variance cluster receives the larger share, and the same logic is then applied within each branch until the process reaches individual assets. If L and R denote two sub-clusters, the split is:

$$w_L = \frac{V_R}{V_L + V_R}, \quad w_R = \frac{V_L}{V_L + V_R}$$

where V_L and V_R are cluster variances. The important feature is not the algebra alone, but how it is applied locally within the hierarchy.

Diversification is imposed in stages, first across broad groups and then within finer groups, so estimation errors are less likely to propagate across the entire portfolio.

Why HRP can be more stable than naive MVO

The survey evidence summarized by Marti et al. (2021) and the subsequent HRP literature point to four practical sources of stability. First, HRP avoids matrix inversion entirely, eliminating the numerical instability that undermines MVO. Second, grouping similar assets provides hierarchical regularization: estimation errors within a cluster partially cancel, so individual-asset misestimates have less impact on the final portfolio. Third, the hierarchical structure itself is relatively stable, yielding more consistent weight assignments across rebalancing dates. Fourth, by ignoring expected returns, HRP eliminates error-maximization at the cost of not expressing directional views.

Limitations and extensions

HRP is not a universal solution. Its basic form does not use return forecasts, so any genuine predictive content in the signal is intentionally ignored. That is often an acceptable trade when forecast error dominates, but it becomes a real opportunity cost when the model has stable directional information. Vanilla HRP is also long-only by construction because the recursive bisection step assigns positive capital shares at every level. Readers working on long-short strategies should treat HRP as a stability template rather than a plug-in allocator. One workaround is to apply hierarchical allocation separately to long and short candidate pools before combining them, though nested clustered optimization provides a cleaner way to express views inside the same general framework.

The method is also sensitive to the clustering recipe. Raffinot (2016) compares several hierarchical variants using bootstrap-based model confidence sets and finds strong out-of-sample performance for the class as a whole, but not a single universally dominant specification. That finding is more useful than a single ranking because it identifies where the method is robust and where design choices still matter. Standard HRP also treats the hierarchy as a sequence of point-in-time clusterings rather than as a dynamic structure with explicit control over turnover, so changes in cluster membership can create a different kind of instability.

Nested Clustered Optimization (NCO) extends the same clustering intuition in a different direction. HRP uses the hierarchy to avoid global optimization and allocate capital through recursive risk splits. NCO instead uses clustering to decompose the optimization problem: it first optimizes within clusters, then across the resulting cluster portfolios. This preserves the ability to express expected-return views, constraints, and alternative objectives, while reducing the dimensionality and instability of the covariance-driven optimization problem. NCO is therefore closer to a clustered, regularized version of MVO than to vanilla HRP.

The trade-off is complexity. HRP is transparent and difficult to overfit because it ignores expected returns and avoids matrix inversion. NCO is more flexible, but it reintroduces the optimizer assumptions and can still overfit noisy expected-return estimates if the inner and outer optimizers are not carefully constrained or validated.

A related line of work, **Schur Complementary Allocation** (Cotton, 2024), connects hierarchical allocation to minimum-variance portfolios by using Schur-complement adjustments to retain selected off-block covariance information. This reframes the HRP-versus-minimum-variance choice as a continuum rather than a binary choice: the practitioner can decide how much covariance information to admit, depending on the reliability of the estimate.

ETF walk-forward results

Running the four allocators on the same GBM-selected ETF universe (top-5 picks at each monthly rebalance, 252-day covariance window, 2010–2023) yields a narrow but consistent ordering in favor of the covariance-aware methods. Ledoit-Wolf shrinkage minimum variance delivers the highest realized Sharpe at 0.8437, HRP follows at 0.8293, inverse-volatility at 0.8074, and equal weight trails at 0.7763. The spread is 0.067, and all four allocators share the same -28% maximum drawdown because the GBM-ranked top-5 selection dominates the overall path.

The cross-section is narrow enough that allocator differences are bounded. With only five names per rebalance, the correlation structure has limited room to express itself, and equal weighting is already close to the inverse-variance solution when the universe is small. Monthly rebalancing also limits how quickly the hierarchy can re-cluster as regimes shift, and GBM-selection concentrates capital in names the signal already ranks highly, so allocator differences reduce to how each weights an already-filtered set. Even so, the covariance-aware methods extract a small edge: the renormalized long-only projection used by Min Variance (LW) keeps the shrinkage signal in the realized weights, and HRP's recursive bisection captures most of that same structure without the matrix inversion. Marti et al. (2021) document how thin out-of-sample margins typically are across hierarchical and non-hierarchical methods, consistent with a 0.067 Sharpe spread on a five-asset universe. HRP's structural advantages (hierarchical regularization, no matrix inversion, no return forecasts) matter most on larger, more heterogeneous universes than the one tested here.

Method	Annual Return	Sharpe	Max DD	Calmar
Min Variance (LW)	11.83%	0.8437	-28%	0.4215
HRP	11.41%	0.8293	-28%	0.4063
Inverse Volatility	10.92%	0.8074	-28%	0.3893
Equal Weight	10.38%	0.7763	-28%	0.3698

Table 17.2: Walk-forward backtest on the GBM-selected top-5 ETF universe (2010–2023)

Implementation: `06_hierarchical_risk_parity` shows the end-to-end HRP pipeline (clustering, quasi-diagonalization, and recursive bisection) with dendrograms, quasi-diagonal covariance heatmaps, and weight-evolution time-series. The walk-forward backtest resolves the selected GBM prediction set from the ETF case-study registry at runtime and applies HRP, inverse-volatility, minimum-variance, and equal-weight sizing to that selection. An `ml4t-diagnostic` tear sheet packages the cumulative return, drawdown, rolling Sharpe ratio, monthly heatmap, and return distribution panels for the HRP allocator.

Now we turn to using deep learning for end-to-end portfolio learning, building on the material from *Chapter 13*.

17.7 Comparing allocator performance

A fair comparison of the allocation approaches introduced so far (heuristics, robust MVO, and hierarchical methods) requires identical inputs, identical backtest protocols, and careful attention to the degrees of freedom each method consumes, while guarding against the subtle overfitting that can arise from "allocator shopping."

Experimental design

A controlled allocator comparison holds everything constant except the allocation method. All allocators should receive the same expected-return forecasts; here, the common input is a ridge-based cross-sectional ETF model, so performance differences can be attributed to sizing and diversification rather than to changes in the predictions. The same principle applies to the backtest protocol. Rebalancing frequency, transaction-cost assumptions, treatment of dividends, and corporate-action handling should all remain fixed.

Constraints and estimation windows require the same discipline. Long-only rules, maximum position sizes, sector caps, leverage limits, and turnover penalties should be aligned across methods wherever the comparison is meant to be head-to-head. Covariance estimation should also be matched. If robust MVO uses a Ledoit-Wolf covariance estimate within a particular lookback window, the competing risk-based allocators should use the same underlying risk information unless the experiment explicitly tests the covariance model itself.

The notebook `09_allocator_comparison` **compares four methods** that represent increasing modeling structure:

- **Equal weight** is the null model: capital is divided evenly across assets regardless of forecast strength or risk, and any sophisticated allocator should clear that hurdle before it is taken seriously.
- **Inverse-volatility** weighting adds a risk estimate but still ignores directional views and cross-asset correlations.
- **Robust MVO** introduces forecasts, covariance structure, position limits, and turnover-aware regularization.
- **HRP** maintains the risk focus while introducing diversification via clustering rather than matrix inversion.

Empirical results for an ETF momentum strategy

The controlled comparison uses identical ML signals on the ETF universe from January 2018 through December 2023. The backtest runs each allocator on the same dates, with the same rebalancing schedule and cost assumptions.

The following table compares key performance metrics:

Method	Annual Return	Annual Vol	Sharpe	Max DD	Avg Turnover
MVO (Ledoit-Wolf)	6.7%	18.0%	0.450	-21.7%	10.5%
Inverse Volatility	6.8%	19.2%	0.439	-23.3%	8.3%
HRP	6.1%	19.3%	0.404	-25.6%	10.1%
Equal Weight	4.6%	19.5%	0.327	-19.7%	6.8%

Table 17.3: Allocator performance metrics

Robust MVO and inverse-volatility achieve similar Sharpe ratios, separated only by a gap of 0.011 (see *Table 17.3*), while equal-weight delivers the shallowest drawdown despite lower Sharpe. Allocator choice changes risk shape and turnover, but often by narrower margins than expected.

The comparison notebook also simulates performance under realistic transaction cost assumptions for the inverse volatility method. In this simulation, the weight-based return (+46.6%) drops to +1.5% after accounting for commission, slippage, and fill timing. *Chapter 18* details this transaction-cost channel.

The cross-case summary (the best allocator per case study, the best-minus-worst Sharpe spread, and the structural reading of when allocator choice is load-bearing) is consolidated in *Section 20.5*, where allocator outcomes are read jointly with cost survival (*Section 20.6*) and risk overlays (*Section 20.7*). The conclusion that carries over from the ETF comparison above is unchanged: allocator gains cannot rescue a weak signal-cost combination.

Figures 17.5 through *17.7* give a cross-case-study preview of the *Section 20.5* analysis. *Figure 17.5* is a Sharpe heatmap across allocators × case studies, where the row-by-row variation shows which case studies are allocator-sensitive and which are not. *Figure 17.6* plots allocator uplift over equal weight against signal strength: the slope answers "when does optimization help?" Uplift correlates positively with signal quality, with the strongest evidence on case studies where the underlying signal already had measurable predictive power. *Figure 17.7* ranks the best allocator Sharpe per case study, showing where allocator choice is load-bearing for the reported result.

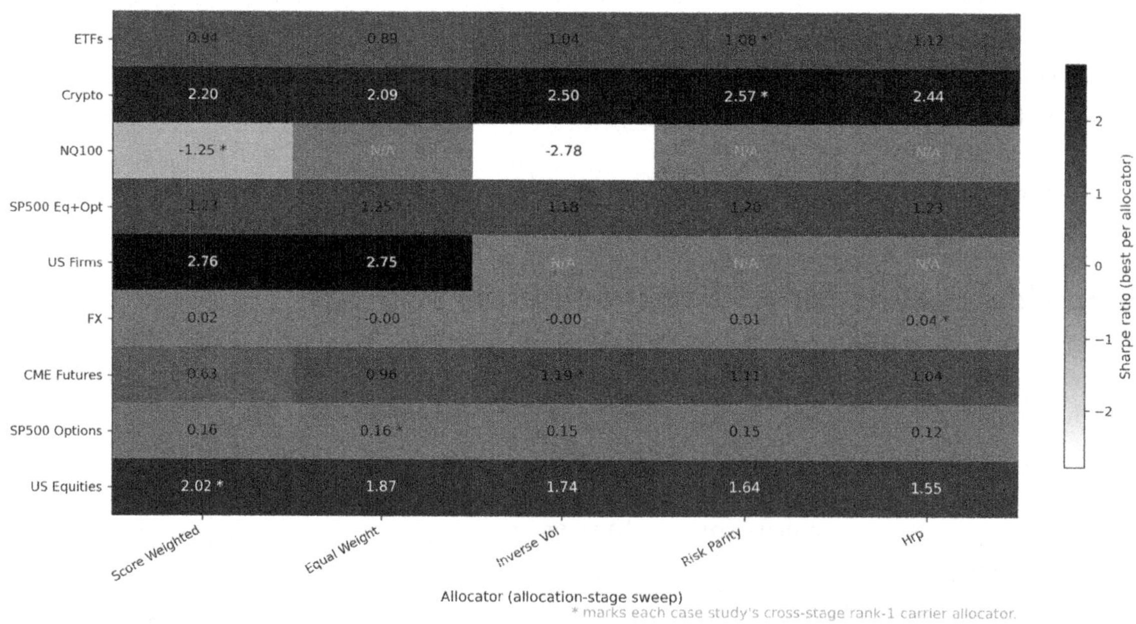

Figure 17.5: Allocator performance heatmap. Each cell shows the Sharpe ratio of one allocator on one case study; darker cells mark stronger allocators on that case study

Figure 17.6 plots allocator uplift over equal weight against signal strength: the slope answers "when does optimization help?" Uplift correlates positively with signal quality, with the strongest evidence on case studies where the underlying signal already had measurable predictive power.

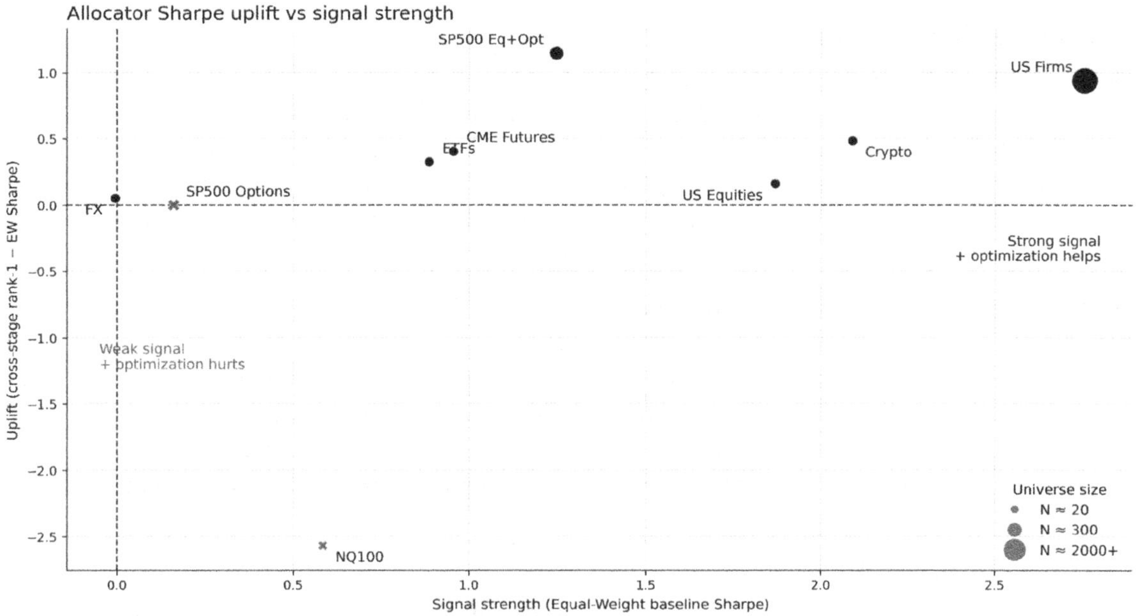

Figure 17.6: When does allocation optimization help? Signal-strength on the x-axis (case-study IC), allocator uplift over equal weight on the y-axis. Allocator choice matters more on case studies with stronger underlying signals

Figure 17.7 ranks the best allocator Sharpe per case study, showing where allocator choice is load-bearing for the reported result.

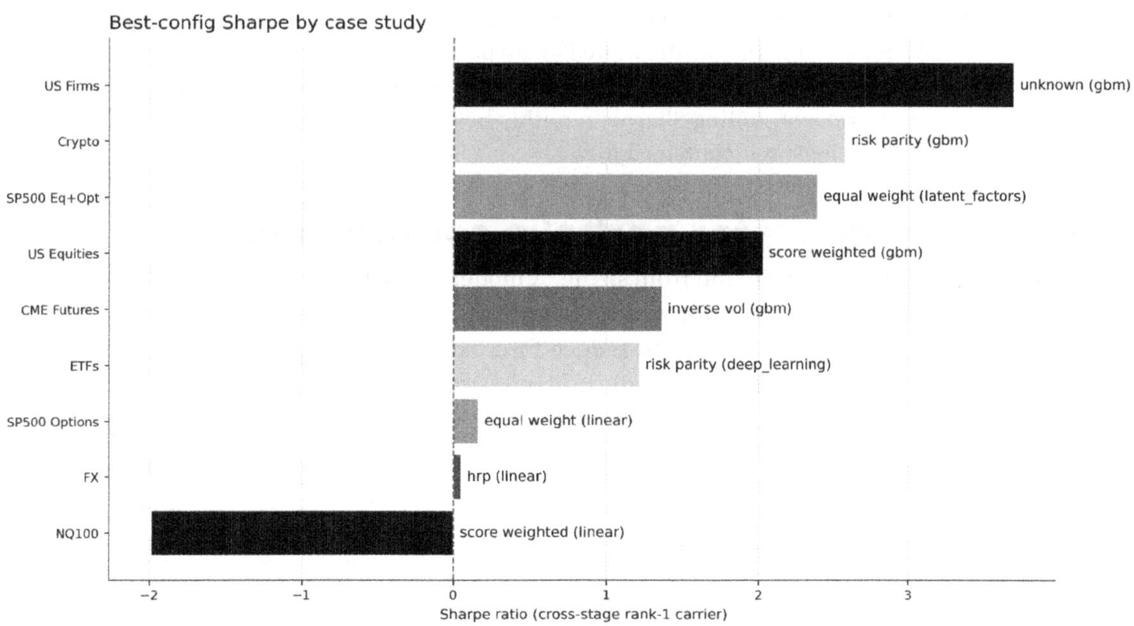

Figure 17.7: Best allocator Sharpe by case study. Horizontal bars show the headline Sharpe achieved by the best-performing allocator on each case study, with the allocator name annotated

The broader lesson

The "best" allocator depends on signal quality, transaction costs, and investor objectives. Strong and stable forecasts can justify score-based tilts or constrained optimization because there is something worth expressing. Weak or noisy forecasts usually call for robust heuristics that resist overreacting to estimation error. HRP occupies a middle ground: more structured than inverse-volatility weighting, less directionally expressive than forecast-driven optimization, and often attractive when the priority is diversification stability rather than maximum aggressiveness.

The broader lesson is humility. Allocation methods often live in narrower performance bands than the predictive models that feed them. In the ETF comparison above, the spread between best and worst Sharpe is only 0.123, and the top two methods differ by 0.011. Those are not meaningless differences, but they are smaller than many researchers implicitly assume before running the test. In practice, more value is often created by improving signal quality and execution realism than by repeatedly re-parameterizing allocator geometry. *Chapter 20* compares allocators across the nine case studies.

Implementation:

- `08_library_comparison` complements the comparison by showing `skfolio`'s `WalkForward` cross-validation and comparing `PyPortfolioOpt`, `Riskfolio-Lib`, and `skfolio` under the same 11-ETF universe – useful when treating the allocator itself as an estimator with proper out-of-sample folds.
- `09_allocator_comparison` implements the controlled allocator comparison reported in this section, with the Ridge-based ETF signal, identical inputs and rebalances across allocators, and the production replay through the `ml4t-backtest` Engine. A `ml4t-diagnostic` tear sheet for the selected allocator (resolved at runtime, not hard-coded) is saved to `output/allocator_comparison/allocator_comparison_<method>_tear_sheet.html`, packaging the cumulative-return, drawdown, rolling-Sharpe, monthly-heatmap, and returns-distribution panels in a single self-contained file.

17.8 Deep learning for portfolio construction

Classical allocators separate prediction from sizing. A model estimates returns or ranks assets; a risk model estimates covariance; an allocator turns both into weights. This separation improves diagnosis, but the losses are not aligned. A model can reduce forecast error while producing signals that are expensive to trade, poorly diversified, or fragile under leverage.

End-to-end portfolio learning replaces this modular pipeline with a policy that maps features directly to positions and trains on a portfolio-level objective. The advantage is alignment: gradients reward the model for improving portfolio returns after risk scaling and costs. The cost is diagnostic opacity. Prediction error, sizing, turnover, and exposure control become entangled in one loss surface.

For that reason, learned allocators should be evaluated on a separate evidence track. They do not consume the same forecast stream as equal weight, inverse volatility, MVO, or HRP, so a direct head-to-head comparison confounds forecasting architecture with allocation logic. The appropriate question is not whether a neural allocator outperforms MVO in isolation, but whether it clears simple heuristics after leakage checks, seed variation, turnover costs, and regime-sliced diagnostics.

The end-to-end pipeline

The end-to-end allocators in this section share a common five-stage structure with gradients flowing backward through every stage:

1. **Inputs:** For each asset i and decision time t, the network receives a fixed-length lookback window $\mathbf{X}_{i,t} = [x_{i,t-L+1}, \dots, x_{i,t}]$ where $x_{i,t} \in \mathbb{R}^F$ is a per-day feature vector. Standard choices are vol-scaled returns over multiple horizons, an EWMA realized-volatility estimate (typically with a 63-day half-life), and a small number of technical indicators, such as multi-scale MACD or normalized momentum. DeePM deliberately restricts itself to closing prices to isolate the contribution of its architectural priors; the Saly-Kaufmann benchmark uses a slightly richer feature set centered on stationarized returns and ticker embeddings.
2. **Sequence encoder:** A sequence model g_ϕ processes the lookback window and produces a fixed-dimensional hidden state $h_{i,t} \in \mathbb{R}^H$. The encoder is the swappable component of the pipeline. Any of the *Chapter 13* architectures (LSTM, xLSTM, PatchTST, iTransformer, TFT, Mamba, Mamba2, or hybrids) can occupy this slot. The encoder is applied per asset with shared weights (channel-independence): the same g_ϕ runs on every asset's lookback window. This is a deliberate regularization that prevents the model from memorizing asset identities through its temporal weights; identity is reintroduced separately, typically through learned ticker embeddings concatenated to the hidden state.
3. **Signal projection:** A small head (a linear layer followed by a hyperbolic tangent) projects the hidden state to a scalar signal:

$$s_{i,t} = \tanh\left(w_{\text{lin}}^\top h_{i,t} + b_{\text{lin}}\right) \in [-1,1]$$

   Reading $s_{i,t}$ as a directional conviction is a deliberate design choice: the interval $[-1,1]$ allows long-short positioning, and the tanh squash bounds the projection so the position layer cannot ask for unbounded exposure. Notebook 11 (Zhang, Zohren, and Roberts, 2020) is the only exception in this section: it ends in a softmax over assets and produces a long-only weight vector. We treat it as a baseline precisely because it sits one architectural choice away from the long-short template the later notebooks adopt.

4. **Position layer:** A volatility-targeting transformation converts the signal into a position size:

$$w_{i,t} = s_{i,t} \cdot \frac{\sigma^*}{\hat{\sigma}_{i,t}}$$

where σ^* is a portfolio volatility target (typically 5–15% annualized depending on the universe; the VLSTM and DeePM ablations in this chapter use 15% in line with the Saly-Kaufmann benchmark, while the closed-form rule is most often stated at 10%) and $\hat{\sigma}_{i,t}$ is an ex-ante asset volatility estimate. The position layer does two things at once. It equalizes risk contributions across assets so that learning is not dominated by the highest-volatility markets, and it makes gross exposure self-scaling: when realized volatility rises, position sizes mechanically shrink, limiting drawdowns without requiring an explicit regime label.

5. **Portfolio aggregation and loss:** Realized portfolio returns are computed within the same computational graph by combining positions with realized asset returns, minus a cost term proportional to the absolute weight changes. Under the equal-risk-capital convention used by the Saly-Kaufmann benchmark, the cross-sectional aggregate is:

$$R_t^{\text{port}} = \frac{1}{K_t}\left[\sum_{i=1}^{K_t} w_{i,t-1}\, r_{i,t} - c\sum_{i=1}^{K_t} \left|w_{i,t-1} - w_{i,t-2}\right|\right]$$

where K_t is the number of active assets and c is a per-unit cost coefficient. The training loss is then a differentiable function of R_t^{port}, typically the negative annualized Sharpe ratio, introduced below.

Figure 17.8 shows how these five stages compose into a single end-to-end graph.

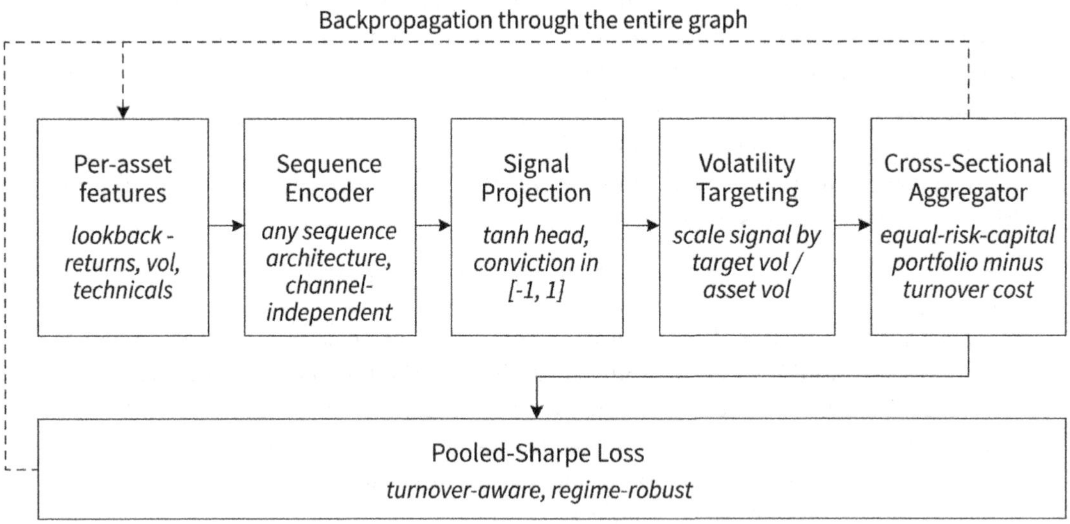

Figure 17.8: The end-to-end portfolio-learning pipeline

Per-asset features pass through a shared sequence encoder (any *Chapter 13* architecture) into a tanh signal head; vol-scaling turns the signal into a position; the cross-sectional aggregator produces a realized portfolio return; the loss is computed on that return and backpropagates through the entire graph.

Training a portfolio objective directly

The standard training loss is the negative annualized Sharpe ratio computed across the training horizon:

$$\mathcal{L}_{\text{SR}}(\theta) = -\sqrt{A} \cdot \frac{\widehat{\mathbb{E}}[R_t^{\text{port}}(\theta)]}{\sqrt{\widehat{\text{Var}}[R_t^{\text{port}}(\theta)] + \varepsilon}}$$

where A is the annualization factor (252 for daily returns) and ε is a small numerical stabilizer. Minimizing $\mathcal{L}_{\text{SR}}$ optimizes the economic quantity the allocator is judged on rather than a proxy that may or may not be aligned with it.

Two refinements are standard practice:

- **Pooled Sharpe** computes the statistic across all training returns concatenated into a single sequence rather than per asset or per training window: per-asset Sharpe encourages the model to specialize in a few easy names, while pooled Sharpe forces the policy to perform across the full universe and is the better proxy for out-of-sample Sharpe (an empirical observation both DeePM and Saly-Kaufmann confirm).
- **Transaction-cost-aware loss** subtracts a turnover penalty inside the numerator so the network internalizes implementation friction during training, rather than producing a strategy that survives only on gross returns.

A subtlety arises in how the loss is computed across mini-batches. **Sharpe is a non-separable objective**: its gradient depends on global statistics, namely the sample mean, and standard deviation of the returns being optimized. Therefore, naive microbatch gradient accumulation yields the wrong gradient: it optimizes the average of mini-batch Sharpe, a different objective from pooled Sharpe over the full batch. DeePM handles this with an exact two-pass procedure:

- A first pass accumulates sufficient statistics (sums of returns and squared returns) without storing activations
- A second pass uses those statistics to compute the correct analytical gradients

Details matter when effective batch sizes need to span multiple years to stabilize the Sharpe estimator.

Average Sharpe over a long sample can also mask periods when the allocator is fragile, even when the long-run statistic is favorable. The DeePM subsection below introduces a SoftMin penalty over rolling sub-windows as the regime-robust counterpart to plain pooled Sharpe.

Architecture under a portfolio objective

The pipeline is encoder-agnostic, which raises an empirical question: which encoders do best when the loss is a portfolio Sharpe rather than a forecast error? Saly-Kaufmann et al. (2026) answer this with a unified benchmark that runs linear baselines, LSTM and xLSTM variants, PatchTST, iTransformer, TFT, Mamba and Mamba2, and several hybrids (VLSTM, VxLSTM, LPatchTST, VSN-Mamba2) through the same volatility-targeted long-short layer and pooled-Sharpe loss on roughly fifteen years of futures, FX, bonds, equity indices, and energy products. All models face the same target, the same evaluation universe, and the same transaction-cost stress test, so Sharpe differences isolate the effect of the temporal inductive bias rather than of the data.

The benchmark's central finding is that **inductive bias matters more than raw capacity.** Linear baselines are unreliable across regimes; generic Transformers are mixed (iTransformer in particular trades too little, posting low turnover but weak economic performance); plain state-space models do not consistently outperform the recurrent class. Recurrent and hybrid architectures lead. The top performer, VLSTM, couples a TFT-style variable-selection network to a shared-weight LSTM encoder; LPatchTST and TFT are close behind, and xLSTM variants offer a favorable balance of return and turnover.

A second, equally important finding is that **robustness reorders the architectures.** VLSTM leads on average Sharpe but is not dominant on every axis: LPatchTST and VxLSTM are comparatively attractive on drawdown and tail-risk measures, and xLSTM often achieves the highest breakeven transaction cost because it trades less aggressively. The "best" architecture therefore depends on whether the objective is maximum average return, downside protection, or implementation robustness.

Variable selection – VLSTM as the case study

The benchmark's top performer, VLSTM, is the chapter's natural architectural case study because the mechanism that distinguishes it from a plain LSTM (the variable-selection network) is also the simplest example of an inductive bias paying its way under a portfolio loss.

Financial features have very uneven signal strength across markets and through time. A 21-day momentum feature can carry a strong signal in one regime and pure noise in another; a volatility-of-volatility feature might matter for FX but not for equities; a slow-moving carry feature might dominate in calm periods and disappear in crises. A plain LSTM that receives all features stacked into its input vector spends part of its capacity learning to ignore the noisy channels at every time step. The TFT-style variable-selection network provides the model with an explicit gating mechanism: each feature is embedded through its own gated residual network (a per-feature non-linear projection with a learned skip), and a softmax gate over features computes a per-time, per-asset weighted combination. The mixture that reaches the LSTM has weights that adapt to each asset's current state rather than being held fixed across the universe.

Notebook `12_vlstm_portfolio` implements the Saly-Kaufmann VLSTM on the ETF universe under the same volatility-targeted long-short layer, the same pooled-Sharpe training loss, and a 5 bps turnover cost internalized inside the loss. On the test window, the VLSTM attains a gross Sharpe of 0.66 with a 17.6% maximum drawdown, closes to 0.55 at the 5 bps cost level used in training, and degrades to 0.44 at 10 bps and 0.22 at 20 bps. Equal-weight is effectively cost-invariant (Sharpe 0.65 → 0.64 across 0–50 bps) because rebalance-to-equal carries near-zero turnover; inverse-volatility decays modestly across the same 0/5/10/20/50 bps grid (0.62 → 0.60 → 0.59 → 0.55 → 0.45), so the VLSTM's relative gap widens monotonically with cost.

Variable selection therefore recovers most of the gap between a softmax long-only LSTM and the benchmark heuristics at gross terms but does not yet clear them at realistic cost. The training diagnostics show the characteristic failure mode: the pooled Sharpe on the training window climbs past 12, while the validation Sharpe collapses within a few dozen epochs. Early stopping protects the out-of-sample metric, but the underlying fragility (overfitting to training-window statistics that do not generalize) is exactly what the next architecture is designed to counter.

DeePM – Structural priors and a regime-robust loss

DeePM (Wood, Roberts, and Zohren, 2026) extends the same end-to-end pipeline with four additional structural components, each motivated by a specific failure mode of the simpler architecture above.

Asynchronous closes corrupt naive cross-sectional attention → Directed Delay (Causal Sieve). A cross-sectional attention layer that lets each asset's representation see all other assets' contemporaneous closes is fine when markets close synchronously, but global futures and FX markets do not. When the Nikkei closes at 06:00 UTC and the S&P closes at 21:00 UTC, an attention layer that gives the Nikkei representation access to the same-date S&P close uses information from the Nikkei's future filtration.

DeePM's Directed Delay shifts the allowed information flow per pair by an amount that respects each market's closing calendar, so each asset's representation only sees other assets' returns realized before its own close. This is a cross-sectional analog of the look-ahead-bias discipline that runs through the entire book. It is what makes a cross-asset attention mechanism deployable in a multi-region universe at all.

Channel-strength heterogeneity beyond what plain VSN handles → V-VSN temporal backbone. DeePM uses a hybrid VSN-LSTM-Attention encoder per asset. The variable-selection block is "vectorized" in that it operates on each lookback time step independently before the LSTM receives the gated feature vector, and the attention block on top of the LSTM lets the per-asset representation attend to its own past at variable horizons.

The combination is a richer per-asset temporal encoder than the VLSTM of the previous subsection: the temporal-encoding equivalent of moving from "weighted feature mixture into an LSTM" to "weighted feature mixture into an LSTM with self-attention on top."

Cross-sectional attention overfits in low-signal regimes → Macro Graph Prior implemented as a GAT. Free cross-sectional attention is permutation-equivariant (the right inductive bias for a portfolio set), but it allows attention weights to form between economically implausible asset pairs and amplifies noise when correlation estimates are unstable.

DeePM constrains attention to a fixed economic adjacency: intra-group cliques inside each macro group (equity indices, rates, energy, metals, agricultural commodities, FX, and more.) plus a small set of cross-group edges capturing economically motivated linkages such as safe-haven flows and supply-chain relationships. Inside that fixed adjacency, a Graph Attention Network learns dynamic edge weights that can upweight the bonds-equity link in risk-off regimes and downweight it in growth regimes. The structural prior fixes *which* edges are admissible while leaving *how strongly* each edge transmits information to the data: the cross-sectional counterpart of how a variable-selection network reasons over features.

Lucky-window overfit on long pooled-Sharpe horizons → SoftMin-augmented loss. A plain pooled Sharpe over a long training horizon can be inflated by a few favorable periods, leaving the policy fragile during the worst windows it has seen. DeePM augments the pooled Sharpe with a SoftMin penalty over rolling sub-windows:

$$\mathcal{L}(\theta) = -\mathrm{SR}_{\mathrm{pool}}(\theta) - \lambda \cdot \mathrm{SoftMin}_{\tau}(\{\mathrm{SR}_b(\theta)\}_{b=1}^{B})$$

where SR_b are Sharpe ratios computed on B non-overlapping training sub-windows (quarterly blocks in the paper) and:

$$\text{SoftMin}_\tau(\{SR_b\}) = -\tau\log\left(\frac{1}{B}\sum_{b=1}^{B}\exp\left(-SR_b/\tau\right)\right)$$

As $\tau \to 0$, the SoftMin approaches the worst sub-window's Sharpe, and the loss reduces to a pure worst-case objective; at moderate τ, it weights the weak sub-windows without collapsing onto a single episode. The objective, therefore, asks the network to perform well on average *and* be tolerable in the worst regime it has seen during training. The mechanism has a distributionally robust optimization interpretation: the SoftMin term is mathematically equivalent to taking the expectation of the negative Sharpe under an adversarial reweighting of the training sub-windows, constrained to a Kullback-Leibler ball around the uniform distribution. The effect on the policy is the same regardless of which interpretation one prefers. The gradient asks the network to invest some of its capacity in the regimes where average-case Sharpe would have let it coast.

`13_deepm_regime_robust` puts these four pieces together on the ETF test window:

- The full DeePM model achieves a Sharpe of 0.98 with a maximum drawdown of −7.5%.
- A no-SoftMin ablation that keeps the structural priors but drops the regime-robust loss reaches Sharpe 0.74 with a −8.9% drawdown.
- The two heuristic baselines have Sharpe ratios of 0.69: equal-weight with maximum drawdown of −18.4% and inverse-volatility with −14.7%.
- The regime-sliced comparison shows the full model's calm-vs-crisis Sharpe gap is +0.21 (calm 1.21, crisis 1.00), compared with +0.69 for the no-SoftMin ablation (calm 1.26, crisis 0.57). SoftMin substantially narrows the regime gap, mostly by lifting crisis-window performance.

On this test window, full DeePM leads on every margin that matters: a Sharpe of 0.98 against 0.69 for both heuristics and 0.74 for the no-SoftMin ablation, a maximum drawdown of −7.5% against −18.4% and −14.7% for equal-weight and inverse-volatility, and a calm-crisis Sharpe gap of 0.21 against 0.69 for the no-SoftMin variant. The contribution of SoftMin is sharply localized: the calm-window Sharpe barely moves (1.26 to 1.21), while the crisis-window Sharpe lifts from 0.57 to 1.00, a +0.43 gain that accounts for almost the entire regime-gap reduction. The result reinforces a recurring lesson of this chapter: **regime-robust training can deliver a Sharpe lift and a drawdown improvement simultaneously**, and the two effects need to be read together rather than traded against one another.

Figure 17.9 shows the resulting drawdown behavior through volatile periods.

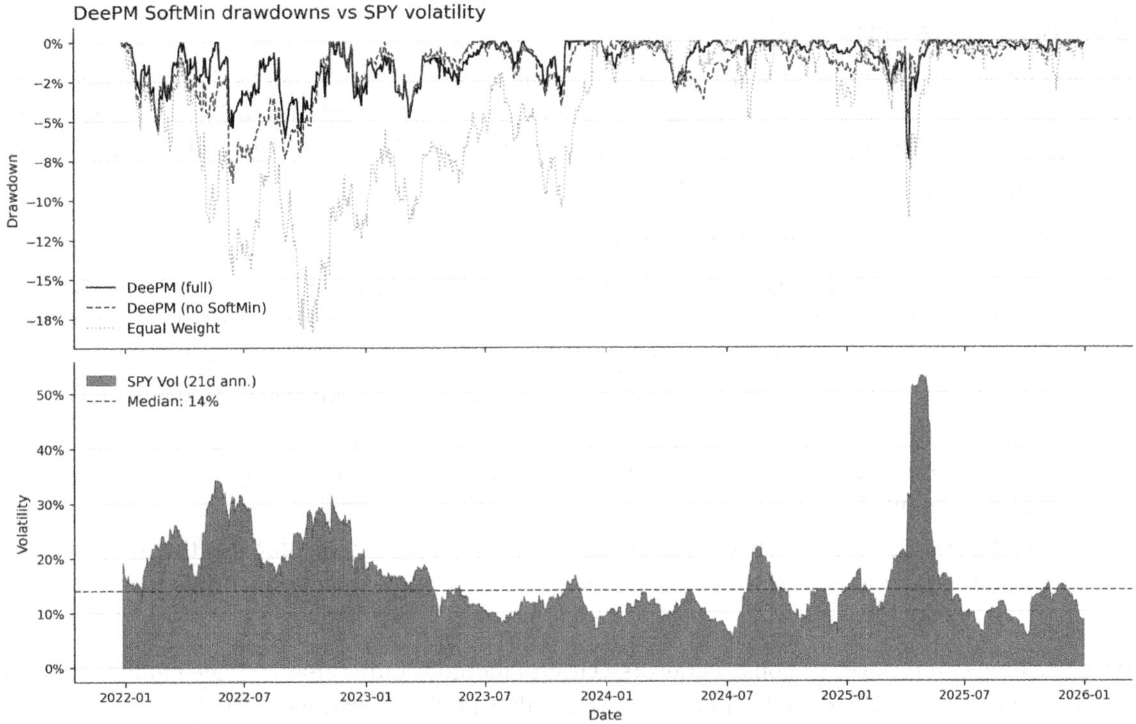

Figure 17.9: DeePM drawdown comparison. A regime-robust allocator should improve the path of losses, not only the average return

The three notebooks together decompose the end-to-end paradigm into separable contributions:

- `11_dl_portfolio_allocation` (Zhang et al.) achieves a Sharpe ratio of 0.48, a faithful softmax-long-only LSTM baseline that trails the heuristics on this universe despite the lowest realized maximum drawdown of the three (−10.9%) at less than half the heuristics' volatility.
- `12_vlstm_portfolio` reaches a gross Sharpe of 0.66 (effectively tying the heuristics in gross terms) but degrades to 0.55 at the 5 bps cost level used in training and 0.22 at 20 bps, while equal-weight is essentially flat (0.65 → 0.65) and inverse-volatility loses 0.07 over the same range (0.62 → 0.55).
- `13_deepm_regime_robust` reaches Sharpe 0.98 with a −7.5% maximum drawdown, exceeding the heuristics on Sharpe by roughly 0.29 while cutting drawdown by more than half.

The 0.48 → 0.66 improvement measures the architectural contribution of variable selection; the 0.66 → 0.98 move (together with the much-improved drawdown profile) measures the joint contribution of the structural priors (Directed Delay, Macro Graph) and the SoftMin regime-robust loss, with the gain showing up in both Sharpe and risk shape on this particular test window.

Evaluating learned allocators

Because end-to-end training optimizes a portfolio objective, learned allocators should be evaluated on allocator metrics rather than forecasting accuracy. *Section 17.3*'s multi-dimensional framework, including Sharpe, drawdown, turnover, concentration, regime-sliced performance, and transaction-cost breakeven, applies without modification.

Three considerations are specific to the learned setting:

- **Seed sensitivity becomes a first-class metric**: The loss surface is non-convex, the gradient depends on global batch statistics, and the variance across random initializations can dominate small differences in performance. Saly-Kaufmann report this explicitly, and an architecture ranking that ignores it can be reordered by changing the random-seed budget.
- **Turnover stops being a post hoc diagnostic**: Architectures with similar gross Sharpe ratios can differ by a factor of two in breakeven cost, so the cost-stress curve matters as much as the headline number.
- **The heuristic comparison stays non-negotiable**: An end-to-end allocator that cannot clear equal weight and inverse volatility on its own test window is not yet competitive, however sophisticated its encoder.

Deep learning enters portfolio construction as a class of methods rather than a single model. Classical allocators remain the right default when signals are stable, and the covariance structure is the binding constraint. End-to-end allocators are the right default when the objective is hard to factor cleanly into forecasting plus optimization: regime robustness, cost-aware sizing, or cross-asset interaction with known structure. DeePM is the chapter's clearest example of the second case.

All three notebooks train end-to-end on raw ETF prices over a sub-universe of the ETF case study; only `13_deepm_regime_robust` uses asset-class group labels for its macro graph. Unlike `06_hierarchical_risk_parity` and `07_conformal_position_sizing`, they do *not* consume the ETF case study's GBM walk-forward predictions. The goal here is to isolate the architectural and loss-design contribution of end-to-end portfolio learning, not to reuse a fixed signal as input. Reusing case-study predictions on top of these encoders is a natural extension but would conflate signal quality with allocator architecture.

Implementation:

- `11_dl_portfolio_allocation` implements the Zhang, Zohren, Roberts softmax long-only LSTM baseline.
- `12_vlstm_portfolio` shows the Saly-Kaufmann VLSTM (TFT-style variable-selection block + LSTM encoder) under the volatility-targeted long-short layer with a 5 bps cost-aware Sharpe loss and a cost-stress sweep over 0/5/10/20/50 bps.
- `13_deepm_regime_robust` shows the full DeePM implementation with Directed Delay, Macro Graph Prior, SoftMin-augmented loss, and regime-sliced (calm versus crisis) evaluation.

17.9 Summary

Portfolio construction translates forecasts into tradable positions: the point at which a signal becomes profit or loss. This chapter established a rigorous framework for making allocation decisions explicit, testable, and comparable. It formalized the allocation problem as a constrained optimization over weights, leverage, and rebalancing frequency, and then introduced the allocator term sheet to ensure every design choice remains auditable. Multi-dimensional evaluation, including Sharpe, drawdown, turnover, concentration, and regime-sliced diagnostics, replaced single-metric comparisons.

The empirical results reinforce a humbling message: simple heuristics set a high bar. Equal weighting and inverse volatility require minimal estimation and frequently match or beat sophisticated optimization out-of-sample. Mean-variance optimization fails without robust fixes. Ledoit-Wolf shrinkage, position constraints, and turnover penalties partially mitigate it but cannot fully overcome the instability inherent in inverting a noisy covariance matrix. Hierarchical Risk Parity avoids matrix inversion entirely and produces portfolios with better drawdown characteristics, at the cost of ignoring return forecasts. Regime-aware adaptation of inputs and constraints offers a middle path between static allocation and fragile regime switching.

End-to-end deep learning allocators bypass the predict-then-optimize pipeline entirely, training directly on the portfolio objective, but sacrifice the modularity and interpretability that make classical approaches debuggable. The chapter-local comparison shows that allocator performance spreads are often narrower than model-performance spreads, while the cross-case results already show that the leading allocator varies by dataset rather than converging on a single universal method. *Chapter 20* provides the full cross-case allocator synthesis.

Chapter 18 develops the transaction-cost dimension that allocation decisions must ultimately confront. *Chapter 19* adds the risk overlays that determine whether allocator differences survive stress, tail events, and leverage constraints. The turnover generated by different allocators has real dollar costs, and the portfolios that look similar on gross Sharpe can separate sharply once costs and risk controls are imposed.

18

Transaction Costs

A strategy that looks brilliant on paper can lose money the moment it trades. Every trade carries a cost: the spread you cross, the market you move, the opportunity you miss. These costs accumulate during a backtest and turn paper profits into real losses. Transaction costs account for most of the gap between theoretical alpha and realized returns.

Cost modeling is a first-class concern in the ML4T workflow. Rather than treating costs as an afterthought (a percentage shaved off at the end), we integrate them from signal evaluation through to live execution. The goal is not to *eliminate* costs, which is impossible, but to understand them well enough to make informed trade-offs: Is this factor's IC worth its turnover? Can this strategy scale to meaningful AUM? When does execution quality matter more than signal quality?

After completing this chapter, you will be able to:

- Map where transaction costs enter each stage of the ML4T pipeline, from factor evaluation through risk management.
- Classify costs into explicit, implicit, and capacity components and identify which dominate for a given strategy type.
- Parameterize three baseline backtest cost models (spread, linear slippage, and square-root impact), with guidance on when each applies.
- Evaluate execution algorithms (TWAP, VWAP, Almgren-Chriss) as controls that shape the impact-timing trade-off rather than solutions that eliminate costs.
- Design a transaction cost analysis (TCA) framework that decomposes realized costs, validates ex-ante models, and closes the feedback loop.
- Apply cost-based guardrails (break-even turnover, minimum required edge, capacity analysis, and kill-switch criteria) to assess the strategy's feasibility before deployment.

We will begin by mapping cost integration points across the workflow (*Section 18.1*), then develop a practitioner cost taxonomy (*Section 18.2*) and connect it to microstructure regimes (*Section 18.3*). Three baseline cost models for backtesting follow (*Section 18.4*). *Sections 18.5* and *18.6* cover execution algorithms and the Almgren-Chriss optimal execution framework. *Section 18.7* introduces TCA as the feedback mechanism that keeps cost models calibrated. We close with practical guardrails that determine when costs should kill a strategy (*Section 18.8*).

18.1 Where costs enter the ML4T workflow

A factor that clears the gross-return hurdle can still fail once it trades in size. This section identifies where transaction costs enter the ML4T workflow so that each stage evaluates net returns. The following list introduces each stage in turn:

1. Costs first bite in **feature evaluation**. A feature with a slightly higher IC is not better if it requires ten times the turnover. The strategies covered in *Chapters 7* and *8*, therefore, need cost-aware signal thresholds because forecast quality and trading intensity must be judged together.
2. Costs become explicit in **strategy simulation**. *Chapter 16* converts signals into orders, holdings, and realized PnL. If that stage assumes frictionless execution, the backtest approves strategies whose gross alpha was never large enough to survive spread, slippage, and impact.
3. **Portfolio construction** is also a cost decision. *Chapter 17*'s turnover constraints, position limits, and rebalance rules are not cosmetic. They regularize the optimizer to mitigate costly portfolio churn and keep desired weights within the market's liquidity budget.
4. The downstream chapters inherit the same constraint. *Chapter 19* treats capacity and execution stress as risk limits, while *Chapter 20* folds net-of-cost monitoring into the production loop.

Figure 18.1 maps those links across the full research-to-production pipeline:

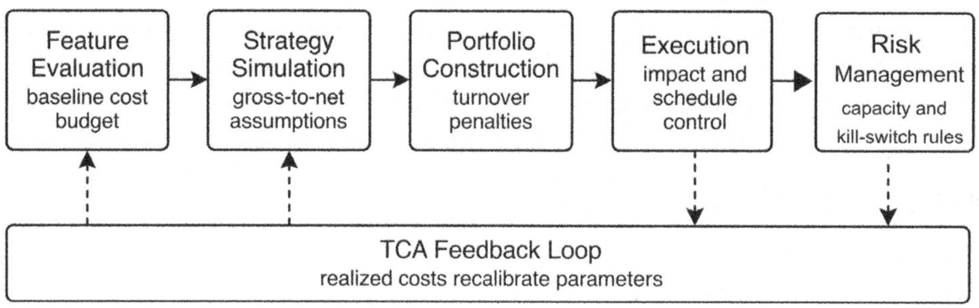

Figure 18.1: Cost integration across the ML4T pipeline. Transaction costs constrain every stage, from factor evaluation to risk management, with TCA feedback recalibrating ex ante parameters

Cost analysis operates through two lenses. Ex ante models forecast the cost of hypothetical trades for backtests and portfolio design. Ex post transaction cost analysis (TCA) measures the actual costs incurred by the desk. The first lens prevents naive simulations. The second prevents stale parameters. The workflow is circular: estimate, trade, measure, recalibrate.

The false positive problem

Ignoring costs produces false positives. The sign of the bias is easy to understand: every turnover-heavy strategy looks better before spread, slippage, and impact are accounted for. The bias is large enough to erase many published gross-return effects:

- Frazzini et al. (2018) show why the calibration source matters. Using $1.7 trillion of live institutional executions across 21 developed equity markets, they find that patient execution costs are far below the estimates often inferred from TAQ data. TAQ describes the average trade; it does not isolate a patient allocator using schedule control, passive liquidity, and venue selection.

- Retail execution shows the same point from the other side. Schwarz et al. (2022) document large execution-price differences across retail brokers even when commissions are zero and orders are matched on observable characteristics. The implication is not that one universal cost number exists. It is the routing, urgency, and execution style that decide whether an edge survives.

These findings create two symmetric errors. TAQ-based costs can reject viable strategies that would survive patient execution. Zero-cost assumptions approve strategies that fail the moment they trade. The fix is conservative calibration when execution data is absent and continuous TCA-based recalibration when execution data is available.

The remaining sections provide tools to avoid both failure modes: a cost taxonomy (*Section 18.2*), regime-aware baseline models (*Section 18.4*), and TCA-based validation frameworks (*Section 18.7*). The goal is to make cost-aware research the default, beginning with the cost components themselves.

> **Implementation:** See `01_cost_taxonomy` for cross-asset fee schedules and breakeven analysis, and `03_market_impact_calibration` for impact model calibration.

18.2 A cost taxonomy for practitioners

Transaction costs have structure. That structure determines which terms belong in the model and which components dominate for a given strategy. *Figure 18.2* organizes the taxonomy into three branches (explicit, implicit, and capacity), each requiring distinct modeling approaches.

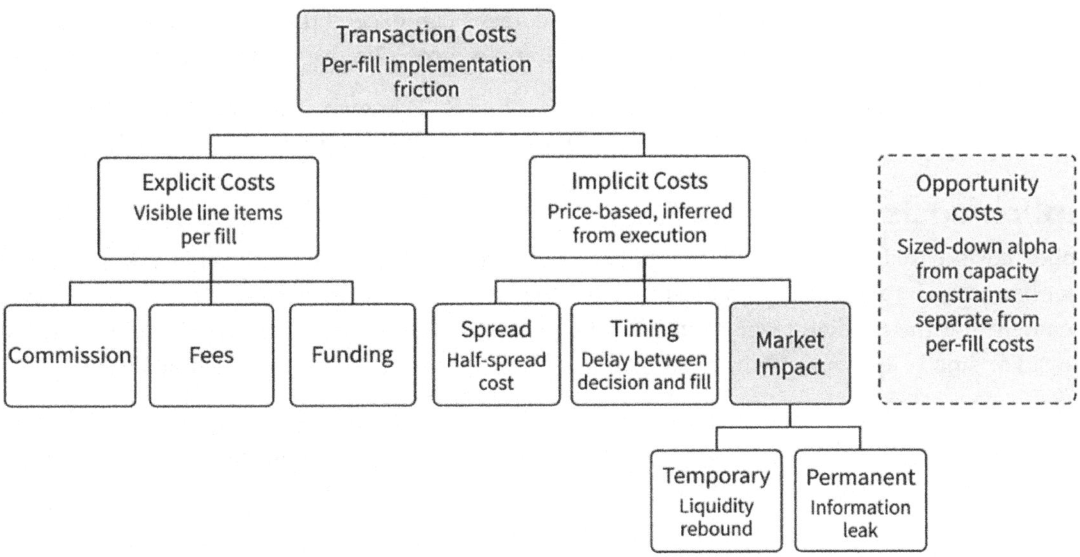

Figure 18.2: Transaction cost taxonomy

Convention note: Throughout this section, costs are expressed in basis points (bps) of notional value, one-way unless explicitly stated as round-trip. One basis point equals 0.01% of trade value. Impact model outputs (C_{impact}) represent expected price movement as a fraction of price, which converts directly to bps when multiplied by 10,000.

Explicit costs

Explicit costs are contractually defined and accounted for exactly. Commissions, exchange fees, and clearing charges belong in this bucket. They are often small for liquid cash equities but still meaningful for futures, options, and high-turnover strategies, where a few basis points, repeated thousands of times, become material.

Regulatory fees also belong here. They scale mechanically with notional or share count and should be modeled as fixed-schedule inputs rather than left in an undifferentiated slippage term. For a strategy that sells large notional amounts every day, individually tiny fees add up to a visible annual drag.

Financing costs are explicit as well, even though they are easy to overlook. Margin interest, borrow fees on shorts, and futures roll all convert gross alpha into carry decisions. An instrument with sub-basis-point trading friction can still be expensive to hold if financing terms deteriorate. Borrow deserves special attention because it is broker-specific, time-varying, and often the dominant cost on the short side. A conservative backtest, therefore, needs either historical borrowing data or a defensible proxy based on market cap, float, and short-interest pressure.

Transaction taxes are the clearest example of a mechanical first-order wedge. In markets that impose stamp duties or securities transaction taxes, those levies can exceed the spread for the most liquid names. Any cross-market comparison that omits them is wrong before the first trade is simulated.

Explicit costs should be inserted exactly where the schedule is known. The modeling error is usually not in this bucket; it is in treating the exact, visible costs as if they were the whole problem.

Implicit costs

Implicit costs arise from the interaction between the order and the market. The bid-ask spread is the lower bound on implicit cost. A round-trip trade that buys at the ask and sells at the bid pays the full spread, even if the market never moves. For liquid large-cap equities, that may be only a few basis points. For small-caps, options, or stressed markets, it can be an order of magnitude larger.

Slippage is the gap between the intended execution benchmark and the actual fill. That gap reflects quote drift during transmission, queue position, partial fills, and adverse selection. Spread is paid immediately. Slippage accumulates while the order is being executed.

Market impact is the price movement caused by trading itself. Kyle (1985) provides the canonical linear-impact framework: the market maker learns from order flow, so larger and more informative trades move the price more.

For attribution, it is useful to distinguish between temporary and permanent impacts:

- **Temporary impact** is the price pressure created during execution that partially reverts once the order is complete; it reflects liquidity consumption and dealer inventory effects
- **Permanent impact** is the information footprint of the trade: if the order reveals information, the market revises its value estimate, and the price move does not fully revert

Amihud (2002) showed that illiquidity, measured as the ratio of absolute return to dollar volume, helps explain cross-sectional differences in returns and serves as a practical proxy for this broader impact channel. The distinction matters because temporary impact is the part the trader should seek to reduce through scheduling and venue choice, while permanent impact reflects how visible and informative the order has become. Hasbrouck (1991) provides the basic empirical framework for measuring that informational component.

Capacity costs

Capacity costs appear when the strategy scales into the market's liquidity budget. Participation is the first term. Trading 0.25% of ADV and trading 5% of ADV are different businesses. Frazzini et al. (2018) show that impact increases in a concave fashion with trade size, which is why the square-root rule is the default practical model.

Crowding is the second term. Chordia, Roll, and Subrahmanyam (2000) show that liquidity co-moves across names and sectors. Capacity is therefore not a static property of the signal. It depends on who else is trying to trade the same idea and when they arrive.

Opportunity cost closes the stack. Slower execution reduces impact but increases the chance that the market moves before the order is complete. Capacity is therefore a joint property of signal decay, order size, and execution urgency.

The cost stack

For practical modeling, costs combine into a stack:

$$C_{total} = C_{explicit} + C_{spread} + C_{slippage} + C_{impact}$$

The relative importance varies by strategy:

Strategy Type	Dominant Costs
High-frequency	Spread, exchange fees
Daily rebalancing	Spread, slippage
Weekly/monthly	Market impact
Low-turnover	Explicit fees, opportunity cost

Table 18.1: Dominant costs by strategy

To anchor the taxonomy in concrete magnitudes, the following table shows typical one-way all-in costs across the asset classes covered by this book's case studies. The two-orders-of-magnitude range, from under 1 basis point for liquid ETFs to over 100 basis points for illiquid options, is driven primarily by market structure rather than asset fundamentals.

Asset Class	Retail (bps, one-way)	Institutional (bps)	Dominant Component
US large-cap equities	1–5	5–15	Spread + execution quality
US small-cap equities	10–30	20–50	Spread + impact
Liquid ETFs (SPY, QQQ)	0.5–3	1–5	Spread
Equity options	10–100+ (of premium)	3–20	Spread (no Rule 605 transparency)
Index futures (ES, NQ)	0.7–1.5	0.5–1.0	Tick-constrained spread
FX spot (major pairs)	5–30	0.5–3	Venue segmentation
Crypto perps (CEX)	5–50	2–10	Fee tier + volatility regime
IG corporate bonds	30–80	5–20	Embedded markup

Table 18.2: Trading cost rules of thumb; depend on market/venue and broker

Dominant costs determine modeling effort. A daily signal needs spread and slippage estimates that move with the regime. A slower, larger allocator needs impact and financing terms that scale with position size and holding period.

Implementation: See `01_cost_taxonomy` for cost component breakdowns across strategy types, `02_spread_estimation` for empirical spread estimation, and `12_commission_slippage_comparison` for side-by-side commission and slippage model comparisons across asset classes.

18.3 The microstructure regime link

Transaction costs are not stationary. Spread, slippage, and impact move with market state, so constant parameters are wrong by construction. This section links the microstructure ideas from *Chapter 3* to the conditioning variables that belong in cost models.

Intraday liquidity patterns

Liquidity follows predictable intraday patterns that directly affect execution costs (see *Chapter 3*):

- **Market open (9:30-10:00 ET for US equities):** High volatility, wide spreads, and thin depth as the market processes overnight information. Impact costs peak as participants compete to establish positions. Executing during this window is materially more expensive than executing at midday.
- **Midday (11:00-14:00 ET):** Lowest volatility and tightest spreads. Market makers provide maximum depth. This window offers the lowest execution costs for patient traders but may introduce timing risk for urgent orders.
- **Market close (15:30-16:00 ET):** Volume tends to concentrate as index funds rebalance and traders close intraday positions. Spreads tighten, but depth can be consumed quickly. Auction mechanisms (closing auctions) offer execution certainty at the cost of price impact.

Karnaukh et al. (2015) documented similar patterns in FX markets, where liquidity concentrates during overlapping trading sessions (London/New York) and deteriorates during Asia-only hours.

Volatility and spread dynamics

Spreads widen predictably with volatility. Market makers face adverse selection: informed traders are more likely to trade when they have private information, which tends to coincide with periods of volatility. To compensate for this risk, market makers widen spreads.

This proportionality follows from inventory-based market-making models (for example, Ho and Stoll 1981): the market maker sets spreads to compensate for price risk over the expected time between trades. The relationship is approximately:

$$Spread \propto \sigma \cdot \sqrt{\Delta t}$$

where σ is return volatility and Δt is the time between quote updates. During high-volatility events such as earnings releases and macro announcements, spreads widen materially relative to normal levels.

Impact costs also scale with volatility. The standard square-root impact model includes volatility explicitly:

$$Impact = \sigma \cdot \eta \cdot \sqrt{\frac{Q}{V}}$$

where η is the impact coefficient, Q is order size, and V is average daily volume. Higher volatility means higher impact for the same participation rate.

Regime transitions

Markets also shift between regimes abruptly. Stress episodes compress depth, widen spreads, and increase impact fast enough to invalidate parameters estimated from quiet periods. March 2020 is the template: across rates, credit, and equities, execution costs moved by multiples rather than percentages. Any systematic strategy forced to rebalance during stress will pay those stressed costs, not the trailing average.

One mechanism is information asymmetry. Faster participants detect regime shifts sooner and widen the gap between patient and urgent execution. A second mechanism is market inelasticity. Bouchaud (2022) argues that aggregate demand is less price-elastic than standard models assume, so the same flow causes larger price moves when liquidity withdraws.

The practical question is not which single indicator defines the regime. It is the indicators that jointly describe execution conditions. Implied volatility, relative volume, quote-depth imbalance, and spread-normalized-to-history should be read together. A high VIX print without spread widening does not imply the same execution response as a high VIX print with depth collapse and one-sided order-book imbalance.

Implications for cost modeling

Regime dependence changes four modeling decisions. Parameters should be estimated separately by volatility bucket and trading window, rather than pooled into a single average. When the regime is ambiguous, stressed parameters are the safer default because cost underestimation can lead to false positives. Production systems should monitor the same indicators in real time and adjust participation when spreads or depth move outside normal bounds. Historical backtests should also use contemporaneous regimes, so that crisis periods incur crisis-level costs rather than a diluted full-sample average.

The regime lens prevents the assumption that today's costs predict tomorrow's. Cost models are only as good as their conditioning on market state.

> **Implementation:** See `02_spread_estimation` for regime-conditioned spread analysis and `03_market_impact_calibration` for impact coefficient estimation by VIX regime.

18.4 Baseline backtesting cost models

Every researcher needs implementable cost models for backtesting. This section presents three baseline models of increasing realism and shows when each one is adequate.

A unified view of impact models

A trade schedule specifies how a parent order is divided over time. Let x_t denote the remaining inventory to be executed at time t, and let:

$$v_t = -\dot{x}_t$$

denote the signed trading rate. For a buy order, $v_t > 0$; for a sell order, $v_t < 0$. A faster schedule concentrates volume into a shorter interval, while a slower schedule spreads the same parent order over a longer horizon.

Market impact models differ in how they map this schedule into price pressure and execution cost. A useful way to organize many transient-impact models is to separate three ingredients:

1. An instantaneous impact function $f(\cdot)$, which maps trading intensity into immediate price pressure.
2. A decay kernel $G(\cdot)$, often called the propagator, which determines how past impact persists or fades.
3. A market-specific scale parameter κ, which captures liquidity, volatility, spread, depth, and other market conditions.

Under this representation, the transient price impact at time t, measured as a fraction of price, can be written as:

$$I_t = \kappa \int_0^t f(v_s) G(t-s)\, ds$$

The expected impact cost of executing the schedule over the horizon T, normalized by total traded notional, is then obtained by integrating the current trading rate against the impact already present while the trade is being executed:

$$C_{\text{impact}} = \frac{1}{Q}\int_0^T v_t\, I_t\, dt, \qquad Q = \int_0^T |v_t|\, dt$$

This distinction matters. The single integral of I_t represents the price pressure remaining at a given point in time. The cost of execution depends on the impact incurred throughout the schedule, which is why the cost expression involves the trading rate and the evolving impact process.

For backtesting, however, researchers usually do not estimate a full propagator model. They use reduced-form approximations that map observable trade size, volatility, volume, and spread into expected cost. Different assumptions about the impact function, decay behavior, and execution horizon produce the canonical models summarized in *Table 18.3*.

Model	Core Assumption	Typical Reduced-Form Unit Cost	When to Use
Spread	The main cost is crossing the bid-ask spread.	Half-spread, plus commissions or fees where relevant	Small orders in liquid markets
Linear participation	Impact rises approximately linearly with participation or order size relative to volume.	$C_{\text{impact}} \propto Q/V$	Medium-sized orders, conservative baseline, theoretical benchmark
Square-root metaorder	Impact increases in a concave manner with order size and scales with volatility.	$C_{\text{impact}} \propto \sigma\sqrt{Q/V}$	Large orders, institutional-style execution, empirical baseline
Transient linear impact	Impact is linear in trading rate but decays over time as liquidity replenishes.	Depends on the execution horizon relative to market resilience	Multi-period execution where schedule timing matters
Propagator models	Impact from past trades decays slowly and may interact with concave impact functions.	Model-dependent; often calibrated to reproduce concave metaorder impact	High-frequency, multi-period, or execution-focused research

Table 18.3: Market impact model overview

This framing is useful because the models are not competing philosophical categories; they are progressively richer approximations to the same execution problem. Let's think more about the different types of model:

- A spread model is a lower bound. It assumes that the main cost is simply crossing the bid-ask spread and ignores the effect of the order on subsequent prices.

- A linear model is a simple participation-based extension. It penalizes larger trades relative to available volume and is easy to implement, but it can overstate the cost of large orders when impact is empirically concave.
- A square-root model is the empirical workhorse for meaningful order sizes. It captures the robust finding that impact tends to increase less than proportionally with order size, often scaling with volatility and the square root of the order's share of market volume.
- Transient-impact and propagator models become relevant when execution timing matters. They distinguish between the immediate price pressure caused by trading and the persistence of that pressure as liquidity replenishes. These models are more realistic for multi-period execution, but they also require stronger assumptions and more calibration data.

The remainder of this section implements the first three models: spread costs, linear participation costs, and square-root impact costs. These are the most useful baselines for strategy backtests because they require limited data, are transparent to audit, and cover the main regimes encountered in practical research. More detailed transient-impact models are better treated as execution models than as default backtest cost models.

The spread model

The simplest cost model charges half the bid-ask spread per trade:

$$C_{spread} = \frac{1}{2} \cdot \text{Spread}_t$$

For a round-trip, the full spread is paid. This model captures the minimum cost of crossing the spread to execute.

Parameterization approaches:

- Historical quotes: Calculate time-weighted average spreads from TAQ or similar data, conditioned on volatility regime
- Volume-weighted spread: Weight spread observations by trading volume to reflect when trades actually occur
- Conservative default: For US large-cap equities, 5-10 basis points; for small-caps, 20-50 basis points; for emerging markets or illiquid names, 50-100+ basis points

The spread model underestimates costs for large orders (which face impact beyond the spread) but provides a useful lower bound.

The linear slippage model

The linear slippage model adds execution friction that scales with participation:

$$C_{slippage} = C_{spread} + \alpha \cdot \frac{Q}{V}$$

where α is the slippage coefficient in basis points per unit participation (order size Q relative to daily volume V). This captures costs from market moves during execution, partial fills, and queue position.

Bear the following in mind during calibration:

- Compare execution prices to mid-quotes at order submission across historical trades
- Condition on volatility regime: slippage is typically 2–3x higher during volatile periods
- Conservative defaults: 5 basis points for liquid large-caps; 15-25 basis points for mid- and small-caps; but these figures are only starting points, vary with the market, and require research

The linear model works well for moderate order sizes, where impact scales roughly linearly with value. It fails for large orders where the impact is concave.

The square-root impact model

For meaningful order sizes, market impact dominates, and scales sublinearly with participation. The square-root model, grounded in theoretical, and empirical work, captures this relationship:

$$C_{impact} = \sigma \cdot \eta \cdot \sqrt{\frac{Q}{V}}$$

where:

- σ = daily return volatility
- η = impact coefficient (typically 0.1–0.5)
- Q = order quantity in shares
- V = average daily volume in shares

The square-root law has strong empirical support. Sato and Kanazawa (2024) find exponents near 0.5 across multiple asset classes. Toth et al. (2011) connect that regularity to order-book dynamics, and Cont et al. (2014) show that the realized coefficient still depends on current depth, imbalance, and recent flow.

The key practical point is concavity. Doubling order size does not double the impact, but it still increases the total cost enough that schedule design matters. *Figure 18.3* compares linear, square-root, and power-law assumptions on a 100,000-share order: linear charges 330 bps, square-root 103 bps, power-law 850 bps. The square-root model is a better default because it captures both cross-asset heterogeneity and the concave increase in cost with size. Once a cost model is selected, the relevant question for a strategy is whether realized gross alpha survives the resulting drag.

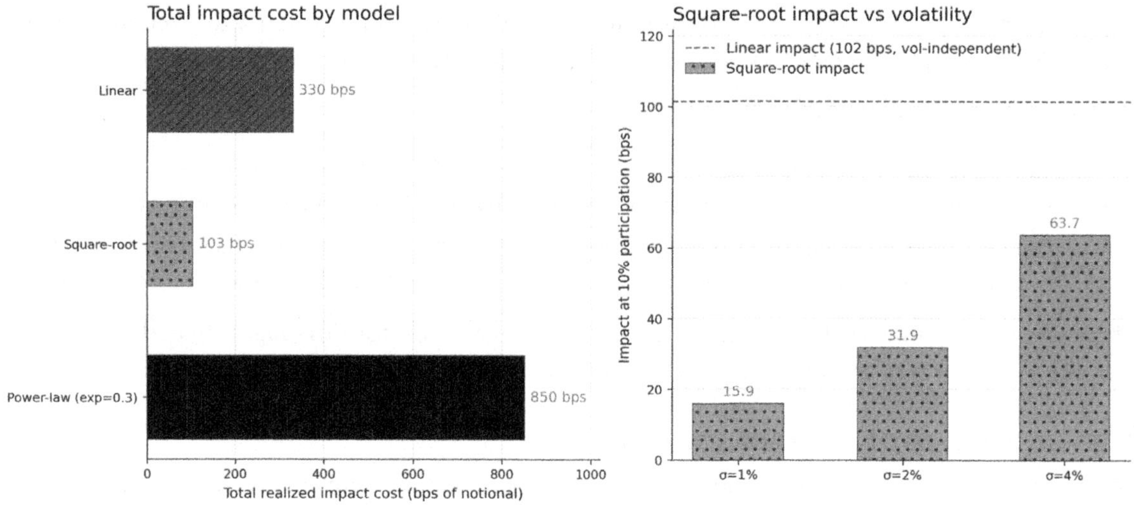

Figure 18.3: Left: total realized impact cost on a 100,000-share parent order at $100 under linear, square-root, and concave power-law (exp=0.3) impact models, in bps of notional. Right: square-root impact at 10% participation across volatility regimes (sigma = 1%, 2%, 4%), with the vol-independent linear reference (102 bps) overlaid. Impact cost rises with model convexity and with volatility

Figure 18.4 maps that drag across eight of the chapter's case studies: gross-to-net Sharpe degradation at the headline cost configuration of each case study, with the breakeven cost level annotated alongside.

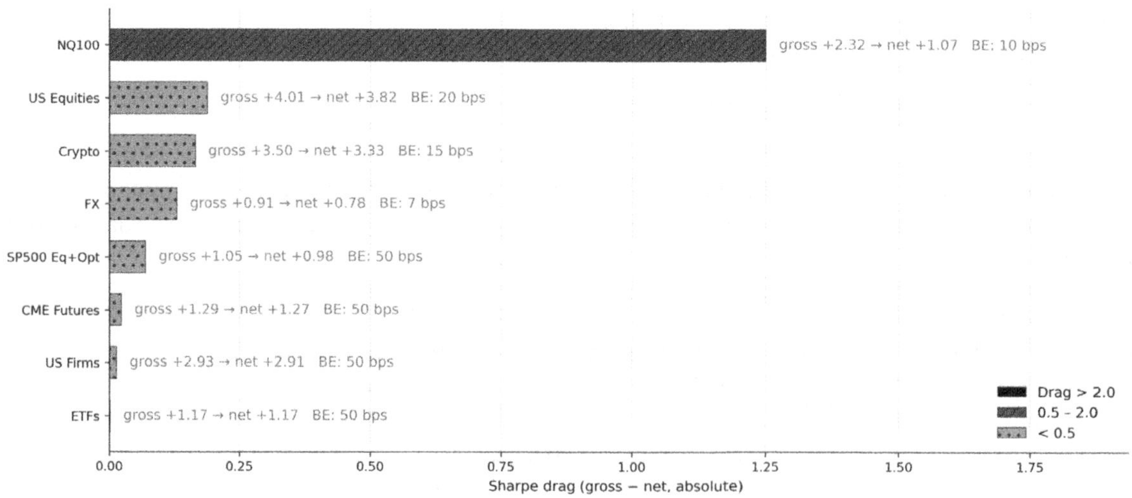

Figure 18.4: Gross-to-net Sharpe degradation by case study at headline cost configurations. The annotated breakeven column shows how much further the model could absorb before realized Sharpe crosses zero

To use the square-root model in a backtest, it helps to distinguish three related tasks: assembling a full one-way cost estimate, calibrating the impact coefficient, and deciding when the model is an appropriate baseline.

A practical one-way specification combines explicit fees, half the bid-ask spread, and temporary market impact:

$$C_{total} = C_{explicit} + \frac{1}{2}\text{Spread} + \sigma \cdot \eta \cdot \sqrt{\frac{Q}{V}}$$

This decomposition is useful because the three terms capture different mechanisms. $C_{explicit}$ covers commissions, exchange fees, and taxes. The half-spread term captures the immediate cost of demanding liquidity. The square-root term captures temporary impact that rises with participation but does so in concave rather than linear form. For small trades, spread and explicit fees may dominate. As order size increases, the impact term usually becomes the larger component.

The impact coefficient η is not a universal constant. It varies with asset class, liquidity, volatility, market regime, and execution style. *Table 18.4* therefore provides starting ranges rather than fixed values.

Asset Type	**Typical η Range**
Large-cap equities	0.1–0.3
Mid-cap equities	0.2–0.4
Small-cap equities	0.3-0.6
Liquid futures	0.1–0.2
FX majors	0.05–0.15

Table 18.4: Impact coefficients by asset class

In practice, η should be estimated from transaction-cost analysis, broker execution data, or comparable historical trades whenever possible. Taranto et al. (2018) show that realized impact also depends on recent order flow and market state, so even a well-estimated coefficient is only an average summary. For backtesting, it is usually better to err on the conservative side and use values from the upper half, or upper quartile, of the range that fits the relevant asset class and liquidity bucket.

Choosing and stress testing a baseline cost model

Model choice should follow expected participation. For very small orders, a spread model often provides an adequate lower bound. For moderate participation, a linear slippage model is a reasonable simplification. For larger trades, the square-root specification is the better default because it reflects the concave empirical relationship between size and impact.

Participation Rate	Recommended Model
< 0.5% of ADV	Spread model
0.5% - 2% of ADV	Linear slippage
>2% of ADV	Square-root impact

Table 18.5: Impact model by participation rate

These thresholds are rules of thumb, not hard boundaries. Their purpose is to keep the backtest from using a model that is structurally too optimistic. A spread-only model may be acceptable for a low-turnover strategy trading small fractions of daily volume, but it will materially understate costs for a strategy that repeatedly trades several percent of dollar volume.

When historical execution data is unavailable, initialize the model conservatively: at least the quoted spread, a slippage allowance that widens in volatile periods, and an impact coefficient chosen from the more expensive end of the plausible range. These inputs are initial assumptions to be challenged later, not final estimates.

The limits of these baseline models should also be explicit. The square-root model can break down in stressed markets, where impact may steepen sharply; for very small trades, where fixed costs dominate; and in fragmented or queue-driven microstructure, where execution priority matters. The model should therefore be treated as a robust baseline for backtesting, not as a precise forecast of realized execution cost. Validation through transaction-cost analysis, discussed in *Section 18.7*, remains essential.

A second limitation is the choice of cost base. The baseline models in this section express costs in basis points of notional value, which works well for cash equities, FX, and futures. It does not work well for instruments whose traded price is only a small fraction of the notional exposure. As the S&P500 Options case study shows, for a short at-the-money straddle on an index constituent, for example, the option premium may be only 3 to 5% of the underlying notional, while the bid-ask spread on that premium may be another 5 to 15% of the premium itself. That translates to roughly 15 to 75 basis points of underlying notional per side, far above the single-digit basis-point assumptions that may be reasonable for equities. *Section 18.8* shows how this mismatch can drive the same strategy from strongly negative to modestly positive Sharpe depending on how spread crossing and universe filtering are modeled. The broader lesson is that when traded price and notional exposure are not proportional, the baseline notional-bps framework should be replaced by a price-scaled model calibrated to the instrument.

Costs as portfolio regularizer

Mean-variance optimization is unstable, in part, because the frictionless version assumes that rebalancing is free. Add realistic trading costs, and the optimizer becomes less willing to chase small forecast changes with large weight changes. In that sense, transaction costs regularize portfolio weights. That is why *Chapter 17*'s practical MVO belongs in the same conversation as *Chapter 18*'s execution models.

Implementation: See `03_market_impact_calibration` for parameter calibration and model comparison, and `06_ml4t_execution_demo` for the API of the `ml4t.backtest.execution` module.

18.5 Execution algorithms as controls

Execution algorithms control the trade-off between impact and timing risk. They do not eliminate transaction costs. The important question is therefore which benchmark an algorithm optimizes and which risks it leaves behind, not whether it is "optimal" in the abstract.

Time-weighted average price

Time-weighted average price (**TWAP**) divides an order into equal slices executed at regular intervals:

$$\text{Slice}_i = \frac{Q}{N} \text{ executed at time } t_i$$

TWAP optimizes simplicity and schedule certainty. It is easy to implement, easy to audit, and useful as a baseline benchmark. Its weakness is equally clear: equal time slices ignore intraday volume patterns, do not respond to spread blowouts, and expose the full order to timing risk during the execution window. TWAP is acceptable when urgency is low and liquidity is roughly stable. It should not be the default for orders whose cost depends materially on the timing of their execution.

Volume-weighted average price (VWAP)

Volume-weighted average price (**VWAP**) shapes execution to match historical volume patterns:

$$\text{Slice}_i \propto \text{ExpectedVolume}_i$$

More shares execute during high-volume periods, which usually reduces per-slice impact. VWAP therefore optimizes benchmark tracking rather than pure cost minimization. It works well when historical volume profiles are stable, and the trader cares about matching the market's average execution level. It fails when the realized session departs from the expected profile, when spreads widen suddenly, or when the benchmark itself is a poor proxy for execution quality.

Obizhaeva and Wang (2013) showed that optimal trading strategies must account for order book resilience (how quickly depth replenishes after a trade) beyond simple volume matching.

Both TWAP and VWAP are static schedules. They commit to a path before the market reveals whether the session will be calm, stressed, or information-heavy. That is the real limitation. A static schedule continues through regime changes, unexpected news, and liquidity vacuums unless a separate rule interrupts it.

Regime-aware participation

A practical improvement over static schedules incorporates real-time regime signals:

$$\text{ParticipationRate} = \text{BaseRate} \cdot f(\text{Spread}, \text{Volatility}, \text{Depth})$$

where f is a dampening function that reduces participation when spreads widen, volatility spikes, or visible depth disappears. This is the simplest practical upgrade to static execution: trade less when liquidity is expensive, accept slower completion, and make the impact-versus-timing trade explicit.

Nevmyvaka, Feng, and Kearns (2006) show that adaptive execution policies can outperform static VWAP-style schedules once the policy conditions on real-time market state. The conceptual lesson matters more than the exact algorithm: regime awareness belongs inside execution, not outside it.

The trade-off is explicit: aggressive execution minimizes timing risk but maximizes impact; passive execution minimizes impact but accepts timing risk. The optimal balance depends on the strategy's alpha decay rate: fast-decaying signals require aggressive execution despite costs.

Sophisticated execution systems use a receding-horizon approach: optimize a multi-period execution plan, execute only the first period, then re-optimize with updated market state. This is identical to model predictive control (MPC) in control engineering. The market state (order book depth, recent volume, price trajectory) is the system state; the execution schedule is the control input; the objective trades off expected shortfall, risk, and impact costs. It explains why institutional desks do not simply follow textbook Almgren-Chriss trajectories but continuously replan as conditions evolve.

Execution as strategy design input

Execution, therefore, feeds back into strategy design. A high-turnover signal needs cheap execution just to survive. Capacity limits are execution limits stated in portfolio language. Holding period determines urgency: slow alpha can wait for liquidity, while fast alpha must pay for immediacy.

Avellaneda and Stoikov (2008) make the complementary point from the market-maker side: inventory risk and spread capture are the mirror image of the trader's urgency-versus-impact trade-off. Strategy design must therefore assume the execution problem it will actually face, not a frictionless benchmark.

Implementation:

- `04_vwap_twap_execution` compares TWAP and VWAP execution.
- `07_ml4t_volume_participation` shows participation-gated execution mechanics.
- `08_ml_dynamic_execution` demonstrates ML-based adaptive execution.

18.6 Optimizing execution with Almgren–Chriss as a unifying framework

The **Almgren-Chriss** framework turns execution into a quantitative risk-cost trade-off. Even when a desk does not implement the full model, the framework remains useful because it makes the risks of urgency, impact, and timing explicit.

Every execution faces the same trade-off. Trading quickly reduces exposure to adverse price moves but increases immediate impact. Trading slowly reduces immediate impact but leaves the order exposed to price drift. Optimal execution chooses a schedule on that frontier rather than pretending the trade-off does not exist.

Almgren and Chriss (2001) formalized optimal execution as minimizing expected cost plus a risk penalty:

$$\min_{x} E[C(x)] + \lambda \cdot \mathrm{Var}[C(x)]$$

where x is the execution trajectory, $E[C(x)]$ is expected impact cost, $\mathrm{Var}[C(x)]$ captures timing risk, and λ is the urgency parameter. Larger λ corresponds to a stronger preference for completion certainty and a more front-loaded schedule.

Model components

The framework requires a small set of inputs with clear economic interpretation. Volatility σ determines timing risk: the more volatile the asset, the larger the penalty for waiting. Temporary impact η captures the price pressure created during execution that then partially reverts. A common specification is:

$$\text{TempImpact} = \eta \cdot \frac{v}{V}$$

where v is the trading rate and V is the market volume.

Permanent impact γ captures the price change that persists after the trade because the market learns from order flow:

$$\text{PermImpact} = \gamma \cdot \frac{Q}{V}$$

where Q is the total order size. Eisler et al. (2010) reinforce the same practical point at the order-book level: the price effect of trading depends on market state, so the parameters in the objective are not constants.

The optimal trajectory

Under the standard linear-impact, Brownian-price assumptions, the optimal inventory path is:

$$x(t) = X_0 \frac{\sinh\big(\kappa(T - t)\big)}{\sinh(\kappa T)}$$

with:

$$\kappa = \sqrt{\frac{\lambda\sigma^2}{\eta}}$$

for the simplified case without permanent-impact feedback. The shape is not TWAP. Higher volatility or stronger urgency raises κ directly; a shorter horizon enters only through κT. All three front-load execution.

Regime-dependent parameters

The framework is only as good as its inputs. Volatility should reflect the execution horizon, not a stale annual estimate, so recent realized volatility, implied volatility, and known event risk all matter. Impact coefficients also move with time of day, stress, and crowding. Chan (2022) shows that impact decay and capacity interact over days, meaning an execution schedule can look feasible under a same-day model but still be too aggressive once lingering impact is included.

Given parameter uncertainty, practitioners should not rely on single-point estimates. Instead, generate schedules under multiple scenarios:

Scenario	Volatility	Impact	Risk Aversion
Base case	Historical avg	Calibrated	Medium
High vol	+50%	+30%	Higher
Low liquidity	+20%	+50%	Higher
Benign	-20%	-20%	Lower

Table 18.6: Scenario examples

Donnelly (2022) emphasizes that robust execution accounts for model uncertainty rather than optimizing under assumed-known parameters. If optimal trajectories vary dramatically across scenarios, the trade is fragile to miscalibration. In that case, a blended or conservative approach is preferable to false precision. The scenarios above use stylized stress multipliers; in practice, they should be tied to the asset class's observed regime distribution.

What Almgren-Chriss means for research

For research, the framework delivers four durable lessons. Execution cost depends on how the order is traded, not only on what is traded. The execution problem has its own frontier: impact buys immediacy, while patience buys a lower market footprint. Capacity is endogenous to the execution style, so the same signal may be viable under patient trading and infeasible under urgent liquidation. Urgency should also be tied to alpha decay. A signal with a half-life measured in minutes should not be paired with a schedule designed for daily rebalancing.

The principal contribution of Almgren-Chriss is therefore organizational: it converts execution from ad hoc judgment into a model with named inputs and observable trade-offs.

Figure 18.5 visualizes this directly: as risk aversion rises, optimal trajectories front-load execution, reducing timing variance while increasing immediate impact.

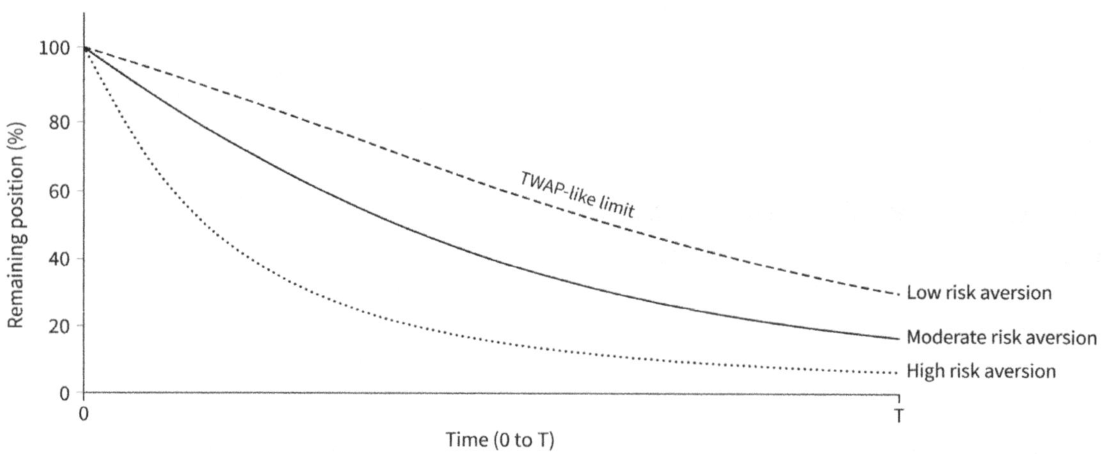

Figure 18.5: Almgren-Chriss optimal trajectories by risk aversion

The original framework assumes a linear, permanent impact, and an instantaneous, temporary impact. Later transient-impact and limit-order extensions relax those assumptions and are most relevant to live execution systems with tighter microstructure control. For research backtests, Almgren-Chriss remains the right baseline because it captures the main urgency-versus-impact trade-off without requiring a full execution stack. That makes it the natural bridge from transaction-cost estimation to the viability checks in the next section.

Implementation: See `05_almgren_chriss_optimal_execution` for scenario-based execution planning.

18.7 Transaction cost analysis and model validation

Transaction cost analysis (**TCA**) turns fills into model feedback. TCA measures realized execution cost, attributes that cost to identifiable sources, and shows whether a bad outcome came from the market or from the execution policy. That feedback loop is what keeps ex-ante models calibrated.

Implementation shortfall

Implementation shortfall (**IS**) is the standard TCA metric, measuring the difference between the decision price and the execution price:

$$IS = \frac{P_{execution} - P_{decision}}{P_{decision}}$$

For a buy order, a positive IS indicates execution cost (paid more than intended). For sell orders, negate the numerator: $IS = (P_{decision} - P_{execution})/P_{decision}$. For multi-leg trades, compute IS per leg and aggregate by notional weight.

The implementation shortfall captures spread, slippage, impact, and timing in a single metric. Madhavan (2002) made it the institutional default because it measures the quantity that matters operationally: the difference between the paper portfolio and the executed portfolio.

Cost decomposition

TCA becomes diagnostic only after the shortfall is decomposed. Spread cost measures the immediate payment for liquidity:

$$C_{spread} = \frac{P_{first_fill} - P_{arrival_mid}}{P_{decision}}$$

Impact cost measures the price movement created by the order itself:

$$C_{impact} = \frac{P_{avg_fill} - P_{arrival_mid}}{P_{decision}} - C_{spread}$$

Timing cost measures the market move during the execution window:

$$C_{timing} = \frac{P_{end_mid} - P_{arrival_mid}}{P_{decision}}$$

Timing can help or hurt. That sign matters because it separates bad luck from bad scheduling. Opportunity cost captures the unfilled remainder:

$$C_{opportunity} = (1 - \text{FillRate}) \cdot \frac{P_{close} - P_{decision}}{P_{decision}}$$

Said (2022) emphasizes exactly this distinction between market-driven and execution-driven price moves. Without that separation, TCA becomes descriptive accounting rather than a calibration tool.

Component	Value (bps)	Share
Total IS	2.83	100%
Spread cost	1.00	35%
Impact cost	0.63	22%
Timing/slippage cost	0.50	18%
Explicit fees	0.70	25%

Table 18.7: Example TCA decomposition

In this illustrative decomposition (Perold, 1988; Wagner and Edwards, 1993), spread and explicit fees are the largest contributors, while impact remains material. This pattern implies that execution quality (for example, venue selection and schedule design) and fee minimization can both improve net performance before changing strategy logic.

Figure 18.6 presents this decomposition as a waterfall from decision benchmark to realized execution, with spread, impact, timing/slippage, and explicit-fee terms, to isolate market-driven effects from execution-driven ones, making attribution additive and operational for daily monitoring.

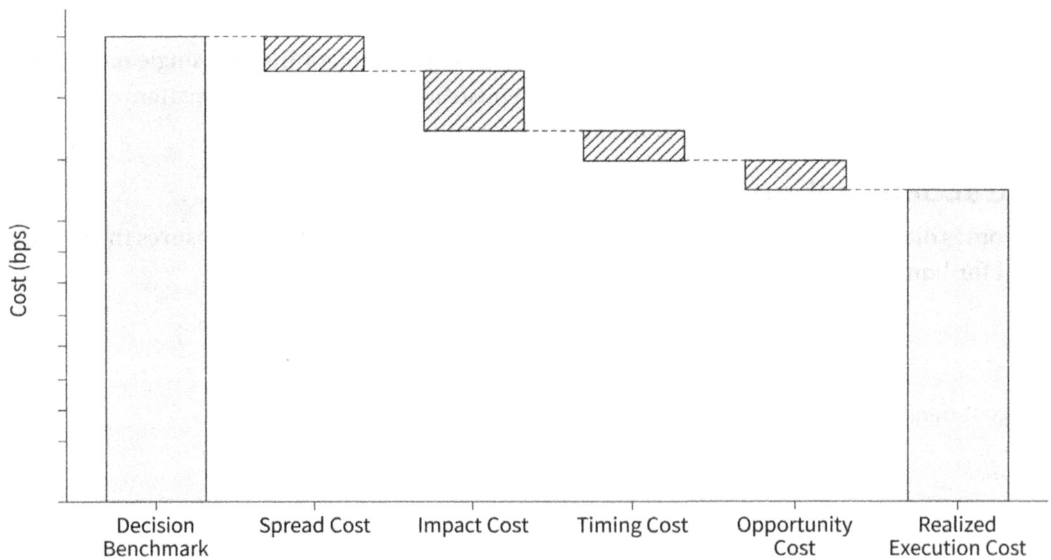

Figure 18.6: TCA decomposition waterfall

A useful TCA report, therefore, asks one question before anything else: was the cost market-driven or execution-driven? Market-driven costs arise when volatility spikes, news arrives, or market-wide liquidity deteriorates during the order window. Execution-driven costs arise when participation is overly aggressive relative to available depth, parameters are stale, or the schedule is poorly timed. The distinction decides the remedy. Market-driven losses call for better regime conditioning. Execution-driven losses call for policy changes.

Regime context in TCA

TCA should be conditioned on the market regime. "Bad fills" during a high-volatility period may represent good execution given the conditions, whereas the same fills during a calm period indicate execution failure.

Regime tags make the comparison set fair. A useful report groups orders by volatility bucket, liquidity state, event calendar, and intraday window. Comparing stressed open-auction fills with calm midday fills produces noise, not evidence.

Closing the loop

TCA's highest-value use is parameter updating. Estimate the model, trade, measure realized cost, compare the prediction to the outcome, then update the model. Systematic underestimation means the coefficients are too low. Regime-specific residuals mean conditioning is missing. Size-specific residuals mean the impact function is misspecified.

The strongest calibration test compares backtested net PnL with realized live PnL over the same strategy logic. If the two diverge persistently, the cost model is wrong. Vendor coefficients are starting values, not authority.

Hautsch and Huang (2012) studied limit order flow and market impact, demonstrating that execution data can inform optimal order sizing and timing decisions.

The hidden costs of risk-model-driven turnover

TCA should also expose turnover created by the risk model rather than the signal. If the covariance estimate shifts between windows, the optimizer can trigger rebalancing even when expected returns remain unchanged. Paleologo (2025) treats this as a hidden implementation cost of unstable portfolio construction.

A simple diagnostic is to hold the alpha signal fixed and recompute weights as only the covariance matrix changes. Large turnover under that null experiment indicates that the risk model is creating trades with no informational content. The Frobenius norm of the change in factor-mimicking portfolios, $\| \mathbf{P}_t - \mathbf{P}_{t-1} \|_F$, is one compact summary statistic. This links directly to *Chapter 14*'s eigenvector-stability problem: unstable loadings become unnecessary turnover unless the estimation method is stabilized. The notebook `10_gross_vs_net_performance` plots the null-turnover decay.

TCA report elements

A practical TCA report should support decisions, not just record history. It needs summary statistics such as average implementation shortfall, fill rate, and completion time; attribution that separates spread, impact, timing, and missed fills; regime slices by volatility, time of day, and size bucket; and a validation page comparing predicted with realized costs. If the report cannot tell the desk which parameters to change, it is incomplete.

For implementation, several starting points exist: `pyfolio` includes a transaction cost analysis module, and open-source libraries such as `tca-tools` provide basic IS decomposition. At the institutional level, Bloomberg TCA and Virtu Analytics (formerly ITG) produce standardized FIX-protocol (see *Chapter 3*) reports that integrate with order management systems. The notebook accompanying this section demonstrates a lightweight TCA implementation suitable for research backtests.

Implementation: See `01_cost_taxonomy` for decomposition primitives and baseline attribution, and `10_gross_vs_net_performance` for turnover-linked cost diagnostics.

18.8 Designing practical cost guardrails

Not every strategy that looks profitable in research survives the impact of trading costs. This section provides the diagnostics that decide whether a strategy is deployable, scalable, or unprofitable once friction is accounted for.

Break-even turnover

This heuristic provides a quick sanity check, not a precise cutoff, for the turnover a strategy can sustain before trading costs absorb expected gross return:

$$\text{Turnover}_{\text{max}} = \frac{E\left[R_{\text{gross}}\right]}{\text{Cost per unit turnover}}$$

For a strategy with a 5% expected annual gross return and 25 basis points of round-trip cost per unit of turnover:

$$\text{Turnover}_{\text{max}} = \frac{0.05}{0.0025} = 20$$

This implies that the strategy can sustain an annual turnover of about 20 times capital before estimated trading costs consume its expected gross return. The exact mapping from this number to trading frequency depends on the turnover convention used, so the formula is best read as an order-of-magnitude diagnostic rather than a literal rebalancing schedule.

A more conservative formulation incorporates the Sharpe ratio:

$$\text{Turnover}_{max} = \frac{SR \cdot \sigma}{\text{Cost per trade}}$$

where SR is the Sharpe ratio and σ is strategy volatility. This accounts for risk-adjusted returns, recognizing that higher-volatility strategies can sustain higher turnover given the same Sharpe ratio.

Figure 18.7 shows the same break-even logic as a surface over turnover and one-way trading cost. The message is immediate: once turnover moves into the high single digits, even modest execution costs demand implausibly large pre-cost alpha.

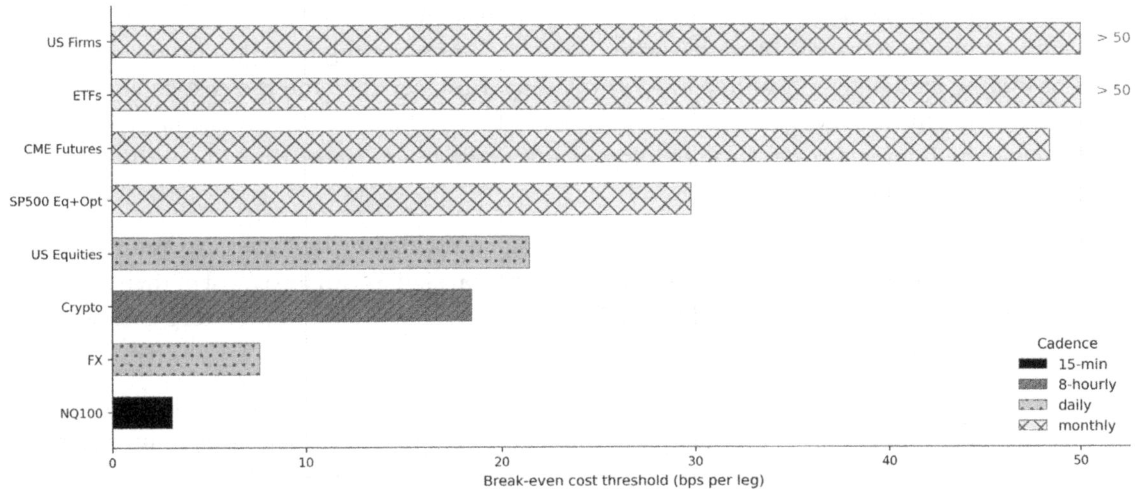

Figure 18.7: Break-even alpha rises quickly with turnover and one-way cost

Strategies with fast rebalancing need much larger gross edges to survive realistic frictions.

Minimum required edge

The same constraint can be written from the other direction: given estimated costs, what return per trade is required?

$$\text{Edge}_{min} = \frac{\text{Total cost}}{\text{Avg holding period}}$$

For a strategy paying 20 basis points per round-trip with a 5-day average holding period:

$$\text{Edge}_{min} = \frac{0.0020}{5} = 4 \text{ bps/day}$$

The strategy must therefore generate at least 4 basis points per day just to cover trading costs. If the signal is only worth 2 basis points per day, it is not viable at that cadence. Break-even turnover and minimum required edge are the same constraint expressed in different algebraic forms. Use both. If they disagree, either the turnover estimate or the cost estimate is wrong.

Gabaix and Koijen (2021) strengthen the same intuition at the market level. If markets are more inelastic than standard models assume, order flow moves prices more than expected, and the required edge rises accordingly.

Alpha-to-go – What a signal is worth after costs

The break-even and minimum-edge heuristics above treat expected return as a static input. But if rebalancing is costly, the relevant quantity is not today's expected return but the *cumulative cost-discounted expected return over the holding period*: **the signal's value after accounting for the cost of building the position and eventually unwinding it** (Paleologo, 2025).

Consider a signal that follows an AR(1) process with persistence ϕ (close to 1 for slowly decaying momentum; close to 0 for fast mean-reverting signals). When trading costs are proportional to a speed-of-trading parameter Γ that depends on volatility, risk aversion, and the cost coefficient, the alpha-to-go discounts the raw signal by a factor that depends on both ϕ and Γ. A fast-decaying signal (small ϕ) with high impact costs (large Γ) has very low alpha-to-go: by the time the position is built, the signal has disappeared.

This lens changes how signals should be ranked. Slow signals with long half-lives can amortize entry costs and retain most of their raw alpha. Fast mean-reversion signals can lose most of their apparent value before the position is fully established. The useful ranking metric is therefore cost-adjusted signal quality, not raw IC in isolation.

In the ML4T workflow, alpha-to-go sits between model output (*Chapters 11–14*) and allocation (*Chapter 17*). It is the cost-aware filter that determines how much of the predicted alpha is actually capturable. Strategy evaluation (*Chapter 16*) should use cost-discounted returns, not raw returns, when assessing profitability, particularly for strategies where signal decay and cost magnitude are of the same order.

Capacity analysis

Capacity is not a fixed number: it depends on execution approach and acceptable cost degradation. More precisely, a strategy's Sharpe ratio is a decreasing function of assets under management (AUM): as AUM grows, market impact increases and net-of-cost performance degrades. Capacity is the AUM at which the Sharpe ratio drops below a minimum threshold (typically $SR_{min} = 0.5$ or the hurdle rate).

The shape of this $SR(\text{AUM})$ curve depends on the cost model: linear costs produce linear SR degradation, while square-root costs produce concave degradation; capacity increases less-than-linearly with AUM. For ML4T case studies, an order-of-magnitude capacity estimate follows from computing the AUM at which daily trading volume would exceed 1% of the average daily volume across the traded universe.

Participation-based capacity: A simple first-pass capacity estimate limits the strategy's daily traded dollars to a fixed fraction of average daily dollar volume (ADDV):

$$\text{Daily trading capacity} = \text{MaxParticipation} \times \text{ADDV}$$

If the strategy turns over a fraction τ of portfolio capital per day, the corresponding AUM capacity is approximately:

$$\text{AUM Capacity} \approx \frac{\text{MaxParticipation} \times \text{ADDV}}{\tau}$$

For example, if the maximum acceptable participation rate is 5% and the traded universe has \$1B of average daily dollar volume, then a fully rebalanced daily strategy ($\tau \approx 1$) has an approximate capacity of \$50M. If average daily turnover is only 20% of capital ($\tau = 0.2$), capacity rises to about \$250M. The key point is that participation caps constrain daily trading flow first; portfolio capacity follows only after turnover is specified.

Impact-adjusted capacity: A more refined estimate starts from a square-root impact model. If trading a daily notional Q generates expected impact:

$$I(Q) = \eta\sigma\sqrt{\frac{Q}{V}},$$

where V is daily dollar volume, σ is daily volatility, and η is an empirical impact coefficient, then imposing a maximum acceptable impact I_{max} implies:

$$Q_{\text{max}} = V\left(\frac{I_{\text{max}}}{\eta\sigma}\right)^2$$

This quantity is the maximum daily traded notional, not yet the maximum portfolio AUM. Converting it into strategy capacity again requires a turnover assumption:

$$\text{AUM Capacity} \approx \frac{Q_{\text{max}}}{\tau}$$

This formulation makes the economics explicit: impact models determine how much can be traded per day within a cost budget, and turnover determines how that daily trading budget translates into deployable capital.

Capacity studies across major anomalies find dramatic variation. Low-turnover strategies like size and profitability can absorb much larger capital bases before becoming unprofitable, while momentum capacity decays at substantially lower AUM; high-frequency strategies that remain profitable after spreads typically have capacities an order of magnitude smaller.

Across the case studies, the same pattern appears. High-turnover intraday designs often fail net of cost even when gross backtests look attractive, while slower strategies preserve more of their edge. *Chapter 20* consolidates the cross-case survival tables; the guardrail logic developed here explains those outcomes.

Figure 18.8 summarizes capacity as a frontier: net Sharpe decays with scale, and the viable region is bounded by the minimum acceptable post-cost Sharpe threshold.

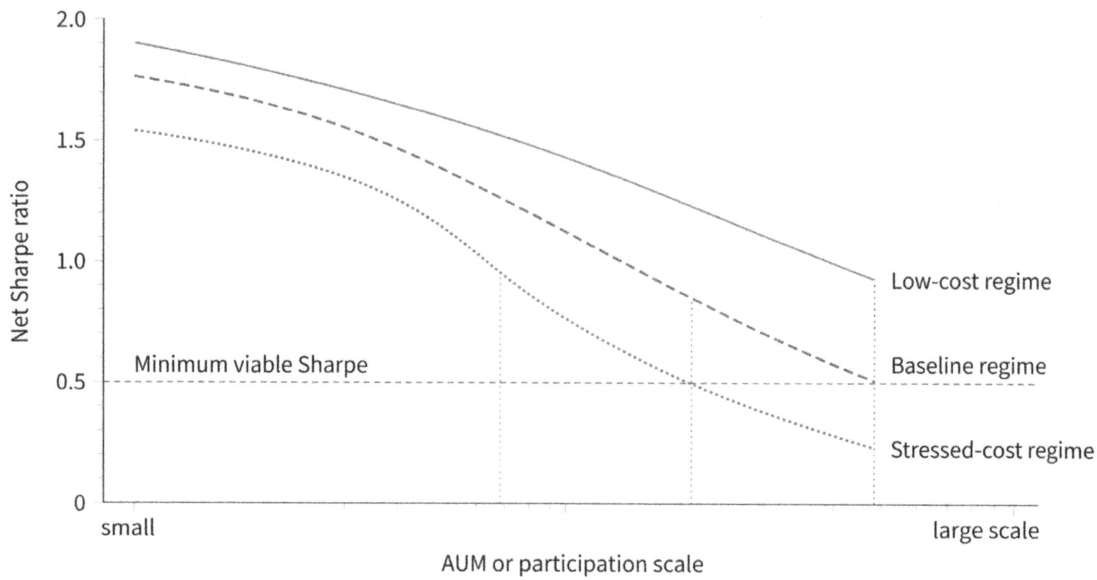

Figure 18.8: Capacity frontier under transaction costs: net Sharpe degrades with scale; feasible capacity depends on cost model and turnover

Net Sharpe declines as the AUM/participation scale rises, and feasible capacity is the point at which it intersects with a minimum viability threshold.

Kill switch criteria

Define kill criteria before deployment, not during stress. Absolute triggers capture slow bleed, such as sustained negative net returns, repeated implementation shortfall far above budget, or chronic underfilling. Relative triggers compare realized costs to the model; for example, a rolling overshoot relative to the forecast or a cost-adjusted Sharpe ratio that falls below the minimum acceptable threshold. The common feature is precommitment: the strategy is stopped because it violates a published operating rule, not because we later lost confidence.

Cost guardrails connect back to the rest of the workflow. *Chapter 8* should score factors against break-even turnover, not raw IC alone. *Chapter 17* should embed cost-aware turnover constraints in the optimizer. *Chapter 19* should treat capacity limits as risk limits, because exceeding capacity is not only costly but also destabilizing in adverse market conditions.

When to abandon rather than modify

A failed cost test does not always mean immediate abandonment. The first repairs are obvious: reduce turnover, improve execution, narrow the universe to more liquid names, or accept lower capacity. Those changes are worth attempting because they target the implementation channel directly rather than pretending the research signal changed. If they still cannot produce acceptable net performance, the strategy should be dropped regardless of gross backtest quality. A strategy that cannot clear its own friction is not deployable.

A practical example – Cost mitigation for options

The S&P 500 options case study (*Chapter 20*) illustrates how much of a strategy's apparent success or failure is driven by execution discipline rather than by the signal itself. The illustrative strategy is a systematic short-straddle sell on S&P 500 constituents with daily delta hedging of the underlying, a textbook volatility-risk-premium harvest. Single-name options carry wide round-trip bid-ask spreads, so small differences in how the strategy transacts translate directly into large differences in net Sharpe. The same signal, evaluated under three increasingly disciplined execution regimes, yields three qualitatively distinct conclusions (see `case_studies/sp500_options/14_costs.ipynb` for the worked cascade):

1. **Rung 1: Naive round-trip.** Enter each cohort on Friday, hold ten trading days, and close at the market. Both entry and exit legs cross the bid-ask spread on call and put contracts, with commission paid on each leg. This is the default a reader would implement with no thought given to option microstructure. Under that discipline, the strategy is decisively unprofitable as specified: cumulative entry-leg cost is comparable in magnitude to the position notional itself, so the option bid-ask consumes the volatility-risk premium before any signal is realized, leaving validation and holdout net Sharpes well into negative territory.
2. **Rung 2: Hold to expiry.** O'Donovan and Yu (2024) observe that holding each short-option position to its natural expiration eliminates the second leg of the round trip: the contract settles at intrinsic value, no market exit is required, and the exit bid-ask is never paid. The same strategy under that single change (same model, same delta hedge, same universe) moves from decisively unprofitable to negative net Sharpe within a wide bootstrap confidence interval. Cumulative cost falls materially because half of the round-trip spread is no longer crossed, but cumulative entry-leg cost on the full ~612-symbol universe remains large enough that the strategy is indistinguishable from flat at best.
3. **Rung 3: Hold to expiry plus liquid-universe filter.** Restricting the execution set at each rebalance date to the bottom quintile of relative half-spread (the tightest-quoted 20% of that day's candidate straddles, roughly 120 of the ~600 names) is the second of the two mitigations in the O'Donovan-Yu cascade, applied here more strictly than the paper's own bottom-four-deciles (~40%) screen. Within sp500_options the selected configuration under this discipline (signal-stage, equal-weighted top-5, linear/ridge, label `ret_to_expiry`, `universe_filter=liquid`) lifts validation Sharpe to +0.160 with a 95% bootstrap interval [−0.975, +1.778] and holdout Sharpe to +0.974 with interval [−0.836, +3.135]. Both intervals straddle zero, and the paired-bootstrap difference against the equal-weight holdout benchmark is −1.574 [−3.801, +0.730]. The selected strategy sits below the +2.714 EW universe Sharpe on the 2021 holdout. The same signal, the same model, and the same cost accounting produce a different qualitative conclusion simply because the execution set is cleaner.

These net Sharpes assume best-case algorithmic execution: the cost model charges only 20.3% of the quoted option half-spread, the at-the-money ratio Muravyev and Pearson (2020) estimate (roughly 2.6 ¢ effective against a 12.8 ¢ quoted half-spread), and that O'Donovan and Yu (2024) adopt via Heston et al. (2023). That fraction is the lenient, strategy-favorable end of the execution-cost range rather than a neutral average (newer auction-based evidence puts the realized fraction materially higher), so the rung-3 holdout survival is conditional on that assumption.

This is why *Section 20.6* sweeps the spread fraction (0.203, 0.5, 0.75, 1.0) rather than fixing a single point: the lesson is the strategy's survival *across* the cost grid, not a claim that it earns a specific Sharpe at the most favorable execution assumption.

Three features of this cascade deserve attention. First, the cascade is monotonic: each additional discipline rung makes a real improvement, and the holdout point estimate crosses zero only once both are applied. Second, the improvement is not subtle—it is large enough to flip the strategy's qualitative deployability conclusion, even though the holdout bootstrap interval still straddles zero. Third, the mitigation does not compose without limit: tightening the universe past the bottom quintile leaves an execution set too thin to diversify across, and the top-5 portfolio concentrates onto too few names. The mitigations are a short staircase, not a parameter that can be pushed without limit.

The holdout improvement requires a caveat. Annualized Sharpe on a twelve-month window carries a standard error of roughly ±1, so the rung-3 holdout point estimate is not a precise number; the meaningful shift is from "indistinguishable from a sizable loser" to "indistinguishable from flat," a change in the qualitative conclusion about deployability, not a claim that the strategy earns a specific positive Sharpe in production. The deflated-Sharpe logic of *Section 20.5* still applies. But the direction matters: the difference between rung 1 and rung 3 is not a small effect that disappears under multiple-testing adjustment. It is the difference between an execution discipline that fits the instrument's microstructure and one that does not. When transaction costs scale with the traded price rather than with the notional amount, the practical lesson is the same: modify the execution before abandoning the signal.

Comparing fixed and relative cost regimes

The options cascade above is about whether the strategy survives a *real* friction stack. The complementary lesson, visible in the broad US equities case study (~3,200 names, 2000–2015 validation, 2016–2018 holdout), is that the *cost model itself* can dominate the conclusion when it is poorly matched to the universe. The risk is worth making explicit: when diagnosing a strategy's apparent survival, ask whether the cost model fits the data before debating the signal.

The case study sweeps two cost regimes: relative and fixed costs. The first applies an 11-point basis-point grid from 0 to 50 bps total per leg, a size-invariant fraction of the share price. The second walks a six-point-per-share grid from 0¢ to 10¢, a fixed-dollar charge per share that scales inversely with price. The validation Sharpe is similar across regimes at low cost (bps mean 1.93 at 10 bps, per-share mean 1.90 at 1¢ half-spread) because the median post-2001 adjusted price (~$18.44) makes a 1¢ half-spread roughly half a basis point of notional. However, the two regimes diverge as the cost rises. The bps grid keeps the strategy in positive territory through 20 bps (mean: 0.86) and remains barely positive through 30 bps (mean: 0.01). The per-share grid decays sharply through 2.5¢ (mean 0.66) and is modestly negative at 5¢ (mean −0.29).

The disagreement results from applying a constant per-share charge to adjusted historical prices that span a wide nominal range. The same position that costs 5 bps at a price of $200 costs 50 bps when the same name's adjusted history prints at $20, and 200 bps if a 1990s split sequence pushed the adjusted print to $5. The 5¢ breakeven point in the case study's adjusted price distribution implies a round-trip cost of near 55 bps for the median name.

As a practical rule for a global cost regime, use bps-of-notional when the universe spans a wide adjusted-price range. Use fixed per-share-plus-spread only when (a) prices are relatively stable in nominal terms or (b) measure per-asset spreads from quote data. Use both for sensitivity analysis. When the two regimes disagree about whether the strategy survives, the disagreement is a diagnostic about the cost model, not a finding about the signal.

See `case_studies/us_equities_panel/18_costs.ipynb` and `case_studies/sp500_equity_option_analytics/16_costs.ipynb` for the dual-regime sweeps, and `case_studies/etfs/16_costs.ipynb` for the per-share example with tiered commissions.

Implementation: See `03_market_impact_calibration` for the empirical η coefficient feeding the square-root impact capacity formula, `09_frequency_tradeoff` for cadence-versus-cost trade-offs, `10_gross_vs_net_performance` for break-even and capacity diagnostics, and `11_cost_cliff` for high-frequency viability stress tests.

18.9 Summary

Transaction costs are binding constraints throughout the ML4T workflow. They separate into explicit fees, implicit frictions, and capacity effects; they move with the market regime; and they admit a ladder of backtest models from spread to square-root impact. Execution algorithms control the impact-versus-timing trade-off rather than removing it, and TCA is the mechanism that validates and updates those ex-ante assumptions.

The practical message is asymmetric. Overestimating costs can reject viable ideas; underestimating them destroys real capital. Break-even turnover, minimum required edge, and capacity analysis are therefore feasibility tests, not optional diagnostics. Cost-based kill criteria make that discipline operational, forcing the strategy to justify its friction continuously rather than only in research.

Chapter 19 develops the risk management framework, incorporating cost-based capacity limits and execution risk alongside the traditional dimensions of market, credit, and operational risk.

19

Risk Management

A strategy that survives rigorous cross-validation (*Chapter 7*), proves stable across regimes (*Chapter 8*), and avoids the pitfalls of time-series leakage (*Chapters 7* and *11*) has earned a seat at the table. Portfolio construction (*Chapter 17*) gave it position sizes; realistic cost modeling (*Chapter 18*) told us what we actually keep. Yet none of this answers a deceptively simple question: *what happens when things go wrong?*

Risk management is not a reporting layer bolted on after research. It is system design: a set of constraints, controls, and governance artifacts that define what the strategy is *allowed* to do when conditions deteriorate. A strategy without explicit risk controls is not a tradable system; it is a hypothesis awaiting its first stress test.

After completing this chapter, you will be able to:

- Measure tail risk with VaR and CVaR, including regime-conditional estimates and liquidity-aware interpretation.
- Evaluate path risk using drawdown depth, drawdown duration, recovery time, and related path-dependent metrics.
- Decompose portfolio risk into market, factor, sector, geographic, and macro exposures to distinguish intended from unintended bets.
- Design and interpret historical, hypothetical, and reverse stress tests that challenge return, cost, volatility, and correlation assumptions together.
- Build adaptive risk controls, including volatility targeting, exposure caps, and position-level exits, using only information available at decision time.
- Specify kill switches, drift monitoring, and governance artifacts that turn a backtested strategy into a deployable trading system.

Section 19.1 establishes the risk management mandate within the ML4T workflow. *Section 19.2* provides a practical taxonomy mapping each risk type to observable proxies and controls. *Sections 19.3–19.4* cover tail risk measurement (VaR, CVaR) and path risk (drawdowns, recovery). *Section 19.5* decomposes risk into factor, sector, and macro sources. *Section 19.6* introduces stress testing and scenario analysis. *Section 19.7* builds adaptive controls that adjust to conditions without lookahead. *Section 19.8* defines kill switches and risk governance.

19.1 Turning your backtest winner into a tradable system

López de Prado (2018) emphasizes that strategy risk extends beyond market exposure to encompass model risk, overfitting risk, and operational failures that no backtest can fully anticipate. Federal Reserve (2011) guidance on model risk management applies as much to quantitative trading as to bank credit models: every model requires documented assumptions, identified limitations, ongoing monitoring, and a clear owner responsible for its behavior.

Three principles guide this chapter:

1. **Constraints must be implementable without lookahead.** Every adaptive control (volatility scaling, exposure caps, pause rules) must use only information available at decision time. A risk limit that implicitly conditions on future volatility introduces the same leakage we spent *Chapters 7* and *11* eliminating.
2. **Controls must be auditable.** When a drawdown occurs, the post-mortem must trace exactly which signals triggered which actions. "The model decided" is not an acceptable answer. This requires logging, versioning, and clear escalation paths.
3. **Governance artifacts must exist before deployment.** The strategy definition introduced in *Chapter 6* is augmented with explicit thresholds for acceptable drawdown, leverage limits, concentration bounds, and the conditions under which trading pauses or stops entirely.

A risk-managed strategy differs from a backtested model in several concrete ways:

Aspect	Backtested Model	Risk-Managed System
Position limits	Implicit (data-driven)	Explicit caps by name, sector, factor
Leverage	Whatever optimizer is chosen	Hard ceiling with regime-conditional tightening
Drawdown response	None	Predefined de-risking triggers
Failure mode	Undefined	Kill switches with escalation rules
Documentation	Research notebook	Risk term sheet, monitoring dashboard

Table 19.1: Active risk management versus simple backtests

Risk management sits at the interface between research and execution:

- The feature and label validation discipline from *Chapters 7–9* ensures we are not fooling ourselves about expected returns
- Portfolio construction (*Chapter 17*) translates signals into positions
- Cost modeling (*Chapter 18*) reveals the friction between gross and net performance

Risk management asks: *given all of this, what can still kill us?* The answer spans multiple dimensions (market moves, factor exposures, liquidity evaporation, model breakdowns, operational failures), each requiring its own measurement and control.

Implementation: See `01_var_cvar` and `06_stress_testing` for the risk metrics underlying this framework.

19.2 A practical risk taxonomy for quant strategies

A practical taxonomy maps each risk type to an observable proxy and a control mechanism. Abstract categories become actionable only when translated into specific metrics and thresholds.

Four stylized facts of asset returns, documented across markets and decades, constrain which risk metrics are estimable and which modeling choices are appropriate (Cont, 2001):

1. Daily returns show little serial correlation, which is why point return prediction is difficult, and *Chapter 11-14*'s IC values remain modest.
2. Squared and absolute returns, however, are strongly autocorrelated, so volatility is often more predictable than direction.
3. Return distributions also exhibit heavy tails, with tail indices that make Gaussian assumptions especially unreliable in the extremes. Parametric VaR based on normality is therefore not just imprecise; it is structurally biased in the part of the distribution that matters most for risk control. Volatility clustering adds a second constraint and a second opportunity. High-volatility periods tend to follow high-volatility periods, while calm tends to follow calm. That persistence is what makes GARCH, EWMA, and related models operationally useful in *Section 19.7*.
4. At the same time, return distributions become more nearly Gaussian as the horizon lengthens from daily to weekly or monthly frequencies. Risk models are therefore generally more reliable at lower frequencies than at intraday or daily horizons.

The practical consequence is narrow but important: variance is the highest moment of returns that can usually be estimated with confidence from ordinary historical samples. Anything beyond it, including skewness, kurtosis, and deep quantiles, requires either much more data or stronger assumptions.

Market risk

Market risk is the most familiar category. For long-short equity, net market exposure or beta to a broad index captures directional risk; for rates strategies, duration and convexity matter. Market risk is not inherently good or bad. It is either intended or unintended. A long-biased equity strategy wants market beta because the equity risk premium is part of the thesis. A market-neutral strategy treats residual beta as a hedging failure. The same 0.1 beta that is irrelevant to the first strategy is a meaningful unintended exposure for the second. The relevant proxies are portfolio beta, net exposure as a share of NAV, and duration-style sensitivities, while the corresponding controls are exposure limits, hedging overlays, and explicit neutrality constraints in the optimizer.

Factor risk

Strategies also carry exposure to style factors such as value, momentum, size, quality, and volatility. Daniel and Moskowitz (2016) document how severe momentum crashes can be when the factor reverses. Unintended factor tilts therefore inherit risks that the research process may never have stress-tested directly. The usual proxies are factor loadings from regressions on standard factor portfolios, whether Fama-French, Barra, or a custom internal system. The usual controls are exposure limits, explicit hedges, or multi-factor constraints embedded in portfolio construction.

Leverage risk

Leverage amplifies both returns and losses. A 2x leveraged strategy changes path dependency, increases margin-call probability, and interacts with financing costs that can spike during stress. Because volatility is time-varying (Schwert, 1989), leverage multiplies a moving target rather than a fixed one. The main proxies are gross exposure as a multiple of NAV, margin utilization, and sensitivity to financing costs. The corresponding controls are hard leverage caps and dynamic deleveraging triggers tied to volatility or liquidity regimes.

Concentration risk

Diversification protects only to the extent positions are actually spread. A portfolio of 100 names dominated by five positions is not diversified; it is five concentrated bets wearing a diversified costume. Concentration risk applies not only to single names, but also to sectors, countries, and shared factor exposures. Practical proxies include the Herfindahl-Hirschman Index of position weights, maximum single-name weight, and sector or country concentration. The matching controls are position limits, sector caps, and minimum effective-number-of-position thresholds.

Liquidity and capacity risks

A strategy that works at $10 million may fail at $100 million if it trades illiquid names or requires excessive turnover. *Chapter 18* quantifies the cost channel; here the point is that liquidity is also a risk category in its own right. Liquidity risk has two faces. Exogenous liquidity reflects market-wide conditions that affect everyone, while endogenous liquidity reflects the strategy's own impact on prices. The proxies include position size relative to ADV, estimated market impact, bid-ask spreads, and stress indicators such as VIX or credit spreads. The controls differ accordingly: exogenous liquidity calls for regime-aware trading pauses, while endogenous liquidity calls for ADV limits, capacity estimates, and turnover ceilings.

Model risk

Model risk arises from incorrect assumptions, incorrect data, incorrect implementation, or overfitting to historical patterns. Federal Reserve (2011) defines it as errors in model development, implementation, or use. A strategy that passed backtesting may still fail because the model was validated on patterns that do not recur, or because the implementation no longer aligns with the research objective. The relevant proxies are out-of-sample degradation, regime-slice instability, and excessive sensitivity to hyperparameters. The controls are holdout validation, ongoing benchmark monitoring, documented model limitations, and explicit re-research triggers.

Operational risk

Operational risk encompasses everything outside the model: data feed failures, execution errors, reconciliation breaks, and human errors. A strategy can be analytically sound and still lose money because a sign was flipped in production or a corporate action was mishandled. A short book accidentally converted into a long book or a stock split misread as a price collapse can create large unintended exposures without any change in the underlying signal. The main proxies are execution-error rates, reconciliation breaks, system uptime, and manual override frequency. The controls are automated reconciliation, dual entry for critical parameters, pre-trade compliance checks, and formal incident review.

The risk control matrix

The following table synthesizes these categories into a single point of reference:

Risk Type	Proxy	Control	Monitoring Frequency
Market	Net beta, duration	Exposure limits, hedges	Daily
Factor	Factor loadings	Factor constraints	Weekly
Leverage	Gross/NAV ratio	Hard caps, vol triggers	Intraday
Concentration	HHI, max weight	Position limits	Daily
Liquidity	ADV coverage, spreads	Capacity limits	Weekly
Model	OOS degradation	Re-research triggers	Monthly
Operational	Error rates	Automated checks	Continuous

Table 19.2: Risk category overview

Other categories (counterparty risk, regulatory risk, and technology/infrastructure risk) may apply depending on the strategy's execution venue and institutional context. This taxonomy covers those most relevant to systematic strategies. *Figure 19.1* organizes the risk types and their key proxies; *Table 19.2* pairs each proxy with its control mechanism and monitoring cadence.

Figure 19.1: Risk taxonomy for systematic strategies

Each major risk class is useful only when linked to an observable proxy and a control that can be enforced in production.

Implementation: See `04_factor_exposure` for factor decomposition and `06_stress_testing` for liquidity stress scenarios.

19.3 Measuring the tail – VaR and CVaR

Standard deviation tells us about typical fluctuations. But strategies do not fail during typical periods. They fail during extremes. Tail risk metrics attempt to quantify what happens in the worst cases, and how bad "worst" actually gets.

Value at risk

Value-at-Risk (VaR) answers a specific question: what is the maximum loss we expect over a given horizon at a given confidence level? Formally, VaR at confidence level α is the α-quantile of the loss distribution:

$$\text{VaR}_\alpha = \inf\{l : P(L > l) \leq 1 - \alpha\}$$

For example, a daily 95% VaR of 2% means: "We expect to lose more than 2% on only 5% of trading days." This is a threshold, not a prediction of what happens beyond it.

The main estimation approaches differ in how much structure they impose. Historical simulation uses the empirical distribution of past returns. It is simple and largely assumption-free, but its answer depends heavily on the sample period. Parametric VaR assumes a distribution, often normal, and estimates the required parameters. It is fast and convenient, but it becomes misleading when returns are non-normal. Extreme Value Theory focuses directly on the tail and is usually better suited to deep-loss estimation, though it requires careful threshold selection and more modeling judgment. VaR's popularity stems from its intuitive interpretation, but it has a critical flaw: it tells us nothing about losses beyond the threshold. A strategy with 95% VaR of 2% might lose 3% when the threshold is breached or 20%; VaR treats those cases as equivalent.

Conditional value-at-risk

Conditional VaR (CVaR), also called Expected Shortfall, addresses this limitation. CVaR asks: given that we exceed the VaR threshold, what is the expected loss?

$$\text{CVaR}_\alpha = \mathbb{E}[L \mid L > \text{VaR}_\alpha]$$

Rockafellar and Uryasev (2000) showed that CVaR has a crucial property VaR lacks: subadditivity. A risk measure is subadditive if the risk of a portfolio is at most the sum of the risks of its components. Subadditivity means portfolio CVaR cannot exceed the sum of component CVaRs, a property consistent with diversification benefits, unlike VaR, which can pathologically increase when combining positions (Artzner et al., 1999).

In the companion analysis (`01_var_cvar`), an equal-weighted basket of SPY, AGG, GLD, EFA, and EEM (US equities, US aggregate bonds, gold, developed international, emerging markets) shows that diversification reduces portfolio VaR by about 24% relative to the weighted sum of individual asset VaRs over 2006–2024. *Figure 19.2* compares the tail estimates from historical, parametric, and Cornish-Fisher methods on the same portfolio.

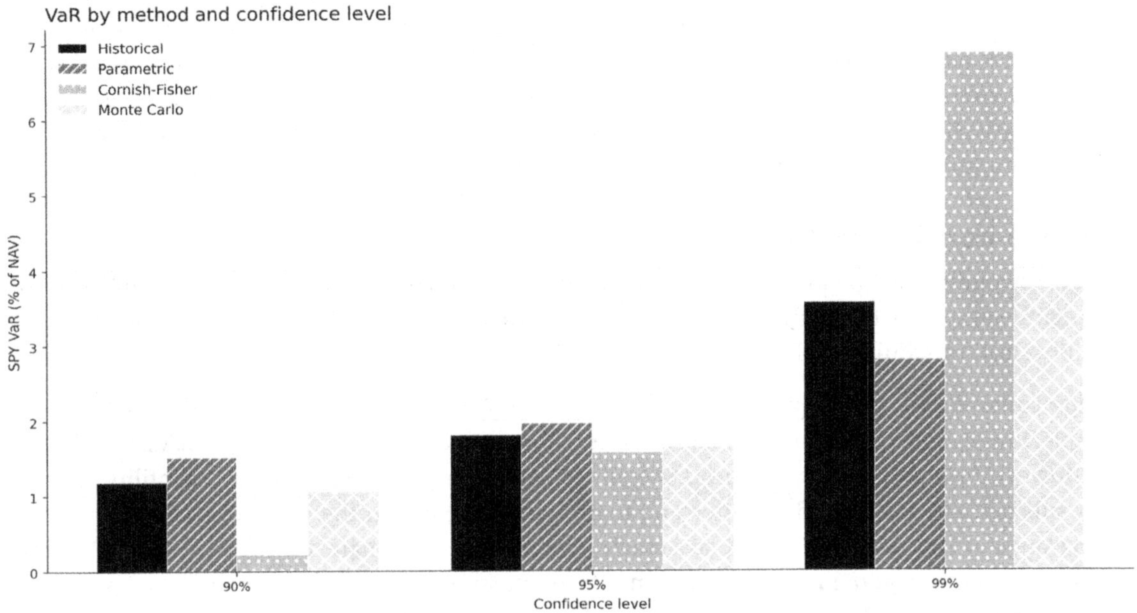

Figure 19.2: VaR-method comparison on the same portfolio

Historical, parametric, and Cornish-Fisher estimates differ most where distributional assumptions are least reliable.

The practical interpretation: if your daily 95% CVaR is 3%, then on the 5% of worst days, you expect to lose 3% on average. This captures the severity of tail events, not just their frequency.

A distribution-free loss bound

The Cantelli inequality provides a model-free complement to VaR that requires no distributional assumptions, only finite variance. For any portfolio, the probability of a shortfall exceeding k standard deviations below the mean is bounded by $P(\text{shortfall} > k\sigma) \leq 1/(1+k^2)$. Because the mean return equals $SR \cdot \sigma$, a losing period (a return below zero) is a shortfall of SR standard deviations, so a portfolio with Sharpe ratio SR has at most a $1/(1+SR^2)$ probability of a losing period: 50% at $SR = 1.0$ and 20% at $SR = 2.0$. Compare this to Gaussian VaR, which gives 16% and 2.3% respectively. The Cantelli bound is far more conservative, but it holds for any return distribution with finite variance. When fat tails or regime shifts make parametric VaR unreliable, this inequality provides a hard floor on loss probability from nothing more than the strategy's risk-adjusted return; Cont (2001) documents that fat tails are the rule rather than the exception in asset returns.

Why VaR understates real risk

Both VaR and CVaR are typically computed on historical returns that assume normal trading conditions. Tail events rarely occur in isolation. During stress, liquidity evaporates, so spreads widen, market impact spikes, and the cost of exiting positions rises precisely when exit is most urgent. Correlations also break in the wrong direction. Ang and Timmermann (2011) show that exceedance correlations, conditional on both assets experiencing extreme returns, are materially higher in downside tails than in upside tails. Diversification benefits therefore shrink when they are most needed. At the same time, *Chapter 18*'s cost parameters, often estimated from ordinary periods, can become several times larger in crisis. Bianchi et al. (2023) document how fat-tailed return behavior makes parametric VaR especially unreliable in these environments, with stressed losses often materially underestimated.

Regime-conditional risk metrics

A single unconditional VaR or CVaR masks the variation across market regimes. Khang (2022) shows that regime-aware risk forecasts substantially outperform unconditional estimates. The insight is that volatility clusters: calm periods predict calm periods, and periods of stress predict periods of stress.

Regime-conditional risk computes separate VaR and CVaR estimates for each identified regime, for example, low-volatility, normal, and high-volatility states based on realized volatility or VIX levels (Shu and Mulvey, 2025). Empirical work on U.S. equities documents that high- and low-volatility regimes differ substantially in realized variance and that regimes persist on the order of months once they begin (Ang and Timmermann, 2011), so a single unconditional estimate averages over very different states of the world. *Figure 19.3* shows this amplification: stressed regimes widen both VaR and CVaR, but the gap is larger for CVaR, the quantity a risk manager cares about when deciding how to de-risk.

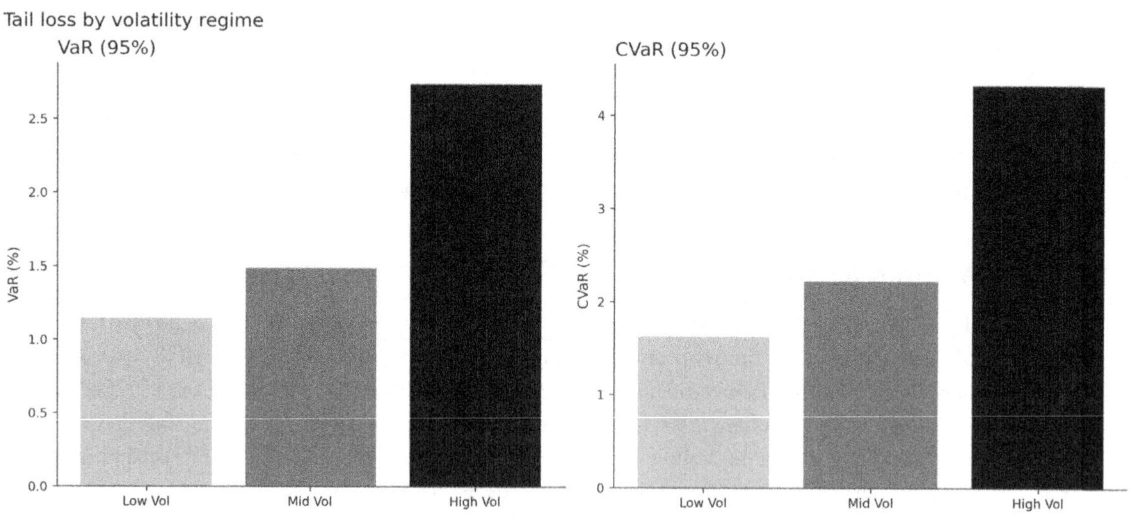

Figure 19.3: Regime-conditional tail risk

The conditional estimates show several patterns. Tail risk is amplified in stressed states: in `01_var_cvar`, the SPY high-volatility regime CVaR (95%) of 4.33% is about 2.7x the low-volatility regime value of 1.63%. Some strategies also show strongly asymmetric exposure, with stable risk in calm markets but explosive tails in stress, so the worst regime combines higher risk with worse compensation. The most dangerous moments are often regime transitions rather than established crisis periods, because controls calibrated to the old state fail before the new one is fully recognized.

Incorporating liquidity haircuts

To make tail risk estimates realistic, the cost parameters from *Chapter 18* should be stressed alongside the return distribution. That usually means doubling or tripling spread assumptions in the stress scenario, increasing market impact in line with the historical ratio of crisis-to-normal impact, and reducing assumed ADV to reflect lower participation in stressed markets. The resulting liquidity-adjusted VaR captures not just the price move but the cost of responding to it. For strategies with meaningful turnover or position sizes, that adjustment can increase effective VaR by 50-100%.

Evaluating risk model quality

The preceding metrics (VaR, CVaR, regime-conditional estimates) all depend on a volatility forecast. But how do you know whether your volatility model is any good? The fundamental difficulty is that "true" volatility is never observed. We observe proxies: squared daily returns, realized variance from intraday data, or range-based estimators. Each proxy introduces its own noise, and a naive comparison (computing mean squared error against a chosen proxy) can reverse model rankings when a different proxy is used. The model that looks best against squared returns may look worst against 5-minute realized variance.

Hansen and Lunde (2006) resolved this problem by identifying loss functions that preserve model rankings regardless of which volatility proxy is used. Two functions have that rank-robustness property. The first is MSE of variance:

$$L = \left(\hat{\sigma}^2 - \sigma^2_{\text{proxy}}\right)^2$$

which operates on variance rather than volatility; that distinction matters because variance MSE is proxy-robust while volatility MSE is not. The second is QLIKE:

$$L = \log(\hat{\sigma}^2) + \sigma^2_{\text{proxy}}/\hat{\sigma}^2$$

whose asymmetry penalizes under-prediction of variance more heavily than over-prediction. For risk management, where underestimating risk is more dangerous than overestimating it, that asymmetry is a feature rather than a defect.

Patton (2011) extended these results to broader families of loss functions, establishing that QLIKE and MSE are effectively the only practical choices that guarantee consistent model ranking across arbitrary volatility proxies. In application, compare competing volatility models, including GARCH, EWMA, realized variance, and ML-based forecasts, by computing average QLIKE and MSE against either squared daily returns or 5-minute realized variance. The model with the lowest average loss is preferred, and the ranking holds whichever proxy is chosen.

For risk management, where under-prediction carries asymmetric consequences, QLIKE is the natural choice. For alpha research, where unbiased forecasts matter more than conservatism, MSE is preferred. Both should be computed when evaluating the volatility inputs that feed *Chapter 17*'s allocation models and *Chapter 18*'s cost models. A risk model that systematically underestimates volatility produces over-leveraged portfolios and optimistic cost projections; the pipeline compounds the error downstream. Paleologo (2025) gives a practitioner-oriented discussion of these robust loss functions in production risk systems.

Practical guidance

Report both VaR and CVaR: VaR is familiar to stakeholders; CVaR captures tail severity. Use historical simulation for robustness, supplemented by parametric estimates for sensitivity analysis. On real SPY returns the Kupiec backtest in `01_var_cvar` favors historical VaR (exception ratio 1.11x, Kupiec p=0.10) over both parametric (1.17x, p=0.012) and Cornish-Fisher (1.45x, p<0.001) at 95% coverage; the Cornish-Fisher polynomial becomes unstable at this confidence level when realized excess kurtosis is in the double digits, which is typical for daily equity index returns.

Compute regime-conditional metrics and present the worst-regime CVaR prominently. Apply liquidity haircuts to avoid false comfort from frictionless backtests. Risk metrics describe the past, not the future.

Implementation: See `01_var_cvar` for VaR/CVaR computation and regime-conditional analysis.

19.4 Drawdowns, path risk, and time to recovery

VaR and CVaR measure point-in-time tail risk. But strategies do not exist at points in time—they travel paths. A strategy that loses 2% per day for 30 consecutive days may never breach a daily 5% VaR threshold, yet its investors experience a 45% drawdown. Path risk captures what point-in-time metrics miss: the cumulative damage and the time required to recover.

Maximum drawdown

Maximum drawdown (MDD) measures the largest peak-to-trough decline over a period:

$$MDD = \max_{t\in[0,T]} \left(\frac{\max_{s\in[0,t]} P_s - P_t}{\max_{s\in[0,t]} P_s} \right)$$

where P_t is the portfolio value at time t. Unlike volatility, which averages over all observations, MDD captures the single worst experience an investor would have endured.

MDD has operational significance: it determines the point of maximum regret, the moment when allocation decisions are most tested. A strategy with a 30% drawdown requires a 43% gain to recover. A 50% drawdown requires 100%. The asymmetry is punishing.

Institutional allocators operate under constraints that make path risk decisive. Many face hard drawdown limits (10% or 15% is common), where breaching triggers mandated redemption regardless of expected recovery. Investment professionals often cannot survive drawdowns that exceed peer norms, even if subsequent performance is excellent; career risk makes path risk personal.

Capital withdrawn during a drawdown misses the recovery. The realized return for an investor who redeems mid-drawdown is worse than the strategy's theoretical return, a gap that widens with drawdown severity. Leveraged strategies compound the problem: margin calls during drawdowns force deleveraging at the worst possible moment, converting temporary losses into permanent impairment.

Maximum drawdown tells us the depth but not the duration. Two drawdowns of equal magnitude differ dramatically if one lasts two months and the other two years. Drawdown duration measures the time from peak to trough; recovery time measures the additional time from trough back to the prior peak.

Ulcer Index incorporates both depth and duration by computing the quadratic mean of drawdowns over a period:

$$UI = \sqrt{\frac{1}{n}\sum_{i=1}^{n} D_i^2}$$

where D_i is the drawdown at time i. Unlike MDD, the Ulcer Index reflects the cumulative burden of being underwater, giving higher weight to prolonged drawdowns.

The historical record – 150 years of drawdowns

Alankar et al. (2023) provide a sobering catalog of downside tail events. Examining U.S. equity returns from 1871 to 2022, they identify 23 peak-to-trough declines exceeding 15%. These events cluster into two distinct types: gamma events that are fast and sharp and delta events that are slower and deeper. The distinction matters for hedging: gamma events, such as the 1987 crash or March 2020, respond well to option protection, while delta events, such as the 2008 financial crisis or the dot-com bust, require duration-based defenses.

Conditional drawdown analysis

Just as VaR varies by regime, drawdowns cluster. A strategy that shows modest drawdowns in backtesting may experience its worst losses during conditions the backtest undersampled. The 2008 financial crisis, the 2020 COVID crash, and the 2022 rate shock each stress different exposures.

Conditional drawdown analysis partitions the equity curve by regime and computes:

- Maximum drawdown within each regime
- Average drawdown duration by regime
- Recovery time conditional on the regime in which the drawdown began

Daniel and Moskowitz (2016) illustrate the pattern with momentum crashes: momentum strategies showed modest drawdowns for decades, then experienced 50%+ crashes during market reversals. Unconditional drawdown statistics understate the tail risk embedded in factor timing.

Two companion notebooks connect these path-risk ideas to trade construction. The fixed-stop comparison in `02_exit_strategies` produces *Figure 19.4*, which shows how different stop widths redistribute exit outcomes: tighter rules cut losses sooner, but they also increase the share of trades closed before the thesis has time to recover. The MAE/MFE excursion analysis in `03_position_sizing_mae_mfe` produces *Figure 19.8*, which calibrates stop and take-profit distances against the realized adverse and favorable excursions of historical trades, turning generic rules into strategy-specific sizing and exit policies. Both views express the same general lesson: controls should be calibrated to the strategy's realized behavior rather than chosen from generic preference, and they should be judged by how they change realized exit behavior, not only by the headline maximum drawdown they target.

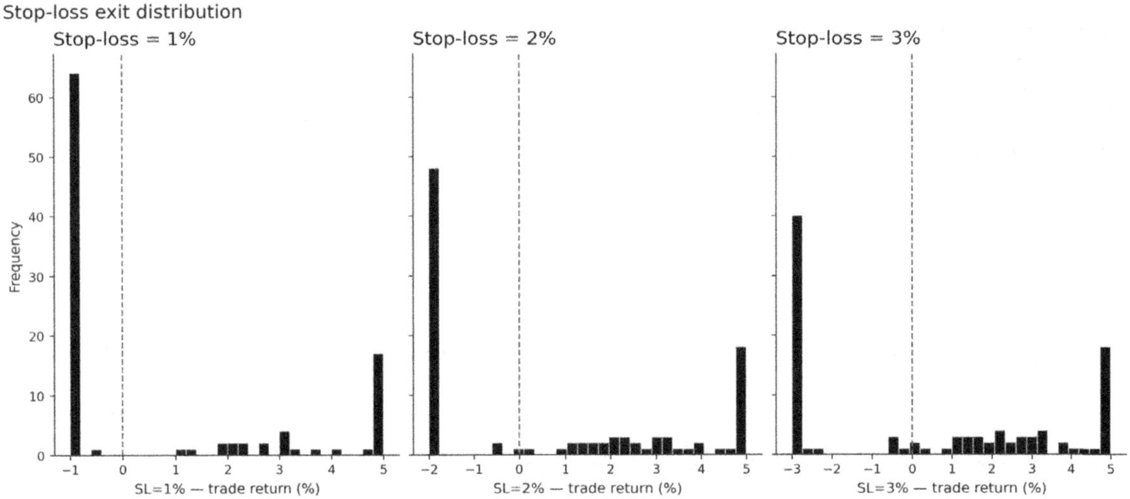

Figure 19.4: Stop-loss exit distribution under alternative rules

Linking drawdowns to kill switches

Drawdown thresholds serve as natural kill switch triggers. A strategy that breaches its ex-ante maximum acceptable drawdown has entered territory where continued operation requires explicit review. A graduated escalation framework (five levels at 5%, 10%, 15%, 20%, and 30% drawdown, each with predefined action and approver) is developed in *Section19.8* (*Table 19.7*), and is preferable to a single binary cutoff. The thresholds should be set before deployment, documented in the risk term sheet, and enforced automatically where possible.

Metric	Measures	Use Case
Maximum Drawdown	Worst peak-to-trough loss	Mandate limits, allocator communication
Drawdown Duration	Time in drawdown	Investor patience, career risk
Recovery Time	Time to regain peak	Capital planning, reinvestment timing
Ulcer Index	Integrated drawdown pain	Holistic path risk comparison
Calmar Ratio	Return / MDD	Risk-adjusted return focusing on path

Table 19.3: Common risk metrics

Implementation: See `01_var_cvar` for SPY drawdown depth and time-to-recovery (the 2007–2012 GFC drawdown reaches –55.2% over 355 trading days with an 869-day recovery), `02_exit_strategies` for the stop-distance comparison that anchors *Figure 19.4*, `03_position_sizing_mae_mfe` for the MAE/MFE excursion calibration that anchors *Figure 19.8*, and `10_ml4t_backtest_risk_demo` for the `ml4t.backtest.risk` module, which provides production-ready implementations of `StopLoss`, `TrailingStop`, `TighteningTrailingStop`, and `ScaledExit` rules that compose via `RuleChain`, `AllOf`, and `AnyOf` patterns.

19.5 Decomposing factor, sector, and macro exposures

A strategy's total risk is an aggregate that obscures its sources. A portfolio with 15% annual volatility might derive that risk from market beta, factor tilts, sector concentration, or idiosyncratic name bets, each with different implications for diversification, hedging, and regime sensitivity. Risk decomposition reveals the structure beneath the aggregate. In production, this decomposition serves as a diagnostic tool: monitoring factor exposures over time detects drift before it causes losses, and comparing current exposures to historical norms flags emerging risks.

The factor model framework

The foundation of risk decomposition is a factor model that expresses portfolio returns as a linear combination of systematic factors plus a residual:

$$r_p = \alpha + \sum_{k=1}^{K} \beta_k F_k + \epsilon$$

where r_p is portfolio return, β_k is the exposure to factor k, F_k is the factor return, and ϵ is the idiosyncratic residual. The β_k coefficients tell us how much of the portfolio's movement is explained by each systematic source.

Common factor frameworks include:

- **Fama-French:** Market, size, value (3-factor); adds momentum and profitability (5-factor)
- **Barra/MSCI:** Comprehensive models with 10-20 style and industry factors
- **Macro factors:** Rates, credit spreads, VIX, dollar, oil, particularly relevant for multi-asset strategies

The choice of factor model depends on the asset class and strategy type. An equity long-short strategy naturally maps to equity style factors; a macro strategy requires explicit macro factor exposures.

Intended and unintended exposures

Factor decomposition distinguishes between the exposures the strategy intends to take and those it acquires incidentally. A momentum strategy *intends* momentum exposure. But if the current momentum portfolio happens to be overweight technology stocks, it carries unintended sector exposure. If those tech stocks are also high-beta, it carries unintended market exposure.

Unintended exposures are dangerous because:

- They are not compensated in the strategy's investment thesis
- They may reverse unexpectedly
- They complicate attribution and risk management

Paleologo (2025) emphasizes that effective risk management requires separating signal-driven exposures from mechanical exposures that arise from portfolio construction. A momentum strategy with unintended value exposure should either hedge the value tilt or document it as an accepted risk.

Exposure stability across regimes

Factor exposures are not static. A strategy's beta to the market or to momentum drifts over time, and the variation often correlates with regime. Brixton et al. (2022) document that the stock-bond correlation, long assumed to be negative, turned positive during the 2022 inflation shock. Strategies built on diversification assumptions that had held for decades experienced unexpected, correlated drawdowns.

Rolling factor regressions surface these drifts directly. In `04_factor_exposure`, IWM's rolling one-year HML loading climbs from roughly 0.1 to 0.3 over 2015–2024, a structural shift in small-cap value tilt that an unconditional regression would average away. The implication for risk management is operational: factor exposures must be monitored on a rolling basis, and any hedge or risk budget built on a static loading silently becomes mis-sized as the underlying tilt drifts. Exposures that appear hedged in normal times may also become directional in stress, so the rolling window should be short enough to catch regime transitions but long enough to suppress estimation noise.

Sector and geographic decomposition

Beyond style factors, sector and geographic concentration carry their own risks. A U.S. equity strategy with 40% in technology is not just about stock selection: it is a technology sector bet. A global strategy with 70% in U.S. equities is making a bet on the U.S. dollar and the U.S. economy.

Useful concentration metrics:

- **Sector weights** versus benchmark
- **Active sector bets** (portfolio weight - benchmark weight)
- **Geographic exposure** for global strategies
- **Single-name concentration** (top 10 weights, HHI)

These exposures should be explicit in the risk term sheet. If the strategy intends to overweight technology, document it. If the overweight is incidental, consider rebalancing or hedging.

Macro factor sensitivities

For strategies with cross-asset exposure, macro factors provide additional insight:

- **Rate sensitivity**: Duration, convexity
- **Credit sensitivity**: Spread duration, default risk
- **Volatility sensitivity**: Vega, variance swap exposure

- **Currency sensitivity:** FX exposure by currency pair
- **Commodity sensitivity:** Energy, metals, agricultural products

Harvey et al. (2022) show that crypto assets carry hidden exposures to risk-on/risk-off dynamics and liquidity conditions that standard equity factors miss. Any strategy spanning multiple asset classes requires a factor model that covers all of them: an equity factor model applied to a portfolio holding crypto and commodities will attribute those exposures to alpha, inflating the apparent skill.

Attribution and decomposition in practice

Risk decomposition enables:

- **Performance attribution:** How much return came from each factor versus alpha?
- **Risk budgeting:** How much risk is allocated to each factor?
- **Hedging decisions:** Which exposures should be neutralized?
- **Crowding risk detection:** If the strategy's factor exposures are highly correlated with popular smart-beta ETFs or widely-held factor portfolios, liquidation risk increases: when crowded trades unwind, correlated positions sell simultaneously.

A strategy that generates an 8% annual return, with factor exposures accounting for 6%, is not an alpha strategy: it is a factor portfolio with modest alpha. This distinction matters for fees, benchmarking, and realistic expectations.

In `04_factor_exposure`, a Fama-French three-factor regression on a representative SPY/QQQ/IWM/VTV/VUG ETF portfolio (40/20/15/15/10 weights) yields R^2 of 0.995: systematic factors explain 99.5% of variance, leaving only 0.47% annualized alpha unexplained. The result is typical for diversified portfolios: apparent "alpha" is factor exposure in disguise. Concentrated strategies, or strategies driven by alternative data, may show lower R^2 and more genuine idiosyncratic returns.

Attribution uncertainty and why point estimates are not enough

Standard factor attribution reports deterministic decompositions: "40% of PnL came from momentum, 30% from value, 30% idiosyncratic." But factor returns are estimated from cross-sectional regressions, and that estimation error propagates into the attribution. A factor that explains 40% plus or minus 25% of PnL is very different from one that explains 40% plus or minus 5%, yet the standard tear sheet treats both as equally informative (Paleologo, 2025).

The remedy is to compute HAC (Newey-West) standard errors for each attributed PnL component, which absorb the serial correlation typical of daily factor returns. Factor return estimation produces errors with covariance approximately $(B^T \Omega_\epsilon^{-1} B)^{-1}$, where B is the factor loadings matrix and Ω_ϵ is the idiosyncratic covariance. The standard error of a factor's PnL contribution is $\text{SE(factor PnL)} = |w \cdot b_k| \times \text{SE}(f_k)$, where w is the portfolio weight vector, b_k is the vector of loadings on factor k, and $\text{SE}(f_k)$ is the factor return standard error. Reports should read "Momentum contributed +2.3% ± 0.8%" rather than a bare "+2.3%." On the SPY/QQQ/IWM/VTV/VUG portfolio in 04_factor_exposure, the FF5 attribution under HAC inference shows market dominates the +13.02% annualized return contribution, while SMB, HML, RMW, and CMA contributions are statistically indistinguishable from zero, a result that a point estimate alone would have hidden.

When attribution standard errors are large relative to the attributed PnL, the decomposition is uninformative: you cannot distinguish factor from idiosyncratic contribution with any confidence. This is especially common in portfolios with few assets, weak factor structure, or short evaluation windows. If the confidence interval on a factor's PnL contribution spans zero, claiming that factor "drove" performance is not supported by the data. Always present attribution with confidence bands and interpret them with the same rigor applied to any statistical estimate.

Detecting hidden dependencies in residuals

After removing factor exposures, idiosyncratic residuals should, in principle, be uncorrelated, but in practice they often are not. Significant pairwise correlations among residuals indicate latent sub-factors not captured by the model: industry sub-sectors, supply-chain linkages, or shared exposures to unmeasured variables.

Correlation thresholding provides a simple diagnostic: compute pairwise correlations among the idiosyncratic residuals and flag pairs that exceed a threshold (for example, $|\rho| > 0.15$). Grouping these pairs reveals clusters of assets that move together for reasons the factor model cannot explain, such as payment processors, semiconductor suppliers, or regional bank groups. Even on a tightly-modeled ETF basket, residual correlations can be striking: in `04_factor_exposure`, the FF5 idiosyncratic residual correlation between VTV and VUG is -0.73 and between QQQ and VUG is $+0.54$, both well above the $|\rho| > 0.15$ threshold and signaling latent style or sector factors that FF5 does not span. The technique bridges factor modeling and unsupervised ML: it effectively clusters using the factor model's residual correlation matrix, identifying structure the model misses and that contributes to an underestimation of portfolio risk.

Precision matrix quality – The Mahalanobis-distance variance diagnostic

Factor decomposition and portfolio optimization both depend on the covariance matrix and its inverse (the precision matrix). But a covariance matrix that predicts portfolio variance well may still yield an unstable inverse, and the inverse drives mean-variance optimization weights.

The variance of the Mahalanobis distance provides a portfolio-independent diagnostic: for each day t, compute $d_t^2 = r_t^T \hat{\Omega}^{-1} r_t$, the squared Mahalanobis distance of the return vector under the estimated precision matrix. If the model is well calibrated, d_t^2 should have an approximately constant expected value (equal to the dimensionality of the return vector, here 5). The diagnostic measures the temporal variance of d_t^2: low values indicate a stable, reliable precision matrix, while high values signal instability that will propagate into erratic optimizer weights. The ETF basket in `04_factor_exposure` returns a mean d^2 of 6.88 against an expectation of 5 with $\text{Var}(d^2) = 1457$, tripping a HIGH flag, a clear warning that the raw precision matrix needs shrinkage before being fed into a mean-variance optimizer. Monitoring this variance over time flags periods of covariance model degradation before they corrupt portfolio construction.

Resolving attribution ambiguity via factor rotation

When factors are correlated, naive attribution spreads PnL across factors in a way that depends on the factor representation rather than economic reality. Rotating the factor basis changes the decomposition without altering the portfolio or its risk, a sign that the attribution reflects a mathematical convention rather than economic substance.

Maximal attribution resolves this ambiguity by finding the rotation that maximizes PnL for a prioritized set of factor groups. A practitioner might first attribute to market exposure, then to sectors, then to styles. The procedure sequentially orthogonalizes each group against those already attributed, yielding a unique hierarchical decomposition in which each factor group's contribution reflects the PnL it would generate if the remaining factors were at their conditional expectations. This technique is most valuable in multi-factor settings where naive regression-based attribution produces implausible sign flips depending on which factors are included.

Trade-level SHAP as a diagnostic tool

Factor decomposition operates at the portfolio level; trade-level SHAP diagnostics operate at the individual position level. When a trade fails unexpectedly (the model predicted positive returns but realized losses), SHAP values identify which features drove the incorrect prediction.

Analyzing the SHAP profiles of the worst trades reveals recurring error patterns: momentum reversals, volatility regime mismatches, or liquidity-driven artifacts. This diagnostic loop (backtest → identify failures → explain with SHAP → cluster patterns → generate improvement hypotheses) systematically converts post-hoc trade analysis into actionable model improvements. See `05_trade_shap_diagnostics` for the full workflow using `TradeShapAnalyzer`.

Implementation: See `04_factor_exposure` for factor decomposition and regime-conditional analysis, and `05_trade_shap_diagnostics` for trade-level SHAP forensics.

19.6 Stress testing and scenario analysis

Historical risk metrics assume the future resembles the past, a reasonable baseline that fails precisely when it matters most. Stress testing asks a different question: how does the strategy behave under conditions that may be rare, unprecedented, or explicitly constructed to challenge our assumptions?

Historical crises as regime examples

The simplest stress test replays historical crisis periods:

Crisis	Period	Key Characteristics
2008 financial crisis	Sep 2008–Mar 2009	Credit freeze, correlation spike, liquidity collapse
2010 Flash Crash	May 6, 2010	Intraday liquidity vacuum, microstructure failure
2015 CNY devaluation	Aug 2015	EM contagion, volatility spike

Crisis	Period	Key Characteristics
2020 COVID crash	Feb–Mar 2020	Fastest 30% decline in history, V-shaped recovery
2022 Rate Shock	Jan–Oct 2022	Stock-bond correlation flip, duration pain

Table 19.5: Historical crises timeline

Each crisis stresses different exposures. A strategy that survived 2008 may fail in 2022 if its risk profile depends on negative stock-bond correlation. Zumbach and Zumbach (2025) advocate using these historical episodes not as predictions but as regime exemplars, samples of the parameter space that reveal vulnerabilities.

Replaying these crises in `06_stress_testing` on a balanced 60/40 portfolio shows substantial losses in both episodes: the 2008 GFC is -29.2% and the 2020 COVID crash is -21.5%, with the COVID decline concentrated in a shorter window.

Stressing cost parameters

Historical replay captures price moves but may understate execution damage. *Chapter 18*'s cost models use parameters estimated from normal markets. During stress:

- **Spreads widen:** 3-10x normal in severe crises
- **Market impact increases:** Order flow imbalance reduces effective liquidity
- **Participation drops:** Fewer counterparties, smaller ADV

A complete stress test applies these stressed cost parameters to the portfolio's holdings during the crisis period. A strategy that shows -15% return in historical simulation may show -25% when forced to trade at crisis spreads.

Scenario matrix construction

Beyond historical replay, scenario analysis constructs hypothetical but plausible combinations of shocks.

Some base scenarios include:

- Volatility doubles (VIX from 15 to 30)
- Spreads widen 3x
- Market impact increases 2x
- Correlations converge to 0.7

Combined scenarios stress multiple parameters simultaneously:

Scenario	Vol	Spreads	Impact	Correlations
Moderate Stress	1.5x	2x	1.5x	+0.2
Severe Stress	2x	3x	2x	+0.3
Crisis	3x	5x	3x	0.7 universal
Liquidity Crisis	1.5x	10x	5x	+0.2

Table 19.6: Combined stress scenarios

The scenario matrix need not be exhaustive: its purpose is to reveal how the strategy degrades as conditions worsen. A strategy that fails only under extreme scenarios is robust. One that fails under moderate stress requires rethinking.

A univariate Monte Carlo that resamples portfolio returns from a heavy-tailed Student-t distribution yields complementary insights: for the defensive diversified allocation in `06_stress_testing`, the 20-day 95% VaR is -4.5% and 95% CVaR is -5.9%; for the 60/40 portfolio, the same metrics are materially worse at -7.1% and -9.3%.

Factor-specific stress tests

Factor-exposed strategies require factor-specific scenarios:

- **Momentum reversal:** Historical episodes in which momentum crashed, including 2009 Q1 and 2020 Q1, illustrate what happens when the factor reverses. Daniel and Moskowitz (2016) document that momentum crashes cluster after market declines and volatility spikes.
- **Value compression:** Periods where cheap stocks got cheaper (2019-2020 growth dominance) stress value strategies.
- **Rate shock:** 2022's rate rise stressed anything with duration: not just bonds, but long-duration equities. The historical replay in `06_stress_testing` quantifies the cross-allocation impact: the 60/40 portfolio lost 20% in 2022, the defensive allocation 20%, the aggressive allocation 25%, and an All Weather allocation 26%, measured portfolio damage, not just the ~230 bps headline rate move.
- **Credit stress:** 2008 and March 2020 show what happens when credit spreads blow out.

Implementing factor-specific stress tests requires mapping historical factor shocks to current holdings. For momentum reversal, identify the worst momentum-factor drawdown period (2009 Q1 saw a -40% momentum factor return), extract the daily factor returns during that window, and apply them to the portfolio's current momentum loading. For rate shocks, use the historical yield curve shifts from 2022 (the 10-year yield rose ~230bps in nine months) and compute duration-weighted losses on current holdings. The key is that factor stress tests are *conditional* on the portfolio's current exposures: the same crisis affects different portfolios in different ways.

Reverse stress testing

Standard stress testing asks, "What happens if X?" Reverse stress testing asks, "What would cause the strategy to breach a critical threshold?"

Starting from a defined failure point (for example, 30% drawdown), work backward:

1. What combination of factor moves would cause this loss?
2. How plausible is that combination?
3. What would we observe before it happened?

This approach often reveals hidden vulnerabilities. A market-neutral strategy might appear safe until reverse stress testing reveals that a simultaneous value crash and momentum crash (both factors it holds long) would breach the drawdown limit.

Connecting stress results to controls

Stress testing is diagnostic, not cosmetic. Each stress test that reveals a vulnerability should map to either:

- **Accepted risk:** Documented in the risk term sheet, communicated to allocators
- **Hedged exposure:** Explicit overlay to neutralize the risk
- **Reduced exposure:** Smaller position sizes or tighter limits
- **Kill switch trigger:** Automatic de-risking if early warning indicators fire

A stress test that reveals problems but triggers no action is wasted effort; the value of stress testing lies in the decisions it informs.

A practical discipline: after each quarterly stress test, require a one-page memo documenting (a) the scenarios run, (b) the vulnerabilities identified, and (c) the specific changes made to limits, hedges, or monitoring as a result. If the memo's third section is empty, the stress test failed its purpose.

> **Implementation:** See `06_stress_testing` for historical replay and scenario analysis.

19.7 Adaptive risk controls without leakage

Static risk limits assume risk is constant. In live markets, it is not. A conservative position size in calm regimes can become reckless after a volatility shock. Adaptive controls are, therefore, necessary but also a common source of lookahead bias.

The governing rule is simple and strict: a control signal at time t may use only information available at $t-1$ or earlier. That rule applies to volatility estimates, regime labels, liquidity proxies, and any downstream transformation of those inputs.

Temporal discipline is easiest to enforce when controls are built from observable series and fixed protocols. Lagged realized volatility is valid; same-day realized volatility is not. Thresholds on published indicators, such as the VIX or credit spreads, are auditable; ex-post regime labels are not. Historical depth and quote-based proxies are valid; same-day execution outcomes are not.

The subtle failure mode is model-inferred regimes. Hidden-state models can leak future information if they are fit on the full sample or if smoothed probabilities are used in backtests. Even online implementations can leak when the full historical state path is re-estimated after each new observation. The result is a regime label at time t that depends partly on data from $t+1$ and beyond.

GARCH and EWMA as operational volatility engines

Most adaptive overlays rely on conditional volatility estimates. The two workhorses are GARCH(1,1) and EWMA. GARCH (see *Chapter 9* for more detail) can be written as:

$$\hat{\sigma}_t^2 = \omega + \alpha r_{t-1}^2 + \beta \hat{\sigma}_{t-1}^2$$

EWMA is the anchor-free special case that reacts quickly to new shocks. GARCH's mean-reverting anchor can stabilize longer-horizon baseline risk estimates, while EWMA is often preferred for short-horizon reactivity (Bollerslev, 1986). In production, the two are often combined rather than treated as substitutes.

Volatility targeting

Volatility targeting scales exposure inversely with estimated volatility:

$$w_t = w^* \cdot \frac{\sigma_{\text{target}}}{\hat{\sigma}_{t-1}}$$

Here w^* is baseline exposure, σ_{target} is target volatility, and $\hat{\sigma}_{t-1}$ is a lagged estimate. Evidence in Moreira and Muir (2017), Browne et al. (2023), and Paleologo (2025) shows that this overlay can improve risk-adjusted outcomes when implemented with realistic lags and leverage caps.

Operationally, the method is straightforward: choose a trailing window, enforce a one-step lag, cap the scaling factor in low-volatility states, and keep the rule fixed during evaluation. Risk parity extends the same idea across assets by equalizing risk contributions (Hurst, 2010).

Short-term volatility updates for crisis response

Slow covariance half-lives provide stable estimates in normal markets but adapt too late in stress. **Short-Term Volatility Updating (STVU)** addresses this by preserving slow correlation structure while scaling volatility with a fast multiplier:

$$m_t = \frac{\text{short-horizon realized vol}}{\text{baseline predicted vol}}$$

The multiplier is typically smoothed with short-horizon EWMA and applied to both factor and idiosyncratic volatility components (Paleologo, 2025). Conceptually, STVU creates a fast lane for volatility level updates without forcing full covariance re-estimation at crisis frequencies.

This matters most for leveraged or volatility-targeted books, where stale risk estimates mechanically produce oversized positions. During shock periods, STVU can trigger deleveraging materially earlier than slow-only models while preserving the baseline model in calm regimes.

Regime-triggered exposure caps

Regime caps are a stronger intervention than continuous volatility scaling. Exposure limits can step down as stress signals move from normal to elevated to severe conditions. A typical pattern is gross exposure near 200% in calm states, around 150% in elevated stress, and near 100% in severe stress, with state transitions tied to published indicators such as VIX, credit spreads, and spread-widening proxies.

The key requirement is pre-definition. Thresholds and transition rules must be specified before performance evaluation; otherwise, the cap logic itself becomes an overfitted strategy parameter.

Concentration and turnover limits

Adaptive control should also tighten concentration and turnover as market quality deteriorates. Name caps can be compressed across stress states, turnover ceilings reduced as spreads widen, and sector limits tightened when cross-sectional correlations rise. These controls reduce the chance that a volatility shock and a liquidity shock are taken simultaneously through the same crowded exposures.

Position-level controls

Portfolio overlays are not sufficient without position-level exits. Fixed stops are transparent but can be brittle when volatility changes. Trailing stops protect accrued gains but can still trigger whipsaw exits in noisy markets. The design variable is stop width: tighter stops reduce loss per trade but increase the probability of premature exit.

ATR-scaled stops and MAE/MFE-calibrated thresholds are often superior to fixed percentages because they adapt to the strategy's realized excursion profile. In `02_exit_strategies`, tighter fixed stops generate more frequent stop-outs, while calibrated and volatility-aware rules better balance loss control against avoidable churn.

Figure 19.5 extends the same calibration logic to learned exits in `08_ml_exit_signals`, where signal-strength-conditioned barriers change the mix of barrier outcomes across entry-quality buckets.

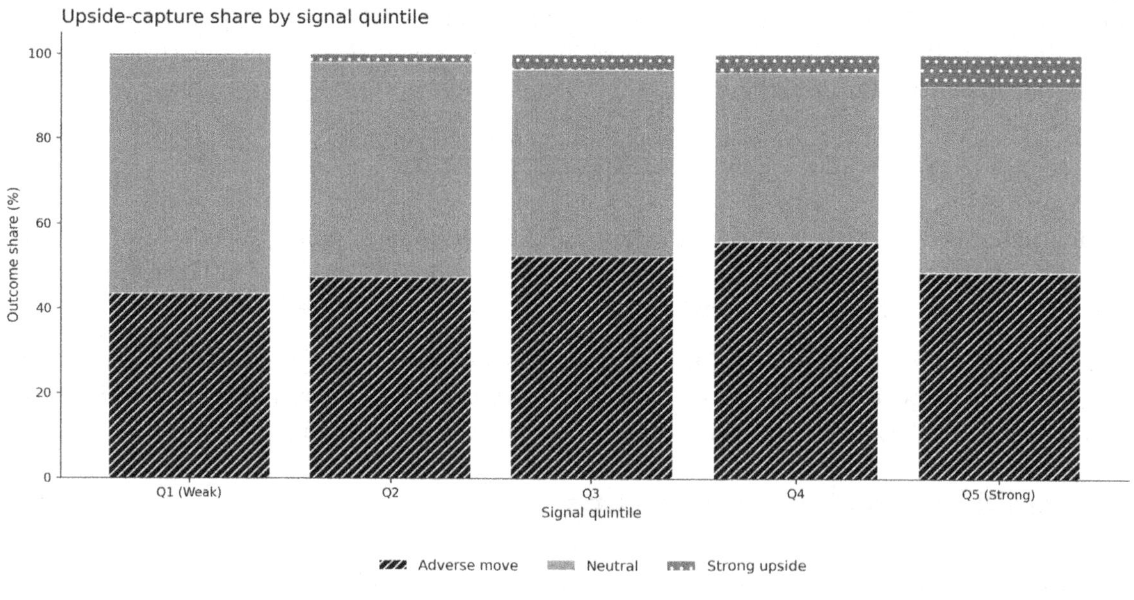

Figure 19.5: Barrier outcomes by signal strength

Exit rules change both realized loss control and the fraction of trades closed before the original thesis can recover. The signal-strength buckets in *Figure 19.5* also reveal that the lift comes from upside selection rather than downside protection: the top-quintile trades earn meaningfully more on the upside than bottom-quintile trades lose on the downside, so the discriminant power is asymmetric. Treat learned exit signals as a tool for sizing winners, not as a substitute for explicit stops on losers.

The learned-exit notebook needs careful interpretation. It is best read as evidence that exit behavior can be conditioned on signal quality, not as evidence that a learned exit model will always outperform a simpler baseline on a prediction metric such as AUC. The practical point is that position-level controls belong to the same calibration workflow as portfolio overlays: they should be judged by their effect on realized trade paths, not by generic classification scores in isolation.

Notebook `11_systematic_risk_sweep` pushes the same calibration problem further by sweeping stop-loss and take-profit rules over a broad grid. *Figure 19.6* shows that the one-dimensional performance surfaces are uneven rather than monotone, and *Figure 19.7* adds the joint stop-loss/take-profit surface. *Figure 19.8*, from the MAE/MFE excursion analysis in `03_position_sizing_mae_mfe`, then turns those excursion profiles into an operational sizing rule. The point is not that one grid point is universally optimal. The point is that stop logic should be chosen as part of a calibration workflow that weighs drawdown control against avoidable churn.

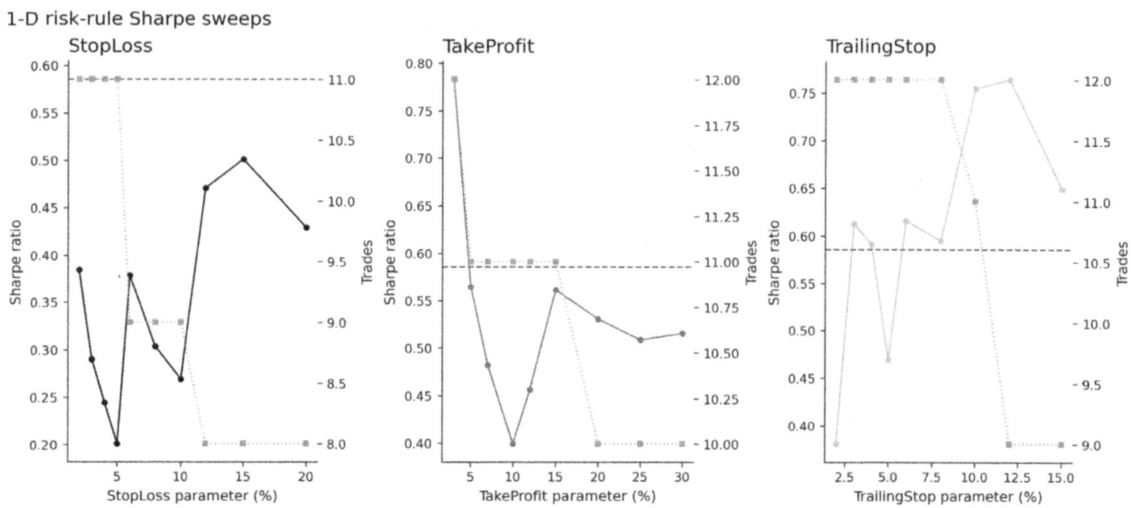

Figure 19.6: One-dimensional risk-rule sweeps shown in three line graphs

Performance is uneven rather than monotone, which is why stop design must be calibrated rather than chosen from a generic preference for tighter exits.

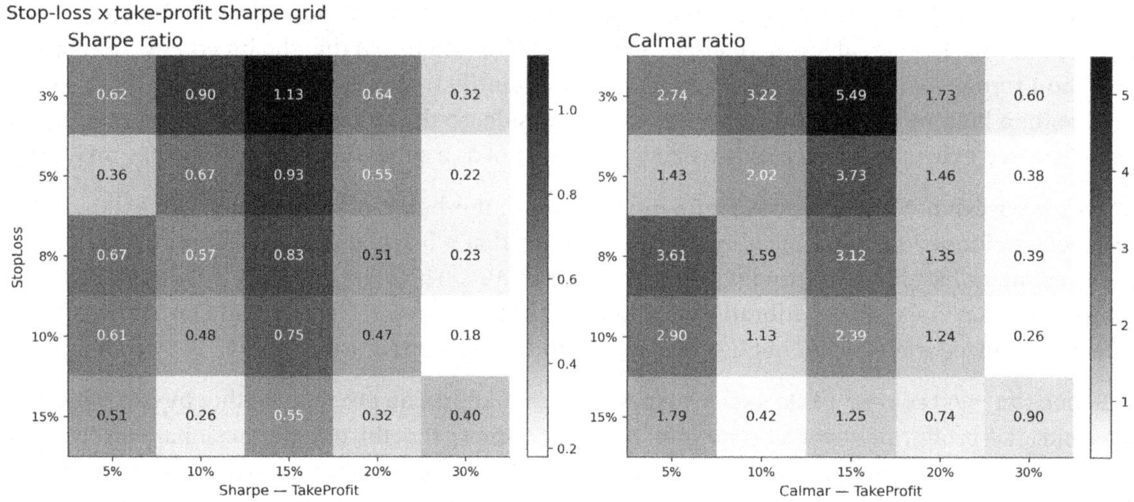

Figure 19.7: Joint stop-loss and take-profit surface, shown in two heatmaps

The interaction between the two controls matters more than any single threshold chosen in isolation.

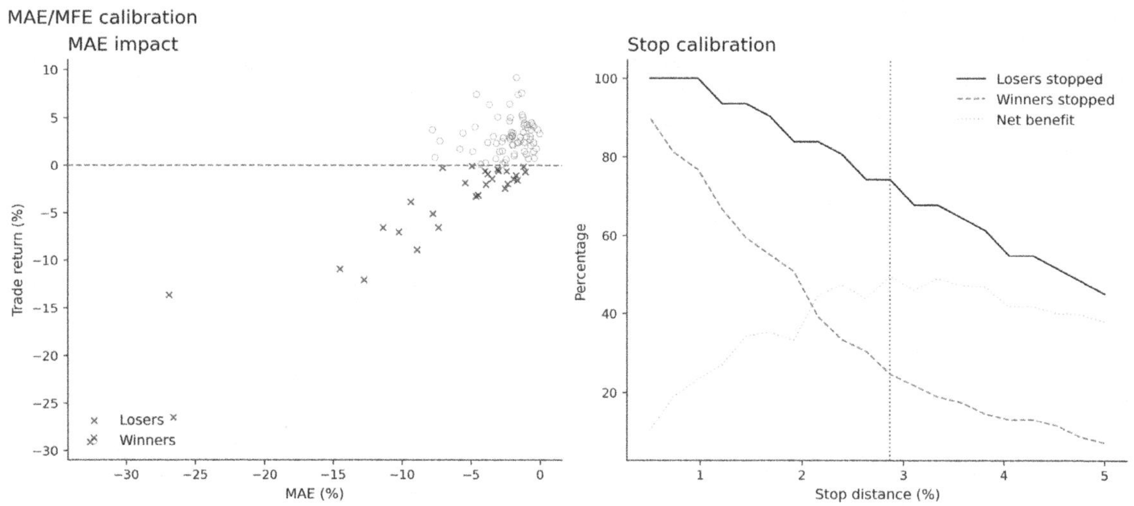

Figure 19.8: MAE/MFE calibration for position-level controls

Excursion analysis turns generic stop rules into strategy-specific sizing and exit policies.

When the underlying allocator is itself uncertainty-aware (the conformal inverse-width allocator of *Section 17.4* sizes positions by $1/\Delta_i$ from per-asset calibrated prediction-interval widths), the controls in this section compose with it orthogonally. The allocator decides how much capital each name receives; the rules calibrated here decide when an open position should exit. The *Section 17.4* validation evidence shows that conformal sizing on its own does not displace the baseline with the highest cross-stage validation Sharpe; the gap reflects the value the overlays in this section add on top of any sizing rule, conformal or otherwise.

From rule-based controls to learned hedging policies

Buehler et al. (2019) formulate hedging as direct optimization of a risk objective, learning position updates from market state and current holdings. With transaction costs as the objective, learned policies can produce no-transaction regions, consistent with classical asymptotic results (Whalley and Wilmott, 1997).

For CVaR-trained policies, the Rockafellar-Uryasev (2000) representation provides a differentiable objective:

$$\mathrm{CVaR}_\alpha(L) = \min_w \left[w + \frac{1}{1-\alpha} \mathbb{E}(L-w)^+ \right]$$

The potential benefit is tighter objective-level hedging under realistic frictions. The governance cost is lower transparency and a higher model-risk management burden. In practice, the safest deployment pattern is hybrid: a learned policy within hard, deterministic envelopes defined by traditional controls.

The notebook `09_deep_hedging` illustrates this pattern. The evidence is most useful as a demonstration of how tail-risk objectives and transaction costs can be optimized jointly, not as a blanket claim that learned hedging always dominates simpler policies on every operational dimension.

Anti-patterns to avoid

The recurring failure modes are consistent across implementations: thresholds mined from in-sample performance, control parameters tuned on evaluation windows, kill switches calibrated with hindsight, and the use of same-day signals that violate tradable timing. Each one can make a weak control look strong in a backtest and fragile in production. The common defect is not mathematical sophistication but broken governance. A control that cannot be specified ex ante and reconstructed after the fact is not a valid control.

Walk-forward validation and auditability

Adaptive controls require the same walk-forward discipline used elsewhere in the book. Define the rule first, tune only inside nested training loops, and evaluate on untouched forward windows with strict timestamp integrity.

A production-ready control stack is auditable end-to-end. Rule logic should be frozen and documented before deployment; historical signal values should be reproducible; each position change should be traceable to a specific control input; and overrides should be recorded with explicit rationale. If a control cannot be reconstructed, it cannot be trusted.

Implementation: `02_exit_strategies` (stop-rule comparison and MAE/MFE), `06_stress_testing` (regime-conditional volatility for the volatility-targeting overlay), `07_drift_detection` (drift signals that anchor adaptive thresholds), `08_ml_exit_signals` (signal-strength-conditioned exits in *Figure 19.5*), `09_deep_hedging` (deep-hedging as a learned policy under transaction costs), `10_ml4t_backtest_risk_demo` (composable rule structures from `ml4t.backtest.risk`), `11_systematic_risk_sweep` (the stop-loss/take-profit grids that anchor *Figures 19.6* and *19.7*), and `03_position_sizing_mae_mfe` (the MAE/MFE excursion calibration behind *Figure 19.8*).

19.8 Applying kill switches and risk governance

Kill switches define the conditions under which a strategy must reduce risk, pause trading, or trigger formal review. A strategy without explicit failure conditions is forced to improvise under stress, which is exactly when discretion is least reliable.

Kill switches must be defined before deployment, documented in the risk term sheet, and tested in the same way as any other strategy rule. In practice, the triggers usually fall into three groups. Performance-based triggers respond to drawdown, rolling underperformance, or abnormal loss streaks. Behavior-based triggers respond to turnover explosions, execution slippage, or a widening gap between live and expected tracking behavior. Market-state triggers respond to conditions such as severe spread widening, liquidity withdrawal, or stress indicators moving beyond predefined bands.

The important point is not the specific threshold but the structure around it. Every trigger needs a metric, a threshold, an action, an escalation path, and a reinstatement condition. Without that surrounding logic, a kill switch is not a governance rule; it is only a number on a dashboard.

Escalation and review cadence

Well-designed kill switches are rarely binary. A graduated framework is usually more robust because it separates early warning from full shutdown:

Level	Trigger	Action	Decision Authority
1 - Watch	5% drawdown	Increased monitoring	PM
2 - Caution	10% drawdown	50% position reduction	PM + Risk
3 - Review	15% drawdown	New positions halted	CIO
4 - Pause	20% drawdown	Full position unwind	CIO + Board
5 - Terminate	30% drawdown	Strategy shuttered	Board

Table 19.7: Illustrative kill switch specifications

The thresholds and actions are illustrative: each strategy requires calibration to its expected volatility and investor tolerance. A high-volatility strategy might have wider bands; a low-vol strategy, tighter.

The drawdown rule paradox

Varma (2025) documents a troubling pattern: mechanical drawdown rules often lock in losses that a subsequent recovery would have erased. Across ETF and portfolio data from 1993 to 2022, traditional drawdown triggers frequently amplified losses.

The asymmetry is straightforward. Drawdown rules often trigger when prices are already depressed, and expected returns are higher than usual. A sequence of smaller drawdowns followed by repeated forced exits can therefore do more damage than a single managed drawdown that is allowed to recover. That evidence argues against a single universal cutoff and in favor of context-aware escalation, cross-asset confirmation, and review of the broader market state before capital is removed.

Context matters: a 10% drawdown during elevated VIX carries different implications than the same drawdown in calm conditions. Simultaneous drawdowns across assets signal systematic risk; isolated drawdowns in single positions may be worth riding out.

Some failures indicate that the model is broken rather than temporarily unlucky. Persistent underperformance, a clear change in factor behavior, repeated cost overruns, or a structural change in data or market design should trigger formal re-research. That process is corrective rather than punitive: models have shelf lives, and the same validation discipline used earlier in the workflow must be applied again once the environment changes materially.

Drift detection as early warning

For production ML models, drift detection provides early warning that the trading environment has shifted. The Population Stability Index (PSI) offers interpretable thresholds: PSI < 0.10 indicates minimal drift, 0.10-0.25 suggests moderate drift that warrants investigation, and PSI greater than 0.25 signals significant drift that requires model retraining. These are rules of thumb, not universal constants; appropriate thresholds depend on feature distributions, sample sizes, and the model's sensitivity to distributional shifts. Calibrate thresholds on historical regime transitions before deployment.

In `07_drift_detection`, the monitoring demo is best read as a workflow illustration; on the real crypto perpetuals panel, the domain-classifier AUC saturates near 1.0 because funding and volatility regimes drift continuously, so per-feature PSI is the more reliable trigger until the AUC threshold is calibrated on the strategy's own data.

Model risk management documentation

Federal Reserve (2011) treats this documentation burden as part of model risk management rather than as auxiliary paperwork. A deployable risk addendum, therefore, needs to record the model's assumptions, its known limitations, the metrics used for ongoing monitoring, and clear ownership of the strategy and its controls. That document should also summarize the actual kill-switch thresholds, the authorities responsible for each escalation level, and the conditions under which trading may resume after a pause.

The exact contents vary by strategy. A high-frequency execution model may require latency and inventory limits that are irrelevant to a monthly allocator, while a leveraged multi-asset portfolio may require much more detail on financing, counterparty concentration, and crisis deleveraging. The value lies less in a universal template than in the discipline of writing down the assumptions and responses before the strategy is exposed to stress.

Governance as a competitive advantage

Good governance is a competitive advantage, though the mechanism is indirect. Allocators conducting due diligence routinely reject strategies that lack documented risk frameworks: the absence signals operational immaturity regardless of return quality. Internally, explicit rules replace discretionary judgments, enabling the strategy to scale without requiring a proportional increase in human oversight. The discipline of documenting failure modes before deployment forces clarity about what the strategy actually does, often revealing risks that the research process missed.

Implementation: See `07_drift_detection` for monitoring dashboards and `10_ml4t_backtest_risk_demo` for portfolio-level limits. The `ml4t.backtest.risk` module provides `MaxDrawdownLimit`, `DailyLossLimit`, `MaxPositionsLimit`, and `GrossExposureLimit` classes that implement these kill switches programmatically, each with configurable thresholds and actions (warn, reduce, halt).

19.9 Summary

Risk management is system design, not a reporting layer. We transformed the validated strategy from earlier chapters into a tradable system with explicit constraints, adaptive controls, and governance artifacts. Every control must be implementable without lookahead, auditable after the fact, and documented before deployment. Tail risk is regime-dependent: unconditional VaR and CVaR mask materially higher exposure in stressed states, and path risk (drawdown depth, duration, and recovery time) determines whether a strategy survives long enough for its edge to compound.

The deliverables of a risk-managed system are concrete: a risk term sheet addendum with calibrated thresholds and escalation paths; regime-conditional VaR and CVaR estimates that reveal the true tail exposure; stress test results that map vulnerabilities to specific controls; and a monitoring dashboard with drift detection that provides early warning before losses materialize. Together, these artifacts transform a validated backtest into a system that an allocator can underwrite and a portfolio manager can operate.

Chapter 20 synthesizes the full pipeline (from signal definition through risk management) into a single assessment of each case study's viability, comparing the incremental contribution of every stage.

20

Strategy Synthesis

Chapters 6 through *19* applied the ML4T research workflow to nine case studies, from defining the trading objective, engineering labels and features, and training several model families to generating predictions, constructing portfolios, imposing transaction costs, and testing under risk controls. Each chapter asked how a specific technique performs inside that pipeline.

This chapter inverts the question. Across nine case studies spanning seven asset classes (from 15-minute NASDAQ-100 microstructure to monthly firm-characteristic strategies, FX majors, crypto derivatives, and large-scale US equities), what do the first-pass results, taken together, say about translating ML predictions into trading strategies?

After completing this chapter, you will be able to:

- Read a feature triage ledger as a screen for downstream strategy work, and recognize where feature-level survival predicts strategy-level survival and where it does not.
- Distinguish signal quality, portfolio translation, cost survival, and temporal stability as separate evaluation stages.
- Compare how model families behave after the full pipeline, and identify when several configurations cluster within measurement error of one another.
- Diagnose differences between validation and holdout through prediction quality, portfolio translation, and structural break as distinct mechanisms.
- Evaluate strategies under realistic constraints, including instrument-appropriate cost models, capacity limits, and multiple testing adjustments.
- Identify next-iteration priorities (label redesign, ensembling, feature engineering, allocator research) inside the ML4T iterative workflow.
- Identify the binding constraint in each case study and the specific next research step the evidence suggests.

Section 20.1 reviews each case study's performance from signal to portfolio to holdout. *Section 20.2* revisits upstream feature triage across the nine studies and asks whether feature-level survival forecasts translate into strategy-level survival. *Section 20.3* and *Section 20.4* examine why prediction quality alone does not determine strategy performance and which model families translate consistently across the pipeline. *Section 20.5* isolates the allocator layer. *Section 20.6* imposes cost-survival realism and *Section 20.7* the risk-overlay layer. *Section 20.8* adds a causal lens. *Section 20.9* reads the case studies for what worked, what constrained performance, and the specific next research step each case suggests.

Box 20.1: What these results measure, and what they do not

The nine case studies share a deliberately middle-of-the-road design. Each draws on standard model configurations, standard backtest assumptions, and a feature set tailored to the instrument but not further tuned; none represents an attempt to extract the maximum achievable Sharpe ratio. The design is also static over time: each strategy's model is chosen by walk-forward validation, then applied across its one- to two-year holdout period as a single fit, with no retraining within that window and no response to a drawdown or a stretch of poor performance.

That schedule keeps nine parallel case studies tractable; a live research program would refit more often and step in when a strategy stopped working, so the holdout figures understate what a more adaptive process could reach. The single largest constraint is data. Almost every case study runs on price and returns alone: no fundamentals for most equity universes, no order-book depth for the intraday strategies, no macro or rate-differential series for FX, no on-chain activity for crypto. The two case studies built on richer-than-price inputs are the exception: US firm characteristics and the S&P 500 equity-plus-options analytics, and the largest validation Sharpe in the test bed, US firm characteristics, is one of them.

A thorough research program would iterate where this pass does not, adding alternative data, engineering features across several cycles, and widening each universe; *Section 20.9* names the highest-value next move for each strategy. The outcomes that follow reflect an application of the workflow under tight constraints, not a measure of what the methods can ultimately deliver.

20.1 First-pass results across nine case studies

The nine case studies share the same research workflow but differ in data, horizon, market logic, and execution constraints. This section walks each case study's arc from prediction to portfolio to holdout. *Table 20.1* summarizes the design facts; *Chapter 6* and the accompanying code repository carry the full setup.

Case Study	Asset Class	Period	Frequency	Universe	Horizon
US Firm Characteristics	Equity	1990–2016	Monthly	~2,500	1 month
US Equities Panel	Equity	1990–2018	Daily	~3,200	5 days
ETFs	Cross-asset	2007–2025	Daily	100	21 days
CME Futures	Futures	2011–2025	Daily	30	5 days

Case Study	Asset Class	Period	Frequency	Universe	Horizon
S&P 500 Eq+Options	Equity	2017–2021	Daily	633	5 days
FX Pairs	FX	2011–2025	Daily	20	21 days
Crypto Perpetuals	Crypto	2020–2025	8-hourly	19	24 hours
S&P 500 Options	Options	2017–2021	Weekly	~500	To expire
NASDAQ-100 Microstructure	Equity	2020–2021	15 min	114	60 min

Table 20.1: Case-study setup. Period covers training, validation, and holdout windows combined

The universe is the average count of tradable assets. Horizon is the forecasting target carried to the holdout.

Evaluation metrics

Every case study reports the same set of metrics. The daily cross-sectional information coefficient (IC) is the Spearman rank correlation between model scores and realized returns across traded assets, averaged across sessions in the window, with a 95% HAC-robust confidence interval (Newey–West, *Chapter 7*). ICIR is the ratio of the mean daily IC to its standard error across walk-forward folds. Sharpe ratio is the daily geometric mean return divided by daily volatility, annualized by the square root of the number of annual trading periods, reported with its probabilistic Sharpe ratio (Bailey and López de Prado, 2014) and a 95% confidence interval. Annualized return, maximum drawdown, turnover, and trade count come from the same backtest as the Sharpe ratio. Throughout, ** marks values significantly different from zero at the 1%-level and * at the 5%-level, two-sided.

Headline outcomes

Three numbers carry the most weight: the strongest predictive signal each case study produced, the strongest validation-period strategy performance that signal supported, and how the selected configuration behaved during the holdout period. *Table 20.2* collects these for the nine cases.

Case Study	Rebalance	Daily IC	Val. Sharpe	Holdout Sharpe
US Firm Characteristics	Monthly	+0.037**	+2.75**	+1.77
US Equities Panel	Weekly	+0.036**	+2.03**	−0.49
S&P 500 Eq+Options	Weekly	+0.041**	+2.39**	−0.73
CME Futures	Weekly	+0.032*	+1.36**	+1.11
ETFs	Monthly	+0.085**	+1.36**	+1.00
Crypto Perpetuals	24-hour	+0.026**	+2.57**	−0.13
S&P 500 options	Weekly	−0.002	+0.16	+0.97
FX Pairs	Daily	+0.012	+0.05	+0.19
NASDAQ-100 Microstructure	15-min	+0.004	+1.13	+0.53

Table 20.2: First-pass modeling and strategy outcomes for the selected configuration in each case study

Daily IC is the mean daily cross-sectional IC; significance is HAC-robust against zero. Validation and Holdout Sharpe are for the same configuration, the one with the highest validation Sharpe across the signal, allocation, and risk-overlay stages.

The six case studies that produced positive validation performance are shown below with a performance figure; the three that resolved flat keep their *Table 20.2* line and a sentence. *Section 20.9* compiles the per-case readings into specific next steps for further research.

Cases that hold or decay

US Firm Characteristics is the only case whose validation edge continues to the holdout with both its Sharpe point estimate and its drawdown profile intact (*Figure 20.1*). The best-performing configuration (a gradient-boosted model that assigns equal weight to 50 names) posts a validation Sharpe ratio of +2.75 [+2.33, +3.37] and stays at +1.77 on the 2016 holdout, where the holdout daily IC of +0.048 [+0.031, +0.065] still excludes zero. A concentrated 10-name alternative on a higher-IC model achieves a nearly identical validation Sharpe ratio but a −34% holdout drawdown, compared with this configuration's −8.6%, so diversification, not signal strength, is what survives out of sample. The binding question is realized capacity: the long leg tilts toward smaller names whose bottom-quartile spreads commonly run 100 to 500 basis points, so universe-mean spreads understate friction.

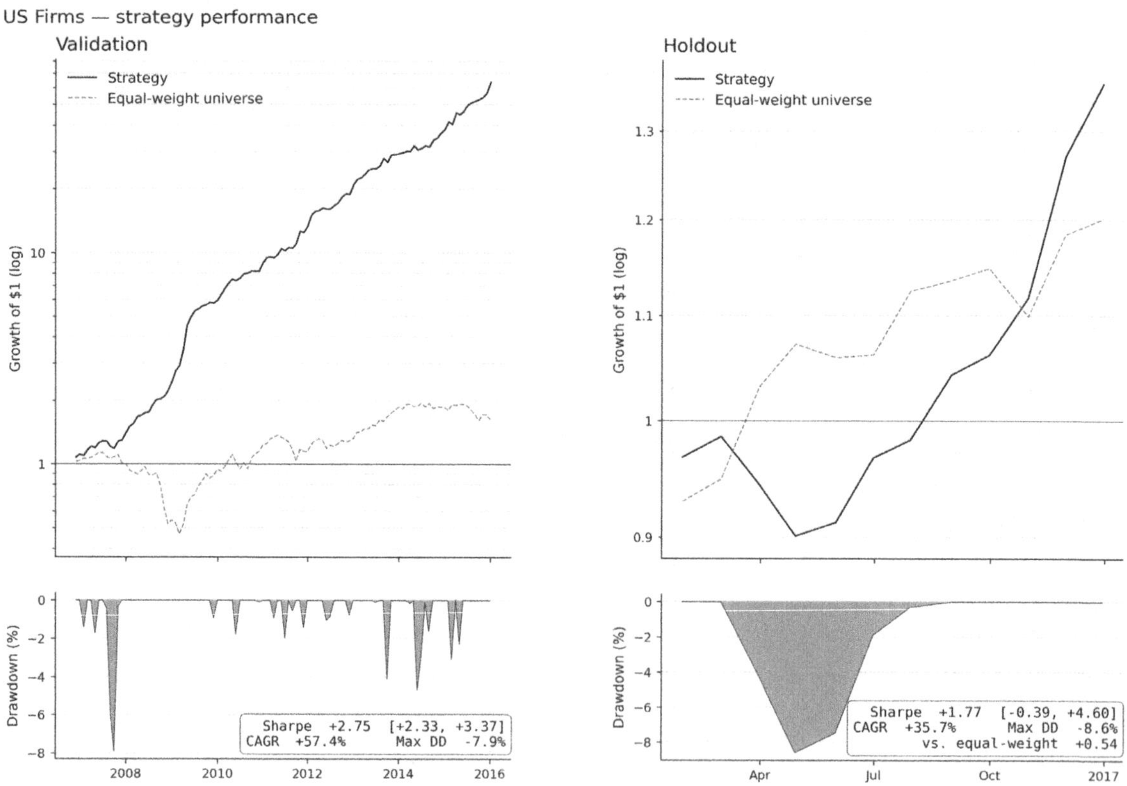

Figure 20.1: US Firms, validation (left) and holdout (right). Top: cumulative return of the highest-validation-Sharpe strategy versus the equal-weight universe benchmark, log scale; bottom: the strategy's drawdown, shaded

The metrics panel reports annualized Sharpe (95% CI), CAGR, maximum drawdown, and the strategy-minus-benchmark paired-bootstrap Sharpe difference. The validation edge continues into the holdout with the Sharpe point estimate and the drawdown profile intact.

The US Equities Panel has the longest validation period among all case studies (16 walk-forward folds over 4,000 trading days) yet still fails out of sample (*Figure 20.2*). The 2016–2018Q1 holdout sign-flips: daily IC turns slightly negative, validation Sharpe of +2.03 [+1.46, +2.55] lands at −0.49 with a 48% drawdown, and the strategy underperforms an equal-weight US-equities benchmark that produces a Sharpe ratio of +1.82 over the same window. Both prediction quality and portfolio translation degrade, making this the chapter's anchor for the takeaway that a strong validation Sharpe does not guarantee a holdout Sharpe.

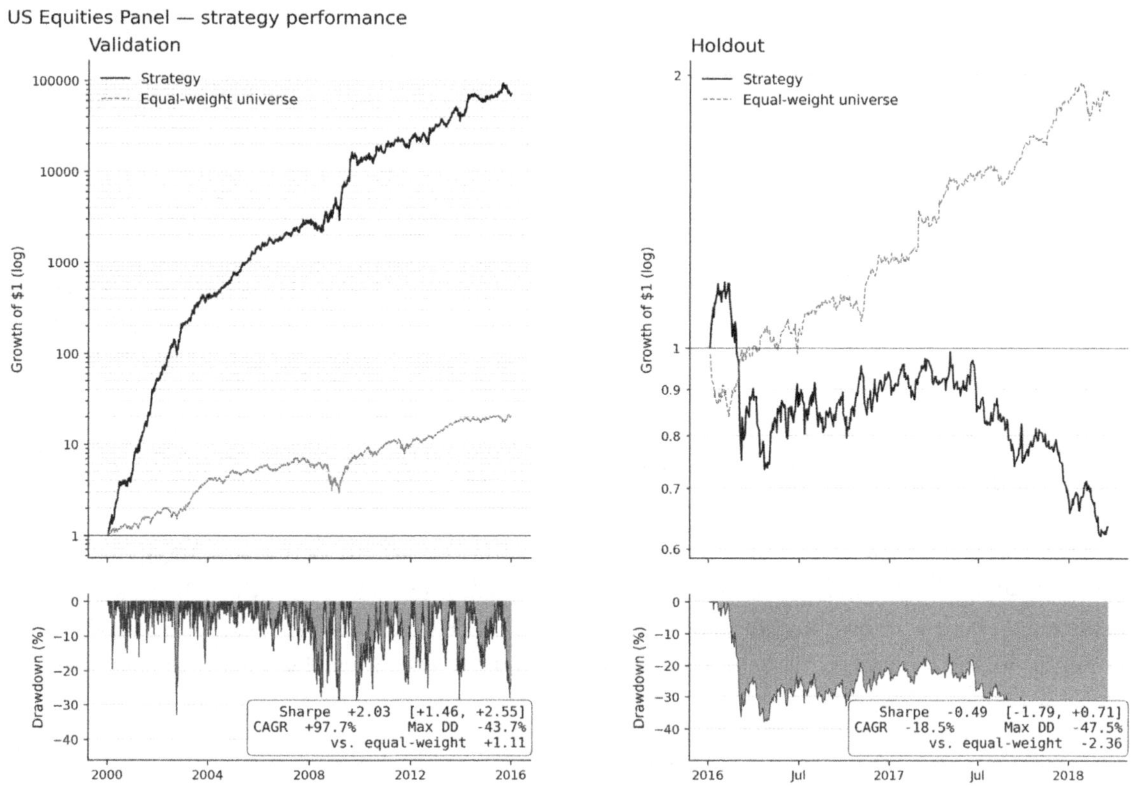

Figure 20.2: US Equities Panel: the validation (left) cumulative return climbs steeply while the holdout curve (right) gives the gains back and the drawdown deepens to nearly half of capital: a credible validation edge that sign-flips out of sample

S&P 500 Equity-plus-Options combines 633 stocks with option-implied analytics under an IPCA latent-factor model, the only credible cross-sectional signal at the risk-adjusted 5-day label (*Figure 20.3*). Validation Sharpe of +2.39 [+1.21, +3.51] carries the tightest selection-bias adjustment, but the 2021 holdout decays to −0.73 against an equal-weight benchmark Sharpe of +1.82. Confounding diagnostics (*Section 20.8*) flag the option-implied features as entangled with momentum and volatility, so the failure suggests regime sensitivity at least as much as overfitting.

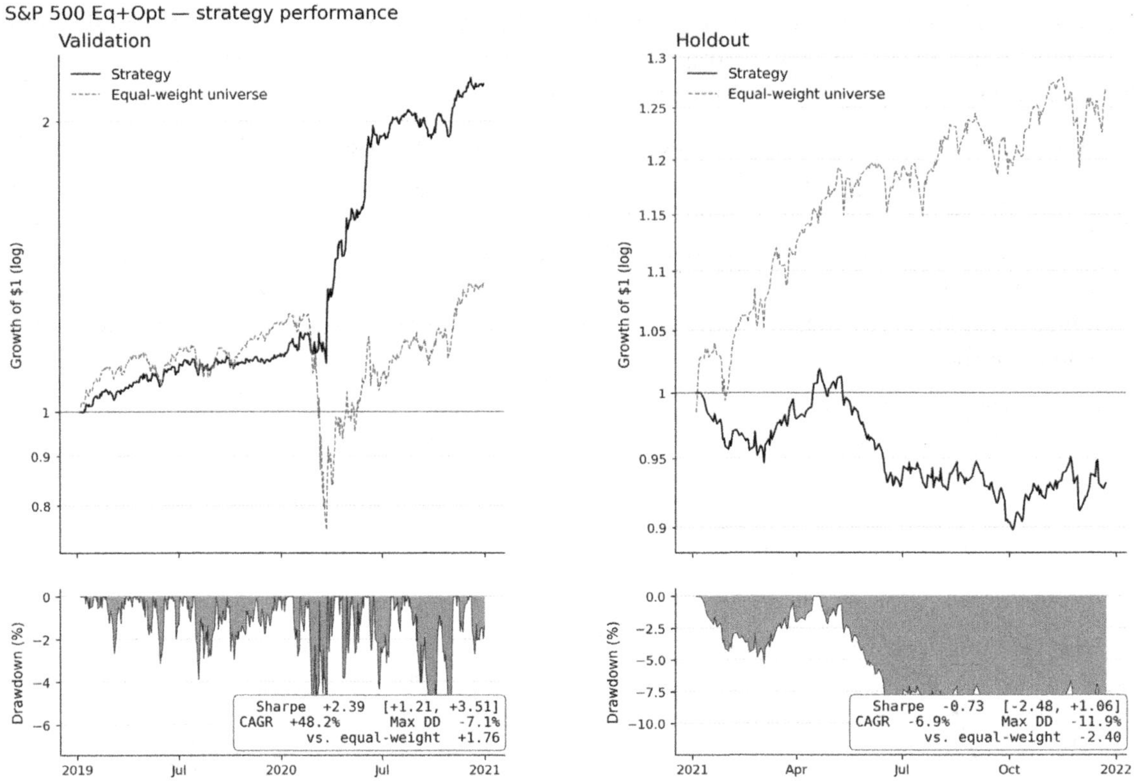

Figure 20.3: S&P 500 Eq+Options, validation (left) and holdout (right), same layout as Figure 20.1. The 2021 holdout reverses a strong validation curve; the equal-weight benchmark outperforms the selected book over the same window

CME Futures is the case where data construction shapes the result just as much as the model family (*Figure 20.4*). The 5-day label is built on a ratio-adjusted continuous series. Daily IC clears the 5% threshold on both windows, and validation Sharpe of +1.36 [+0.50, +2.14] holds at +1.11 [−0.43, +2.77] on the 2024–2025 holdout, close to validation, though the window is too short to resolve the gap.

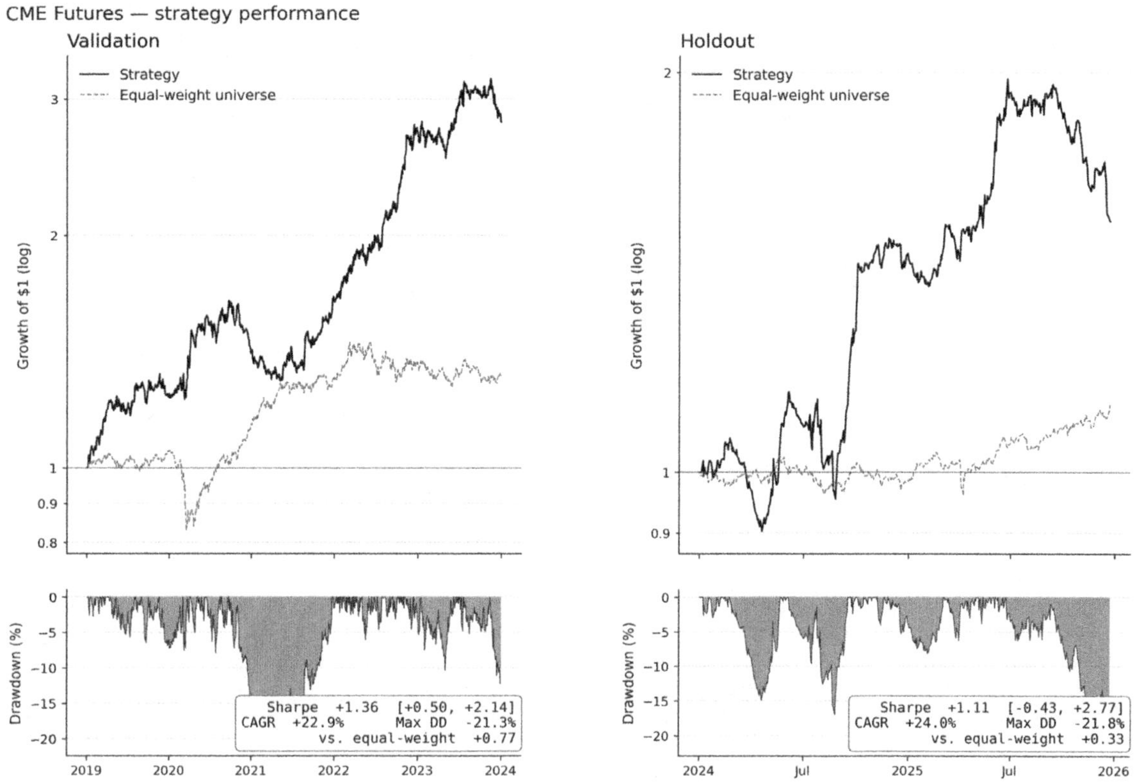

Figure 20.4: CME Futures, validation (left) and holdout (right). The holdout cumulative return and drawdown track the validation profile; because the holdout window is short, its Sharpe ratio is wide

ETFs produced the strongest per-name signal among case studies, with a validation daily IC of +0.085 [+0.051, +0.119] and a validation Sharpe of +1.36, which holds at +1.00 on the holdout and is statistically indistinguishable under a paired bootstrap (*Figure 20.5*). The strategy nonetheless trails an equal-weight cross-asset benchmark that ran +1.33 during the 2024–2025 mega-cap rally; a Fama-French five-factor-plus-momentum attribution returns a 6.7% annualized alpha (HAC $t = 2.77$) with market and CMA loadings dominating, so the relative shortfall traces to residual market exposure in a regime that favored mega-cap beta.

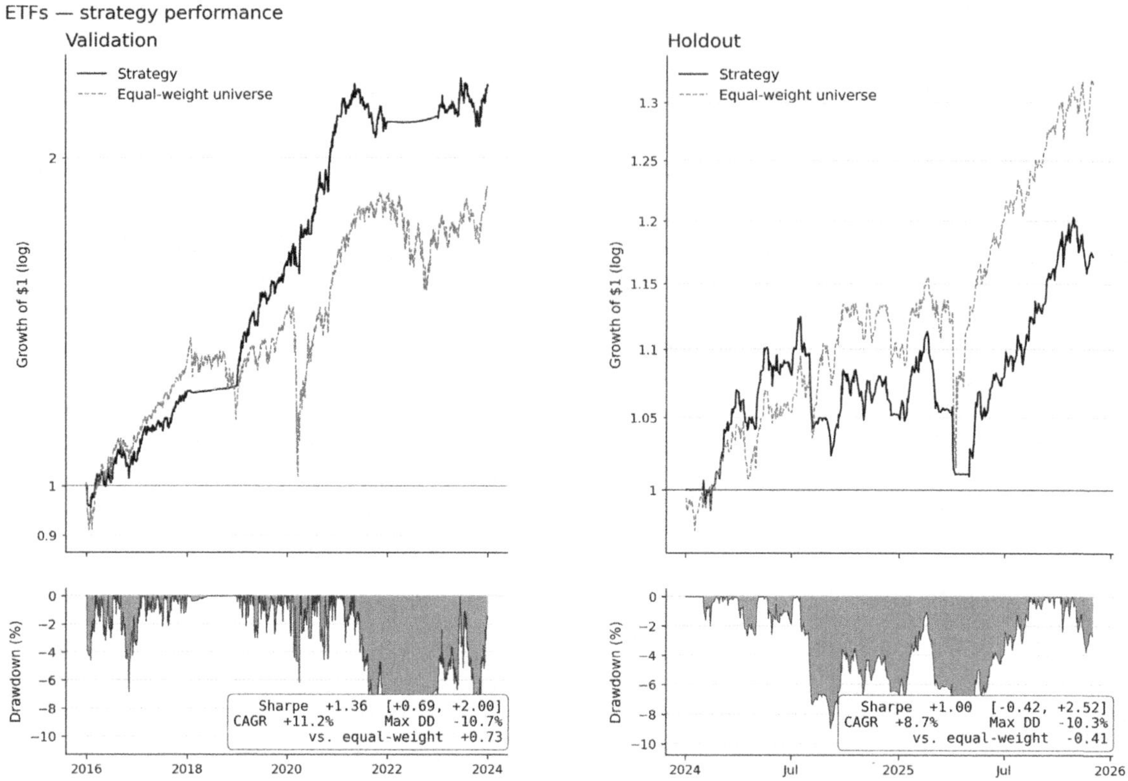

Figure 20.5: ETFs, validation (left) and holdout (right). The validation Sharpe carries to the holdout Sharpe even as the holdout daily IC weakens; the cap-weighted benchmark still outpaces the strategy in a mega-cap regime

Crypto Perpetuals ran a long-short funding-rate signal whose validation edge was real and selection-adjusted but did not transfer (*Figure 20.6*). Validation Sharpe of +2.57 [+1.06, +4.32] reverses to −0.13 with a −65% drawdown, and the holdout daily IC turns negatively significant at −0.029. The equal-weight perpetual universe also ran near zero on the 2024–2025 tape, so the strategy is not underperforming a passive baseline so much as the cross-sectional funding pattern itself decayed; regime persistence, not cost, is the binding constraint.

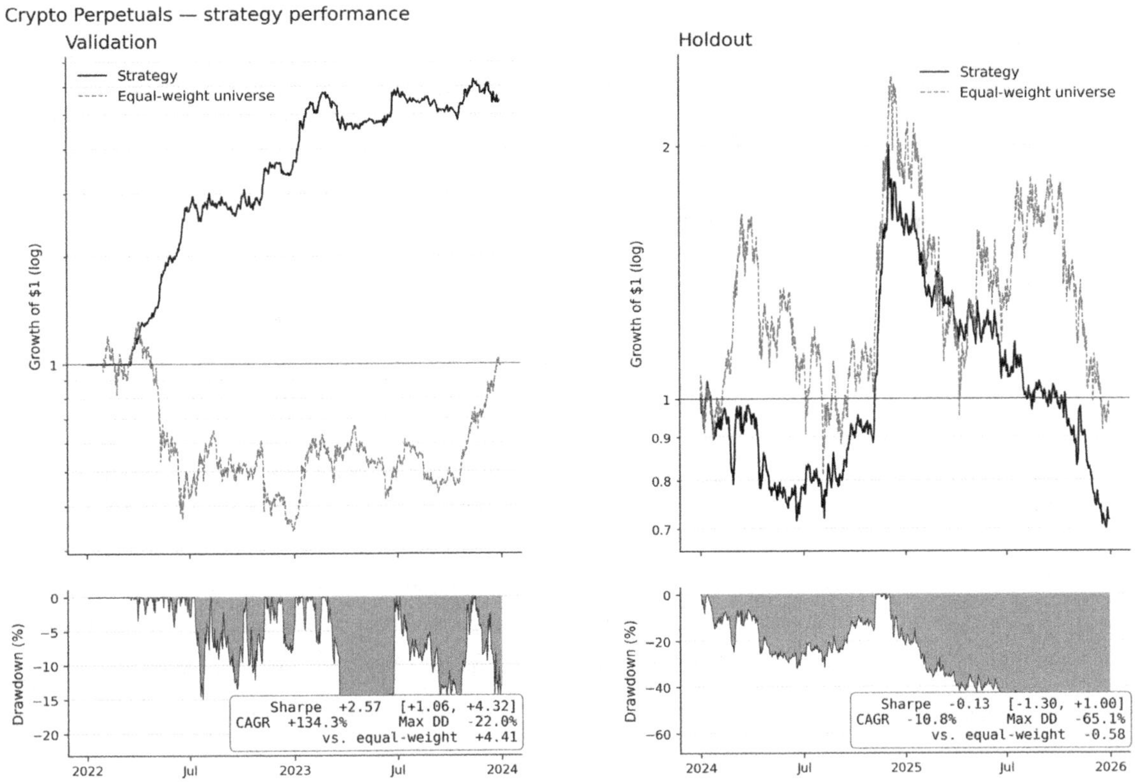

Figure 20.6: Crypto Perpetuals, validation (left) and holdout (right). The holdout yields a steep validation gain and reaches a –65% drawdown as the funding pattern decays amid the macro regime shift

Case studies that show little to no edge

Three cases produced no cross-sectional edge using the first-iteration setup:

- **S&P 500 Options** runs a systematic short straddle whose daily validation IC straddles zero and whose validation Sharpe of +0.16 comes with a wide confidence interval; the 2021 holdout yields a Sharpe ratio of +0.97, but an equal-weight short-straddle benchmark ran +2.55 over the same window, so the positive holdout reflects the structural short-volatility premium surviving execution rather than model selection.
- **FX Pairs** selected a linear ridge model on the 21-day forward return, long-short on cross-sectional rank: validation daily IC is +0.012 [–0.036, +0.061] and validation Sharpe is +0.05 [–0.56, +0.73], an interval spanning zero that fails the validation gate, and no model family at any horizon clears the IC threshold (*Section 20.3*). The holdout Sharpe point estimate is +0.19 [–0.92, +1.31], but it performs worse than an equal-weighted FX benchmark, which achieves a higher Sharpe ratio in both windows.

- **NASDAQ-100 Microstructure** turns positive after a cost-feasibility screen: restricting the 114-name universe to names whose measured half-spread leaves room for an intraday edge moves validation Sharpe from a full-universe collapse to +1.13 and holdout to +0.53, but both intervals cross zero, and the screened strategy trails a passive benchmark on the same screened universe across both windows.

From validation to holdout

The cases split into five patterns:

- US Firm Characteristics, CME Futures, and ETFs hold close to validation through the holdout period: the validation Sharpe interval excludes zero, the holdout Sharpe interval stays within sampling error of the validation interval, and the selection-bias adjustment is robust at every cohort granularity.
- US Equities Panel, S&P 500 Eq+Options, Crypto Perpetuals: decay or sign-flip from a credible validation edge. Both validation Sharpe and IC exclude zero, but the holdout flips Sharpe negative, and the strategy underperforms a passive benchmark.
- S&P 500 Options strengthens on point estimate under a structural premium.
- FX Pairs never produced a resolvable validation edge and lands near zero on the holdout.
- NASDAQ-100 Microstructure reaches a marginal positive only behind a cost-feasibility screen.

Figure 20.7 sorts the nine cases by the signed change in the Sharpe ratio from validation to holdout.

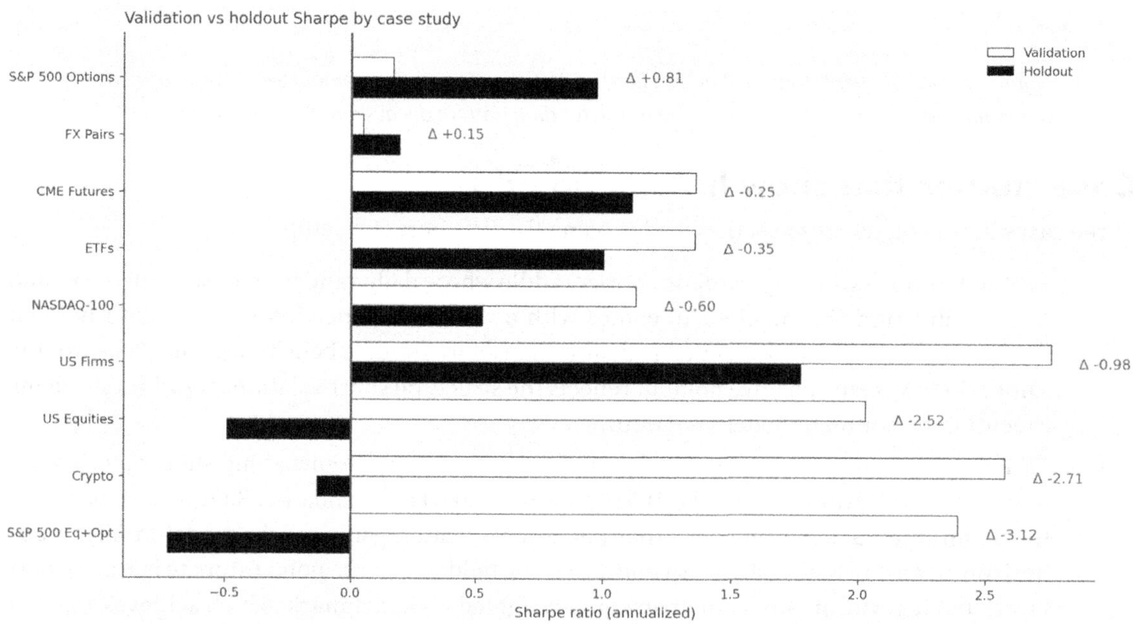

Figure 20.7: Validation versus holdout Sharpe across the nine case studies, sorted by signed change (Δ is holdout minus validation); the validation bar is the selected configuration's cross-stage best, matching Table 20.2. Three cases hold close to validation, three decay sharply or sign-flip, one strengthens on the holdout, one resolves near zero, and one reaches a marginal positive only after a cost-feasibility screen

Where in the workflow a strategy loses value carries more diagnostic weight than the headline number. When a holdout drifts below validation, the change tends to take one of three forms, and most cases show a mix of them:

- Prediction-quality drift describes a signal that weakens out-of-sample, as in US Equities Panel and Crypto Perpetuals, where daily IC sign-flips alongside Sharpe; the response is to revisit features, labels, horizons, or model selection.
- Portfolio-translation drift describes prediction quality that holds while portfolio construction loses value disproportionately, as in ETFs, where holdout Sharpe holds within sampling error against a benchmark that still outpaces it; a different allocator or regime-conditional weighting recovers more value than retraining.
- Regime change describes a shift that renders the fitted relationships less informative, as in S&P 500 Equity-plus-Options on the 2021 cap-weighted tape and Crypto Perpetuals on the 2024–2025 macro tape; regime detection, shorter retraining windows, or explicitly regime-conditional models are candidate responses the standardized pipeline does not apply.

A first diagnostic pass after a disappointing holdout should determine which mechanism best fits the case rather than rerunning the same pipeline with different hyperparameters. The next sections examine why prediction quality alone does not determine strategy performance (*Section 20.3*, *Section 20.4*), how allocator and cost choices interact with the signal (*Section 20.5*, *Section 20.6*), how realistic risk overlays change the out-of-sample picture (*Section 20.7*), and what causal diagnostics add (*Section 20.8*). *Section 20.9* compiles the per-case readings into specific next steps for research.

20.2 Setup and feature evaluation

Before any model trains, every case study runs a false-discovery rate (FDR) controlled triage pass on its candidate feature menu following the procedure of *Chapter 8*: hypothesis-driven candidates are scored individually, the cross-section is corrected for multiplicity, and each feature is classified as PROCEED, REVISE, or STOP based on FDR significance, fold-sign stability, and monotonicity in forward returns.

Under that common triage protocol, the PROCEED rate spans roughly two orders of magnitude across the test bed. Two case studies (Crypto and US Firms) clear the FDR hurdle for roughly two-thirds of their candidate features. Six (ETFs, CME Futures, FX Pairs, S&P 500 Options, S&P 500 Eq+Opt, and NASDAQ-100) sit between 4 and 25%; one of those six produces zero FDR-significant features but still earns a handful of PROCEED decisions through fold-sign stability and monotonicity. US Equities Panel produces no FDR-significant features and no PROCEED decisions on its 73-feature menu.

Case Study	Candidates	FDR-significant	PROCEED	% PROCEED
Crypto	45	32	32	71.1
US Firms	57	38	40	70.2
ETFs	71	1	17	23.9
CME Futures	69	6	13	18.8
FX Pairs	61	4	10	16.4

Case Study	Candidates	FDR-significant	PROCEED	% PROCEED
S&P 500 options	51	4	6	11.8
S&P 500 Eq+Opt	49	0	4	8.2
NASDAQ-100	88	4	4	4.5
US Equities	73	0	0	0.0

Table 20.3: Triage funnel by case study

The candidate column counts hypothesis-driven features authored from domain reasoning; FDR-significant counts those that clear the Benjamini-Hochberg threshold at 5% on daily IC; PROCEED additionally requires fold-sign stability and a monotone IC profile across rank deciles.

The procedure is identical across all nine; what varies is the asset class and the underlying signal-to-noise ratio of the feature menu relative to the chosen target.

Feature survival and strategy survival

The triage ledger is upstream of every model and backtest. To test its forecast value, we pair each case study's PROCEED rate with the holdout Sharpe ratio of the configuration that yields the highest validation Sharpe, which emerges from the full pipeline.

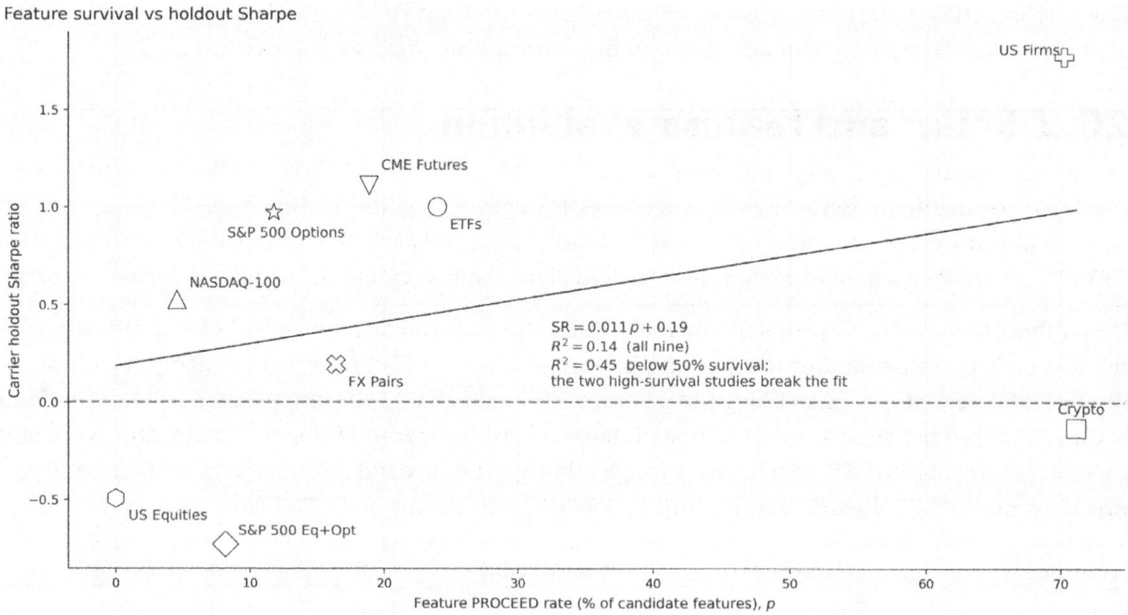

Figure 20.8: Feature-level survival rate against the highest-validation-Sharpe configuration's holdout Sharpe. A least-squares fit across all nine case studies is weakly positive (R-squared 0.14), tightening to 0.45 among the seven with below-50 % survival; the two high-survival case studies bracket the holdout-Sharpe range and break the fit. The case study at zero PROCEED lands in the negative-Sharpe band

The two case studies with high PROCEED rates (above 70%) span most of the holdout-Sharpe range: US Firms at +1.77 and Crypto at −0.13. Two near-identical feature funnels produce strategy outcomes that differ by nearly two units of Sharpe. The moderate-PROCEED band (4–25%) is similarly split: CME Futures, ETFs, S&P 500 Options, and NASDAQ-100 produce positive holdout Sharpes (+1.11, +1.00, +0.97, and +0.53 on the cost-feasible universe); FX Pairs resolves flat at +0.19, below its passive benchmark; and S&P 500 Eq+Opt produces a negative −0.73. US Equities yields zero PROCEED with a holdout Sharpe of −0.49, consistent with its sign-flip diagnosis in *Section 20.1*.

Two interpretations follow. Feature-level FDR survival is a screen, not a predictor of strategy-level survival. The screen filters out features whose IC is not statistically distinguishable from zero on a given horizon and label definition, but it does not capture feature interactions, economic effect size, persistence at the rebalancing cadence, or interaction with the allocator and cost model. What matters more than the count of surviving features is the collective economic value of those features relative to per-period frictions and to how they are turned into positions. The analysis of global feature importance in the model context and of local importance for outlier trade results can yield insights for further development beyond the initial setups evaluated during this first pass. *Sections 20.3* and *20.4* take that comparison into the model evidence and the IC-to-Sharpe translation.

20.3 Signal quality and prediction uncertainty

The information coefficient is standard for evaluating the predictive performance of ML models, but the nine case studies show it is incomplete as a single measure of signal quality. The more complete picture comes from a small diagnostic bundle (level, stability, and selection sensitivity) that describes the signal's shape across folds, horizons, and checkpoints.

Table 20.4 maps the signal landscape across the test bed. No model class is uniformly best. GBM produces the highest best-in-family IC on four case studies, latent factors lead three, and deep-learning sequence models lead the remaining two. What matters more than the ranking is the dispersion across families: a family that looks like the natural default in one trading context can be mediocre in another.

Case Study	Linear	GBM	Tabular DL	Deep Learning	Latent Factors
US firms	-0.004	0.080	0.031	—	0.062
ETFs	0.054	0.037	0.041	0.062	0.085
CME Futures	0.017	0.032	0.004	-0.001	0.037
US equities	0.015	0.032	0.017	0.007	0.005
Crypto	0.009	0.011	0.003	0.029	—
S&P 500 Options	0.007	0.018	0.002	0.013	—
S&P 500 Eq+Opt	-0.006	0.006	0.011	0.011	0.012
FX Pairs	0.005	0.002	0.007	0.011	—
NASDAQ-100	0.005	0.006	—	0.005	—

Table 20.4: Best-in-family validation daily IC by case study and model family on each case study's primary label (max across configurations within each family; some combinations did not run)

The row maximum refers to the case study's primary label. It does not always coincide with the "Best Daily IC" column of *Table 20.2*, which scans across all labels and configurations: where the highest-validation-Sharpe configuration trains on a secondary label or a directional formulation (US Equities, S&P 500 Eq+Opt), the *Table 20.2* figure exceeds the primary-label maximum here. US Firms peaks at GBM +0.080, ETFs at latent factors +0.085 with deep learning +0.062 and linear +0.053 trailing, CME Futures at latent factors +0.037 with GBM +0.032 close behind, and the primary-label ceiling sits near +0.085.

The noisy link from model to strategy performance

Across the test bed, IC and realized Sharpe are weakly but positively related: the per-variant correlation is 0.34, so IC explains only about an eighth of the cross-variant variation in Sharpe and predicts it noisily. In ETFs, the latent-factor SDF specifications lead the daily IC field at +0.085, while the highest-signal-stage Sharpe lies with an LSTM configuration at +0.89, whose daily IC is only +0.052; IC leader and signal-Sharpe leader are distinct configurations within the same case study's top cluster. S&P 500 Eq+Opt shows the disconnect from the other direction: small per-family daily ICs (none above +0.014) combine with a validation Sharpe of +2.39 that decays sharply to a holdout Sharpe of −0.73 whose strategy-versus-EW confidence interval [−4.17, −0.75] excludes zero on the negative side. NASDAQ-100 has the weakest daily IC in the test bed (around +0.005); on the full 114-name universe, its signal-stage Sharpe is deeply negative, and only after screening to the cost-feasible names does the configuration reach a marginal +1.13, which says that breadth alone cannot compensate for a per-bar edge smaller than execution friction unless the tail is screened out first.

With nine heterogeneous observations, these are small-sample patterns, but they are consistent enough to carry a practical lesson: IC measures average prediction quality across the cross-section, while Sharpe measures risk-adjusted portfolio return after construction, costs, and signal timing interact. The gap between the two is mediated by cadence, breadth, allocator choice, and cost structure, taken up in *Section 20.4*.

Best-family daily IC tops out near +0.085 across the entire test bed. No model, label, or feature set in the nine studies pushes past that ceiling. The pattern is consistent with the academic consensus that predicting financial returns is a low-signal-to-noise problem (Gu, Kelly, and Xiu, 2020). Trying to tune a single model past this level is unlikely to yield meaningful gains; the path to better strategies runs through breadth, ensembles, and portfolio construction.

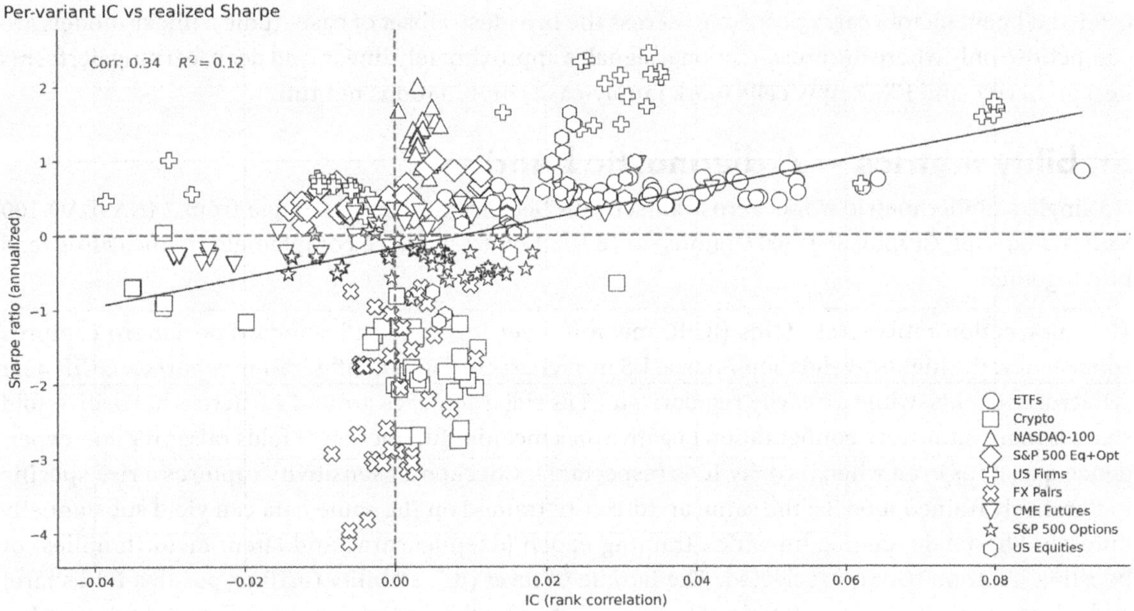

Figure 20.9: Per-variant IC versus validation-stage Sharpe across all case studies, with the least-squares trend

The positive association is weak (correlation of 0.34): the conversion from signal to strategy is noisy and pipeline-dependent, as shown in *Figure 20.9*.

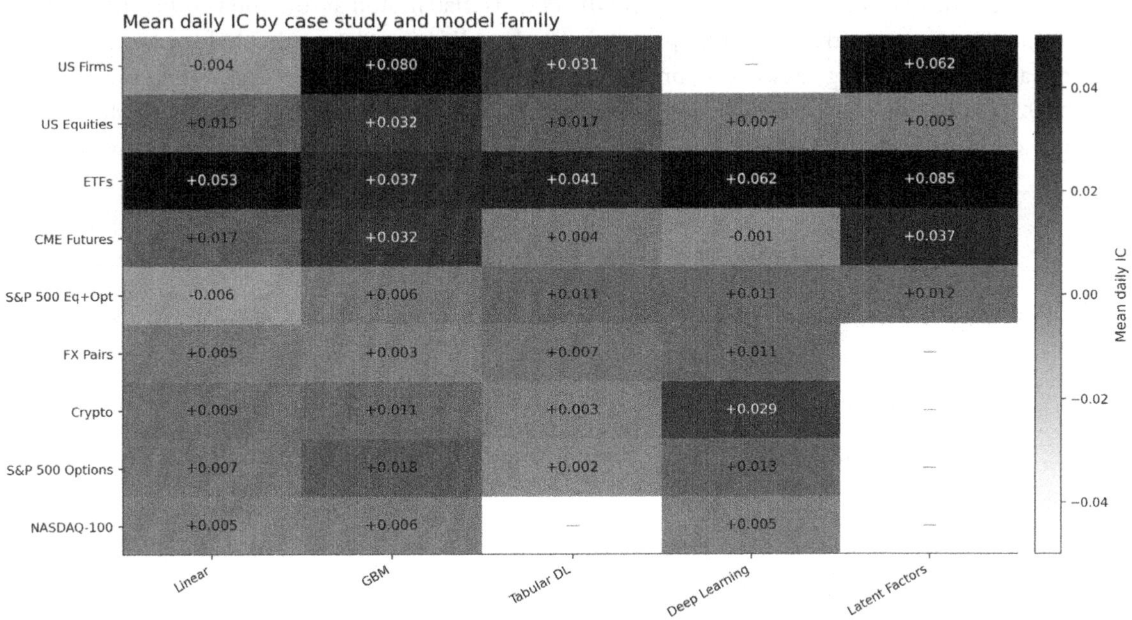

Figure 20.10: Mean daily cross-sectional information coefficient by case study and model family

GBM and latent factors carry positive IC across the broadest subset of case studies; linear models are competitive only where the cross-sectional signal is approximately linear, and deep learning performs best on Crypto and FX. Empty cells mark family-case combinations not run.

Stability metrics – A diagnostic bundle

No single stability metric works across all settings because fold counts range from 2 (NASDAQ-100, S&P 500 Eq+Opt, Crypto, S&P 500 Options) to 16 (US Equities). Three complementary measures read best together.

The information ratio across folds (ICIR, mean IC over its cross-fold standard deviation) captures consistency: the highest-validation-Sharpe US firm characteristics configuration reports an ICIR near 2.1 across 10 folds, while a heavily regularized ETFs ridge achieves around 1.3 across 8. Positive-fold share is more intuitive: a configuration negative on a meaningful fraction of folds raises regime-dependence questions even when its daily IC is respectable. Checkpoint sensitivity captures a risk specific to iteratively trained models: the same architecture trained on the same data can yield substantially different Sharpe depending on which training epoch (deep-learning and latent-factor families) or boosting iteration (GBM) is selected. The bundle of level (IC), stability (ICIR or positive-fold share), and selection sensitivity (per-iteration Sharpe trajectory) is the unit of signal quality; no single number captures all three.

Stability also has a time dimension that fold summaries flatten. *Figure 20.11* traces the CME Futures strategy's rolling 12-month Sharpe ratio and daily IC together across the validation and holdout windows, with both lookbacks set to a year so that each tracks its annualized full-period average on the same footing. The two series move in step, and the edge is distributed across the window rather than concentrated in a few months, painting a picture behind a validation Sharpe that holds into the holdout rather than a strong average resting on one regime. The rolling edge is weakest in the year after the March 2020 COVID dislocation, where it dips below zero, and runs strongest through the March 2022 rate-hike cycle, both marked on the axis, but it sits above its annual average for most of the window.

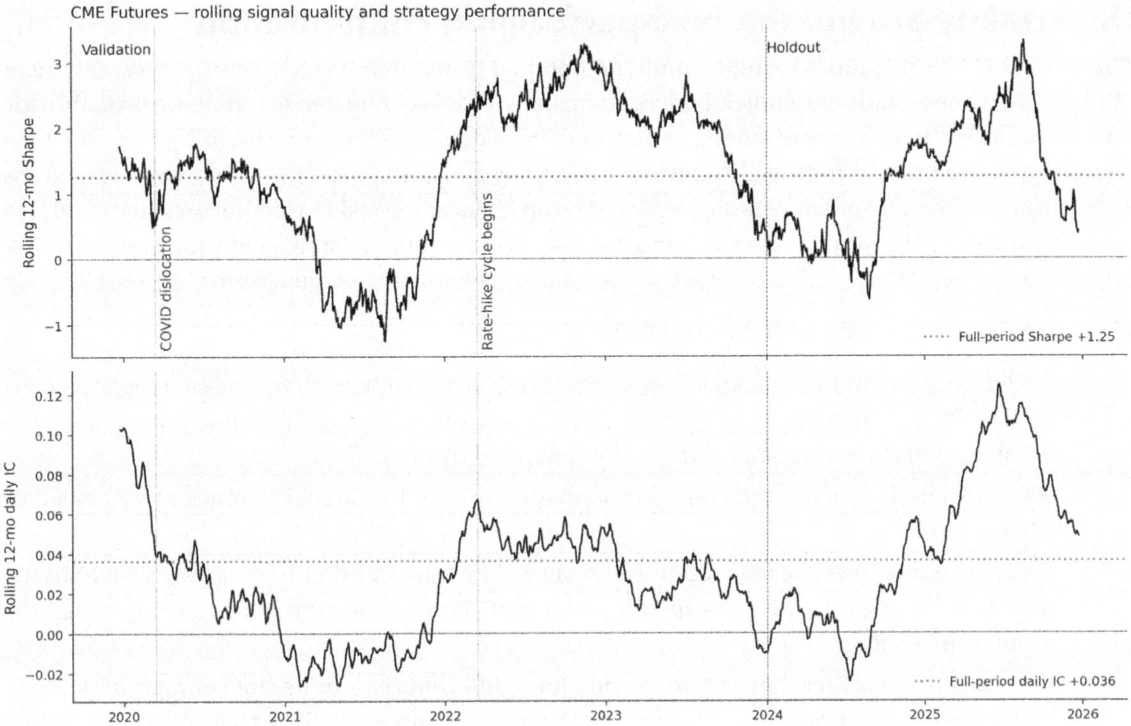

Figure 20.11: Rolling twelve-month annualized Sharpe (top) and rolling twelve-month daily cross-sectional IC (bottom) for the CME Futures strategy

Finally, the empirical finding from per-iteration trajectories is that no single iteration count is optimal across case studies. Some GBM trajectories peak early and plateau (well before the default cap), while others continue improving even after the budget runs out, and a third group degrades after an early peak as training continues. This dispersion is structural rather than noise: cost regime, signal cadence, and label horizon each shape where the validation Sharpe ratio peaks. Checkpoint selection is therefore a per-case-study research decision, not a hyperparameter that generalizes across asset classes. Two production-grade alternatives are available: an ensemble across the top-three checkpoints, with validation Sharpe damping the per-iteration noise that several trajectories show even within their best region; a nested cross-validation over the iteration grid is methodologically cleaner but computationally costly. Either step belongs in the next iteration under the *Chapter 6* workflow.

Uncertainty around the best-performing configuration

The validation Sharpe ratio is a single number computed from the validation return series. Its uncertainty arises from a **stationary block bootstrap** on daily returns and from the analytic **probabilistic Sharpe ratio** (PSR); the ranking among configurations is therefore best interpreted against the bootstrap confidence interval for the difference between any two configurations rather than against the point estimates alone. For case studies where the top cluster lies inside that uncertainty band, the highest-validation-Sharpe configuration and its closest competitor are statistically indistinguishable; elsewhere, the highest-validation-Sharpe configuration is genuinely separated from the rest of the field.

The pattern across the case studies reflects this:

- US Firms places its highest- and tenth-validation-Sharpe configurations only 0.04 Sharpe apart, well inside the bootstrap envelope. Hence, the best-validation configuration is a member of a small top cluster rather than statistically separated from the field.
- ETFs are similarly tight: ten configurations spanning all five model families fit within a 0.08 Sharpe band.
- CME Futures shows a wider top-to-tenth spread of 0.39, but that is roughly its fold-Sharpe standard error, so its highest-validation-Sharpe GBM specification is not cleanly separated from its field either.
- NASDAQ-100's cost-feasible cohort is wide for a different reason: its slot configurations span roughly +0.2 to +1.4 validation Sharpe, and the field maximum is a linear five-slot configuration at +2.11 sitting far above that band. That maximum does not survive the holdout. Out-of-sample, the same configuration drops to a holdout Sharpe ratio of −0.21. The demonstrated collapse, not its distance from the rest of the cohort, is what disqualifies it: its high validation Sharpe reflects a single configuration that fit the validation window rather than a separated leader. The gradient-boosted ensemble at +1.13 is deployed instead because it yields positive out-of-sample (holdout) Sharpe +0.53, whereas the individual configurations do not.

The cluster diagnostic is descriptive, not a basis for selection: where the top cluster contains numerous candidates, the highest-validation-Sharpe configuration is one realization of a near-tied set, and the ensembling discussion of *Section 20.4* trades a small amount of peak Sharpe for a measurable reduction in dispersion under exactly those conditions.

Label choice as a first-order decision

Label engineering often yields a higher return on research effort than model architecture work. Three patterns recur across the test bed:

- On classification versus regression, the continuous return label is the more dependable choice. Every case study that reached a deployable signal ran on it, and where both label types were tried, it produced the higher portfolio Sharpe ratio. US firm characteristics is the instructive exception: its direction label produces a markedly higher daily IC across the sweep, but that edge reverses under portfolio construction, where the continuous label still posts the higher Sharpe. The choice interacts with the allocator because classification signals translate into portfolio weights differently than continuous scores do.

- On horizon scaling, FX GBM daily IC improves materially from the 1-day to the 21-day horizon, and ETFs improves modestly at the longer horizon; longer horizons also reduce turnover, which reduces cost drag, making horizon a first-order design decision rather than a preprocessing detail.
- On winsorization, heavy-tailed return distributions distort the rank-return relationship IC measures: in US firm characteristics, winsorizing the monthly return label at the 1st and 99th percentiles produces substantially larger daily IC than the unwinsorized label across a hyperparameter sweep.

The general point holds across case studies: label preprocessing is consequential, and within-family IC differences driven by label choice can match or exceed the differences between model architectures on the same label.

Section 20.9 returns to these levers as part of the deliberate-constraints inventory. The narrower point here is that optimizing model architecture while treating the label as fixed misallocates research effort. A GBM on a well-engineered label can produce stronger daily IC and stronger fold consistency than a more complex model on raw forward returns.

20.4 From signals to strategies

With IC treated as one diagnostic among several, the practical question becomes how to convert whatever predictive content remains into portfolio-level performance, and which model families translate consistently across the full pipeline. The Fundamental Law of Active Management gives the organizing framework: $IR \approx IC \times \sqrt{BR}$, where BR is the number of independent bets per period (Grinold and Kahn, 2000). The nine case studies ground that formula empirically and show where the translation gains or loses value.

The fundamental law, empirically

Breadth is proxied by the product of rebalancing frequency, universe size, and portfolio concentration (top-K), recognizing that correlation within the universe reduces effective breadth below the nominal count, particularly for the NASDAQ-100, where 114 stocks move largely as a single market. The proxy is directional rather than calibrated, and the figure reads as a heuristic lens rather than a formal validation of the law.

With only nine heterogeneous observations, IC alone already tracks holdout Sharpe moderately (correlation 0.61), while scaling by the crude breadth proxy degrades that link toward zero rather than tightening it: the case studies differ too much in cost structure, regime exposure, and portfolio design for the simple proxy to add value.

The Fundamental Law nonetheless helps interpret individual case studies:

- US firm characteristics pair a high best-in-family daily IC (+0.080, GBM) with moderate breadth at a monthly cadence, and the retrained highest-validation-Sharpe configuration performs robustly at a holdout Sharpe of +1.77.

- NASDAQ-100 has the weakest best-in-family IC (around +0.006) paired with very high nominal breadth at a 15-minute cadence; on the full universe, breadth fails to compensate for execution friction, and the signal-stage Sharpe is deeply negative, and only after screening to the cost-feasible names does the selected configuration reach a marginal validation Sharpe of +1.13 that stays at +0.53 on the holdout.
- FX Pairs has a modest deep-learning best-in-family IC (+0.011) and a 20-pair universe that sharply caps breadth; its highest-validation-Sharpe configuration is a linear ridge model whose validation Sharpe of +0.05 carries a CI that crosses zero and whose holdout Sharpe of +0.19 sits below its equal-weight benchmark. Breadth contributes only when execution friction does not offset it first.

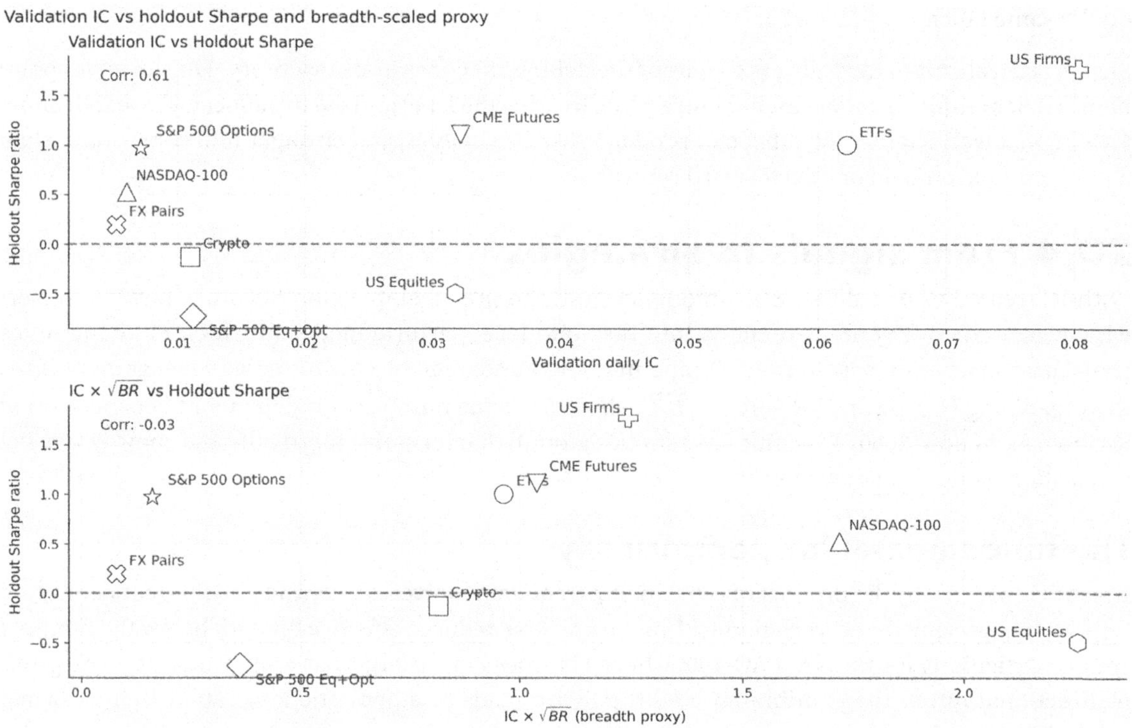

Figure 20.12: Fundamental Law diagnostic. Left: IC alone versus holdout Sharpe. Right: IC adjusted for breadth (rebalance frequency × top-K). All nine case studies are shown; NASDAQ-100's raw breadth is the largest, but its small IC places it mid-cluster on the breadth-scaled axis, so it does not distort the scale

Cadence and effective breadth

Aggregating across the test bed by rebalancing cadence shows the same pattern at scale. The monthly strategy (US firm characteristics) has the largest signal-stage Sharpe at +2.75. Daily-cadence strategies span a wide range: US Equities +1.87, S&P 500 Eq+Opt +1.25, CME Futures +0.96, ETFs +0.89, S&P 500 Options +0.16, and FX Pairs slightly negative at −0.09. The 8-hourly Crypto signal is +2.09 at the signal stage but decays to −0.13 on holdout; the 15-minute NASDAQ-100 configuration reaches +1.13, but only in the cost-feasible universe; the same signal on the full 114-name universe is deeply negative.

The NASDAQ-100 result makes the breadth mechanism explicit: nominal breadth is the highest in the test bed, yet per-bar friction overwhelms the edge until the universe is screened down to the most-liquid names with the lowest spread. Whether the screened configuration extends to coarser cadences is an open question for a second iteration.

Cadence interacts with costs in both directions: higher frequency multiplies breadth but also multiplies turnover. The optimal cadence is the point at which the marginal Sharpe contribution from an additional rebalancing period equals the marginal cost of the trade that realizes it. Selectivity, the number of top-ranked names the portfolio retains, adds a further dimension. Sweeping the top-K parameter from tight (top-5) to broad (top-50) shows a case-study-specific response: studies with substantive positive signal tend to produce higher median Sharpe at broader K, while studies with weak or negative underlying signal show no systematic Sharpe response to K. The appropriate K is a function of signal strength and universe breadth, not a hyperparameter with a universal optimum.

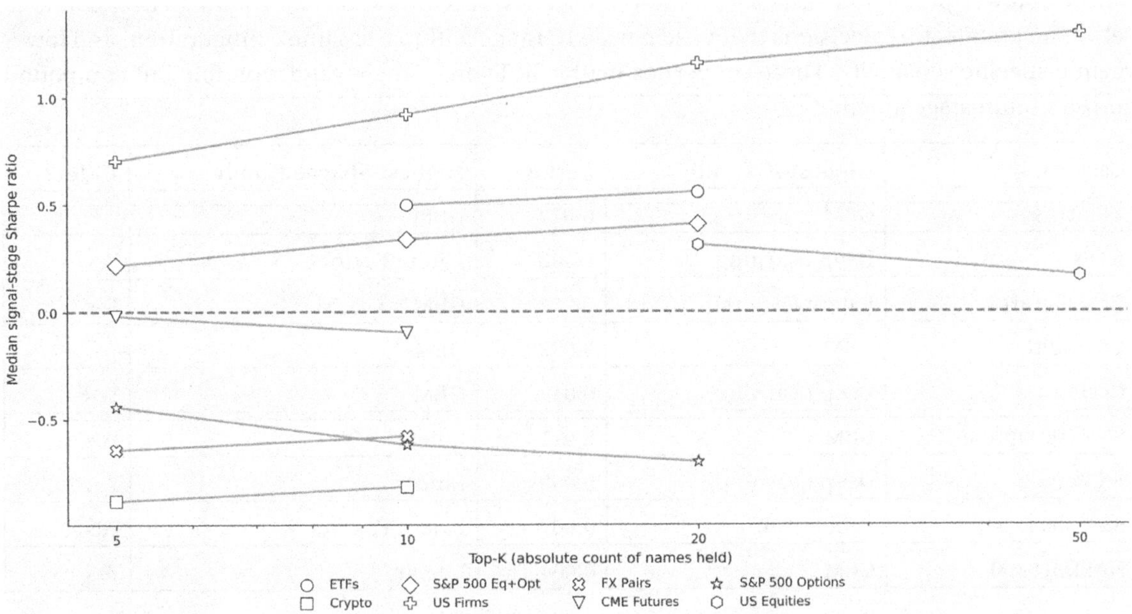

Figure 20.13: Median signal-stage Sharpe as top-K grows, per case study. The NASDAQ-100 is omitted: equal-weight top-K is not its selected method (a slot-persistence rule is), and those alternative configurations score roughly −10 to −22, far below this scale

Win rate and payoff asymmetry

Win rates (the fraction of rebalancing periods in which the strategy produces a positive return) cluster near half for the intraday and daily strategies, from just under half in FX Pairs and Crypto Perpetuals through the low-to-mid fifties for most case studies, and rise to roughly 81 for US firm characteristics. The gap is largely mechanical: a monthly cadence produces many fewer evaluation periods than an intraday one, and the monthly aggregate averages over the individual losing days that would otherwise lower a higher-frequency win rate. It is also partly a function of payoff shape: the high-frequency strategies (FX Pairs and Crypto Perpetuals near 48, NASDAQ-100 near 52) sit close to half their periods and depend on the size of winning periods relative to losing ones, while US firm characteristics produce positive returns in most months with moderate per-period gains.

The distinction matters for risk management. A strategy with a low win rate requires appropriate position sizing and a long evaluation horizon to weather the arithmetically inevitable losing streaks, while a high-win-rate monthly strategy faces a different risk: a single bad month can erase several good ones if position sizing ignores tail risk.

Family rankings shift across the pipeline

At the IC stage, the family producing the highest mean daily IC varies across case studies: GBM in four (US firms, US equities, S&P 500 options, NASDAQ-100); deep-learning specifications in three (Crypto, FX pairs, ETFs); and tabular DL and latent factors taking the highest mean IC in one apiece (S&P 500 Eq+Opt and CME futures, respectively). After predictions pass through portfolio construction, cost filtering, and risk overlays, GBM produces the highest allocation-stage Sharpe in four of the nine case studies, including two in which a different family had the highest IC. The mechanism is consistent with lower prediction variance and fewer selection risks. GBM has no training checkpoints to select, no architecture decisions that yield a wide IC range within the same configuration, and lower regime-specific sensitivity. These properties matter little on a single validation fold but compound across a multi-stage pipeline.

Case Study	Highest-IC Family	Best IC	Highest-Sharpe Family	Differ?
US firms	GBM	0.047	GBM	—
ETFs	Deep Learning	0.043	Latent Factors	Yes
CME Futures	Latent Factors	0.024	GBM	Yes
US Equities	GBM	0.023	GBM	—
Crypto	Deep Learning	0.012	GBM	Yes
S&P 500 Options	GBM	0.011	Linear	Yes
FX Pairs	Deep Learning	0.008	Linear	Yes
S&P 500 Eq+Opt	Tabular DL	0.007	Latent Factors	Yes
NASDAQ-100	GBM	0.004	Linear	Yes

Table 20.5: Model family cascade

The highest-IC family differs from the highest-Sharpe downstream family in seven of nine case studies: the choices that maximize signal quality and those that maximize post-construction Sharpe diverge in most of the tested settings. The "Best IC" column is the family's primary-label daily IC averaged across all in-family configurations, which sits 0.002–0.033 below the per-family maximum of *Table 20.4*; the broader scope shifts the family ranking for ETFs and S&P 500 Eq+Opt.

Ensembling the top clusters

When several configurations are statistically indistinguishable (their validation Sharpe confidence intervals overlap, and the paired bootstrap on the daily return difference straddles zero), averaging their predictions is the natural response. For each case study, the three highest-validation-Sharpe training runs are z-scored cross-sectionally at each timestamp and averaged into an ensemble score, which then feeds the highest-Sharpe configuration's strategy specification at the same top-K, cadence, and cost regime.

Two patterns emerge:

1. Ensembling does not raise peak Sharpe; it trades a small amount of it for a measurable reduction in dispersion when configurations are genuinely close.
2. The benefit concentrates where the top cluster is tight relative to Sharpe standard error.

CME Futures and S&P 500 Options, with top-to-tenth Sharpe spreads roughly equal to the fold-Sharpe standard error, see little benefit from ensembling; the case studies whose top cluster falls within the bootstrap noise band (US Firms, ETFs, US Equities, FX pairs) stabilize without sacrificing much of their peak performance.

NASDAQ-100 is the case where the stability trade performs best: the highest-validation configuration, a linear five-slot at +2.11, collapses to a holdout Sharpe of −0.21, and a broad holdout sweep across the model panel finds individual configurations mostly negative out of sample (linear median −0.31, gradient-boosted median −0.42), so no single model generalizes. The 12-model gradient-boosted ensemble at +1.13 validation is deployed because it outperforms the holdout by +0.53, whereas the individual configurations do not.

Ensembling is a stability tool, not a universal Sharpe booster, and the cluster diagnostic of *Section 20.3* identifies the case studies where it pays off.

When deep learning helps

Deep learning is not uniformly superior: it plays a distinctive role when the signal lies in temporal structure or nonlinear interactions that trees cannot capture. CME futures provides a partial nonlinearity diagnostic. On the primary 5-day forward return, linear models top out at a best-in-family daily IC of +0.017, tabular deep learning reaches +0.004, GBM reaches +0.032, deep learning is essentially zero (−0.001), and latent factors take the highest case-study IC at +0.037 (SDF). The flat-to-negative deep-learning result on the primary horizon undercuts a clean nonlinearity gradient: the signal that exists is captured by GBM and latent factors, not by sequence models. GBM nonetheless produces the highest signal-stage Sharpe through stable portfolio translation, which fits the chapter's broader pattern. When a linear IC is compared with a GBM IC in the same case study, the signal is approximately linear, and additional model complexity is unlikely to help.

Crypto perpetuals cautions against reading family rankings too confidently on thin evidence. Best-in-family deep-learning IC of +0.029 exceeds GBM's +0.011, but both are small in absolute terms, and the training set spans only two cross-validation folds. Minor perturbations to the feature set or the training window can reshape the family ranking under that kind of evidence base. Family rankings are sensitive to upstream data and feature choices and should not be locked in after a single iteration.

A coverage caveat on the family-ranking claim is warranted: deep learning was not trained for US firm characteristics (the case study with the tightest fold-level dispersion), and coverage was reduced for some other studies due to computational cost. GBM's downstream-ranking advantage is real, but partly because GBM was tested more than deep learning. The practical default is to start with GBM across all settings and invest in deep learning only when there is positive evidence of structural nonlinearity, either from the linear-versus-GBM IC gap or from the temporal structure of the trading problem.

Complementary Roles

Latent-factor models and linear models play complementary diagnostic roles. On ETFs, the latent-factor SDF achieves the highest daily IC at the primary horizon (+0.085, $t_{HAC} = 4.89$) and carries through to the selected cross-stage strategy after allocation and risk overlay (validation Sharpe +1.36); the deep-learning LSTM has the highest signal-stage Sharpe (+0.89) but ranks below the latent factors on daily IC. For US equities, GBM at the 21-day horizon has the highest daily IC, and IPCA contributes a complementary latent-factor signal at the same horizon that a second iteration could test in a label-compatible ensemble. Whether latent factors are better read as signal generators or as portfolio-construction inputs is a question these experiments leave open: the ETFs result places SDF in the signal-generator role at the primary horizon, while the residual ensemble value of SAE and ridge configurations in the same top cluster on daily IC keeps the portfolio-construction reading on the table.

Linear models play a different role: a positive linear daily IC confirms a first-order linear structure in the feature space, and their smoother predictions generate lower median validation-stage turnover than GBM in five of eight measurable case studies (Crypto, S&P 500 Eq+Opt, FX pairs, CME futures, and US equities, by 28 to 55), with ETFs and US Firms tied within a few percent and NASDAQ-100 the lone counter-example. Where the linear IC is competitive with the tree-based ranking, linear is a cost-efficient alternative.

Even the model families most consistent across the pipeline still face hard market constraints: spreads, turnover, allocator-signal interplay, and capacity limits. *Section 20.5* covers the allocator layer in detail; *Section 20.6* covers costs.

20.5 Portfolio allocation across the case studies

A single allocator per case study carried the signals of *Section 20.4* into portfolios. This section isolates the allocator layer: the highest-validation-Sharpe signal is held fixed on each case study and routed through as many as six allocators: equal weight, inverse volatility, score weight, mean-variance optimization with Ledoit-Wolf shrinkage, risk parity, and hierarchical risk parity. The four moment-based methods require a per-symbol price or covariance estimate, so on the returns-only US Firms panel only equal weight and score weight apply. The best-minus-worst Sharpe spread within that fixed signal quantifies the headroom the allocator alone has to move the result.

Case Study	Signal	Best Allocator	Best SR	Worst Allocator	Worst SR	Spread
US firms	GBM	equal weight	+2.75	score weight	+2.51	0.25
Crypto	GBM	RP	+2.57	SW	+1.88	0.69
US Equities	GBM	SW	+2.02	HRP	+1.49	0.53
S&P 500 Eq+Opt	Latent factors	equal weight	+1.25	MVO	+0.73	0.52
CME Futures	GBM	inverse vol	+1.19	SW	+0.63	0.56
ETFs	Latent factors	HRP	+1.12	SW	+0.68	0.44

Case Study	Signal	Best Allocator	Best SR	Worst Allocator	Worst SR	Spread
S&P 500 Options	Linear	HRP	+0.17	risk parity	+0.15	0.02
FX Pairs	Linear	HRP	+0.04	MVO	−0.42	0.46
NASDAQ-100	n/a	n/a	n/a	n/a	n/a	n/a

Table 20.6: Per-case-study best and worst allocator with the highest-validation-Sharpe signal held fixed, on validation

Spread is the within-signal envelope, taken as the maximum across rebalance and top-K variants. NASDAQ-100 carries no allocation-stage entry: its strategy is a signal-stage slot rule on the cost-feasible universe (the slot mechanism is the sizing rule), and the allocation sweep ran on the full universe, not on the selected configuration.

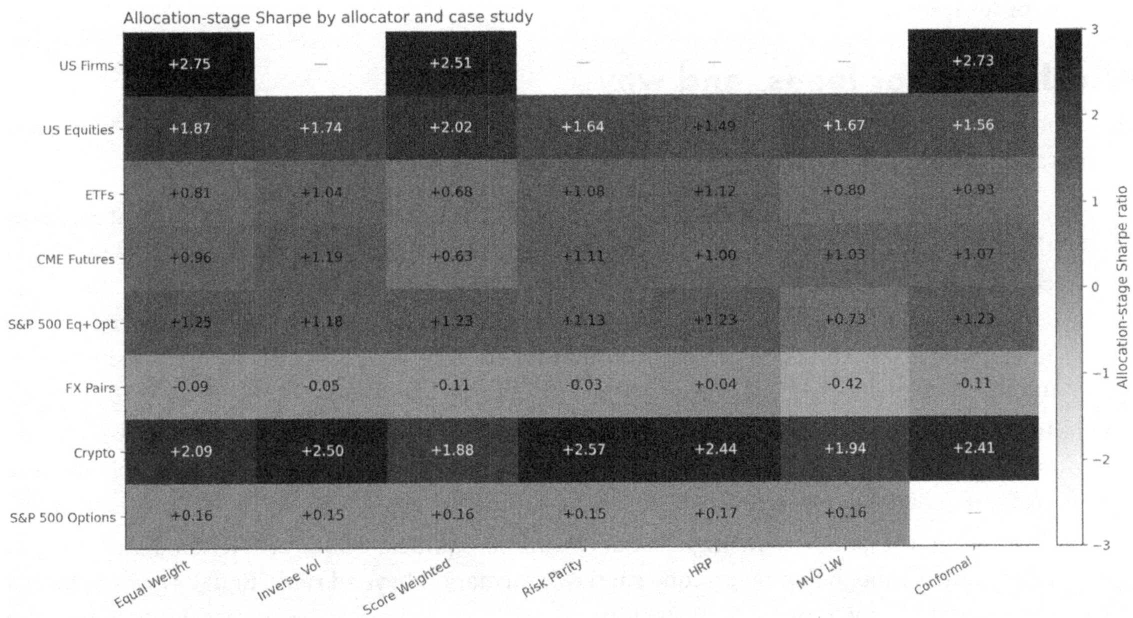

Figure 20.14: Allocation-stage Sharpe across case studies (rows) and allocators (columns), all on the highest-validation-Sharpe signal configuration

Figure 20.14 shows risk-parity and inverse-volatility methods achieve the highest Sharpe on vol-heterogeneous universes (Crypto, ETFs, CME Futures); score weighting achieves the highest Sharpe where prediction magnitudes carry information (US Equities); equal weight achieves the highest Sharpe on S&P 500 Eq+Opt where the signal broadcasts thinly across the universe, and on US Firms, whose returns-only monthly panel has no per-symbol price series: the four moment allocators are undefined there and appear as blank cells; hierarchical risk parity achieves the highest Sharpe on FX Pairs, on a signal that barely clears the noise floor. FX is bounded just above zero. No allocator rescues a failing signal. NASDAQ-100 carries no allocation-stage entry: its strategy is a signal-stage slot rule and the allocation sweep ran on the full universe, not on the selected configuration.

How much the allocator moves the result

The within-signal spreads vary substantially. The median is 0.49 Sharpe, roughly an order of magnitude smaller than the cross-signal range of *Section 20.4*. The widest are Crypto (0.69) and CME Futures (0.56), vol-heterogeneous universes where a covariance- or volatility-aware allocator has the most room to differentiate names. The tightest is S&P 500 Options at 0.02, where the leading allocators cluster near +0.16 because the liquid-universe filter leaves few names to differentiate. FX Pairs shows a moderate 0.46 spread on a structurally weak signal (signal-stage Sharpe −0.09): the allocator controls how fast a flat signal bleeds (best HRP +0.04 against worst MVO −0.42), not whether it has an edge.

The results confirm *Section 17.7* on a smaller within-chapter comparison: allocator choice changes risk shape, turnover, and the marginal Sharpe contribution, but rarely by margins that approach the variation produced by signal choice or by the cost-aware accounting of *Section 20.6*. The allocator is a second-order lever once the signal is fixed.

Which allocator leads, and why

The allocator that achieves the highest Sharpe is not constant across the test bed, but the pattern is structural:

- Risk parity achieves the highest Sharpe ratio on Crypto, and its hierarchical variant achieves the highest Sharpe ratio on ETFs: vol-heterogeneous universes with sufficient cross-sectional correlation appear to favor equal risk contribution over a full covariance inversion. US Firms is a special case: its returns-only monthly panel provides no per-symbol price series, so the four moment-based allocators are undefined and excluded, and among the lookback-free allocators, equal-weight edges score-based weights by 0.25 Sharpe.
- Inverse-volatility achieves the highest Sharpe ratio on CME Futures, where cross-sectional volatility heterogeneity across sectors (bonds, energy, grains) rewards a per-symbol volatility scaler that captures the relevant differences without inverting a noisy covariance matrix.
- Score-weighted achieves the highest Sharpe on US Equities, whose prediction distribution is heavy-tailed enough that magnitude carries information beyond rank. Equal weight achieves the highest Sharpe ratio on S&P 500 Eq+Opt, where the signal is broadcast thinly across the universe and signal noise dominates the weighting decision, so the lowest-assumption allocator does best.
- Hierarchical risk parity achieves the highest Sharpe on FX Pairs by clustering correlated pairs in the 20-name universe before allocating; on a configuration whose signal-stage Sharpe is −0.09, this lifts the allocation stage to roughly +0.04, and the *Section 20.7* time-exit overlay nudges the managed Sharpe to +0.05. The allocator de-risks a flat signal rather than amplifying an edge.
- Mean-variance optimization with Ledoit-Wolf shrinkage never strictly exceeds the highest-Sharpe allocator on any case study (it comes within a rounding margin of the lead only at S&P 500 Options' +0.16 noise floor) and posts the lowest Sharpe on S&P 500 Eq+Opt and FX Pairs.

The best-allocator pattern, therefore, tracks a structural property of the universe (size, correlation density, signal heaviness) more than a property of the allocator family, consistent with the portfolio-construction literature and with *Section 17.6*: matrix-inversion methods suffer when covariance estimates are noisy; risk-parity-flavored methods achieve the highest Sharpe when the relevant signal is risk; score weighting achieves the highest Sharpe when magnitudes carry information.

Allocator selection is a defensible second-order optimization once the signal and the cost regime are fixed. The within-signal spread on positive signals suggests roughly 0.02 to 0.69 Sharpe of available headroom: real but bounded, and wider on the vol-heterogeneous universes (CME Futures, Crypto) than on the more uniform ones. No allocator rescues a failing signal: on FX Pairs (signal-stage Sharpe −0.09), the best within-signal allocator reaches only +0.04 and the worst falls to −0.42; the allocator controls the rate of loss, not the sign of the edge. The *Section 20.6* cost-survival analysis carries the allocator-signal pairs into dollar accounting, where the picture sometimes reverses again.

20.6 Trading realism – Costs, capacity, and execution

Costs are a design input that shapes universe selection, rebalancing cadence, and position sizing long before a backtest is run. Frazzini, Israel, and Moskowitz (2018) and Novy-Marx and Velikov (2016) document how quickly an apparent edge erodes once realistic frictions are applied, particularly as turnover and participation rise.

The breakeven costs implied by the backtests span a wide range:

- ETFs, US firms, and US equities retain positive Sharpe at the 50-basis-point sweep ceiling, so their breakeven lies above the grid rather than at any specific value within it.
- CME futures and S&P 500 Eq+Opt break even near 30 basis points per leg and crypto perpetuals near 15, all above their assumed schedules.
- FX pairs have a thin breakeven of roughly 7 basis points per leg, only a few basis points above the assumed spread on cross-currency pairs.
- NASDAQ-100 microstructure illustrates a cost decision made by universe selection rather than a basis-point breakeven: on the full 114-name universe, the signal trades at a negative gross Sharpe (−0.78 before any cost is applied), while screening to the cost-feasible names (those whose measured half-spread leaves room for the intraday edge) produces the positive result of *Section 20.1*.
- S&P 500 options require a cost model that scales with the premium rather than the notional, as addressed below.

Case Study	Assumed Per-Leg Cost	Breakeven (bps)	Interpretation
ETFs	per-share + half-spread	50+	Wide margin
Crypto Perpetuals	3–4 bps (taker/maker)	15	Positive margin
NASDAQ-100	per-share + measured spread	~10	On cost-feasible names; breakeven on bps companion grid
S&P 500 Eq+Opt	6.5 bps	30	Positive margin

Case Study	Assumed Per-Leg Cost	Breakeven (bps)	Interpretation
US firms	12.5 bps	50+	Wide margin
FX Pairs	1–8 bps (pair-tier)	7	Thin margin
CME Futures	≈10 bps (tick implied)	30	Positive margin
S&P 500 options	premium-scaled	n/a	See HTM analysis below
US equities	12.5 bps	50+	Wide margin

Table 20.7: Breakeven-cost scorecard

Breakeven is the highest per-leg basis-point cost at which the highest-validation-Sharpe configuration retains positive Sharpe; the sweep grid runs from 0 to 50 basis points, so "50+" denotes a strategy whose breakeven exceeds the sweep ceiling. NASDAQ-100's strategy lives on the cost-feasible names (the universe screen sets which names are tradable) and on the bps companion grid that configuration breaks even near 10 basis points per leg, a thin but real cushion (on the full universe the signal is already negative at zero cost). ETFs and NASDAQ-100 use per-share commission plus a half-spread instead of a flat basis-point assumption; the table reports their breakeven against the bps companion grid run alongside the primary cost regime.

The cost survival landscape

Each breakeven number, which indicates the cost level at which the strategy stops making money, must be interpreted in light of the strategy's structural cost exposure. The stricter bar is the benchmark Sharpe ratios of *Section 20.1*, which several configurations fail to clear on the holdout even when they survive the cost grid on validation. Furthermore, constructing a clean benchmark is itself difficult outside the index-linked case studies, where an equal-weight buy-and-hold is the natural comparison.

Among the monthly and daily equity strategies, ETFs (monthly), S&P 500 Eq+Opt (monthly), and US equities panel (daily) all retain positive Sharpe ratios well into the basis-point grid: ETFs and US equities to the 50 bps ceiling, and S&P 500 Eq+Opt to roughly 30 bps. The cushion at the 6.5 to 12.5 basis-point per-leg assumption used in the signal stage is generous on average, but the cost reality varies substantially across symbols: daily and monthly equity universes mix liquid large-caps with illiquid small-caps, and the mean bps understates the friction the illiquid tail of the portfolio actually faces. US firm characteristics carry the largest validation Sharpe in the test bed (signal-stage validation +2.75, retrained holdout +1.77) and survive the basis-point sweep to its 50 bps ceiling with net Sharpe still above +2.2, but the binding constraint is universe liquidity rather than per-leg cost: the long leg concentrates in bottom-quartile market-capitalization names where spreads commonly run 100 to 500 basis points, well outside the grid.

Among derivatives strategies, CME futures retains positive Sharpe to roughly 30 basis points per leg, three times the tick-implied cost; the highest-validation-Sharpe inverse-volatility configuration holds a net Sharpe near +0.5 at 30 bps but turns slightly negative by 50. The strategy passes the cost gate with room to spare on a flat-bps reading, though product-level liquidity and roll costs are second-iteration questions the bps grid does not resolve. Crypto perpetuals break even near 15 basis points per leg with gross Sharpe above +3.5, well above the 3-to-4-basis-point taker/maker schedule on Binance; net Sharpe falls from +3.3 at 1 bp to +0.66 at 15 bps and turns negative by 20, so any deterioration in fee tier or rebate access reverses the conclusion quickly. The 8-hourly cadence raises a critical question about capacity and potential market impact.

The remaining three case studies fail or require an instrument-specific cost model:

- FX pairs break even at roughly 7 basis points per leg, within the 1-to-8-basis-point per-leg spread implied by the major-versus-cross pair tiers. The 20-pair universe with daily rebalancing and the configuration with the highest validation Sharpe produce a tight margin in which execution quality, not model choice, governs viability.
- For the full universe, the NASDAQ-100 microstructure starts with a negative gross Sharpe ratio, so a full-universe basis-point breakeven does not exist. Arguably, the cost-sensitive 15-minute cadence makes the blunt bps framing the wrong instrument in the first place: a per-share fixed commission of a fixed fraction of a cent (modeled on Interactive Brokers fees) is a more precise model for intraday execution (for a second iteration). Regardless, the cost-feasibility screen in *Section 20.1* leads to a positive result for the strategy. The liquidity-screened universe comes with a measurable cushion: on the bps grid, it stays positive by roughly 10 basis points per leg, with a net Sharpe ratio of +0.29, and then turns negative by 15.
- S&P 500 options highlights that the cost model must fit the instrument. Option transaction costs scale with the premium, not with the notional, so a basis-point sweep against the notional measures the wrong quantity. Under daily mark-to-market hold-to-expiry accounting on the full universe, the strategy fails the cost gate; *Section 18.8* presents the three-rung cost-mitigation cascade that restricts execution to the bottom-quintile half-spread cohort and lifts the retrained holdout Sharpe to +0.97.

Cost fragility tracks two observable inputs: rebalancing cadence and universe liquidity. High turnover produces the steepest cost gradient in the test bed: crypto perpetuals (8-hourly) lose roughly two-tenths of a Sharpe point per basis-point increment and NASDAQ-100 (15-minute) close to one-tenth on its cost-feasible configuration, both far faster than the monthly-rebalance strategies. Moving to a longer cadence is usually a higher-return implementation change than tuning the model. Blanket basis-point assumptions fit poorly for options, micro-cap equities, and high-frequency strategies, where per-share or per-trade models better reflect execution economics. Evaluation must match the instrument.

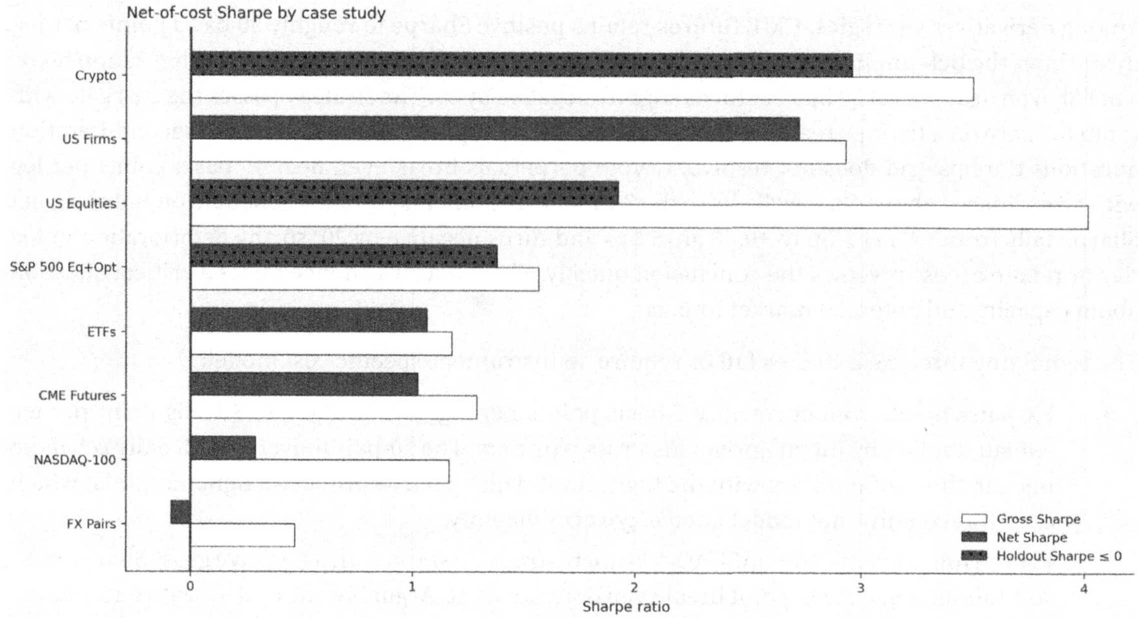

Figure 20.15: Gross Sharpe at zero cost versus net Sharpe at each case study's actual cost regime, both read from the same cost-sensitivity sweep so net never exceeds gross; bars whose holdout Sharpe is non-positive are hatched

Capacity and concentration

Among case studies, apparent edges concentrate where capacity is most constrained. The US firm characteristics case study concentrates its long leg heavily in bottom-quartile market-capitalization names; a conservative capacity estimate computes the minimum average daily volume across portfolio constituents and applies a 1-to-5 participation rate, at which point the participation constraint becomes binding at moderate asset levels. Avramov, Cheng, and Metzker (2020) find the same pattern across the broader ML-for-asset-pricing literature: reported profitability erodes once economic restrictions (short-sale constraints, liquidity filters, transaction costs) are imposed. ETFs and FX operate in highly liquid markets where capacity is not the binding constraint; their signal-stage edges are correspondingly thinner.

Cost survival is one of several filters. *Section 20.7* examines temporal stability and risk overlays: whether the signal-plus-cost picture holds across different market regimes and time periods, and whether path-risk overlays add or subtract value relative to the underlying signal.

20.7 Risk overlays

Risk overlays refine strategies that already have signal and a cost buffer; they cannot redeem a strategy that lacks predictive edge. The cross-case sweep covers position-level overlays: trailing stops on adverse price excursions and time-based exits on stale positions.

Three case studies achieve their highest-validation-Sharpe with a position-level overlay. S&P 500 equity-plus-options stands apart: a 3% trailing stop lifts the Sharpe ratio from +1.25 at the signal stage to +2.39 and cuts maximum drawdown from −43% to −7%. ETFs and CME futures post modest Sharpe lifts of +0.24 and +0.17 over their allocator baselines. ETFs use a 4.3% trailing stop tuned to the 25th percentile of the 20-bar maximum-adverse-excursion distribution, which reduces drawdown from −28% to −11%; CME futures use a 5% trailing stop that lifts Sharpe but leaves drawdown slightly deeper at −21% versus −18%, because the avoided-loss against missed-recovery balance is sensitive around the threshold.

Four case studies see no Sharpe improvement from any overlay. Crypto perpetuals (20-bar time exit at an 8-hourly cadence) and US equities (40-bar time exit at a daily cadence) show risk-overlay Sharpe ratios within ±0.02 of their allocator baselines, with drawdowns unchanged; the overlay window matches the natural holding period of the highest-validation-Sharpe configuration in each case. FX pairs use a 20-bar time exit on the linear-ridge long-short configuration that lifts Sharpe by +0.01 (from +0.04 at the allocation stage to +0.05). Neither the price path nor the position duration exposes an asymmetry the overlay can profitably intercept, so the overlay is a near-neutral pass-through. NASDAQ-100's cost-feasible configuration was swept across the same overlay grid: its best variant, a 20% trailing stop, holds managed Sharpe at +1.06 against a +1.13 no-overlay baseline, and every tighter stop or shorter time exit reduces Sharpe further: no overlay improves it, confirming that cost, not overlay choice, is its binding constraint.

Two case studies do not use risk overlays due to data limitations: S&P 500 options' highest-validation-Sharpe configuration is held to expiry, and the data does not contain daily highs and lows; and the US firm characteristics case study does not have price data at all.

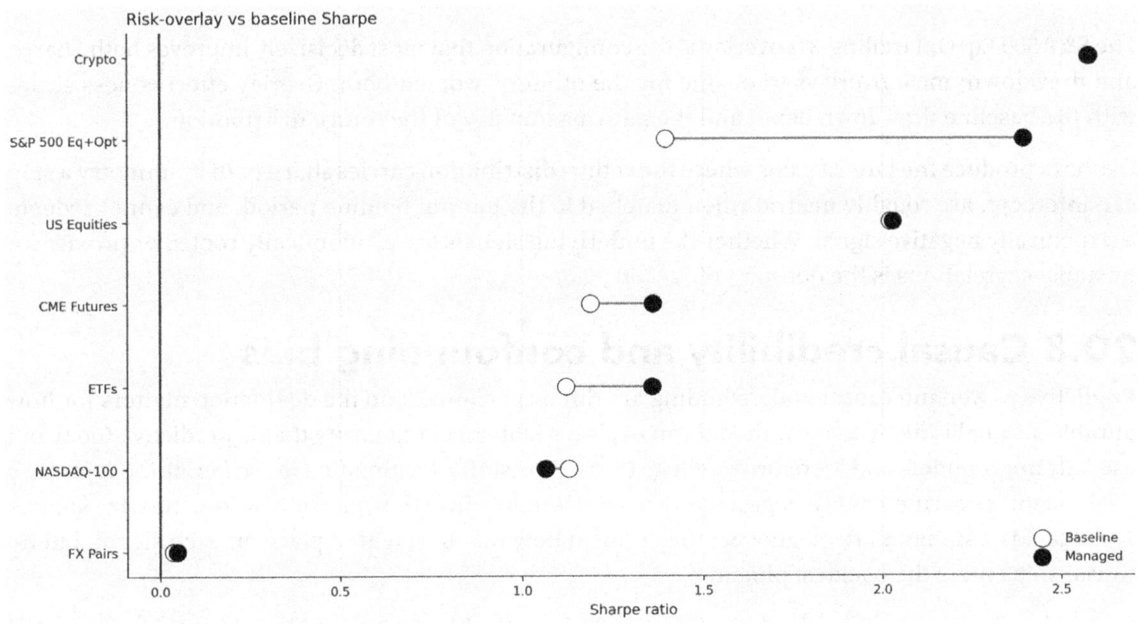

Figure 20.16: Allocation-stage versus risk-stage Sharpe across the seven case studies with overlay rows on their highest-validation-Sharpe lineage

Trailing stops on path-asymmetric return distributions produce the largest gains; time-exit overlays matched to the natural holding period are near-neutral.

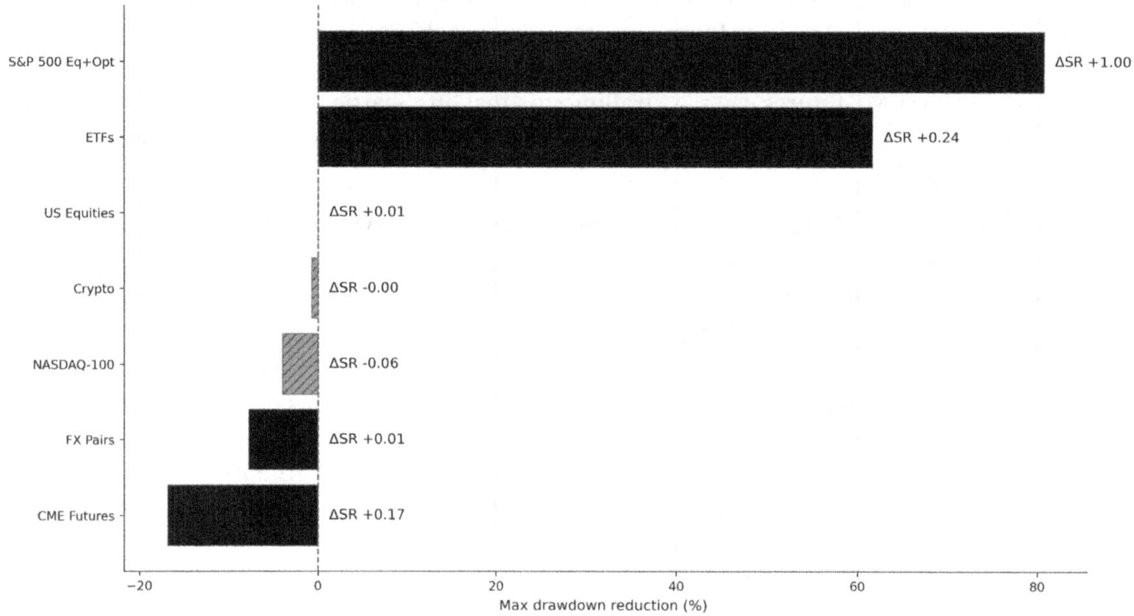

Figure 20.17: Maximum-drawdown reduction (in percentage points) per overlay row on the highest-validation-Sharpe lineage, with the Sharpe delta versus the allocator baseline annotated on each bar

The S&P 500 Eq+Opt trailing-3% overlay is the configuration that most decisively improves both Sharpe and drawdown; most overlays trade one for the other or worsen both. Overlay effectiveness scales with the baseline drawdown depth and the path asymmetry of the return distribution.

Overlays produce the largest gains where the return distribution carries sharp path asymmetry a stop can intercept, are roughly neutral when matched to the natural holding period, and cannot redeem a structurally negative signal. Whether the underlying signals are economically rooted or proxies for unstable correlations is the question of *Section 20.8*.

20.8 Causal credibility and confounding bias

Predictive power and causal understanding are different claims, and the distinction matters for how durable a signal is likely to be. A model can exploit a statistical regularity that is predictive today but causally ungrounded, and therefore fragile to the regime shifts documented in *Section 20.1*. *Chapter 15*'s dual machine-learning analysis provides a partial window into this question across the case studies. The dual ML estimates are diagnostic; they inform how much weight to place on each signal, but no causal step enters the backtest pipeline.

Across the nine case studies, the dual ML estimator and the block-permutation refutation are applied as specified in *Sections 15.4–15.6*; standard risk-factor controls (market, momentum, volatility) and the engineered confounders from each case study's feature pipeline form the nuisance set. The credibility summary reported below combines four quantities:

- The DML effect direction and magnitude
- The HAC p-value on the second-stage coefficient
- The refutation p-value from the time-shuffled re-fit
- The percentage gap between the naive regression coefficient and the DML coefficient

Each estimate is computed on the forward-return label the case study actually deploys, so the screen speaks to the signal as traded rather than to a separate reporting horizon. Significance at $p < 0.05$ and refutation stability at refutation $p < 0.05$ define the two reporting thresholds.

Case Study	Candidate Treatment	DML Effect	p (HAC)	Refutation p	Bias %
ETFs	momentum (skip-recent 6, 1)	−0.058	0.000	0.00	+33
S&P 500 Options	variance risk premium 21d	−0.123	0.000	0.03	+50
US firms	momentum 12–2	+0.009	0.003	1.00	+103
US Equities	momentum 12-1	−0.001	0.454	0.35	+354
SP500 Eq+Opt	IV–RV spread	−0.003	0.168	0.12	+133
Crypto Perps	premium z-score 14d	−0.001	0.530	1.00	+53
NASDAQ-100	signed volume share	≈ 0	0.966	0.99	−142
CME Futures	carry percent	≈ 0	0.454	0.19	−60
FX Pairs	momentum (skip-recent)	−0.004	0.468	0.06	−82

Table 20.8: Dual ML estimates on each case study's deployed forward-return label, the horizon the strategy actually trades

The candidate treatment is the strongest model feature for that case study after the controls (factor returns, volatility, the chapter's engineered confounders) are held constant. Large absolute bias percentages on rows where the DML effect is near zero (NASDAQ-100, CME Futures, FX Pairs) reflect tiny denominators rather than strong confounding effects.

Two case studies clear both thresholds on the label they deploy: ETFs and S&P 500 Options. These are also the two signals with the clearest economic rationale (the cross-sectional momentum premium in ETFs and the variance-risk premium in S&P 500 options), and the causal screen is consistent with that rationale, since each survives the HAC significance test and the block-permutation refutation. US Firms reaches significance ($p = 0.003$), but its refutation companion fails to reject the time-shuffled null (refutation $p = 1.00$), so the estimate cannot be separated from a spurious fit. The remaining six signals do not clear the significance threshold at the horizon they trade. Each of these earned its place in the deployed strategy on validation Sharpe, so each is predictive; what the dual ML screen adds is that their edge is empirical rather than causally identified at the traded label. That separation, two economically grounded signals from a larger set whose edge is statistical, is an input to position sizing and monitoring, not a determination of whether a signal should be traded.

Confounding bias should be reported alongside Sharpe as a complementary fragility metric. Bias quantifies the extent to which the naive effect is explained by observable confounders such as momentum, volatility, and market factors. High absolute bias means the signal is sensitive to shifts in those confounders: if the relationship between momentum and returns changes, a high-bias signal is more likely to break. That risk dimension differs from holdout decay, which captures all sources of deterioration including data snooping and regime change. Whether confounding bias predicts holdout decay is an open empirical question (nine observations are too few to establish a pattern), but even without that link, bias is informative as a fragility indicator. Predictive signals without causal identification can still be deployed for trading provided that appropriate risk management is in place. For inference about *why* a strategy works or how durable it is likely to be, causal evidence matters more, and that distinction informs both position sizing and monitoring intensity: high-bias strategies warrant tighter risk budgets and more frequent re-evaluation.

Because most of these signals are only partially understood, the next research step on each case study is concrete. *Section 20.9* collects those per-case next steps.

20.9 Next steps after the first research iteration

Every result in this book comes from a single pass through a standardized pipeline, and the chapter frames each case study as the *first* iteration of the *Chapter 6* strategy research workflow. This closing section names, for each of the nine cases, the concrete next research step. The diagnostic readings of *Section 20.3* through *Section 20.8* each pointed to a specific upstream or downstream lever; those are collected in the following list as per-case next iterations:

- **US firm characteristics:** Filter the universe to the top three quartiles by market capitalization and re-run to see how Sharpe behaves under realistic capacity. The signal-stage edge is the largest in the test bed, but the long leg concentrates in bottom-quartile names whose spreads commonly run 100 to 500 basis points; liquidity, not signal, is the binding constraint.
- **US equities panel:** Decompose the validation-to-holdout sign flip (+2.03 to −0.49 on the highest-validation-Sharpe GBM) by sector and calendar period to determine whether the decay is gradual or concentrated in a specific regime. If the sign flip concentrates in small-cap technology names during a particular rate regime, engineer sector-specific features, extend the horizon to 21 days to reduce turnover, and ensemble with the IPCA signal.
- **ETFs:** Ensemble the latent-factor SDF, deep-learning NLinear, and linear ridge configurations from the validation top cluster and evaluate whether the combined signal stabilizes the +0.046 holdout daily IC. The daily validation IC ceiling of +0.085 on the standard feature set suggests broader feature inputs (sentiment, fundamentals, cross-asset signals) are a higher-impact lever than deeper architectures.

- **CME futures:** Verify the interaction-based signal on a second data source or an alternative back-adjustment method. The continuous-series construction shapes the family rankings more than the model choice does, so robustness against that construction is the highest-value next test.
- **S&P 500 equity-plus-options:** Test checkpoint ensembling on the latent-factor highest-validation-Sharpe configuration to characterize the per-configuration IC range and whether averaging across configurations stabilizes the holdout result, which decayed from validation Sharpe +2.39 to holdout −0.73 with strategy-versus-EW confidence interval [−4.17, −0.75] excluding zero on the negative side.
- **FX pairs:** No model family clears the IC threshold at any horizon, so the open question is whether a cross-sectional signal exists in this 20-pair universe at all, not how to execute one: the linear-ridge configuration resolves flat (validation +0.05, holdout +0.19, both below the equal-weight benchmark). The higher-value next steps are richer inputs (rate differentials, macro releases, positioning data) and a slower cadence to widen the thin 7-basis-point cost margin, before any further pipeline tuning.
- **Crypto perpetuals:** Add explicit regime detection or shorter retraining windows before any second-iteration backtest. The cross-sectional funding pattern is genuine but unstable over the observed holdout: the highest-validation-Sharpe GBM clears +2.57 validation Sharpe but decays to −0.13 on holdout, a validation-to-holdout Sharpe difference whose 95% bootstrap interval excludes zero on the negative side. Deepening the cross-section beyond 19 contracts is a parallel line of research.
- **S&P 500 options:** Retain the bottom-quintile half-spread execution discipline (*Section 20.6*, *Section 18.8*) as the candidate path forward, with the understanding that the resulting +0.97 retrained holdout Sharpe sits within a wide one-year confidence interval and has not been confirmed at the bottom-decile spread restriction. The next iteration's question is whether the same model produces a positive net Sharpe at institutional spreads and size.
- **NASDAQ-100 microstructure:** The cost-feasibility screen converts a full-universe failure into a marginal positive result (validation +1.13, holdout +0.53), though the edge is not statistically resolved and trails a passive benchmark on the same screened universe. Test the screen's sensitivity by widening and tightening the cost-feasible cutoff, and search the rebalancing-cadence axis (30-minute, hourly, daily) under the per-share cost model to see whether a coarser cadence lifts the screened strategy clear of per-bar friction.

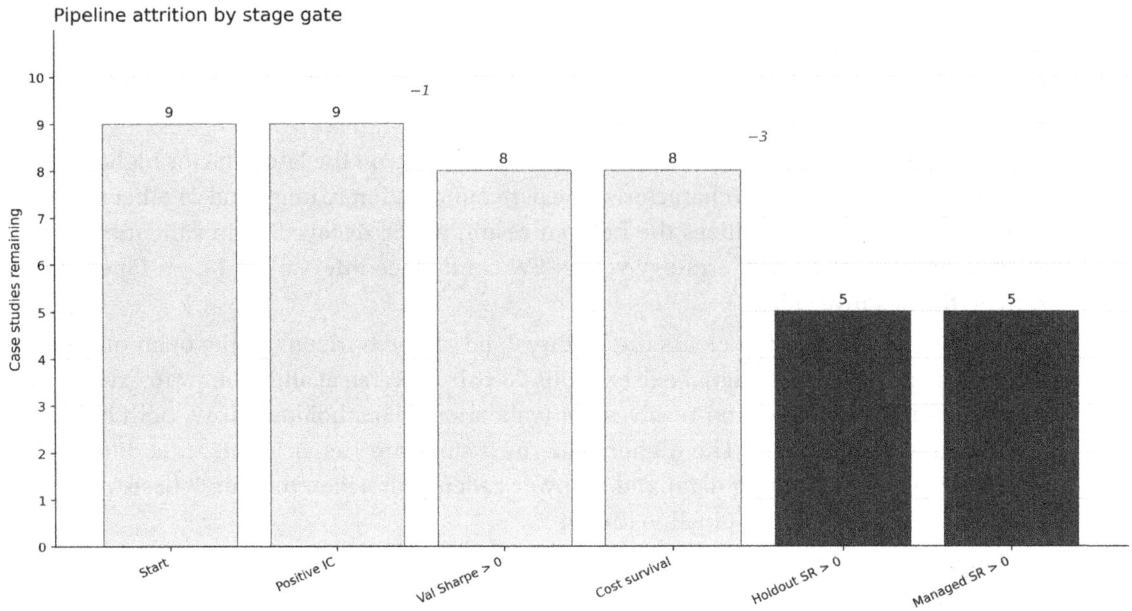

Figure 20.18: Pipeline attrition across the evaluation gates

All nine case studies show positive validation IC; eight clear the validation-Sharpe gate (FX pairs drop, its validation Sharpe spanning zero); eight survive the cost gate; five retain a positive holdout Sharpe; and all five hold through risk-overlay management. The attrition concentrates at the holdout gate (eight strategies enter it and five emerge) rather than at validation, and motivates the per-case next-iteration agenda above.

20.10 Summary

The nine case studies taken together show that a standardized ML-for-trading pipeline (applied once, with off-the-shelf features, simple allocators, static cost assumptions, and no retraining inside the holdout) leaves five of the nine strategies with a resolved positive holdout Sharpe, gradated from the stronger results of ETFs, CME futures, and US firm characteristics, through the marginal NASDAQ-100 (+0.53), to the execution-cost-conditional S&P 500 options (+0.97). Three decay to a negative holdout, and FX pairs resolves flat: its +0.19 holdout point estimate spans zero and sits below the passive benchmark. The holdout intervals are wide in every case, and one strategy is structurally below the cost line under realistic accounting. The best-family daily IC across the test bed tops out near +0.08; measurement-error analysis finds the highest-validation-Sharpe and near-top configurations statistically indistinguishable in most cases, and the ensemble demonstration of *Section 20.4* shows that averaging across those top configurations trades peak Sharpe for fold-to-fold stability. None of the nine studies produces a strategy that should be carried directly to capital; each is one iteration through the *Chapter 6* workflow.

The workflow is the book's contribution. The nine case studies are one application of it; a reader's own iteration (on a different universe, with richer features, on a longer horizon, through multiple cycles) is where the evidence becomes useful. *Chapter 6* is the reference for how that iteration proceeds.

Chapter 21 turns to reinforcement learning, where a one-shot prediction-then-allocate pipeline gives way to policies that act, observe, and adapt: execution scheduling, inventory-aware hedging, and position sizing as learned behaviors rather than static rules. The remaining chapters in Part V extend the toolkit further (retrieval-augmented research, knowledge graphs, autonomous agents, and live-trading infrastructure in *Chapters 22* through *27*), but the workflow of diagnostic rigor, implementation realism, and frozen holdout validation does not change. The methods expand; the discipline holds.

21

Reinforcement Learning

Prediction alone does not generate returns. Traders must translate forecasts into actions that navigate market impact, transaction costs, inventory risk, and model uncertainty. Reinforcement learning (RL) addresses this gap by learning policies for sequential decisions under feedback and delay. Supervised learning predicts what is likely to happen next; RL chooses the action that is justified now, given a longer-horizon objective.

This chapter focuses on the financial settings where that framing applies most cleanly: execution, market making, and derivatives hedging. In each case, the action itself is the optimization target, and the reward is tied directly to implementation shortfall, inventory-aware spread capture, or hedging error under costs. The chapter also covers inverse reinforcement learning for inferring objectives from observed behavior, while emphasizing practical limits rather than algorithmic breadth.

After working through the chapter and its notebooks, you will be able to:

- Formulate execution, market-making, and derivatives hedging problems as partially observed Markov Decision Processes with economically coherent state, action, reward, and constraint designs.
- Match value-based and actor-critic RL methods to financial tasks based on action-space structure, sample-efficiency needs, and stability requirements.
- Benchmark RL execution policies against TWAP and Almgren-Chriss-style schedules in controlled simulated and crypto-data settings, and interpret apparent gains with appropriate caution.
- Compare deep hedging results with delta hedging and Whalley-Wilmott-style benchmarks under transaction costs using PnL distributions and tail-risk metrics.
- Distinguish inverse reinforcement learning from behavior cloning and explain what reward inference can and cannot recover from observed trading behavior.
- Diagnose the simulation-to-reality risks that govern deployability, including non-stationarity, reward hacking, market impact, partial observability, latency, and benchmark mismatch.

Sections 21.1–21.3 establish the decision-theoretic framing, the MDP formulation, and the core algorithm families. *Sections 21.4–21.7* apply that machinery to execution, market making, deep hedging, and inverse RL. *Section 21.8* closes on the simulation-to-reality gap, which separates a promising simulator result from a deployable policy.

21.1 The sequential decision-making paradigm in finance

Reinforcement learning reframes the central question from prediction to sequential action under uncertainty, with direct consequences for trading system design (Sun et al., 2023). Supervised models treat prediction and action as separate problems, ignoring the feedback loop in which actions alter the environment being modeled (Hambly et al., 2023). A strategy built on price forecasts will, through its execution, move prices, a dynamic that static prediction models cannot capture.

RL is goal-directed: an agent interacts with a dynamic environment over time, learning a *policy* that maps situations to actions that maximize cumulative reward (Kolm and Ritter, 2019). The framework handles sequential decisions in which actions influence future states, and feedback is delayed, sparse, or indirect.

The temporal credit assignment problem

RL must attribute a final outcome to the sequence of actions that produced it. In trading, a profitable exit may follow a dozen decisions made over the preceding days or weeks. Supervised models get immediate feedback for each prediction; an RL agent learns from delayed, aggregated rewards.

This is the temporal credit assignment problem, and RL's value function is the machinery that solves it. The value function $V(s)$ is the total expected future reward starting from state s and following the current policy thereafter. That long-horizon objective aligns with the targets of portfolio managers and institutional traders, who optimize multi-period PnL rather than one-step accuracy.

End-to-end optimization

RL collapses the "predict then act" pipeline into a single optimization: the agent learns a policy that maps market states directly to trading actions, targeting the financial objective rather than an intermediate proxy (Hambly et al., 2023). The policy requires fewer explicit assumptions about return distributions, volatility dynamics, or impact functions, so it can fit dynamics that classical parametric models miss. "Model-free" means only that the algorithm does not require a transition model. State design, reward shaping, and simulator construction still embed substantial modeling choices.

RL introduces a trade-off absent from supervised learning: exploit actions known to be profitable, or explore untried actions that might do better. In non-stationary markets, pure exploitation is brittle: a strategy that only repeats past patterns fails when regimes shift. Disciplined exploration matters, but in finance it has to run through simulators, offline data, or strict risk controls rather than unconstrained live trading (Hambly et al., 2023; Halperin, Kolm, and Ritter, 2025).

Why this chapter focuses on execution rather than alpha

RL is often expected to learn directional trading strategies that discover alpha from price movements. In practice, alpha-seeking RL faces severe obstacles: non-stationarity erodes learned patterns across regimes, exploration-driven market impact is costly and irreversible, and reward functions based on short-window Sharpe ratios invite overfitting and reward hacking. Surveys and simplified trading demonstrations reach the same conclusion: these setups serve as proofs of concept but remain far from the decision problems institutions must deploy (Millea, 2021). The predict-then-act pipeline in *Chapters 11–14*, combined with the portfolio construction and risk management in *Chapters 16–19*, handles alpha generation on firmer ground.

RL's comparative advantage lies in domains where the *action itself* is the optimization target (minimizing execution cost, managing inventory, hedging derivatives) and where the reward is well-defined and directly measurable: implementation shortfall, inventory-penalized spread capture, hedging PnL.

The next section introduces the Markov Decision Process, the formal structure that underpins every algorithm and application in this chapter.

21.2 Financial markets as Markov decision processes

Applying RL to finance requires translating trading problems into **Markov Decision Processes (MDPs)**, the formal framework for sequential decision-making in stochastic environments (Hambly et al., 2023). State design, reward shape, and action granularity determine what the agent can learn more than the algorithm itself does. In finance, these choices embed hypotheses about market dynamics, about which features carry signal, and about which horizons matter.

The MDP framework

Figure 21.1 illustrates the MDP loop: the agent observes market state, selects an action (trade size, spread, hedge ratio), receives a reward (PnL, risk-adjusted return), and transitions to a new state as the market evolves. Repeating this loop thousands of times during training is how the agent learns a policy.

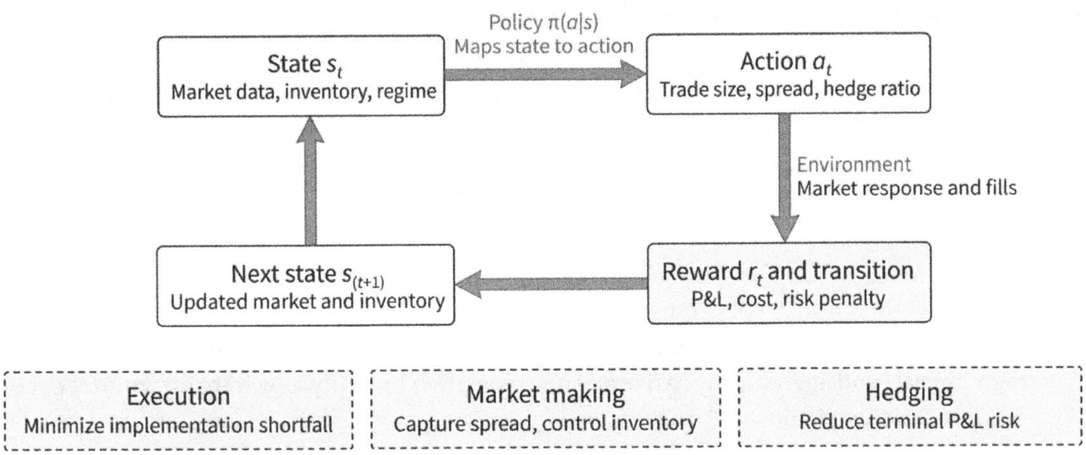

Figure 21.1: Conceptual MDP loop for financial reinforcement learning across execution, market making, and hedging tasks

An MDP is formally defined by a five-element tuple $\langle S, A, P, R, \gamma \rangle$: a state space, an action space, transition dynamics, a reward function, and a discount factor. *Figure 21.1* shows the corresponding state, action, and reward at each step. The central tenet is the **Markov property**: the future is conditionally independent of the past given the present. In other words, the probability of transitioning to the next state s_{t+1} depends only on the current state s_t and action a_t, not on the entire history of preceding states and actions (Kolm and Ritter, 2019).

In practice, financial states are rarely Markovian: current price and volume alone do not capture regime, momentum, or microstructure dynamics. Practitioners address this by stacking recent observations into the state vector and adding rolling statistics (volatility, spread averages, order flow momentum) that summarize recent history. The feature categories below reflect this principle: each one encodes information that makes the current state a better summary of the relevant past.

Partial observability in financial markets

Financial environments are partially observable: a trader executing a large order cannot see other participants' intentions, hidden liquidity in dark pools, or pending news releases. The agent receives observations o_t that provide incomplete information about the true state s_t (Halperin et al., 2025).

Partial observability is why state engineering carries so much weight in financial RL. Each additional feature (order book depth, volatility regime indicators, time-of-day effects) supplies information about latent market conditions. Richer state representations do more than improve performance; they bring the problem closer to the fully observable MDP that algorithms assume. Recurrent architectures (LSTMs or GRUs; see *Chapter 13*) offer an alternative: an internal memory that implicitly constructs a belief state from the observation sequence.

State representation

The state space, S, defines the agent's view of the world. Early approaches used low-dimensional states consisting of a lookback window of historical prices and portfolio values. Production systems now use richer representations (Hambly et al., 2023):

- **Public market data** forms the foundation: bid-ask spread, depth at multiple price levels, order flow imbalance, and other features derived from the limit order book (LOB). For execution and market making, these microstructure features are the most informative predictors of short-term price dynamics.
- **Private agent information** captures the agent's internal state: current inventory or portfolio holdings, unrealized PnL, and time remaining until a terminal horizon. These path-dependent features are essential for risk-aware decision-making.
- **Regime indicators** capture the current market regime: rolling volatility, spread levels, depth ratios, and time-of-day effects. Including these features means the optimal policy π^* is inherently regime-conditioned. The agent learns to trade passively in fragile conditions (low liquidity, high impact) and aggressively in deep conditions (high liquidity, low impact) without explicit regime-switching logic.

Action space design

The action space, A, defines the agent's choice set, and its structure determines which algorithms apply:

- **Discrete actions** give the simplest formulation: {Buy, Sell, Hold} for a directional trader, or a discrete set of spread levels for a market maker. Value-based algorithms such as DQN handle these by estimating action values.
- **Continuous actions** are more realistic for many financial decisions: the quantity of shares in an execution slice, the limit-order price, or portfolio allocation weights. These require actor-critic algorithms such as PPO or SAC that produce continuous action vectors directly (Hambly et al., 2023).
- **Action constraints** are ubiquitous in finance: position limits, maximum order sizes, participation rate caps, and inventory bounds. These can be enforced through action clipping, penalty terms in the reward, or constrained MDP formulations. Hard constraints (kill switches, regulatory limits) should never rely solely on learned behavior.

Reward engineering

The reward function R is the load-bearing piece of an MDP: the scalar signal that drives learning. The agent will optimize whatever this signal rewards, so reward engineering, not algorithm choice, is what aligns the learned policy with the financial objective (Kolm and Ritter, 2019). Consider the following factors:

- **Naive PnL rewards** (the per-step change in portfolio value) are intuitive but noisy, and can encourage high-variance strategies that chase expected return without regard for risk.
- **Risk-adjusted returns** shape more conservative policies by optimizing a performance metric directly: Sharpe, Sortino (penalizing downside only), or Calmar (return relative to maximum drawdown). This aligns the agent's objective with the risk-return trade-off that institutions optimize.
- **Task-specific rewards** match each application's objective:

Task	Objective	Reward Function
Optimal execution	Minimize implementation shortfall	$R_t = -(p_{\text{arrival}} - p_{\text{exec}}) \times v$
Market making	Balance spread capture and inventory risk	$R_t = \text{PnL}_t - \lambda \cdot I_t^2$
Deep hedging	Minimize terminal risk	$R_T = -\text{CVaR}_\alpha(\text{PnL}_T)$
Portfolio allocation	Maximize risk-adjusted returns	$R_t = \Delta\text{SR}$ or $r_t - \lambda\sigma_t$

Table 21.1: Objectives and rewards by task

These reward designs connect to economic theory. Kolm and Ritter (2019) showed that a quadratic per-step reward (penalizing deviations of the wealth increment from its mean, scaled by a risk-aversion parameter λ) produces agents that approximately maximize mean-variance utility. This equivalence holds beyond Gaussian returns, covering all elliptical distributions and certain asymmetric families (Halperin et al., 2025). The quadratic reward form also makes the Q-function analytically tractable, enabling solutions without neural network approximation, the insight underlying the QLBS framework in *Section 21.6*. Kolm and Ritter (2019) give the full derivation.

The risk-aversion parameter λ controls the return-versus-risk trade-off. For market making, asymmetrically dampened rewards (penalizing speculative gains more than spread-capture gains) discourage trend-following and improve learning stability.

Transition dynamics and discount factors

The transition model $P(s' \mid s, a)$ is unknown in finance: the market response emerges from a multi-agent system. Financial RL therefore relies on model-free algorithms that learn policies directly from experience, with neural networks generalizing across the high-dimensional state spaces that feature engineering produces (Mnih et al., 2015). The discount factor γ sets the planning horizon: values near 1.0 (0.99–0.999) encourage the far-sighted optimization that execution and hedging require.

The next section surveys the families of algorithms that solve such MDPs, from value-based methods like DQN to actor-critic architectures that handle continuous action spaces.

Implementation: See `02_optimal_execution_ppo` and `03_market_making_ppo` for complete MDP formulations.

21.3 Core algorithms – From DQN to actor-critic

Actor-critic architectures have become the practical default in financial RL: they handle continuous actions natively and trade off stability against flexibility well (Hambly et al., 2023). The progression from value-based to actor-critic methods exposes the choices that drive algorithm selection. The best textbook reference for RL algorithms remains Sutton and Barto (2018).

The Bellman equation

All value-based RL methods rest on a recursive relationship known as the **Bellman optimality equation.** The optimal action-value function $Q^*(s, a)$ that expresses the maximum expected cumulative reward from taking action a in state s and acting optimally thereafter satisfies:

$$Q^*(s,a) = \mathbb{E}\left[R_{t+1} + \gamma \max_{a'} Q^*(s_{t+1}, a') \mid S_t = s, A_t = a\right]$$

This equation states that the value of a state-action pair equals the expected immediate reward plus the discounted value of the best action in the next state. The recursive structure enables **temporal difference (TD) learning:** rather than waiting for a complete episode to evaluate an action, the agent updates its Q-estimate after each step using the observed reward and its current estimate of the next state's value. **Q-learning**, the classical algorithm, performs these updates using a simple tabular representation. The transition to deep RL replaces the table with a neural network, enabling generalization across the high-dimensional, continuous state spaces that characterize financial markets.

Deep Q-networks

Value-based algorithms focus on learning the optimal action-value function $Q^*(s, a)$. The policy is derived implicitly by selecting the action that maximizes the Q-function: $\pi(s) = \text{argmax}_a Q^*(s, a)$.

Deep Q-Networks (**DQN**) approximate the Q-function with a neural network (Mnih et al., 2015). Two innovations stabilize training: experience replay breaks temporal correlations by randomly sampling past transitions, and target networks provide stable regression targets via slowly updated Q-network copies. DQN is restricted to discrete actions: buy/sell/hold or quoting at fixed price levels. van Hasselt et al. (2015) showed that **Double DQN** reduces Q-value overestimation by decoupling action selection from value estimation; **Dueling DQN** separately estimates state value and action advantage (Wang et al., 2016).

Actor-critic – On-policy

Policy-based methods directly parameterize and optimize the policy $\pi_\theta(a \mid s)$. The policy parameters θ are updated using policy gradient methods, adjusting in the direction that increases expected return (Sutton et al., 2000). In practice, **Proximal Policy Optimization** (**PPO**) uses a learned value-function baseline to reduce variance, making it an actor-critic method, though it originated in the policy-gradient tradition.

PPO constrains policy updates via a clipped surrogate objective, preventing the performance collapse common in unconstrained policy-gradient methods (Schulman et al., 2017). That stability makes PPO the default starting point for financial applications, including portfolio management and general trading. The drawback is on-policy learning: past experience must be discarded after each update, making PPO less sample-efficient than off-policy alternatives, a real cost when high-quality financial data is scarce.

Actor-critic – Off-policy

Actor-critic algorithms combine value-based and policy-based ideas. An *actor* network learns the policy $\pi_\theta(a \mid s)$; a *critic* network learns a value function that evaluates the actor's actions. The critic provides a low-variance learning signal that guides actor updates, stabilizing training (Konda and Tsitsiklis, 1999).

Deep Deterministic Policy Gradient (**DDPG**) extends DQN to continuous action spaces via a deterministic actor policy while retaining experience replay and target networks. DDPG is sensitive to hyperparameters; **TD3** mitigates this sensitivity through clipped double Q-learning, delayed policy updates, and target policy smoothing.

Soft Actor-Critic (**SAC**) adds entropy maximization to the actor-critic objective: the agent maximizes expected return while keeping its policy as stochastic as possible (Haarnoja et al., 2018). The entropy term encourages exploration, prevents premature convergence, and produces policies resilient to perturbation, properties that suit market making and dynamic hedging. The cost is tuning complexity: the entropy coefficient and learning rates require careful calibration, especially in non-stationary financial environments where PPO's simpler update rule is more forgiving.

Algorithm	Type	Policy	Action Space	Sample Efficiency	Best Financial Use Cases
DQN	Value-based	Off-policy	Discrete	Moderate	Simple trading, discretized execution
PPO	Actor-Critic	On-policy	Both	Lower	Portfolio allocation, execution, general trading
DDPG/TD3	Actor-Critic	Off-policy	Continuous	Higher	Execution, hedging, continuous allocation
SAC	Actor-Critic	Off-policy	Continuous	Highest	Market making, dynamic hedging, microstructure

Table 21.2: Algorithm selection for finance

Risk-aware RL

Standard RL maximizes expected cumulative reward, the mean of the return distribution. This *risk-neutral* formulation ignores variance, tail risk, and higher moments, and is therefore insufficient for financial applications where risk management matters as much as return generation (Halperin et al., 2025). Three extensions address this gap.

Mean-variance RL incorporates both expected return and variance into the objective: $\text{Reward} = \mathbb{E}[\text{Return}] - \lambda \cdot \text{Var}[\text{Return}]$ Because this remains an expectation (of a risk-adjusted quantity), the standard RL machinery still applies: the variance penalty is absorbed into the reward definition. When the reward takes the quadratic form discussed in *Section 21.2*, the Q-function becomes analytically tractable and can be solved without neural networks (Kolm and Ritter, 2019). The limitation is that variance penalizes upside and downside deviations equally.

CVaR-based RL directly optimizes tail risk by using Conditional Value at Risk (the expected loss in the worst $\alpha\%$ of outcomes) as the risk penalty. This focuses the agent on downside protection, which aligns with how institutions evaluate risk. Unlike mean-variance RL, CVaR-based methods generally require deep neural networks for function approximation.

Distributional RL changes the target: rather than learning the expected return, algorithms like Quantile Regression DQN (QR-DQN) and Implicit Quantile Networks (IQN) learn the **full probability distribution** of cumulative future rewards. With the distribution in hand, any risk measure (VaR, CVaR, skewness) can be computed at decision time, making risk preferences configurable without retraining. For tail-risk-driven applications, distributional methods give the richest representation of uncertainty.

Model-based and model-free approaches

The algorithms above are *model-free*: they learn policies directly from experience without modeling the environment's transition dynamics. *Model-based RL* takes the other route: first learn a model of how the environment responds to actions, then plan against that model. Model-based methods are more sample-efficient, but only as good as the learned model.

In practice, financial RL spans both paradigms. Execution and market-making agents are typically model-free, learning from simulated or historical interactions without modeling price dynamics explicitly. Deep hedging, by contrast, is model-based: it learns optimal hedging policies **for a given stochastic process** (for example, Heston, SABR) used to simulate the underlying asset. Changing the simulation model requires retraining the hedging network, a dependency that model-free approaches avoid.

Practical algorithm selection

Actor-critic methods dominate financial RL because execution sizes, portfolio weights, and hedge ratios are continuous. The choice between on-policy (PPO) and off-policy (SAC/TD3) turns on the stability-versus-efficiency trade-off: SAC's sample efficiency dominates when a high-fidelity simulator makes data generation cheap; PPO's robustness is preferable with limited historical data. Hybrid workflows (off-policy pre-training in simulation, on-policy fine-tuning for deployment) combine the advantages of both.

Figures 21.2 and *21.3* compare the three algorithms implemented in the teaching notebook on a standardized discrete-action trading environment: DQN, PPO, and A2C. In a compact simulator, raw wealth paths can become unstable and are highly seed-sensitive, so *Figure 21.2* is best read as a diagnostic of differing learning dynamics rather than a fixed performance ranking.

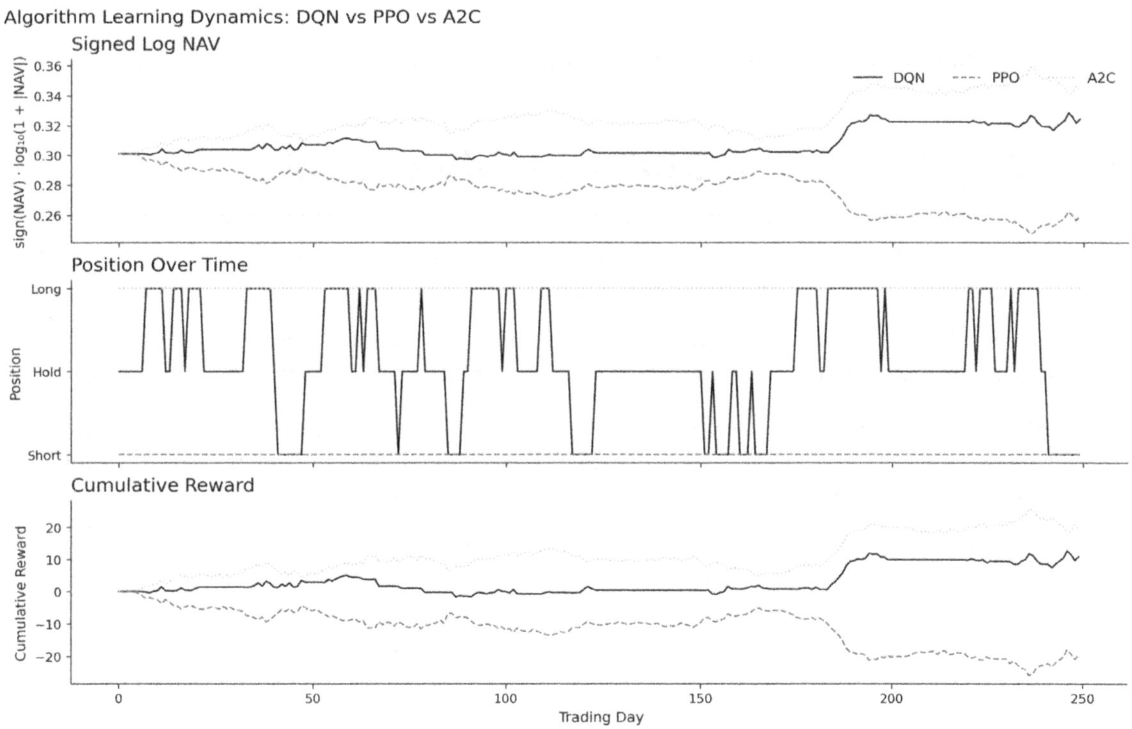

Figure 21.2: DQN, PPO, and A2C learning dynamics in the standardized teaching environment

Figure 21.3 shows that the three methods induce visibly different position-occupancy patterns: algorithm choice shapes policy style even before moving to richer market environments.

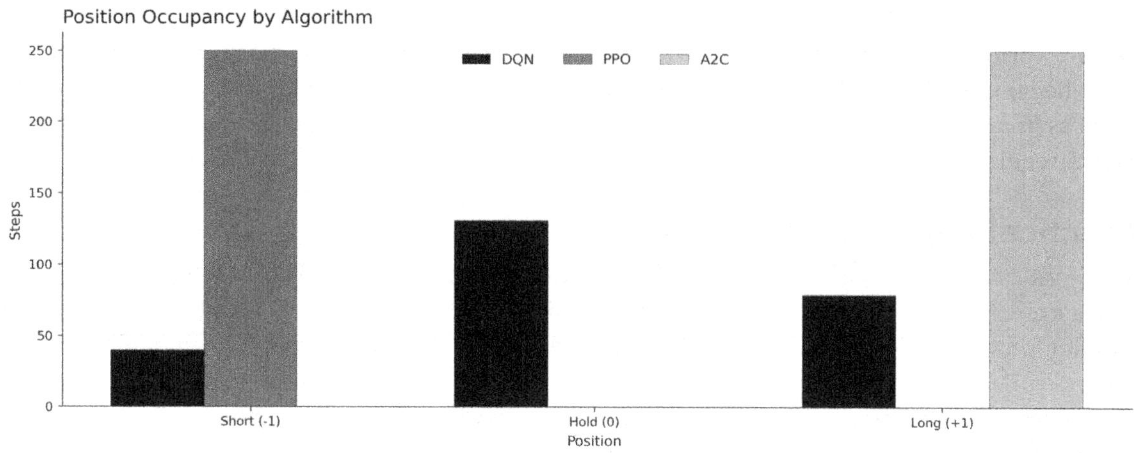

Figure 21.3: Position-occupancy patterns induced by the three algorithms

The remaining sections apply these algorithms to the financial tasks motivated in *Section 21.1*, beginning with optimal trade execution, the application with the clearest evidence of institutional deployment.

> **Implementation:** See `algorithms_comparison` for the side-by-side implementation.

21.4 Application I – Optimal trade execution

Optimal execution (liquidating or acquiring a large position over a specified time horizon) is among the most commercially mature RL use cases in finance. Public disclosures are limited, but execution is the application area with the clearest evidence of live institutional deployment (Hafsi and Vittori, 2025).

A large parent order (for example, selling one million shares of a liquid equity) is broken down into smaller child orders over time. The trader faces a trade-off between two costs:

- **Market impact** arises from executing too quickly. Large orders consume liquidity and move the price against the trader. Executing the full position at once pushes the order through the book and results in significant slippage.
- **Timing risk** arises from executing too slowly. Spreading the trade over time reduces instantaneous impact but exposes the trader to adverse price drift. If the market moves against the position during execution, the average fill price can be worse than immediate execution would have achieved.

The standard metric for evaluating execution quality is **implementation shortfall** (IS): the difference between the asset's price at the time of the decision (the arrival price) and the final average execution price. Minimizing IS requires dynamically balancing impact against timing risk as market conditions evolve.

Classical benchmarking with Almgren-Chriss

The foundational analytical solution to this problem is the Almgren-Chriss model (Almgren and Chriss, 2001), covered in depth in *Chapter 18*, which derives optimal execution schedules by balancing expected impact cost against execution-risk variance. The result is an efficient frontier of trading trajectories, ranging from more uniform schedules to more front-loaded liquidation as risk aversion rises.

The model's limitations stem from its assumptions: constant market impact parameters, constant volatility, and a predetermined schedule that cannot adapt to real-time changes in liquidity or order flow. In reality, these conditions shift throughout the day, particularly around news events, market open, and close.

The RL approach to execution

Reinforcement learning reformulates optimal execution as a sequential decision problem. Instead of computing a fixed schedule upfront, the agent learns a policy that maps market state, remaining inventory, and time-to-deadline to the next trade decision. This can outperform a static schedule when liquidity, volatility, and impact vary in ways the analytical model does not capture.

State representation is high-dimensional, typically combining remaining inventory and time-to-deadline, recent volatility and return patterns, limit-order-book features (spread, depth at multiple levels, order flow imbalance), and private execution metrics such as average price achieved and cost incurred.

Actions specify what the agent does each step. The agent may set the size of the next child order (continuous) or select from a menu of order types and aggressiveness levels (discrete). Continuous order sizes are often discretized into bins (0%, 10%, 20%, ... of remaining inventory) to enable DQN-based approaches. Actions can also include the choice between market orders (guaranteed execution, higher impact) and limit orders (possible price improvement, execution uncertainty).

Rewards are designed to minimize implementation shortfall while discouraging pathological behavior. A common formulation combines realized execution cost with penalties for residual inventory, impact, or delayed completion. Reward design is the central difficulty: misaligned penalties produce policies that satisfy the coded reward but make no economic sense.

Industry evidence – J.P. Morgan LOXM

A prominent real-world example is J.P. Morgan's **LOXM** system, which has optimized equity order execution since 2017. J.P. Morgan built LOXM with deep reinforcement learning, training it on billions of historical and simulated trades to fill client orders quickly at the best available price and to exit large positions without moving the market (Financial Times, 2017). The system's mandate is deliberately narrow: it decides how to execute an order, not what to buy or sell, and it runs within the bank's existing electronic trading risk controls. The bank first deployed it in European equities in 2017, then extended it to Asia and the United States, and reported pricing better than its internal benchmark.

These accounts leave the training details and independent performance evidence proprietary. That makes it useful as a signal of institutional interest, but not as a source of reproducible benchmark numbers.

The academic evidence is clearer than the industry evidence. Kearns and Nevmyvaka (2013) survey the broader landscape of ML for microstructure and execution, while Nevmyvaka, Feng, and Kearns (2006) remains an early empirical demonstration that RL can improve execution policies on historical data, even though production implementations today are disclosed only selectively.

High-fidelity simulation requirements

Training an execution agent on simple price replay is insufficient; the agent must experience realistic market impact and queue dynamics.

Multi-agent simulators like Agent-Based Interactive Discrete Event Simulation (**ABIDES**; Byrd, Hybinette, and Balch, 2020) populate the market with algorithmic and noise traders. Training in these environments enables the agent to learn under realistic market impact and reflexive participant behavior, in which other traders react to the agent's orders (Hafsi and Vittori, 2025). Other environment families use historical replay or benchmark suites built from real-market data. The right choice depends on whether the priority is endogenous agent interaction, close historical reconstruction, or reproducible benchmarking.

The simulator must model:

- **Order book mechanics**: how limit orders queue and fill
- **Market impact**: how trades move prices
- **Queue priority**: time and price priority for limit order execution
- **Partial fills**: orders that execute only partially
- **Latency**: delays between decision and execution

Without these elements, the agent may learn policies that exploit unrealistic assumptions (such as instantaneous fills at the bid or ask) and fail in live markets.

Figure 21.4 compares the PPO execution policy with TWAP and an Almgren-Chriss-style schedule in the teaching environment, averaged across evaluation episodes rather than a single rollout.

The PPO policy combines a constrained action space with a soft penalty for deviations from a reference schedule, which keeps the agent on a paced trajectory rather than allowing it to liquidate instantaneously. PPO achieves the lowest mean implementation shortfall of the three (about 44 bps versus 53 for TWAP and 52 for Almgren-Chriss) and follows a schedule that sits between the uniform TWAP profile and the more back-loaded Almgren-Chriss path. Read the figure as modest positive evidence that state-dependent pacing can improve on simple schedules in a compact simulator, and as a reminder that the result is sensitive to simulator design.

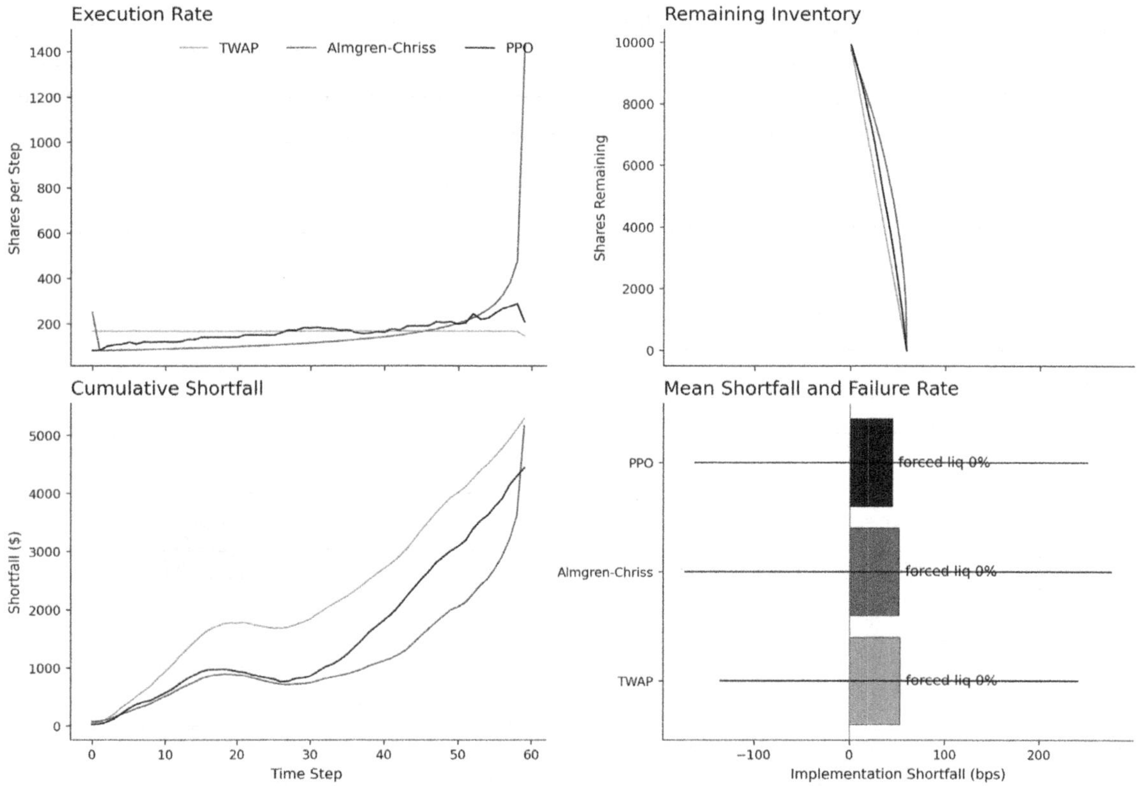

Figure 21.4: Average execution profile comparison in the teaching environment

A practical caveat is that execution agents are highly sensitive to reward shaping, hyperparameter tuning, and the random seed. Pinning the seed makes any single run reproducible, but the policy's character (uniform, back-loaded, or somewhere in between) varies across seeds; the published figure represents one fixed point on that distribution. More generally, an under-constrained reward can yield policies that undertrade early, overtrade early, or oscillate between extremes; the simulator and reward both have to penalize these behaviors in economically coherent ways. This is a concrete instance of the reward-hacking problem discussed in *Section 21.8*: a policy can satisfy the coded objective yet fail to match the intended execution style.

Figure 21.5 extends the analysis to crypto perpetuals using hourly Binance data and the premium index as a state feature. The PPO policy here uses the same paced action space and reference-schedule penalty as the synthetic-environment version, and on this evaluation outperforms both TWAP and a simple premium-aware heuristic on mean shortfall (about −123 bps versus −90 and −89, respectively; negative values reflect sales above the arrival price in trending market conditions, so larger magnitudes are more favorable for a seller).

The learned policy shows clear premium conditioning: average hourly volume is about 4.4 shares during high-premium periods versus 3.7 during low-premium periods. It trades less aggressively near funding settlement (about 3.6 shares per hour within two hours of funding versus 4.4 outside that window). The figure is a stylized but reproducible demonstration that microstructure features can carry signal for an execution policy; the benchmark is too small to support production claims.

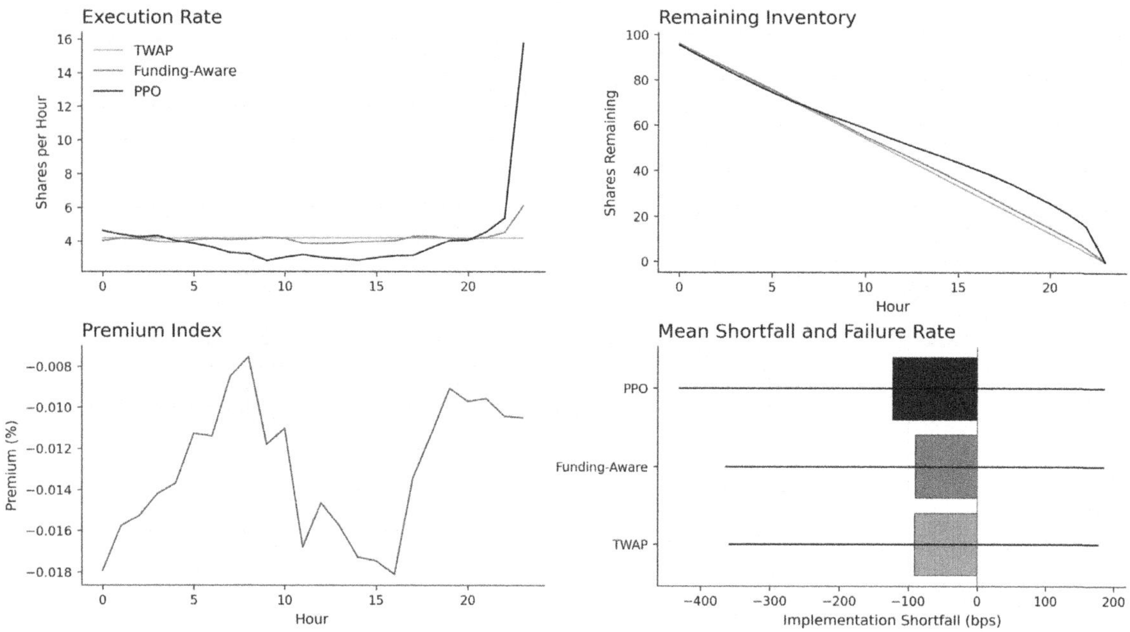

Figure 21.5: Average crypto execution comparison from the notebook evaluation set

The next application turns from liquidation to liquidity provision, where the control problem is no longer how fast to trade a parent order but how to quote continuously while managing inventory risk.

Implementation: `02_optimal_execution_ppo` runs the PPO agent against TWAP and an Almgren-Chriss-style schedule in a Gymnasium environment; `04_crypto_execution_rl` applies the same framing to crypto perpetuals with premium-index features.

21.5 Application II – Market making

A market maker provides liquidity by continuously posting bid and ask limit orders, profiting from the spread while managing inventory and adverse selection risk. The continuous adaptation and dynamic objective balancing make market-making a natural application of RL (Hambly et al., 2023).

The profit engine is **spread capture**: buy at the bid, sell at the ask, collect the difference. With balanced order flow and no price drift, the strategy would earn steady profits from uninformed flow.

Two complications, introduced in *Chapter 3*, change the picture:

- **Inventory risk** arises when buy orders fill more frequently than sell orders, or vice versa. The market maker accumulates a directional position (long or short) and becomes exposed to adverse price movements. A 1000-share long position can be erased by a 1% price drop, wiping out dozens of trades' worth of spread profit.
- **Adverse selection risk** comes from informed traders. When a counterparty with superior information about future price movements trades against the market maker, the fill is not random: it is an informed counterparty exploiting stale quotes. A market maker who does not account for this systematically loses money to informed flow.

The central challenge is adjusting quotes (both spread width and quoted sizes) to maximize spread capture while controlling inventory and adverse selection risks.

Classical benchmark – Avellaneda-Stoikov

The **Avellaneda-Stoikov model** (Avellaneda and Stoikov, 2008) gives a closed-form solution for optimal bid and ask quotes. It introduces a **reservation price**: an indifference price that deviates from the market mid-price as a function of current inventory.

When the market maker is long (positive inventory), the reservation price shifts below the mid-price, producing more aggressive sell quotes (encouraging fills that reduce inventory) and less aggressive buy quotes (discouraging accumulation). The optimal spread around this reservation price is set by market volatility and the Avellaneda-Stoikov risk-aversion parameter γ_{AS} (distinct from the MDP discount factor γ).

The model requires explicit assumptions about order arrival rates, volatility dynamics, and the relationship between inventory and optimal quotes. Real markets exhibit non-stationary order flow, varying informed-trader activity, and regime-dependent dynamics that these assumptions do not cover.

The RL approach to market making

Reinforcement learning learns a quoting strategy directly from interaction with a limit-order-book environment, without explicit assumptions on arrival rates or inventory dynamics.

State representation must capture the information relevant to quoting decisions:

- Current inventory (the most critical variable for risk management)
- Features of the limit order book: current spread, depth at multiple levels, order imbalance
- Recent price volatility and momentum
- Time-of-day effects (liquidity varies systematically through the trading day)
- Fill rates and adverse selection indicators

Actions define the quoting strategy. The agent decides how far from the mid-price to place bid and ask quotes, typically expressed as $(\delta_{\text{bid}}, \delta_{\text{ask}})$, the offsets from the mid-price. Actions may also include the size to quote at each level or whether to quote at all during unfavorable conditions.

Rewards must balance the competing objectives of profitability and risk management. The standard formulation combines realized PnL from spread capture with a quadratic penalty for holding inventory:

$$R_t = \text{PnL}_t - \lambda \cdot \text{Inventory}_t^2$$

The risk-aversion parameter λ controls how aggressively the agent prioritizes inventory neutrality over raw profits. Higher λ produces tighter inventory control at the expense of potentially missing profitable trading opportunities.

Asymmetrically dampened rewards (penalizing speculative gains more than spread-capture gains) improves learning stability by discouraging trend-following behavior that is inappropriate for market makers. In high-frequency market making, latency is a first-order concern: encoding order hold times and placement timing into the state and action spaces teaches the agent that a quote's value depends not only on its price but on how quickly it reaches the exchange (Kolm and Ritter, 2019).

Production deployment remains proprietary: market makers have strong incentives not to disclose methods. Public evidence is therefore concentrated in academic simulators and benchmark studies. Multi-agent environments such as ABIDES provide standardized settings with explicit exchange mechanics, latency, and interacting agents, making them useful laboratories for testing inventory-aware policies before any live deployment (Byrd, Hybinette, and Balch, 2020).

Learned risk management behaviors

Evaluation tracks terminal liquidated wealth (the value of holding the inventory at the closing mid-price plus accrued spread profit) and compares the learned policy against reservation-price baselines using tight, base, and wide spreads. On that evidence, the main qualitative result is not dominance but policy shape: the policy responds to inventory in the right direction, yet it also carries somewhat more residual inventory and much larger wealth dispersion than the analytical baselines.

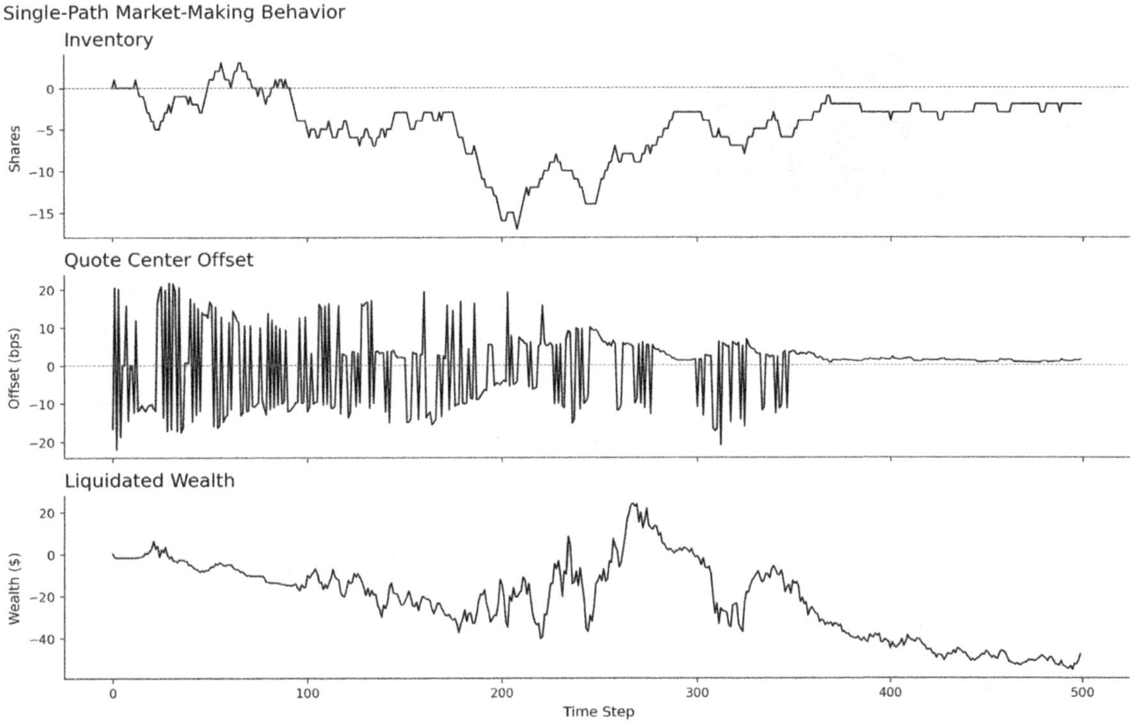

Figure 21.6: Representative market-making episode showing inventory, quote-center offset, and liquidated wealth under the learned policy

Figure 21.6 is therefore best read as a single-path diagnostic. In the representative episode, the learned policy shifts its quote center away from the current inventory, echoing the reservation-price logic of Avellaneda-Stoikov. When inventory becomes short, the quotes move upward to discourage further selling and attract buy-side replenishment; when inventory moves long, the offset turns back toward the ask side. This is the economically relevant behavior to inspect in a pedagogical simulator, not whether one episode happens to earn more than another.

Figure 21.7 aggregates the exported notebook history by inventory bucket and plots the average quote-center offset rather than the raw spread. Buckets force zero as an explicit boundary, so the short and long sides appear in separate bins rather than collapsing into a single zero-straddling bucket. The statistic is closer to the reservation-price object in the benchmark model. The average offsets are small, within roughly ± 2 bps across all inventory buckets (which now span about -24 to $+10$ contracts), and only weakly and noisily related to inventory rather than cleanly monotonic. The peak positive offset, under $+2$ bps, falls in the moderately short buckets, while the most-short and the long buckets sit near or slightly below zero. The inventory-dependent quote skew in this run is therefore weak and noisy rather than a clean monotonic relationship.

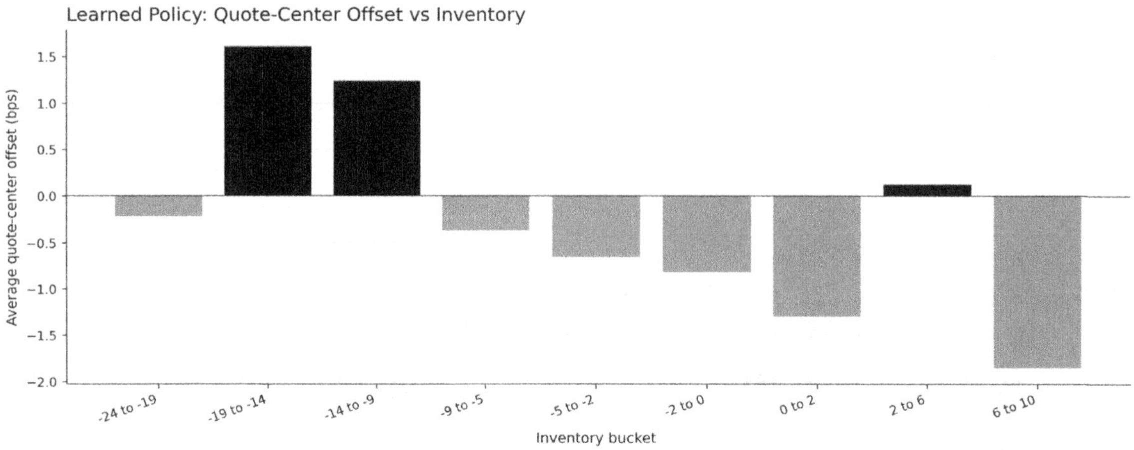

Figure 21.7: Average quote-center offset by inventory bucket in the notebook environment

The notebook's summary statistics are more cautious than the pathwise figure. After 300K training steps, the PPO policy reaches average liquidated wealth comparable to the reservation-price baselines, but with much larger dispersion and somewhat larger terminal inventory. The current implementation illustrates adaptive quote control but does not prove that the learned policy reliably dominates a well-specified analytical benchmark.

Execution and market making both design explicit reward functions: implementation shortfall and inventory-penalized spread capture, respectively. The next application, deep hedging, uses the same learned-policy machinery but shifts the objective to minimizing the tail risk of terminal hedging PnL under transaction costs.

Implementation: `03_market_making_ppo` benchmarks a PPO market-making agent against reservation-price policies with fixed spread widths.

21.6 Application III – Deep hedging for derivatives

The **Deep Hedging** framework extends the risk measures and hedging concepts from *Chapter 19* to learned policies. Instead of relying on analytical formulas derived under idealized assumptions, Deep Hedging parameterizes the hedge with a neural network and trains it on simulated or historical scenarios that include explicit market frictions. Buehler et al. (2019) framed the problem as direct optimization of a risk measure on terminal hedging PnL, folding transaction costs, discrete rebalancing, and model misspecification into the objective rather than treating them as afterthoughts.

Overcoming classical hedging limitations

Classical delta hedging holds a position equal to the option's delta ($\partial V / \partial S$). It achieves perfect replication only under three conditions: continuous rebalancing, zero transaction costs, and correct volatility specification. All three fail in practice. Transaction costs make continuous rebalancing prohibitive. Discrete rebalancing introduces accumulating hedging error. The constant-volatility assumption produces systematically misspecified Greeks. Under realistic frictions, discrete delta hedging is provably suboptimal, motivating a learned alternative.

Deep hedging, introduced by Buehler et al. (2019), reframes derivative risk management as risk minimization under frictions. The shift is from exact replication to control of residual risk: instead of matching the option payoff path by path, the goal is to find the hedge policy that minimizes a chosen risk measure of terminal PnL after transaction costs. The policy maps market state to the next hedge position, and its parameters are optimized end-to-end against a scenario generator. The setup aligns with reinforcement learning, but the objective is terminal hedging rather than a generic cumulative reward.

MDP formulation for deep hedging

The deep hedging framework maps naturally to an MDP structure, though with some distinctive features:

State representation includes:

- Current price of the underlying asset
- Time remaining until option expiration
- Current hedge position
- Volatility features, which may be model-implied, realized, or scenario-specific
- Any path-dependent characteristics of the derivative

Actions are the target hedge positions to hold until the next rebalancing time. This is a continuous action space, so the policy's output is usually a hedge ratio rather than a discrete buy or sell decision.

Rewards differ from typical RL applications. Deep hedging is episodic, and the economically relevant signal is terminal hedging PnL, so the objective is usually specified as a risk measure of the terminal distribution rather than as a dense step-by-step reward. Common choices are:

- **Variance:** Minimize $\mathrm{Var}[\mathrm{PnL}_T]$
- **Expected Shortfall (CVaR):** Minimize the expected loss in the worst $\alpha\%$ of outcomes
- **Mean-variance utility:** Minimize $\mathbb{E}[C] + \lambda \cdot \mathrm{Var}[C]$ where C is the cost

The choice of risk measure encodes the hedger's preferences. CVaR is the natural choice when downside tail risk is the quantity that drives risk management and capital allocation decisions.

The no-transaction band

A common behavior of cost-aware deep hedging policies is a **no-transaction band**. Rather than continuously rebalancing, the policy tolerates small deviations from a reference hedge and trades only when the expected reduction in risk justifies the transaction cost.

This behavior is economically intuitive: when the portfolio is already close to the desired hedge, the cost of a small adjustment can exceed its marginal benefit. The effective band can depend on current market conditions, time to expiry, and option sensitivity.

Classical approaches can derive such bands only in restricted settings. For example, Whalley-Wilmott-style asymptotics provide an analytical no-transaction region for small proportional costs, but their derivation relies on strong assumptions. Learned hedging is attractive because the same logic can be extended to richer dynamics and more complex payoffs. In the notebook, *Figure 21.8* should be read as a single-path diagnostic comparing the learned hedge with the Black-Scholes delta and a Whalley-Wilmott benchmark. It illustrates how a cost-aware hedge can move more selectively than raw delta, but by itself, it is not proof of dominance.

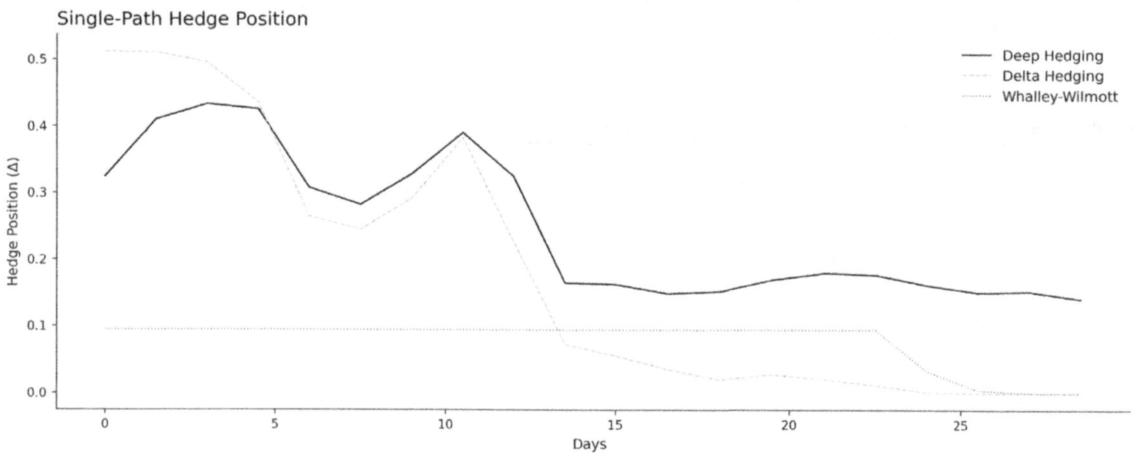

Figure 21.8: Illustrative single-path hedge trajectory for deep hedging, Black-Scholes delta, and a Whalley-Wilmott benchmark

Implementation with pfhedge

The **pfhedge** library provides a mature open-source implementation of the Deep Hedging framework in PyTorch. It includes:

- Stochastic process models for simulating underlying assets (GBM, Heston, and so on)
- Derivative instruments (European and American options, lookbacks, barriers)
- Hedging networks with customizable architectures
- Training utilities with various risk measures, including expected shortfall

Using pfhedge, practitioners can train deep hedging agents for specific derivatives, scenario models, and cost structures, then compare the resulting PnL distributions against analytical hedging rules. The accompanying notebook `05_deep_hedging_pfhedge` uses a stylized European call with proportional costs, a Heston-style stochastic-volatility scenario generator, an expected-shortfall objective, and matched self-financing accounting across all methods. This is a compact pedagogical setup, not a full reproduction of Buehler et al. (2019), whose experiments also include richer market settings and historical S&P 500 data.

Q-Learner in Black-Scholes – A value-based alternative

An alternative value-based approach, **Q-Learner in Black-Scholes** (**QLBS**), offers complementary insights into discrete-time hedging (Halperin, 2019).

QLBS applies Q-learning to the hedging problem, learning both a hedge policy and an implied option value within a mean-variance control problem.

The key innovation is to formulate hedging with a **quadratic (mean-variance) reward**, which makes the Q-function analytically tractable. Under this formulation, the Q-function satisfies a modified Bellman equation that can be solved without neural network approximation in simple cases or with function approximation for complex derivatives.

QLBS learns price as a byproduct of optimal hedging. In that formulation, option value is tied to the optimal hedging strategy under the agent's risk preferences and transaction costs rather than derived solely from frictionless replication.

Comparing the two approaches:

Aspect	Deep Hedging	QLBS
Method	Direct policy optimization	Value-based (Q-learning)
Learns	Hedging policy directly	Q-function → derives policy
Price	External input	Emergent from hedging cost
Reward	General (CVaR, variance)	Quadratic (mean-variance)
Tractability	Requires neural networks	Analytical in simple cases

Table 21.3: Comparing deep hedging with QLBS

Both approaches relax the exact replication logic of Black-Scholes, but each remains only as realistic as the scenario generator and objective behind it, a caveat that constrains how notebook evidence should be read.

Figure 21.9 compares PnL distributions for a European call hedged under proportional transaction costs. In the current notebook, discrete delta hedging is the strongest method for dispersion and 5% CVaR, with deep hedging competitive but not dominant.

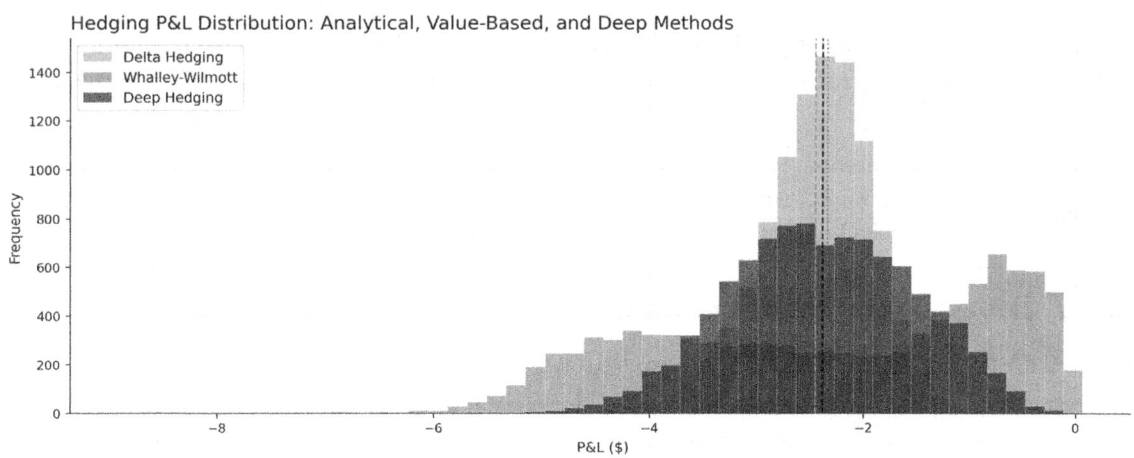

Figure 21.9: Terminal PnL distribution for deep hedging, Whalley-Wilmott, and discrete delta hedging under the notebook's transaction-cost assumptions

Figure 21.10 extends the comparison to the Whalley-Wilmott analytical benchmark and the tabular Q-learning baseline. Under these notebook assumptions, deep hedging improves on the value-based tabular baseline and sits between delta hedging and Whalley-Wilmott on the reported risk metrics. The lesson is not that deep hedging always produces the lowest dispersion or CVaR, but that fair comparison requires matched accounting, a friction-aware benchmark set, and an objective aligned with the reported statistics.

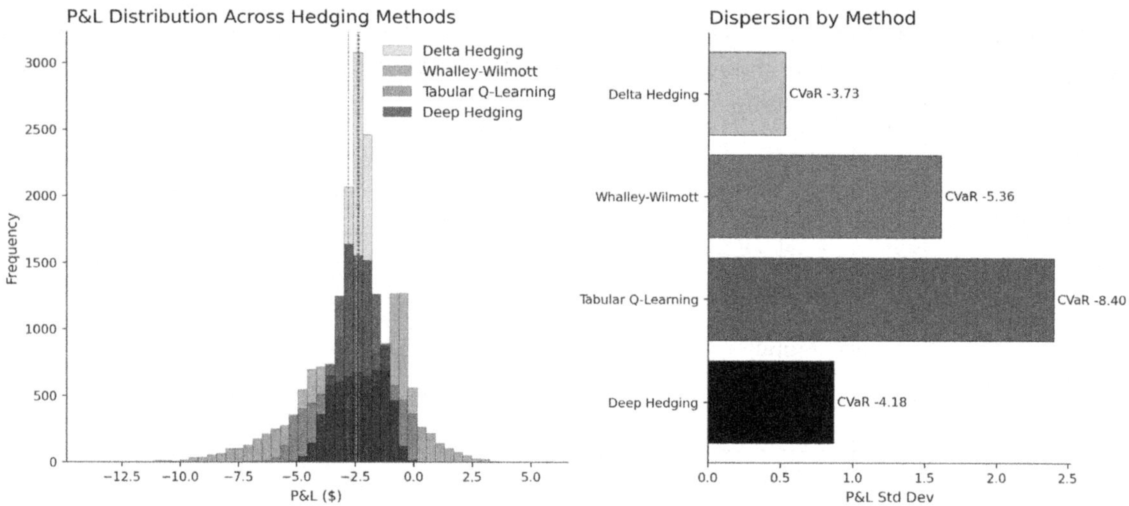

Figure 21.10: Deep hedging, QLBS-style tabular hedging, Whalley-Wilmott, and delta hedging under identical notebook assumptions

Buehler et al. (2019) show that deep hedging becomes most informative when the hedge problem departs materially from the Black-Scholes idealization: richer dynamics, stronger frictions, additional hedge instruments, or objectives that target tail risk rather than variance alone. A compact teaching notebook can illustrate the workflow but should not be treated as a competitive benchmark study.

The next section turns from designed reward functions, such as implementation shortfall, inventory control, and tail-risk hedging, to the inverse problem of inferring the reward from observed expert behavior.

> **Implementation:** See `05_deep_hedging_pfhedge` for a compact implementation using `pfhedge`, training a hedging network under an expected-shortfall objective and comparing it with delta hedging, Whalley-Wilmott, and a tabular Q-learning baseline.

21.7 Inverse reinforcement learning – Learning from observed behavior

The preceding applications (optimal execution, market making, and deep hedging) share a common assumption: the reward function is known in advance. Implementation shortfall, inventory-penalized spread capture, and CVaR-adjusted hedging PnL are explicit objectives that practitioners design from domain knowledge. The next problem is learning the reward function itself from observed expert behavior.

Inverse Reinforcement Learning (**IRL**) inverts the standard RL problem: given observed behavior, infer the reward function that rationalizes it (Ziebart et al., 2008). It supports strategy identification, expert imitation, and surveillance-oriented anomaly analysis. Relative to direct policy imitation, reward inference can offer a more portable representation of behavior, but only insofar as the assumptions about the reward model and environment hold.

Consider an execution algorithm that trades aggressively in some conditions, slows during volatility spikes, and adjusts by time of day. The actions are visible; the objective is hidden. IRL estimates a reward specification that best explains the observed behavior under the chosen model class (Arora and Doshi, 2021). Unlike direct action imitation, that representation can transfer to new environments or diagnostics, though the transfer is never guaranteed.

The IRL framework

IRL begins with expert demonstrations: a dataset of state-action trajectories collected from an expert policy π^*. The goal is to find a reward function $R(s, a)$under which the demonstrated behavior is optimal.

Maximum Entropy IRL (Ziebart et al., 2008) addresses the ill-posed nature of this inference by finding the reward function that makes the demonstrations most likely while remaining maximally non-committal about behavior not observed. This corresponds to maximum likelihood estimation, where the policy distribution takes the form:

$$P(\tau \mid R) \propto \exp\left(\sum_t R\,(s_t, a_t)\right)$$

The optimization finds reward weights that maximize the likelihood of the observed trajectories. Recent theoretical advances have strengthened the foundations of MaxEnt IRL, establishing connections to f-divergence minimization and improving both sample efficiency and computational tractability (Snoswell et al., 2020).

Adversarial approaches scale IRL to high-dimensional settings. **Generative Adversarial Imitation Learning** (**GAIL**) (Ho and Ermon, 2016) frames imitation as a game between a generator (the learning policy) and a discriminator (that distinguishes expert from generated trajectories). The generator learns to fool the discriminator, implicitly recovering the expert's objective. **Adversarial IRL** (**AIRL**) extends this by explicitly recovering a transferable reward function rather than merely matching behavior.

Behavior cloning versus reward inference

A simpler alternative to IRL is **behavior cloning**: treat demonstration data as supervised learning, mapping states directly to actions. The approach is computationally straightforward: train a neural network to predict expert actions from states.

Behavior cloning has three limitations:

- **Distribution shift** causes compounding errors: when the cloned policy makes a small mistake, it enters states the expert never visited, and errors cascade.

- **No reward recovery** limits generalization: behavior cloning copies actions, not objectives, so changes in the environment (for example, new transaction costs) require entirely new demonstrations. IRL recovers the underlying objective, enabling retraining under new conditions.
- **Suboptimal experts** confound imitation: behavior cloning faithfully reproduces mistakes, whereas IRL methods like T-REX learn from ranked demonstrations and can recover reward functions that exceed those of any individual demonstrator (Arora and Doshi, 2021).

Financial applications

IRL has been applied across several financial domains:

- **Strategy identification from order flow** is among the earliest financial IRL applications. Yang et al. (2015) applied Gaussian Process IRL to high-frequency trading data, clustering algorithms by their inferred objective functions. The approach identified distinct strategy types (momentum, mean-reversion, inventory management) from order flow alone, without access to traders' actual strategies.
- **Goal-based wealth management** is a proposed use case for preference inference. The G-Learner and GIRL frameworks (Dixon and Halperin, 2020) formulate wealth management in a way that can infer client preferences from observed choices over time, with the goal of adapting recommendations to revealed rather than purely stated preferences.
- **Imitation learning for market making** bridges the gap between IRL and direct policy learning. FlowHFT (Li et al., 2025) uses flow matching to learn market-making policies from historical data without explicit reward specification, a continuous-time imitation approach that models trajectory distributions more directly than pointwise action cloning.

Practical considerations

IRL success depends on three factors: demonstration quality (noisy or irrational experts produce unreliable rewards), reward parameterization (the feature basis constrains what objectives can be expressed), and computational cost (MaxEnt IRL solves a full RL problem in its inner loop, making it expensive for large state spaces). In practice, this means linear reward models can miss the nonlinear preferences that matter in microstructure settings, so richer function classes or stronger structural assumptions may be necessary (Arora and Doshi, 2021). Despite these constraints, IRL complements standard RL: one infers what to optimize, the other optimizes it.

Figures 21.11 and *21.12* illustrate an IRL workflow using simplified TWAP demonstrations. *Figure 21.11* shows the reward weights inferred by the notebook's linear MaxEnt IRL setup; read them qualitatively as a decomposition of uniform-rate execution incentives, not as a uniquely identified structural reward.

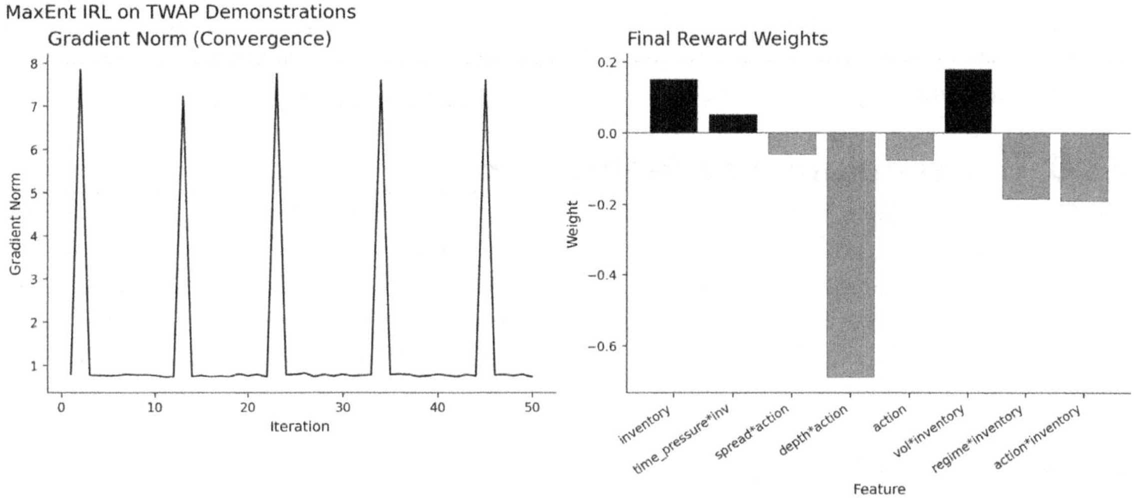

Figure 21.11: Reward weights inferred by the notebook's linear MaxEnt IRL example

Figure 21.12 compares the action distribution generated by the IRL-derived policy against the expert demonstrations it learned from. It is a behavioral sanity check, not proof that the latent objective has been recovered. The figure contrasts only the expert (the matching target) against the IRL-derived policy; behavior cloning is discussed above but not visualized because its absolute action distribution is not on a directly comparable scale.

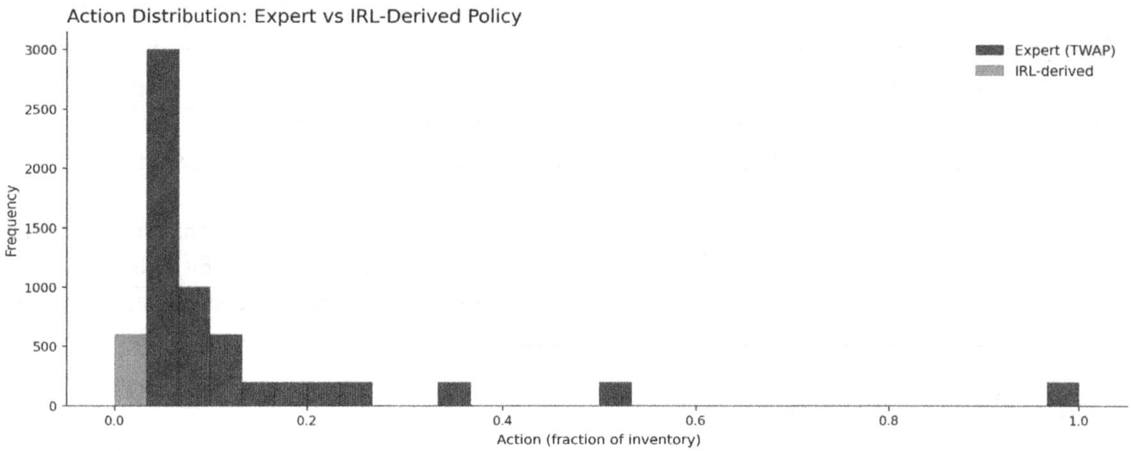

Figure 21.12: Action distributions from the expert and the IRL-derived policy

Implementation: `inverse_reinforcement_learning` walks through behavior cloning and linear MaxEnt IRL on execution data, using TWAP demonstrations to show how inferred reward features can be interpreted.

Whether the reward is designed (*Section 21.4–21.6*) or inferred (*Section 21.7*), the practical barrier is the same: policies trained in simulation must hold up in live markets. The next section examines the simulation-to-reality gap between teaching exercises and deployable systems.

21.8 The simulation-to-reality gap

Reinforcement learning has theoretical promise and applied potential in finance, but the transition from research prototype to live trading performance remains the main barrier to wider adoption. The "sim-to-real gap," the repeated failure of strategies that perform well in simulation once exposed to live markets, remains one of the main obstacles (Hambly et al., 2023). Millea (2021) adds the related point that many published trading results are hard to compare because datasets, cost models, and execution assumptions are inconsistent.

Sources of failure

Four causes drive the gap between simulation and reality:

- **Non-stationarity** is the most basic challenge. The statistical properties of asset returns (volatility, correlation, liquidity) change over time in response to macroeconomic events, policy changes, and shifts in market structure. These regime shifts violate the MDP assumption of a stationary transition function. A policy learned in one regime may be inappropriate in the next.
- **Overfitting and spurious correlation** exploit the low signal-to-noise ratio of financial data. The vast parameter space of deep neural networks makes it easy for an RL agent to overfit specific training patterns, a complex form of data snooping with no out-of-sample predictive power.
- **Market impact and reflexivity** break the link between backtests and reality. A simple backtest assumes the agent is a passive observer of historical prices. In reality, the agent's trades move prices. Large orders consume liquidity and cause slippage. Other market participants observe and react to the agent's activity. A backtest that ignores this feedback loop overestimates performance.
- **Latency and execution frictions** add another layer of reality that simulations often miss. Real-world trading systems face delays in receiving market data and in having orders acknowledged by exchanges. An agent trained assuming zero latency makes decisions based on stale information and receives fills at worse-than-expected prices.

High-fidelity simulation

Bridging the sim-to-real gap begins with more realistic training environments. Instead of simple price replay, serious RL research for trading requires richer market simulators. The chapter notebooks make this point directly: execution policy character depends on whether the action space, schedule penalty, and cost terms together encode the intended trade-off; deep hedging becomes interpretable only when the objective, accounting convention, and benchmark set are aligned.

Multi-agent simulators like ABIDES (introduced in *Section 21.4*) are a leading approach. Training RL agents within such environments (where other agents react to the learner's orders by widening spreads, piling into momentum, or pulling liquidity) lets the agent learn under reflexive market impact rather than meeting it for the first time in live trading.

For hedging, the same lesson applies: deep hedging becomes more informative when training environments incorporate realistic frictions, discrete rebalancing, and richer state information rather than frictionless toy dynamics (Buehler et al., 2019; Zheng, He, and Yang, 2023).

Domain randomization complements simulator fidelity by varying environment parameters during training: impact coefficients, latency distributions, spread dynamics, and fee schedules across episodes. Instead of calibrating a single "correct" environment, domain randomization trains the agent across a distribution of plausible market conditions. Fast, vectorized simulators make this practical by enabling many parallel rollouts with diverse parameter settings.

Offline reinforcement learning

Offline RL learns effective policies from static historical datasets without live interaction, avoiding the risks and costs of "trial-and-error" in real markets. Financial institutions possess massive archives of tick-by-tick data that can serve as training datasets.

The central challenge is **distributional shift:** the historical data were collected by past trading strategies that may differ from the optimal policy the agent seeks to learn. Practical offline RL methods, therefore, either penalize out-of-distribution actions or constrain learning toward behavior well supported by the data, reducing the risk of exploiting states and actions never observed historically.

Decision Transformers reframe offline RL as sequence modeling (Chen et al., 2021). A trajectory of return-to-go, state, and action triples can be modeled autoregressively, and conditioning on a target return-to-go yields actions associated with that return level in the training data. In finance, Decision Transformers reuse mature sequence-modeling infrastructure on large historical archives, though they still inherit the usual dependence on data coverage and objective specification.

RL-specific backtesting pitfalls

Beyond the general challenges of financial backtesting (look-ahead bias, survivorship bias, transaction costs), RL introduces its own category of pitfalls:

- **State information leakage:** future-looking features enter the state representation. Including the day's closing price in the state for an intraday agent is the classic example: the closing price is unavailable during the day, but a backtest that includes it shows unrealistic performance.
- **Reward hacking:** the agent maximizes the coded reward in ways that violate the objective's spirit. An agent with a penalty for negative returns might learn to avoid trading entirely, earning zero returns and zero penalties, rather than seeking positive returns with some volatility.
- **Ignoring market impact:** training without realistic impact modeling lets the agent place arbitrarily large orders because it never experiences the price moving against it. Live deployment with real impact fails.
- **Order fill assumptions:** assuming limit orders fill instantly and completely at the quoted price ignores queue priority, partial fills, and order-book dynamics and overstates strategy performance.

Deployment checklist

Moving an RL agent from simulation to live trading proceeds in four phases:

1. **Pre-flight validation:** Out-of-sample testing across distinct market regimes, validation in a simulator with realistic impact, offline policy evaluation (OPE) using methods such as importance weighting or doubly robust estimation, and independent model review before any real-capital deployment.
2. **Staged deployment:** Paper trading first, then limited-capital deployment with strict position and loss limits. Define quantitative go/no-go criteria before scaling.
3. **Real-time controls:** Hard-coded risk limits that cannot be overridden by the agent, a manual kill switch accessible to the trading desk, continuous monitoring of execution latency and realized slippage versus simulation assumptions, and human oversight with authority to halt the agent.
4. **Ongoing governance:** Scheduled retraining at a cadence matched to strategy horizon and regime-shift frequency, performance decay monitoring with automatic alerts, and complete model versioning for regulatory audit.

> **Implementation:** See `backtest_with_impact` for a concrete example of how market-impact assumptions erode strategy performance.

Figure 21.13 isolates the one variable that governs market impact: order size relative to available liquidity. It applies the same long-only momentum strategy and the same five-million-dollar order to real US equities from 2010 to 2016, using split- and dividend-adjusted prices, across stocks spanning five orders of magnitude in daily volume. The square-root impact model follows the Almgren-Chriss form, scaling with the participation rate (the order divided by average daily volume), so the same order is a sliver of a mega-cap's volume and a large multiple of a micro-cap's. Stocks are chosen by liquidity measured over a formation window before the test, and the demonstration is scoped to names where the momentum signal is profitable before costs, so the figure shows what impact it has on a strategy that works on paper; the names are representative of their liquidity tiers rather than selected on outcome. The left panel plots net return against order participation under no, low, medium, and high impact; the right panel plots the high-impact erosion, the return given up relative to the no-impact baseline.

The contrast is the lesson. For the mega-cap, the order is roughly 1.5% of daily volume, and the strategy stays clearly profitable even under the strongest impact assumption. For the micro-cap, the same order is many times daily volume, and the strongest assumption turns a large paper gain into a near-total loss. Erosion grows monotonically as the order consumes more of daily volume, tracing the square-root law, and below a liquidity threshold a profitable strategy becomes a reliable loser: across a sample of profitable-on-paper names, the strong impact assumption flips essentially every thin-stock winner (those whose orders exceed a day's volume) into a loser, while most liquid-stock winners survive. This is the documented reason small-cap alpha resists scaling, and the motivation for execution that adapts to the liquidity actually available (*Section 21.4*). The figure is a diagnostic of how impact assumptions interact with liquidity, not a calibrated estimate of deployable size or a substitute for formal transaction-cost analysis.

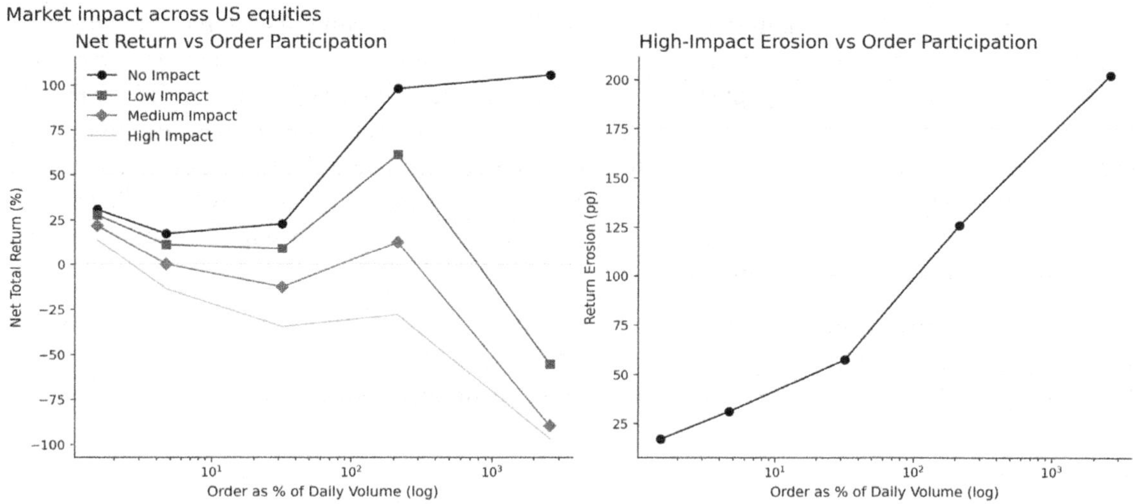

Figure 21.13: The same order across the liquidity spectrum. Left: net return versus order participation under progressively stronger square-root impact. Right: high-impact return erosion rising with participation

Explainability and regulation

Deep RL's opacity creates regulatory and risk management challenges. In Europe, MiFID II's algorithmic-trading provisions in Articles 17 and 48 directly require resilient systems, testing, controls, and monitoring for automated trading infrastructure. The EU AI Act introduces a broader governance framework for AI systems, but algorithmic trading is not singled out as a separate high-risk category in Annex III. Partial transparency is achievable through SHAP analysis of state-action mappings, surrogate decision trees that approximate the learned policy with interpretable rules, and counterfactual trajectory analysis. *Chapter 24* covers explainability for autonomous agents in depth.

21.9 Summary

Reinforcement learning is most persuasive in finance when the action itself is the object of optimization. Execution, market making, and hedging fit that requirement more cleanly than generic alpha discovery because the state, action, and reward can be tied to observable economic objectives: implementation shortfall, inventory control, or risk-sensitive hedging error. The chapter's notebooks make that point unevenly. The execution examples produce paced liquidation policies that are economically interpretable but back-loaded relative to a uniform schedule. The market-making notebook shows inventory-aware quote control without establishing superiority of the learned policy over reservation-price baselines. The deep-hedging notebook is a workflow example: with matched accounting and friction-aware benchmarks, it places learned hedging between delta and Whalley-Wilmott on the reported risk metrics rather than asserting universal outperformance. Inverse reinforcement learning extends the framework by asking what objective is implicit in observed behavior, but it inherits the same dependence on modeling assumptions and data quality.

The practical limit is the simulation-to-reality gap. Financial environments are partially observed, non-stationary, and reflexive, so simulated success does not automatically carry over to live trading. Realistic simulators, offline RL, explicit impact modeling, and stronger governance narrow the gap but do not eliminate it. The lesson is methodological: benchmark selection, accounting consistency, export provenance, and figure design determine whether an RL result is illustrative or defensible. RL is structurally well-matched to execution, market making, and hedging (domains with explicit reward signals and a controllable action surface), but the same methodological discipline applies whether the agent's claims are modest or ambitious.

The next chapter turns from sequential control to grounded language systems. *Chapter 22* shows how retrieval-augmented generation constrains large language models with verifiable evidence, enabling them to support financial research without relying on unsupported synthesis.

22

RAG for Financial Research

Large language models (LLMs) can synthesize complex financial documents, but they can also fabricate details with persuasive fluency. In finance, that failure mode is not a nuisance; it is a deployment blocker. **Retrieval-augmented generation** (**RAG**) addresses the problem by grounding each answer in a controlled evidence base whose contents, timestamps, and citations can be inspected directly.

This chapter develops a financial RAG system as an engineering stack rather than a prompt trick. After completing this chapter, you will be able to:

- Explain why hallucination makes ungrounded LLM use unacceptable in finance and why retrieval-augmented generation is the core architectural response.
- Design a financial RAG pipeline from document ingestion through retrieval and grounded generation, including structure-aware parsing, chunking, metadata, embeddings, and citation support.
- Compare generic and domain-specific embedding models and evaluate retrieval quality on a target corpus using practical retrieval metrics and latency trade-offs.
- Build a retrieval stack that combines semantic search, lexical search, metadata filtering, and re-ranking to improve precision and recall on financial documents.
- Use constraint-based prompting, citation checks, and tool-verified computation to make generated answers more faithful, auditable, and numerically reliable.
- Diagnose RAG failures by separating retrieval, context, synthesis, computation, and abstention errors, and apply targeted evaluation methods to improve each component.
- Distinguish when to use RAG versus fine-tuning for financial applications, and explain how RAG functions as one tool within broader agentic workflows.

Sections 22.1-22.2 frame the problem and the core architectural solution. *Sections 22.3-22.6* build the stack from document ingestion through prompting and tool-verified computation. *Section 22.7* introduces the evaluation framework for systematically debugging RAG. *Section 22.8* compares practical applications and the strategic boundary between RAG and fine-tuning, while *Section 22.9* shows how RAG becomes one tool inside broader agent workflows.

22.1 From feature extraction to generation

Chapter 10 built a toolkit for extracting structured features from financial text—sentiment scores, risk categories, feature vectors—using domain-adapted transformers such as FinBERT (Huang, Wang, and Yang, 2020) and earlier lexicon-based approaches, such as the Loughran-McDonald dictionary (Loughran and McDonald, 2011). These outputs feed directly into trading signals and risk models, but classification has a ceiling.

A fine-tuned FinBERT model can tell you *if* a sentence in a 10-K filing is negative, but it cannot explain *why*. It cannot synthesize information from disparate sections, answer multi-hop questions, or generate a narrative summary. The practitioner's interaction is limited to a fixed taxonomy. But a human analyst's job is to ask questions like: *"What drove the revenue increase in the European segment, and what risks were cited for those operations?"* A discriminative classifier cannot answer this.

Modern Large Language Models shift the practitioner's goal from "extract a feature" to "ask a complex question" (Saha et al., 2025). Built on the Transformer architecture (Vaswani et al., 2017) and refined through instruction tuning, LLMs are designed for *generation*: their primary output is human-readable content—summaries, analyses, answers—not numeric features.

These capabilities—multi-step synthesis, in-context learning, and instruction following—improve sharply with scale and instruction tuning (Wei et al., 2023). In finance, LLMs can generalize from a few prompt examples to perform complex sentiment analysis without domain-specific fine-tuning (Xie et al., 2024; Lopez-Lira and Tang, 2025). The model effectively learns a new task from context, enabling analytical work previously exclusive to human experts: summarizing Management's Discussion and Analysis (MD&A) sections, drafting investment theses, or identifying risk factors in dense regulatory filings.

This power comes with an inherent flaw: **hallucination.** LLMs produce outputs that are plausible, confident, and grammatically correct but factually wrong or entirely fabricated (Lopez-Lira, Tang, and Zhu, 2025). Hallucination is an intrinsic property of a probabilistic model trained to predict the next most likely token, not a bug to be patched.

In finance, this risk is unacceptable. A single hallucinated fact, such as an invented revenue figure, a fabricated regulatory requirement, or a misattributed CEO quote, can lead to flawed investment decisions, compliance breaches, or legal liability. Recent finance-specific research has documented adjacent failure modes that reinforce the same operational lesson: LLMs can exhibit systematic bias in investment analysis and can appear more reliable than they are when memorization contaminates forecasting tasks (Lee et al., 2025; Lopez-Lira, Tang, and Zhu, 2025). The exact failure pattern depends on the task and evaluation protocol, but the implication is stable. Fluent output is not self-verifying, and even occasional unsupported claims are unacceptable in high-stakes settings.

Post-hoc fact-checking does not scale and fails to address the root cause: the model's generation process is opaque, so correcting one output leaves the underlying flawed logic intact. The solution must be *architectural*—a framework that constrains the LLM to generate only over trusted, verifiable information. This is the core principle behind Retrieval-Augmented Generation.

22.2 Grounding LLMs with retrieval-augmented generation

Retrieval-Augmented Generation (RAG), first formalized by Lewis et al. (2020), addresses hallucination at the architectural level. Instead of trusting the model's parametric knowledge (information encoded in its weights during pre-training), RAG constrains the LLM to rely on *non-parametric* knowledge—an external, curated knowledge base that the system controls and can verify. Because generation draws on retrieved context, every claim can, in principle, be linked back to a specific source document, page, or passage. Achieving reliable provenance in practice requires the citation-verification techniques discussed in *Section 22.6*.

The index-retrieve-generate pipeline

A RAG system combines an information retrieval system with a large language model in three stages:

1. **Index (Offline):** This is the preparatory stage where the knowledge base is created. The system ingests and processes a corpus of trusted documents, for example, SEC filings, earnings call transcripts, research reports, or regulatory guidelines, and converts it into a searchable format. Each document is parsed and split into smaller, manageable chunks of text. Each chunk is then passed through an **embedding model**, which converts the text into a dense numerical vector representation. These vectors, along with their corresponding text chunks and metadata (source file, page number, section header), are stored in a **vector database** optimized for similarity search.
2. **Retrieve (Online):** When a user submits a query, the retrieval stage is initiated. The user's natural-language question is converted into a vector embedding using the same model used during indexing. The vector database is then queried to find the k text chunks whose vectors are most semantically similar to the query vector, typically measured by cosine similarity. These top-k chunks constitute the retrieved context—the set of source documents that the system believes are most relevant to answering the question.
3. **Generate (Online):** In the final stage, the retrieved text chunks are combined with the original query into a single, comprehensive prompt. This augmented prompt is sent to an LLM with a crucial instruction: **synthesize an answer based only on the provided context**. This constraint is the architectural mechanism that enforces grounding. The LLM is explicitly told not to rely on its internal knowledge but to act as a synthesis engine over the supplied evidence. The output is a generated answer, ideally accompanied by citations pointing back to the source chunks that support each claim.

Figure 22.1 illustrates this three-stage architecture, showing how documents flow through parsing, embedding, and storage during the offline phase, and how queries trigger retrieval and LLM-powered synthesis during the online phase.

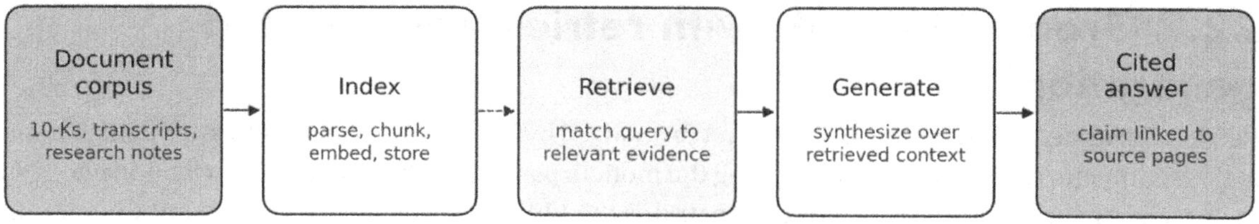

Figure 22.1: RAG indexes documents offline, retrieves evidence online, and generates only over retrieved context

The orchestration layer

Frameworks such as **LlamaIndex** (optimized for RAG pipelines: ingestion, indexing, retrieval) and **LangChain** (a general-purpose LLM application framework with modular chain and agent patterns) abstract the plumbing that connects parsers, embedding models, vector databases, and LLMs. Both are open-source and evolving rapidly; the choice depends on whether the workflow is RAG-centric (LlamaIndex) or part of a broader agent architecture (LangChain). Newer entrants like **Haystack** offer alternatives.

The simplicity of this paradigm is both its strength and its limitation. A naive implementation that uses fixed-size chunks, a generic embedding model, and simple vector search fails on the complex, jargon-filled documents common in finance. Production systems require advanced techniques at every stage: structure-aware parsing, domain-specific embeddings, hybrid retrieval, re-ranking, and constraint-based prompting. The remaining sections build this stack from the bottom up.

22.3 Intelligent document ingestion

The performance of any RAG system is capped by the quality of its knowledge base, and that quality begins with document ingestion. Financial documents—SEC 10-K and 10-Q filings (whose structure is introduced in *Chapter 4*), earnings call transcripts, prospectuses, and regulatory guidelines—are long and dense, containing a heterogeneous mix of prose, tables, embedded images, and hierarchical structures. Naive ingestion destroys this structure and degrades retrieval.

The failure of naïve chunking

The simplest ingestion method is fixed-size chunking: splitting a document into blocks of 500 or 1,000 characters with some overlap. This approach is computationally cheap but semantically destructive. Financial tables—a critical source of quantitative data—are arbitrarily fragmented, with column headers separated from their values. Section headers like "Item 7. Management's Discussion and Analysis" are divorced from the paragraphs they introduce. Risk factor bullet points are split across chunks, losing their logical grouping.

The result is what practitioners call "context confusion." When the retrieval system fetches these fragmented chunks and passes them to the LLM, the model may conflate information from different fiscal years, misattribute statements to the wrong sections, or fail to synthesize a coherent answer because the necessary context is scattered across unrelated chunks. Naive chunking violates the very premise of RAG: that retrieved context provides a reliable grounding for generation.

Chunk size – The fundamental trade-off

Chunk size is among the most consequential hyperparameters in RAG system design, yet it receives comparatively little attention.

Small chunks of about 200–300 tokens have higher retrieval precision—the system can pinpoint the exact relevant sentence or paragraph. But small chunks lack context. A sentence stating "Revenue grew 15%" is meaningless without knowing which segment, which period, and whether this was organic or acquisition-driven. Small chunks force the retrieval system to fetch many pieces and hope the LLM can reassemble them correctly.

Large chunks of 1,000–2,000 tokens, however, have more self-contained context per chunk, reducing the need for cross-chunk synthesis. But larger chunks dilute relevance—if only one paragraph in a 1,500-token chunk is relevant, the embedding represents an average of relevant and irrelevant content, potentially harming retrieval accuracy. Large chunks also consume more of the LLM's context window.

A common starting point is 400–600 tokens for financial documents, with 50–100-token overlap, but these are defaults, not universal answers. The optimal size depends on the document types, query patterns, and the LLM's context budget. Treat chunk size as a hyperparameter: evaluate retrieval recall across a grid of sizes (256, 512, 768, 1024) on an evaluation set before committing. *Figure 22.2* compares fixed-size, semantic, and structure-aware chunking strategies, illustrating the trade-off between speed and quality.

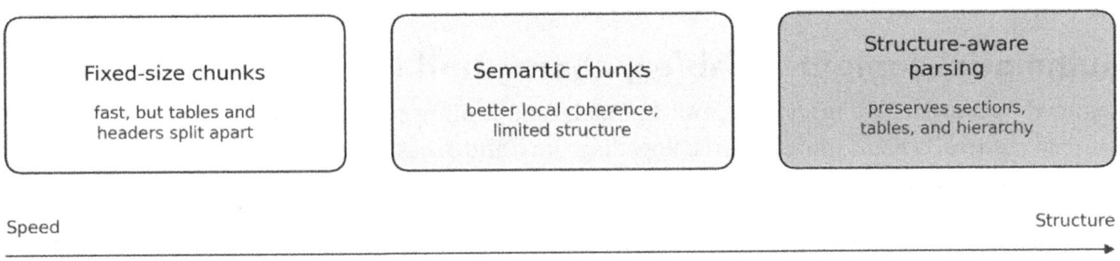

Figure 22.2: Fixed-size chunks are cheapest, while structure-aware parsing preserves the most usable context

A practical resolution is **Parent Document Retrieval** ("small-to-big"): retrieve using small, precise chunks but pass the larger parent section to the LLM. Each paragraph gets its own embedding for retrieval precision, but when a paragraph matches, the system returns the full subsection. This captures precise matching with rich context at the cost of maintaining a chunk-to-parent mapping during ingestion.

Structure-aware parsing

The solution to naive chunking is **structure-aware parsing:** tools that understand a document's semantic layout. Rather than treating a PDF as a character stream, these tools identify and preserve section boundaries, paragraph groupings, table layouts, and list hierarchies.

LlamaParse, developed by the creators of LlamaIndex, is a representative example. It uses a combination of vision models and LLMs to intelligently reconstruct a document's logical structure from its visual rendering. Tables are extracted not as fragmented text but as structured Markdown or JSON, preserving rows, columns, and headers. Charts can be processed by a vision model to generate textual summaries of their content. Hierarchical relationships between sections and subsections are preserved, enabling retrieval systems to recognize that a paragraph discussing "European revenue" belongs within the broader context of "Geographic Segment Analysis."

Docling (created by IBM) provides an open-source alternative with a hybrid parser that combines layout detection, table recognition, and text extraction. **Marker** focuses on high-fidelity PDF-to-Markdown conversion. The tooling landscape evolves rapidly; by the time of publication, newer options may have emerged. The stable principle is structure preservation—evaluate tools on that criterion rather than brand loyalty.

These tools are not infallible. Scanned PDFs require **optical character recognition** (**OCR**) as a preprocessing step, which can introduce transcription errors. Filings with non-standard layouts—nested tables, multi-column sections, footnotes spanning page breaks—can confuse even vision-based parsers. Tables rendered as images rather than HTML are particularly problematic: the parser must detect (via OCR) and reconstruct the table structure, a pipeline in which errors compound. Validate parser output on representative documents before trusting it at scale. In financial RAG, ingestion errors are effectively irreversible downstream: once tables, headings, or temporal markers are lost, later retrieval and generation stages cannot reliably reconstruct them.

Multimodal content – Tables, charts, and images

Financial documents are inherently multi-modal. A 10-K filing contains not just prose but tables of financial metrics, organizational charts, flow diagrams, and occasionally embedded images. Ignoring this content sacrifices significant information density.

Tables are particularly critical—they often contain the quantitative facts analysts most frequently query. Structure-aware parsers convert tables into Markdown or JSON while preserving row-column relationships. The challenge is that tables in PDFs are often visually rendered without an underlying structure, requiring vision models to reconstruct the logical layout.

Charts and figures may contain information absent from the surrounding text—for example, a revenue-by-segment bar chart may be the only place where segment growth rates appear. Vision-language models, both closed and open-weight, generate textual descriptions that are indexed alongside prose. The cost is non-trivial: each image requires a vision-model API call during ingestion, adding latency and expense. A practical heuristic: always process tables (high information density, structured output); process figures selectively when they contain quantitative data not duplicated in the text.

An emerging alternative bypasses text extraction entirely: **vision-first retrieval** models like ColPali (Faysse et al., 2025) index document pages as images and retrieve them using vision-language embeddings. This sidesteps parsing errors but sacrifices structured metadata such as section hierarchy, statement type, or fiscal periods that financial RAG depends on for filtered retrieval and verifiable citations. Text-extraction pipelines remain the production default; vision-first approaches are worth monitoring as models mature.

Metadata – The key to verifiable citations

Beyond content parsing, the ingestion stage must tag each chunk with rich **metadata**. At minimum: source document name, page number, and section header (for example, "Item 1A. Risk Factors"). For financial documents, **temporal metadata is critical**: fiscal year, fiscal quarter, filing date, and period end date. A query about "Apple's 2023 risk factors" must not retrieve 2022 disclosures, and a question about "most recent guidance" must prefer the latest filing.

Without explicit temporal tagging, the retrieval system cannot distinguish between current and stale information—a particularly dangerous failure mode in finance where outdated data can be worse than no data at all. Beyond fiscal year and quarter, ingestion should enforce **point-in-time integrity** by tracking the filing publication date, the fiscal period referenced, and the ingestion timestamp. These fields are not interchangeable: a 2024 fiscal-period disclosure may only become public in 2025. Historical queries and backtests must filter by publication availability, not period labels alone, to prevent information leakage.

Each indexed unit should also include sufficient provenance to support later citation checks, namely its structural role (prose, table cell, footnote, figure caption) and extraction method. Without this modality-aware metadata, citation formatting may appear precise yet still fail to achieve claim-evidence alignment.

This metadata serves two purposes:

1. It enables filtered retrieval: a user asking about "Apple's 2023 risk factors" can have the system automatically restrict search to chunks tagged with the correct company and fiscal year, improving precision.
2. It enables verifiable citations: when the LLM generates an answer, it can include page and section references that let analysts navigate directly to the source and verify the information—closing the trust loop essential for any high-stakes financial application.

Metadata tagging is not optional for production-grade financial RAG. The quality of ingestion determines the semantic units available for embedding, and embeddings, which we discuss next, determine what retrieval can find.

Implementation: `01_sec_filing_pipeline.py` walks the end-to-end ingestion pipeline for five SP100 issuers: it resolves tickers via `edgartools`, lists the ten target 10-K filings in roughly 2.6 seconds, with filing date and accession number on every record, and then runs a side-by-side parser comparison that quantifies the structure-aware lift. Table preservation roughly doubles (0.45 → 0.85), layout fidelity nearly doubles (0.40 → 0.88), and parse latency increases by about 70%—the cost-versus-fidelity envelope this section frames qualitatively.

The notebook also reports a metadata-integrity audit: filing date and ingestion timestamp populate at 100% on the `edgartools` listing object, while `fiscal_year_end` is absent and must be enriched from the document body downstream, illustrating the point-in-time-integrity discipline emphasized above.

22.4 Domain-specific embeddings

The retrieval stage hinges on embedding models—neural networks that convert text into dense vector representations where semantic similarity corresponds to geometric proximity. A query about "interest rate sensitivity" should map to a vector near passages discussing "duration risk" or "yield curve exposure," even if those exact words don't appear. But this understanding is learned from training data, and for finance, that creates a gap.

General-purpose embedding models like OpenAI's `text-embedding-3-small` (as of early 2026) or open-source sentence-transformer alternatives (Reimers and Gurevych, 2019) perform well on broad retrieval tasks but are not fluent in the specialized vocabulary, acronyms, and semantic relationships of finance. The term "alpha" means something entirely different in a portfolio context than in general language. Ticker symbols like "AAPL" or "NVDA" may have weak or noisy representations. Nuanced concepts—"forward P/E," "covenant compliance," "buyback yield"—are unlikely to be well captured by models trained predominantly on Wikipedia and Reddit.

The problem runs deeper than vocabulary. A passage stating "the Fed raised rates by 75 basis points" is semantically connected to "mortgage affordability pressure" and "duration losses in bond portfolios"—but only if the model has learned these causal chains from financial data.

The FinMTEB benchmark

The **Finance Massive Text Embedding Benchmark** (**FinMTEB**) provides quantitative evidence of this gap (Tang and Yang, 2025). Modeled on the general-purpose **Massive Text Embedding Benchmark** (**MTEB**) that has become the standard for embedding evaluation, FinMTEB evaluates models across retrieval from SEC filings and earnings calls, semantic similarity of financial sentence pairs, downstream classification tasks like sentiment detection, and document clustering by theme or sector.

The benchmark reveals consistent gaps: on retrieval tasks involving financial jargon, cross-document reasoning, or temporal references, generalist models lag domain-adapted alternatives by a substantial margin. The difference is particularly acute for queries involving quantitative concepts ("compare gross margin trends") or regulatory specifics such as describing fair-value disclosure requirements under SFAS 157 (the Statement of Financial Accounting Standards on fair-value measurement).

Domain-adapted embedding models

For production financial RAG, the embedding model should be selected using finance-specific evaluation rather than relying solely on a general leaderboard. While FinMTEB shows that domain-adapted models can outperform general-purpose embeddings on financial text, the ranking is not stable across tasks: retrieval over filings, classification of financial news, semantic similarity, reranking, and summarization can favor different models.

The current shortlist (mid-2026) spans both managed APIs and open/self-hosted models:

- Among commercial options, Voyage remains a leading candidate for financial retrieval, with voyage-finance-2 still positioned as a finance-specific model and the newer Voyage 4 family relevant for high-quality general retrieval. Other managed options worth benchmarking include Gemini Embedding, Cohere Embed 4, and OpenAI text-embedding-3-large, especially where enterprise reliability, latency, deployment controls, or multimodal document handling matter.

- Among open or locally deployable models, Fin-E5 remains the finance-adapted reference model from the FinMTEB paper, while Qwen3-Embedding, Qwen3 rerankers, BGE-M3, BGE-en-ICL, and E5/Mistral-derived models are current practical candidates depending on hardware, licensing, language coverage, and latency constraints.

Treat any published ranking as a shortlist. The embedding and reranking landscape changes quickly, and leaderboard averages can hide the task that matters most for the financial RAG system you are aiming to build. For production use, benchmark several candidates on a representative local corpus of filings, earnings call transcripts, research notes, news, and the actual query types the application will serve, then evaluate retrieval recall, citation precision, latency, vector size, cost, and reindexing burden before standardizing on a model.

Embedding dimensions and quantization

One practical consideration is often overlooked: embedding dimensionality directly impacts storage, memory, and latency. High-dimensional embeddings (1536 or 3072 dimensions) capture more nuance but require proportionally more resources from the vector database. For large corpora—millions of chunks from thousands of filings—the choice matters.

Modern practice increasingly adopts **Matryoshka embeddings** (Kusupati et al., 2022), in which the training objective explicitly packs useful information into the leading dimensions of each vector, so that truncating to the first 256 (or 512, or 1024) dimensions still yields a usable representation. Naive truncation of a conventionally trained embedding does not behave this way; the property has to be trained in. When it is, practitioners can serve shorter vectors to meet latency and storage budgets without retraining. Similarly, **binary quantization** compresses 32-bit float vectors to 1-bit representations—a 32× memory reduction—though the accuracy trade-off depends on corpus and query distribution and should be validated empirically.

Evaluating embedding models on the target corpus

Public leaderboards like FinMTEB generate a shortlist, but they do not guarantee rank ordering on a specific filing corpus, query mix, or latency budget. "Best on public benchmark" is a hypothesis, not a deployment conclusion. Evaluate empirically on the target corpus using the following checklist:

1. **Sample 50–100 representative queries** that the RAG system will face in production.
2. **Create ground-truth relevance labels** for the top-10 passages each query should retrieve.
3. **Compare candidate models** using Recall@k, Mean Reciprocal Rank (MRR), and latency.
4. **Select by measured trade-offs** between domain-specific and generic models on the deployed document types.
5. **Rerun after shifts** in corpus composition or query distribution.

The incremental cost of this evaluation is modest relative to the payoff. A retrieval system that misses the most relevant passages propagates errors downstream to generation. No amount of prompt engineering compensates for poor retrieval. With strong embeddings in place, the next question is how to search them—and why a single retrieval method is rarely enough.

Implementation: `02_domain_embeddings_comparison.py` runs the protocol above on a 191-passage 10-K corpus with a 15-query workload spanning risk, technical, and general questions. `BAAI/bge-large-en-v1.5` (1024-d) edges `all-MiniLM-L6-v2` (384-d) by 14.0% on mean reciprocal rank (0.675 versus 0.592) and by 11.1% on Precision@3 (44.4 versus 40.0%). The per-query-type breakdown reveals the more important asymmetry: bge-large leads on technical queries (MRR 0.90 versus 0.73) and on risk queries (0.61 versus 0.48), while MiniLM edges ahead only on the general-business slice (0.56 versus 0.51).

The 14% aggregate MRR spread between the two models is comparable to the variance across query types within a single model, which is exactly why "best on public benchmark" is a hypothesis that has to be validated on your own corpus and query mix.

22.5 Hybrid retrieval and vector databases

Pure semantic search has a blind spot, even with domain-specific embeddings. Vector similarity excels at finding conceptually related passages—for example, "profitability concerns" surfaces "margin compression" or "cost overruns." But it struggles with exact matches: specific tickers, regulatory codes, or quoted figures. A query for "Form 4 filings for TSLA" may retrieve passages about insider trading in general while missing documents containing Tesla's ticker. In finance, where analysts routinely search for specific companies, dates, and terms, this failure mode is acute.

Hybrid search combines two complementary retrieval paradigms (Weller et al., 2025):

- **Semantic (Vector) Search:** Finds passages *conceptually* similar to the query, even if they use different words. Handles synonyms and intent well.
- **Keyword (Lexical) Search:** Finds passages containing *exact terms* in the query. The classic algorithm is **BM25** (Best Match 25), a refined variant of term-frequency–inverse-document-frequency (TF-IDF) scoring that has been the workhorse of information retrieval for decades (Robertson and Zaragoza, 2009). BM25 excels at matching tickers, entity names, and regulatory codes.

By running both in parallel and fusing results, hybrid search balances conceptual relevance with keyword precision. The analyst asking about "AAPL's capital return program" benefits from semantic search understanding "capital return" as related to "buybacks and dividends," while BM25 ensures passages containing "AAPL" are appropriately boosted.

Reciprocal rank fusion

The fusion step typically uses **Reciprocal Rank Fusion (RRF)** (Cormack, Clarke, and Buettcher, 2009). A document that ranks highly in *both* methods is more likely to be relevant than one that ranks highly in only one. RRF assigns each document a score inversely proportional to its rank in each list, then sums across methods:

$$\mathrm{RRF}(d) = \sum_{r \in R} \frac{1}{k + \mathrm{rank}_r(d)}$$

where R is the set of ranking methods, $\text{rank}_r(d)$ is the document's rank in method r, and k is a smoothing constant (typically 60). Documents absent from a ranking contribute zero to that sum.

As a worked example, suppose three documents are retrieved for the query "AAPL supply chain," with ranks:

Document	**BM25 rank**	**Semantic rank**
A (exact ticker match)	1	15
B (supply-chain discussion)	10	2
C (loose AAPL mention)	50	8

Table 22.1: Rank fusion example

With $k = 60$, the RRF scores are:

- $\text{RRF}(A) = 1/61 + 1/75 \approx 0.0297$
- $\text{RRF}(B) = 1/70 + 1/62 \approx 0.0304$
- $\text{RRF}(C) = 1/110 + 1/68 \approx 0.0238$

Document B ranks first. Its consistent presence in both lists beats A's top-1 BM25 rank, undermined by a weak semantic rank. This is RRF's characteristic bias: it favors documents well-ranked by *multiple* signals over documents that dominate one signal and fade in another.

RRF is simple and robust, requiring no training and adapting automatically to different query types. Learned fusion—training a model to optimally weight retrieval scores—typically offers only marginal improvement while adding complexity. On a 200-passage 10-K corpus with a 15-query workload mixing entity-heavy and conceptual queries, `03_hybrid_retrieval.py` measures Hybrid (RRF) at MRR 0.443 against BM25's 0.349, a 27% advantage that holds on precision and recall as well. A generic web-trained cross-encoder rerank stage, by contrast, degrades MRR by 36% relative to Hybrid alone—a useful warning that off-the-shelf rerankers can be miscalibrated on financial passages. *Figure 22.3* visualizes the parallel vector and keyword search merging through RRF.

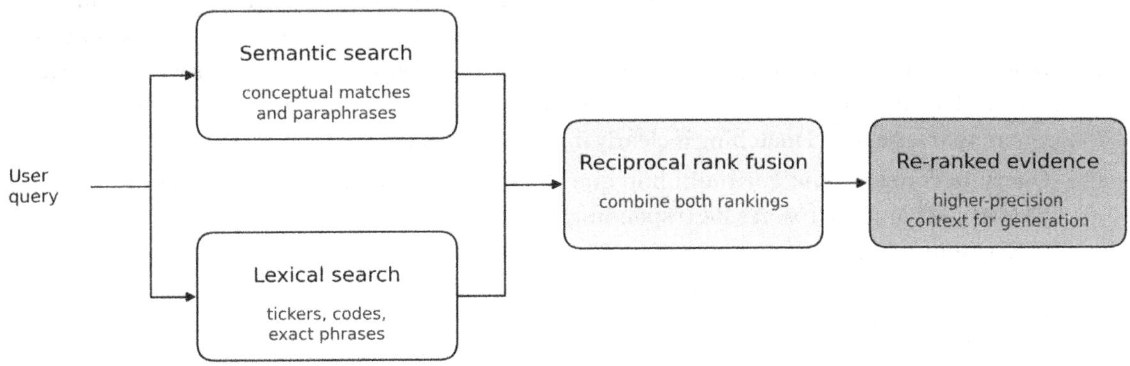

Figure 22.3: Hybrid retrieval merges semantic and lexical rankings before generation

Beyond bi-encoders – The retrieval architecture spectrum

Dense retrieval in production typically uses a **bi-encoder**—a model that embeds the query and every document independently into a single vector each, so similarity scoring reduces to a fast dot product over precomputed vectors. Bi-encoders are efficient but lose fine-grained token-level alignment; a **cross-encoder** (introduced in *Section 22.6*) recovers that signal at much higher cost.

Between these two extremes lies **late-interaction retrieval**, exemplified by **Contextualized Late Interaction over BERT (ColBERT)** and its descendants. These models store per-token embeddings for every document and compute similarity at query time as a sum of per-query-token maxima over document tokens (the "MaxSim" operation). Late-interaction models capture token-level matching that single-vector bi-encoders miss at a fraction of cross-encoder cost, making them practical for first-stage retrieval over large corpora. The trade-off is index size: storing per-token vectors requires substantially more storage than single-vector approaches.

For most financial RAG deployments, bi-encoder retrieval followed by cross-encoder re-ranking (*Section 22.6*) remains the pragmatic choice; late-interaction is worth evaluating when single-vector embeddings consistently miss relevant passages despite tuning.

Query enhancement techniques

Raw user queries are often suboptimal for retrieval. An analyst might ask: "What happened with their China business?" The retrieval system must resolve "their" to a company, match "China business" to "Asia-Pacific segment" or "People's Republic of China (PRC) revenue," and handle temporal vagueness. Several techniques address this:

- **Query Expansion:** Automatically add synonyms or related terms. "China business" expands to "PRC," "Asia-Pacific," "Greater China." Domain-specific expansion dictionaries (mapping "buyback" to "share repurchase" and "capital return") are particularly valuable.
- **Hypothetical Document Embeddings (HyDE):** Instead of embedding the query directly, use an LLM to generate a hypothetical answer, then embed that answer (Gao et al. 2023). The hypothesis "The company's China business experienced a 15% decline due to regulatory headwinds" may retrieve more relevant passages than the sparse original query. HyDE adds latency (an LLM call before retrieval) and introduces a risk: if the hypothetical answer is wrong, retrieval is biased toward incorrect passages. Use HyDE selectively for complex, conversational queries where sparse keyword matching is clearly insufficient, and empirically validate retrieval quality.
- **Query Decomposition:** For multi-hop questions, break the query into sub-questions. "Compare Apple's and Microsoft's R&D spending trends" is split into two separate retrieval queries, with results merged before generation. This prevents the retrieval system from having to find passages that simultaneously discuss both companies—such passages may not exist, even if the information is available in separate sections.

Vector database selection

The indexed embeddings and metadata must be stored in a system optimized for similarity search. In practice, teams choose among managed services, self-hosted vector databases, lightweight local options, and database extensions such as `pgvector`. Product names change more slowly than feature matrices, so durable selection criteria matter more than any point-in-time comparison table. For financial RAG, ask three questions first: does the system support metadata filtering before **approximate nearest neighbor** (**ANN**) search, can it participate cleanly in a hybrid retrieval stack, and does it fit the organization's existing operational footprint?

For production-ready financial RAG, databases with native hybrid search (Weaviate, Pinecone, Milvus, Qdrant) simplify the architecture. For prototyping, ChromaDB with a separate BM25 index provides a cost-effective alternative. Organizations already invested in PostgreSQL can use pgvector to avoid new infrastructure; similarly, enterprises running OpenSearch or Elasticsearch can leverage their native hybrid search with first-class RRF support rather than introducing a separate vector database.

Filtered retrieval

Financial queries often include implicit or explicit filters: "Apple's 2023 10-K," "risk factors from the most recent filing." Rather than relying solely on similarity, **pre-filtering** by metadata improves precision.

Modern vector databases natively support filtered search: apply metadata constraints (`company = "AAPL", fiscal_year = 2023, document_type = "10-K"`) *before* computing similarity scores. The implementation matters: pre-filtering (applying metadata constraints before ANN search) preserves recall because the search operates only over the relevant subset.

Post-filtering (searching the full index, then discarding non-matching results) can severely reduce recall if the relevant subset is small relative to the corpus. Most production vector databases now natively support pre-filtering. At minimum, tag each chunk with: company identifier, fiscal year, fiscal quarter, document type (10-K, 10-Q, earnings call), filing date, section header, and page number. This metadata schema enables the most common financial filters and supports the citation formatting discussed in *Section 22.6*.

A concrete example illustrates the risk: an analyst asking "What guidance did management provide for 2024?" without a fiscal-year constraint might retrieve 2022 forward-looking statements that happen to mention 2024—plausible, well-cited, and dangerously stale.

Retrieval is the foundation of RAG quality. No amount of prompt engineering compensates for passages that the retrieval stage failed to find. But retrieval returns a ranked set of candidates, not a verified answer. The next section addresses the final two stages—re-ranking the candidate set for precision and constraining the LLM's generation to produce only grounded, citable responses.

22.6 Re-ranking and constraint-based prompting

Retrieval optimizes for recall—casting a wide net to ensure relevant documents are captured. The initial retrieval may return 20–50 candidate chunks, some highly relevant, others noise. Two techniques close this gap: re-ranking to sharpen precision and constraint-based prompting to enforce grounding.

Cross-encoder reranking

A **reranking** step acts as a refinement filter between retrieval and generation. While initial retrieval uses fast but approximate methods (such as vector similarity or BM25), re-ranking employs a more powerful model to re-score each candidate for precise relevance.

The typical architecture uses a **cross-encoder**—a model that takes the query-document pair as a single input and outputs a relevance score (Nogueira and Cho, 2020). Unlike bi-encoders (which embed query and document independently), cross-encoders attend to fine-grained token-level interactions, yielding more accurate relevance judgments at the cost of pairwise computation:

1. **Initial retrieval:** Fast search returns the top 50 candidate chunks.
2. **Re-ranking:** Cross-encoder scores each chunk against the query.
3. **Selection:** Top-5 highest-scoring chunks pass to the LLM.

The latency cost of re-ranking 50 chunks is typically 100–200ms—acceptable for analytical applications but potentially prohibitive for real-time use cases. Options include Cohere's Rerank API, open-source cross-encoders from the Sentence-Transformers library, and domain-specific re-rankers fine-tuned on financial Q&A datasets.

Context window management

Modern LLMs offer context windows of 128K to 1M+ tokens, raising a tempting question: why not pass an entire 10-K filing and let the model find what it needs?

This "long-context" approach has three significant drawbacks. First, LLMs struggle to attend to information in the middle of very long contexts—Liu et al. (2024) document strong primacy and recency effects rather than uniform use of the full window. Second, inference cost scales with input tokens: passing 200K tokens when 5K would suffice increases cost substantially with no guaranteed accuracy improvement. Third, time-to-first-token increases substantially. The "lost in the middle" effect is model- and version-dependent; newer architectures may partially mitigate it. Benchmark on the target model before assuming a specific failure pattern.

The pragmatic recommendation: use long context windows as a fallback for complex multi-hop queries, but maintain focused retrieval as the default. A 5–10K-token context of precisely relevant chunks typically outperforms a 100K+-token context of loosely relevant material.

Constraint-based prompting

The final defense against hallucination is the generation prompt itself. A production-grade RAG prompt imposes explicit constraints that enforce grounding and verifiability:

- **Role assignment:** "You are an expert financial analyst conducting due diligence on SEC filings."
- **Context constraint:** "Answer based ONLY on the provided context. Do not use outside knowledge."
- **Uncertainty handling:** "If the context lacks sufficient information, state clearly that the information is not available."

- **Citation instruction**: "For each factual claim, include an inline citation in the format [Page X, Section Y]."
- **Structured output**: "Structure your response as: (1) Direct answer, (2) Supporting evidence with citations, (3) Caveats or limitations."

A critical caveat: **citations are not automatically faithful**. LLMs can cite passages that do not support the claim, blend information across chunks, or generate plausible page numbers that do not exist. Production systems should verify citation fidelity—for example, by requiring the model to quote a supporting phrase alongside each citation, or by implementing automated claim-evidence alignment that validates each citation against the retrieved context. A lightweight verification step: extract each cited passage by its page/section reference, compute semantic similarity between the claim and the cited text, and flag pairs below a threshold for human review. This catches the most common failure—plausible but unsupported citations—without requiring a second LLM call. *Section 22.7* covers how to systematically measure citation fidelity.

The companion notebook `05_10k_rag_assistant.py` demonstrates the narrower but more relevant production pattern used in this chapter: citation-constrained answering, explicit abstention when context is insufficient, and lightweight checks for retrieval coverage and citation presence.

Numeric reliability and tool-verified computation

Financial queries frequently require not just text retrieval but arithmetic: "What was the year-over-year change in operating margin?" or "How does the current ratio compare to the industry median?" LLMs retrieve the right evidence but routinely make calculation errors—a failure mode distinct from hallucination because the source passages are correct, but the derived answer is wrong.

The reliable pattern for numeric questions is a four-stage pipeline:

1. Retrieve evidence, including table slices.
2. Extract numbers into a structured schema (cells, units, period, segment).
3. Compute via code or tooling rather than the LLM.
4. Generate a narrative explanation with citations and a reproducible calculation trace.

This "retrieve-extract-compute-narrate" pattern delegates arithmetic to deterministic tools and constrains the LLM to what it does well: synthesis and explanation. Agentic frameworks (*Section 22.9*) formalize this by giving the LLM access to a code interpreter as an explicit tool. Even without a full agent architecture, requiring structured numeric output (JSON with extracted values and computed results) and programmatically validating the arithmetic catches most common quantitative errors.

Programmatic output validation

Prompt-level constraints are necessary but insufficient for production financial systems. Programmatic validation adds a second layer: structured output parsing (JSON mode, function calling) ensures the LLM's response conforms to a schema; claim-level verification pipelines check each assertion against retrieved context; and guardrail frameworks (such as NeMo Guardrails, Guardrails AI) enforce output constraints—topic adherence, toxicity filtering, format compliance—through code rather than prompt instructions alone. The combination of prompt constraints and programmatic validation is increasingly common in production deployments.

The prompt as contract

This constraint-based approach transforms the LLM from a generative oracle into a synthesis engine. The model's task is not to "know" the answer but to articulate what the provided evidence supports. When combined with properly parsed, metadata-tagged, and precisely retrieved context, this architecture produces answers *designed* to be verifiable—the analyst can trace cited claims back to their sources and independently confirm them. The gap between "designed to be verifiable" and "automatically verified" is where production engineering effort concentrates.

The prompt is a contract between the system and the LLM. A vague prompt invites hallucination; a precise, constraining prompt enforces grounding. With the full RAG stack in place, the next challenge is to treat it like any ML system: define metrics, build evaluation sets, and iterate on data.

22.7 Diagnosing RAG pipeline bottlenecks

Without systematic evaluation, a RAG system is an opaque pipeline that resists debugging. It might retrieve irrelevant documents, miss key information, or hallucinate despite having the correct context. Anecdotal success on a handful of test queries provides false confidence. Diagnosing *where* the pipeline fails—retrieval, context, synthesis, computation, or abstention—determines *what* to fix.

Failure modes

RAG failures fall into distinct categories, each requiring different remediation:

- **Retrieval failure** (low-context recall): The correct information exists in the knowledge base, but the retrieval stage fails to retrieve it. The answer is wrong, and manual corpus search reveals relevant passages that were not retrieved.

  Fix: Improve embeddings, tune hybrid search weighting, or refine chunking.

- **Context failure** (low context precision): Retrieval finds some relevant documents but includes too much noise, diluting the signal. The retrieved context contains tangentially related material but omits key details.

  Fix: Tune re-ranker thresholds, improve metadata filtering, or adjust chunk granularity.

- **Synthesis failure** (low faithfulness): Retrieval succeeds, and context is accurate, but the LLM generates an incorrect or hallucinated answer—misinterpreting context, failing to synthesize, or ignoring the grounding constraint.

  Fix: Refine prompts, switch to a more capable LLM, or implement answer verification.

- **Computation failure** (correct evidence, wrong arithmetic): A variant of synthesis failure specific to quantitative queries. The system retrieves the right table or passage, but the LLM miscalculates a derived value—reporting an incorrect year-over-year change or misapplying a formula. This failure is invisible to standard faithfulness metrics because the cited evidence is correct; only the computation is wrong.

  Fix: Delegate arithmetic to code (*Section 22.6*) and validate numeric outputs programmatically.

- **Abstention failure**: Some questions have no answer in the indexed documents—the user is asking about a company not in the knowledge base, a time period not covered, or information that simply wasn't disclosed. A well-calibrated system should abstain rather than fabricate. Evaluate refusal quality alongside the other metrics: does the system correctly identify when it lacks sufficient information, and does it communicate uncertainty appropriately?

Figure 22.4 summarizes the five failure classes and the diagnostics that separate them.

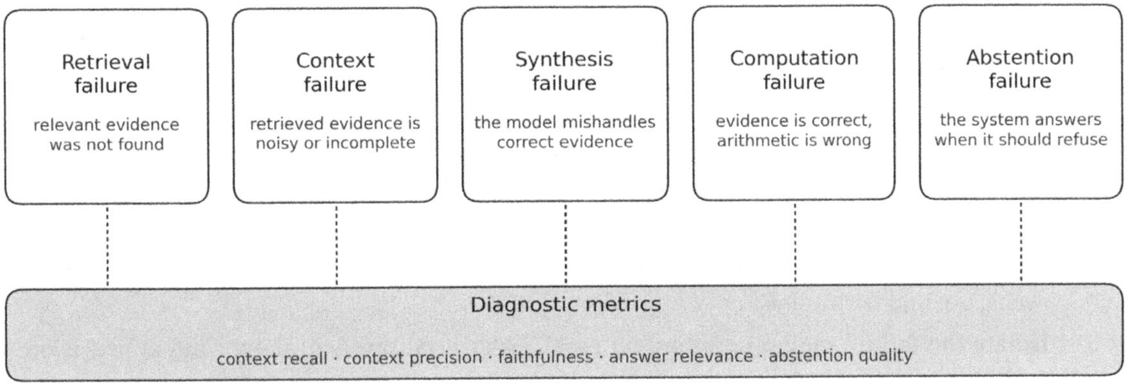

Figure 22.4: Retrieval, context, synthesis, computation, and abstention failures each call for different diagnostics and fixes

RAGAs and claim-level evaluation

Retrieval-Augmented Generation Assessment (**RAGA**) provides automated metrics for each failure mode (Es et al., 2024). Datasets like FinDER (Choi et al., 2025) supply ground-truth question-answer pairs specifically designed for financial RAG evaluation:

Metric	What It Measures	Failure Mode
Context precision	Are retrieved chunks relevant to the query?	Context failure
Context recall	Did retrieval return all necessary information?	Retrieval failure
Faithfulness	Is the answer grounded in context (no hallucination)?	Synthesis failure
Answer relevance	Does the answer address the user's question?	Synthesis failure
Abstention quality	Does the system refuse when evidence is insufficient?	Unanswerable query

Table 22.2: RAGA metrics

These metrics are computed by using an LLM (often GPT-4) as a judge to evaluate the quality of retrieved context and generated answers against ground-truth annotations or through automated reasoning. While not perfect, they provide a scalable way to benchmark pipeline performance and track improvements over time.

RAGAs measure answer-level quality, but high-stakes financial applications benefit from finer-grained diagnosis. **RAGChecker** (Ru et al. 2024) decomposes generated answers into atomic claims and checks each claim's entailment against retrieved evidence, yielding an **unsupported claim rate**—the fraction of claims not supported by any retrieved passage.

This complements RAGAs: a response may score high on overall faithfulness while containing one unsupported numeric claim that matters most. For production deployments, track unsupported claim rate alongside RAGA metrics, and calibrate LLM-as-judge scores against a human-labeled subset to prevent false confidence. `04_ragas_evaluation.py` instantiates this four-axis harness on a small fixture set and shows the failure-mode separation in action: retrieval scores 0.33 (the weakest stage), grounded-answer quality 0.65, abstention F1 0.50, and security robustness 0.67, with an unsupported-claim rate of 0.50 versus an unsafe-action rate of 0.17—a useful reminder that ungrounded text generation is typically the more frequent failure and the place to invest guardrail effort first.

The diagnostic workflow has five steps:

1. **Build an evaluation set**: 50–100 representative queries with ground-truth answers and source passages. Stratify by difficulty (single-hop factual, multi-hop reasoning, comparative) and document type. Include 10–20% unanswerable queries. Have domain experts validate ground truth—automated generation introduces the same biases the harness is meant to detect.
2. **Compute baseline metrics**: Run RAGAs on the evaluation set to establish context recall, context precision, and faithfulness.
3. **Isolate the failure mode**: Low context recall → retrieval problem. Low context precision → ranking problem. Low faithfulness → synthesis problem.
4. **Apply targeted fixes**: Address the weakest component—improve embeddings, tune re-ranker, or refine prompts—rather than making untargeted changes.
5. **Monitor continuously**: Use observability tools such as TruLens to track RAG performance in production and detect degradation over time (for example, due to corpus drift or new query patterns).

This diagnostic capability transforms RAG from an opaque pipeline into an engineering system that can be systematically debugged and improved. Without measurement, tuning is guesswork; with measurement, changes can be evaluated against observable trade-offs. Financial workflows add one requirement to the workflow above: **citation traceability**, the ability to tie every factual claim back to a specific source passage. Score it alongside the RAGA metrics in every evaluation cycle.

Extending the harness to adversarial inputs

The failure modes discussed so far assume benign inputs. A qualitatively different threat arises when the corpus itself contains malicious instructions (such as might come from prompt injection via poisoned documents) or when users craft adversarial queries designed to bypass grounding constraints. If the system includes tool-use capabilities (*Section 22.9*), the attack surface expands further. Security belongs in the same evaluation harness as accuracy rather than in a separate audit: reuse the diagnostic metrics—unsupported-claim rate, citation-failure rate, and abstention behavior—under adversarial prompts so that a regression in robustness looks the same as a regression in accuracy. The notebook `08_rag_security.py` implements a stress-test suite covering prompt injection, retrieval poisoning, and action injection scenarios. On a four-fixture attack set, simple defenses (input sanitization plus retrieval-aware refusal) drive the unsafe-action rate from 0.50 to 0.00 and reduce the unsupported-claim rate from 1.00 to 0.25 (a 75% relative reduction)—a useful demonstration that meaningful robustness gains do not require a model swap, while the residual 0.25 unsupported-claim rate diagnoses what the defense stack still misses.

Iterative correction loops

The workflow above assumes a human reviews metrics and decides what to fix. An emerging pattern closes this loop automatically: **corrective RAG (CRAG)** and **self-RAG** architectures use the LLM itself to evaluate retrieval quality and re-query when initial results are insufficient. If retrieved context scores are below a confidence threshold, the system reformulates the query, broadens the search, or invokes a different retrieval strategy before generating an answer. This turns the static retrieve-then-generate pipeline into an iterative loop—a natural bridge to the agentic frameworks in *Section 22.9*. The trade-off is latency: each correction cycle adds an LLM call. Limit correction rounds for interactive applications; for batch analytical tasks, the additional latency is typically acceptable.

With the evaluation framework established, the next section turns to deployment: applying the full RAG stack to real financial workflows and making the strategic choice between RAG and fine-tuning for different use cases.

22.8 Applications and strategic choices

This section applies the RAG architecture from *Sections 22.2–22.7* to three financial use cases, then draws a strategic comparison with fine-tuning.

The 10-K due diligence assistant

The primary use case for financial RAG is a due diligence assistant for long, dense regulatory filings. An SEC 10-K annual report for a large corporation can span 200–300 pages of financial statements, management discussion, risk factors, legal proceedings, and segment analyses (Lopez-Lira, 2023). Manually searching for specific information—comparing revenue drivers across years, tracing risk disclosures to performance, extracting quantitative commitments—takes hours.

A well-designed RAG system transforms this process. The analyst poses complex, multi-hop questions and receives synthesized answers with page-number citations.

Example query:

```
Based on the MD&A and Risk Factors sections, what were the primary drivers of
the 10% revenue increase, and what risks were cited that could threaten this
growth?
```

This question forces the system to connect two different filing regions: the MD&A discussion of what drove growth and the Risk Factors discussion of what could undermine it. A naive pipeline struggles because fragmented chunks obscure the cross-section relationship and a loose retrieval pass may surface only one side of the story. In production, the remedy is the full stack developed earlier in the chapter: structure-aware ingestion, precise retrieval, and citation-constrained generation. The defining feature is **verifiability**: every factual claim in the generated answer should point back to a page or section the analyst can inspect directly.

Implementation: See `05_10k_rag_assistant.py` for a compact chapter-scale assistant that demonstrates local filing ingestion, top-*k* retrieval, citation-constrained prompting, and lightweight retrieval/citation diagnostics. The notebook notes LlamaParse and richer retrieval backends as production upgrades, rather than as already implemented. The companion `01_sec_filing_pipeline.py` covers EDGAR access and the metadata needed for point-in-time filtering and citation traceability.

Production deployment requires governance controls beyond the technical pipeline: access controls, audit logging of prompts and retrieved context, retention policies, and human-in-the-loop review for externally shared outputs (*Chapter 26*). Security considerations—prompt injection, retrieval poisoning, citation misuse—are evaluated using the diagnostic framework in *Section 22.7*; `08_rag_security.py` implements a dedicated stress-test harness.

Comparative case study – ESG analysis

ESG analysis illustrates the contrast between the classification paradigm of *Chapter 10* and the reasoning paradigm of RAG.

First, recap the **Fine-Tuned Classification** approach (as seen in *Chapter 10*): a discriminative transformer fine-tuned on labeled ESG text (Baltussen et al. 2025; Zhao, Li, and Zheng, 2020) classifies news articles or disclosure snippets into predefined taxonomies, such as "Environmental-Risk", "Social-Opportunity", or "Governance Concern."

The workflow: collect a labeled dataset, fine-tune a transformer with a classification head, run on incoming documents, and output category labels and confidence scores. This approach is scalable because it turns open-ended text into compact signals that can feed screening, factor construction, and portfolio constraints. The limitation is structural: the model operates within a fixed taxonomy and cannot explain *why* it classified a document or why it answered follow-up questions. The output is a score, not an evidence trail.

RAG-based due diligence builds a RAG system over a company's full-text sustainability reports—the 100+ page documents detailing carbon emissions, supply chain practices, diversity metrics, and governance structures. The workflow: parse and index the sustainability report with structure-aware chunking, build a RAG query engine with domain-specific embeddings, enable the analyst to ask open-ended questions in natural language, and output narrative answers with citations to specific pages and sections.

Example query:

```
Summarize the company's Scope 2 emissions reduction strategy, list their key
performance indicators (KPIs), and identify stated five-year targets—with page
references.
```

This approach enables deep qualitative analysis: the analyst can explore nuances, ask follow-up questions, and receive cited answers that can be verified. It augments the human analyst's judgment rather than replacing it with a score. The limitation is operational rather than conceptual: it requires a maintained document corpus, retrieval infrastructure, and stronger controls around citations, abstention, and governance, and it does not naturally emit the scalable numeric time series that systematic strategies demand. The trade-offs are shown in the following table:

Dimension	Fine-Tuned Classifier	RAG-Based Q&A
Primary output	Numeric scores, labels	Narrative answers with citations
Scalability	High (batch processing)	Medium (per-query)
Flexibility	Low (fixed taxonomy)	High (open-ended questions)
Verifiability	Indirect (model confidence)	Direct (source citations)
Knowledge updates	Requires retraining	Update corpus, no retraining
Best use case	Systematic factor construction	Fundamental due diligence

Table 22.3: The strategic trade-off

A quantitative fund building a systematic ESG strategy—screening thousands of stocks daily based on ESG risk signals—would choose the classifier. The output is a number that feeds directly into portfolio optimization. A fundamental analyst at a long/short equity fund investigating a specific company's sustainability commitments—preparing for a management meeting or building an investment thesis—would choose the RAG system. The output is insight, not a score.

Sophisticated firms employ both classification for breadth and RAG for depth. The classifier identifies *which* companies warrant attention; the RAG system enables *understanding* what those companies are actually doing. *Figure 22.5* presents this decision framework visually.

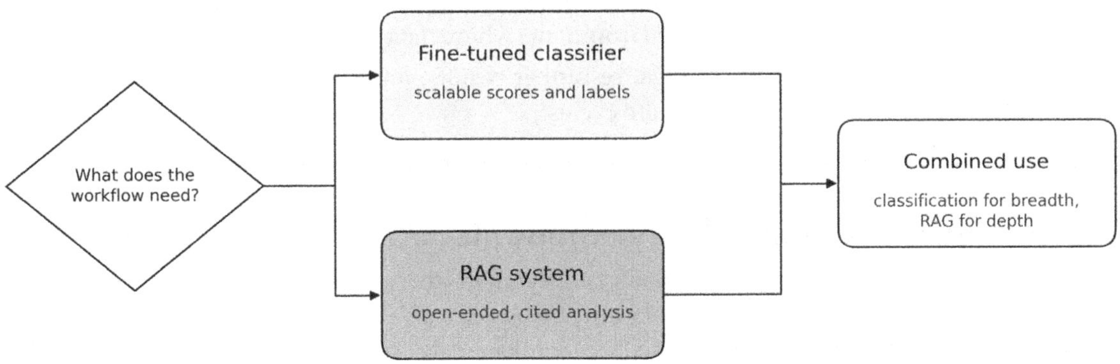

Figure 22.5: Fine-tuning serves scalable scoring, while RAG serves cited, open-ended analysis

Implementation: See `06_esg_rag_vs_finetune.py` for a stylized side-by-side comparison. The notebook is designed to clarify the architectural trade-off between label-producing classifiers and cited narrative workflows, not to serve as a production latency benchmark.

Generation model selection

The strategic choice extends beyond RAG versus fine-tuning to the generation model itself. **Commercial APIs** (such as GPT, Claude, Gemini) offer the highest capability but require sending documents to external servers—a non-starter for many financial institutions with strict data residency requirements. Open-weight models (such as Llama 3, Mistral, DeepSeek, Qwen) can run on-premise or in private cloud environments, preserving data sovereignty at the cost of lower capability on complex tasks.

The gap is narrowing: **open-weight models** increasingly approach commercial API quality for well-constrained RAG tasks where context provides most of the required information. Choose based on four criteria: capability (does the model follow grounding constraints reliably?), cost (per-query economics at expected volume), latency (acceptable for the use case?), and data residency (can proprietary documents leave the infrastructure?).

Many production deployments use a tiered approach: open-weight for high-volume, routine queries; commercial APIs for complex analytical tasks that require stronger synthesis.

Production lifecycle

After the demo works, teams spend most of their time on operational concerns that the pipeline architecture does not address:

- **Incremental indexing:** Detect new filings, restatements, and revisions; update embeddings only for changed spans rather than reindexing the full corpus.
- **Corpus versioning and reproducibility:** Version the corpus snapshot, embedding model, re-ranker, prompt templates, and generation model together. Store a compact "retrieval bundle" (query, retrieved chunks, evidence spans, model versions, answer) per response to support audit and reproducibility.
- **Deletions and retention:** Implement tombstoning, legal holds, and retention rules with audit logs—requirements in regulated environments where data cannot simply be deleted.
- **Caching:** Cache query embeddings, re-ranker results, and frequently asked answers with staleness policies tied to filing update cycles.

These concerns are prerequisites for production deployment, not afterthoughts.

Deployment in regulated environments

Financial RAG systems operate under regulatory expectations that generic AI deployments do not face. Broker-dealer supervisors and the EU AI Act now treat generative AI as in scope for documentation, oversight, and transparency obligations, and large-bank model risk supervision is separately evolving as regulators work out how to distinguish conventional models from generative and agentic systems.

The specifics vary by jurisdiction and entity type, but the design-time implication is stable: build for auditability and provenance from the start—access logs, versioned retrieval bundles, retention and tombstoning—because retrofitting these controls into a live system is far more expensive than designing them in. A full treatment of governance and MLOps appears in *Chapter 26*; the principle here is to involve compliance and model-risk teams early, not after deployment.

Structured data extraction – Institutional holdings

RAG techniques extend naturally beyond free-text Q&A to structured data extraction from regulatory filings. SEC 13F filings—quarterly disclosures of institutional equity holdings—provide a rich source of signals for quantitative strategies. Parsing these filings programmatically and constructing co-ownership graphs reveals crowding patterns, institutional momentum, and network-based features that complement traditional price-volume signals. Co-ownership features capture slow-moving institutional positioning that price-volume data cannot: when multiple large funds hold concentrated positions in the same stocks, the resulting crowding risk creates co-liquidation vulnerability invisible to standard momentum or value factors. The bipartite graph of institutions and stocks also provides a natural input to the graph neural network methods in *Chapter 23*, where message passing over the ownership network can propagate information about institutional behavior across connected securities.

Each application discussed in this section treats the RAG pipeline as a static retrieve-then-generate sequence. The next section introduces agentic frameworks, in which the LLM can decide *when* to retrieve, *which* tools to invoke, and *how* to decompose multi-step research questions—transforming RAG from a fixed pipeline into a component of an autonomous reasoning loop.

> **Implementation:** `07_institutional_holdings_graph.py` shows a pipeline that fetches 13F filings via EDGAR, constructs co-ownership networks, and engineers cross-sectional features.

22.9 Introducing agentic frameworks

The RAG systems in this chapter are passive: they wait for a question, retrieve context, and generate an answer. The next evolution moves from question-answering to **autonomous action**—AI agents that plan, use tools, and achieve goals.

An **AI agent** is a system where an LLM serves as the controller for an autonomous process that can plan, use tools, and take actions. The core components are:

- **LLM Controller**: The reasoning engine that interprets goals, plans steps, and decides on actions
- **Tools**: External capabilities the agent can invoke—a RAG system for document retrieval, a web search API, a code interpreter for numerical calculations and statistical analysis, a database query interface, or financial APIs for real-time market data and fundamentals
- **Memory**: Context that persists across interactions, allowing the agent to maintain state, learn from past actions, and build up knowledge over a session

This architecture enables multi-step problem solving that goes well beyond what a static RAG pipeline can achieve. Rather than answering a single question, the agent can decompose a complex goal into subgoals, execute them sequentially or in parallel, handle failures, and synthesize results.

The ReAct paradigm

The foundational framework for LLM agents is **ReAct** (derived from *Reason* and *Act*) (Yao et al., 2023), which structures behavior as an iterative loop:

1. **Thought:** The agent reasons about what it knows and what it needs to do next.
2. **Action:** Based on this reasoning, the agent invokes a tool or takes an action.
3. **Observation:** The agent observes the result of its action.
4. **Repeat:** The loop continues until the agent determines it has achieved the goal or needs to ask for clarification.

This cycle of reasoning, tool invocation, and observation becomes the starting point for the fuller agent architectures in *Chapter 24*.

The pattern scales to complex analytical workflows: decomposing a research question into sub-queries, invoking the appropriate tool for each (such as document retrieval, API calls, calculations), observing the results, and iterating until a comprehensive answer emerges.

RAG as an agent tool

A sophisticated agent does not replace RAG; it *uses* RAG as one tool among many. The RAG system built in this chapter—with its parsed knowledge base, hybrid retrieval, and citation-generating prompts—becomes part of the "Document Analysis" tool in the agent's toolkit alongside web search, code interpreter, database query, and financial APIs.

The agent's LLM controller orchestrates these tools, deciding which to invoke based on the user's goal and the results of previous actions. The value of multi-tool orchestration emerges when a question cannot be answered from documents alone. "What is Company X's current EV/EBITDA (enterprise value to earnings before interest, taxes, depreciation, and amortization) relative to its five-year average?" requires document retrieval for qualitative context, a database query for historical fundamentals, and a calculation for the ratio and comparison. No single RAG pipeline handles all three; an agent routes each sub-task to the appropriate tool.

Not every problem requires an agent—well-designed LLM workflows often outperform agents for structured, predictable tasks, reserving agentic architectures for truly open-ended exploration (Bowne-Anderson, 2025).

Industry adoption

Financial institutions are moving from experimentation to early deployment, but the frontier is narrower than public claims suggest. Internal research assistants, document-triage tools, and analyst-facing retrieval systems are now in limited production at a growing number of firms.

Multi-agent architectures—specialized agents for documents, databases, and calculations coordinated by a supervisor—are well-described in the research literature (Saha et al., 2025; Yu et al., 2024; Kong et al., 2024), but most deployed agentic systems in regulated finance still hold a **human-in-the-loop** at every action that touches external state: order placement, client communications, or account changes.

Man Group has publicly discussed using agentic AI to generate quantitative trading signals (Fang and Moore, 2025)—notable because it is one of the few cases where a firm has publicly tied an agentic system to a live signal-generation workflow rather than to a pure research-assistant use case. The trajectory is clear—from features to synthesis to action—but the gap between benchmark demos and audited, production-grade agentic pipelines remains substantial.

RAG provides the foundation—grounded knowledge retrieval—upon which agentic systems are built. *Chapter 24* will deliver the full implementation.

22.10 Summary

Retrieval-augmented generation is the core architecture for using large language models in financial research without treating model output as self-authenticating. The central design principle is simple: the model should synthesize over retrieved evidence, not over whatever it happens to remember. But making that principle work in practice requires more than a vector store and a prompt. Financial documents demand structure-aware ingestion, domain-sensitive embeddings, hybrid retrieval, re-ranking, constraint-based prompting, and deterministic handling of numeric computation. The result is not an opaque oracle but an auditable research tool whose claims can be traced to specific sources.

A strategic boundary separates RAG from fine-tuning. Fine-tuning is appropriate when the goal is a repeatable skill, such as classification or extraction over stable labels. RAG is appropriate when the goal is evidence-grounded analysis over changing documents and questions. Once that distinction is clear, evaluation becomes equally clear: diagnose failures in retrieval, context, synthesis, computation, and abstention separately, and judge systems by grounded usefulness rather than surface fluency.

The next chapter introduces knowledge graphs, which make entities and relationships explicit when questions depend on paths, networks, and temporal structure rather than on narrative evidence alone.

23

Knowledge Graphs

Retrieval-augmented generation (Lewis et al., 2020) has made evidence-grounded financial question answering practical, but vector retrieval still operates on isolated chunks. When a question depends on ownership chains, supplier networks, contagion paths, or the timing of relationship changes, similarity search alone is not enough. Those questions require explicit relational structure (see *Figure 23.1*).

A knowledge graph provides that structure by representing entities as nodes, relationships as typed edges, and identifiers, timestamps, and provenance as properties attached to nodes and edges. This chapter concentrates on explicit financial knowledge graphs built for deterministic traversal and auditable answers, rather than on broad community-summary GraphRAG systems whose primary value lies in thematic synthesis. After completing this chapter, you will be able to:

- Distinguish financial questions that genuinely require graph structure from those better served by tabular databases or vector retrieval.
- Design a compact, typed, and auditable financial knowledge graph with stable entity identity, finite relationship vocabularies, and edge-level provenance.
- Build and validate LLM-assisted extraction pipelines that convert disclosures into replayable graph objects while controlling schema, duplication, and temporal consistency.
- Explain how Graph RAG differs from vector retrieval and implement safe relational query workflows using constrained text-to-query generation and deterministic database execution.
- Transform graph structure into leakage-aware machine learning features, including topology, crowding, concentration, and cross-graph interaction features.
- Evaluate explicit knowledge graphs, statistical financial networks, and learned graph representations pragmatically for forecasting, portfolio construction, and risk analysis.
- Apply a three-timestamp framework and disclosure-time cutoff rules to prevent temporal leakage in graph queries, feature generation, and backtests.
- Make sound engineering choices about graph databases, ontology scope, query safety, and schema evolution for production-oriented financial systems.

Section 23.1 establishes when graphs justify their overhead. *Sections 23.2-23.3* cover graph construction and relational retrieval. *Sections 23.4-23.5* turn graph structure into features and network-based portfolio inputs. *Section 23.6* addresses temporal integrity, and *Section 23.7* closes with the engineering decisions needed to keep the system auditable and stable.

23.1 When relational structure justifies a graph

Not every financial question benefits from a graph. Schema design, extraction, and graph maintenance carry overhead that is justified only when the analytical task is genuinely relational: when the answer depends on paths between entities, not on properties of entities in isolation.

When graphs add value

Three conditions reliably justify the use of graph infrastructure: relationships that span multiple entities, involve complex links, and evolve over time.

Multi-hop dependency queries

Questions that require joining facts across multiple entities are the clearest use case. "Which companies share critical suppliers with Nvidia, and which of those suppliers sit in geopolitically concentrated regions?" requires traversing supplier edges, intersecting with competitor supplier edges, and filtering by geographic properties. A graph database executes this as a pattern match; a relational database requires recursive self-joins that grow unwieldy beyond two hops; a vector retrieval system must infer the path from disconnected text fragments, exactly where high-impact errors enter.

One financial motivation is **contagion analysis**. Haldane and May (2011) showed that the stability of financial systems depends on the architecture of interconnections, the "robust-yet-fragile" property of scale-free networks. A single node failure propagates through hub-and-spoke structures in ways that per-entity risk metrics cannot capture. Supply chain graphs, interbank lending networks, and cross-holding structures all exhibit this topology.

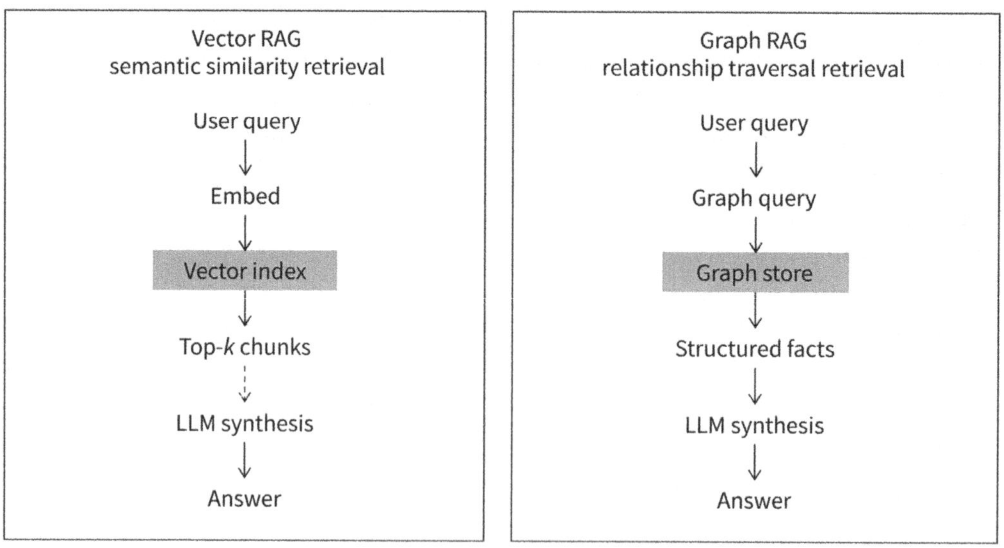

Figure 23.1: Vector RAG retrieves similar chunks; Graph RAG traverses explicit relations

Structural crowding and co-ownership

Institutional ownership data from SEC 13F filings form a bipartite network: institutions hold securities, and securities are held by institutions. Projecting this network onto the security dimension reveals co-ownership patterns that predict return correlations beyond what fundamental factors explain.

Antón and Polk (2014) showed that stocks connected through common institutional ownership exhibit excess return comovement: returns correlate not because the firms are fundamentally similar, but because the same investors trade them simultaneously. Greenwood and Thesmar (2011) extended this to price fragility: securities with concentrated institutional ownership face fire-sale risk because forced liquidation by a single holder triggers correlated selling by others holding similar portfolios.

Computing co-ownership Jaccard similarity, crowding scores, and ownership concentration requires traversing the institution-security bipartite graph. The features that encode fragility and crowding are inherently relational: they measure a stock's position in the ownership network, not its standalone characteristics. Konstantinov and Fabozzi (2025) provide recent evidence that causal spillover effects across asset networks convey risk information beyond what standard correlation models capture.

Temporal relationship evolution

Relationships change. A supplier becomes a competitor after vertical integration. An institution builds a position over multiple quarters before it becomes visible. Executive migration between firms creates hidden information channels. These dynamics appear in edge patterns before they surface in price data.

Li and Passino (2024) constructed dynamic financial knowledge graphs from news corpora and showed that temporal edge patterns (relationship formation, dissolution, and type transitions) carry thematic signals useful for trend detection. Evolving graph structure encodes regime shifts, strategic repositioning, and emerging competitive dynamics that static cross-sectional features miss. For these signals to be tradable, edge timestamps must distinguish between when an event occurred, when it was publicly disclosed, and when the extraction pipeline observed it, a three-timestamp model detailed in *Section 23.6*.

What distinguishes temporal graph signals from conventional time-series features is that they encode **topological change**: not shifts in entity attributes, but changes in the structure of relationships. A new supplier link, a dissolved partnership, or a shift in institutional ownership alters the network's information-propagation properties, and these structural events are difficult to capture in tabular features because they involve relationships between entities, not the entities themselves.

When graphs do not help

Three conditions consistently fail to justify the need for graph infrastructure.

Single-entity attribute lookup

If the question is "What was Apple's revenue last quarter?" the answer lives in a single record. A graph adds storage and query overhead without analytical benefit. A common mistake in early KG projects is encoding entity attributes as graph relationships (for example, `Company -HAS_REVENUE-> $500B`), which complicates queries without adding relational insight.

Narrative synthesis over broad corpora

When the task is "Summarize the main themes in 500 analyst reports," the bottleneck is text comprehension, not relational traversal. Community-summary approaches like GraphRAG (edge et al., 2024) address this by building statistical summaries of entity communities, but their core value lies in summarization rather than in graph structure. Vector retrieval with clustering and re-ranking often achieves comparable quality with lower infrastructure overhead.

Sparse graphs with few relationships

Graph analytics assume reasonable density. If the knowledge graph has 10,000 entities but only 500 edges, centrality metrics become unstable, community detection produces degenerate clusters, and network features add noise rather than signal. As a rough heuristic, if the average node degree falls below 2–3, most topology metrics are unreliable.

Sparsity is often a symptom of extraction failure rather than a property of the domain: if the supply chain graph of S&P 100 companies has fewer than 200 edges, the extraction pipeline needs improvement before the graph infrastructure becomes useful.

Practical decision framework

A useful test: restate the question as a path pattern. If it naturally decomposes into "find entities connected through relationship chains," a graph representation is likely justified. If the question concerns the properties of individual entities or requires summarizing large collections of text, simpler tools are more appropriate.

The rest of this chapter assumes the graph path is justified and addresses the practical challenges: constructing reliable graph objects from financial disclosures (*Section 23.2*), querying them for relational reasoning (*Section 23.3*), extracting features for machine learning (*Sections 23.4–23.5*), maintaining temporal integrity (*Section 23.6*), and engineering the supporting infrastructure (*Section 23.7*).

Implementation: See `09_knowledge_graph_features.py` for notebook-scale relational features derived from compact supply-chain and holdings graphs, and `10_network_portfolio_construction.py` for market-network structure derived from real return data.

23.2 Constructing financial knowledge graphs

The central change in knowledge-graph practice is not that LLMs can extract triples; older systems could do that. The change is that modern models can map long, noisy disclosures into structured outputs with enough flexibility to replace large portions of handcrafted parsing logic. That shift changes project economics and lets teams iterate on real corpora quickly.

Speed alone is not sufficient in finance. A graph that cannot be replayed, audited, and corrected is a liability. The practical requirement is twofold: use LLMs for extraction throughput and pair them with data contracts that keep outputs stable across model versions and data updates.

From legacy pipelines to directed extraction

Before LLMs, most teams used one of two approaches. Rule-based systems used regular expressions and keyword grammars: precise on narrow templates, brittle outside them. Supervised relation-extraction models performed better across linguistic variation, but required expensive labeled data and recurring retraining as document styles changed. Elhammadi et al. (2020) achieved 78% precision on the top-100 extractions using a pre-LLM pipeline that combined NER, dependency parsing, and pattern matching on financial news, a strong result for its time but one that required substantial per-corpus engineering.

Both approaches shared a structural weakness: extraction and schema design were loosely coupled. Engineers often normalized text first and then tried to coerce it into graph objects. That ordering produced recurring failure modes: duplicate entities, drifting relation names, and sparse provenance fields.

LLM-based extraction reverses the order. The schema is defined first. Prompting and structured output constraints force the model to emit graph-ready objects directly, moving engineering effort from parsing cleanup to validation and monitoring.

Governance before prompt

A robust extraction run starts with three contracts covering identity, schema, and provenance.

Identity contract

Mentions are not identities. "Apple," "Apple Inc.," and "AAPL" may refer to the same company and, therefore, should never persist as independent canonical nodes. The extraction layer should preserve mentions while resolving canonical identifiers (CIK, ticker, LEI, CUSIP/ISIN, where relevant) in a separate canonicalization step.

Identity resolution in financial data is harder than simple deduplication. Tickers change (Facebook → Meta), mergers create new entities from old ones (Dow/DuPont → Corteva + DowDuPont), and the same name can refer to different entities across jurisdictions. A practical canonicalization strategy uses stable identifiers (such as CIK or LEI) as primary keys and stores tickers as time-varying attributes with validity intervals. Corporate actions (mergers, spinoffs, name changes) should be treated as first-class events that update identity attributes rather than exceptions handled ad hoc.

Schema contract

Relationship vocabulary should be finite and typed. In practice, this means an allowlist of relation types with explicit source-target constraints. If a generated edge violates those constraints, it is rejected or routed for review.

Provenance contract

Every accepted node and edge must carry enough metadata to answer two questions: "where did this claim come from?" and "when did it become publicly available?" At minimum, store source document ID, filing/public date, source location (section/page/span), extraction timestamp, and extractor version.

These contracts make high-coverage extraction maintainable and keep downstream analytics interpretable.

A five-stage extraction workflow

A production-oriented workflow usually includes five stages:

1. **Targeted document slicing.** Focus extraction on relationship-dense filing segments. For 10-K pipelines, Items 1, 1A, and 7 are common starting points. This excludes boilerplate sections that rarely contain relation-level evidence.
2. **Schema-constrained generation.** Use JSON Schema or typed function output modes so that emitted objects can be validated without fragile text parsing.
3. **Canonicalization and deduplication.** Resolve aliases, collapse duplicates, and preserve mention-level evidence.
4. **Rule validation.** Enforce relation allowlists, type constraints, date sanity checks, and provenance completeness.
5. **Human review queue.** Route low-confidence or rule-violating objects for analyst adjudication.

Each stage should emit diagnostics and failure counts to enable iterative quality improvement. The pipeline should be idempotent: reprocessing the same filing with the same extractor version should produce identical graph objects.

Reflection-driven correction, as shown by FinReflectKG (Arun et al., 2025a), can improve compliance by having the model critique and revise its own extractions before validation. The reflection loop works in three steps: extract candidate triples, evaluate them against schema rules, and propose fixes for violations. This iterate-until-convergence pattern is particularly effective for entity normalization (for example, splitting "John Ternus, CEO of Apple" into separate Person and Role entities) and for enforcing relationship type constraints.

Error taxonomy and monitoring

Teams often monitor extraction precision and stop there. For graph workloads, four additional metrics matter:

- **Schema-valid rate:** Fraction of generated objects satisfying type constraints
- **Provenance coverage:** Fraction of accepted edges with complete evidence metadata
- **Duplicate-node rate:** Unresolved aliases mapping to separate canonical nodes
- **Temporal-consistency rate:** Edges with coherent event/public/extraction timestamps

These metrics reveal different failure classes. A model can produce high lexical quality but still degrade graph usability if identity or provenance quality collapses. Tracking these across extraction runs also reveals model regression: a prompt change that improves entity extraction but degrades temporal consistency would be invisible to standard NLP evaluation, but visible in graph quality metrics.

A practical monitoring target: schema-valid rate above 90% and provenance coverage above 95% for edges entering production graphs. Beyond automated metrics, routinely sample extracted edges and have analysts score correctness and provenance adequacy. Maintain a frozen "gold subset" of filings and verify that extraction outputs remain stable across prompt and model updates. This regression testing catches quality degradation that aggregate metrics can mask.

Supply chain schema example

Consider constructing a supply chain graph from 10-K filings. The objective is to extract three relationship families (supplier dependencies, customer concentration links, and competitive relationships) for the S&P 100.

The schema should be small, typed, and versioned:

Object	Core Fields	Purpose
Company node	canonical ID, name, ticker, sector	Identity stability across filings
Filing node	accession, form, filing date	Source traceability
HAS_SUPPLIER edge	evidence span, public date, extractor version	Dependency analysis and auditability
HAS_CUSTOMER edge	evidence span, public date	Concentration analysis
COMPETES_WITH edge	evidence span, public date	Market structure queries

Table 23.1: Sample schema

The flow is shown in the following diagram:

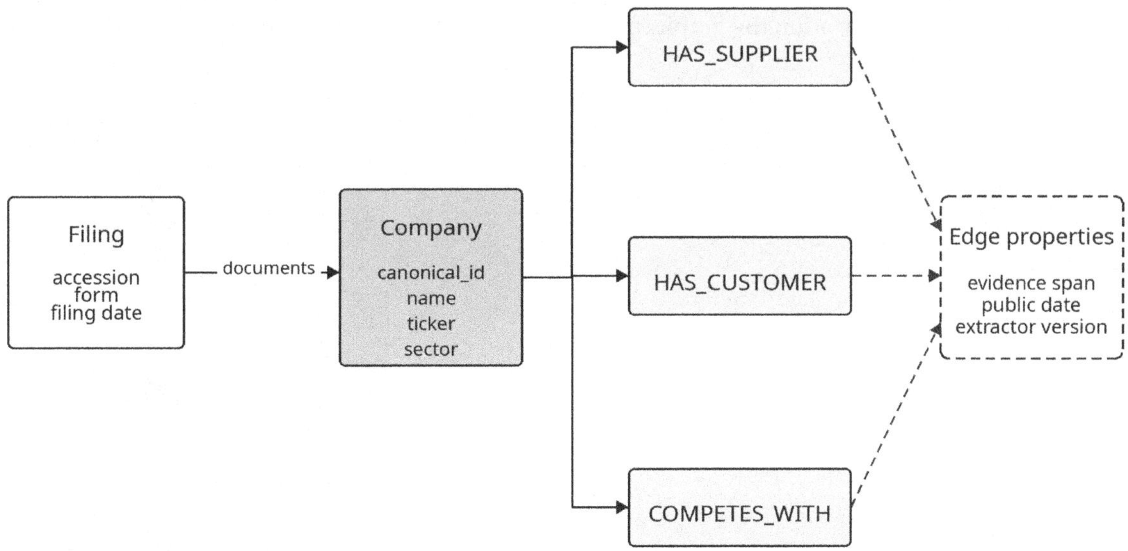

Figure 23.2: Minimal supply-chain schema linking companies, filings, and typed relationship edges

The design principle is to store evidence with the edge. A relationship without a source context is difficult to verify, correct, or trust in downstream models. This schema is deliberately small: five object types cover the core analytical use cases. Larger schemas can be built incrementally as extraction pipelines mature, but starting with a compact schema reduces validation complexity and makes error diagnosis tractable.

An important caveat: **supply chain relationships disclosed in 10-K filings are partial, selective, and sometimes intentionally vague**. Companies disclose relationships they are required to report or choose to highlight; they do not provide a complete supplier inventory. This makes 10-K extraction a high-precision, low-recall source. A separate noise source enters at the LLM extraction step: generic placeholder entities such as "leaf merchants," "vendors," or "third parties" surface as candidate suppliers and require a curated stop list during canonicalization to keep the graph clean. When a use case requires broader coverage, layer in structured or vendor datasets and reconcile them through the identity contract. The KG schema accommodates this: edges from different sources carry different provenance metadata, and downstream consumers can filter by source confidence.

The pipeline acquires 10-K filings from EDGAR, stages them as per-ticker parquet files, and rebuilds a consolidated reference artifact from the local cache before extraction. Text is sliced from sections that carry relationship signals, especially Item 1 (Business), Item 1A (Risk Factors), and Item 7 (MD&A). Targeted slicing reduces extraction noise and lowers per-filing cost. The extraction stage applies the workflow described above, with entity normalization collapsing common aliases, dropping generic placeholder entities, and linking each accepted edge to source filing metadata.

When the extracted graph is visualized, structural concentration becomes easier to inspect than in raw triples alone. In the current notebook-scale run, shared suppliers such as TSMC, Foxconn, and Samsung emerge as bridge nodes connecting multiple downstream firms. That pattern is exactly the kind of relational concentration the graph representation is intended to expose.

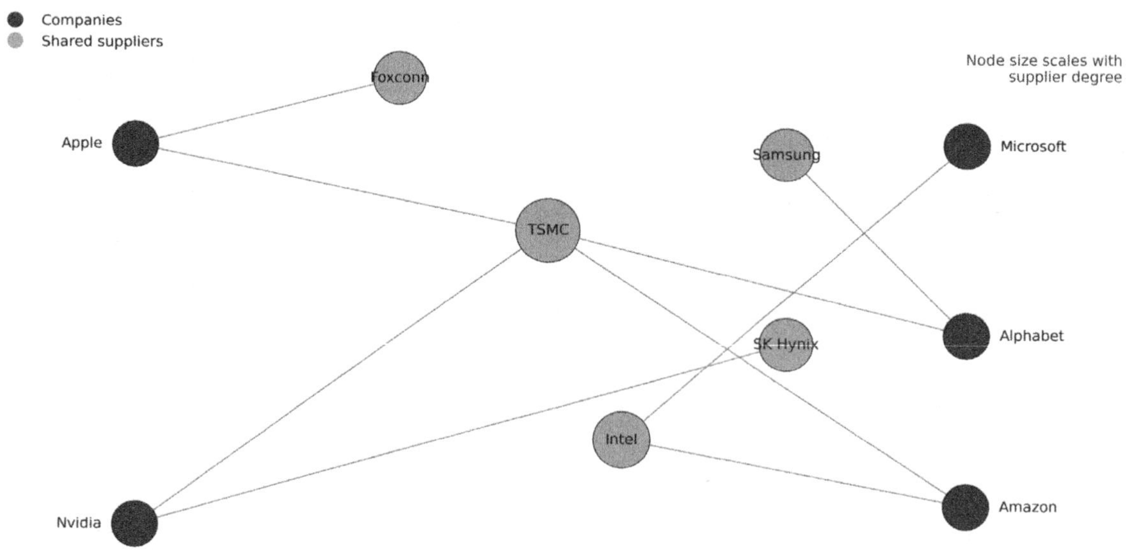

Figure 23.3: Notebook-scale extraction highlights shared suppliers as concentration nodes linking multiple downstream firms

Idempotent writes keep reruns stable and enable versioned refreshes. In practice, that means using merge-style loading logic keyed on canonical node identity and relationship type, then updating edge-level provenance fields such as source document, source section, source span, public date, extraction time, and extractor version. The important property is behavioral rather than syntactic: reprocessing the same filing should update the same relationship record, not create a parallel copy that inflates downstream path counts.

Graph RAG, graph-derived ML features, and temporal graph analytics all depend on this foundation. If extraction does not preserve identity and evidence, downstream systems inherit hidden error. If it does, the same filing corpus becomes a reusable relational substrate for many analyses. LLMs are not replacing data discipline: they make disciplined graph construction scalable. With graph objects in place, the next question is how to query them. *Section 23.3* shows how Graph RAG delegates relational logic to the database while keeping language generation in the model.

Implementation: See `01_sp100_sec_download.py` for SEC EDGAR filing acquisition and `02_supply_chain_kg_construction.py` for the extraction and loading pipeline. The notebook works with the staged EDGAR cache, a live Neo4j instance, and a local LLM extraction path.

The staged run processes 601 10-K filings covering 101 S&P 100 companies and extracts 1,057 unique typed relationships after deduplication (276 supplier, 472 competitor, and 309 customer edges) across 127 distinct subject companies, and surfaces TSMC, Foxconn, and Samsung as the three most connected suppliers, serving 61, 33, and 28 downstream companies, respectively. The cached parquet ships with an `extracted_triples.meta.json` file that pins the content hash, schema, row count, and extractor identity.

23.3 Deterministic relational reasoning with graph RAG

Graph RAG uses an LLM for language understanding and a graph database for relational retrieval. Multi-hop joins are executed by the database engine, so the analyst can iterate on questions without re-engineering prompt chains each time.

Graph RAG is strongest for questions whose answer depends on explicit relationship paths:

- "Which competitors share suppliers with company X?"
- "Which institutions hold both a company and its key suppliers?"
- "Which exposures were visible before date T?"

Vector retrieval remains better for narrative and open-ended questions. The question "What are the main risks facing semiconductor companies?" is better served by vector retrieval across risk-factor disclosures than by graph traversal. In practice, most production systems are hybrid: graph retrieval for relational structure, document retrieval for narrative evidence. The query routing stage determines which path is appropriate for each incoming question.

End-to-end architecture

A robust Graph RAG path includes five stages:

1. **Query routing.** Classify incoming questions as graph, document, or hybrid. This reduces unnecessary text-to-Cypher generation and improves answer quality for non-relational questions.
2. **Text-to-Cypher generation.** Generate Cypher from a compact schema representation and explicit query policy. The schema should include only the labels, relationships, and properties that the query interface is allowed to use. Not all questions are well-suited to free-form query generation; many production teams use parameterized template libraries with an LLM router that selects and fills the appropriate template, rather than generating arbitrary Cypher. This reduces the attack surface and simplifies validation.
3. **Query safety validation.** Validate generated queries before execution. This is a structural requirement for financial deployment, not optional hardening. The validation layer should enforce: read-only database role, allowlisted labels and relationships, parameterized values (never string interpolation), timeout and row-limit guards, and write/admin keyword blocking.
4. **Deterministic retrieval.** Execute validated Cypher and return structured rows with provenance metadata. The database handles relational joins; the LLM does not need to infer connection paths from text fragments.
5. **Grounded synthesis.** Compose the final answer from retrieved rows and cite source evidence. The synthesis prompt should include retrieved rows verbatim and instruct the model to cite specific rows when making claims. Because edges carry evidence pointers (such as document ID, section, span offsets), the system can fetch the original text snippets that justified each relationship and include them alongside the graph result. This two-layer citation (graph row plus underlying disclosure text) prevents a common failure mode where "the KG says X" without showing the original evidence.

This division of labor keeps retrieval logic in the database and language generation in the model, making errors easier to localize during debugging.

Example query flow

Consider the question, "Which companies compete with Apple and share its suppliers?" In a Graph RAG system, the model does not answer that by narrating over loosely related passages. It routes the request to a constrained text-to-Cypher path, generates a read-only query over the `COMPETES_WITH` and `HAS_SUPPLIER` relationships, and applies a cutoff-date filter so that only relationships public at the time of the query are eligible. The database returns structured rows such as competitor names and shared suppliers; the model then turns those rows into prose while preserving the underlying evidence links. The cutoff-date filter is not an implementation detail. In finance, it is the mechanism that keeps historical analysis from leaking post-cutoff information.

In the current teaching workflow, the same pattern is applied to the real institutional holdings graph. Questions such as "Which institutions hold both Apple and Microsoft?" or "What are Berkshire Hathaway's largest positions?" are routed to a compact, validated set of Cypher templates rather than to unconstrained query generation. This is a narrower interface than a fully general Graph RAG agent, but it is closer to how audited production systems are usually deployed.

Comparing explicit KG graph RAG to community-summary GraphRAG

Two graph retrieval families are common in practice, as surveyed by Peng et al. (2024). **Explicit domain KG Graph RAG** uses typed entities and deterministic traversal, well-suited for regulated financial workflows where provenance and replay are required. **Community-summary GraphRAG** (Edge et al., 2024) constructs graph abstractions from corpus themes to enable broad summarization. It excels at thematic synthesis but is less direct for schema-governed relational queries where audit trails matter. The two approaches are complementary. This chapter emphasizes explicit domain KGs because they map directly to auditable financial reasoning and downstream feature workflows.

Evaluation and failure modes

A useful Graph RAG evaluation harness checks three properties: query validity (syntax and schema compliance of generated Cypher), provenance coverage (share of returned claims linked to source evidence), and temporal correctness (accuracy under historical cutoff constraints).

Two recent benchmarks provide standardized evaluation with real financial data. FinDER (Choi et al., 2025) offers 5,703 expert-annotated query-evidence-answer triplets from S&P 500 10-K filings. Its queries reflect real analyst search behavior: abbreviated, ambiguous, and domain-specific. FinDER evaluates retrieval broadly (both sparse and dense methods), not Graph RAG specifically, but its finding that generation quality is strongly limited by retrieval quality reinforces the case for structured graph retrieval on relational questions.

FinReflectKG-MultiHop (Arun et al., 2025b) tests the specific claim that KG-guided evidence outperforms text-window retrieval for multi-hop financial reasoning. Built on the FinReflectKG knowledge graph derived from S&P 100 filings (2022–2024), it generates analyst-style questions that require 2–3-hop reasoning across companies, years, and filing sections. KG-guided retrieval improved correctness by approximately 24% while reducing token consumption by roughly 85% compared to page-window retrieval. The efficiency gain shows that structured retrieval is not just more accurate but also more economical: the model spends tokens reasoning over pre-selected facts rather than navigating noisy context.

Common failure modes include invented labels or properties in generated Cypher, overly broad traversals that return noisy rows, missing cutoff filters in historical queries, and synthesis drift, where generated text exceeds the evidence returned. These are engineering problems: strict validation gates, conservative query templates, and regression test suites address most of them. Most production deployments route relational questions to the graph path and narrative questions to vector retrieval. When graph and vector results conflict, temporal metadata usually resolves the discrepancy: the more recent evidence takes precedence, provided timestamps are reliable.

Graph RAG is a different retrieval contract from vector RAG: the database executes relational logic, and the model explains results. When that contract is enforced, multi-hop financial questions move from heuristic synthesis toward repeatable analysis. Graph RAG answers questions about the existing structure; the next section turns that same structure into tabular features that can feed gradient-boosted models and factor regressions.

The same pattern is visible in the notebook's head-to-head benchmark on the live 13F holdings graph. Across seven analyst-style questions spanning holder lookup, co-ownership joins, and portfolio composition, structured graph retrieval achieves perfect support recall (1.00) against an embedding baseline that averages 0.13. Vector retrieval fails entirely on holdings-lookup queries (recall 0.00) and returns only a fraction of the relevant co-ownership rows (0.17) and direct-holder rows (0.30). Graph retrieval also uses roughly a third as many tokens per query (82 versus 267) because the traversal returns only the rows that match the schema rather than a broad set of candidate chunks. The magnitude of that gap depends on corpus and question type, but the direction is consistent with the FinReflectKG-MultiHop finding: on relational questions, structured retrieval is both more accurate and cheaper per answer.

Implementation: See `03_graph_rag_qa.py` for the text-to-Cypher pipeline over the 13F holdings graph, and `04_rag_comparison_benchmark.py` for the graph-versus-embedding comparison on 10,624 holdings rows covering 10 institutions and 250 stocks.

23.4 From graphs to machine learning features

The knowledge graphs constructed in previous sections (supply chain relationships from 10-K filings, institutional holdings from 13F) encode structural information that traditional price-based features do not capture. Graph analytics transform that structure into tabular features for gradient boosting (*Chapter 12*) and factor models (*Chapter 14*).

These algorithms extract scalar features from network structure. Prior studies report predictive value from text-derived network features (Kertkeidkachorn et al., 2023), though effect sizes depend on dataset design and evaluation protocol.

Network topology features

Core features derive from centrality measures that quantify each node's structural importance:

Feature	Calculation	Financial Interpretation
PageRank	Iterative influence propagation	Supply chain importance—companies depended upon by many others
Betweenness	Fraction of shortest paths through node	Bottleneck position where disruption propagates widely
Clustering Coefficient	Local connectivity density	Redundancy—high clustering suggests alternative paths exist
Degree	Direct connection count	Immediate network exposure—more connections, more transmission channels

Table 23.2: Network topology features

Different centrality measures carry different information. **PageRank** identifies systemically important firms weighted by the importance of their dependents. **Betweenness** identifies bottleneck firms whose failure would disconnect parts of the network. Using multiple centrality measures as separate features lets the downstream model learn which structural role matters for a given prediction task.

Supply chain risk features

Beyond topology, the supply chain KG enables the development of domain-specific risk indicators. In the notebook workflow, these are derived from the extracted graph itself rather than from a hand-labeled supplier master. Examples include supplier count, shared-supplier count, single-source count, supplier-overlap ratio, and supplier-dependency score. Together, these features distinguish firms with diversified supply relationships from firms whose risk is concentrated in a small set of disclosed counterparties.

A company that depends on a few shared upstream suppliers is structurally fragile, even if no single disclosure directly states that risk. The graph makes that concentration measurable, and it does so in a form that can be joined to other feature families.

Institutional crowding features

The 13F holdings knowledge graph reveals ownership patterns that carry predictive information about price dynamics. **Four feature families** are derived from the institution-security bipartite network:

1. **Crowding score.** Institutional holder count relative to the cross-sectional median measures how crowded a position is. Stocks with high crowding face correlated selling pressure during market stress: forced liquidation by one holder triggers cascading sales by others (Greenwood and Thesmar, 2011).
2. **Smart money concentration.** Value-weighted share held by top-performing institutions signals informed conviction, reflecting analytical judgment rather than index tracking.
3. **Ownership Herfindahl Index** (see *Chapter 17*). Concentration of holdings across institutions predicts fire-sale risk. A stock held by three large funds is more fragile than one held by thirty small funds, even at the same total institutional ownership.
4. **Co-ownership Jaccard.** The Jaccard similarity between two stocks' institutional-holder sets predicts return correlation beyond what fundamental factors alone explain. Antón and Polk (2014) showed that this co-ownership effect is economically significant: stocks linked by common institutional ownership exhibit excess comovement driven by correlated trading activity rather than shared fundamentals.

Konstantinov and Fabozzi (2025) provide recent evidence that network-based causal spillover metrics carry risk information beyond simple correlation models. Treat exact magnitudes as study-specific unless reproduced on your own corpus and split definitions.

Three temporal considerations affect how these features are computed for backtesting. First, 13F filings are quarterly with a 45-day reporting delay: a holding is tradable information only after the public filing date, not the quarter-end date. Second, large institutions sometimes request confidential treatment for positions they are building; masked positions appear in later amendments, creating gaps in real-time analysis. Third, derived relationships, such as portfolio similarity, should be recomputed quarterly as holdings change; they represent computational artifacts, not disclosed relationships.

Cross-graph integration and temporal dynamics

The distinctive value of knowledge graph features comes from combining information across graph layers. A stock with both concentrated supplier dependence (supply chain KG) and high crowding (holdings KG) faces compound risk: operational disruption would coincide with correlated institutional selling. The `supply_chain_crowding` interaction feature captures this by multiplying a supplier-overlap measure with institutional crowding.

Unlike traditional factor models, where factors are assumed to be independent, KG features can directly encode structural dependencies. Other cross-graph features include concentrated dependency risk (supplier dependency score multiplied by ownership concentration) and systemic exposure (betweenness multiplied by holder count).

Graph structure also encodes *dynamic* information propagation. Cheng et al. (2020) showed that events affecting upstream entities in a supply chain KG propagate to downstream firms at different speeds depending on the industrial chain: a raw material shock reaches component manufacturers before final assemblers. Their KG-based event embedding framework exploits these lead-lag relationships, showing that graph topology determines the timing of information transmission, not just whether it occurs. A supply chain graph with temporal event data can generate lead-lag features: the weighted average of upstream event severity, lagged by estimated propagation delay, becomes a predictive feature for downstream firms.

The supply-chain graph is a single snapshot, whereas the staged 13F holdings panel spans four quarterly vintages, covering Q1 through Q4 2025. The companion notebook uses this history to compute three vintage-aware ownership features: the mean Jaccard distance between the institutional-holder sets of consecutive vintages (ownership churn), the coefficient of variation of total reported position value across vintages, and the count of new institutional holders who entered the position between the two most recent vintages. These populate for the 78 of 127 entities with a 13F CUSIP match; the supply-chain churn columns remain at the zero baseline until multiple supply-graph vintages are materialized.

Features tracking network changes over time capture evolving structure that static snapshots miss:

- Relationship churn (edge turnover rate)
- Centrality momentum (change in PageRank over time)
- Supplier change (net change in supplier count)

A company whose supplier count declines while competitor connections grow signals that it is undergoing strategic repositioning, information not reflected in quarterly financials until later. The companion notebook produces features in wide format (one row per company, ready for gradient boosting or factor regression) and long format (stacked feature names and values, convenient for information coefficient calculation). The features derived so far rely on explicitly stated relationships; *Section 23.5* adds a complementary perspective from statistical financial networks built on return correlations and assesses where graph neural networks fit in practice.

Implementation: See `09_knowledge_graph_features.py` for the complete feature engineering pipeline and `05_institutional_holdings_kg.py` for the ownership graph construction. Both notebooks operate on staged real data. `09_knowledge_graph_features.py` joins the live supply-chain graph in Neo4j (127 source companies, 1,057 typed relationships) with the staged 13F holdings artifacts (201,145 raw rows), matches 80 of the 127 supply companies to the holdings universe, and produces a 31-column feature matrix spanning five families: topology (5 columns), supply (7), holdings (9), temporal (6), and cross-graph (4), joinable with the price-based features from earlier chapters.

23.5 Correlations and portfolios in financial networks

Knowledge graphs encode explicitly stated relationships: supplier links from 10-K filings, holdings from 13F. But financial networks also arise from statistical relationships. Correlation-based networks, minimum spanning trees, and hierarchical clustering of return series have been studied for over 25 years and provide a complementary perspective on market structure. This section connects the established financial networks literature to the knowledge graph features developed earlier, then assesses where graph neural networks fit in practice.

The established tradition

Mantegna (1999) introduced **minimum spanning trees** (MSTs) constructed from stock return correlations as a tool for revealing hierarchical structure in financial markets. The approach converts a correlation matrix into a distance metric, constructs the MST, and interprets the resulting tree as a map of market organization: clusters of related stocks, hub securities that connect sectors, and peripheral assets with distinct dynamics.

This line of research matured over two decades. Marti et al. (2021) reviewed the full trajectory, from correlation-based networks and hierarchical clustering to random matrix theory filtering and modern applications in portfolio construction and risk management. Their survey identifies what works (MSTs reliably recover sector structure and detect regime changes) and what remains unstable: community detection algorithms are sensitive to estimation window and filtering method, and hierarchical structures can shift substantially across adjacent time periods.

Correlation-based networks are useful for visualization, cluster identification, and diversification analysis, but their structural features require careful treatment in predictive models. Network topology metrics computed from correlation graphs are noisier than the same metrics from explicitly stated relationships because the underlying edges are estimated rather than observed. The choice of filtering method (MSTs, planar maximally filtered graphs, or random matrix theory) determines which relationships survive and, therefore, which community structures and centrality rankings emerge. Practitioners should match the filter to their analytical goal rather than treating this choice as a preprocessing detail.

From minimum spanning trees to portfolio construction

The companion notebook builds MSTs from `us_equities` return data and shows how network structure informs portfolio construction, following Konstantinov, Aldridge, and Kazemi (2023), who showed that network-based allocation can improve diversification relative to naïve equal-weight and minimum-variance portfolios.

Stocks that occupy central positions in the correlation network are more connected to the broader market and contribute less marginal diversification. Peripheral stocks, those at the edges of the MST, tend to offer more independent return streams. Network-aware allocation exploits this by giving peripheral assets greater weight.

Whether this translates to superior risk-adjusted returns after transaction costs depends on rebalancing frequency, estimation window, and the stability of network structure across regimes. MST structure can shift substantially between adjacent estimation windows, creating turnover that erodes theoretical diversification gains.

The notebook `10_network_portfolio_construction.py` evaluates this empirically on a 100-stock universe from 2015–2018 (504-day correlation lookback, average pairwise correlation 0.24). Equal-weight, inverse-volatility, and network-diversified portfolios produce Sharpe ratios of 1.58, 1.51, and 1.54, respectively, with maximum drawdowns of −10.3%, −10.6%, and −10.1%, close enough that the summary metrics do not separate the three at this universe size. The structural argument for the network-diversified construction emerges from the contagion simulation: a shock propagated from the highest-centrality node (BRK.B) affects the portfolio roughly 3.8 times more severely (−87.3%) than the same shock originating at a peripheral node (AAL, −23.0%), illustrating that topology governs contagion reach more than shock magnitude.

GNN maturity assessment

Graph Neural Networks (**GNNs**) extend deep learning to graph-structured data through message-passing: a node's representation is iteratively updated by aggregating information from its neighbors. Common architectures include Graph Convolutional Networks (Kipf and Welling, 2017), Graph Attention Networks (Velickovic et al., 2018), and GraphSAGE (Hamilton, Ying, and Leskovec, 2017).

GNN applications in finance exist on a maturity spectrum. The clearest production-adjacent success case remains **transaction-graph fraud detection**. Weber et al. (2019) showed that graph neural methods can separate suspicious Bitcoin flows from ordinary activity on the Elliptic dataset, which is why fraud detection falls into a different maturity bucket than alpha generation.

Domain	Maturity	Evidence
Fraud Detection	Production-ready	Elliptic Bitcoin dataset (Weber et al., 2019); deployed at scale
Systemic Risk	Emerging	Academic research, regulatory pilot programs
Alpha Generation	Experimental	Limited reproducible evidence after costs

Table 23.3: Graph Neural Network applications

Fraud detection succeeds because transaction networks have high signal-to-noise ratios (distinctive fraudulent topologies), clear labels, and real-time requirements that GNN inference can meet.

Alpha generation from price correlations remains challenging due to market efficiency, regime non-stationarity, and the reproducibility gap in academic claims.

The pragmatic recommendation

For the financial use cases in this book, hand-crafted graph features are the first-choice baseline. They are easier to audit, easier to debug, and more stable under governance constraints. Consider 13F holdings data: crowding scores, ownership HHI, and co-ownership Jaccard, computed directly from the graph structure, are transparent, explainable to regulators, and robust across regimes. GNNs add complexity without proportional benefit for these structured relationships.

The companion GNN notebook illustrates this on the correlation network of a 200-stock universe, with the graph estimated ex-ante on returns strictly before the 21-day target window: 480 edges at a correlation threshold of 0.5, a graph density of 2.41%, and pairwise correlations ranging from −0.32 to 0.99, with a mean of 0.21. Four GAT embedding dimensions are concatenated with eight tabular factors and fed to a ridge regression. On this sample, the hybrid model's cross-sectional information coefficient (0.215) lands roughly 7.7% below the tabular-only baseline (0.233). The comparison is in-sample and scale-limited, but the direction aligns with the broader literature's concern about GNN alpha generation: added architectural complexity does not translate into reliable improvements in structured equity forecasting problems at this scale.

For teams that want learned graph representations without the full GNN complexity, simpler graph embedding methods (such as node2vec or metapath2vec) provide an intermediate step: they produce vector representations from random walks on the graph, are faster to train than message-passing architectures, and can serve as features alongside hand-crafted metrics.

The **recommended path** is:

1. Start with graph analytics and hand-crafted features (*Section 23.4*).
2. Use network-based portfolio methods with explicit structure (such as MSTs or community detection).
3. Add GNN or graph embedding features only if they improve out-of-sample metrics after accounting for transaction costs and temporal leakage.
4. Keep learned graph features supplemental, not the default architecture.

Dynamic knowledge graphs, such as FinDKG (Li and Passino, 2024), represent an emerging direction in which temporal edge patterns carry thematic signals. The framework is promising but should be evaluated against simpler temporal features before adopting the full GNN apparatus, as discussed in the next section.

> **Implementation:** See `10_network_portfolio_construction.py` for MST construction, centrality-driven portfolio weighting, and the contagion simulation; see `06_gnn_feature_engineering.py` for the GAT-on-correlation-network versus tabular-ridge comparison.

23.6 Temporal integrity and leakage-safe evaluation

Static knowledge graphs answer the question "What relationships exist?" Temporal graphs answer "when did those relationships become observable?" That second question is central in finance because the timing of availability determines whether a signal is tradable.

The three-timestamp model

Every relationship in a financial knowledge graph should carry three timestamps:

- **Event time:** when the underlying event occurred (for example, an executive departed)
- **Disclosure time:** when the information became publicly available (for example, the 8-K was filed)
- **Extraction time:** when the pipeline processed the source document

The critical distinction is between event time and disclosure time. An acquisition may be agreed in March but filed in April; a supplier relationship may exist for years before appearing in a 10-K. Feature generation and historical queries must use disclosure time as the visibility gate: information that was true economically but not yet disclosed cannot enter the model.

8-K filings as a temporal case study

SEC Form 8-K illustrates the three-timestamp model concretely. Companies must disclose material events within 4 business days, including acquisitions, leadership changes, earnings announcements, and strategic shifts. The gap between event and disclosure varies by event type:

Item	Event Type	Typical Disclosure Lag
1.01	Material Agreement	1–4 business days
2.01	Acquisition/Disposition	1–4 business days
5.02	Executive Changes	1–4 business days
7.01	Regulation FD	Same day (by definition)
8.01	Other Events	Variable

Table 23.4: Disclosure lag by event type

The disclosure lag matters for backtesting: an executive departure on March 1 filed on March 5 should not be available to a model evaluated on March 3. The current notebook implementation persists event date, public filing date, and extraction date directly on the event graph, so leakage-safe filtering becomes a graph query condition rather than a manual bookkeeping step.

Executive turnover clustering is a temporal signal that surfaces from 8-K event graphs. When multiple companies in a sector replace executives simultaneously, it may signal industry-wide disruption or competitive pressure. This pattern is visible only when event timestamps are aggregated across the graph; individual filings reveal individual changes, but the cluster is a structural observation. The extraction methodology should follow reflection-driven approaches (Arun et al., 2025a) to improve compliance, particularly for entity normalization in event-dense filing periods.

13F temporal considerations

Institutional holdings data from 13F filings introduces additional temporal complexity through three mechanisms:

- **Quarterly lag.** 13F filings are reported quarterly with a 45-day delay. Holdings become tradable information only after the public filing date, not the quarter-end date. A December 31 snapshot filed on February 14 should be added to the graph on the filing date.
- **Position masking.** Large institutions sometimes request confidential treatment for positions they are in the process of building. Masked positions appear in later amendments, creating gaps in real-time analysis. Any crowding or co-ownership feature computed during the masking period will be biased downward.
- **Confidential treatment gaps.** When an institution's full 13F is withheld and released months later, the delayed disclosure creates a temporal inconsistency: either exclude the institution during the gap or use the amendment date as the effective disclosure time.

Snapshot construction and dynamic features

A common workflow uses rolling windows, treating each window as a dated analytical view:

1. Filter edges visible at cutoff (using disclosure time).
2. Build windowed subgraphs.
3. Compute additions and removals versus the previous window.
4. Compute window-level diagnostics such as churn, centrality drift, and concentration.

Quarterly windows align with fundamental disclosures. Shorter windows capture event-driven structure but increase noise and computation cost. The important constraint is consistency: once a window policy is chosen, keep it stable throughout evaluation.

The visibility-safe query pattern enforces temporal discipline by filtering every edge on disclosure time before any aggregation occurs. In concrete terms, a supplier query should return only relationships whose public timestamp is on or before the cutoff date, regardless of when the underlying relationship began economically. This distinction is what prevents post-cutoff information from entering the analysis.

Temporal graphs produce several candidate features for predictive modeling:

- **Relationship churn**: Edge turnover rate (new + dropped edges/total), measuring network stability and identifying restructuring periods
- **Centrality momentum**: Change in PageRank or betweenness over time, identifying entities gaining or losing structural importance
- **Concentration drift**: Shift in supplier or ownership concentration, capturing evolving risk exposure
- **Theme acceleration**: Tagged relation frequency over time, identifying emerging trends before they consolidate

Dynamic financial knowledge graphs, such as FinDKG (Li and Passino, 2024), and temporal relation construction approaches (Miao et al., 2019) systematically explore these dynamics. Both show that temporal edge patterns carry thematic and structural signals, though translating pattern detection into tradable alpha requires the same walk-forward validation and cost controls applied to any other feature candidate.

Leakage-safe evaluation protocol

Temporal experiments fail most often due to evaluation hygiene. A minimum protocol includes five rules:

- **Split by disclosure time, not event time:** Prevents using information that was true but not yet public
- Embargo observations **near split boundaries:** Prevents leakage through the gap between event and disclosure
- **Enforce cutoff filtering in every query path:** No exceptions
- **Log snapshot hash and extractor version:** Enables replay and audit of historical feature values
- **Compare against simpler baselines:** Both non-graph variants (tabular only) and static-graph variants (no temporal features)

Without these controls, performance estimates are unreliable. Temporal KG features require more evaluation infrastructure than static features, but the infrastructure is reusable across feature families and strategies. Enforcing temporal discipline requires supporting infrastructure. *Section 23.7* addresses database selection, ontology strategy, query safety, and schema evolution.

Implementation: See `07_dynamic_kg_temporal.py` for temporal snapshot construction and leakage-safe query patterns, and `08_8k_event_extraction.py` for the event extraction pipeline. Both notebooks run on the staged 8-K event graph. In the current notebook-scale run, the temporal notebook loads roughly 2,400 timestamped events from 207 companies, applies a 2025-11-01 disclosure-time cutoff that hides about 200 events, and retains roughly 2,200 in the visible snapshot, measures a mean disclosure lag near a week against a mean extraction lag of roughly three years, and verifies that no post-cutoff disclosures enter the visible graph. Alongside the parquet outputs, the notebook writes a `snapshot_manifest.json` that records the cutoff, window, upstream-extractor identity, and per-parquet SHA-256, the audit anchor for the **Log snapshot hash and the extractor version** protocol bullet above.

The extraction notebook processes 50 8-K filings with the Qwen2.5-7B model under FinReflectKG reflection; the critic–corrector loop lifts the validation rate by several percentage points through tens of corrections across the extracted events, and the typed relationships that emerge load idempotently to Neo4j. Counts vary run-to-run at the temperature=0.1 setting; the directional shift, not the exact tally, is the methodological claim.

23.7 Building a KG-ready pipeline

Reliable knowledge-graph workflows depend on supporting engineering infrastructure: database selection, ontology strategy, query safety, and schema evolution.

Engine and query language selection

For book workflows, Neo4j with Cypher is the default because it offers mature tooling and a low-friction path from prototype to medium-scale deployment. The decision framework for other contexts:

Engine Type	When to Choose	Key Trade-off
Neo4j (self-managed or Aura)	Teaching, research, medium-scale production	Strong developer tooling; operational tuning at scale
Managed cloud graph (Neptune, for example)	Teams optimizing for operations	Managed scaling and IAM; tighter cloud coupling
Distributed graph engine (TigerGraph, for example)	Very large graph analytics	High throughput on massive workloads; steeper complexity

Table 23.5: Graph database decision framework

For teams with existing relational infrastructure, PostgreSQL with recursive **Common Table Expressions** (CTE) can handle moderate graph workloads, particularly when the graph is narrow (few relationship types) and queries rarely exceed 3–4 hops. This avoids adding a new database to the stack, though query syntax becomes unwieldy for complex path patterns.

The practical selection rule: choose the engine that supports strict access boundaries, query guards, and stable schema metadata for text-to-Cypher controls. If those requirements are met, the specific engine matters less than the governance layer built on top of it. Cypher is the default for teaching because path patterns are concise and readable; Gremlin provides imperative traversal control in the AWS/Azure ecosystems; SPARQL is standard in RDF and linked data contexts. The structural thinking (node identity, typed relationships, and constraint-aware query design) carries over across languages.

Ontology strategy

Financial teams rarely adopt large-scale ontologies in a single step. The **Financial Industry Business Ontology** (FIBO) defines over 1,200 classes, a comprehensive standard but an impractical starting point for most implementations. Teams that attempt full FIBO adoption often stall during early iteration because the ontology's breadth obscures the analytical goal.

A pragmatic middle path captures interoperability benefits without engineering paralysis: align core entity classes with established identifiers (CIK, CUSIP, LEI) where natural, keep task-specific relationship vocabulary compact (most financial KG implementations use approximately 8–15 relationship types), and codify type constraints and validation rules in code rather than ontology management tools. A supply chain KG might use `Company`, `Filing`, and three relationship types (supplier, competitor, customer), small enough to reason about, large enough to support multi-hop analysis. When integration with external systems requires FIBO alignment, the mapping can be added incrementally without restructuring the core graph.

Query safety controls

Text-to-Cypher interfaces require runtime controls beyond database access management. A production-grade safety layer should enforce:

- **Read-only credentials for all natural-language query paths**: Write access should never be reachable from a text-to-Cypher interface
- **Allowlisted labels, relationships, and properties**: The LLM generates queries only against the declared schema, not the full database catalog
- **Query parameterization rather than string interpolation**: Prevents injection attacks and improves caching
- **Execution limits on timeout, row cap, and traversal depth**: Prevent runaway queries from degrading the database
- **Query logging for replay and audit**: Every generated and executed query should be traceable

These controls are architectural requirements, not optional hardening. Research on financial knowledge graph query interfaces (Zehra et al., 2021) confirms that query safety and explainability are first-order concerns for regulated deployment.

Schema versioning

Knowledge graphs evolve as extraction pipelines improve and analytical needs expand. Schema evolution without breaking existing queries requires discipline: additive changes (such as new node labels, relationship types, properties) are safe and should be the default pattern; renames or removals require migration scripts and downstream query audits; version metadata on edges (such as extractor version, schema version) enable coexistence of old and new extraction formats during transition periods.

A practical pattern is to tag each extraction run with a schema version and include version filters in queries when reproducibility is required. The minimal production architecture comprises an ingestion layer, a schema-constrained extraction layer, a canonicalization service, a graph database with read/write separation, a retrieval layer for safe text-to-Cypher execution, and an evaluation harness for query validity, provenance coverage, and temporal correctness.

Implementation: See `02_supply_chain_kg_construction.py` for schema and loading patterns.

23.8 Summary

Knowledge graphs earn their complexity only when the question is genuinely relational. That is the chapter's central discipline. When the answer depends on paths across entities, relationship types, and disclosure timing, graphs provide something vector retrieval cannot: explicit structure that can be traversed, audited, and reused. Graph construction is therefore as much a governance problem as an extraction problem. Identity resolution, schema constraints, provenance tracking, and temporal metadata are what turn noisy filings into graph objects that can support deterministic retrieval and downstream modeling.

Once that foundation is in place, graph workflows serve two distinct purposes. Graph RAG supports multi-hop reasoning by delegating relational logic to the database and language generation to the model, while graph analytics convert network structure into features that capture concentration, crowding, and contagion pathways invisible to standalone entity attributes. The companion notebooks ground each of these workflows empirically: the supply-chain extraction pipeline produces over a thousand typed relationships from S&P 100 filings, the RAG benchmark compares graph and vector retrieval on real institutional holdings questions, and the cross-graph feature pipeline combines supply-chain topology with 13F ownership signals into a unified feature matrix.

Throughout, the three-timestamp model remains decisive: without disclosure-time discipline, graph-derived signals are no more trustworthy than any other feature contaminated by look-ahead bias.

The next chapter uses some of the same ingredients in a different role. *Chapter 24* turns structured retrieval, memory, and evidence tracking into autonomous agent workflows for financial research and forecasting.

24

Autonomous Agents

Quantitative finance increasingly relies on systems that do more than evaluate fixed prediction functions. Earlier chapters focused on ML models that estimate returns and other targets from structured data. This chapter turns to agentic workflows: systems that gather evidence, use tools, maintain state, coordinate intermediate steps, and produce artifacts that can be reviewed, replayed, scored, and audited.

These workflows are useful beyond forecasting. In practice, agentic systems can support research, coding, data management, experiment tracking, report generation, monitoring, compliance review, and other tasks where the inputs are incomplete, heterogeneous, or changing. Their value does not come from replacing statistical models. It comes from organizing work around goals, evidence, tool use, provenance, and bounded autonomy.

The chapter therefore treats agents as engineering systems rather than chat interfaces. The core use case is decision support: collect market, document, and research evidence; turn that evidence into structured outputs; preserve enough state for replay and evaluation; and expose the controls that determine whether the result is trustworthy. This chapter does not cover autonomous trade execution. The systems here may search, read, compute, write sandboxed artifacts, and produce structured recommendations, but they do not place orders or commit capital. Execution and order routing require a stricter operational layer and are addressed in *Chapter 25*.

Two capstones make the architecture concrete. The first uses forecasting agents because event forecasting is evidence-rich, probabilistic, and externally scorable. A Bridgewater AIA-style system provides the motivating pattern: agents retrieve evidence, produce probability estimates, aggregate independent views, calibrate outputs, and preserve artifacts for later scoring. The second capstone generalizes the same primitives to the ML4T research process: an operator that uses coding, data, registry, and skill-retrieval tools to iterate on case-study research lines under bounded, replayable conditions.

After completing this chapter, you will be able to:

- Explain when agentic workflows add value in quantitative finance and when conventional statistical, rules-based, or batch pipelines remain the better choice.

- Distinguish the roles of ReAct, Tree of Thoughts, and Reflexion, and choose appropriate reasoning budgets for evidence-driven financial tasks.
- Design explicit state and memory schemas that support provenance, checkpointing, replay, schema evolution, and post-outcome evaluation.
- Specify robust tool contracts, structured outputs, source policies, and context-engineering rules for research, forecasting, and workflow agents.
- Compare single-agent, multi-agent, and operator-style architectures, and define a migration path from notebook prototypes to operational services without sacrificing visibility and control.
- Build an evidence-first forecasting workflow with structured output extraction, trace inspection, replayable artifacts, aggregation, calibration, and evaluation.
- Design a bounded research-iteration operator that uses coding, data, registry, and skill-retrieval tools while preserving auditability and human review.
- Define the operational, statistical, and security controls required to make agent outputs decision-grade, including point-in-time integrity, contamination-aware testing, observability, policy gates, sandboxing, and human approval boundaries.

The discussion moves from cognitive architectures to memory, tool integration, framework choices, and three implementations: a single-agent forecasting researcher, a multi-agent forecasting workflow, and an ML4T research-iteration operator. It closes with the controls that separate notebook demos from decision-grade systems, including point-in-time integrity, contamination-aware evaluation, observability, security policy, and human approval boundaries. *Section 24.1* begins with the structural shift from fixed prediction functions to adaptive agentic workflows.

24.1 From prediction functions to agentic workflows

Large language models change the structure of quantitative work (Korinek, 2025). Traditional pipelines map engineered features to outputs through fixed transformations: a model receives a feature vector and returns a prediction. **Agentic pipelines add an adaptive layer** that can inspect evidence, decide what information is missing, call tools to retrieve it, and update a persistent state before producing an output.

This shift does not replace statistical modeling; it changes where automation happens. Earlier chapters estimate returns, risk, and allocations using prepared datasets in which inputs are clean, and schemas are fixed. Agentic systems driven by large language models extend that pipeline upstream, into messier territory where raw evidence is noisy, heterogeneous, and incomplete. Kong et al. (2024) survey LLMs in investment management and identify retrieval augmentation and point-in-time discipline as prerequisites for reliable deployment, themes that recur throughout this chapter. In finance, this upstream layer includes filings, earnings transcripts, event calendars, policy statements, and market-implied probabilities: sources that vary in format, arrive on different schedules, and require relevance judgment before they can inform a decision.

Figure 24.1 shows the high-level architecture as a five-phase loop, from Perception and Reasoning to Planning, Action, and Observation.

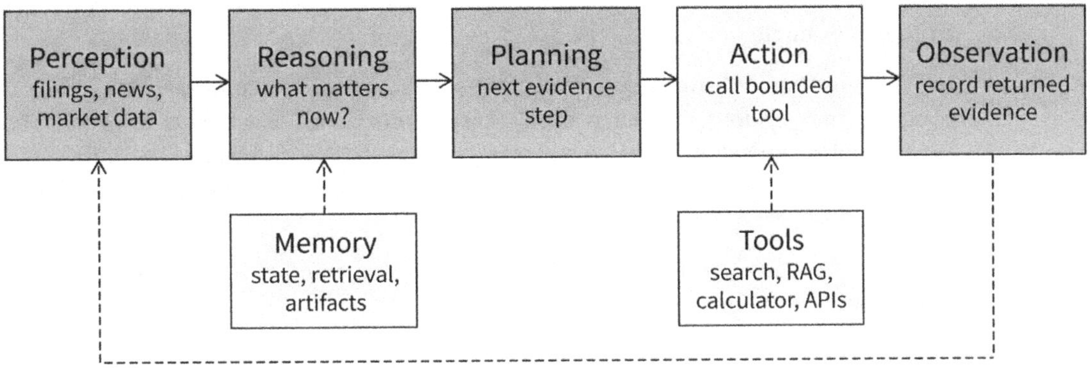

Figure 24.1: Non-trading agent loop from perception through observation, with tools and memory attached to the core workflow

In this chapter, "action" means **information actions**: calling a market-data API, querying a filing index, retrieving evidence from a vector store, requesting a calculation, or writing a structured artifact, not order execution. This boundary is a design choice: **read-only systems** are easier to secure and evaluate. It also aligns with the most credible public prototypes in the literature, including Bridgewater's **AIA Forecaster** and **AlphaAgents** (by authors from BlackRock), which treat agent workflows as research and forecasting systems rather than as autonomous execution engines (Alur et al., 2025; Zhao et al., 2025).

Ang et al. (2026) present the **Self-Driving Portfolio**, an agentic architecture for institutional asset management that coordinates approximately fifty specialized agents through a full strategic asset allocation pipeline from macro regime classification, capital market assumptions, and portfolio construction to peer review with voting and CIO-level ensemble combination. The paper shows how multi-agent architectures can compress workflows that traditionally require teams of specialists working over days into automated runs completed in minutes. Their pipeline operates at the analysis-and-recommendation boundary, not at the execution boundary, reinforcing the non-trading design principle.

Financial decisions are constrained by three properties that generic chatbot applications rarely face:

1. Outputs should be probabilities with calibration diagnostics, not narratives. Uncertainty quantification is not optional when capital is at risk.
2. The system must respect what was knowable at the decision date; any leakage of future information invalidates the entire output.
3. Every claim must map to specific evidence and tool traces, as regulatory and compliance reviews require an audit trail that connects conclusions to their sources.

Agentic systems derive their complexity from decisions that depend on the acquisition and synthesis of evidence rather than on fixed feature transformations: tasks such as event forecasting, due diligence workflows, and structured research support.

A running example

The running example estimates the probability that a prediction-market question resolves positively. The questions span macro events, corporate earnings, geopolitical developments, and technology milestones: heterogeneous, evidence-rich forecasting tasks where agentic workflows add genuine value over fixed pipelines. The complete workflow proceeds through **six stages:**

1. The system ingests the question and a decision cutoff date, enforcing point-in-time discipline.
2. It then gathers evidence through a web search limited to the cutoff date.
3. Multiple research agents produce independent probability forecasts from the evidence they each discover.
4. Those forecasts are aggregated using principled combination rules and calibrated against historical reliability.
5. The system persists all artifacts (evidence, reasoning traces, and probability estimates) so they can be replayed.
6. Finally, after the event has resolved, scoring functions evaluate forecast accuracy using appropriate scoring rules.

Every major section of the chapter maps to one stage of this pipeline, and the accompanying notebooks implement each stage progressively:

- `01_react_reasoning` builds the provider abstraction and ReAct loop.
- `02_tool_contracts` adds typed schemas and provenance.
- `03_state_and_memory` introduces checkpointed state and quality gates.
- `04_research_agent` composes these into a single-agent research workflow.
- `05_aggregation_math` through `08_forecasting_pipeline` construct the multi-agent system.
- `09_evaluation_and_governance` scores forecasts, runs ablations, and applies security controls.
- An optional `10_framework_comparison` contrasts the same pipeline in three framework styles.

Where agentic workflows do not help

Agentic orchestration is not a universal replacement for traditional pipelines, and recognizing the boundary prevents costly overengineering. When labels are stable and fully structured, the adaptive evidence-gathering loop adds latency and non-determinism without improving accuracy. When the task is latency-critical (for example, execution at microsecond granularity), the overhead of language model inference is prohibitive. When no external evidence retrieval is required and model decisions can be implemented as fixed transformations, the entire reasoning loop is unnecessary machinery. In these settings, simpler statistical or rules-based systems deliver better reliability-to-cost tradeoffs. Agents are best treated as an additional layer for evidence-rich tasks, not as a default replacement for existing model stacks.

Autonomy levels and realistic deployment boundaries

Agent deployments range from passive summarization (L0) through decision support with probability estimates (L1), constrained actions gated by human approval (L2), and progressively autonomous operation (L3–L4).

Most practical financial deployments remain at L1–L2 because the economics are asymmetric: a forecasting error is expensive, but a policy-free execution error can be catastrophic. A broad survey of agentic AI in finance confirms this pattern and documents the escalating systemic risk that accompanies higher autonomy (Aldridge et al., 2025). The notebooks in this chapter operate at L1, producing structured forecasts for human review.

Interface with reinforcement learning

Chapter 21 covers policy learning under reward signals, in which agents learn what to *do* from interactions with the environment. This chapter addresses a different layer: stateful research orchestration, in which the agent decides what to *know* before producing output.

The two layers are complementary: a research agent might produce probability estimates that feed an RL policy for position sizing, or an RL execution agent might query a research agent for updated fundamental context. Readers should treat this chapter's outputs as structured inputs to the simulation and deployment stages in *Chapters 16–21* and *25*. With the agentic workflow framed, *Section 24.2* turns to the reasoning patterns that drive it.

24.2 Cognitive architectures – How agents reason

Reasoning patterns are foundational to agent design, but they are only one layer of the system. The patterns discussed here build on chain-of-thought prompting (Wei et al., 2023), which showed that externalizing intermediate reasoning steps improves multi-step accuracy without fine-tuning. Li et al. (2025) survey the full spectrum of reasoning architectures in LLMs, from fast pattern matching to deliberate multi-step search. In production, the quality of reasoning also depends on tool contracts, state visibility, and evaluation infrastructure, topics addressed in later sections. This section introduces three key frameworks as building blocks and clarifies where each one earns its complexity.

The ReAct framework

ReAct (**Reason + Act**; Yao et al., 2023a) is the default pattern for evidence-grounded tasks. As *Figure 24.2* illustrates, it alternates between reasoning and tool use in a tight loop. The agent first identifies its next information need in a thought step, then selects and calls a tool, integrates the returned observation into its working context, and repeats until it judges the evidence sufficient for a response.

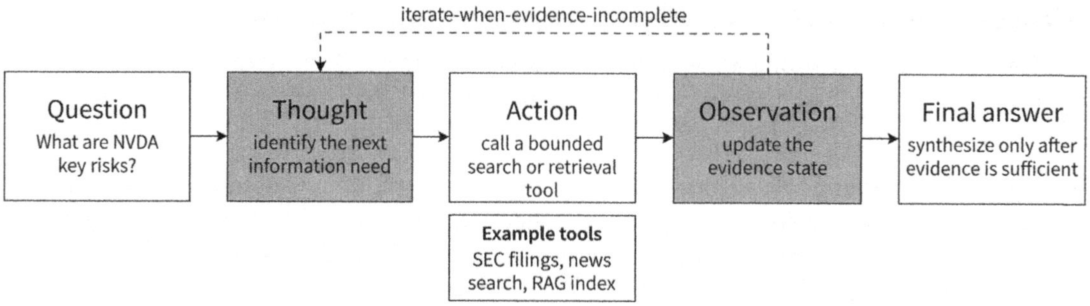

Figure 24.2: A flow diagram showing how ReAct alternates thought, tool use, and observation until the evidence is sufficient for an answer

The main benefit is **traceability**. Each intermediate claim can be linked to a specific tool call and observation, creating an audit trail that connects conclusions to sources. This property is valuable for compliance and debugging, especially when outputs are probabilistic forecasts that downstream systems consume.

ReAct also has predictable failure modes that practitioners should anticipate:

- **Repetitive tool loops** occur when the agent cannot determine that it has already retrieved the relevant evidence
- **Premature synthesis** occurs when the agent jumps to a conclusion based on a single observation rather than gathering corroborating data
- **Brittle behavior** follows from vague tool schemas: if the agent cannot distinguish between two tools with overlapping descriptions, it routes calls incorrectly
- **Hidden contradictions** accumulate when early and late observations conflict, but the agent never explicitly reconciles them

These failures are manageable when the workflow imposes iteration limits, evidence-sufficiency checks, and explicit state validators, all of which are shown in the accompanying notebooks.

> **Implementation:** `01_react_reasoning` builds the full ReAct loop with a provider-agnostic `LLMClient` protocol that decouples agent logic from any specific LLM service. The agent emits structured JSON decisions at each step rather than relying on fragile text parsing, producing an execution trace of thought-action-observation triplets that the reader can inspect for auditability.
>
> The same notebook switches providers without changing the agent code: the same loop runs against a deterministic mock, a local Ollama model, or a commercial API, establishing the abstraction that later notebooks inherit. Tree of Thoughts and Reflexion are presented as design patterns rather than dedicated notebook implementations; the capstone notebooks apply these ideas selectively within the multi-agent pipeline.

Tree of thoughts

Tree of Thoughts (ToT) (Yao et al., 2023b) expands reasoning by exploring multiple candidate paths in parallel before selecting one. Where ReAct follows a single evidence chain, ToT branches at decision points and evaluates alternatives before committing. This is useful when decisions depend on strategic branches rather than linear accumulation of evidence: for instance, scenario planning around divergent policy regimes, stress-testing allocation alternatives under different macro assumptions, or evaluating multiple hypothesis families before deciding which retrieval queries to run.

For example, an agent analyzing the impact of a central-bank rate decision might branch into a hawkish scenario (such as a higher terminal rate or a sector rotation toward financials), and a dovish scenario (for example, rate cuts or duration-sensitive growth stocks), retrieving different evidence sets for each branch before selecting the better-supported path. Without branching, the agent would commit to a single narrative early and retrieve only confirming evidence.

The cost is compute and complexity. ToT multiplies the number of model calls by the branching factor and introduces state management to track, score, and prune candidate paths. It should be reserved for situations in which branch exploration materially changes decisions. In a typical financial research workflow, this means high-stakes strategic questions where the cost of premature commitment outweighs the cost of additional inference.

Reflexion

Reflexion (Shinn et al., 2023) adds a post-run critique layer. After completing a task, the system records compact lessons (observations about what worked, what failed, and why) that can condition future behavior without full retraining. The method is attractive because it offers an adaptation mechanism that is lighter than fine-tuning but more persistent than single-conversation learning.

In practice, Reflexion helps only when memory policies are explicit. Lessons must carry provenance metadata that records when and under what conditions they were generated. Each lesson needs a validity horizon: a regime-change observation from a rising-rate environment should not persist indefinitely into a low-rate regime. Decay and pruning rules must retire stale lessons before they become persistent bias. And a rollback mechanism must handle the case where new evidence contradicts a stored lesson. Without these controls, Reflexion can convert temporary heuristics into durable analytical blind spots. *Section 24.3* formalizes the memory hierarchy that supports these policies.

Choosing and composing reasoning patterns

A practical selection rule starts with ReAct as the baseline, adds ToT only for branch-heavy decisions where parallel hypothesis evaluation improves outcomes, and layers in Reflexion only after the core evaluation pipeline is stable enough to reliably identify which lessons are worth persisting. This sequence aligns engineering effort with measurable benefit: ReAct is cheap and auditable, ToT adds cost proportional to the number of branches, and Reflexion requires the most infrastructure investment.

In real workflows, these patterns are usually composed rather than used in isolation. A common composition for forecasting tasks begins with ReAct for initial evidence gathering, branches into a brief ToT exploration when observations conflict and competing interpretations require explicit comparison, and optionally records a Reflexion note after scoring once outcomes are resolved. Composition should remain shallow (one layer of each) unless evaluation shows clear gains from deeper nesting. Deeply nested compositions increase trace complexity and make failure analysis substantially harder.

A practical guardrail is to define a maximum reasoning budget per run: a cap on total tool calls, a limit on branch count, and a ceiling on reconciliation rounds. When the budget is exhausted, the system should return a bounded output with explicit uncertainty rather than continue exploratory reasoning indefinitely. *Section 24.7* applies these budgets to the multi-agent capstone.

The following table compares the mechanisms, strengths, and best applications of each framework.

Framework	Mechanism	Strengths	Best For
ReAct	Thought-Action-Observation loop	Grounded, auditable	Interactive research, due diligence
Tree of Thoughts	Parallel path exploration	Strategic depth	Scenario analysis, portfolio alternatives
Reflexion	Post-run critique and memory	Adaptive behavior	Iterative workflow refinement

Table 24.1: Reasoning frameworks: mechanism, strengths, and finance applications

These frameworks are complementary. The chapter capstones use ReAct-style evidence loops as the default and add multi-agent and evaluation layers only where they provide measurable incremental value. Reasoning patterns determine how an agent thinks; *Section 24.3* addresses what it remembers.

24.3 Agent memory – State, persistence, and replay

After selecting a reasoning pattern, the next design task is memory. In agentic finance workflows, memory determines whether the system is testable and auditable. A one-shot prompt can produce a plausible answer, but a durable workflow requires explicit memory across multiple timescales: within a single reasoning step, across a task session, and between sessions over weeks or months.

The memory hierarchy

Figure 24.3 separates three timescales:

1. *Working* memory is the model context for the current reasoning step: prompt instructions, current state fields, recent tool outputs, and any retrieved evidence. It is bounded by the model's context window and refreshed at every turn.
2. *Short-term* memory spans the task session, storing attempted actions, unresolved questions, temporary conclusions, and recent failures so the agent does not repeat dead-end searches or lose track of partial results.
3. *Long-term* memory is persistent storage that survives across sessions: retrieval indices, run artifacts, scored outcomes, and calibration history that the system can query as needed.

The memory types are shown in the following flow diagram:

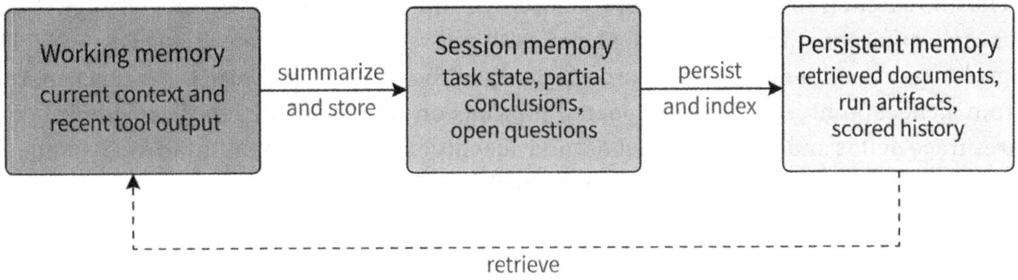

Figure 24.3: Working, session, and persistent memory support replay, audit, and disciplined reuse

Yu et al. (2025) operationalize this hierarchy in **FINMEM**, a trading agent with layered memory and profiled character traits that adapts risk tolerance across market regimes. Their results show that explicit memory structure improves both performance and interpretability: the agent can explain which stored observations informed its current decision.

The main engineering risk is conflating these layers. When long-lived facts are kept only in context windows, reproducibility fails: the same question asked in a different conversation yields a different answer because the evidence has scrolled out of context. When transient reasoning is written directly to long-term memory without validation, stale assumptions accumulate, biasing future runs.

Why explicit state is mandatory

Implicit chat history is convenient for prototypes but inadequate for production. A conversation transcript mixes instructions, evidence, reasoning, and tool outputs into an undifferentiated stream. Extracting any specific artifact (say, the evidence that supported a particular probability estimate) requires parsing free text, which is fragile and unreproducible.

Typed state objects solve this by making transitions explicit. A minimal state schema for a forecasting agent includes run and question identifiers, plus `as_of_date` and `cutoff_date`, which enforce point-in-time discipline. The remaining fields record evidence, reasoning, and intermediate outputs: structured evidence records with source metadata and timestamps; a list of unresolved sub-tasks; a tool-call trace with status codes and error messages; intermediate probability estimates with associated confidence; and a decision artifact status that tracks whether the output is a draft, under review, or finalized.

These fields serve two purposes: they enable static and runtime validation before outputs are accepted, and they provide the substrate for replay and evaluation. Without them, debugging reduces to rereading conversation logs and guessing where the reasoning went wrong.

Checkpointing, replay, and diagnosis

Checkpointing should be tied to decision boundaries rather than arbitrary intervals. The natural checkpoints for a forecasting workflow fall after initial evidence collection (when the agent has gathered its inputs), after contradiction resolution (when conflicting observations have been reconciled), before final synthesis (when intermediate probabilities are about to be combined), and before any high-impact downstream handoff (when the output will feed another system). **Each checkpoint captures the full state object**, all tool outputs received so far, and the metadata required for faithful replay.

Replay is the core debugging mechanism for non-deterministic systems. Because language models are stochastic, a failing run cannot be reproduced by simply re-running the same prompt: the model may generate different reasoning paths. The objective of replay is to **isolate changes in model behavior** from changes in evidence. A useful protocol freezes the tool outputs from the target run, restores state from a checkpoint, reruns with updated prompts or policies while holding evidence constant, compares trace deltas and evaluation deltas, and accepts only changes that improve defined metrics. Without this discipline, teams routinely mistake evidence drift for prompt improvements, concluding that a reworded system prompt fixed a problem when in fact the underlying data shifted.

Memory lifecycle and governance

Long-term memory requires governance because not all stored information should be reused indefinitely. Each artifact type needs a retention window: raw tool outputs might persist for the scoring horizon plus a buffer, while intermediate reasoning traces might expire after evaluation. Eviction rules must retire stale lessons before they become persistent bias. Provenance requirements ensure that reusable evidence carries enough metadata to verify its point-in-time validity. And conflict-handling policies must specify what happens when a new observation contradicts stored material: does the old artifact get flagged, archived, or deleted?

These policies are especially important for adaptive memory methods such as Reflexion (*Section 24.2*). A lesson tied to a specific volatility regime or policy environment should expire when conditions change. FinCon (Yu et al., 2024) takes a related approach: a multi-agent system that stores investment beliefs as natural-language summaries and re-injects them across episodes, using conceptual verbal reinforcement to improve sequential decisions without full retraining. The critical implementation detail is that stored beliefs carry regime tags and can be pruned when the tagged conditions no longer hold.

State schemas evolve as workflows mature. Every checkpoint should carry an explicit schema version with migration rules between adjacent versions, so that historical artifacts remain comparable across refactoring boundaries.

Memory and evaluation are coupled

Forecast evaluation depends on memory quality in ways that are easy to underestimate. Calibration requires historical forecast-outcome pairs stored with enough resolution to verify whether events rated at 70% actually occurred roughly 70% of the time. Ablation analysis (testing whether removing a tool or evidence source changes outcomes) requires that intermediate artifacts from the original run be preserved. If artifact persistence is incomplete, evaluation shifts from systematic analysis to anecdotal review, rendering the agent's claimed accuracy unverifiable. *Section 24.7* develops the full evaluation methodology.

Agent reliability depends on explicit state, disciplined persistence, and replayable diagnostics. Fluent output does not substitute for any of them, and memory design therefore belongs as much to model risk control as to software architecture.

Implementation: `03_state_and_memory` makes these principles concrete. The notebook defines an `AgentState` dataclass that carries a run identifier, a forecast question, a cut-off date, an evidence list with source metadata and timestamps, a tool-call trace, open sub-questions, quality-gate results, and a synthesis status field.

Three quality gates enforce evidence discipline before the agent may advance to synthesis: a coverage gate that verifies all required evidence types are present, a freshness gate that rejects evidence outside the allowed time window, and a consistency gate that detects ticker mismatches and post-cutoff data leakage. The notebook also exercises checkpoint round-trip serialization (writing state to JSON, restoring it, and verifying that the restored object passes the same gates), establishing the replay substrate that *Section 24.6* applies in a full research agent workflow and that *Section 24.7* extends to multi-agent evaluation.

With state and memory in place, the next control surface is how the agent interacts with the outside world. *Section 24.4* formalizes tool contracts, provenance, and context engineering.

24.4 Tool integration – Contracts, controls, and context engineering

With an explicit state defined, tool integration becomes the next control surface. Tools convert language-model reasoning into verifiable operations: retrieving a stock quote, querying a filing index, or computing a rolling statistic. In finance, tool design is often the dominant determinant of agent quality, outweighing prompt engineering and even model selection.

Tool categories for research and forecasting

A forecasting agent typically requires four classes of tools:

1. Market data tools retrieve prices, implied signals such as option-derived volatility, and event metadata like earnings dates and dividend announcements.
2. Document tools access filings, earnings transcripts, and analyst reports, either from local storage or through retrieval-augmented generation pipelines.
3. Search tools find recent external evidence (news articles, regulatory announcements, macroeconomic releases) subject to source controls that limit which domains the agent may query.
4. Deterministic calculation tools handle statistics and transformations that should not depend on language model stochasticity: computing returns, running regressions, or evaluating scoring functions.

Execution tools (order placement, portfolio rebalancing) constitute a separate layer with substantially stricter controls. They are not required for this chapter, which operates at the read-only boundary established in *Section 24.1*.

Tool contracts and selection quality

A tool contract specifies purpose and scope, required arguments with their types and allowed value ranges, error semantics that distinguish transient failures from permanent ones, and provenance fields that every response must carry. Weak contracts push complexity into prompt text: if the model must infer from a vague description whether a tool returns adjusted or unadjusted prices, it will sometimes guess wrong. Strong contracts move constraints into typed interfaces and validation logic, where they can be checked statically before a call is dispatched.

High-quality tool descriptions include three parts: what the tool returns, when to call it, and when *not* to call it. The negative guidance matters because failures in tool selection are among the most common agent bugs. Typical patterns include selecting a broad tool when a scoped alternative exists (querying a general news API when a filing-specific tool would return more precise results), repeating calls after definitive errors, calling tools with incomplete arguments that trigger silent defaults rather than explicit failures, and mixing stale and current evidence without checking timestamps. Mitigations include argument validators that reject malformed calls before execution, retry policies that vary by error class, and state-based guardrails that block reasoning transitions until required fields are present.

Context engineering

Context engineering is the controlled design of model-visible information across reasoning steps. Rather than sending the full accumulated context into every step (a common anti-pattern that wastes tokens and introduces noise), each step should expose only the state fields relevant to its task, make available only the tools appropriate for its phase, restrict evidence sources to those consistent with the current point-in-time boundary, and require a specific output schema that downstream steps can parse deterministically.

This principle applies at every scale. Within a single ReAct loop, the agent's system prompt should specify which tools are active for that phase. Across a multi-agent pipeline, each specialist should receive only the evidence relevant to their analytical perspective, not the full research dossier. The result is reduced ambiguity, improved reproducibility, and lower cost: three properties that compound as agent complexity grows.

Provenance and structured output

Whenever downstream components are code rather than humans reading prose, agent outputs should be structured objects: evidence records with source metadata, specialist forecast objects with probability estimates and reasoning summaries, uncertainty quantifications, and final decision artifacts. Structured outputs support deterministic parsing, schema validation, and consistent logging, all prerequisites for the replay infrastructure described in *Section 24.3*.

Tool responses should carry provenance by default. A practical response schema includes a source identifier, publication and retrieval timestamps, a document span or record key that localizes the evidence, policy flags such as allowlist status, and quality annotations when available. These fields make it possible to answer three operational questions quickly: Was this evidence available at the decision date? Which tool and source produced this value? Can the claim be reproduced from stored artifacts? When provenance is absent, errors propagate silently and are expensive to diagnose after the fact.

Enforcing structured output

Typed output contracts are only as reliable as the enforcement mechanism. Major providers now offer built-in structured-output modes: JSON mode constrains generation to valid JSON, tool-use forcing requires the model to emit a function call rather than free text, and schema-validated generation checks outputs against a JSON Schema before returning them to the caller. These mechanisms move validation from post hoc parsing into the generation loop itself, eliminating an entire class of deserialization failures.

For the forecasting pipeline in this chapter, enforcement matters at two boundaries. Specialist agents must emit structured forecast objects with typed probability fields, not prose that downstream code must parse with regex. The supervisor must emit a final decision artifact that passes schema validation before it enters the persistence layer. When a model cannot satisfy the schema because the evidence is insufficient or the question is ambiguous, the enforcement layer should surface a structured error or abstention object rather than silently falling back to unstructured text. The chapter notebooks apply a lighter-weight version of this discipline: `01_react_reasoning.py` uses JSON-mode responses for tool decisions, while later notebooks move forecast artifacts into typed dataclass schemas and explicit validation logic in the orchestration layer. The design principle is the contract, not a particular validation library.

Source policy

Search and retrieval tools require an explicit source policy. Domain allowlists restrict the agent to trusted sources. Date constraints tied to the run's cutoff date enforce point-in-time discipline at the tool level rather than relying on the model to self-police. Source metadata must be present in every returned item so that downstream evaluation can trace claims to origins.

The FinDER benchmark (Choi et al., 2025) underscores this dependence in financial question answering over 10-K filings: retrieval quality is a binding constraint on downstream generation quality, which makes source policy a first-order determinant of agent output accuracy.

Error handling and graceful degradation

Not all tool failures should trigger hard stops. A robust agent distinguishes transient failures that warrant retries, persistent tool failures that require a fallback path, policy violations that must be denied and escalated, and missing critical evidence that should result in an explicit abstention rather than a fabricated answer. Graceful degradation means returning a bounded output with explicit uncertainty rather than manufacturing false confidence, a property that matters more in financial applications than in most other domains.

Model Context Protocol (**MCP**) standardizes tool access across providers and runtimes. A pragmatic strategy is to start with direct integrations for core tools where latency matters, and to adopt MCP selectively where interoperability benefits outweigh the overhead. The *Chapter 22* RAG pipeline applies this pattern for document retrieval tools.

In finance, tool integration is a systems-design problem. Reliable results require strong contracts, narrow permissions, explicit exposure of context, and structured outputs. Prompt quality matters, but tool quality sets the ceiling. With reasoning, memory, and tools defined, *Section 24.5* addresses the framework and engineering stack that hosts them.

> **Implementation:** `02_tool_contracts` applies these principles with a ToolDefinition class that exports typed JSON schemas in both Anthropic and OpenAI formats from a single definition, eliminating provider-specific boilerplate. Every tool response is wrapped in a provenance-enriched result that carries a source identifier, publication, and retrieval timestamps, and policy-compliance metadata.
>
> The notebook enforces a domain allowlist that restricts retrieval to approved sources and logs blocked calls with the policy that triggered the denial. Argument validation rejects malformed requests before execution, and the full execution log is structured for downstream replay and audit.

24.5 The engineering stack – Frameworks and migration

Given the tool and state requirements established in the preceding sections, the choice of framework becomes an implementation question. Framework discussion is often presented as a ranking problem: which library posts the highest benchmark score? For agentic finance workflows, this framing is usually unhelpful because the binding constraints are not benchmark accuracy but state visibility, replay capability, and policy enforcement. The better question is which framework best supports the controls required by the target workflow.

Start from constraints, not preferences

Industry experience reinforces this constraint-first perspective. Recent practitioner write-ups describe agentic systems that are useful only when tightly integrated with proprietary tools, data controls, and evaluation loops, rather than being treated as stand-alone chat products (Fang and Moore, 2025). The common lesson is that workflow value comes from domain integration and governance, not from the choice of framework by itself.

A cautionary note: framework ecosystems evolve rapidly, and the landscape in early 2026 may differ from what readers encounter. The principles in *Sections 24.3-24.4*, namely explicit state, typed contracts, and replay support, outlast any specific library. If a framework enforces these properties with less boilerplate, adopt it; if it obscures them, avoid it regardless of benchmark claims.

Framework choice should follow from explicit constraints: the required state visibility; whether the team needs replay and checkpoint support for debugging non-deterministic runs; the complexity of the retrieval pipeline; whether a single agent with well-designed tools suffices or multi-agent orchestration is necessary; the debugging and observability infrastructure that must be in place before production; and deployment constraints such as team size, existing infrastructure, and maintenance budget. When these constraints are stated clearly, many choices become straightforward.

Need	Preferred Style	Typical Fit
Minimal overhead, full custom control	Native SDK and typed schemas	Small or tightly scoped agents
Quick ReAct/tool orchestration	Lightweight agent framework	Prototypes and teaching labs
Retrieval-centric applications	Retrieval-first framework abstractions	RAG-heavy workflows
Explicit state and durable execution	State-graph framework with persistence and replay	Production research pipelines
Complex multi-role collaboration	Multi-agent orchestration framework with role models	Specialized collaboration tasks

Table 24.2: Design-choice matrix

From notebook pattern to production demo

The notebooks build toward the production demo. Early notebooks isolate provider abstractions, tool contracts, state, and aggregation so readers can see each control surface clearly. Later notebooks compose those pieces into a forecasting workflow. The final step is to place the same logic within a stricter software boundary that includes configuration, connectors, storage, evaluation jobs, and publishing. In this chapter, that culmination is the `aia-forecaster` implementation, which turns the notebook patterns into a runnable forecasting service rather than a sequence of disconnected examples.

This progression also clarifies what a "framework comparison" can and cannot establish. `10_framework_comparison.py` compares how the same forecasting task looks when expressed as explicit Python, CrewAI-style role orchestration, and a LangGraph-style state graph. That comparison is useful because it explains the migration path into the production demo: start with explicit control flow, add stateful orchestration only where it helps, then wrap the resulting workflow in a packaged application boundary. The production forecaster is therefore not a different architectural idea; it is the end of the notebook sequence with stronger operational constraints.

Migration sequence that reduces rework

A practical migration sequence keeps complexity proportional to measured benefit. Start by building a minimal baseline with native SDK calls and typed output schemas: this establishes the core data flow and makes the agent's behavior testable from the first day. Next, add explicit state objects and trace capture so that every reasoning step is logged and inspectable. Then add checkpoints and replay hooks to support the debugging protocol from *Section 24.3*. Finally, add multi-agent orchestration only when evaluation shows that specialist diversity or adversarial debate produces measurable improvement over the single-agent baseline.

This incremental approach avoids a common set of anti-patterns: adopting multi-agent abstractions before a single-agent baseline shows the task is feasible; relying on framework defaults for security controls that should be explicit; postponing observability until after deployment, when debugging costs are highest; and treating framework migration as a substitute for evaluation methodology. Framework changes can improve ergonomics, such as better graph visualization and more convenient checkpointing APIs, but they rarely fix weak state design or poor scoring practices.

Comparing frameworks locally

If a direct comparison is needed, compare one reproducible task using a single fixed dataset and metric suite, keeping prompts, tools, and policies constant so that differences reflect framework behavior rather than configuration drift. Report traceability quality, failure rates, and debug effort alongside task accuracy.

For this chapter, the comparison is intentionally narrow. The notebook contrasts a fully executable native SDK implementation with two framework-style expressions of the same pipeline. That makes it useful for reasoning about migration and state visibility, but not for producing a head-to-head vendor ranking.

Pattern	State Handling	Chapter Status	Best Fit
Native SDK	Explicit Python objects and functions	Fully executable	Small or linear pipelines that need full control
CrewAI-style roles/tasks	Framework-managed task orchestration	Illustrative pseudocode	Role-based collaboration and fast prototyping
LangGraph-style state graph	Explicit graph state and node transitions	Illustrative pseudocode	Branching workflows that benefit from durable state
Packaged application layer	Config, storage, connectors, jobs, and publishing around an agent core	Implemented in companion repo	Operational forecasting services

Table 24.3: Framework patterns compared in the chapter

Framework selection also has team-operating implications. Explicit graph-based orchestration often improves code review and incident triage because state transitions are visible in the graph definition rather than buried in conversation history. More implicit orchestration may accelerate prototyping, but can increase debugging costs when failures occur in opaque internal routing. Multi-agent abstractions improve modularity and separation of concerns, but they require stronger integration testing and clearer ownership boundaries to prevent coordination failures. Once a workflow becomes operational, another layer appears above the orchestration framework: profile-aware configuration, artifact versioning, connector health, storage migrations, and scheduled jobs. These are software-engineering concerns, but they determine whether the agent can be evaluated and maintained over time.

Implementation: `10_framework_comparison` includes a fully executable native SDK, along with CrewAI- and LangGraph-style pseudocode for the same forecasting task. The native variant runs end-to-end with the same `LLMClient` and `ToolExecutor` used throughout the chapter; the framework variants are illustrative patterns that show how role definitions, task orchestration, and state-graph nodes can express the same logic. The comparison reveals concrete trade-offs: the native SDK offers maximum debuggability and state visibility at the cost of manual orchestration, while graph-based frameworks provide persistence and visualization at the cost of framework coupling.

Operational deployment is handled by the companion `aia-forecaster` repository, which wraps the same forecasting pipeline in configuration profiles, prediction-market connectors (such as Manifold or Polymarket), persistent run and forecast storage, scheduled evaluation commands, and a publishing layer that emits forecast feeds and evidence ledgers.

Framework choice is an architecture decision, not a performance claim. The right selection enforces state discipline, replayability, and policy controls for the specific workflow. *Section 24.6* applies all of these building blocks in the chapter's first capstone: a stateful research agent.

24.6 Designing the research agent at the heart of the pipeline

This section operationalizes the design patterns from the preceding sections in a single-agent setting. The workflow remains read-only and evidence-driven. The objective is to produce a calibrated probability forecast for a prediction-market question using web search as the sole evidence tool. Every claim in the output must trace to a specific search query and its results, and the system must persist enough artifacts for replay and inspection. This notebook is the first capstone in the chapter's progression toward the production forecasting demo: it keeps the scope narrow so that state, output extraction, and trace inspection remain legible before those same controls are embedded in a larger multi-agent pipeline.

Architecture and toolset

The agent combines a single constrained tool, explicit ReAct-loop control flow, structured output extraction, and persistent traces for replay. The sole tool is web search: the same design choice made by the AIA Forecaster, where limiting the agent to a single tool class simplifies the contract surface and focuses evaluation on reasoning quality rather than tool-routing accuracy. The search tool enforces a cutoff date at the tool boundary, preventing post-cutoff evidence from entering the context. Execution tools are deliberately excluded. This agent produces probability estimates, not orders.

The agent emits structured JSON at every step, choosing between two actions: `search` (issue a query) or `forecast` (produce a probability with rationale). This two-action schema is minimal by design: it eliminates the tool-selection ambiguity that causes routing failures in richer tool sets. The step prompt provides the question, optional market context, and the action schema; the agent must output exactly one valid JSON action per step.

ReAct loop and rich output extraction

The workflow follows the ReAct pattern from *Section 24.2*. The agent begins by assessing what information it needs, issues search queries to gather evidence, and terminates with a forecast action when it judges the evidence sufficient. A configurable step limit (default: five) prevents unbounded exploration. If the agent exhausts its budget without forecasting, the system records a forced default with explicit uncertainty rather than manufacturing confidence.

After the agent produces a forecast, the system extracts rich metadata beyond the raw probability. Confidence is either explicit (if the LLM includes it) or inferred from probability extremity $\text{confidence} = 2 \cdot |p_{\text{yes}} - 0.5|$. Sentiment maps the probability to a five-level scale from strongly bearish to strongly bullish. Key findings and uncertainties are extracted from the rationale text. Evidence quality is assessed from the number of search queries and sources consulted. The result is an `AgentForecastArtifact` that captures not just the prediction but the full provenance chain: traces, token usage, confidence, sentiment, evidence quality, and reasoning.

The quality gates from *Section 24.3* apply here as well. The state and memory notebook establishes the pattern: coverage gates verify that sufficient evidence was gathered, freshness gates check that evidence falls within the allowed window, and consistency gates detect post-cutoff leakage. These gates use the same mechanism as the multi-agent pipeline. The difference is that, at the single-agent level, gate failures are easy to diagnose and fix.

Trace inspection and replay

Every step of the ReAct loop is captured in an `AgentTrace` object: the step number, the action taken, the search query (if any), the results returned, and the raw LLM output. This trace makes the agent's reasoning path fully inspectable after the run completes. The full artifact (including traces, extracted metadata, and token usage) can be serialized to JSON for checkpoint round-tripping and comparison across runs.

In the production demo, the same discipline is carried into persistent run and forecast records. The important continuity is not the storage mechanism itself but the fact that every later scoring and audit step depends on artifacts that can be reconstructed without re-reading free-form transcripts.

Walkthrough of a typical run

A typical run unfolds as a short sequence of bounded transitions. The agent receives a prediction-market question and an optional market-implied probability, searches for relevant evidence using one to three queries, and produces a forecast with a rationale grounded in the evidence it finds. The full trace and serialized artifact are then available for inspection.

This sequence matters because it isolates failure points. If forecast quality is poor, the trace reveals whether the root cause was insufficient search queries, irrelevant results, JSON parsing failures, or flawed reasoning. In practice, the most common failures in this implementation are search queries that miss the key evidence, LLM outputs that fail JSON parsing, or rationales that ignore retrieved evidence in favor of prior knowledge. Those are exactly the failure classes that later grow more expensive in a multi-agent system, which is why the chapter addresses them here first.

Evaluation and acceptance criteria

Before promoting to multi-agent workflows, the single-agent baseline should show stable task success across repeated runs, evidence groundedness above a predefined threshold, a low forced-default rate, reproducible artifacts from stored traces, and reasonable token efficiency. These criteria prevent premature escalation to more complex architectures, a common mistake when prototype results look promising but reproducibility has not been verified. *Section 24.7* develops the full evaluation methodology and extends this single-agent pattern into the production-oriented forecasting workflow.

When results are weak, debug in this order: tool contracts and search quality first, then JSON parsing and output extraction, then prompt wording. Most reliability failures originate in tool and parsing design, not in language generation. *Section 24.7* extends this single-agent baseline to a multi-agent forecasting system that incorporates agent diversity, aggregation, debate, and calibrated evaluation.

> **Implementation:** `04_research_agent` builds the complete `ResearchAgent` class that is reused throughout the rest of the chapter. The agent runs a ReAct loop on a live prediction-market question (fetched from Polymarket or a resolved evaluation panel), using web search as its sole evidence tool. Each step produces structured JSON: either a search action with a query or a forecast action with a probability and rationale.
>
> The notebook records rich output extraction (confidence, sentiment, key findings, uncertainties, and evidence quality), all captured in an `AgentForecastArtifact` with full provenance. The execution trace shows every search query, its results, and the final reasoning path. When run in mock mode (the default for CI), responses are deterministic and reproducible; when run with a live LLM provider, the agent performs real web searches and produces genuine forecasts. Readers can modify the provider, step limit, or search parameters through the Papermill parameters cell and observe how the agent adapts its search strategy and forecast quality.

24.7 Multi-agent forecasting systems

Section 24.6 established a single-agent research baseline. This section extends that baseline to a multi-agent forecasting architecture designed for probability quality, traceability, and reproducible evaluation. The capstone is a forecasting system, not an autonomous trading engine. Its design draws on two public architectures:

- **AIA Forecaster** combines agentic search, supervisor reconciliation, and calibration in a read-only prediction-market workflow (Alur et al., 2025)

- **AlphaAgents** emphasizes specialist roles and debate for equity decision support (Zhao et al., 2025)

The chapter implements the AIA-style pipeline: parallel research agents, aggregation, optional debate, supervisor review, calibration, and persisted forecast artifacts. The outputs remain probability forecasts and scored artifacts, and their value is measured after event resolution rather than at the time of narrative generation.

Architecture – From agent ensemble to production pipeline

The architecture is easiest to understand in terms of six layers, each producing artifacts that make the system evaluable and debuggable at every stage. The intake layer loads open questions, resolution criteria, and market baseline signals from prediction-market connectors. It records the decision timestamp and the cutoff date used for the downstream retrieval policy. That step defines the point-in-time envelope that every subsequent tool call must respect.

The research layer then runs parallel agents under the same cutoff policy. The AIA Forecaster proposes that **agents** sharing a single prompt still produce useful variation because each issues its own search queries and reasons over whatever those queries return (Alur et al., 2025); stochastic sampling sends them down different retrieval paths rather than role specialization. The chapter notebooks test how much that variation matters and find the answer depends on the question. On `06_multi_agent_research`, three Claude Sonnet 4 agents forecast whether the US will enter a recession by the end of 2026, a question whose public evidence points in one direction. Their search paths still differed: one agent weighted current low-risk model readouts, the others leaned on historical base rates. The three forecasts nonetheless clustered at probabilities of 0.12, 0.22, and 0.22, close to the market price of 0.175. When the evidence is one-directional, independent agents reach similar probabilities, and that agreement is the expected outcome.

A genuinely contested question produces a wider spread for the same reason. On `07_adversarial_debate`, the agents forecast whether the Fed will hike in 2026, where credible evidence supports both sides; the same three-agent setup returned 0.35, 0.58, and 0.38, and the assigned bull and bear roles held a gap near 0.4 across three rounds without reaching consensus. The condition worth watching for is the opposite of either outcome: identical search results, identical reasoning, and an identical forecast across agents would signal a broken sampling temperature or a structural bug that suppressed the variation. That uniformity is the case to debug; similar numbers on a one-directional question are not. Forecast spread tracks how contested a question's evidence is, not a sampling setting the operator can turn up on demand.

Debate and role specialization are therefore configuration choices to evaluate against the target question set, not fixes for a failure mode. An adversarial bull-bear stage and specialist mandates incur added latency on two-sided questions, where surfacing and stress-testing the disagreement move the aggregate; on one-directional questions, they add cost without changing the answer. Specialist-role architectures such as AlphaAgents (Zhao et al., 2025) and the institutional SAA pipeline of Ang, Azimbayev, and Kim (2026), which assigns distinct macro, asset-class, portfolio-construction, and risk mandates across roughly fifty agents, extend the same logic: explicit structure buys diversity that sampling alone does not, and whether it pays is empirical.

If specialist roles produce measurably better calibration on the target questions, they justify their complexity; otherwise, a single research role plus an optional debate stage is the simpler default.

The next four layers convert those agent outputs into a forecast that can be tracked over time:

- **Aggregation** combines the independent probabilities into a pre-supervisor estimate. An optional debate stage stress-tests that estimate when the configuration enables bull-bear reconciliation.
- The **supervisor** layer identifies disagreements, performs clarifying searches, and may override the aggregate only when its confidence clears a policy threshold. The final calibration layer transforms the probability into the published forecast.
- The **persistence** and **scoring** layers store all intermediate and final artifacts so that calibration monitoring, baseline comparison, and ablation analysis can proceed after events resolve. Without this final layer, the system cannot learn from its own history.

The pipeline is shown in the following figure:

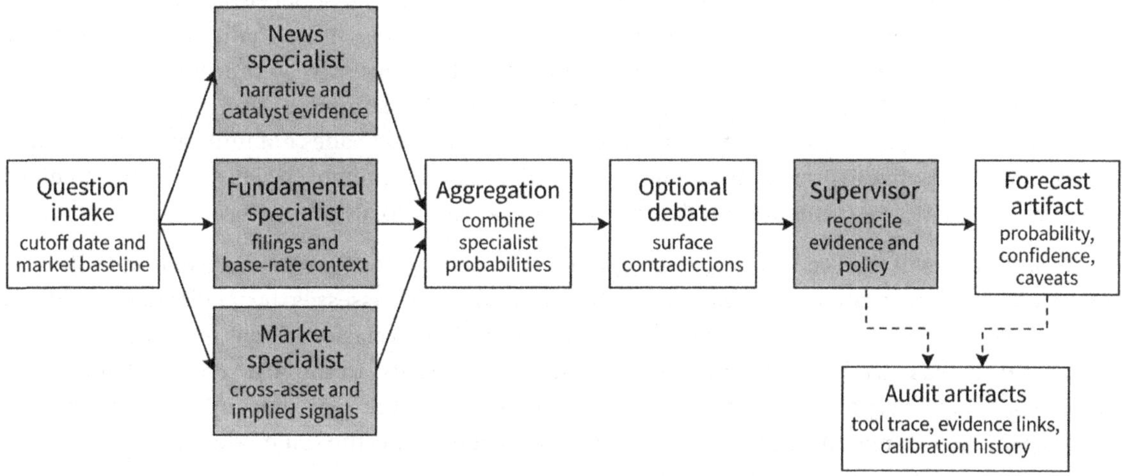

Figure 24.4: Multi-agent forecasting pipeline with research agents, aggregation, debate, and supervisor stages

Aggregation and extremization

Aggregation encodes assumptions about dependence and is not a cosmetic step. Options range from simple averaging to weighted combinations based on historical reliability or evidence quality. The notebook demo exposes these choices as configuration rather than burying them inside prompts: mean, median, trimmed mean, and **Neyman-style extremization** are all explicit policies. A more principled approach is to apply extremization, which amplifies deviations from the base rate when forecaster diversity is genuinely high. One form is:

$$p_{\text{extreme}} = \text{base} + d \times (p_{\text{mean}} - \text{base})$$

where $d > 1$ increases the distance from the base rate. Neyman's extremization factor under an equicorrelated model is $d = \sqrt{n/(1 + (n - 1)\rho)}$, where n is the number of forecasters and ρ is their average pairwise correlation. When agents are perfectly independent ($\rho = 0$), $d = \sqrt{n}$ and extremization is aggressive. When they are highly correlated ($\rho \to 1$), $d \to 1$, and the mean passes through unmodified. This correctly reflects the fact that correlated agents contribute less independent information.

`05_aggregation_math` visualizes this relationship directly: a sensitivity plot shows how the extremization factor d varies with correlation ρ for different numbers of forecasters, making clear that adding correlated agents provides diminishing marginal information. The notebook also implements Platt scaling and compares calibrated against uncalibrated aggregates. This relationship exposes a fundamental design tension: adding more agents improves forecasts only if they bring genuinely diverse evidence, not just different phrasings of the same analysis.

The debate-supervisor pattern

Some systems insert an adversarial debate between aggregation and supervisor review. A minimal design has a bull agent presenting the strongest positive case, a bear agent challenging assumptions and the source's quality, an optional second round focused on unresolved contradictions, and a supervisor who reconciles the outcome. Debate can surface weak assumptions and improve the quality of synthesis, but it should remain optional and measurable. If debate does not improve out-of-sample scoring metrics relative to its cost and latency overhead, it should be removed. This is why the notebook demo treats debate as a configuration flag rather than as mandatory architecture.

The supervisor itself is a reconciliation stage, not a replacement for agent evidence. It identifies the agreement and disagreement structure across the research agents, assesses the quality of the evidence and the severity of contradictions, determines whether additional clarification is needed, and produces the final forecast artifact with an explicit rationale and caveats. In the AIA-style implementation, supervisor override is policy-bound: the supervisor may replace the aggregate only when it returns a forecast with high confidence. That rule matters because it prevents the last model call in the pipeline from automatically dominating the rest of the evidence.

Probability calibration

Raw model probabilities are often miscalibrated. As Alur et al. (2025) observe, LLMs are "fundamentally miscalibrated for probabilistic prediction under uncertainty" and tend to hedge toward base rates. Calibration aligns forecast probabilities with realized outcome frequencies so that events rated at 70% by the system actually occur roughly 70% of the time.

A common post hoc method is **Platt scaling**, which fits a logistic transformation:

$$\hat{p} = \sigma\big(a \cdot \operatorname{logit}(p) + b\big)$$

Calibration and aggregation are distinct operations, and their interaction matters. If aggregation already extremizes probabilities, applying Platt scaling on top can compound overconfidence unless the calibration window is disjoint from the aggregation training data. This is not only a statistical concern but also an implementation concern: the production demo explicitly warns when both extremizing aggregation and post hoc calibration are enabled, because the combination can overshoot without validation on held-out data.

A practical calibration workflow reserves a historical window of resolved events, fits calibration parameters on that window only, evaluates on a disjoint holdout window, and monitors drift with an explicit refit cadence. Common pitfalls include fitting on too few resolved events, overlapping calibration and evaluation windows, recalibrating too frequently without evidence of drift, and interpreting improved **expected calibration error (ECE)** as overall improvement when sharpness has collapsed. The remedies are procedural: define minimum sample sizes for recalibration, isolate temporal windows, jointly monitor calibration and sharpness, and version-control the calibration model to ensure historical comparisons remain valid.

Evaluation, ablation, and baselines

A forecasting system should be judged by the quality of its probabilities, not by the quality of its narrative. The core metrics are Brier score, log score, expected calibration error, reliability diagnostics, and sharpness. Lower Brier and log scores indicate better overall forecast accuracy. Lower ECE indicates better calibration. Higher sharpness (the variance of forecast probabilities) is desirable only when calibration remains acceptable; a sharp but miscalibrated system is dangerous.

Ablation analysis identifies which components add measurable value. At a minimum, the evaluation should compare raw agent probabilities against the aggregated pre-calibration forecast, the aggregated post-calibration forecast, a variant without supervisor review, a variant with fewer agents, and the market baseline. Useful ablation questions include whether debate improves scores after cost adjustment, whether supervisor override reduces large errors or adds noise, whether calibration improves reliability without collapsing sharpness, and whether agent diversity provides genuinely incremental information. Ablations should be interpreted jointly with cost and latency: a component that slightly improves score quality but doubles runtime may still be justified for low-frequency, high-value decisions, but not for high-throughput workflows.

Diagnostic checklist: Beyond aggregate metrics

Aggregate metrics can hide systematic errors. Diagnostic analysis should examine error concentration by event type, overconfidence rates in high-probability bins, the contribution of supervisor overrides to large misses, and patterns of agent disagreement preceding forecast failures. These diagnostics clarify whether the next improvement should target retrieval quality, aggregation assumptions, calibration methodology, or override policy.

The most defensible claim is incremental information relative to a robust baseline, typically market consensus for the same event universe. Two cautions about interpreting that comparison:

1. For unresolved questions, both the market price and the agent forecast are estimates of the same future probability; neither can be declared correct in advance without an unwarranted assumption that the market is the ground truth.
2. On a resolved-outcome panel sufficient to compute Brier or log score, contamination is the dominant operational risk: the agent's search tools may retrieve articles dated after the question's natural cutoff, so apparent outperformance can reflect leakage rather than skill.

The defensible workflow is to evaluate on time-disjoint windows with explicit cutoff enforcement, report ranges across calibration variants and seeds rather than point estimates, and treat single-panel "wins" as illustrative of the scoring methodology rather than as definitive evidence of the superior approach. If, after that discipline, the model does not add incremental information at a stable cost/latency envelope, the architecture needs revision; calling it sophisticated is not a defense.

Apply a retention rubric to each component: Does it improve resolved-outcome metrics? Is the improvement stable across event subsets? Is the cost and latency overhead acceptable? Does it increase policy risk or operational fragility? Components that fail should be demoted or removed.

Component	Description
Research agents	N parallel agents that search and reason independently; forecast spread reflects how contested the question's evidence is, not the sampling temperature
Debate	Optional bull/bear reconciliation stage
Supervisor	Policy-bound synthesis and override logic
Aggregation	Mean/median/weighted/extremized combination rules
Calibration	Post hoc probability calibration
Search	Bounded, date-filtered retrieval with source policy
Persistence	Run artifacts, trace metadata, and scored outcomes
Evaluation	Brier/log/ECE, reliability diagnostics, and ablations

Table 24.4: Implementation architecture

Production optimizations include asynchronous agent execution, response caching with cutoff-aware keys, and replay modes for rapid iteration. They also require persistent run records, forecast rows, and later-evaluation rows so that the system can transition from a single notebook run to a track record. *Section 24.9* turns to the operational controls that make these forecast quality claims decision-grade.

Implementation: The multi-agent forecasting pipeline is built progressively across five notebooks:

- `05_aggregation_math` covers the pure mathematics of Neyman extremization and Platt scaling with sensitivity analysis across correlation and forecaster-count parameters.
- `06_multi_agent_research` runs three `ResearchAgent` instances on the pinned recession question and reports the result described above: when the evidence points one way, the agents' independent search paths still land on close forecasts (0.12 to 0.22), near the market price. The notebook compares aggregation methods (simple mean, Neyman extremization, and confidence-weighted Neyman) and analyzes sensitivity to the correlation parameter, so readers can see what aggregation can and cannot add when the inputs already agree.

- `07_adversarial_debate` implements the bull-bear debate, tracking the probability gap across rounds with consensus detection that terminates early when positions align.
- `08_forecasting_pipeline` assembles the full agent-aggregation-debate-supervisor pipeline into the `AIAForecaster` class, runs it across multiple forecast questions, and reports token-cost analysis per question alongside persisted state.
- `09_evaluation_and_governance` scores a ten-question resolved panel spanning US macro (Fed rate decisions, CPI), corporate milestones (NVIDIA earnings, Tesla deliveries, Apple product events), market levels (S&P 500 targets, tech IPO timing), crypto price thresholds (Bitcoin), geopolitical events (tariff policy), and technology releases (GPT-5). Metrics include Brier, log, ECE, and sharpness; the notebook also produces a reliability curve and runs ablation experiments comparing the full pipeline against mean-only aggregation, a single agent, and market-baseline prices.

When run in mock mode (the default for CI), responses are deterministic and the metric values illustrate the evaluation methodology. When run with a live LLM provider, the notebooks perform real web searches on current prediction-market questions and produce genuine forecasts. The companion `aia-forecaster` repository provides the supporting operational machinery (configuration profiles, prediction-market connectors, persistent storage, and scheduled evaluation) needed to build a real track record over time.

24.8 The ML4T research agent

The forecasting workflows in *Sections 24.6* and *24.7* stop when an agent returns a calibrated probability. They are valuable systems, and a live multi-agent forecaster runs on the book's website, but their deliverables sit closer to event prediction than to the systematic-trading research process this book has developed across its earlier parts. *Chapter 20* ran that process to its first decision point on nine case studies.

Each case study now exists as a research artifact: a fixed dataset, a labeling and feature pipeline, a comparable set of models, a portfolio construction rule, a backtest with explicit cost and risk treatment, and a registry of validation and holdout results. *Section 20.9* closes each case study with a sketch of the most informative experiment to run next. The agent in this section is what executes that sentence end-to-end against the artifacts the case study left behind.

The operator's shape

Research-line iteration looks different from prediction-market forecasting. Every case study has its own follow-up, and that follow-up is rarely a parameter sweep: it is a small amount of code that wires together the chapter's libraries against a real run-log registry. Pre-enumerating the catalog of moves a researcher might make across nine case studies would either grow without limit or constrain the agent from making the moves that matter.

The shape that fits this task is the one that production coding agents have converged on, and that this chapter calls the **operator**: a small orchestrator that hands a language model a handful of general-purpose tools (read and write files, run bash, query a SQLite registry, read a Parquet file, list and read a corpus of how-to skills) and then steps out of the way. The operator that runs the notebook is roughly 880 lines and exposes 10 such tools. The language model accesses them via `run_bash` when it decides the moment has come.

Skills are the task-specific knowledge layer

The skills repository is the second pillar of this section, and a key feature of the book as a whole. Earlier chapters teach the methodology (point-in-time discipline, deflated Sharpe, cross-sectional information coefficient computation, walk-forward design, cost-aware backtest specification) in long-form prose alongside production code. The skills repo distills that methodology into a corpus that the agent can consult at runtime. The companion `skills` repository ships 56 concept-first Markdown files organized into nine categories: concepts, validation, infrastructure, features, data, backtest, and so on. Each file is short and structured:

- A problem statement
- A WRONG and CORRECT example pair
- A Production Implementation block that names the exact `ml4t-data`, `ml4t-engineer`, `ml4t-diagnostic`, or `ml4t-backtest` function to call

The operator's prompt does not embed any of this. Instead, two of its ten tools are `list_skills`, which returns a one-line summary across the catalog, and `read_skill`, which fetches the full text of one file. When the agent reaches a method-choice decision point ("should I deflate this Sharpe?", "How do I compute IC across a panel without leakage?", "Which library function applies the next-step suggestion?"), it reads the relevant skill on demand.

The discipline that prevents look-ahead bias, mishandled cross-section ICs, or naive Sharpe arithmetic lives in those files, and the libraries the operator's bash subprocess imports enforce the rest. This is the inversion that makes the operator pattern work: the agent's prompt stays short and stable while the corpus the agent can consult grows with the methodology the chapter has been teaching.

The forecasting workflows in *Sections 24.6* and *24.7* do not need this layer because their action space is bounded by the search and forecast schemas; the workflow agent in *Section 24.8* is exactly where skills incur their cost.

Two example runs of the ML4T research loop

The notebook replays two complete runs against the captured DeepSeek v4 Pro traces.

The first run targets the ETFs case study, whose *Section 20.9* next step is to ensemble the strongest gradient-boosting, tabular deep-learning, and convolutional autoencoder predictions and check whether the combined signal stabilizes the holdout Sharpe of the LSTM baseline. The operator did exactly that: it queried the registry to identify the prediction set with the highest validation Sharpe in each model family, read the skills on IC computation and deflated Sharpe, z-score-averaged the three signals cross-sectionally, recovered the LSTM baseline's exact backtest specification from the `backtest_runs.spec_json` field, and re-ran the cost-aware backtest under that identical configuration.

The ensemble produced the highest information coefficient in the case study (0.065 versus the LSTM's 0.052), but its validation-window Sharpe was lower (0.56 versus 0.92 on the same window). Per-fold IC instability (three of nine folds were negative) was amplified by the score-weighted top-k allocator, eroding the IC advantage at the portfolio level. The registry carries holdout predictions only for the LSTM, so this validation comparison cannot displace the holdout ranking; promoting the ensemble there would require retraining or generating holdout predictions for its three constituents. The agent diagnosed the gap and reported a clean negative. The run took 39 tool-use turns and roughly $1.25 in OpenRouter spend.

The second run targets the US firm characteristics case study, whose *Section 20.1* prose flags that the selected strategy's long/short legs cluster heavily in small-cap names and whose *Section 20.9* suggests filtering the universe to its top three market-capitalization quartiles. The operator located the lagged market equity column in the case study's feature parquet, computed monthly mcap-quartile cutoffs, signal-filtered the selected model's predictions to the top three quartiles, recovered the matching backtest specification from the registry, and re-ran it.

Sharpe collapsed from 4.27 to 2.24 (a 48% drop) while maximum drawdown deepened from −15% to −52% and IC fell from 0.074 to 0.048. Turnover was unchanged, confirming the move was a signal-level filter rather than a portfolio-construction artifact. The chapter's small-cap binding-constraint claim is now a quantified one: the strategy retains genuine alpha after the capacity filter (Probability of Backtest Overfitting near zero), but roughly half of the reported Sharpe is a small-cap residual the static cost assumption did not absorb. Twenty-seven turns, about $0.95.

What the runs share and where the limits sit

The two outcomes deliver opposite results: a clean negative and a quantified concern, as one might obtain from regular research. The runs share the property that makes the operator pattern portable: extending it to a different case study is one entry in `CASE_STUDY_TASKS` and a different value for `RESEARCH_OPERATOR_CASE_STUDY`. The same agent loop, the same tool surface, and the same skills repository handle both runs without code changes. The reason this works is that the methodology is not in the operator. It is in the libraries that the operator's bash subprocess imports, and in the skills that the model reads when a method choice arises. That separation of concerns is also what makes the loop auditable: the trace records every tool call, every skill read, and every script the model wrote, so a reviewer can replay the decision path just as the demo notebook replays the captured run.

The failure modes worth watching are model-side: a confabulated improvement, a `done()` declared before the experiment finished, and an overaggressive interpretation of an inconclusive result.

The structural protections (sandboxed writes, a read-only working copy of the registry, a bounded turn count, a fixed model) are necessary but not sufficient. Production deployment of this pattern requires the controls in *Section 24.9* to be wrapped around the operator: replay receipts, contamination tracking, deterministic seeds, and the operational gates that separate a notebook demonstration from a service.

Key Takeaways

The Research Agent reuses the architectural primitives the rest of this chapter built (typed traces, structured artifacts, an explicit ReAct loop, a replay-first persistence model) and re-points them from the open web to the deterministic ml4t stack.

The deliverable changes: a forecast resolves and earns a Brier score, while a research-line iteration produces a recommendation about the line and a registry-attached experiment record that future iterations are accountable to. Both deliverables are trustworthy only when the system that produces them is bounded, replayable, and inspectable, and the case for the operator pattern is that these properties carry over from a narrow forecasting agent to a workflow agent operating on a real research artifact.

The next section turns to the production controls (replay, contamination tracking, and the operational gates) that any executor downstream of an iteration agent will need before it can be trusted to act on a research note without a human in the loop.

Implementation: `11_research_operator` replays the two runs end-to-end from saved traces. Toggling `REPLAY_TRACE = False` runs the operator live against a sandboxed copy of either case study (~$1, ~8 minutes per run on DeepSeek v4 Pro via OpenRouter).

Switching the model is a single parameter; switching the case study is a single entry in `CASE_STUDY_TASKS`. The notebook prints the tool surface, shows skill discovery, replays both runs, and tabulates the side-by-side outcomes.

24.9 Preparing for production

A forecasting-agent prototype can look strong in notebooks and still fail in production. Common causes are non-determinism, hidden data leakage, weak observability, and uncontrolled cost. After defining the capstone architecture, the next design challenge is operational robustness: the controls that make forecast quality claims decision-grade. In this chapter, that transition is not hypothetical. The notebook sequence culminates in a production demo that wraps the forecasting pipeline in configuration profiles, prediction-market connectors, persistent storage, evaluation commands, and publishing jobs.

The reliability gap and observability

Agents are non-deterministic systems. Identical prompts can yield different tool sequences and different conclusions across runs. Reliability, therefore, requires process controls rather than single-run confidence. Bounded retries classified by failure type prevent the system from hammering a broken tool. Fallback strategies produce explicit low-confidence outputs when primary paths fail, instead of fabricating answers. Checkpoint recovery allows restarts from the last known-good state rather than re-running entire workflows. Deterministic validators around tool outputs catch schema violations and missing fields before they propagate downstream. The target is stable workflow behavior under variation, not exact token-level reproducibility.

Every run should produce a complete operational trace. At minimum, traces must capture run identifiers and timestamps, the input prompt and policy context, every tool call with arguments and outputs, state transitions and gate outcomes, model outputs and structured artifacts, latency and token cost telemetry, and final status with error classification. Without this trace, incident diagnosis is mostly guesswork. The production demo turns this requirement into data structures rather than prose guidance: run records persist configuration snapshots, agent artifacts, aggregation and supervisor outputs, token counts, search counts, and duration; forecast records persist the published probabilities and the market price observed at forecast time; evaluation records persist post-resolution scores.

Observability should support two distinct views:

- An engineering view for tool failures, latency spikes, and state-transition anomalies
- A research view for calibration drift, baseline deltas, and ablation sensitivity

Separating these views prevents teams from conflating operational incidents with model-quality issues. Fabozzi and López de Prado (2025) reinforce this point: prompts, retrieval corpora, and model versions must be treated as regulated artifacts because an LLM-assisted output that cannot be reproduced months later creates compliance risk regardless of its accuracy.

Statistical testing and point-in-time integrity

Deterministic assertions are insufficient for agent systems. Testing should include repeated trials with distribution-aware thresholds: a success rate above a defined level across N runs, a policy-violation rate below tolerance, the variance of forecast outputs under controlled inputs, and the stability of calibration metrics over rolling windows.

Point-in-time integrity is a first-class requirement. Every run should carry a `cutoff_date` that propagates to all tool calls; retrieval tools must apply date filters that exclude post-cutoff evidence, and downstream components should revalidate publication timestamps. The replay protocol from *Section 24.3* applies directly. In the production demo, the same boundary appears as an explicit backtest cutoff that is propagated into research-agent search and supervisor-clarifying queries, which is the correct level at which to enforce the rule: the tool boundary, not the model narrative.

Contamination-resistant evaluation

Backtests can overstate performance when models have latent exposure to historical periods. Lopez-Lira, Tang, and Zhu (2025) show that LLMs can appear to forecast economic variables pre-cutoff by memorizing realized outcomes from their training data, rendering pre-cutoff evaluation fundamentally non-identifiable. Contamination-aware evaluation should therefore apply strict temporal splits with a gap between training and evaluation periods, time-shift tests that assess whether model performance degrades as the evaluation window moves further from the training data, event windows designed to avoid leakage from post-event coverage, and baseline comparisons on the same event set to anchor interpretation. Claims of outperformance should be rejected when they are not stable across these controls. When contamination analysis and demo performance disagree, the contamination analysis should take precedence.

Evaluation metric stack

The evaluation stack spans three dimensions:

1. Research agent quality is measured by task success rate, citation faithfulness (does each claim link to stored evidence?), tool-call validity, abstention quality when gates fail, and latency and cost per successful run.
2. Forecasting quality is measured by Brier score, log score, expected calibration error, reliability diagnostics, and sharpness.
3. Operational health is tracked through incident rate, policy violation rate, replay pass/fail rate, and drift alerts on key metrics.

Benchmark evidence helps calibrate realistic thresholds. The FinBen evaluation (Xie et al., 2024) tests LLMs across 42 financial datasets and 24 tasks, finding that extraction and classification are relatively reliable, while forecasting and numeric reasoning remain weak. This is a useful reference for setting expectations by task type. However, static benchmarks measure isolated LLM capability, not agent behavior. Evaluating agents is fundamentally harder because outputs depend on dynamic tool interactions, state transitions, and multi-step reasoning chains that vary across runs.

Resolution-based scoring platforms, in which forecasts are evaluated against real-world event outcomes after a defined waiting period, provide a more rigorous evaluation protocol. The key advantage is that they test the full pipeline under conditions less prone to memorization-driven overstatement, making them a natural complement to the contamination controls described above.

Implementation: `09_evaluation_and_governance` illustrates this logic on a ten-question resolved panel spanning US macro (Fed rate decisions, CPI), corporate milestones (NVIDIA earnings, Tesla deliveries, Apple product events), market levels (S&P 500 targets, tech IPO timing), crypto (Bitcoin), geopolitical events (tariff policy), and technology releases (GPT-5). The notebook produces Brier, log, ECE, and sharpness scores, a reliability curve, and an ablation comparison that together make the evaluation workflow structure concrete. In mock mode, the specific metric values illustrate the scoring methodology; when run with a live LLM, the same scoring pipeline evaluates real forecasts. The production `aia-forecaster` provides the necessary machinery to accumulate a real track record over time.

Cost, latency, and deployment fit

Current LLM latency makes agent workflows unsuitable for microsecond-sensitive execution. The stronger near-term fit is research support, event forecasting, and lower-frequency decision preparation. This constraint should be explicit in system design and reader expectations.

Cost should be measured at the workflow level, not by token price alone. The most effective lever is model cascading: routing sub-tasks to the cheapest model that meets quality requirements. In a typical forecasting pipeline, evidence extraction, formatting, and tool-argument construction are well-suited to smaller, faster models, while probability synthesis, contradiction resolution, and supervisor reconciliation benefit from frontier-model capabilities.

A practical cascading architecture assigns a model tier to each pipeline phase and monitors per-phase error rates to detect when a cheaper tier degrades output quality. In practice, cascading often materially lowers costs, but the gain has to be measured phase by phase rather than assumed.

Additional cost controls include caching with cutoff-aware keys that avoid redundant retrieval, context compression before model calls, early-exit logic when confidence is sufficient, and per-forecast budgets that cap total expenditure. Cost optimization that degrades calibration or increases policy violations is not a valid trade.

Release process and monitoring

A lightweight release protocol improves stability without adding excessive ceremony. Before deployment, run replay and ablation checks on a fixed validation panel, compare score, calibration, and policy metrics against the prior release, require explicit sign-off for any regressions, and deploy behind a canary or shadow run when possible. Incident response should classify failures by root cause: retrieval or policy failures, connector or runtime failures, state-transition failures, or calibration drift, so that remediation is targeted and postmortem quality improves over time.

Operational packaging helps here as much as model quality does. Configuration profiles separate local, backtest, and production settings without rewriting prompts or code. A scheduler can run pull, forecast, and track jobs on different cadences. A publisher can emit a feed, per-market histories, and evidence ledgers for external inspection. None of these features directly improves probability, but together they determine whether the workflow can be monitored, replayed, and governed as a living service rather than a one-off notebook run. The governance document that constrains the pipeline need not be bespoke: Ang, Azimbayev, and Kim (2026) show that the Investment Policy Statement (already a legal and regulatory requirement for institutional investors) can serve as the operational boundary for an entire multi-agent pipeline, analogous to the operational design domain in autonomous driving. Repurposing an existing governance artifact rather than inventing a new one reduces adoption friction and aligns agent constraints with the same document that constrains human portfolio managers.

A production workflow should expose a compact dashboard spanning forecast quality (including Brier, log score, ECE, and sharpness), baseline deltas, policy violations, latency, cost, and metric drift. Alert thresholds should be policy-driven (triggering on sustained ECE increases, rising unsupported-claim rates, post-cutoff retrieval attempts, or latency violations) and coupled with run-level trace links for triage.

Collective effects and risk posture

As agent usage rises across the industry, feedback loops can amplify market fragility. Lopez-Lira (2025) shows this in market simulations where LLM agents built on similar foundation models exhibit correlated behavior, producing bubbles, and liquidity crises that would not emerge from heterogeneous agents. This motivates a conservative deployment posture: clear action boundaries, explicit approvals for high-impact decisions, and strong monitoring for correlated failure patterns across agent instances.

Production quality is achieved through controls that make behavior measurable: point-in-time integrity, replayability, contamination-resistant evaluation, trace-complete observability, and durable operational artifacts. Without these controls, claims about forecast quality are not decision-grade. *Section 24.10* formalizes the security and governance layer that protects these controls from adversarial interference.

24.10 Security and governance

Building on the production controls in *Section 24.9*, this section formalizes security and governance requirements for financial agent systems. Security begins with architecture: the chapter defaults to read-only forecasting and research, thereby reducing the attack surface and simplifying policy enforcement. The production demo preserves that boundary. It pulls markets, searches for evidence, stores forecasts, and publishes artifacts, but it does not place trades or commit capital automatically. The controls described here apply regardless of the chosen framework and should be treated as prerequisites for any deployment that touches financial data or produces outputs consumed by decision-makers.

Threat model – Where failures originate

A practical threat model identifies attack surfaces by workflow layer. At the input layer, malicious user prompts and malformed queries can steer the agent toward unauthorized behavior. At the retrieval layer, prompt injection embedded in documents and poisoned indices can hijack reasoning, a risk amplified in finance because retrieved text often contains imperative language and speculative narratives. At the tool layer, excessive permissions, argument abuse, and tool shadowing (substituting a malicious tool for a legitimate one) create execution risks. At the state layer, corrupted artifacts, stale memory reuse, and loss of provenance undermine reproducibility. At the output layer, unsupported claims, overconfident probabilities, and policy bypass can mislead downstream consumers.

An additional risk cuts across all layers: latent model bias. Lee et al. (2025) show that LLMs exhibit systematic investment preferences (favoring certain sectors, styles, or contrarian positions) and display confirmation bias when evidence conflicts with these latent preferences. These biases are invisible to standard accuracy metrics and require dedicated stress tests that present the same evidence framed from opposing perspectives. Agent diversity in *Section 24.7* partly mitigates this risk, but only if agents use different foundation models or receive deliberately varied framing.

Prompt injection and retrieval defenses

Prompt injection remains the primary risk in tool-connected systems, as documented by OWASP (2025). Defenses require strict separation of instructions from retrieved data so that injected text cannot override system prompts. Content sanitization and pattern filters should strip known injection patterns before evidence enters the reasoning context. Evidence gating should verify that claims in the synthesis phase link to specific retrieved artifacts rather than to injected instructions. Citation verification checks that every referenced source actually exists in the evidence store. The chapter notebook illustrates this with a simple pattern-based sanitizer. The production demo adds another practical layer by restricting search with explicit allowlists and blocklists, thereby reducing the set of documents that can reach the model in the first place.

Retrieval poisoning targets the evidence pipeline rather than the prompt. Mitigations include index governance: source controls on what enters the retrieval corpus, ingestion checks that validate document provenance, and periodic integrity scans that detect unauthorized modifications to the index.

Least privilege and the warden pattern

Excessive capability is a preventable risk. If a workflow requires read-only data access, write and execution privileges should not exist in that runtime. The default control set includes read-only credentials for all data access, scoped API keys that limit each tool to its intended domain, tool-specific argument constraints that reject out-of-range values, domain allowlists for retrieval sources with optional denylists for known-bad domains, and network and filesystem sandboxing where the environment supports it. Least-privilege enforcement should be verified through automated policy checks, not trusted solely on documentation. In the production demo, this principle is concrete rather than aspirational: market connectors are read-only, search access is configurable and source-bound, and credentials are scoped per provider rather than shared across the entire workflow.

For operations that can change state outside the workflow boundary (sending a notification, writing to a shared database, or triggering a downstream process), the **Warden** pattern interposes a policy proxy between agent output and runtime execution. The Warden validates each operation against an allowlist, rejects blocklisted patterns, validates arguments and value ranges, enforces timeout and resource limits, and logs every allow or deny decision to immutable storage.

`09_evaluation_and_governance` implements this pattern with three concrete policies: a no-write policy that blocks trade-execution tools (such as `execute_trade`, `send_order`, and `modify_position`), a domain-allowlist policy that rejects search queries containing terms indicating misuse (such as "hack", "exploit", "bypass", or "credentials"), and a rate-limit policy placeholder. The notebook exercises the Warden across four test calls: two benign search queries (one on NVIDIA earnings, one on the Federal Reserve rate decision) pass through, while a search query for "hack admin credentials" and a trade-execution request are blocked with logged denials. The same notebook tests prompt-injection defense with five payloads covering role-override attempts ("ignore all previous instructions"), tool-call injection (embedded JSON trade commands), and data-exfiltration prompts, detecting all three attack classes while passing clean financial text through unmodified. This pattern does not eliminate risk, but it reduces risk concentration and creates enforceable policy boundaries that are auditable in retrospect.

In this chapter, the Warden appears as a teaching example because the production demo remains read-only. In practice, a sensible order is: first, prove the forecasting workflow under bounded permissions, then add stronger action controls only if the use case truly requires side effects.

Human-in-the-loop controls and governance artifacts

For consequential actions, human approval is a governance requirement, not an optional nicety. An approval queue routes high-impact actions to designated reviewers. Threshold gates trigger human review when risk, cost, or exposure exceeds defined levels. Dual sign-off is required for exceptional overrides that fall outside normal operating parameters. Anomaly escalation flags unusual action sequences, such as a sudden spike in tool calls or an unexpected topic shift, for human inspection. All approval decisions should be logged with a rationale to support later review. For the read-only forecasting workflow in this chapter, the practical approval points are release management and publication: configuration changes, provider changes, and forecast publication policies should be reviewed even when the system does not execute trades.

A compliant workflow generates reusable governance artifacts: the full run trace; an evidence index with provenance metadata; the policy evaluation log showing which controls were applied and their outcomes; the forecast artifact with confidence assessments and caveats; and a post-resolution score record linking the forecast to its outcome. In the production demo, these artifacts extend to persisted run records, forecast histories, and evidence ledgers that can be published or audited independently of the model runtime. Later deployment and MLOps chapters (*Chapters 25-26*) scale these control patterns into full operating frameworks.

Security testing and metrics

Security controls should be tested with adversarial scenarios, not only nominal runs. A practical test suite includes prompt-injection payloads embedded in retrieved text, malformed tool arguments that probe validation boundaries, tool-name collisions and shadowing attempts, stale-source and post-cutoff retrieval attempts, and supervisor-override requests outside policy bounds. Each test should specify the expected allow/deny behavior and the required log fields, thereby converting security posture from narrative assurance to measurable system behavior.

Note that several security metrics overlap with the operational health metrics in *Section 24.9*. In production, these should be monitored through a unified trace infrastructure rather than separate systems, with security-specific alert thresholds layered on top.

Security metrics close the feedback loop. Key measurements include prompt-injection success rate (ideally zero but monitored continuously), unsupported-claim rate, policy-violation attempt rate, blocked privileged-call rate, false-positive rejection rate for valid calls, and mean time to incident diagnosis from trace data. These metrics integrate with the same run artifacts used for forecasting evaluation, so security monitoring does not require a separate infrastructure.

In financial agent systems, security is a property of the workflow. Read-only boundaries, explicit policy gates, immutable traces, and measured control performance are required for decision-grade use.

Category	Control	Implementation	Verification
Input	Sanitization	Strip injection patterns from user input	Adversarial prompt test suite
Permissions	Least privilege	Read-only tools and scoped credentials	Permission audit per deployment
Retrieval	Domain policy	Allowlisted sources and date constraints	Post-cutoff retrieval attempt rate
Execution	Warden proxy	Validate tool calls against policy rules	Blocked-call log review
High-stakes	HITL	Require human approval above thresholds	Approval queue latency monitoring
Observability	Full tracing	Log every message, tool call, and decision	Trace completeness checks
Audit	Immutable Logs	Write-once storage for compliance	Periodic integrity verification

Table 24.5: Financial agent security checklist

24.11 Summary

This chapter argued that financial agents should be designed as workflows rather than personalities. Reasoning patterns such as ReAct, Tree of Thoughts, and Reflexion matter only when they are embedded in explicit state, typed tool contracts, bounded autonomy, and replayable artifacts. The chapter's capstones applied that principle progressively: first in a single-agent research workflow that can be inspected step by step, then in a multi-agent forecasting pipeline that accumulates evidence, aggregates views, reconciles disagreement, and publishes probabilities that can later be scored.

The deeper lesson is that forecasting support and market execution are different system classes. This chapter remained deliberately read-only because evidence acquisition, probability estimation, calibration, persistence, and post-outcome evaluation already impose demanding engineering and governance requirements. Point-in-time integrity, contamination-aware testing, observability, and security policy are what make any claim of forecast quality defensible, whether the workflow is presented in a notebook or wrapped as a production forecasting service.

The companion `aia-forecaster` repository carries the notebook workflow into an operational forecasting service with configuration profiles, prediction-market connectors, persistent storage, evaluation commands, and a publishing layer—the operational starting point for moving from exercises to a running system.

The next chapter moves from research workflows to deployment infrastructure. *Chapter 25* shows how disciplined artifacts from agent and model pipelines enter live trading systems with stronger operational controls, monitoring, and failure handling.

25

Live Trading Systems

The transition from profitable backtest to live execution is where most algorithmic trading projects fail. Not because the strategy lacks edge, but because the production system diverges from the research environment in subtle ways that erode returns—a feature is calculated slightly differently, a fill assumption that doesn't match reality, a timing mismatch between signals and execution. Research on **backtest overfitting** shows that even correctly implemented strategies suffer significant performance degradation when moving to live trading (Bailey et al., 2015)—and this assumes the live implementation matches the backtest exactly.

The solution is a unified framework that runs **identical code in both backtest and live modes**, eliminating technical divergence by construction. The strategy classes, allocation logic, cost parameters, and risk controls built in *Chapters 16–19* are not prototypes to be rewritten—they port directly to live execution through the same `ml4t-backtest` library, with only the data source and execution destination changing. This chapter builds the remaining production infrastructure—broker integration, order management, pipeline verification, and operational procedures—needed to deploy these strategies with confidence.

After completing this chapter, you will be able to:

- Explain why technical divergence between research and production is a primary failure mode in live trading, and how a unified framework reduces that risk.
- Design a dual-mode, event-driven trading architecture in which deterministic strategy logic runs unchanged in backtest, paper, and live execution.
- Compare broker, exchange, and managed-platform deployment paths and evaluate them based on asset coverage, execution quality, operational burden, and control.
- Model order handling as an explicit state machine that supports partial fills, cancellations, rejections, reconciliation, and idempotent crash recovery.
- Verify technical parity across the full pipeline, from raw data and features to predictions, sizing decisions, and generated orders.
- Plan a staged live rollout using pre-flight checks, shadow or paper trading, kill switches, reconciliation procedures, and awareness of venue and jurisdictional constraints.

Section 25.1 introduces the unified framework that lets identical strategy code run in both backtest and live modes. *Sections 25.2–25.3* integrate two broker APIs—Interactive Brokers for global multi-asset access and Alpaca for developer-friendly US equity and crypto trading—while *Section 25.4* evaluates managed platforms as an alternative path. *Section 25.5* models the order lifecycle as an explicit state machine, and *Section 25.6* establishes pipeline verification methods that ensure technical parity before deployment. *Section 25.7* covers operational readiness—kill switches, graduated paper-to-live transitions, and the regulatory landscape that constrains what can be deployed where.

25.1 The unified research-to-production framework

Quantitative strategy development often follows a convenient but error-prone path. Research happens in Jupyter notebooks using historical data. The promising strategy then gets rewritten for production in a different language or framework, possibly by a different team. This creates two parallel implementations of the same logic—and two opportunities for implementation bugs to hide.

The problems compound over time. A researcher improves the feature engineering; the production team must replicate the change. The production system hits an edge case; the fix doesn't propagate back to research. Six months later, the backtest shows a 15% annual return, while live trading delivers only a 3% return. The discrepancy is real, but its sources can be difficult and time-consuming to diagnose.

Technical divergence

Technical divergence occurs when the same inputs produce different outputs in backtest versus live execution. Unlike statistical decay—where the market genuinely changes—technical divergence is entirely self-inflicted.

The most common source is **differences in feature calculation**: a moving average computed on adjusted closing prices in research but on unadjusted prices in production, or a volatility estimate using a slightly different lookback window. These differences often go undetected until cumulative divergence becomes material.

Timing assumptions create a second class of divergence. Research code calculates signals at market close and assumes execution at the next open. Production code receives data with varying delays and executes asynchronously. The backtest assumes perfect synchronization that never exists in practice.

Data handling edge cases—missing prices, corporate actions, ticker changes—compound the problem. Research code often ignores these complications; production must handle them gracefully. Even **order translation** introduces divergence: converting a signal ("+0.05 target weight for AAPL") into actual orders involves rounding to valid lot sizes and respecting available liquidity, and different implementations make different choices.

The unified framework solution

A unified framework eliminates technical divergence by construction. The same code—literally the same source files—runs in both modes:

- In **backtest mode**, the framework feeds historical data through the strategy, simulates order execution with configurable assumptions, and records positions and returns—traditional backtesting, but using production code.
- In **live mode**, the framework connects to broker APIs, feeds real-time data through the identical strategy logic, and routes orders to execution. No translation layer, no second implementation of the strategy itself.

In the ML4T stack, this pattern is split across two companion libraries. `ml4t-backtest` provides the event-driven research and validation engine introduced in *Chapters 16–19*. `ml4t-live` provides the same `Strategy` interface for both paper and live trading, via broker adapters, live data feeds, and safety controls. The key continuity is at the strategy layer: the decision logic stays the same even though live deployment adds broker, feed, and risk-management infrastructure around it.

Architecture for dual-mode operation

The architecture rests on four design principles:

1. **Abstract interfaces for data and execution** hide the source: the strategy receives market data through an interface that is indifferent to whether the source is a historical database or a live WebSocket feed, and orders pass through an execution interface that routes them to a simulator for backtesting or to a broker for production.
2. **Signal generation must be deterministic**—given the same market state, the strategy produces identical signals. This means avoiding system time dependencies, random seeds that differ between runs, or external state that varies between environments.
3. **Both modes share an event-driven core.** In backtest, events replay from history; in live trading, events arrive from market data feeds. The same event handlers process both.
4. **Position state, order state, and strategy state** are maintained identically in both modes. The framework handles persistence and recovery, ensuring a restarted live system can resume from a saved state.

Figure 25.1 shows the dual-mode architecture: the same `Strategy` component connects to either the backtest engine (historical data and simulated execution) or the live engine (market data feeds and broker APIs), with the strategy code unchanged across both modes.

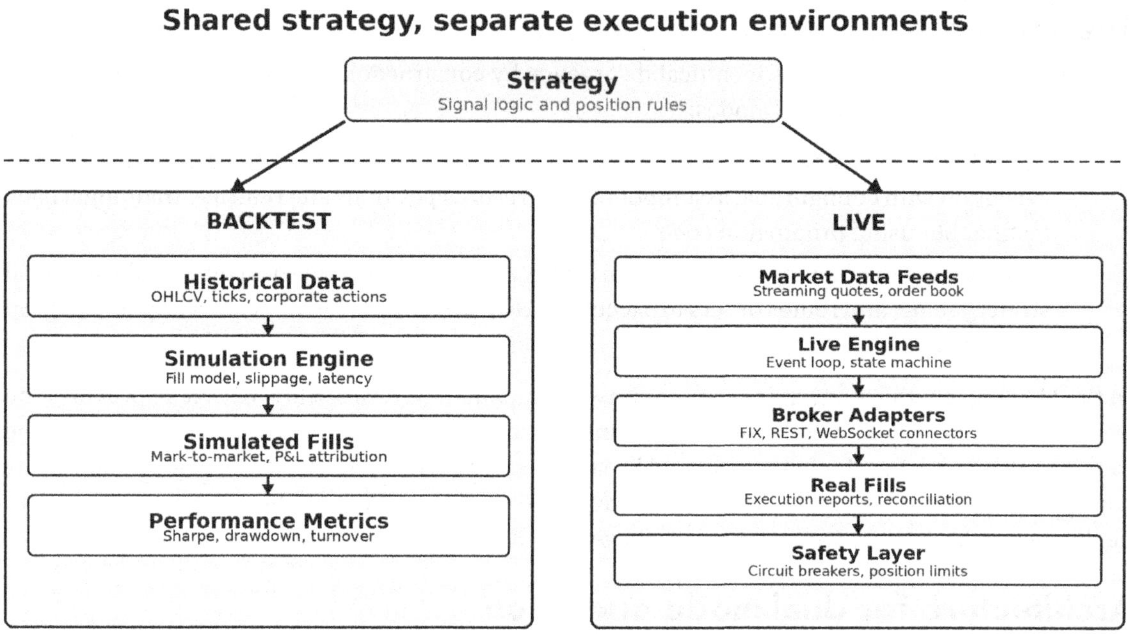

Figure 25.1: Unified framework architecture. The same strategy logic applies to both historical replay and live feeds, while execution, broker, and safety infrastructure differ by mode

From simulation to live

The strategies simulated in *Chapters 16–19* are production code waiting for a live data source. In those chapters, each case study defines a `Strategy` subclass with an `on_data()` method that receives market data, computes signals, and submits orders through the framework's execution interface. The `Engine` runs this strategy against historical data in backtest mode: the ETF momentum strategy in *Chapter 16* uses the same `MLSignalStrategy` class through allocation (*Chapter 17*), transaction cost modeling (*Chapter 18*), and risk management (*Chapter 19*), accumulating layers of portfolio construction logic, cost-aware constraints, and adaptive risk controls.

Going live means keeping the same strategy class while replacing the historical runtime with `ml4t-live`'s `LiveEngine`, broker adapters, and live data feeds. The `on_data()` logic, allocation rules, and portfolio intent carry over unchanged. Around that strategy, the live stack adds the operational pieces that a backtest does not need: asynchronous broker connectivity, startup checks, shadow mode, persistent risk state, and guarded order submission. *Chapter 17*'s `WeightFollowerStrategy`—which translates model-generated target weights into rebalancing orders—becomes the live execution strategy. *Chapter 18*'s cost model parameters (spread estimates, impact coefficients, turnover constraints) become the live cost budget against which realized execution is measured. *Chapter 19*'s kill-switch levels and drawdown thresholds become live safety controls enforced by the broker wrapper, rather than assumptions within a simulator.

This continuity is the payoff of the unified framework. The nine case studies—ETFs, crypto perpetuals, futures, FX, equities, and options—each define a complete pipeline from features through risk-managed execution. Any of these pipelines can move from backtest into a live runtime without rewriting the strategy logic, provided the pipeline verification tests introduced in *Section 25.6* confirm technical parity.

The framework provides the strategy interface; what remains is to connect it to specific brokers. The next two sections integrate Interactive Brokers and Alpaca, the two broker APIs most relevant to practitioners deploying the strategies from this book, especially in the US.

Implementation: `01_unified_framework_demo` demonstrates signal parity on a shared historical replay: the same `DualMAStrategy` produces matching signals in both backtest and live-style execution with zero strategy-code changes—the unified framework's central claim, reduced to a side-by-side comparison.

`02_etfs_deployment_loop` is the chapter's anchor demonstration of the full re-train-and-deploy cycle on real ETF data: it refreshes the ETF panel via `ml4t-data`, retrains the Ridge regressor identified in the ETF case study, and replays the live window via `ml4t.backtest.Engine` to produce an offline reference signal tape, and submits the latest top-K basket through Alpaca paper equities—reconciling the live broker submission against the offline tape symbol by symbol. It is referenced again in *Section 25.7* as the deployment-loop reference implementation.

25.2 Integrating with Interactive Brokers

Interactive Brokers (**IBKR**) provides global multi-asset access via the **Trader Workstation** (TWS) app or the IB Gateway socket API, the Client Portal API, and institutional interfaces such as FIX/CTCI. IBKR Pro's tiered US equity and ETFs commissions start at around $0.0035/share, and eligible US securities accounts can apply for portfolio margin once the account's equity reaches $100,000 (per regulation), or more (per broker risk limit). For systematic traders who need broad instrument coverage, IBKR remains one of the most flexible retail-accessible broker stacks.

TWS versus IB Gateway

For retail accounts, IBKR provides two connection options, each suited to different use cases:

- **TWS** is the full desktop application. It provides a graphical interface for manual trading, as well as API access. TWS requires a physical (or virtual) display to run, which complicates headless server deployments. However, its visual feedback proves valuable during development and debugging.
- **IB Gateway** provides access to the same API without the graphical overhead. It runs headlessly on servers, consuming fewer resources than TWS. For production deployments, IB Gateway is typically the better choice.

Both require authentication that must be refreshed periodically. Automated login solutions exist but require careful security consideration—the credentials provide full account access.

Connection patterns

The main retail and developer workflow uses IBKR's event-driven, long-lived socket connection. The `ib_async` library makes the low-level, callback-driven socket API easier to use by providing a higher-level Python interface that feels closer to normal synchronous or `asyncio` programming. Each connection is identified by a client ID unique to each process on the account—using the same ID from multiple processes causes disconnection conflicts. By default, TWS listens on port 7496 (live) or 7497 (paper); IB Gateway uses 4001 (live) or 4002 (paper).

The TWS/Gateway API uses a long-lived socket connection, so the trading system must actively detect broken or stale connectivity. Use a lightweight heartbeat, such as periodic `reqCurrentTime()` calls, and treat missed or delayed responses as a failure that can affect order management. When connectivity drops, or IBKR reports a reset, reconnect with exponential backoff, re-subscribe to market data as needed, and reconcile broker state by reloading open orders, completed orders, executions, positions, and account values before resuming trading.

Order types and execution

IBKR supports extensive order types. For algorithmic trading, the essential ones are (see also *Chapter 3*):

- Market orders execute immediately at the best available price but should be used sparingly—Harris (2003) documents how they incur both spread costs and market impact, with the latter increasing in order size relative to available liquidity (see also *Chapter 18*)
- Limit orders specify a maximum buy or minimum sell price, providing price certainty at the cost of execution certainty
- Stop orders become market orders when the trigger price is reached, which is useful for stop-loss logic but can lead to significant slippage in fast markets

IBKR Pro's SmartRouting scans multiple venues for best execution, functionally replicating institutional smart order routing—and critically, it does not sell order flow to wholesalers. Schwarz et al. (2022) measured round-trip execution costs across five US brokers using 85,000 simultaneous market orders and found dispersion ranging from 0.07% to 0.46%, with payment for order flow explaining only 3.4% of the variation. The takeaway: broker routing choices can matter more than the direct commissions.

IBKR's adaptive orders extend this by balancing urgency against price based on market conditions, reflecting the execution trade-off formalized by Almgren and Chriss (2001): executing quickly minimizes timing risk but increases market impact, while executing slowly reduces impact but exposes the position to adverse price movements.

Order attributes further modify behavior—**Good-Till-Cancelled** (GTC) orders persist across sessions, **Immediate-or-Cancel** (IOC) orders fill immediately or cancel, and **All-or-None** (AON) orders require complete fills. Review IBRK's documentation to get an overview of the diverse order tools available across asset classes.

Position and account management

Accurate position tracking requires attention to several data flows:

- Position updates arrive through the `position()` callback (requested via `reqPositions()`) and reflect the broker's authoritative view—reconcile internal tracking against these at session start and periodically throughout the day
- Account values (equity, margin, buying power, PnL) flow through `updateAccountValue()`, requested via `reqAccountUpdates()`; monitor margin utilization to avoid forced liquidations
- Execution reports are delivered via `execDetails()` for each fill, including price, quantity, commission, and timing—essential for trade analysis and reconciliation

Error handling

IBKR's error messages are delivered via the `error()` callback as numeric error codes. Implement a centralized error handler that logs all errors and escalates critical ones to alerting systems—errors often indicate problems that worsen over time.

IBKR error codes include:

Code	Meaning	Action
502	Cannot connect	Gateway/TWS not running or not accepting connections
504	Not connected	Connection dropped; reconnect and reconcile state
201	Order rejected	Parse message for reason (margin, symbol, market hours)
202	Order cancelled	Client- or broker-initiated (for example, end-of-day GTC)
162	Historical data pacing	Rate limit hit; implement request queuing with delays

Table 25.1: Important IBKR error codes

Historical data access

IBKR provides historical bar data via `reqHistoricalData()`, and access may require a subscription. There are several limitations:

- **Pacing restrictions:** Historical data requests are rate-limited and the exact limits depend on your request pattern. Implement request queuing with appropriate delays rather than assuming an unlimited pull rate.
- **Data availability:** Historical data availability varies by instrument and exchange. Verify data exists before depending on it.
- **Bar sizes:** Available intervals range from 1 second to 1 month. Not all sizes are available for all instruments.

For strategies that require extensive historical data, consider supplementing IBKR data with data from dedicated vendors. Use IBKR primarily for recent data and verification against your primary source.

IBKR's depth comes with complexity; the next section covers Alpaca, which trades a narrower universe through a simpler API and serves as the faster on-ramp for readers running their first live experiments.

Implementation: See `03_ib_paper_trading_demo`, which shows IB connectivity, warm-up data requests, and shadow-mode order flow when a paper-trading session is available.

25.3 Integrating with Alpaca

Alpaca provides commission-free US stock, options, and ETF trading, plus API access to crypto markets, through a clean REST and streaming interface with generous paper-trading access. For many readers, it is the easiest broker path for early live-trading experiments. "**Commission-free**" does not mean cost-free: routing quality, spread capture, and venue selection still determine realized execution cost.

Alpaca also offers a paid plan geared more toward execution quality and infrastructure than toward zero-fee simplicity. The paid plan also lifts rate limits and expands data coverage.

REST and WebSocket APIs

The REST API handles synchronous operations—submitting orders, querying positions, and fetching account information. The streaming interfaces deliver asynchronous updates, such as fills, position changes, and market data events, after subscribing to the relevant channels. In production, use request-response calls for commands and persistent streams for status updates.

Paper trading mode

Alpaca's paper trading requires no account funding—create an account, generate paper trading API keys, and begin immediately. The paper environment uses the same general account and order workflow but simulates fills rather than negotiating against real liquidity. That makes paper trading useful for integration testing, not for measuring live slippage, market impact, or partial-fill behavior.

Use paper trading extensively before risking real capital. Run the complete system in paper mode for several trading sessions, observing that orders execute correctly, positions track accurately, and reconciliation works as expected.

Key differences from IBKR

Traders migrating from IBKR should note several differences:

Broker	Alpaca	IBKR
Asset classes	US equities and ETFs, listed options, crypto	170 markets, all asset classes
Order types	Market, limit, stop, stop-limit (more on paid plan)	Adaptive, pegged, conditional, and many more
Rate limits	200 requests/min (unlimited on paid plan)	50 messages/second on TWS API
Authentication	API key/secret (no expiry)	Session-based; periodic renewal required

Broker	Alpaca	IBKR
Data costs	Basic data included; consolidated and real-time requires a subscription	Separate charges per exchange and data type
Execution routing	PFOF to wholesalers (standard); smart routing (paid tier)	SmartRouting across venues; no PFOF (Pro)

Table 25.2: IBKR and Alpaca, compared (as of June 2026)

For multi-asset strategies, IBKR remains necessary. For most systematic strategies trading US equities or crypto, Alpaca's simpler order types suffice.

Both Alpaca and IBKR provide cryptocurrency trading through the same API, with 24/7 trading hours that require an always-on system design. Alpaca's USD-quoted spot subset covers eleven of the nineteen Binance USDT perpetual contracts the crypto case study trades; ADA, APT, ATOM, BNB, COMP, INJ, NEAR, and SUI are not Alpaca-tradeable, so a strategy ported from the Binance perp universe must either route the missing names to another venue or log them signal-only. Crypto orders accept fractional quantities (for example, 0.005 BTC); Alpaca also supports **fractional equity** shares. For strategies spanning both asset classes, the unified API simplifies integration compared to maintaining separate exchange connections. **Broker offerings continue to evolve**; always check the latest information on the broker's website.

Direct crypto exchange APIs

For crypto derivatives—perpetual futures, options, and leveraged positions—broker-mediated access through Alpaca or IBKR is insufficient. Major crypto exchanges (such as Binance, Bybit, OKX, and Deribit) operate as both venues and counterparties, exposing REST and WebSocket APIs that provide direct order book access. This is the closest analog to direct market access available to retail traders, though the exchange itself serves as both a matching engine and a custodian—a structural counterparty risk absent in traditional finance, where the broker, exchange, and clearinghouse are distinct entities.

The **crypto funding-rate case study** in *Section 25.6* deploys to OKX, which provides an instructive example of a direct exchange API. OKX's v5 API covers spot, perpetual swaps, futures, and options through one interface and offers separate live and demo workflows. The exact authentication requirements, fee schedule, and rate limits can change, so production deployments should read the venue's current documentation rather than hard-code operational assumptions from a notebook.

Geographic restrictions are the binding constraint. Exchange availability, derivatives access, and leverage terms vary by jurisdiction and change frequently. Treat venue eligibility as a legal and operational prerequisite, not as a detail to verify after the strategy is finished. The CCXT library provides a unified Python interface that abstracts away exchange-specific authentication and rate limiting, reducing the integration cost of multi-exchange strategies.

Implementation: See `04_alpaca_paper_trading_demo` for paper-trading connectivity and shadow-mode execution, `05_alpaca_crypto_live_demo` for the crypto path through Alpaca's API, and `09_crypto_funding_deployment_loop` for the split-venue deployment of the *Chapter 12* funding-rate workflow—OKX for live data (bars and 8-hour funding rates), Alpaca paper crypto for execution on the USD-quoted spot subset.

Error handling

Alpaca errors arrive as HTTP status codes with JSON error bodies:

- **403 Forbidden:** Authentication failed. Verify the API keys and check that both paper and live keys match the endpoint.
- **422 Unprocessable Entity:** Order validation failed. The response body explains why—insufficient buying power, an invalid symbol, or the market is closed.
- **429 Too Many Requests:** Rate limit exceeded. Implement exponential backoff and request queuing.
- **500/503 Server Errors:** Alpaca infrastructure issues. Retry with backoff; if persistent, check Alpaca's status page.

Parse error responses carefully. The `message` field typically explains the problem clearly enough to determine the appropriate action.

Idempotency keys

Alpaca supports client-provided order IDs (`client_order_id`) for idempotent order submission. Use this feature:

- **Generate unique IDs:** Use UUIDs or deterministic IDs based on strategy, symbol, and signal timestamp. Store the mapping between your internal order references and `client_order_ids`.
- **Retry safely:** If an order submission times out, retry with the same `client_order_id`. If the original succeeded, Alpaca returns the existing order. If it failed, Alpaca creates the new order.
- **Prevent duplicates:** The system should never create duplicate orders due to network issues or crash recovery. Client order IDs make this guarantee possible.

This idempotency pattern is essential for production reliability and applies equally to IBKR integration.

Building and maintaining broker connectivity is not the only path; the next section evaluates managed platforms that bundle infrastructure, data, and execution into a hosted service—a trade-off between convenience and control that practitioners should assess before committing to either model.

25.4 QuantConnect and managed platforms

Building and maintaining trading infrastructure demands substantial engineering effort. Managed platforms offer an alternative: let someone else handle the infrastructure while you focus on strategy development. QuantConnect, built on the open-source LEAN engine, exemplifies this approach.

The platform approach versus self-hosted

Managed platforms bundle infrastructure (servers, networking, and monitoring), pre-built broker integrations that update when APIs change, historical and real-time data feeds, and optimized backtest engines. The trade-off is between convenience and speed-to-market and flexibility and control—platforms constrain data sources, supported brokers, and available order types, but dramatically reduce implementation effort.

This chapter's earlier sections describe a different path: self-hosting with `ml4t-backtest` for research and validation, then `ml4t-live` for paper or live execution using the same strategy interface. That stack preserves direct control over code, data pipelines, and broker connectivity, but it also leaves operational responsibility with the practitioner. QuantConnect and LEAN offer integrated infrastructure and managed convenience, with less control over the surrounding environment.

LEAN engine overview

LEAN, the engine powering QuantConnect, is open source (Apache 2.0 license). This creates a hybrid option:

- **Cloud deployment**: Deploy strategies on QuantConnect's infrastructure. Pay based on usage; benefit from managed operations.
- **Local development**: Run LEAN locally during research. Full control over the environment; no cloud costs during development.
- **Self-hosted production**: Deploy LEAN on your own infrastructure. Same engine as QuantConnect, but on servers you control (and pay for).

LEAN supports multiple asset classes (such as equities, options, futures, forex, crypto) and brokers (including Alpaca, IBKR, and others). Strategies written in C# or Python can backtest on years of data and deploy to production with minimal code changes. Its main attraction is integration rather than raw speed: it combines backtesting, vendor-managed data, broker connectivity, and deployment infrastructure into a single platform.

The LEAN architecture follows event-driven principles similar to those discussed in *Chapter 16*. Data handlers feed the algorithm; the algorithm generates orders; an execution handler routes to brokers. The framework manages state persistence, position tracking, and reconciliation.

Trade-offs – Convenience versus flexibility versus cost

Evaluate platforms against self-hosted systems across several dimensions:

- **Development speed**: Platforms accelerate initial development. No infrastructure setup, pre-configured data access, or example algorithms to start from. Self-hosted systems, such as an `ml4t-backtest` plus `ml4t-live` workflow, require more upfront investment before trading begins.
- **Flexibility**: Self-hosted systems can integrate any data source, connect to any broker, and implement any execution logic. Platforms limit you to their supported options. If your strategy needs something the platform doesn't offer, you're stuck.

- **Cost structure:** Platforms charge subscription fees, per-algorithm fees, or profit sharing. At a small scale, these fees are modest. At a large scale, self-hosted infrastructure often costs less. Calculate the crossover point for your expected capital deployment.
- **Intellectual property:** Platform deployment means your strategy code resides on third-party infrastructure. Reputable platforms like QuantConnect implement access controls, but risks remain. Self-hosted systems keep strategy logic on your infrastructure.
- **Operational burden:** Platforms handle monitoring, alerting, updates, and incident response. Self-hosted systems require you to build and maintain these capabilities.

When platforms make sense

Platforms are a good fit for a variety of situations. They suit retail-scale operations, where infrastructure costs dominate; rapid prototyping before committing to a full build-out; teams with limited engineering bandwidth and where development time is more valuable than operational control; and simpler strategies that trade liquid instruments through supported brokers.

They also serve as effective learning environments for understanding algorithmic trading before building custom infrastructure. A self-hosted stack is the better fit when custom data handling or tighter control over live operations (including lower latency) matter more than managed convenience.

Migration considerations

Platform lock-in is a legitimate concern. Plan for potential migration:

- Keep strategy logic separable from platform-specific boilerplate and document which features are portable.
- Maintain independent relationships with data vendors rather than relying solely on platform data.
- Some platforms allow exporting strategy code—test that exports run on alternative infrastructure before depending on migration. Consider hybrid operation across platforms or a platform-versus-self-hosted split to reduce the risk of a single point of failure.

Whether self-hosted or managed, every live system must handle orders that fail, partially fill, or arrive out of sequence. The next section models the order lifecycle as an explicit state machine—the layer that sits between strategy signals and broker execution, regardless of which infrastructure path you choose.

> **Implementation:** See `06_quantconnect_case_study` for exporting ETF case-study predictions to QuantConnect's Object Store and consuming them from a LEAN algorithm.

25.5 Order lifecycle management

An order's journey from strategy signal to final fill involves multiple state transitions, any of which can fail, time out, or produce unexpected results. Managing this lifecycle correctly separates robust trading systems from fragile ones. The steps of the typical lifecycle are as follows:

1. The strategy first produces an internal target—"increase AAPL weight to 5%"—based on current market data.
2. This signal then becomes a concrete order ("buy 150 shares of AAPL at market") through position sizing, lot-size rounding, and order-type selection, where the choice between market and limit orders reflects the urgency-versus-impact trade-off formalized by Almgren and Chriss (2001).
3. The order is transmitted to the broker, but until acknowledgment arrives, its existence is uncertain—a network failure during submission leaves it unclear whether the order reached the broker.
4. Once the broker confirms receipt and assigns an order ID, the order is "working" at the exchange.
5. Execution may be immediate (a market order in a liquid stock) or delayed (a limit order away from the market), and partial fills create intermediate states. Madhavan (2002) provides a comprehensive framework for the microstructure dynamics that determine execution quality.
6. After fills, internal position records update, and reconciliation confirms alignment with broker records.

Each step offers opportunities for failure. Robust systems detect failures early and respond appropriately, rather than allowing undetected discrepancies to accumulate.

State machine for order status

A state machine is a model that represents a process as a set of discrete states and rules governing how events can trigger valid transitions between states. It provides a disciplined way to model the order lifecycle because every live trading system must know exactly where each order stands, which events are valid at that point, and which actions are no longer allowed. The **seven primary states** are:

1. *Created*: Exists internally, not yet submitted.
2. *Submitted*: Sent to broker, awaiting acknowledgment.
3. *Acknowledged*: Broker confirmed receipt, order is working.
4. *Partially Filled*: Some quantity executed, remainder working.
5. *Filled*: Complete execution, terminal.
6. *Canceled*: Removed before full execution, terminal.
7. *Rejected*: Broker refused, terminal.

Figure 25.2 visualizes the complete state machine with 10 states and valid transitions between them. **Terminal states** (Filled, Canceled, Rejected) have no outgoing transitions, while working states allow progression through fills or cancellation. Note how this resembles the logic of the NASDAQ ITCH order flow messages we analyzed in *Chapter 3*.

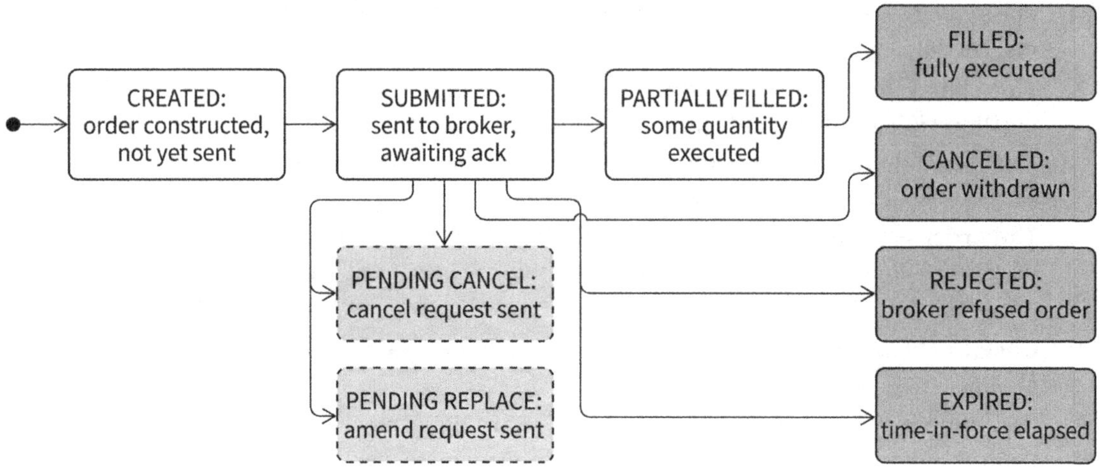

Figure 25.2: Order state machine. Explicit working and terminal states make asynchronous broker callbacks auditable and constrain legal transitions

The state machine is the critical integration point between the unified framework from *Section 25.1* and the broker APIs from *Sections 25.2–25.3*.

There are two modes:

- In **backtest mode**, the framework simulates state transitions instantaneously
- In **live mode**, the same state machine processes asynchronous broker callbacks

Because both modes share the state machine logic, order-handling behavior is verified in backtests and reproduced exactly in production. State transitions must handle edge cases:

- **Out-of-order messages:** A fill notification may arrive before acknowledgment. The state machine must accept valid transitions regardless of message order.
- **Concurrent events:** A cancel request sent just as the order fills creates a race condition. The order moves to `PENDING_CANCEL` while the cancelation is in flight; the fill notification then arrives ahead of the cancel acknowledgment, the in-flight cancel is discarded, and the audit trail records the `PENDING_CANCEL` → `FILLED` transition so the resolution remains reconstructible after the fact.
- **Network timeouts:** Submissions without acknowledgment within the timeout period require querying the broker state before deciding whether to retry.

Handling partial fills, rejections, and cancellations

Partial fills require running calculations: cumulative filled quantity, volume-weighted average price across fills, and remaining quantity. Each fill event triggers position updates and may also trigger new orders if the strategy targets a specific position size.

Rejections demand understanding the cause. Insufficient buying power? Retry after other orders free capital. Invalid symbol? Log the error and investigate. Market closed? Wait for the market to open. Don't blindly retry rejections.

Cancellations may be trader-initiated or broker-initiated. End-of-day cancellation of day orders is expected. Midday cancellation by the broker indicates a problem that requires investigation.

End-of-day reconciliation

Daily reconciliation compares internal records against broker statements:

- **Position reconciliation:** Internal position quantities versus broker-reported positions. Discrepancies indicate missed fills, erroneous calculations, or trades made outside the system.
- **Order reconciliation:** Internal open order list versus broker open orders. Orphaned broker orders (not tracked internally) present danger—they can fill unexpectedly.
- **Cash reconciliation:** Expected cash balance versus reported balance. Differences indicate missed fills, fee miscalculations, or deposits/withdrawals outside the system.

When reconciliation detects discrepancies, halt automated trading until the discrepancies are resolved. Automatic correction risks turning record-keeping errors into trading errors. Manual review before adjustment is safer.

Idempotency for crash recovery

System crashes create a particularly dangerous failure mode. The system submitted an order, then crashed before recording the submission. After a restart, should it submit again?

Client order IDs solve this problem. Before submission, generate and persist a unique ID for the order. Include this ID in the submission request. After recovery:

1. Check if the order ID exists in pending orders.
2. Query the broker using the client order ID.
3. If the broker has the order, update the internal state to match.
4. If the broker doesn't, the submission failed; retry with the same ID.

This pattern ensures orders are never duplicated due to crashes. The client order ID acts as an idempotency key—submitting the same ID twice returns the existing order rather than creating a duplicate.

Correct order handling is necessary but not sufficient—the entire signal generation pipeline must also produce identical outputs in backtest and live modes. The next section establishes a systematic verification methodology that tests parity at every stage from raw data through final orders.

Implementation: The notebook `07_order_state_machine` implements 10 order states, 19 valid state-event transitions, and demonstrates complete lifecycle tracking via audit trails.

25.6 Ensuring technical parity through pipeline verification

Live trading failures have two different sources:

- The first is a *technical failure*: the pipeline diverges from the backtest, so the same inputs produce different outputs. This is a bug and should be detected before deployment.
- The second is a *statistical failure*: the pipeline is technically correct, but out-of-sample performance differs from the backtest because markets changed or the backtest was overfit.

Bailey et al. (2015) provide a framework for estimating the probability of backtest overfitting (discussed in *Chapter 16*), but even that analysis assumes technical parity. The present section addresses parity; *Chapter 26* addresses the ongoing monitoring required after parity has been verified.

Technical parity verification ensures your live system does exactly what your backtest simulated. Until you've verified parity, live performance deviations could stem from either bugs or market conditions—making diagnosis impossible.

The verification methodology

Verification proceeds step by step through the signal generation pipeline. At each stage, feed identical inputs to backtest and live systems, then compare outputs. Any difference indicates a technical divergence that requires investigation.

Figure 25.3 shows parallel backtest and live pipelines with comparison checkpoints at each stage, enabling a binary search for divergence: when the outputs differ, check each intermediate stage to isolate the source of the divergence.

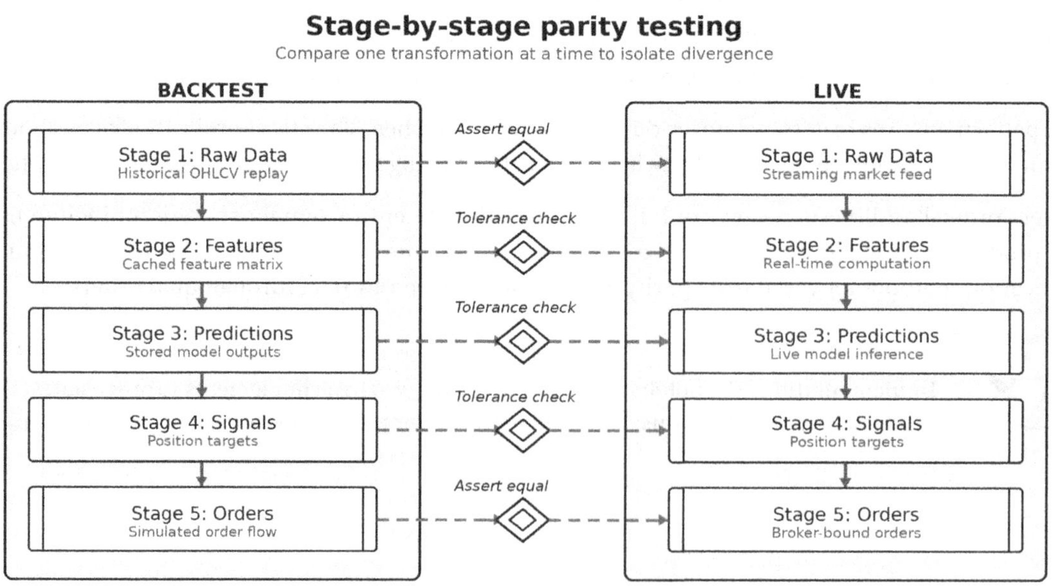

Figure 25.3: Pipeline verification flow. Comparing raw data, features, predictions, signals, and orders stage by stage isolates technical divergence before live capital is at risk

The pipeline stages for a typical ML-based strategy:

1. **Raw data → Features:** Market data transforms into model features. A momentum factor calculated on adjusted closes should produce identical values whether computed in backtest replay or from live data snapshots.
2. **Features → Predictions:** For ML-based strategies, the model transforms features into return forecasts. The same feature vector must produce the same prediction in both environments.
3. **Predictions → Signals:** Forecasts combine with risk model and constraints to produce target positions. Given identical predictions and current positions, the optimizer should output identical targets.
4. **Signals → Orders:** Target positions translate into actual orders, accounting for lot sizes, existing positions, and execution constraints. The same signal should generate the same orders.

Aim for automated tests at every stage to verify pipeline integrity and identify regressions.

Feature parity testing

Feature verification uses point-in-time historical data. Choose a historical decision date, run the backtest up to that point, extract the feature values computed for that timestamp, feed the same as-of raw data into the live feature pipeline, and compare the resulting feature vectors.

Differences reveal implementation divergence. Common culprits:

- **Look-ahead bias in backtesting:** The backtest inadvertently uses future data unavailable at the time of the decision. The live system, correctly using only past data, computes different features. López de Prado (2018) identifies look-ahead bias as a critical backtesting pitfall that inflates apparent performance.
- **Data adjustment differences:** The backtest uses split-adjusted data throughout. The live system receives unadjusted prices, which can lead to price jumps not present in the adjusted history.
- **Missing data handling:** The backtest forward-fills missing prices; the live system raises an error, uses a different fill method, or just passes the missing values to the model.
- **Timezone confusion:** The backtest interprets timestamps in one timezone; the live system uses another.

Create automated tests that verify feature parity across multiple historical dates. Run these tests continuously—data feed changes, library updates, or code modifications can introduce divergence.

Prediction consistency testing

For ML strategies, verify that the trained model produces identical predictions in both environments. Extract a feature vector from the backtest at a specific historical point, pass that same vector through the model in the backtest environment and in the production environment, and compare the outputs directly.

Model divergence sources include:

- **Serialization differences:** The model saved from research doesn't deserialize identically in production. Different library versions, missing dependencies, or platform differences can cause subtle changes.
- **Preprocessing mismatch:** The production pipeline applies preprocessing (scaling, encoding) slightly differently than research.
- **Random state:** If the model is stochastic, ensure production uses the same random seed or a deterministic mode.
- **Numerical precision:** Float32 rather than float64 computation can cause tiny differences that accumulate through deep networks.

Again, automate testing of your model prediction workflow to catch deviations without delay.

Sizing logic verification

Position sizing and portfolio optimization introduce additional complexity. Given the same predictions and current portfolio, run the optimizer in both environments and compare the target positions directly.

Divergence sources include:

- **Optimizer configuration:** Slight variations in constraint tolerances or solver settings yield different optimal points
- **Risk model differences:** Using different covariance estimates or risk factor loadings can change optimal positions
- **Universe differences:** The backtest and live systems operate on different instrument universes due to data availability or listing status

Automated regression tests

Automate verification with a custom test suite rather than relying on manual spot-checking. For a daily strategy, for example, the system should check each morning whether the previous day's live signals match what the backtest would have produced from the same information set. Any mismatch should halt trading until it is explained.

Before deployment, per-commit tests should compare features and predictions against a ground truth of cases. In addition, the complete live pipeline should periodically be replayed on historical data and compared with backtest results to catch integration errors that unit tests may miss.

The `08_pipeline_verification` harness operationalizes this discipline: on the deterministic test tape, five gated parity tests pass end-to-end (features, predictions, signals, order count, order details), the feature count is annotated `EXPECTED_DIFFERENCE` so warm-up window mismatches surface informationally rather than failing the CI gate, and zero tests are skipped because the harness emits explicit SKIP semantics when the async live pipeline cannot run—closing off the silent-pass-against-empty-live-log failure mode.

Diagnosing divergence points

When tests detect divergence, diagnosis should proceed systematically through the pipeline. Start by verifying that the inputs are identical; a data-feed issue can easily look like a computation bug. If the end-to-end outputs still differ, compare the intermediate artifacts, stage by stage.

Matching features but different predictions point to the model layer, while matching predictions but different signals point to the optimization layer. Also, check dependency versions, since library updates can change edge-case behavior. Logging inputs and outputs at each pipeline boundary speeds up this process by showing where the two environments first diverge.

Unified data sources

A subtle but critical source of divergence is **exchange-level differences**. Training on historical data from one exchange while running live inference on another creates a distribution shift that no amount of code verification can detect:

- **Quote conventions differ**: bid-ask spreads, price rounding, and timestamp alignment vary across exchanges. Features computed on Binance historical data may exhibit slightly different distributional properties than the same features computed on Coinbase live data.
- **Fee structures affect signals**: Trading costs embedded in exchange data differ. A funding rate signal trained on exchange A's funding structure may not generalize to exchange B's different rate calculation methodology.
- **Liquidity profiles vary**: Volume patterns, market depth, and order flow characteristics differ across exchanges. Cross-sectional features that rank assets by volume can yield different rankings across exchanges.

The first preference is straightforward: use the same venue for both training and inference. Mixing historical data from one exchange with live data from another introduces a distribution shift. When matching venues is impossible, treat the mismatch as an explicit verification problem.

The crypto perpetual materials illustrate this practical complication. The *Chapter 12* model artifacts are rooted in Binance-derived training data, while the live deployment demo connects to OKX market data. That makes venue comparison part of the verification task: feature definitions may match while exchange conventions still differ. The operational lesson is that mismatches must be measured and documented before live deployment.

Historical data depth may require pragmatic choices—a single exchange's public API may provide only 90 days of history, whereas archived datasets offer years of data. When mixing sources, verify that feature distributions are comparable before training on combined data.

Funding rate strategy – Live deployment

The **crypto perpetuals case study** demonstrates the complete ML-to-live pipeline. The *Chapter 12* LightGBM classifier uses 13 features: three funding-rate features (premium z-score, 8h momentum, and 24h momentum) plus ten supporting price features covering momentum at multiple horizons, rolling volatility, and technical indicators. The core hypothesis, that extreme funding rates reflect crowded positioning prone to mean reversion, is detailed in *Chapter 6* (see also the book's GitHub repo); here, the focus is on deploying the trained model into a live-execution workflow.

For live trading, the notebooks deploy to OKX, which provides real-time funding rate data on an 8-hour settlement cycle, OHLCV candles at minute and hourly resolution, and broad API accessibility for both data retrieval and order execution.

Each minute, the live pipeline:

1. *Fetches* hourly bars and funding rate history from OKX.
2. *Computes* all 13 features to match the training schema and transformations as closely as the live venue permits.
3. *Predicts* using the trained LightGBM classifier (3-class: `stop_loss`, `timeout`, `profit_take`).
4. *Decides* entry, hold, or exit based on prediction probabilities.

Two exit mechanisms protect capital:

- **Prediction-flip exit:** When P(profit) drops below the exit threshold, indicating the funding rate opportunity has closed or conditions changed, exit the position
- **Stop-loss exit:** If the price moves against the position by more than, for example, 1%, exit immediately, regardless of the model's prediction

This architecture shows that ML models can be deployed at higher frequencies than they were trained for, provided feature computation remains consistent (but predictive performance may differ). That is the chapter's central principle: the same feature definitions must survive the transition from research to inference. The verification suite described earlier in this section provides the tooling to systematically confirm this parity.

Parity versus regime stability

Technical parity is the chapter's main concern: the live pipeline must compute exactly what the backtest computed. But a parity-verified pipeline can still lose money when market structure shifts after training. The crypto funding-rate case illustrates this distinction directly.

The research loop trained the LightGBM classifier on 2020–2023 data and evaluated it across validation and holdout windows extending into 2025. Validation performance suggested a positive edge; holdout performance, which includes the late 2025 crypto drawdown, did not. A natural reaction is to suspect a bug—some subtle feature shift or leakage. The verification discipline in this section rules that out: features, predictions, and signals match across environments.

The explanation is structural. Funding-rate signals prescribe a specific cross-sectional allocation: long tokens with unusually negative funding (where shorts appear crowded and are expected to mean-revert up), short tokens with unusually positive funding. In the case-study universe of nineteen perpetual swaps, that prescription loaded the long leg onto smaller-cap tokens (COMP, DOT, SUI, AVAX) at roughly 10% weight each and the short leg onto majors (BTC, ETH). When the 2025 drawdown compressed the entire crypto asset class, the long-alt leg drew down considerably harder than the short-major leg paid out. The signal itself remained internally consistent; the implied factor exposure (alts over majors) swung against the strategy.

The holdout losses are spread across the entire long leg rather than concentrated in a handful of blow-up names: the top three loss-contributing tokens together account for only about 8% of total losses. Universe filtering—for example, restricting the universe to majors—would not fix this: removing the long-alt leg leaves an unhedged short position, which is not the strategy the signal prescribes.

Let's delineate the responsibilities of *Chapter 25* versus *Chapter 26*:

- *Chapter 25* asks: Does the live system compute the same quantities as the backtest? Here, yes.
- *Chapter 26* asks: Should the system continue trading given current regime characteristics? That is a monitoring question—tracking whether funding-rate means, cross-sectional dispersion, and realized correlations still resemble the training distribution—and it can trigger a pause even on a technically correct pipeline.

The OKX demonstration in this chapter, therefore, treats the crypto pipeline as a parity artifact rather than a profitable strategy. The value of the demo is that it exposes every live-trading mechanic: authenticated and unauthenticated endpoints, asynchronous feed orchestration, the trained-model-to-order pathway, and kill-switch behavior under adverse PnL conditions. Whether the current funding-rate regime rewards the signal is a separate question that this chapter does not attempt to answer.

A contrasting deployment – FX daily signals

The FX case study offers a complement. Its holdout performance remained consistent with validation—no sign flip, no concentrated exposure to a single macro factor that swung against the strategy during the out-of-sample window. Its live-deployment characteristics are also forgiving: daily decision cadence, quote-driven venues with narrow spreads, and continuous weekday markets available through Interactive Brokers' IDEALPRO desk on a paper account.

The FX notebook wires the *Chapter 12* FX model into a paper-trading loop that rebalances daily across majors and carry-cross pairs. The verification discipline still applies—features computed from live tick data must match what the backtest computed from end-of-day bars—but regime stability is a weaker concern because the strategy's implied factor exposure (a blend of carry and short-horizon momentum) is less tightly coupled to a single market-wide drawdown.

Taken together, the two demos frame the two sides of parity:

- The OKX deployment shows how a pipeline survives the transition from research to inference even when the regime no longer rewards the signal
- The IB IDEALPRO deployment shows what live execution looks like when pipeline and regime cooperate

A third demonstration carries the parity discussion into the **basket-rebalance setting.** The IB basket-rebalance notebook ranks a 20-name US large-cap universe by a 20-day momentum signal and routes the resulting basket through a single `IBBroker` paper session. Two of its choices are worth flagging because they are exactly the kind of parity gaps that a live deployment reveals:

1. The **warmup bars** are pulled from `IBBroker.reqHistoricalDataAsync` rather than from a research-time loader, sourcing rank inputs and `SafeBroker`'s order-value reference prices from the same session that will execute the orders. Using a research-time loader would risk ranking names based on stale prices and computing position sizes relative to historical levels, leading to a feature-parity failure. The cost is operational: IB pacing limits and per-contract qualification add latency to the warmup step and require parallelizing the per-symbol requests through `asyncio.gather`.
2. The **post-submission state** is reconciled by polling `IBBroker.get_positions_async` rather than by subscribing to `ib.execDetailsEvent`. Polling is simpler and sufficient for a daily rebalance, but it adds latency and can miss fills that land between intervals; an event-driven reconciliation is the production-grade alternative.

Both choices are documented in the notebook, so you can see the trade-off rather than work around it.

Technical parity is a prerequisite, but a verified pipeline still needs operational discipline to survive in production. The next section establishes the pre-flight checklists, kill switches, and graduated deployment procedures that protect live capital once technical parity has been confirmed.

Implementation: `08_pipeline_verification` uses a deterministic parity harness and live wrappers to test feature, prediction, and signal consistency.

`09_crypto_funding_deployment_loop` is the complete ML-to-live pipeline on crypto perpetuals—training a LightGBM three-class direction model on the *Chapter 12* funding-rate panel, fetching live OHLCV bars and 8-hour funding rates from OKX's public API, scoring all 19 perps, and routing the resulting basket through Alpaca paper crypto on the eleven USD-quoted spot pairs Alpaca lists (the remaining perps are logged signal-only; requires Alpaca account).

`11_fx_deployment_loop` is the single-venue contrast: a Ridge regressor trained on the *Chapter 12* 20-pair FX panel, deployed through Interactive Brokers' paper account on IDEALPRO—IB serves as both the live data plane (daily FX bars via `reqHistoricalDataAsync`) and the execution plane (Forex spot orders), since FX is one of the few asset classes where a single retail broker can cover both (requires IBKR account).

`12_ib_basket_rebalance_demo` extends the discussion into a live IB paper basket-rebalance setting and is referenced again in *Section 25.7* for its startup-reconciliation pattern.

25.7 Operational readiness

A system that passes all verification tests can still fail in production due to operational gaps. This section covers the pre-launch requirements and ongoing practices that separate reliable trading from catastrophic surprises.

Preflight checklist

Operational readiness begins with a startup gate, not with the first signal. Before the strategy is allowed to trade, several checks need to pass:

1. The **runtime environment** must demonstrate that the container or server is healthy, network paths to the broker are open, data feeds are current, and that supporting services, such as databases and monitoring, are available. A strategy that starts from a partially degraded environment is already in an abnormal state before it places an order.
2. **Authentication is a separate gate.** Credentials must be valid, the paper or live setting must match the intended environment, and the account must have the permissions needed for the planned orders and data sources. These checks are easy to ignore in notebooks because a missing credential often fails loudly. In production, the more dangerous case is partial success: the session authenticates, but to the wrong account, the wrong environment, or a limited permission set.
3. The **trading algo's state must be coherent** before trading begins. Internal positions should match broker positions, cash balances should reconcile, no orphaned orders should remain from the prior session, and the previous reconciliation cycle should have completed cleanly. Without this baseline, the strategy is no longer extending yesterday's state; it is compounding an unknown discrepancy.
4. **Market context** is part of the same startup gate. The system should confirm that the venue is open when required, that no exchange restrictions or circuit breakers are active, and that prices are current rather than stale.
5. **Configuration** belongs in this gate as well: risk limits, order-size caps, and kill-switch access should be verified before the first automated action

These checks should run automatically at startup, produce a short human-readable report, and block trading if any required condition fails.

Kill switches and emergency procedures

Verification reduces risk; it does not remove the need for intervention. When systems misbehave, **the response should be graded:**

- The first level is to pause new signals while allowing existing orders to finish. This is the right response when behavior is suspicious but not yet clearly dangerous.
- The second level is to cancel all working orders while leaving positions unchanged. This is appropriate when order routing or order logic is suspect, but inventory is still acceptable.
- The third level is to flatten positions and return the portfolio to cash. This is the correct choice when continuing to hold risk is no longer justified by the confidence in the system state.
- The final level is a full shutdown of the trading process and any dependent automation. That level is reserved for infrastructure failures, corrupted state, or situations in which operator trust in the system has completely broken down.

Each action should be executable via a single clear control: a command, a shortcut, or a button that has already been tested. Under stress, multi-step emergency procedures fail because they ask the operator to reason clearly at the moment when the system is least trustworthy. The kill switch should also remain independent of the component it controls. If the strategy engine hangs, the operator still needs a broker-side or infrastructure-side path to cancel orders and flatten risk.

Enforced safety in the live runtime

The pre-flight requirements are not aspirational. In `ml4t-live`, `SafeBroker` is the single point that enforces these requirements, and the runtime distinguishes documented limits from active controls. The position-value cap, the per-order cap, the daily-loss kill switch, and the maximum data-staleness threshold are all checked on every order intent before it reaches the broker adapter; an order that would breach any of them raises rather than ships.

Two of those controls deserve specific attention because they fail open without persistence:

- The **daily-loss kill switch** is useful only if it survives an engine restart during a trading day; otherwise, a crash and reconnect reset the loss counter and re-enable trading at the worst possible moment. `SafeBroker` writes the daily-loss state to a state file on every transition and reloads it on reconnect, so a same-day restart resumes with the kill-switch state intact.
- The **data-staleness check**, similarly, requires a known timestamp for the last bar received per asset; the engine maintains that per-asset snapshot and rejects orders whose freshest market data exceeds the configured threshold.

These two together prevent two of the most common live-trading failure modes: trading on a stale feed during a venue outage and re-entering positions after the kill switch was supposed to be latched.

Startup reconciliation closes the third of the common failure modes. When `SafeBroker.connect()` runs, it diffs the persisted snapshot from the previous session—positions and pending orders the engine knew about at last shutdown—against the broker's current authoritative state. A clean report means the two agree. A non-clean report means something changed between sessions: an after-hours order was finally filled, a manual flatten occurred in the GUI, an order was canceled out-of-band, or a partial fill landed after the last persist. The reconciliation report is exposed to the caller, and any production launcher should refuse to start a new trading cycle until either the report is clean or the operator has explicitly reset the persisted state. The `12_ib_basket_rebalance_demo` follows that pattern verbatim.

The deployment loop in `02_etfs_deployment_loop` enforces two further invariants the runtime checks but cannot infer from configuration. A **training-cutoff guard** pins `LABEL_AVAILABLE_AS_OF = LIVE_WINDOW_START - forward_horizon_days`, so no `fwd_ret_h` training label reads prices from the live window—a 21-day forward return on a 2025-01-01 live window forces training to cut at 2024-11-29 rather than 2024-12-31. Both `feature_cutoff_date` and `label_available_as_of` are persisted in `training_metadata.json` alongside the run record, so the *Chapter 26* monitoring loop can audit the invariant after the fact without re-running training. The **basket disposition** is partitioned across `intended_basket`, `attempted_basket`, `accepted_basket`, and `failed_basket` and persisted separately on each run rather than collapsed into a single status string. The *Chapter 26* monitor alerts on a non-empty `failed_basket` without re-parsing exec records, and the dry-run path used in this chapter's CI (`SUBMIT_PAPER_ORDERS=false`) keeps the full basket in `intended_basket` so the disposition itself remains testable in the absence of a live broker.

The broker-independent operator surface comes from the `ml4t-live` CLI:

- `ml4t-live status` reads the persisted state file and reports the current daily-loss counter, the kill-switch latch, the persisted position snapshot, and any pending orders the previous session knew about
- `ml4t-live shadow <strategy>` runs a strategy in shadow mode for a bounded duration, with the same risk surface but virtual fills, and reports a small set of health states:
    - `ok` when bars are arriving
    - `waiting_for_data` before the first bar
    - `feed_silent` when bars stop arriving inside the configured silence window
    - `idle_market_closed` when no fresh data is expected
    - `broker_disconnected` when the broker connection has dropped

The states listed here are what a watchdog or supervisor process should *consume*; they are not a substitute for it.

Transitioning from paper to live trading

Paper trading validates integration, but it does not validate market impact, live commissions, or the operational pressure of real money. In the ML4T stack, this transition begins with `ml4t-live` in shadow mode or paper mode, using the same strategy logic that passed backtest verification. A sensible transition starts with an extended paper phase long enough to observe routine behavior: orders should route correctly, reconciliation should pass daily, and no unexplained drift should appear between the strategy and the broker.

The first live deployment should use a fraction of the intended capital. The purpose is not to prove profitability; it is to verify that live fills, fees, and position updates behave as expected when money is at risk. If that phase remains clean, capital can be increased gradually. Each step up in size is another test of whether the strategy remains operationally stable under higher stakes.

Parallel operation can make this transition more informative. Running the live and paper versions side by side, or keeping a shadow portfolio alongside the executing book, exposes divergence in signals, order timing, and realized fills. Those differences are often more useful diagnostically than the raw PnL of either book during the transition window.

Regulatory and jurisdictional considerations

Live trading means interacting with regulated financial markets. The rules governing algorithmic trading vary dramatically by jurisdiction, and aspiring traders must understand the requirements that apply in their operating environment before deploying any automated system. This section provides a practical overview—not legal advice—of the landscape as of early 2026.

United States

The US imposes no special registration or approval requirement on retail individuals running algorithmic strategies through a broker. However, several rules shape the practical environment:

- The **Pattern Day Trader rule** requires $25,000 minimum equity for accounts executing four or more day trades within five business days—a binding constraint for smaller accounts running intraday strategies.
- **SEC Rule 15c3-5 (the Market Access Rule)** requires broker-dealers to implement pre-trade risk controls on all orders, whether manual or algorithmic, effectively prohibiting unfiltered "naked" market access.
- **FINRA Rule 3110** imposes supervision obligations on firms. For most strategies in this book—rebalancing at daily or lower frequency through standard broker APIs—these rules are largely transparent: the broker's infrastructure handles pre-trade checks, and position sizes are far below the thresholds that trigger enhanced scrutiny.

European Union

MiFID II Article 17 requires investment firms engaged in algorithmic trading to notify their national competent authority, maintain effective risk controls, and ensure trading systems are resilient with appropriate thresholds and limits. Firms must implement pre-trade controls, including price collars, maximum order values, and kill buttons.

These obligations apply to regulated investment firms, not to retail individuals trading through a licensed broker. However, a retail trader who scales to manage external capital will enter regulated territory and face regulatory requirements.

India

India has moved toward one of the most prescriptive retail-algorithmic regimes. SEBI and the exchanges now expect broker-mediated approval workflows and exchange-assigned identifiers for many automated retail deployments.

The exact operational details have changed repeatedly, so Indian-market strategies should be checked directly against current broker and exchange guidance before launch rather than inferred from older blog posts or sample code.

Transaction taxes and access constraints

Beyond formal approval, geography determines trading costs and product availability in ways that can dominate all other considerations. Transaction taxes, leverage caps, and venue access can turn an otherwise attractive backtest into an untradeable strategy. UK stamp duty, European financial-transaction taxes, and product-level crypto restrictions are common examples. A crypto-perpetuals strategy and a US ETF rotation strategy do not face the same legal or economic constraints, even if their implementation looks quite similar.

There is no global solution because legal systems are national in nature. Before deploying any strategy live, verify four things in the target jurisdiction:

1. Whether the product is legal to trade.
2. Whether the broker supports automated access for it.
3. What taxes or market-access fees apply.

4. Which leverage or margin rules govern the account.

Those checks belong in the deployment checklist, not in an appendix after the strategy is already built.

Monitoring handoff to Chapter 26

With the system live and technically verified, the core question changes. The issue is no longer whether the code runs as designed, but whether live performance remains within expectation, input distributions remain stable, and model behavior stays interpretable over time. *Chapter 26* addresses the problems of monitoring and adaptation.

Implementation:

- `10_safety_risk_demo` walks the configurable risk surface in isolation—order and position caps, rate limiting, the manual kill switch, shadow-mode order routing through `VirtualPortfolio`, and the asset-restriction filter.
- `12_ib_basket_rebalance_demo` carries the same controls into a live IB paper session and operationalizes the startup-reconciliation pattern: `SafeBroker.connect()` is called before the basket loop, and the notebook refuses to launch unless the reconciliation report is clean.
- `13_runtime_safety_showcase` drives the corresponding runtime-trust contract under failure: stale-data rejection from a `MarketSnapshot` past the configured threshold, automatic kill-switch activation on a simulated daily-loss breach with latch survival across `SafeBroker` reconstruction, a non-clean `reconciliation_report` produced from a deliberately divergent persisted state file, and the `LiveEngine` health-state transitions narrated above.

25.8 Summary

This chapter addressed the most common failure mode in algorithmic trading: technical divergence between backtest and live systems. The unified framework pattern—where the same strategy code runs unchanged in both modes—eliminates an entire class of bugs by construction. We integrated three execution models with distinct trade-offs: Interactive Brokers for professional-grade global access with SmartRouting and portfolio margin, Alpaca for developer-friendly US equity and crypto trading, and direct crypto exchange APIs for derivatives strategies that require venue-level access. Broker selection is itself an execution-quality decision—routing architecture determines realized cost more than posted commissions do—and geographic constraints on product availability, transaction taxes, and leverage caps further shape what is deployable where. Managed platforms offer a fourth path for traders who prioritize convenience over full control.

On the execution side, we modeled the order lifecycle as an explicit state machine with 10 states and 19 valid transitions, handling partial fills, race conditions, and crash recovery through idempotent client order IDs. Pipeline verification—systematic parity testing of features, predictions, and signals between backtest and live systems—ensures that the first category of live trading failures (technical bugs) is caught before deployment. Operational readiness procedures, from four-level kill switches to graduated paper-to-live transitions, provide the discipline needed for production operation.

Going live is an achievement, but it is the beginning of a new challenge: markets change, and models decay. *Chapter 26* addresses the monitoring and adaptation infrastructure—drift detection, circuit breakers, safe model rollout—needed to maintain performance over time.

26

MLOps and Governance

A model has cleared every backtest, and the deployment verification covered in *Chapter 25* has taken the system live, executing real trades with real capital. Keeping it working is the next problem.

Every deployed model decays. Market regimes shift, competitors discover similar signals, and the statistical relationships the model learned gradually erode. The difference between a profitable trading operation and a capital-destroying one often comes down to how quickly we detect this decay and how safely we respond.

This chapter builds the post-deployment infrastructure that separates production-grade trading systems from research prototypes. Where *Chapter 25* ensured the system launched correctly, the task now is to keep it correct, or to fail gracefully when it cannot. The governance model has three layers: detection through data validation gates, rolling metrics, and drift analysis; response through shadow evaluation and staged rollouts; and automated safety through circuit breakers that halt trading when losses or conditions breach limits. The supporting MLOps infrastructure, including feature stores, model registries, and CI/CD, should be right-sized to the team's maturity rather than adopted wholesale.

After completing this chapter, you will be able to:

- Distinguish technical pipeline divergence from statistical performance decay and choose the corresponding diagnostic and response workflow.
- Build a live-monitoring framework that combines data-integrity gates, rolling performance metrics, backtest-to-live comparison, and execution-quality checks.
- Apply drift diagnostics to production artifacts, including PSI, K-S, SHAP-based feature monitoring, and online detectors such as Adaptive Windowing (ADWIN) and the Drift Detection Method (DDM).
- Design a safe model-update workflow using shadow mode, incumbent-versus-candidate evaluation, explicit promotion criteria, staged rollout gates, and tested rollback procedures.
- Implement multi-level circuit breakers across trade, strategy, portfolio, and system layers, with clear recovery and override discipline.
- Evaluate and right-size the supporting MLOps stack, including feature stores, data versioning and lineage, model registries, experiment tracking, and CI/CD controls.

The technical-versus-statistical failure taxonomy in *Section 26.1* organizes what follows: detection (*Sections 26.2* and *26.3*), response (*Section 26.4*), automated safety (*Section 26.5*), and the supporting MLOps infrastructure (*Section 26.6*).

The monitoring, drift, and rollout notebooks work from real case-study artifacts: the `us_equities_panel` holdout boundary, stored prediction streams, real feature panels, and the SQLite registry that tracks every training run. The circuit-breaker notebook drives its market-risk rules with the real SPY 2020 H1 path through the COVID crash; only the infrastructure-latency stream remains synthetic, scoped to make the latency breaker's rolling-average trip inspectable. The remaining infrastructure notebooks operate on the same local Parquet and SQLite stores. Broker connectivity is out of scope; alert logic, data lineage, and promotion gates are grounded in actual workflow outputs.

26.1 Two sources of live trading failure

Live trading failures fall into two categories that demand different diagnoses and responses. Confusing them wastes time and capital.

Technical failure caused by pipeline divergence

A *technical* failure occurs when the live system computes something differently than the backtest. The same inputs should produce the same outputs, but they do not. Common causes include data format mismatches (the backtest used adjusted prices while the live feed provides unadjusted ones), timing errors (features computed at market close in backtesting arrive with slight delays in production, so a "20-day volatility" spans different windows), and implementation bugs (such as a sign error, an off-by-one index, or a missing normalization step that runs without errors but produces subtly wrong results).

Technical failures are *verification problems*. *Chapter 25* addressed these: reconciliation between backtest and live systems should catch pipeline divergence. When a live system produces different outputs for identical inputs, the cause is a bug to fix.

Statistical failure caused by performance decay

Statistical failure occurs when the system works exactly as designed (the same inputs produce the same outputs), but the outputs no longer predict returns. The implementation is correct; the model has decayed.

Four mechanisms cause statistical decay:

- *Overfitting*: The model learned patterns from the training data that do not generalize to new data. Backtest performance reflected in-sample noise rather than out-of-sample signal. Every strategy risks this; validation mitigates but does not eliminate it. Harvey, Liu, and Zhu (2016) showed how multiple hypothesis testing inflates backtested performance across finance research, and the same risk applies to individual strategy development.
- *Look-ahead bias*: Subtle information leakage inflated backtest results. Perhaps the features were computed using future data that would not have been available in real time. Perhaps survivorship bias excluded delisted securities from the universe.

- *Regime change*: Market structure shifted. Volatility regimes changed, correlations broke down, or the relationship between features and returns evolved. What worked in the training period does not work in the current market.
- *Alpha decay*: The strategy became crowded. Other participants, human or algorithmic, discovered similar patterns. The captured alpha attracted competition, and returns were arbitraged away. McLean and Pontiff (2016) documented this empirically: once anomalies became public, their profitability fell sharply, consistent with a mix of data-mining bias and post-publication arbitrage.

Why the distinction matters

Different failures demand different responses:

Failure type	Diagnosis	Response
Technical	Same inputs → different outputs	Fix the bug
Statistical	Same inputs → same outputs → poor returns	Retrain, redesign, or retire

Table 26.1: Responses by failure type

Treating statistical decay as a bug leads to futile debugging. Treating bugs as statistical decay leads to unnecessary model changes. The first step in any investigation is determining which category applies.

Capponi et al. (2025) formalize how nonstationarity erodes model reliability: the question is not whether performance will degrade, but when, and whether detection arrives in time to respond. The monitoring framework in the following sections assumes decay will happen and builds systematic detection accordingly.

Implementation: `01_drift_monitoring` (statistical drift detection), `06_mlflow_experiments` (experiment tracking and model registry workflows).

26.2 Performance monitoring

A systematic monitoring framework tracks multiple performance dimensions, compares live results to backtest expectations, and triggers alerts when metrics breach meaningful thresholds. The goal is to detect decay early enough to respond before losses accumulate.

Data integrity gates

Before monitoring model performance, validate the data feeding it. A large fraction of apparent drift incidents in live trading are silent data defects: stale prices, corporate action mishandling, broken joins, timezone misalignment, missing bars, or duplicated rows. These are technical failures in the taxonomy of *Section 26.1*, but they surface first as statistical anomalies in downstream metrics.

A lightweight data contract layer catches these defects at ingest, before they propagate to feature computation, inference, or execution. Schema validation libraries such as Pandera enforce type constraints, null bounds, monotonic timestamp ordering, and uniqueness keys on each incoming DataFrame. Great Expectations offers a similar approach, with human-readable validation artifacts that are useful for team collaboration.

The key design choice is a *fail-closed* policy for execution-critical feeds: if market data fails validation, do not trade on it. Non-critical analytics pipelines can fail open with warnings. Integrate validation outcomes into the same tiered alert system described below: a schema violation on a primary data feed should trigger a critical alert, while a minor anomaly on a secondary feed warrants a watch-level notification.

The rolling metrics framework

Point-in-time metrics hide trends. A strategy with an acceptable overall Sharpe ratio may show alarming decay in recent windows. Rolling calculations can reveal nuances that aggregate statistics obscure.

For a trailing window of w trading days ending at time t, the basic monitoring formulas are:

$$\widehat{SR}_{t,w} = \frac{\sqrt{252}\,\bar{r}_{t-w+1:t}}{s_{t-w+1:t}}, \qquad DD_t = 1 - \frac{V_t}{\max\limits_{u \le t} V_u}, \qquad HR_{t,w} = \frac{1}{w} \sum_{i=t-w+1}^{t} \mathbf{1}\,(r_i > 0)$$

where $\bar{r}$ is mean daily strategy return net of costs, s is its sample standard deviation, V_t is portfolio value, and HR is hit rate. These are simple diagnostics, not sufficient statistics; the point is to compute them consistently on live, net-of-cost returns and compare them with the same quantities from validation. The following key metrics were introduced in earlier chapters.

Rolling Sharpe ratio

Compute Sharpe over trailing windows (for example, 30-, 60-, and 90-day) and plot them alongside backtest expectations. The gap between backtested and realized Sharpe ratios is often a critical monitoring metric.

A well-calibrated strategy should show live Sharpe within a reasonable range of backtested Sharpe, accounting for estimation uncertainty. Persistent underperformance (live Sharpe consistently 0.5 or more below expectation) signals either overfitting in the backtest or a regime change in the market.

Information coefficient

The correlation between your predictions and subsequent returns. While Sharpe measures aggregate performance, IC measures predictive accuracy at the signal level.

Monitor rolling IC to catch prediction decay before it fully manifests in returns. A strategy might temporarily maintain acceptable returns due to favorable market conditions, even as IC declines. When conditions normalize, the degraded predictions will produce losses.

Hit rate and win/loss ratio

The hit rate and win/loss ratios answer: What fraction of trades are profitable? When trades win, how much? When they lose, how much? These metrics decompose Sharpe into interpretable components.

A declining hit rate with a stable win/loss ratio suggests the model's directional predictions are weakening. Stable hit rate with a deteriorating win/loss ratio suggests correct direction but poor magnitude estimation or worsening execution.

Drawdown depth and duration

Maximum drawdown measures the largest peak-to-trough decline. Drawdown duration measures how long recovery takes.

Extended drawdowns beyond historical norms (both deeper and longer than those observed in backtesting) suggest the strategy has entered unfamiliar territory. The model may be operating in a regime it wasn't trained for.

Alert thresholds

Monitoring generates continuous data; alerts require thresholds. Thresholds too tight generate noise and alert fatigue. Thresholds too loose allow damage before detection.

Design tiered thresholds:

- **Watch** (yellow): Metrics outside normal range but not alarming. Log for review; no action required. Example: Rolling 30-day Sharpe ratio drops below 1.0 when the expected value is 1.5.
- **Warning** (orange): Metrics deteriorated significantly. Investigate promptly; consider reducing exposure. Example: Rolling Sharpe drops below 0.5 for two consecutive weeks.
- **Critical** (red): Metrics breach hard limits. Take protective action; may trigger automated response. Example: Rolling Sharpe negative for 30+ days, or drawdown exceeds historical maximum.

Calibrate thresholds empirically from your backtest: what metric levels preceded historical degradation episodes? What values would have given you sufficient warning to act?

Threshold design must also prevent alert fatigue. A monitoring system that pings the team every day trains them to ignore it. Stick to alerts with a defined action, measure false-positive rates from historical data, and review alert thresholds whenever you add a new metric. If a threshold fires often but never changes exposure, retraining cadence, or diagnostic priority, it is noise masquerading as rigor.

Visual dashboards

A production monitoring dashboard should display five panels, whether built in Grafana with a Prometheus backend or in a simpler stack like Streamlit against flat files:

- **Real-time PnL**: Cumulative and daily returns versus benchmark, with a backtest overlay showing expected versus realized equity.

- **Rolling metrics:** Sharpe, IC, and hit rate across 30-, 60-, and 90-day windows. Multiple windows distinguish temporary noise (short window drops, long window stable) from persistent decay (all windows declining).
- **Drawdown tracker:** Current depth and duration as time series, with horizontal lines marking historical maximum and circuit-breaker threshold.
- **Alert status:** Color-coded indicators (green/yellow/orange/red) with timestamps of the last state change. A single glance should convey system health.
- **Backtest comparison:** Live equity overlaid on backtested equity curve: the gap between these lines is a central visual diagnostic.

Figure 26.1 shows a representative monitoring dashboard layout with these five panels.

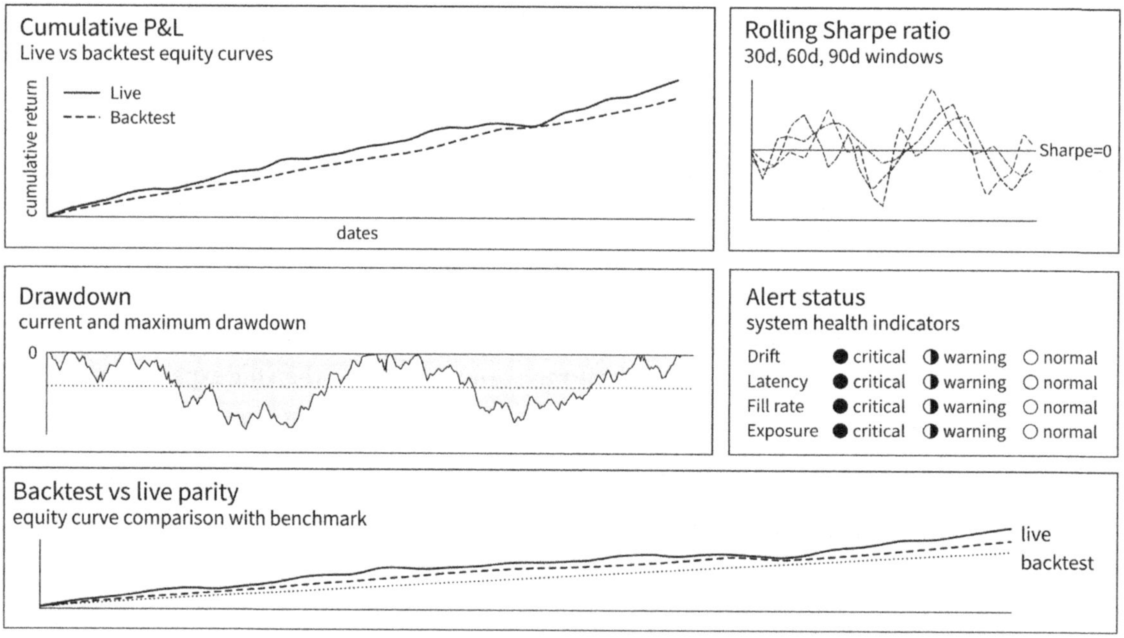

Figure 26.1: Trading system monitoring dashboard. Live-versus-backtest equity, rolling diagnostics, drawdown, alerts, and benchmark comparison support daily operational review

Comparison to backtesting expectations

The backtest provides your performance hypothesis; live trading tests that hypothesis. Systematic comparison reveals whether reality matches expectations.

For each metric, track:

- **Backtested value:** What did validation predict?
- **Live value:** What are you actually observing?
- **Deviation:** How far apart are they?
- **Significance:** Is the deviation larger than expected from estimation noise?

Some deviation is inevitable because backtest estimates carry confidence intervals. Persistent, large deviations in one direction indicate that something systematic has changed.

Compute the backtest-to-live ratio for key metrics. A strategy backtested at Sharpe 2.0 running live at Sharpe 1.5 has a 0.75 realization ratio. Track this ratio over time. Declining realization ratio (even if absolute performance remains acceptable) suggests ongoing degradation.

Execution quality monitoring

Model performance metrics capture signal quality, but *execution quality* often dominates short-horizon PnL variability and can masquerade as model decay. Widening spreads, declining fill rates, increasing slippage, or broker throttling all reduce realized returns without changing the model's predictions.

Monitor execution alongside model metrics: slippage relative to backtest assumptions, spread paid versus quoted, fill ratio and partial-fill behavior, and latency distributions from signal generation to order fill. Compute a realized-versus-simulated transaction cost ratio analogous to the backtest realization ratio described above. If execution costs consistently exceed backtest assumptions, the problem is market microstructure or infrastructure, not the model, and retraining would be the wrong response.

Example monitoring workflow

The notebook material uses the real `us_equities_panel` holdout stream rather than a simulated monitoring record. The reference slice comes from the last pre-holdout year; the current slice comes from the most recent holdout window. Beyond that boundary, the notebook computes PSI and K-S checks for the monitored features, tracks the distribution of stored model scores, and rolls IC, hit rate, and error metrics across the live-style window. The operating logic is the same as that used by a production desk: start with baseline expectations, compare current behavior to those baselines, and escalate only when deterioration is persistent enough to warrant a change in decision.

Figure 26.2 renders the operational view produced by this workflow. The dashboard combines a PSI bar chart over the monitored features, a prediction-score histogram comparing reference and current windows, a rolling IC panel, and a rolling hit-rate panel. Read together, the four panels separate input-side shifts (PSI bars, score histogram) from output-side performance (rolling IC, rolling hit rate), so an operator can tell whether a metric move reflects changing inputs, changing relationships, or both. *Section 26.3* covers the drift-detection algorithms behind the PSI and histogram panels in detail.

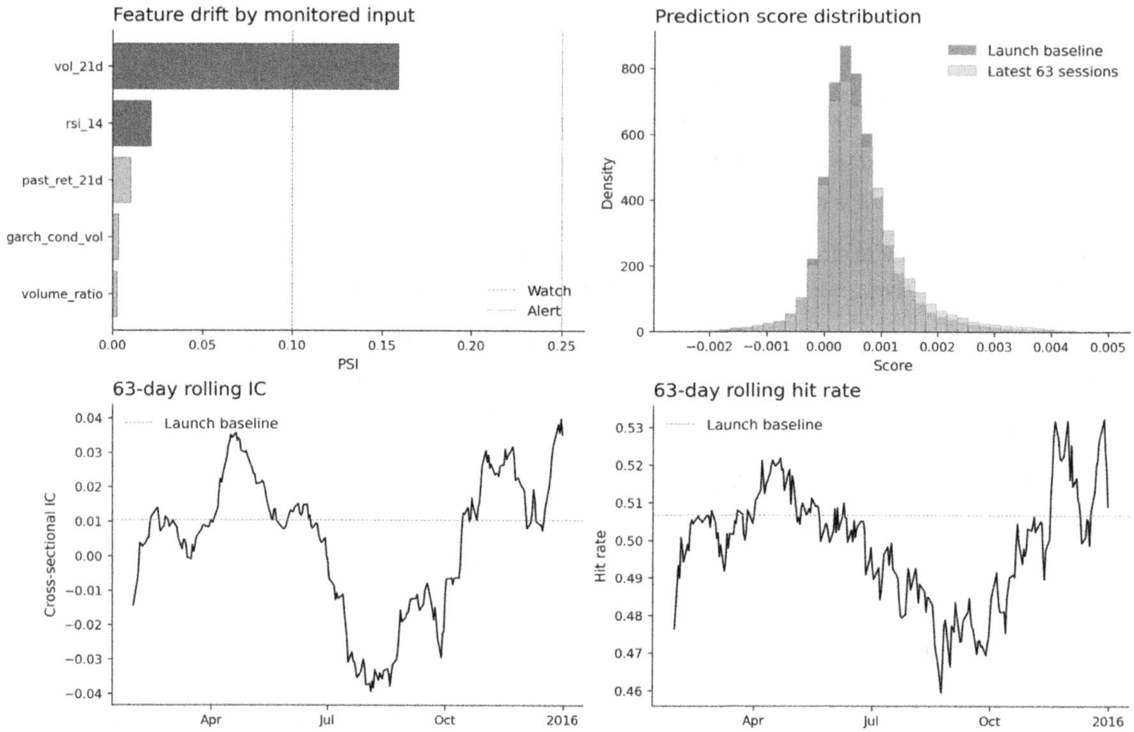

Figure 26.2: Drift-monitoring dashboard on the us_equities_panel holdout stream. PSI bars, prediction-score histogram, rolling IC, and rolling hit-rate panels combine input-side and output-side diagnostics in a single operational view

The practical sequence is simple: monitor the metric gap, determine whether the issue is technical or statistical, diagnose the likely mechanism, and only then adjust exposure or initiate a model-update workflow. A mild drop in rolling Sharpe may justify observation. A sustained drop paired with worse IC, deeper drawdowns, or execution-cost inflation justifies intervention. What matters is that monitoring links each metric breach to an explicit response.

Monitoring tells you *that* performance changed; the next section adds drift detection to diagnose *what* changed: whether the shift lies in input distributions, feature importance, or the feature-target relationship itself.

Implementation: `01_drift_monitoring` illustrates rolling metrics, thresholding, and a compact dashboard on the real `us_equities_panel` holdout artifacts. `06_mlflow_experiments` shows how the same review workflow can be tied to the local experiment registry and its stored artifacts.

26.3 Drift detection

Performance monitoring tells you *that* something changed. Drift detection tells you *what* changed. By tracking shifts in input distributions, feature importance, and feature-target relationships, you can diagnose decay before it fully manifests in returns.

Data drift caused by input distribution changes

Data drift occurs when the statistical properties of your input features shift from their training distribution. The model receives data that it was not trained on.

The Population Stability Index (PSI) quantifies the distribution shift:

$$PSI = \sum_i (A_i - E_i) \cdot \ln \frac{A_i}{E_i}$$

where A_i is the actual proportion in bin i and E_i is the expected proportion from training. A common heuristic interpretation is:

- **PSI** < 0.1: No significant shift. Model inputs remain stable
- **PSI 0.1–0.25**: Moderate shift. Investigate, but the model is not yet failing
- **PSI** > 0.25: Significant shift. Model predictions likely unreliable

Compute PSI for each key feature by comparing recent production data with the training reference set. Spikes in PSI often precede performance degradation, so they provide a warning before returns deteriorate. The chapter notebook does this directly on the `us_equities_panel` feature artifacts, comparing the last available year of holdout predictions against the prior reference window.

The **Kolmogorov-Smirnov test (K-S test)** complements PSI for continuous features by measuring the maximum distance between cumulative distribution functions. Unlike PSI, K-S makes no binning assumptions and directly tests whether two samples came from the same distribution, making it the preferred choice for continuous features where binning would discard information.

Feature drift caused by importance shift

Even when input distributions remain stable, the *importance* of features can change. A feature that historically drove predictions may become less influential while other features gain prominence. SHAP value monitoring (Lundberg and Lee, 2017) tracks each feature's contribution over time by decomposing predictions into additive attributions and aggregating across the live window. Three summaries matter: mean absolute SHAP (average magnitude), SHAP variance (stability of the contribution), and relative ranking (whether the importance hierarchy has shifted). Persistent rank changes and a collapsing contribution from a core feature are early warnings that the model is leaning on a relationship the market no longer rewards. *Section 26.2* covers how these summaries surface in the operational drift dashboard alongside performance metrics.

Concept drift caused by relationship changes

The most insidious form of drift arises from changes in the relationship between features and the target. Inputs look similar, but they no longer predict outcomes the same way. This is **concept drift**: the underlying data-generating process has changed. Lu et al. (2018) provide a taxonomy of concept drift types (sudden, gradual, incremental, and recurring), each requiring different detection and adaptation strategies. Hinder, Vaquet, and Hammer (2023) survey the state of the art in drift detection, situating ADWIN and DDM within a broader taxonomy of methods and their operational trade-offs.

Regime shifts are a leading instance of concept drift. When markets transition from trending to mean-reverting, the same momentum signal that previously predicted positive returns now predicts negative returns. The feature distribution may be unchanged; the feature-target relationship has inverted.

Production teams often rely on online drift libraries such as `river` to monitor concept drift in real time. The notebook uses lightweight detector logic on the stored validation error stream to keep the alert behavior transparent.

Adaptive Windowing (**ADWIN**) (Bifet and Gavaldà, 2007) maintains a variable-length window of observations. It continuously tests whether recent observations differ statistically from older observations. When drift is detected, the window shrinks to include only post-drift data.

Apply ADWIN to your strategy's prediction errors, the difference between predicted and realized returns. If the error distribution changes significantly, something about the prediction problem has changed.

Drift Detection Method (**DDM**) (Gama et al., 2004) monitors the error rate over time. It maintains running statistics for error rate and standard deviation, signaling a warning when the error rate increases moderately and a drift warning when it increases substantially.

DDM is simpler than ADWIN but less adaptive, offering a lightweight alternative when computational overhead is the binding constraint. The online-drift notebook compares ADWIN-style and DDM behavior on the final real validation year before the sealed holdout, relating alert clusters to a market-stress proxy rather than to synthetic change points.

Practical workflow

Not everything needs monitoring. Focus on:

- **High-importance features:** Features with historically large SHAP contributions. If these drift, model performance will likely follow.
- **Volatile features:** Features with historically variable distributions. These are more likely to drift.
- **Domain-sensitive features:** Features known to change with market regimes: volatility measures, correlation metrics, liquidity indicators.
- **Monitoring frequency:** Balance responsiveness against noise. *Table 26.2* summarizes a practical cadence that separates daily checks from slower, more computationally expensive diagnostics.

Method	Frequency	Typical Trigger
PSI on key production features	Daily	PSI $>$ 0.25 on high-importance inputs
K-S test on continuous features	Daily or weekly	p-value $<$ 0.05 on recent versus reference sample
SHAP importance monitoring	Weekly	Rank reordering or large drop in a core feature's mean absolute SHAP
ADWIN/DDM on prediction errors	Continuous	Warning or drift state on the live error stream

Table 26.2: Key monitoring methods

Alert integration: Connect drift detection to your alerting system. PSI greater than 0.25 on a key feature should trigger an investigation. An ADWIN drift signal should escalate to warning status.

The detector itself also needs monitoring. The online-drift notebook tracks alert frequency, warning streaks, and related health signals, enabling recalibration of ADWIN or DDM sensitivity before they overwhelm operators with false positives. Treat detector health like any other production metric: if it pages constantly without changing decisions, it has stopped being useful.

From detection to diagnosis

Drift detection tells you something changed; diagnosis tells you whether it matters:

Drift detected?	Performance decay?	Interpretation	Response
Yes	No	Robust model; distribution shifted, but the relationship holds	Monitor; no action required
No	Yes	Incomplete drift coverage or gradual concept drift	Expand monitoring; check for untracked features
Yes	Yes	Feature drift explains decay	Retrain on recent data or switch to a regime-specific model
No	No	Healthy operation	Continue normal monitoring

Table 26.3: Drift detection responses

The diagnostic workflow: detect drift, correlate with performance, hypothesize a mechanism, and validate with targeted analysis. This systematic approach prevents both under-reaction (ignoring real problems) and over-reaction (changing models based on noise).

Detection and diagnosis identify when and why a model is decaying; the next section addresses *what to do about it*: safe model updates that protect capital while allowing model evolution.

Implementation: `01_drift_monitoring` illustrates PSI, K-S, prediction-distribution drift, and alert-state summaries on the real holdout monitoring artifacts.

`02_online_drift_detection` compares ADWIN-style and DDM alerts on real chronological error streams from the final validation year before promotion.

26.4 Safe model updates

Monitoring detected decay. Diagnosis identified the cause. Now the model has to be updated without replacing one failure with another. The replacement may perform worse than the decayed original. Safe update workflows protect capital while still allowing model evolution.

When to retrain

There are two basic approaches:

- **Scheduled retraining** updates models at fixed intervals: weekly, monthly, quarterly. The schedule should reflect your strategy's expected decay rate. High-frequency strategies operating in fast-changing markets may need weekly updates; long-term strategies may retrain quarterly.
- **Triggered retraining** updates models when monitoring signals warrant. When rolling Sharpe drops below the threshold, or PSI exceeds the limits, or ADWIN signals drift, trigger the retraining pipeline.

Scheduled retraining provides predictability but may update unnecessarily (if nothing has changed) or too late (if decay has accelerated). Triggered retraining responds to actual conditions but requires robust monitoring to avoid false triggers. You can combine both approaches: scheduled as baseline, triggered for exceptional conditions.

Shadow mode evaluation

Before any new model touches capital, run it in **shadow mode**: process live data, generate predictions, but do not trade. Shadow mode provides validation under realistic conditions. We implement this directly in `ml4t-live`, where the strategy runs against live feeds while a virtual portfolio records hypothetical positions and PnL. The chapter notebook reconstructs this logic from the real `us_equities_panel` artifacts: it selects an incumbent from the historical validation record, replays a shadow window on the next release year, and records the candidate's hypothetical outcomes before any allocation increases.

Deploy the new model (the **candidate**) alongside the production model (the **incumbent**). Both receive identical live data feeds and generate predictions in real time. Only the incumbent executes trades. Three comparison metrics anchor the decision:

- **Prediction agreement**: how often the incumbent and candidate agree on direction. Disagreement is not necessarily bad, but its source should be understood before promotion.
- **Hypothetical returns**: the returns the candidate would have generated if it had traded, computed under realistic execution assumptions.
- **Risk characteristics**: whether the candidate takes similar or different risks. Unexpected risk-profile changes warrant investigation.

Figure 26.3 presents the full rollout protocol. The top row reports shadow-mode diagnostics: the cumulative net return of the candidate relative to the incumbent over the shadow window, and the realized correlation of 0.61 between their per-name signal scores. The bottom row shows the staged transition: a capital-capped A/B test in which the candidate trades a small fraction of total capital, and the allocation path stepping the candidate share from 10% to 25%. The candidate need not dominate every day; what matters is that disagreement becomes observable, attributable, and reviewable at each stage before its capital share grows.

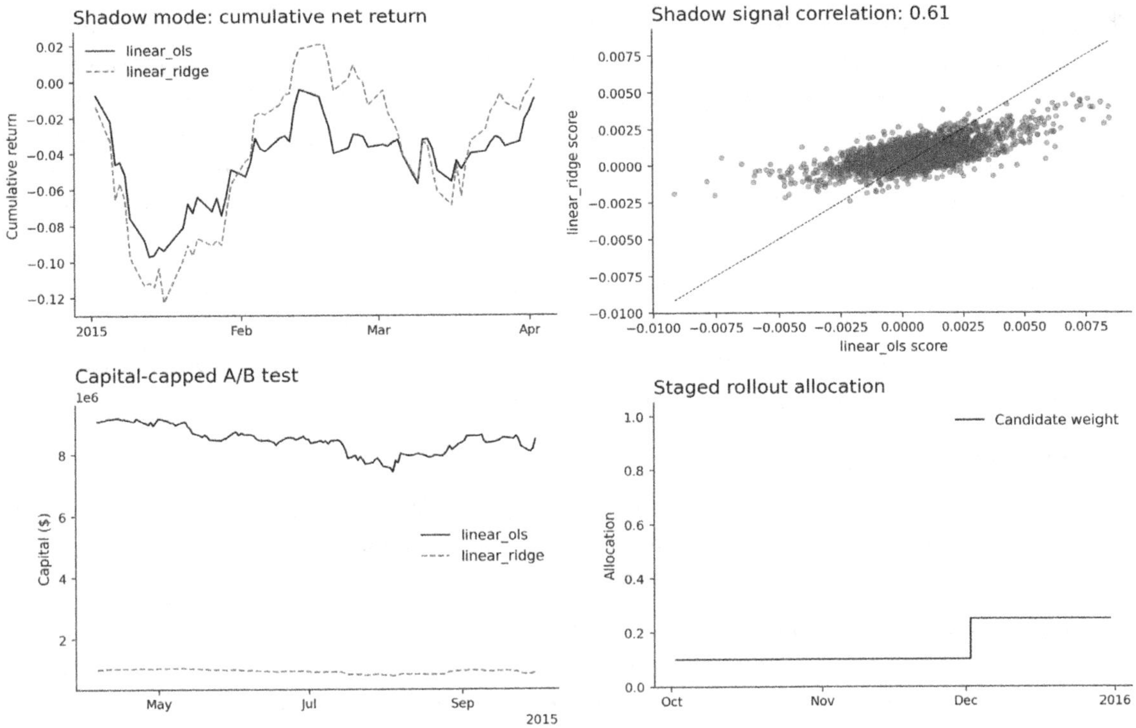

Figure 26.3: Staged rollout dashboard

Figure 26.3 shows the staged rollout dashboard for the incumbent and candidate models across the three stages—shadow mode (top row), capital-capped A/B test (bottom left), and staged allocation increase (bottom right).

Deciding duration

Shadow periods should span a sufficient range of market conditions to validate robustness. A candidate that looks better during trending markets may fail in choppy conditions. A common default is a 60-day shadow period (long enough to capture multiple market regimes and short enough to maintain deployment velocity), though the appropriate window depends on strategy **rebalance frequency**: a monthly strategy needs at least two rebalance cycles in shadow.

Statistical testing

Visual inspection of performance is not sufficient. Statistical tests assess whether the candidate genuinely outperforms or whether the observed difference is attributable to noise. A paired test on daily return differences can establish whether the candidate has a higher mean return over the same dates, while Sharpe-ratio comparisons require methods that account for both mean and volatility, as well as the correlation between the two return series.

The classic test compares the difference in Sharpe ratios. If $\widehat{SR}_C - \widehat{SR}_P$ is the observed difference, its standard error determines whether the gap is statistically meaningful. The original **Jobson-Korkie test** provides an early framework for this comparison, but it relies on restrictive assumptions about identically, independently, and normally distributed returns; later corrections and robust alternatives relax some of these assumptions. Bailey and López de Prado (2014) propose a **deflated Sharpe ratio** that is especially useful when the candidate was selected after many experiments because it adjusts for estimation error, multiple testing, and non-normal returns.

Bootstrap methods provide a practical alternative. Resample paired return observations, or use a block bootstrap when returns are serially dependent, then compute the Sharpe-ratio difference for each sample. The resulting distribution provides confidence intervals and an empirical estimate of how often the candidate's apparent advantage could arise by chance.

Effect size matters

A statistically significant 0.05 Sharpe improvement may not justify deployment risk. Define a minimum effect size for promotion (for example, a Sharpe improvement of 0.2-0.3) below which you do not promote regardless of statistical significance.

Statistical power matters as much as the test itself. Short shadow windows can neither confirm nor reject modest improvements with much confidence, especially when returns are noisy, autocorrelated, or fat-tailed. López de Prado, Lipton, and Zoonekynd (2025) show why naive Sharpe comparisons over short samples are unstable and quantify the observation counts required for reliable inference at a given effect size. If the effect size of interest is small, extend the shadow period or use bootstrap power analysis before declaring the candidate better.

Phased rollouts

If shadow mode validates the candidate, do not immediately replace the incumbent. Phase the transition:

- **Capital-capped A/B testing:** allocate a small fraction of capital (for example, 5% to 10%) to the candidate. The system now measures real performance, including execution costs, slippage, and market impact. The incumbent continues trading the remainder. A/B testing with real capital reveals issues that shadow mode misses: the candidate's signals may cluster in illiquid names, or its sizing may create market impact. These effects only appear when capital is actually deployed.
- **Gradual increase:** if A/B results validate, increase the candidate's allocation progressively through gates such as 10% to 25%, 25% to 50%, and 50% to 100%, each requiring a minimum observation period and continued outperformance before the next promotion. A complete transition typically spans 60 to 90 days, depending on rebalancing frequency and market conditions.
- **Promotion criteria:** define explicit thresholds rather than relying on discretionary judgment. An illustrative set requires the candidate's Sharpe ratio to exceed the incumbent's by at least 0.2, with statistical significance at the 10% level, and no drawdown exceeding the strategy's historical maximum during any stage. These values are rule-of-thumb starting points; calibrate them to the strategy's turnover and signal noise.

Rollback procedures

Every deployment should be reversible. Before promoting a new model:

- **Archive the incumbent:** store the current production model with full versioning, so that it can be restored instantly.
- **Define rollback triggers:** specify the conditions that trigger automatic rollback: drawdown exceeding a threshold, consecutive losing days, or system errors, for example.
- **Test rollback mechanism:** before deploying the candidate, verify that rollback actually works. A theoretical rollback procedure that fails under pressure is useless.
- **Decide between automatic or manual rollback:** Lower-level triggers (system errors, data feed failures) should roll back automatically: speed matters more than nuance. Higher-level triggers (performance degradation) may warrant manual confirmation to avoid over-reaction to noise.

> **Implementation:** `03_safe_model_rollout` demonstrates shadow mode, A/B testing, and staged promotion on real incumbent-candidate prediction artifacts from `us_equities_panel`.
>
> `06_mlflow_experiments` adds the experiment-ranking, artifact-logging, and registry workflows needed to manage these promotion decisions systematically.

Safe updates handle gradual decay; the next section addresses sudden failure: circuit breakers that halt trading automatically when losses or infrastructure conditions breach hard limits, before human review can intervene.

26.5 Circuit breakers and safety

Monitoring and safe updates address gradual decay. Circuit breakers address sudden failure: when something goes catastrophically wrong, and speed matters more than nuance. These are your automated safety nets: simple, hard-coded rules that protect capital when sophisticated systems fail.

Multi-level protection

Defense in depth: multiple independent safety layers, each catching different failure modes. The circuit breaker architecture implements four hierarchical levels:

- *Per-trade* (individual order validation)
- *Per-strategy* (exposure limits for a single strategy)
- *Portfolio* (aggregate risk across all strategies)
- *System* (infrastructure health and latency monitoring)

Each level operates independently: a breach at any level halts the relevant scope without requiring higher-level intervention. *Figure 26.4* illustrates this layered defense architecture.

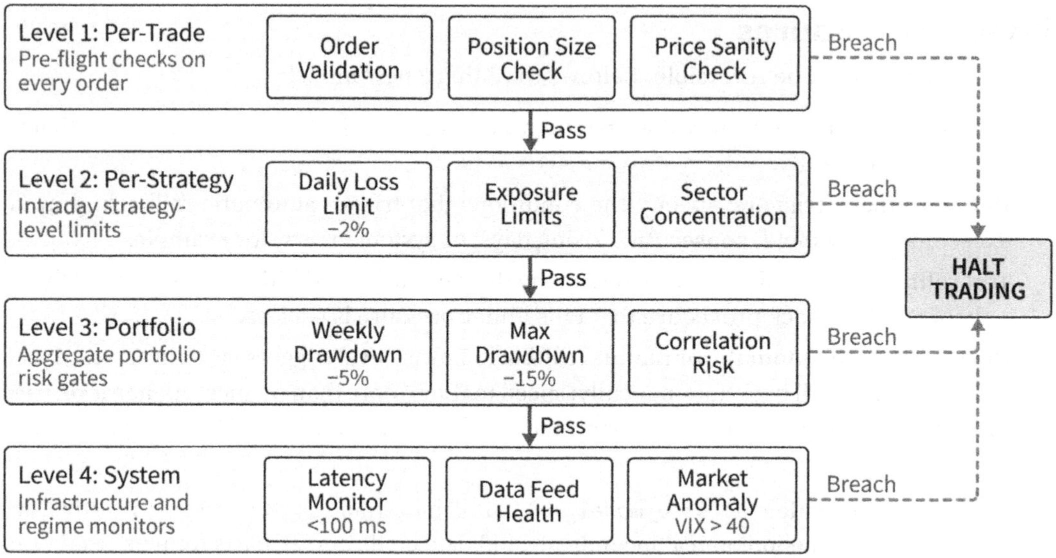

Figure 26.4: Circuit breaker architecture. Per-trade, strategy, portfolio, and system layers provide independent failure containment

Three breaker types matter most.

Loss-based breakers

The most important category: Halt trading when losses exceed thresholds:

- Daily drawdown limit (for example, -2%): Protects against single-day disasters
- Weekly drawdown limit (for example, -5%): Catches sustained bleeding
- Maximum drawdown from peak (for example, -10% to -15%): Ultimate circuit breaker

Drawdown-based rules have a long history in portfolio management (Korn, Möller, and Schwehm, 2022), but they need careful calibration. Varma (2025) argues that fixed drawdown cutoffs are blunt instruments, so drawdown breakers work best when combined with other signals such as exposure, liquidity, and market stress. When losses breach genuinely hard limits, halt trading immediately. Don't wait for human review. Don't try to "trade out" of the hole. Stop the bleeding first.

Position-based breakers

This mechanism prevents dangerous concentrations:

- Maximum position size per asset (for example, 5% of portfolio)
- Maximum sector exposure (for example, 20% in any sector)
- Maximum correlation (avoid multiple positions moving together)

Position limits catch situations where the model becomes overconfident in specific bets. Even if each trade looks reasonable individually, aggregate exposure may be dangerous.

Anomaly-based breakers

This breaker responds to unusual market conditions:

- Extreme volatility (for example, VIX > 40)
- Liquidity collapse (for example, bid-ask spreads 3× normal)
- Price dislocations (for example, any asset moves 10%+ intraday)

During market stress, normal relationships break down. Models trained on normal conditions may produce nonsense in extreme conditions. Stepping aside during anomalies is often the prudent response.

Notebook `04_circuit_breakers` implements drawdown, daily-loss, consecutive-loss, and latency breakers; the position-based and anomaly-based categories above extend the same state machine with different trip conditions.

The trading circuit breakers above are risk controls: rules about when to stop trading based on PnL, positions, or market conditions. The software circuit breaker pattern described below serves a different purpose: **infrastructure resilience.** It prevents cascading failures when system dependencies (data feeds, execution APIs) become unreliable. Both are necessary; they protect against different failure modes.

Implementation patterns and libraries

The notebook implements a custom circuit-breaker state machine to make the control logic explicit. In production, a library such as `pybreaker` can provide the same CLOSED/OPEN/HALF_OPEN lifecycle for infrastructure dependencies without changing the underlying policy design.

The breaker operates in three states:

- **Closed** (normal): Calls pass through to the underlying function. The breaker counts failures.
- **Open** (tripped): After exceeding the failure threshold (for example, 5 consecutive failures), all calls fail immediately without executing. This prevents wasted resources on a known-broken dependency.
- **Half-open** (probing): After a timeout period (for example, 30 seconds), the breaker allows a single call through. If it succeeds, the breaker returns to the Closed position. If it fails, the breaker reopens.

This three-state model prevents cascading failures. If your data feed is down, you don't want every prediction request to time out while waiting for data. The circuit breaker fails fast, preserving system resources and preventing zombie processes.

Whether you use a custom implementation or `pybreaker`, every CLOSED→OPEN transition should trigger an alert, and every OPEN→HALF_OPEN→CLOSED recovery should be logged for post-incident review. These events form the basis of your circuit breaker monitoring dashboard.

System-level monitors halt trading when infrastructure degrades. A typical threshold of 100ms end-to-end latency catches data feed delays, execution system slowdowns, or network issues before they cause stale-data trading. When latency exceeds the threshold, the breaker opens and trading halts until the system recovers.

Recovery procedures

Tripping a circuit breaker is the beginning, not the end. You need clear recovery protocols, grouped as the immediate response, investigating the problem, and resuming trade.

Immediate actions:

1. **Acknowledge the alert**, using PagerDuty, Slack, or whichever platform you use.
2. **Assess the situation:** What triggered the breaker? What's the current exposure?
3. **Secure the position:** If you are partially exposed, decide whether to close or hedge.

Diagnostic questions:

- Was this a technical failure (data feed, execution system) or model failure (wrong predictions)?
- Is the market experiencing unusual conditions that triggered anomaly breakers?
- What was the sequence of events leading to the trigger?

Resume criteria:

Define what must be true before trading resumes:

- All system components are healthy
- Data feeds validated
- Market conditions normalized (if anomaly-triggered)
- Root cause identified and either fixed or determined nonthreatening

Gradual restart:

Don't resume at full capacity immediately. Start with reduced position sizes or paper trading. Verify systems behave correctly before scaling back up.

Manual override considerations

Circuit breakers should be automatic: speed matters during failure. But they should also be overridable by authorized personnel, for cases where the breaker triggers incorrectly.

Override discipline requires logging every override (who, when, why), requiring explicit risk acknowledgment, time-limiting the override (for example, one hour unless renewed), and reviewing all overrides after the fact. Making overrides too easy defeats the purpose; making them impossible prevents response to genuine false positives. The balance depends on your risk tolerance and operational maturity.

With monitoring, drift detection, safe updates, and automated safety in place, the next section surveys the supporting MLOps infrastructure (feature stores, model registries, and CI/CD) that these governance layers depend on in a production deployment.

Implementation: `04_circuit_breakers` demonstrates a custom circuit-breaker state machine, layered safety rules, and recovery procedures.

26.6 MLOps infrastructure overview

The preceding sections focused on monitoring and safety, the most critical aspects of production governance. The supporting infrastructure tools are useful but not central; small teams can start with minimal infrastructure and add complexity as needs grow.

Preventing training-serving skew with feature stores

Feature stores ensure that features computed during training exactly match those computed during inference. Without this consistency, your live system receives different inputs than your backtest, a technical failure waiting to happen.

The core problem is that, in research, you compute features from historical data with complete freedom. In production, you must compute the same features in real-time, from streaming data, with strict latency constraints. Subtle differences (date handling, normalization windows, default values for missing data) create training-serving skew that silently degrades performance. Sculley et al. (2015) documented how such "hidden technical debt" compounds across ML systems, making feature consistency a first-order concern. Paleyes, Urma, and Lawrence (2023) survey deployment challenges across industries and highlight data quality, monitoring, and system integration as recurring operational bottlenecks, reinforcing the need for early investment in feature stores and drift detection.

Feast (`feast.dev`) provides a unified feature registry. Define features once; Feast handles both historical retrieval (for training) and online serving (for inference). Key benefits:

- **Consistency:** The same feature definition serves both training and production
- **Point-in-time correctness:** Feast manages temporal joins to prevent look-ahead bias
- **Versioning:** Feature definitions are versioned alongside models

Feast separates **offline** and **online** stores. The offline store (typically Parquet, BigQuery, or Redshift) holds historical feature values for training, potentially years of data across thousands of entities. The online store (Redis, DynamoDB) holds only the most recent feature values for low-latency inference. Feast automatically materializes features from offline to online, ensuring consistency between training and serving.

For trading systems, this architecture solves a common problem: you compute rolling features (20-day volatility, 60-day momentum) during backtesting using pandas with full hindsight. In production, you must compute the same features incrementally as new data arrives. Feast's feature definitions ensure the computation is identical; the online store ensures serving latency stays under milliseconds.

Feature stores scale from small experiments, such as a handful of tickers and features, to production deployments with thousands of features across large universes. Our notebook shows the control logic directly on the real `us_equities_panel` feature tables: it defines feature views against the stored Parquet sources, performs a point-in-time offline join for training, reconstructs an online-style as-of snapshot for inference, and measures the skew created by an incorrect timestamp rule. The key concept is still training-serving consistency rather than a specific vendor setup.

Data versioning and lineage

Feature stores ensure consistency between training and serving, but they do not answer the question: *which exact dataset produced this model?* When a model fails in production and you need to distinguish data corruption from genuine regime shift, you must be able to reproduce the exact training data. Without data versioning, diagnosis is guesswork and rollback is risky.

At minimum, every training run should record a *run manifest*: a JSON artifact logging the git commit hash, dataset snapshot identifier (a content hash or partition version), feature set version, model registry version, and configuration hash. DVC (`dvc.org`) provides a Git-like interface for versioning large data and model files alongside code, enabling small teams to achieve reproducibility and rollbacks without a dedicated metadata platform. Attach the manifest to each MLflow run as a tagged artifact so that any deployed model can be traced back to its exact inputs.

Experiment tracking with model registries

Model registries provides version control for models: tracking which model version is deployed, what training data was used, and how it performed in testing.

MLflow (`mlflow.org`) offers a lightweight solution combining:

- **Experiment tracking:** Log hyperparameters, metrics, and artifacts for every training run
- **Model versioning:** Store trained models with full lineage (including training data, code version, dependencies)
- **Deployment staging:** Manage transitions from "Staging" to "Production" status

For the safe update workflow described in *Section 26.4*, MLflow tracks which model is the current incumbent, which is the candidate in shadow mode, and the performance comparison between them. During training, MLflow automatically logs metrics such as IC and Sharpe. These logged metrics become the basis for ranking candidates during promotion.

Model registries also support auditability. When regulators or risk officers ask, "Why did the model make this decision?" you need to know exactly which model version was deployed, when, trained on what data, and with what hyperparameters. The CRISP-ML(Q) framework (Studer et al., 2021) and the Federal Reserve's SR 11-7 guidance (Board of Governors, 2011) on model risk management both emphasize model lineage and reproducibility as regulatory necessities.

The registry entry is only part of the governance record. Production teams also need durable review artifacts: a model card summarizing intended use and known limitations, an independent validation memo, and a current monitoring report showing live performance, drift status, and open incidents. The notebook shows the adjacent MLflow pieces, namely artifact logging, experiment summaries, and registry stages, but those records do not replace the governance artifacts themselves. SR 11-7's core requirements (effective challenge, ongoing monitoring, and documented governance) are hard to satisfy if these materials live only in chat threads or ad hoc dashboards.

CI/CD for trading models

Continuous Integration/Continuous Deployment adapts to ML with specific considerations. Standard CI/CD includes unit tests for feature computation and signal generation, integration tests for pipeline components, validation tests to confirm model performance exceeds minimum thresholds, and smoke tests after deployment. The ML-specific addition is automated deployment gates: no model reaches production unless validation metrics pass, shadow-mode comparison shows no regression, and rollback has been verified. GitHub Actions, GitLab CI, or similar tools orchestrate these checks so that no human needs to remember to run validations.

Right-sizing your stack

Not every team needs enterprise-grade infrastructure. A sensible progression:

Minimal (solo or small team):

- Feature computation in pandas/numpy with careful documentation
- Models saved to versioned directories (Git LFS for large files)
- Cron or systemd timers for scheduled pipelines
- Manual deployment with a checklist
- Monitoring via simple dashboards (Streamlit, basic Grafana)

Intermediate (growing team):

- Feast for feature consistency
- MLflow for experiment tracking and DVC for data versioning
- Prefect (`prefect.io`) or Dagster (`dagster.io`) for workflow orchestration with retries and observability
- GitHub Actions for automated testing
- Prometheus and Grafana for monitoring
- Structured logs with consistent correlation IDs (run, strategy, order) for incident diagnosis

The Prometheus-Grafana stack is the standard observability pairing: Prometheus scrapes custom trading metrics (`strategy_sharpe_30d`, `signal_ic_rolling`) at 15–30-second intervals, while Alertmanager routes threshold breaches to Slack or PagerDuty with configurable escalation policies.

Mature (production at scale):

- Full-featured store with real-time serving
- Model registry with approval workflows
- Kubernetes for deployment orchestration
- OpenTelemetry (`opentelemetry.io`) for correlated logs, metrics, and traces across the full signal-to-execution pipeline

Start simpler than you think you need. Infrastructure serves the trading system, not the reverse. The sections on monitoring (*26.2–26.3*) and safety (*26.5*) matter more than tooling choices. Get those right first; optimize infrastructure as constraints demand.

Implementation:

- `05_feast_feature_store` demonstrates feature-store concepts, point-in-time joins, and feature lineage through the real case-study feature tables.
- `05b_feast_live` extends the same workflow to use a live Feast integration with the same artifacts.
- `06_mlflow_experiments` demonstrates experiment tracking, artifact logging, and registry-style promotion workflows through the local SQLite registry and content-addressed run bundles.

The following summary draws together the detection, response, and safety layers into the three-layer governance model that keeps a deployed trading system operating correctly or failing gracefully when it cannot.

26.7 Summary

We built the post-deployment infrastructure that separates production-grade trading systems from research prototypes. The central insight is diagnostic: technical failures (pipeline bugs that produce incorrect outputs) and statistical failures (correct outputs that no longer predict returns) demand different responses. Conflating them wastes time and capital.

The three-layer governance model runs from detection to response to automated safety. Detection begins with data quality gates and continues through rolling performance metrics, execution-quality monitoring, and drift diagnostics that separate input shifts (PSI, K-S), feature-importance changes (SHAP), and concept drift (ADWIN, DDM). Response uses shadow mode, capital-capped A/B testing, and staged rollouts to replace decayed models without swapping one failure for another. Automated safety provides the last line of defense through multi-level circuit breakers that halt trading when losses, exposures, or infrastructure conditions breach hard limits. The supporting MLOps infrastructure (*Section 26.6*), spanning feature stores, data versioning, model registries, and workflow orchestration, should be right-sized to operational maturity rather than adopted wholesale.

Chapter 27 steps back from implementation to reflect on the systematic edge that arises when the entire pipeline (from data through modeling, deployment, and governance) operates as a coherent, continuously validated system.

27

The Systematic Edge

Throughout this book, you have worked the five stages of the ML4T workflow, from strategy hypothesis through data engineering, signal research, portfolio construction, and deployment. You now have the techniques. The most important lesson is not any one of them: *your process is your edge*.

This closing chapter turns from method to direction. It maps the career paths open to a systematic practitioner, the resources worth your continued study, the emerging technologies that warrant attention, and a practical plan for the years ahead. The end of the book is the start of that work.

27.1 The systematic edge – From techniques to philosophy

The workflow is more than a development method; it is a blueprint for an alpha factory—a repeatable way to generate, test, and deploy strategies across a career. Models decay, alpha erodes, and markets keep changing. A single successful strategy is a temporary advantage. A process that produces a diversified portfolio of strategies over time is durable value (Harvey, 2021).

That process is also your main defense against the cognitive biases that pervade financial markets. Confirmation bias leads researchers to find the patterns they expect; overfitting produces strategies that fail in production; data mining turns spurious correlations into apparent alpha (Lopez de Prado, 2018). A systematic workflow imposes discipline through falsifiable hypotheses, out-of-sample testing, and corrections for multiple testing.

The shift now is from **learning the steps** to **embodying the systematic mindset**. Technical skills set your entry point; systematic thinking sets your trajectory. As machine learning spreads through quantitative finance, practitioners who pair that skill with disciplined process compound their advantage over the course of their careers.

27.2 The modern quant career

The quantitative finance industry has changed over the past decade. Boundaries between roles are blurring as machine learning becomes standard, and hybrid positions are emerging between systematic and fundamental approaches. Knowing the landscape helps you make deliberate career decisions.

Five core roles

Five roles define most of the modern quant landscape, each with distinct skills and compensation:

- **Quantitative researchers** formulate and validate trading hypotheses, combining statistics, ML, and market intuition to find predictive signals. Senior researchers at top-tier firms command $200K to $1M+ annually.
- **Quantitative traders** manage live strategies, optimize execution, and react to real-time dynamics. Strong programming skills are now essential. Compensation: $250K to $2M+ at leading firms.
- **Quantitative developers** ("strats") build and maintain the technology stack, from data pipelines to execution gateways. Compensation: $180K to $800K.
- **Portfolio managers** carry PnL responsibility, deciding which strategies to deploy and at what size. Compensation: $300K to $10M+ at top funds.
- **Risk managers** model and monitor portfolio risk within defined limits, which calls for statistical expertise and regulatory knowledge. Compensation: $150K to $600K.

A notable trend is the rise of "quantamental" approaches, hybrid strategies that blend systematic techniques with fundamental analysis (Chin, 2025). Quantamental analysts use NLP to parse earnings calls while building traditional financial models, and practitioners who bridge both worlds command premium compensation. AI foundation models are accelerating this convergence, letting systematic strategies absorb unstructured data that was once the preserve of discretionary managers (Fabozzi and Prado, 2025).

Institutional ecosystems

The type of firm shapes the work as much as the role itself:

Firm Type	Characteristics	Example Firms
Hedge funds	External capital, focus on scalability, rigorous risk reporting	Millennium, Citadel, Two Sigma
Proprietary trading	Own capital, higher risk tolerance, capacity-constrained strategies	Jane Street, Optiver, Jump Trading
Investment banks	Client-facing roles, structured environment, heavy regulation	Goldman Sachs, JPMorgan, Morgan Stanley
Asset managers	Long-term focus, large-scale factor investing	BlackRock, Vanguard, AQR

Table 27.1: A table comparing the characteristics of different types of trading firms

This choice often matters more than the initial choice of role. A researcher at a high-frequency prop shop develops entirely different skills than one at a multi-billion-dollar asset manager.

Geographic dynamics

New York remains the dominant hub, but Miami has become a significant center. London keeps its importance despite Brexit uncertainty, with Amsterdam and Dublin gaining ground. Singapore and Hong Kong anchor the Asia-Pacific markets.

Figure 27.1 shows typical career progressions across these environments, from entry-level roles to senior positions.

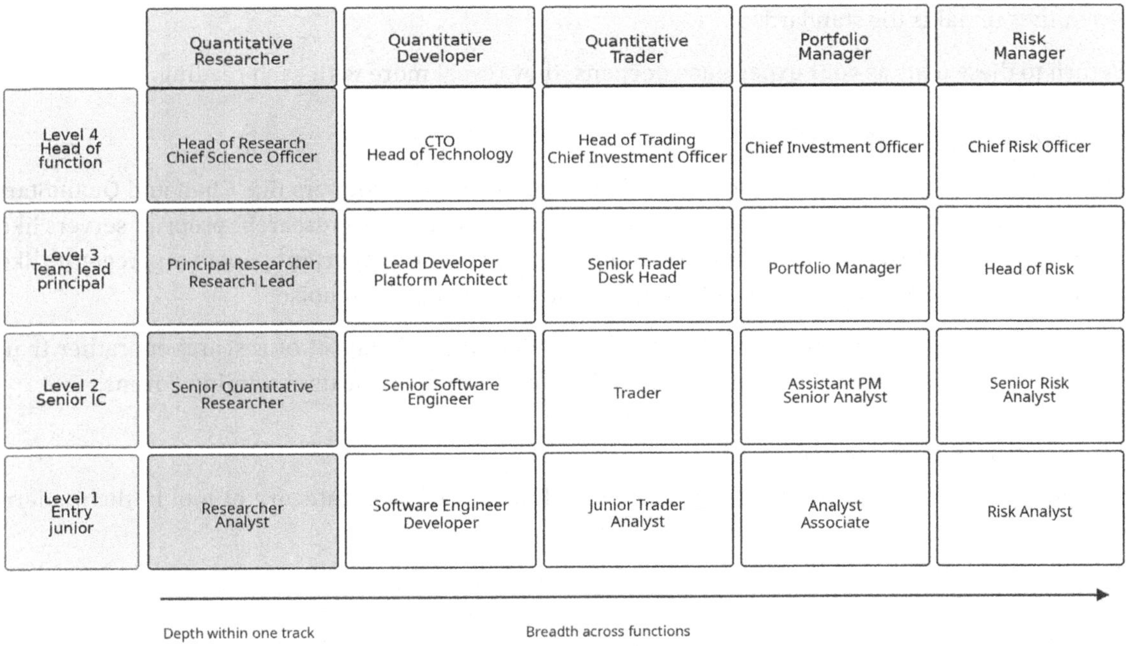

Figure 27.1: Typical career progressions across trading environments, from entry-level roles to senior positions

The strongest practitioners develop "T-shaped" expertise: deep knowledge in their primary function alongside a broad understanding of the whole trading lifecycle (Cerniglia and Fabozzi, 2022). A developer who grasps alpha decay, or a researcher who appreciates system latency, is far more valuable than a narrow specialist. That cross-functional fluency matters more as the line between alpha research and execution continues to blur.

27.3 Building a learning practice

Information overload is a real career risk. The body of quantitative-finance material is vast and of variable quality. Continuous learning works best when it is curated: a balance of foundational knowledge, current developments, and active participation in a community.

The foundational library

Begin with the texts that provide both theory and practitioner experience. Ernest Chan's *Quantitative Trading* offers practical guidance on building trading systems. Marcos Lopez de Prado's *Advances in Financial Machine Learning* (2018) addresses implementation challenges that academic treatments often overlook. Andrew Ang's *Asset Management: A Systematic Approach to Factor Investing* (2014) provides the framework for systematic strategies across asset classes. Larry Harris's *Trading and Exchanges* (2003) remains essential for market microstructure. For derivatives, John Hull's *Options, Futures, and Other Derivatives* remains the standard.

Return to these texts as your experience deepens; they reveal more with each reading.

Staying current online

Much of the field's current thinking lives online. Blogs from practitioners like Chan and QuantStart offer technical tutorials grounded in real trading experience. For new research, preprint servers like arXiv (especially the q-fin section) and SSRN offer early access to important papers. Aggregators like Quantocracy curate the quant web, which helps you filter signal from noise.

Set up alerts for key authors and topics. Follow a small, high-signal set of researchers rather than attempting comprehensive coverage; deep reading of a few papers beats skimming dozens.

Mastering the toolchain

Rather than chasing every new library, understand the *role* of each category of tool in the modern quant stack:

Workflow Stage	Core Capability
Data ingestion and storage	Handling diverse sources, ensuring data quality
High-performance analysis	Processing large datasets efficiently
Statistical and ML modeling	Building and validating predictive models
Portfolio and risk analysis	Optimizing allocations, managing exposures
Backtesting	Realistic simulation with proper methods
Production MLOps	Deployment, monitoring, model lifecycle

Table 27.2: A table comparing the capabilities required from tools at each stage in the workflow

Fluency across these categories enables effective collaboration; it is as much a communication skill as a technical one.

Structured learning pathways

Use free resources for exploration; invest in formal learning for career pivots. Online platforms from Stanford, MIT, and Columbia offer rigorous foundations. The **Certificate in Quantitative Finance (CQF)** provides practitioner-focused training that employers value, often more than a second academic degree for those already in the workforce.

Pursue an advanced degree (MFE, PhD) only if you are targeting top-tier research roles where deep theoretical expertise matters.

The book's companion repository and website host the full codebase, data and library updates, and additional guided material for readers who want structured practice beyond the text.

Community and brand building

Treat community participation as a career activity, not only a learning one. Contributing to open-source projects builds visible proof of expertise. Publishing through personal blogs, guest posts, or arXiv preprints establishes a professional profile and sharpens your own understanding.

Engage on QuantNet forums and specialized communities. Attend conferences like QuantMinds International, not just for the content but for the relationships that accelerate a career. Teaching others, whether through meetup presentations or written tutorials, compounds your own learning while expanding your network.

Crowdsourced prediction platforms offer a low-barrier way to apply these skills against live capital and build a public track record. Numerai, the best-funded modern descendant of the Quantopian crowdsourcing model, pays data scientists for return forecasts on an obfuscated feature set and lets them stake a cryptocurrency on their out-of-sample performance; CrunchDAO runs a comparable tournament and other research competitions tied to the ADIA Lab research community. Neither replaces a research role, but both let you test models against real money and accumulate evidence of skill that employers can see.

27.4 Navigating the frontiers – Quantum, DeFi, and ethical AI

The quantitative finance landscape keeps changing. Three frontiers warrant attention: quantum computing (long-term potential), decentralized finance (immediate opportunity), and AI ethics (a required competency). The task is to separate hype from reality and allocate attention accordingly.

Quantum computing – Promise versus reality

Quantum computing draws intense interest from the financial sector. Nearly 80% of major banks are exploring its potential, and JPMorgan Chase has invested $100 million in Quantinuum. The potential applications are significant: quantum algorithms could solve optimization problems intractable for classical computers and break modern cryptographic systems.

The reality check

The field remains in the Noisy Intermediate-Scale Quantum (NISQ) era. Industry analyses suggest that meaningful quantum advantage in derivatives pricing requires thousands of logical qubits and tens of millions of operations, far beyond current capabilities. Major quantum hardware vendors and financial institutions project commercial viability in the 2030-2040 timeframe, with most experts targeting the mid-2030s as the earliest realistic milestone.

Practical implications

For working quants, quantum computing is a frontier to monitor, not to prepare for. The immediate concern is *defensive*: institutions should plan transitions to quantum-resistant cryptographic standards. Develop skills elsewhere.

DeFi – A live market

Where quantum is a long-term prospect, decentralized finance is a live, multi-billion-dollar market generating new data and alpha *today*. Unlike traditional finance's opaque, siloed data, public blockchains provide transparent, real-time, granular ledgers of every transaction.

This on-chain data is a new source of alternative data. Transaction flows, wallet concentrations, protocol lending rates, and liquidity-pool dynamics offer signals unavailable through conventional channels.

Quants are already developing strategies native to this market:

- Automated market making (AMM) optimization
- Yield farming across protocols
- Cross-exchange arbitrage
- MEV (maximal extractable value) capture

These strategies carry novel risk factors. Smart-contract vulnerabilities can drain capital in an instant. Impermanent loss affects the economics of liquidity provision. Regulatory uncertainty adds jurisdictional risk.

The skills required—blockchain data engineering, smart-contract interaction, modeling new market mechanics—are natural extensions of the ML4T toolkit. DeFi is perhaps the most accessible of these frontiers for practitioners seeking new alpha.

AI ethics – From philosophy to compliance

AI ethics has moved from philosophy to a quantitative discipline. The EU AI Act mandates explainability for high-risk financial AI, with compliance costs averaging €29,277 per system annually. Regulators worldwide are intensifying their focus on algorithmic governance.

Practitioners must now show proficiency in:

Area	Key Techniques
Interpretability	SHAP, LIME, attention visualization
Bias detection	Fairness metrics, disparate impact analysis
Robustness	Adversarial testing, distribution shift detection
Auditability	Model documentation, decision logging

Table 27.3: A table showing areas of proficiency required from modern practitioners

These capabilities build on *Chapter 14*'s treatment of model explainability but extend into governance frameworks. The ability to articulate *why* a model makes specific predictions—and to show that those predictions do not systematically disadvantage protected groups—becomes a professional requirement. As AI agents take on more autonomous roles in research and trading (Korinek, 2025), the governance requirements will only intensify.

Framing ethics through a quantitative lens provides a practical method. Just as we measure and manage financial risk, we can measure and manage model risk across fairness, robustness, and transparency.

Strategic prioritization

Allocate attention accordingly: DeFi and AI governance offer immediate opportunities and requirements; quantum computing warrants monitoring but not immediate skill investment. The systematic mindset applies to career strategy too: put resources where they generate near-term returns while keeping an eye on long-term disruptions.

27.5 Building your path forward

Long-term success means moving from passive learning to active career design: deliberate practice, accountability, and personal sustainability.

Conduct a skills assessment

Begin with a candid self-evaluation. Map your current capabilities against the quant roles from *Section 27.2*. Identify gaps that limit progression, but prioritize the weaknesses that *complement* existing strengths over starting entirely new skill tracks.

Ask yourself: which role fits my interests and aptitudes? Where does my skill profile fall short? What single improvement would most accelerate my trajectory?

Design a learning system

Knowledge without application has limited value. For every new technique you learn, find a use for it in your current role or a personal project. Build a portfolio that shows not just understanding but results. The following key elements are vital:

- **Daily habits:** Even 30 minutes a day spent on research papers, new approaches, or market analysis compounds over time. Microlearning works well: focus on specific skills relevant to current projects rather than attempting comprehensive courses.
- **Personal knowledge management:** Use tools like Obsidian or Notion to externalize your learning. Document not just what works but what does not; failed experiments often provide the most valuable lessons. Keep a searchable repository of code snippets, research notes, and lessons learned.
- **Accountability:** External accountability improves follow-through. Whether through mentorship, study groups, or public commitments to learning goals, build structures that encourage consistency.

Avoid common pitfalls

Four failure modes recur across quant careers. Over-specialization creates vulnerability to shifts in approach. Underestimating soft skills limits advancement despite technical strength. Ignoring regulatory change leaves you unprepared. Perpetual learning without application generates knowledge that never compounds into expertise.

Ground your learning in practical applications and measurable results. The most sophisticated model provides no value unless it translates to better investment outcomes.

27.6 Summary

This closing chapter turns the ML4T workflow into a broader career philosophy. The central lesson is that your process is your edge: individual models decay, signals weaken, and markets change, but a disciplined approach to generating, testing, combining, and deploying strategies can keep producing value over time. The chapter connects that mindset to the modern quant career landscape, where researchers, traders, developers, portfolio managers, and risk professionals increasingly need both deep technical skill and broad fluency across the full trading lifecycle.

The chapter also lays out how to keep building after the book ends. A strong learning practice combines foundational texts, current research, practical projects, community participation, and a visible record of work. Emerging areas such as DeFi and AI governance already matter, while quantum computing is worth monitoring as a longer-term frontier. The practical message is to keep learning deliberately, apply new ideas to real problems, and build a sustainable career around systematic thinking rather than any single technique or strategy.

Other Books You May Enjoy

If you enjoyed this book, you may be interested in these other books by Packt:

Python for Algorithmic Trading Cookbook, Second Edition

Jason Strimpel

ISBN: 978-1-80666-203-6

- Acquire equities, futures, and options data using OpenBB and FMP
- Process and analyze time series data efficiently with pandas and Polars
- Store and query massive datasets with ArcticDB, DuckDB, and Parquet
- Visualize trading data using Matplotlib, Seaborn, and Plotly Dash
- Engineer alpha factors using PCA, regression, and Fama-French models
- Backtest strategies with VectorBT and Zipline Reloaded frameworks
- Evaluate performance and risk using Alphalens Reloaded and PyFolio
- Deploy and automate live trades using the Interactive Brokers API

Python for Finance Cookbook, Second Edition

Eryk Lewinson

ISBN: 978-1-80324-319-1

- Preprocess, analyze, and visualize financial data
- Explore time series modeling with statistical (exponential smoothing, ARIMA) and machine learning models
- Uncover advanced time series forecasting algorithms such as Meta's Prophet
- Use Monte Carlo simulations for derivatives valuation and risk assessment
- Explore volatility modeling using univariate and multivariate GARCH models
- Investigate various approaches to asset allocation
- Learn how to approach ML-projects using an example of default prediction
- Explore modern deep learning models such as Google's TabNet, Amazon's DeepAR and NeuralProphet

Packt is searching for authors like you

If you're interested in becoming an author for Packt, please visit `authors.packt.com` and apply today. We have worked with thousands of developers and tech professionals, just like you, to help them share their insight with the global tech community. You can make a general application, apply for a specific hot topic that we are recruiting an author for, or submit your own idea.

Share your thoughts

Now you've finished *Machine Learning for Trading, Third Edition*, we'd love to hear your thoughts! If you purchased the book from Amazon, please `click here to go straight to the Amazon review` page for this book and share your feedback or leave a review on the site that you purchased it from.

Your review is important to us and the tech community and will help us make sure we're delivering excellent quality content.

Index

Symbols

A

B

C

D

E

F

H

I

M

N

O

S

T

U

V

W

X

Y

Z

Made in the USA
Monee, IL
23 August 2026

61081586R00453